legal liability and risk management for public and private entities

SPORT AND PHYSICAL EDUCATION

LEISURE SERVICES, RECREATION AND PARKS

CAMPING AND ADVENTURE ACTIVITIES

legal liability and risk management for public and private entities

Betty van der Smissen, J.D.

ANDERSON PUBLISHING CO./CINCINNATI

VAN DER SMISSEN, LEGAL LIABILITY AND RISK MANAGEMENT FOR PUBLIC AND PRIVATE ENTITIES

© 1990 by Anderson Publishing Co.

Library of Congress Cataloging-in-Publication Data

Van der Smissen, Betty, 1927-
     Legal liability and risk management for public and private entities: sport and physical
education, leisure services, recreation and parks, camping and adventure activities / Betty Van Der
Smissen.
        p.   cm.
     Includes index.
     ISBN 0-87084-914-X
     1. Liability for sports accidents — United States. 2. Tort liability of parks — United States. 3.
Tort liability of recreation agencies — United States. 4. Sports — Law and legislation — United
States. 5. Parks — Law and legislation — United States. 6. Recreation — Law and legislation —
United States. I. Title. KF1290. S66V363   1990
346.7303'22 — dc20   90-692
[347.306322]   CIP

Contents

PART A
LEGAL CONCEPTS OF NEGLIGENCE

Chapter 2 — *Concluded*

Section

Chapter 3   Who is Liable? — The Doctrine of Respondeat Superior

Section

Chapter 4   Approaches to Immunity and Limiting Liability

Section

Chapter 4 — *Concluded*

Section

Chapter 5   Defenses

Section

PART D
RISK MANAGEMENT

Chapter 24 — *Concluded*

Section

Chapter 25   Management of Financial Risks Through Retention and Transfer

Section

INDEX

Preface

This work is a comprehensive treatise on negligence as applied particularly to the fields of physical education and sport, parks and recreation, leisure services, and camping and adventure activities. It is an authoritative source of information based upon primary data of case and statutory law; however, it is not held out to be an exhaustive compilation. Additional cases can be obtained in the opinions of the cases and through legal bibliographical resources. Only cases of supreme and appellate court record are included. It is acknowledged that there are lower court decisions, as well as many insurance claims and law suits filed which are settled out-of-court. While these impact upon operations, they do not formulate the law.

Also, the ever-changing law and its interpretation and application is recognized; thus, it is mandatory that the reader endeavor to update with current case decisions and statutory enactments. Periodic supplements to this book will be issued to assist. Furthermore, inasmuch as the law of negligence is based in the states and there are differences among states, this work presents the points of law as evidenced in the cases, but in no way has attempted an interpretation of statutes or case law in any specific state. It is essential that attorneys, who are members of the Bar in the specific state, be consulted for such advisement. To facilitate determination of the law in each state, cases and statutes are cited by state in the Appendix, rather than a master alphabetical listing of cases.

The law is presented in three approaches. Part A (Chapters 2 to 5) sets forth some basic legal concepts of negligence, utilizing illustrative cases from the professional fields encompassed. Part B (Chapters 6 to 14) identifies cases and selected legislation for specific sports and leisure services and activities, while Part C (Chapters 15 to 22) presents cases in accord with situations which give rise to law suits. However, there is no commentary drawing implications for operations or safety practices; it is believed that these are self-evident. Part D (Chapters 23 to 25) discusses risk management. All parts are equally applicable to public agencies, private non-profit organizations, and commercial enterprises.

Chapter 1 is an overview of legal aspects pertinent to the professional fields toward which this book is directed, both to provide a frame of reference for the field of negligence within the larger legal field, and to give some understanding of the scope and pervasiveness of law in physical education and sport, parks and recreation, leisure services, and camping and adventure activities. Chapter 1 is so presented that this book may be used as a text for both undergraduate and graduate courses in legal aspects and as a primary resource in management, administration, programming, facilities, outdoor recreation, camping et al. courses. (See last section in Chapter 1 for suggestions regarding use with students.) Law students, and others who have access to a law library, should augment Chapter 1 topics with law review articles and readings from ALR and other legal references.

As a valuable resource, this set should be in the professional library of all practitioners in the fields encompassed. Lawyers servicing these fields also will find this book an indispensable source of legal information.

Chapter 1.   Legal Aspects Overview

USE OF BOOK WITH STUDENTS

The law is all-pervasive in the administration and conduct of physical education and sports, parks and leisure services, and camping. Although it has been estimated that "conservatively, perhaps 75 to 80 percent of the daily legal issues presented in this field involve tort law,"[1] — the subject of this volume — to give the professional practitioner and student[2] a better perspective and understanding of this pervasiveness and the substance of the various aspects, Chapter 1 presents an overview of legal aspects, especially pertinent to the professional practitioner. Supplemental readings are given to augment the overview for students.[3]

The first four sections deal with legal liability. Legal liability infers a responsibility or obligation between parties which courts recognize and enforce. This liability may arise because of an agreement between parties, such as a contract; or, it may be created by the U.S. Constitution or statutes requiring certain actions, such as human rights legislation. A liability, too, may be occasioned by an act against society in the form of a criminal act against an individual, such as murder, robbery, and rape. Torts, wrongs against a person's body, property, or reputation, also give rise to a liability for damages. While there are many types of liability in the legal field, only these four areas will be discussed briefly to provide a frame of reference and distinguish negligence among the types of liability. Table 1.1 contrasts the four areas; the introductions to the specified sections augment that table. Subsequent sections set forth these liabilities in more detail.

The final two sections of the chapter discuss some pertinent aspects of property law and business operations. Business law in general is not included.

§ 1.1 Contractual liability

Although the law of contracts has become increasingly important in sport and recreation, the purpose of this section is *not* to provide a treatise on contracts, but to put

---

[1] Michael I. Ashe, educator and practicing trial attorney, in a book review. JOPERD October 1984 at p. 86. "This field" refers to parks and recreation.

[2] See the end of the chapter for suggested use of book with students.

[3] It is recommended that these books be placed in Library Reserve for college students. Only the author is given in footnote citations (introduced by boldfaced words); full citations at end of chapter in "Use of Book with Students." Law students should utilize legal bibliographic tools for identifying additional legal commentary in law reviews, ALR, et al.

Table 1.1   Types of Liability

Type	Nature of Act	Who Brings Action	Outcome
Contractual §1.1	an agreement between two parties which creates an obligation to do or not to do a particular thing, *e.g.*, perform a service, provide a product	the person injured due to the breach of agreement (contract) sues the other party	the court orders performance or monetary compensatory actual damages be given to the injured party
Criminal §1.2	an act against an individual which offends society, and thus is considered an act against society; most reprehensible — felonies, e.g. murder, rape, robbery; "lesser" crimes — misdemeanors	the public defender (government) investigates and brings action against offender on behalf of the injured victim	misdemeanors — fine and/or jail; felonies usually imprisonment without compensation to victim; however, some states have a statute providing for monetary compensation to victim
Human Rights §1.3	violation of statute or Constitutional provision guaranteeing certain rights to individuals	the government sues for compliance with statute; injured person can sue for restitution; an organization can sue on behalf of a person, e.g., ACLU	restitution (dollars, position or both) to person whose rights violated; compliance mandated; may be fine or withholding of government funds from entity which violated rights
Torts §1.4	injury to person's body, property, or reputation by another individual	unintentional acts (negligence) — injured sues one who injured (tortfeasor) as individual or corporate entity (doctrine of respondeat superior) or both; all who had anything to do with the situation likely to be sued intentional act — usually injured sues tortfeasor, doctrine not applicable	actual monetary compensatory damages; intentional torts may additionally assess punitive damages

it in perspective in regard to the various liabilities and to call attention to the field of contracts in general.

§ 1.11　Elements of contract

The basic law of contracts is as old as time itself and is rooted in common law, although statutorily, the Uniform Commercial Code (UCC) has been enacted in nearly every state. It applies primarily to business and commercial transactions, including the sale and transfer of goods, negotiable instruments (checks, bills, notes) and secured commercial transactions, banking practices and credit, warehousing, et al.

A contract is an agreement between two parties involving a promise or set of promises which the law will enforce. The parties may be referred to as promisor and promisee, offeror and offeree, or seller and buyer. The task of the law is to provide adequate remedies to persons who are injured when others fail to perform their promises. The injured party brings suit against the person who failed to perform. The remedy may be to: (1) decree specific performance in delivering a product or service (almost never required for personal services contracts, although a person may be enjoined from performing for others), (2) payment of compensatory monetary damages, (3) rescission and restitution (attempting to restore parties to original status), or (4) restoration, where mutual mistake has been made (rewriting a contract to conform to the true intention of the parties).

Contracts may be express or implied and bilateral or unilateral. The basic elements of a contract include an offer and an acceptance. There are technical considerations in what an offer is and what an acceptance is; but, the critical aspects are that if you are making an offer, it should be very specific, and if you are accepting an offer you should read the details and "fine print" very carefully. Whereas oral agreements were common place and the "gentleman's agreement" honored without question in past years, it is very desirable that every detail should be written and the document appropriately reviewed and signed by the parties involved. Under the UCC, with certain exceptions, sale of goods for $500 or more and sale of personal property of more than $5,000 must be written. Nevertheless, an oral contract can be binding when the parties reach proper agreement. A prospective assistant football coach alleged breach of oral contract and brought action against the University and head coach. Although the head coach could be a proper agent for the University, evidence indicated that the head coach did not extend employment contract (did not meet requirements of a contract).[4]

In addition to an offer and an acceptance, there must be consideration for a valid contract. Sometimes it is said that an agreement becomes a binding contract when consideration is given. Consideration is a "benefit" to one party and a "detriment" to the other. Consideration can be other than money, as long as it has value.

Not all contracts are enforceable; there must be the capacity to perform (*e.g..*, minor cannot contract) and the contract must be legal (*e.g.*, cannot violate statutory or Constitutional law). Also, contracts of adhesion (unequal bargaining power or unfair

---

[4] Bruner v. Univ. of Southern Mississippi, 510 So. 2d 1113 (Miss. 1987).

and thus against public policy) are considered unconscionable. (See §16.1 for further discussion of elements of a valid contract, as applied to exculpatory agreements.) Other unconscionable provisions include certain provisions in leases of property and sales contracts, et al., such as restrictive covenants which discriminate against persons of other races or religions.

The term "privity of contract" sometimes is used. Privity refers to the relationship which exists between the contracting parties. However, with the enactment of warranty statutes and the acceptance in some states for certain actions of the doctrine of strict liability, the absence of privity is no longer a viable defense in such situations, and third party beneficiaries and even bystanders may be able to sue for damages. (See §21.1 as related to products liability.) In a 1984 Iowa case,[5] a novelty store owner was found not to be a direct beneficiary (third party) of a contract between a basketball referee and the Big Ten. The referee made a last minute call in a game, alleged losing the game for the University of Iowa and therewith extensive novelty sales. The court held that the store owners could not maintain a cause of action. Contractual rights generally are considered assignable unless of a personal nature; however, a health spa member's exculpatory agreement was held assignable, although of a personal nature.[6]

§ 1.12   Applications of contract

The law of contracts permeates every aspect of operations. The importance of contracts rests in their everyday use in administering recreation and park systems or physical education and sport programs. Two categories of contracting are briefly described as illustrative application of contract liabilities: (1) employment contracts and (2) contracts for services and products. However, one of the most important aspects of contract law is those contracts which seek to shift financial and negligence liability. Insurance for buildings, vehicles, and operations in general, including programs and activities, is contractual and is discussed in §25.3. There, also, is transfer of financial risk by non-insurance contracts, such as indemnification clauses and requirements in contracts for insurance endorsements (see §25.2) and independent contractor relationships (see §3.12). Another contractual method of avoiding liability for negligence is through the exculpatory clause with a participant (see §16.1). See also §1.6 Business Operations and §17.41 Consumer Protection Laws.

§ 1.121   Employment contracts

Employment contracts are an essential in any operation for they set forth the terms of employment, the salary and benefits, the responsibilities and obligations. Perhaps the most visible aspect of contract, in terms of public media, is that of professional athletes' contracts; however, few individuals are involved in such contracts.[7]

---

[5] Bain v. Gillispie, 357 N.W. 2d 47 (Iowa App. 1984); for discussion of officiating malpractice, see §15.3.

[6] Petry v. Cosmopolitan Spa, Int'l, 641 S.W. 2d 202 (Tenn. App. 1982).

[7] For extensive discussion of professional contracts and collective bargaining, see Berry and Wong, Vol. I; and Weistart and Lowell. For contract application's to amateur athletic's, see Wong, Chapter 3.

One area of litigation has been that of the continuing teaching contract and extracurricular responsibilities, particularly coaching, in a school system.[8] The questions involve whether a teacher can be assigned against one's will a coaching responsibility when qualified, whether a teacher who has been coaching can be terminated from coaching when the original contract was for teaching and coaching, (*i.e.*, is a contract divisible and at whose option) and whether tenure and the continuing contract laws extend to extracurricular activities (coaching). Cases also have been brought on "due process," that is, termination without procedural due process (see also §1.34 Human rights). Generally the school administration has the right to assign extracurricular responsibilities; and, coaching assignments are not protected under state laws providing for continuing contracts; such protection is for employment, not specific tasks.

Labor relations is another aspect of contract especially as related to collective bargaining agreements between school districts or other employer and the employee. In the *Pittston* case,[9] an arbitrator's interpretation of two specific sections of a labor agreement was sustained and the school board had to pay teachers who engaged in

[8] For general discussion related to teaching and coaching in high school and college, see Arnold, Chapter 12 Staffing the Interscholastic Athletic Program; and Clement, Chapter 11 Contracts.

For example, Alabama State Tenure Comm. v. Dudley, 448 So. 2d 376 (Ala. App. 1984); Board of Educ., City of Asbury Park v. Asbury Park Educ. Assoc., 145 N.J. Super 495, 368 A. 2d 396 (1976), modified 382 A. 2d 392 (1977); Bowman v. Pulaski Co. Special School Dist., 723 F. 2d 640 (1983); Brown v. Board of Educ., Morgan Co. School Dist., 560 P. 2d 1129 (Utah 1977); Chiodo v. Board of Educ., Special School Dist. No. 1, 298 Minn. 380, 215 N.W. 2d 806 (1974); Coco v. School Comm. of Boylston, 392 Mass. 221, 466 N.E. 2d 118 (1984); DePaoli v. Board of Educ., 92 A.D. 2d 894, 459 N.Y.S. 2d 883 (1983); Dist. 300 Educ. Assoc. v. Board of Educ., Dundee Comm. School Dist. No. 300 of Kane et al. Counties, 31 Ill. App. 3d 550, 334 N.E. 2d 165 (1975); Fairchild v. Vermont State Colleges, 141 Vt. 362, 449 A. 2d 932 (1982); George v. School Dist. No. 8R, Umatilla Co., 490 P. 2d 1009 (Ore. App. 1971); Hachiya v. Board of Education, 750 P. 2d 383 (Kan. 1988); Hood v. Alabama State Tenure Comm., 418 So. 2d 131 (Ala. App. 1982); Irvin v. Board of Educ. of Holt Co., 215 Neb. 794, 340 N.W. 2d 877 (1983); Hooker v. Tufts Univ., 581 F. Supp. 104 (1983); Jackson v. Hazlehurst Municipal Separate School Dist., 427 So. 2d 134 (Miss. 1983); Knapp v. Whitaker, 577 F. Supp. 1265 (1983); Kirk v. Miller, 83 Wash. 2d 777, 522 P. 2d 843 (1974); Kondos v. W. Va. Board of Regents, 318 F. Supp. 394 (1974); Lamar School Dist. No. 39 v. Kinder, 278 Ark. 1, 642 S.W. 2d 885 (1982); Lee v. Ozark City Board of Educ., 517 F. Supp. 686 (1981) racial disc. also charged; Leone v. Kimmel, 335 A. 2d 290 (Del. Super. 1975); Lindsey v. Univ. of Arizona, 150 Ariz. 184, 722 P. 2d 352 (1986) 157 Ariz. 48, 754 P. 2d 1152 (1988); Los Angeles Comm. College Guild, Amer.

Fed. of Teachers v. Los Angeles Comm. College Dist., 150 Cal. App. 3d 88, 198 Cal. Rptr. 20 (1984); Malynn v. Morgan Hill Unified School Dist., 137 Cal. App. 30 785, 187 Cal. Rptr. 303 (1982); McCullough v. Cashmere School Dist. No. 222, Chelan Co., 15 Wash. App. 730, 551 P.2d 1046 (1976); McGrath v. Burkhard, 131 Cal. App. 2d 367, 280 P. 2d 864 (1955); Milton v. Espey, 356 So. 2d 1201 (Ala. 1978) hiring contract University Student Center; Monaco v. Raymond, 471 N.Y.S. 2d 225 (1984); Munger v. Jesup Comm. School Dist., 325 N.W. 2d 377 (Iowa 1982); Neal v. School Dist. of York, 205 Neb. 558, 288 N.W. 2d 725 (1980); Parrish v. Moss, 107 N.Y.S. 2d 580 (1951); Richards v. Board of Educ., Joint School Dist. No. 1, City of Sheboygan, 58 Wis.2d 444, 206 N.W. 2d 597 (1973); Roberts v. Wake Forest Univ., 55 N.C. App. 430, 286 S.E. 2d 120 (1982), aff'd. 292 S.E. 2d 571; Salinas v. Central Education Agency, 706 S.W. 2d 791 (Tex. App. 1986); Saraceno v. Foothills-De Anza Comm. College Dist., 127 Cal. App. 3d 850, 179 Cal. Rptr. 742 (1982); Shenefield v. Sheridan Co. School Dist., 544 P. 2d 870 (Wyo. 1976); Smith v. Board of Educ., Urbana School Dist. No. 116, Champaign Co., 708 F. 2d 258 (1983); Stang v. Indp. School Dist. No. 191 , 256 N.W. 2d 82 (Minn. 1977); State ex rel. Hawkins v. Tyler Co. Board of Educ., 275 S.E. 2d 908 (W. Va. App. 1981); Swager v. Board of Educ., Unified School Dist. 412, 9 Kan. App. 2d 648, 688 P. 2d 270 (1984); Tate v. Livingston Parish School Board, 391 So. 2d 1240 (La. App. 1980); Vail v. Board of Educ., Paris Union School Dist., No. 95, 706 F. 2d 1435 78 L. Ed. 2d 81 (1983), pet. cert. granted 80 L. Ed. 2d 377, 104 S. Ct. 66 (1984), aff'd. 104 S. Ct 2144; West Shore Education Assoc. v. West Shore School Dist., 72 Pa. Cmwlth. 374, 456 A. 2d 715 (1983); White v. Banks, 614 S.W. 2d 331 (Tenn. 1981).

[9] Pittston Area School Dist. v. Pittston Area Fed. of Teachers, 456 A. 2d 1148 (Penn. 1983).

extracurricular sports-related school activities at the extracurricular compensation rate established in the labor contract (see also §1.341 Labor relations/unions).

The nature of the employment contract also is at issue in determining workers' compensation, especially as related to sport officials and athletes (see §§25.341 and 25.343) and for all employees, whether they were within the scope of their employment (see §25.34).

§ 1.122   Contracts for services and products

While employment contracts are contracts for service, there are other types of contracts for service pertinent and important to recreation and sport enterprises. For example, there are contracts for providing a program, such as a musical;[10] for disc jockey service for a junior high prom;[11] for constructing or repairing a facility or working on an area, such as a dam and the clearing of brush and trees from the reservoir basin;[12] for maintaining vehicles or transportation (see §22.1). Tickets to events represent a type of contract between the sponsor and the participant.[13] A football player sought to hold that a football scholarship was a contractual relationship;[14] and the administratrix of estate of a student athlete brought action on contract, alleging that the president of the University, athletic director, and head football coach breached an oral contract to insure the life of student killed in a plane crash while on a recruiting trip with the coach.[15] A gymnastic varsity athlete who became a quadraplegic brought suit on contract when the University stopped payments to him for medical expenses when he sued the University.[16] Property use and rental are primary areas for contracts. In contracts for service, the relationship, whether independent contractor or lessor/lessee, determines the nature of the liability (see §3.11, 3.12).

Contracts for products are essential, particularly the purchase and sale of supplies, materials, and equipment. The setting forth of specifications of the product is critical to purchase/sale performance. Political subdivisions and schools may be controlled by state laws, particularly the bidding process and requirements thereof. Further, a number

[10] Kerner v. Hughes Tool Co., 56 Cal. App. 3d 924, 128 Cal. Rptr. 839 (1976); see also, Projects, Inc. v. Wilder, 60 N.C. App. 182, 298 S.E. 2d 434 (1982) money-making project failure and company sued for contract price. The travel & tourism industry is heavily based in contract law as related to services; for further discussion, see Cournoyer & Marshall, Chapter 8.

[11] Hebert v. Livingston Parish School Board, 438 So. 2d 1141 (La. App. 1983).

[12] Seaman Unified School Dist. No. 345, Shawnee Co. v. Casson Const. Co., 3 Kan. App. 2d 289, 594 P. 2d 241 (1979); Van Meter v. Bent Const. Co., 46 Cal. 2d 588, 297 P. 2d 644 (1956); see also, Kutztown State College v. Degler-Whiting, Inc., 76 Pa. Cmwlth. 180, 463 A. 2d 1206 (1983) scoreboard; Manshul Const. Corp. v. Dormitory Authority, 111 Misc. 2d 209, 444 N.Y.S. 2d 792 (1981) construction physical educ. building; Marston's Inc. v. Roman Catholic Church, 132 Ariz. 90, 644 P. 2d 244 (1982) synthetic gym floor installation.

[13] Circuit Court of Twelfth Judicial Circuit v. Dept. of Natural Resources, 317 So. 2d 772 (Fla. App. 1975), 339 So. 2d 1113 (1976) state park lake; Furlon v. Haystack Mountain Ski Area, 136 Vt. 266, 388 A. 2d 403 (1978) ski lift; Kearney v. Roman Catholic Church, 31 A.D. 2d 541, 295 N.Y.S. 2d 186 (1968) scout troop; Sims v. Etowah Co. Board of Educ. et al., 337 So. 2d 1310 (Ala. 1976) football spectator; Taggie v. Dept. of Natural Resources, 87 Mich. App. 752, 276 N.W. 2d 485 (1979) state park.

[14] Taylor v. Wake Forest Univ., 16 N.C. App. 117, 191 S.E. 2d 379 (1972).

[15] Greenhill v. Carpenter, 718 S.W. 2d 268 (Tenn. App. 1986) barred by doctrine of sovereign immunity. For further discussion of student-athlete contractual relationships, see Schubert, et al., §3.1 Contractual rights and obligations.

[16] Cardamone v. Univ. of Pittsburgh, 384 A. 2d 1228 (Pa. 1978).

of federal agencies, such as the Consumer Product Safety Commission, may control various products through safety regulations. Product liability suits, also, may be brought on breach of warranty (see §21.12).

In contracting or purchasing supplies, equipment, et al., because of conflict of interest, it is not desirable to purchase where one gains a personal financial benefit. Some states have laws related thereto, such as Ohio[17] which states that "A superintendent, supervisor, principal, or teacher employed...shall not act as sales agent, either directly or indirectly, for any person, firm, or corporation...for school apparatus or equipment of any kind for use in the public schools. A violation of this section shall work a forfeiture of their certificates to teach in the public schools."

§ 1.2 Criminal liability

Of increasing concern to both sport administrators and park managers is crime. Criminal liability arises out of an act against society, that is, the act against an individual is of such character as to offend society, too. Because of such character, the government prosecutes the criminal in behalf of the public, protecting common interests, rather than the individual wronged suing or attempting to bring the criminal to justice. Most individuals, additionally, would not have the money to conduct the necessary investigation to apprehend a criminal who has committed a felony.

Crimes usually are classified as felonies or misdemeanors, depending upon the nature and severity of the act. Felonies are the "most reprehensible" offenses and include murder, rape, burglary, grand larceny, robbery, and arson, while misdemeanors are the "lesser" crimes and include disorderly conduct, petit larceny, violations of fish and game laws or other outdoor use laws, traffic offenses, and various municipal ordinances. Felonies usually are punishable by state prison incarceration, while misdemeanors may result in fines or jail imprisonment or both. Normally the injured has not received compensation; however, many states[18] have passed crime victim compensation acts. Attempting to get relief, a teacher sued the school for the value of the property taken when she was robbed in the classroom at gunpoint. The issue was whether the school breached its statutory duty to provide a "reasonably safe" work environment. The robber had entered the school grounds through a hole in the fence. Held that the school could not reasonably foresee that the unrepaired hole would lead to armed robbery and thus was not liable for the teacher's loss.[19]

There is a dual system of criminal justice with both the states and the federal government having penal codes and a court system with prescribed procedures. Federal crimes involve acts against federal officials or institutions, while all other offenses usually are considered of concern to the states. However, whether state or federal offenses, or misdemeanors or felonies, the individual's rights are protected as related to arrest, evidence, et al. A person must be proven guilty "beyond a reasonable doubt."[20]

[17] Ohio Rev. Code Ann. §3329.10.

[18] For example, the federal Victims and Witness Protection Act, California, Illinois, Maryland, Massachusetts, Minnesota, New Jersey, Ohio, Nebraska. According to the National Organization for Victims

Assistance, approximately four-fifths of the states have some type of restitution or victim compensation (1983).

[19] Kavanaugh v. Orleans Parish School Board, 487 So. 2d 533 (La. App. 1986).

[20] For further understanding of the criminal justice

This section focuses primarily upon the protection and control responsibilities of a sponsoring agency as related to criminal acts and to violation of law, rather than upon crimes which might be committed by such agency or its employees. There are four aspects of particular importance to park and recreation operations and amateur and professional sport: (1) protection against felonies, (2) misdemeanors and enforcement of laws, (3) crimes of moral turpitude, and (4) violence (assault and battery). It should be noted that *where there is a duty to protect or control against crime, the failure to do so is **negligence** and the injured party may bring a suit on such basis (see §1.4 Tort liability). Most of the cases cited in this section are brought on such basis (negligence). The holdings in the cases give some guidance for operations management.*

§ 1.21 Protection against felonies

Crimes of violence against individuals, such as acts of murder, rape, and robbery, committed on public recreation and park areas or in public facilities, including schools and professional athletic facilities, became a major concern in the decade of the '80s. While most efforts to combat such violence are taken at the local level, some state legislatures have responded in a variety of ways, such as empowering park rangers with certain police powers,[21] giving designated benefits to citizens who endeavor to prevent certain crimes,[22] and authorizing use of force under specific conditions.[23] Nevertheless, it should be noted that the school, municipality, or other entity responsible for the safety of invitees/patrons may be held liable for negligence, failure to provide a safe environment.

Whereas, in 1974, the California court said that there was no duty to warn against criminal conduct for the public is aware of such incidence in unlit and little used places and further that "the disquieting spectre of warning signs for such, would not be unlike leper's bell,"[24] a decade later the California court extended the liability of public schools to criminal actions on campuses.[25] A college student was attacked in daylight by a man who jumped from behind thick, untrimmed foilage and attempted to rape her. The court said that where there were prior incidents in the same area, the school should have warned the women and trimmed the foilage; however, the court also noted that the school could raise as a defense, factors such as the probability and gravity of potential injury versus the practicality and cost of protecting against the risk of injury. After a college basketball game, a cheerleader was abducted and taken to a rock quarry where she was raped and murdered. Foreseeability and security measures taken by the college were important issues. The court held that where evidence did not show "repeated

system, see Clement, Chapter 2 The Legal System (pp. 7-19) and Woody and Associates, Chapter 2 Criminal Law (pp. 39-82) and Chapter 3 Juvenile Law (pp. 83-112); and crime as related to parks, see Frakt and Rankin at pp. 255-264 criminal law.

[21] For example, Massachusetts, Ohio, Oklahoma, South Carolina.

[22] For example, California, Delaware.

[23] For example, Alaska.

[24] Hayes v. State, 11 Cal. 3d 469, 113 Cal. Rptr. 599, 521 P. 2d 855 (1974) criminal attack on beach.

[25] Peterson v. San Francisco Comm. College Dist., 141 Cal. App. 3d 456, 190 Cal. Rtpr. 335, 36 Cal. 3d 799, 205 Cal. Rptr. 842, 685 P. 2d 1193 (1984); see also, Donnell v. Calif. Western School of Law, 200 Cal. App. 3d 715 (1988) no duty to protect adult student from attack by third party on dark, adjoining city sidewalk or to mount exterior monitors on building walls, since did not have control over sidewalks. For further discussion, see Ferrito, Leonard, and Max Bromley, *Hospital and College Security Liability*, Columbia, MD: Hanrow Press, 1987.

course of criminal activity" which would have imposed a particular duty, the security employed, specifically, at least one security officer on duty each hour of the day and regular patrol of the campus by members of the sheriff's department, was adequate.[26] The foreseeability criterion was applied in a 1984 case.[27] The court held for the plaintiff when she was attacked by an unidentified male assailant in the women's locker room on the premises of the YMCA. It was held that the defendant was aware of the potential risk to those using the locker facilities if they were left unattended and, thus, were negligent in providing such security. And, in a state park bath house a woman was criminally attacked. Inadequate lighting (both lighting not working and poorly lit) and security for park users to prevent criminal attacks were alleged.[28] Further, in a 1986 case in Hawaii, the court held that the state park owed no duty to warn or protect campers from criminal conduct when such assailants were unknown and not under state's control.[29]

Failure to provide security as related to the state tort claims acts was at issue in two additional cases.[30] In the New Jersey situation, a college student was attacked without provocation and stabbed in the abdomen. He had left the basketball game at half time when rioting broke out between black and white students to return to his dormitory. The court held that plaintiff was barred from recovery and that the college was not liable in tort for failure to protect against criminal propensity of a third person. In the other situation, two young women after a class in a building located in a remote, outlying area of the campus, about 7:20 p.m., walked to their car parked near the building entrance where they were assaulted by three men who abducted them, drove them to a secluded area, and murdered them. Again, recovery was barred by sovereign immunity, the court holding that the University's decision to provide security guards, et al. was a discretionary decision, partially based upon budgetary limitations controlled by the legislature. A ten-year-old also was murdered; she was found on a one-acre unimproved urban parcel adjacent to the park. There was no fence and park users frequently wandered onto the land, which had mounds of weed-covered dirt and patches of tall weeds and brush. The court said that such condition in itself did not pose a risk of death and failure to warn or fence off property did not constitute gross negligence, under the statute.[31]

[26] Brown v. North Carolina Wesleyan College, 309 S.E. 2d 701 (N.C. App. 1983).

[27] Montag v. YMCA of Oneida Co., 482 N.Y.S. 2d 613 (1984); see also Haddox v. Suburban Lanes, Inc., 349 S.E. 2d 910 (W. Va. 1986) shooting of patrons in bowling alley.

[28] Trevathan v. State, 740 S.W. 2d 500 (Tex. App. 1987) state protected by immunity under Tort Claims Act.

[29] Wolsk v. State, 711 P. 2d 1300 (Hawaii 1986).

[30] Relyea v. State, 385 So. 2d 1378 (Fla. App. 1980); Setrin v. Glassboro State College, 136 N.J. Super. 329, 346 A. 2d 102 (1975); see also Casey v. Geiger, 499 A. 2d 606 (Pa. Super. 1985) rape of 10-year-old in park, forcibly taken when walking in park after swim lesson, overgrown underbrush; Culter v. Board of Regents, 459 So. 2d 413 (Fla. App. 1984) security against assault and rape in dormitory; Duffy v.

City of Phila., 580 F. Supp. 164 (1983) city-owned stadium, pro football game; Rainey v. Wilmington Parking Authority, 488 A. 2d 906 (Del. Supp. 1984) assault & robbery, municipal parking facility, alleged lack of security, not barred by gov't immunity; Rodrigues v. N.J. Sport & Exposition Authority, 193 N.J. Super. 39, 472 A. 2d 146 (1983) racetrack patron robbed in parking lot; Taylor v. Centennial Bowl, 65 Cal. 2d 114, 52 Cal. Rptr. 561, 416 P. 2d 793 (1966) assaulted in bowling center parking lot; Vann v. Board of Educ., Phila., 464 A. 2d 684 (Pa. Cmwlth. 1983) unsecured fence and inadequate lighting, school property, assaulted and beaten, not foreseeable.

[31] Thomason v. Olive Branch Masonic Temple, 156 Mich. App. 736, 401 N.W. 2d 911 (1986) defendant protected by recreational user statute, weeds did not constitute willful conduct.

In a 1984 Illinois case,[32] the court held that the Village owed a duty to protect its business invitee (attendee at a rock concert), inasmuch as there was sufficient advance warning of potential trouble. The plaintiff was criminally attacked as he went to the parking area. The nature of the duty of the police was distinguished between the duty of police to preserve a community's well-being wherein the duty is general, owed to the community at large, and for which the municipality is generally not liable for failure to supply general police protection, and the undertaking of special protection to specific members of the community, which was the situation in this case. This was a voluntary undertaking for which the police then were held to owe a duty to protect against criminal attack.

Knowledge of a prior incident just 15 days earlier was a critical point in determining foreseeable risk which would hold the school liable for physical and emotional injuries arising from assault and rape on school grounds before classes. The school's duty to supervise also was in issue. A 15-year-old girl, about ready to enter the building, was grabbed from behind and dragged to some nearby bushes, where she was beaten and raped.[33] In another case[34] teachers were escorting second graders from homeroom to physical education class. The seven-year-old girl did not arrive; one of the students said she had gone back to the classroom to retrieve something. The classroom teacher, after turning the other students over to the physical education teacher, checked the homeroom and not finding her there, assumed she had returned to physical education class. In fact, she had been abducted by an unknown trespasser who took her to a nearby abandoned house and sexually assaulted her. Plaintiff recovered $51,000 in general damages. And, in a 1987 case,[35] a high school girls' basketball coach was charged with second degree sexual abuse. While traveling by bus to a game, he allegedly touched a team member on the thigh area and between her breasts. Court held for the coach, stating that the touched parts were not "intimate or sexual parts" under the statute.

The City had employed an independent contractor to operate the Convention Center. A security guard employed by the independent contractor was battered and raped while on the midnight shift (2:30 a.m.). The City was not held liable[36] (see §3.12 Independent contractor).

Two 1986 cases[37] involved shootings. In the federal case a black high school player was shot allegedly by an unknown white assailant while participating in a football game with a neighboring school. Plaintiff, who was paralyzed, brought action against the officials for failure to provide adequate security at interracial school events, alleging violation of due process rights under §1983. Court held that complaint failed to state a cause of action in that only simple negligence was alleged and the officials were not directly responsible for security at athletic field. Further, there was no allegation that the officials had knowledge of either impending attack of racial violence at previous athletic

32 Comastro v. Village of Rosemont, 122 Ill. App. 3d 405, 78 Ill. Dec. 32, 461 N.E. 2d 616 (1984).

33 Fazzolari v. Portland School Dist., 78 Or. App. 608, 717 P. 2d 1210 (1986) pet. rev. allowed 301 Or. 338, 722 P. 2d 737 (1986) aff'd. 303 Or. 1, 734 P. 2d 1326 (1987).

34 McGraw v. Orleans Parish School Board, 519 So. 2d 847 (La. App. 1988).

35 State of Oregon v. Woodley, 88 Or. App. 493, 746 P. 2d 227 (1987).

36 Rowley v. City of Baltimore, 484 A.2d 306 (Md.App. 1984).

37 Moye v. A. G. Gaston Motels, Inc., 499 So. 2d 1368 (Ala. 1986) details of events following the dance outside described in case; Williams v. Boston, 599 F. Supp. 363 (1984) aff'd. 784 F. 2d 430 (1986).

events. In the other situation, a teenager was shot as the youths were dispersing after a dance, which was sponsored by the local radio station at a motel. There had been four security guards and the facilities, including the parking lot and area in front of the motel, were checked for persons not coming to the dance and each person who entered was searched for drugs, alcohol, and weapons. The shooting occurred as a group of boys who had been at the dance drove away in their car and one shot back, hitting the decedent. Held for defendant; there was insufficient evidence to put owner on notice that criminal acts were likely to occur and thereby impose an additional duty to protect.

§ 1.22   Misdemeanors and enforcement of the law

There are two types of laws involved — those which concern anti-social behaviors, such as littering, vandalism, lewdness and indecent exposure, public drunkenness, disorderly conduct, traffic violations, and petit larceny, and those which relate directly to area and facility use, such as joggers must wear reflectorized clothing ½ hour after sunset and before sunrise, youth curfews (constitutionality upheld in *City of Milwaukee v. K.F,* 145 Wis.2d 24, 426 N.W.2d 329 (1988)), building improper fires, hiking in prohibited areas, violation of hunting and fishing laws, park regulations et al. Particularly in the latter type, often there may be a lack of notice, while in the first there may be vagueness in the law, that is, a lack of specificity as to the nature of the behavior to which the law is directed. Nevertheless, the enforcement of the law is essential to preserving the values and quality of the recreation experience and the physical resources. Not all professional personnel have authority to make arrests; only those park police, stadium security personnel, game wardens or forest rangers, et al. who are appropriately deputized can make arrests; however, all personnel can call attention to violations and should be concerned about law enforcement (see also §1.532).

Hazing. It should be noted that at least 12 states as of 1985 had passed laws that make it a crime to allow hazing. Additionally, some of these states also established civil liability, where a person who is hazed may sue the person who did the hazing, the organization involved, and the college administrators who knew or should have known the hazing would take place. *Harden v. U.S.,* 485 F. Supp. 380 (1980), relates both to hazing and act of a park ranger in shooting a 15-year-old being hazed by a fraternity. The hazing took place in a campground in a reservior management area operated by the Corps of Engineers. The ranger had been called by the occupants of the campground. The court held for the plaintiff, saying that the ranger failed to exercise ordinary care and diligence when he thrust a loaded, cocked revolver from window of moving vehicle in attempt to fire "warning shot" which hit boy when vehicle stalled. The Corps had provided little or no formal training to ranger. The victim was found to be 25% of the proximate cause of his own fatal injury.[38]

§ 1.221   Intoxication

Intoxication is a problem of long-standing in recreation and sport situations, and

----

[38] See also §10.22 on hazing as related to school activities.

efforts to give responsibility for injuries which occur to the vendor, employer, or social host date back to the turn of the century.[39] Concern in the mid-'80s has focused upon the injuries occasioned by vehicle accidents due to intoxication; however, of equal importance to recreation and sport are the injuries inflicted by spectators and patrons to themselves and others. The various states have attempted to curtail injuries through alcohol beverage control statutes, including dramshop acts, "driving under the influence" (DUI) statutes, host liquor laws, boating-while-intoxicated laws, and age restrictions related to purchase/drinking laws. (See Appendix for some statute citations.) Liability of commerical vendors, employers, and social hosts for torts of the intoxicated has been imposed under two theories of negligence: (a) negligence *per se* for violations of the alcohol beverage control statutes, and (b) common law negligence.[40]

Intoxication can be an intervening cause releasing defendant from liability. Such was the situation in *Craine v. U.S.*[41] The Government had rented a boat, but failed to warn boater of the dam spillway and a couple of days later the boat was swept over the dam. However, it was found that the intervening sole proximate cause was the intoxication of the operator which "excused" the negligence of the Government. The Coast Guard estimated in 1985 that approximately one-half of the annual boating accidents were alcohol-related. By 1985, 16 states had passed laws related to boating-while-intoxicated, and another 16 states had bills pending. The toughest laws have been enacted by Florida, Maryland, and Pennsylvania.

In the late '80s there was court activity relating to determination that alcoholism is a willful misconduct[42] and, on the other hand, that alcoholism is a disease. Either determination has considerable impact on plaintiff's recovery of awards and on defendant responsibilities.[43]

§ 1.2211   Dramshop Laws

In the mid-1980s approximately two-thirds of the states had dramshop laws making the vendor of alcoholic beverages liable for the actions of their patrons under certain situations. While bars and liquor stores are the target of the laws, the term bar

[39] Mastad v. Swedish Brethren, 83 Minn. 40, 85 N.W. 913 (1901) defendant held picnic at lake, sold tickets, undertook to protect persons so invited from assaults by drunken people, judgment for plaintiff, one who sells liquor to one in attendance, thereby rendering him drunk and disorderly, foreseeable that assault be committed.

[40] See Erickson, Jon R., and Donna H. Hamilton. Comments: Liability of Commerical Vendors, Employers, and Social Hosts for Torts of the Intoxicated. 19 *Wake Forest Law Review* 1013-1048 (1983). For further discussion, see Cournoy v. Marshall, Chapter 12.

[41] Craine v. U.S., 722 F. 2d 1523 (1984).

[42] For example, Zavala v. Regents of the Univ. of Calif., 125 Cal. App. 3d 646, 178 Cal. Rptr. 185 (1981) plaintiff and friend went to a private informal party at a dormitory on college campus; after an evening of

drinking asked directions to the rest-room, but decided to go outside and went through door at end of hallway marked "exit"; door lead to stairway from fourth floor to concrete balcony halfway between floors; balcony had a 43" concrete wall, 8" thick, which plaintiff 5'4" tall fell over; the jury question raised was whether plaintiff by voluntary intoxication was guilty of willful misconduct when he was a young and inexperienced drinker who did not understand effect alcohol would have on him. Court stated that willful misconduct did not bar application of comparative negligence doctrine.

[43] Check for developments. See discussion on drug testing as related to similar testing for alcohol as concerns invasion of privacy (§§1.331, 1.4121). This is to be distinguished from drunken driving testing. Also, alcohol abuse and alcohol rules for athletes should be distinguished from intoxication as presented in this section.

encompasses those operated by recreation and sport enterprises, whether public or private. Some states[44] have license laws specific to recreation and sport enterprises. Dramshop laws generally are applicable only to commerical vendors; however, some broadly worded acts[45] include employers and social hosts. Insurance usually is used to cover liability (see §25.3).

In order for liability to exist, it is usually required that the defendant sold or provided alcoholic beverages to an intoxicated person or a person underage, that the alcohol caused or contributed to, in part or whole, to the impairment of the individual, and that the plaintiff's injury was proximately caused by the impairment of the intoxicated individual. The imposition of liability of commerical vendors is a matter of social philosophy by legislatures, in that such liability should be a deterrent to sale of alcohol to the two classes of persons (minors and intoxicated) and in that it is more equitable to impose the cost of injuries on those making a profit from the sale of the beverage which caused the intoxication (which in turn caused the injury) than on an innocent, injured third party. While damages may be sought against the intoxicated person (tortfeasor), only too often such person is judgment proof (has no money!).

In a 1984 Pennsylvania case,[46] a minor became intoxicated on an evening cruise, which was part of an annual community entertainment event. She was seriously injured in a one-car accident as she drove home and sued the festival sponsor, the ferry system, and the city police and fire departments. The court found a cause of action against the festival sponsor with determination of proximate cause for the jury. The plaintiff had alleged negligence *per se* for the sponsor selling liquor to a minor. However, where the sale was to a minor not intoxicated, who gave the liquor to the driver, there was no liability.[47]

Most dramshop actions involve vehicle accidents; however, in a Michigan case[48] it was a shooting. Both dramshop and common law negligence actions were brought against school district, its booster club, and a bar for the death of decedent, who was killed by an allegedly visibly intoxicated person who had been served alcoholic beverages by a high school athletic booster organization at its fundraiser, as well as at the bar. Decedent was estranged from her husband and attended the event with another person, who had accompanied her to a bar prior to and following the event. Decedent and companion returned to her home, went to the bedroom and an argument ensued, whereupon companion shot decedent and then killed himself. Plaintiffs' alleged the companion was visibly intoxicated at the fundraiser and at the bar and should not have been sold drinks, which was the proximate cause of decedent's death at the hand of the companion. The court held that the school district could be held vicariously liable under

44 e.g., Connecticut.
45 e.g., Iowa, Minnesota. Nearly one-half of the states enacted or amended dram shop laws in 1986 and 1987. A model act was drafted in 1985 — the Model Alcoholic Beverage Retail License Act of 1985; for text and commentary, see 12:2 *Western State Univ. Law Review* 442-517, spring 1985.
46 Torres v. Salty Sea Days, Inc., 36 Wash. App. 668, 676 P. 2d 512 (1984); see also, Maro v. Potash, 220 N.J. Super. 90, 531 A. 2d 407 (1987) sports tickeᵗ

holder assaulted and harassed by another ticket holder at sports complex; stadium concessionaire sued for serving alcoholic beverages to one who assaulted plaintiff.
47 Strang v. Cabrol, 37 Cal. 3d 720, 209 Cal. Rptr. 347, 691 P. 2d 1013 (1984); see also Duluth Superior Excursions, Inc. v. Makela, 623 F. 2d 1251 (1980).
48 Kerry v. Turnage, 154 Mich. App. 275, 397 N.W. 2d 543 (1986).

dramshop provision of the State Liquor Control Act for actions of the athletic booster club. It was further held that no common law action existed for negligence, as the dramshop action was exclusive remedy.

In some states[49] commercial vendors may be held liable for accidents caused by drunken customers even in the absence of a statute on the basis of common law negligence. Where an otherwise valid exculpatory clause may have been signed (see §16.1), such was held unenforceable as against public policy if the state had a dramshop act.[50]

§ 1.2212   Host liquor liability

While host liquor liability usually is applied to social hosts and private parties, it has been applied to employee parties and sponsored social functions. There are two aspects of host liquor liability as related to employees, when an intoxicated employee injures a third party and when the intoxicated employee injures oneself. The employee becomes intoxicated on alcoholic beverages served by the employer, usually at a social event. In a 1983 case[51] an 18-year-old employee was served alcoholic beverage at the company-sponsored Christmas party and he became intoxicated. He obtained his car keys from a company employee and on his way home collided with another vehicle, resulting in his total and permanent disability. The court found the company liable on negligence *per se*, distinguishing that this was a minor and noting that the Pennsylvania Crimes Code regarding an adult supplying a minor alcoholic beverages was violated. However, the court noted that in Pennsylvania, an 18-year-old can be both presumptively capable of negligence and liable as an adult for the summary offense of consuming alcohol. Liability was found in a California case,[52] where an employee became intoxicated, also at a Christmas party, and on the way home, due to drunken driving, injured plaintiff. The court held that such injury was reasonably foreseeable, and although it occurred away from the premises, it was held to be within his scope of employment, and the doctrine of respondeat superior applied (see §3.41).

The social host law was applied to a school district in Michigan, insulating the school from liability, and precluding plaintiff's action on lack of supervision. The vocational technical school held a bowl-a-thon at a local bowling alley from 11 p.m. to 2:30 a.m. It was sponsored by the student senate to raise money for school functions. The advisor to the student senate was the only faculty member present. No other members of the general public were bowling at the time. The two fellows (plaintiffs) were seen that evening to be obviously intoxicated while attempting to bowl and were requested to

[49] e.g., in 1984 courts in Arizona, Minnesota, North Carolina, Oregon, Wyoming so held; for example, Hawkins v. Conklin, 87 Or. App. 392, 742 P. 2d 672 (1987).

[50] Scheff v. Homestretch, Inc., 60 Ill. App. 3d 424, 18 Ill. Dec. 152, 377 N.E. 2d 305 (1978).

[51] Congini v. Portersville Valve Co., 312 Pa. Sup. 461, 458 2d 1384 (1983) modified 470 A. 2d 515 (Pa. 1983); discussed in 57 Temple Law Quarterly 453-464 (1984).

[52] Harris v. Trojan Fireworks Co., 120 Cal. App. 3d 157, 174 Cal. Rptr. 452 (1981); discussed in 19 Wake Forest Law Review 1013 (1983) at p. 1026; see also Gariup Constr. Co. v. Foster, 497 NE. 2d 924 (Ind. App. 1986) Christmas party, employee engaged in "drinking game" consuming 6-8 shots of 80 proof whiskey in 30-40 minute period, then immediately left to pick up wife, auto accident enroute, injured in other car brought action against company.

leave by the bowling alley manager and the faculty advisor helped remove the two young men; however, later he denied noticing any evidence of intoxication. Shortly after the removal, police found the fellows in a one-car roll-over accident.[53]

The school district had requested two deputies from the Parish sheriff's office to be assigned to a high school dance being held following a football game. Despite rules forbidding students to consume alcoholic beverages during school-sponsored events, plaintiff did so and became intoxicated. Toward the end of the evening, he went to the parking lot where he became sick. He was sitting on a truck and was told to get off. When driver later returned to his truck, he was not aware plaintiff had fallen under the truck and ran over him, severely injuring him. There was no liability on the part of the deputies for failure to detect presence of student under the truck as their duty was to a general public and not to individuals; plaintiff did not show that a special duty was owed him.[54]

Many states have enacted tougher criminal penalties and civil sanctions related to drunken-driving, and in 1984 the courts appeared to join the legislatures in broadly applying host liquor laws and the liability of those who serve gratuitous drinks.[55] Some states,[56] however, have not extended liability to non-commercial hosts, relying on the old common law rule. It holds that it is the negligent consumption of alcohol, not the sale or provision, that causes intoxicated people to injure themselves and others. A 1985 California case[57] applied some basic legal principles, stating a social host has the right to have negligence apportioned under comparative negligence, may be more than one negligent act contributing to proximate cause, and the effect of nonfeasance.

§ 1.2213   Responsibility toward students and youth participants

The responsibility of schools and youth organizations for enforcement of the state alcoholic beverage control statutes, specifically as applicable to minors, is affected by the mores of the times and the changing role of such institutions and agencies. A college-student relationship in the decade of the '80s is no longer that of *in loco parentis* (see §2.1112).[58] Also, the control of student off-campus activities is very difficult.[59] The

[53] Beseke v. Garden Center, Inc., 401 N.W. 2d 428 (Minn. App. 1987).

[54] Lowe v. Patterson, 492 So. 2d 110 (La. App. 1986) writ denied 496 So. 2d 355 (La. 1986).

[55] e.g., in New Jersey, as indicated in cases of preceding paragraph. Mitseff v. Wheeler, 38 Ohio St. 3d 112, 526 N.E. 2d 798 (1988) social host has duty to refrain from furnishing alcohol to minor and may be liable for damages to third person injured in auto accident involving minor.

[56] e.g., California passed legislation eliminating social host liability for injuries resulting from intoxication of guest; some states, e.g., New Jersey, modified the law; check your own state.

[57] Sagadin v. Ripper, 175 Cal. App. 3d 1141, 221 Cal. Rptr. 675 (1985); see also Murphy v. Muskegon County, 162 Mich. App. 609, 413 N.W. 2d 73 (1987) motorcyclists sued county for injuries when cycles hit cable on abandoned county road, the two intoxicated

were held 96% and 99% negligent under comparative negligence.

[58] Campbell v. Board of Trustees, Wabash College, 495 N.E. 2d 227 (Ind. App. 1986) after having consumed alcoholic beverages (purchased by male friend) all night in male friend's fraternity room, plaintiff was injured in auto accident enroute back to her own room at nearby college, her male friend driving was intoxicated, court held for college and fraternity stating that they were "not expected to assume a role anything akin to in loco parentis or a general insurer." Beach v. Univ. of Utah, 726 P. 2d 413 (Utah 1986) no special relationship requiring protection, 20-year-old student wandered from campsite and fell off cliff at night when on university-sponsored field trip from voluntary intoxication, on free time, behavior not of type to alert leaders to give rise to duty.

[59] Irani, Rita Mankovich. Torts — Negligent Supervision — College Liability — Student Intoxica-

vendor of the alcoholic beverage was held liable, but the college was not held liable when the driver lost control of his vehicle due to intoxication of his passenger, another student, who was injured. He was returning from the annual sophomore class picnic and was 18 years of age. The class president, also under the legal drinking age, purchased the beer. Publicity on the picnic (flyers posted over campus) contained prominently displayed beer mugs. No faculty advisor or other faculty member of the college attended the picnic, although the advisor participated in planning and signed the check which was subsequently used to purchase the beer. The court discussed the rights and privileges accorded persons over 18 and distinguished responsibility for younger youth and children. It also discussed notice for the need to supervise[60] (see also §15.333). In a 1981 California college situation, the court did not hold the college liable for injuries sustained in a speed contest which occurred after drinking on University premises. The court said that even though the University had the right to terminate a student's occupancy in the dormitory on short notice for violation of rules, including rules against drinking, the University was not liable for damages suffered by plaintiff, where conduct of students, with no known violent propensities and without knowledge that they would drink to excess and thereafter operate motor vehicles, did not rise to the level of foreseeable harm.[61]

A fraternity was held liable ($250,000) in the death of a pledge due to acute alcohol intoxication with a terminal aspiration of his gastric contents. The entire initiation party involved drinking in a variety of activities (detailed in the case opinion) where the pledges were forced by harassment and psychological manipulation to consume enormous quantities of alcoholic beverages. When decedent passed out, he was placed on a couch. One and a half hours later, although fraternity brothers discussed taking him to the infirmary due to his pale color and lack of responsiveness, he was left lying face down and unconscious on the couch. In the morning he was found dead.[62]

A high school was held not liable for an injury which occurred due to intoxication at a party on the basis that the activity in which the student was engaged was ultra vires and that no "special relationship" was established to make the school liable. In this 1985 case,[63] the court noted that under the State of Washington's statute abrogating immunity, school districts are liable according to "normal rules of tort law." The seniors had a "release day" and it was at this event that the drinking took place. The court said that mere knowledge by faculty advisor and principal that the students had planned a party at which alcohol was to be consumed could not render the school district liable in negligence for death of student in automobile accident upon returning from such party, where no district employee or agent was present at party or participated in any way with its planning, and faculty advisor had in fact expressly registered her

---

tion Injury. 19 *Duquesne Law Review* 381-395 (1981); discusses Bradshaw case. Territo and Bromley (cited in footnote 25) sets forth four roles of universities as related to alcohol and student conduct: supervisor of student conduct, proprietor, seller, and social host.

[60] Bradshaw v. Rawlings, 464 F. Supp. 175 (1979), 612 F. 2d 135 (1979), cert. denied 100 S. Ct. 1836 (1980). Wiener v. Gamma Phi Chpt. of ATO, 485 P. 2d 18 (Ore. 1971) serving alcohol to minor guest at ranch

party knowing would be driving home held unreasonable.

[61] Baldwin v. Zoradi, 123 Cal. App. 3d 275, 176 Cal. Rptr. 809 (1981).

[62] Ballou v. Sigma Nu General Fraternity, 352 S.E. 2d 488 (S.C. App. 1986).

[63] Rhea v. Grandview School Dist., 694 P. 2d 666 (Wash. App. 1985); see also Beseke case in preceding subsection.

disapproval of students' plans and reported the incident to the principal. The school had been authorized to totally release the seniors from custody and control under the "noninstructional purposes" provision of statute authorizing release of seniors during last five school days, and thus the activity was considered out of the scope of school's authority. It was acknowledged that liability attaches when schools supervise and exercise control over extracurricular activities. The court said further that exceptions to the general rule of nonliability for furnishing intoxicants to able-bodied persons exist for obviously intoxicated persons, persons in state of helplessness, or persons in special relationship to furnisher of intoxicants.

Of concern is drinking in a park, and a 1985 Washington case[64] addressed this issue. Three minors paid $1 fee to enter park and drove to an isolated area out of view of park personnel where others were drinking alcoholic beverages. They consumed 48 12-ounce cans of beer, about equally divided among them. At closing time the park official gave notice to the youths and others of the park's impending closure and directed their transportation to the public roadway. About three to four miles outside the park, the intoxicated youth turned into the path of an oncoming motorcyle driven by the plaintiff. The county officials knew the area was used regularly by many people, including minors, for the consumption of alcoholic beverages; a sign was posted notifying visitors that liquor was banned from the park. The caretaker told people it was banned and the three youths were aware of the ban. It was conceded that it was difficult to apprehend violators because they could easily see approaching law enforcement officers from a long distance. The court held that: (1) the county did not have the common-law duty to prevent the minor from becoming intoxicated in the park; (2) the liquor control statutes did not impose a duty upon the county to prevent the minor from drinking in the park so as to establish that the failure to do so amounted to negligence *per se* for violation of law; (3) the motorcyclist was not within the class of persons protected by the statute; and (4) the county was not liable for the actions of the minor where there was no allegation or evidence that any county employee made direct contact with the minor individually and assumed responsibility for his conduct.

Disciplining youth for drinking, also, is a concern of administration, both in terms of Constitutional right of due process[65] and appropriateness of the punishment.[66] Three students consumed alcohol en route to a high school football game and were suspended from school, in the *Claiborne* case. The school policy that provided that any student using alcohol "prior to" coming on school grounds or to school sponsored events would be expelled from school for one semester was held to be unconstitutionally vague and overbroad. In the *Tomlinson* case two students were expelled for ten days, directed to participate in a ten-week counseling program (external to the school), and could not

---

[64] Hostetler v. Ward, 41 Wash. App. 343, 704 P. 2d 1193 (1985); case also discusses nuisance theory, public-duty doctrine, actionable negligence.

[65] Wood v. Strickland, 348 F. Supp. 244, rev./remanded 485 F. 2d 186, 420 U.S. 308, 95 S. Ct. 992 (1975), rehearing denied 421 U.S. 921, 95 S. Ct. 1589 (1975); Claiborne v. Beebe School Dist., 687 F. Supp. 1358 (1988).

[66] Tomlinson v. Pleasant Valley School Dist., 479

A. 2d 1169 (Pa. Cmwlth. 1984); Katzman v. Cumberland Valley School Dist., 479 A. 2d 671 (Pa. Cmwlth. 1984); in Blaine v. Moffat County School Dist., 709 P. 2d 96 (Colo. App. 1986) aff'd. 748 P. 2d 1280 (Colo. 1988) teacher dismissed for neglect of duty when she allowed cheerleaders, including underaged, to drink beer at motel room where they were staying, and drank beer with them.

participate in extra-curricular activities the remainder of the school year for drinking a soft drink containing whiskey; the court modified the penalty on the basis of its being excessive. The girls were cheerleaders and at the junior varsity football game they were offered a drink from a Pepsi-Cola bottle by a student from a different school. Each girl took a sip and, realizing that the soft drink was mixed with whiskey, they, nevertheless, each took a second sip. Their cheerleading coach was informed of this and promptly reported them to the proper authorities, who issued an immediate ten-day suspension; and, after a hearing was held before the Board, the other penalties were instituted. The girls were good students with no prior discipline problems. The penalty was modified by lifting the suspension and, providing that the girls attend a counseling program within the school, they could continue in activities. In the *Katzman* case, an eleventh grade student while on a field trip joined four other students in ordering and drinking a glass of wine in a restaurant. On later questioning by the school authorities, she admitted the incident, whereupon she was suspended for five days, excluded from classes, expelled from the cheerleading squad, prohibited from taking part in school activities during the suspension period, permanently expelled from the National Honor Society, and reduced grades in all classes by two percentage points for each day of suspension (10 points). The court held that the reduction of grades was a misrepresentation by a school board of a student's academic achievement for reasons irrelevant to academic achievement being graded. She was to have had an option of Saturday work as an alternative to lowering grades, but this had been denied to her.

§ 1.2214   Protecting the intoxicated and patrons

Considerations in protecting the intoxicated and patrons include protecting the patron against injury to oneself because of impaired functioning due to intoxication, protecting against other intoxicated patrons who are participating, and protecting against other patrons who attack or become more violent in injuring another person. Generally, one who conducts activity is expected to note the condition of the participant and take precautions regarding the safety of that individual (see §19.13). Most of the cases, however, do not come in conducted activity, but when one is engaged in activity as an individual. The question, then, is what duty does the supervising person have. A number of cases[67] involve diving into water which is too shallow for the dive. The results have been varied. Where there is a duty owed, the intoxicated swimmer's action may be held to be contributorily negligent. In the *Denham* case, the plaintiff was held 30% contributorily negligent under comparative negligence law when he dived into a lake; and, the question also was raised as to contributory negligence in the *Rainey* case in which plaintiff dived into the shallow end of the city pool while at a private night swim party. In another private party at a health club, plaintiff also dived into the shallow end. The court also held plaintiff guilty of contributory negligence and stated that there was

---

[67] Brown v. Southern Ventures Corp., 331 So. 2d 207 (La. App. 1976) motel swim pool coping or slanted tile border loose; Chidester v. U.S., 646 F. Supp. 189 (1986) California law applied, dived into creek in national forest; Denham v. U.S., 646 F. Supp. 1021 (1986) aff'd. 834 F. 2d 518 (1987) lake swimmer, Texas law applied; Mullery v. Ro-Mill Constr. Corp., 76 A.D. 2d 802, 429 N.Y.S. 2d 200 (1980) private health club; Rainey v. East Point, 173 Ga. App. 893, 328, S.E. 2d 567 (1985) city pool.

insufficient evidence to establish any special duty on the part of club toward member, that is, the club did not know nor should it have known that the member was so intoxicated that he was unable to take care of himself so as to impose that special duty. When the dive is into a natural body of water, then statutes may determine the liability, such as in the *Chidester* and *Denham* cases. Under the various statutes, one usually has to prove that the defendant was grossly negligent or the act was willful and malicious (see §12.1 and Chapter 14). Where there is a defective premise, such as in the *Brown* situation, liability will rest in negligence for such defective premise as the proximate cause of injury. In a 1987 case,[68] which did not involve water, the question was whether the defendant's alleged negligence was the proximate cause of injury. An intoxicated student, while patron at football game at the University stadium, vaulted over a 4' wall and fell approximately 30' onto concrete steps. The court held that the University's failure or inability to enforce its prohibition of alcoholic beverages in stadium was not solely responsible for injuries.

When a patron is intoxicated, there is a tendency just to "throw them out." The decedent and friend paid the admission fee and entered the roller rink. At that time it was obvious that decedent was in a drug and/or alcohol induced state of mental and physical incapacitation. As they sat at the snack bar, such incapacitation also was obvious; nevertheless, the manager ejected decedent from the premises. His social companions aided him into his automobile and drove the car to a location 300' from the premises. The friends left decedent in the car asleep or unconscious in the back of the vehicle as they went back to skate. The manager permitted the friends to return to the car to check without requiring payment for readmission. The decedent remained in the back of the unheated automobile into the early morning hours in February (Michigan). Then, when on one visit to the car, the friends found decedent had gone. The manager and some friends drove in a car looking for him for a while, then abandoned the search until the next day. Decedent was found behind a nearby building, lying face down in the snow. Autopsy revealed he died of shock and exposure from the cold. The court held that the roller rink defendant owed no duty to aid individual who came onto premises in incapacitated condition due to consumption of alcohol and who was escorted from premises by his social companions who were not in such condition. Acts of defendant did not place incapacited individual in worse situation.[69]

When an invitee comes upon a commerical premises of another and passes out cold on the floor, whether through illness, injury or drunkenness, the owner or operator of the premises cannot ignore the inert figure lying in a dangerous place and has an affirmative duty to take at least some minimal steps to safeguard the inert figure. However, the owner is not required to take any action beyond that which is reasonable under the circumstances, which usually for injury or illness is to give first aid and turn over to appropriate persons who will look after the person. There is no requirement to give aid to one who is in the hands of apparently competent persons who have taken charge or whose friends are present and apparently in a position to give necessary assistance. In

[68] Allen v. Rutgers, State University of N.J., 216 N.J. Super. 189, 523 A. 2d 262 (1987).

[69] Dumka v. Quaderer, 151 Mich. App. 68, 390 N.W. 2d 200 (1986); see also Martin v. Philadelphia Gardens, 348 Pa. 232, 35 A. 2d 317 (1944).

Personal Representative v. Fisherman's Pier,[70] the court held that there was a cause of action when a drunken, passed-out customer (Starling) was left alone lying on a commerical pier in early hours of the morning close to the ocean and in imminent danger of rolling over unrestrained into water with full knowledge of defendant's employee, and in fact customer did so fall in and was drowned. Total incapacity of drunk rendered duty on operator.

In a 1987 case,[71] a 16-year-old suffered a disabling spinal injury while attending a rock concert and dance at defendant's sports pavilion. During the first two nights of the concert, one or more fights erupted and on both nights there was evidence of alcoholic beverages being consumed on the premises even though many of the concert-goers were minors. On this evening, plaintiff, a friend of the band, to heighten the frenzied atmosphere, as he had done previous nights, donned a wolf's head mask and simulated banging his head in an attempt to get the crowd involved. Plaintiff was joined by members of the audience in simulating group head-banging. While this ritual was in progress, plaintiff was approached from behind by a person, obviously intoxicated, to supposedly perform the ritual, too, but who shook plaintiff violently, allegedly causing a severe spinal cord injury. The court held that the owner had no duty to protect dancer plaintiff against how allegedly intoxicated patron danced and did not proximately cause injuries.

What is the duty owed when intoxicated patrons attack other patrons outside the building? The patrons were attending a "midnight madness" bowling extravaganza. One group, the plaintiffs, and another group had heated and loud repartee and at the end two members of plaintiffs' group went to tell the manager on duty and indicated the other group was drunk, loud, unruly, et al. and requested that the manager "keep an eye" on them. Thereafter, the one group continued to harass, taunt, and cause some difficulty. When the alley closed at 2:30 a.m., the plaintiff's group delayed until the other group had left the building and were the last patrons to leave. A violent melee occurred in the parking lot when the other group, which had waited, accosted plaintiff's group and plaintiff was beaten into unconsciousness. The manager and his assistant took little action either inside or outside. Plaintiff brought action alleging that proprietor of alley was negligent in failing to insure safety and welfare of patrons on premises, as required by Georgia law. It was for jury to determine whether proprietor should have been aware of potential physical altercation between the two groups of patrons before it actually occurred; if so, then there was a duty to take action to avoid such altercation.[72]

See §15.1232 for discussion regarding actions of intoxicated spectators. Although there is a duty to protect, go to the aid of an intoxicated person in danger, as described in the preceding paragraph, the Vermont court held in a 1981 case[73] that its Aid to Endangered Act did not create a duty to try to stop a fight.

[70] Personal Representative, Estate of Starling v. Fisherman's Pier, 401 So. 2d 1136 (Fla. App. 1981). Discussed in Kushner, Roberta. Liability of Commercial Premises Owners to Injured Invitees: Estate of Starling v. Fisherman's Pier. 6 *Nova Law Journal* 535-522 (1982).

[71] Levangie v. Dunn, 182 Ga. App. 439, 356 S.E. 2d 88 (1987).

[72] Bishop v. Fair Lanes Georgia Bowling, Inc., 803 F. 2d 1548 (1986) Georgia law applied; see also Maksinczak v. Salliotte, 140 Mich. App. 537, 364 N.W. 2d 737 (1985) woman was attacked by an intoxicated woman while attending a fireworks display organized by the city and park owner, plaintiff failed to show existence of duty to prevent the attack.

[73] State v. Joyce, 139 Vt. 638, 433 A. 2d 271 (1981).

§ 1.23   Crimes of moral turpitude

There are two types of moral turpitude behavior presented in this section. The first, gambling and bribery, while sometimes involving athletes, is primarily the behavior of other persons; while the second, drugs, is oriented essentially to the athletes.

§ 1.231   Gambling and bribery

Both amateur and professional sports are concerned with gambling and bribery. Gambling related to sporting events is of long standing and there has been considerable public regulation thereof.[74] Bribery is closely related and, also, has been subject to federal and state laws.[75] In Rhode Island, whereas bribing a public official is a misdemeanor, it is a felony with a possible seven-year jail sentence for bribing a basketball referee. New Hampshire also makes bribery of a sports official a felony.

§ 1.232   Drugs

The concern of the sports world related to drugs is of two dimensions. One is the use of drugs to enhance performance and the other is chemical dependency by the athletes. The drug testing program of the Olympics and related tournaments and meets for amateur athletes is well-known. The use of performance enhancing drugs usually is not subject to criminal prosecution; however, increasingly in the late '80s, states are passing laws relating to the use and dispensing of anabolic steroids; for example, Florida, Indiana, Louisiana (see statutes of states in Appendix). See §1.331 for further discussion of drug testing athletes.

Particularly in the decade of the '80s, both collegiate and professional sports have endeavored to identify chemically dependent athletes. While some athletes are dismissed from the team, efforts are made to place addicted athletes in a treatment program. The National Basketball Assocation and its Player Association in 1983 signed a pact as an addendum to the collective bargaining agreement which provides for drug tests and disciplinary action. Because chemical dependency is a chronic relapsing disorder, follow-up counselling programs are being established for recovering addicts. In fall 1984, the National Federation of State High School Federation Associations began seminars on chemical health education for coaches, officials, and students. In mid-1985 Commissioner Ueberroth instituted a mandatory drug testing program for major league personnel from owners to bat boys and secretaries. Testing of players is controlled in agreement with the Players' Association.[76]

Chemical dependency also includes use of alcoholic beverages (see §1.221). In substance abuse, whether drugs or alcohol, it must be remembered that when there is violation of any law, the athlete, as any non-athlete, is subject to prosecution. Treatment and rehabilitation programs instituted are reflective of the concern for the athlete and the

[74] For further discussion with references, see Weistart and Lowell at §2.20, Berry and Wong, Vol. II, sec. 5.70 et seq.; and Wong, pp. 647-656.

[75] For example, Alabama, California, Colorado, Maryland, Nevada, New Hampshire, New York, North Dakota, Oregon, Rhode Island.

[76] For further discussion, see Berry and Wong, Vol. II, sec. 5.60 et seq., and Wong, Chapter 12.

image of sport by the team management. They are not legally mandated, although a judge may order a rehabilitation program for an offender of the law brought to court.

Another aspect of concern to the sport world, especially professional sports, is that of drug trafficking. As of mid-1985 a number of professional past and present star athletes have been sentenced on criminal charges related to drug trafficking. There have been charges of entrapment by the government officials in order to obtain evidence.[77]

Not to be overlooked is drug testing in the workplace. (See §1.342).

§ 1.24 Violence (criminal assault and battery)

Assault and battery are acts which can be either or both a crime and an intentional tort (see §1.4132), that is, the same act may be both a tort against an individual and a crime against the state. In such instances there may be both a civil tort action and a criminal prosecution for the same offense. The term aggravated battery is sometimes used for battery of a criminal nature, inasmuch as there is an unlawful act of violent injury punishable as a felony. And, assault may be a crime when the assault is done with intent to commit a crime. While assault and battery, the crime and the tort, may be tried successively or at the same time, a decision for or against the defendant in one is not conclusive as to the other.

While assault and battery of public "servants" is made a specific crime in some states,[78] the assault and battery by third persons of users of park and recreation areas and facilities is of concern and appropriate general supervision to deter such must be provided (see §18.323), the focus of this section is violence in sport. Acts of assault and battery in sport can be directed toward the spectators, the officials, and the players by the spectators, officials, and players. For situations relating to injuries to spectators by spectators, see §15.123, by players §15.15, by employees §15.16, and by officials §15.312; and for injuries to officials, see §15.322. These assault and battery actions are nearly all in the field of intentional tort. Some states,[79] though, have enacted laws making attacks on sport officials a crime. However, it is player violence, player against player, that has given rise, beginning particularly in the mid-'70s, to the question of criminal actions for injuries due to such violence. There have been extensive writings on the subject.[80]

Injuries to one player by another have traditionally been handled under civil law, either negligence and the doctrine of assumption of risk (see §5.22 and specific sports) or the intentional tort of assault and battery (see §1.41322), specifically, reckless disregard for the safety of others. The suggestions that injuries be dealt with in the

---

[77] E.g., Johnson v. State, 446 So. 2d 103 aff'd. 447 So. 2d 284 (Fla. App. 1983) affirms Rotenberry v. State of Florida, 429 So. 2d 378 (Fla. App. 1983).

[78] For example, Illinois, Massachusetts.

[79] For example, Oklahoma (1978) provides for up to 6 months in the county jail or $500 fine or both, extends to reporters, players, coaches, et al.

[80] See Berry and Wong, Vol. II Chapter 5 and Wong, pp. 290-297. For further discussion and bibliographical and case citations, see: Carroll, John F, Torts in Sports — "I'll See You in Court!" 16 Akron Law Review 537-565, winter 1983; Horrow, Rick, Sports Violence: The Interaction Between Private Lawmaking and the Criminal Law, Arlington, Va.: Carrollton Press, 1980; Rains, Cameron J., Sports Violence: A Matter of Societal Concern, 55 The Notre Dame Lawyer 796-813, June 1980; Zupanec, Donald M. Annotation: Liability of Participant in Team Athletic Competition for Injury to or Death of Another Participant, 77 ALR 3d 1300-1309.

criminal courts indicate the inadequacy of sport controls and disciplinary mechanisms by sport itself and that some form of increased deterrence is needed. To that end, the Sports Violence Act of 1980, was introduced into Congress,[81] and the American Bar Association formed a Sports Violence Task Force for the ABA Sports Forum Committee.

The appropriateness and effectiveness of bringing player against player violence actions in the criminal field is a matter of meeting the criteria of criminal law and the role of sport in society, that is, how society perceives sport and how it wants its sports played, particularly at the professional level. Excessive violence is defined by society. Particularly ice hockey and football are aggressive sports of physical contact, and intimidation by physical means is often a part of the strategy of play. Violence appears to be not only an accepted, but also a desired part of the game by many spectators; and, the players are performers for the spectators. Thus, players in professional hockey and football tend to accept fighting and violence as a part of the game. "If society wants a game to be played in a certain way, it must tolerate certain harms....if society does not choose to accept these harms, it may demand that the game be played in a different way....if requiring the players to consider the consequences of their acts will prevent the sport from being played in the way society desires it to be played, then society may not hold players who knowingly inflict injury on their opponents criminally responsible.[82] This concept has been referred to as *Socialadäquanz* or "social adequacy".

Because of the aggressive nature of the game and the societal expectations with which the players endeavor to comply (at least to some extent), violence in sport appears to be an exception from the usual criteria for consent and intent. It is argued that players do not participate or deal physical blows that injure out of a malicious intent to injure or desire to harm an opponent, and that players who freely participate in games where such conduct is commonplace do indeed consent to such acts. Also, it is repugnant to the societal perception of athletic contests in which there is not intent to injure. (See citations in this subsection for discussions on consent and intent.)

Most actions of player violence against another player have not been brought as a criminal action, but as a civil action (see §1.41322). *State v. Forbes*,[83] involving Minnesota criminal assault statutes, was an action by an ice hockey player who was hit with a hockey stick, causing serious injury to face and eyes. However, the jury could not agree on a verdict and the prosecutor chose not to retry the case. Three National Hockey League players were tried for criminal assault, but acquitted in the Candian courts.[84] The effort to bring criminal action is of longstanding, dating to 1878 when the defendant

---

[81] See Berry and Wong, Vol. II, sec. 5.20 et seq. Students may wish to read the testimony at the hearings on the bill H.R. 7903; H.R. 5079 and 2263 in 1981, comparable proposals to 7903; check for subsequent legislation and any hearings.

[82] See Consent in Criminal Law: Violence in Sport, 75 *Mich. Law Rev.* 148-179 (November 1976).

[83] State v. Forbes, Dist. Ct. No. 63280 (Jan. 14, 1975) (dismissed Aug. 12, 1975); Minn. Stat. Ann. §609.11 and 609.225(2).

[84] Regina v. Green (1971) 16 D.L.R. 2d 137 (1970); Regina v. Maki (1971) 14 D.L.R. 2d 164 (1970); Regina v. Maloney, 28 C.C.C. 2d 323 (Ont. 1976); see also, Regina v. Leyte (1973) 13 Can. Crim. Case. (n.s.) 458 (Kent Provincial Ct.), one handball player hit another with his fist, breaking the other's nose, and judge distinguished the time interval between termination of play and the blows struck and that such blows much later are not part of the aggressiveness of the game. Self-defense was a factor in the Maki and Leyte cases.

player had kneed the deceased in the stomach in a soccer game.[85] Defendant was acquitted.

In a 1976 New York case,[86] the defendant was convicted of assault in third degree. The defendant was carrying the football when plaintiff tackled him. Allegedly, the plaintiff threw a punch to the throat of the defendant while tackling the defendant. Both fell to the ground and there was a pile up of players. After all the players got off defendant, he punched plaintiff in the eye with "intent to cause physical injury." Plaintiff sustained an eye laceration which required plastic surgery. It should be noted that the punch occurred after play had ceased, not during play. The case was brought under the Penal Law. In the opinion of the case, the court discussed the two defenses generally used related to assaultive attacks by participants in sporting events: (1) that the act was consented to as being part of the game, referred to as the "consent defense," and (2) that the act was justified as an act of "self-defense." The *Maki* and *Green* cases cited in the preceding paragraph were referenced.

§ 1.3 Human Rights Liability

While the American people have been concerned about human rights for many years (*e.g.*, Civil Rights Act of 1872), the decade of the 1970s saw considerable increase in federal and state statutory and regulatory law directed toward not only protection of employees in their work place but also preserving human rights of individuals in general. That individual rights were paramount during the era of the late 1960s and the 1970s and reflected in the legislation is evidenced also in the negligence law (see Chapter 4).

The government has the right to regulate certain activities and enterprises — and compliance is expected. Violation of such laws brings a legal liability and an action by the government against the operating entity. Failure to comply may result in being "closed-down" and/or fines or restitution. The scope of such regulatory action is broad. There also has been in the late '70s and into the decade of the '80s increasingly non-public regulation of amateur athletics and professional sport activities and challenges in the courts.[87]

The legal question most often posed is whether such regulation, whether public or non-public, is in violation of the constitutional rights of individuals. To be distinguished is whether the behavior or action is a "right" or a "privilege." A right is something guaranteed to all by the Constitution, while a privilege is an opportunity made available

[85] Regina v. Bradshaw, 14 Cox Crim. Cas. 83 (1878); see also, Regina v. Moore, 14 L.T.R. 229 (1898); Regina v. Coney, 8 Q.B.D. 534 (1882). All cases tend to support the argument that sport is an exception as related to consent and intent.

[86] People, State of N.Y. v. Freer, 86 Misc. 2d 280, 381 N.Y.S. 2d 976 (1976).

[87] For further discussion on regulation of sport, see Berry and Wong, Vol. II, Chapter 1 Amateur Athletic Associations; Wong, Chapter 4 Amateur Athletic Asso-

ciations; Weistart and Lowell, Chapter 1 Regulations of Amateur Sports; both give considerable attention to this topic. For example, illustrative cases where such regulation was alleged unconstitutional (in violation of rights), Kite v. Marshall, 494 F. Supp. 227 (1980); NCAA v. Univ. of Nevada, 624 P. 2d 10 (Nev. 1981); Univ. Interscholastic League v. Green, 583 S.W. 2d 907 (Tex. 1979); Watkins v. Louisiana H.S. Athletic Assoc., 301 So. 2d 695 (La. App. 1974).

at the rightful discretion of another. Actions are most commonly brought under the Fifth and Fourteenth Amendments to the U.S. Constitution which provide that no person shall be deprived of life, liberty, or property without due process of law and that no person shall be denied equal protection of the laws, that is, all persons who are similarly situated are treated the same in respect to the purpose of the statute or regulation. There are two types of due process — substantive due process, which sets forth the rights of individuals and the circumstances under which those rights may be restricted; and, procedural due process, which relates to the process of the application of the law, that in the administration and application of the law is it reasonable, fair, and equitable.[88] In addition to due process, the Fourteenth Amendment provides for "equal protection;" and, it is under this clause that a great deal of the legal action has been brought regarding participation of and opportunities for females in sport.

A second area of human rights for both participants and personnel is addressed under the First Amendment, in respect to the freedoms of speech, press, religion, assembly, et al. and to the redress of grievance. With the concern in the late '80s for drug testing of both athletes and employees, the Fourth Amendment has become a focal point of human rights related thereto, the right of privacy and unreasonable search.

U.S. Constitutional Amendments Specific to Human Rights

Amendment I

Congress shall make no law respecting an establishment of religion, or prohibiting the free exercise thereof; or abridging the freedom of speech, or of the press; or the right of the people peaceably to assemble, and to petition the Government for the redress of grievance.

Amendment IV

The right of the people to be secure in their persons, house, papers, and effects, against unreasonable searches and seizures, shall not be violated, and no warrants shall issue, but upon probable cause, supported by oath or affirmation, and particularly describing the place to be searched, and the persons or things to be seized.

Amendment V

...; nor shall any person be subject for the same offense to be twice put in jeopardy of life or limb, nor shall be compelled in any criminal case to be a witness against himself, nor be deprived of life, liberty, or property without due process of law; nor shall private property be taken for public use without just compensation.

[88] For discussion as related to sport, see Appenzeller, *(Contemporary Issues)* §2.2 Sports, the Law and Due Process; Arnold, Chapter 15 Examining Allegations of Denial of Fourteenth Amendment Rights: Due Process and Equal Protection (pp. 246-282); Clement, (@ Chapter 10 Fourteenth Amendment to the Constitution; Schubert, et al., §3.3A Procedural due process @ pp. 63-74; Waicukauski, Chapter 1 Due Process in the Enforcement of Amateur Sports Rules (pp. 1-39). Wong, pp. 145-158.

Amendment XIV §1

...No state shall make or enforce any law which shall abridge the privileges or immunities of citizens of the United States; nor shall any State deprive any person of life, liberty, or property, without due process of law, nor deny to any person within its jurisdiction the equal protection of the laws.

This section only overviews the field of human rights in respect to those aspects most pertinent to and which have had the greatest impact in the fields of athletics and sport, recreation and parks. Some excellent readings are cited to give the details in this most important area of law. Human rights legislation, both statutes and regulatory acts, is constantly being modified; latest updating is essential from legislative reports, professional periodicals, and offices which administer the regulations. For liability of officers and board members for violation of civil rights of students, participants, or employees, see §3.2.

§ 1.31   Discrimination in sport and recreation participation

While in athletics and sport, one most frequently thinks of gender discrimination, not only in sport but also other leisure services, there may be evidenced discrimination based on age, religion, race, et al.

§ 1.311   Gender

Foremost in sport, both in the schools and non-school settings was Title IX[89] on sex discrimination.[90] It affected both the offerings and the nature of participation in sport

---

[89] Title IX of the Educational Amendments of 1972, 20 U.S.C. §1681, 1682 (Supp. Ill, 1973).

[90] For further discussion see: Arnold, Chapter 16 Sex Discrimination in Interscholastic Athletics (pp. 283-319); Berry and Wong, Vol. II Chapter 3 Sex Discrimination in Athletics; Clement, at pp. 135 et seq., excellent Title IX equal opportunities for females; Waicukauski, Chapter 3 Legal Approaches to Sex Discrimination in Amateur Athletics: The First Decade (pp. 95-113); Wong, Chapter 8 Sex Discrimination Issues. Extensive early review: Rubin, Richard Alan, Comment: Sex Discrimination in Interscholastic High School Athletics, 25 *Syracuse Law Review* 535-574, spring 1974, see also sections on civil liberties, employment, property, and rights of the handicapped.

For example, selected cases since 1980, prior to 1988 amendment: Bennett v. West Texas State Univ., 525 F. Supp. 77 (1981) rev. 698 F. 2d 1215 (1983) 799 F. 2d 155 (1986) basketball; Blair v. Washington State University, 108 Wash. 2d 558, 740 P. 2d 1379 (Wash. 1987) women's athletics class action; Burkey v. Marshall Co. Board of Educ., 513 F. Supp. 1084 (1981); Caulfield v. Board of Educ., NYC, 632 F. 2d 999 (1980); Clark v. Arizona Interscholastic Assoc., 695 F. 2d 1126 (1982); Croteau v. Fair, 686 F. Supp. 552 (1988)

baseball; Force v. Pierce City R-VI School Dist., 570 F. Supp. 1020 (1983) football; Habetz v. Louisiana H.S.A.A., 842 F. 2d 136 (1988); Haffer v. Temple Univ., 524 F. Supp. 531 (1981), aff'd. 688 F. 2d 14 (1982) aff'd. 678 F. Supp. 517 (1987) women's inter-collegiate athletic program; Hillsdale College v. Bell, 696 F. 2d 418 (1982); Lafler v. Athletic Board of Control, 536 F. Supp. 104 (1982) boxing; Lantz v. Ambach, 620 F. Supp. 663 (1985) football; Mularadelis v. Haldane Central School Board, 427 N.Y.S. 2d 458 (1980) males denied playing on girls' volleyball team; N. Haven Board of Educ. v. Bell, 102 S. Ct. 1912 (1982); O'Connor v. Board of Educ., 101 S. Ct. 72 (1980), 645 F. 2d 578 (1981), on remand 545 F. Supp. 376 (1982); O'Connor v. Peru State College, 781 F. 2d 632 (1986); Othen v. Ann Arbor School Board, 507 F. Supp. 1376 (1981), aff'd. 699 F. 2d 309 (1982); Ridgeway v. Montana High School Assoc., 633 F. Supp. 1546 (1986) 638 F. Supp. 326 (1986) class action; Saint v. Nebraska School Activities Assoc., 684 F. Supp. 626 (1988) wrestling; Univ. of Richmond v. Bell, 543 F. Supp. 321 (1982); Yellow Springs Exempted Village School Dist. v. Ohio H.S.A.A., 443 F. Supp. 753 (1978) rev'd. 647 F. 2d 651 (1981) basketball.

Illustrative cases prior to 1980: Atty. Gen. v. Mass.

for males and females. The regulations endeavoring to bring compliance with the statute were fraught with disagreement and law suits as to interpretation. The impact has been heavily financial and reaches from the local school district and municipal recreation programs to the National Collegiate Athletic Association (NCAA). Some states passed sex discrimination laws specific to athletics.[91]

The legal issue in sex discrimination in sport participation is equal opportunity for females to participate, that is, a *right to compete* for a position on a team on equal terms with others, including males. The mandate related to equal opportunity does not give a female a right to a position on a team; and, the courts recognize differences in talents and abilities among individuals. The issue of female discrimination has arisen in youngsters' recreational teams through intercollegiate varsity teams. Distinctions have been made in the nature of the sport, such as football, as to the appropriateness of both males and females to participate on the same team. Some have argued for "separate but equal," but the issue then continues as to what is equal if separate, in terms of equity of facility use, number of coaches (and salaries), travel accommodations, extent of scholarships, et al. If a girl has a right to "try out" for a team which is male, can a boy seek to play on a team which is female? (See §1.342 for gender discrimination in employment.)

While Title IX was the mainstay of law suits regarding gender discrimination, the 1984 case[92] involving Grove City College negated the effectiveness of the statute because of the interpretation that the law was applicable only if the specific program (rather than any aspect in the institution) for which sex discrimination was alleged received federal funds. Few athletic programs receive federal funds. To re-establish the apparent original intent of the statute and negate the effect of the *Grove City* case, federal legislation was passed in 1988.[93] Not finding relief on the federal level after the

---

I.A.A., 393 N.E. 2d 284 (Mass. 1979); Bednar v. Nebraska School Activities Assoc., 531 F. 2d 922 (1976); Brenden v. Indp. School Dist., 477 F. 2d 1292 (1973) tennis, cross-country ski, running; Bucha v. Illinois H.S.A., 351 F. Supp. 69 (1972); Cape v. Tenn. Sec. School Athletic Assoc., 563 F. 2d 793 (1977) basketball; Cannon v. Univ. of Chicago, 99 S. Ct. 1946 (1979); Carnes v. Tennessee Secondary School Athletic Assoc., 415 F. Supp. 569 (1976); Clinton v. Nagy, 411 F. Supp. 1396 (1974) football; Commonwealth, Packel v. P.I.A.A. 18 Pa. Cmwlth. 45, 334 A. 2d 839 (1975) challenged const. of by-laws; Darrin v. Gould, 85 Wash. 2d 859, 540 P. 2d 882 (1975) football; Fortin v. Darlington Little League, 514 F. 2d 344 (1975); Gilpin v. Kansas State School Activities Assoc., 377 F. Supp. 1233 (1974) cross-country track; Gomes v. R.I. Interscholastic League, 604 F. 2d 733 (1979) reverse discrimination, boy on girls' volleyball team; Haas v. South Bend Comm. School Corp., 289 N.E. 2d 495 (Ind. 1972) golf; Hoover v. Meiklejohn, 430 F. Supp. 164 (1977); Leffel v. Wisc. Interscholastic Athletic Assoc., 444 F. Supp. 1117 (1978); Moody v. Cronin, 484 F. Supp. 270 (1979); Magill v. Avonworth Baseball Conference, 364 F. Supp. 1212 (1973) 516 F. 2d 1328

(1975) Little League; Morris v. Michigan State Board of Education, 472 F. 2d 1207 (1973) tennis; N.O.W. v. Little League Baseball, 127 N.J. Super. 522, 318 A. 2d 33 (1974); Opinion of Justices to House of Rep., 371 N.E. 2d 426 (1977); Petrie v. Illinois High School Association, 75 Ill. App. 3d 980, 394 N.E. 2d 855 (1979) males denied playing on girls' tennis team; Reed v. Neb. School Act. Assoc., 341 F. Supp. 258 (1972) golf; Ritacco v. Norwin School Dist., 361 F. Supp. 930 (1973) class action; Ruman v. Eskew, 333 N.E. 2d 138 (Ind. App. 1975) tennis.

[91] For example, Minnesota.

[92] Grove City College v. Bell, 687 F. 2d 684 (1982), pet cert. granted 103 S. Ct. 1181, aff'd. 465 U.S. 555, 104 S. Ct. 1211 (1984) lengthy opinions. As of early 1985, over 60 cases of discrimination were suspended or closed by the Dept. of Education, pending Congressional action.

[93] P.L. 100-259, Civil Rights Restoration Act of 1987 (passed March 1988) encompasses civil rights from four prior statutes: Title IX, 1972 Education Amendments; Title VI, Civil Rights Act of 1964; Age Discrimination Act of 1975; Sec. 504, 1973 Rehabilitation Act.

Grove City case, some individuals began to turn to the state civil rights statutes and the U.S. Constitution equal rights protection.[94]

An extensive body of literature has been written on sex discrimination in sport.[95]

Gender discrimination is not only in sport participation but also in other leisure services. A male brought action under the state law against discrimination for sex discrimination in price-ticketing practices by the corporation operating the professional basketball team (Seattle Sonics). Plaintiff alleged that "ladies night" reduced prices for tickets for women was sex discrimination. The court held that it was not discrimination, since by purchasing tickets for his wife and woman guest he benefitted from the price reduction.[96] At issue in a 1987 case[97] also was discrimination against males in respect to price of alcoholic beverages sold at dance club. A Community Relations Board had found the club in violation of city antidiscrimination ordinance and the club brought suit appealing the finding. The Club allowed only female patrons to join group which received discounted prices for drinks. The court found that this policy did violate the ordinance, but said that it "found such discrimination was 'innocuous' and actually designed to ultimately benefit males." Elite all-male dining clubs, prestigious gathering places for business and relaxation, have been subject to discrimination suits in the latter part of the '80s. In *N.Y. State Club Ass'n v. N.Y.C.*, 118 A.D.2d 392, 505 N.Y.S.2d 152 (1986) aff'd. 69 N.Y.2d 211, 505 N.E.2d 915 (1987), a consortium of private clubs sought to have declared unconstitutional a city law prohibiting discrimination by clubs which provide benefits to business entities and to persons other than their own members, thereby assuming sufficient public character so as to forfeit "distinctly private" exemption from the city anti-discrimination law. The court held that the law was a valid constitutional exercise of police power and that it did not violate club members' rights to privacy, free speech and association under the Federal Constitution.

In a bit different approach, a health club filed a complaint that a county public accommodation ordinance, proscribing discrimination in places of public accommodation, was unconstitutional and asked for interlocutory injunction staying proceedings of County Human Relations Commission on complaint alleging discrimination by health club. Three men, who were members of the Spa, were denied admission to an aerobic class held at the Spa; they filed complaint with the Commission, which found reasonable grounds existed for believing there was discrimination. Court held that the

---

[94] For example, Blair v. Washington State University, 108 Wash. 2d 558, 740 P. 2d 1379 (1987); B.C. v. Cumberland Regional School Dist., 531 A. 2d 1059 (N.J. Super. 1987); Isbister v. Boys' Club of Santa Cruz, Inc., 40 Cal. 3d 72, 219 Cal. Rptr. 150, 707 P. 2d 212 (1985) mod. 40 Cal. 3d 585.

[95] For example, Czapanskiy, Karen. Grove City College v. Bell: Touchdown or Touchback? 43 *Maryland Law Review* 379-412 (1984); Krakora, Joseph E. Note: The Application of Title IX to School Athletic Programs. 68 *Cornell Law Review* 222-235 (1983); Sex Discrimination in High School Athletics: An Examination of Applicable Legal Doctrines, 66 *Minnesota Law Review* 1115-1140 (1982); Lemaire, Lyn. Women and

Athletics: Toward a Physicality Perspective. 5 *Harvard Women's Law Journal* 121-142 (1982); Richardson, Kristen v. Touchdown, but a Flag on the Play: Antidiscrimination in Collegiate Athletics and Recovery of Public Interest Attorney Fees Under Blair v. Washington State University. 24 *Williamette Law Review* (2) 525-538, spring, 1988. Check legal bibliographic sources for updating.

[96] MacLean v. First Northwest Industries of America, 24 Wash.App. 161, 600 P. 2d 1027 (1979), rev'd./remanded 635 P. 2d 683 (1981).

[97] Clearwater v. Studebaker's Dance Club, 516 So. 2d 1106 (Fla. App. 1987).

ordinance was valid exercise of "police power" of a charter county and lack of defining the term "discrimination" did not render the ordinance unconstitutionally vague. The denial of the injunction stood.[98]

§ 1.312   Age, race, religion, et al.

There, also, may be discrimination on the basis of age, race, religion,[99] disability,[100] martial status, national origin and residence[101] — not only in participation, but also in the use of public accommodations. Some states, in addition to the antidiscrimination federal regulations, have enacted legislation of their own or established Human Relations Commissions.[102] The landmark case on racial segregation is *Brown v. Board of Education*, 347 U.S. 483 (1954); and while it involved public schools specifically, by implication other segregated public facilities were inherently unequal and therefore violated the equal protection rights of the Constitution. The various Civil Rights Acts, also, impacted upon park and recreation facilities, programs, and services; and, law suits were brought to enforce these Acts and the rights of individuals.[103] While there remains in the mid-'80s some Congressional and legal action related to schools and the forms of desegregation, the law suits as related to availability of sport and recreation facilities and services are minimal.

Several black football players were removed from the university football team after they boycotted practices in protest of alleged racial discrimination by coaching staff and administration. They brought action, alleging free speech, liberty, and property right violations, and breach of contract. In *Hysaw v. Washburn University*, 690 F. Supp. 940 (1987), the court held that the players did not have a property interest protected by due process in playing football or liberty interest by due process in pursuing college football careers, so as to support action alleging violation of civil rights statute; however, it did hold that there were genuine issues of material fact on claimed violations based on alleged violation of First Amendment right to free speech by removing players from team after they protested racial mistreatment.

Racial discrimination also can come in employment (see §1.342).

§ 1.32   Right to participate in recreation and sport

There are primarily two aspects of right to participate, one as related to the handicapped and the various disabilities, and the other in terms of controlling eligibility

98 Holiday Universal Club of Rockville, Inc. v. Montgomery County, 67 Md. App. 568, 508 A. 2d 491 (1986) dis'md. for want of jurisdiction 307 Md. 260, 107 S. Ct. 920 (1987).

99 Menora v. Illinois H.S. Assoc., 527 F. Supp. 637 (1981) basketball headgear; see also §1.33.

100 For example, Poole v. South Plainfield Board of Education, 490 F. Supp. 948 (1980); Wright v. Columbia Univ., 520 F. Supp. 789 (1981); see also §1.32.

101 For example, Sea Isle City v. Caterina, 123 N.J. Super. 422, 303 A. 2d 351 (1973); see also §1.323 Eligibility.

102 For example, Oregon, Minnesota.

103 For a brief discussion, see Frakt and Rankin, at pp. 182-188; Schubert, et al., at pp. 95-98. See also due process citation, footnote 88. In Williams v. City of Boston, 784 F. 2d 430 (1986) black athlete shot while participating in high school football game with rival school, alleged failure to provide security for potential racial situation and post-shooting coverup of facts, violating constitutionally protected liberty interest.

for participation in sport. Actions on the right to participate, also, have been brought on denial of "property right without due process" in that not to play would diminish the opportunity to earn college athletic scholarships. The courts have held that to play sports is not a constitutionally-protected entitlement, only an expectation.[104] In *Haverkamp v. Unified School Dist. No. 380,* 689 F. Supp. 1055 (1986), a cheerleader alleged deprivation of property interest, as well as violation of free speech rights under the First Amendment. The plaintiff had been removed as head cheerleader after she had gone to another city to "cut an album." The court held that the cheerleading did not rise to level of constitutionally protected property interest; plaintiff also failed to state substantive due process claim. Corporal punishment to violate due process must be arbitrary, capricious, or wholly unrelated to legitimate goal of maintaining an atmosphere of learning.

Applying Kansas law, the court held in 1986 that viewing a basketball game and attending high school extracurricular activities was not a constitutionally protected right and that due process had been followed. There were two separate incidents involved. In one, the grade school was vandalized and the high school students were suspended for three days from school and the nonstudents were told they could not attend high schhol extracurricular events. In the other incident, students, while attending a basketball game, were reprimanded by the athletic director for unsportsmanlike conduct, but ignored the reprimand; so, the next day they were informed by the principal they were not to attend the next game. The youths and their parents sued for violation of due process as they were not afforded a hearing.[105]

In the challenge to the constitutionality of U.S. Department of Interior regulation banning nude bathing at Cape Code National Seashore, the court held that nude bathing at remote piece of federal land which was readily frequented by general public and which had been used traditionally for such purpose was entitled to some constitutional protection as a personal liberty right protected by due process clause of Fifth Amendment, but that the regulation was constitutional in view of environmental problems in the area classified as a "natural environment area," in which area the nude bathing was taking place.[106] Nude dancing also has been protected under the First Amendment as freedom of expression, that is, an expressive activity (conveying a message).[107] Generally, sports have not been considered expressive activities protected under the First Amendment.[108]

Another aspect of the right to play is the legality of charging a fee to participate in athletics and other extracurricular activities. While this has been commonplace with municipal and youth organization activities, schools have generally not charged special participation fees. This consideration of charging a fee by schools has come about

---

[104] Adamek v. PIAA, 59 Pa. Cmwlth. 261, 426 A. 2d 1206 (Pa. Cmwlth. 1981); Davenport v. Randolph Co. Board of Educ., 730 F. 2d 1395 (1984) Alabama; Walsh v. Louisiana H.S.A.A., 616 F. 2d 152 (1980); Stock v. Texas Catholic Interscholastic League, 364 F. Supp. 362 (1973).

[105] Boster v. Philpot, 645 F. Supp. 798 (1986).

[106] Williams v. Hathaway, 400 F. Supp. 122 (1975).

[107] Schad v. Borough of Mount Ephraim, 452 U.S.

61 (1981); see also BSA, Inc. v. King County, 804 F. 2d 1104 (1986) held barroom nude dancing expressive activity entitled to First Amendment protection; adult entertainment featuring topless dancing in "bar" that sold only non-alcoholic beverages, thus not under county ordinance prohibiting nude exposure.

[108] See note, Selfridge v. Carey: The First Amendment's Applicability to Sporting Events, 46 *Albany L. Rev.* 937 (1982).

because of the tight budgets and school boards see the fee as a special source of income. A 1982 California case[109] held that schools cannot charge fees unless specifically authorized by law. Further, when sport and other activities are considered a part of basic education and a "right" of education, extra fees cannot be imposed upon students; the financial burden should be upon the schools, not the individual student participant. However, in a 1980 case,[110] North Carolina upheld student fees even though there was a state constitutional requirement that public education should be free. However, sport most often is considered a "privilege" rather than a "right" (see introduction to §1.3 and §1.323).

§ 1.321 The disabled athlete

Some individuals with physical disabilities may be excellent athletes, yet because of their disability they are disqualified from participating in certain sports. These athletes should be distinguished from those disabled persons who desire to participate in recreation and sport (see next subsection §1.322). Physical conditions for which individuals have been disqualified include, but are not limited to, vision in only one eye, diabetes, one kidney, epilepsy, impaired hearing, and loss of one or more limbs. These individuals (and their parents) contend that they should be able to participate if they can meet the physical performance criteria for an athletic team and have sued for the right to play. Such suits[111] have been successful, for example, for an interscholastic wrestler with one kidney, a girl with congenital cataract in one eye, and high school freshman with defective vision in one eye. In the 1980s the number of suits extensively increased. Most actions were brought under Section 504 of the Rehabilitation Act of 1973 (29 U.S.C.A. 3794),[112] which provides that a person should not be discriminated against on the basis of being handicapped.[113] There are four elements which the court[114] has delineated for action under Section 504: (1) that the person is a "handicapped" person under the Act, (2) that the person is otherwise qualified for the athletic activity, (3) that the person is being excluded solely because of the handicap, and (4) the school is receiving federal financial assistance. Where there is a rule of disqualification due to disability, the reasonableness and rationale for such rule is considered. The basis of such rule frequently has been the 1976 guidelines set forth by the American Medical Association's document *Disqualifying Conditions for Sports Participation*.[115] However, there is evidence that the constitutional right to participate broadens the opportunities

[109] Hartzell v. Connell, 137 Cal. App. 30196, 186 Cal. Rptr. 852 (1982).

[110] Snead v. Board of Education, 299 N.C. 609, 264 S.E. 2d 106 (1980); Michigan also has so ruled.

[111] For example, Colombo v. Sewanhaka Central H.S. Dist. No. 287 Misc. 2d 48, 383 N.Y.S. 2d 518 (1976) hearing deficiency, football/lacrosse/soccer; Kampmeier v. Harris, 93 Misc. 2d 1032, 403 N.Y.S. 2d 638 (1978), rev'd. 66 A.D. 2d 1014, 411 N.Y.S. 2d 744 (1978) vision, basketball; Poole v. S. Plainfield Board of Educ., 490 F. Supp. 948 (1980) one kidney, wrestling; Swiderski v. Board of Educ., Albany, 95 Misc. 2d 931, 408 N.Y.S. 2d 744 (1978) defective vision, athletic

program in general; Wright v. Columbia University, 520 F. Supp. 789 (1981) eye impairment since birth, football.

[112] In 1988 the Act was integrated into the Civil Rights Restoration Act.

[113] May also sue on state laws, such as in New York.

[114] Doe v. NYU, 666 F. 2d 761 (1981).

[115] In 1988 new suggested guidelines were issued by the American Academy of Pediatricians as a Policy Statement; see "Recommendations for Participation in Competitive Sports," *Pediatrics* 81:737-739 (May 1988).

for the physically disabled. Where there is appropriate authority for rule decision-making, the courts do not like to interfere.[116] For further discussion, see §17.34 and references in footnote.[117]

§ 1.322   Programming and barrier-free facilities for the handicapped

The right to participate extends both to being able to have access to areas and facilities in order to engage in recreational and educational activities and to have programs in which persons of mental and physical disabilities can participate. In addition to the Constitutional Amendments and the Civil Rights Restoration Act of 1987, referenced in the preceding section, the authority or the mandate for these rights of the handicapped are embodied particularly in P.L. 94-142 Education for All Handicapped Children Act (20 U.S.C.A. §1401 et seq.) and in the Architectural Barriers Act of 1968 (P.L. 90-480).

P.L. 94-142 specifically refers to physical education in the public schools and is the only curricular area specifically designated within the description of special education. The implementing rules and regulations for P.L. 94-142 define physical education as including the development of physical and motor fitness, fundamental motor skills and patterns, and skills in aquatics, dance, and individual and lifetime sports. The law also requires that an Individualized Education Program, known as an IEP, be designed for every handicapped child and such IEP must be written for physical education, too. Additionally, an individual with special needs must be placed in the "least restrictive environment," that is, in the most normal environment in which they can potentially succeed. "Mainstreaming" is not required, unless that is the least restrictive environment for that person.[118]

Wheelchair athletes brought action when denied the right to participate in the New York City Marathon. Although the State Rights Board affirmed the State Division of Human Rights, finding that there was unlawful discrimination, the court did not uphold the finding of the State agencies.[119]

The law regarding AIDS was developing in the late '80s, but there appeared to be some indication that AIDS may be considered a handicap under Section 504 and its successor, the Civil Rights Restoration Act.[120]

The Architectural Barriers Act mandates that any building or facility constructed in whole or in part by federal funds must be made accessible to and usable by the

[116] Colombo v. Sewanhaka Central H.S. Dist. No. 2, 87 Misc.2d 48, 383 N.Y.S. 2d 518 (1976).

[117] For further information: Appenzeller, *(Contemporary Issues)* §4.3 The Athlete with Disabilities; Kathleen De Santis, The Disabled Student Athlete: Gaining a Place on the Playing Field, *Comm/Ent.* vol. 5, no. 3, spring 1983, pp. 517-548 *(Journal of Communications & Entertainment Law);* Cavallaro v. Ambach, 575 F. Supp. 171 (1983) N.Y. law 19-year-olds not permitted to participate interscholastic wrestling, no exception to be made for neurologically impaired who sued on discrimination action.

[118] For further discussion, see: Appenzeller, *(The*

Right) Chapter 5 Legal Mandates, pp. 93-142; Clement, Chapter 12 Handicapped legislation. For legislative, regulatory, and case law developments related to all types of mental and physical disability, see *Mental and Physical Disability Law Reporter.* One must keep up-to-date with annual legislative enactments and regulatory developments.

[119] N.Y. Roadrunners Club v. State Division of Human Rights, 55 N.Y. 2d 122, 432 N.E. 2d 780 (1982).

[120] *Mental and Physical Disability Law Reporter,* January-February, 1988.

physically handicapped. Many states and municipalities also have a comparable law. This includes not only schools but also public recreation facilities and areas.[121]

§ 1.323 Eligibility to participate in sport

Rules for eligibility to participate in sport are usually made by the governing body, whether it be the NCAA, NAIA, a state high school athletic association, the university or college, the local school district, Little League or other youth sport organization, the municipal recreation department, the AAU, or the USOC, et al.[122] Interscholastic participation is generally considered a privilege accorded under the specified rules; the expectation of obtaining a college athletic scholarship does not give a property right to the student, although a collegiate top-ranking player may be found to have a property right in his future professional career. The legal question usually is whether the rule is reasonable, and, if so, then the courts tend not to interfere in the internal controls of the governing body.[123] Suits[124] regarding high school eligibility have encompassed over-

[121] The American National Standards Institute (ANSI) has national architectural standards of accessibility.

[122] The authority and associations to which local entities belong has not only been in contention, but also such associations have been the defendant in a variety of types of law suits. See §3.13. For further discussion, see: Arnold, Chapter 11; Berry and Wong, Chapters 1 and 2; Schubert, et al. at §§1.2, 2.1 Regulations governing eligibility; Waicukauski, Chapters 1, 4, and 7; Weistart & Lowell, Chapter 1; Wong, pp. 172-249.

[123] Clear, Delbert K. Participation in Interscholastic Athletics. *Phi Delta Kappan* Nov. 1982 conceptual discussion with case citations; see also Greene, Linda A., The New NCAA Rules of the Game: Academic Integrity of Racism. 28 *Saint Louis Univ. Law Journal* 101-151 (1984). Some case examples: Admek v. Penn. Interscholastic Assoc., 426 A. 2d 1206 (1981); Blue v. Univ. Interscholastic League, 503 F. Supp. 1030 (1980) Texas; Brown v. Wells, 181 N.W. 2d 708 (Minn. 1970); Florida H.S.A.A. v. Thoms, 409 So. 2d 245 (Fla. App. 1982) Association rule on number of players for post season play held unconstitutional; Kissick v. Garland Indp. School Dist., 330 S.W. 2d 708 (Tex. 1959); Kriss v. Indiana H.S.A.A., 390 N.E. 2d 193 (1979); Kulovitz v. Illinois H.S.A., 462 F. Supp. 875 (1978); Snow v. N.H.I.A.A., 449 A. 2d 1223 (N.H. 1982); State ex rel. Evans v. Fry, 11 Ohio Misc. 231, 230 N.E. 2d 363 (1967); Yellow Springs v. Ohio H.S.A.A., 443 F. Supp. 753 (1978), rev'd. 647 F. 2d 651 (1981) found OSHSAA rule unconstitutional.

[124] For example, *age:* Barrett v. Phillips, 223 S.E. 2d 918 (N.C. App. 1976); Blue v. Univ. Interscholastic League, 503 F. Supp. 1030 (1980); Cavallaro v. Ambach, 575 F. Supp. 171 (1983); Mahan v. Agee, 652 P. 2d 765 (Okla. 1982); Robinson v. Illinois H.S.A., 45 Ill. App. 2d 277, 195 N.E. 2d 38 (1963).

Red-shirting: Lee v. Florida H.S.A.A., 291 So. 2d

636 (Fla. App. 1974); Murtaugh v. Nyquist, 358 N.Y.S. 2d 595 (1974).

Transferring: ABC League v. Missouri State H.S.A.A., 530 F. Supp. 1033 (1982); Bruce v. So. Car. H.S.A.A., 189 S.E. 2d 817 (1972); Doe v. Marshall, 459 F. Supp. 1190 (1978), 622 F. 2d 118 (1980) Texas; English v. NCAA & Tulane Univ., 439 So. 2d 1218 (La. 1983); Florida H.S.A.A. v. Temple Baptist Church, 509 So. 2d 1381 (Fla. App. 1987); Griffin H.S. v. Illinois High School Association, 822 F. 2d 671 (1987); Hardy v. Univ. Interscholastic League, 759 F. 2d 1233 (1985) Texas; Harrisburg School Dist. v. PIAA, 309 A. 2d 363 (Pa. 1973); Kent v. Calif, Interscholastic Federation, 222 Cal. Rptr. 355 (1986); Palmer v. Bloomfield Hills Board of Education, 164 Mich. App. 573, 417 N.W. 2d 505 (1987); PIAA v. Greater Johnstown School, 463 A. 2d 1198 (Pa. Cmwlth. 1983); Rogers v. Board of Educ. of Little Rock, 281 F. Supp. 39 (1968); Sullivan v. Univ. Athletic League, 599 S.W. 2d 860 (Tex. Civ. App. 1980) aff'd./rev'd. in part 616 S.W. 2d 170 (Texas 1981); Walsh v. Louisiana H.S.A.A., 616 F. 2d 152 (1980); Weiss v. Eastern College Athletic Assoc. and NCAA, 563 F. Supp. 192 (1983); see also 15 ALR 4th 885.

Semester limitation: Ala. H.S.A.A. v. Meddars, 456 So. 2d 284 (Ala. 1984); PIAA v. Geisinger and Orlando, 474 A. 2d 62 (Pa. Cmwlth. 1984); Spath v. N.C.A.A., 728 F. 2d 25 (1984).

Residence: Ala. H.S.A.A. v. Rose, 446 So. 2d 1 (Ala. 1984); Scott v. Kilpatrick, 237 So. 2d 652 (Ala. 1970).

Married: Bell v. Lone Oak Indp. School Dist., 507 S.W. 2d 636 (Tx. 1974); Board of Educ., Davis Co., 14 Utah 2d 227, 281 P. 2d 718 (1963); Cochrane v. Board of Educ., Mesick Consl. School Dist., 360 Mich. 390, 103 N.W. 2d 569 (1960); Davis v. Meek, 344 F. Supp. 298 (1972) Ohio; Holt v. Shelton, 341 F. Supp. 821 (1972); Indiana H.S.A.A. v. Raike, 164 Ind. App. 169, 329 N.E. 2d 66 (1975); Moran v. Yellowstone Co., 350 F. Supp. 1180 (1972) Montana.

aged athletes, number of semesters or years one can participate (red-shirting), transfer and residence, and being married. Eligibility, also, may rest in certain restrictive rules of the governing body, such as a high school athlete not being able to participate in practice with or against any college athletic squad, playing on a nonschool team in a recreational situation, going to a non-sanctioned sport camp in summer.[125] The question still is whether the rule is for the overall good of the high school athletic program and the athletes participating.

Eligibility as related to academic standards (projected g.p.a., grades, and "normal progress") is another legal issue and, also, goes to the discriminatory nature of the rule, as well as the "right" of an individual to fully participate in school athletics.[126] A basketball team player for three years, plaintiff had enrolled in a non-baccalaureate program and was denied admission to a degree program when he applied. Conference rules required that the player be a candidate for a degree and he was declared ineligible, although his g.p.a. and credit accumulation were adequate. Degree admission apparently was denied on the basis of a confidential memorandum indicating copying work of others and dropping any course in danger of failing. The player's application was handled in a manner different from other students. The court ordered the University to admit the athlete to a degree program, as the player had been recruited as an athlete and had "lived up to" his scholarship requirements. Denial of his senior year would mean deprivation opportunity for considerable monetary compensation in the professional draft, projected dropping from second to sixth round draft choice.[127]

Whereas most of the foregoing discussion relates to rules and requirements placed upon a school by the governing body, eligibility also may be a matter of compliance with training rules, academic requirements, and code of conduct. The control of an athlete's behavior as a condition for participation when the nature of such control involves civil liberties is discussed in §1.331. For both association rules and local school rules, the courts seem to distinguish between ineligiblity reasons beyond the personal control of the player (e.g., exemptions from age and transfer rules because of illnesses, handicaps, and parental residence), which are the most vulnerable in court, and those wherein the player is in control of one's own destiny (e.g., behavior, attendance, academic grades).[128] But whichever type of ruling, it is essential that each player be dealt with fairly and equitably. Particularly when a player has been suspended or declared ineligible because of a violation of a rule, the athlete must be accorded "due

[125] For example, Brown v. Wells, 288 Minn. 468, 181 N.W. 2d 708 (1970) summer camp; Kite v. Marshall, 494 F. Supp. 227 (1980), rev'd. 661 F. 2d 1027 (1981) Texas summer camp; Morrison v. Roberts, 183 Okla. 559, 82 P. 2d 1023 (1938) awarded little gold football; Robin v. N.Y. State Public H.S.A.A., 420 N.Y.S. 2d 394 (1979) practiced with college team.

[126] See Waicukauski, Chapter 5 The Regulation of Academic Standards in Intercollegiate Athletics, pp. 161-190; Jones v. Wichita State Univ., 698 F. 2d 1082 (1983); Greene, Linda S., The New NCAA Rules of the Game: Academic Integrity of Racism: 28 Saint Louis Univ. Law Journal 101-151 (1984). Academic eligibility regulations have been enacted by a number of states wherein a student must pass all courses in order to

participate in extracurricular activities, including athletics. See: Bailey v. Truby, 321 S.E. 2d 302 (W. Va. App. 1984) law did not violate constitutional rights of due process (procedural and substantive) and equal protection; in related case State Superintendent of Schools sought injunction to prohibit enforcement of law, Truby v. Broadwater, 332 S.E. 2d 284 (W. Va. App. 1985); see also Spring Branch Indp. School v. Stamos, 695 S.W. 2d 556 (Tex. 1985) also held Texas law constitutional.

[127] Hall v. Univ. of Minnesota, 530 F.Supp. 104 (1982); see also § 1.411.

[128] See Clear, Delbert K. Participation in Interscholastic Athletics. Phi Delta Kappan, Nov. 1982.

process," a constitutionally-guaranteed right. There must be meaningful and timely hearings. Sometimes it is alleged that the rule is ambiguous or vague or was not communicated properly, falling short of the due process requirement of clarity. The *Bunger* case[129] discusses the authority of the State H.S.A.A. and the school and distinguishes eligibility to participate and suspension from school.[130]

§ 1.33   Civil liberties

The nature of civil liberties germane to sport and recreation is essentially of two types, the control of the conduct/behavior of the athlete in order to participate and the use of public areas and facilities. However, civil liberties may be at issue in the right **not** to participate, as was the situation in *Matter of Hickey*.[131] The father of a 16-year-old girl refused to permit her to attend physical education classes on the basis of religious beliefs. The father was brought to court on educational neglect proceedings. It was held that the girl being 16 was not required by statute to attend school and her father's action or inaction could not constitute educational neglect. Religion and the First Amendment also was at issue in *Clayton by Clayton v. Place,* 690 F. Supp. 850 (1988). Action was brought against the school board and school superintendent, challenging the school district rule prohibiting dances on school property. The court held that the rule was an impermissable establishment of religion, advancing community's "no dance" religious beliefs, rather than being a reflection of the community's "cultural conservatism," as claimed by the school officials.

Students brought First Amendment action against their high school principal for banning school's Confederate logo. The ban came after meetings with Black students who viewed the Confederate symbols as a persistent affront, given the association between the symbols and the history of slavery. The athletic teams were known as "Rebels" and the symbols (version of Confederate flag and caricature of "Johnny Reb") had been in use since 1930s. At the district court hearing the action was dismissed as "frivolous" and ordered plaintiffs to pay $1,800 in defendant's attorneys' fees. This, however, was reversed and remanded for determination regarding First Amendment rights.[132]

Most of the actions are brought under the First Amendment, except for drug testing, which is brought also under the Fourth Amendment. See also confidentiality of records §1.35 and invasion of privacy §1.41. For discussion of mental patients' legal rights, see Robert Henley Woody and Associates, *The Law and the Practice of Human Services,* San Francisco: Jossey-Bass Publishers, 1984, Chapter 8 Rights of Institutionalized Patients, pp. 289-340.

[129] For example, Bunger v. Iowa H.S.A.A., 197 N.W. 2d 555 (Iowa 1972); Braesch v. DePasquale, 200 Neb. 726, 265 N.W. 2d 842 (1978); Dallam v. Cumberland Valley School District, 391 F. Supp. 358 (1975) transfer of residence; Duffley v. N.H.I.A.A., 446 A. 2d 462 (N.H. 1982); Dumez v. Louisiana H.S.A. A., 334 So. 2d 494 (La. App. 1976) participated on non-school team; Goss v. Lopez, 419 U.S. 565, 95 S. Ct. 729 (1975); Hamilton v. Tenn. Secondary School Athletic Assoc., 552 F. 2d 681 (1976); Quimette v. Babbie, 405 F. Supp. 525 (1975) refusal to attend phy. educ. class.

[130] For further discussion, see: Arnold, Chapter 15 Examining Allegations of Denial of Fourteenth Amendment Rights, Due Process and Equal Protection, pp. 246-282; Wong, pp. 145-161; Staton, Richard. Recent Cases Concerning the Rights of Student Athletes. 10 *J. of College & Univ. Law* 209-224 (1983-84).

[131] Matter of Hickey, 124 Misc. 2d 669, 477 N.Y.S. 2d 258 (Family Ct., Suffold Co. 1984).

[132] Crosby v. Holsinger, 816 F. 2d 162 (1987).

§ 1.331   Control of an athlete's behavior as condition for participation[133]

Most athletic teams have training rules which are established presumably for the enhancement of the quality of play — one conditions in a certain way, eats certain foods at specified times, goes to bed at a certain time, et al. These rules are seldom challenged substantively, although when suspension occurs due to violation,[134] due process may be at issue (see §1.323). However, when the control of behavior extends to aspects which do not directly affect performance, then such control may be alleged to violate constitutional rights. In subsequent paragraphs are some controls which have been challenged.

Grooming. In the late '60s and early '70s the traditional appearance decorum of young people particularly changed and in reaction thereto grooming or appearance codes for athletes were established, particularly as related to hairstyle.[135] Law suits were brought alleging that such codes were a violation of the personal rights, the civil liberties of the athlete, and were not directly related to athletic performance. The schools and coaches argued that conformity with rules is essential, while the athlete and parents argued enfringement of personal rights and that the regulations were "arbitrary, capricious, and unreasonable."[136] A 1984 case[137] supported a school's right to regulate grooming (clean shaven); plaintiffs could not prove policy was unreasonable or arbitrary. Dress codes, also, have extended to officials and two football players who officiated baseball brought action against the Baseball Umpires' Association successfully.[138]

Married. At about the same time, the regulation restricting participation of married students in sports and other extracurricular activities in high school was challenged. The purpose of the regulation was at issue, with the schools arguing that it was for the good of the individual and the student alleging discrimination and violation of civil liberties and right to fully participate in all aspects of the school program.[139]

Free speech. Violation of right to free speech was alleged by members of the women's basketball team at the University of Oklahoma when their athletic scholarships were terminated. These students had voiced support for the assistant coach over the head coach. The court held that the players' comments were not of public concern and, thus, not constitutionally protected.[140] The question is whether there was dismissal only

---

[133] For further discussion, see: Berry and Wong, Vol. II, §2.30 Discipline of individual athletes; Clement, Chapter 9 First and Fourth Amendments to the Constitution; Schubert et al., §3.3C First Amendment Rights; Wong, pp. 250-265; see also references cited in §§1.31, 1.32.

[134] Makanui v. Dept. of Education, 721 P. 2d 165 (Hawaii App. 1986) athlete forbidden to participate in state track meet due to shooting off fireworks in the parking lot, deemed conduct unbecoming.

[135] For brief discussion of hairstyles (cases), see Appenzeller, Sports and the Courts, at pp. 58-67.

[136] For example, see: Corley v. Daunhauer, 312 F. Supp. 811 (1970); Dostert v. Berthold Public School Dist. No. 54, 391 F. Supp. 171 (1975); Jacobs v. Benedict, 35 Ohio Misc. 92, 301 N.E. 2d 723 (1973); Trent v. Perritt, 391 F.Supp. 171 (1975) brought in Title

IX and sex discrimination as related to grooming; Zeller v. Donegal School Dist. Board of Educ., 517 F. 2d 600 (1975).

[137] Davenport v. Randolph Co. Board of Educ., 730 F. 2d 1395 (1984) Alabama; Humphries v. Lincoln Parish School Board, 467 So. 2d 870 (La. App. 1985).

[138] Action brought in Denver District Court; see Narol, Melvin S. and Stuart Dedopoulos, Beards — Are They a Clear and Present Danger? *Referee*, Nov. 1979, pp. 36,51.

[139] For brief discussion on married students' participation restrictions, see: Arnold, at pp. 273-277. See also §1.323.

[140] Marcum v. Dahl, 658 F. 2d 731 (1981); see also Bowman v. Pulaski Co. Special School Dist., 723 F. 2d 640 (1983).

for the remarks or because of the behavior which disrupted the harmony of the program, where the first would be protected constitutionally, but the latter would not. The court does not like to interfere in internal matters. The students also alleged unsuccessfully, denial of due process before being deprived of their scholarships.

Attendance. Attendance at practices as a requirement to participate was challenged in an Illinois case[141] on grounds of religious freedom. There was a policy that only two situations would be excuses from practice, illness or death in the family. The elementary school youngster was to attend catechism one day a week. The court held that it was too great a burden to change a practice schedule to permit the child to practice and also attend the catechism.

Religion. In a 1982 case,[142] the court upheld the high school association rule forbidding basketball players to wear hats or other headgear, except headbands, when playing. Jewish student-athletes challenged the ruling under First Amendment, alleging violation of freedom of practicing their religion by wearing yarmulkes during games. Religion also was in issue in a 1986 Pennsylvania case.[143] The school required a tetanus shot as condition for participation in interscholastic baseball. Plaintiff alleged this violated his religious beliefs and under the First Amendment he was denied freedom of religion and under the Fourteenth Amendment equal protection. The court held that interscholastic sports is a privilege and not a constitutionally protected interest; and, further, that while a person may not be compelled to choose between exercise of religion (First Amendment right) and participation in an otherwise available public program, participation in interscholastic sports did not rise to level of important government benefit. The court held in favor of the school and its regulation.

Dress. Violation of a civil liberty also can occur in other than team sport. A town ordinance prohibiting shirtless jogging except on the beach or private property was held not to violate any constitutional rights such as right to dress, freedom of expression, due process, and was reasonable exercise of police power.[144]

Drug testing. A major issue in controlling both amateur and professional athletes' behavior in the late '80s is that of drug testing and freedom from drugs in the body. There really are two types of drugs concerned, those for body building, steroids, and other drugs. The NCAA and other regulatory organizations have a list of "banned drugs" for which they test. The time of testing varies from at random in season to only medal winners after individual competition and final team championship athletes. Actions are brought primarily on invasion of privacy based on individual rights under the First and Fourth Amendments.[145] Drug testing and the right to search and seize

[141] Keller v. Gardner Comm. Cons. Grade School Dist. 72C, 552 F. Supp. 512 (1982).

[142] Menora v. Illinois High School Association, 527 F. Supp. 637 (1981), 683 F. 2d 1030 (1982); see also *Keller* case in preceding paragraph.

[143] Calandra v. State College Area School Dist., 99 Pa. Cmwlth. 223, 512 A. 2d 809 (1986).

[144] DeWeese v. Town of Palm Beach, 688 F. 2d 731, 616 F. Supp. 971 (1985).

[145] For further discussion, see: Berry and Wong. Vol. II, §§5.60 et seq. at pp. 436-477 Drug abuse,

testing, and enforcement; Wong, chapter 12 Drug testing in amateur athletics; see also law review articles: Lock, Ethan, and Marianne Jennings. The Constitutionality of Mandatory Student-Athlete Drug Testing Programs: The Bounds of Privacy. 38 *Univ. of Florida Law Review* 581-613 (1986); Meloch, Sally Lynn. An Analysis of Public College Athlete Drug Testing Programs Through the Unconstitutional Condition Doctrine and the Fourth Amendment. 60 *Southern California Law Review* 815-850 (1987); Scanlan, John A. Playing the Drug-Testing Game: College Athletes,

extends into the school system, other than athletics, as part of the "war against drugs."[146]

§ 1.332   Use of public areas and facilities

Freedom of speech and religion are the two primary civil liberties at issue in situations involving use of public areas and facilities. Frequently schools and municipalities permit use, either free or by rental agreement, of their gymnasiums or sports arena, their athletic fields or open park areas, and their theaters and other facilities and areas. In most situations there is no question as to the right to permit use, but rather whether the criteria or regulations for such use violate a person or organization's right to free speech or religion. That is, the criteria must be non-discriminatory or what is referred to as "content neutral." It is appropriate to have classifications of groups, organizations, or persons with criteria related to each, but the criteria must apply equally to all within the classification. For example, if political groups are permitted to use a facility, then all political groups must be under the same rules; one group cannot be denied use because the school board, for example, does not like their point of view. The regulations should provide little discretion by the administrator acting upon an application for use, so as to protect against bias, prejudice, and favoritism. Regulations are authorized under the police power of the government to protect or provide for the health, safety, morals, and welfare of the people. Regulations can be directed toward time, place, and manner of use, but must meet the "least restrictive means" test and avoid vagueness. The basis of the suits is enfringement of the First Amendment, which provides that there shall be free exercise of religion and freedom of speech, as well as the right of the people to peaceably assemble. The courts have held that as related to local and state government, the Fourteenth Amendment encompasses the liberties set forth in the First Amendment.[147] The 1984 Equal Access Act, P.L. 98-377, instructs all public secondary schools to grant equal access to meeting rooms for all student-initiated groups to discuss "religious, political, philosophical, or other content....at the meeting."[148] Also in 1984 were a number of law suits[149] challenging the constitutionality of placing a creche in a public park at Christmastime. The Supreme Court held that erecting a creche did not violate the First Amendment.[150] However, in a 1988 case, *ACLU v. Allegheny Co.*, 842 F.2d 655 (1988), there was an opposite result. The court held that placement of creche and menorah violated First Amendment, as each display was located at or in public building

---

Regulatory Institutions, and the Structures of Constitutional Argument. 62 *Indiana Law Journal* 863-984 (1987). Keep up-to-date through *NCAA News,* newsletters cited at the end of this chapter, and other professional and legal literature. See also cases: O'Halloran v. Univ. of Wash., 679 F. Supp. 997 (1988); Schaill by Kross v. Tippecanoe County School Corp., 679 F. Supp. 833 (1988).

[146] Clement, @ pp. 120-125.

[147] For further discussion, see: Appenzeller at pp. 259-268; Frakt & Rankin at pp. 162-182. See also

Hennessey v. Indp. School Dist., 552 P. 2d 1141 (Oka. 1976).

[148] Clark v. Dallas Indp. School Dist., 671 F. Supp. 1119 (1987) was brought under the Equal Assess Act and involved use of school for religious purposes immediately before and after school time; held that establishment clause interests of district prevailed over free exercise interests of students.

[149] e.g., McCreary v. Stone, 739 F. 2d 716 (1984).

[150] Lynch v. Donnelly, 104 S. Ct. 1355 (1984) and, notwithstanding the Supreme Court decision, continues to be challenged.

devoted to "core functions" of government, neither display was subsumed by larger display of nonreligious items. The court set forth criteria for displays. Separation of church and state also was at issue involving a monolith containing text of Ten Commandments displayed in city park, based on First Amendment.[151]

Whereas at mid-century there was racial segregation of facilities in some parts of the United States and use of facilities often discriminatorily denied, after *Brown v. Board of Education*, 347 U.S. 483 (1954), increased legal action, for the most part, has opened all athletic and recreation facilities and park areas to persons of all races.[152]

See also §15.12 introduction for comment on lawful assembly.

§ 1.34　Employment

There are many aspects of the law which are involved in employee-employer relationships, including labor relations, civil rights, workers' compensation, contract, and protective laws and regulations. For brief discussion of contract, see §1.121, and for workers' compensation, see §25.34; see also §1.35 on records. There are many other legal aspects of the field of personnel administration which have considerable ramification for recreation and park systems, camping, and sport operations.[153] It is very important to keep up-to-date with state and local regulations, as well as the federal statutes and regulations. Check with various government offices responsible for administering the regulations, as well as professional personnel administrators for larger companies and organizations.

§ 1.341　Labor relations/unions

Labor law and unionization go back a century and play an important role in personnel relations, not only in private enterprise and professional sports but also in schools and governmental operations. The right to unionize and to strike has been won by most all classifications of employees, and with the right to unionize also comes the right of collective bargaining for wages, working conditions, and benefits. The legislation affecting labor relations is extensive and the labor contracts complex. Perhaps because of the mass media and sports stars being in the public domain, the most visible evidence of the impact of labor negotiations and the impact of the right to strike is in professional sports.[154] The differences between players in team sports, such as baseball and football, and the individual sports, such as tennis and golf, should be recognized. Professional athletes in team sports have a basic contract negotiated by the players' association and then each may bargain specific salary and certain benefits. In individual sports there are basic benefits negotiated, then there is no salary, but the player receives whatever is earned in terms of placement (*i.e.*, first, second, et al.). Professional sports officials

[151] Freedom From Religion Foundation v. Zielke, 663 F. Supp. 606 (1987) held that none of plaintiffs had "standing" to bring action.

[152] See Frakt & Rankin at pp. 182-188.

[153] In general, legal aspects of personnel administration are not included in this chapter; only selected aspects of human rights are presented in this section.

[154] See Berry and Wong, Vol. I, Professional Sports Leagues; Schubert, et al., Chapter 6 Labor law: developments in professional sports; Weistart and Lowell (several chapters). All three have extensive treatment of the subject. See also Wong, pp. 538-553.

have unionized for a number of sports, such as football and baseball. Maintenance and clerical personnel, both in sport and non-sport areas, and the skill trades have long had unions, but unionization of professional personnel, such as teachers, is unfamiliar to many. Unions for maintenance employees, secretarial personnel, and other groups of employees are quite different from professional athletes in that the contract is all-encompassing and individuals have no right for individual negotiating for themselves. Most management personnel in leisure services and sport enterprises will have a great deal to do with unions and their employees who are unionized and should seek to both understand the nature and appreciate the role of unions.[155]

§ 1.342   Civil rights

While one thinks first of discrimination as related to employment, there are a number of other civil rights involved, such as freedom of speech, freedom from sexual harassment, due process, invasion of privacy in drug testing, and rights related to personal information (see §1.35). Most law allegations of suits involve more than one civil rights violation, such as due process, First Amendment, and equal protection.

Discrimination. The human rights of employees include areas of discrimination similar to those for participants and users. These rights include equal opportunity for employment, equity of salary and working conditions, and due process for termination or change in employment status.[156]

The bases of equal opportunities for employment include the Fifth and Fourteenth Amendments,[157] Title VII of the Civil Rights Act of 1964, as amended, and Executive Order 11246 and Revised Order No. 4. Employment discrimination is prohibited on the basis of race, color, religion, sex, or national origin. The Vocational Rehabilitation Act of 1973 and the Age Discrimination in Employment Act of 1967 prohibit discrimination on the basis of handicap and age, respectively.[158] Veterans, also, are given preference by statute. A position is not guaranteed to one of the classes specified, only the right to have equal opportunity to apply; the qualifications for the position still must be met. A factor in determining whether equal opportunity has been complied with is the available pool of qualified persons in the appropriate geographical area and the amount of time given for such qualified persons to learn of a position and apply. Announcement of positions must be in a manner whereby those qualified, but of the special populations, would see such announcements. Also, in the interview and application processes, there are certain protections of human rights. The aforementioned acts and executive orders provide that one cannot ask about religion, gender, national origin, age or handicapped unless as employment criteria they are "bona fide occupational qualifications necessary....", known as BFOQ. The court held in Illinois that sex (male) was a BFOQ

---

[155] See Frakt and Rankin, at pp. 207-219. Has general discussion of labor relations.

[156] For further discussion, see: Appenzeller, Chapter 7; Berry and Wong, Vol. II, sec. 3.40; Frakt and Rankin at pp. 219-238; Woody and Associates, Chapter 6 Employment Discrimination Law.

[157] Text of Amendments V and XIV is in §1.3 introduction.

[158] P.L. 100-259, The Civil Rights Restoration Act of 1987 encompassed/integrated Title IX, 1972 Education Amendments; Title VI, Civil Rights Act of 1964; Age Discrimination Act of 1975; and Sec. 504, 1973 Rehabilitation Act, restoring full coverage of these acts as intended by the Congress initially.

factor where a home economics teacher brought suit to "bump" a male physical education teacher with less seniority. His responsibilities included supervising male students in locker room.[159] The focus of job qualifications must be on those skills and attributes for successful performance of the task. Further, any educational standard has to have a demonstrable relationship to successful job performance.[160] One is cautioned that in zealousness not to discriminate against minorities that care be taken against "reverse discrimination,"[161] particularly against white males. In sport, the most common allegation of discrimination is gender, discrimination against women.[162] When one sees on a position announcement "Equal opportunity employer", it means that the foregoing process for providing equal opportunity to all persons to apply for the position has been followed. Frequently one hears the term "affirmative action"; affirmative action should be distinguished from the process of equal opportunity. Affirmative action is when there is a plan to bring into better balance the number of minorities employed as related to all employees. When an agency or institution has a plan, then designated minorities to bring balance, who are in the available pool of qualified persons, are given priority in being hired.

Discrimination also can come after hire in tenure and promotion, as evidenced in an Alabama[163] and an Arkansas case.[164] In the *Cross* case, a highly successful black coach alleged that he had been bypassed as head football coach and athletic director because he was black. The court found for the plaintiff and ordered that he be promoted and that he receive back pay. In the *Lee* case, however, the court found that the person hired had qualifications based upon stated criteria superior to plaintiff's and upheld the school's not hiring plaintiff. Although dismissal actions are more frequently brought on due process, an assistant basketball coach alleged that his contract, after six years, was not renewed in retaliation for having filed an EEOC claim, which University officials thought detrimental to the institution.[165] And, in *Sennewald v. Univ. of Minnesota,* 847 F. 2d 472 (1988) a female assistant softball coach unsuccessfully brought action on gender discrimination as related to promotion under Title VII. The court held that "sex-neutral" criteria had been used in not giving her full-time status, namely programmatic and budgetary.

The Equal Pay Act of 1973 deals with equity of pay, prohibiting discrimination in the payment of wages on the basis of sex "for equal work on jobs...performed under similar working conditions." Some actions of equity were brought under Title IX of the Education Amendments of 1972, although it did not specifically refer to employment, but provided for increased emphasis on female sports and the elements of equity for

159 Zink v. Board of Education, Chrisman, 146 Ill. App. 3d 1016, 100 Ill. Dec. 657, 497 N.E. 2d 835 (1986).

160 Padilla v. Stringer, 395 F. Supp. 495 (1974) high school education requirement for zookeepers violated VII, discriminated against Hispanics.

161 McConnell, David M. Title VII at Twenty — The Unsettled Dilemma of "Reverse" Discrimination. 19 *Wake Forest Law Review* 1973-1103 (1983).

162 For example, Oates v. D.C., 824 F. 2d 87 (1987) female high school physical education teacher wanted to be head football coach; see also citations in subsequent paragraphs.

163 Lee v. Attala City School System, 588 F. 2d 499 (1979).

164 Cross v. Board of Education of Dollarway, Arkansas School Dist., 395 F. Supp. 531 (1975); see also for race discrimination in employment of coach: Hardman v. Board of Educ., Dollarway Ark. School Dist., 714 F. 2d 823 (1983); Harris v. Birmingham Board of Educ., 712 F. 2d 1377 (1983) Alabama; Lujan v. Franklin Co. Board of Educ., 766 F. 2d 917 (1985); Peques v. Morehead Parish School Board, 632 F. 2d 1279 (1980), aff'd. 706 F. 2d 735 (1983).

165 Greenwood v. Ross, 778 F. 2d 448 (1985).

sports for girls and women with boys and men do include that of the coaches. Two women coaches in Pennsylvania brought action under Title VII, alleging unequal pay for coaching in comparison with the men coaching; however, the men who coached women's sports received the same as women who coached women's sports and the court did not uphold the allegation of discrimination.[166] In a 1987 Illinois case,[167] a woman coach of girls' high school and junior high school volleyball teams asked for review of employment discrimination based on gender. Held that pay differential of coaches was based on sex of participants, not coach, and the job requirement of skill, effort and responsibilities.

Freedom of speech. The Alabama Education Association and four teachers brought a civil rights action[168] challenging the constitutionality of an Alabama statute providing for forfeiture of pay increases by teachers who engage in specified activity, namely in this situation, an extracurricular demonstration. Plaintiffs alleged that such statute violated the First Amendment rights of free speech. The court held that the statute was "overbroad" and thus unconstitutional. In another case about the same time, the plaintiff part-time coaching assistant also alleged denial of right of free speech and expression as guaranteed by the First Amendment.[169] Plaintiff had written several articles in the school paper criticizing the athletic department's rules and was dismissed from his position on the basis that his personal views seriously conflicted with his assignment in the athletic department. The court did not uphold his allegation. Free speech was held to be abridged in two 1983 cases[170] and coach was re-instated. In the Knapp case it was held unconstitutional to force a teacher to go through the superintendent to reach the Board of Education; while in the McGee situation, the coach wrote a letter to the town newspaper outlining his reasons for keeping the junior high school track program.

Freedom from sexual harassment. Another civil liberty related to working conditions is that of freedom from sexual harassment. Actions are brought under Title VII.[171] A policy related to sexual harassment and procedures for handling violations should be part of personnel practices manual.

Due process. Another legal aspect of employment is that of the constitutional right of due process, particularly as related to termination of employment or change in an

[166] Jackson v. Armstrong School Dist., 430 F. Supp. 1050 (1977); see also, Civ. Rights Div. v. Amphitheater Unified School, 140 Ariz. 83, 680 P. 2d 517 (1983); Enstad v. N. Cent. of Barnes Public School Dist. No. 65, 268 N.W. 2d 126 (N.D. 1978); Hill v. Nettleton, 455 F. Sup. 514 (1978); Hooker v. Tufts Univ., 581 F. Supp. 104 (1983) Massachusetts; Kenneveg v. Hampton Twsp. School Dist., 438 F. Supp. 575 (1977); N. Haven Board of Educ. v. Bell, 102 S. Ct. 1927 (1982); School Dist., Twshp. Mill Creek v. Commonwealth Human Relations Comm'r, 368 A. 2d 901 (Pa. Cmwlth. 1977).

See also, Dessem, R. Lawrence. Sex Discrimination in Coaching. 3 *Harvard Women's Law Journal* 97-117 (spring 1980); Stacy, Donald R., and Clarence L. Holland, Jr. Legal and Statistical Problems in Litigating Sex Discrimination Claims in Higher Edu-

cation, 11 *Journal of College and University Law* 107-177 (1984); Wildman, Stephanie M. The Legitimation of Sex Discrimination: A Critical Response to Supreme Court Jurisprudence. 63 *Oregon Law Review* 265-307 (1984). Citation content extends beyond sport participation.

[167] McCullar v. Human Rights Comm., 158 Ill. App. 3d 1011, 111 Ill. Dec. 80, 511 N.E. 2d 1375 (1987).

[168] Alabama Educ. Assoc. v. Wallace, 362 F. Supp. 682 (1973).

[169] Parker v. Graves, 340 F. Supp. 586 (1972).

[170] Knapp v. Whitaker, 577 F. Supp. 1265 (1983), aff'd./remanded 757 F. 2d 827 (1985) Illinois; McGee v. South Pemiscot School Dist.-R-V, 712 F.2d 339 (1983) Missouri newspaper letter.

[171] For further discussion, see: Law Review II, pp. 5-7.

employment contract.[172] Further, in a 1984 New York case,[173] a tenured school district administrator received a letter of reprimand relieving him from duties supervising the interscholastic athletic program. He brought proceedings for order annulling and removing the latter from his personnel file. However, the court held that the action was not a deprivation of a property right (termination, suspension, or salary reduction) and hence no due process hearing was required. The letter did not charge the administrator with incompetence or misconduct, nor accuse of any criminal conduct. The court also held no property interest in noneconomic benefits, such as work assignment, when an athletic coach/head football coach was reassigned duties.[174] However, a physical education teacher was held to have a property interest when suspended for three days without pay.[175]

It is essential that personnel policies be established, communicated, and consistently adhered to, including both the procedures and the reasons for termination or change in assignment. Teachers are expected to adhere to a standard of conduct. Just a few examples; see references and updating periodicals for additional cases. A high school basketball coach brought action for reinstatement, alleging that he was arbitrarily dismissed; however, the overwhelming evidence indicated that the coach admitted to knowingly inflicting corporal punishment on students and holding basketball practices before allowable date, notwithstanding that other school employees had allegedly not been penalized for similar violations.[176] A guidance counselor, who also served as wrestling coach, was terminated due to admitted wrongdoing, namely, instructing a freshman wrestler to misrepresent his status by weighing in for an older wrestler, who was overweight. The law provided for dismissal due to "immorality."[177] Based upon the regulation requiring teachers to use reasonable care to look out for safety of students during trip, five sixth grade teachers were dismissed following a drowning death of a student when on a field trip to some caverns. The regulation was held to be mandatory and not unduly vague; the teachers gave no instructions to the students following the tour of the caverns. One of the students had brought an inflatable raft, the students were not required to wear life jackets, and the swimmers and nonswimmers were not separated.[178] The conduct of the teachers also was in issue as the head coach and assistant coach for the boys' wrestling team were dismissed. The two teachers took six high school students to the state wrestling meet. Four female students and one adult female chaperone, the mother of one of the students, also were present; the girls were cheerleaders for the wrestling team during the year, but were not officially acting as cheerleaders at the tournament. Evidence that the teachers had left the students unsupervised while the teachers attended a party and drank alcoholic beverages and had allowed male and female students to sleep in the same rooms during school athletic excursion was sufficient to support determination that teachers had engaged in immoral conduct which rendered them unfit to teach.[179] A junior high physical education teacher

---

[172] See §1.121.

[173] Monaco v. Raymond, 471 N.Y.S. 2d 225 (1984).

[174] Jett v. Dallas Indpt. School Dist., 798 F. 2d 748 (1986).

[175] Jones v. Board of Educ., 651 F. Supp. 760 (1986).

[176] Alabama State Tenure Commission v. Bir-

mingham Board of Education, 500 So. 2d 1155 (Ala. Civ. App. 1986).

[177] Florian v. Highland Local School Dist., 24 Ohio App. 3d 41, 493 N.E. 2d 249 (1983).

[178] Westbrook v. Board of Educ., St. Louis, 724 S.W. 2d 698 (Mo. App. 1987).

[179] Schmidt v. Board of Educ., 712 S.W. 2d 45 (Mo. App. 1986).

was dismissed for "neglect of duty." While participating in a dodgeball game with her students, the teacher was hit with a ball thrown from behind. She reacted in anger, admittedly lost her self-control, grabbed the offending student and kicked her twice in the thigh, leaving substantial bruises. After the class ended, the students and teacher retired to the locker room where there was a verbal exchange, the nature of which is in dispute. The school board ordered the superintendent to investigate; he recommended dismissal. A Fair Dismissal Appeals Board panel held a hearing with the finding that the locker room incident (verbal harassment) did not constitute subject for dismissal or action, but the kicking incident evidenced neglect of duty but did not otherwise support statutory grounds for dismissal.[180] Insubordination of the high school football coach was the reason for nonrenewal of his contract. The court held that the decision was not arbitrary, capricious or discriminatory in light of evidence that coach repeatedly permitted noncertified volunteers to coach at games in violation of clearly expressed school board policy.[181]

Mandatory testing. As of the late '80s, the law related to drug, alcohol, and AIDS mandatory testing in the workplace was unsettled. The issues are essentially the same as for athletes (see §1.331), violation of the Fourth Amendment and due process. A body of case law is developing and also, there is considerable legal commentary.

§ 1.343 Protective laws and regulations

In recreation and camping, particularly, consideration must be given to Child Labor Laws[182] and to the appropriateness of workers' unemployment compensation to seasonal employees.[183] OSHA regulations and other laws and regulations related to working conditions also must be complied with. Provision of smoke-free and abestos-free environment also might be included in this section; however, many jurisdictions do not have environmental quality laws or regulations. In a D.C. case[184] an employee was terminated because she refused to work in an area occupied by other employees who smoked. The court stated that the employer owes a duty to provide all employees with a resonably safe environment, but does not owe a duty to adapt the workplace to particular sensitivities of an individual employee.

§ 1.35 Confidentiality of records

An administrator of personnel must be aware of the protection afforded personnel files. There are two federal acts which relate thereto,[185] namely, the Federal Freedom of Information Act (FOIA)[186] and the Federal Privacy Act of 1974.[187] Under the FOIA an individual has an enforceable right of access to agency records, including one's own

[180] Thomas v. Cascade Union H.S. Dist. No. 5, 80 Or. App. 736, 724 P. 2d 330 (1986).

[181] King v. Elkins Public Schools, 22 Ark. App. 52, 733 S.W. 2d 417 (1987).

[182] For example, Gabin v. Skyline Cabana Club, 54 N.J. 550, 258 A. 2d 6 (1969).

[183] The American Camping Association, Bradford Woods, Martinsville, Indiana 46151 has done considerable work in this regard.

[184] Gordon v. Raven Systems & Research, 462 A. 2d 10 (D.C. App. 1983).

[185] Waitsman, Vickie. Notes: Administrative Law — Privacy Act Exemption (j) (2)... Freedom of Information Act... 56 *Temple Law Quarterly* 127-161 (1983).

[186] 5 U.S.C. §552 (1976).

[187] 5 U.S.C. §5522a (1976).

personnel file, unless the information is covered by one of the Act's nine exemptions. While the FOIA mandates full disclosure, the Privacy Act restricts the disclosure of personal information. The agency may not release without permission of the employee personal information in one's personnel file. In the case of teachers, a vitae is considered public information, but evaluations of performance are not. The two laws differ in scope, procedure, and effect, and sometimes may not be consistent.

State and local legislation known as "Sunshine" laws also affect school board, recreation and park board, municipal governing bodies, and any other public entities' meetings. These laws basically say that deliberations and decisions must be made at open-meetings, subject to public scrutiny. However, matters of personnel because of the impact on the persons involved are often discussed in "executive session" and then the decision officially acted upon in open meeting.

The same rights accorded employees as to the "right to know" and confidentiality or privacy of personal files are given students and their records, including transcripts and disciplinary actions. Federal funds can be denied from any institution which violates the privacy provisions of the Privacy Act.[188] States, also, may have their own statutes. In an Arkansas case,[189] a newspaper sued Southern State College and the Conference of which it was a member to compel access to the financial records regarding the amount of money member institutions disbursed to student athletes. The court held that since the Conference is partially supported by public funds through institutional dues that it was subject to the Arkansas Freedom of Information Act. The court found that the information sought by the newspaper was not within the "scholastic records" exception of the Act, nor within the meaning of "educational records" protected by the State Family Education Act, specifically, that the scholastic exception of the Act is limited to individual records and disclosure of the information would not violate a student's reasonable expectation of privacy. There is serious question, however, about the narrow interpretation of "scholastic record."[190] The Buckley Amendment was held inapplicable. The Family Educational Rights and Privacy Act of 1974 (20 U.S. C.A. §1232g), known as the Buckley Amendment, has given legal protection to student records since its enactment. The implementation of the Act is primarily through the regulations issued by the U.S. Department of Education.

Six members of the University of Maryland varsity basketball team brought action against the newspaper publishers and reporters for invasion of privacy and intentional infliction of mental distress. Both the *Washington Star* and the student newspaper, *Diamondback*, were sued. The newspaper stories were in reference to the athletes' academic eligibility to play. The court held that information concerning scholastic standing of team members did not constitute tortious invasion of privacy, inasmuch as they were "public figures." The case also dealt with the "shield statute" or protection of a reporter's source.[191] The applicablity of the Texas Open Records Act to the NCAA and

---

[188] 20 U.S.C. §1230(g) to 1232(i).

[189] Arkansas Gazette Co. v. Southern State College, 273 Ark. 248, 620 S.W. 2d 258 (1981), appeal dismissed 102 S. Ct. 1416 (1982).

[190] Staton, Richard. Recent Cases Concerning the Rights of Student Athletes. 10 *J. of College & Univ. Law* 209-224 @ 221 (1983-84); see also §1.4121 Invasion of privacy.

[191] Bilney v. Evening Star Newspaper Co., 43 Md. App. 560, 406 A. 2d 652 (1979).

Southwest Athletic Conference was at issue in three separate cases[192] brought on the same issue in 1986. Various broadcasters and newspapers requested they be allowed to inspect and copy certain information relating to infractions or possible infractions of NCAA regulations by various Southwest Athletic Conference members. The court held: (1) that the Act had extraterritorial application, (2) that the Act was constitutional and did not infringe upon any academic freedom or freedom of association, and (3) that the NCAA and SWC were not educational institutions for purpose of Buckley Amendment and public had a legitimate interest in the requested information which outweighed privacy interest of others.

In the physical condition area, whether it be in an athlete's injury treatment file maintained by an athletic trainer, the fitness status and progress files of a client in a health spa, the health record of a camper, et al., these records are subject to privacy just as much as educational records are and must be so maintained.

§ 1.4 Tort Liability

The word tort means wrong. It comes from the Latin derivative "tortus," meaning twisted. At one time it was in common usage in the English language, being used as a synonym for wrong. Although the word is still used in the French, it has faded from general usage in the English and has gradually acquired a technical legal meaning.

It is difficult to give a precise definition of tort liability. A tort is a civil wrong, in contrast to a criminal act. Whereas criminal liability (see §1.2) is directed toward the protection of interests common to the public and the person committing the crime is punished, the field of torts focuses upon the compensation of individuals for losses which they have suffered in respect to their legally recognized interests. The compensation is provided by the tortfeasor (wrongdoer). These losses arising out of human activities cover a very wide scope and, thus, so does the field of tort. Generally, liability is based upon the unreasonable interference with the interests of others, but what is unreasonable is subject to much interpretation according to the situation at hand.

The field of tort liablity may be divided into three categories: (1) intentional acts to harm, (2) unintentional acts which harm or negligence, and (3) strict liability or liability without proof of fault.

§ 1.41 Intentional acts to harm

There are three elements of intentional torts — the act as the proximate cause of the injury, the intent to bring about the injury, and the injury. The intent does not have to be a hostile intent or an intent to do harm, but rather an intent to bring about the harm in a way in which the law will not sanction. Intent should be distinguished from motive. Motive is the reason for the behavior, while intent is a state of mind, a desire to act in a

---

[192] Kneeland v. N.C.A.A., 650 F. Supp. 1047 (1986) Open Records Act applicable; Kneeland v. N.C.A.A., 650 F. Supp. 1064 (1986) Act Constitu-tional; Kneeland v. N.C.A.A., 650 F. Supp. 1076 (1986) Buckley Amendment not applicable.

way that will bring about the consequences. The motive may serve to aggravate, mitigate, or excuse the wrong; for example, acting with malice may permit assessment of punitive damages, while acting in self-defense may be a complete defense.

The doctrine of respondeat superior (see Chapter 3), wherein the employer is responsible for the results of the actions of employees or volunteers, usually is not applicable when the person commits an intentional tort.[193] The employee or volunteer is individually responsible (see §3.41).

Very closely related to intentional acts to harm, and often with the same results, is "willful and wanton misconduct" (see §§2.241, 3.41); and, it is this phrase which is used in nearly all statutes providing immunity or limited immunity. Immunity does not attach if there is such conduct (see §§12.152, 17.1,4.234). Willful and wanton conduct may not be indulged in for the direct intent to harm, but by the very nature of the conduct the results are substantially certain to occur and therefore inferred to have been intended.[194] Reckless misconduct also has been held to intend the consequences (see §1.41322).

Intentional torts may be categorized into three types: interference with property, interference (physical) with person, and disturbance of intangible interests (mental and emotional).

§ 1.411 Interference with property

Violation of property interests include interference both with the rights of possession, such as trespass to land, and with the rights of use and enjoyment, such as private nuisance.[195] Trespass generally is in relation to private property, since public parks and community facilities usually are open to the public and thus one is not a trespasser. However, there can be trespass when areas/buildings are closed, and such trespass may be brought under violation of an ordinance or statute and prosecuted as a crime by the government, rather than as a civil wrong where compensation is given the owner. There, also, is trespass to chattels, where goods are damaged or destroyed, used in an unpermitted way, or moved to another place. Trespass can bring to the trespasser both a civil and a criminal action (see §1.22). Of particular concern to the professional involved in providing services and managing property is what duty is owed to a trespasser and the rights of a trespasser (see §2.123, §12.13).

Conversion is another type of property interest violation. Essentially it is the civil action paralleling the criminal action for theft/stealing, interferring with or retaining property so the rightful owner cannot use it appropriately. For example, in an Illinois case[196] the coach was relieved of his coaching duties on Dec. 18 and was requested by the Athletic Director on Friday, January 15 to remove part of his coaching reference material from the file cabinet. On that day, plaintiff took two boxes to the area and

[193] Willis v. Dade Co. School Board, 411 So. 2d 245 (Fla. App. 1982), pet. denied 418 So. 2d 1278 (1982).

[194] Wanton and willful misconduct was an issue in, for example: Bernesak v. Catholic Bishop of Chicago, 87 Ill. App. 3d 681, 42 Ill. Dec. 672, 409 N.E. 2d 287 (1980) playground crack-the-whip, first aid; Fessenden v. Smith, 255 Iowa 847, 124 N.W. 2d 554 (1964); Jarvis

v. Herrin City Park Dist., 6 Ill. App. 3d 516, 285 N.E. 2d 564 (1972) sliding board on playground; Maloney v. Elmhurst Park Dist., 47 Ill. 2d 367, 265 N.E. 2d 654 (1971) artificial hill in park.

[195] For brief discussion, see Frakt and Rankin at pp. 32-36, 110-113; see §4.4 for discussion of nuisance.

[196] Williams v. Board of Educ., 52 Ill. App. 3d 328, 10 Ill. Dec. 161, 367 N.E. 2d 549 (1977).

determined they would not hold all of the material, so on Monday the 28th he took additional boxes to remove the materials and found the drawers of the file cabinet empty. Subsequently, on February 8, plaintiff, accompanied by the Athletic Director, discovered a small quantity of the material, primarily non-coaching material. Later that day 85 empty manila folders, which had contained the material and were labeled, were found. The labels were used to itemize the nature of the materials taken. The files had been cleared on two separate occasions by the student manager on direction of the athletic director and the principal. The first time he was to put the material in a box, the second "to get rid of it." The janitor removed the boxes found on the floor on two consecutive evenings (January 28 and 29), but the second night the boxes were put in the janitor's room and were not discarded until two days later. The superintendent testified that the teachers could rely upon security and assume that their property would be safe. The coach alleged that his files had been developed over many years of coaching and were essential to doing a good coaching job; he sought $50,000 for the materials destroyed. Court held for the coach for damages for loss of personal coaching library; however, there was difficulty in establishing the amount of damages. Under trover and conversion, property converted is ordinarily measured in terms of fair market value, but, of course, a coach's professional papers are not typically sold in the market place, so the burden was on the plaintiff to give rationale for support of the amount of damages. The school was found not to be immune from tort liability under the State Tort Immunity Act. The jury returned a verdict for $32,500.

Interference with a "property right," meaning a commodity from which one makes money, also has been subject to suit (see also introduction §1.3). At a county fair a reporter filmed a performer, which picture was shown on the news without permission. The court distinguished between newsworthiness and "professional property" from which a living was made. Judgment for plaintiff on violation of Constitutional right.[197] Misappropriation of one's name, photos, logos, et al. is subject to damages.[198]

§ 1.412   Disturbances of intangible interests (emotional and mental)

Particularly public figures, such as athletes and coaches, are subject to disturbances of intangible interests, such as invasion of privacy, defamation (libel and slander), and misrepresentation. Another type of disturbance is that of inflicting mental stress or emotional harm to an individual. Direct physical harm may exist to a nominal amount, but there is extensive emotional damage to the individual; and, there is physiological response to emotional stress. Damages for mental stress is of more recent origin than physical and economic damages (see §2.4). The conduct of defendant must be extreme and outrageous, beyond the boundaries of societal decency; mere insulting or offensive language is not subject to liability.[199]

---

[197] Zacchini v. Scripps-Howard Broadcasting Co., 47 Ohio St. 2d 224, 351 N.E. 2d 454, rev'd. 433 U.S. 562, 97 S. Ct. 2849 (1977); see also Joe Namath case in next section, and Virgil J. Time, Inc., 527 F. 2d 1122 (1975) photos unauthorized used to illustrate article.

[198] For example, Cepeda v. Swift & Co., 291 F. Supp. 242, aff'd. 415 F. 2d 1205 (1969); Gautier v. Pro-Football, Inc., 278 A.D. 431, 106 N.Y.S. 2d 553 (1951); Palmer v. Schonhorn Enterprises, 96 N.J. Supr. 72, 232 A. 2d 458 (1967); Uhlaender v. Henricksen, 316 F. Supp. 1277 (1970).

[199] For brief discussion, see Woody and Associates at pp. 161-162; see also: Prosser and Keeton at pp. 54-66 Infliction of Mental Distress.

§ 1.4121   Invasion of privacy

Invasion of privacy, the intentional tort, should be distinguished from the right to privacy, a human right (see §1.35). There are several aspects of invasion of privacy, including appropriation of person's name or likeness, intrusion upon one's solitude or seclusion, public disclosure of private facts and publicity which places the individual in a false light in the public eye.[200] Drug testing involves the constitutional invasion of privacy. (See §§1.331).

Joe Namath (football) sued *Sports Illustrated* for $2,250,000 for violating his rights to privacy for using his photograph unauthorized. The court held that he was seeking damages, not for violating his privacy but because of a property right which had been violated; that is, he was deprived of income from an endorsement. *Sports Illustrated* had used his picture in a subscription promotion. The court dismissed the case, stating that freedom of speech and press transcended right to privacy in this situation inasmuch as he was newsworthy and his picture had appeared in the magazine for many years in connection with cover and feature stories.[201] However, commercialization or appropriation of another's name or likeness for one's own benefit is an action for which one may recover.[202]

Warren Spahn (baseball) recovered money damages and injunctive relief for publication of a fictitious biography in that it constituted an unauthorized exploitation;[203] however, the court in a subsequent case[204] questioned the decision as related to false reports.

Invasion of privacy also was involved in a field trip discipline situation in *Webb v. McCullough*, 828 F. 2d 1151 (1987). The court held that the principal's search of student's hotel room for alcohol was reasonable on basis of his authority as principal and especially in view of the principal's in loco parentis authority on the trip; however, the student's constitutional rights were violated when the principal broke through locked bathroom door in her hotel room, knocking her against wall.

§ 1.4122   Defamation — libel and slander

Defamation is communication which tends to injure one's reputation, that is, diminishes the esteem, respect, goodwill or confidence in which the plaintiff is held. Slander is communication of an oral (spoken) nature, while libel is communication through one of the forms of publication. Communication requires involvement of a third person(s) in order for the defamatory statement to be actionable. Truth is a complete defense; however, the plaintiff may not recover if the statement was "fair comment" regarding a public figure, which includes coaches, athletes, and player agents. The

[200] For brief discussion, see Berry and Wong, Vol. II. at §4.15; Schubert, et al. at §7.2(5) pp. 194-197; Weistart and Lowell at pp. 1028-1030, §8.17; see also: Prosser and Keeton at Chapter 20 Privacy.

[201] Namath v. Sports Illustrated, 80 Misc. 2d 531, 363 N.Y.S. 2d 276 (1975), aff'd. 48 A.D. 2d 487, 371 N.Y.S. 2d 10 (1975), aff'd. 39 N.Y.S. 2d 897, 352 N.E. 2d 584 (1976).

[202] Martin Luther King, Jr. Center for Social

Change v. American Heritage Products, 250 Ga. 135, 296 S.E. 697 (1982).

[203] Spahn v. Julian Messner, Inc., 43 Misc. 2d 219, 250 N.Y.S. 2d 529 (1964), 18 N.Y. 2d 324, 274 N.Y.S. 2d 877, 221 N.E. 2d 543 (1966), app. dism'd. 393 U.S. 1046, 89 S. Ct. 676 (1969).

[204] Time, Inc. v. Hill, 385 U.S. 374, 87 S. Ct. 534 (1967); see also Time, Inc. v. Johnston, 448 F. 2d 378 (1971).

comment, though, must involve activities of the sporting world or of whatever area of professional endeavor in which the public figure is engaged. Fair comment and malice to injure statements must be distinguished. Freedom of speech and press as a constitutionally protected right, also, has been applied.[205] A baseball umpire brought defamation action against the owner of a major league baseball team for owner's alleged defamatory statements to the media. The owner criticized the umpire as incompetent and biased and referred to certain calls made by umpire as factual support for statement. Court held that these statements fell within ambit of "pure opinion" and found for defendant.[206]

A former high school varsity football coach brought action for defamation in connection with a letter and statements issued by superintendent concerning student's death while participating in a football game. The superintendent said to the press that she would officially reprimand each member of the high school football coaching staff who had not followed required procedures, namely, a required physical examination had not been performed, nor had parental consent been obtained prior to the student's participation. The court held for the superintendent saying that her statement was protected by qualified privilege due to interest in providing public with information as to what steps were being taken to prevent reoccurrence of tragic incident. The coach failed to prove that the superintendent's statements were motivated by malice, such as would overcome the superintendent's defense of qualified privilege.[207] In another New York case,[208] a coach brought action regarding two letters which had been written regarding two incidents of his behavior at campus parties in which he was allegedly in a "severely intoxicated state," for damages to his reputation as a coach. The letters were written two years after the incidents to the University president and Board of Trustees. The defendant newspaper featured the letters which had been provided to it by one of the board of trustees.

In *Kondos v. West Virginia Board of Regents*,[209] the football coach brought action against the University president for allegedly saying untrue, slanderous, malicious and defamatory statements. In *Johnson v. Corinthian Television Corp.*,[210] the Oklahoma court held a wrestling coach and school teacher to be a public figure; and Washington held similarly regarding a basketball coach.[211] In the 1984 case,[212] the basketball coach sued *Sports Illustrated* for libel and a player for slander. The player accused the coach as

[205] For brief readings and additional cases related to sport, see Appenzeller and Appenzeller at pp. 108-110, 174-178, 192-195; Baley and Matthews at pp. 6-7; Berry & Wong, II, at §4.14; Clement, at pp. 91-94; Schubert, et al. at §7.2(4) pp. 192-194; Weistart and Lowell at pp. 1024-1027; see also: Prosser & Keeton at Chapter 19. The lead case establishing the standard on freedom of the press and public figure is N.Y. Times Co. v. Sullivan, 376 U.S. 254, 84 S. Ct. 710 (1964).

[206] Parks v. Steinbrenner, 520 N.Y.S. 2d 374 (1987).

[207] Santavicca v. City of Yonkers, 132 A.D. 2d 656, 518 N.Y.S. 2d 29 (1987).See also, Mahoney v. Adirondack Publ. Co., 123 A.D. 2d 10, 509 N.Y.S. 2d 193 (1986) rev'd/dism'd. 71 N.Y.2d 31, 523 N.Y.S. 2d 480, 517 N.E. 2d 1365 (1987) H.S. football coach, newspaper report on behavior, no malice proven.

[208] Talbot v. Johnson Newspaper Corp., 123 A.D. 2d 147, 511 N.Y.S. 2d 152, aff'd. 71 N.Y. 2d 827, 527 N.Y.S. 2d 729 (1988).

[209] Kondos v. West Virginia Board of Regents, 318 F. Supp. 394 (1970).

[210] Johnston v. Corinthian Television Corp., 583 P. 2d 1101 (Okla. 1978).

[211] Grayson v. Curtis Publishing Co., 72 Wash. 2d 999, 436 P. 2d 756 (1967); see also Basarich v. Rodegherd, 24 Ill. App. 2d 889, 321 N.E. 2d 739 (1974) h.s. coach; Curtis Publishing Co. v. Butts, 388 U.S. 130, 87 S. Ct. 1975 (1967), reh. denied 389 U.S. 889, 88 S. Ct. 11; Vandenburg v. Newsweek, Inc., 507 F. 2d 1024 (1975) track coach.

[212] Barry v. Time, Inc., 584 F. Supp. 1110 (1984).

involved in a NCAA violation and the magazine printed it. Plaintiff failed to plead actual malice with sufficient specificity and the magazine was protected by privilege of neutral reportage. The coach, also, can be the defendant, as was the situation in a Michigan case[213] which held that the coach could criticize a suspended player. The basketball coach was sued for defamation by the player (team captain) when he suspended him and made statements regarding the captain's loyalty. The court held that the coach could be liable only if his statements were made with actual malice and activated by improper motives and ill will. In a 1983 case[214] a well-known baseball player's agent was held to be a "public figure."

Actions on defamation (libel) have been brought by participants against the publisher of a magazine, but there has to be proof of malice and falseness beyond "fair comment."[215] Once a public figure, seemingly always a public figure. Johnston lost his case against *Sports Illustrated,* even though he had not played for 12 years. The court held that the passing of time did not change the status.[216] Statements of a libelous nature usually are in relation to a single individual; however, action was brought against the publisher regarding a statement that the Oklahoma football team used drugs.[217]

Psychology of sport is an important element in sport competition. In *Institute of Athletic Motivation v. University of Illinois,*[218] the authors of a motivation assessment instrument brought a libel and slander action against a university professor who was critical of the instrument. In this particular situation, the professor was not found guilty.

There has been some concern regarding student recommendations and personnel evaluations in the mid-80s. There appears to be qualified privilege of opinion where evaluation is a part of the job; however, there is no protection if the person making the statements knew they were false or acted in reckless disregard for the truth. The burden is on the plaintiff to prove malice, not on the defendant to prove truthfulness. Since whether or not one is defamed depends on the effect the "publication" had upon those who received it, the statement must be capable of conveying a defamatory meaning to the hearer; therefore the focus must be upon the statement and its predictable effect upon those who receive the publication.[219]

While the preponderance of cases relate to sport, parks and recreation also have been subject to libel and slander. In *Moresi v. Teche Publishing Company,*[220] the alleged

213 Iacco v. Bohannon, 70 Mich. App. 463, 245 N.W. 2d 791 (1976).

214 Woy v. Turner, 573 F. Supp. 35 (1983).

215 Bell v. Associated Press, 584 F. Supp. 128 (1984) football; Cepeda v. Cowles Magazines & Broadcasting, 392 F. 2d 417 (1968), cert. denied 393 U.S. 840, 89 S. Ct. 117 (1968) baseball; Cohen v. Cowles Publishing Co., 42 Wash. 262, 273 P. 2d 893 (1954) jockey; Dempsey v. Time, Inc., 43 Misc. 2d 754, 252 N.Y.S. 2d 186 (1964) aff'd. 254 N.Y.S. 2d 80 (1964) boxing; Gomez v. Murdoch, 193 N.J. Super. 595, 475 A. 2d 622 (1984) jockey; King v. Burris, 588 F. Supp. 1152 (1984) baseball; Milkovich v. News-Herald, 15 Oh. St. 3d 292 (1984) wrestling coach; Smith v. McMullen, 589 F. Supp. 642 (1984) slander, baseball general manager.

216 Time, Inc. v. Johnston, 448 F. 2d 378 (1971).

217 Fawcett Publications, Inc. v. Morris, 377 P. 2d 42 (Okla. 1962), cert. denied 376 U.S. 513, 84 S. Ct. 964 (1964).

218 Institute of Athletic Motivation v. University of Illinois, 114 Cal. App. 3d 1, 170 Cal. Rptr. 411(1980).

219 For example, Belliveau v. Rerick 504 A. 2d 1360 (R.I. 1986) professor sued department chair for libel on statement when professor seeking promotion; Colson v. Stieg, 86 Ill. App. 3d 993, 42 Ill. Dec. 53, 408 N.E. 2d 431, aff'd./remanded 89 Ill. 2d 205, 60 Ill. Dec. 449, 433 N.E. 2d 246 (1982) department chair statement to university personnel committee, sued for slander; True v. Ladner, 513 A. 2d 257 (Me. 1986) superintendent of schools found guilty of slander for teacher recommendation.

220 Moresi v. Teche Publishing Co., 298 So. 2d 901 (La. App. 1974), writ refused 302 So. 2d 309 (1974).

defamatory statement was printed in the Sunday and Friday newspaper editions locally and went out on the UP wire service. The statement was that the beach would be closed on Fourth of July because of water pollution. The plaintiff, who operated the campground and store on property leased from the State and also operated the beach as a concession from the State, alleged that the statement caused him to lose a tremendous number of visitors and hence income. The reporter who wrote the story said that a person in the Parish Health Unit told him that there were E. coli bacteria in the water and, therefore, he could not recommend swimming or water contact sports. On the basis of such information, the reporter stated that the water was polluted. Plaintiff could not recover because he could not show that the stories were untrue (in fact they were true about the bacteria and the court said that a newspaper has a duty to provide the public with such information about a public beach), were defamatory (no malice and portions of the story were complimentary to the plaintiff's enterprise), or were written with a reckless disregard for the truth.

Saturday 6 a.m. parents brought eight-year-old son to the emergency room of the hospital for treatment of a head cut he had received on a camping trip. The doctor refused treatment and they eventually went to another hospital where 15 stitches were taken to close the cut. The parents wrote a letter to the paper regarding the situation and raising questions of medical treatment and ethics. The doctor sued the letterwriters and newspaper which published the letter. The charges were substantially true and the defendant had acted without malice, only to bring to public attention the concern. Judgment for defendant.[221]

§ 1.4123　Misrepresentation/deceit/fraud

While the three words — misrepresentation, deceit, and fraud — are used interchangeably in many contexts, they do have broad and varied meanings, and frequently one is used to define the other. Fraud might be considered a generic term, the most vague of the terms, and whose meaning must be defined in the context in which it is being used. The law of misrepresentation may be divided into three categories: (1) action for deceit, (2) action based upon negligence, and (3) action based upon strict liability. It is acknowledged that there is some overlapping of these bases or theories, and there are a good number of areas of law which have some aspect of misrepresentation, that is, of a false statement.

The five elements of the tort cause of action in deceit are:
1. false representation of material fact or concealed material fact
2. such representation was known to be false by the one making it or it was made recklessly without any knowledge of its truthfulness
3. such representation was made with intention that another rely upon it and to induce or refrain from action
4. that one did reasonably rely upon the false representation and took action based thereon

[221] Alleman v. Vermilion Publishing Corp., 316 So. 2d 837 (La. App. 1975).

5.   damage or injury occurred from such reliance

Each of the four illustrative cases[222] set forth these elements.

In the *Merten* case an exculpatory contract with a riding stable was in issue. As part of the contract, there was a misrepresentation in regard to insurance. Such false statement rendered the exculpatory contract unenforceable. The plaintiff had relied upon the untrue statement in making the contract.

The court said in the *Beeck* case that while the false statement may have been made innocently and mistakenly made, when such statement is recklessly asserted, an intent to defraud will be implied. In this situation the misrepresentation was in regard to the manufacturer of a water slide whereby the plaintiff lost a valid cause of action against the actual manufacturer.

In the third situation, the court held that the team and team physician had an obligation to disclose information regarding the nature of a player's injury and that there was fraudulent concealment of medical information, and had this information been known by plaintiff a different course of action might have been taken. Intentional concealment of material fact is actionable fraud only if there is a fiduciary relationship giving right to duty to disclose it; the court held that the relationship between physician and patient (player) is fiduciary in nature and created such a duty. The team physician was obligated to disclose all information to the patient/player for such person to make knowledgable decision of proposed treatment.

There was a different result in the *Whitlock* case, for the plaintiff did not rely upon information or fact which might have been represented or concealed. The plaintiff was a participant in a simulated deep dive experiment and was highly educated and had information and did not rely upon other fact or information.

§ 1.413   Interference with person (physical)

Perhaps the most extensive intentional tort interfering with the person is that of assault and battery. However, another type of interference is that of false imprisonment.

§ 1.4131   False imprisonment

False imprisonment is applicable both to sport and to parks and recreation, as well as camping. False imprisonment is confinement of an individual, improper detention or restraint. It does not have to be incarceration, but a wrongful restriction of the freedom of an individual to move about. There must be intent to confine, but there does not have to be malice; it must be against the will of the one confined. If the plaintiff consents to go somewhere or remain in a certain area, this may be used as a defense. Confinement (preventing leaving an area) can come in a variety of ways, such as: (1) actual or apparent physical barriers, physical force or threats of force (express or implied), duress

---

[222] Beeck v. Aquaslide 'N' Dive Corp., 350 N.W. 2d 149 (Iowa 1984); Krueger v. San Francisco Forty Niners, 189 Cal. App. 3d 875, 234 Cal. Rptr. 579 (1987); Merton v. Nathan, 108 Wis. 2d 205, 321 N.W. 2d 173 (1982) Whitlock v. Duke Univ., 637 F. Supp. 1463 (1986) aff'd. 829 F. 2d 1340 (1987). See also, Valcin v. Public Health, 473 So. 2d 1297 (Fla. App. 1984) fraudulent misrepresentation overcomes presumption of valid medical consent.

sufficient to vitiate consent, or under color of legal authority (sometimes called false arrest; plaintiff believes defendant has such power and submits against one's own will, when in fact defendant has no such power); and (2) originally properly restrained, but now has right to depart, defendant continues to hold, that is fails to perform legal duty to release plaintiff or show means of exit; an unknown exit is comparable to none.[223] The defendant must show legal justification, once the fact of intentional confinement is shown.[224]

§ 1.4132   Assault and battery

While usually the two terms assault and battery are used together, they are separate and distinct torts. One may exist without the other. In a simplified distinction, assault is the threat (non-contact) to use force while battery is the actual use (contact) of force, the unlawful application of force to the person of another. Assault is basically a "mental invasion," while a battery is a physical invasion. The key to assault is "apprehension." However, the apprehension cannot be just fear; it must be an "offer" to use force and an apparent ability and opportunity to carry out the threat immediately. Mere words, no matter how threatening for the future or insulting to the present, do not constitute an assault. And, there must be intent on the part of the defendant to arouse apprehension and interfere with the plaintiff's personal integrity. To commit a battery there must be some positive, affirmative act resulting in an unpermitted touching or contact with the person, but there does not need to be excessive force.[225] It does not have to be a direct application of force, such as a fist hitting a person, as so often is visualized as a battery. The defendant can set in motion the act or force which ultimately produces the desired intentional result. There does not have to be a hostile intent on the part of the defendant, but rather the intent to bring about contact and the absence of consent to the contact on the part of the plaintiff.[226] The defense to battery is consent by the injured person.[227]

A trespass to the person cannot become lawful by being done with good intentions; the least touching of the body of another against one's will constitutes a battery. For example, at a roller skating rink, skater sustained a fracture of her left arm and was taken to the first aid room. In the face of protest by injured plaintiff and her husband, a person acting in behalf of the rink manipulated and pulled her arm with "heavy force" causing pain. He was not a physician or person trained in emergency care, but a former prize fight manager. Even with a physician, the consent of the individual is essential.[228]

Criminal assault and battery must be distinguished from civil assault and battery (see §1.24). The same act can have both actions. Where does negligence fit in? There can be

[223] An old case, Talcott case in §15.122, points out that where police prevented plaintiff, who was at the baseball stadium to purchase tickets, from exiting the regular way because of crowds and did not point out other means of egress and plaintiff did not know how to get out, was guilty of falsely imprisoning him on failing to help him find his way out.

[224] For brief discussion, Frakt and Rankin at pp. 112-113; Woody and Associates at pp. 160-161; see also: Prosser and Keeton at pp. 47-54.

[225] Rodriquez v. Johnson, 132 Misc. 2d 555, 504

N.Y.S. 2d 379 (1986) school bus matron struck child, liable for battery although slap was not an excessive use of force.

[226] See Prosser & Keeton at pp. 39-47.

[227] McQuiggan v. Boy Scouts of America, 73 Md. App. 705, 536 A. 2d 137 (1988) plaintiff injured at Scout meeting, the boys were shooting paper clips at each other, hit eye, held plaintiff consented.

[228] Clayton v. New Dreamland Roller Skating Rink, 14 N.J. Super. 390, 82 A. 2d 458 (1951).

no negligence assault and battery because assault and battery requires intent, while negligence has an absence of intent to injure (see §1.42). *The action of both criminal and civil assault and battery is against the individual who allegedly committed such assault and battery, while action in negligence may be brought against a person or entity who had a duty to protect the plaintiff from unreasonable risk of harm (see §2.1), that is, from being assaulted and battered.* When youngsters get into a fight, whether in school or a recreational setting, seldom is an action brought on assault and battery, but usually on negligence for inadequate supervision (see §18.32).[229]

There are no established categories of assault and battery, but it would be appropriate to discuss this tort by who commits the tort and against whom. First are injuries to spectators, which may occur by actions of employees (see §15.16), of players (see §15.15), and of other spectators and third parties (see §15.1231). The location of assault and battery against spectators can take place not only in the stands but also adjacent to the stands,[230] in the rest rooms,[231] and on parking areas.[232] Although many of these cases involved assault and battery, many also involved negligence in terms of protection of the spectators and, hence, are contained in Chapter 15.[233] Another aspect of assault and battery, which appeared to increase at the beginning of the decade of the '80s, is that concerning sports officials.[234] For a discussion of this aspect, see §15.3 Sports officials. See also §1.21 Protection against felonies for attacks on individuals in different situations, such as parking lots.[235]

Also of concern are assaults by third persons, such as at a bowling alley.[236] Patrons are to be protected, but there must be some reason to believe that a person has violent propensity. In the *Gustaveson* case the management was trying to curb rude, abusive and

[229] For example, Comuntiz v. Pinellas County School Board, 508 So. 2d 750 (Fla. App. 1987) high school student physically beaten during school lunch hour just outside school cafeteria, no teacher posted for cafeteria supervision; Broward County School Board v. Ruiz, 493 So. 2d 474 (Fla. App. 1986) plaintiff attacked and beaten by three students while waiting in cafeteria for ride after school, no supervision specifically assigned to this area although there was a comprehensive supervisory plan which evidenced school's recognitiion for supervision at that place and time, court held school owed duty to provide adequate security.

[230] For example, St. Pierre v. Lombard, 512 So. 2d 1206 (La. App. 1987) fatal stabbing behind the stands at high school football game, duty does not extend to unforeseeable criminal act of independent third party unless constructive notice of intended conduct.

[231] For example, Townsley v. Cincinnati Gardens, Inc., 39 Ohio App. 2d 5, 314 N.E. 2d 409 (1974) rev'd. 39 Ohio Misc. 1, 314 N.E. 2d 406 (1973) dimly lit restroom, basketball event, not insurer of safety but security had admitted was their area for security responsibility, defendant liable.

[232] For example, Boyd v. Gulfport Municipal Separate School Dist., 821 F. 2d 308 (1987) plaintiff attacked in parking lot of school stadium after attending football game.

[233] For example, Cook v. School Dist. VH3J & Amity School Dist., 83 Or. App. 292, 731 P. 2d 443 (1987) intense rival high schools, basketball game, plaintiff attacked by three students; for brief discussion of nature of spectator violence as different type from player violence and crowd control, see Baley and Matthews at pp. 113-114.

[234] For example, high school football game referee assaulted by game spectator sued high school and principal, plaintiff failed to make factual allegations to connect alleged negligent acts of school and principal to harm suffered, Litomisky v. St. Charles H.S., 482 So. 2d 30 (La. App. 1986).

[235] Liability for public entities rests in the Tort Claims Act. Delaware court held action not barred in Rainey v. Wilmington Parking Authority, 488 A. 2d 906 (Del. Sup. 1984) plaintiff assaulted and robbed; but two Pennsylvania cases gave protection: Chevalier v. Philadelphia, 91 Pa. Cmwlth. 36, 496 A. 2d 900, rev'd. 532 A. 2d 411 (Pa. 1987) city not liable for criminal acts performed by third parties, plaintiff alleged inadequate lighting made a dangerous condition; Rhoads v. Lancaster Parking Authority, 520 A. 2d 122 (Pa. Cmwlth. 1987) plaintiff beaten and stabbed by three intoxicated assailants.

[236] Gustaveson v. Gregg, 655 P. 2d 693 (Utah 1982). Just one example.

vulgar behavior by curtailing drinking and in other ways. There was considerable animosity. It was after some comments and other action that plaintiff was struck in the jaw, fracturing it, breaking his dentures, and causing nerve damage. Neither of the parties to the fracas had exhibited violent tendencies before. The court held that in the absence of such, the violence of these two was not foreseeable; however, the court did say that the proprietor must use ordinary care and diligence to protect patrons, but the duty does not extend to becoming an insurer of safety. Often a fracas resulting in assault and battery will occur when patrons become intoxicated (see §1.221).

In a 1988 case, *Leger v. Stockton Unified School Dist.*, 249 Cal. Rptr. 688 (1988), a student member of the wrestling team sued the school district, high school principal, and team coach for injuries sustained when he was assaulted by a non-student in an unsupervised restroom, where he had gone to change clothes for wrestling practice. It was alleged that defendants failed to protect plaintiff, when they knew or reasonably should have known that the restroom was unsafe and attacks by non-students were likely to occur. The court held that the constitutional (state) provision giving students and staff of public schools right to attend safe, secure, and peaceful campuses was not self-executing so as to provide right to sue for damages; that school authorities owed student duty of care; that school authorities were liable to student for injury; and that the statute providing for immunity of public entity or public employee was not applicable. The court stated that while school districts nor their employees are insurers of safety of their students, a student is owed a duty for them to use a degree of care which persons of ordinary prudence, charged with comparable duties, would exercise in same circumstances, particularly where injury was allegedly foreseeable. Neither schools nor their restrooms are dangerous places per se and students are not at risk merely because they are at school. School authorities who know of threats of violence that they believe are well-founded may not refrain from taking reasonable preventive measures simply because violence has yet to occur. The California statute regarding public entity providing police protection service also was discussed.

Teachers, too, not infrequently are the subject of assaults by students. The courts have held that the remedy was workers' compensation.[237]

§ 1.41321   Corporal punishment and physical discipline

Discipline and disciplining is discussed in §18.324. The topic of corporal punishment, however, is included under assault and battery inasmuch as it is a matter of degree and intent as to whether physical punishment is justifiable and appropriate discipline or it is, indeed, assault and battery.[238] While physical disciplining can take place in other settings, corporal punishment is most often thought of in terms of schools. Local schools usually have regulations regarding a teacher's use of corporal punishment; and, some states have legislation regarding corporal punishment.[239]

---

[237] Halliman v. L.A. Unified School Dist., 209 Cal. Rptr. 175 (1984). Illustrative case only.

[238] For brief discussion, see Arnold at pp. 91-93, using corporal or exercise punishment.

[239] e.g., Fla.Stat.Ann. §232.27; Maine Rev. Stat. Ann. tit. 20 §918; Ill.Rev.Stat.Ann. chp. 122 §24-24, 34-84a.

Usually "reasonable" force is permitted, but what is such force is a jury question. In the well-known *Ingraham* case[240] the court set forth some "considerations": seriousness of the offense, the attitude and past behavior of the child, the nature and severity of the punishment, the age and strength of the child, and the availability of less severe but equally effective means of discipline. Efforts have been made to bring action under the Eighth (prohibition against cruel and inhumane punishment) and Fourteenth Amendments (due process); however, such actions have not been successful, particularly when corporal punishment has been authorized by a school system or the state.[241] For decades, reasonable corporal punishment has been upheld by the courts on the legal concept of *in loco parentis* (see §2.1112). Successful actions have alleged excessive force, as evidenced in the cases; described in subsequent paragraphs.

In *LaFrentz v. Gallagher*,[242] action was brought for assault and battery when the teacher in a softball class pushed the pupil against the backstop after the student had made some comments. The court held that the act of the teacher was necessary to maintain discipline in the future and did not constitute assault and battery. Two Louisiana cases against physical education teachers did find liability for assault and battery. In one,[243] a 14-year-old boy sustained a broken arm when his physical education teacher, who was a large person, grabbed him, lifted him up, and shook him — held excessive physical force. In the other case,[244] the physical education instructor severely beat a high school pupil with a wooden paddle so that he was hospitalized for three days. In a 1981 case,[245] a teacher was sued for both alleged slanderous remarks and assaults and batteries.

Poolside discipline in a physical education swim class was at issue in *Metzger v. Osbeck,* 841 F. 2d 518 (1988). Plaintiff, during class, was trading baseball cards with several fellow students on the pool deck. Several feet away the defendant instructor was talking to a student teacher when he overheard plaintiff using inappropriate language in a conversation with a female student. The instructor walked to where plaintiff was standing, and, standing behind him, placed his arms around plaintiff's neck and shoulder area. The instructor asked him quietly "Was that you using foul language?", to which he got no response, so said "That kind of language is unacceptable in this class. Do you understand me?" In the course of the questioning, the instructor's arm moved slightly upward, from plaintiff's Adam's apple to under his chin; and, at some point plaintiff felt pressure on the underneath portion of the chin and had to stand up on his toes. The instructor then released plaintiff, intending to turn him around. Instead, plaintiff, who had lost consciousness at some point, fell face down onto the pool deck, suffering lacerations to his lower lip, a broken nose, fractured teeth and other injuries requiring hospitalization. Plaintiff brought civil rights action, alleging that the instructor's excessive force and appreciable physical pain therefrom constituted invasion of Fifth Amendment liberty interest in his personal security and a violation of

---

[240] Ingraham v. Wright, 498 F. 2d 248, rev'd. 525 F. 2d 909, aff'd. 430 U.S. 651, 97 S. Ct. 1401 (1977) lengthy opinion giving historical background of corporal punishment.

[241] See Ingraham case preceding footnote.

[242] LaFrentz v. Gallagher, 105 Ariz. 255, 462 P. 2d 804 (1969).

[243] Frank v. Orleans Parish School Board, 195 So. 2d 451 (La. App. 1967), writ refused 250 La. 635, 197 So. 2d 653 (1967).

[244] Johnson v. Horace Mann Mutual Insurance Co., 241 So. 2d 588 (La. App. 1970).

[245] McIntosh v. Becker, 111 Mich. App. 692, 314 N.W. 2d 728 (1981).

substantive due process prohibited by the Fourteenth Amendment. The court stated that a decision to discipline, if accomplished through excessive force and appreciable physical pain may constitute violation of constitutional rights; however, the case was remanded for determination of facts, specifically, did the restraints employed by instructor exceed the degree of force needed to correct student's behavior and did the instructor intend harm to the student. It was undisputed that the instructor intentionally placed his arms around student's neck and shoulders, and it was recognized that instructor disclaims any ill-will and that he was motivated by a legitimate disciplinary desire to admonish; however, the instructor was a wrestling coach and was aware of the inherent risks of restraining in such manner. The allegation of violation of due process was not sustained.

In a 1982 Florida case,[246] the plaintiff alleged that the physical education teacher maliciously assaulted and battered her during regular school hours and caused her injury. The action was brought against the school district, rather than the teacher. The court held that under the state immunity statute, the school district would not be liable when an employee does not act within the scope of employment or acts in bad faith or with malicious purpose; however, the statute did not bar suit against the school district for the negligent hiring or retention of a teacher, since the hiring is an operational function. Plaintiff would have to allege facts showing that employer was put on notice of harmful propensities of employee.

A teacher, charged with third-degree assault and endangering the welfare of a child, in *Malte v. State*, 125 A.D.2d 958, 510 N.Y.S.2d 353 (1986) denied 69 N.Y.2d 607, 514 N.Y.S.2d 1024 (1987), brought action for false arrest and malicious prosecution against the State. Plaintiff was a fourth grade teacher who, in response to the misbehavior of a 10-year-old girl in his class, picked her up, placed her on the floor, straddled her legs, and hit her backside approximately 12 times. A State trooper investigating, using a jurisdictionally defective arrest warrant, arrested plaintiff at school, embarassing him in front of his students and peers. The trooper required plaintiff to be fingerprinted, photographed and arraigned, and when plaintiff could not make the $1,000 bail, he was taken to the county jail where he remained for approximately 10 hours, after being strip-searched and issued a prison uniform. Further, the arresting officer gave an interview to a local television station wherein plaintiff was characterized as having beaten the child. The court held that the teacher was not guilty of either third-degree assault or endangering welfare of child; mere evidence of being struck and suffering red mark or black eye are insufficient for crime of assault. The court further held that the teacher had a claim for false arrest, but not for malicious prosecution.

A coach may be sued on assault and battery for the manner in which practice is held. In *Hogenson v. Williams*,[247] action was brought against the seventh grade football team

---

[246] Willis v. Dade Co. School Board, 411 So. 2d 245 (Fla. App. 1982) pet. for rev. den. 418 So. 2d 1278 (1982); in Thomas v. Cascade Union H.S. Dist., 80 Or. App. 736, 724 P. 2d 330 (1986), a junior high physical education teacher was dismissed for "neglect of duty," specifically when in class the students were playing dodgeball and the teacher got hit from behind, she reacted in anger, lost her self-control, grabbed the offending student and kicked her twice in the thigh, leaving substantial bruises, teacher was suing for unfair dismissal.

[247] Hogenson v. Williams, 542 S.W. 2d 456 (Tex. Civ. App. 1976); for physical punishment, see also Bowman v. Pulaski Co. Special School Dist., 723 F. 2d 640 (1983).

coach when he became displeased with the player's blocking assignment performance and struck the student player's helmet with sufficient force to knock the player to the ground, then grabbed the face mask and pulled him around. The player suffered severe cervical sprain and bruising of the brachial plexus. He was discharged after eight days in the hospital, but it took several months to completely recover. The court stated in discussing criminal and civil assault[248] that the definition is the same in that both require intent. The court further discussed "privileged force," as applied to civil assault, stating that any force used by a teacher must be that which the teacher reasonably believes necessary to enforce compliance with a proper command issued for the purpose of controlling, training, or educating the child or to punish the child for prohibited conduct; in either case, the force or physical contact must be reasonable and not disproportionate to the activity of the offense. A teacher may not use physical violence against a child merely because the child is unable or fails to perform, either academically or athletically, at a desired level of ability, even though the teacher considers such violence to be "instruction and encouragement."

One of the more highly publicized cases was that of a college football coach's relationship with a player; however, only a portion of this case involved assault and battery.[249]

While the foregoing case discussions are school-oriented, assault and battery may occur in park and recreational settings by the person in charge. In *Jones v. Knight*,[250] it was alleged that a park ranger assaulted and battered the plaintiff when he directed verbal abuse and nasty language and then suddenly and without provocation or warning sprayed him with mace, thereby injuring him.

§ 1.41322 Player against another player in sports

One of the greatest concerns related to sport in the latter half of the '70s and the decade of the '80s is player violence; however, it is not a new phenomenon. In the mid-'50s actions were brought on assault and battery for injury of one player by another. Plaintiff, 19 years of age, was playing center for an amateur basketball team. Plaintiff was standing in the free throw area with his back to the basket, while defendant was guarding him by standing directly in back of him. When plaintiff was about to receive a pass of the ball from a teammate, it was alleged that the defendant pushed him, struck him in the face with his fist and as plaintiff fell, struck him again, knocking him unconscious. It was alleged further that the defendant was swearing profusely and challenged plaintiff who was unconscious on the floor to get up. Plaintiff was in the hospital several weeks and subsequently had constant headaches and his eyes were "going bad so that he must wear glasses." Because of the injury he had to drop out of school, which he was attending on a scholarship covering tuition and incidental fees.

[248] While assault and battery are two separate torts, as discussed in a preceding paragraph, many courts and writings refer only to assault, considering it inclusive of assault and battery.
[249] Rutledge v. Arizona Board of Trustees (and Kush, the coach), 660 F. 2d 1345 (1981), aff'd. 460 U.S. 719, 103 S. Ct. 1483 (1983), aff'd. 711 P. 2d 1207 (Ariz. App. 1985).
[250] Jones v. Knight, 373 So. 2d 254 (Miss. 1979).

Plaintiff was awarded damages for this "unprovoked assault."[251] And, in *Averill v. Luttrell*, [252] a baseball player assaulted another player, rendering him unconscious and fracturing his jaw. There was recovery against the catcher who delivered the blow, but not the baseball team, on the basis that an assault is a willful independent act entirely outside the scope of the duty of the team management.

There are really three approaches toward injuries to a player caused by another player. It is a question of consent and intent and where the line should be drawn on the continuum. Whereas generally in battery intent to act is sufficient, apparently because of the aggressiveness of sport, intent to injure also is a requirement for battery to be held in sport. The first approach is that of negligence, in which there is no intent at all to injure (see §1.42). As related to consent by the player, there is the concept of assumption of risk by the player (see §5.22). Consent is to contacts and restrictions as permitted by rules or common usage; there is no consent to contacts prohibited if designed to protect the participant.[253] Consent, also, relates to when the aggressiveness occurs. Whether the act took place during the on-going game play or "after the whistle had blown" and play had stopped is often the key factor in establishing intent to injure. There, too, is the issue of proper conduct of the activity for the protection from injury of the players.[254] The second approach is that of civil assault and battery, the focus of this section.[255] Intent must be proven, but it is difficult when physical contact is often a part of the game; however, the question also is "when does reckless disregard for safety of others" or "the deliberate, willful and reckless violation of rules" become civil assault and battery. Does, can the injured player consent to such conduct of another because it is "commonly done" among players? There is the defense of player consent, but to what degree can the injured consent? There, also, is the defense of self-defense, a valid defense for assault and battery (see introduction §1.41 related to motive and intent). Generally, the doctrine of respondeat superior is held not applicable for intentional torts (see §3.41); notwithstanding, the California court[256] indicated a public corporate entity would be liable under the State Tort Claims Act if the player were an employee. A University basketball player struck plaintiff with his fist. Plaintiff sued the University, athletic director and basketball coach, and sought to establish an employer-employee relationship between the University and varsity player inasmuch as athletics was "big business"; but, the court held that the player was not an employee within meaning of Tort

[251] Griggas v. Clauson, 6 Ill. App. 2d 412, 128 N.E. 2d 363 (1955).

[252] Averill v. Luttrell, 44 Tenn. App. 56, 311 S.W. 2d 812 (1957).

[253] Kabella v. Bouschelle, 100 N.M. 461, 672 P. 2d 290 (1983) friendly game of tackle football, participation implied consent but not where prohibited by rules. See also, Ramos v. City of Countryside, 137 Ill. App. 3d 1028, 92 Ill. Dec. 607, 485 N.E. 2d 418 (1985) eight-year-old boy injured by 14-year-old while playing "bombardment".

[254] For cases of approach one, see specific sports in Chapters 6, 7, and 8. See also, §18.3 Nature of supervision, and §19.2 The activity.

[255] There are considerable writings; see, for example: Holfeld, Albert F. Athletes — Their Rights and Correlative Duties. *Trial Lawyer's Guide* (1975) pp. 383-406; Spevacek, Charles E. Notes: Injuries Resulting from Nonintentional Acts in Organized Contact Sports: The Theories of Recovery Available to the Injured Athlete. 12 *Indiana Law Review* 687-711 (1979) deals also with intentional torts and cases cited in this section; Turro, Andrew J. Tort Liability in Professional Sports. 44 *Albany Law Review* 696-718 (1980); also, see references cited in §1.24.

[256] Townsend v. State of Calif., 191 Cal. App. 3d 1530, 237 Cal. Rptr. 146 (1987).

Claims Act. In personal injury suit, against the player who hit plaintiff, jury had awarded plaintiff $25,000. The cases which have been brought are primarily from the professional team sports arena, as evidence by subsequently cited cases. The third approach is that of action for criminal assault and battery, discussed in previous §1.24, where malicious intent is required and consent to lawful and to criminal acts is distinguished. (For further discussion of the legal concepts, see the law reviews cited in the footnote.)

Six cases provide the foundation for recovery on tort for injuries by one player to another in sports.[257] In an amateur high school soccer situation, the goaltender sued for injury. The plaintiff goaltender acquired possession of the ball in the penalty area and had gone down on his left knee, received and pulled the ball to his chest. While in that position, the defendant forward of the opposing team, who had been charging the ball, kicked plaintiff in the head. A soccer rule prohibits all opposing players from making any contact with the goalkeeper when he is in possession of the ball in the penalty area. Plaintiff alleged that the defendant had ample time to avoid the contact. As a result of the injury, plaintiff suffered permanent damage to his skull and brain and must wear a plate in his head and take daily medication for seizures. The court held that a player is liable in tort if his conduct is either deliberate, willful or with a reckless disregard for the safety of others.[258] There appears to be some evidence that in sport the standard may be reckless disregard or misconduct, rather than the willful intent and motive required for assault and battery, for the one injuring another player to be held liable.[259] Two 1988 cases (*Annonio* v. *Balzano*, 139 A.D.2d 943, 527 N.Y.S.2d 923 (1988); Ordway v. *Superior Court*, 198 Cal. App. 3d 98, 243 Cal. Rptr. 536 (1988)), also reference reckless conduct, but as a bar to the defense of assumption of risk. Both of these situations involved jockeys. The California court stated that reasonable implied assumption of risk remains a viable defense after adoption of comparative fault, even though another jockey was in violation of the rules, unless that jockey's conduct was "reckless", in which situation the defense of assumption of risk would be precluded. The court considered reckless conduct a form of intentional conduct. Participants do not consent to acts by others which are reckless or intentional.

Two cases[260] involving softball were decided in 1976, with opposite results. In the Missouri case, the plaintiff was running from first base to second base and the defendant shortshop ran across the infield and collided with the plaintiff. No recovery.

---

[257] Because there is extensive discussion of the cases in the readings cited, only brief facts of the cases are given.

[258] Nabozny v. Barnhill, 31 Ill. App. 3d 212, 334 N.E. 2d 258 (1975). For early discussion of case, see: Goldstein, Lynn A. Participant's Liability for Injury to a Fellow Participant in an Organized Athletic Event. 53 *Chicago-Kent Law Review* 97-108 (1976). See also Moore v. Jones, 120 Ga. App. 521, 171 S.E. 2d 390 (1969) 16-year-old playing soccer in physical education class, plaintiff failed to allege willful and wanton act of opposing player, which was only basis for recovery, plaintiff assumed the risk from ordinary negligent act of opposing player during game play.

[259] See also comment on *Hackbart* case in subse-

quent paragraph; Hanson v. Kynast, 24 Ohio St. 3d 171, 494 N.E. 2d 109 (1986) aff'd. 38 Ohio App. 3d 58, 526 N.E. 2d 327 (1987) lacrosse player twisted and flipped opponent over player's back, causing injury resulting in paralysis, court held no liability short of intentional tort and player not immune from liability for intentional tort; see also Kabella v. Bouschelle, 100 N.M. 461, 672 P. 2d 290 (1983) friendly game of tackle football; and §2.241.

[260] Bourque v. Duplechin, 331 So. 2d 40 (La. App. 1976), cert. denied 334 So. 2d 210 (1976), writ of review not considered, not timely filed 334 So. 2d 230 (1976); Niemczyk v. Burleson, 538 S.W. 2d 737 (Mo. App. 1976).

However, the plaintiff did recover in the Louisiana case. In this situation the plaintiff was the second baseman and the defendant the runner. The defendant ran at full speed five feet out of his way (base path) to run into plaintiff. In the first case the court held that the plaintiff assumed this inherent risk of the game; however, in the second case the plaintiff did not; the defendant was under duty to play softball in ordinary fashion without unsportsmanlike conduct or wanton injury to his fellow players.

Probably the best known of the six cases is *Hackbart v. Cincinnati Bengals*,[261] a case involving professional football. Plaintiff Hackbart, a defensive back for the Denver Broncos, was injured by Clark, an offensive back of the defendant Bengals. Hackbart attempted to block Clark by throwing his body in front of him. He remained on the ground and turned, with one knee on the ground, watching the play. Clark stepped forward and struck a blow with his right forearm to the back of the kneeling plaintiff's head and neck with sufficient force to cause both players to fall forward to the ground. An NFL rule prohibited striking of an opponent in such manner. Both players returned to the sidelines; the officials had not seen the players and no penalty was called. The next day plaintiff Hackbart was in pain and could not play golf; he reported the pain to the team trainer. He played on two successive Sundays on the specialty teams, but then was released on waivers. It was when he sought medical help at this time that the serious neck fracture was identified. It was held that under Colorado law that just because the intentional blow occurred during a game did not make the injury uncompensable. Further, it was stated that where there was an intentional blow, the appropriate standard in personal injury suits was that of recklessness, rather than assault and battery. Assault and battery calls for an intent, as does recklessness; however, in recklessness the intent is to do the act, but without an intent to cause the particular harm; it is enough if the person knows that there is a strong probability that harm will result. Colorado had a six-year limitation period on injuries arising from recklessness. The court held liability on the part of the Bengals and Clark and that reckless misconduct was the proper standard for determining liability.

Another 1979 case[262] was *Tomjanovich v. California Sports, Inc.*, involving professional basketball. The Lakers and Rockets were playing when Washington and another player began to fight. Tomjanovich ran to them and tried to mediate the confrontation, but without looking to see who it was, Washington whirled around and punched Tomjanovich in the face. He suffered fractures of the face and skull, a broken nose, separated upper jaw, cerebral concussion, and severe lacerations around the mouth. Tomjanovich sued the Los Angeles Lakers (Calif. Sports, Inc.) on the basis of the doctrine of respondeat superior and negligent supervision. After a jury trial at which Tomjanovich was awarded $3.2 million, just before the appeal was to be heard, an out-of-court settlement was negotiated of unreported amount.

The sixth case, *Polonich v. A-P-A Sports*,[263] an ice hockey stick-swinging brawl,

[261] Hackbart v. Cincinnati Bengals, 435 F. Supp. 352 (1977), rev'd. 601 F. 2d 516 (1979), cert. denied 444 U.S. 931, 100 S. Ct. 275 (1979).

[262] Tomjanovich v. Calif. Sports, Inc., No. H-78-243 (S.D. Texas Aug. 17, 1979). As reported in Carroll, John F. Torts in Sports — "I'll See You in Court." 16 *Akron Law Review* 537-565 (winter 1983) at p. 542-3.

[263] Polonich v. A-P-A Sports, No. 80-74635 (E.D. Mich. 8/25/82) On appeal. As reported in Carroll at p. 539.

resulted in both compensatory ($500,000) and exemplary ($350,000) damages. When Polonich attempted to clear the puck away from the net his stick hit an opposing hockey player in the face. This player quickly reacted by swinging his stick, hitting Polonich on the bridge of his nose and causing facial injuries. In a Canadian ice hockey case,[264] a player body-checked plaintiff, took possession of the puck and started to skate with it. Plaintiff attempted to delay player by hooking him with his stick and in so doing hit defendant player a painful blow on the back of the neck, upon which defendant stopped, turned, and holding his stick with both hands, brought it down on plaintiff's face, hitting him with the blade between the nose and right eye, rendering plaintiff unconscious. The court stated that a blow struck in the course of a lawful sport is not normally actionable, since those who take part are presumed in law to assume willingly the risk of harm. But a retaliatory blow, struck in anger, even though provoked, may go beyond the immunity conferred by this principle and amount to actionable negligence. Judgment for plaintiff. However, where a fight occurred between members of the two teams after the game had ended, no such assumption of risk existed. In this situation,[265] while there was indeed a melee, the plaintiff had remained on the bench and was hit in an unprovoked circumstance. Such fighting, also, was contrary to association rules. Defendant was held liable for intentional battery.

§ 1.4133   Physical and sexual child abuse

Of concern in the decade of the '80s has been the increasing physical and sexual child abuse. In *Schultz v. Boy Scouts of America*, 102 A.D.2d 100, 476 N.Y.S.2d 309, aff'd. 65 N.Y.2d 189, 491 N.Y.S. 2d 90, 480 N.E.2d 679 (1985), plaintiffs alleged sexual abuse of two boys while at camp, with one subsequently committing suicide, allegedly due to the psychological stress of the situation, including threats after returning to the School. One of the issues was the employment check into the background of the leader who was charged with the abuse. A 13-year-old girl was allegedly sexually "group" molested when she entered the boys' locker room against the rules. She had previously gone into the locker room four times without incident. The question for the jury was whether the girl assumed the risk of group molestation by so entering the locker room, in *Campbell v. Montgomery Co. Board of Education*, 73 Md. App. 54, 533 A.2d 9 (1987). An assistant girls' basketball coach, who also was a school counselor, allegedly sexually abused a girl who was a member of the team and who had come to him for her chemical dependency problems, in *Horace Mann Ins. Co. v. Indp. School Dist.*, 355 N.W. 2d 413 (Minn. 1984). In *Randi F v. High Ridge YMCA*, 170 Ill. App. 3d 962, 120 Ill. Dec. 784, 524 N.E.2d 966 (1988), a teacher's aide at a day care center allegedly beat and sexually assaulted a 3-year-old child. The court held, as generally is true under the doctrine of respondeat superior, that such conduct on the part of the aide was a deviation from the scope of the employment and having no relation to the business of the day care center, and thus the YMCA sponsor of the center was not liable for the acts of the aide. In a Florida case, *Landis v. Allstate Ins. Co.*, 516 So. 2d 307 (Fla. App. 1987), it was held

---

[264] Agar v. Canning, 54 W.W.R. 302 (Manitoba 1965), aff'd. 55 W.W.R. 384 (1966).

[265] Overall v. Kadella, 138 Mich. App. 351, 361 N.W. 2d 352 (1984).

that acts of child molestation at the day care center were clearly intentional or deliberate acts and thus there was no insurance coverage pursuant to the intentional acts exclusion within the policy. The organization was not held liable in *Big Brother/Big Sister of Metro. Atlanta v. Terrell,* for the acts of a volunteer who sexually abused a child; the organization was found not negligent in its selection of the volunteer. The sexual abuse was perpetrated, in *Morris v. Canipe,* 528 So. 2d 1057 (La. App. 1988), by another participant (child), rather than the staff. The school was aware of alleged sexual misconduct problems of one of its students, but the court held that it was not under any duty to report such to or warn the parents of children who were potential victims, but who were not students and were away from the school grounds during the summer recess.

§ 1.42   Unintentional acts which harm — negligence

Whereas negligence was hardly recognized as a special area of torts before the early part of the nineteenth century, today it is seldom disputed as a distinct field of liability as the basis for unintended torts. Legal writers and the courts have attempted to define just what negligence is. They agree on the general concepts, but differ considerably in the development of these concepts. One of the more concise definitions used by a number is "Negligence is an unintentional breach of a legal duty causing damage reasonably foreseeable without which breach the damage would not have occurred."

Whereas intentional torts has three elements (see introduction §1.41), unintentional torts or negligence has four, and the difference between the elements evidences the distinctiveness of the two types of torts. The elements[266] of negligence are embodied in the foregoing definition: (1) a duty to provide a safe environment, (2) an act which breaches the duty of failure to perform to the appropriate standard of care so as not to expose an individual to an unreasonable risk of injury, (3) the substandard act was the cause of the injury, and (4) damage or injury did in fact occur. In negligence there is a duty to protect according to the relationship occasioned in the situation, while in intentional torts there is no duty toward anyone. When one does not properly protect, including protecting against intentional torts and criminal acts, one is said to be negligent. There is an intent to injure in an intentional tort, while in negligence there is no intent at all to injure; the injury is wholly unintentional. Negligence is a matter of conduct, while intentional torts is a state of mind (see introduction §1.41). In both intentional torts and negligence, the act done must be the proximate cause of the injury and injury or damage must have occurred. The injury in both types of torts is to the person or property of the plaintiff, and, thus, the compensation goes to the injured or plaintiff. The tortfeasor (individual only) of an intentional tort must pay the compensation, while under the doctrine of respondeat superior (see Chapter 3), the employer of an employee who was negligent also may have to pay compensation. Normally only compensatory damages are awarded for negligence, while both compensatory and punitive damages may be assessed for intentional torts (see

---

[266] The meaning of the elements is described in detail in Chapter 2.

introduction §1.41 and §2.41). The defenses differ, too. The primary defenses for an intentional tort are consent and self-defense, while there are a number of defenses for negligence (see Chapter 5).

The components and ramifications of negligence are the subject of this book.

§ 1.421   Unavoidable accident

For a person to be negligent, unless there is strict liability (see §1.43), there must be foreseeability (see §2.23) of the risk of injury. Generally speaking, an unavoidable accident is one which could not be foreseen under all the circumstances and, therefore, could not be prevented by the exercise of reasonable precautions. It causes an unintentional injury for which the law does not impose liability. A few case illustrations follow; many more are described in subsequent chapters.

In *Ellis v. Burns Valley School District*,[267] a boy in the eighth grade, age 13 and weighing 75 pounds, was injured when he collided with a sixth grade student, age 15 and weighing over 200 pounds, while playing the game "Black Man" or "King King Calico" in a required physical education class. This was held to be an unavoidable accident. A similar decision was reached in a Washington case,[268] where a high school boy was injured in a physical education class in the gymnasium while playing "touch" football.

In two basketball cases,[269] the court held that the injuries occurred due to physical contact which was considered a normal part of the game and which could not have been controlled by supervision. In one instance two boys bumped heads when they went up for a jump-shot, while in the other they bumped heads when they both went after a ball on the floor.

There are many accidental injuries on the playgrounds. In a Wisconsin case,[270] the injured and another boy, each about ten years old, were playing marbles on the school grounds during recess. The defendant was playing tag with the older boys and accidentally ran into plaintiff causing permanent injury. The court held "if there may be liability for the multitude of trivial injuries which are accidentally inflicted by children on each other in the course of their lawful games, this would open up a vast field of personal injury litigation. We decline to act as pioneers in this almost limitless field."

It should be noted, however, that the line of demarcation between what is an unavoidable accident and what is foreseeable, especially the result of improper selection of activities or inadequate supervision, is not distinct (see especially Chapter 18 Supervision and Chapter 19 Conduct of Activities).

---

[267] Ellis v. Burns Valley School Dist., 128 Cal. App. 550, 18 P. 2d 79 (1933).

[268] Read v. School Dist., 7 Wash. 2d 502, 110 P. 2d 179 (1941).

[269] Albers v. Indp. School Dist., 94 Idaho 342, 487 P. 2d 936 (1971); Kaufman v. New York, 30 Misc. 2d 285, 214 N.Y.S. 2d 767 (1961) latter case overturned by legislation.

[270] Briese v. Maechtle, 146 Wis. 89, 130 N.W. 893 (1911).

§ 1.43   Strict liability[271]

The preceding two categories of tort are based in fault. This third category of strict liability is really absolute liability or liability without fault. It is generally thought that strict liability was the prevailing rule of the early common law. First, intentional torts became a separate category, and then the fault ethic became predominant; but, there have remained certain situations wherein the historically-rooted strict liability was preserved. While there is dispute as to whether there should be any liability without fault, it should be noted that legal fault is not the same as moral blame. The defendant may be morally blameless and the act fully unintentional; but, nevertheless, the defendant will be legally at fault. Strict liability is promulgated for the protection of society and the standard of conduct is absolute. The focus of strict liability is on the dangerousness of the activity or product, rather than on the conduct or intent of the defendant, as is so for negligence and intentional torts, respectively. The activities which give rise to strict liability are not so unreasonable as to be prohibited altogether, but they are sufficiently dangerous or provide unusual risks so that the law requires them to be conducted at the peril of the one sponsoring the activity. Persons choosing to be engaged in such activity should bear the consequences of their choice which provides an extraordinary threat to the safety of society. Further, society believes that the one creating the potential danger rather than the injured person, should be responsible and bear the cost of damages. Strict liability holds that mere due care is not adequate protection and that those who create the threat are in the best position to monitor the threat of injury. Four strict liability situations are particularly pertinent to sport and to recreation and parks.

Animals. In the parks and recreation field, most strict liability cases involve animals kept in the park or zoo; however, the case holdings are inconsistent. *Mangum v. Brownlee*[272] is a case in point holding to the doctrine of absolute liability. A 1987 case, *Burns v. Gleason*, 819 F. 2d 555 (1987), in which a 9-year-old boy was mauled by a jaguar at the zoo, the Louisiana law, keeper of wild animal is absolutely liable without regard to fault for any damage done, was applied in holding defendant zoo owner liable. Kansas, Alabama, and California, however, have cases[273] holding that maintaining of wild animals in the park or zoo is a governmental function without liability. A New York case[274] states that while the policy is strict liability, where the animals are kept for the education and entertainment of the public by an institution which holds a charter for that purpose, liability is imposed only if there is negligence. *Byrnes v. Jackson*[275] holds the

---

[271] See Prosser and Keeton, Chapter 13 Strict Liability. Dobbs, Dan B. *Torts and Compensation*. St. Paul, MN: West Publishing Co., 1985, Chapters 7 and 8.

[272] Mangum v. Brownlee, 181 Okla. 515, 75 P. 2d 174 (1938).

[273] Hibbard v. Wichita, 98 Kan. 498, 159 P. 399 (1916); McKinney v. San Francisco, 190 Cal. App. 2d 844, 241 P. 2d 1060 (1952); Smith v. Birmingham, 270 Ala. 681, 121 So. 2d 867 (1960).

[274] Hyde v. Utica, 259 A.D. 477, 20 N.Y.S. 2d 335 (1940).

[275] 140 Miss. 656, 105 So. 861 (1925).

keeping of animals to be a proprietary function with the proof of negligence necessary for recovery by the plaintiff. The court in Texas[276] implied a proprietary function, but held the keeping of animals, in this specific case, to be a nuisance. Two 1970 cases[277] had allegations by the plaintiff of strict liability for ferocious animals; however, the court held that liability should be (and was) based on negligence.

The difference in liability between individuals maintaining wild animals and an appropriate entity maintaining a zoo or wild animal preserve should be noted. Further, the liability of a governmental entity has been subject to change in the decade of the '70s particularly and continues to change. Most of the cited cases are prior to such time. See §4.2 particularly for the changing status of states. Also see §11.4 Zoos for situations involved in the cited cases and others.

Abnormally dangerous things and activities. The primary activity which is conducted by recreation and parks and which would fall into this category is fireworks. Fireworks have a high degree of care required,[278] and there is indication that some jurisdictions[279] appear to have what might be termed strict liability. For further cases and discussion, see §11.26.

Efforts have been made to apply the doctrine of strict liability to other activities, but unsuccessfully. For example, the plaintiff endeavored to apply the doctrine in a golf case.[280] A novice golfer was taking lessons 200 to 220 yards from first tee and 40 to 50 yards to left of first fairway when another golfer's teed off drive hooked and hit the novice golfer on the forehead. The court held that golfers are not strictly liable without fault to innocent persons who are injured by their golfing activities. In a 1986 case, *Fallon v. Indian Trail School,* 148 Ill. App. 3d 931, 102 Ill. Dec. 479, 500 N.E. 2d 101 (1986), the court held that a trampoline was not abnormally dangerous for purpose of imposing strict liability upon the school district. The theory of strict liability, also, was unsuccessful for the defendant in a river tubing situation, in *Tobey v. State of Louisiana,* 454 So. 2d 144 (La. App. 1984). Failure, however, was on the basis that the state-owned river was not in the custody of the campground. The plaintiff struck a submerged object in the river.

The doctrine also was sought to be applied when a minor plaintiff stepped on hot coals in or near a barbecue pit maintained by the county in its park.[281] The court held that such pits were not unreasonably dangerous, and thus strict liability was not imposed.

When the Vermont ski case[282] in 1978 held an award of $1,500,000 for a novice skier, there was fear that this portended strict liability for ski area operators. This did not occur, however. See §8.41 Duties and responsibilities of ski area operators.

For discussion of duty owed in terms of "not an insurer of safety," see §2.2.

[276] Ft. Worth v. Wiggins, 5 S.W. 2d 761 (Tex. Civ. App. 1928).

[277] Kennedy v. Denver, 29 Colo.App. 15, 476 P. 2d 762 (1970), 31 Colo.App. 561, 506 P. 2d 764 (1972); Willis v. Dept. of Conservation & Economic Dev., 55 N.J. 534, 264 A. 2d 34 (1970).

[278] Olson v. Babbitt, 29 Minn. 105, 189 N.W. 2d 701 (1971).

[279] For example, Haddon v. Lotito, 399 Pa. 521, 161 A. 2d 160 (1960); Harris v. Findlay, 59 Ohio App.

345, 13 Ohio Op. 172, 18 N.E. 2d 413 (1938).

[280] Carrigan v. Roussell, 177 N.J. Super. 272, 426 A. 2d 517 (1981).

[281] Petersen v. Honolulu, 496 P. 2d 4 (Hawaii 1972); see also Lanclos v. Tomlinson, 351 So. 2d 1218 (La. App. 1977) pedestrian fell crossing wooden bridge spanning roadside ditch, defective plank, strict liability not imposed.

[282] Sunday v. Stratton Corp., 136 Vt. 293, 390 A. 2d 398 (1978).

Employers' liability. "The outstanding statutory application of the principle of strict liability is in the workers' compensation acts, which have very largely preempted the whole field of the liability of employers for injuries to their employees. Basically the acts do not rest upon any theory of tort liability, but upon one of social insurance."[283] For further discussion of workers' compensation, see §25.34. While under the doctrine of respondeat superior (see Chapter 3) the negligence of the employee is imputed to the employer and the employer is held liable therefor, this generally is not referred to as employers' strict liability.

Products liability. One of the bases of products liability is that of the doctrine of strict liability. For further discussion, see §21.13.

§ 1.5 Real Property Law

While property law is a large field of law, there are certain aspects to which the attention of professionals in physical education and sport, parks and recreation, and camping should be drawn. This section does not include management, planning and design, or premises liability of the landowner. Liability and operational implications related to areas and facilities are dealt with in other sections of this book, specifically, Chapter 20 and selected sections of the chapters in Part B relating to specific activities or operations. (See table of contents of chapters.) Other sections, also, deal with interference with and use of property, such as nuisance (§4.4); (attractive nuisance §2.1231 should be distinguished), intentional interference with property (§1.411), and recreational use of private (and in certain states also public) property (§12.1). In this section a brief overview is presented on selected aspects of acquisition modes, possession rights, land use controls, and environmental, natural resources, and public land law.

§ 1.51 Acquisition modes

While there are many different modes for the acquisition of property, three are discussed briefly in subsequent paragraphs: purchase, gift, and condemnation.

Purchase. Among the various modes of acquisition, the most common one, of course, is purchase. One should be particularly aware of any restrictions on the title. Public entities have a variety of sources for money, depending upon the state and federal law, including bonds, general appropriation funds, special tax, and matching state and federal grants. If one is interested in a piece of property, one might consider an option to buy or first right of refusal agreement. Such agreements are often made when one is leasing property, so that if the owner wishes to sell, you as the lessee has an opportunity for purchase. Property, also, may be picked up at tax sales.

For public entities, the title is held by the ultimate authority governing unit, for example, the city rather than the recreation board. Only when the governing unit is an independent board of a recreation and/or park district or authority does the park and recreation managing unit hold title. Similarly, where a camp is part of a voluntary

---

[283] See Prosser and Keeton at p. 568.

organization or church, the title is held by the corporate entity, not the camp board, unless the camp is separately incorporated from the parent organization.

Gifts. A gift can be made in a number of ways and it is important if one is soliciting gifts that a person knowledgable about tax law be involved, whether the gift is currently being given outright, is part of an annuity program, or is a part of a person's will as a devise (see §1.52). The key principle in acquiring property gifts is that it is a mutually beneficial arrangement. If the title is not given in fee simple (see §1.52), one must be aware particularly of restrictions placed on the title. This includes use requirements and possible reversion of property if appropriate use is not made of the property, as well as the gift being given upon some contingency that the recipient will perform some function or service. Especially where some specific use is mandated, care must be taken, so that if such use becomes no longer feasible or appropriate that there is the right of resale, rather than reversion. Because some property would require a use not within the objectives of the organization, be it a location not within the overall master plan or inappropriate, or demand so much money in maintenance and operation or for initial renovation in order to use, it is important that one realize that *a gift can be rejected*. It may take some good public relations work if a gift is rejected — of course, working with the donor initially before the gift is best or if the gift has already been made, such as by will, the courts sometimes can help.

Property, also, can be acquired by public entities by statutory dedication, particularly where required for land development. Because dedication is in fact economic contribution by the developer, the review of subdivision plats requiring mandatory dedication of land or money-in-lieu-of-land for park development may bring considerable controversy. Who determines which lands will be so dedicated also can bring controversy.[284] It has been alleged that the mandatory requirement of recreational lands is a "taking" of private property for a public purpose without just compensation (see next paragraph subsection).

While not strictly a gift, different lands can be acquired by transfer, that is, a trading of property. A park parcel, for example, can be released for one purpose, contingent upon receiving another comparable parcel of land. One primary problem with transfer of lands is that of location and typology, for seldom can a comparable piece of land be found.

Condemnation — eminent domain. The acquisition of property by condemnation, a forced sale, gains its authority in the power of eminent domain which governmental agencies have. While the power is inherent in sovereignty and is accorded not only the federal and state governments, but also subdivisions, including schools, municipalities, and other entities, it is not conferred by constitutions; however, federal and state constitutions limit the power and protect the rights of private citizens by requiring that due process be adhered to and just compensation be made to the owner whose property

---

[284] For example, Eyde Bros. Develop. Co. v. Ros-Common Co. Bd. of Road Com'rs., 161 Mich. App. 654, 411 N.W. 2d 814 (1987); Messer v. Town of Chapel Hill, 59 N.C. App. 692, 297 S.E. 2d 632 (N.C. App. 1982); Riegert Apartments Corp. v. Planning Board of the Town of Clarkstown, 57 N.Y. 2d 206, 441 N.E. 2d 1076 (N.Y. 1982). Prisk v. City of Poulsbo, 46 Wash. App. 793, 732 P. 2d 1013 (1987). These cases discussed in *Law Review II* at pp. 12-13. See also Frakt and Rankin at pp. 46-48 for brief discussion of dedication and additional cases.

is being taken. Two questions are integral to eminent domain — what is public use; and, what is just compensation? The term "public use" is defined differently in the various state jurisdictions and changes to meet new social conditions. Generally, however, uses for public parks and recreation areas and facilities and athletic fields are included. Just compensation is usually the current fair market value.[285] The "taking" of property may be found at all levels, from the local small park or playground to the federal government for national park expansion.

Condemnation under the power of eminent domain should be distinguished from "inverse condemnation." Inverse condemnation is when the government does some act which lowers the owner's property value. This may come about by abandoned condemnation proceedings (the government changing its mind), a prolonged condemnation action, or by placing a public use on the property such as use of air space with excessive noise, which causes the property to decline in value. However, proof under inverse condemnation is very difficult inasmuch as a property owner does not have a "property right" in the value of one's property.[286]

§ 1.52 Possession rights

What one can do with property, as well as what one's responsibilities are related to the property, depends upon the "possession rights" of the individual. While there are many sub-classifications which can be made, for more simple approach only four generalized categories are presented: (1) freehold estates, (2) future estates, (3) landlord and tenant, and (4) rights in another's land.

Freehold estates — fee simple, life estates. Freehold estates is one type of present estates. A freehold estate is the real possession of land of uncertain duration, that is either of inheritance or for life. "Of inheritance" does not mean that one has inherited the property, but rather that one has all the rights to a piece of property and it is inheritable. Under such conditions, it is usually referred to as holding title in *fee simple absolute*.[287] This is normally the best type of interest to have in real property, for then one is in full control of the property, except as use is controlled by the government or common law (see §1.53), and can sell, use, or develop the property as one wishes.

When one holds title to property with a life estate, one is not free to sell, use, or develop the property, except as the person who holds the life interest permits. The title is so encumbered for the life of such person. To give property with a life estate to a public or non-profit entity may be a way for the donor to obtain considerable tax benefits and yet know that upon death the property will go as desired. The donor retains a life interest in the property, which usually would mean that as long as that person lives, they may use the property. They normally keep the premises in repair, pay ordinary taxes, and are liable for "waste" (see §1.53). This technique has been used to acquire "inholdings" in public recreational lands — the private person may continue to reside within the lands for their lifetime.

---

[285] For cases and discussion, see *Law Review II* at pp. 8-10; Frakt and Rankin at 39-40.

[286] See *Law Review II* at p. 10; see Hillcrest Golf &

Country Club v. Altoona, 135 Wis. 2d 431, 400 N.W. 2d 493 (1986).

[287] See Frakt and Rankin at p. 38.

Future estates — executory devise. While future estates include reversions and remainders, the most common is that of the executory interest. A gift of personal property by will is termed a bequest, while a gift of real property is termed a devise. Sometimes the word bequeath is used synonymously with devise. Obviously, no interest is vested in the person or corporate entity designated in the will as the recipient until death of the donor. And, of course, the donor may change one's will at any time.

There are two other forms of future interests of which one should be aware, particularly when soliciting financial support. One is the placement of property in a trust under specified conditions, and the other is a gift upon some contingency.

Landlord and tenant. This is important to physical education and sport and to recreation and parks, as well as camping, from both the perspective of being the landlord and leasing or otherwise permitting others to use the property and of being the tenant or lessee. This is considered a non-freehold estate and one can enjoy a tenancy for years, from period to period (meaning year to year, month to month, or even week to week), or at will.[288] The length of term for a tenancy for years can be a critical element in whether one will or can build or place improvements upon property. One has heard of "ninety-nine year" leases — then one can usually put capital improvements upon the land; but, governmental policies generally no longer permit such long-term leases. Some public entities are restricted from capital improvements if the term is less than 25 years. The right to renew the option to lease, also, should be a provision of a lease, if one is putting capital improvements on property. Athletic stadiums are an example of tenancy arrangements, as are camps using governmental property for their sites. The appropriateness of arrangements by public entities with non-profit organizations and with private commercial corporations has been raised; it appears to be a matter of social and economic philosophy. The structure and provisions of a legal agreement are critical to the rights and responsibilities of each party.

For liability in lessor/lessee arrangements as related to operations, see §3.11.

Rights in another's land — easements. There are essentially two types of easements, affirmative and negative.[289] The affirmative easement gives a right of use over the property of another, that is, the owner permits something to be done thereon, for example, such as passing over property as an access to fishing or to get to another parcel of land or water body.[290] In addition to a right of way, another commonly known easement is that of power lines going over property.[291] An easement gives the right to do

[288] In City of Bloomington v. Kuruzovich, 517 N.E. 2d 408 (Ind. App. 1987), a softball player tripped over a manhole cover as he chased a fly ball. The city had continued to maintain park after expiration of a written lease, thus the city as a holdover tenant controlling the property was considered a tenant-at-will and owed a duty to softball player as public invitee.

[289] See Frakt and Rankin at pp. 41-43.

[290] For example, Collins v. Tippett, 156 Cal. App. 3d 1017, 203 Cal. Rptr. 366 (1984) landowner opening property for recreational use subject to public easement; Terrell v. U.S., 783 F. 2d 1562 (1986) Florida law applied, roadway easement involved, old bridge used as fishing pier, plaintiff stepped in hole between bridge and crumbling roadway to bridge.

[291] Kirschner v. Louisville Gas & Electric Co., 743 S.W. 2d 840 (Ky. 1988) power company had easement over open field in neighborhood; 15-year-old climbed high voltage transmission tower, constructed wooden platform, and was injured by arcing electricity, held trespasser and propensity of electricity to arc was not a concealed, dangerous condition, although power company knew children played in the field, did not know children were climbing tower, warning signs were posted on ladder the children were climbing, no liability. Colvin v. Southern California Edison Co., 194 Cal. App. 3d 1306, 240 Cal. Rptr. 142 (1987) two friends rode bikes to creek, crossing place washed too deep so went up stream, one boy pulled guy wire dangling from pole and wire touched electrical conduc-

some act on the property which otherwise might be unlawful (*e.g.*, trespassing). An easement should be distinguished from a license, which merely confers personal privilege to do some act on the land, but does not confer any property interest. An easement usually runs with the title.[292]

A negative easement is of much more recent origin than the affirmative easement and the primary use in parks and recreation in as conservation easements. The Iowa law (Iowa Code Ann. §111D. Conservation easements) sets forth the purpose and definition:

> The department, any county conservation board, and any city or agency of a city may acquire by purchase, gift, contract, or other voluntary means, but not by eminent domain, conservation easements in land to preserve scenic beauty, wildlife habitat, riparian lands, wet lands, or forests, promote outdoor recreation, or otherwise conserve for the benefit of the public and natural beauty, natural resources, and public recreation facilities of the state.

> "Conservation easement" means an easement in, servitude upon, restriction upon the use of, or other interest in land owned by another, created for any of the purposes set forth in section 111D.1. A conservation easement shall be transferable to any other public body authorized to acquire conservation easements. A conservation easement shall be perpetual unless expressly limited to a lesser term, or unless released by the holder, or unless a change of circumstances renders the easement no longer beneficial to the public. No comparative economic test shall be used to determine whether a conservation easement is beneficial to the public.

> A conservation easement may be held by a private, nonprofit organization for public benefit if the instrument granting the easement or the bylaws of the organization provide that the easement will be transferred either to a public body or another private, nonprofit organization upon the dissolution of the private, nonprofit organization.

An easement also is a land use tool to preserve certain environmental qualities, such as a scenic easement would prevent a landowner from constructing some object which would interfere with the enjoyment of others of the scenery.

Rights in another's land may be acquired by adverse possession. Adverse possession is when someone takes actual possession to exclusion of others, such as a structure in the forest or a parcel of land, and has the intent to do so. The owner has knowledge of the assertion of ownership, in that it is open. This possession continues for the statutory period of time (length of time varies considerably in different states, ranging from 5 to 20 years). At the end of this time, the person who has been *de facto* possessor gains title.

---

tor as pole anchor had washed out, recreational user statute applicable.

292 Bergen Ditch & Reservoir Co. v. Barnes, 683 P. 2d 365 (Colo. App. 1984) holder of easement for overflow and use of reservoir as part of lake brought action for trespass and injunctive relief against owner of portion of reservoir bed which was subject to the easement; easement dated back to 1892; court held easement, although distinct from ownership, is an interest in land, and where conveying instrument does not characterize easement as "exclusive" right to use, the grantor (owner) retains right to use the property in common with grantee. Thus plaintiff lost and easement holder could continue to use surface of reservoir waters.

Title by adverse possession should be distinguished from prescriptive easement.[293] The two are similar in that there is open, adverse, and continuous use for the statutory period; however, a prescriptive easement results only in the adverse user acquiring an easement and not a title.

There can be loss of an easement by abandonment; that is, there is some conduct inconsistent with the existence of the easement and it continues for the statutory period of time. A temporary or occasional adverse action related to the easement does not result in abandonment of an easement. There, also, can be abandonment of property, that is, relinquishing all rights and possession with intention of not reclaiming it or resuming possession or enjoyment thereof; and, the property may be appropriated by another. This is a virtual intent to "throw away" the property.

§ 1.53 Land use controls

There are common law devices to control use and statutory controls which derive their authority from the Constitution.

§ 1.531 Common law devices

Common law devices controlling use of property include the concept of "waste" and the public trust doctrine; invasion by others of one's property (trespass) and strict liability for abnormally dangerous activities on the property; and, the creation of a nuisance.[294] Several of these are discussed in other sections. For nuisance, see §4.2; for strict liability, see §1.43; and for trespass, see §1.411. There, also, is liability under the Tort Claims Acts for dangerous conditions which exist on property; see §4.2. While dangerous conditions has been codified in some jurisdictions, it essentially is based in common law liability.

The concept of waste arises from protection of the fee simple owner's rights as against a life tenant or a tenant for years. Waste is an act which is not consistent with good husbandry. There are four types of waste: (1) voluntary waste which is an affirmative act of the tenant which damages the property value; (2) permissive waste wherein the tenant fails to act when there is a duty to do so, such as making ordinary repairs; (3) ameliorating waste, for which a tenant normally is not liable, because there is a change in physical characteristics of the property by an unauthorized act of the tenant, but which act in fact enhances the value of the property; and (4) equitable waste, which usually arises when there is an expression in the agreement "without

---

[293] Ellis v. Municipal Reserve & Bond Co., 60 Or. App. 567, 655 P. 2d 204 (1982) plaintiff claimed ownership of some parcels of land by adverse possession in a quiet title action; defendants denied plaintiff's claim of adverse possession and counterclaimed alleging that they and their predecessors in interest, through use of the parcels, had established a prescriptive recreational easement for the public; held that defendants did not have "standing" to contest plaintiff's claim of title by adverse possession, and further that their proof was not sufficiently clear and positive to establish a prescriptive easement over the property for sunbathing, picnicking, and nature studies. Only parties with standing to contest claim were the record title holder, anyone claiming under the record title holder, and anyone claiming title by some other means (claim to prescriptive easement not a title claim); also to claim such easement, defendants needed to prove their use of property was adverse to and not permitted by plaintiffs.

[294] See Frakt and Rankin at pp. 32-38.

impeachment of waste." This means that the tenant can use the premises as a fee simple owner might and there would be no restitution in a court of law; however, if the use is inconsistent with good stewardship of the property, then a court of equity can bring relief to the actual fee simple owner.

§ 1.5311 Public trust doctrine

The public trust doctrine is probably the most important common law concept for the protection of park and recreation natural resources, such as water and land. The underlying principle is that there are certain natural resources which belong to the public domain. The doctrine, then, provides that the government should hold these resources in trust for the good of society and future generations and administer them for the enjoyment of all. The duty of a trustee is to preserve the corpus (natural resource) and to protect it against diminution, dissipation, or loss. Those who would wish to modify this trust and despoil the resource have the burden of proving that such change is for the promotion of public benefit and consistent with the public trust. As a common law doctrine, the interpretation of what is good for the public benefit is a matter of case law, although a number of states, e.g., Oregon, California, Maryland, have enacted statutes which define, extend, re-enforce, or attempt to restrict the doctrine. A few cases are described to illustrate the application of the doctrine.

Historically, the doctrine was applied primarily to water and submerged lands under navigable waters. The ownership of the subaqueous land was in the government, with dispute as to whether high or low water mark was the boundary. The government was to hold in trust for use and benefit of all people. Under the trust, there can be no diversion of ownership or use permitted except as in aid of commerce, navigation, or for public purposes. Public purposes include parks and recreation. In *People v. Hecker,*[295] it was held that improvements by way of a public park to develop the beach area was not violative of the public trust. In a quite early case,[296] the public trust doctrine was enforced when there was an attempt to reclaim wetlands, which had been used for fishing and hunting purposes, for agricultural land. The Wisconsin court[297] quite some years later did permit the City of Madison to modify a park by filling certain portions of a lagoon and a lakebed to use it for the parking of cars and to make other changes. The court's rationale was that the proposed changes would increase rather than decrease public usage, and it established five criteria: (1) public bodies will control the use of the area, (2) areas devoted to public purposes and open to the public, (3) diminution of lake area very small when compared with whole of the lake, (4) no one of the public uses of the lake as a lake will be destroyed or greatly impaired, and (5) disappointment of those members of the public who may desire to boat, fish, or swim in the area to be filled is negligible when compared with the greater convenience afforded those members of the public who use the park. About the same time, the Wisconsin court[298] also permitted a

---

[295] People v. Hecker, 179 Cal. App. 2d 823, 4 Cal. Rptr. 334 (1960).

[296] Re Crawford County Levee & Drainage Dist., 182 Wis. 404, 196 N.W. 874 (1924), cert. den. 264 U.S. 598, 44 S. Ct. 454.

[297] State v. Public Service Com., 275 Wis. 112, 81 N.W. 2d 71 (1957).

[298] Madison v. State, 1 Wis. 2d 252 Wis. 112, 83 N.W. 2d 71 (1957).

civic auditorium and museum and boating facilities to be built on and over a state-owned lake with the reasoning emphasizing the public use and control of the public structures to be built. Applying the doctrine, the State legislature of Virginia repealed a special act endeavoring to sell some submerged land to developers.

In a 1972 New Jersey case,[299] the doctrine was applied to a municipally-owned dry sand beach immediately landward of the high water mark, particularly as related to accessibility and fee differential between residents and non-residents of the city. Six years later, the New Jersey court[300] held similarly that the general public had a right to use a municipally-owned dry sand beach even though it had been dedicated for use of residents only, on the grounds that the public trust doctrine required that the general public be afforded the right to enjoy such beach. And, in a 1984 New Jersey case,[301] it was the right of the public to cross private lands to enable the public to swim in the ocean and to sue the foreshore in connection therewith. The court stated, however, that precisely what privately-owned upland (dry) sand area was to be available to satisfy the public's rights under the public trust doctrine depends upon the circumstances of the specific situation and that the court was not holding that the public has an unrestricted right to cross at will over any and all property bordering on the common property. As related to use of dry sand areas, several courts have applied the doctrine of custom. In an Idaho case,[302] the court protected the rights of the privately-owned waterfront property of Lake Coeur d'Alene, but in a Maryland situation,[303] the court did not apply the doctrine, primarily because of failure to show "ancient" use by members of the public. An earlier Oregon case[304] did protect the rights of the public in use of the 500-mile beach on the basis of the doctrine of custom. Private landowners were prevented from enclosing the dry sand area to which they had title. The court found that all of the criteria of the doctrine were present — ancient, without interruption, peaceable and free from dispute, reasonable, certain, obligatory, and not repugnant or inconsistent with other custom or law.

The court held that the public had a right to use a navigable river and defined the river as navigable if it is capable of recreational use, such as floating canoes or fishing in flat-bottomed boats; the river does not have to have a commerical function. However, riparian landowners have the right to prohibit the public from crossing their property to reach such a stream.[305]

Whereas ordinarily the government may not dispose of public lands held in trust, the California court[306] did permit the State to convey title on certain nontidal navigable-in-fact lakes and streams to private persons, but the title is subject to the trust and the private owner is required to preserve the lands and allow the public to use the lands and the waters over the lands for recreational purposes.

The application of the public trust doctrine to parks is of long-standing. Regardless

[299] Neptune City v. Avon-By-The-Sea, 61 N.J. 296, 294 A. 2d 47 (1972).

[300] Van Ness v. Deal, 78 N.J. 174, 393 A. 2d 571 (1978).

[301] Mattews v. Bay Head Improvement Assoc., 95 N.J. 306 471 A. 2d 355 (1984).

[302] State ex rel. Haman v. Fox, 100 Idaho 140, 594 P. 2d 1093 (1979).

[303] Dept. of Natural Resources v. Ocean City, 274 Md. 1, 332 A. 2d 630 (1975).

[304] State ex rel. Thornton v. Hay, 254 Or. 584, 462 P. 2d 671 (1969).

[305] State v. McIlroy, 268 Ark. 227, 595 S.W. 2d 659 (1980), cert. den. 449 U.S. 843, 101 S. Ct. 124.

[306] State v. Superior Court of Lake County, 29 Cal. 3d 210, 625 P. 2d 239, 172 Cal. Rptr. 696 (1981).

of the holder of title, parks have consistently been recognized as held in trust for the use of the public.

§ 1.532   Regulatory controls under "Police Power" authority

Police power is an inherent power of the states as a sovereign entity under the Tenth Amendment of the Constitution, which reserves to the states all powers not delegated to the United States (federal) by the Constitution, nor prohibited by it to the states. The municipalities have no inherent police powers, only those delegated to them by the states through state constitutional provisions, statutes or charters.[307] However, municipalities generally are vested with broad police powers.

Police power is the authority to place restraints on personal freedom and property rights of individual persons for the greater good of promoting order, safety, health, morals and general welfare of the people as a whole. This broad authority, which includes also the promotion of the public convenience and general prosperity, is subject to the limitations of the federal and state constitutions, especially due process. However, in respect to private property rights, whereas the power of eminent domain (see §1.51) is an actual appropriation of property for which just compensation must be made to the owner, police power is not considered a "taking," but rather a non-compensable regulation of private property in the public interest, even though the property may be destroyed or its value impaired, since the property is not actually taken for public use.

Exercise of police power usually manifests itself in the form of statutes and regulations by the state and of ordinances by a municipality. Ordinances must be in compliance with state statutes and conform to both state and federal constitutions. Ordinances to be valid must meet the test of reasonableness of public necessity, as determined by the courts. They, also, come under the equal protection clause of the Fourteenth Amendment, that is, the ordinance must apply with equal force and effect to all parties within the classification to which the ordinance applies. The classification, too, must be related to the purpose of the ordinance and cannot be arbitrary and capricious. There can be no discriminatory aspects; an ordinance must operate uniformly as to all similarly situated. These same requirements apply to state exercise of police power through statutes and regulations.

Police power includes authority to enforce, including prohibiting and regulating, seizures, forfeitures and destruction, and fines and other punishments. Regulation may include issuance of permits subject to compliance by the applicant with prescribed conditions. While seizure and destruction may occur, such as in connection with illegal fishing, illegal sale of liquor, and gambling, destruction of property of considerable value may not be permitted if such punishment is not in proportion to the violation involved. Under "due process," an individual generally must be given notice and some form of hearing before being deprived of a protected property interest. Notice only may be adequate in a situation such as abatement of a nuisance, *e.g.*, failure to cut grass and weeds. The penalty prescribed by an ordinance cannot exceed that set forth by state law.

[307] Blue Sky Bar v. Town of Stratford, 4 Conn. App. 261, 493 A. 2d 908 (1985) aff'd. 203 Conn. 14, 523 A. 2d 467 (1987) town had statutory authority to pass ordinance regulating manner of merchandising products (selling ice cream from motorized vehicles).

Statutes and ordinances promulgated by state and municipalities under authority of "police power" reach into every aspect of sport, recreation and parks operations. The court has ruled on the applicability of police power authority in situations, such as the following: control of waters and beaches adjacent to municipal boundaries, including prohibiting certain conduct such as nudity; requirement that individuals must purchase weekly permits in the form of badges in order to use the beach held to be revenue raising measure, rather than for the public welfare; regulation of waterskiing, surfing, and boating; ordinance prohibiting persons convicted of specified offenses from entering any city-owned park or stadium during sporting events was invalid use of police power; prohibition of horseback riding within city limits or on any public way or park, except where expressly designated; the Sunday laws, including banning operation of power boats on a lake located within the city limits; regulating the sale of alcoholic beverages to minors, prescribing hours during which beverages may be sold, and restricting sale within certain distance of church or school; regulation and control, including requiring permits or licenses, for public amusements and entertainment, such as theaters, dance halls and schools, circuses and carnivals, rock concerts, amusement parks, miniature golf courses; and, swimming pools, both public and private regulated. The erection of billboards and signs and distribution of handbills and other advertising matter, also, are subject to regulation under police power authority, as is peddling and canvassing for making money. Permits to hold parades may be required; and, sound trucks may be controlled by noise (decibel) limit or banned from certain locations or times of day. All health and sanitation statutes and ordinances come under the authority of police power. Building codes, including electrical and plumbing requirements, are usually enacted for the protection and welfare of the people. As illustrated, there is little which cannot be regulated under the police power authority.

§ 1.5321   Zoning[308]

While some of the foregoing uses of police power do relate to property use, one of the most important police power applications to property development is zoning. Zoning is the dividing of a municipality into geographical districts or zones and then regulating the nature and use of land in the various zones. The regulation extends to both the development of the land itself and the structures placed thereon and the activities which can be engaged in or the use of the land. Zoning extends to all property within the jurisdictional limits, including both public and private ownership. The focus of zoning is on the land, not with the person or entity who owns or occupies the land or the form of ownership.

While the authority to zone is an application of police power, it is not to be inferred from a grant of general police power to a municipality. The authority to zone usually

[308] This section based upon Chp. 26 Zoning and Planning in Charles S. Rhyne's extensive volume, *The Law of Local Government Operations*. Washington, D.C.: The Law of Local Government Operations Project, Government Law Series, Suite 800, 1000 Connecticut Ave., N.W. 1980, 1314 pp. Persons involved with municipal government will find this volume useful for a number of other aspects presented in Chapter 1. See also, J. Benjamin Gailey, editor, *1984 Zoning and Planning Law Handbook,* N.Y.: Clark Boardman Co., 1984.

must be delegated specifically by the state through statutory or other forms of authorization; it is commonly done through enabling acts. Zoning is primarily a legislative function of the municipality and represents judgment of the elected governing body as to how land should be utilized within its jurisdiction. Zoning regulations are not the same as placing restrictive covenants on property, as such covenants are a matter of contract. Zoning ordinances, however, do place a legal restraint on an owner's use of property, based upon the municipality's power to protect the public health, safety, morals, and welfare of the community.

The scope of the authority is, indeed, broad — for example, public health includes requirements for securing better light and air, preventing overcrowding; safety of the community encompasses reduction of fire hazards by certain building requirements, traffic congestion alleviation regulations, and protection from flooding; morals involve the classification of land near schools and residential areas to remove activities which might distract children and lead them to delinquency, including adult bookstores and entertainment and establishments which essentially are taverns or bars; and welfare deals with promotion of community prosperity and protection and conservation of building and land values, preservation of the character of a neighborhood and orderly development of an area, taking into consideration ecological and environmental factors and problems. Zoning seeks to both suppress offensive or harmful uses and promote desirable uses. Whatever restrictions or requirements are set forth in zoning ordinances, they must be in the public interest and not for the benefit of certain property owners. Zoning cannot be used to create special privileges or private rights through what is known as exclusionary zoning, although zoning for the elderly has been upheld, but not zoning to keep out families with children or low income individuals. The classification of uses in a zone or district must be uniformly applied to both commercial and residential and not be discriminatory. In enacting zoning ordinances, strict procedures for due process related to hearings, notice, publication, et al. must be followed to protect the rights of the people, as individuals and as business and industry entities.

Zoning regulations, including amendments, special permits and exceptions, generally are required to be promulgated in accordance with a comprehensive plan in order to avoid arbitrary, unreasonable, discriminatory, piecemeal zoning and to provide for the use and development of property according to present and future public needs. To handle individual requests for special consideration, zoning hearing boards are established to listen and rule on requests for variances and on appeals. Changes in a zoning plan must be based upon change of conditions, substantial change in character of neighborhood, correction of a mistake, large increase in traffic, et al.

§ 1.53211   Control of activities

The control of activities, the use of property, is at the heart of zoning; and, such directly affect leisure services and sport. Uses are classified in zoning regulations and these classifications must have a substantial relationship to the public safety, health, morals or welfare. Some uses also are controlled by licenses or permits. The fact that a zoning ordinance permits use (activity) in a particular district does not authorize such property use where a license or permit is required; similarly, even though one may be able to obtain a license or permit for a specific activity, that activity cannot be conducted if it violates a zoning ordinance. Further, a zoning ordinance which permits a use is invalid if there is another ordinance or statute barring such use (or activity) generally. Both residential and commercial (industry and business) uses are subject to zoning regulation. Accessory or incidental uses (not zoned) to the principal use zoned are usually permitted, if customary to the principal use.

In regard to educational uses, usually zoning cannot exclude schools from residential areas, inasmuch as zoning cannot interfere with the discharge of governmental functions. Where public schools have been permitted in a residential zone and private or parochial schools excluded, the zoning regulation has been held invalid; however, ordinances have been upheld where they treat parochial and private schools as a distinct class. Schools, though, have been held to have to comply with a city ordinance requiring provision of off-street parking proportional to auditorium capacity for a proposed high school gymnasium addition.[309] What is a school, however, has been at issue. For example, kindergarten and nursery schools have been held to be an educational use; but there is a disagreement as to whether a day care center is such educational use. The term "school" usually has not been extended to recreational uses, such as a day camp, even if held on the school premises.[310] Normally, athletic facilities[311] of a school are permitted as an accessory use, even though such sport activity might otherwise violate a zoning ordinance. However, whereas state colleges and universities are generally held to be protected from local zoning restrictions as an instrumentality of the state, action was brought against Ohio State University in 1982 for violation of zoning ordinances when it erected outdoor basketball courts with a chain-link fence within 14' of the private citizen's residence.[312]

Recreational activities vary in terms of zoning applications. Where the state regulates an activity, then the municipality is preempted. Also, where an activity may be noncommercial residential, such property use usually is distinguished from commerical use of the land for the same activity. For example, an outdoor residential swimming pool ordinarily is a use customarily incidental to a permitted use, and, where public parks and playgrounds are permitted in a residential area, swimming pools, also, are allowed as part of that recreational facility/area. Pools, however, would have to meet requirements, such as filtration systems, even though a hardship might be found. Tennis courts, too, have been held to be an accessory use to residences, and a variance for an indoor tennis center was upheld as in character with the community. However, a zoning ordinance prohibiting commerical recreational facilities kept an

[309] Robinson v. Indianola Municipal Separate School District, 467 So. 2d 911 (Miss. 1985).
[310] For example, Brookville v. Paulgene Realty Corp., 9 A.D. 2d 770 192 N.Y.S. 2d 988, 200 N.Y.S. 2d 126 (1960); Inc. Village of Brookville v. Paulgene Realty Corp., 9 A.D. 2d 770, 192 N.Y.S. 2d 988, 200 N.Y.S. 2d 126 (1960); Margo Operating Corp. v. Great Neck, 129 N.Y.S. 2d 436 (1954); Warminster Area Day Camp Ass'n., Inc. v. Upper Southhampton Zoning Hearing Board, 35 Pa. Comwlth. 541, 386 A. 2d 1076 (1978).
[311] Carine v. Cliffside Park Board of Educ., 161 N.J. Super. 137, 390 A. 2d 1228 (1978); New York Institute of Technology, Inc. v. Ruckgaber, 65 Misc. 2d 241, 317 N.Y.S. 2d 89 (1970); State v. Gerris, 304 S.W. 2d 896 (Mo. 1957); Yancey v. Haefner, 268 N.C. 163, 150 S.E. 2d 440 (1966).
[312] Beatley v. Board of Trustees, Ohio State Univ., 4 Ohio App. 3d 1, 446 N.E. 2d 182 (Ohio App. 1982).

apartment complex owner from building a tennis court for the free use of the tenants. A use permit for a commercial tennis club zoned for single-family dwellings was held to constitute illegal spot zoning. Whether a use is public or private sponsored, also, may make a difference in whether a special permit for such use is approved, as was the situation when the court distinguished a community center and a private club. Permission was sought to extend use of land in a residential area, which already had athletic fields and an indoor swimming pool, to provide indoor tennis, squash, handball, sauna baths (requiring erection of a new building) and to permit the lessee to operate the facilities as a club for its members and guests only. The court held that the proposed facility would be a private club and not a community center facility operated by a local community organization within the zoning regulation allowing a special exception in one-family detached dwelling areas.[313] Golf driving ranges and a miniature golf course have been permitted as special uses in single family housing areas, but the use of property as a par-3 golf course by a motel was not considered an accessory use. Where a golf course was shown to have been a hazardous element, the denial of a special permit to operate the course was upheld. However, in another situation, the location of a golf course in a residential district as a "country club" was permitted.[314]

Where lake shore property falls within municipal jurisdiction, there may be zoning regulation of use of beaches for recreational purposes. This includes activities, such as boat rentals and marinas and commerical recreation facilities. Again, a distinction may be made between residential recreational use and commercial uses. Use of land for trap and skeet shooting has varied, too. In one situation the prohibition of use of residential land for trap and skeet shooting was upheld, while in another a shooting range was held to be within the scope of club uses in a residential area. Similarly, a special exception to operate a trap shooting range in a rural district was held valid, while in an agricultural district, a commerical skeet shooting range was held not to be entitled to a conditional use permit. Permitted use or variance also has been at issue in campground (tent and trailer) uses in rural residential and farm/forest districts.[315]

Where religious institutions have been permitted in a residential district, recreation fields and gymnasiums have been considered accessory uses. As for social clubs and voluntary associations, zoning classifications may distinguish between social clubs and non-profit organizations and between profit-seeking and non-profit clubs. A number of cases have held the YMCA to be a private club permitted in a residential area; however, a YMCA has been denied an increase of facilities permit where there was insufficient parking area and the property was presently overcrowded.[316]

What about conducting commercial activities out of one's home; is such activity or "home occupation" accessory or incidental to the primary residential use? Appropriateness of such activities varies, but in most approved situations the activity must be carried on by an individual who maintains residence in the dwelling and the

[313] Stewart v. D.C. Board of Zoning Adjustment, 305 A. 2d 516 (D.C. App. 1973).
[314] For some case documentation, see Rhyne at pp. 908-910.
[315] For some case documentation, see Rhyne at pp. 910-911.
[316] For some case documentation, see Rhyne at pp. 886-887, 913.

employment of others is generally not permissible. For example, dance instruction was held a "home occupation," but a dancing school was not, nor was a karate school.[317]

Whereas most of the foregoing commentary has related primarily to special permit and accessory uses for recreational activities, it should be taken for granted that where there is a commerical recreation enterprise, it must be in the appropriate zoning district for such commercial enterprises. On the basis of protecting morals, establishments, such as liquor outlets, taverns and cocktail lounges (restaurants which serve beer usually are not included) or "adult entertainment," zoning ordinances may restrict the location away from schools and churches.[318]

In a 1984 case,[319] a zoning ordinance prohibited recreational dancing in a retail zoned district. The plaintiff tavern owner sued, alleging that the dancing prohibition violated the First Amendment of freedom of expression. The court held that while dancing for an audience has First Amendment protection as an expression of freedom, dancing for recreation is not a protected right.

§ 1.53212   Land use planning and development

Zoning can be used as a tool to facilitate land use planning and development objectives; however, planning should be distinguished from zoning. Planning is the broader function. As previously indicated, zoning regulations should be based upon a comprehensive plan. Such plan is especially important for orderly development of an area and for growth control to ensure adequate water supply, sewer facilities, and other governmental and utility services.

As a part of the "promoting the health" authorization for zoning, regulations regarding structures on land have been enacted. These often include floor area provisions, height of building, frontage and minimum lot area, side and rear setback restrictions, portion of lot used for building, et al. And, using the "safety of community" basis, similar structural and lot requirements are made for reduction of fire hazard. Layout, also, may be directed to reduce traffic congestion. Safety is the basis of requirements protecting from flooding, especially flood plain zoning.

"General welfare" authorization for zoning enables ordinances to be enacted which relate to open space preservation and setting aside land areas for recreational use. Techniques used for subdivision control include cluster zoning, transfer of development rights, and planned unit development (PUDs). Mandatory dedication is another device (see §1.51). Preservation and protection of historic areas is within the concept of "general welfare." Aesthetics, for such purpose alone, is not a valid exercise of police power; although desirable and commendable, it is not essential. However, under circumstances related to economic enhancement, such as vacation areas, aesthetics control is justifiable zoning. While the courts vary, there appears to be a trend in the '80s toward aesthetics as a proper basis of land use regulation under certain situations. Design control through requiring architectural review board approval usually has been

[317] For some case documentation, see Rhyne at pp. 895-897.
[318] For some case documentation, see Rhyne at pp. 874-875, 880-881.
[319] Kent's Lounge v. New York, 478 N.Y.S. 2d 928 (1984).

maintained as in the economic and general well-being of the people, and under this authorization there is some aesthetics control. Signs and billboards are a proper subject of zoning ordinances, but is an improper exercise of power if the regulation is solely or primarily on aesthetic grounds.[320]

In a Rhode Island case,[321] the court distinguished between changes in the official comprehensive plan which required a hearing on development of a piece of vacant property for the public's recreational needs, in this instance, a baseball field, which was within the city's authority.

§ 1.54   Environmental, Natural Resources, and Public Land Law

Environmental, natural resources, and public land law is a broad, extensive field in itself and beyond the scope of this chapter; however, it is an important aspect of property law.[322]

Beginning with the enactment of the National Environmental Policy Act of 1969 (NEPA),[323] the decade of the '70s was the era of new environmental quality policy and action, which impacted greatly on parks and outdoor recreation. Among the Act's most significant provisions is the mandating of Environmental Impact Statements (EIS) for Federal actions significantly affecting the quality of the human environment. The Act also created the Council on Environmental Quality (CEQ). Under the subsequent Environmental Quality Improvement Act of 1970[324] and federal executive orders, the Council was directed to develop environmental quality standards and criteria and guidelines for EIS's. An annual report on the state of the nation's environment is issued. The primary acts are the Clean Air Act[325] and the Clean Water Act.[326] Most states have comparable legislation to that of the federal environmental quality acts.[327]

The protection and use of natural resources and public lands also are of paramount importance to parks and recreation, because of both the use of these resources and lands for outdoor recreation and their conservation for future generations. These resources and lands encompass the national forests, national park system, range lands, wilderness areas, rivers, and wildlife. The Property Clause of the U.S. Constitution[328] authorizes Congress to dispose and regulate lands, and the Supreme Court interpreted this to include wildlife. The federal holdings represent approximately one-third of the nation's lands; and, in 1970 a landmark report entitled *One Third of Our Nation* was issued by the Public Land Law Review Commission. State and local governments, also, hold substantial lands. The Land and Water Conservation Fund (LWCF) gave significant impetus through allocation of funds to acquisition and development of public lands at all levels, federal, state, and local.[329]

320 See Frakt and Rankin at pp. 44-48; also, for further commentary and some case documentation, see Rhyne at pp. 727-734, 736-738, 780-781, 783-784, 787-804, 918-919, 922-933.

321 Roy v. Woonsocket, 116 R.I. 745, 360 A. 2d 565 (1976).

322 See Chapter 3, Frakt and Rankin for a good overview.

323 42 U.S.C.A. §4331 et seq.

324 42 U.S.C.A. §4371-4374.

325 42 U.S.C.A. §7701 et seq.

326 33 U.S.C.A. §1251 et seq.

327 For discussion of environmental quality, see Frakt and Rankin at pp. 56-65, 93-99.

328 "The Congress shall have power to dispose of and make all needful rules and regulations respecting the Territory or other property belonging to the United States"; Art. IV, sec. 3, cl.2.

329 See Frakt and Rankin at pp. 65-93 for discussion of the major resources held by the government and pertinent legislation with some focus on issues.

§ 1.6 Business operations

This section is not a business law overview;[330] however, there are a few topics of interest related to business operations and general comment and referral citations are made in reference thereto.

§ 1.61 Antitrust violation

Violation of the Sherman Antitrust Act,[331] *i.e.*, in restraint of interstate commerce, has been a legal issue in professional sport for many years. Antitrust suits were brought against baseball at the beginning of the century and in the early '20s in a landmark case,[332] it gained an exemption from antitrust law. The charges dealt with player restraints. While there were some cases in the '60s, it was not until the decade of the '70s that professional leagues involved in football, basketball and hockey became heavily embroiled in antitrust litigation. These sports have never had the exemption baseball enjoyed. With the advent of extensive collective bargaining by players, the relationship between antitrust litigation as related to player restraint and collective bargaining has been raised.[333]

A second area of antitrust litigation for professional sports is in the control of franchise locations and moving franchises. Since the existing franchise holders make the decision on franchise allocations, the question is raised as to whether this may not be improper control of the market in restraint of interstate commerce and the Sherman Antitrust Act.[334]

Allegations of violation of the Sherman Antitrust Act at the turn of the decade of the '80s has extended to amateur sport, specifically the National Collegiate Athletic Association (NCAA). The Association for Intercollegiate Athletics for Women (AIAW) sued the NCAA in regard to women's sports, particularly tournaments, actually forcing the demise of the Association.[335] And, the University of Georgia and the University of Oklahoma sued for control of television rights to football games.[336]

Antitrust violations also have been raised in regard to the sanctioning of athletic events and eligibility of players by both amateur and professional associations.[337]

---

[330] Citations should be updated with current information. *The Chronicle of Higher Education* reports quite extensively on NCAA and other collegiate sport activities. *Newletters Sports Industry News* is directed toward regulation and litigation of the sport industry, and *Sports and the Courts* provides information on current happenings in sport and physical education. A magazine *Sports, Inc.* reports a good deal on business aspects. Recommended that students take a course in business law if they expect to go into commercial enterprise or top level administration of public and private organizations and institutions.

[331] Sherman Antitrust Act, 15 U.S.C. §1 et seq. (1970).

[332] Federal Baseball Club of Baltimore, Inc. v. National League of Professional Baseball Clubs, 269 F. 681 (1920), aff'd. 259 U.S. 200 (1922).

[333] Extensive legal discussion in Weistart and Lowell, Chapter 5 Antitrust Aspects of Sports Activ-

ities; see also, Kempf, Donald G., Jr. The Misapplication of Antitrust Law to Professional Sports Leagues. 32 *DePaul Law Review* 625-633 (1983); Flood v. Kuhn, 407 U.S. 258, 92 S. Ct. 2099 (1972) challenged the reserve system in baseball.

[334] See Weistart and Lowell at §5.11; L.A. Memorial Coliseum Comm. v. Nat'l Football League, 484 F.Supp. 1274; rev'd./remanded 634 F. 2d 1197 (1980) Raiders to L.A.

[335] AIAW v. NCAA, 558 F. Supp. 487 (1983).

[336] Board of Regents v. NCAA, 546 F. Supp. 1276 (1982), aff'd./remanded in part 707 F. 2d 1147, stay granted 104 S. Ct. 1, 104 S. Ct. 272, 104 S. Ct. 1208, aff'd. 104 S. Ct. 2948 (1984). See also Assoc. of Independent Television Stations v. College Football Assoc., 637 F. Supp. 1289 (1986).

[337] See Weistart and Lowell at §5.10; McCormack v. NCAA, 845 F. 2d 1338 (1988) University alumni, football players, and cheerleaders brought unsuc-

Antitrust has not been the exclusive domain of sport. With the controlling authority of local government and some of the services provided, there has been some movement regarding antitrust activities of local government. In the 98th Congress a Local Government Antitrust Act of 1984 (H.R. 6027) was considered.

§ 1.62 Broadcasting rights

For many years sport has been broadcast on radio, and then on television. The court frequently has had to settle questions about who owns the right to broadcast sports news. The property rights of the teams playing and their parent organization or institution is at issue, particularly with the large dollars. Property rights should be distinguished from antitrust violations.[338] The most noted case is *Board of Regents v. NCAA*,[339] in which the Universities of Georgia and Oklahoma sued for the right to contract for their own televised games.

§ 1.63 Player agents

The role and legal responsibilities and liabilities of a player's agent in the '80s has taken on increasing importance.[340] As of the late '80s, approximately one-third of the states had enacted legislation regulating sports agents.[341]

§ 1.64 Copyrights and trademarks

The University of Pittsburgh sued Champion Products on infringement of its logo. The court held that the University had waited too long to sue and that Champion's use of long standing could be continued.[342] Trademark infringement can be brought alleging unfair competition under Lanham Trade-Mark Act and state deceptive trade practices states. Terms presented for trademark protection roughly fit into four categories: generic or common descriptive, merely descriptive, suggestive, and arbitrary or fanciful.[343]

cessfully action against the NCAA for violations of antitrust and civil rights laws by promulgating and enforcing rules that restricted benefits to be awarded student athletes, held alumni and cheerleaders lacked antitrust standing, Association's eligibility rules did not violate antitrust laws.

[338] See Arnold at pp. 189-190; Garrett, Robert Alan, and Philip R. Hochberg. Sports Broadcasting and the Law. 59 *Indiana Law Journal* 155-193 (1984); see also Berry and Wong, Vol. II Chapter 6, Sports and the media; Wong, Chapter 9 Television and media broadcasting.

[339] Board of Regents v. NCAA, 546 F. Supp. 1276 (1982), aff'd./remanded in part 707 F. 2d 1147, stay granted 104 S. Ct. 1, 104 S. Ct. 272, 104 S. Ct. 1208, aff'd. 104 S. Ct. 2948 (1984); see also Regents of the Univ. of Calif. v. A.B.C. 747 F. 2d 511 (1984); case and implications discussed at some length in Weistart and Lowell, 1985 supplement §5.12.

[340] See Berry and Wong, Vol. I; Wong, pp. 553-594; see also Crandall, Jeffrey P. The Agent-Athlete Relationship in Professional and Amateur Sports: The Inherent Potential for Abuse and the Need for Regulation. 30 *Buffalo Law Review* 815-849 (1981); as an illustrative case, see Detroit Lions v. Argovitz, 580 F. Supp. 542 (1984) player's agent violated fiduciary relationship when negotiating contract.

[341] For example, Alabama, California, Georgia, Indiana, Iowa, Louisiana, Minnesota, Ohio, Oklahoma, Tennessee, Texas.

[342] Univ. of Pittsburg v. Champion Products, Inc., 529 F. Supp. 464 (1982), 566 F. Supp. 711 (1983).

[343] Henri's Food Products Co. v. Tasty Snacks, Inc., 642 F. Supp. 255 (1986) discusses briefly the four categories and statutory law, not a creation or sport trademark.

Infringement of copyrights has become of increasing concern with the ease of reproduction and the use of television as a medium. Materials which are subject to copyright infringement include both reproduction of written and visual materials and use of recorded music without paying royalties.[344]

USE OF BOOK WITH STUDENTS

While this book was not written as a text, its organization and content are such that it can serve well as both a resource to administration and programming courses and a text to a course in legal aspects of one or more of the fields of Physical Education, Sport Management, Parks and Recreation or Leisure Services, and Camping. Depending on the class composition (*i.e.*, physical education or recreation and park majors only, leisure services, sport management, fitness-oriented, et al.), the instructor will select those materials most pertinent for inclusion and emphasis. Assignments and student expectations will vary, too, by whether an upper or lower-level undergraduate class or a graduate class. The materials presented in this book provide great opportunity for practical application of legal concepts to operations, as well as indepth study of a particular aspect of the law.

The use of this book for law students will vary considerably from its use for students in the professional fields encompassed by the book. The book provides excellent resource for study of legal concepts' application to sport law, private leisure services, and natural environment resource/outdoor recreation services, et al., as well as further study of basic negligence concepts. Rather than using the professional books cited, except for Berry and Wong, and Weistart and Lowell, law students will want to supplement the topics by law review articles, reading the case opinions (and shepardizing), et al. Lawyers and law students will find the book a most valuable resource.

The Preface of the book describes its organization. Briefly, Part A provides the basic concepts of negligence, while chapters in Part C contain material on various operational areas related to negligence. Part D covers risk management. Substantively, these parts on negligence are complete in themselves. Chapter 1 presents an overview of other legal aspects (see chapter table of contents for topical outline) with suggested supplemental readings from professional books cited in the footnotes, with the referencing word in boldface to highlight. Each author has an emphasis and offers special expertise on different topics. The best from the books has been selected for each topic in Chapter 1. No text can be adequate in all areas to be covered in a course. Chapter 1 presentation endeavors to take advantage of the expertise of other authors. It also is good instructional methodology to give students supplemental readings and familiarize them with professional "updating" resources. Instructors should be alert for both new editions of the cited books and supplements issued.

[344] See Baley at 127-128; Frakt and Rankin at pp. 264-268; Law Review II at pp. 1-4; Wong, Chapter 10 Trademark law.

Books Recommended for Library Reserve

Appenzeller, Herb. *The Right to Participate*. Charlottesville, VA: The Michie Company, 1983, 405 pp.

Appenzeller, Herb, and Thomas Appenzeller. *Sports and the Courts*. Charlottesville, VA: The Michie Company, 1979, 423 pp.

Appenzeller, Herb, editor. *Sports and Law: Contemporary Issues*. Charlottesville, VA: The Michie Company, 1985. Series of articles written by leaders in sport and the law.

Arnold, Don E. *Legal Considerations in the Administration of Public School Physical Education and Athletic Programs*. Springfield, IL: Charles C. Thomas, 1983, 358 pp.

Baley, James A., and David L. Matthews. *Law and Liability in Athletics, Physical Education, and Recreation*. Dubuque Iowa: Wm. C. Brown Publishing, 1989, second edition, 467 pp.

Berry, Robert C., and Glenn M. Wong. *Law and Business of the Sports Industries*. Vol. I Professional Sports Leagues; Vol. II Common Issues in Amateur and Professional Sports. Dover, MA: Auburn House Publishing Company, 1986.

Clement, Annie. *Law on Sport and Physical Activity*. Indianapolis: Benchmark Press, 1988, 214 pp.

Frakt, Arthur N., and Janna S. Rankin. *The Law of Parks, Recreation Resources, and Leisure Services*. Salt Lake City: Brighton Publishing Company, 1982, 315 pp.

Kaiser, Ronald. *Liability and Law in Recreation, Parks, and Sports*. Englewood Cliffs, NJ: Prentice-Hall, 1986.

Schubert, George W., Rodney K. Smith, and Jessie Trendeau. *Sport Law*. St. Paul: West Publishing Co., 1986, 396 pp.

Waicukauski, Ronald J., editor. *The Law and Amateur Sport*. Bloomington: Indiana University Press, 1982, 298 pp. Chapters are based on presentation at a sport law conference, Indiana University.

Weistart, John C., and Cym H. Lowell. *The Law and Sports*. New York: Bobbs-Merrill Company, Inc., 1979, 1154 pp.; 1985 supplement.

Wong, Glenn M. *Essentials of Amateur Sports Law*. Dover, MA: Auburn House Publ. Co., 1988, 724 pp.

Woody, Robert Henley, and Associates. *The Law and the Practice of Human Services*. San Francisco: Jossey-Bass, Inc., Publishers, 1984, 459 pp.

Additional Resources

Athletic Director & Coach

— former Coach's Legal Report merged into this periodical

— 8 pages on athletics; couple pages each issue "From the Courts"
— monthly
— Professional Publications, Inc. 3690 N. Peachtree Road, Suite 200, Atlanta, GA 30341

Exercise Standards and Malpractice Reporter

— 16 pages on fitness, athletic training, health spas, exercise testing; amount of legal each issue varies, but usually considerable
— monthly
— Professional Reports Corporation, 4571 Stephen Circle NW, Canton, OH 44718

Law Review

— issues referred to as I, II; annual compilation of law-related articles appearing in *Parks and Recreation* magazine, but only two issued to date
— National Recreation & Parks Association, 3101 Park Center Drive, Alexandria, VA 22302

Mental and Physical Disability Law Reporter

— broad scope on legal topics of mental and physical disability
— bi-monthly; size varies approximately 80-110 pages
— Commission on Mentally Disabled, American Bar Association, 1800 M Street, N.W., Washington, DC 20036

Perspective

— focus on campus legal issues
— monthly, 8 pages
— Magna Publications, Inc., 2718 Dryden Drive, Madison, WI 53704

Proceedings, Law and Sports Conference

— annually sponsored; began 1983
— appendices have useful operational materials (examples)
— emphasizes athletics, physical education
— Sports & the Courts, Dr. Herb Appenzeller, Guilford College, Greensboro, NC 27140

Recreation and Parks Law Reporter (RPLR)

— quarterly review of approximately 12 court decisions each issue
— approximately 40-50 pages each issue
— heavy on parks with some recreation, public-oriented
— National Recreation & Parks Association, 3101 Park Center Drive, Alexandria, VA 22302

Sports and the Courts

— quarterly, varies 8-16 pages
— focuses on physical education and athletics; lists current cases and news items of law suits

— Sports & the Courts, Inc., P.O. Box 2836, Winston-Salem, NC 27102

Sports Industry News

— bi-weekly, approximately 8 pages
— focuses on sport as business, predominately pro sports
— Business Publishers, Inc., 951 Pershing Drive, Silver Springs, MD 20910

The Sports Medicine Standards and Malpractice Reporter

— quarterly
— New 1989
— Professional Reports Corp., 4571 Stephen Circle N.W. Canton, OH 44718

Sports, Parks, & Recreation Law Reporter

— monthly, 16 pages
— heavy on sport and physical education, although some applicable to recreation; limited on parks — began June 1987, so mix may change
— Professional Reports Corporation, 4571 Stephen Circle NW, Canton, OH 44718

Sports Medicine Standards and Malpractice Reporter

— 18-20 pages focusing on sport medicine; amount of legal aspects in each issue varies, but usually considerable
— monthly
— Professional Reports Corporation, 4571 Stephen Circle NW, Canton, OH 44718

Hospitality Law

— 8 pages directed toward "preventive-law information" for the lodging industry
— monthly
— Hospitality Law, 2718 Dryden Drive, Madison, WI 53704-3006

As with all courses, reading of articles from professional periodical literature should be required. Because such literature should be current and also selected in accord with the course emphasis and student composition, no citations are given.

Usually students enjoy reading case decisions and researching additional cases. For a guide to legal research for students, see Arnold, appendix B, pp. 336-345; Clement, Chapter 3, pp. 19-26; Frakt and Rankin, appendices, pp. 281-300; and Woody and Associates, pp. 24-35.

Two topics which should be reviewed in a course on Legal Aspects are not included in Chapter 1. The first is the American legal system, including the court system and the nature of a law suit. These references have useful information: Appenzeller, Right to Handicapped, Chapter 4, pp. 79-92; Appenzeller, Sports & the Courts, Chapter 1, pp. 1-10; Arnold, Chapter 2, pp. 7-17; Baley, Chapter 2, pp. 17-37; Clement, Chapter 2, pp. 7-18; Frakt and Rankin, pp. 1-16; Wong, Chapter 2; and Woody and Associates, pp. 1-24.

The second topic is the legal authority under which the different entities providing the various programs, services, et al. operate. It should be understood that private enterprise and private non-profit organizations incorporate under state statutes and thereby certain controls are placed on the corporation, as well as certain responsibilities and privileges accorded. Schools, as an "arm of the state," act under a different legal authority of the state than do municipalities or special park and recreation districts, which usually operate under statutes specifically designating the powers or a charter, which does likewise. Except for limited information in Frakt and Rankin, pp. 16-28, and Kaiser, Chapter 3, the resource books do not cover this topic; however, many physical education and parks and recreation administration books do in respect only to governmental agencies and could be utilized.

A second, but most important aspect of the second topic is the nature of regulation of sport by both private and public entities. Weistart and Lowell, updated by 1985 supplement, discusses this aspect in some detail in Chapter 1 Regulation of Amateur Athletics and Chapter 2 Public Regulation of Sports Activities (especially §1.02, 1.14, 1.15, 1.15.1, 1.28, 1.29; 2.02, 2.03, 2.04), as does Berry and Wong, Vol. II, Chapter 1, Amateur Athletic Associations (approximately 100 pages). See also, Wong, Chapter 4, Amateur Athletic Association (87 pp.)

Part A
Legal Concepts of Negligence

Legal liability based in negligence pervades throughout the operations of sport and physical education, leisure services, recreation and parks, and camping and adventure activities, whether under the auspices of a private nonprofit organization, a commercial enterprise, or a governmental agency. However, for the most part, the law of negligence is not specific to these areas, but rather, the general law is applied to these fields; *e.g.*, reference is sometimes made to "sport law" — it really is law as applied to sport. Therefore, it is essential that professionals have some overall understanding of certain legal concepts, terminology, and principles. This Part endeavors to provide the foundation for this understanding. It is directed toward the professional, not toward lawyers who already have these basic understandings. For this reason, then, illustrations used are from cases and statutes concerned with sport and physical education, leisure services, recreation and parks, and camping and adventure activities. However, this type of treatment of the legal concepts should provide a most valuable resource for lawyers in advisement regarding risk management practices and in settlement and litigation of cases from the respective fields. This Part is not meant to be exhaustive or complete within itself. The citations are only illustrative of the legal concept being described. Consult with your local attorney for elaborations and clarifications.

Both common law and statutory law are included in this book. Common law has been created by the judiciary, while statutory law rests with the legislatures of the states. There is an interesting interaction between the two, as described in the chapters; for example, the change away from the doctrine of governmental immunity was instigated by the courts and modified by the legislatures, whereas the change to comparative negligence and limited liability statutes has been dominantly occasioned by the legislatures, with the courts providing interpretive applications.

Since negligence law lies primarily in the domain of the states, there are differences among states; but, a book of this type cannot presume to give individual state idiosyncrasies, technicalities, or interpretations — only basic principles with some notation of variations. Further, inasmuch as the law is responsive to the people, although basically stable, there will be modifications made through court decisions and legislative enactments from time to time. Both statutes and court decisions must be updated regularly. **It is absolutely essential that local attorneys be consulted on specific application of legal concepts and the ramifications of statutes and court decisions in any specific state.**

The four elements of negligence are presented in Chapter 2: (1) the duty owed, including the origin of such duty and the persons to whom that duty is owed; (2) the nature of the act (standard of care), which must be done to protect a person from undue risk of harm; (3) proximate cause; and (4) damage, including type and apportionment of damages.

Chapter 3 sets forth the doctrine of respondeat superior and principles for determining who is liable. The liability of the corporate entity, board members as individuals, administrative officials and supervisory personnel, employees, volunteers, trainees, et al, is discussed. There also are sections related to lessor/lessee relationships, independent contractors, joint programming, and membership clubs.

The fourth chapter is directed toward approaches to immunity and limiting liability, specifically the doctrines of sovereign/governmental immunity and charitable immunity and the state tort claims acts. The status regarding liability of the 50 states is summarized in terms of the statutory approach taken, the jurisdictional scope, insurance and risk management, and procedural requirements. Particular attention is given to discretionary acts. Additional legal concepts limiting liability are discussed in some detail in other chapters, specifically: statutes limiting liability of volunteers §3.5, ski responsibility statutes §8.4, recreational user statutes §12.1, exculpatory clauses §16.1, and Good Samaritan statutes §17.1. The concept of nuisance is also in chapter 4.

And what are the defenses one has if there is a law suit? Chapter 5 discusses defenses related to the defendants' and the plaintiffs' acts, and those defenses not especially related to either the defendants' or the plaintiffs' acts. Special attention is given to the concepts of assumption of risk and contributory negligence in relation to comparative negligence.

Chapter 2.   The Duty

The elements of a cause of action based on negligence are embodied in the definition of negligence — *negligence is an unintentional breach of a legal duty causing damage reasonably foreseeable without which breach the damage would not have occurred —*

1

and are essentially four.[1] The rules of law relating thereto apply to actions of both governmental and non-governmental entities. These elements are:

1. **A Duty**
   A duty or obligation recognized by the law requiring a person to conform to a certain standard of conduct for the protection of others against unreasonable risks.

2. **The Act**
   A failure on the part of such person to conform to the standard required.

3. **Proximate Cause**
   A reasonably close causal connection between the conduct (failure to conform to appropriate standard) and the resulting injury.

4. **Damages**
   Actual loss or damage to the interests of another.

Each of these elements is discussed in subsequent sections of this chapter.

To establish that a defendant is negligent and thus the injured plaintiff can recover, all four elements must be proven. To establish that defendant is **not** negligent, it need be shown only that one of the elements was not met, that is, that defendant owed no duty to plaintiff in first instance, or that there was no breach of duty owed, or if there was a breach of duty (standard of care not adequate) that it was not the proximate cause of the injuries, or that there was not, in fact, any damage done to plaintiff by defendant's act or failure to act.

§ 2.1 Duty

Duty to act was virtually not considered in the early English law. The tortfeasor was often held liable without regard to fault because the requirements of conduct were absolute and the fact that injury had occurred through the tortfeasor's misconduct was sufficient to establish liability. In the decade of the '80s such concept of absolute wrong is part of the intentional tort and criminal law field, except as related to strict liability (see §1.143) and negligence per se (see §2.1131), rather than part of actions in tort based on negligence.

Negligent conduct in itself is not enough to create liability. It must be shown that the party charged with negligence owed a duty to exercise care toward the party injured. *Duty is a particular status or a special relationship to others.*[2] For negligence to be

---

[1] Keeton, W. Page. *Prosser and Keeton on Torts*. St. Paul: West Publishing Company. Fifth edition. 1984. at p. 164. See also Dumka v. Quaderer, 151 Mich. App. 68, 390 N.W. 2d 200 (1986) rollerskating rink case.

[2] Beach v. Univ. of Utah, 726 P.2d 413 (Utah 1986); Bradshaw v. Rawlings, 464 F. Supp. 175 (1979), 612 F. 2d 135 (1979), cert. denied 100 S. Ct. 1836 (1980); Eichhorn v. Lamphere School Dist., 166 Mich. App. 527, 421 N.W.2d 230 (1988); Flynn v. U.S., 681 F. Supp. 1500 (1988) Utah law applied; Fuhrer v. Gearhart by the Sea, 79 Or. App. 550, 719 P.2d 1305 (1986) pet. rev. allowed 303 Or. 173, 734 P.2d 1348 (1987) aff'd. 87 Or. App. 219, 742 P.2d 58 (1987); McKinley v. Slenderella Systems of Camden, 63 N.J. Super, 571, 165 A. 2d 207 (1960).

actionable, there must be a violation of some legally recognized duty to another person.[3] Often the term "duty" is used for a requirement to do an act, such as "duty to inspect," "duty to warn" or "duty to supervise," but this is incorrect when referring to duty as an element of negligence, for such duty relates to a legally enforceable obligation to exercise care. Also, one should not confuse "no duty" because of lack of foreseeability (see §2.23) and "no duty" because of no special relationship. Duty as an element of negligence refers to a responsibility toward others to protect them from unreasonable risk of injury, arising from a relationship between parties (plaintiffs and defendants). Where there is no such relationship, there is no "duty" or responsibility to perform any act to protect from unreasonable risk. When there is no such duty and hence no requirement to act is discussed in various chapters; for example, as related to supervision, see §18.11; and to warning, see §§12.1, 20.33. A duty can arise in different ways (§2.11 Bases or origins of duty), as well as toward different persons (§2.12 Categories of persons to whom duty is owed). By whom the duty is owed (who is liable?) is discussed in Chapter 3. Whether or not a duty is owed to another usually is a question of law decided by the court (judge) and not by the jury.[4] *If it is determined that no duty was owed, then the case is not actionable.* For illustration, see subsequent discussion.

The concept of duty is an ever evolving one, inasmuch as law is societal-based; and, the legally-imposed obligation, arising by virtue of a relationship between persons whereby one party must conform to a standard of care to protect or for the benefit of another, changes with society's changing value system and desired social policies. This will be evidenced throughout this book, and is especially evident in concepts of governmental immunity, assumption of risk and comparative negligence, landowner limited liability statutes, duty toward trespassers, individual rights and responsibilities, accident-safety levels in products liability, et al.

§ 2.11 Bases or origins of duty

Duty may derive from either statutory or common law. (Moreland v. La Palata Co., 725 P. 2d 1 (Colo. App. 1985)). There are three primary origins: (1) the relationship is one inherent in the situation; however, there is a question as to whether inaction or nonfeasance can result in liability; (2) voluntary assumption of interpersonal relationships resultant in legally enforceable liability; and (3) duty required by statute, which brings a responsibility for exercising reasonable care toward another person.

[3] Bain v. Gillispie, 357 N.W.2d 47 (Iowa App. 1984); Ballard v. Polly, 387 F. Supp. 895 (1975); Berman v. Radnor Rolls, Inc., 542 Pa. Super. 525, 542 A.2d 525 (1988); Cook v. Bennett, 94 Mich. App. 93, 288 N.W. 2d 609 (1979); Ramos by Ramos v. City of Countryside, 137 Ill. App. 3d 1028, 92 Ill. Dec. 607, 485 N.E.2d 418 (1985); State v. Kallio, 92 Nev. 665, 557 P. 2d 705 (1976); Swearinger v. Fall River Joint Unified School Dist., 166 Cal. App. 3d 335, 212 Cal. Rptr. 400 (1985), pet. rev. granted 215 Cal. Rptr. 854, 701 P. 2d 1172 (1985); Wicina v. Strecker, 747 P. 2d 167 (Kan. 1987).

[4] Chavez v. Tolleson Elem. School Dist., 122 Ariz. 472, 595 P. 2d 1017 (1979); Cook v. Bennett, 94 Mich. App. 93, 288 N.W. 2d 609 (1979); Mitchell v. Cleveland Electric Illuminating Co., 30 Ohio St. 3d 92, 507 N.E.2d 352 (1987); Rabel v. Ill. Wesleyan Univ., 161 Ill. App.3d 348, 122 Ill. Dec. 889, 514 N.E. 2d 552 (1987); see also Lawrence-Berry, Robert E. The Proper Judicial Role in Neligence Actions: The *Fazzolari* Triology Redefines "Negligence." 24 *Willamette Law Review* 24:443-462 (1988).

§ 2.111   Inherent in the situation

The existence of duty is inherent in nearly every situation in which a teacher, coach, recreation leader, fitness specialist, administrator, supervisor, manager, or executive, et al. might be actively engaged. This is quite obvious throughout this entire book. For example, in operating a golf course there is the ordinary duty of the manager toward the patron to exercise reasonable care,[5] and certainly there is a special relationship between teachers and their students.[6] However, to what extent a person who is passively involved, in contrast to actively involved with the plaintiff, owes a duty is in question and is discussed in the next sub-section (§2.1111).

There are situations, however, in which the courts have held that the relationship between injured and the defendant was not sufficient to establish a legal relationship requiring responsibility to protect the participant. In illustration, a few cases are cited. An injured hayride passenger brought personal injury action against driver and owner of tractor pulling wagon. The court held that in this situation the driver did not have a duty to control horseplay of adults on wagon; there was no special relationship between the driver and the injured passenger; the driver was not responsible for the activities, only driving safely.[7]

A student brought action against University for injuries sustained in a trampoline accident at a fraternity house. The court held that the student-University relationship was not the type of special relationship that would give rise to duty to Unviersity to take reasonable measures to protect student from injuries sustained. The fraternity owned the trampoline and the premises were leased from the University.[8] In another school situation, the court held that the student, who organized a recreational baseball practice in the city park and for which there was no professional coaching assistance or supervision, was not the University's agent acting in its behalf, nor did the school have any duty to control conduct of this student, although a member of the varsity baseball team, and thus there was no special relationship between the student injured during such practice and the University.[9]

Just because someone is on the premises, or has been on recently, does not give rise automatically to a relationship. A third grade boy was injured when he pedaled his bike past eight to ten fellow students waiting on the playground for transportation to a Cub Scout meeting. The court held that there was no duty to supervise inasmuch as scouting was not a school function and there was no knowledge that scouts waited for transportation on the school premises. Usually an adult was waiting for the scouts and there was no delay, and there was usually no congestion of the passageway.[10] A child had

[5] McRoberts v. Maxwell, 40 Ill. App. 3d 766, 353 N.E. 2d 159 (1976).

[6] Foster v. Houston Gen. Ins., 407 So. 2d 759 (La. App. 1981), writ den. 409 So. 2d 660 (1982); Wagenblast v. Odessa School Dist., 110 Wash. 2d 845, 758 P.2d 968 (1988).

[7] Moore v. Hill, 155 Ill. App. 3d 1, 107 Ill. Dec. 945, 507 N.E. 2d 1314 (1987) cert. denied 508 N.E. 2d 1245.

[8] University of Denver v. Whitlock, 712 P. 2d 1072

(Colo. App. 1985) rev'd. 744 P. 2d 54 (Colo. 1987); see also Chidester v. U.S., 646 F. Supp. 189 (1986) individual injured when dived into creek in national forest on land under special use permit to county by U.S. government, U.S. owed no duty; (see §3.11 lessee/lessor).

[9] Swanson v. Wabash College, 504 N.E. 2d 327 (Ind. App. 1987).

[10] Hill v. Board of Educ., 18 A.D. 2d 953, 237 N.Y.S. 2d 404 (1963).

left the playground and was injured on nearby railroad tracks. There was no showing of defect or condition of the playground that might invite children playing in the playground to enter tracks from playground or to use the tracks as an extension of their playground. Held no duty to child so injured.[11] When children are the participants, frequently one hears that a leader's relationship is similar to parent and child with the duty that of a parent, that the leader is acting in the same manner as a parent. This is often referred to as the doctrine of *in loco parentis*, and is discussed in the second subsection (§2.1112).

Where there may have been a duty due to a special relationship, when the person who was subsequently injured is turned over to appropriate, responsible others, then that relationship also may cease; for example, when a mother or parent assumed responsibilities for their child[12] or friends for an intoxicated person.[13] There, also, may be an implied contract inherent in the situation, which gives rise to a duty. See §2.1113.

§ 2.1111   Active and passive involvement
(misfeasance-nonfeasance dichotomy)

The misfeasance-nonfeasance dichotomy as related to duty is a complex one fraught with moral, as well as economic benefit overtones.[14] The question is "Can a duty arise from passive involvement with a participant, as well as from active involvement?" Can a wrong be committed when the individual is not directly involved (nonfeasance), as well as when an individual is directly and actively involved (misfeasance)? The duty is well established when there is active involvement; however, the courts have been reluctant to find liability for passive inaction or a failure to take steps to protect another from harm when there is not a direct, active involvement. As a general rule in the law of torts, persons have no duty to come to the aid of another, even if they could render assistance with no risk of harm to themselves, if there is no special relationship established.[15] This rule is derived from the common law distinction between misfeasance and nonfeasance. Illinois has codified it by providing in its statutes that the Chicago Park District shall not be liable for passive negligence. A Massachusetts case[16] also held that a coach should not be held for nonfeasance, whereas there is liability for misfeasance.

Misfeasance is sometimes defined as action (acts of commission) or inaction (acts of

---

[11] Abdur-Rashid v. Consolidated Rail Corp., 524 N.Y.S. 2d 716 (1988).

[12] Griffith v. N.Y.C., 123 A.D. 2d 830, 507 N.Y.S. 2d 445 (1986) asthmatic student who did not receive treatment in school, when at home fell from apartment window; Saga Bay Property Owners' Assoc. v. Askew, 513 So. 2d 691 (Fla. App. 1987) owner of lake not liable, absent hidden dangerous condition, responsibility for care remained with parents.

[13] Dumka v. Quaderer, 151 Mich. App. 68, 390 N.W. 2d 200 (1986) individual came onto the roller rink premises in intoxicated condition and was escorted from premises by social companions who were not in such condition, acts of defendant did not place inca-

pacitated individual in worse condition (see §1.2214 as to when there is a duty).

[14] Davis, Victoria J. Sports Liability: Blowing the Whistle on the Referees, 12 *Pacific Law Journal* 937-964 at 942, 1981; Vogan, Joseph John. Negligence — Duty to Aid — Special Relationship Between Companions Engaged in a Common Undertaking. 23 *Wayne Law Review* 1339-1349, 1977; Weinrib, Ernest J. The Case For a Duty to Rescue. 90 *Yale Law Journal* 247-293, December 1980. See also footnote 63 citations.

[15] *Restatement (Second) of Torts* §323, 324 (1966).

[16] Marcy v. Town of Sangus, 22 Mass. App. 972, 495 N.E. 2d 569 (1986).

omission) that positively harms the plaintiff and is actionable, while nonfeasance is passive inaction (acts of omission) that causes a negative harm, but seldom civil liability.[17] In a 1982 case[18] the court said that "usually, a party is considered 'actively negligent' if he participates in some manner in conduct or omission which caused the injury;. . ." and citing another case, went on, "passive negligence exists where one person negligently brings about a condition or an occasion and...another party acts upon that condition. . ." In the same thought, Weinrib[19] stated that "Participation by the defendant in the creation of the risk, even if such participation is innocent, is thus the crucial factor in distinguishing misfeasance from nonfeasance...even though a risk may have arisen independently of a defendant, he is responsible for aggravation of the danger, that is, for substantially increasing the likelihood that it will materialize in harm."

In *Ragnone v. Portland School Dist. No. 1J*[20] the court discussed the concept of active versus passive negligence when applied to the occupier of land. It stated that such distinction is a misnomer when applied to the activities of an occupier, but then went on to say that active negligence is not to be equated with commission and passive negligence with omission; but, rather, active or affirmative negligence refers to the negligent conduct of activities upon the land for which a duty of reasonable care is owed, and the term passive negligence refers to hazards arising from the physical condition of the land, the existence of which normally does not create liability in favor of an injured person.

Another aspect of liability of nonfeasance relates to government nonfeasance. "Because government attempts so much more today than it did in the past, it is increasingly likely that injury will be caused not so much by the government *doing* something wrong but by its *failing* to do something. This tortious failure to act by the government or a public officer is the problem of public nonfeasance."[21] Wangerin goes on to say that although courts may have conceptual difficulties linking an injury with defendant's inaction, one important connecting element is the plaintiff's reliance on the completion of activities undertaken by the defendant. Most of the cases fall into six categories: failure to supervise, inspect, license, protect, warn or repair. Another category extensively litigated is failure to promote constitutionally protected civil rights. These issues discussed by Wangerin are applied to the fields of recreation and

[17] Alfonso v. Lowney, 416 N.E. 2d 516 (Mass. App. 1981); Bank v. Brainerd School Dist., 49 Minn 106, 51 N.W. 814 (1892); Herring v. Mathis Certified Dairy Co., 118 Ga. App. 132, 162 S.E. 2d 863 (1968), 225 Ga. 67, 166 S.E. 2d 89 (1969), 119 Ga. App. 226, 166 S.E. 2d 607, 225 Ga. 653, 171 S.E. 2d 124 (1969), 121 Ga. App. 373, 173 S.E. 2d 716 (1970); Selph v. Morristown, 16 N.J. Misc. 19, 195 A. 862 (1938); Thompson v. Board of Educ., 11 N.J. 207, 94 A. 2d 206 (1953); Indianapolis v. Baker, 72 Ind. App. 323, 125 N.E. 52 (1919).

[18] Johnson v. Hoover Water Well Service, 108 Ill. App. 3d 994 64 Ill. Dec. 476, 439 N.E. 2d 1284 (1982) not a sport, physical education, recreation case; see also Sagadino v. Ripper, 175 Cal. App. 3d 1141, 221 Cal. Rptr. 675 (1985) to violate law regarding furnishing of alcohol, must be an affirmative action; Univ. of

Denver v. Whitlock, 712 P. 2d 1072 (Colo. App. 1985) rev'd. 744 P. 2d 54 (Colo. 1987) quotes Keeton, trampoline at fraternity house (described in preceding section), no liability.

[19] Id, Weinrib at pp. 256, 257.

[20] Ragnone v. Portland School Dist. No. 1J, 44 Or. App. 347, 605 P. 2d 1217 (1980), 289 Or. 339, 613 P.2d 1032 (1980), aff'd. 47 Or. App. 656, 615 P. 2d 1077 (1980), rev'd. 633 P. 2d 1287 (Or. 1981); see also Johnson v. Sunshine Mining Co., 106 Idaho 866, 684 P. 2d 268 (1984) motorcycle; Brown v. Scott Paper Co., 684 F. Supp. 1392 (1987) swimmer dived into water-filled gravel pit; see §12.1 landowner limited liability.

[21] Wangerin, Paul T. Actions and Remedies Against Government Units and Public Officers for Nonfeasance. 11 *Loyola Univ. L. J.* 102 (1979).

parks, physical education and sport, and camping and adventure activities in other sections of this book, but in nearly all situations the failure to perform is not so much nonfeasance as misfeasance acts of omission. See §2.21 for further discussion.

Liability for nonfeasance first appeared regarding those engaged in "public" callings and the idea still adheres in the obligation of common carriers, innkeepers, et al. Whereas an affirmative act to render aid may be morally sound, it must be recognized that legal duty is not coextensive with moral duty. The fear of potential liability also has restricted the voluntary rendering of aid, and to counter this fear a number of states have enacted limited liability statutes. (See §2.112 Voluntary assumption of duty, §2.113 Statutory requirement, and §17.2 on first aid). To eliminate the distinction between misfeasance and nonfeasance and impose a general duty to aid would indeed be a difficult concept to administer by the court in deterimation of the balance between victim's peril and defendant's risk.[22]

The nature of the negligence may have an effect upon indemnity, although the active-passive tests to determine when indemnification will be allowed by one party has in practice proven elusive and difficult of fair application. In the *Sanchez* case,[23] plaintiff was bringing action on products liability and sued the manufacturer of the volleyball standard, the sporting goods store which sold it, and the city which used it in activity. While all three were held jointly and severally liable, under the Contribution Among Tortfeasors Act, the passive wrongdoer should be indemnified by the active wrongdoer. In this situation, the sporting goods store was considered a passive wrongdoer. A more accurate terminology would be that the passive wrongdoer is really a secondary wrongdoer and not a joint tortfeasor at all. The Illinois court, in *AMF, Inc.* v. *Victor J. Andrew High School,* 172 Ill. App. 3d 337, 122 Ill. Dec. 325, 526 N.E.2d 584 (1988), in distinguishing contribution and indemnification, stated that the theory of active/passive negligence did not survive enactment of Contribution Act.

§ 2.1112 Doctrine of *in loco parentis*

The doctrine of *in loco parentis* in essence means that the individual or agency which is providing for a child stands in the place of a parent and is charged with a parent's rights, duties, and responsibilities. A camp, a school, a recreation center, et al., when they accept children assume certain parental responsibilities and must act in relation to the child as the "reasonably prudent parent" would, protecting the child from dangers and preventing the child from engaging in self-injury and irresponsibilities. Thus, a duty can arise from the parental relationship assumed.

The applicability of the doctrine of *in loco parentis* to duty should be distinguished from negligence as related to the activity in which the child is engaged. *In loco parentis* does not extend beyond matters of conduct and discipline.[24] A teacher may discipline to maintain control in the future, but undue force that would bring the act under assault and

---

[22] See Vogan for further discussion.

[23] Sanchez v. City of Espanola, 94 N.M. 676, 615 P. 2d 993 (1980).

[24] Breen v. Kahl, 419 F. 2d 1034 (1969); Guerrieri v. Tyson, 147 Pa. Super. 239, 24 A. 2d 468 (1942); Smith v. Consolidated School Dist. No. 2, 408 S.W. 2d 50 (Mo. 1966).

battery is cautioned.[25] The Ohio court[26] has stated that although a teacher may stand *in loco parentis* as regards enforcement of authority, the teacher does not stand *in loco parentis* with regard to one's negligent acts and the teacher is not accorded the same tort immunity given parents. A teacher, however, is not held in strict accountability as an insurer of safety of pupils; strict application of laws of negligence may be tempered by social desiderata.[27]

The doctrine of *in loco parentis* as applied to college students went out in the late '60s.[28] This is not to say, however, that rules and regulations and supervision are not required for the protection against unreasonable risks. A 1987 case[29] discusses the custodial relationship between university and student, which may give rise to a duty, especially duty as related to security.

Very few of the cases related to physical education and sport, recreation and parks, or camping and adventure activities have allegations of *in loco parentis*.[30] Most of the cases in the late '70s come out of the State of Illinois,[31] seeking interpretation of a 1975 law.[32] In *Kobylanski v. Chicago Board of Education*[33] the court held that the School Code sections dealing with the duty of teachers to maintain discipline were intended to confer the status of *in loco parentis* on teachers in nondisciplinary as well as disciplinary matters. However, this interpretation definitely stands alone among states. For elaboration of situations and responsibilities involving discipline, see §18.32.

There is another facet of the doctrine of *in loco parentis* which has arisen particularly in the 1970's, and that is regarding the "constitutionalization" of children's rights. Action was brought in a 1987 case[34] when the teacher searched the hotel room of students while on a field trip. The court held that the search was reasonable in view of principal's *in loco parentis* authority (disciplinary) over students during the trip, but violation of the Fourteenth Amendment rights was an issue for the jury. Whereas ordinarily a child cannot sue a parent for damages, the traditional rules are being

[25] LaFrentz v. Gallagher, 105 Ariz. 255, 462 P. 2d 804 (1969).

[26] Baird v. Hosmer, 46 Ohio St. 2d 273, 75 Ohio Ops. 2d 323, 347 N.E. 2d 553 (1976).

[27] Segerman v. Jones, 256 Md. 109, 259 A. 2d 794 (1969).

[28] For example, Buttny v. Smiley, 281 F. Supp. 280 (1968); Moore v. Student Affairs Comm. of Troy State Univ., 284 F. Supp. 725 (1968); Pratz v. Louisiana Polytechnical Inst., 316 F. Supp. 872 (1970); see also Bradshaw v. Rawlings, 464 F. Supp. 175 (1979), 612 F. 2d 135 (1979), cert. denied 100 S. Ct. 1836 (1980) discusses duty in terms of special relationship.

[29] Rabel v. Illinois Wesleyan Univ., 161 Ill. App. 3d 348, 112 Ill. Dec. 889, 514 N.E. 2d 552 (1987); see also University of Denver v. Whitlock, 712 P. 2d 1072 (Colo. App. 1985) rev'd. 744 P. 2d 54 (Colo. 1987); see also §§1.21 and 1.2213.

[30] Hale v. Davies, 8 Ga. App. 126, 70 S.E. 2d 923 (1952); Montague v. School Board, Thornton Fr. Tp., 57 Ill. App. 3d 828, 15 Ill. Dec. 373, 373 N.E. 2d 719 (1978); Spearman v. University City Public School Dist., Mo., 617 S.W. 2d 68 (1981).

[31] Wille, James A. The in Loco Parentis Status of Illinois Schoolteachers: an Unjustifiably Broad Extension of Immunity. 10 *John Marshall J. of Practice and Procedure* 599-628.

[32] Ill. Rev. Stat. Ch. 122, §§24-24, 34-84a (1975).

[33] Kobylanski v. Chicago Board of Education, 63 Ill. 2d 165, 347 N.E. 2d 705 (1976); see also Ausmus v. Chicago Board of Education, 155 Ill. App. 3d 705, 108 Ill. Dec. 137, 508 N.E. 2d 298 (1987); Hilgendorf v. First Baptist Church of Danville, 157 Ill. App. 3d 428, 109 Ill. Dec. 659, 510 N.E. 2d 527 (1987); Kain v. Rockridge Comm. Unit School Dist. #300, 117 Ill. App. 3d 681, 72 Ill. Dec. 813, 453 H.E. 2d 118 (1983); O'Brien v. Twshp. H.S. Dist. #214, 73 Ill. App. 3d 618, 29 Ill. Dec. 918, 392 N.E. 2d 615 (1979), aff'd./rev'd. in part, 83 Ill. 2d 462, 47 Ill. Dec. 702, 415 N.E. 2d 1015 (1980).

[34] Webb v. McCullough, 828 F. 2d 1151 (1987).

modified and the *in loco parentis* status of agencies servicing children cannot be used to overcome a child's constitutional rights[35] (see §1.13 on Human rights).

§ 2.1113   Implied contract giving rise to duty

A 1983 case,[36] held that a public employee's act falls within the scope of employment only if the duty is imposed because of public employment. Plaintiff alleged that the purchase of a ticket to a football game was an implied contract that gave rise to a duty to furnish a safe and proper place from which to view the game. However, there was distinction made as to whether action was brought to recover on breach of implied contract for which the county board would be liable or on breach of duty in tort for which the board would be immune.[37]

Just because defendant operated a recreational facility for adult boating on a lake and rented boats, there was no duty to provide the plaintiff a lifeguard by virtue of his renting the canoe.[38]

§ 2.112   Voluntary assumption

If one does not owe a duty because of a relationship inherent in the situation (see §2.111) and there is no statute which requires an affirmative act (duty) (see §2.113), then at common law there is no duty owed, and hence no liability, not even when failure to come to the aid of another might cost the life of that person.[39]

"This idea of voluntary assumption of a duty by affirmative conduct runs through a variety of cases. Just when the duty is undertaken, when it ends, and what conduct is required, are nowhere clearly defined, and perhaps cannot be."[40] It may therefore be suggested that whether or not the situation has been made worse is only one fact to be considered, as bearing upon what the reasonable person would do under the circumstances. A 1983 case,[41] after stating that "a duty voluntarily assumed must be performed with due care," said that ". . . voluntarily undertaking to render a service is not sufficient to impose a duty. It must also be shown that either (a) the failure to exercise due care increased the risk of harm, or (b) the harm is suffered because of the (person's) reliance on the undertaking."

Most of the voluntary assumption of a duty situations relate to management of outdoor areas. It was held that a municipality, making an ice skating rink available to the general public without charge, had no duty to provide supervision for those participating

[35] Rose, Carol M. *Some Emerging Issues in Legal Liability of Children's Agencies.* New York: Child Welfare League of America. 1978. pp. 5-9.

[36] Pope v. McIntyre, 333 N.W. 2d 612 (Mich. App. 1983).

[37] Sims v. Etowah Co. Board of Educ., 337 So. 2d 1310 (Ala. 1976)

[38] Christian Appalachian Project v. Berry, 487 S.W. 2d 951 (Ky. 1972).

[39] Handiboe v. McCarthy, 114 Ga. App. 541, 151 S.E. 2d 905 (1966); Osterlind v. Hill, 263 Mass. 73, 160 N.E. 301 (1928); Yania v. Bigan, 397 Pa. 316, 155 A. 2d 343 (1959).

[40] Keeton at pp. 379.

[41] Mullins v. Pine Manor College, 389 Mass. 35, 449 N.E. 2d 331 (1983); see also Thompson v. U.S., 595 F. 2d 1104 (1979).

in games on ice and no duty to provide equipment for such games; but, when it assumed such duties, it then also assumed the duty to apply reasonable care in the performance of such duties.[42] This protective reponsibility or duty, also, was the basis of a 1982 Hawaii case.[43] The court held that where there was no duty to provide lifeguarding services, if the city/county voluntarily assumed this protective responsibility, then it must perform with reasonable care. A 1982 California case[44] held similarly in regard to providing lifeguard and police protective services on a beach which was an unimproved publically-held property. The federal government, also, was held to a duty of reasonable care when it decided to patrol a beach area; further, it was not absolved of liability on claim of discretionary function for manner in which it executed the decision, a ministerial act.[45] A University which operated a lake facility was held not to be immune from liability once it decided to provide services, and such facility had to be operated with reasonable care.[46] While the city was not held liable under the California statute regarding dangerous natural conditions of unimproved public property, the court dicta did say that the statute is not a bar to liability if the public entity voluntarily assumed a duty to protect the public from a hazardous condition and then negligently performed. In this situation, the natural area was a cave.[47] A 1987 California case held similarly regarding voluntarily providing warnings at cliffs in a recreational area.[48]

The concept of voluntary assumption of duty extends to private as well as public agencies. A church once it decided voluntarily to provide transportation had imposed upon it a duty of care toward persons transported;[49] and, where the church undertook to inspect the farmland, on which a snowmobile party was to be held, for conditions which might be dangerous, the church assumed a duty of making an adequate inspection.[50] In a situation involving the YWCA subleasing its auditorium for a musical comedy and a participant was injured in dance rehearsal, the court stated that if a person voluntarily assumes a duty or undertakes to render services to another that should have been seen as necessary for the other's protection, that person may be liable for harm caused by negligent performance of the undertaking. (*Thorson v. Mandell*, 402 Mass. 744, 525 N.E.2d 375 (1988).)

The court[51] held that a mere gratuitous promise does not give rise to a duty imposing a tort obligation on promissor even though promisee may rely on it and suffer damage. In this situation, a high school graduate sued the basketball coach and school district for negligence and violation of civil rights in failure to timely furnish referral and recommendation to college, allegedly resulting in plaintiff's losing opportunity to receive athletic scholarship.

[42] Diker v. City of St. Louis Park, 286 Minn. 461, 130 N.W. 2d 113 (1964).

[43] Kaczmarcsyk v. City & Co. of Honolulu, 656 P. 2d 89 (Hawaii 1982); see also Augustus v. Joseph A. Craig Elem. School, 459 So. 2d 665 (La. App. 1984).

[44] Gonzales v. San Diego, 182 Cal. Rptr. 73 (1982).

[45] Caraballo v. U.S., 830 F. 2d 19 (1987) New York law applied.

[46] Brown v. Florida State Board of Regents, 513 So. 2d 184 (Fla. App. 1987).

[47] Winterburn v. City of Pomona, 186 Cal. App. 3d 878, 231 Cal. Rptr. 105 (1986).

[48] McCauley v. City of San Diego, 190 Cal. App. 3d 981, 235 Cal. Rptr. 732 (1987).

[49] Malloy v. Fong, 220 P. 2d 48, rev'd. 37 Cal. 2d 356, 232 P. 2d 241 (1951).

[50] Isler v. Burman, 305 Minn. 288, 232 N.W. 2d 818 (1975).

[51] Hunt v. Scotia-Glenville Central School District, 92 A.D. 2d 680, 460 N.Y.S. 2d 205 (1983).

§ 2.1121   Limited liability statutes

Because of the reluctance to countenance nonfeasance as a basis of liability (see §2.1111), the courts through application of common law have persistently refused to recognize the moral obligation of common decency and common humanity, and some of the decisions have been shocking. For example, the defendant rented a canoe to an intoxicated person, who subsequently upset the canoe and was drowned — the defendant refused to give aid and was held to have no duty to do so.[52] One would like to urge assumption of a moral responsibility to save those in peril; however, because of the nature of society in the decades of the '70s and '80s, specifically, the tendency to sue others when there is any type of injury, regardless of relationship or fault, many individuals no longer feel that the potential liability suit and the impersonalness and ingratitude of the receipient are worth the effort to be helpful to others.

To encourage individuals who have skills related to first aid, et al., some legislatures have enacted Good Samaritan Laws and limited liability laws for those rendering CPR and other emergency treatment (see §17.1). Also, to encourage citizens to give assistance to crime victims and protect teachers and others who report child or drug abuse, limited liability statutes have been enacted. Further, to encourage the opening of private lands for public recreation, nearly all states have enacted recreational user statutes (see §12.1).

The federal court, in *Creasy* v. *U.S.*, 645 F. Supp. 853 (1986), gave a new definition to Good Samaritan law. It held the Farmers' Home Administration liable, under Virginia's good samaritan doctrine, to plaintiff who was injured in fall when rotten subflooring of her kitchen gave way, saying that there is liability for negligent performance of voluntary undertaking.

§ 2.1122   Last clear chance and rescue doctrines

Last clear chance doctrine. What is the last clear chance doctrine? If the injured (plaintiff) through one's own negligence puts oneself into a dangerous position from which one cannot help oneself out of danger, and the defendant seeing the plaintiff's peril and having the last clear opportunity to avoid the inflicting of the injury by ordinary care, fails to so exercise such care, the defendant is responsible. In other words, although the defendant had no original duty to the plaintiff, the doctrine creates a new duty to act. When the defendant discovers the plaintiff in a perilous situation and realizes that the plaintiff cannot extricate oneself from the situation without aid and the defendant can render such aid, there is a duty imposed upon the defendant to use the means at one's disposal to avoid injuring the plaintiff. Because the defendant must discover the perilous situation, the doctrine also has been called the "discovered peril" doctrine.

Plaintiff was unsuccessful because the criterion that defendant "discover" or know of

---

[52] Osterlind v. Hill, 263 Mass. 73, 160 N.E. 301 (1928); see §1.2214, however, for responsibility to intoxicated in decade of 1980s.

the peril was not met. A number of boys before Scouting meeting were shooting paper clips, when one was injured in the eye; the adult leaders were at the other end of a 80' to 90' long room, setting up for the meeting.[53] Another criterion is that the failure to render the aid or to render it properly must be the proximate cause of the injury to the plaintiff. Just such was the situation in a fraternity hazing incident. The jury instruction regarding last clear chance doctrine was held appropriate where inference was present that members of fraternity furnished alcohol to pledge, that they induced him to drink excessive quantities within short period of time and as a result, he became acutely intoxicated and helplessly unconscious, and that though members were aware of pledge's dangerous condition they cancelled whatever chance of recovery from acute intoxication he might have had due to failure to render him assistance by taking him to medical facility.[54]

Schweitzer v. Gilmore, 251 F. 2d 171 (1958), in holding the doctrine inapplicable, stated that the last clear chance doctrine requires a showing that (a) injured party was in a position of peril, (b) defendant knew or ought to have known of that fact and the fact that injured party could not or would not escape from position of danger, and (c) defendant then had an opportunity to avert the accident, but failed to act; the doctrine requires a supervening or intervening negligence. In another case[55] it was stated that the last clear chance doctrine was an exception to barring recovery on contributory negligence, and the plaintiff did recover in spite of contributory negligence.

The doctrine of last clear chance has been unsuccessfully alleged due to governmental immunity,[56] and in several cases[57] the court held that the doctrine was not applicable.

Rescue doctrine. Whereas the last clear chance doctrine is concerned with the contributory negligence of the victim with a duty owed by the defendant to extricate such victim, the rescue doctrine relates to the contributory negligence of the defendant who attempted a rescue and in the process was contributorily negligent. In referring to a "rescue rule adaptation" to the Wisconsin comparative negligence doctrine, the court stated that one is not guilty of contributory negligence in exposing oneself to danger of a rescue unless the intervention was performed under circumstances which would make it rash or reckless or wanton in the judgment of the ordinarily prudent person.[58] The action (act) of the plaintiff should be distinct from the subsequent act of the defendant in order to apply the doctrine of rescue.[59] The court also tried to distinguish the rescue rule from the sudden emergency rule. Sudden emergency doctrine was in issue in a situation where a dance instructor was involved in an automobile accident. The court held that motorist whose view of stopped vehicle was allegedly obstructed by third party could

[53] McQuiggan v. Boy Scouts of America, 73 Md. App. 705, 536 A. 2d 137 (1988).

[54] Ballou v. Sigma Nu General Fraternity, 352 S.E. 2d 488 (S.C. App. 1986).

[55] Williams v. Baton Rouge, 252 La. 770, 214 So. 2d 138 (1968).

[56] Vaughn v. Alcoa, 194 Tenn. 449, 251 S.W. 2d 304 (1952).

[57] Cox v. Barnes, 469 S.W. 2d 61 (Ky. App. 1971); Chapman v. State, 6 Wash. App. 316, 492 P. 2d 607 (1972); Fraley v. Lake Winnepesaukah, 631 F. Supp. 160 (1986) amusement ride; Keough v. Royal Canadian Legion et al., 6 W.W.R. 335 (1978) snowmobile race spectator; Shuman v. Mashburn, 137 Ga. App. 231, 223 S.E. 2d 268 (1976).

[58] Cords v. Anderson, 80 Wis. 2d 525, 259 N.W. 2d 672 (1977), rehearing denied 82 Wis. 2d 321, 262 N.W. 2d 141 (1978).

[59] Hunt v. Sun Valley Co., 561 F. 2d 744 (1977).

not invoke sudden emergency doctrine to overcome presumption of negligence after motorist collided with rear of stopped vehicle. The dance instructor was entitled to $50,000 in general damages.[60]

A real question is raised under the rescue doctrine as to the duty owed the rescuer, which arises even when the defendant (rescuer) endangers no one's safety but one's own. While most of the cases involve attempts by the injured rescuer to recover from some third person whose negligence allegedly imperiled the victim and required the rescue, a few have dealt with the question whether the rescued person may be liable to the rescuer. It seems that the rescuer may recover from the person being saved for such person was negligent in imperiling oneself.[61]

Although the case[62] references the doctrine of "rescue," the approach is slightly different in that the defendant is liable for damage or injury suffered by the rescuer. The court held that such liability exists only in those situations in which the defendant might invite the person to rescue and that injury was caused by defendant's negligence. In this situation the defendant operated and maintained a summer youth camp and locked the camp when not in use. After several incidents of burglary and vandalism at the camp, the decedent, living next door to the camp, voluntarily requested deputization in order to protect the camp. Death resulted from gunshot wounds sustained when investigating an incident of vandalism at the camp. Held that the defendant had no duty to take additional precautions for the protection of the decedent and such event was not foreseeable.

The imposition of the duty to rescue is really a moral decision — and what, then, should be the legal consequences if one does respond and injury occurs. "Am I my brother's keeper?"[63] The Brady article states that current case laws imposes a duty only in three limited circumstances: (1) public callings, e.g., common carriers, innkeepers, to rescue patrons in peril; (2) special status relationship, e.g., employers to aid employees; and (3) those who create a perilous situation by their own negligent actions have a duty to rescue the victim of their negligence. Because of the costs of emergency rescue, some states have passed statutes relating thereto.[64]

§ 2.113 Required by statute

A duty to take positive action to protect another may be imposed by statute. This

[60] Fontenot v. Boehm, 512 So. 2d 1192 (La. App. 1987).

[61] No cases in point related to parks and recreation, camping and adventure activities; but for discussion of the concept, see Crais, W.C. III. Rescue Doctrine: Negligence and Contributory Negligence in Suit by Rescuer Against Rescued Person. 4 A.L.R. 3d 558-564; see also The Rescue Principle Revisited. 126 The Solicitors' Journal 335-336, May 21, 1982; for further discussion as related to intervening cause, see Keeton at p. 301 et seq.

[62] Neff v. Woodmen of World Life Insur. Society, 87 N.M. 68, 529 P. 2d 294 (1974), cert. writ denied 87 N.M. 48, 529 P. 2d 274 (1974).

[63] Woozley, A.D. A Duty to Rescue: Some Thoughts on Criminal Liability. 69 Va. L. Rev.

1273-1300 (1983); Brady, Viola C. Notes — The Duty to Rescue in Tort Law; Implications of Research on Altruism. 55 Ind. Law J. 551-561 (1980); Prentice, R. Expanding the Duty to Rescue. 19 Suffolk Univ. Law Review 15-54 (1985); Radcliffe, C. A Duty to Rescue: the Good, the Bad and the Indifferent — The Bystanders' Dilemma. 13 Pepperdine Law Review 387-404 (1986); Silver, J. The Duty to Rescue: a Reexamination and Proposal. 26 William and Mary Law Review 423-448 (1985); Theisen, D. The Duty to Rescue and the Good Samaritan Statute. 8 Hamline Law Review 231-253 (1985).

[64] For example, Alaska; see also Bunting v. U.S., 662 F. Supp. 971 (1987).

often is referred to as requiring an affirmative obligation because the duty is to do some definite act rather than merely to use care to prevent immediate acts in the on-going activity from harming others. Most statutory duties referring to schools or municipalities are imposed upon the board as a whole. These statutory duties may be specific in the statute or implied in the general authorization to conduct an educational or recreational program. These duties include the establishment of rules and regulations as may be necessary for program operation and participant discipline,[65] maintenance of premises or facilities in a reasonable safe condition,[66] selection of suitable and competent leadership,[67] and provision for supervision.[68] Some states hold that the school or municipality is not liable unless such liability is imposed by statute.[69] However, it should be noted that legislative enactments may impose a duty on private parties as well as public, such as in the case[70] where the defendant failed to carry out the corporation's responsibilities with regard to water safety under the applicable city ordinances. Such failure was held to constitute more than a mere nonfeasance and amounted in fact to an actionable misfeasance. One must distinguish between statutes which impose a duty to act and those which are regulatory in nature, that is, certain building code or other construction requirements, equipment specifications, health regulations, safety standards, protective device requirements, et al. There are a great many regulatory statutes and administrative regulations, but very few statutes which set forth a duty. Violations of regulatory statutes tend to be alleged as negligence *per se* or evidence of negligence.

Not every person who may be injured while the alleged negligent one was violating a statute gains a right of action in tort. In order for statutory violation to be actionable negligence, two criteria must be satisfied. First, the injured person must be of the class specifically intended to be protected as individuals and not merely as a member of the general public which is being protected by the statute. Such is the situation in cases which hold that the injured person must be a user, and properly using the area or facility.[71] This also may be referred to as the duty being owed privately, as distinguished from a duty to the general public.[72] Secondly, the injury suffered by the plaintiff must be

[65] Gammon v. Edwardsville Comm. Unit School Dist. No. 7, 82 Ill. App. 3d 586, 38 Ill. Dec. 28, 403 N.E. 2d 43 (1980); Garber v. Central School Dist., 251 A.D. 214, 295 N.Y.S. 850 (1937); Govel v. Board of Educ. (two cases), 267 A.D. 621, 48 N.Y.S. 2d 299 (1944); Luce v. Board of Educ., 2 A.D. 2d 502, 157 N.Y.S. 2d 123 (1956); Ostrowski v. Board of Educ., 31 A.D. 2d 571, 294 N.Y.S. 2d 871 (1968); Williams v. Cotton, 346 So. 2d 1039 (Fla. App. 1977).

[66] Florey v. Burlington, 247 Iowa 316, 73 N.W. 2d 770 (1955); Schmitt v. Cheviot, 31 Ohio Op. 12 (1933); Shaw v. Boston American League Baseball Co., 325 Mass. 419, 90 N.E. 2d 840 (1950).

[67] Garber v. Central School Dist., 251 A.D. 214, 295 N.Y.S. 850 (1937); Kolar v. Union Free School Dist., 8 N.Y.S. 2d 985 (Madison Co. Ct. 1939); Luce v. Board of Educ., 2 A.D. 2d 502, 157 N.Y.S. 2d 123 (1956); Shannon v. Fleischhacker, 116 Cal. App. 258, 2 P. 2d 835 (1931).

[68] Graff v. Board of Educ., 258 A.D. 813, 15 N.Y.S. 2d 941 (1939); Miller v. Board of Educ., (two cases) 291 N.Y. 25, 50 N.E. 2d 529 (1943).

[69] Koehn v. Board of Educ., 193 Kan 263, 392 P. 2d 949 (1964); Rhoades v. School Dist., 115 Mont. 352, 142 P. 2d 890 (1943).

[70] Herring v. Mathis Certified Dairy Co., 118 Ga. App. 132, 162 S.E. 2d 863 (1968), 225 Ga. 67, 166 S.E. 2d 89 (1969), 119 Ga. App. 226, 166 S.E. 2d 607, 225 Ga. 653, 171 S.E. 2d 124 (1969), 121 Ga. App. 373, 173 S.E. 2d 716 (1970).

[71] Belt v. Los Angeles, 55 Cal. App. 2d 31, 130 P. 2d 163 (1942); Caldwell v. Island Park, 304 N.Y. 268, 107 N.E. 2d 441 (1952); Howard v. Fresno, 22 Cal. App. 2d 41, 70 P. 2d 502 (1937).

[72] Piasecny v. Manchester, 82 N.H. 458, 136 A. 357 (1926); Smith v. Iowa City, 213 Iowa 391, 239 N.W. 29 (1931).

within the same general class of risks to which the statute is directed, that is, the statute should have been enacted to protect against the injury which occurred, and the plaintiff's injuries were a reasonably foreseeable consequence of and proximately caused[73] by a violation of the statute.[74]

The statutory duty may be imposed upon an individual.[75] Illustration of this is *Hudson v. Craft*.[76] The California code provided that a boxing referee shall stop the contest or match when either of the contestants shows a marked superiority or if apparently outclassed. The court held that the explicit language created a statutory duty toward the plaintiff, injured boxer.

§ 2.1131 Negligence *per se*

If a statute is determined to be applicable, that is, it is interpreted as designed to protect the class of persons which includes the plaintiff against the type of risk occasioned (as described in the preceding section), and the violation is not excused, the great majority of courts hold that the jury must be directed that such unexcused violation is conclusive on the issue of negligence. This is usually referred to as negligence *per se* or negligence in itself. An excused violation is one, for example, where an emergency might make it more dangerous to comply with the statute or that the violation is a recognized reasonable act. There may be some statutes for which there is no excused violation, and neither reasonable ignorance nor all proper care will avoid liability — in such case the defendant may become liable on the mere basis of violation — such properly falls under the heading of strict liability, although frequently the courts refer to negligence *per se*.[77] Sometimes the statutes specify; *e.g.*, South Carolina states that there be strict liability for injuries by traps or trapping devices, while North Carolina provides that violation of special provisions for motorcycles should not be considered negligence *per se*.

In addition to the person injured being one of the class of persons for whose benefit the statute was adopted, the violation of statutes must proximately cause the injury. In *Fredette v. City of Long Beach*, 187 Cal. App. 3d 122, 231 Cal. Rptr. 598 (1986), the plaintiff was injured when he dove off pier and struck his head. The building code had been violated regarding fencing construction sites.

Two illustrative cases[78] involve swimming pools. In the California case, there was

---

[73] Fredette v. City of Long Beach, 187 Cal. App. 3d 122, 231 Cal. Rptr. 598 (1986) dive from pier under construction, violated building code to fence construction sites; Utesch v. Atlas Motor Inns, 687 F. 2d 20 (1982) Virgin Islands swim pool, violated building code.

[74] For further discussion of both private and public parties, see Municipal Tort Liability and the Public Duty Rule: A Matter of Statutory Analysis, 6 *William Mitchell Law Review* 391-412 (1980); Laughlin, Ann T., Municipal Corporations — Tort Liability — Municipality Held Not Liable for Negligent Inspection Absent a Special Duty to Individual Members of the Public, 3

Hamline Law Review 231-242 (1980); both articles based on Cracraft v. City of St. Louis Park, 279 N.W. 2d 801 (Minn. 1979).

[75] Davis, Victoria J. Sports Liability: Blowing the Whistle on the Referees. 12 *Pacific Law Journal* 937-964 at 944, 1981.

[76] Hudson v. Craft, 33 Cal. 2d 654, 204 P. 2d 1 (1949).

[77] Keeton, at pp. 227-231.

[78] Lucas v. Hesperia Golf & Country Club, 225 Cal. App. 2d 241, 63 Cal. Rptr. 189 (1967); Ward v. Thompson Heights Swimming Club, 27 N.C. App. 218, 219 S.E. 2d 73 (1975)

failure to post phone numbers in compliance with statutes and regulations regarding emergency procedures. In the other case, the plaintiff was suing for the death by electrocution of a substitute lifeguard. The wiring in the pumphouse was not properly installed by National Electric Code standards. A statute required installation in conformity with the Code. The question for the jury in a Georgia case[79] was whether the 14-year old hotel guest who was physically strong and an experienced swimmer was guilty of lack of ordinary care for his own safety so as to preclude recovery for his death which was allegedly the result of negligence *per se* on the part of the hotel owner for violating an ordinance requiring provision of a lifeguard and certain rescue equipment.

The plaintiff, a young lady 11-years-old, was walking a horse, subsequent to having ridden the horse, when the 14-year-old defendant rode his mini-bike into the field. The horse became scared and bounded away, dragging the youngster a distance, severely injuring her. Plaintiff alleged that there had been a violation of the statute which stated that a person of less than 16 could not operate a mini-bike unless accompanied by another person 18 years of age or older, who is properly licensed, and asked that it be held that such violation is negligence as a matter of law. The court held that in this situation it was not negligence *per se* for the parents to have entrusted the mini-bike to the young rider. The rider was not irresponsible or reckless in prior operation of the vehicle.[80] A contrary result was reached in an early case[81] in camp. A 12-year-old had soup spilled on his back when a camper of the same age, who had volunteered to be a substitute waiter, tripped. The State's labor law stated that no child under the age of 14 should be employed in connection with any business or occupation carried on for pecuniary gain. The court held that the violation of the law was evidence of negligence *per se* from which a jury might find liability. The Pennsylvania court, though, held that the host was negligent *per se* in serving alcohol to the point of intoxication to a person less than 21 years of age, and thus was liable for injuries proximately resulting from minor's intoxication. The plaintiff was an employee of the defendant company, which held a Christmas party for its employees at which alcoholic beverages were served.[82] Although aware of the intoxicated condition, the keys to the car were given to plaintiff who wanted to drive from the plant to his home.

However, the Florida court[83] pointed out that the reverse may not be true, that is, that compliance with the Code is not, as a matter of law, a presumption of no negligence. The conditions and circumstances existing at the time of the accident may require a greater care than that indicated in the Code.

§ 2.1132   Mandatory and permissive statutory duties

The concept of mandatory and permissive duties as a basis of liability relates

[79] Henry Grady Hotel Corp. v. Watts, 119 Ga. App. 251, 167 S.E. 2d 205 (1969).

[80] Crabtree v. Shultz, 57 Ohio App. 2d 33, 11 Ohio Op. 3d 31, 384 N.E. 2d 1294 (1977).

[81] Spear v. Koslelle, 150 Misc. 305, 269 N.Y.S. 391 (1934).

[82] Congini v. Portersville Valve Co., 312 Pa.Super. 461, 458 A.2d 1384 (1983); modified 470 A.2d 515 (Pa. 1983).

[83] Fries v. Florida Power and Light Co., 402 So. 2d 1229 (Fla. App. 1981).

primarily to the doctrine of governmental immunity (see §4.2), and the following commentary is based on early cases and provides a historical frame of reference. "...where the corporation exercises powers and privileges, which are permissive and not mandatory,...then the municipality acts in a proprietary or private capacity... The right is permissive rather than mandatory and we think, when the city undertakes to maintain a park...it must be held to be duty of the city to maintain the park in a reasonably safe condition for those lawfully using the same."[84]

An Iowa court[85] followed similar reasoning in that a city is under a duty to maintain a park in a reasonably safe condition if it chooses to have a park as permitted under statute. Two New York cases also refer to operation under permissive statutes.[86] The corollary to this would then be that a mandatory duty would come under the doctrine of governmental immunity.[87] However, a contrary result was reached when a statute imposing certain duties was discounted in favor of precedents from other jurisdictions.[88] However, most courts do not recognize the permissive-mandatory distinction for tort liability. A governmental function is more often determined by its character than whether it is mandatory or voluntary; the fact that the duty may be undertaken voluntarily and not under compulsion of statute is of no consequence.[89]

In making a distinction as to the nature of the mandatory duty, one of the aspects is to whom the duty is owed. A New York committee said that where the statute imports an intention to protect the interests of an individual as such, liability, but where the statute does not import such intention but rather to protect a person only as a member of the general public, no liability.[90]

It has always been understood that is was essential for a plaintiff to show the breach of duty privately, as distinguished from one owed to the public.[91] No agrument is required to establish the fact that municipal playgrounds, like schools, are public institutions open to enjoyment by all the people from which the city in its corporate capacity receives no special advantage. There is nothing in the facts stated in the reserved case from which it could be found that the defendant owed the plaintiff any other duty than that which is owed to all members of the public for whose benefit the playground in question was maintained. For the non-performance of this duty there can be no recovery under the foregoing rule.[92]

Another way of expressing to whom the duty is owed is when the relation between the parties is that of governor and governed and the officer of the municipality is negligent

[84] Sapula v. Young, 147 Okla. 179, 296 P. 418 (1931).

[85] Florey v. Burlington, 247 Iowa 316, 73 N.W. 2d 770 (1955).

[86] Augustine v. Brant, 249 N.Y. 198, 163 N.E. 732 (1928); Edinger v. Buffalo, 213 N.Y. 674, 107 N.E. 1076 (1914).

[87] R.A.C., "Notes: Liability of Municipal Corporations for Negligence in Connection with Recreational Facilities," 24 Va. L. Rev. 430 (1938); "Municipal Liability — A Proposal," 23 Iowa L. Rev. 392 (1937); Ft. Worth v. Wiggins, 5 S.W. 2d 761 (Tex. App. 1928).

[88] Honaman v. Philadelphia, 322 Pa. 535, 185 A. 750 (1936).

[89] Alder v. Salt Lake City, 64 Utah 568, 231 P. 1102 (1924); Bolster v. Lawrence, 225 Mass. 387, 114 N.E. 722 (1917); Gebhardt v. LaGrange Park, 354 Ill. 234, 188 N.E. 372 (1933); Hannon v. Waterbury, 106 Conn. 13, 136 A. 876 (1927).

[90] First Interim Report of the Joint Legislative Committee on Municipal Tort Liability, State of New York, Legislative Document (1955) No. 42, Williams Press, Albany, New York 1955, p. 17.

[91] Cracraft v. St. Louis Park, Minn., 279 N.W. 2d 801 (1979) distinguish from public invitee (see §2.12112).

[92] Piasecny v. Manchester, 82 N.H. 458, 136 A. 357 (1926).

in discharge of his duty, no liability arises, but when the relation between the municipality and the injured party is that of one proprietor to another, liability may arise.[93] In another Wisconsin case, recovery was allowed against the city under the nuisance theory because the relationship between the city and the injured party was not that of governor and governed.[94]

Another facet to statutory breach was discussed by an Iowa case.[95] It was held that although Iowa usually follows the governmental view of immunity, where injury is caused by public servants while negligently performing their governmental functions there is no liability, but where injury is caused by dangerous conditions due to the municipality's own negligent failure to perform its duty as required by statute, there is liability. This type of holding is specifically treated by the California Code.[96]

§ 2.12 Categories of persons to whom duty owed (plaintiffs)

While a duty may be created on one of the three bases described in the preceding section (§2.11), *the nature of that duty depends upon the relationship between the individual (plaintiff) and the person allegedly negligent (defendant).* In the legal literature, relationships most commonly are defined in terms of the status of the plaintiff, whether an invitee, a licensee, or a trespasser. In *Mitchell* v. *McArthur,* 743 S.W.2d 604 (Mo.App. 1988), a situation in which a softball player slid into home plate, the court held that the petition did not state negligence cause of action against operators of softball field, as it did not contain allegation as to player's statuts as either invitee, licensee, or trespasser, and thus did not allege what duty, if any, was owed to her.

This system of somewhat rigid categories into which the plaintiff must fit has been in disfavor for some time with legal writers and some judges. In response, following the adoption in England in 1957 of a statute which abrogated the distinction between invitee and licensee, but retained the category of trespasser, a number of state courts and legislatures have abolished the categories in common law.[97] The first of these was the California court[98], in 1968, when it held that whether the plaintiff was a trespasser, a licensee or an invitee made no difference as to the duty of reasonable care owed to plaintiff, but nature of the duty was to be considered only on the issue of what was reasonable care. The Hawaii court[99] followed a year later. The New York court[100] stated it this way: "Law is not concerned with distinctions between duties owed trespassers,

[93] Virovatz v. Cudahy, 211 Wis. 357, 247 N.W. 341 (1933).

[94] Robb v. Milwaukee, 241 Wis. 432, 6 N.W. 2d 222 (1942).

[95] Florey v. Burlington, 247 Iowa 316, 73 N.W. 2d 770 (1955).

[96] West's Ann. Calif. Code, Government Div. 3.6 Part II (1963).

[97] For example, Colorado, Illinois, Minnesota, Massachusetts, New York, Rhode Island, Wisconsin.

[98] Rowland v. Christian, 69 Cal. App. 2d 108, 70 Cal. Rptr. 97, 443 P. 2d 561 (1968); subsequent cases: Beauchamp v. LosGatos Golf Course, 275 Cal. App. 2d 25, 77 Cal. Rptr. 914 (1969); Chase v. Shasta Lake Union School, 66 Cal. Rptr. 517 (1968); Carlson v. Ross, 271 Cal. App. 2d 29, 76 Cal. Rptr. 209 (1969); Fitch v. LeBeau, 1 Cal. App. 3d 320, 81 Cal. Rptr. 722 (1969); Smith v. Americania Motor Lodge, 39 Cal. App. 3d 1, 113 Cal. Rptr. 771 (1974).

[99] Pickard v. Honolulu, 51 Hawaii 134, 452 P. 2d 445 (1969); also, Gibo v. Honolulu, 51 Hawaii 299, 459 P. 2d 198 (1969).

[100] Basso v. Miller, 47 A.D. 2d 812, 366 N.Y.S. 2d 1009, aff'd. 386 N.Y.S. 2d 564, 40 N.Y. 2d 233, 352 N.E. 2d 868 (1976); Scurti v. City of N.Y., 40 N.Y. 2d 433, 354 N.E. 2d 794 (1976); Supples v. Canadian National Ry Co., 386 N.Y.S. 2d 489 (1976).

licensees and invitees, but rather with application of standard of reasonable care under circumstances whereby foreseeability shall be the measure of liability." And the Wisconsin court[101] held that the common-law distinction between a landowner's duty to licensees and the duty to invitees was abolished, that the duty of the landowner or occupier to those who come upon the land was that of ordinary care under the circumstances. The Tennessee court in a 1984 case[102] set forth this approach to classifications, thusly:

> Common-law classifications of one injured on land of another as an "invitee" or "licensee" are no longer determinative in jurisdiction in assessing duty of care owed by landowner to the person injured; duty owed by landowner is one of reasonable care under all of the attendant circumstances, with foreseeability of the presence of the visitor and likelihood of harm to him being one of the principal factors in assessing liability... "Care" exhibited by landowner toward visitor that is reasonable in one context may be wholly unreasonable or more than reasonable in a different context.

The distinction of the status of persons and the repudiation of the categories has come about primarily as related to premises liability,[103] as noted in the Wisconsin and Tennessee statements which referred to landowners. Illinois was more direct in passing its Premises Liability Act, and its court[104] distinguished, thusly:

> Under Illinois common law, the duty a property owner owes to a person who enters his premises depends upon whether the entrant is an invitee, licensee, or a trespasser... The "premises doctrine," however, has been abolished... Under this statute, there is no longer a distinction between the invitee and the licensee, such that the landowner owes to all persons entering his premises with his express or implied consent the duty of reasonable care regardless of the purpose of the visit;... The duty owed to the trespasser, including the trespassing child entrant upon the premises, has not been changed by the Act.

The abolishment of the distinction among entrants in terms of status, thus, is primarily as related to premises or landowner liability, and, even then, many of the recreational user statutes and some subsequent cases deny this application in referencing the nature of the duty owed (see §§12.14, 12.152). Further, as the English statute did and the Tennessee and Illinois courts indicated, the status of trespasser effectively remains and the distinction abolished is that between invitee and licensee. This concept is reinforced when nature of duty is discussed by the courts; the distinction is between duty owed

---

[101] Antoniewicz v. Reszcynski, 70 Wisc. 2d 836, 236 N.W. 2d 1 (1975).

[102] Hudson v. Gaitan, 675 S.W. 2d 699 (Tenn. 1984).

[103] Hawkins, Carl S. Premises Liability After Repudiation of the Status Categories: Allocation of Judge and Jury Functions. 15(1) *Utah Law Review* 15-63, 1981.

[104] O'Donnell v. Electro-motive Div. of General Motors Corp., 148 Ill. App. 3d 627, 102 Ill. Dec. 51, 499 N.E. 2d 608 (1986) motorcyclist crashed into cables which divided parking lot, accident at night, cables not illuminated; see also Sumner v. Hebenstreit 167 Ill. App. 3d 881, 118 Ill. Dec. 888, 522 N.E.2d 343 (1988) plaintiff dived into water-filled sandpit, set forth the 3 categories and duty owed each by landowner.

trespassers and duty owed licensees. The invitee usually is not referenced.[105] To state that the distinction among all three categories of invitee, licensee, and trespasser has been abolished is not really correct. A health spa case[106] set forth the categories of persons entering on land and the duty related to each, to wit:

> (1) a trespasser is one who enters the premises without the permission of the occupier or without a legal right to do so; and towards the trespasser no duty exists in most instances except to refrain from willfully or wantonly injuring him and (2) a licensee is one who enters the premises with the occupier's express or implied permission, but only....for his own purposes which are unconnected with the occupant's interests and to him in addition to the duty owed to a trespasser, is owed the duty of warning the licensee of latent dangers of the premises if actually known by the occupier.

Key to the nature of duty in all of the states which have abrogated the categories is what is reasonable under the circumstances, and the circumstances do take into consideration how the plaintiff got there and for what purpose; each situation is to be taken on its own merits. Notwithstanding the statements of abrogation, the preponderance of states still adhere to the differentiation of plaintiff's status in assigning "reasonableness under the circumstances." Further, criteria similar to those previously applied to the three categories are utilized in determining the nature of duty and resultant liability. Therefore, this section addresses the nature of duty in terms of the three categories of invitees, licensees, and trespassers. The *Denham* case stated that "The distinction between the duties owed to a licensee and to a trespasser is that while one always has the duty to warn the former of a known hazard, one must warn the latter only if the failure to do so would be grossly negligent." The use of the terms "grossly negligent" and "willfully and wantonly" in the two definitions should be noted, for they are the basis of liability under most limited liability statutes.

What is the distinction among the three categories of invitee, licensee and trespasser? The Illinois court in the *O'Donnell* case defined the three categories, thusly:

> **An invitee**...one who enters upon the premises with the owners implied or express consent, for the mutual benefit of himself and the owner, or a purpose connected with the business in which the owner is engaged or permits to be carried on upon the premises.

> **A licensee**...one who enters upon the premises of another with the owner's express or implied consent "to satisfy his own purposes rather than for the mutual benefit of himself and the owner or a purpose connected with the business in which the owner is engaged or permits to be carried on upon the premises."

---

[105] For example, in addition to the O'Donnell and Duncan cases, see Denham v. U.S., 646 F. Supp. 102 (1986) aff'd. 834 F. 2d 518 (1987) applying Texas law, swimmer dived into lake.

[106] Duncan v. World Wide Health Studios, Inc., 232 So. 2d 835 (La. App. 1970).

A trespasser is one who enters upon the premises of another with neither permission nor invitation.

It must be recognized that an entrant may change status while on the property, with consequent change in duty owed. An invitee who begins to pursue one's own purposes may become a licensee, while a trespasser who is "discovered" and permitted to remain on the property may become a licensee. Subsequent sections describe in more detail the status of and duty owed to invitees (§2.121), licensees (§2.122) and trespassers (§2.123). It should be noted that almost all situations of negligence, as related to the fields of sport and physical education, parks and recreation, leisure services, and camping and adventure activities, involve invitees, for indeed, individuals are invited to participate and to use facilities and services. The situations where licensees and trespassers are involved are almost entirely limited to use of premises (a building or outdoor area) for unsponsored recreational activities.

§ 2.121   Invitees

There are three considerations relating to liability toward invitees — an invitation for a particular purpose, an invitation to a specific area, and the duty owed the invitee.

§ 2.1211   Invitation for a particular purpose

An invitation to enter or remain on the property must be issued to the person specificially for a particular purpose in order for an individual to be considered an invitee. Social guests usually are considered as licensees (see §2.122).

§ 2.12111   Business invitee

Traditionally, if the "particular purpose" involved some economic benefit to the owner, then the person was a "business invitee." Obviously, when one pays admission to see an athletic or other event, this places the individual in the business invitee category. In discussing the use of a University gymnasium by member of public without fee, the Ohio court[107] distinguished a business invitee and a licensee, stating that business invitees are persons who come upon premises of another, by express or implied invitation, for some purpose which is beneficial to owner, while a licensee is a person who enters premises of another by permission or acquiescence, for one's own pleasure or benefit, and not by invitation. The court held that the plaintiff was a licensee. The Texas court also distinguished a business invitee and a licensee in *Vela v. Cameron Co.,* 703 S.W.2d 721 (Tex. App. 1985). Parents of swimmer brought suit against county and State under wrongful death and survival acts for drowning, which occurred below mean low tide line and thus did not occur on premises of county, even though the county

---

[107] Light v. Ohio Univ., 28 Ohio St. 3d 66, 502 N.E. 2d 611 (1986).

controlled the beach area beginning above mean low tide line. The court held that the
county owed no duty to warn of hazardous undertow where swimmer did not pay for use
of county beach and thus was a licensee rather than a business invitee. Had the swimmer
been a business licensee the applicable standard was that a landowner has a duty to warn
of hazards on adjoining premises, the court noted.

A spectator at a PGA-sponsored golf tournament was held to be a business invitee.
The Professional Golfers Association was sued, also.[108] A participant, member of high
school basketball team, in an invitational tournament which charged spectators
admission was held to be a business invitee.[109] In another case, a 16½-year-old boy
dived into a city swim pool where the water was only 6'8" deep instead of 9' to 10' as it
should have been, and injured himself. The swimmer had paid an admission fee, and
hence the court considered him a business invitee; it was held that the pool with
inadequate water was a dangerous instrumentality.[110] In another business invitee
case,[111] the plaintiff paid admission to attend a basketball game and after the game went
to the school catefeferia to buy food. While seated at a table, the chair gave way and she
sustained injuries. Since the chair was in full control of the defendant and was furnished
to the plaintiff as a business invitee, a *prima facie* showing of negligence was made out
when shown that the chair collapsed while in ordinary use by plaintiff.

A patron (business invitee) fell on the slippery floor of the restaurant in the golf club
house. Both the city who owned the golf course and the restaurant management which
had leased the restaurant aspect for operation were sued.[112] Two girls, 15 and 16 years of
age, drowned when marine operators failed to replace ropes indicating a hidden drop-
off. They were held to be business invitees although they had paid no fee to swim
because of the expectation of economic benefit from boat rentals and other marine sales;
in fact, the father of one was waiting at the time to rent a boat.[113]

A Texas case[114] addressed the situation as to the status of a club (health spa) member.
The court said that:

> Persons who have been treated as invitees include patrons of restaurants,
> banks, theatres, and places of amusement... The difference between those
> business relationships and this one is...a continuing right to return to the spa
> from time to time...relationship to the spa was something less than that of a
> tenant whose landlord is under a contractual obligation to make needed
> repairs. She was more like a person who holds a season ticket to a number of

108 Duffy v. Midlothian Country Club, 92 Ill. App.
3d 193, 47 Ill. Dec. 786, 415 N.E. 2d 1099 (1980) aff'd.
135 Ill. App. 3d 429, 90 Ill. Dec. 237, 481 N.E.2d 1037
(1985).

109 Nunez v. Isidore Newman H.S., 306 So. 2d 457
(La. App. 1975).

110 Cummings v. Nazareth, 430 P. 255, 242 A. 2d
460 (1968). Two additional swimming pool cases held
that the participants who had paid a fee were business
invitees and were owed a duty of care: Campbell v.
Peru, 48 Ill. App. 2d 267, 198 N.E. 2d 719 (1964);
Rumsey v. Salt Lake City, 16 Utah 2d 310, 400 P. 2d 205
(1965).

111 Raffa v. Central School Dist., 16 A.D. 2d 855,
227 N.Y.S. 2d 723 (1962).

112 Lightner v. Balow, 159 Wash. Dec. 869, 370 P.
2d 982 (1962).

113 Kesner v. Trenton, 216 S.E. 2d 880 (W. Va.
1975); see also Haugen v. Central Lutheran Church, 58
Wash. 2d 166, 361 P. 2d 637 (1961) in a somewhat
unusual result, a member of a congregation donating his
labor in construction of the church building was held to
be a business invitee of the church.

114 Adam Dante Corp. v. Sharpe, 468 S.W. 2d 167
(Tex. Civ. App. 1971), aff'd. 483 S.W. 2d 462 (1972).

separate performances or a meal ticket which can be used from time to time. Club membership has been held to create an invitee relationship.

See additional cases in subsequent sections.

§ 2.12112   Public Invitee

The "business invitee" concept was found to be too narrow to encompass the entire spectrum of cases in which invitee status is justified; therefore, the courts have gradually developed a second test, referred to as "public invitees." This status is accorded individuals where the defendant extends an invitation to the public or a segment of the public to enter the premises (event) and the plaintiff did enter for the purpose for which the invitation was extended. Except where there is definite economic benefit (profit), this classification includes the majority of activities and events sponsored by schools, municipalities, voluntary organizations, et al. in the recreation and parks, physical activity and sport, and individual/family camping field.

When a municipality invites the general public, whether from within the city limits or from without,[115] to use the parks and recreation areas and facilities, those who respond to such invitations are invitees.[116] After all, the purpose of such areas and facilities is for the use of the general public. When a softball player, who went to the municipal park to participate in a softball game as member of a team belonging to the municipal league, and who was using the park facilities for one of the uses that the park had been held open to public at the time, fell in a hole in the park's parking lot and was injured, he was held to be a public invitee.[117]

What action results in an "invitation" may be in dispute, but the courts have held that the invitation may be implied as well as express. In *Gregaydis v. Watervliet Civic Chest, Inc.*[118] it was held that even if a person, as a guest of a member of the charitable organization which sponsored the recreation center, was a licensee when he entered, he became entitled to benefit of reasonable care when the director of the center undertook to instruct him as to use of a chinning bar. It was acknowledged that the member was an invitee, but no determination was made as to whether the guest was an invitee or licensee. A Girl Scout leader who was injured when she tripped over a sprinkler on the premises of a savings and loan association while attending a scout meeting which was held in the association's building was held to be an invitee of the association rather than a licensee inasmuch as the association had invited the public to use its building for group

115 Norberg v. Hagna, 46 S.D. 568 195 N.W. 438 (1923); Thrasher v. Cincinnati, 28 Ohio Op. 97 (1944); Vaughn v. Alcoa, 194 Tenn. 449, 251 S.W. 2d 304 (1952).

116 Becker v. Newark, 72 N.J. Super 355, 178 A. 2d 364 (1962); Burnett v. San Diego, 127 Cal. App. 2d 191, 273 P. 2d 345 (1954); Caldwell v. Island Park, 304 N.Y. 268, 107 N.E. 2d 441 (1952); Glenn v. Raleigh, 246 N.C. 469, 248 N.C. 378, 103 S.E. 2d 482 (1958); Lindstrom v. Mason City, 126 N.W. 2d (1964); Rhoades v. Palo Alto, 100 Cal. App. 2d 336, 223 P. 2d 639

(1950); Sanders v. Long Beach, 54 Cal. App. 2d 651, 129 P. 2d 511 (1942); State ex rel. Kansas City v. Ellison, 281 Mo. 667, 220 S.W. 498 (1920); Terranella v. Union Bldg. & Const. Co., 3 N.J. 443, 70 A. 2d 753 (1950); Tweedale v. St. Petersburg, 125 So. 2d 920 (Fla. 1961).

117 Treps v. City of Racine, 73 Wis. 2d 611, 243 N.W. 2d 520 (1976).

118 Gregaydis v. Watervliet Civic Chest, Inc., 14 A.D. 2d 623, 218 N.Y.S. 2d 383 (1961).

meetings.[119] An opposite result was reached in an Ohio case.[120] The plaintiff went to the defendant's home for the sole purpose of paying for dinner tickets to fashion show sponsored by women's club of which plaintiff was not a member; thus, plaintiff came to defendant's home to confer a benefit upon the club and upon defendant's wife, a member of the club. The court held that plaintiff was therefore an invitee, notwithstanding that plaintiff had been invited in for a cup of coffee, and not a social guest, which category usually is considered similar to that of a licensee. The court said that the *status of the plaintiff upon property is determined by the circumstances which bring plaintiff to the property*, and defined invitee as one who is on the premises to confer some benefits upon the invitor other than purely social.

The recreational user statutes have been held to be applicable only to public invitees (see §§12.14, 12.151). One of the stipulations in the statutes is that the use must be gratuitous; the owner cannot receive any remuneration.

See additional cases cited in next two sections.

§ 2.1212   Invitation to a specific area

One of the elements which differentiates a licensee from an invitee is that the invitee is using a specific area for the purpose designated. The invitation, however, may extend not only to portions of the premises which invitees are especially invited to use but also to portions to which it appears from the particular circumstances of a case that the invitation is reasonably extended.[121]

In two maintenance-related cases, the plaintiff was held to be an invitee. In one, the plaintiff was injured when she slipped in a special education class by reason of a substance on the gym floor.[122] The court held that while there was a duty as to an invitee, there had been no notice of the defective condition. In the other, the plaintiff slipped on an icy patch while entering a door of the clubhouse.[123] In this situation the plaintiff, using the front entrance rather than another entrance because there was no sign otherwise, was deemed an invitee and was owed a duty of reasonable care. She had not gone where not "invited." A similar circumstance occurred in Iowa when the plaintiff and his date, as they were leaving a dance at the municipal golf course club house, went around the building to find a dark spot, went off the sidewalk about 9' and fell into an open basement entrance due to damp, slick grass on the steep incline. It was held that while the plaintiff was an invitee to the clubhouse, he was not an invitee in this location which was not related to the dance and no duty was owed him to protect him from absolute danger.[124]

The obligation, however, to render the premises safe exists only while the visitor is upon the part of the premises to which the invitation is extended. Two novices went

[119] McKinnon v. Wash. Fed. Savings & Loan Assn., 68 Wash. 2d 644, 414 P. 2d 773 (1966).

[120] Daggett v. Di Trani, 194 N.J. Super. 185, 476 A. 2d 809 (1984) plaintiff slipped, fell, injured on driveway of residence.

[121] Lamb v. Redemptorist Fathers of Georgia, 111 Ga. App. 491, 142 S.E. 2d 278 (1965).

[122] Cumberland College v. Gaines, 432 S.W. 2d 650 (Ky. 1968).

[123] Madisonville v. Poole, 249 S.W. 2d 133 (Ky. 1952).

[124] Cox v. Des Moines, 235 Iowa 178, 16 N.W. 2d 234 (1944).

skiing and decided to try an area not open for skiing. They were injured when they went over a ledge; held no recovery because there was no general invitation to the public to use that area for skiing; the skiers were not invitees owed a duty, but licensees who took the premises as they found them.[125] In another "area of invitation" case,[126] a student was held to be an invitee to a park. He was using a hill for tobagganing; there had been, but were not presently, signs stating "Toboggan Slide Closed," "Danger No Sliding." However, no negligence was proven.

There was implied invitation in a water supply reservoir case.[127] The lake's primary purpose was water supply, but it also was used for recreation; however, when the decedent left the area of implied invitation to another location, he lost his status of invitee.

It should be emphasized that where individuals are invited to a park, it means the duty is owed for any portion of the park the individuals might seek to use, as long as that use is one for which they were invited.[128] Such appropriate use, in the case of a golf course, includes caddying.[129] A caddy was held to be an invitee to whom the city owed a duty of reasonable care. Where a patron of the restaurant of the clubhouse on the minicipal golf course was injured, he was held to be a business invitee owed a duty of reasonable care.[130]

Certain natural conditions may or may not give rise to a duty. Even though a pond was not constructed for the purpose of swimming, but was created by heavy rains, if it is in a recreational area for children, such children are invitees to the area and owed a duty of reasonable care in posting signs prohibiting use or erecting guard rails around the dangerous pool.[131] Other types of natural conditions may not give rise to such a duty.[132] Two children, ages eight and ten, were skating in the park when they broke through the ice. Held that they were not invited to use the pond for skating and that the risk of thin ice arose because of the weather, a natural condition for which the city was not held liable.

Where no invitation was extended, the injured party was not owed the duty of an invitee. In this case the city owned a tract of land; however, it was not a public park with recreation facilities to which the public was invited. It did have a pond, but this was not held out as a swimming area. A 14-year-old boy lost his life swimming. It was held that there was neither as express or implied invitation to swim and hence the municipality did not owe a duty to protect by erecting guards around the pond.[133] A similar result was obtained in a situation where the park was under construction and the public was not yet invited to use the area.[134]

---

[125] Balaas v. Hartford, 126 Conn. 510, 12 A. 2d 765 (1940).

[126] Beccue v. Rockford Park Dist., 94 Ill. App. 2d 179, 236 N.E. 2d 105 (1968).

[127] Dumond v. Mattoon, 60 Ill. App. 2d 83, 207 N.E. 2d 320 (1965).

[128] Anadarko v. Swain, 42 Okla. 741, 142 P. 1104 (1914).

[129] Lowe v. Gastonia, 211 N.C. 564, 191 S.E. 7 (1937).

[130] Lightner v. Balow, 59 Wash. 2d 856, 370 P. 2d 982 (1962).

[131] Nation v. St. Joseph, 5 S.W. 2d 1106 (Mo. App. 1928); Streickler v. N.Y. Board of Educ., 225 N.Y.S. 2d 602 (1962) patch of ice on playground; see §2.1231 for attractive nuisance.

[132] Cleveland v. Walker, 52 Ohio App. 477, 6 Ohio Op. 138, 3 N.E. 2d 990 (1936).

[133] Toledo v. Cummings, 121 Ohio St. 37, 166 N.E. 897 (1929); see §20.3321 Hazard warning.

[134] Mangum v. Powell, 196 Okla. 306, 165 P. 2d 136 (1946).

Furthermore, to owe a duty, the invitation to participate must be extended by the person who owes the duty. The city leased the ball park to the softball association. It was held that the association, not the city, invited the injured to play ball; therefore, the municipality did not owe a duty and was not liable.[135] As a lessor the city was concerned with the premises, not the conduct of the activity. Had the injury occurred due to a dangerous condition of the premises, a different result would have been reached and the city held liable.[136]

§ 2.1213   Duty owed an invitee

The duty owed an invitee is that of "reasonable care," and what is reasonable care is usually a matter for the jury. The duty, however, is the greatest owed of the three classifications — invitee, licensee, and trespasser. *The duty owed an invitee is to perform an affirmative action to protect from unreasonable risk of harm* and to avoid affirmative acts which make the situation worse.[137] The duty to invitees is nondelegable.[138] While the owner on whose premise the invitee has come is not a guarantor of the invitee's safety, there must be an affirmative action in anticipation of foreseeable hazards which might harm, and this includes actions of both employees and an independent contractor (see §3.12 Independent contractors). The 1987 Florida court[139] stated that a landowner owes two duties to an invitee: (1) to use reasonable care in maintaining the premises in a reasonably safe condition; and (2) to give the invitee warning of concealed perils which are or should be known to the landowner and which are unknown to the invitee and cannot be discovered by the invitee through exercise of due care. The Indiana court[140] referred to the public invitee rule, saying that a city maintaining a park open to general public incurred duty under public invitee rule to design park safely for children and adults and to keep it free from hazards. The duty owed to a business invitee is similar to that owed a public invitee — ordinary and reasonable care;[141] however, under Illinois law, a business invitee need not establish, in order to recover in negligence, that landowner had actual or constructive knowledge of defective condition, where instrumentality causing injury was an integral part of the business enterprise, and where it may reasonably be inferred that defective condition was due to negligence of landowner, rather than actions of third party.[142] In *Berman* v.

[135] Whealen v. St. Louis Softball Assn., 356 Mo. 622, 202 S.W. 2d 891 (1947).

[136] Harllee v. Gulfport, 120 F. 2d 41 (1941); see §3.11 Lessor/lessee relationships.

[137] Dumka v. Quaderer, 151 Mich. App. 68, 390 N.W. 2d 200 (1986) intoxicated person, roller rink.

[138] Baker v. Mid Maine Medical Center, 499 A. 2d 464 (Me. 1985) country club golf exhibition.

[139] City of Milton v. Broxson, 514 So. 2d 1116 (Fla. App. 1987) softball spectator city park.

[140] City of Bloomington v. Kuruzovich, 517 N.E. 2d 408 (Ind. App. 1987) player tripped over manhole cover as he chased fly ball.

[141] For example, Duffy v. Midlothian Country Club, 92 Ill. App. 3d 193, 47 Ill. Dec. 786, 415 N.E. 2d 1099 (1980) aff'd. 135 Ill. App. 3d 429, 90 Ill. Dec. 237, 481 N.E.2d 1037 (1985); Haddox v. Suburban Lanes, Inc., 349 S.E.2d 910 (W. Va. 1986); Kesner v. Trenton, W. Va., 216 S.E. 2d 880 (1975); Martin v. United States, 392 F. Supp. 243 (1975); Nunez v. Isidore Newman H.S., 306 So. 2d 457 (La. App. 1975); Schreiber v. Walt Disney World Co., 389 So. 2d 1040 (Fla. App. 1980); Smith v. United States, 546 F. 2d 872 (1976); Wright v. Mt. Mansfield Lift, 96 F. Supp. 786 (1951); Yania v. Bigan, 397 P. 316, 155 A. 2d 343 (1959).

[142] Higgins v. White Sox Baseball Club, 787 F. 2d 1125 (1986) concession stand door came loose and struck plaintiff.

Radnor Rolls, Inc., 542 Pa. Super. 525, 542 A.2d 525 (1988), a roller rink situation, the Pennsylvania court endeavored to distinguish a "no duty" concept and assumption of risk, where the landowner had no duty toward a business invitee to guard against obvious dangers or the risks of an activity generally known to be dangerous and the plaintiff assumed the risk of injuries by voluntarily encountering a known danger. The "no duty" concept involves a finding that the defendant had no duty to the plaintiff and, therefore, was not negligent, while under assumption of risk the defendant owes a duty but may be relieved of liability because the plaintiff assumed the risk. Further, the Florida court[143] stated that a prerequisite to the duty of a landowner to warn was that the defendant's knowledge of danger must be superior to that of business invitee. It should be noted that while the cases cited relate to duty of a landowner and an invitee, *the same standard of reasonable care is applied to the conduct of activity and provision of services.* The standard of care is discussed in §2.2.

The question is sometimes raised as to whether the duty extends to protection of the invitee against criminal violence by third persons on the premises. The authorities are divided. In a 1980 case,[144] plaintiff was attending a football game and during the third quarter left his seat to go to the washroom. As he began to descend the stairs, without warning, he noticed a hand reaching into his front pocket where he kept his money clip. Plaintiff suffered serious injury when he turned to see what was happening and was thrown over the railing onto the ground below by two men. Assailants were not apprehended. Plaintiff sued and court held that the municipal corporation which owned the stadium and the football club which leased it owed no duty to protect plaintiff against the type of harm suffered absent evidence that the attack was reasonablly foreseeable. Another 1980 case[145] held similarly that in absence of foreseeability of violent assaults on a campus, there was no duty to protect. (For further discussion, see §1.21.)

The holder of a complimentary pass to a high school football game was considered an invitee to whom was owed a duty of reasonable care by the school district. He was knocked to the ground by a group of children engaged in horseplay.[146] And, in another school case, while attending a father-son event, a father was injured when another student went to retrieve a basketball and collided with him. Having come upon the school's premise at the school's invitation to attend a specific event, the father was an invitee to whom the school owed a duty of reasonable care.[147]

In *Stevens v. Central School Dist.*,[148] an adult person was participating in a community recreation basketball game in the school gym when he was injured when he crashed through a glass door panel. The glass was ordinary glass and the player was not aware that it was not safety glass. Defense alleged that the player was a licensee and thus could not recover for defect in design of building, but if he were considered an invitee,

---

[143] City of Milton v. Broxson, 514 So. 2d 1116 (Fla. App. 1987) softball spectator in city park.

[144] Gill v. Chicago Park District, 85 Ill. App. 3d 903, 41 Ill. Dec. 173, 407 N. E. 2d 671 (1980).

[145] Relyea v. State, 385 So. 2d 1378 (Fla. App. 1980).

[146] Tanari v. School Directors, 69 Ill. 2d 630, 14 Ill. Dec. 874, 373 N.E. 2d 5 (1977).

[147] Borushek v. Kincaid, 33 Ill. Dec. 839, 78 Ill. App. 3d 295, 397 N.E. 2d 172 (1979).

[148] 25 A.D. 2d 871, 270 N.Y.S. 2d 23 (1966), aff'd. 21 N.Y. 2d 780, 288 N.Y.S. 2d 475, 235 N.E. 2d 448 (1968).

the only duty defendant owed was a warning that the door did not have safety glass. The court held, however, that the player was an invitee to whom a duty of reasonable care was owed and this included provision of safety glass or proper informing of the appreciation by the player of risks involved with ordinary glass.[149]

A 15-year-old boy sleeping in a Forest Service campground was also deemed to be an invitee since he had an express invitation to use the premises.[150] A limb fell on him while he was sleeping, seriously injuring him. Court held that there was a duty of ordinary care to eliminate dangerous conditions. The operator of the premises must exercise reasonable care for the protection of such invitees. This includes not only warning visitors of dangers which are known, but also inspecting the premises to discover possible defects and hazards. In a 1980 health spa situation, the member plaintiff slipped and fell inside a whirlpool bath and injured her back. She alleged improper maintenance of the premises, failure to warn of a danger, and faulty steps. The court stated that the duty of reasonable and ordinary care owed to an invitee includes the discovery of reasonably discoverable conditions on the premises which may be unreasonably dangerous and the correction thereof or a warning to the invitee of the danger. No negligence found; judgment for defendant.[151] The owner, however, is not expected to and cannot guarantee against injury, particularly injury by third persons[152] or by the failure of the injured person to exercise proper care for one's own safety.

The same holds true for the recreational use of playgrounds after school hours. In leaving the facility open, it is an invitation for children to use the apparatus; they are invitees and owed a duty of reasonable care for seeing that the premises are safe.[153] However, the injured must use ordinary care for one's own safety. A 16-year-old boy, engaged in touch football on the playground, ran backwards into a merry-go-round pivot post. The court[154] held that he caused his own injury and the city did not have a duty to protect him in such situation.

Where the school permits use of its facilities for a community center, participants are invitees and a duty of reasonable care for their safety is required, even though they are not students.[155] There was a similar holding were the school permitted use of its building for Bluebirds.[156] The school unsuccessfully alleged the injured to be a licensee to whom they would not owe such a duty.

---

[149] In a comparable situation of injury to 17-year-old senior who ran into large glass window behind basketball goal, the court held similarly. Clary v. Alexander County Board of Education, 19 N.C. App. 637, 199 S.E. 2d 738 (1973), 285 N.C. 188, 203 S.E. 2d 820 (1974). See §§20.1 and 20.2.

[150] Smith v. United States, 117 F. Supp. 525 (1953).

[151] Sevin v. Shape Spa for Health & Beauty, Inc., 384 So. 2d 1011 (La. App. 1980).

[152] Plaza v. San Mateo, 123 Cal. App. 2d 103, 266 P. 2d 523 (1954); Whittaker v. Franklinville, 265 N.Y. 11, 191 N.E. 716 (1934).

[153] Cheyenne, 34 Wyo. 67, 241 P. 710 (1925).

[154] Iacono v. Fitzpatrick, 61 R.I. 28, 199 A. 689 (1938).

[155] Kelley v. Board of Educ., 191 A.D. 251, 180 N.Y.S. 796 (1920); Slovin v. Gauger, 200 A. 2d 565 (Del., 1964); see also, Aaser v. Charlotte, 265 N.C. 494, 144 S.E. 2d 610 (1965).

[156] Kidwell v. School Dist., 53 Wash. 2d 672, 335 P. 2d 805 (1959).

§ 2.122   Licensees[157]

The Nebraska court[158] defined a licensee and the duty owed, thusly:

One who, solely for his own personal pleasure, convenience, or benefit, enters the premises of another with the consent of the latter but without an invitation, express or implied, is a bare licensee.... The owner or occupant of property owes to a licensee the duty only to refrain from injuring him by willful or wanton negligence or a designed injury, or by failure to warn of a hidden danger or peril known to the owner or occupant but unknown to or unobservable by the licensee in the exercise of ordinary care.

The Alabama court[159] added in regard to duty that:

owes licensee duty not...to negligently injure him after discovering his peril...no duty to warn licensee of potentially dangerous condition unless he does some positive act which creates new hidden danger, pitfall, or trap, which is condition that person could not avoid by use of reasonable care and skills; landowner is not liable unless he does some act which goes beyond mere negligence.

The federal court,[160] referencing Missouri law, applied the concept of licensee and duty thereto to park users. It said that persons who enter federal park to take part in planned, organized park programs are invitees, while those who use only property and none of the facilities, programs, or personnel of park are mere licensees. In the opinion, the court distinguished the nature of the park in question (Ozark National Scenic Riverways Park) with publicly held property of a more commercial nature, specifically a municipal golf course, stating that the vast majority of individuals come to wilderness areas such as the Park for their own pleasure rather than to participate in planned, organized, and supervised activity. Further, it said that there is no way for park personnel to even know how many visitors are in the Park, much less what activities they may be engaged in, and to hold that all visitors to the Park are invitees would be an "absurb miscarriage of justice." The federal court[161] two years earlier held similarly, applying Indiana law, in finding that widow and decedent were not invited guests of park, but, rather, licensees, having entered park and used facilities for their own entertainment.

---

[157] Licensee is not to be confused with one who is issued a license by a governmental agency. The term licensee is used because one is given "license" or privilege to enter.

[158] McCurrey v. YMCA, 210 Neb. 278, 313 N.W. 2d 689 (1981) plaintiff injured when fell while playing basketball on an outdoor asphalt playground owned by defendant, plaintiff not member of organization.

[159] Edwards v. City of Birmingham, 447 So. 2d 704 (Ala. 1984) plaintiff injured when trying to catch

foul ball, stepped in hole in baseball field in public park, danger open and obvious; Brown v. Scott Paper Co., 684 F. Supp. 1392 (1987) applied Miss. law, swimmer dived into water-filled gravel pit, implied licensee.

[160] Will v. U.S., 656 F. Supp. 776 (1987) plaintiff dived from tree into swim hole in river.

[161] Clem v. U.S., 601 F. Supp. 835 (1985) drowning at unguarded beach in national park.

Under Indiana law, a licensee was one held to enter premises of another for one's own convenience, curiosity or entertainment. In a third federal case,[162] this time applying Georgia law, the court found the injured swimmer to be a bare licensee and no duty toward plaintiff to make premises safe or to warn of conditions alleged to have caused injured. There was no evidence suggesting that any benefits were conferred on landowner by presence of injured person. However, a distinction was made between landowner's duty to licensee under the Georgia Recreational Property Act and that under negligence statutes, with the duty owed under the Act more narrow than the duty owed under negligence statutes. Special attention should be given to suits brought under the recreational user statutes (see §21.14 Status of entrant).

In addition to park users, as just described, there are many other situations which give rise to the plaintiff being a licensee. Among the common types of persons who fall in this category of licensee are those who take short cuts across property, who make permissive use of property, who sightsee or spectate without invitation, social guests, et al. For example, the plaintiff was held to be a "mere licensee" because he was playing in a school yard, not during the school term or during a summer program, for which reason there was no supervision or organized play, when he was injured from shattering glass from a bottle thrown by three older boys.[163] And, the court[164] held that the plaintiff was a "bare licensee" when 14-year-old plaintiff, a Scout, was climbing a tree on the defendant's property and a limb broke, hurling him to the ground. A 13-year-old boy was held to have a status "no greater than that of licensee" when, while playing ball on defendant's vacant lot, was injured when his hand became entangled in defendant's open and unguarded conveyor belt while he was attempting to retrieve a ball.[165] However, the defendant was unsuccessful in holding that a "pass" ticket for a ballgame made a youngster a licensee, rather than an invitee.[166] And, a four-year-old child who had been playing with the son of the defendant owner of premises was held to be a licensee when he drowned in the pool.[167] The status of licensee also was designated for a man who took a leaky boat and drowned.[168] Additional situations in which the plaintiff was held to be a licensee are described in subsequent paragraphs discussing duty.

Social guests, also, are usually designated as licensees.[169] The reasoning given is that the guests understand that when they come, they are to be placed on the same footing as one of the family, and must take the premises as the occupier uses them.[170] This status

[162] Nye v. Union Camp Corp., 677 F. Supp. 1220 (1987) swimmer struck head on submerged object in lake (stumps).
[163] Crossen v. Board of Education, 45 A.D. 2d 952, 359 N.Y.S. 2d 316 (1974).
[164] Davis v. Shelton, 33 A.D. 2d 707, 304 N.Y.S. 2d 722, (1969), app. dismd. 26 N.Y. 2d 829, 309 N.Y.S. 2d 358, 257 N.E. 2d 902.
[165] Washington v. Trend Mills, Inc., 121 App. 659, 175 S.E. 2d 111 (1970).
[166] Stroud v. Bridges, 275 S.W. 2d 503 (Tex. Civ. App. 1955).
[167] Handiboe v. McCarthy, 114 Ga. App. 541, 151 S.E. 2d 905 (1966).
[168] Venable v. Langford, 116 Ga. App. 251, 157 S.E. 2d 34 (1967).

[169] Crabtree v. Shultz, 57 Ohio App. 2d 33, 384 N.E. 2d 1297 (1977); Ferguson v. Kasbohm, 131 Ill. App. 3d 424, 86 Ill. Dec. 608, 475 N.E. 2d 984 (1985); Hager v. Griesse, 29 Ohio App. 3d 329, 505 N.E. 2d 982 (1985); Latimer v. Latimer, 66 Ill. App. 3d 685, 23 Ill. Dec. 471, 384 N.E. 2d 107 (1978); LePoidevin v. Wilson, 107 Wis. 2d 745, 322 N.E. 2d 699, rev'd./ remanded Ill. Wis. 2d 116, 330 N.W. 2d 555 (1983); Pashinian v. Haritonoff, 79 Ill. App. 3d 1203, aff'd. 81 Ill. 2d 377, 43 Ill. Dec. 21, 410 N.E. 2d 21 (1980); Robles v. Severyn, 19 Ariz. App. 61, 504 P. 2d 1284 (1973).
[170] Keeton at pp. 414-415.

is accorded even though the guest may perform gratuitously services for the host. However, as related to motor vehicles, in some states, the standard of care owed a social invitee may be that of an invitee (see §22.123).

While the licensee has in common with the invitee the element of consent, the licensee does not enjoy the same duty owed. Rather, the nature of the duty owed is more like that owed a trespasser, in that there is no duty to seek out dangers and take affirmative action to protect. Reasonable care must be exercised to warn the licensee of any concealed dangerous conditions or activities which are known or changes in the condition of the premise which the licensee may not know and which may be dangerous to him.[171] The Connecticut court said, in reference to a situation involving a tobogganer licensee, that a possessor of land is liable for bodily harm caused to a gratuitous licensee by natural or artificial conditions thereon if, but only if, he: (a) knows of condition, realizes that it involves an unreasonable risk to licensee and has reason to believe that licensee will not discover condition or realize the risk, and (b) invites or permits licensee to enter or remain on land, without exercising reasonable care to make condition reasonably safe or to warn licensee of condition and risk involved therein.[172] The licensee must not be injured by willful, wanton, or gross negligence.[173] The licensee-invitee distinction is of particular importance in cases involving limited liability for landowners in terms of the duty owed, that is, the only duty owed licensees is not to willfully or wantonly injure the person; the licensee takes the land as finds it.[174] Some illustrative cases follow.

In two Pennsylvania cases,[175] the injured parties were held to be gratuitous licensees and in a Connecticut case[176] a licensee. In the *Miller* case a ten-year-old boy was injured one Saturday morning when he went with his Sunday School class to the park. He was descending a sloping trail 5' wide, constructed of stones and with logs forming steps. The trail connected two paths. Plaintiff contends that he slipped on a loose stone and, losing his balance, began to run down the 50' toward the other trail, fell on the level part of the lower trail, and rolled over and down a slope 23' to a stream. It was further alleged that rain the day before made the stones slick. It was held that the boy was a gratuitous licensee and that the city was liable only if it knew of the condition and realized that it

[171] Slovin v. Gauger, 193 A. 2d 452 (Del. 1963), aff'd 57 Del. 378, 200 A. 2d 565 (Del. 1964).
[172] Dougherty v. Graham, 161 Conn. 248, 287 A. 2d 383 (1971).
[173] Lower Neches Valley Authority v. Murphy, 529 S.W. 2d 816, rev'd. 536 S.W. 2d 561 (Tex. 1976); Walker v. Reed, 180 Ga. App. 165, 348 S.E. 2d 707 (1986); Wight v. State, 93 Misc. 2d 560, 403 N.Y.S. 2d 450 (1978).
[174] Barbre v. Indianapolis Water Co., 200 N.E. 2d 1142 (Ind. App. 1980); Bickford v. Int'l Speedway Corp., 654 F. 2d 1028 (1981) good discussion of invitee, licensee, and trespasser and duty owed; see also, Lister v. Campbell, 371 So. 2d 133 (Fla. App. 1979); Moore v. Burn Constr. Co., 98 N.M. 190, 646 P. 2d 1264 (1982); Taylor v. Mathews, 40 Mich. App. 74, 198 N.W. 2d 843 (1972); see legal article citations, §2.1231; and James,

John F., Premises Liability: Private Road Owner's Liability to Implied Invitees, 31 Ark.L.Rv. 335-344 (1977); Shipley, W.E. Comment Note — Duty to Take Affirmative Action to Avoid Injury to Trespasser in Position of Peril Through No Fault of Landowner, 70 A.L.R. 3d 1125-1134; Strenkowski, Edward A., Tort Liability of Owners and Possessors of Land — A Single Standard of Reasonable Care Under the Circumstances Towards Invitee and Licensees, 33 Ark.L.Rv. 194-210 (1979); see also 12.1.
[175] Miller v. Philadelphia, 345 Pa. 1, 25 A. 2d 185 (1942); Onstott v. Allegheny County, 338 Pa. 206, 12 A. 2d 785 (1940).
[176] Balaas v. Hartford, 126 Conn. 510, 12 A. 2d 765 (1940).

involved an unreasonable risk which there was reason to believe the boy would not discover or realize. Such was not the case.

The *Balaas* case has already been described wherein the novice skiers went to a part of the park not set out for skiing; therefore, they were not invitees, but were licensees who must take the premises as they found them. The premises were not found to be of such a hazardous nature that notice of danger was required. Also in the previously cited *Toledo* case (§2.1212), the injured used a portion of land not set out for recreational use, swimming. While the injured was on the land with the consent of the city, he was not invited on and was hence a licensee who took the premises as he found them. *Blair v. Mt. Hood Meadows Development Corp.*[177] also involved skiing. In this 1981 case, the skier left the ski run when the run branched sharply to the right and then to the left, but the skier skied straight ahead. Plaintiff was an experienced skier, but had not skied this particular run before. The court in remanding the case stated that if the skier was negligent in leaving the designated ski run, he lost his status as an invitee and became a licensee, but if it was the operator's negligence in not marking the run appropriately, thus being responsible for the skier's mistaking the route, the status of invitee was retained.

Plaintiff was injured when she started down a dark stairway and missed a step near the bottom as she was going to a county home demonstration meeting in the community room in the basement of the high school. There was a vigorous dissent that the woman was an invitee.[178] In a somewhat similar case,[179] a woman who came for a Brownie meeting was injured in a recessed area on the premises. The court held that she was a licensee because the function was not connected with the purpose of the parochial school, that there was no benefit to the invitor, and hence the plaintiff must take the premises as they are.

The plaintiff was held to be a licensee to whom the defendant owed no greater duty than to avoid maintenance of traps and hidden dangers in *Goldstein v. Board of Educ.*[180] A company installing a 250-pound horizontal ladder had dug holes and assembled the ladder, then at the end of the day left it lying on the playground. Plaintiff, an eight-year-old while attempting to lift the ladder with other children, was injured when the ladder fell on him. The court held that the horizontal ladder on the ground was not inherently dangerous.

In a 1974 case[181] the court indicated that there was no duty to erect safeguards (two children picking berries fell in drainage ditch) to protect children who were not invitees (but trespassers or licensees), but if the city had invited the children, then it was operating a playground or park in a governmental capacity.

---

[177] Blair v. Mt. Hood Meadows Development Corp., 48 Or. App. 109, 616 P. 2d 535 (1981), rev'd. 291 Or. 293, 630 P. 2d 827 (1981), rehearing denied, opinion modified 291 Or. 703, 634 P. 2d 241 (1981).

[178] Smith v. Board of Educ., 204 Kan. 580, 464 P. 2d 571 (1970).

[179] Gruhalla v. George Moeller Constr. Co., 391 S.W. 2d 585 (St. L. Ct. App. 1965) school was joined with construction company.

[180] 24 A.D. 2d 1015, 266 N.Y.S. 2d 1 (1965), aff'd. 18 N.Y. 2d 991, 278 N.Y.S. 2d 224, 224 N.E. 2d 729 (1966).

[181] Bailey v. Mobile, 296 So. 2d 149 (Ala. 1974).

§ 2.123 Trespassers

A trespasser is one who enters or remains upon the premises without the consent, actual or implied, of the owner. The general rule regarding duty to a trespasser is that there is no duty to exercise reasonable care; one who is wrongfully on the premises must take the premises as one finds them and "be aware" for one's own safety. However, there are several limitations on such freedom from duty.

First, the owner's privilege does not extend to intentional torts, that is, to intentional and reckless misconduct that injures the trespasser. For example, the mother was not barred from recovery for the death of her child when he was involved in theft of the contents of cigarette vending machine and was killed when the storekeeper had rigged the machine with dynamite. The storekeeper was guilty of willfully and intentionally injuring the trespassing son. Mother recovered on wrongful death action.[182]

Where there are frequent trespassers on a limited area, such as entering at a specific point and traversing a small area, there is a duty to discover and protect them from the activities of the owner and to dangerous passive conditions, such as concealed high tension wires or a bull in a pasture near a path. The reasoning seems to be that where there is continued tolerance of intruders there is some duty for care, on the rationale that the defendant's responsibility outweighs the inconvenience of guarding against injury to the trespasser.[183]

Second, and related to the foregoing paragraph, is the limitation concerning highly dangerous activities, which requires the owner to use care for the safety of other human beings. For example, this might be when a firing range is adjacent to a children's camp. However, there is no duty to warn adult trespassers who are already aware of obviously dangerous natural and artificial conditions on the property.[184]

Third, once a trespasser is discovered, there is a trend toward changing the status to that of licensee, with its incumbent duty to warn or otherwise protect from hazardous conditions. A discovered trespasser, if left on the premises, remains with the consent of the owner. In a 1982 case[185] the plaintiff, ignoring signs, dived (as he had done many times before) from the bridge into the river at a recreation area. The court said that the duty owed by landowner to uninvited licensee or discovered trespasser is essentially the same: to avoid willful and wanton harm to him, and to warn him of defect or condition known by landowner to be dangerous when such danger is not open to ordinary observation by licensee of trespasser. The landowner carries a duty to see that the hazardous conditions do not become an instrument of harm to others.[186]

---

[182] McKinsey v. Wade, 136 Ga. App. 109, 220 S.E. 2d 30 (1975); see also Kirschner v. Louisville Gas & Electric Co., 743 S.W. 2d 840 (Ky. 1988).

[183] Keeton at pp. 393-399. See Smith v. Goldman, 53 Ill. App. 3d 632, 11 Ill. Dec. 444, 368 N.E. 2d 1052 (1977) referenced discovered trespasser or trespasser on limited area subject to frequent trespass, bicyclist.

[184] Watters v. Buckbee Mears Co., 354 N.W. 2d 848 (Min. App. 1984).

[185] Dougherty v. Hernando Co., 419 So. 2d 679 (Fla. App. 1982); see also Grant v. City of Duluth, 526 F. Supp. 15 (1981) rev'd. 672 F.2d 677 (1982) Minn. law applied; Holland Builders, Inc. v. Leck, 395 So. 2d 579 (Fla. App. 1981) pet. dism'd. 402 So. 2d 610 (Fla. 1981); Johnson v. Rinker Materials, Inc., 520 So. 2d 684 (Fla. App. 1988) and Morris v. Florentes, 421 So. 2d 582 (Fla. App. 1982).

[186] See cases cited in foregoing section on Licensees.

Fourth, one of the limitations on responsibility (in contrast to freedom from duty) is that of natural conditions. It has been held by the courts[187] that there is no duty on the part of the landowner to protect either adult or child trespasser from natural conditions existing on the land. The landowner is liable only for those perils or hazards created. Of particular protection in this regard are some of the state statutes (see §12.1). However, under the recreational user acts or limited liability landowner laws, there is no protection when the landowner deliberately creates the hazard.[188] On the other hand, giving permission to enter under the limited liability landowner laws does not change the status of the user in terms of the nature of duty owed to that of licensee from trespasser.

Fifth is a consideration which both limits the duty and the responsibility, depending upon who is involved. The defendant landowner, of course, would be liable for those in one's employ, as well as those who have been invited upon the property; but, the landowner is not liable for the acts of a trespasser acting without one's knowledge, until there has been reasonable opportunity to discover the situation, at which time, then, a duty to exercise proper care to prevent harm to others arises. The reckless conduct of a trespasser may be held an unforeseeable superceding event absolving owner/lessee of liability.[189]

The law subdivides trespassers into adults and children. Children often are deemed to need special care by virtue of their age, and the doctrine of attractive nuisance is frequently applied (see next sub-section.) In *Schofield v. Merrill*[190] 23-year-old plaintiff was injured when he jumped into the water of a quarry from a height of about 20', hitting a ledge of rock below the water surface. The court distinguished the duty as to child trespassers and adult trespassers, thusly: an occupier of land will be held to a duty of ordinary care to certain foreseeable child trespassers, but landowners are not liable to an adult trespasser for injuries sustained by trespasser on landowners' land, even if injuries resulted from negligence of landowners. A trespasser is entitled to no greater duty from one with a right of control over land than that he refrain from willful, wanton or reckless disregard for the trespasser's safety. Except for cases relating to the limited liability laws for private land and water owners enacted by the majority of states, there are few cases involving trespassing adults.

§ 2.1231   Trespassing children and the attractive nuisance doctrine

Under old common law rule, a landowner owed no duty of care toward trespassers; the occupier of the land could leave all kinds of dangerous conditions on the premises, even if immediately adjacent to a school playground. However, even before the turn of the century, this rule was modified as to trespassers who were children. A special concept as to legal cause developed, generally known as the attractive nuisance doctrine. Occasionally, the concept is referred to, and perhaps more accurately, as the

[187] Odar v. Chase Manhattan Bank, 138 N. J. Super. 464, 351 A. 2d 389 (1976)

[188] Krevics v. Ayars, 141 N. J. Super. 511, 358 A. 2d 844 (1976).

[189] Boltax v. Joy Day Camp, 113 A.D. 2d 859, 493 N.Y.S. 2d 590 (1985), aff'd. 67 N.Y. 2d 617, 489 N.Y.S. 2d 660, 490 N.E. 2d 527 (1986) swimming pool.

[190] Schofield v. Merrill, 386 Mass. 244, 435 N.E. 2d 339 (1982).

attractive-place doctrine.[191] The doctrine has sometimes been named the "turntable doctrine" because the leading case involved a six-year-old boy playing on a railroad turntable; the railroad employees knew of his presence and had previously forbidden him to play there; nevertheless, the boy was injured and recovered damages.[192] It was held that the railroad failed to exercise the requisite care in keeping its premises free from dangerous conditions. A second case[193] about the same time, and also involving a railroad turntable, rationalized its result on the theory that the turntable had attracted the child onto the defendant's land and thus the defendant, having induced the trespass, would not be permitted to set it up as a defense. From this idea, the doctrine acquired the title "attractive nuisance,"[194] a label which continues to persist.

Undoubtedly because of the governmental immunity doctrine, many early attempts were made to circumvent such immunity by seeking recovery against the municipality under this doctrine of attractive nuisance for injuries arising out of parks and playgrounds.[195] Such attempts, however, were usually based on a misunderstanding of the doctrine. The doctrine cannot be applied in the public park and playground cases because the first essential element that the child be a trespasser is lacking.[196] A patron of a municipal park or playground is very seldom a trespasser for such areas and facilities are usually held out for public use and such child is an invitee. In a Wisconsin case,[197] the court held that the attractive nuisance doctrine had no applicability because the child was not a trespasser; Salmo Pond was a public facility, and thus the child could not be a trespasser. In a 1982 case, the Illinois court spoke to the doctrine of attractive nuisance and school district immunity from liability in that state, stating that the doctrine did not negate the statutory immunity;[198] however, as related to recreational user statutes, the statutes do not negate the doctrine. Where a child is injured and the elements for attractive nuisance have been met, the landowner is liable.[199]

[191] Doran v. Kansas City, 241 Mo. App. 156, 237 S.W. 2d 907 (1951).

[192] Sioux City & Pac. R. Co. v. Stout, 17 Wall. 657, 21 L. Ed. 745 (1873).

[193] Keffe v. Milwaukee & St. P. Rx., 21 Minn. 207 (1875).

[194] Attractive nuisance should be distinguished from nuisance, see §4.4.

[195] Big Stone Gap v. Johnson, 184 Va. 375, 35 S.E. 2d 71 (1945); Caywood v. Comm'rs. of Sedgwick Co., 194 Kan. 419, 399 P. 2d 561 (1965); Davis v. Provo City Corp., 1 Utah 2d 244, 265 P. 2d 415 (1953); Godfrey v. Shreveport, 6 La. App. 356 (1927); McCall v. McCallie, 48 Ga. App. 99, 171 S.E. 843 (1933); Murphy v. Carlsbad, 66 N.M. 376, 348 P. 2d 492 (1960); Royston v. Charlotte, 278 Mich. 255, 270 N.W. 288 (1936); Smith v. Iowa City, 213 Iowa 391, 239 N.W. 29 (1931); State ex rel. Kansas City v. Ellison, 281 Mo. 667, 220 S.W. 498 (1920).

[196] Lovin v. Hamlet, 243 NC 399, 90 S.E.(2d) 760 (1956); Solomon v. Red River Lumber Co., 56 Cal. App. 742, 206 Pac 498 (1928); Smith v. Iowa City, 213 Iowa 391, 239 N.W. 29 (1931); Williams v. Primary School Dist., 3 Mich. App. 468, 142 N.W.2d 894 (1966).

[197] Wirth v. Ehly, 93 Wis. 2d 433, 287 N.W. 2d 140 (1980); see also Caine v. New Castle County, 379 A. 2d 1112 (1977) Hamilton v. Turner, 273 So. 2d 590 (La. App. 1973) the stock pond was so located that children could not be attracted to it until after they had been trespassers, pond held not an attractive nuisance; Massey v. Wright, 447 So. 2d 169 (Ala. 1984) swimming pool, child held not a trespasser and doctrine, thus, did not apply.

[198] Jackson v. Board of Educ., Chicago, 109 Ill. App. 3d 716, 65 Ill. Dec. 328, 441 N.E. 2d 120 (1982). Illinois law had been based upon 1955 playground swing case, Kahn v. James Burton Co., 5 Ill. 2d 614, 126 N.E. 2d 836 (1955). Applicability to child falling into ditch in park addressed in Corcoran v. Village of Libertyville, 49 Ill. App. 3d 818, 7 Ill. Dec. 306, 364 N.E. 2d 467, aff'd. 73 Ill. 2d 316, 22 Ill. Dec. 701, 383 N.E. 2d 177 (1978).

[199] For example, Adams v. Louisiana, 525 So. 2d 55 (La. App. 1988); Graham v. Gratiot Co., 126 Mich. App. 385, 337 N.W. 2d 73 (1983); Hughes v. Quarve Anderson Co., 338 N.W. 2d 442 (Minn. 1983); see §21.143.

Keeton[200] discusses, citing cases, the four conditions for liability as set forth by the *Restatement of Torts 339:* (1) the place where the condition is found must be one upon which the possessor knows or has reason to know that children are likely to trespass; (2) the condition must be one which the occupier should recognize as involving an unreasonable risk of harm to such children; (3) the child, because of immaturity, either does not discover the condition or does not in fact appreciate the danger involved; and (4) the utility to the possessor of maintaining the condition must be slight as compared with the risk to children involved. This last condition appears to be of primary significance. Negligence is to be determined by weighing the probability and the gravity of the possible harm against utility of the defendant's conduct. In general, the public interest in the free use of land is such that the owner will not be required to take precautions which are so burdensome or expensive as to be unreasonable in light of the risk or to make the premises "childproof."[201] The Minnesota court added a fifth element: the possessor fails to exercise reasonable care to eliminate the danger or otherwise to protect the children. Some states, also, have legislated regarding the standard of care owed children. A Massachusetts statute sets forth five specifications as to when a person who maintains an artificial condition upon one's own land is liable for physical harm to children trespassing thereon.

The third condition, maturity of the child trespasser, was in issue when a 13-year-old girl slipped and fell while walking to bank on a pipe which was formerly part of substructure of a pier near lake. The court held that the child was not too young to understand and avoid the danger, that she had above average intelligence, and that, with full knowledge and appreciation of danger, she walked a wet pipe. Appreciation of the risk by the injured goes to assumption of risk and contributory negligence defenses (see §5.21 and §5.22).[202]

Cases involving drownings in swimming pools, ponds, creeks, rivers, lakes, etc., have particularly sought to apply the doctrine.[203] The great weight of authority, however,

[200] Keeton, pp. 398-412, Trespassing Children; see also Alegre v. Shurkey, 396 So. 2d 247 (Fla. App. 1981); Boehne v. Elgin Packing Co., 8 Ill. App. 153, 289 N.E. 2d 283 (1972); Ibieta v. Phoenix of Hartford Ins. Co., 267 So. 2d 748 (La. 1972); Kempen v. Green Bay and Mississippi Canal Co., 66 Wis. 2d 185, 224 N.W. 2d 202 (1974); Latimer v. Clovis, 83 N.M. 610, 495 P. 2d 788 (1972); McWilliam v. Guzinski, 71 Wis. 2d 57, 237 N.W. 2d 437 (1976); Ochampaugh v. Seattle, 91 Wash., 2d 514, 588 P. 2d 1351 (1979); O'Keefe v. South End Rowing Club, 64 Cal. 2d 729, 51 Cal. Rptr. 534, 414 P. 2d 830 (1966); Saul v. Roman Catholic Church, 75 N.M. 160, 402 P. 2d 48 (1965); Schneider v. Seattle, 24 Wash. App. 251, 600 P. 2d 666 (1979); Smith v. Crown-Zellerbach, Inc., 638 F. 2d 883 (La. 1981); Yeske v. Avon Old Farms School, 1 Conn. App. 195, 470 A. 2d 705 (1984).

[201] Guillot v. Fisherman's Paradise, 422 So. 2d 1194 (La. App.) 437 So. 2d 840 (La. 1983) 2 ½ and 8-year-old boys weekend at camp on reservoir with grandparents, younger brother wandered away and drowned in nearby oxidation pond, held risk of drowning could have been easily eliminated by installation of fence or other enclosure sufficient to keep children out. Guenther v. G. Grant Dickson & Sons, 170 Ill. App. 3d 538, 121 Ill. Dec. 393, 525 N.E.2d 199 (1988) 13-year-old riding 3-wheeled ATV collided with another vehicle on path, apparently due to her line of sight being obscured by overgrown vegetation — was expense of remedying condition slight compared to risk of children? no landowner liability.

[202] Richards v. Marlow, 347 So. 2d 281 (La. App. 1977) writ denied 350 So.2d 676 (La. 1977); some cases dealing with attractive nuisance: Beechy v. Oak Forest, 16 Ill. App. 3d 240, 305 N.E. 257 (1973); Christians v. Homestake Enterprises, 97 Wis. 2d 638, 294 N.W. 2d 534 (1980), rev'd./remanded 101 Wis. 2d 25, 303 N.W. 2d 608 (1981); Petersen v. Honolulu, 53 Hawaii 440, 462 P. 2d 1007 (1970), aff'd. 53 Hawaii 499, 496 P. 2d 4 (1972); Soule v. Mass. Electric Co., Mass., 390 N.E. 2d 716 (1979); Washington v. Trend Mills, Inc., 121 Ga. App. 659, 175 S.E. 2d 111 (1970); for additional citations, see 16 A.L.R. 3d 25.

[203] Anneker v. Quinn-Robbins Co., 80 Idaho 1, 323 P. 2d 1073 (1958); Belt v. Los Angeles, 55 Cal. App. 2d 31, 130 P. 2d 163 (1942); Betts v. San

is that the doctrine cannot be applied where a child drowns in a body of water, unless there is some unusual element of danger present,[204] or conditions that are artificial and uncommon.[205] In 1971 Burnett[206] stated that 11 states followed the Mississippi rule, that impounded waters of all types (creek, pond, lake, swim pool) are excluded from the attractive nuisance doctrine, and that 13 states placed water hazards in a special category and allowed recovery only under special circumstances. This point of view of exclusion was sustained in the 1970s[207] and appears well established.[208] While initially natural water areas were an exception to the doctrine, this has been expanded to residential pools, at least in Georgia.[209] For a discussion of water-related cases, see Chapters 9 and 14, swimming in Pools and Water-based Recreation, respectively.

Two late 1980s cases relate to a child as a trespasser without particular application of the attractive nuisance doctrine, apparently shifting from the historical attractive nuisance theory to foreseeability of harm (see §2.23) and the duty to protect. A 14-year-old boy was injured when he fell from a tree in a campground, rendering him a quadriplegic. The court[210] stated that the customary rules of ordinary negligence are

Francisco, 108 Cal. App. 2d 701, 239 P. 2d 456 (1952); Doran v. Kansas City, 241 Mo. App. 156, 237 S.W. 2d 907 (1951); Early v. Ethyl Employees Recreation Assoc., 101 So. 2d 716 (1958, La. App.); Fedearowicz v. Amsterdam, 268 App. Div. 803, 49 NYS 2d 16 (1944), aff'd 293 N.Y. 814, 59 N.E.2d 178; Gilliland v. Topeka, 124 Kan. 726, 262 P. 493 (1928); Handley v. City of Hope, 137 F. Supp. 442 (1956); Harper v. Topeka, 92 Kan. 11, 139 P. 1018 (1914); Henroid v. Gregson Hot Springs Co., 52 Mont. 447, 158 P. 824 (1916); Mangum v. Powell, 196 Okla. 306, 165 P. 2d 136 (1946); Kitto v. Minot Park District, 224 N.W. 2d 795 (N.D. 1974); McCallister v. Homestead, 322 Pa. 341, 185 A. 583 (1936); McGraw v. District of Columbia, 3 App. D.C. 405, 25 L.R.A. 691 (1894); Robbins v. Omaha, 100 Neb. 439, 160 N.W. 749 (1916); Rose v. Wichita, 148 Kan. 317, 80 P. 2d 1078 (1938); Sroufe v. Garden City, 148 Kan. 874, 84 P. 2d 845 (1938); Staley v. Security Athletic Ass'n, 152 Colo. 19, 380 P. 2d 53 (1963); Vaughn v. Alcoa, 194 Tenn. 449, 251 S.W. 2d 304 (1952); Vanderford v. Houston, 286 S.W. 568 (Tex. Civ. App. 1926); Venable v. Langford, 116 Ga. App. 257, 157 S.E. 2d 34 (1967); Williams v. Morristown, 32 Tenn. App. 274, 222 S.W. 2d 607 (1949); for additional citations, see 16 A.L.R. 3d 25.

204 Fickling v. City Council, 110 Ga. App. 330, 138 S.E. 2d 437 (1964); Gordon v. C.H.C.Corp., 236 So. 2d 733 (Miss. 1970); Guillot v. Fisherman's Paradise, 437 So. 2d 840 (La. 1983) unenclosed oxidation pond held attractive nuisance for 2-year-old; Madher v. Casper, 67 Wyo. 268, 219 P. 2d 125 (1950); McGill v. Laurel, 252 Miss. 740, 173 So. 2d 892 (1965); Van Alst v. K.C., 239 Mo. App. 346, 186 S.W. 2d 762 (1945); Vincent v. Barnhill, 203 Miss. 740, 34 So. 2d 363 (1948).

205 Weber v. Springville City, 725 P. 2d 1360 (Utah 1986) creek was held to be natural watercourse and not irrigation ditch.

206 Gerald F. Burnett. "The Exclusion of Artificial Water Hazards from the Attractive Nuisance Doc-

trine." 42 *Miss L.J.* 355-373, summer 1971.

207 Ausmer v. Suman, 336 So. 2d 730 (Miss. 1976); Bailey v. Mobile, 292 Ala. 436, 296 So. 2d 149 (1974); Blair v. U.S., 433 F. Supp. 217 (1977); Clifford v. Recreation & Park Com., 289 So. 2d 373 (La. App. 1973), cert. den. 293 So. 2d 168; Cooper v. Diesel Service, Inc., 254 Ark. 743, 496 S.W. 2d 383 (1973); Earnest v. Regent Pool, Inc., 288 Ala. 63, 257 So. 2d 313 (1972); Hunter v. Evergreen Presbyterian Vocational School, 338 So. 2d 164 (La. App. 1976); McWilliam v. Guzinski, 71 Wis. 2d 57, 237 N.W. 2d 437 (1976); Montega Corp. v. Grooms, 128 Ga. App. 333, 196 S.E. 2d 459 (1973); Ochampaugh v. Seattle, 91 Wash. 2d 514, 588 P. 2d 1351 (1979); Oliver v. Atlanta, 147 Ga. App. 790, 250 S.E. 2d 519 (1978); for additional citations, see 16 A.L.R. 3d 25.

208 Glover v. Mobile, 417 So. 2d 175 (Ala. 1982); Locke v. Liquid Air Corp., 725 F. 2d 1331 (1984); Wren v. Harrison, 165 Ga. App. 847, 303 S.E. 2d 67 (1983).

209 Gregory v. Johnson, 159 Ga. App. 320, 283 S.E. 2d 357, rev'd. 249 Ga. 151, 289 S.E. 2d 232 (1982), aff'd. 290 S.E. 2d 560 (Ga. App. 1982); see also Carlson v. Tucson Racquet & Swim Club, 127 Ariz. 247, 619 P. 2d 756 (1980) club pool — attractive nuisance not applicable to 16-year-old trespasser of age and intelligence to understand pool dangers; similarly, not applicable to 14-year-old diving into 2' of water, gravel pit in Lister v. Campbell, 371 So. 2d 133 (Fla. App. 1979), cert. denied 348 So. 2d 346 (1979).

210 Batzek v. Betz, 165 Ill. App. 3d 399, 116 Ill. Dec. 497, 519 N.E. 2d 87 (1988) campground child fell from tree; see also Friedman v. Park Dist., Highland Park, 151 Ill. App. 3d 374, 104 Ill. Dec. 329, 520 N.E. 2d 826 (1986); sledding hill, hit fence; Melerine v. State of Louisiana, 505 So. 2d 79 (La App. 1987) writ denied 507 So. 2d 226 (1987) fell from tree platform in state park.

211 Walt Disney World v. Goode, 425 So. 2d 1151 (1982) 436 So. 2d 101 (1983), aff'd. 501 So. 2d 622 (Fla. App. 1986).

applicable in cases dealing with personal injury to children; however, the criteria specified are similar to those for attractive nuisance.

> The rule of liability…a child is injured is the foreseeability of harm to the child. An injury is deemed foreseeable, and the duty will be imposed…, only if (1) the landowner or person in possession knows or should have known that children frequent the premises, (2) if the cause of the child's injury was a dangerous condition on the premises, and (3) the expense or inconvenience of remedying the condition is slight compared to the risk to the children.

> In regard to the second element, a "dangerous condition" is one likely to cause injury to a child who, by reason of his or her immaturity, might not be capable of comprehending or avoiding the attendant risks…. If the condition involves obvious risks that children generally would be expected to appreciate and avoid, there is no duty to remedy the condition…. Since children are expected to avoid dangers that are obvious, there is no reasonably foreseeable risk of harm. The law does not require the landowner or possessor of land to protect against the possibility children will injure themselves on obvious or common conditions.

The court identified three obvious or common conditions: fire, water, and falling from heights. Thus, the court held that there was no duty to the child when he fell from a tree. In a Florida case,[211] the court held that the ordinary rules of negligence, as applied to business invitee at place of public amusement, were to determine liability of Walt Disney World for four-year-old child who drowned in moat. The question was whether the duty of reasonable care was breached by the fence not being sufficient to prevent children from gaining access.

In an early Michigan case,[212] a seven-year-old boy had his eye put out on a municipal golf course when struck by a golf ball while he and other small children were playing in the middle of the fairway of the 13th hole. The court held that there was a responsibility to trespassers to minimize likelihood of dangers; the municipality, knowing children played on the fairway, did nothing to protect them. Signs and inadequate fences did not suffice. In a very early New York case,[213] a teacher failed to lock the gym doors. A moveable basketball backstop constructed so that it could be bolted to the floor, but was not, toppled over onto a young boy and killed him. The deceased was a trespasser in the gym for he had been forbidden to enter the gym. The school was not required to anticipate that the basketball backstop would be used for climbing purposes and hence was not liable. Whether access is "open" or "closed" can be a critical issue of fact regarding whether a person is a trespasser or not. Such was the situation in *Caine v. New Castle County,* 379 A. 2d 1112 (Del. 1977), when an 11-year-old boy was fatally injured on a sledding hill when he hit a metal post which had been erected on which to fasten the chain link fence, but the fence had not yet been installed.

[212] Lyshak v. Detroit, 351 Mich 230, 88 N.W. 2d 596 (1958).

[213] Longo v. Bd. of Educ. of New York City, 235 A.D. 733, 255 N.Y.S. 719 (1932).

§ 2.2   The Act — Standard of Care

Once it is established that a duty is owed to the plaintiff, then the next question relates to "the act," for the duty requires that the plaintiff not be exposed to an "unreasonable risk of harm." To fulfill the duty owed, the defendant must have exhibited certain behavior or conduct. The nature of the act can be described in terms of being misfeasance, nonfeasance, or malfeasance. "The reasonable and prudent man" and reasonable care concepts are the bases of the standard of care, while foreseeability of harm is the key in determination of the scope of liability negligence. The degrees of negligence provide an indicator of the extent of negligence. Each of these aspects is discussed in subsequent sections.

§ 2.21   Nature of the act — misfeasance, malfeasance, nonfeasance

Negligent conduct may occur because of the manner in which a person acted (an act of commission) or because a person failed to act (an act of omission). Often used synonomously with acts of commission and acts of omission are misfeasance and nonfeasance, respectively. This use is technically incorrect, since misfeasance may include both acts of commission and omission. The distinguishing factor is the nature of the person's (defendant) participation in the enterprise (activity), that is, whether passive (nonfeasance) or active (misfeasance) participation. For additional discussion of nonfeasance and misfeasance as relates to Duty, see §2.1111.

Malfeasance. As defined by Black, [214] malfeasance is:

> the commission of some act which is positively unlawful; the doing of an act which is wholly wrongful and unlawful; the doing of an act which person ought not to do at all or the unjust performance of some act which the party had no right or which he had contracted not to do...no legal right to do, or any wrongful conduct which affects, interrupts, or interferes with performance of official duty, or an act for which there is no authority or warrant of law or which a person ought not to do at all....

In providing for indemnification or legal defense of an employee, some of the state laws specifically exclude such coverage when the act of the employee is considered malfeasance. [215]

Nonfeasance. Nonfeasance is the neglect of duty when passively involved. The law has been reluctant to use nonfeasance as a basis of liability, since the tortfeasor has committed no active wrong, although inaction may not be in accord with social and moral obligations. [216] In order for an act of omission or failure to act to result in liability for negligence, a duty to take positive action, to do a specific act, must be established. This may be established by statute or by the relationship between the party standing

---

[214] Black's Law Dictionary, Fifth edition.

[215] For example, Indiana, Nebraska; see §4.2. Horace Mann Ins. Co. v. Indp. School Dist., 355 N.W.2d 413 (Minn. 1984) sexual contact by male ass't girls' basketball coach who also was school counselor.

[216] Moore v. Murphy, 254 Iowa 969, 119 N.W. 2d 759 (1963).

aside inactive and the party or parties involved in the enterprise. This relationship is of such character that the rules of society demand an affirmative act, in opposition to inaction, that is legally enforceable. An example of nonfeasance: a societal demand for an affirmative act is reflected in the law of some states which require the first person upon an accident to stop and render aid in some manner; failure to do so would be nonfeasance (as well as statutory violation). This relationship often has in it an element of advantage or benefit for the one standing by (defendant), usually economic, which benefit justifies the requirement of special obligations of action.

The parents of a boy who drowned after taking a boat in camp sued the president (officer) of the church corporation sponsoring the camp. The defense for him was that plaintiff did not allege any misfeasance or malfeasance on the part of the president, and that all he is charged with is nonfeasance or the omission of certain duties for which he should not be held liable. The parents entrusted their child to the encampment, not to the president as an individual. All the president's acts were done in connection with his official position.[217] In a 1977 Massachusetts case[218] a public officer was involved and the court held that public officers are liable only for their own acts of misfeasance in connection with ministerial functions, and that negligence amounting to nothing more than nonfeasance creates no liability on the part of the public officer. In this situation a student, who was blind in one eye and had limited vision in the other, was injured by an allegedly defective door.[219]

The defense alleged that quality of wrestling instruction involved nonfeasance for which there should not be liability; not so, the court held.[220] Regarding the liability of individual members of a board, it was held in the *Iseminger case*[221] that as long as the acts were governmental duties, they were not liable for nonfeasance. The individual board members, also, were charged with nonfeasance by the plaintiffs, who said that the board members failed to inspect the school premises, to provide deceased with safe playground area, and failed to inspect, repair, and anchor the swing set, allowing it to remain as a "death trap." The court held for the defendants; the school board members were not liable.[222]

In a case[223] where action was brought by a mother of her deceased 14-year-old son who drowned at a Sunday School picnic while swimming, it was stated that an agent ordinarily is not liable for mere nonfeasance, but is liable for misfeasance. Massachusetts also distinguished misfeasance and nonfeasance and held the superintendent of parks not liable if no direct role.[224]

Misfeasance. When a person is actively engaged in some enterprise, a duty arises to

[217] McQuire v. Louisiana Baptist Encampment, Inc. 199 So. 192 (La. App. 1940).

[218] Whitney v. City of Worcester, 373 Mass. 208, 366 N.E. 2d 1210 (1977).

[219] For public officer involved in nonfeasance, see also Brooks v. Jacobs, 139 Md. 371, 31 A. 2d 414 (1943); Fulgoni v. Johnston, 302 Mass. 421, 19 N.E. 2d 542 (1939); Moore v. Murphy, 254 Iowa 969, 119 N.W. 2d 759 (1963).

[220] Smith v. Consolidated School Dist., 408 S.W. 2d 50 (Mo. 1966).

[221] Iseminger v. Black Hawk County, 175 N.W. 2d 374 (Iowa 1970).

[222] Rennie v. Belleview School Dist., 521 S.W. 2d 423 (Mo. 1975).

[223] See p. 2-5 Herring v. Mathis Certified Dairy Co., 118 Ga. App. 132, 162 S.E. 2d 863 (1968), aff'd./ rev'd. 225 Ga. 67, 166 S.E. 2d 89 (1969) 119 Ga. App. 226, 166 S.E. 607, 225 Ga. 653, 171 S.E. 2d 124 (1969), 121 Ga. App. 373, 173 S.E. 2d 716 (1970).

[224] Alfonso v. Lowney, 416 N.E. 2d 516 (Mass. App. 1981).

conduct the enterprise with due care for the rights of others. Failure to do so, whether this is failure to perform an act (act of omission) or the improper performance of an act (act of commission), constitutes misfeasance. This assumes that the act is lawful. For example, a swimmer reported to the lifeguard in a boat in the pool that a 14-year-old girl had gone under the water; the lifeguard, however, did not go because he did not really believe the girl was under. This was misfeasance, an act of omission. He should have acted, but failed to do so.[225] In another drowning incident,[226] artificial respiration was applied, but ineffectively (due to being incorrect). This was also misfeasance, but an act of commission. The distinction between misfeasance and nonfeasance is important in some jurisdictions. Some jurisdictions adhere to the view that a municipality may be held liable for its misfeasance, but not for nonfeasance;[227] while in other jurisdictions, the liability of the agent may be limited to acts of misfeasance. However, nearly all negligence cases involve misfeasance; the number which have nonfeasance in issue are very few.

§ 2.22 The reasonable and prudent professional and "reasonable care" concepts

The standard of care required is not that of an insurer of safety,[228] but rather to act reasonably in view of the probability, not possibility, of injury to others.[229] A 14-year-old boy was injured when he fell from a slide in the city park. The court held that the city is not an insurer of children's safety, but it is responsible to provide reasonably safe premises given the nature and conduct of children.[230] This is the general holding in schools, too. The court held in two swimming pool cases[231] involving diving that the pool operator was not an insurer of the safety of the swimmers. Several horseback riding cases,[232] similarly, have held that one is not an insurer of safety. In a 1980 case[233] which involved an injured ankle on a footpath in a national park, the court also held that one is not an insurer of safety.

[225] Pierce v. Ravena, 264 A.D. 457, 36 N.Y.S. 2d 42 (1942).

[226] De Simone v. Philadelphia, 380 Pa. 137, 110 A. 2d 431 (1955).

[227] Bank v. Brainerd School Dist., 49 Minn. 106, 51 N.W. 814 (1892); Indianapolis v. Baker, 72 Ind. App. 323, 125 N.E. 52 (1919); Selph v. Morristown, 16 N.J. Misc. 19, 195 A. 862 (1938); Thompson v. Board of Educ., 11 N.J. 207, 94 A. 2d 206 (1953).

[228] Applebaum v. Nemon, 678 S.W. 2d 533 (Tex. App. 1984) day care center, 2-year-old playing outdoors; Clark v. Furch, 567 S.W. 2d 457 (Mo. App. 1978) physical education class, 6-year-old on playground jungle gym; Haddox v. Suburban Lanes, Inc., 349 S.E. 2d 910 (W. Va. 1986) husband came into bowling alley, shooting wife who was bowling; Henretig v. U.S., 490 F. Supp. 398 (1980) footpath in national park; Jefferson v. YMCA, 354 Pa. 563, 47 A. 2d 653 (1946) decedent wandered from locker room into fully lighted, unoccupied pool; Ware v. Cincinnati, 98 N.E. 2d 102 (1951) child in park wandered across 4' wall and between concrete disc and ventilator.

[229] Springer v. St. Bernard Parish School Board, 521 So. 2d 461 (La. App. 1988); see also Bolkhir v. N.C. State Univ., 85 N.C. App. 521, 355 S.E. 2d 786 rev'd./remanded 365 S.E. 2d 898 (N.C. 1988); McKinley v. Slenderella Systems of Camden, N.J., 63 N.J. Super. 571, 165 A. 2d 207 (1960).

[230] Mills v. American Playground Device Co., Ind. App., 405 N.E. 2d 621 (1980); see also Rollins v. Concordia Parish School Board, 465 So. 2d 213 (La. App. 1985) merry-go-round on school grounds; Townsley v. Cincinnati Gardens, 39 Ohio App. 2d 5, 314 N.E. 2d 409 (1974), rev'd. 39 Ohio Misc. 1, 314 N.E. 2d 406 (1973) assault in dimly lit public rest-room at basketball event.

[231] Lincoln v. Wilcox, 111 Ga. App. 365, 141 S.E. 2d 765 (1965); Smith v. American Flyers, Inc., 540 P. 2d 1212 (Okla. App. 1975).

[232] Alfonso v. Market Facilities of Houston, 356 So. 2d 86 (La. App. 1978), cert. writ denied 357 So. 2d 1169 (1978); Christian v. Elden, 107 N.H. 229, 221 A. 2d 784 (1966); Fredrickson v. Mackey, 196 Kan. 542, 413 P. 2d 86 (1966).

[233] Henretig v. U.S., 490 F. Supp. 398 (1980).

...express invitation demands exercise of reasonable care.[234] ...owed the plaintiff a duty to exercise reasonable care in conducting the tests.[235] ...must keep parks reasonably safe for all persons using them.[236] ...failing to use reasonable care to prevent aggravation of the injury.[237] ...highly dangerous activities require greater care.[238] ...not required to exercise the same degree of care for the safety of pedestrians in parkways as on public streets and sidewalks.[239] ...to use reasonable care not to injure.[240] ...in the exercise of ordinary care should have known.[241] ...held to the same degree of care as private persons.[242] ...a reasonably prudent person would have known.[243]

These phrases from the holdings in ten cases indicate that the key aspect in negligence liability is the standard of care exercised. Whether one is negligent depends upon how one acted. But to determine how one should act is not an easy matter! Is it negligence for a lifeguard to be gone from his post for five minutes while he escorts some rowdy boys out, gets a drink on a hot day, or talks with a friend?[244] Is it negligence for a coach to rely upon the word of an 18-year-old boy who says he has recovered from a shoulder injury to permit him to play football without a doctor's opinion?[245] Is it negligence to fail to post signs or other warning devices along a trail in a park?[246] Is it negligence for a teacher to supervise the playground from inside the building?[247]

A California case[248] said that the standard of care required is that which a person of ordinary prudence, charged with the stated duties, would exercise under similar circumstances; but, what is this reasonable and prudent person?[249] One legal writer says that:[250]

..., this reasonable man is a creature of the law's imagination. He is an abstraction. He has long been the subject of homely phrase and witty epigram. He is no man who has ever lived and is not to be identified with any of the parties nor with any member of the jury....

Now this reasonably prudent person is not infallible or perfect. In foresight,

---

[234] Anadarko v. Swain, 42 Okla. 741, 142 P. 1104 (1914).

[235] Brittan v. New York State, 200 Misc. 743, 103 N.Y.S. 2d 485 (1951).

[236] Capp v. St. Louis, 251 Mo. 345, 158 S.W. 616 (1913).

[237] Briscoe v. School Dist. No. 123, 32 Wash. 2d 353, 201 P. 2d 697 (1949); Welch v. Dunsmuir Joint Union High Sch. Dist., 326 P. 2d 633 (Cal. App. 1958).

[238] Bucholz v. Sioux Falls, 77 S.D. 322, 91 N.W. 2d 606 (1958); Smith v. Vernon Parish School Board, 442 So. 2d 1319 (La. App. 1983) refers to "greater degree of care" standard.

[239] Dramstadt v. West Palm Beach, 81 So. 2d 484 (Fla 1955).

[240] Evansville v. Blue, 212 Ind. 130, 8 N.E. 2d 224 (1937).

[241] Felt v. Toledo, 47 Ohio App. 461, 192 N.E. 11 (1933).

[242] Ide v. St. Cloud, 150 Fla. 806, 8 So. 2d 924 (1942) affirmed 13 So. 2d 448 (Fla. 1943).

[243] Orrison v. Rapid City, 76 S.D. 145, 74 N.W. 2d 489 (1956).

[244] See lifeguard situations §9.42.

[245] See medical considerations §§17.2 and 17.3.

[246] See warnings of danger §20.332.

[247] See Chapter 18 Supervision.

[248] Pirkle v. Oakdale Union Grammar School Dist., 40 Cal. 2d 207, 253 P. 2d 1 (1953).

[249] Caltavuturo v. Passaic, 124 N.J. Super. 361, 307 A. 2d 114 (1973); Capers v. Orleans Parish School Bd., 365 So. 2d 23 (La. App. 1978); Dailey v. Los Angeles Unified School Dist., 2 Cal.3d 741, 87 Cal. Rptr. 376, 470 P. 2d 360 (1970) hold similarly.

[250] Harper, Fowler v., Fleming James, Jr., and Oscar S. Gray. The Law of Torts, Boston: Little, Brown, and Co., 1986, second edition. p. 389.

caution, courage, judgment, self-control, altruism and the like he represents, and does not excel, the general average of the community. He is capable of making mistakes and errors of judgment, of being selfish, of being afraid — but only to the extent that any such shortcoming embodies the normal standard of community behavior. On the other hand, the general practice of the community, in any given particular, does not necessarily reflect what is careful. The practice itself may be negligent.... Thus the standard represents the general level of moral judgment of the community, (what it feels ought ordinarily to be done), and not necessarily what is ordinarily done, although in practice the two would very often come to the same thing.

The Utah court[251] in 1987 said that "Standards in deciding if risk is unreasonable are those found in life of community; unreasonable risks are those which society, in general, considers sufficiently great to demand preventive measure." In respect to schools, the New York court[252] said that a school district owes duty to its students to exercise same degree of care toward them as would reasonably prudent parents under similar circumstances.

However, to perform the standard of care as would a prudent citizen or a prudent parent is not adequate, for it is not the standard of care required "for the situation." It is further required that the degree of skill be exercised which the general class of persons engaged in that profession would have.[253] *Thus, the standard of care required is that of a reasonable and prudent **professional**.* This would mean, for example, that a physical education instructor would have to act, not only as any ordinary reasonable and prudent person, but also in the conduct of activity and provision of facilities and areas as a reasonable and prudent physical educator. The same would be true for a recreation leader, a coach, a park superintendent, etc. *The standard of care would be measured by the moral qualities, judgment, knowledge, experience, perception of risk and skill that a person in the capacity of a professional would have.* It should be emphasized that the standard is not that of a person with the actual qualifications of the individual, but of a person competent for the position for which the individual holds oneself to be qualified. For example, if a person is employed to teach physical education and undertakes to do some apparatus work, but in fact has neither training nor adequate knowledge of apparatus to be fully aware of the hazards of activity, that person is, nevertheless, held to the standard of safety precautions, including adequate instructions, of a physical educator competent in apparatus, not the standard of one with limited background. A hockey coach, as a person of substantial experience, was held to a higher standard of care than an "average person."[254] The standard of care provided must be that of the best professional practices. Thus, standard of care is relevant to custom, as indicated in a case involving lifeguards and posting regulations at a campground lake.[255] Trade

---

[251] Wagoner v. Waterslide, Inc., 744 P. 2d 1012 (Utah App. 1987).

[252] Merkley v. Palmyra-Macedon Cent. School Dist., 130 A.D. 2d 937, 515 N.Y.S. 2d 932 (1987) shot put dropped on plaintiff's hand.

[253] Lee v. Sun Valley Company, 107 Idaho 976, 695 P. 2d 361 (1984); Whitehurst v. Boehm, 41 N.C. App. 670, 255 S.E. 2d 761 (1979).

[254] Everett v. Bucky Warren, Inc., 376 Mass. 280, 380 N.E. 2d 653 (1978).

[255] McClure v. Suter, 63 Ill. App. 3d 378, 20 Ill. Dec. 308, 379 N.E. 2d 1376 (1978).

standards, also, may be considered, as well as the "state-of-the-art"; but, such standards may not always be accepted as the standard of care required.[256]

There is a second aspect to the standard of care and that is "the reasonable care" concept. Negligence is the failure to exercise that degree of care which is reasonable under the circumstances.[257] What is reasonable is situational. *Reasonableness is usually determined by three situational elements — the activity, the environmental conditions, and the participants.* Regarding the participants, for example, in a Louisiana case[258] the court held that where youngsters participating in Special Olympics were involved, the duty not to expose to unreasonable risk "becomes more onerous." Further, in respect to schools, the Louisiana court[259] said that schools were required to follow a reasonable standard of care commensurate with age of children under attendance circumstances.

As to environmental conditions, the court[260] held that the degree of care required is commensurate with the situation to keep premises in a reasonably safe condition. In this situation (wet floor of a connecting way from poolside to men's dressing room) a higher degree of care was required. The rubber safety mats had been removed by someone. In a 1972 case[261] it was held that where an inhalator as a safety device at a pool was not required by law, reasonable care had been taken when all lifeguards were qualified and properly positioned. In another case,[262] the court held that it was reasonable in this day of television and football that a person would be knowledgable of sideline hazards, and thus a chalk line marking the spectators' sideline area and a schoolboy patrol were reasonable care and that it was unreasonable expense to require permanent barriers, especially when the area had multiple uses. Again, reasonable care was the duty owed in a golf case where a patron toppled over on a bench.[263] The bench was of ordinary design; the patron had plenty of time to observe the bench and its stability on the terrain. No amount of superintendence could have prevented the accident. In a 1979 New Jersey case,[264] the plaintiff was injured when he was playing behind the backstop of a baseball field and fell and injured his eye on glass debris. The court referred to "palpably unreasonable," the term which the New Jersey Tort Claims Statute uses.

An additional word should be said about the standard of care required. In negligence action, reasonableness of defendant's conduct is question for jury.[265] Although certainly expert witnesses can testify, in the final analysis, a jury of laymen and not professional physical educators, coaches, recreation leaders, outdoor managers, fitness specialists, et al. determine whether the standard of "reasonable care" has been met. There are many factors involved in this determination, and it is not always as a jury of professionals would decide. Sometimes the procedures taken for educational purposes

[256] Upham v. Chateau De Ville Dinner Theatre, 380 Mass. 350, 403 N.E. 2d 384 (1980); see also §21.1 introduction, paragraph on standards.

[257] O'Leary v. Jacob Miller Co., 473 N.E. 2d 200, 19 Mass. App. 947 (1985).

[258] Foster v. Houston General Insurance Co., 407 So. 2d 759 (La. App. 1981).

[259] Drueding v. St. Paul Fire & Marine Insurance Co., 482 So. 2d 83 (La. App. 1986); Patterson v. Orleans Parish School Board, 461 So. 2d 386 (La. App. 1984); Rollins v. Concordia Parish School Board, 465 So. 2d 213 (La. App. 1985).

[260] Tulsa v. Goins, 437 P. 2d 257 (Okla. 1967).

[261] Schulte v. Graff, 481 S.W. 2d 596 (Mo. App. 1972).

[262] Turner v. Caddo Parish School Board, 252 La. 810, 214 So. 2d 153 (1968).

[263] Panoz v. Gulf & Bay Corp., 208 So. 2d 297 (Fla. 1968).

[264] Williams v. Town of Phillipsburg, 171 N.J. Super. 278, 408 A. 2d 827 (1979).

[265] Merkley v. Palmyra-Macedon Cent. School Dist., 130 A.D. 2d 937, 515 N.Y.S. 2d 932 (1987).

are not always understood, and neither are the technical aspects of many physical education and athletic activities, and leisure services and outdoor area management. Reasonableness also is interconnected with public policy. Part C, especially Chapters 18, 19 and 20, is directed toward the required standard of care in terms of what the reasonable and prudent *professional* should do for that given *situation* as determined by the jury in the many cases described.

§ 2.23   The test of foreseeability

An important consideration in establishing want of reasonable care is that of foreseeability.[266] *The scope of liability is whether there is a foreseeable risk of injury. Conduct cannot be considered unreasonable, if the risk is not foreseeable.* If act is not to be reasonably anticipated, or if its occurrence would, in eyes of reasonable people, be unlikely, it cannot be said that event was foreseeable and, if it was not foreseeable, there is no duty to provide against it.[267] Where reasonable people could differ as to the foreseeability, the question is one of fact for the jury.[268] Negligence is based upon those unintentional acts which harm, but wherein the person does not wish to bring about the consequences which follow, nor does that person believe that they will occur, but in fact such consequences could have been foreseen by a reasonable and prudent professional in the same situation and action to guard against them should have been taken. The reason for failure to foresee the consequences, whether it be carelessness, bad judgment, excitement, simple inattention, inexperience, ignorance, stupidity, or forgetfulness, is immaterial, even though acting in good faith.

The test of foreseeability is foresight, not a test of proximate cause, which is hindsight.[269]*The "reasonable and prudent professional" must be able to foresee from the circumstances a danger to the participant, a danger which presents an "unreasonable risk of harm" against which the participant must be protected.* A few illustrative cases are cited in subsequent paragraphs.

The question in a case[270] against a church was whether the scout troop advisor should have foreseen the injury which might occur by the boys playing a particular game with thin rope and lack of mats on a bare concrete floor. In another New York case[271] it was held foreseeable that students would use unpaved paths and thus an inspection of a wooded area with a footbridge (which was in bad condition) should have been done. In a summer camp it was held that a camper might kick open a stuck door and be injured; in fact, the hook on the door did strike another camper when the door was kicked.[272]

[266] Duarte v. California, 84 Cal. App.3d 705, 148 Cal. Rptr. 804 (1978).

[267] Roberts v. Town of Colchester, 134 Misc. 2d 109, 509 N.Y.S. 2d 975 (1986) dived off bridge, hit bottom; see also Caraballo v. U.S., 830 F. 2d 19 (1987) dived into shallow water at beach in national park, New York law applied.

[268] Boltrax v. Joy Day Camp, 493 N.Y.S. 2d 590 (1985); Markowitz v. Arizona Park Board, 146 Ariz. 260, 705 P. 2d 937, rev'd. 146 Ariz. 352, 706 P. 2d 364 (1985).

[269] Dellwo v. Pearson, 259 Minn. 452, 107 N.W. 2d 859 (1961). See also Bolkhir v. N.C. State Univ., 85 N.C. App. 521, 355 S.E. 2d 786 rev'd./remanded 365 S.E. 2d 898 (N.C. 1988); Haddox v. Suburban Lanes, Inc., 349 S.E. 2d 910 (W. Va. 1986).

[270] Kearney v. Roman Catholic Church of St. Paul, 31 A.D. 2d 541, 295 N.Y.S. 2d 186 (1968).

[271] Meyer v. New York, 92 Misc. 2d 996, 403 N.Y.S. 2d 420 (1978).

[272] Obshatcko v. YM & YWHA of Williamsburg, 45 A.D. 2d 1023, 358 N.Y.S. 2d 43 (1974).

In a city park situation, it was held that the city should have foreseen the danger presented by an open 10″ by 12″ hole in the parking lot customarily used by the softball players to "warm up" before games.[273] A contrary result was reached when a young boy removed a loose copper coil from the water fountain in the city park and struck a girl when he threw it at her.[274] Foreseeability was the ultimate test of duty of an electric company to insulate or locate appropriately its electrical wire to prevent a scaffold being used to replace bulbs in lights on outdoor courts (30′ high) from coming in contact therewith and injuring persons replacing bulbs.[275]

It was a question of foreseeability when a spectator at a golf tournament was struck at concession stand placed between two fairways.[276] In another golf case it was held that the instructors should have foreseen the intervening act of a ninth grade student who fatally struck a classmate with a golf club during physical education class.[277] Lack of foreseeability was a factor when a badly hooked golf shot struck adjacent property owner.[278]

A California case[279] held that it was not necessary that the exact injuries which occurred should have been foreseeable; it is enough that a reasonably prudent person would have foreseen that injuries of the same general type would be likely to occur in the absence of safeguards. In this situation a 16-year-old high school student was killed on the playground when injuries were sustained as a result of "slap boxing." In another California case,[280] a 12-year-old boy suffered fatal injuries while playing a skateboard version of crack-the-whip. The court held that even though a harm may be foreseeable, a concomitant duty to forestall and prevent the harm does not automatically follow; rather, the question is whether the risk of harm is sufficiently high and the amount of activity needed to protect against harm sufficiently low to bring the duty into existence. The court must decide foreseeability not only on existence of risk of harm but also on magnitude and probability.[281]

In several cases it was alleged that there was foreseeable harm which required appropriate action, specifically, more supervision,[282] setting forth of rules and regulations to control conduct,[283] and excusing a student from certain exercises.[284] In

[273] Treps v. Racine, 73 Wis. 2d 611, 243 N.W. 2d 520 (1976).

[274] Jenkins v. Miami Beach, 389 So. 2d 1195 (Fla. App. 1980).

[275]Bush v. Alabama Power Co., 457 So. 2d 350 (Ala. 1984).

[276] Duffy v. Midlothian Country Club, 92 Ill. App.3d 193, 415 N.E. 2d 1099, 47 Ill. Dec. 786, (1980). aff'd. 135 Ill. App. 3d 429, 90 Ill. Dec. 237, 481 N.E. 2d 1037 (1985).

[277] Brahatcek v. Millard School Dist., 202 Neb. 86, 273 N.W. 2d 680 (1979).

[278] Nussbaum v. Lacopo, 27 N.Y. 2d 311, 265 N.E. 2d 762 (1970).

[279] Dailey v. Los Angeles Unified School District, 2 Cal. 3d 741l, 87 Cal. Rptr. 376, 470 P. 2d 360 (1970); see also Koprowski v. Manatee Co., 519 So. 2d 78 (Fla. App. 1988) walking on beach, hit by wind-blown rescue board which had been propped on lifeguard stand.

[280] Bartell v. Palos Verdes Peninsula School Dist., 147 Cal. Rptr. 898, 83 Cal. App. 3d 492 (1978).

[281] See also McKinley v. Slenderella Systems of Camden, N.J., 63 N.J. Super. 571, 165 A. 2d 207 (1960) reducing salon "treatments"; Springer v. St. Bernard Parish School Board, 521 So. 2d 461 (La. App. 1988) volunteer track coach jumped over playground fence, slipped on wet grass.

[282] Grant v. Lake Oswego School District, 515 P. 2d 947 (Or. App. 1973); Hanley v. Hornbeck, 127 A.D. 2d 905, 512 N.Y.S. 2d 262 (1987); Morris v. Douglas Co. School Dist., 241 Or. 23, 403 P. 2d 775 (1965).

[283] Stilwell v. Louisville, 455 S.W. 2d 56 (Ky. 1970).

[284] Summers v. Milwaukee Union H.S. Dist., 481 P. 2d 369 (Or. App. 1971).

the *Summers* case, the court held that a person (teacher) is bound not only by what is known but also by what might have been known had ordinary diligence been exercised. A physical education instructor is required to exercise reasonable care for the protection of students under supervision. Foreseeability of harm gives rise to a duty to take reasonable care to avoid harm. Harm in the *Summers* case was held foreseeable. Similarly in a 1983 case,[285] the court held that it was foreseeable that injury would occur when the fitness testing course was not laid out according to the manual, specifically that there should be at least 14' of unobstructed space beyond the start and finish lines so that pupils could run at top speed past the finish line without danger of running into the gymnasium wall or colliding with other students. However, in another fitness case,[286] the situation was held not foreseeable, that is, that an inexperienced athlete with an experienced friend would utilize the advanced athletic equipment without proper supervision and instruction.

Similar foreseeability and responsibility was at issue in a case[287] 12 years later. In this situation it was assumed that the faculty advisor knew of the student club's reputation, planning session for club initiation ceremony, and the planned hazing ceremony; and, thus, without taking further action of controlling the initiation, it was foreseeable that injury might occur. In the process of the hazing ceremony, the plaintiff severed his spinal cord and became permanently paralyzed from the neck down. In a college situation about the same time, the court held that the action of the students was not foreseeable. Student plaintiff sued for injuries sustained in an auto speed contest which occurred after drinking on University premises. The court said that it was not foreseeable that there would be harm where the students had no known violent propensities to the University and that there was no reason to believe that they would drink to excess and thereafter operate motor vehicles in a speed contest.[288] The court also held injuries unforeseeable when university students took, without permission, cafeteria trays for sliding down a hill. It said that proximate cause of injuries was the careless activity of the students.[289]

However, where circumstances are to occur which should give reason to anticipate dangers, then the management is responsible for taking precautions to control a crowd. The court held that the hotel, at which one of the teams headquartered for the Army-Notre Dame game, should have been aware of the probable congestion and hilarity of patrons. Plaintiff was awarded damages on the basis that negligence is gauged by the ability to anticipate and that where one assembles a crowd to financial gain, one also must give care to protection of such patrons.[290] In *Rotz v. City of New York*, 532 N.Y.S.2d 245 (1988), 25-year-old plaintiff was attending a concert in the park. There was a "tremendous crowd". A commotion ensued and everybody panicked and started to run. While the crowd was running, there were shouts of "get out of the way, there's a

[285] Ehlinger v. Board of Education, New Hartford, 96 A.D. 2d 708, 465 N.Y.S. 2d 378 (1983).

[286] Duncan v. World Wide Health Studios, Inc., 232 So. 2d 835 (La. App. 1970).

[287] Rupp v. Bryant, 399 So. 2d 417 (Fla. App. 1981), aff'd. 417 So. 2d 658 (1982).

[288] Baldwin v. Zoradi, 123 Cal. App. 3d 275, 176 Cal. Rptr. 809 (1981).

[289] Pizzola v. State of New York, 130 A.D. 2d 796, 515 N.Y.S. 2d 129 (1987).

[290] Schubart v. Hotel Astor, Inc., 168 Misc. 431, 5 N.Y.S. 2d 203 (1938).

lion, a lion". In the course of this stampede, plaintiff was unable to move, and was knocked down and trampled upon, suffering serious leg fracture. The court stated that the city owed a duty to provide adequate degree of general supervision of crowd invited by exercising reasonable care against foreseeable dangers under circumstances prevailing.

In a swimming pool accident, the danger was held not foreseeable when plaintiff dived from pool edge into path of three racing swimmers.[291] Harm also was not foreseeable when one 12-year-old boy was assaulted by other children.[292] Foreseeability was at issue, too, when a youth was participating in an indoor "sleep-in" at the Y and was struck by a heavy object falling from a rack from which the counselor was attempting to remove pillows as plaintiff was sleeping on floor, as directed.[293] Whether or not it was foreseeable that a five-year-old would wander away from his mother and climb through a hole in a fence of a pool one-half block away, drowning in 6″ of rain water, that is, whether a child was likely to trespass, was a crucial consideration in a New Mexico case.[294]

Foreseeability as related to maintenance and notice of the potentially dangerous condition was at issue when plaintiff fell in men's locker room at the University due to a slippery condition from water on the floor. The court said that persistent accumulation of water on floor of locker room created a foreseeable risk, and that the State had notice of the condition through its employees, and that the state did not use reasonable care to eliminate the hazard.[295] In a 1981 case[296] it was held foreseeable that plaintiff would be injured when a nut and bolt was not in place which secured a railing around the platform in the school gymnasium. And, in another New York case (1980),[297] involving the facility, glass doors located at one end of the gymnasium constituted a dangerous condition and foreseeable injury. Armed robbery of a teacher in classroom when the felon came through a hole in the playground fence was held to be an unforeseeable result of such hole.[298] The duty to protect does not extend to unforeseeable or unanticipated criminal acts of independent third person.[299]

The court[300] held no foreseeability when a piano, pushed and pulled toward the front of a stage by two 13-year-old boys, went over the edge and onto a business invitee at the recreational resort. The boys had moved it from rear of stage to find a lost dart. The circumstances of the handling of the piano by the boys was not a danger known to the

---

[291] Benoit v. Hartford Accident and Indemnity Co., 169 So. 2d 925 (1964).

[292] Mancha v. Field Museum, 5 Ill. App. 3d 699, 283 N.E. 2d 899 (1972).

[293] Willis v. YMCA, 34 A.D. 2d 583, 307 N.Y.S. 2d 967 (1970), rev'd. 28 N.Y. 2d 375, 321 N.Y.S. 2d 895, 270 N.E. 2d 717 (1971).

[294] Latimer v. Clovis, 83 N.M. 610, 495 P. 2d 788 (1972).

[295] Van Stry v. State of N.Y., 479 N.Y.S. 2d 258 (1984).

[296] Woodring v. Board of Education, Manhasset Union Free School District, 79 A.D. 2d 1022, 435 N.Y.S. 2d 52 (1981).

[297] Eddy v. Syracuse Univ., 78 A.D. 2d 989, 433 N.Y.S. 2d 923 (1980), pet. denied 52 N.Y. 2d 705, 437 N.Y.S. 2d 1028 (1981).

[298] Kavanaugh v. Orleans Parish School Board, 487 So. 2d 533 (La. App. 1986).

[299] St. Pierre v. Lombard, 512 So. 2d 1206 (La. App. 1987) spectator fatally stabbed at high school football game (see §1.21).

[300] Richter v. Adobe Creek Lodge, 143 Cal. App. 2d 514, 299 P. 2d 941 (1956).

resort owner, nor one which he had a duty to anticipate and guard against. A high school student was injured when a fellow student kicked a classroom stool upon which she was seated, causing her to fall to the floor. It was alleged that the principal and teacher were negligent in purchasing or authorizing stools of this design which they knew or should have known were improperly designed and not safe for use, and further, that the teacher was negligent in not maintaining proper control over the students. The court held that the stool was not defective and that the incident and resulting injury were not foreseeable from the standpoint of the teacher.[301]

Injury was held not foreseeable in a day camp when one of the campers was injured when another camper swung a bat (not at the plaintiff) and accidentally hit plaintiff.[302] Similarly, there was no foreseeability of injury when an 8″ to 10″ stump, 6″ in diameter, was left on an area about 14′ from an adjacent lot on which children played football.[303] Normally the children had not run into the area where the stump was left.

There is one circumstance in which foreseeable risk does not give rise to a duty of reasonable care to protect, and that is when the risk is open and obvious, both to adults and to children.[304] This is particularly true of natural environmental conditions (see §2.1231 Trespassing children and attractive nuisance doctrine and §20.332 Warning of natural area dangerous conditions). The rationale is that while there is the possibility of injury, it is not foreseeable that an individual would expose oneself to the risk of injury to an open and obvious hazard, that is, while there is a possibility of injury, there is no expected probability. For example, in *Sperr by Sperr* v. *Ramsey County,* 429 N.W.2d 315 (Minn. App. 1988), a 10-year-old child went ice skating at the ice arena. While running to his father's car after leaving the arena, he hit a low-hanging tree branch and sustained severe eye injuries. The tree was not overhanging a sidewalk; and, the fact that the county maintenance personnel sometimes trimmed branches so that they would not interfere with mowing grass did not give rise to a legal duty to trim the branches so that they pose no possible danger to children. The court held that it was not foreseeable that the branch might cause injury, in that it was in plain view and obvious.

§ 2.24 Character of conduct — ordinary and gross negligence

When considering liability as related to the act (§2.2), the character of the conduct of the defendant is a critical component. In the mid- and late 1980s, consideration of ordinary negligent conduct only does not suffice, particularly as related to statutory immunities and other efforts to limit liability (see Chapter 4). One must consider the character of the conduct. Conduct might be scaled from "not negligent" to felonious intent.

[301] Boyer v. Jablonski, 70 Ohio App. 2d 141, 435 N.E. 2d 436 (1980).

[302] Crohn v. Congregation B'nai Zion, 22 Ill. App. 2d 625, 317 N.E. 3d 637 (1974).

[303] Johnson v. Kreuger, 36 Colo. App. 242, 539 P. 2d 1296 (1975).

[304] For example, Durham v. Forest Preserve Dist. of Cook Co., 152 Ill. App. 3d 472, 105 Ill. Dec. 614, 504 N.E. 2d 899 (1987).

Figure 2.1   Character of Defendant's Conduct and Liability

Character of Conduct

not negligent	ordinary negligence	gross negligence	reckless disregard or willful "negligence"	willful and wanton misconduct	willful and malicious misconduct	felonious intent

Liability of Conduct

no liability	unintentional tort liability		intent implied liability	intentional tort liability		criminal act
	certain immunity statutes provide liability only if gross negligence; exculpatory clauses may not be valid, nor doctrine of respondeat superior applicable if gross negligence		standard applied to some player violence	certain immunity statutes provide liability only if this type of misconduct; defamation requires malice; exculpatory agreements not valid; doctrine of respondeat superior not applicable		

A three-element formula has been used by some of the courts[305] in discussing the distinction between ordinary negligence and willful and wanton misconduct: (1) knowledge of a situation requiring the exercise of ordinary care and diligence to avert injury to another; (2) ability to avoid the resulting harm by ordinary care and diligence in the use of the means at hand; and (3) the omission to use such care and diligence to avert the threatened danger, when to the ordinary mind it must be apparent that the result is likely to prove disastrous to another. The first two elements are present in ordinary negligence, and can be recognized as foreseeability of an unreasonable risk (§2.23) and application of reasonable care in protecting against that risk (§2.22), respectively. When danger is foreseeable and one fails to use reasonable care, one is negligent. The third element is added for willful misconduct, that is, one does not exercise reasonable care when it is quite apparent that disastrous injury will occur. As indicated on the foregoing Figure 2.1, there are gradations between ordinary negligence and willful/malicious misconduct. The importance of gross negligence, reckless disregard or willful "negligence," and willful and wanton/malicious misconduct is discussed in subsequent paragraphs and subsections.

Degree of care and degree of negligence should be distinguished. The degree of care relates to the amount of care, that is, the conduct which is reasonable for a given situation, which is dependent upon various factors, including the relationship between the parties, the nature and extent of the risk inherent in that situation, and whether the participant is a minor. To speak of degree of negligence is to consider degree of legal fault. The most common distinctions are labeled slight, ordinary and gross negligence.[306] **Slight negligence** is absence of the care the circumstances would normally demand, just a little less care than ordinary negligence, but not that which should be given for the circumstances. This degree of negligence is seldom referred to in physical education, sport, recreation, park, and camping cases. **Ordinary negligence** is that most commonly identified and is failure to perform with the degree of care the circumstances require, the omission of that care which a person of prudence usually would be expected to give, or the want of "ordinary care." While the result (injury) is not intended, one should know what the results might be. One who exhibits ordinary negligence might be said to be a "careless person."

Gross negligence. It is gross negligence which into the 1980s has the greatest impact upon immunity and liability, for it is in the statutes that the exception of gross negligence is made regarding immunity for certain situations set forth in the Tort Claims Acts (see §4.2), the landowner liability or recreational user acts (see §12.1) and the limited liability acts relating to CPR, first aid, emergency care, et al. (see §17.1). Also, gross negligence opens the door for exemplary damages.[307] Gross negligence is defined as "very great negligence" or failure to exercise even that care which a careless person would use. Most courts consider that gross negligence falls just short of a reckless disregard of consequences and that it differs from ordinary negligence only in

[305] Dinger v. Dept. of Natural Resources, 147 Mich. App. 164, 383 N.W. 2d 606 (1986); Rosa v. U.S. 613 F. Supp. 469 (1985) applying Pennsylvania law.
[306] Kionka, Edward J. Torts in a Nutshell. St. Paul; West Publishing Co., 1977 at 113-6; Keeton, at 208-217.
[307] Rawlings Sporting Goods, Inc. v. Daniels, 619 S.W. 2d 435 (Tex. Civ. App. 1981).

degree, not in kind (see next sub-section on recklessness); it is of an aggravated character as distinguished from the mere failure to exercise ordinary care of ordinary negligence. A few illustrative cases are cited; see the next sub-section and the foregoing indicated sections for further citations and detail.

It was held that the defendants were guilty of gross negligence or willful and wanton misconduct in failing to fence an area and deny access thereto or take other steps to avert danger to children at the water-filled gravel pit.[308] The acts of the baseball coach, athletic director, and buildings and grounds supervisor were allegedly grossly negligent when plaintiff fell on glass while running laps on the outdoor track.[309] Gross negligence was alleged in a case where a nine-year-old fell from defendant's dock and drowned.[310] And a fourth case, also relating to a landowner, had an allegation of gross negligence when snowmobilers were killed when they struck a guy wire of utility pole at night.[311] In a situation where the mast of a sailboat came in contact with a power line, the court distinguished awarding of exemplary damages as a punishment for gross negligence from compensation to the injured party, based upon the state statute.[312]

§ 2.241 Recklessness, willful and wanton behavior

While ordinary negligence is usually the result of carelessness, it is not undue disregard for the rights of others. On the other hand, gross negligence is almost akin to recklessness. The *Restatement of Torts §282* distinguishes recklessness and negligence when it defines negligence: any conduct, except conduct recklessly disregardful of the interest of others, which falls below the standard established by the law for the protection of others against unreasonable risk of harm. Recklessness denotes a greater degree of misconduct, bordering on intent, for the tortfeasor is aware that one's conduct may cause injury to others, yet proceeds to act heedlessly, willfully, and wantonly. In *Ordway* v. *Superior Court,* 198 Cal. App. 3d 98, 243 Cal. Rptr. 536 (1988), it is stated that recklessness is a form of intentional conduct and that participants do not consent to acts by others which are reckless or intentional, thus assumption of risk as a defense has little or no application. The exact status of recklessness, though, differs from jurisdiction to jurisdiction and from legal writer to legal writer. Some would use recklessness and gross negligence synonymously. However, wherein recklessness has such substantial certainty of harm that it is inseparable from intent itself, others hold that it should be dealt with as if the harm were actually intended; but, to use the term "willful negligence" is contradictory, since negligence does not imply intent to harm. Nevertheless the term is used. In either situation, it remains that recklessness is conduct of an unreasonable character from which it is highly probable that harm would result. In some jurisdictions, reckless conduct is held to justify liability even though there would not be liability for ordinary negligence, to negate the defense of contributory negligence, to impose

---

[308] Taylor v. Mathews, 40 Mich. App. 74, 198 N.W. 2d 843 (1972).

[309] Short v. Griffitts, 220 Va. 53, 255 S.E. 2d 479 (1979).

[310] Magerowski v. Standard Oil Co., 274 F. Supp. 246 (D.C. 1967).

[311] Burnett v. City of Adrian, 414 Mich. 448, 326 N.W. 2d 810 (1982); Thomas' Estate v. Consumers Power Co., 58 Mich. App. 486, 228 N.W. 2d 786 (1975).

[312] Pedernales Elec. Co-op, Inc. v. Schulz, 583 S.W. 2d 882 (Tex. Civ. App., 1979).

punitive damages, and to consider such conduct the legal cause even though ordinary negligence would not have been so considered.

In a 1981 case,[313] while being hazed at a student club initiation ceremony, plaintiff severed his spinal cord, resulting in paralysis from the neck down. There were school regulations requiring approval of the principal for outings outside school hours, prohibiting hazing, and requiring a faculty member present at all club activities and meetings. The club advisor was not present. Further, allegedly the club had a well-known reputation for violating regulations, particularly consumption of alcoholic beverages, and the advisor knew of this reputation and the planned hazing ceremony. Under Florida governmental unit tort law, suit is permitted against an employee if one's conduct exhibited wanton or willful disregard of human rights, safety, or property. The court held that the allegation of gross and reckless conduct was within the ambit of the phrase "wanton and willful misconduct." Willful and wanton misconduct also was held when a youngster fell from slide with loose and slippery handrails; notwithstanding prior injuries to other children, the defendants failed to replace the handrail. The court said that this was a dangerous condition from which children must be protected, particularly children generally who, by reason of age and immaturity, would not be expected to comprehend and avoid attendant risks.[314]

The Nebraska court[315] endeavored to differentiate "willful misconduct" and "willful negligence," stating that to constitute willful misconduct there must be actual knowledge, or its legal equivalent of peril to be apprehended, coupled with conscious failure to avert injury, and to constitute willful negligence, act done or omitted must be intended or must involve such reckless disregard of security and right as to imply bad faith. It further stated that for action to be willful or wanton, evidence must show that one acted with actual knowledge that danger existed and that one intentionally failed to act to prevent harm which was reasonably likely to result. In a 1981 Illinois case[316] the court discussed the "negligence standard" in contrast to the "willful-and-wanton-misconduct standard." The youngsters had been playing "tackle-the-football," an amalgamation of football, keep away, and soccer. The game had stopped, but defendant continued to play catch with the football and collided with a girl who was bystanding. The importance of the difference was related to the ability to recover in Illinois. The jury found that defendant was negligent as related to the duty toward the bystander. This was an informal youth-at-play situation, not organized sport. The coach was not found guilty of willful and wanton misconduct in directing a student to use ladder (instead of a scaffold) to change scoreboard in a 1987 Illinois case.[317] The court said that for willful and wanton injury there must have been intention or the act must have been committed under circumstances exhibiting reckless disregard for safety of others, such as failure, after knowledge of impending danger, to exercise ordinary care to prevent it or failure to

[313] Bryant v. School Board of Duval Co., 399 So. 2d 417 (Fla. App. 1981).

[314] Scarano v. Town of Ela, 116 Ill. App. 3d 184, 117 Ill. Dec. 72, 520 N.E. 2d 62 (1988).

[315] Garreans by Garreans v. City of Omaha, 216 Neb. 487, 345 N.W. 2d 309 (1984) explosion of drum, camper in public park next to a "trash" drum.

[316] Osborne v. Sprowls, 84 Ill. 2d 390, 50 Ill. Dec. 645, 419 N.E. 2d 913 (1981).

[317] Braun v. Board of Education, Red Bud Comm. Unit School Dist., 151 Ill. App. 3d 787, 104 Ill. Dec. 416, 502 N.E. 2d 1076 (1987).

discover danger through recklessness or carelessness when it could have been discovered by ordinary care.

When an act is committed under circumstances exhibiting a reckless disregard for the safety of others, such as a failure after knowledge of impending danger to exercise ordinary care to prevent it or a failure to discover the danger through recklessness or carelessness when it could have been discovered by the exercise of ordinary care, there is a tendency to label this conduct as willful and wanton and permit the plaintiff to recover even though certain defenses would have prevented recovery for ordinary negligence.[318] Further, when a participant in sport assumes known dangers or risks which inhere in the activity, it does not relieve others involved of the duty to refrain from causing injury through wanton, reckless or intentional conduct.[319]

A 1984 Kansas case[320] endeavored to distinguish negligence, recklessness, and gross and wanton in an effort to determine what was immunity and what was liability under the State Tort Claims Act. The situation involved installation and maintenance of a baseball diamond fence; the court held that the conduct by the City was not "gross and wanton." The court stated, proof of willingness (intent) is not necessary in establishing gross and wanton negligence because a wanton act is something more than ordinary negligence but is something less than willful injury. To constitute wantonness, act must indicate a realization of imminence of danger and a reckless disregard or a complete indifference or an unconcern for the probable consequences of the wrongful act. And, as set forth in *McClendon* v. *Norwood,* 179 Ga. App. 176, 346 S.E. 2d 1 (1986), under most state tort claim acts, board members and administrators sued in their official capacity or for acting in areas where they were vested with discretion are not liable unless they acted willfully, wantonly or outside scope of their authority. See §§4.13 and 4.234.

Willful and wanton misconduct also has consequences on defenses. For example, exculpatory agreements are held invalid as against public policy where the defendant engages in willful and wanton behavior. This also is true in most jurisdictions where there is gross negligence.[321] And, recreational user acts do not protect landowners who act willfully and maliciously (see §12.152). However, in a case which held voluntary intoxication willful misconduct, the court held that willful misconduct did not bar application of comparative negligence doctrine.[322] For further discussion of willful and wanton, see §1.41, and for intentional nuisance, see §4.4.

§ 2.242   *Res ipsa loquitur*

In establishing negligence, the plaintiff sometimes alleges that the standard of care

[318] For example, Rosa v. U.S., 613 F. Supp. 469 (1985) Pennsylvania law applied; Stephens v. U.S., 472 F. Supp. 998 (1979).

[319] Kabella v. Bouschelle, 100 N.M. 461, 672 P. 2d 290 (1983); Turcotte v. Fell, 123 Misc. 2d 877, 474 N.Y.S. 2d 893 (1984); see §1.41322.

[320] Willard v. Kansas City, 235 Kan. 655, 681 P. 2d 1067 (1984).

[321] For example, Adams v. Roark, 686 S.W. 2d 73

(Tenn. 1983); Gillespie v. Papale, 541 F. Supp. 1042 (1982); Lee v. Beauchene, 337 N.W. 2d 827 (S.D. 1983); Milligan v. Big Valley Corp., 754 P. 2d 1063 (Wyo. 1988); Randle v. Hinckley Parachute Center, Inc., 141 Ill. App. 3d 660, 96 Ill. Dec. 5, 490 N.E. 2d 1041 (1986); Smith v. Golden Triangle Raceway, 708 S.W. 2d 574 (Tex. App. 1986).

[322] Zavala v. Regents of Univ. of Calif., 125 Cal. App. 3d 646, 178 Cal. Rptr. 1985(1981).

was such that "the thing speaks for itself" and the recovery should be granted without further proof.[323] This is known as the doctrine of *res ipsa loquitur*. The risk is so great, so unreasonable, that the danger is obvious. It is immaterial whether or not this unreasonable risk was a breach of statutory duty; however, some attempt to invoke the doctrine without further question for any breach of statutory duty. But, all statutory breaches do not result in an unreasonable risk or an obligation to the injured. *Res ipsa loquitur* is a rule of evidence which, when applied, permits but does not compel an inference that the defendant was negligent.

To apply the doctrine two factors are necessary, although the presence of the two factors does not infer negligence: (1) the instrumentality must be under the exclusive control and management of the defendant, and (2) the occurrence must be such that in the ordinary course of things it would not have happened if defendant had used reasonable care.[324] In three[325] of four cases, the doctrine of *res ipsa loquitur* was held to be inapplicable. In the one case[326] the collapse of bleachers (which do not ordinarily collapse) sustained the imposition of liability on *res ipsa loquitur* theory. Both of the factors were met in the Boyer case, but they were not met in the other three cases. The *Cumberland College* case further stated that where the condition is created by the possessor, no proof of notice is necessary; however, where the condition was created otherwise, then it must be shown that there was notice (constructive or actual) of the defect. In a 1982 baseball case[327] the doctrine was held applicable. The plaintiff was hit by a foul ball, which went through the protective screening behind home plate. The court said that there were four elements of *res ipsa loquitur:* (1) event must be of kind which ordinarily does not occur in absence of someone's negligence; (2) event must be caused by agency or instrumentality within exclusive control of defendant; (3) event must not be due to any voluntary action or contribution on part of plaintifff; and (4) evidence as to true explanation of event must be more readily accessible to defendant than to plaintiff.

The doctrine of *res ipsa loquitur* also has been attempted to be applied in drowning cases. An 11-year-old boy drowned while participating in a swimming class. The plaintiff alleged incompetent lifeguards and sought a ruling that such made the occurrence a situation where the doctrine should be applicable. The court held that there are various factors which could account for a drowning and that drowning is not such an

[323] Aurora v. Weeks, 384 P. 2d 90 (Colo. 1963); Cleveland v. Pine, 123 Ohio St. 578, 176 N.E. 229 (1931); Felt v. Toledo, 47 Ohio App. 461, 192 N.E. 11 (1933); Litzmann v. Humbolt County, 127 Cal. App. 2d 86, 273 P. 2d 82 (1954); Novack v. Los Angeles School Dist., 92 Cal. App. 2d 169, 206 P. 2d 403 (1940); Nussbaum v. Lacopo, 27 N.Y. 2d 311, 265 N.E. 2d 762 (1970); Refson v. State, 52 Misc. 2d 498, 276 N.Y.S. 2d 176 (1966); Rome v. London & Lancashire Indem. Co., 169 So. 132 (La. App. 1936); St. John v. St. Paul, 179 Minn. 12, 228 N.W. 170 (1929); Swiontek v. New York City, 108 N.Y.S. 2d 844 (1951).

[324] Funez v. Jefferson Parish School Board, 528 So. 2d 1057 (La. App. 1988); Johnson v. Dept. of Mental Retardation & Developmental Disabilities, 35 Ohio Misc. 2d 18, 520 N.E. 2d 29 (1987); O'Connor v.

Chandris Lines, 566 F. Supp. 1275 (1983); Pietz v. Oskaloosa, 250 Iowa 374, 92 N.W. 2d 577 (1958).

[325] Akins v. Sonoma Co., 60 Cal. Rptr. 499, 430 P. 2d 57 (1967); Cumberland College v. Gaines, 432 S.W. 2d 650 (Ky. 1968); Gill v. United States Fidelity & Co., 257 So. 2d 437 (La. 1972); see also Woolbright v. Six Flags Over Georgia, 172 Ga. App. 41, 321 S.E. 2d 787 (1984) amusement park roller coaster.

[326] Boyer v. Iowa H.S. Athletic Assoc., 260 Iowa 1061, 152 N.W. 2d 293 (1967); see also bleacher cases Lawson v. Clawson, 177 Md. 333, 9 A. 2d 755 (1939); Parker v. Warren and Warren v. Nailling (two cases), 503 S.W. 2d 938 (Tenn. App. 1973).

[327] Uzdavines v. Metro. Baseball Club, Inc., 115 Misc. 2d 343, 454 N.Y.S. 2d 238 (1982).

occurrence which in the ordinary course of things happens only if there is negligence.[328] In the dictum of a much earlier case,[329] the Iowa court stated that application of the *res ipsa loquitur* rule to drowning accidents would be carrying the doctrine beyond its recognized limits. The *Rome* case cited previously did follow the doctrine, but subsequently was overruled by the *Gill* case, also cited previously. In another swimming case,[330] but in Virginia, the doctrine of *res ipsa loquitur* also was rejected. The doctrine, however, was held applicable in an Arkansas case[331] when the plaintiff was thrown off the sled of a toboggan-type water slide. The wheels of the sled jumped out of the grooves on the runway of the track. The court held that the defect in the track should have been known to the defendant and remedied.

Res ipsa loquitur also was raised in two cases[332] concerned with golf carts. The doctrine was held not applicable in both. The plaintiff was unsuccessful in raising the doctrine in five cases[333] involving injuries on ski lifts. However, the plaintiff was successful in the *Refson* case when he was injured when a stone ledge fell from its position on a lodge. The court held that the doctrine of *res ipsa loquitur* relieves a plaintiff from burden of producing direct evidence of negligence, but does not relieve him from burden of proving that person charged with negligence was at fault. Plaintiff did, though, establish an inference of negligence against State sufficient to make a prima facie case for court's consideration.[334] Five cases[335] involved horseback riding, three involving slipping of the saddle. The court held in three of the cases that the doctrine of *res ipsa loquitur* was inapplicable under the situation of the accident, but in the *Rafter* case, the court said that defendant had exclusive control of the saddle at the time when the negligence in fastening the saddle on occurred and held the doctrine applicable.

§ 2.243 Prima facie case

Another legal concept related to evidence and conduct of defendant is that of prima facie case. A case which presents evidence that is sufficient "on its face" to establish a given fact, in the situations under consideration, negligence, and which, if not rebutted or contradicted will remain sufficient, is said to be a prima facie case. In 1987 the New

[328] Wong v. Waterloo Community School, 232 N.W. 2d 865 (Iowa 1975).

[329] Hecht v. Des Moines Playground & Recreation Association, 227 Iowa 81, 287 N.W. 259 (1939); see also Evansville v. Blue, 212 Ind. 130, 8 N.E. 2d 224 (1937); McKeever v. Phoenix Jewish Community Center, 92 Ariz. 121, 374 P. 2d 875 (1962).

[330] S & C Co. v. Horne, 281 Va. 124, 235 S.E. 2d 456 (1977).

[331] Dickson v. Bounds, 190 Ark. 86, 77 S.W. 2d 456 (1934).

[332] Gillespie v. Chevy Chase Golf Club, 187 Cal. App. 2d 52, 9 Cal. Rptr. 437 (1960); Hutchins v. Southview Golf Club, 343 S.W. 2d 223 (Mo. App., 1960).

[333] Albert v. State, 80 Misc. 2d 105, 362 N.Y.S. 2d 341 (1974); Cowen v. Tyrolean Ski Area, Inc., 127 N.H.

397, 506 A. 2d 690 (1985); Houser v. Floyd, 220 Cal. App. 2d, 34 Cal. Rptr. 96 (1963); Jordon v. Loveland Skiing Corp., 503 P. 2d 1034 (Colo. App. 1972); Lawrence v. Davos, 46 A.D. 2d 41, 360 N.Y.S. 2d 730 (1974); Refson v. State, 52 Misc. 2d 498, 276 N.Y.S. 2d 176 (1966); Albert v. State, 80 Misc. 2d 105, 362 N.Y.S. 2d 341 (1974).

[334] Refson v. State, 52 Misc. 2d 498, 276 N.Y.S. 2d 176 (1966).

[335] Heath v. Madsen, 273 Wis. 628, 79 N.W. 2d 73 (1956); Lewellyn v. Lookout Saddle Co., 315 So. 2d 69 (La. App. 1975); Rafter v. Dubrock's Riding Academy, 75 Cal. App. 2d 621, 171 P. 2d 459 (1946); Tezon v. Perkins, 240 Mo. App. 696, 214 S.W. 2d 732 (1948); Williams v. Hawkins, 304 So. 2d 75 (La. App. 1974), appl. den. 307 So. 2d 373.

York court[336] stated that to establish prima facie case of negligence, plaintiff was required only to demonstrate that the defendant's negligence was a substantial factor bringing about the injury; plaintiff was not required to eliminate all of the potential causes, but simply to provide the sufficient evidentiary basis from which causation could reasonably be inferred. Having an instructor without certification for a scuba diving check-out class was sufficient to establish a prima facie case of negligence[337] as was a situation in which an injury occurred to a sleeping youth (on the floor) when a heavy object fell from a rack while a counselor was seeking to reach some pillows.[338] Since the chair which collapsed when plaintiff sat upon it in the cafeteria after a basketball game was in full control of the defendant and collapsed in ordinary use, a prima facie showing of negligence was held.[339] A prima facie case, also, was established when a horse saddle turned due to failure to properly cinch it.[340] A prima facie case was established when the plaintiff's son was electrocuted in a pool.[341]

A prima facie case failed to be established in a case involving maintaining a water ski area in safe condition,[342] as well as in a situation where a boy struck his head on the bottom when diving from post into gravel pit.[343] Both of these involved consideration of a statutory duty. A prima facie case also was not established in a situation where the plaintiff was struck by a speeding car as he left a fireworks display at the park,[344] and in a basketball situation where there was a dirty floor.[345]

§ 2.244 Doctrine of exclusive control

At a day care center, a child returning from the play area was crying and said his head hurt. Cold compresses were put on, the child was put to bed for a nap and later was given lunch. After lunch the child was sent to the school nurse, and the mother picked him up shortly before three. Noting a patch over one eye, the mother took the child to an eye hospital where it was determined that there had been a severe injury to the eye. The court held that the allegation of liability based on the doctrine of exclusive control did not apply, and further stated that this doctrine was dangerous because it raises an inference of negligence and shifts to the defendant the responsibility of going forth with evidence. The court specified five elements, all which must be present, to apply the doctrine: (1) where thing that caused accident is under exclusive control or manufacture of defendant; (2) accident or injury would ordinarily not happen if defendant exercised due care or

---

[336] Locilento v. John A. Coleman Catholic High School, 523 N.Y.S. 2d 198 (1987) intramural tackle football case; see also Fleming v. Kings Ridge Recreation Park, 138 A.D. 2d 451, 525 N.Y.S. 2d 866 (1988) handrails on 3 meter diving board.

[337] Leno v. YMCA, 17 Cal. App. 3d 651, 95 Cal. Rptr. 96 (1971).

[338] Willis v. YMCA, 34 A.D. 2d 583, 307 N.Y.S. 2d 967 (1970), rev'd. 28 N.Y. 2d 375, 321 N.Y.S. 2d 895, 270 N.E. 2d 717 (1971).

[339] Raffa v. Central School Dist., A.D. 2d 855, 227 N.Y.S. 2d 723 (1962).

[340] Rafter v. Dubrock's Riding Academy, 75 Cal. App. 2d 621, 171 P. 2d 459 (1946).

[341] Travelers Ins. Co. v. Stanley, 252 F. 2d 115 (1958).

[342] Marlow v. Columbia Heights, 284 N.W. 2d 389 (Minn. 1979). By statute, Ohio provides that violation of the watercraft regulations (statutes) resulting in injury shall constitute prima facie evidence of negligence.

[343] Lister v. Campbell, 371 So. 2d 133 (Fla. App. 1979), cert. denied 378 So. 2d 346 (1979).

[344] Ziginow v. Redford Jaycees, 133 Mich. App. 259, 349 N.W. 2d 153 (1983).

[345] Pederson v. Joliet Park Dist., 136 Ill. App. 3d 172, 90 Ill. Dec. 874, 483 N.E. 2d 21 (1985).

made (manufactured) article with due care; (3) where evidence of cause of injury or accident not equally available to both parties but exclusively accessible to and within possession of defendant; (4) the accident itself is very unusual or exceptional and the likelihood of harm to plaintiff or one of his class could reasonably have been foreseeable and prevented by due care; and (5) general principles of negligence have not theretofore been applied to such facts.[346]

The doctrine of exclusive control also was attempted to be applied in a fireworks case.[347]

§ 2.3   Proximate Cause[348]

Before one can be held liable for alleged negligent conduct, it must be proved that the negligent act in fact caused the injury. Mere occurrence of an accident, standing alone, cannot support an inference that the defendant was negligent[349] and that the negligence proximately caused the injury. The burden is on the plaintiff to produce competent evidence that the defendant was negligent and that the negligence was the proximate cause of the injury.[350] In most cases the test for actual causation is whether plaintiff has established that the harm would not have occurred but for the negligent conduct of defendant.[351] In most of the recreation and park, physical education and athletic cases, the act is not difficult to prove as the cause-in-fact. In the landmark *Welch* case,[352] the injured football player was able to move parts of his body before being moved from the field, but subsequent to moving was paralyzed; the moving in an improper manner caused further injury resulting in paralysis. Maintenence cases are particularly obvious as to direct causation. A pile of hot ashes is left — a child is burned; a slide structure becomes loose — a child is injured; a decayed limb is not taken care of — a person is hit and injured; a hole in a walk is not repaired — a woman steps into it and is injured.[353] A piece of apparatus is insecurely fastened to the joist and comes down causing injury to the participant.[354] A student who was boxing was injured because he was not taught the art of defense.[355]

There are also some cases in which an act is alleged to be the causal factor, but is not.[356] For example, a job applicant over-exerted on a strength test injuring himself; the

[346] Greathouse v. Horowitz, 439 Pa. 62, 264 A. 2d 665 (1970).

[347] Haddon v. Lotito, 299 Pa. 521, 161 A. 2d 160 (1960).

[348] Note: Legal cause and proximate cause are used synonomously in this treatise (65 C.J.S. Negligence Sec. 103 at p. 649).

[349] Murphy v. Chestnut Mountain Lodge, 124 Ill. App. 3d 508, 79 Ill. Dec. 914, 464 N.E. 2d 818 (1984) rental skis did not have antifriction devices. Fleming v. Kings Ridge Recreation Park, 138 A.D. 2d 451, 525 N.Y.S. 2d 866 (1988) 11-year-old child fell from 3-meter diving board, did not show low handrails (lower than recommended standard by Nat'l Spa & Pool Institute) were substantial cause of fall.

[350] Wu v. Town of Fairfield, 204 Conn. 435, 528 A. 2d 364 (1987) held plaintiff failed to present sufficient evidence that any breach of duty on part of town's lifeguards was proximate cause of death.

[351] Salk v. Alpine Ski Shop, Inc., 342 A. 2d 622 (R.I. 1975) ski binding release situation in which court opinion made statements regarding proximate cause.

[352] Welch v. Dunsmuir Joint Union High Sch. Dist., 326 P. 2d 633 (Calif. App. 1958).

[353] See §20.2 Condition of premises.

[354] Johnson City Bd. of Educ. v. Ray, 154 Tenn. 179, 289 S.W. 502 (1926).

[355] LaValley v. Stanford, 272 A.D. 183, 70 N.Y.S. 2d 460 (1947); see also Parmentier v. McGinnis, 157 Wash. 596, 147 N.W. 1007 (1914) boxing not proximate cause of death.

[356] See also §18.1 Supervision and proximate cause.

device was not defective as alleged.[357] A ferris wheel in defective condition injured a child; the alleged violation of the Child Labor Law as the cause was not upheld.[358] A spectator was injured when the bleachers collapsed, proximate cause of bleacher failure was cadence swaying of exuberant fans, not negligent erection.[359] The court held that a drowning at the county park was caused by decedent's own negligence in swimming in area after close of park when she in fact did not know how to swim, rather than being caused by a breach of duty owed by the county.[360] In a Pennsylvania case it also was the action of the injured plaintiff in diving into a pool, rather than the design of the pool, that was the proximate cause of the injury, hence no liability on the part of the manufacturer and retailer.[361] Similarly, the plaintiff's act of diving into an open and obvious danger (shallow water) was held proximate cause, rather than failure to warn or failure to have depth markers.[362] In other cases a kick at the door and not a defective door was deemed the proximate cause of injury,[363] the injured student and the student who threw a discus also were found to be the proximate cause of injury,[364] and a 12-year-old was the cause of her own injury when she rushed toward a glass paneled door with hand outreached for the "panic bar" while looking in another direction.[365] And, in a Minnesota case,[366] the plaintiff could not prove that defendant's conduct was the cause of injury. Plaintiff had cut his foot on an object in the lakebed, but could not show that the broken glass jar, broken beer bottle, or rusty beer can found near the location was either the object that made the cut or thrown in by defendant. Failure to post warnings was found not to be the proximate cause of injury when plaintiff dived into shallow water at a state recreational area in Arizona.[367]

However, there are some instances in which proving or disproving a causal relationship is more difficult; for example, the absence of a lifeguard. The lifeguard was temporarily absent when he escorted a group of small boys to the dressing room; during the absence a member of the college swim team in company of three other swim team members went under in the pool. Was the absence of the guard the proximate cause? Held no; with an additional guard (the swim team members had taken care of pulling him out) the result would have been no different.[368] However, in a Utah case,[369] the

[357] Williams v. Alhambra, 131 Cal. App. 2d 262, 280 P. 2d 177 (1955).

[358] Shannon v. Fleishhacker, 116 Cal. App. 258, 2 P. 2d 835 (1931).

[359] Richards v. School Dist., 348 Mich. 490, 83 N.W. 2d 643 (1957).

[360] McPhee v. Dade Co., 362 So. 2d 74 (Fla. App. 1978).

[361] Colosimo v. May Dept. Store Co., 325 F. Supp. 609, rev'd. 466 F. 2d 1234 (1972); see also product liability §§21.1 et seq.

[362] Belling v. Haugh's Pools, Inc., 126 A.D. 2d 958, 511 N.Y.S. 2d 732 (1987) motion denied 70 N.Y. 2d 602, 512 N.E. 2d 550 (1987) dismissed as untimely 70 N.Y. 2d 748, 514 N.E. 2d 393 (1987); Caris v. Mele, 521 N.Y.S. 2d 260 (1987); Murphy v. D'Youville Condominium Ass'n., 175 Ga. App. 156, 333 S.E. 2d 1 (1985); Palumbo v. State Game & Fresh Water Fish Comm., 487 So. 2d 352 (Fla. App. 1986) warnings

about alligators ignored; Smith v. Stark, 111 A.D. 2d 913, 490 N.Y.S. 2d 811 (1985), aff'd. 67 N.Y. 2d 693, 499 N.Y.S. 2d 922, 490 N.E. 2d 841 (1986); see also, §20.3321 and next section §2.31 Intervening cause.

[363] Obshatcko v. YM & YWHA of Williamsburg, 45 A.D. 2d 1023, 358 N.Y.S. 2d 43 (1974).

[364] Marques v. Riverside Military Academy, 87 Ga. App. 370, 73 S.E. 2d 574 (1952).

[365] Tyler v. Jefferson Parish School Board, La. App. 258 So. 2d 206 (1972).

[366] Marlow v. Columbia Heights, 284 N.W. 2d 389 (Minn. 1979).

[367] Markowitz v. Arizona Parks Board, 705 P. 2d 937, rev'd. 706 P. 2d 364 (Ariz. 1985).

[368] Curcio v. New York, 275 N.Y. 20, 9 N.E. 2d 760 (1937).

[369] Griffin v. Salt Lake City, 111 Utah 94, 176 P. 2d 156 (1947); see also, Newport v. Ford, 393 S.W. 2d 760 (Tenn. 1965).

guard's absence was held to be the proximate cause. Three children had worked themselves along the handrail to the deep water. One became frightened, let go, and drowned. Although the guard was there immediately it was held that if he had not been absent he would have noticed the three children prior to the drowning, and could have warned them and watched. In another case[370] the guard was not absent physically, but was talking to a girl friend and not paying attention. A boy drowned, but no one knew how it occurred. The lack of attention by the guard was sufficient cause to permit recovery.

In determining whether an act is the proximate cause, some courts follow the **probable consequences** rule. According to this rule, a defendant is liable for injuries which are the natural and probable consequences of one's negligent act. In another swimming pool case,[371] a bottle vending machine was kept in the dressing room; it was held that it was the natural and probable consequences that bottles would break, causing injury to a patron.

What is a natural and probable consequence is sometimes difficult to say. How far will the law go? In a seemingly far-fetched very early case,[372] a fall (fracturing a hip) on a women's dressing room steps at a swimming area was held to be the proximate cause of pneumonia which resulted in death two months after the accident. It is also questioned whether the probable consequences rule is limited by the doctrine of foreseeability. It was held that a city should anticipate (was foreseeable) that an iron rod sticking up some 3″ from the center of a cement post of a partly demolished bench in a public square used as a playground would be dangerous to children and hence was liable for injuries to a seven-year-old child.[373] However, there was no liability on the basis that the injured was not a foreseeable plaintiff when a woman looking out of a second floor window was struck by a ball (resulting in removal of an eye) hit by boys playing in the street below.[374]

A little different approach to probable consequences is a 1982 Michigan case.[375] Plaintiff spectator was struck by a batted ball while attending a baseball game and alleged that the stadium owner should have warned her of the high risk from batted balls; however, there was no evidence presented that if proper warning had been given, plaintiff would have taken any precautions to prevent the injury.

Rather than discussing probable cause, the Texas court[376] stated that the elements of proximate cause may be inferred from circumstances surrounding the event, and the jury is to be allowed latitude in making the determination regarding proximate cause. In this situation it was held that an employee in a health spa shouting at plaintiff, who was on the treadmill and fell, was the proximate cause. In another case[377] medical testimony

---

[370] Rome v. London & Lancashire Indem. Co. of America, 169 So. 132 (La. App. 1936).

[371] Orrison v. Rapid City, 76 S.D. 145, 74 N.W. 2d 489 (1956).

[372] Kuenzel v. St. Louis, 278 Mo. 277, 212 S.W. 876 (1919).

[373] Bonczek v. Philadelphia, 338 Pa. 484, 13 A. 2d 414 (1940).

[374] Wildman v. New York, 254 A.D. 591, 3 N.Y.S. 2d 37 (1938); see also, Vitetta v. Albany, 4 A.D. 2d 797, 164 N.Y.S. 2d 416 (1957).

[375] Falkner v. John E. Fetzer, Inc., 113 Mich. App. 500, 317 N.W. 2d 337 (1982).

[376] Figure World v. Farley, 680 S.W. 2d 33 (Tex. App. 1984).

[377] Marcantel v. Allen Parish School Board, 484 So. 2d 322 (La. App. 1986) modified and aff'd. 490 So. 2d 1162 (La. App. 1986) writ cert. denied 496 So. 2d 328 (1986).

hypothesized that the phenomenon (shortening of the leg) was the body's reaction to the trauma experienced (another student fell on leg, fracturing it, in physical education class) and thus the incident was held to have a causal connection to the shortening of the leg. However, in another medical case,[378] plaintiff failed to provide adequate evidence by medical expert that a college football injury was probable cause of subsequent physical problems several years later (after college).

A number of courts have adopted the **substantial factor** test, and when applied to the fact of causation alone, it is of assistance. The law of legal causation does not require that one's negligent act be the sole cause of the injury; it is possible that several factors independent of each other contributed to the harm done. Generally, the test employed in determining whether an individual can be held liable for one's negligent conduct is whether such conduct was a substantial factor in bringing about the injury.[379] A substantial factor has usually been interpreted to mean any such factor which in and by itself would have caused the injury. The jury must answer the question: would the injury have occurred had it not been for the defendant's conduct? The *Second Restatement of Torts* §433 has adopted the substantial factor test, but has limited its application to the fact of causation. The Kentucky court held that the coach's action was "the last and only substantial factor" in causing death by electrocution. A student athlete was using a whirlpool bath at school; the coach had modified the whirlpool bath and did not install a ground fault interrupter in wiring, as required by the national electric code. Plaintiff also had brought action against the independent contractors and inspector.[380] There may, however, be more than one negligent act which contributes concurrently as proximate cause of injury, such as held in a California case.[381] This situation involved a social host serving alcoholic beverages and the automobile manufacturer on design of the automobile. The New York court[382] referred to a "contributing proximate cause" in an injury due to collision of bicycle racer with pedestrian on the highway on which the race was being conducted. Held that the State permitting bicyclist association to conduct races on state highway without exercising reasonable care to abate known dangers to pedestrians was a contributing proximate cause.

In a 1982 Connecticut case[383] it was a matter of supervision of a YMCA volleyball tournament. In prior years supervision had been provided, but none this year. It was hot and humid and the final game, characterized as a "blood game." In the game the plaintiff was knocked to the ground and suffered a severe and permanent disabling injury. The court held that the lack of supervision of the tournament was not a substantial factor in bringing about the plaintiff's injury. In a Washington case[384] a ten-year-old pupil was injured when struck by an automobile driven by one of the teachers when the car was being moved from the parking lot and the class was being dismissed from a

---

[378] Eberhart v. Morris Brown College, 181 Ga. App. 516, 352 S.E. 2d 832 (1987).

[379] Leslie v. City of Bonesteel, 303 N.W. 2d 117 (S.D. 1981) draining municipal pool.

[380] Massie v. Persson, 729 S.W. 2d 448 (Ky. App. 1987).

[381] Sagadin v. Ripper, 175 Cal. App. 3d 1141, 221 Cal. Rptr. 675 (1985).

[382] O'Connor v. State, 126 A.D. 2d 120, 512 N.Y.S. 2d 536 (1987).

[383] Hearl v. Waterbury YMCA, 187 Conn. 1, 444 A. 2d 211 (1982); see also Bruss v. Milwaukee Sporting Goods Co., 34 Wis. 2d 688, 150 N.W. 2d 337 (1967) bleachers collapse, substantial factor test.

[384] Gattavara v. Lundin, 166 Wash. 548, 7 P. 2d 958 (1932).

nearby door. Held that lack of supervision at this time on the grounds was the proximate cause. An 11-year-old girl suffered a misplaced vertebra in a physical education class while attempting a headstand.[385] The proximate cause of injury was failure on the part of the instructor to give proper strengthening exercises before attempting the headstand. Negligence in erecting a slide in the pool (a V-shaped opening in the side of the slide on which the injured's thumb caught) was the proximate cause in a Texas case.[386] Inadequate lighting in a room in which students were playing badminton was held to be the proximate cause of a foreseeable injury to the plaintiff who was struck in the eye.[387] A contributing cause in the injury of the plaintiff in a New York case was a missing see-saw handle.[388]

There are an equal number of cases holding that certain factors are not substantial in causing the injury. The failure to have the bottom of a pool painted white was held not to be the proximate cause of a drowning.[389] An allegation of proximate cause was unsuccessful where there was only one attendant at a horse merry-go-round.[390] A similar result was found on an allegation that the golf course layout was the proximate cause of injury when a golfer on an adjacent fairway was injured; in fact, the proximate cause was the act of the player hooking the ball.[391] A 13-year-old boy died from meningitis shortly after boxing.[392] It was held that failure to give a physical exam, not giving instruction in self-defense, and not warning of the dangers after a heavy meal were not the proximate cause of death. A child was injured in the act of climbing over a wire fence separating two parts of the playground.[393] Failure to provide "unclimbable" barrier held not to be the proximate cause. Failure to provide proper rules and regulations was alleged in two cases to be the proximate cause of injury; the court did not so hold.[394] Neither was the violation of athletic association rules held to be the proximate cause in a high school football case.[395] However, failure to enforce its own rules was held to be the proximate cause of injury to a third grader playing softball.[396] In another case,[397] the boy's inability or inexperience in swimming was held to be the proximate cause of his drowning, not the attractiveness of the water. Failure to provide sufficient lifeguards,[398] requiring student to participate barefoot when he failed to bring his sneakers,[399] and failure to attach pad properly on a trampoline[400] were in issue as to whether such was the proximate cause of injury. In a 1983 New York case[401] it was at

[385] Gardner v. State (two cases), 281 N.Y. 212, 22 N.E. 2d 344 (1939).
[386] Belton v. Ellis, 254 S.W. 1023 (Tex. Civ. App. 1923).
[387] Styer v. Reading, 360 Pa. 212, 61 A. 2d 382 (1948).
[388] Lezoli v. New York, 9 A.D. 2d 906, 195 N.Y.S. 2d 78 (1959).
[389] Evansville v. Blue, 212 Ind. 130, 8 N.E. 2d 224 (1937).
[390] Carr v. City and County of San Francisco, 170 Cal. App. 2d 48, 338 P. 2d 509 (1959).
[391] Campion v. Chicago Landscape Co., 295 Ill. App. 225, 14 N.E. 2d 879 (1938).
[392] Iacona v. Board of Educ., 285 A.D. 1168, 140 N.Y.S. 2d 539 (1955).
[393] Brown v. Scranton, 313 Pa. 230, 169 A. 435 (1933).

[394] Berner v. Board of Educ., 286 N.Y. 174, 36 N.E. 2d 100 (1941); Ferguson v. Payne, 306 N.Y. 590, 115 N.E. 2d 687 (1952), aff'd. 279 A.D. 968, 111 N.Y.S. 2d 531 (1953).
[395] Barrett v. Phillips, 29 N.C. App. 220, 223 S.E. 2d 918 (1976).
[396] Tashjian v. North Colonie Central School Dist. No. 5, 50 A.D. 2d 691, 375 N.Y.S. 2d 467 (1975).
[397] McGill v. Laurel, 252 Miss. 740, 173 So. 2d 892 (1965).
[398] YMCA of Metro. Atlanta v. Bailey, 107 Ga. App. 417, 130 S.E. 2d 242 (1963).
[399] Brod v. Central School Dist., 386 N.Y.S. 2d 125 (1976).
[400] Kungle v. Austin, 380 S.W. 2d 354 (Mo. 1964).
[401] Ehlinger v. Board of Education, New Hartford, 465 N.Y.S. 2d 378 (1983).

issue whether the teacher's failure to layout the course for a fitness speed test according to the recommendations in the manual was the proximate cause of the student's injury when she crashed into the wall.

Of particular importance is the treatment of supervision as proximate cause. Often the plaintiff alleges lack of supervision as the causal factor; however, the courts are taking a close look and are holding that the lack of supervision must indeed be in fact the cause of the injury.[402] In seven cases the court held that lack of supervision was not the proximate cause and the plaintiff did not recover. The situations included boys playing basketball during Christmas holiday in a gym without supervision (they had been let in by the custodian) and the injury occurred when two boys went for the ball;[403] another basketball situation where two boys went up for a jump-shot and their heads bumped;[404] a six-year-old injured when struck by a sled while waiting in line for his turn to slide in a public playground;[405] a third-grader injured when he pedaled his bike past eight to ten fellow students waiting after school to be picked up on the playground for a meeting and one grabbed him causing him to fall;[406] at noon recess the teacher had gone to answer the phone and an eight-year-old returning from lunch was hit by another who batted a stone;[407] a teacher left the room temporarily and a thrown pencil hit plaintiff in eye;[408] supervision of first grader, youngster caught hand in closing restroom door,[409] and an eighth grader attending a school dance fell from a stair landing.[410] In three other cases, the court held that supervision would have prevented the accident,[411] that there was no negligent supervision and hence lack of supervision was not the proximate cause,[412] and that the length of time the supervisor was absent was insufficient to show such absence or lack of supervision to be the proximate cause of injury.[413] In Texas, plaintiff tried to circumvent Tort Claims Act as related to immunity of teachers by alleging negligent act related to use or operation of school bus, since plaintiff suffered severe convulsions on the bus on way home, although she had been injured earlier in school. No; the court held the injury was not proximate result of use or operation of school bus.[414]

[402] Borushek v. Kincaid, 78 Ill. App. 3d 295, 33 Ill. Dec. 839, 397 N.E. 2d 172 (1979); Brahatcek v. Millard School Dist., 202 Neb. 86, 273 N.W. 2d 680 (1979); Dailey v. Los Angeles Unified School District, 2 Cal. 3d 741, 87 Cal. Rptr. 376, 470 P. 2d 360 (1970); Ely v. Northumberland General Ins. Co., 378 So. 2d 1024 (La. App. 1979); Fagen v. Summers, 498 P. 2d 1227 (Wyo. 1972); Leone v. City of Utica, 66 A.D. 2d 463, 414 N.Y.S. 2d 412 (1979), aff'd. 49 N.Y. 2d 811, 426 N.Y.S. 2d 980, 403 N.E. 2d 964 (1979); Raleigh v. Indp. School District No. 625, 275 N.W. 2d 572 (N.C. 1978); Sharp v. Fairbanks North Start Borough, 569 P. 2d 178 (Alaska 1977); Shields v. Watervliet, 41 A.D. 2d 170, 341 N.Y.S. 2d 699 (1973); Sly v. Board of Education, 213 Kan. 415, 516 P. 2d 895 (1973); Tanari v. School, 69 Ill. 2d 630, 14 Ill. Dec. 874, 373 N.E. 2d 5 (1977); Verhel v. Indp. School Dist., 359 N.W. 2d 579 (Minn. 1984); see also §18.4; Ulm v. Gitz, 286 So. 2d 720 (La. App. 1973).

[403] Albers v. Independent School Dist., 94 Idaho 342, 487 P. 2d 936 (1971).

[404] Kaufman v. New York, 30 Misc. 2d 285, 214 N.Y.S. 2d 767 (1961).

[405] Brady v. Buffalo, 34 A.D. 2d 878, 312 N.Y.S. 2d 446 (1970).

[406] Hill v. Board of Educ., 18 A.D. 2d 953, 237 N.Y.S. 2d 404 (1963).

[407] Wilber v. Binghamton, 271 A.D. 402, 66 N.Y.S. 2d 250 (1946), aff'd. 296 N.Y. 950, 73 N.E. 2d 263 (1947); see also Nichter v. City of Buffalo, 74 A.D. 2d 996, 427 N.Y.S. 2d 101 (1980).

[408] Ohman v. Board of Educ., 300 N.Y. 306, 90 N.E. 2d 474 (1949).

[409] Patterson v. Orleans Parish School Board, 461 So. 2d 386 (La. App. 1984).

[410] Ziegler v. Santa Cruz City H.S. Dist., 168 Cal. App. 2d 277, 335 P. 2d 709 (1959).

[411] Sheehan v. St. Peter's Catholic School, 188 N.Y. 2d 868 (Minn. 1971).

[412] Coates v. Tacoma School Dist., 55 Wash. 2d 392, 347 P. 2d 1093 (1960).

[413] Segerman v. Jones, 256 Md. 109, 259 A. 2d 794 (1969).

[414] Hopkins v. Spring Indp. School Dist., 706 S.W. 2d 325, aff'd. 736 S.W. 2d 617 (Tex. 1987).

Whether or not certain physical conditions were the proximate cause of injury also has been at issue in a number of cases. In one case[415] the condition was that of rocks under playground equipment, and in another[416] concealed weeds at end of playground. A slippery floor in a camp bunk house,[417] failure to maintain a water fountain,[418] and not covering a drain pipe in a pool[419] are other physical conditions raising the question of proximate cause. Determination of proximate cause also involved whether a reservoir was in a dangerous condition[420] and failure to warn regarding the condition of a beach[421] and diving off a pier.[422]

There are many additional cases in which the issue of proximate cause was raised; the foregoing cases are illustrative only.

§ 2.31 Intervening Act

In spite of what has been said previously about the test of probable consequences and foreseeability, the test of foreseeability does seem to apply where a subsequent intervening act causes the injury. It is possible for one to be negligent yet some unforeseeable and independent act might be the direct cause of the injury. In such situations there is no liability as far as the original tortfeasor is concerned.[423] Such was the situation in a 1984 boating case.[424] The Federal Government had rented a boat to some persons, but failed to warn regarding the dam spillway, and the children of the parent plaintiffs were drowned when the boat was swept over the dam. However, the sole proximate cause of the deaths was held to be the intoxication of the operator of the boat, thus "excusing" the negligence of the Government in failing to warn.

To qualify as an intervening or supervening cause which breaks the causal nexus between act of defendant's negligence and resulting injury, cutting off the possible liability for the original negligence, at least three requirements must be met: (1) intervening act must be independent of original act, (2) the act must be adequate in itself to bring about the resultant injury, and (3) it must not have been a reasonably foreseeable event.[425] Intervening is used in a time sense; it refers to later events. An intervening

---

[415] Robbins v. Camp Sussex, Inc., 28 Misc. 2d 16, 216 N.Y.S. 2d 176 (1960), aff'd. 218 N.Y.S. 2d 695 (1961).

[416] Sears v. Springhill, 303 So. 2d 602 (La. App. 1974), writ refused 307 So. 2d 371.

[417] Soares v. Lakeville Baseball Camp, 343 N.E. 2d 840 (Mass. 1976).

[418] Jenkins v. Miami Beach, 389 So. 2d 1195 (Fla. App. 1980).

[419] Brown v. United States, 99 F. Supp. 685 (1951).

[420] Trimblett v. State, 156 N.J. Super. 291, 383 A. 2d 1146 (1977).

[421] Buchanan v. Newport Beach, 50 Cal. App. 3d 221, 123 Cal. Rptr. 338 (1975).

[422] Warner v. Bay St. Louis, 408 F. Supp. 375, motion denied 526 F. 2d 1211 (1975).

[423] Beck v. San Francisco School Dist., 225 Cal. App. 2d 503, 37 Cal. Rptr. 471 (1964); Lemak v. Pittsburgh, 147 Pa. Super 62, 23 A. 2d 354 (1942);

Lottes v. Pessina, 174 S.W. 2d 893 (Mo. App. 1943); Mangum v. Brownlee, 181 Okla. 515, 75 P. 2d 174 (1938); May v. Board of Educ., 269 A.D. 959, 58 N.Y.S. 2d 127 (1945); McLeod v. Grant County School Dist., 42 Wash. 2d 316, 255 P. 2d 360 (1953); Munson v. Board of Educ., 17 A.D. 2d 687, 230 N.Y.S. 2d 919 (1962), aff'd. 13 N.Y. 2d 854, 242 N.Y.S. 2d 492, 192 N.E. 2d 272; Petrich v. New Orleans City Park Improvement Assn., 188 So. 199 (La. App. 1939); Whittaker v. Franklinville, 265 N.Y. 11, 191 N.E. 716 (1934).

[424] Craine v. U.S., 722 F. 2d 1523 (1984).

[425] Marquardt v. Cernocky, 18 Ill. App. 2d 135, 151 N.E. 2d 109 (1958) picnic grounds parking; Minor v. Zidell Trust, 618 P. 2d 392 (Okla. 1980); Sharp v. Fairbanks North Star Borough, 569 P. 2d 178 (Alaska 1977) wrestling tournament, mother took son and friend, auto refueling.

cause is one which comes into active operation in producing the result *after* the act of the defendant.

A 15-year-old boy was waiting for his turn to caddy when the defendant's chauffeur negligently backed over a flag pole which had been taken down and placed across the driveway. When the car hit the pole it caused the pole to strike the plaintiff in the back causing serious injury. It was held that the negligent placing of a flag pole across the driveway was not the proximate cause of the injury; the chauffeur's negligence in backing, an intervening cause, was the proximate cause. The court said that it was not sufficient that the negligence charged furnished the condition by which the injury was made possible, inasmuch as the injury itself was dependent upon the act of a third person.[426]

An intervening act was insufficient cause to negate the original negligent act. The plaintiff was injured when he fell from the bleachers due to being thrown off balance by another person who was trying to regain his own balance after they had both stood up to see at the football game. It was held that the negligence of the defendant, in maintaining an insecure seat plank, was also the cause of the involuntary act of the third person which was the direct cause of the plaintiff's fall.[427]

An unforeseeable act of a third party was held to be the proximate cause.[428] The city exercised reasonable care in employing men to remove bottles, broken glass and litter strewn in the park by the public and the fact that there was litter was not the proximate cause of injury when a small girl was struck in the eye by a broken piece of bottle thrown by a boy.

With therapeutic recreation in mental hospitals, a 1982 Georgia case[429] is pertinent. The plaintiff's father was voluntarily admitted to a private mental hospital and against the general practice was issued an unrestricted weekend pass privilege. While away from the institution, the father confronted his wife and shot her; subsequently he was convicted on two counts of murder. Plaintiffs instituted this wrongful death action on the basis that their father's criminal act was reasonably foreseeable and the death of their mother was proximately caused by defendant's negligence in issuing the weekend pass and failing to exercise proper control over their father's freedom to leave the premises. The court held that the general rule that the intervening criminal act of a third person will insulate a defendant from liability for an original act of negligence does not apply when it is alleged that the defendant had reason to anticipate the criminal act; where one takes charge of a third person who he knows or should know to be likely to cause bodily harm to others if not controlled, there is a duty to exercise reasonable care to control the third person to prevent him from doing such harm.

In *Akins v. Sonoma County*,[430] it was held that failure of parents to supervise a two-year-old whom they had taken to the top row of bleachers while attending a roller derby

[426] Seenbock v. Omaha Country Club, 110 Neb. 794, 195 N.W. 117 (1923).

[427] City of Jackson v. McFadden, 181 Miss. 71, 177 So. 755 (1937).

[428] Clark v. Buffalo, 288 N.Y. 62, 41 N.E. 2d 459 (1942).

[429] Bradley Center v. Wessner, 161 Ga. App. 576, 287 S.E. 2d 716, aff'd. 250 Ga. 199, 296 S.E. 2d 693 (1982).

[430] Akins v. Sonoma County, 60 Cal. Rptr. 499, 430 P. 2d 57 (1967).

exhibition at the fairgrounds was a "superintervening cause" not foreseeable, nor was the type of injury it caused foreseeable. No recovery was given. A parent also was an intervening cause when a child entered a pool area through a hole in the fence and drowned. The court held the mother should have watched to see where her child was.[431] Bat throwing was considered an independent intervening cause of injury when plaintiff acting as catcher was struck in the face by a bat which the batter slung behind her after hitting the ball. It also was held that no amount of supervision could have prevented such accident; hence lack of supervision was not the proximate cause of injury.[432] The cause of injury was an independent, intentional act of the defendent who after school threw a high-jump bar at his sister, who had laughed at him when he missed on a jump. The bar missed her but hit her boyfriend plaintiff in the eye.[433] In another playground case,[434] a seven-year-old was injured when a fellow student threw a small rock which hit a larger rock and rebounded hitting the plaintiff. This was considered by the court as an intervening act of the student; the school had general supervision, which was all that was required. An intervening act by the student was also held to be the proximate cause; a student in the senior play picked up a gun being used as a prop, inserted a live bullet, and fired upon another cast member. The court held that no supervisor could monitor every detail and that the intervening act of a third party was not foreseeable.[435] In a Wisconsin case[436] the teacher was absent from class; however, it was held that the rowdyism and intentional conduct of the student was an intervening cause.

Even though there may be an intervening act, the original negligent person may be liable for damages if the intervening cause is foreseeable; and, if the harm that occurred is within the scope of danger of risk attributable to defendant's negligent conduct, then it is deemed foreseeable. In *Rupp v. Bryant,*[437] the failure of the school board and its agents (especially the club faculty advisor) to implement its policy, particularly failure of adviser to attend Club initiation ceremony, had as its foreseeable consequence the immediate proximate cause, hazing. During the hazing activity the plaintiff sustained injuries which permanently paralyzed him from the neck down. Foreseeability of intervening cause also was an issue when a four-year-old climbed a fence from the play area adjacent to where the mother was sitting at a table, crossed a walkway, and climbed over a second fence to get to the waterway (moat) running around the castle at the amusement park. The defendants alleged that the mother's negligence was an intervening cause which should shield them from liability. Not so, the court said; parent's negligent supervision of their children was foreseeable by the park.[438] As stated in a 1984 Tennessee case,[439] an intervening negligence charge should clearly distinguish

[431] Latimer v. Clovis, 83 N.M. 610, 495 P. 2d 788 (1972).

[432] Brackman v. Adrian, 472 S.W. 2d 735 (Tenn. App. 1971).

[433] Bush v. Smith, 289 N.E. 2d 800 (Ind. 1972).

[434] Fagan v. Summers, 498 P. 2d 1227 (Wyo. 1972).

[435] Ferreira v. Sanchez, 79 N.M. 768, 449 P. 2d 784 (1969); see also D.C. v. Cassidy, 465 A. 2d 395 (D.C. App. 1983).

[436] Cirillo v. Milwaukee, 34 Wis. 2d 705, 150 N.Y. 2d 460 (1967).

[437] Rupp and Bryant, 417 So. 2d 658 (1982), appeal of Bryant v. School Board of Duval Co., 399 So. 2d 417 (Fla. App. 1981).

[438] Walt Disney World Co. v. Goode, 425 So. 2d 1151 (Fla. App. 1982), pet. den. 436 So. 2d 101 (1983) aff'd. 501 So. 2d 622 (Fla. App. 1986).

[439] Abbott v. American Honda Motor Co., 682 S.W. 2d 206 (Tenn. App. 1984) three-wheeler motorcycle; see also Rotz v. City of New York, 532 N.Y.S. 2d 245 (1988) crowd control at park concert.

between a foreseeable intervening act which would not bar defendant's potential liability, and an unforeseeable intervening act which would bar defendants' liability.

In 1986 the New York court[440] stated that a defendant is relieved of liability where, after one's negligence, an unforeseeable superceding force intervenes which breaks the chain of causal connection and itself causes the injury. Further, a plaintiff's own conduct may be a superceding force absolving a negligent defendant from liability. However, in order to be a superceding cause, a plaintiff's negligence must be more than mere contributory negligence, which would be relevant in apportioning culpable conduct. Rather, such conduct, in addition to being foreseeable, must rise to such a level of culpability as to replace the defendant's negligence as the legal cause of the accident. This approach by the New York courts has been applied primarily in situations where plaintiff dived into open and obvious danger, that is, shallow water.

§ 2.32   *Vis major* (act of God)

No liability attaches when the proximate cause is an act of God, a condition caused by the natural elements.[441] Lightning, or a bolt or strike of lightning, occurring in the atmosphere during storms is an act of God. However, appropriate protective action must be taken. The golf club was not negligent in maintaining the weather shelter on the course, which had a gabled roof peaked about 10' above the ground, where the ground elevation 87' away from shelter was higher than the shelter.[442] And, in an Ohio case[443] the court also stated that protective action must be taken; but, in this situation, the park and recreation board failed to install a lightning protection system on a metal-roofed picnic shelter. The shelter had been rented for a family picnic. A thunderstorm approached and as the picnickers were packing apparently lightning struck the metal roof, resulting in the death of one and injuries to some others. Defendants alleged that the lightning was an "act of God" for which they should not be held liable; however, where proper care and diligence would have avoided the act, it is not excusable as an act of God. If the failure to install lightning rods was a concurrent cause of the death and injuries, then the park and recreation board could be held liable.

Wind might seem to be an "act of God"; however, the defendant still was held liable

---

[440] Mesick v. State of New York, 118 A.D. 2d 214, 504 N.Y.S. 2d 279 (1986) plaintiff injured when fell onto jagged rocks due to a slip or trip as tried to grasp a rope to swing out into the water; see also plaintiff's conduct not so culpable as to supersede State's negligence; see also Boltrax v. Joy Day Camp, 113 A.D. 2d 859, 493 N.Y.S. 2d 590 (1985) aff'd. 67 N.Y. 2d 617, 489 N.Y.S. 2d 660, 490 N.E. 2d 527 (1986) pool, plaintiff dived from lifeguard chair into shallow water, plaintiff so careless that defendant absolved of responsibility, such conduct unforeseeable; Howard v. Poseidon Pools, 133 Misc. 2d 43, 506 N.Y.S. 2d 519, motion granted 133 Misc. 2d 50, 506 N.Y.S. 2d 523 (1986) motion denied 133 Misc. 2d 874, 508 N.Y.S. 2d 834 (1986) aff'd./rev'd. in part 522 N.Y.S. 2d 388 (1987) plaintiff dived into shallow above-ground pool; Smith v. Stark and Pal Pools, 111 A.D. 2d 913, 490

N.Y.S. 2d 811 (1985) aff'd. 67 N.Y. 2d 693, 499 N.Y.S. 2d 922, 490 N.E. 2d 841 (1986) plaintiff's dive took place in the shallow end of an inground pool where the plaintiff saw several people standing in the pool; see also comment on these cases in preceding section.

[441] Cleveland v. Walker, 52 Ohio App. 477, 6 Ohio Op. 138, 3 N.E. 2d 990 (1936); Whitcher v. Board of Educ., 233 A.D. 184, 251 N.Y.S. 611 (1931).

[442] Davis v. Country Club, 381 S.W. 2d 308 (Tenn. App. 1963). The concept of climatological immunity is discussed in McGowan v. Borough of Eatontown, 151 N.J. Super. 440, 376 A. 2d 1327 (1977) auto accident caused by ice.

[443] Bier v. City of New Philadelphia, 11 Ohio St. 3d 134, 464 N.E. 2d 147 (1984).

because of negligence which permitted the wind to blow an umbrella away. An umbrella on a lifeguard's stand was not fastened tightly and when it blew down, a rib pierced the temple of a 14-year-old, killing him.[444] In another case,[445] a sudden gust of wind caught an umbrella mounted on a table near a pool, throwing the table into the plaintiff, who was injured. The Club knew of the frequent upset of tables and the injury was foreseeable.

At a children's Halloween parade, a parade watcher was injured by a runaway vehicle when the driver suffered a heart attack. The court said that no one can be held liable for an accident not reasonably foreseeable or prevented by exercise of reasonable care.[446]

§ 2.4 Damage

The fourth element of negligence which must be proven in order to recover is that of damage. In some way the plaintiff must be injured in person and/or property, and the basic remedy is in compensatory monetary damages for such injury. And, common law rules of damage for physical harm hold that justice requires that the plaintiff be restored to pre-injury condition, so far as it is possible to do so with money. Of course, in the very serious physical conditions, such as being a quadriplegic, money is a poor substitute for mobility, but certainly with appropriate handling and motivation, a quadriplegic can lead a most useful and contributing life.

Where the plaintiff proves a compensable injury to his person, recovery may be had for all adverse physical and mental consequences of that injury, although the specific elements of damage for which recovery may be had vary somewhat among the torts and from jurisdiction to jurisdiction. There are four commonly compensable types of harms.[447]

1. **Economic loss**[448] for past and future pecuniary losses and out-of-pocket expenses, including such items as (a) medical expenses — doctor, hospital, nursing, medicines, physical therapy, travel to obtain services, et al.; (b) lost occupational earnings; (c) costs incurred by required substitute hired to do work injured would normally do; and (d) custodial care, if any, required because the injured is partially or wholly incapable of caring for oneself. Because compensation is normally awarded at the time of trial, the lump sum must include both present and future losses. This requires a projection for the estimated lifetime of the injured. Expert testimony is often needed to estimate impaired earning capacity, as well as physical/medical needs. Negligence cases normally recover primarily if not solely economic losses.

2. **Physical pain and suffering** may be compensable, and within broad limits, its valuation is left largely to the jury's discretion.

---

[444] Brewer v. U.S., 108 F. Supp. 889 (1952).

[445] Blue v. St. Clair Country Club, 7 Ill. 2d 359, 131 N.E. 2d 31 (1955); see also Koprowski v. Manatee County, 519 So. 2d 78 (Fla. App. 1988) plaintiff walking on beach struck by wind-blown rescue board which had been propped against lifeguard stand.

[446] Luke v. Anoka, 277 Minn. 1, 151 N.W. 2d 429 (1967).

[447] Cases cited are illustrative only.

[448] Colonial Park Country Club v. Joan of Arc, 746 F. 2d 1425 (1984) N.M. law applied, purely economic loss cannot be covered in products liability case (see §21.1); National Crane Corp. v. Ohio Steel Tube Co., 213 Neb. 782, 332 N.W. 2d 39 (1983).

3. **Emotional distress**[449] is another frequent category of claim in tort cases, although not always compensable in negligence cases. Except as provided in some wrongful death statutes, compensation for this type of loss has not been in favor, although in the decade of the 1980s there has been increased awarding of such damages. Damages may be allowable for harms such as (a) fright and shock; (b) anxiety; (c) loss of peace of mind and happiness; (d) humiliation and embarrassment caused by the injury, such as disfigurement and disability; (e) distress from loss of ability to enjoy a normal life; and (f) inconvenience caused by injury. Emotional distress, resultant from physical injury, should be distinguished from infliction of emotional distress, the act, as in harassment and intentional infliction as discipline.[450]

4. **Physical impairment** may be compensated by a base compensation on the physical impairment itself in lieu of compensation for emotional distress. This would cover both temporary and permanent impairments, as well as partial or total impairment; for example, eyesight, hearing, or use of an extremity.

§ 2.41 Punitive and exemplary damages

Punitive damages may be assessed to punish the wrongdoer on the premise that perhaps such monetary civil fine will deter others from similar conduct in the future. Sometimes such damages are referred to as exemplary or vindictive damages. Punitive damages are of common law origin and generally are not recoverable as a matter of right, but only in the discretion of the jury.[451] The right to recover varies state to state,

---

[449] Battalla v. State, 26 A.D. 2d 203, 272 N.Y.S. 2d 28 (1966) ski chair; Cunningham v. Lockard, 736 P.2d 305 (Wash. App. 1987) parents crossing road to go to soccer game struck by car, claim of minor children's emotional distress not upheld as children were not present at incident; Delta Farms Reclamation Dist. v. Sup. Ct. of Co. San Joaquin, 125 Cal. App. 3d 662, 178 Cal. Rptr. 401 (1982) 33 Cal. 3d 699, 190 Cal. Rptr. 494, 660 P. 2d 1168 (1983) emotional stress witnessing drowning; Fazzolari v. Portland School Dist., 78 Or. App. 608, 717 P. 2d 1210 (1986) pet. allowed 301 Or. 338, 722 P. 2d 737 (1986), aff'd. 303 Or. 1, 734 P. 2d 1326 (1987) assault and rape on school grounds; Garfield v. U.S., 297 F. Supp. 891 (1969); Goodwin v. Reilley, 176 Cal. App. 3d 86, 221 Cal. Rptr. 374 (1985) intoxicated motorcyclist not liable for emotional distress of parent whose son was injured because not percipient witnesses to accident; Landreth v. Reed, 570 S.W. 2d 486 (Tex. Civ. App. 1978) also witnessing of drowning, parents awarded $25,000, 14-month-old infant plaintiff received $30,000, annotated in 10 *Texas L. Rv.* 1167 (1979); McGraw v. Orleans Parish School, 519 So. 2d 847 (La. App. 1988) seven-year-old girl abducted from school grounds on way to physical education class and sexually molested; Wells v. Colorado College, 478 F. 2d 158 (1973) court held award not excessive in view that could not enjoy normal life, judo case; Williams v. U.S., 660 F. Supp. 699 (1987) Ark. law applied, father award $100,000 mental grief when

16-year-old son drowned at air force base swimming pool when on base for R.O.T.C. leadership program.

[450] Jackson v. City of Wooster, Board of Education, 29 Ohio App. 3d 210, 504 N.E. 2d 1144 (1985) eighth grade physical education class discipline; Sitomer v. Half Hollow Hills Central School Dist., 133 A.D. 2d 748, 520 N.Y.S. 2d 37 (1987) school physician said student not physiologically mature enough to try out for tennis team; Strachan v. John F. Kennedy Memorial Hospital, 209 N.J. Super. 300, 507 A. 2d 718 (1986) stated that infliction of emotional distress is not tort, but rather item of damages which must be related proximately to breach of duty, held that $35,000 to each of suicide victim's parents were well outside outer limit fixed as emotional distress damages recoverable by bystanders; Tilton v. Franklin, 24 Mass. App. 110, 506 N.E. 2d 897 (1987) rev. denied 509 N.E. 2d 1202 (1987) reckless infliction of emotional distress barred by tort claim act because not specifically waived (see though §4.2), student editor of high school yearbook falsely accused of fraud related to advertising.

[451] Chuy v. Phila. Eagles Football Club, 431 F. Supp. 254 (1977) held that assessment of punitive damages on emotional stress claim proper; Leichtamer v. Amer. Motors Corp., 67 Ohio St. 2d 456, 424 N.E. 2d 568 (1981) jeep at off-road recreation facility — must be sufficient evidence of malice before question of punitive damages will be submitted to jury; Rawlings Sporting Goods, Inc. v. Daniels, 619 S.W. 2d 435

and about one-half of the states with tort claims acts make reference thereto, with about two-fifths of the states specifically not permitting punitive damages. A few states do permit such damages, but limit the amount[452] (see §4.243). Some states restrict punitive damages to certain types of actions, such as products liability, and to when there are elements of fraud, malice, gross negligence or oppression.[453]

In order to justify an award of punitive damages, the tortfeasor must have acted from a wrongful motive, or at least with gross or knowing indifference to the rights and safety of another. It is this element of intent that usually prevents recovery in negligence cases, since negligence is based on unintentional wrongs. Usually even gross negligence is not enough on which to recover; ordinarily must be reckless or willful and wanton misconduct. With a finding of gross negligence, the plaintiffs were awarded exemplary damages when the mast of their sailboat hit a 7200-volt power line which was too low.[454] Interestingly, in two 1980 Minnesota cases,[455] it was held that although exemplary damages were statutorily prohibited, no similar prohibition existed with respect to liability of municipal employees and officers. It also appears that in some states there is an attempt to circumvent the maximum damages imposed by statute by interpreting the statute to mean compensatory, not exemplary or punitive. There is question as to whether certain punitive damages are insurable; however, the Iowa court[456] held that the insurance company had to pay punitive damages under the insurance policy (false arrest).

§ 2.42   Amount of damages recoverable

Generally the awarded damages are figured at present value, although there may be an inflation figure included. Usually compensatory damages are tax exempt. This enumeration of losses and damages from the largest award at that time (1974) gives illustration of how the dollar amount is determined.[457]

(Tex. Civ. App. 1981) football helmet — gross negligence entitled to award exemplary damages; Truelove v. Wilson, 159 Ga. App. 906, 285 S.E. 2d 556 (1981) held that punitive damages not available in wrongful death action; Wussow v. Commercial Mechanism, Inc., 90 Wis. 2d 136, 279 N.W. 2d 503 (1979), rev'd. 97 Wis. 2d 136, 293 N.W. 2d 897 (1980) pitching machine — conduct of manufacturer and its purchaser was deemed outrageous and warranted punitive damages.

[452] Smith, Joel E. Recovery of Exemplary or Punitive Damages from Municipal Corporation. 1 ALR 4th 448-474.

[453] For example, Gorman v. Saf-T-Mate, Inc., 513 F. Supp. 1028 (1981) motorboat, breach of warranty,

Indiana law applied; Ehrhardt v. Brunswick, Inc., 186 Cal. App. 3d 734, 231 Cal. Rptr. 60 (1986) motorboat used for waterskiing, products liability, punitive damages not recovered.

[454] Pedernales Elec. Co-op v. Schulz, 583 S.W. 2d 882 (Tex. Civ. App. 1979).

[455] Paradise v. Minneapolis, 297 N.W. 2d 152 (Minn. 1980); Wilson v. Eagan, 297 N.W. 2d 146 (Minn. 1980).

[456] Cedar Rapids v. Northwest Insurance Co., 304 N.W. 2d 228 (Iowa 1981).

[457] Niles v. City of San Rafael, 42 Cal. App. 3d 230, 116 Cal. Rptr. 733 (1974).

Lost earnings	$ 503,570
Past medical expenses	86,240
Future medical expenses	196,902
Cost of medical supplies & equipment	41,637
Medical emergency fund	50,000
Tutoring and instruction	242,643
Attendant care	1,299,637
Total economic loss	$2,420,629
General damages	1,604,371
Total awarded	$4,025,000

Each item of future expense was supported through use of expert testimony documenting the boy's life expectancy, the current cost of the various services adjusted by estimates of future inflation and utilizing U.S. Department of Labor studies, commercial investment studies, Federal Reserve System studies, and statistics from the U.S. Savings and Loan League. Plaintiff was a high school football player who became a quadriplegic.

The excessiveness of damages was discussed in *Hooks v. Washington Sheraton Corp.*[458] Eighteen-year-old plaintiff was rendered a quadriplegic when he dived from a three-meter diving board, which was equipped with a high performance board that propelled him into shallow water where he struck his head on the bottom. The jury awarded $6 million to plaintiff and $1 million to his parents. Life earnings, taxes, and costs of maintenance were considered. Award was reduced to $4.5 million to plaintiff and $180,000 to parents. And, in another pool case,[459] an award of $1,250,000 was deemed "beyond range of reasonable compensation" and reduced to $1,000,000.

With multi-million dollar cases, has sport become too costly to have? — this question has been responded to by the states through their tort claims acts. At least 35 states have placed maximums on awards against governmental agencies and their employees (see §4.243). The Constitutionality of this limitation in the face of the due process and equal protection clauses of the Constitution has been before the courts.[460] The tendency is to hold that the right to recover against a governmental entity is a privilege, rather than a right, and a "rational basis test" was applied defining the risk exposure of the governmental entity.

[458] Hooks v. Washington Sheraton Corp., 578 F. 2d 313 (1977); Kirk v. Washington State Univ., 109 Wash. 2d 448, 746 P.2d 285 (1987) permanent injury to elbow of cheerleader, $353,791 held "not so excessive as to shock conscience of court"; Murray v. Ramada Inns, Inc., 821 F. 2d 272 certified to La. Sup. Ct., 521 So. 2d 1123 (La. 1988) 843 F. 2d 831 (1988) swimmer diving into shallow water of pool, held $250,000 excessive, reduced to $25,000.

[459] Gaston v. Aquaslide 'N' Dive Corp., 487 F. Supp. 16 (1980) pool slide.

[460] Cargill v. Rochester, 119 N.H. 661, 406 A. 2d 704 (1979).

Except in governmental agency situations where the statute waives immunity to the extent of insurance carried (see §4.2), the amount of insurance carried does not act as the maximum amount which can be recovered on a judgment. If a judgment is for $1.5 million and insurance covers only $1 million, the balance must be forthcoming from other sources. Insurance pays only for the amount insured. The court can award damages in any amount appropriate.

For further discussion of damages, see Chapter 25 on insurance, §5.23 comparative negligence and §4.24 insurance and risk management under Tort Claims Acts.

§ 2.43 Apportionment of damages[461]

The defendant is not relieved of liability merely because others also are responsible for the same harm. In fact, to the contrary, an individual may be held for the total damages although others also were at fault. This is referred to as **joint and several liability**. If more than one person (entity) is a party defendant and found liable, the court does not limit the injured party's recovery against each of them to a proportionate share of fault. The injured party can recover the entire judgment from either one or all of them at its option. This can lead to what may seem like an unfair result. For example, in *Walt Disney World Co.* v. *Wood*, 489 So. 2d 61 (Fla. App. 1986) aff'd. 515 So. 2d 198 (Fla. 1987), Walt Disney World was ordered to pay 86% of the damages to a patron, even though it was found to be only 1% to blame for the accident. Plaintiff was found to be 14% at fault. The court said that viability of the doctrine of joint and several liability was a matter to be decided by the legislature. Joint and several liability is not modified under comparative negligence statutes;[462] however, a number of states in their tort reforms of the mid to late 1980s have modified joint and several liability so that the defendants are liable only for their proportionate share as a tortfeasor (see §4.26). The apportionment is between the plaintiff and tortfeasors. However, the plaintiff is entitled to but one compensation for the loss. There cannot be unjust enrichment. When the judgment has been paid in full, it is referred to as satisfaction of the judgment, and the plaintiff cannot recover further from any of the tortfeasors, regardless of how much each of them paid toward the judgment.

---

[461] Some additional illustrative cases: Aalco Manufacturing Company v. City of Espanola, 615 P. 2d 993 (N.M. App. 1980), rev'd. 95 N.M. 66, 618 P. 2d 1230 (1980) volleyball net standards, manufacturer and sporting goods store; Carr v. Karkow Rodeos, 610 F. Supp. 25 (1985), vacated with direction 788 F. 2d 485 (1986) South Dakota law applied, bareback bronco rodeo rider, settled out of court with several defendants, distinguished pro rata and pro tanto; Contino v. Lucille Roberts Health Spa, 125 A.D. 2d 437, 509 N.Y.S. 2d 369 (1986) aerobic dance, chiropractor's advice; Harper v. Liggett racquetball racquet; McCormick v. Maplehurst Winter Sports, Ltd., 166 Ill. App. 3d 93, 116 Ill. Dec. 577, 519 N.E. 2d 469 (1988) snow tubing; Ogg v. City of Springfield, 121 Ill. App. 3d 25, 76 Ill. Dec. 531, 458 N.E. 2d 1331 (1984) sailboat collision with power line; Thurston Metals and Supply Co., Inc. v. Taylor, 230 Va. 475, 339 S.E. 2d 538 (1986) golfer lost eye, hit by another golfer's backswing. See also §5.23 Comparative negligence; apportionment of damages is determined by the jury.

[462] *E.g.*, by statute see Florida, Idaho, Michigan, Montana, Nevada, New Jersey, North Dakota, Ohio, Oregon, Pennsylvania, Texas, Utah, Wyoming; by case interpretation Arkansas, California, Colorado, Connecticut, Minnesota, Oklahoma, Washington, Wisconsin. Some states have passed the Uniform Contribution Among Tortfeasors Act, *e.g.*, Hawaii. American Motorcycle Ass'n v. Superior Court, 146 Cal. Rptr. 182, 20 Cal. 3d 578, P. 2d 899 (1978) discusses quite detailed joint and several tortfeasors as related to comparative negligence.

There is also frequently settlement out-of-court. Boys ages 8 and 11, were playing basketball as part of the school recreation program when the city fire truck came to put out a dumpster fire on the school playground. The kids ran to the truck, climbed all over the ladder truck, were ordered off, but then got back on. When they tried to jump off, as the truck turned into the street, they fell under the truck and were seriously injured when the wheels ran over them. Prior to the trial, the plaintiffs (boys and guardians) settled with the defendant city. However, the court found the school board 75% negligent and the city 25% negligent. Also, the court held that all plaintiffs but one were barred from recovery, since the amounts they had already received in settlement from the city exceeded the damages awarded them by the jury. The award which was over the amount allocated by the jury was reduced in accordance with the jury's ascertainment of damages. Since the city paid the pre-trial settlement, it could seek contribution from the defendant school board.[463]

One of the defendants may come under a Tort Claims Act with a maximum amount specified. Such was the situation in *Trinity River Authority v. Williams*, a 1983 Texas case.[464] Decedent was drowned below the restricted area of a dam when his boat was caught and sunk in back currents. It was held that the City was a "joint operator" of the dam project with the River Authority. The River Authority came under the State Tort Claims Act and had a limit of damages of $100,000; however, the City's function in supplying water was considered a proprietary function not protected by the Tort Claims Act, and hence, the City had no maximum on damages which could be levied. The City and River Authority were held jointly and severally liable for $500,000 to decedent's wife, with the River Authority paying only its limit of $100,000 and the City $400,000.

A release by the plaintiff should be distinguished from satisfaction. Whereas satisfaction is receipt of full compensation for the injury, a release is actually a surrender of the cause of action, which may be done on a gratuitous basis or for an inadequate or partial consideration for injury received. There are some differences in the laws of the states as to whether a release of one or more tortfeasors is in fact a release against all for that cause of action.[465] In *Lincoln v. Gupta,* 142 Mich. App. 615, 370 N.W.2d 312 (1985), involving whose duty it was to obtain an informed consent, the hospital or the physician, the opinion set forth these principles under Michigan law: "Release of one of several joint tortfeasors does not release other joint tortfeasors unless terms of release so provide; however, where master or principal's liability is based solely on doctrine of respondeat superior, master or principal and servant or agent are technically not joint tortfeasors." It was held that the physician had the duty to obtain the informed consent, and that the physician and hospital were not joint tortfeasors. Further, "… there is distinction between convenant not to sue and release of liability. Covenant not to sue agent does not release principal from liability."

With the "joint and several" rule, it is entirely possible that one tortfeasor might have paid the total judgment, or that the various tortfeasors paid a disproportionate amount.

[463] Law v. Newark Board of Education, 175 N.J. Super. 26, 417 A. 2d 560 (1980).
[464] Trinity River Authority v. Williams, 659 S.W. 2d 714 (Tex. App. 1983).

[465] Cash v. Street & Trail, Inc., 136 Ga. App. 462, 221 S.E. 2d 640 (1975); Lee v. State of Alaska, 490 P. 2d 1206 (Ala. 1971).

What is the right of one tortfeasor against another? The early common law was that there was no right of contribution; but, at the beginning of the 1980s, most states have enacted statutes which now provide for **contribution among joint tortfeasors** in equitable, not necessarily equal, portions. To gain such contribution, one tortfeasor would have to sue another, in a separate action. In a case[466] involving an accident with a golf cart, the golf pro sought contribution from the county, which owned and operated the golf course. It was held that while the right of contribution does arise at time of concurring independent acts, nevertheless until one of the joint tortfeasors pays more than one's proportionate share of the underlying claim, the right remains contingent and inchoate, and it is not until the tortfeasor pays more than one's proportionate share that the right ripens into the cause of action and any statutory time limits begin to run. And, in a New Jersey case,[467] defendant county park commission had right to implead and seek contribution from borough under the joint tortfeasor contribution law. Plaintiff had dived into a water area near a falls, which area ownership had been indicated by tax assessor to plaintiff as the county, when it was in fact the borough which owned it. Judgment was entered by the trial court against three defendants (the city, manufacturer of volleyball net standards, and sporting goods store which sold standard to city) jointly and severally liable, assessing one-half of judgment against city and one-half against sporting goods store and manufacturer. The appellate court reapportioned damages, requiring manufacturer to pay two-thirds and city one-third; then, the supreme court reversed the appellate court and reinstated the trial court division for payment of the judgment.[468]

In another case[469] the court held that where there is a pending action, a contribution claim should be asserted by counterclaim or by a third-party claim in that action, and where such claim was not asserted, the joint tortfeasor did not have standing to appeal dismissal of other joint tortfeasors pursuant to pre-trial settlement. In this situation a high school student was permanently paralyzed by injury suffered while she was somersaulting on a minitrampoline during physical education class. Plaintiff brought suit against the school district, high school, and manufacturer. Prior to trial the school district and high school entered into a $1.6 million settlement. The jury awarded plaintiff $5 million, but the $1.6 million was offset, leaving an award of $3.4 million for the manufacturer to pay. Now, after judgment had been rendered, the manufacturer could not appeal dismissal of the district and school.

The owner and operator of boat against whom the judgment was made brought suit

[466] Albert v. Dietz, 283 F. Supp. 854 (Hawaii 1968). See also Law v. Newark Board of Education, 175 N.J. Super. 26, 417 A. 2d 560 (1980) see text for footnote 463; Home Insurance Co. v. Advanced Machine Co., 443 So. 2d 165 (Fla. App. 1983) insurer, which settled for distributor of malfunctioning electric pitching machine, brought contribution action against remaining codefendants city, original manufacturer and its successor corp., $1.1M settlement, contribution claimant must prove that contribution defendant is jointly negligent, as well as fact that settlement amount was not in excess of what is reasonable; Almli v. Santora, 154 Mich. App. 60, 397 N.W.2d 216 (1986)

defendant motorist, landowners, and county board of road commissioners counter-claimed plaintiff parents of child injured while sliding down snow-covered hill for contribution based on negligent supervision of parents, court barred such contribution.
[467] Dambro v. Union Co. Park Comm., 130 N.J. Super. 450, 327 A. 2d 446 (1974).
[468] Aalco Mfg. Co. v. City of Espanola, 615 P. 2d 993 (N.M. App. 1980), rev'd. 95 N.M. 66, 618 P. 2d 1230 (1980); second case, same situation Sanchez v. City of Espanola, 94 N.M. 676, 615 P. 2d 993 (1980).
[469] Pell v. Victor J. Andrew H.S., 123 Ill. App. 3d 423, 78 Ill. Dec. 739, 462 N.E. 2d 858 (1984).

against two companions of plaintiff for contribution; court held that the companions' negligence was so slight that owner and operator were not entitled to contribution from them. A tortfeasor liable for the injuries sustained by another is not entitled to contribution from a party whose conduct has been adjudged less negligent than that of the injured party.[470]

Contribution should be distinguished from indemnification. Contribution distributes the loss among the tortfeasors by requiring each to pay a proportionate share, while indemnification[471] shifts the entire loss from one tortfeasor who has been compelled to pay it to another who should bear it instead. In *AMF, Inc.* v. *Victor J. Andrew High School*, 172 Ill. App. 3d 337, 122 Ill. Dec. 325, 526 N.E. 2d 584 (1988), a mini-trampoline manufacturer sued the high school, seeking indemnification. The court distinguished indemnification and contribution, thusly: "Whereas contribution involves sharing of payment of damage awards by those whose combined actions brought about common injury, indemnity provides for complete shifting of liability upon a showing of pretort relationship between guilty parties and qualitative distinction between their conduct; indemnification claim may be filed in pending action by third-party complaint or as separate action after original action is over and judgment has been entered against party or party has settled claim made against him." A good number of the Tort Claims Acts (see §4.2) authorize indemnification of employees by the governmental entity, that is, if a judgment is against an employee, the corporate entity would "indemnify" or pay the judgment. Some statutes refer to "hold harmless" the employee, e.g., New Jersey requires a school corporate entity to "hold harmless" teachers. One also may contract to indemnify another and this is frequently done when one's facilities or areas are used by another agency or when an independent contractor is used to perform certain responsibilities.

The county superintendents of schools for four counties entered into a written agreement for the formation of a joint science and conservation education program. A student was seriously injured and brought action against the superintendents. The superintendents joined in a stipulation for settlement ($1.2M) of the action, but then raised claims for contribution or indemnity aganst each other. The court held that the contract to conduct the program was appropriate and held the four counties equally liable, and also jointly and severally liable. Since the present case was against only two of the school superintendents, the court said that these two defendants would have to sue the other two schools to establish participation and the right of contribution. The agreement did not contain any language of indemnification (see §4.43 and §25.21).[472]

There are many ramifications regarding the apportionment of damages; the foregoing sets forth only some of the basic concepts.[473]

---

[470] Horton by Horton v. Orbeth, 342 N.W. 2d 112 (Minn. 1984).

[471] See also §§16.3 and 25.21; Bjorklund v. Hantz, 296 Minn. 298, 208 N.W. 2d 722 (1973) snowmobile.

[472] Ross v. Campbell Union School Dist., 70 Cal. App. 3d 113, 138 Cal. Rptr. 557 (1977).

[473] For further information see legal periodicals; see also *Keeton* at 322-355.

Chapter 3.   Who is Liable?
— The Doctrine of Respondeat Superior

The first concern of any person injured is "Who can I sue?" and of the sponsoring agency and its personnel, "Am I liable?" In the decade of the '80s, everyone associated in any way with the incident of injury seemed to be not only subject to suit but also actually sued, whereas before the '70s, the "deep pocket," the corporate entity, an impersonalized entity, primarily was sued. All "persons" from the corporate entity, the administrator or supervisor, the program and service personnel, to the volunteer and student trainee are joined in suit for the court to determine just who is liable and to what extent. In *Lovitt v. Concord School District*[1] the school district, superintendent of schools, principal and coaches were joined in suit; while in another football case,[2] the school district, athletic trainer, and three coaches were sued. And, it was the athletic director, football coach, athletic trainer, helmet manufacturer, and the helmet seller who were sued in a college defective helmet 1982 case.[3] The county school board, the athletic director, and the baseball coach/buildings and grounds supervisor were sued in a 1979

---

[1] Lovitt v. Concord School District, 58 Mich. App. 593, 228 N.W. 2d 479 (1975).

[2] Garza v. Edinburg Consol. Indept. School Dist., 576 S.W. 2d 916 (Tex. Civ. App. 1979).

[3] Hemphill v. Sayers, 552 F. Supp. 685 (1982) applying Illinois law.

Virginia suit.[4] And, after a student was forbidden to participate in state track meet, a dozen different organizations and persons were sued, ranging from the Governor to the High School Athletic Association to the track coach.[5] In a golf injury case, the county, who owned the golf course, the Recreation Board, who operated the course, the voluntary association of golf course users, and the golf pro and course manager were all sued.[6] Those sued in a situation where a seven-year-old drowned in a river located in a public park included the two boys playing with the deceased at the time and their parents, the city owning the park, and five employees of the city (foreman of the park, city forester, assistant superintendent of parks, director of recreation, and director of parks and recreation).[7] In another water-related (pond) case,[8] the city, the summer program director, the swimming program supervisor, and the lifeguards were all sued when a guest was injured in a diving accident in a private lake, plaintiff brought suit against more than 200 defendants, including three neighborhood associations and individual subdivision lot owners.[9]

Whether a public or semi-public agency, a charitable organization, a private-not-for-profit corporation, or commercial-for-profit business enterprise, the doctrine of respondeat superior applies. The doctrine states that the *negligence of the employee is imputed to the corporate entity if employee was acting within scope of responsibility and authority, and if not a willful and wanton act to injure another.* Under the doctrine the "superior" or corporate entity must respond or be accountable for the actions of its employees. If those who are internal to the agency (administrators/supervisors, employees, or volunteers/trainees) act in a negligent way, then their negligence is imputed to the corporate entity, as well as being individually liable for their wrong doing. At the same time, the corollary also is true; that is, if the employee is found not negligent, then the corporate entity could not be held liable,[10] unless there was a separate, personal negligence.[11] The members of a board of directors of an organization generally are immune for their discretionary acts, that is, their policy and planning decisions, but may be held liable for fiscal mismanagement and noncompliance with human rights requirements. The members of a membership organization, which is incorporated, generally are not held liable as individuals.

The imputing of negligence to "the superior" is not a line staff relationship. The liabilities incurred by the negligent act of an employee will not necessarily be imputed to the administrator or supervisor. The line of responsibility for negligent acts is depicted in Figure 3.1.

[4] Short v. Griffitts, 220 Va. 53, 255 S.E. 2d 479 (1979).

[5] Makanui v. Dept. of Educ., 721 P. 2d 165 (Hawaii App. 1986).

[6] Jopes v. Salt Lake County, 9 Utah 2d 297, 343 P. 2d 728 (1959).

[7] Boucher v. Fuhlbruck, 26 Conn. Sup. 79, 213 A. 2d 455 (1965).

[8] Sanders v. City of Ansonia, 33 Conn. Sup. 195, 369 A. 2d 1129 (1976).

[9] Yahrling v. Belle Lake Assoc., 145 Mich. App.

620, 378 N.W. 2d 772 (1985) rev'd. 429 Mich. 66, 412 N.W. 2d 213 (1987).

[10] Benton v. School Board of Broward Co., 386 So. 2d 831 (Fla. App. 1980); Dobbins v. Board of Educ. of Henry Hudson Regional High School, 133 N.J. Super. 13, 335 A. 2d 58 (1974), aff'd. 67 N.J. 69, 335 A. 2d 23 (1975); Lincoln v. Gupta, 142 Mich. App. 615, 370 N.W. 2d 312 (1985).

[11] Shelton v. Planet Insur. Co., 280 So. 2d 380 (La. App. 1973).

Figure 3.1   Line of Responsibility for Negligent Acts under Doctrine of Respondeat Superior

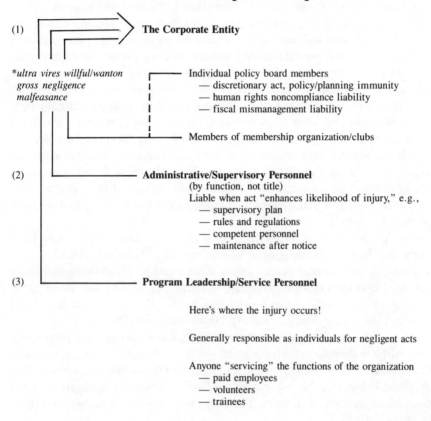

(1)   The Corporate Entity

*ultra vires willful/wanton
gross negligence
malfeasance*

Individual policy board members
— discretionary act, policy/planning immunity
— human rights noncompliance liability
— fiscal mismanagement liability

Members of membership organization/clubs

(2)   **Administrative/Supervisory Personnel**
(by function, not title)
Liable when act "enhances likelihood of injury," e.g.,
— supervisory plan
— rules and regulations
— competent personnel
— maintenance after notice

(3)   **Program Leadership/Service Personnel**

Here's where the injury occurs!

Generally responsible as individuals for negligent acts

Anyone "servicing" the functions of the organization
— paid employees
— volunteers
— trainees

these acts break the line of corporate responsiblity for acts of its employees; see §§2.21, 2.24, 2.41, and 3.411.

There are three basic levels at which responsibility rests:
(1)   the corporate entity (school board, municipal council, recreation or park board or commission, owner, board of directors of a corporation, et al.) and the policy board members as individuals (see §3.2); members of membership organization (see §3.14)
(2)   administrative officials and supervisors (superintendents of schools or parks and recreation, principals, facility general managers, head athletic trainers, community center and fitness directors, head lifeguards, pool and golf course managers, athletic directors, camp director, trip leader, head counselor, et al.); see §3.3 and
(3)   individuals engaged in direct leadership (teachers, coaches, athletic trainers, recreation leaders, camp counselors, lifeguards, et al.) or services (grounds keepers, maintenance staff, athletic equipment "managers," locker room

attendants, vehicle drivers, concessionnaires, camp kitchen staff, et al.); and, also included are sports officials. These persons may be paid employees (see §3.4), volunteers (see §3.5), or trainees (see §3.6), and they may be part- or full-time, seasonal or year-round.

There are different roles and responsibilities incumbent upon the persons at each of these three basic levels and, thus, different liabilities. The court in deciding a case must make a determination regarding the specific liabilities. For example, in *Berg v. Merricks*[12] action was brought against the physical education instructor, principal, superintendent, county, school board, and individual members of the board for injury to a student in a trampoline accident. The court had to consider each separately and found that the instructor was not negligent in the manner in which he supervised the physical education class or instructed the students to perform; that the high school principal was not negligent in view of the fact that the physical education department was a responsibility of the county supervisor of physical education; that the superintendent was not immune from suit, but was not negligent; and that the county and board of education were immune from suit.

This chapter deals with the nature of the liability of these persons on each of the three levels. There are, however, some general determinants of "Who is Liable?"

1.   The first element of negligence, a duty owed, must be present (see §2.1). The person(s) who owes this duty is liable. The nature of the duty may differ on the administrative/supervisory and employee levels. The duty owed is a direct responsibility to the injured plaintiff, establishing liability.

2.   Once the fact that a duty is owed is established, then not only is the person who must perform the duty to the participant with the standard required, individually liable, but also those persons or entities employing the individuals who owed the duty are liable, that is, whomever the "superior" is, in application of the doctrine of respondeat superior. The duty owed is imputed to the "superior," bringing liability.

3.   The next determinant is whether or not there is some common law doctrine or statutory limitation which negates or abridges the responsibility (duty). Do the doctrines of governmental/sovereign immunity or charitable immunity apply? (See §§4.1, 4.3.) Or, is there a limited liability law related to the nature of the act (see §4.5), such as use of private lands (see §12.1) or rendering emergency care (see §17.1)? If yes, and the person or entity being sued can qualify coming under such doctrines or statutes, then the duty owed is abrogated, resulting in no liability. The liability as related to persons other than those internal to the sponsoring organization (the "superior") is discussed in various sections and chapters, such as private landowners §12.1; spectators, passers-by, and sport officials Chapter 15; and lessor/lessee relationships and independent contractors in this chapter §§3.11 and 3.12, respectively.

In the legal field various terms are used relating to liability of a corporate entity. The doctrine of respondeat superior also is known as vicarious liability, that is, a corporate entity is vicariously liable under the doctrine of respondeat superior. Vicarious liability

---

[12] Berg v. Merricks, 20 Md.App. 666, 318 A. 2d 220 (1974), cert. denied 272 Md. 737 (1974).

imposes liability for a tortious act upon a person or entity who was not personally negligent, but is held liable because of the relationship of the person or entity with the individual who committed the negligent act. Vicarious liablity describes the existence of a relationship, not a cause of action.[13] The most typical relationships which give rise to liability are employer-employee, master-servant, and principal-agent. The foregoing paragraphs illustrate the employer-employee relationship. Under the master-servant relationship, a "servant" is one who is in the employ of another and subject to that person's control. When the California legislature amended a statute removing the term "agent" and substituting the term "servant," the court[14] explained, thus:

> For purposes of the Restatement Second of Agency, the terms "employee" and "servant" are synonyms and refer to those agents whose acts give rise to respondeat superior liability of their employer or principal; agents who are outside of that master-servant relationship are independent contractors.

> Effect of amendment removing the term "agent" and substituting the term "servant"…was to remove the possible inference that agents or independent contractors might be within the ambit of vicarious liability.

While historically the common law has referenced the master-servant relationship, as related to governmental entities, the State Tort Claim Acts (see §4.2) use the term employer-employee. The California court[15] pointed this out in elaborating upon its earlier distinction; and, in addition, stated that "servant" is more restrictive than "agent" and that "in the eyes of the community" one does not like to refer to a person as a servant when the individual is a part of the employer's working staff. For this reason, in this book, relationships are referred to as employer-employee, not master-servant. As in most Tort Claim Acts, the term employee encompasses those paid and those who serve without pay.

There also is some confusion regarding the principal-agent dichotomy and vicarious liability and the doctrine of respondeat superior. A 1985 Texas case[16] stated that "an agency relationship must exist in order for party to be held liable under respondeat superior." The Indiana court[17] in 1987 discussed both master-servant and principal-agent relationships and used agent in the more common parlance of agency law:

---

[13] Kerry v. Turnage, 154 Mich. App. 275, 397 N.W. 2d 543 (1986) high school athletic booster club held agent and school vicariously liable for serving liquor to a visibly intoxicated person who later killed plaintiff's decedent.

[14] Swearingen v. Fall River Joint Unified School Dist., 166 Cal. App. 3d 335, 212 Cal. Rptr. 400 (1985) 215 Cal. Rptr. 854, 701 P. 2d 1172 (1985) 40 Cal. 3d 445, 220 Cal. Rptr. 627, 709 P. 2d 430 (1985) auto accident, student riding with host family off-campus basketball game.

[15] Townsend v. State of Calif., 191 Cal. App. 3d 1530, 237 Cal. Rptr. 146 (1987) university basketball player who struck another player held to be neither a servant nor an employee.

[16] Pierson v. Houston Indp. School Dist., 698 S.W. 2d 377 (Tex. App. 1985) explosion on homecoming float, no agency relationship between state FFA and local sponsors.

[17] Swanson v. Wabash College, 504 N.E. 2d 327 (Ind. App. 1987) recreational baseball practice in city park; see also Ginn v. Renaldo, Inc., 183 Ga. App. 618, 359 S.E. 2d 390 (1987) unidentified patron, who slammed door on hand of plaintiff, not agent of club; Hanson v. Kynast, 24 Ohio St. 3d 171, 494 N.E. 2d 1091 (1986) aff'd. 38 Ohio App. 3d 58, 526 N.E. 2d 327 (1987) lacrosse player who injured another player not agent of university; McGarr v. Boy Scouts of America, 74 Md. App. 127, 536 A. 2d 728 (Md. App. 1988) 11-year-old scout fell over precipice, status of scoutmaster at issue; Souza v. Narragansett Council, B.S.A., 488 A. 2d 713 (R.I. 1985) scout boxing match, scoutmaster held not an agent or employee of council.

Agency is a relationship resulting from manifestation of consent by one party to another that the latter will act as an agent for the former, and agent must acquiesce to arrangement and be subject to principal's control.

Apparent agency is initiated by manifestation of principal; however, necessary manifestation is one made by principal to third party who in turn is instilled with reasonable belief that another individual is agent of principal, and it is essential that there be some form of communication, direct or indirect, by principal, which instills a reasonable belief in mind of third party. Statements or manifestations made by agent are not sufficient to create an apparent agency relationship.

...

Test for determining a master-servant relationship, for purposes of doctrine of respondeat superior, is whether one has right to direct and control conduct of alleged servant at time of incident.

(quoting a previous Indiana decision) The general rule of liability that presupposes authorization of the acts of the agent in order to bind the principal applies to a principal's contractual or nontort liability. The tort liability of the principal expressed in the doctrine of respondeat superior is based not upon the agency relationship (authorization or ratification) but upon the employer-employee relationship. Thus, the touchstone for the principal's liability for the tortious acts of his agent is merely whether they are done within the course and scope of employment.

...

The test for determining a master-servant relationship is whether one has the right to direct and control the conduct of the alleged servant at the time of the incident. The primary consideration in an employment setting is whether there was an intent that a contract of employment, express or implied, did exist. In other words, there must be a mutual belief that an employer-employee relationship did exist.

In general, the term "agent" is used in this book as related to the law of agency, and not synonymously for employee. However, one must be cognizant of how the term is used in their own state jurisdiction, and in reporting cases, the terminology in the opinion is used.

One also must distinguish between agent and independent contractor, for the entity for which a person is an agent is liable for the acts of the agent, whereas there would not be liability for the acts of an independent contractor, except under certain circumstances (see §3.12). In a situation where plaintiff's injury occurred while on a tour to the South Pacific, plaintiff sought damages from the tour planner/seller on the basis that the cruise company was an agent of the tour planner/seller; but, the court held that the cruise company was an independent contractor, for whose negligence the tour planner/seller was not liable.[18]

§ 3.1   The corporate entity

Under the doctrine of respondeat superior, the corporate entity is responsible for the negligent acts of those who represent it in the conduct of activities which it sponsors or facilities and areas which it maintains. The negligence is imputed to the corporate entity. In *Gorsuch v. Springfield*, 43 Ohio L. Abs.83, 61 N.E. 2d 898 (1945) the park superintendent negligently attempted to relight the pilot light of a gas heater in the golf course clubhouse. The city was held liable for such negligence. A school district was held liable when at an annual play-day a student was injured when a defective blanket was used for blanket tossing, declared to be an unsafe game. The board's argument that it should not be held liable because it had hired competent teachers and supervisors was to no avail; the doctrine of respondeat superior applied.[19] And, a passer-by was struck on the head by a ball thrown out of the ball park by a player, who had dropped a pop fly and the winning run scored. The court held that the team sponsor was responsible, saying that the player was an agent of the sponsor and had acted in the scope of his employment.[20] Similarly, a spectator was struck by a basketball thrown toward the spectators by a member of the defendant's basketball team. Held the player was acting in the course of his employment.[21] However, in amateur sport, the result usually is the opposite; that is, the player who may have injured another player does not hold the status of employee or agent, and so the corporate entity is not liable. For example, in a lacrosse game, a player was held not an agent of the university (*Hanson v. Kynast,* 24 Ohio St. 3d 171, 494 N.E.2d 1091 (1986) aff'd 38 Ohio App. 3d 58, 526 N.E.2d 327 (1987)), and in a basketball game, the player who injured another player was held not an employee or "servant" within the Tort Claims Act (*Townsend v. State of California,* 191 Cal. App. 3d 1530, 327 Cal. Rptr. 146 (1987)). Throughout the various chapters the principle of the doctrine of respondeat superior is well illustrated as most cases are based upon it.

If negligence is imputed from the employee to the corporate entity, then the reverse should be true, also — that there can be no corporate negligence if the employee is not negligent. Action was brought against the physical education teacher and school board on behalf of a student injured when she slipped on loose gravel while running during gym class on macadam driveway of the school parking lot. The court held that where the teacher was free of negligence, no negligence could be imputed to the school board.[22] In order for the negligence of the employee to be imputed to the corporate entity, the employee must be acting within scope of duty. An act outside the scope of authority or responsibility is referred to as an *ultra vires* act, and may be used as a defense. The city was not liable when the foreman without authorization removed from a playground a slide and placed it temporarily on some private property. The city did not authorize use of equipment or area as public playground. There was to be no liability, as mere ownership cannot establish liability.[23] However, if an employee is acting outside the

[18] Lavine v. General Mills, Inc., 519 F. Supp. 332 (1981).

[19] Rook v. State (two cases), 254 A.D. 67, 4 N.Y.S. 2d 116 (1938).

[20] Bonetti v. Double Play Tavern, 126 Cal. App. 2d 848, 274 P. 2d 751 (1954).

[21] McFatridge v. Harlem Globe Trotters, 69 N.M. 271, 365 P. 2d 918 (1961).

[22] Dobbins v. Board of Education, 133 N.J. Super. 13, 335 A. 2d 58 (1974).

[23] Vecchio v. Pittsburgh, 114 Pa. Super. 326, 173 A. 468 (1934).

scope of responsibility, but the corporate entity had "notice" or knew about these *ultra vires* acts, then the corporate entity is deemed to have condoned or given tacit approval to the acts, and the negligence is imputed to the corporate entity. Where a lifeguard struck a child in throwing a horseshoe, but the Board had notice of his acts (he had been throwing horseshoes for two weeks), the doctrine of respondeat superior applied.[24] In addition, if the employee willfully and wantonly injures a person, the corporate entity is not liable for this intentional misconduct. For further discussion of both willful and wanton conduct and *ultra vires acts*, see §§3.4 and 5.13.

More than one employee may have committed a tortious act or negligence in fulfilling the duties owed the injured person, and while one employee is not liable for the acts of another employee, the corporate entity is liable for each and all. As indicated in the introduction to this chapter, the plaintiff may sue each of the persons individually, as well as the corporate entity. In only limited situations will a corporate entity seek to recover from an employee (see §3.43). However, where there are joint tortfeasors, that is, more than one wrongdoer, most states provide for Contribution of Joint Tortfeasors. These laws are usually used when the joint tortfeasors are corporate entities and not all corporate entities are sued, so that those who are not sued do not pay their "fair share"[25] — so, the corporate entity which the court ordered to pay by virtue of finding negligence brings action against those who were not used for their pro rata share. Similarly, if there were a number of individuals who contributed toward the injury (negligent), but some were not included in the suit, those who were held negligent and had to pay can sue those who were joint tortfeasors for their pro rata share.[26]

Where governmental agencies are involved, whether municipalities, school districts, or state agencies, in those jurisdictions which do adhere to the doctrine of governmental or sovereign immunity,[27] the doctrine of *respondeat superior* does not apply. Becoming more common, however, especially under State Tort Claim Acts, is a modification wherein the doctrine of *respondeat superior* does apply to ministerial acts with resultant liability of the corporate entity, but it does not apply to discretionary acts

[24] Rafsky v. New York City, 257 A.D. 855, 12 N.Y.S. 2d 560 (1939).

[25] This is known as "joint and several" liability, meaning that the plaintiff may sue one or all and recover the full amount, and similarly, a corporate entity or person who is negligent can be held liable for the full amount of damages although others also may have been negligent. This is one of the aspects of liability always considered for possible tort reform, and as of the late 1980s about one-half of the states have modified their laws to allow recovery only for the pro rata share (see §4.2).

[26] e.g., Aalco Mfg. Co. v. City of Espanolo, 615 P. 2d 993 (N.M. App. 1980) rev'd. 95 N.M. 66, 618 P. 2d 1230 (1980) volleyball standards products liability; Carr v. Karkow Rodeos, 610 F. Supp. 25 (1985) vacated with direction 788 F. 2d 485 (1986) bare bronco rodeo riding, pro tanto v. pro rata share; Contino v. Lucille Roberts Health Spa, 125 A.D. 2d 437, 509 N.Y.S. 2d 369 (1986) aerobic dance, chiropractor's advice; Harper v. Liggett Group, 459 So. 2d 1260 (La. App. 1984)

cert. denied 462 So. 2d 655 (La. 1985) imported racquetball racquet, products liability; McCormick v. Maplehurst Winter Sports, Ltd., 166 Ill. App. 3d 93, 116 Ill. Dec. 577, 519 N.E. 2d 469 (1988) snow tubing, hit by tow rope; Ogg v. City of Springfield, 121 Ill. App. 3d 25, 76 Ill. Dec. 531, 458 N.E. 2d 1331 (1984) sailboat hit electric power line; Thurston Metals & Supply Co., Inc. v. Taylor, 230 Va. 475, 339 S.E. 2d 538 (1986) golfer struck by club swung by another golfer; Walt Disney World v. Goode, 425 So. 2d 1151 (Fla. App. 1982) pet. for rev. denied 436 So. 2d 101 (1983) aff'd. 501 So. 2d 622 (Fla. App. 1986) child drowned in moat at amusement park.

[27] Graff v. Board of Educ., 258 A.D. 813, 15 N.Y.S. 2d 941 (1939); Harris v. Des Moines, 202 Iowa 53, 209 N.W. 454 (1926); Katterchinsky v. Board of Educ., 215 A.D. 695, 212 N.Y.S. 424 (1925); Mocha v. Cedar Rapids, 204 Iowa 51, 214 N.W. 587 (1927); Smith v. Hefner, 235 N.C.1, 68 S.E. 2d 783 (1952).

and immunity is retained.[28] Included in the next chapter's discussion of the doctrines of governmental and sovereign immunity is the relationship of employee torts to governmental liability.

§ 3.11   Lessor/lessee relationships

It is very common practice in sport, parks and recreation either to permit others to use one's facilities and areas or to utilize the facilities and areas of others. Such usage may be a part of the services and available without charge just by signing up; or, there may be a formal lease agreement with a number of specifications regarding responsibilities of the lessee and lessor. Whatever the arrangement or agreement, the principles of law are the same, and these are discussed by use of case illustrations in this section. There are two basic questions. First, was the injury premise-related or activity-related? If the injury is premise-related, the owner or lessor of the premise usually remains liable for unsafe premises, as well as the entity conducting the activity, unless the contract has specified lessee responsibility for that particular aspect of the premises which gave rise to the injury. Second, if the injury was activity-related, did the owner retain any control over the activity or the use of the premises? Even though the owner of the premise is not directly conducting the activity, if such owner retains any control whatsoever over the activity or use, usually there is a relationship established between participant and lessor, and liability is retained for the negligent conduct of the activity. That is, for the lessor to be liable to the injured, there must be a special relationship of the lessor/property owner to the injured which gives rise to a duty not to expose to an unreasonable risk (see §2.1). This principle was established early in *Brown v. Cleveland Baseball Co.,* 158 Ohio St. 1, 106 N.E.2d 632 (1952), a situation where the temporary bleachers collapsed at a professional football game held in a park owned by the defendants but leased to the football club, when the court said:

> One having neither occupation nor control of premises ordinarily has no legal duty to invitee of another with respect to condition or use of those premises. In order to have the occupation or control of premises necessary to impose such legal duty with respect to the condition or use of those premises, one must ordinarily have the power and the right to admit such individuals to the premises or to exclude them from the premises. Where a lessor has not substantially relinquished to his lessee all occupation of and control over a portion of the leased premises and where such lessor has actually exercised his right of occupation of or control over such portion, such lessor is under the duty to exercise ordinary care with respect to the condition of such portion and that duty extends to invitees of the lessee. In such an instance, the duty with respect to the condition of such portion of the premises, owed by the lessor to an invitee of the lessee, is the same duty which any occupier of premises would owe to his own invitees.

---

[28] Boucher v. Fuhlbruck, 26 Conn.Sup. 79, 213 A. 2d 455 (1965).

In a 1987 Colorado case,[29] a fraternity member sustained an injury on a trampoline resulting in quadriplegia. The fraternity-owned trampoline was kept on the front yard of the fraternity which rented the house from the university. The court held that the relationship between university and fraternity, arising from fraternity's renting house from university, and university's actions pursuant to its rights under lease, provided no basis of dependence by fraternity members upon which special relationship could be found to exist between university and the student that would give rise to duty on part of university to protect student from injuries sustained while jumping on trampoline at fraternity. In another 1987 case,[30] a student was stabbed while attending a high school football game, and his parents sued the school board which had rented the stadium to the high school, a private parochial school. Under the lease, the school board assumed no duty under contract to provide security for event. The court held that "as a general rule, lessor's liability to third party, other than lessee, who is injured on premises must be based on negligence, and not on strict liability. . . . Defendant is liable to plaintiff in negligence, only if he has breached some duty owing to plaintiff." (See also, §14.25 Concessionnaires and Marinas; §§16.134 and 16.3 for indemnification and exculpatory provisions in lease agreements for both equipment rental and facility use).

In a situation of after-school "shooting baskets" sponsored by the city on a school facility, the court held that where the school board's only connection with the incident was that it owned the building, and no defect in the premises was suggested, it was not liable for plaintiff's injuries. Plaintiff alleged that the injuries were due to inadequate supervision.[31] A similar result was reached in a much earlier case,[32] when the plaintiff was injured in an after-school tumbling class held by the city in the school gymnasium. Again, the injury was not caused by a defect in the premises, but alleged due to the negligence of the instructor.

A minor was injured when she was struck by a thrown baseball while attending a high school baseball game. Among the defendants sued were the borough, which leased the baseball field from an electric company, and the lessor electric company. The electric company did not charge for use of the field and was held to come under protection of the recreational user statute (see §17.1). As for the borough, and also the school district of the visiting team and the township in which the field was located, there was no liability, absent showing that these defendants were in possession of the field within meaning of the State Tort Claims Act.[33] In another case[34] the city leased its park to the Soft Ball Association, an independent organization not under the control or supervision of the city. Even though the city reserved the right to use the field at certain times, the court held that the city did not owe a duty to the plaintiff who was injured when playing softball, because it did not invite him to play, the Association did. In a third ball game case,[35] the plaintiff was injured when struck by a baseball in play by the

29 University of Denver v. Whitlock, 712 P. 2d 1072 (Colo. App. 1985) rev'd. 744 P. 2d 54 (Colo. 1987).

30 St. Pierre v. Lombard, 512 So. 2d 1206 (La. App. 1987).

31 Morris v. Jersey City, 179 N.J. Super. 460, 432 A. 2d 553 (1981).

32 Walter v. Everett School Dist., 195 Wash. 45, 79 P. 2d 689 (1938).

33 Lowman v. Indiana Area School Dist., 96 Pa. Cmwlth. 389, 507 A. 2d 1270 (1986).

34 Whealen v. St. Louis Soft Ball Assn., 356 Mo. 622, 202 S.W. 2d 891 (1947).

35 Pollan v. Dothan, 243 Ala.99, 8 So. 2d 813 (1942).

team leasing the stadium. It was held that the city did not owe a duty to invitees entering the stadium, unless the injury was caused by the city's negligence. It was further held that the negligence of the person in possession and control of the premises at the time of injury, rather than the owner or right of possession thereof, is the basis of liability in such situations. A similar decision resulted in holding the lessee liable when it failed to warn a 23-year-old boy, a business invitee, about the condition of the pool (depth and a device for diving).[36] In another pool case,[37] an 11-year-old boy was drowned when he went with his 4-H group to the pool operated by the city. Except for providing two lifeguards, as requested, the city had no other involvement in the conduct of the swimming activity. It was held that the city owed only reasonable care in the safety of the pool. In a Connecticut case,[38] the city leased all swimming pool facilities to two individuals; the city retained the right to inspect the premises and furnished all equipment. The lessees merely operated the facilities. The city was held liable. In 1988 case, *Thorson v. Mandrell*, 402 Mass. 744, 525 N.E.2d 375 (1988), illustrates some common issues. A theater company had subleased an auditorium from the YWCA, and during rehearsals, one of the performers was injured when she did a dance maneuver backflip on hardwood floor, resulting in permanent paralysis. The YWCA had a policy of no gymnastics within the auditorium and no performance of gymnastics unsupervised by a trained gymnast. The business manager who approved the lease tried to get an idea of what the users of the auditorium would be doing, but had not linked theater to gymnastics. Plaintiff alleged that the YWCA violated its duty owed to her by failing to enforce its policy against gymnastics in the auditorium and failing to inquire into the renter's qualifications, and thus subjected her to an unreasonable risk of harm. Not so, the court held; the YWCA did not undertake to render service or assume a duty for the protection of its users by adopting the policy, nor was it negligent in failing to investigate competence of director of theater company and staff where there was no evidence which would have put the YWCA on notice of any of the staff's inadequacies. Further, the conditions which caused injury were not created by the YWCA (owner of auditorium), but by the director and those participating in the dance maneuver; and, even if the YWCA knew that gymnastic-like dance maneuvers would be involved in the rehearsal of the musical comedy and that its own policy against gymnastics maneuvers would be applicable, it had no duty to warn of dangers inherent in attempting the maneuvers, since the dangers were obvious.

The sponsor of the activity may be responsible for the condition of the premises, as well as the activity, for a duty is owed to participants/spectators to protect from harm, and this includes environmental conditions. As is often the situation, in a 1984 case,[39] the school had put down plastic strips on the gymnasium floor to protect the hardwood surface during a wrestling exhibition. The 3' wide strips were placed around the wrestling ring; and, "little strips of masking tape" were used to hold the heavy plastic

[36] Fort Worth v. Barlow, 313 S.W. 2d 906 (Tex. Civ. App. 1958).

[37] Hecht v. Des Moines Playground and Recreation Assn., 227 Iowa 81, 287 N.W. 259 (1939).

[38] Carta v. Norwalk, 108 Conn. 697, 145 Atl. 158 (1929); see also Novak v. Delavan, 31 Wis. 2d 200, 143 N.W. 2d 6 (1966); additional cases regarding premise-related v. activity-related injuries are described in §§19.23 and 20.2.

[39] Begin v. Georgia Championship Wrestling, Inc., 172 Ga. App. 293, 322 S.E. 2d 737 (1984).

strips together, instead of running the tape on the joint, closing it totally. Plaintiff's foot got in between two seams and she fell; she was wearing low heeled shoes with rubber soles. She suffered a ruptured disc in her spine, necessitating an operation. Plaintiff sued the promoter of the exhibition, rather than the school. The court stated that an occupier of the premises is under duty to inspect premises to discover possible dangerous conditions of which one does know and to take reasonable precautions to protect invitee from dangers which are foreseeable from arrangement and use of premises. The premises do not have to be continuously patrolled to discover defects; a "reasonable" time is allowed to exercise care, but liability can be based upon actual or constructive notice of defects.[40] On the other hand, an invitee must exercise ordinary care for one's own safety.

A school or municipality as lessor of either a building facility or an area, including any equipment, under most circumstances is liable for maintaining the premises in a safe condition.[41] Jury awarded nearly $150,000 (reduced to $20,000 statutory maximum for charitable organizations) to plaintiff when motion picture screen fell on her. She was a part of a family reunion and Christmas party for which the religious organization had made the school available without charge.[42] In *Harllee v. Gulfport*, 120 F. 2d 41 (1941), the city granted permission to a city softball league to play games at night at the city playground and use the bleachers. The city was held liable for failure to maintain the bleachers in safe condition. In an Arizona case,[43] a school had leased its stadium to another school district for a high school football game. The lessor school was held liable when a railing around the grandstand (known to be in disrepair) broke and a patron was injured. In *Guymon v. Finicum*, 265 P. 2d 706 (Okla. 1953), the grandstand at a ball park on city property had been constructed by a private person. However, the town ball team did not have authorization to use the land or place the bleachers thereon. Nevertheless, the court held that there was some "deal" between the city and the ball club which was in the furtherance of public interest in that the property was being used for the amusement and entertainment of the public. The court held that the city owed a duty to maintain parks, including grandstands owned and erected thereon by third parties and used in public interest, in a reasonably safe condition for intended use.

In an Iowa case,[44] the school leased certain playgrounds to the city via a written agreement. A child was injured on a merry-go-round when he stuck his finger into the open area caused by a missing center cover plate and had it badly mangled. The court held that the city had notice of this condition (missing center cover plate), and as lessee (tenant) it stood as qualified owner and occupier, and thus took the demised premises as it found them. Recovery was for plaintiff.

[40] Schimenti v. Nansen Properties, Inc. 20 A.D. 2d 653, 246 N.Y.S. 2d 273 (1964) also holds notice with reasonable time to repair needed for liability.
[41] Barrett v. Lake Ontario Beach Imp. Co., 174 N.Y. 310, 66 N.E. 968 (1903) a legal principle of long standing!, lessor of public toboggan slide, which was defective, who fails to furnish proper protection to persons using it, is liable; Gibson v. Shelby Co. Fair Assoc., 44 N.W. 2d 363 (Iowa 1950) barriers on county fair grounds constructed for harness horse racing and

unsuitable for hot rod auto racing, thus races thereon were inherently dangerous to spectators.
[42] Mason v. Southern New England Conf. Ass'n of Seventh-Day Adventists, 696 F. 2d 135 (1982).
[43] Sawaya v. Tucson High School Dist. No. 1, 78 Ariz. 389, 281 P. 2d 105 (1955).
[44] Fetters v. Des Moines, 260 Iowa 490, 149 N.W. 2d 815 (1967).

In the *Boyer* case[45] the Association had leased a facility, wherein they had exclusive control and management of the bleachers for the state basketball tournament. Plaintiff was injured when the bleachers collapsed. As tenant of the property, the Association was presumptively regarded as owner for the time-being and subject to all the responsibilities of one in possession to one who enters by invitation. Further, the fact of exclusive control, together with the fact that bleachers do not ordinarily collapse, sustained the imposition of liability on *res ipsa loquitur* theory.[46]

The nature of the control by the lessor was also in issue where the city leased the arena for hockey, but retained a substantial measure of use and control over the corridors even while the lessee was using them. Upon proof of negligence, the city would be liable.[47] An earlier case[48] held that the municipality had a right to lease to the Odd Fellows the third floor of a school house and retain control of the rest of the premises; however, it was stated that common passageways must be kept reasonably safe. In a 1987 case[49] the court held that the City created the Stadium Authority and gave it title and possession, as well as the obligation for care and maintenance; the City and the Authority were two separate entities and the City was not held liable when spectators at a baseball game were injured by errant fireworks.

The obligation to maintain safe premises extends only to those areas which are leased and to which the individual is invited. A golf course club house was leased to a group of dancers of which the injured plaintiff was a member. After the dance, the plaintiff went around the building to a darkened area (seeking the dark with his date) and fell into a basement stairway. There was held to be no liability.[50] A school had leased its auditorium to a dance school for a "dance revue." About half-way through the program, a nine-year-old and his ten-year-old cousin went to get a drink at the water fountain in the lobby. From there they could see into the gymnasium, which was adjacent to the lobby and the lights were on. Looking in they saw several boys playing on the gymnastic rings. The ten-year-old recognized one of the boys and went into the gym to talk with him. The nine-year-old, by standing on a chair provided by one of the youths, grabbed onto the rings. The other boys pulled him back by the feet and let him go. As he was swinging forward, the rings came to an abrupt halt, causing him to fall to the floor and injure himself. It was school policy that the rings be tied up to keep the students from playing on them. The court held that the risk of harm which was posed by the set of gymnastic rings in an unlocked and unsupervised gymnasium, accessible to nine-year-old child, who attended a dance recital with his parents in adjacent auditorium and who strayed from auditorium into gymnasium, was not an unreasonable risk when rings were considered in context of their normal use and, not being within scope of school board's

---

[45] Boyer v. Iowa H.S. Athletic Assoc., 138 N.W.2d 914 (Iowa 1965), aff'd. 260 Iowa 1061, 152 N.W. 2d 293 (1967).

[46] Responsibility of the owner for the condition of bleachers and grandstands is upheld in most jurisdications, and is a long standing legal concept; e.g., Folkman v. Lauer, 244 Pa. 605, 91 A. 218 (1914) baseball park grandstand; Lusk v. Peck, 132 A.D. 426, 116 N.Y.S. 1051 (1909), aff'd. 199 N.Y. 546, 93 N.E. 377 (1910) football bleachers; Tulsa Entertainment Co.

v. Greenlees, 205 P. 179 (Okla. 1922); see also §15.131 Bleachers.

[47] Aaser v. Charlotte, 265 N.C. 494, 144 S.E. 2d 610 (1965).

[48] Douglas v. Hollis, 86 N.H. 578, 172 A. 433 (1934).

[49] Costello v. Pittsburgh Athletic Co., 652 F. Supp. 1579 (1987).

[50] Cox v Des Moines, 235 Iowa 178, 16 N.W. 2d 234 (1944).

duty to remedy an otherwise unreasonably dangerous condition, was not a basis for imposing liability upon school board for injuries sustained. Court further stated that failure to lock doors on gymnasium may have been a cause-in-fact of accident, but such was not basis for imposing liability without a further determination as to what duty was imposed on school board related thereto.[51]

In an Oregon situation, the fairgrounds arena had been leased for an "Indian powwow" by the school. Plaintiff was injured by horses boarded on adjacent fairgrounds. The Court held that the county, owner of the fairgrounds, had a responsibility to take reasonable steps to insure the safety of those coming within areas under one's control; and, that the school had no obligation to control horses found elsewhere on the fairgrounds.[52] Landlord-tenant relationship was also the subject of the *Hughes* case.[53] The Orthopedic Guild conducted an annual style show in the high school. Plaintiff was injured while performing duties in the kitchen when she slipped and fell due to a recessed area. The court held that the lessee takes the premises as one finds them. There was no faulty design or construction, and the lessee knew of the recessed area. Further, the landlord owes no greater duty to a third person than to the tenant. In another case[54] the Thalian Association had rented a theater from the city. After the performance, while lights still dimmed, a patron walked forward and fell into the depressed orchestra pit. The court held there was no inherent danger in construction of a pit; and since the city had relinquished control of premises, plaintiff did not recover.

Where the city leased land to a private corporation for holding a festival and the festival corporation built bleachers, although the city inspected the bleachers, the city was not liable when the bleachers collapsed. The inspection duty was held a governmental function and the city as lessor of the premises received no compensation or had an express contract for the use of the land.[55] However, a different result was reached when the city permitted the Chamber of Commerce to operate a carnival in the city park under a plan whereby the city shared in the proceeds which went for improvement of park facilities. The plaintiff, a paying patron, was injured on a "ride" found to be defective. The negligence of those actually operating the device was imputed to the city.[56] On another mechanical ride device,[57] also found defective, the city was found liable as lessor. The lessor retained considerable control over the activities of the amusement park through the board of directors. The lease had a non-liability clause in that the fair association was to protect and save harmless the city from loss, cost or expense arising or accruing on account of any real or asserted damage or injury to person or property, which was negated by the retention of control. One cannot retain

[51] Dunne v. Orleans Parish School Board, 444 So. 2d 1317 (La. App. 1984), review granted 447 So. 2d 1074 (1984), rev'd. 463 So. 2d 1267 (La. 1985).

[52] Baker v. State Board of Higher Educ., 20 Or. App. 277, 531 P. 2d 716 (1975).

[53] Hughes v. Chehalis School Dist., 61 Wash. 2d 222, 377 P. 2d 642 (1963).

[54] Toothe v. Wilmnington, 8 N.C. App. 171, 174 S.E. 2d 286 (1970).

[55] Tyler v. Ingram, 139 Tex. 600, 164 S.W. 2d 516 (1942).

[56] Scroggins v. Harlingen, 131 Tex. 237, 112 S.W. 2d 1035 (1938).

[57] Davis v. Atlanta, 84 Ga. App. 572, 66 S.E. 2d 188 (1951). However, when property was leased for an amusement park, lessor was found not liable in Fraley v. Lake Winnepesaukah, 631 F. Supp. 160 (1986) and Grant v. City of Duluth, 526 F. Supp. 15 (1981) rev'd 672 F. 2d 677 (1982), applying Georgia and Minnesota law, respectively.

control of an operation and contract away its obligation to exercise reasonable care for the safety of those participating in the activity.

Control also was a factor in where the city leased part of a lake bank in a public park to a private person, who kept a number of his own rowboats for boating and fishing upon the lake. An 11-year-old boy drowned when a dilapidated boat sank. It was alleged that the city reserved the right to control the lake and boating by virtue of an ordinance; however, the ordinance did not authorize the city agents to take action with respect to the boats, their protection or moorings, or set up any standards whatsoever. No liability was held.[58] The plaintiff was injured while sitting in his campsite at the city's campground when a horse on which there was an inexperienced rider ran him down. The campground was operated by a concessionnaire, and both the city and the concession-naire knew horses frequented the site and of the danger, but did not take steps to avoid the danger. Although the concessionnaire had an agreement for indemnification of the city, the court held that the city itself was negligent.[59]

Exclusiveness of control was argued in a California case.[60] The District had leased the reservoir to the county as a recreational facility where water skiing took place, however, the District specified that no use shall interfere with the operation of the dam and that the raising and lowering of the water was the exclusive domain of the District. Thus, the county knew neither when nor how much the water would be raised or lowered. Although the lease had a clause holding harmless the District and indemnify-ing it against any injury to persons or property, the court held that one cannot contract away liability to third persons for one's own active negligence. The court held that the District retained control of the water level and knew or should have known that lowering the water created a dangerous condition of which water skiers were entitled to be warned, or at least to which the county should have been warned. The lessor in *Ward v. U.S.*,[61] also, was not absolved of liability in another aquatic situation involving provision of a lifeguard and retention of control.

The law varies slightly when a natural area is leased. Plaintiff was injured when he dived into a creek in national forest, which was on land under special use permit to California county. He sued the federal government. The court applied California law and held that under California rule that lessor of land is generally not subject to liability to lessee or others coming on to land with consent of lessee for physical harm caused by any dangerous condition which comes into existence after lessee has taken possession.[62] For situations involving natural areas, see Chapters 12, 13, 14 and especially §12.1 as relates to recreational user statutes.

The nonperformance of a duty established by the contract also can bring liability. For example, in a Missouri situation the private pool operator and not the county recreation supervisors were liable for failure to provide proper rescue equipment;[63] and, in an

[58] White v. Centralia, 8 Ill. App. 2d 483, 131 N.E. 2d 825 (1956).

[59] Zimmerman v. Baca, 346 F. Supp. 172 (1972).

[60] Larson v. Santa Clara Valley Water Conservation Dist., 218 Cal. App. 2d 515, 32 Cal. Rptr. 875 (1963).

[61] Ward v. U.S., 208 F. Supp. 118 (1962).

[62] Chidester v. U.S., 646 F. Supp. 189 (1986).

[63] Schulte v. Graff, 481 S.W. 2d 596 (Mo. App. 1972); see also for another equatic non-performance case, Baroco v. Araserv, Inc., 621 F. 2d 189 (1980), rehearing denied 627 F. 2d 239 (1980).

Illinois case[64] the team and not the league had agreed to protect the crowd. In a park maintenance situation, the state as lessor was immune from suit, but the judgment went against the lessee.[65] But, in a 1985 Louisiana case,[66] the court held that the leasing of the school auditorium was an educational purpose, not recreational, and therefore the limited liability of landowners for recreational purposes was not available to the school. However, when the recreational user statutes are applicable, the lessee is considered same as owner and has limited liability.[67] The doctrine of governmental immunity does not appear to be affected by leasing. Under most Tort Claim Acts there is liability for dangerous conditions.[68]

In a very early case,[69] the court held that the owner cannot avoid liability where it is foreseen that the lessee will continue to put the premises to a use that has been determined to be a nuisance. In this situation, the nuisance was an improperly guarded shooting gallery which had a path near the park grounds.

Even though a formal lease may have expired, a lessee may continue to be liable. In a 1987 Indiana case,[70] the city entered into a written lease with a private developer for a park area. During the time of lease the city generally maintained the park and installed a ball diamond during the period of the written lease. The injured plaintiff was a softball player who had gone to the field with his team and was warming up outside the first base line. In attempting to catch a fly ball he turned and backpedaled the last few steps. As he backpedaled he tripped over a manhole cover which was approximately 19′ from the ball field and 9″ above ground level. The manhole which caused the accident was part of a sewer system originally built as part of the private development; the sewer was dedicated to the city long before the accident. The court awarded damages to the plaintiff in holding that the city remained a tenant-at-will under deemed renewal of lease for a year because it continued to maintain and use the park after expiration of the written lease. Lease, which is renewed when tenant holds over past term of lease, contains same terms and is subject to same conditions as original lease.

The difference between a "lease" and a "license" was addressed in a case[71] involving a landowner. A motocyclist drove off the "blind sheer end" of a pile of dirt. The landowner was temporarily stockpiling the dirt for another, and therefore the use of property for this purpose was a license, not a lease. A lease gives exclusive possession of premises against others, while a license confers a privilege to occupy under the

[64] Riley v. Chicago Cougars Hockey Club, 100 Ill. App. 3d 664, 56 Ill. Dec. 210, 427 N.E. 2d 290 (1981).

[65] Thomas v. Jeane & State of Louisiana, 411 So. 2d 744 (La. App. 1982).

[66] Dunne v. Orleans Parish School Board, 444 So. 2d 1317 (La. App. 1984), review granted 447 So. 2d 1074 (1984), rev'd. 463 So. 2d 1267 (1985).

[67] Abdin v. Fischer, 374 So. 2d 1379 (Fla. 1979); see for further discussion §12.112.

[68] Atlanta v. Garner, 192 S.E. 841 (Ga. App. 1937); Granat v. Mayor et al. Savannah 200 S.E. 311 (Ga. App. 1938); Plemmons v. Gastonia, 62 N.C. App. 470, 302 S.E. 2d 905 (1983), cert. den. 309 N.C. 322, 307 S.E. 2d 165 (1983); see §4.2 on governmental/sovereign immunity.

[69] Larson v. Calder's Park Co., 180 P. 599 (Utah 1919).

[70] City of Bloomington v. Kuruzovich, 517 N.E. 2d 408 (Ind. App. 1987).

[71] O'Shea v. Claude C. Wood Co., 97 Cal. App. 3d 903, 159 Cal. Rptr. 125 (1979). See also Rotz v. City of New York, 532 N.Y.S. 2d 245 (1988) plaintiff trampled by crowd at concert in park, producer of concert had permit agreement with city Dept. of Parks and Recreation, which provided that producer responsible for all arrangements, including security with civil commotion and riot specified.

owner. The use of lease arrangements in this perspective relates to recreational use of landowner's property primarily (see §12.1). In a 1972 case,[72] a girl drowned in a body of water on a nine-hole par-3 golf course which had previously been a public park. The defendant had a leasehold interest in the golf course and had constructed the body of water. Although the agreement referred to a "license," the court held that in fact the right was that of leaseholder because of the exclusiveness of possession. However, no negligence was found, hence no recovery.

§ 3.12 Independent contractor relationships

Independent contractors include individuals, companies, and concessionnaires. Whereas the general rule has been that liability can be shifted when an independent contractor is employed to perform a particular task, the employer must exercise reasonable care to select a competent, experienced, and careful contractor with proper equipment and appropriate safety precautions to protect employees and the public invited. There has been a continuing erosion of the general rule of non-liability.[73] The rationale for non-liability has been that since the employer has no right of control over the manner in which the work is to be done by the independent contractor that the employer should not be held liable for the negligent acts of the independent contractor. However, the employer remains the primary beneficiary of the work and is the one who selects the independent contractor, is financially responsible, and can demand indemnity from the independent contractor. Thus, the courts are holding the employer liable in certain situations, primarily: (1) negligence of the employer related to the work being done, such as proper selection of contractor, reasonable inspection of the work after completed, if on employer's own land to prevent activities or conditions which are dangerous to those outside of it or who enter as invitees; (2) non-delegable duties, such as keeping premises reasonably safe for business invitees and to provide employees with a safe place to work; (3) "inherently dangerous" activities, sometimes referred to as "peculiar risk," such as construction of reservoirs, use or keeping of vicious animals, the exhibition of fireworks, wherein injurious consequences can be expected unless special efforts are made to protect; but not liable for "collateral" negligence, or negligence in the operative details of the work and easily controlled by the contractor. Only limited illustrative cases are described in this section.

A plaintiff may seek to establish that the entity carrying out the activity was an agent of the defendant, rather than an independent contractor in order to recover damages from the defendant for whom the activity was being conducted.[74] In *State Compensation Fund*

[72] Mason v. Carroll, 289 Ala. 610 269 So. 2d 89 (1972).

[73] Castro v. State of Calif., 114 Cal. App. 3d 503, 170 Cal.Rptr. 734 (1981) "peculiar risk" doctrine, employee of construction company employed by State to install pipeline to transport Feather River water across City to a reservoir backed truck into fellow employee plaintiff; Rowley v. Mayor and City Council of Baltimore, 60 Md. App. 680, 484 A. 2d 306 (1984) city hired independent contractor to manage civic center, employee battered and raped; Keeton, W. Page, editor. Prosser and Keeton on Torts, St. Paul: West Publishing Co., Fifth edition, 1984 at §71 Independent Contractors; O'Dell, Christopher C., Employers Beware: You May Be Liable for the Negligence of Your Independent Contractor, 51 *U. Colo. L. Rv.* 275-288 (1980).

[74] Lavine v. General Mills, 519 F. Supp. 332 (1981) tour package seller and planner in relation to cruise company.

v. Le Desma, 23 Ariz. App. 126, 531 P. 2d 171 (1975), employee was injured while on a field trip supervising a group of inner-city youngsters, and filed against the city under workers' compensation. However, the court held that while the city provided funds for the recreational program for inner-city children to a private organization, the ultimate supervision and control of the program vested in the private organization and not the city; and, thus, the private organization was held to be an independent contractor and not merely a subcontractor of the city. Hence, the person who had filed for workers' compensation was not a city employee, but an employee of the private organization.

§ 3.121   Individuals as independent contractor

Among the individuals employed in sport and recreation who may be hired either as an employee of the organization or as an independent contractor are physicians, officials, lifeguard/swimming instructors, aerobic dance instructors, fitness specialists, bus drivers, etc.

Whether a physician who attends a team is an independent contractor or an employee of the school or club depends upon the arrangement. In a professional football situation, where the Club employed the physician on a contractual salary basis, the physician was held to be an employee and not an independent contractor.[75] A similar result was reached when a physician employed by a baseball team for the emergency treatment of spectators did not exercise appropriate professional practices.[76] However, physicians were held not to be employees of the State in a boxing incident.[77] A similar result was reached in *Cramer v. Hoffman,* 390 F.2d 19 (1968), when the court held that in a football injury case the physician was in an independent contractor relationship with the university. However, Florida[78] has held that a university physician acting within the scope of employment comes within the governmental immunity of the university. A Canadian court held a hockey club physician an independent contractor and stated the test as to whether an independent contractor or not as the "degree of control that the club has over the doctor." The doctor made the final decision as to what treatment an injured player would have and whether an injured player would play, without advice from the management of the club; the doctor felt that he served the interests of the players exclusively and that his primary obligation was to them, not the club.[79] In a 1987 New York case,[80] the school physician was an employee of the school. Junior high student brought action against both the physician and the school district, alleging negligence and negligent infliction of emotional distress for determination that student was not physiologically mature enough to try out for the high school tennis team. This determination was based upon results of a screening test designed under the auspices of

[75] Chuy v. Phila. Eagles Football Club, 431 F. Supp. 254 (1977), aff'd. 595 F. 2d 1265 (1979); see also, Cramer v. Hoffman, 390 F. 2d 19 (1968) football physician college independent contractor.

[76] Fish v. Los Angeles Dodgers Baseball Club, 56 Cal. App. 3d 620, 128 Cal. Rptr. 807 (1976).

[77] Rosensweig v. State, 208 Misc. 1065, 146 N.Y.S. 2d 589 (1955), 5 A.D. 2d 293, 171 N.Y.S. 2d 912 (1958), rev'd. on other grounds 5 N.Y. 2d 404, 158

N.E. 2d 229 (1959). See also Classen v. Izquiedo, 137 Misc. 2d 489, 520 N.Y.S. 2d 999 (1987) ringside physician held independent contractor.

[78] Testa v. Pfaff, 464 So. 2d 220 (Fla. App. 1985).

[79] Wilson v. Vancouver Hockey Club, 5 D.L.R. 4th 282 (1983); see §17.33 The physician for further discussion of physical examinations and sport.

[80] Sitmoer v. Half Hollow Hills Central School Dist., 133 A.D. 2d 748, 520 N.Y.S. 2d 37 (1987).

the State Education Department. No negligence found, nor was the physician guilty of malpractice.

The employment relationship, also, can be an important factor of liability for companies with fitness programs with the same principles holding — if an employee of the company, then the company can be held liable for the negligence of the physician or nurse employed, but if an independent contractor, the company normally would not be held liable. In *Panaro v. Electrolux Corp.*, 208 Conn. 589, 545 A.2d 1086 (1988), employee brought malpractice action against company nurse alleging that nurse's failure to exercise reasonable professional care increased severity and risk of harm of stroke employee suffered. Held that the nurse was not an independent contractor because she was a full-time employee of company with regular hours, salary, benefits and was subject to withholding taxes by company. Plaintiff had sought to evade the Workers' Compensation Act exclusivity section precluding employee from bringing suit against fellow employee.

In a school situation, a student suffered a fractured leg while participating in a physical therapy program administered at the elementary school. The 11-year-old was born with a congenital deformity of the spinal column, resulting in some paralysis of his legs. The two physical therapists had been employed by the school district, but just this year the arrangement had changed so that they were paid by the State and were under the direction of the State Services for Crippled Children. They no longer attended school staff meetings and scheduled therapy sessions independent of the school's supervision. The liability of the school focused upon the theory set forth in the *Second Restatement of Torts* §411 that an employer is subject to liability for physical harm to third persons caused by failure to exercise reasonable care in selecting the employee, even if such employee is an independent contractor. While it was admitted that the person conducting the physical therapy was not qualified to do so, there was no evidence that any such deficiency caused a recognized risk of harm to anyone in plaintiff's condition and, therefore, was not proximate cause of plaintiff's injury. School district was not held vicariously liable for negligence of state-employed therapist.[81]

As related to sport officials, golf caddies and golf pros, et al., the question usually is raised in regard to Workers' Compensation, since an independent contractor is not covered under a company's Workers' Compensation. Control by the employing entities is the critical issue. For example, in *Cardello v. Mt. Hermon Ski Area, Inc.*, 372 A. 2d 579 (Me. 1977), the court held that what plaintiff (a national ski patroller) did, when and where he did it and his right to act as patroller were determined by officials of National Ski Patrol and not by owner of ski area, and thus he was not an employee of owner, and therefore not entitled to compensation. Control also was at issue in *Thorson v. Mandell*, 402 Mass. 744, 525 N.E.2d 375 (1988), a situation in which a performer was employed and injured during dance rehearsals when she attempted a dance maneuver backflip on hardwood floor. The court held that she was an employee inasmuch as the proprietor of the theater company directed her participation. (See §25.343.) In *Collegiate Basketball Officials Association, Inc. v. National Labor Relations Board*, 836 F. 2d 143 (1987), the

---

[81] Greening v. School Dist. of Millard, 223 Neb. 729, 393 N.W. 2d 51 (1986).

organization of officials petitioned for review of the NLRB decision that the athletic conference did not violate NLRA by refusing to bargain. Held that referees were independent contractors, not employees, and therefore, refusal to bargain was not unfair labor practice. The officials' organization retained a limited right to fire member officials "not in good standing," a determination not subject to athletic conference review. Because the proprietor of facility where fatal boxing match occurred did not participate in selection of referee, he was not vicariously liable for any negligence of the referee, so the court held in *Classen v. Izquiedo* 137 Misc.2d 489, 520 N.Y.S.2d 999 (1987). For additional lawsuits involving sport officials as defendants, see §15.3.

In *Frankel v. Willow Brook Marina*,[82] an 8½-year-old youngster drowned in a pool operated by the Marina. Minutes before he was found unconscious on the bottom of the pool, he had been one of four children receiving swimming instructions in a class conducted by a lifeguard employed by the Marina. Plaintiff sued both the Marina and the lifeguard, and the Marina cross-claimed against the lifeguard, seeking to be indemnified in the event it were to be held liable solely because of the lifeguard's negligence. The court found that the lifeguard was acting as an agent of the Marina and was not an independent contractor in giving the lessons and that the lifeguard was not guilty of negligence which was a proximate cause of the accident, but that the Marina was guilty of negligence, apart from that of the lifeguard. When the lifeguards were hired, they were told they could supplement their pay by giving swimming lessons at the pool. Evidence indicated that the Marina failed to give adequate instructions to its teenage lifeguards and failed to provide adequate supervision during the pre-opening hours when the pool was being used; the Marina was aware of the various activities going on, including aquatic show practice, as well as the lessons.

The city was held not liable in a golf situation.[83] An individual taking golf lessons from the golf course pro was positioned about 15 yards in front of the tee when another golfer's ball driven from the tee hit and injured plaintiff. The pro was held to be an independent contractor, in regard to such instruction, inasmuch as he retained all fees and full control of the lessons.

And, a school bus driver was held to be an independent contractor when he was additionally hired on a special basis to carry students on a special trip. The *Averette* case[84] presented a definition of an independent contractor:

> An independent contractor is one who renders service in the course of an occupation representing the will of his employer only as to the result of his work, and not as to the means by which it is accomplished.

Another transportation case,[85] in which plaintiff was injured due to a collision between the school bus and a sanitation truck, discussed additional principles of liability as related to independent contractor:

[82] Frankel v. Willow Brook Marina, 275 F. Supp. 320 (1967).

[83] Petrich v. New Orleans City Park Improvement Assn., 188 So. 199 (La. App. 1939).

[84] Averette v. Traveler's Insurance, 174 So. 2d 881 (La. App. 1965); see §22.11 for additional transportation situations.

[85] Settles v. Inc. Village of Freeport, 132 Misc. 2d 240, 503 N.Y.S. 2d 945 (1986).

Generally, party who engages independent contractor is not responsible for negligence of contractor or his employees, and doctrine of respondeat superior does not apply; however, where work involved may be characterized as inherently dangerous, duties of employer are nondelegable and liability attaches for negligence of independent contractor, where lack of due care and performance of work has been demonstrated.

...

Employer remains liable for injuries caused by negligence of independent contractor if employer fails to use reasonable care to select competent contractor, where contractor was in fact incompetent.

In this situation the transportation was not considered inherently dangerous work and the school district was not held liable for the negligence of the independent contractor, the company employed to transport the children.

§ 3.122   Contracting related to premises

Construction and repair should be distinguished. Generally one is not liable for the acts of an independent contractor where there is negligent installation of fixtures which are permanently affixed to and an integral part of the building.[86] In another situation the school brought action against the contractor, engineering company, and architects for water damage to the gymnasium floor, allegedly resulting from improper design and construction of the school. The court found evidence that the contractor's final grading of area surrounding the gymnasium was improper, but found no negligence on the part of the other two defendants.[87] In a third situation, an eight-year-old boy was thrown from a moving merry-go-round on the school playground onto some pipes piled in close proximity thereto, suffering a fractured skull. The pipes were for monkey bars to be assembled later. The contractor was absolved of responsibility. Although this was a new school area, the contractor had turned over the area to the school, and thus the school was liable for any negligence relating to the pile of pipes.[88] In a health spa situation,[89] a false ceiling collapsed. The court, however, held against the health spa because sufficient time had elapsed and the condition was obvious so that it should have been aware of the dangerous condition. They had not notified the contractor.

While the owner of property is generally not liable for negligent acts of an independent contractor, such owner is liable where the nature of the contractor's work is likely to render premises dangerous to invitees of the owner. In an early Massachusetts case[90] the owner of an amusement park was found negligent in designating a walk used

86 O'Gan v. King City Joint Union H.S., 3 Cal. App. 3d 641, 83 Cal. Rptr. 795 (1970).

87 Seaman Unified School Dist. No. 345, Shawnee Co. v. Casson Const. Co., 3 Kan. App. 2d 289, 594 P. 2d 241 (1979).

88 Roman Catholic Church, Diocese of Tucson v. Keenan, 74 Ariz. 20, 243 P. 2d 455 rehearing 74 Ariz. 76, 244 P. 2d 351 (1952).

89 Roman Spa, Inc. v. Lubell, 334 So. 2d 298 (1976), rev'd./remanded 362 So. 2d 922 (1978) op. after remand 364 So. 2d 115 (Fla. App. 1978).

90 Wilson v. Norumbega Park Co., 275 Mass. 422, 176 N.E. 514 (1931).

by pedestrians as a place for driving (riding) ponies managed by an independent contractor. In this situation, a mother was with her six-year-old and was hit from behind by larger ponies being ridden by some boys on the pathway.

A city cannot delegate to an independent contractor its duty to keep its park in safe condition.[91] The lights in a shelter house had gone out. The park department requested the electric company to dig up the wires and repair the defects. The electric company workmen left the area unguarded and without warnings of an open ditch wherein heavily charged electric wires were exposed. A ladder had been laid over the ditch; a boy fell in and hung through the ladder by his shoulders with his legs touching the wires, causing him to be seriously burned. The city was held liable for not maintaining the park in a reasonably safe condition, even though the hazard was caused by an independent contractor.

The city also appears to retain its obligation to maintain safe premises when an activity is hazardous, even though it has engaged an independent contractor.[92] The city sponsored a fireworks exhibition in the park and engaged an independent contractor to manage it. One of the crowd was killed when a mortar fell into the spectators. During the afternoon preceding the evening exhibition, a truck had backed against the mortar and pointed it toward the crowd. The city was held liable on failure to use the degree of care required, which almost appears to be a strict liability for fireworks.

An independent contractor also may be liable for a subcontractor. In *Fisherman's Paradise*[93] an independent contractor had been hired to refurbish a boat. A subcontractor, also an independent contractor, had been employed to install the boat's refrigerator, which broke from its mounting and injured plaintiff. Primary contractor was held liable for subcontractor's negligence. Also, the owner of premises may be held liable for injury to an employee of an independent contractor under certain circumstances, as pointed out in a 1987 Texas case:[94] "(Ordinarily) responsibility for performing or conducting task in safe manner rests with contractor and not premises owner where activity is under control of contractor and danger arises out of employee's performance of task. (However), premises owner may be liable for injuries suffered by employee of independent contractor when owner retains right to control some part of independent contractor's work, but fails to exercise retained control with reasonable care." In this instance, employee fell from work scaffold suspended by discarded rope owner had left on premises; premises owner was held liable, plaintiff being awarded $654,000. There was a similar holding in *Claudy v. City of Sycamore*, 170 Ill. App. 3d

---

[91] Lewis v. Kansas City, 233 Mo. App. 341, 122 S.W. 2d 852 (1938). See also Ellis v. Board of Trustees of Moose Jaw Public School Dist., 2 W.W.R. 19 (1946) plaintiff injured by falling of roofing equipment erected by defendant company engaged in repairing the roof; Price v. U.S., 530 F. Supp. 1010 (1981) U.S. Army Corps of Engineers allowed contractor in charge of dredging undertaken to repair seawall following hurricane to remove sand and thus cause depression near public beach, allegedly cause of drowning, also Corp negligent in designing and supervising warning system around depression.

[92] Arnold v. State, 163 A.D. 253, 148 N.Y.S. 479 (1914) landmark case; Harris v. Findlay, 59 Ohio App. 375, 13 Ohio Op. 172, 18 N.E. 2d 413 (1938); Taylor v. Oakland Scavenger Co., 17 Cal. 2d 594, 110 P. 2d 1044 (1941); see also Costello v. Pittsburgh Athletic Co., 652 F. Supp. 1579 (1987).

[93] Fisherman's Paradise, Inc. v. Greenfield, 417 So. 2d 306 (Fla. App. 1982).

[94] Gulf States Utilities v. Dryden, 735 S.W. 2d 263 (Tex. App. 1987).

990, 120 Ill. Dec. 812, 524 N.E.2d 994 (1988). The widow of employee of tree trimming company, who was electrocuted when he came in contact with power lines while trimming trees pursuant to contract with city, brought action against the city. The court held that: "Employer of independent contractor can be liable for injuries of contractor's employee which result from performance of inherently dangerous activities. Employer of independent contractor is not liable for acts or omissions of the latter; exception to that rule provides that an employer who retains control of any part of the work will be liable for injuries resulting from his failure to exercise his right of control with reasonable care.... City could be held liable... in view of testimony that city retained some control over the tree trimming service company by making inspections of the jobsite and retaining the power to stop work or fire employees if the job was not being done properly."

A little different application of "invitee" was used in a 1984 Alabama case.[95] It was held that an employee of an independent contractor hired by a tennis club to replace bulbs in the lights on its outdoor tennis courts was an invitee of the tennis club.

See Chapter 20 for further cases on premise conditions/maintenance and construction.

§ 3.123   Concessionnaires as independent contractors

A concessionnaire was held to be an independent contractor whose negligence could not be imputed to the United States (National Park Service) to form the basis of tort liability under the Federal Tort Claims Act (however, Nevada law was applied). Alleged negligence was failure to warn of or guard against the flash flood in the canyon. The court distinguished between the independent contractor and an agent. The critical test is the existence of authority to control and supervise the detailed physical performance and day-to-day operations, and not whether the person must comply with standards and regulations. The concession agreement was deemed to have the origin of its provisions in the various rules and regulations issued by the government for "standard" concession agreements, and, as such, are the sort of regulation-mandated contractual restrictions that are designed to secure objectives; and, that despite their restrictive effect on the activities of the contracting party (concessionnaire), do not convert an independent entrepreneur into a principal-agent relationship.[96]

The city leased land to defendant bathing beach company who constructed and operated a swimming pool on the land. A nine-year-old child drowned. The city as lessor was held not liable and the bathing beach company was held to be an independent contractor and liable for negligence.[97] However, in another early Kansas case,[98] in which the city had a contract with the concessionnaire, the concessionnaire was regarded as an employee rather than an independent contractor.

The court held in a North Carolina case[99] that a general concessionnaire at a fair had a

---

[95] Bush v. Alabama Power Co., 457 So. 2d 350 (Ala. 1984).

[96] Ducey v. U.S., 523 F. Supp. 225 (1981), rev'd./ remanded 713 F. 2d 504 (1983) Nevada law applied.

[97] Swan v. Riverside Bathing Beach Co., 128 Kan. 230, 276 P. 796 (1928), 132 Kan. 61, 294 P. 902 (1931).

[98] Warren v. Topeka, 125 Kan. 524, 265 P. 78 (1928).

[99] Dockery v. World of Mirth Shows, 264 N.C. 406, 142 S.E. 2d 29 (1965).

duty, with respect to ride owned and operated by an independent contractor, to inspect and supervise operation of ride if it was one likely to cause injury to passenger; and, the duty could not be delegated to an independent contractor. Where there is a hazardous circumstance, liability cannot be shifted entirely to the independent contractor. However, in a 1981 case[100] it was held that if the contractor is not negligent, there is no negligence imputable to the owner. In this Louisiana case a minor fell into a bed of hot coals under a burned out brush pile during land cleaning operations on land on which impromptu play activity had been permitted, but the right to play and recreation had been withdrawn by the owner when clearing operations began.

In *Caillouette v. Cherokee Beach & Campground, Inc.*, 386 So. 2d 666 (La. App. 1980) writ denied 387 So. 2d 597 (La. 1980), plaintiffs brought suit against defendant for wrongful death of son, who died when he dove into river from bluff after he had rented an inner tube from defendants for "tubing" on river. The court held that persons providing rented inner tubes were not required by law to warn users of tubes of obvious dangers attendant to diving into unknown body of water, and could not be held liable for injuries suffered by one who trespassed on property of third person in order to do so (see §20.332 for further information on warnings).

§ 3.13   Program sponsorship and joint programming; sport associations and leagues

In a high school football conditioning summer program, the plaintiff sued the State High School Athletic Association, as well as the school and its employees. The Association was held liable for having failed to properly communicate and enforce its regulations.[101] An opposite result was reached in a hockey case[102] because in this specific incident the league had no duty by terms of its lease. Thus, where a league has responsibilities toward the plaintiff via its members whom it controls, it can be held liable. Athletic associations, such as the NCAA and the state high school associations control both the conduct of the game and the eligibility of the participants, in short, every aspect of the game. With such control comes challenges in the courts.[103] See especially §1.323 eligibility rule-making.

Plaintiff, a student at a private high school, was severely injured in a game between

[100] Lacombe v. Greathouse, 407 So. 2d 1346 (La. App. 1981).

[101] Peterson v. Multnomah County School Dist. No. 1, 60 Or. App. 81, 668 P. 2d 385 (1983).

[102] Riley v. Chicago Cougars Hockey Club, 100 Ill. App. 3d 664, 56 Ill. Dec. 210, 427 N.E. 2d 290 (1981); an opposite result was reached in Santangelo v. City of N.Y., 66 A.D. 2d 880, 411 N.Y.S. 2d 666 (1978) when court held that supervision was shared by city and hockey league, making both liable.

[103] For example, ABC League v. Missouri State H.S.A.A., 530 F. Supp. 1033 (1982); B.C v. Cumberland Regional School Dist., 220 N.J. Super. 214, 531 A.2d 1059 (1987); Duffley v. N.H.I.A.A., 122 N.H. 484, 446 A. 2d 462 (1982); Florida H.S.A.A. v. Thomas, 409 So. 2d 245 (Fla. App. 1982); Georgia H.S.A.A. v. Waddell, 285 S.E. 2d 7 (Ga. 1981); Makanui v. Dept. of Educ., 721 P. 2d 165 (Hawaii App. 1986); School Dist., Harrisburg v. P.I.A.A., 309 A. 2d 353 (Pa. 1973); Snow v. N.H.I.A.A., 449 A. 2d 1223 (N.H. 1982); Univ. Interscholastic League v. Hardin-Jefferson Indpt. School Dist., 648 S.W. 2d 770 (Tex. Civ. App. 1983); Univ. Interscholastic League v. Payne, 635 S.W. 2d 754 (Tex. 1982). These are not negligence situations, but control challenges. See also Weistart, John C. and Cym H. Lowell, The Law of Sport, Indianapolis: Bobbs-Merrill Co., 1979 with 1985 supplement, Chapter 1 Regulation of Amateur Sport.

two rugby clubs fielded by two high schools, members of the Chicago Catholic High School Athletic League. He sued various defendants, including the League. Under Illinois law, constitution and bylaws of an unincorporated association constitute a contract between association and its member. Plaintiff alleged that the League was negligent on six counts, such as failing to insist upon protective equipment for athletes, allowing member schools to employ coaches with little or no rugby experience, and failing to inform member schools of the risk of serious harm in the game of rugby, even though it knew or should have known that such information was necessary to its member schools. The court held that the League did not have duty to protect student from injury in rugby inasmuch as rugby was not a League sport and was thus not regulated by the League.[104]

There are many organizations which "sponsor" recreational activities or teams. The question regarding liability really rests on whether the person in charge was an "agent" of the organization and whether there was control over the activity and any duty owed. In *Davis v. Shelton*,[105] a scout troop went on an overnight and plaintiff was injured when a tree limb on which he was climbing broke. The court held that the Council and the church sponsoring the troop had fulfilled their obligation by providing competent leadership. In another New York case[106] nearly 15 years later, the court held the corporate "sponsor" did not supervise running of the event (skiing slalom), nor control operation of the event or design of the slope, and hence was not liable. The required special relationship between corporation (Miller Brewing Co.) and plaintiff did not exist.

Where two organizations jointly sponsor an activity, under the "joint and several" rule, each is fully responsible for the negligence which may occur in the activity itself. Or, the court may hold joint sponsors equally responsible, if all are sued, and the right of indemnification depends upon the agreement. For example, four county superintendents of schools entered into a written agreement for the formation of a joint science and conservation education program. A student was seriously injured and the superintendents joined in a stipulation for settlement of the action, but then raised claims for contribution or indemnity against each other. The court held the four groups equally liable with no claim for indemnity.[107] See §2.43 on joint tortfeasors.

What about trade associations, especially as related to product standards? In a New Jersey 1987 case,[108] plaintiff suffered severe injuries when he dived into the shallow end of a residential in-ground swimming pool and brought action against the nonprofit trade association, which had promulgated the minimum standards for construction and design of such pools, as well as other defendants. Held that the trade association in

[104] Perkaus v. Chicago Catholic H.S. Athletic League, 140 Ill. App. 3d 127, 94 Ill. Dec. 624, 488 N.E. 2d 623 (1986); see also Swearingen v. Fall River Joint Unified School Dist., 166 Cal. App. 3d 335, 212 Cal. Rptr. 400 (1985) 215 Cal. Rptr. 854, 701 P. 2d 1172 (1985), 40 Cal. 3d 445, 220 Cal. Rptr. 627, 709 P. 2d 430 (1985) duty for safety of host school for off-campus activity, see also Travelers' Indemnity Co. v. Swearingen, 169 Cal. App. 3d 779, 214 Cal. Rptr. 383 (1985).

[105] Davis v. Shelton, 33 A.D. 2d 707, 304 N.Y.S. 2d 722 (1969), app. dism'd. 26 N.Y. 2d 829, 309 N.Y.S. 2d 358, 257 N.E. 2d 902.
[106] Vogel v. West Mountain Corp., 470 N.Y.S. 2d 475 (1983).
[107] Ross v. Campbell Union School District, 70 Cal. App. 3d 113, 138 Cal. Rptr. 557 (1977).
[108] Meyers v. Donnatacci, 220 N.J. Super. 73, 531 A. 2d 398 (1987); see also introduction to §21.1 Product liability.

setting forth such standards had no duty to warn plaintiff of danger of shallow water diving.

Or, what is the liability of associations which offer training, such as first aid or life saving? (see §17.14).

§ 3.14   Membership clubs; joint ventures/joint enterprises

The liability of members and officers of clubs for injuries to members and third parties and guests, as well as that of the corporate entity, has been in issue for many years. Usually there is no problem with an incorporated club or association, for it is clothed with the status of a legal entity, capable of being sued and suing.

A member of an unincorporated, nonprofit baseball association sued the association, alleging that it had a duty to protect him from foreseeable harm. Plaintiff was conducting baseball tryouts on behalf of the association, was a member of the board and commissioner of the association's "teener" league. During the tryouts, he was injured when he turned from facing the outfield back toward the batter and was struck in the eye by a batted ball. The court held that plaintiff was one of the joint entrepreneurs who were in possession of the ball field and actively conducting the very activity which caused the injury. In addition, plaintiff voluntarily exposed himself to the risks inherent in baseball, being hit by a batted ball.[109] In another 1986 case,[110] a member's guest brought action against the Ridge Runners Club 99 and members for injuries arising from fall of tree cut by members on club's property, and members brought cross-claims against club. It was held that the membership dues paid to recreation club in exchange for rights to use property, to cut trees, and to take wood from club's property constituted "consideration" for such rights and, therefore, brought club within exception to immunity under the New York statute. The club owed a duty of reasonable care to guest who assisted members in cutting wood.

The concern in this section, however, is for the membership of unincorporated clubs and associations. Generally, individual members are personally liable, whether an officer or not, for tortious acts which they either individually commit or participate in or authorize, assent to, or ratify. Liability attaches whether or not there is personal participation in the wrongful act, unless such act is done without knowledge or approval. However, usually liability does not attach merely by virtue of membership where injury was sustained by a third party at a social event sponsored by the association; liability attaches only to those who are shown to have actively participated.[111] The question also is raised as to whether a member who is injured may recover against the association.[112]

[109] Bowser v. Hershey Baseball Assoc., 357 Pa. Super. 435, 516 A. 2d 61 (1986).

[110] Schoonmaker v. Ridge Runners Club 99, 119 A.D. 2d 858, 500 N.Y.S. 2d 562 (1986).

[111] See 14 C.J.S. 1279 et seq. or 6 Am.Jur.2d 427 et seq.; also see cases in Parts B and C, and in §17.4 as related to health spas and fitness clubs. See Buckley, E. T., Member Liability for Dues, Fees, Fines, and Assessments in Non-profit Associations and Corporations. 19 *Univ. of San Francisco Law Review* 393-412, Spring/Summer 1985.

[112] Libby v. Perry, 311 A. 2d 527 (Me. 1973); see also Country Club of Coral Gables v. McHale, 188 So. 2d 405 (Fla. App. 1966) complimentary membership, slipped and fell on outdoor dance floor, considered business invitee; Peterson v. Tam O'Shanter Racquet Club, 90 Ill. App. 3d 1029, 46 Ill. Dec. 459, 414 N.E. 2d 181 (1980) member injured when ran into concrete wall concealed by canvas backdrop while playing tennis, club has affirmative duty to keep premises in safe condition.

Generally, the members of a club are not considered engaged in a "joint venture," in the legal sense, where all are equally liable and equally responsible. In *Ruppa v. American States Ins. Co.*[113] the saddle club put on a horse show. One of the members was negligent. The court stated that members of the nonprofit incorporated saddle club were not engaged in joint venture in holding a horse show in view of lack of any agreement to share profits, and vicarious liability for death of horse show participant could, therefore, not be imposed on members on such basis. However, a 1987 Wyoming case[114] held that the members of an unincorporated club were engaged in a joint enterprise. A member of a gun club was injured during a mock gunfight staged by the unincorporated association and brought suit against the club, its members, the chamber of commerce and the city. He had signed an exculpatory agreement releasing parties from negligence liability. The court held that members of unincorporated association are engaged in a joint enterprise, and negligence of one member acting in furtherance of enterprise is imputable to all; thus, member of such association could not sue another member of such association, as part of the association, as that would be tantamount to allowing that person to sue oneself. The court held further that members of an unincorporated association engaged in joint enterprise are not precluded from suing one another in their individual capacities for individual negligence, as no person may negligently injure another without responsibility. The court also held that the release was held effective, there was not an employment relationship between the chamber of commerce and the member, and the city was not liable.

There, also, is the question as to whether a club officer may sue the club of which he is an officer. The "exalted ruler" of the Elks club arrived early at the club to assist in preparations for a party being hosted by the officers and was injured in a fall in the kitchen. As exalted ruler, plaintiff sat on the board of trustees as an ex-officio, non-voting member. The board did control the management of the club facility, but hired a manager for the actual operation of the facility itself. The club in its defense sought to apply the joint enterprise and master-servant rules, under which plaintiff could not recover. However, the court held joint enterprise inapplicable and stated that they had found no circumstances under which an elected officer of a fraternal organization was considered an employee, and thus that theory, too, was inapplicable.[115]

Joint enterprise, also, should be distinguished from club sponsorship. A yacht club member, who had volunteered to assist in some renovation work, sued the club for injuries when a beam and framework toppled, causing him to fall off a ladder and be injured. In discussing the situation, the court defined common or joint enterprise, thus:

> In law of negligence, term "common" or "joint enterprise" means an association of two or more persons in the pursuit of a common purpose under such circumstances that each has the authority, express or implied, to act for all in respect to control of means or agencies employed to execute such

---

[113] Ruppa v. Amer. States Ins. Co., 91 Wis. 2d 628, 284 N.W. 2d 318 (1979).

[114] Boehm v. Cody Country Chamber of Commerce, 748 P. 2d 704 (Wyo. 1987).

[115] Erdman v. Lower Yakima Valley, Wash., Lodge, No. 2112 of B.P.O.E. 41 Wash. App. 197, 704 P. 2d 150 (1985).

common purpose; as a result of which the negligence of one participant may be imputed to another so as to bar recovery against a negligent defendant.[116]

The club was not liable to member for injury. A different result was reached in *Tanner v. Columbus Lodge No. 11, Moose*, 44 Ohio St.2d 49, 73 Ohio Ops.2d 233, 337 N.E.2d 625 (1975) due to a State statute which permits an unincorporated association to be sued as an entity, and thus a member could sue the association as such entity.

The concept of joint venture or joint enterprise rests in the doctrine of vicarious responsibility and is applied primarily to business arrangements. Its non-business application has been in the field of automobile law.[117] There are four elements for a joint enterprise to be established: (1) an agreement, express or implied, among the members of the group; (2) a common purpose to be carried out by the group, (3) a community of pecuniary interest in that purpose; and (4) an equal right to a voice in the direction of the enterprise. The law of partnership and the principles of agency serve as the foundation for the theory of joint enterprise.[118]

A group of older cases, now very much in the minority and almost totally overruled, found joint enterprise as any association of persons, for any purpose of common interest, including social occasions and pleasure trips.[119] Most cases now set forth the requirement that the purpose be for business, not social/pleasure.[120] Further, a common objective is to be distinguished from common purpose; for example, riding together to a location is a common objective, but not necessarily a common purpose.[121] Control, i.e., equal right to a voice in the direction of the enterprise, is another essential element. If one does not have any control, then one is not part of a joint enterprise.[122] Where there is a joint enterprise, each individual of the enterprise is liable and the negligence of one member is imputed to the others. By the same rationale, if notice is given to one member, such as a warning, then it is held that all have had notice.[123]

In the outdoor adventure/challenge activity literature, there has been indicated that if such activity is conducted as a "joint venture," meaning as indicated in the foregoing

---

[116] Farrar v. Edgewood Yacht Club, 302 A. 2d 782 (R.I. 1973); see also O'Bryant v. V.F.W., 376 N.E. 2d 521 (Ind. App. 1978); Hertzog v. Harrison Island Shores, Inc., 21 A.D. 2d 859, 251 N.Y.S. 2d 164 (1964).

[117] Keeton at §72 Joint Enterprise.

[118] Easter v. McNabb, 97 Idaho 180, 541 P. 2d 604 (1975) three-day fishing trip, companions in auto accident on way home, held not joint venture, lack of pecuniary interest in common purpose of fishing, negligence of driver could not be imputed to passengers; see also Whittington v. Sowela Tech., Inst., 438 So. 2d 236 (La. App. 1983), cert. denied 443 So. 2d 591 (La. 1983).

[119] Keeton at §72.

[120] Campanella v. Zajic, 62 Ill. App. 3d 886, 20 Ill. Dec. 33, 379 N.E. 2d 866 (1978); DeSuza v. Andersack, 63 Cal. App. 3d 694, 133 Cal. Rptr. 920 (1976); Fugate v. Galvin, 84 Ill. App. 3d 573, 40 Ill. Dec. 318, 406 N.E. 2d 19 (1980); Stock v. Fife, 13 Mass.App. 75, 430 N.E. 2d 845 (1982).

[121] Babington v. Bogdanovic, 7 Ill. App. 3d 593, 288 N.E. 2d 40 (1972); Buford v. Horne, 300 So. 2d 913 (1974); Hall v. Blackham, 18 Utah 2d 164, 417 P. 2d 664 (1966); Hilton v. Blose, 297 Pa. 458, 147 A. 100 (1929) riding together or furnishing gas and oil or money for gas and expenses does not make association business enterprises; see also §22.123.

[122] Cecil v. Hardin, 575 S.W. 2d 268 (Tenn. 1978); Freeman v. U.S., 509 F. 2d 626 (1975) mass parachutists; Massey v. Scripter, 401 Mich. 385, 258 N.W. 2d 44 (1977) tandem bicycle. Cases in preceding footnote relate, also, to control, passenger lack of control over driver of vehicle.

[123] Ruth v. Hutchinson Gas Co., 209 Minn. 248, 296 N.W. 136 (1941) hunting trip; in another case involving hunting, Delgado v. Lohmar, 289 N.W. 2d 479 (Minn. 1979), the court held the hunters were not engaged in a joint enterprise inasmuch as they were in a recreational activity on a gratuitous and voluntary basis and there was no sharing of equipment or expenses, each hunter had control of his own gun.

paragraph, an association of persons for common social or pleasure purpose, liability can be evaded by an organization. If it is a true joint venture, then there is no organization sponsorship, and the individuals associating together to go on such activity have equal right to the direction of the activity and equal responsibility; however, where there is sponsorship, just to state that it is an individual venture and participants must organize themselves does not relieve an organization of a duty owed to participants; there has to be *de facto* a joint venture. As some outing clubs do, and thereby be relieved of a duty toward the activity itself, an organization may facilitate individuals getting together in joint venture by making available equipment on a rental or loan basis, by permitting its bulletin board to be used for sign-ups, by allowing the group to meet for organizational purposes in their facility; but, there must be no indication of sponsorship of the activity itself, nor "control" by selecting a coordinator to help the interested persons get organized for the activity.

§ 3.2   Board members as individuals

What is the liability of those citizens who serve on the local school board of education, the city council, the YMCA board of directors, or the local mental health association board? Are they individually liable for the torts of the employees of the organization on whose board they sit? Generally, a board member is not held liable individually for either the directives of the board or the negligence of an employee.[124]

Directives of the board are usually given by the board as a whole and for such actions a board member is not liable individually.[125] The board action, however, must be within the legal scope of authority. To act beyond such scope of responsibility is an *ultra vires* act for which board members are liable individually.[126] Board members also can be liable when they have acted willfully or wantonly,[127] or when they have breached a statutory duty.[128] Two non-delegable duties relate to fiscal management and human rights implementation (§1.3).[129] The management responsibilities are not those of an executive, but rather the board has a duty to make informed policy decisions. There is usually no liability for a seeming *ultra vires* act where the governing board acted within

---

[124] e.g., where teacher was injured while using parking lot, which had loose gravel, for physical education class, the court in Sheldon v. Planet Insur. Co., 280 So. 2d 380 (La. App. 1973) said that the board officers were not individually liable, but the corporate entity inasmuch as it had sole authority to authorize and fund such repairs and renovation.

[125] Adams v. Schneider, 71 Ind. App. 249, 124 N.E. 2d 718 (1919); Johnson City Bd. of Educ. v. Ray, 154 Tenn. 179, 289 S.W. 502 (1926); Medsker v. Etchison, 101 Ind. App. 369, 199 N.E. 429 (1936); Rhoades v. School Dist. No. 9, 115 Mont. 352, 142 P. 2d 890 (1943).

[126] Holgerson v. Devil's Lake, 63 N.D. 155, 246 N.W. 641 (1933); Norberg v. Hagna, 46 S.D. 568, 195 N.W. 438 (1923).

[127] McClendon v. Norwood, 179 Ga. App. 176, 346 S.E. 2d 1 (1986) six-year-old injured allegedly on defective playground equipment, unverified allegations.

[128] Perkins v. Trask, 95 Mont. 1, 23 P. 2d 982 (1933).

[129] In Wood v. Strickland, 420 U.S. 308, 95 S. Ct. 992 (1975), the court said that a school board member is not immune from liability for damages if he knew or reasonably should have shown that the action he took within the sphere of official responsibility would violate the constitutional rights of the student affected, or if he took the action with the malicious intention to cause a deprivation of constitutional rights or other injury to the student.

its general powers, but under a statute which was held unconstitutional or later repealed.[130]

Increasingly, the distinction is made between discretionary and ministerial acts, with no liability for those actions in performance of discretionary duties.[131] Almost all acts of a board are discretionary in nature (see §4.13). The courts also are reluctant to hold board members liable on nonfeasance acts[132] (see §2.21).

The court in Maryland in 1974 held that members of county boards of education were "public officials" and thus immune from tort action.[133] In keeping therewith the legislature of Maryland in the late '70s incorporated into its laws the widespread concern for citizens who might serve on boards, when it said:

> Recent court decisions throughout the country have created new grounds of personal liability of public officers and employees accruing from the discharge of their public duties. As a result it is becoming increasingly difficult to recruit and retain qualified personnel to serve in public positions that involve either the exercise of discretion or dealing with the public at large;....[134]

and many of the states are endeavoring to provide some protection for board members as individuals through indemnification provisions or insurance authorization[135] (see §4.234) or expressly exempting them from personal liability.[136] Such immunity, however, is lost when there is intentional wrongdoing or an *ultra vires* act.[137]

§ 3.3   Administrative officials and supervisory personnel

Suing administrative officials and supervisory personnel appears to be quite commonplace. Some of this increase in suits against officials was initiated as a way to circumvent governmental/sovereign immunity, while other suits are just a result of the increasing practice to join all possible parties. For example, in an Arizona case,[138] not only were the board members as individuals joined, but also the principal, in an action which concerned the conduct of a teacher. Action was dismissed for all but the teacher.

---

[130] Augustine, v. Brant, 249 N.Y. 198, 163 N.E. 732 (1928); Holgerson v. Devil's Lake, 63 N.D. 155, 246 N.W. 641 (1933); Jensen v. Juul, 66 S.D. 1, 278 N.W. 6 (1938); Juntila v. Everett School Dist., 178 Wash, 637, 35 P. 2d 78 (1934); Longwell v. Kansas City, 199 Mo. App. 480, 203 S.W. 657 (1918); Norberg v. Hagna, 46 S.D. 588, 195 N.W. 438 (1923); Petty v. Atlanta, 40 Ga. App. 63, 148 S.E. 747 (1929); Reid v. Atlanta, 39 Ga. App. 519, 147 S.E. 789 (1929); Scroggins v. Harlingen, 131 Tex. 237, 112 S.W. 2d 1035 (1938); Thayer v. St. Joseph, 227 Mo. App. 623, 54 S.W. 2d 442 (1932); Thrasher v. Cincinnati, 28 Ohio Op. 97 (CP. 1944).

[131] Mokovich v. Independent School Dist., 177 Minn. 446, 225 N.W. 292 (1929); Rennie v. Belleview School Dist., 521 S.W. 2d 423 (Mo. 1975); Whitney v. City of Worcester, 373 Mass. 208, 366 N.E. 2d 1210 (1977).

[132] Herring v. R.L. Mathis Certified Dairy Company, 118 Ga. App. 132, 162 S.E. 2d 863 (1968) aff'd./ rev'd. 225 Ga. 67, 166 S.E. 2d 89 (1969), 119 Ga. App. 226, 166 S.E. 2d 607, 225 Ga. 653, 171 S.E. 2d 124 (1969), 121 Ga. App. 373, 173 S.E. 2d 716 (1970); Iseminger v. Black Hawk County, Iowa, 175 N.W. 2d 374 (1970).

[133] Berg v. Merricks, 20 Md. App. 666, 318 A. 2d 220 (1974); cert. den. 272 Md. 737 (1979).

[134] Md. Code Ann., Art. 78A §16C.

[135] e.g., Montana, Vermont.

[136] e.g., Alaska, Arizona, Tennessee, Indiana.

[137] e.g., Georgia.

[138] LaFrentz v. Gallagher, 105 Ariz. 255, 462 P. 2d 804 (1969).

And, obviously, in order for an administrative official to be held liable, such official must be responsible. The city superintendent of parks was held not personally liable when it was shown he had no direct role in the design, construction, or maintenance of the zoo wolf pen.[139] And, a high school football game referee was assaulted by a game spectator and sued the high school and its principal. Court held that plaintiff failed to make factual allegations to connect alleged negligent acts of the principal with harm he suffered.[140] In *Berg v. Merricks*[141] it was held that the supervision in question was the responsibility of the county supervisor of physical education and not the principal.

Insofar as administrative officials, such as a past superintendent, supervisor, superintendent of schools, principal, etc., are concerned, they are, of course, liable for their own acts of negligence as any other employee or individual. These acts of negligence do not include those of subordinates unless the administrators have directed the performance or cooperated in their commission.[142] If this were not so, no individual would undertake certain public offices. Ordinarily where governmental immunity does not protect the corporate entity, the negligence of the employee is imputed directly to the corporate entity, not from the employee to the administrative superior. For example, where a coach was negligent in his supervision of a letter club initiation stunt and a boy was electrocuted, the superintendent was not held liable because he gave permission for use of the gymnasium for the initiation.[143] The relationship between the administrator and that of the employee is not that of master-servant, such as a principal or superintendent of a school and a teacher; therefore, the administrator is not liable for the misfeasance of the school employee, the negligence of a subordinate, but rather is liable for one's own act of personal misfeasance, as described in subsequent paragraphs.[144] Another consideration is whether the act the administrator did is discretionary or ministerial. In most states there is immunity for discretionary acts, but liability for ministerial acts. Most acts of administrators are ministerial because they are "operations" (see §4.13).

Further, there must be a duty owed. Does the executive officer owe an employee safe working conditions? In a situation where injury to teacher was occasioned by loose gravel on parking area, which was being used for physical education class because of lack of other adequate space, the court said that the superintendent did not owe such duty as an individual because the obligation was solely the employer (school corporate entity) inasmuch as it had sole authority to authorize and fund such repairs and renovations.[145] Acts for which an administrator or supervisor is responsible, and for which negligent performance makes one liable because it enhances the likelihood of

[139] Alfonso v. Lowney, 1981 Mass. App. Adv. Sh. 305, 416 N.E. 2d 516 (1981).

[140] Litomisky v. St. Charles High School, 482 So. 2d 30 (La. App. 1986).

[141] Berg v. Merricks, 20 Md. App. 666, 318 A. 2d 220 (1974).

[142] Boucher v. Fuhlbruck, 26 Conn. Sup. 79, 213 A. 2d 455 (1965); Kokomo v. Loy, 185 Ind. 18, 112 N.E. 994 (1916); Luce v. Board of Educ., 2 A.D. 2d 502, 157 N.Y.S. 2d 123 (1956); Medsker v. Etchison, 101 Ind. App. 369, 199 N.E. 429 (1936); Shannon v.

Fleishhacker, 116 Cal. App. 258, 2 P. 2d 835 (1931); Smith v. Consolidated School Dist. No. 2, 408 S.W. 2d 50 (Mo., 1966).

[143] DeGooyer v. Harkness, 70 S.D. 26, 13 N.W. 2d 815 (1944).

[144] Gray v. Wood, 64 A. 2d 191 (R.I. 1949) school principal and school custodian in relation to a slippery floor.

[145] Shelton v. Planet Insur. Co., 280 So. 2d 380 (La. App. 1973).

injury, encompass a wide range of functions. There are five categories of functions:

1. employing competent personnel and discharging employees shown to be unfit
2. providing proper supervision and having a plan of supervision
3. directing certain services as to manner they should be done
4. establishing rules and regulations for safety and complying with policy and statutory requirements
5. remedying dangerous conditions and defective equipment or giving notice of same when there is knowledge of the condition

Each of these categories is addressed in subsequent paragraphs. (Cases cited are illustrative only.)

Employing competent personnel and discharging employees known to be unfit.[146] In a case[147] where a diving equipment store operator contributed his services to the YMCA for instruction in scuba, the court said that it was a nondelegable duty to the participants in the scuba class to exercise reasonable care in selection of instructors and assistant instructors.

In a case settled out of court, a day camp used a college swimming pool for its swimming program for one week. During this week twelve different persons had been employed by the college as lifeguards; however, none of the guards had current Red Cross lifesaving certificates and only four had ever had one (now expired). A camper went down in the pool and subsequently died. The father sued for approximately $15 million, with an out-of-court settlement of slightly under $1 million. There was little question that the administrators of the college and the supervisor of the pool would be held liable for employment of improperly credentialed lifeguards. It should be noted, however, that except in a few states related to first aid and CPR (see §17.14), the holding of a certificate does not protect the one certified. It is what that person does that determines whether the person was negligent or not; but, the employment of a credentialed person can give some protection to the administrator in terms of employing a competent person, until there is actual or constructive notice to the administrator that the person does not measure up to the expectations of a person so credentialed.

Where licensing or certification exists, the responsibility may be shifted for determining what is competent personnel to the state agency, rather than the local hiring agency (school or other entity).[148]

In *Smith v. Consolidated School Dist.*, 408 S.W. 2d 50 (Mo. 1966), the superintendent of schools was not held liable for an injury to a student in wrestling class on a technical point that he recommends but does not employ the instructors. There is also the concept of "negligent hiring" in which the administrator owes a duty to the public to use reasonable care in the selection and retention of employees, particularly as to fitness, *e.g.*, child abuse (see §1.4133), a criminal record. This gives the unenviable

---

[146] Fernelius v. Pierce, 22 Cal. 2d 226, 138 P. 2d 12 (1943).

[147] Leno v. YMCA, 17 Cal. App. 3d 651, 95 Cal. Rptr. 96 (1971).

[148] Berg v. Merricks, 20 Md. App. 666, 318 A. 2d 318 (1974).

choice between invasion of privacy and loss of possible job opportunities, et. al.[149]

Providing proper supervision and having a plan of supervision. This responsibility is based upon the element of reliance. Mandatory schooling forces parents to rely on the government to protect their children. The government repeatedly has been found liable for the failure of teachers to supervise.[150] The question in this section, however, is what is the liability of the administrative official or supervisory personnel? There is some evidence that the supervision of other personnel is a discretionary act for which there is no liability for failure to perform.[151] However, this does not seem to be the prevailing view in light of the very definite duty to provide an environment safe from undue risk of harm.[152] The court stated that the principal and vice-principal could have been held liable for failure to provide supervision, had lack of supervision been found to be the proximate cause of the injury.[153] A New Jersey case[154] and a Michigan case[155] held similarly.

The court indicated in a California case[156] that the high school physical education department head had failed to develop an appropriate supervisory plan for the faculty on duty during the lunch hour. And, in a 1979 case,[157] it was indicated that the principal failed to exercise reasonable care in supervising the curriculum development and an inexperienced physical education instructor. Where a student was fatally injured at the hands of a fellow student while on the way from the locker room to gym class, the court held that although the superintendent and principal were not insurers of safety, they were obliged to exercise ordinary care to supervise and see that the students were supervised.[158]

While the acts in the foregoing cases did not directly occasion the injury, they did enhance the likelihood of injury. Negligence is related to awareness of recognizable risk

---

[149] Schmitt, Marianne Jeannette. Torts — Master and Servant — Negligent Hiring — Employer Owes a Duty to the General Public to Use Reasonable Care in Hiring and Retaining Employees. Evans v. Morsell, 284 Md. 160, 395 A. 2d 480 (1978). 9 Baltimore Law Review 435-452, 1980; see also Cutter v. Town of Farmington, 126 N.H. 836, 498 A. 2d 316 (1985) which holds negligence in performance by employee is not synonymous with incompetence upon employment, a tort of the administrator.

[150] Wangerin, Paul T. Actions and Remedies Against Government Units and Public Officers for Nonfeasance. 11 Loyola University Law Journal 101-143, 1979.

[151] Boucher v. Fuhlbruck, 26 Conn. Sup. 79, 213 A. 2d 455 (1965); Cook v. Bennett, 94 Mich. App. 93, 288 N.W. 2d 609 (1979); a 1986 Michigan case, Webber v. Yeo, 383 N.W. 2d 230 (Mich. App. 1986), however, held supervision a ministerial act.

[152] Ballard v. Polly, 387 F. Supp. 895 (1975) a D.C. case holding assignment of playground supervisors is clearly ministerial rather than discretionary acts and do not warrant the protection of sovereign immunity; Longo v. Santoro, 195 N.J. Super. 507, 480 A. 2d 934

(1984) held that decisions of principal involving the assignment of school personnel for supervision of student lunch hour activities were discretionary operational or less than high-level planning decisions involving allocation of personnel for which principal would be granted immunity under State Tort Claims Act.

[153] Sly v. Board of Education, 213 Kan. 415, 516 P. 2d 895 (1973).

[154] Caltavuturo v. Passaic, 124 N.J. Super 361, 307 A. 2d 114 (1973), cert. denied, 63 N.J. 583, 311 A. 2d 6 (1973); see also Titus v. Lindberg, 49 N.J. 66, 228 A. 2d 65 (1967).

[155] Cook v. Bennett, 94 Mich. App. 93, 288 N.W. 2d 609 (1979); see also, Flournoy v. McComas, 488 P. 2d 1104 (Colo. 1971).

[156] Dailey v. Los Angeles Unified School Dist., 84 Cal. Rptr. 325, vac. 87 Cal. Rptr. 376, 470 P. 2d 360 (1970).

[157] Larson v. Indp. School Dist. Braham, 252 N.W.2d 128 (1977), aff'd. 312 Minn. 583, 289 N.W. 2d 112 (1979), rehearing denied (1980).

[158] Kersey v. Harbin, 531 S.W. 2d 76 (Mo. App. 1975), aff'd. partly and rev'd. partly 591 S.W. 2d 745 (Mo. App. 1979).

of harm. Knowledge of the dangers, constructive or actual notice, also may impute negligence to the administrator.[159]

While the employment of competent personnel may be a non-delegable function, (see preceding subsection), the assignment of proper supervisory personnel may relieve a supervisor/administrator of liablility. In a Kentucky case,[160] both the teacher and the principal were sued when a student was injured by live ammunition when it was not prepared properly by another student. The court held that the principal was not negligent since he had delegated the direction of the play to the teacher.

Directing certain services as to manner they should be done.[161] The athletic director and high school principal were not immune from liability as related to weight lifting training sessions in preparation for high school football team tryouts in the fall. Among allegations was that they failed to see that the program was properly conducted. However, the negligence of the coach could not be imputed to the school superintendent merely because he was in a supervisory postion and there was no evidence of personal neglect as superintendent.[162]

Establishing rules and regulations for safety and complying with policy and statutory requirements. In a drowning case[163] in Kentucky, the principal of a school was found not to have been negligent in regard to a drowning which occurred inasmuch as he had prescribed certain conditions for an all day outing to the beach. In another water situation,[164] a 14-year-old boy drowned at a Sunday School picnic while swimming at a lake resort. The general manager of the resort was charged with responsibility of insuring compliance with city ordinances with regard to water safety; however, the court held that "mere failure to comply with some provisions of county ordinance regulating swimming pools would not be sufficient to support charge of willful and malicious action."

In a 1981 case,[165] the court said that suit is permitted against a governmental employee in his individual capacity if the employee's conduct toward the plaintiff was in bad faith, or with malicious purpose, or in a manner exhibiting wanton or willful disregard of human rights, safety, or property. In this situation the principal failed to carry out his duty to execute and implement without negligence the school board policy, specifically that no outing of student club could occur without permission of the school principal, and, if it occurred, it had to be attended by a faculty advisor. During the club's initiation outing, the plaintiff received injuries, resulting in paralysis from the neck down, from a hazing activity.

In this early case,[166] plaintiff alleged that principal was negligent in failing to promulgate more adequate regulations for the safety of the pupils. Plaintiff fell on

[159] Lynch v. Board of Educ., Collinsville, 72 Ill. App. 3d 317, 28 Ill. Dec. 359, 390 N.E. 2d 526 (1979), aff'd. 45 Ill. Dec. 96, 82 Ill. 2d 415, 412 N.E. 2d 447 (1980).

[160] Welsley v. Page, 514 S.W. 2d 697 (Ky. App. 1974).

[161] Kokomo v. Loy, 185 Ind. 18, 112 N.E. 994 (1916).

[162] Vargo v. Svitchan, 100 Mich. App. 809, 301 N.W. 2d 1 (1980).

[163] Cox v. Barnes, 469 S.W. 2d 61 (Ky. App. 1971).

[164] Herring v. R.L. Mathis Certified Dairy Co., 118 Ga. App. 132, 162 S.E. 2d 863 (1968), aff'd./rev'd. 225 Ga. 67, 166 S.E. 2d 89 (1969), 119 Ga. App. 226, 166 S.E. 2d 607, 225 Ga. 653, 171 S.E. 2d 124 (1969), 121 Ga. App. 373, 173 S.E. 2d 716 (1970).

[165] Bryant v. School Board of Duval Co., 399 So. 2d 417 (Fla. App. 1981).

[166] Thompson v. Board of Educ., 280 N.Y. 92 19 N.E. 2d 796 (1939).

exterior stairway when fellow pupil running down stairway during class dismissal collided with her. Court held that the principal exercised such general supervision as was possible, and he was not required to attend personally to each class at the same time. Rules and regulations also were in issue in a frisbee accident.[167]

Any rules and regulations must be promulgated under appropriate authorization. The court held that the Fish and Game Commission exceeded its authority in adopting a rule that the owner of a watercraft shall be liable for any injury or damage occasioned by the negligent operation of such watercraft, or the failure to observe ordinary care, because the rule went beyond the authorization to make rules and regulations regarding safety and went into the domain of the legislature, the establishment of liability.[168]

Remedying dangerous conditions and defective equipment or giving notice of same when there is knowledge of the condition.[169] Maintenance is a critical function of an administrator or supervisor, as is inspection for dangerous conditions. In a Georgia case,[170] the claim of injured student against principal was for alleged negligence in allowing a dangerous condition to exist at the school under his direct supervision and control. The condition concerned a rug and mat to be placed at a door of the school. The principal, in another case,[171] had actual notice of a jagged, "dangerous" large hole in a rusted chain-link fence partially surrounding the school, but which had some years previous been used for tennis.

A 1986 Michigan case[172] extended the responsibility of the administrator for warning of dangerous conditions to warning parents of such conditions in the school setting, and held that such was a ministerial act for which there was liability. In this situation a boy drowned in a beginning swimming class in school. The court said that the parents should have been informed of the dangerous conditions in the swimming class, specifically condition of the premises, no lifeguard on duty during the class, and lack of constant supervision of students in the class.

While malpractice has been a term primarily associated with the medical field and certain other professional personnel, the lack of proper administration has been termed "managerial malpractice."[173] Some jurisdictions hold that the administrator must be engaged in active negligence for the injured to recover.[174] And while some courts have been reluctant to allow liability for acts of nonfeasance, governmental liability for such acts has been expanding[175] (see §2.212). However, in some jurisdictions to determine whether a suit may be maintained, discretionary acts must be distinguished from ministerial acts.[176] (For discussion of discretionary acts' immunity, see §4.13.) But,

---

[167] Krueger v. Bailey, 406 N.E. 2d 665 (Ind. App. 1980).

[168] Stewart v. Stephens, 118 Ga. App. 811, 165 S.E. 2d 572, aff'd./rev'd. 225 Ga. 185, 166 S.E. 2d 890 (1969).

[169] Dawson v. Tulare Union High School Dist., 98 Cal. App. 138, 276 P. 424 (1929); Shannon v. Fleishhacker, 166 Cal. App. 258 2 P. 2d 835 (1931).

[170] Hennessy v. Webb, 245 Ga. 329, 264 S.E. 2d 878 (1980).

[171] Caltavuturo v. City of Passaic, 124 N.J. Super. 361, 307 A. 2d 114 (1973).

[172] Webber v. Yeo, 383 N.W. 2d 230 (Mich. App. 1986).

[173] See introduction, Chapter 19.

[174] Medsker v. Etchison, 101 Ind. App. 369, 199 N.E. 429 (1936).

[175] Wangerin, Paul T. Actions and Remedies Against Government Units and Public Officers for Nonfeasance. 11 *Loyola University Law Journal* 101-143, 1979.

[176] Vandall, Frank J. Special Contribution: Tort Liability of Public Officials. 29 *Mercer Law Review* 303-322, 1977.

even where there is immunity for discretionary acts, this cloak of immunity is lost when the act is done either with willful intent and malice or outside the scope of authority (an *ultra vires* act). Some courts hold that an officer acting beyond the scope of duty constitutes malfeasance creating personal liability,[177] but this does not appear to be the usual application of malfeasance (see §2.21).

Failure to promote constitutionally protected civil rights has been subject of considerable litigation involving officers (see §1.3).

As suits have increased against officials as individuals, particularly at the state and federal levels, these persons have not wished to assume some of the responsibilities. Therefore, liability gradually has been transferred from the officer to the government by several types of legislative codifications. The statutes have provided for administrative employees at the local, as well as state level. One type provides that the administrative officer shall not be personally liable unless acting outside scope of authority or is acting in a malicious or corrupt way.[178] There was such holding where it was found that the superintendent, assistant and associate superintendents were acting within their discretionary authority and the principal was acting within his ministerial authority. The case involved the falling of a soccer goal fatally injuring a girl in physical education class.[179] But, in a 1984 case,[180] it was held that the Executive Director of the Dept. of Natural Resources was not protected by statutory immunity for willful and malicious acts.

§ 3.4 Employees as individuals

Most acts of negligence involve the employee who has a direct relationship to the participant. As indicated in discussing the doctrine of respondeat superior (introduction to this chapter), it is the negligence of the employee that is imputed to the corporate entity. Whereas some schools and municipalities can seek refuge in the doctrine of governmental immunity (see §4.1), no such immunity cloaks the individual teacher, coach, maintenance man, or recreation leader;[181] as in all non-public entities, the right remains to sue the employee as an individual.[182] After all, the employee did breach the duty, commit the wrong. However, the extent of suits against individuals has never been great, compared to the suits against the corporate entity.[183] Most professional leaders

---

[177] Wilson v. Eberle, 15 Alaska 260 (1954).

[178] E.g., Connecticut, Georgia, New York, Tennessee. See Appendix for citations.

[179] Truelove v. Wilson et al. DeKalb Co. Board of Educ., 159 Ga. App. 906, 285 S.E. 2d 556 (1981).

[180] Hambley v. State Dept. of Natural Resources, 459 So. 2d 408 (Fla. App. 1984); see also Comuntzis v. Pinellas County School Board, aff'd./rev'd. in part and remanded 508 So. 2d 750 (Fla. App. 1987) plaintiff beaten by fellow students during school lunch hour just outside school cafeteria, principal's actions within scope of duty, but school held liable as supervision operational not discretionary.

[181] For persons in public agencies, some State Tort Claims Acts provide some protection or indemnifica-

tion (see §§4.234, 4.242). Cantwell v. Univ. of Mass., 551 F. 2d 879 (1977) Mass. law applied; DeStafney v. Univ. of Alabama, 413 So.2d 391 (Ala. 1982); Kaiser v. Emrich, 40 Ill. Dec. 506, 84 Ill. App. 3d 755, 406 N.E. 2d 207 (1980); Lovitt v. Concord School Dist. 58 Mich. App. 593, 228 N.W. 2d 479 (1975); Spearman v. University City Public School Dist., (Mo. Sup. 1981) 617 S.W. 2d 68.

[182] DeGooyer v. Harkness, 70 S.D. 26, 13 N.W.2d 815 (1944); Esposito v. Emery, 249 F. Supp. 308 (1965).

[183] It is recognized that some suits against teachers, recreation leaders and supervisors as individuals, but not against the corporate entity, may have been omitted from this study.

just do not have extensive financial resources, and there is something more impersonal about seeking a large sum from a corporation. Nevertheless, in the decade of the '80s, there appeared to be an increasing tendency to join employees as individuals as defendants. While some would say that physical education, athletics, and recreation leaders occupy a position in which there is considerable risk, it still remains that the standard of care is that of the reasonable and prudent *professional*.[184] And, after all, in what area of life are there no risks? This section is directed toward the liability of the employee as an individual. The cases are illustrative only.

§ 3.41   The employee "stands alone"

There are times when the doctrine of respondeat superior becomes negated by the actions of the employee, the negligence of the employee is not imputed to the corporate entity, and the employee "stands alone." In such situations, the corporate entity is not liable and the employee usually would have to rely on one's own personal liability insurance coverage. Any immunities granted by the legislature (see §4.2 and §17.1) also usually are negated by these actions. There are four primary actions of the employee which usually result in the employee "standing alone:" *ultra vires* act, willful and wanton conduct, gross negligence, and use of excessive force. The concept of gross negligence is detailed in §2.24.

The use of excessive force, usually in disciplinary situations, borders between negligence and assault and battery, an intentional tort. The use of excessive force for disciplining a school child, when not in the extreme, may be considered negligence. For example, a 230-pound physical education instructor disciplined a young student by "bear hugging" him and then dropping him on the floor, breaking his arm. This the court held was unnecessary and while the instructor had a right to physically discipline, it held this was excessive and, thus, negligence.[185] In *LaFrentz v. Gallagher*[186] action was brought for assault and battery based upon disciplinary action taken by a teacher in a softball class. Excessive force in the discipline of students resulting in bodily injury to students may also abrogate immunities given by statute[187] (see also §§1.141 assault and battery, 18.32 management of behavior, and 15.12 crowd control).

Willful and wanton conduct goes to the intent of the act. Negligence is based upon unintentional acts which harm. However, very poor professional practices can infer that the actions were in essence willful and wanton, as was alleged in a case involving a back somersault maneuver with an obese student.[188] The failure to comply with school board

---

[184] Duda v. Gaines, 12 N.J. Super. 326, 79 A. 2d 695 (1951); Govel v. Board of Educ. (two cases), 267 A.D. 621, 48 N.Y.S. 2d 299 (1944); Hale v. Davies, 86 Ga. App. 126, 70 S.E. 2d 923 (1952); Johnson City Bd. of Educ. v. Ray, 154 Tenn. 179, 289 S.W. 502 (1926); LaValley v. Stanford, 272 A.D. 183, 70 N.Y.S. 2d 460 (1947); Lee v. Board of Educ., 263 A.D. 23, 31 N.Y.S. 2d 113 (1941); Luce v. Board of Educ., 2 A.D. 2d 502, 157 N.Y.S. 2d 123 (1956); McDonell v. Brozo, 285 Mich. 38, 280 N.W. 100 (1938); Mokovich v. Independent School Dist., 177 Minn. 446, 225 N.W. 292

(1929); Sayers v. Ranger, 16 N.J. Super 22, 83 A. 2d 775 (1951).

[185] Frank v. Orleans Parish School Bd., 195 So. 2d 451 (La. App. 1967), writ refused 250 La. 635, 197 So. 2d 653 (1967).

[186] LaFrentz v. Gallagher, 105 Ariz. 255, 462 P. 2d 804 (1969).

[187] e.g., Texas.

[188] Landers v. School Dist., O'Fallon, 66 Ill. App.3d 78, 22 Ill. Dec. 837, 383 N.E. 2d 645 (1978).

policy regarding outings for student clubs was interpreted as being in a manner exhibiting wanton or willful disregard of human rights, safety, or property for which the faculty advisor was liable as an individual.[189] In *Acker v. Spangler*, 500 A. 2d 206 (Pa. Cmwlth. 1985), it was held to be a willful tortious act when the employee pulled a small table out from under a spectator seated thereon. The school was held immune, but the employee liable. Even where a state statute may provide for coverage of an employee, individual suit against an employee, but not against the corporate entity, is possible whenever the employee was not acting within scope of employment or, while within his employment, was acting in bad faith or with malicious purpose or in a manner exhibiting wanton and willful disregard of human rights, safety or property[190] (see §1.141).

§ 3.411   Ultra Vires Act

An *ultra vires* act is one outside the scope of authority or responsibility of the employee. The negligence of an employee is not imputed to the corporate entity where such employee acted beyond the scope of duty.[191] In a 1983 case,[192] the act of the employee was held to be outside this scope of employment. A part-time employee of a boat rental agency took a boat without his employer's permission for his own pleasure riding. He had never operated this specific boat before; however, the keys had been left in it. The court held that the owner was not accountable to a third party who had been injured. Similarly, a zoo employee was held to be outside the scope of employment, when he returned to the zoo to perform an employment task, but after completion of the task and in violation of rules, he took mother and child into the primate night house behind cages, an area off limits to public. The two-year-old child was bitten by an ape.[193] And, in a 1984 case,[194] the court held that the mere presence of police personnel on an evening cruise sponsored by a nonprofit organization which ran an annual community festival was not enough to give rise to the requisite special relationship for purpose of holding city liable on ground of failure to check identification of persons consuming liquor. Members of the police and fire departments served on the board of directors of the organization, but the off-duty policemen were hired to provide security and check identification cards and were not acting in behalf of the police department. Thus, working the cruise was outside the scope of their employment and their actions were not chargeable to the city.

Where a corporate entity, though, enjoys benefits from the *ultra vires* act of the employee or had notice of such *ultra vires* acts, it is rendered liable for negligence. For example, it was held that a lifeguard was acting outside the scope of his employment when he participated in horseshoe throwing at the city bathing beach and struck a child,

[189] Bryant v. School Board of Duval Co., 399 So. 2d 417 (Fla. App. 1981).
[190] Dist. School Board of Lake Co. v. Talmadge, 355 So. 2d 502, aff'd. 381 So. 2d 698 (1980), rev'd. 406 So. 2d 1127 (Fla. App. 1981); Willis v. Dade Co. School Board, 411 So. 2d 245 (Fla. App. 1982) pet. denied 418 So. 2d 1278 (1982).
[191] Cunningham v. Niagara Falls, 242 A.D. 39, 272 N.Y.S. 720 (1934); Sherwood v. Moxee School Dist., 58 Wash. 2d 351, 363 P. 2d 138 (1961).
[192] Palestina v. Fernandez, 701 F. 2d 438 (1983).
[193] Normand v. New Orleans, 363 So. 2d 1220 (La. App. 1978), cert. den. 366 So. 2d 573.
[194] Torres v. Salty Sea Days, Inc., 36 Wash. App. 668, 676 P. 2d 512 (1984).

injuring her. However, because the city had notice of such *ultra vires* acts, it was rendered liable for the injury.[195] However, in *Randi F. v. High Ridge YMCA*, 170 Ill. App. 3d 962, 120 Ill. Dec. 784, 524 N.E. 2d 966 (1988), it was held that a teacher's aide at a day care center was acting outside the scope of employment and that such act had no relation to the business of the day care center or the furtherance thereof. The aide allegedly beat and sexually assaulted a 3-year-old child. The day care center was not held liable. It was stated that if an employee commits an intentional tort with a dual purpose of furthering the employer's interest and venting personal anger, respondeat superior may lie, but if the employee acts purely in one's own interest, liability under respondeat superior is inappropriate. See §22.1 for situations relating to transportation and *ultra vires* acts.

A primary defense for the corporate entity is to allege that the act of the employee was *ultra vires*, not authorized — and if such is true, then frequently the corporate entity can evade liability. A health spa, being sued by a patron, joined its employee as an additional defendant on theory that she acted outside scope of employment.[196] The plaintiff could not recover against corporate entity defendant because employee was held to have been outside scope of his employment when he was on his way home from meeting at restaurant with co-employee and prospective vendor and was involved in an automobile accident. While entertaining prospective vendors was sanctioned, such did not constitute evidence of being in employer's service when he drove home from such entertainment in an allegedly inebriated state.[197] See commentary §3.1 this chapter and §5.13 *ultra vires* acts as a defense.

§ 3.42   Limiting liability and indemnification

As previously indicated, the doctrine of sovereign/governmental immunity does not apply to individual employees, only to the public corporate entity; however, there are efforts to enact legislation which does provide some immunity to an employee. As described in the preceding section (§3.3 Administrative officials), discretionary acts generally are immune from liability if within the scope of authority; however, most employees are not in position to engage in discretionary acts, but rather, they perform ministerial duties which do, indeed, carry liability. Some states do provide specifically by statute that employees shall not be personally liable for damage or injury if in the performance of duties within the scope of responsibilities and if the act is not willful and wanton.[198] There also are limited liability statutes relating to emergency care. For a complete discussion of these, see §17.1.

Indemnification is another approach to protecting the employee. For many years, public agencies generally did not carry insurance in respect to the employee as an

[195] Rafsky v. New York City, 257 A.D. 855, 12 N.Y.S. 2d 560 (1939).
[196] Leidy v. Deseret Enterprizes, Inc., 252 Pa. Super. 162, 381 A. 2d 164 (1977).
[197] Healthdyne v. Odom, 173 Ga. App. 184, 325 S.E. 2d 847 (1984).
[198] e.g., Connecticut, New Jersey, New Mexico, Texas (See Chapter 4 for detailed status); a case

applying Georgia governmental immunity law is True-love v. Wilson et al. DeKalb Co. Board of Education, 159 Ga. App. 906, 285 S.E. 2d 556 (1981) holding principal and teacher acted within scope of authority and without willful and wanton intent to injure; in Lewis v. Beecher School System, 118 Mich. App. 105, 324 N.W. 2d 779 (1982) held employee cloaked with governmental immunity if acting within scope of

individual. This has changed and in the decade of the '80s, most states provide by statute for either indemnification if a judgment should be against an employee or provision of insurance to cover legal defense costs and any judgment. Also, in recognition that there may be conflict of interest between the individual employee and the corporate entity, several states (*e.g.*, New York, Texas) now provide by statute that if deemed desirable in legal defense, private counsel can be obtained for the employee. See both §4.24 and §25.2 for discussion of indemnification and insurance coverage.

Although teachers may stand *in loco parentis* as regards the enforcement of authority (discipline), teachers do not stand *in loco parentis* with regard to their negligent acts, and teachers therefore do not have the same immunity accorded to parents.[199] The same would hold for a recreation leader or camp counselor responsible for children (see §2.1112).

§ 3.43   Recovery against the employee

Nebraska, as part of its Tort Claims Act, provides that a political subdivision may bring an action for recovery from an employee when the political subdivision has made payment of an award of settlement growing out of the employee's act or omission. This is the reverse of indemnification! A number of states do provide for contribution from joint tortfeasors, and particularly where a corporate entity should have been subjected to suit and costs due to *ultra vires* acts of an employee would this apply.

§ 3.5   Volunteers

What is the status of a volunteer working in a program? The usual rule is that if persons are acting in behalf of the agency, whether or not they are receiving monetary reimbursement, they are considered agents of the organization. Therefore, a volunteer's negligence is imputed to the corporation under the doctrine of *respondeat superior*, and the corporation cannot evade responsibility because the individual was a volunteer. However, at the same time, as true for an employee as discussed in the previous section (§3.4), volunteers are liable for their own negligent acts. (Section does not discuss liability for volunteers who are themselves injured while volunteering service and are plaintiffs in the court action.)

A number of states, particularly in the 1980s, have made provisions for volunteers through various statutory approaches; these are discussed in the next sub-section (§3.51). Case precedent essentially applies the doctrine of *respondeat superior* and is discussed in the following sub-section (§3.52).

employment — wrestling in physical education class situation; Pierson v. Indp. School Dist., 698 S.W. 2d 377 (Tx. 1985) regarding explosion on school float held personal immunity not waived if within scope of duties; Schultz v. City of Brentwood, 725 S.W. 2d 157 (Mo. App. 1987) employee of pre-school, day care center held not "public official" with immunity.

[199] Baird v. Hosmer, 46 Ohio St. 2d 273, 75 Ohio Ops. 2d 323, 347 N.E. 2d 533 (1976).

§ 3.51   Statutory provisions

Because of the greater number of lawsuits and the difficulty in obtaining insurance in the mid-1980s, the performance of volunteer service for both public entities and nonprofit organizations appeared to decline. In order to allay fears of liability, particularly as related to nonprofit organizations and especially youth sport programs, in 1986-1988 there was extensive legislative activity. Table 3.1 State Statutes Limiting Liability of Volunteers Serving Nonprofit Corporations summarizes the statutes by state.

Nearly one-half of the states have statutes providing for immunity of nonprofit organization volunteers in general, including officers, directors, and trustees of the organization. Volunteers, of course, are those persons who serve without compensation. Not included in compensation are apppropriate expenses, including meals, lodging, and transportation, and for sports officials, a modest honorarium. Almost all statutes also require that the volunteer be acting "in good faith" and within the scope of function or duties. In nearly all statutes, the immunity of the volunteer is negated by willful and wanton misconduct. Additionally, in some states, immunity is lost for reckless disregard of safety of others and for gross negligence. Personal immunity is provided in most states, although a few do provide only for insurance coverage or indemnification. There are a few exclusions, primarily the operation of motor vehicles or transportation of participants/players. In several of the sport-oriented statutes, care and maintenance of real estate unrelated to practice or playing areas is excluded for immunity of volunteers. While general immunity is provided, this immunity is waived in most states to the extent of insurance coverage. See Table 3.1 for more specific provisions for each state.

While sport programs are encompassed, for the most part, in the statutes covering volunteers in general, ten states have passed laws specific to sport (See Table 3.1 for the states and statutory provisions). Most of these statutes enumerate managers, coaches, umpires, referees, and persons who assist these persons. A couple statutes also immunize financial sponsors, and several require volunteers, in order to take advantage of statutory immunication, to participate in safety orientation and training skills program. Several of the statutes exclude educational institution athletic programs, focusing upon recreational sport programs.

There also are some limited focus statutes. A few of these are indicated on Table 3.1, and others are included in the statutory citations of the appropriate state. Some of the earlier statutes were repealed. The trend appears to be more toward encompassing statutes for a class of people, rather than for a specific service or recreational program. The sport-oriented statutes are an exception to this trend.

In the Tort Claims Acts and related statutes, particularly where there is authorization for insurance or indemnification for employees, a good number of states specifically include volunteers as being covered; and, some by Attorney General Opinions (AGO) (*e.g.*, Missouri, Nevada) construe the term employee to include volunteers (see §4.234 and Table 4.1). To the contrary in a 1981 law, Tennessee defines very narrowly the term government employee for cities and counties; and, Massachusetts does not include public employee for indemnification in its statute.

Efforts have been made to limit the liability of volunteers when rendering emergency care; however, if the volunteer owes a duty to the person to whom care is rendered, just as an employee, the Good Samaritan statutes would not apply (see §17.1). See also §§17.15 and 17.16 as related to physicians who volunteer services to sport teams.

Table 3.1 State Statutes Limiting Liability of Volunteers Serving Nonprofit Corporations[1]

State[2]	Protected Class[3] General	Protected Class[3] Sports	Date Enacted[4]	Applicability[5]	Liability Protection[6]	Exclusions[7]	Volunteer Prerequisites[8]	Negating Behavior[9]	Special Considerations[10]
Alabama			1987	officer, director, trustee, member governing body of not-for-profit organizations	individuals immune; corporate entity not immunized from acts of noncompensated officers	for-profit subsidiary, gambling, games of chance, parimutuel betting	noncompensated	willful, wanton; gross negligence; fraud	example of officers' immunity statute; does not specify volunteers
Alaska			1988						limit liability of directors of corp.
Arizona	X		1988	members, directors, officers, employees, agents, volunteers nonprofit corp. & assoc.	indemnification				enter into contracts or agreements joint purchasing of insurance or pool retention of risk
Arkansas			1981	state & local gov't. volunteers, including schools	liability insurance may be provided to same extent as provided paid staff; volunteers enjoy sovereign immunity same extent as paid staff				

State[2]	Protected Class[3] General	Protected Class[3] Sports	Date Enacted[4]	Applicability[5]	Liability Protection[6]	Exclusions[7]	Volunteer Prerequisites[8]	Negating Behavior[9]	Special Considerations[10]
California			1987	volunteer director or officer of nonprofit corp.	no personal liability to 3rd party for monetary damages; does not limit corp. liability for acts of volunteer		within scope of duty; act performed in good faith; without compensation	reckless, wanton, intentional act; gross negligence	damages covered by liability insurance; or, if good faith effort to obtain insurance unsuccessful, no personal liability
				emergency search & rescue volunteer	immunity from civil damages		possess 1st aid training; good faith	AGO — gross negligence	
Colorado	X	specifies sporting programs or activities	1986	board of directors; leader, assistant, coach, or trainer for any program, org., service group, recreational group or nonprofit corp. serving or providing sporting programs or activities for people 18 years or younger	not liable for civil damages when performs a service, or adopts or enforces a policy or regulation to protect health or safety of another	immunity does not extend to protect such persons from liability for acts or omissions which harm third persons	without compensation or expectation; for benefit of another; in good faith	wanton & willful	performance does not create duty of care to third person
Connecticut			1979	volunteers in state gov't.	liability insurance to same extent as provided salaried employees				

State[2]	Protected Class[3] General	Protected Class[3] Sports	Date Enacted[4]	Applicability[5]	Liability Protection[6]	Exclusions[7]	Volunteer Prerequisites[8]	Negating Behavior[9]	Special Considerations[10]
Delaware		X	1986	member of qualified staff-manager, coach, umpire, referee or assistant to, person who prepares field; nonprofit sports program recognized by NCAA or AAU or organized for recreational purposes; sponsors & operators of programs	not liable for civil damages which exceed insurance coverage or the minimum coverage required by law if no coverage		without compensation	reckless act or omission; grossly negligent	
	X		1986	volunteer — trustee, director, officer, agent, or worker not-for-profit corp. (501 (c))	not subject to suit directly, derivatively or contribution	operation of motor vehicle during activity except limited to extent of insurance coverage	without compensation	willful, wanton; grossly negligent	liability of organization under respondeat superior retained
Florida			1983	state only, volunteers	covered by state liability protection and workers' compensation				
			1988	county gov't. only, volunteers	covered by workers' compensation		own free will, without monetary compensation		does not reference liability or insurance, just "other benefits" as county deems appropriate

State[2]	Protected Class[3] General	Protected Class[3] Sports	Date Enacted[4]	Applicability[5]	Liability Protection[6]	Exclusions[7]	Volunteer Prerequisites[8]	Negating Behavior[9]	Special Considerations[10]
Florida (continued)			1973	volunteers, community-care-for-the-elderly core services	insurance coverage, including excess auto liability protection		within volunteer's assignment		volunteers shall be provided training & supervision
Georgia			1969	member, director, trustee, or officer of board of non-profit, charitable or eleemosynary institution or organization or of any local gov't, agency, board, authority, or entity	immune from civil liability		without compensation; in good faith; within scope of official actions & duties	willful & wanton misconduct	
		X	1988	volunteer (manager, coach, instructor, umpire, referee, or assistant to such persons), employees, officers of nonprofit assoc. conducting or sponsoring sports or safety programs	not liable, except to extent of insurance coverage	transportation of participants; care & maintenance of real estate unrelated to practice, training, or playing areas	within scope of assigned duties	willful & wanton conduct; gross negligence	includes safety programs as related to home, vehicle maintenance & operation, boating, hunting, firearms, self-protection, fire hazards, or other activity which may involve exposures to personal injury; sports programs — competitive sport as recognized by NCAA, AAU, and USOC, and organized for recreational purposes

State[2]	Protected Class[3]		Date Enacted[4]	Applicability[5]	Liability Protection[6]	Exclusions[7]	Volunteer Prerequisites[8]	Negating Behavior[9]	Special Considerations[10]
	General	Sports							
Hawaii			1978	volunteers to state agency	deemed employees of state, who are provided defense; personal liability insurance may be furnished		own free will; no monetary or material gain		nondiscrimination subsection on right to volunteer
Idaho			1987	volunteer officers & directors of charitable corp. or unincorporated membership org. engaged exclusively in charitable activities	personally immune from civil liability except for insurance policy coverage			willful & wanton; fraud; knowing violation of law; breach of fiduciary duty; acts not in good faith which involve intentional misconduct, fraud, knowing law violation; improper personal benefit	organization purpose includes to foster national or international sports competition, but only if no part of activities involve provision of athletic facilities or equipment

State[2]	Protected Class[3]		Date Enacted[4]	Applicability[5]	Liability Protection[6]	Exclusions[7]	Volunteer Prerequisites[8]	Negating Behavior[9]	Special Considerations[10]
	General	Sports							
Illinois		X	1987	volunteer managers, coaches, instructor, umpires or referees, or assist same; sports program — competitive sports program formally recognized by USOC, AAU, NCAA — that portion organized for recreational purposes, primarily for participants 18 years of age or younger, but no age limit for programs for physically handicapped or mentally retarded	not liable for civil damages	transportation of participants or others to or from game, event, or practice; care & maintenance of real estate unrelated to the practice or playing area which persons or nonprofit assoc. own, possess, or control	without compensation	conduct of person falls substantially below the standards generally practiced & accepted in like circumstances; or, when under a recognized duty to another, knowing or having reason to know that an act or omission would create substantial risk of harm; establish conduct well below ordinary standards of care	doctrines of assumption of risk and comparative fault not affected; liability of organization for acts or omissions is not barred
Indiana			1985	member of board or commission of the state or a political subdivision or not-for-profit corp., who sets policy or oversees activities or functional responsibilities	liability limited to that coverage by insurance		without compensation		does not affect corporate entity liability

State[2]	Protected Class[3]		Date Enacted[4]	Applicability[5]	Liability Protection[6]	Exclusions[7]	Volunteer Prerequisites[8]	Negating Behavior[9]	Special Considerations[10]
	General	Sports							
Iowa	X		1987	director, officer, employee, member, trustee, or volunteer of nonprofit organization, including unincorporated club if no part of income distributed to members, directors, or officers	not personally liable		act performed in discharge of duty	intentional misconduct, knowing violation of law, improper personal benefit	
Kansas	X		1987	volunteer — officer, director, trustee or other person who performs services nonprofit org. (501 (c))	if nonprofit org. carries insurance, not liable; or, if volunteer required to be insured, liability only to extent of coverage	not liable for acts of others unless volunteer authorizes, approves, ratifies or otherwise actively participates in the act or omission of officer, director, or other person of the org.; person who delivers health care service to patients in a medical care facility	without compensation	willful or wanton misconduct, intentionally tortious conduct	corporate entity still liable for acts or omissions and are imputed to corp. entity for purpose of apportioning liability for damages to third party

State[2]	Protected Class[3]		Date Enacted[4]	Applicability[5]	Liability Protection[6]	Exclusions[7]	Volunteer Prerequisites[8]	Negating Behavior[9]	Special Considerations[10]
	General	Sports							
Kentucky	X		1988	director, officer, volunteer, or trustee of nonprofit org. exempt under 501 (c) tax code	immune from civil liability		without compensation; acting in good faith; within the scope of official functions & duties	willful or wanton misconduct	
Louisiana			1988	director, officer, trustee, or volunteer worker for inc. & uninc. nonprofit org. which sponsors a fair or festival, or any nonprofit historical org. organized for civic or historical purposes	not individually liable in exercise of judgment, implementation of policy, or management of affairs		in good faith, within scope of official functions & duties	willful or wanton misconduct	also a statute regarding limitation of liability toward persons injured in connection with Mardi Gras, fairs & festivals
		X	1987	volunteer athletic coach, manager, team physician, or sports team official for act directly related to responsibilities while actively participating in sporting activities or in practice thereof	no cause of action against		without compensation (small stipend does not exclude; must participate in safety orientation & training program by league or team — may waive for documented proficiency in first aid & safety	gross negligence	

State[2]	Protected Class[3] General	Protected Class[3] Sports	Date Enacted[4]	Applicability[5]	Liability Protection[6]	Exclusions[7]	Volunteer Prerequisites[8]	Negating Behavior[9]	Special Considerations[10]
Maine	X		1987	director, officer, volunteer of any nonprofit organization organized or incorporated in state or principal place of business in state	immune from civil liability		within course & scope of activities of the organization; act not personal to individual		
Maryland	X	specifies athletic club	1986	director, officer, employee, providing services or performing duties on behalf of athletic club, charitable org.., community assoc., or homeowners' assoc.	not personally liable if assoc. or org. maintains insurance coverage not less than $200,000/$500,000, deductible not greater than $10,000, and if coinsurance, rate of coinsurance not greater than 20%			malice; gross negligence (personal liability beyond insurance coverage)	plaintiff recover damages from assoc. or org. only to extent of insurance coverage; athletic club organized & operated exclusively for recreational purposes, exempt under 501 (c) of tax code
		includes athletics	1987	volunteer in community recreation program as athletic coach, manager, official, program leader, or assistant	volunteer not personally liable; athletic official not liable for any action brought by player, participant, or spectator	"community recreation program" does not include public or private educational institution athletic programs; negligent operation of a motor vehicle		willful, wanton or grossly negligent act; volunteer permitting an unsupervised competition, practice, or activity	athletic official — one who officiates, referees, or umpires interscholastic, intercollegiate or any other amateur athletic contest conducted by nonprofit or governmental body

State[2]	Protected Class[3] General	Protected Class[3] Sports	Date Enacted[4]	Applicability[5]	Liability Protection[6]	Exclusions[7]	Volunteer Prerequisites[8]	Negating Behavior[9]	Special Considerations[10]
Maryland (continued)	X		1987	volunteer, including officer, director, trustee of charitable organization	not liable beyond limits of any personal insurance	health care malpractice	no compensation directly or indirectly	reckless, willful or wanton misconduct; intentional conduct	
Massachusetts		X	1987	volunteer (manager, coach, umpire, referee or assistant to manager or coach), officer, director, trustee or member of a nonprofit corp. or assoc., and the nonprofit assoc. entity; sports program organized for recreational purposes and primarily for participants 18 years of age or younger, except no age limitation on programs for physically handicapped or mentally retarded	not liable for any action in tort	activities primarily commercial in nature, even though revenues primarily for maintaining sports program or other charitable purpose; transportation of participants; care & maintenance of real estate owned, possessed, or controlled used in connection with sports program or any other assoc. activity	without compensation, but umpires & referees modest honorarium	intentional acts to harm, grossly negligent acts	
Michigan									

| State[2] | Protected Class[3] | | Date Enacted[4] | Applicability[5] | Liability Protection[6] | Exclusions[7] | Volunteer Prerequisites[8] | Negating Behavior[9] | Special Considerations[10] |
	General	Sports							
Minnesota		X	1987	athletic coach, manager, or official for sports team organized or performing under a nonprofit charter; community-based voluntary nonprofit athletic assoc.; volunteer of the assoc. — applies to sports competitions, practice & instruction	not liable for money damages to player, participant or spectator	to extent insurance coverage; operation, maintenance or use of motor vehicle; coach, manager, or official as part of public or private educational institution's athletic program		willful & wanton acts or reckless behavior; violation of federal, state, or local law	
Mississippi	X		1988	"qualified" volunteer providing services, goods, or use of property or equipment for volunteer activity for volunteer agency, except agency established primarily for recreational benefit of its stockholders or members	not liable for civil damages; volunteer not vicariously liable for acts of another	negligent operation of motor vehicle, aircraft, boat, or other powered mode of conveyance	without compensation or change, acting within scope of activity	intentional act; willful, wanton or reckless act; grossly negligent	volunteer activity — includes rescue services, enhancement of cultural, civic, religious, educational, scientific or economic resources of community

| State[2] | Protected Class[3] | | Date Enacted[4] | Applicability[5] | Liability Protection[6] | Exclusions[7] | Volunteer Prerequisites[8] | Negating Behavior[9] | Special Considerations[10] |
	General	Sports							
Mississippi (continued)		officials only	1988	sports officials (referees, umpires, linesmen & those in similar capacities) who officiate at any level of competition and duly registered or members of local, state, regional or national org. engaged in educ. & training to sports officials	not liable for acts in relation to officiating duties within confines of facility in which athletic contest being played		acting within scope of activity	intentional, willful, wanton, reckless, malicious, or grossly negligent acts	
Missouri									
Montana	X		1987	officer, director, or volunteer of nonprofit corp.	not individually liable		within scope of official capacity	willful or wanton misconduct	nonprofit corp. liability retained
Nebraska			1923	Boy Scout council, board of directors, scout executive, or others having mgmt. or control of Boy Scouts & those having charge of juniors in similar organizations not organized for pecuniary gain or profit	not liable to juveniles or parents, guardians or any standing in loco parentis				use of juveniles to render service patrolling streets or grounds, aid in maintenance of order at public gatherings (state, city, fair assoc., school, other)

State[2]	Protected Class[3]		Date Enacted[4]	Applicability[5]	Liability Protection[6]	Exclusions[7]	Volunteer Prerequisites[8]	Negating Behavior[9]	Special Considerations[10]
	General	Sports							
Nevada	X		1987 amend.	officer, director, trustee or other person who performs services without compensation	immune from civil damages		services not supervisory in nature	volunteer — intentional, willful, wanton or malicious acts; officer, trustee, director — intentional misconduct, fraud, knowing violation of law	amend. 1987 added "volunteers," to officers; trustees, directors; nonprofit corp., assoc., or organization liability retained
New Hampshire	X	sports specified	1988	volunteer who performs services without compensation for nonprofit organization or governmental entity	volunteer immune from liability; liability of organization limited to $250,000 aggregate per person per occurrence and $1M total per occurrence	transportation; care of organization's premises	athletic coaches or sports officials shall possess proper certification or validation of competence in the rules, procedures, practices, & programs of the athletic activity; volunteer must have prior written approval from the organization to act on behalf of org.	willful, wanton or grossly negligent misconduct	purpose — specifies to foster amateur competition in a sport formally recognized by NCAA
New Jersey	X		1987	trustee, director, officer, other uncompensated volunteers	not liable for damages	negligent operation of motor vehicle		reckless disregard for duties imposed by the position; willful, wanton, or grossly negligent act	this law does not supercede the sport statute (next statute)

State[2]	Protected Class[3] General	Protected Class[3] Sports	Date Enacted[4]	Applicability[5]	Liability Protection[6]	Exclusions[7]	Volunteer Prerequisites[8]	Negating Behavior[9]	Special Considerations[10]
New Jersey (continued)		X	1986	athletic coach, manager, or official for sports team organized or performing pursuant to nonprofit or similar charter or (sponsored/funded) member team in league organized by or affiliated with a county or municipality recreation dept. — encompasses competition, practice & instruction	immunity from civil liability for damages to player, participant or spectator	negligent operation of motor vehicle; person who permits sport competition or practice to be conducted without supervision; coach, manager, official who services public or private educational institution's athletic program	Coach, manager, or official must participate in safety orientation and training skills program (more detail in statute)	willful, wanton or grossly negligent act	financial sponsor not involved in administration not liable to player, participant, coach, official or spectator; sponsor providing goods, services, or other assistance not liable to player or participant unless willful, wanton, or grossly negligent act
New Mexico									
New York									
North Carolina	X		1987	direct service volunteer who performs service for a charitable nonprofit organization (humane & philanthropic objectives)	not liable for civil damages, except to extent of insurance carried by organization or volunteer	operation of motor vehicle	acting in good faith; services rendered were reasonable under the circumstances	gross negligence, wanton conduct, intentional wrong-doing	

State[2]	Protected Class[3] General	Protected Class[3] Sports	Date Enacted[4]	Applicability[5]	Liability Protection[6]	Exclusions[7]	Volunteer Prerequisites[8]	Negating Behavior[9]	Special Considerations[10]
North Dakota	X		1987	volunteer providing services to nonprofit organization	immune from civil liability	negligent operation of a motor vehicle	acting in good faith, with reasonable & ordinary care, in scope of duties	willful misconduct, gross negligence	athletic aspects controlled by next statute
		X	1987	volunteer athletic coach, manager, or official for sports team organized or performing pursuant to nonprofit charter	not liable to player or participant	negligent operation of a motor vehicle; to a person permitting competition or practice without supervision; service as a part of public or private educ. inst. athletic program	acting in good faith, with reasonable & ordinary care, in scope of duties, participate in safety orientation & training program	willful misconduct, gross negligence	
Ohio	X		1986	officer, trustee, other uncompensated volunteer of charitable nonprofit corp., assoc., institution, society with any education-related purpose for both supervisory and nonsupervisory services	not liable in damages in a civil action			willful or wanton misconduct, intentionally tortious conduct	volunteer not liable for actions of officers, et al. or employees unless had prior knowledge & authorized, approved, as actively participated, or ratified
Oklahoma									

State[2]	Protected Class[3] General	Protected Class[3] Sports	Date Enacted[4]	Applicability[5]	Liability Protection[6]	Exclusions[7]	Volunteer Prerequisites[8]	Negating Behavior[9]	Special Considerations[10]
Oregon			1983	volunteers transporting handicapped & older persons	see statute — limitations vary by number of persons being transported; 5 or fewer, 6-16, & 17 or more		valid driver's license	intentional acts, gross negligence, intoxication	
Pennsylvania		X	1986	manager, coach, instructor, umpire or referee or volunteer assisting in sports program of nonprofit assoc.; officer or employee of assoc.; recreational sports programs primarily for participants 18 years of age or younger, but no age limitation for physically handicapped or mentally retarded	no liability for civil damage	transportation of participants or others — game, event, or practice; care & maintenance of real estate unrelated to practice or playing areas owned, possessed or controlled		conduct falls substantially below the standards generally practiced & accepted in like circumstances; did act, under recognized duty, knowing or having reason to know that such act created a substantial risk of actual harm	assumption of risk & contributory fault not affected; sport program — competitive sports formally recognized by AAU or NCAA, but only that part of program organized for recreational purposes

State[2]	Protected Class[3] General	Sports	Date Enacted[4]	Applicability[5]	Liability Protection[6]	Exclusions[7]	Volunteer Prerequisites[8]	Negating Behavior[9]	Special Considerations[10]
Rhode Island		X	1987	manager, coach, instructor, umpire, referee or official or assists same in youth sports program under nonprofit corp.; director, trustee, officer or employee of such corp.; also covered are interscholastic or intramural programs under jurisdiction of school controlling org.	not liable for civil damages			willful, wanton or reckless disregard for safety	school controlling org. — R.I. Interscholastic League, Comm. on Jr. Hi School Athletics, Board of Regents for Elem. & Sec. Educ.; youth sports program — recreational athletic competition or instruction for participants 19 years of age or younger, no age restriction for physically or mentally handicapped
South Carolina									
South Dakota	X		1987	volunteer of nonprofit org. or corp., certain hospitals or governmental entity	immune from civil liability; waiver to extent of insurance or risk sharing pool except for volunteer serving as director, officer or trustee	negligent operation of motor vehicle	in good faith, within scope of official functions and duties	willful & wanton misconduct	
Tennessee									

State[2]	Protected Class[3] General	Protected Class[3] Sports	Date Enacted[4]	Applicability[5]	Liability Protection[6]	Exclusions[7]	Volunteer Prerequisites[8]	Negating Behavior[9]	Special Considerations[10]
Texas	X	youth sports specified as a purpose	1987	director, officer, trustee, & direct-service volunteer of charitable org. (private primary & secondary schools excluded)	immune from civil liability, except waiver to extent of insurance coverage	operation or use of any motor driven equip., including airplane	acting in scope of functions & duties, and in good faith	intentional, willfully or wantonly negligent, or with conscious indifference or reckless disregard for safety of others	liability of employee & organization entity limited to $500,000/$1M per occurrence; organization cannot participate in any political campaign (see statute for additional org. criteria.)
Utah									
Vermont									
Virginia									
Washington									
West Virginia									

State[2]	Protected Class[3] General	Protected Class[3] Sports	Date Enacted[4]	Applicability[5]	Liability Protection[6]	Exclusions[7]	Volunteer Prerequisites[8]	Negating Behavior[9]	Special Considerations[10]
Wisconsin	X		1987	volunteer, provides service to or on behalf of corp. (nonstock) without compensation	not liable	civil or criminal proceeding brought by or on behalf of any gov'tal. unit, authority, or agency; violation of state or federal law where proceeding pursuant to an express private right of action created by statute; negligent operation of auto, truck, train, airplane or other vehicle, violation in scope of practice under volunteer's state license, certificate, permit or registration		a violation of criminal law, unless reasonable cause to believe lawful; willful misconduct	to be used in conjunction with other special statutes relating to volunteer immunity
Wyoming									

Footnotes

1 This table presents only those statutes which specified volunteers serving nonprofit corporations; almost every state has statutes regarding nonprofit corporations which include indemnification and/or insurance coverage for directors, officers, and trustees, who serve uncompensated on the governing body of the corporation. In addition, statutes relating to volunteers in governmental entities should be checked. These include both provisions in state tort claims acts and special focus statutes. See §4.2 and citations in Appendix.

2 Complete citations for statutes are in the Appendix.

3 Most statutes regarding volunteers either protect volunteers as a general class of persons (an X in "general" column) or volunteers specific to sport programs (an X in "sports" column). If the statute is other than these two protected classes, there is no X, but the type of volunteer may be found in the Applicability column.

4 This is the date of original enactment. Many statutes have been amended, even quite a number which were enacted in 1986 and 1987. Be sure to check statutes in a law library or with your local attorney for any updating amendments, or even the repeal of certain statutes. Don't forget to check for new statutes.

5 This column gives the enumeration of the statute as to whom the statute is applicable, including the definition of nonprofit corporation and other descriptive information regarding applicability.

6 This column indicates the nature or type of liability protection afforded by the statute. In almost all states, it is immunity from liability for civil actions/damages. The terminology of the statute is used in this column, as in all columns, should there appear to be some inconsistency.

7 The type of activity or situation which is excluded from the general immunity of the statute is listed in this column.

8 In order to qualify, there often are certain characteristics set forth for the volunteer. These usually are noncompensated, within scope of functions or duties, and performance of act in good faith. In almost all states where defined, expenses include meals, lodging, and travel; modest honoraria for sport officials (umpires, referees) are not considered compensation.

9 Negating behaviors are those acts of the volunteer which prevent the volunteer from being protected by the general authorization of immunity. Almost all states specify willful and wanton misconduct; other frequently listed behaviors include gross negligence and reckless disregard for safety of others.

10 Special considerations are explanatory comments or special provisions. Generally, immunizing a volunteer does not reduce liability of the nonprofit association; the association remains liable under the doctrine of respondeat superior.

§ 3.52 Doctrine of respondeat superior applied to volunteers

The position in the *Restatement of Agency 2d* §225 that one who volunteers services without an agreement for or expectation of reward may be a servant of the one accepting such services is the one most commonly applied in the cases and supports the application of the doctrine of *respondeat superior*. In determining whether the relationship between an unpaid volunteer-tortfeasor and the sponsoring agency (whether public or charitable) is such that the agency is responsible for the acts of the volunteer depends primarily upon whether the volunteer was "within the control of the agency" and was acting within the scope of "employment" or authority/responsibility.[200] Control is determined by a number of factors, including the specific action of the volunteer and how much of it was directed by the agency, the hierarchical organization which may give evidence of the right to control, and the contact before and after the incident between the volunteer and the agency. In a 1985 case[201] it was held that the scoutmasters at this particular camp were not employees for this segment of program as the council had not authority over them.

In *Leno v. YMCA*, 17 Cal. App. 3d 651, 95 Cal. Rptr. 96 (1971), the scuba instructor was a volunteer, but not certified as a scuba instructor. The court held that to select an instructor with care is a nondelegable responsibility of the agency. In another water case[202] where the agency gave the volunteer instructions regarding safety in swimming and what to do in case of an emergency, which directly involved the agency, it was held that the volunteer was an agent of the organization and the doctrine of *respondeat superior* applied. The selection of permitting a person who volunteers to serve in a leadership capacity is an extremely important function of an agency or organization,[203] for a person who is conducting the activities on behalf of such organization must adhere to the same standard of care as an employee who is paid. These persons must give the same standard of care as an employee who is paid, and, thus require the same type of credentials, orientation, and supervision as a paid employee.

The imputing of liability extends from not only instructional service, as just discussed, but also supervisory responsibilities. In one situation[204] a youth at an indoor "sleep-in" was struck by a heavy object falling from a rack from which the counselor was removing pillows while he was sleeping on the floor; and, in another,[205] at an exhibit where there were a number of booths, a parade-sized flag was leaned against the wall with three tacks in the cloth to hold it against the wall. The flag was jostled by a photographer trying to take a picture and it fell on the Plaintiff. It was held that the flag was put up in a negligent manner.

---

[200] Reserved.

[201] Reserved.

[202] Malloy v. Fong, 220 P. 2d 48, rev'd. 37 Cal. 2d 356, 232 P. 2d 241 (1951).

[203] Souza v. Narragansett Council, B.S.A., 488 A. 2d 713 (R.I. 1985).

[204] Garcia v. Herald Tribune Fresh Air Fund, Inc., 80 Misc. 2d 970, 365 N.Y.S. 20 134 (1975), 51 A.D.2d 897, 380 N.Y.S.2d 676 (1976).

[205] Morehouse College v. Russell, 109 Ga. App. 301, 136 S.E. 2d 179 (1964); Young v. Boy Scouts of America, 9 Cal. App. 2d 760, 51 P. 2d 191 (1935).

Volunteer drivers is another area of frequent concern.[206] While the courts vary in interpretation, the general holding appears to be that if the vehicle was being driven as part of the service/activity, then there is liable for negligence. If there is no control and the activity begins at the point of disembarking, with individuals getting their own way to the location, then there may not be liability. See Chapter 22 Transportation.

Frequently in youth organizations young people are elected to positions of self-governance. Such was the situation involving an institution for vocational training for deviant youth. The institution employed an athletic coach and the residents elected nine peers to be athletic leaders, as part of the self-governance program. One of the youth leaders directed the plaintiff to stop playing basketball and to play volleyball in an empty pool. The plaintiff refused and was pushed, causing injury. The court held that the elected athletic youth leader was not an employee relationship to the institution. This holding, however, should be taken with caution in light of attitudes developed in the 1970s toward individual rights and the right of redress.[207]

Sometimes individuals think that a volunteer for a voluntary agency is protected by charitable immunity. In *Wood v. Abell*, 268 Md. 214, 300 A. 2d 665 (1973), the court held that the charitable immunity doctrine did not protect a negligent employee of a charitable institution. In this situation the decedent was killed at a county fair when a tractor around which he was working, its driver having dismounted, rolled backward and over him. In a New York case,[208] a 15-year-old was injured in New Jersey by a chain saw while engaged as a volunteer in clearing property owned by defendant religious organization, which was chartered in New Jersey, which recognizes charitable immunity. The plaintiff was a New York resident, which state does not recognize charitable immunity. Generally the doctrine of *lex loci delicti* is the rule unless there are extraordinary circumstances. The court held that such circumstances existed and that the New York policy of assuring full recourse for injuries applied and was justified under the "center of gravity" or "grouping of contacts" test.

§ 3.6   Trainees, student teachers, aides, and interns

There appears to be increasing use of interns in the recreation and parks field as budgets have tightened in the 1980s; and, also, education seems to be requiring more practicums pre-student teaching, as well as continuing the student teaching experience. Further, the cooperative education programs,[209] as well as "experiential education" programs, particularly as relate to outdoor experiences, have given concern for liability. Then, there are sport management and fitness/health spa internships. In all these

[206] Willis v. YMCA, 34 A.D. 2d 583, 307 N.Y.S. 2d 967 (1970), rev'd. 28 N.Y. 2d 375, 321 N.Y.S. 2d 895, 270 N.E. 2d 717 (1971).

[207] Riker v. Boy Scouts of America, 8 A.D. 2d 565, 183 N.Y.S. 2d 484 (1959).

[208] e.g., Baxter v. Morningside, Inc., 10 Wash. App. 893, 521 P. 2d 946 (1974); Fircrest Poultry Farms Co. v. State of Oregon, 82 Or. App. 695, 728 P. 2d 968 (1986); Manor v. Hanson, 120 Wis. 2d 582, 356 N.W. 2d 925 (1984); Scottsdale Jaycees v. Superior Court of Maricopa Co., 17 Ariz. App. 571, 499 P.2d 185 (1972).

[209] Isom v. California Junior Republic, 33 Cal. App. 2d 299, 91 P. 2d 122 (1939).

settings the concern is for using these neophytes, these inexperienced persons as they are learning and the liability they occasion for both the sponsoring agency in which program they are learning and the school or local agency from which they come. The responsibilities are very clear — *the standard of care required of an inexperienced, unpaid person (or paid) who is learning is the same as that of an experienced person.* (For further discussion, see Chapter 18 Supervision and Chapter 19 Conduct of Activity.) It should be pointed out, too, that the intern, student teacher, aide, or trainee stands in the same relation to the person supervising them, as any other employee. See §3.3 supervisory personnel for enumeration of type of responsibilities the supervisor has for the individual trainee, et al. Of particular importance is the assessment of the individual's capacities, abilities, understandings, and orientation to the situation in which that person is learning. A student teacher or trainee may indeed demonstrate activities, be in charge of an activity, and do other tasks — but they must have been properly instructed prior thereto and the assessment appropriate to the responsibilities which they are asked to assume.

In some instances the agency has paid a nominal salary in order that the person could be considered an employee and come under its insurance coverage. On the other hand, there is increasing request by the local agency accepting interns or student teachers to require the sponsoring agency, usually a college or university, to cover the student with liability insurance; such institution usually requires the student to pay the premium for insurance coverage. Because of the question frequently raised as to the status of student interns and teachers in terms of being "employees" subject to the doctrine of respondeat superior and in terms of being covered under the insurance policy or the right to carry coverage, a number of states have enacted statutes providing that school volunteer aides, student teachers, and interns should be considered "agents" for purposes of liability insurance,[210] while other states approach the problem by stating that student teachers are to be included in the authority to protect school personnel by indemnification or insurance coverage.[211] A student intern is considered like an employee in applying the concept of discretionary-ministerial acts.[212] In a 1987 case,[213] the court held that there was a consensual employment relationship between individual performing services at hospital pursuant to student internship program and the hospital, and that the student could recover for a back injury under Workers' Compensation. In spite of the concern and discussion, few cases have been identified which either include students as defendants or have students as the principal in the injury situation.[214] Some illustrative cases follow.

In a 1980 case,[215] a freshman sued the college for injuries sustained when she was struck by a golf ball driven by a senior student while she was receiving instruction in a golf class. The senior was a major in physical education and was designated as

[210] Rakaric v. Croation Cultural Club, 76 A.D. 2d 619, 430 N.Y.S. 2d 829 (1980).

[211] Wuerffel v. Westinghouse Corp., 148 N.J. Super. 327, 372 A. 2d 659 (1977).

[212] e.g., Maryland.

[213] e.g., Illinois, Connecticut, New York, North Carolina.

[214] Ross v. Consumers Power Co., 420 Mich. 567, 363 N.W. 2d 641 (1984) juvenile care facility swimming outing.

[215] Barragan v. Workers' Compensation Appeal Board, 195 Cal. App. 3d 637, 240 Cal. Rptr. 811 (1987).

"teaching assistant". The case was remanded for determination by a jury on whether the student had assumed the risks and the accident was unavoidable and whether the senior was appropriate to be assisting. The senior was enrolled in a practicum, but was not an expert golfer. There is a duty on the part of the college for supervision and instruction, which duty is not abrogated by reason of the fact that one student participant injures another.

A series of physical tests were being administered as prerequisite to college admission. A physical education instructor was in overall charge, but each test was administered by one senior student, while another recorded the results. Plaintiff was injured at the leg lift test allegedly due to the senior student's inexperience. He had completed a course in tests and measurements during the previous semester in which he had been instructed in the administration of this test, and also the student assistants had been given general group instruction in the administration of the various components of the physical fitness index tests; however, there was evidence that the instruction had not been thorough, complete, and thus proper precaution and instructions to the one being tested were not given.[216]

A graduate student was serving as a student assistant coach for the varsity baseball team. He was an experienced baseball player himself. The student assistant was hitting fungoes and the injured plaintiff was standing nearby to catch the balls coming back in. On the first attempt to hit, the bat slipped out of the assistant's hands and struck plaintiff in the mouth, causing extensive, painful facial injuries which required prolonged treatment, including plastic surgery, but moderate facial disfigurement remained. Held that there was no negligence; judgment for defendants.[217]

In a fourth case[218] a teacher's aide, a mentally handicapped person, was instructed by the teacher to take the class for retarded youngsters outside to play. The aide was allowed to determine the activities in which the children were to play. The aide directed plaintiff to high jump a stick held by herself and one of the classmates. While so doing, plaintiff tripped and his head struck the ground, resulting in a fractured vertebra of the neck. Defendant immune on basis of State statute. The court[219] held that a teacher's aide had rendered appropriate supervision when left with a class. Two children had a history of behavior problems, and aide requested the one inside her classroom to go to his next class, but he thrust his fist through a window, breaking the glass and severely injuring himself. The second student was jumping up and down outside the window.

Three cases[220] focused upon rendering emergency care. In the *Durham* case three

216 Morris, John E. and K. Fred Curtis. Legal Issues Relating to Field-Based Experiences in Teacher Education. 34 *J. of Teacher Educ.* 2-6, March-April, 1983; Swalls, Fred. *The Law On Student Teaching.* Danville, Ill.: Interstate Printers & Publishers, 1976, 69 pp.

217 DeMauro v. Tusculum College, Tenn. 603 S.W. 2d 115 (1980).

218 Brittan v. State, 200 Misc. 743, 103 N.Y.S. 2d 485 (1951); see also Wong v. Waterloo Comm. School Dist., 232 N.W. 2d 865 (Iowa 1975) 15-year-old aide in school summer swimming class.

219 Richmond v. Employers' Fire Ins. Co., 298 So.

2d 118 (La. App. 1974), cert. denied 302 So. 2d 18 (1974).

220 Schumate v. Thompson, 580 S.W. 2d 47 (Tex. Civ. App. 1979); see also teacher aide cases: Edmonson v. Chicago Board of Educ., 62 Ill. App. 3d 211, 19 Ill. Dec. 512, 379 N.E. 2d 27 (1978) lunchroom; Fagan v. Summers, 498 P. 2d 1227 (Wyo. 1972) playground; Marcantel v. Allen Parish School Board, 480 So. 2d 322 (La. App. 1986) mod. & aff'd. 490 So. 2d 1162 (La. App. 1986) writ cert. denied 496 So. 2d 328 (1986) classroom teacher had returned to classroom, which had been left in charge of teacher's aide, so school board not liable for inadequate supervision.

students assisted in bringing up the young man from the pool and in lifting him from the pool, his head "slapped" against the edge of the pool, causing further damage; however, under the circumstances, no actionable negligence was found. In the *O'Brien* situation, a student assistant trainer for the football team was treating an injury of a player. The knee abrasion had been received the day before the first practice when plaintiff fell in a locker room of a public swimming pool, which was neither owned nor used by the school. The plaintiff did not treat the injury at home, but every other day the student trainer would change the bandage at the training room. One of the teachers looked at the injury a couple of times, but said nothing. On Friday of the second week of practice, what is described as a boil developed at the site of the injury. After practice the physical education teacher who was also employed as trainer, looked at it, said it looked like an ingrown hair and that the student trainer would take care of it. He did by putting hot packs on it, opening it, cleaning it, and rebandaging it. The complication developed thereafter. Court said that a cause of action was stated even under the State statute in that the immunity did not shield teachers from liability for allegedly directing an incompetent and untrained student to provide medical and surgical treatment to another student for injuries received off the school property during an activity unrelated to school; any such decision was for the student's parents. This action was outside the teacher's supervisory function. The third case also involved a student trainer (see §17.32 for situation). Plaintiff basketball player sprained his ankle in a practice scrimmage and the coach turned the treatment of the injury over to the student trainer. The court held for the defendant.

Transportation was involved in two additional cases.[221] In the Delaware case, a student soccer player was driving one of two cars to a game when the brakes failed and he rammed into the lead car driven by the coach. The court held that the soccer team coach had not been assigned the duty of inspecting the vehicle provided by the university for transporting the team and thus could not be held liable for injuries sustained by student driver for failure to inspect or test brakes of vehicle, and in absence of showing that coach knew or should have known by exercising due care that the brakes were defective, he was not negligent in allowing the student to operate the vehicle. The student was known as a good driver. In the other transportation case, the student athletes were injured while driving to a doctor's office to obtain a physical examination required to participate in the football program. While the examination was required, the athletes had to obtain their own transportation, and the court declined to extend the doctrine of *respondeat superior* to off-campus, non-competitive activity where one athlete negligently injured another.

A number of legal concepts were embodied in a 1983 Louisiana case[222] in which the husband brought action for the death of his wife in an automobile accident which occurred while his wife was on a school field trip. The driver of the van was a student, who was held to be an agent of the school. Such status is determined by the control the

---

[221] Henix v. George, 465 So. 2d 906 (La. App. 1985).

[222] Durham v. Commonwealth, 406 S.W. 2d 858 (Ky. App. 1966); Gillespie v. Southern Utah College, 669 P. 2d 861 (Utah 1983); O'Brien v. Township H.S. Dist. #214, 73 Ill. App. 3d 618, 29 Ill. Dec. 918, 392 N.E. 2d 615 (1979), aff'd./rev'd. in part 83 Ill. 2d 462, 47 Ill. Dec. 702, 415 N.E. 2d 1015 (1980).

school had and the school did have as much control over the student, who was not compensated, as it had over a compensated employee driver; compensation is not required to be an agent. The issue of the group as "joint venture" was raised; however, the court said that a joint venture is an undertaking by two or more persons to combine property, capital, labor or skill to conduct a particular activity and that the intent to so enter into joint venture was not present; only the enrollment in class bound the group together and the trip was solely attributable to the class. The student driver was found to be negligent in that she was driving at an excessive rate of speed and failed to maintain proper control of the van. Additionally, the school was found negligent in failing to provide a qualified driver for the field trip, *i.e.*, one qualified and trained in transportation of large groups over a long distance on a heavily traveled interstate. The release signed by the students did not meet the criteria for a valid release (see §16.1 exculpatory agreements.) The doctrine of sudden emergency was found inapplicable (see also §22.1 participant transportation.)

[223] Adams v. Kline, 239 A. 2d 230 (Del. 1960); Rawls v. Dugas, 398 So. 2d 630 (La. App. 1981), cert. den. 400 So. 2d 1378 (1981).

[224] Whittington v. Sowela Technical Inst., 438 So. 2d 236 (La. App. 1983), cert. den. 443 So. 2d 591 (La. 1983).

Chapter 4   Approaches to Immunity and Limiting Liability

What Hageman said to the people of Kansas about their Tort Claims Act could be said to people in all states:

> Because of the sweeping changes in the whole area of governmental immunity/liability, the practitioner would be well-advised to forget what he/she knows and approach the Act (this chapter) with a clean slate.[1]

---

[1] Hageman, John A., and Lee A. Johnson. Governmental Liability. The Kansas Tort Claims Act. 19 *Washburn Law Journal* 260 (1979) at p. 260.

The dominant characteristic of the modern era since the late '70s has been change, and nowhere is this more true than in the field of tort liability, especially liability as related to governmental agencies.

There always has been an interplay between the courts and the legislatures. The most notable legislative invasion of the common law sphere has been in the field of torts. While courts have either deferred or defaulted to legislatures in the full development of the common law, the legislatures have similarly invited or, by their inaction, required the courts to decide the most fundamental issues of social policy.[2] What greater area of social policy is there than determination of compensation for injury. "Tort law is a system of reallocating the costs of accidents. When one of the parties in an accident is the government, sovereign immunity in tort may preclude any reallocation."[3]

There appear to be five eras in the evolvement of the approach to immunity and limiting liability as related to governmental and non-profit, charitable organizations. The eras reflect societal attitudes toward government and toward people.

Era #1 — immunity via doctrine of governmental/sovereign immunity

Until the mid-1950s, the predominant approach to immunity for both governmental agencies and charitable organizations was that of the doctrine of governmental/ sovereign immunity and the doctrine of charitable immunity. These are discussed in §§4.1 and 4.3, respectively. Nuisance, as a legal concept, was used in an unsuccessful effort to evade immunity. (See §4.4.)

Era #2 — authorization of insurance

While one underlying factor was the desire that public and charitable funds should not be used for damage awards for injuries, there was a public consciousness that a person who was injured should receive some compensation. Therefore, the reaction of the legislatures in the late '50s and early '60s was to authorize the carrying of insurance by public entities; however, in most states immunity remained where there was no insurance or the insurance coverage was insufficient. Immunity was waived only to the extent of insurance (see §4.24). Generally, employees were not covered; but then, in the '60s, few people sued employees, only the corporate entity or so-called "deep pocket." Further, there were few million dollar awards and insurance coverage was reasonable financially for the entity.

Era #3 — era of human rights

It was in the 1960s that the human rights movement accelerated, and it included the "right" of individuals for compensation for life, if an injury maimed a person seriously, such as quadriplegia. Questions were being asked, such as: Why should an individual have to withstand tremendous financial costs, as well as perhaps career redirection and other "damages," when the injury was occasioned by an employee of a governmental agency, but be able to recover appropriate compensation when the tort was done by a private individual? Why should not the financial costs be spread broadly over a

[2] Bischoff, Ralph F. The Dynamics of Tort Law: Court or Legislature? 4 *Vermont Law Review* 35 (1979); Satter, Robert. Changing Roles of Courts and Legislatures. 11 *Connecticut Law Review* 230 (1979); Silver, Howard, and Richard D. Toth. Torts. 26 *Wayne Law Review* 833 (1980); see also Chapter 1.

[3] Spitzer, Matthew L. An Economic Analysis of Sovereign Immunity in Tort. 50 *Southern California Law Review* 515 (1977) at p. 515.

governmental agency? Why should not a governmental agency have to "pay" for its torts, especially if the activity in which it was engaged was in competition with private enterprise? However, there also appeared to be a societal attitude of "rights without responsibilities" and a mentality of "if I get hurt, I'll sue you!" The finger of wrongdoing became pointed rigidly at the sponsor of the activity in an almost strict liability mode, that is, "if I get injured, regardless of fault, you owe me!" and, further, increasingly individuals were sued as well as the corporate entity. There appeared to be little feeling of community or responsibility one for another; each was "out for oneself;" there was little "I'm my brother's keeper," except to ask for a life-time financial pay-off. Insurance coverage became like a "security blanket." For the most part, legislatures are frequently very slow to respond to social issues and most legislatures appeared reticent to enact legislation to deal with the situation. Therefore, the courts began rendering decisions which did uphold the individual's right to redress the wrongs by governmental agencies, which resulted in injury. Then, the legislatures responded, but with as many variations as states! The concern was not so much for safety and the management of risk as for financial coverage by taking out insurance. Insurance premiums still appeared to be within the financial ability of corporate entities and individuals. Individuals began to take out professional coverage. While the era of human rights brought much in the way of progress for certain human rights, for tort liability it brought financial concern for increasingly larger and larger damage awards, resulting in Era #4.

Era #4 — tort claims acts

The late 1970s and the early 1980s brought a new definition of governmental liability. The legislatures responded with statutory guidelines regarding the right to sue, who would be liable, the size of awards, procedural requirements, risk management, et al. in the form of tort claims acts. Nearly all states revamped their statutes relating to torts and governmental entitites and many passed a whole new revision integrating statutes (see §4.2). One key was the changing concept of immunity from the governmental-proprietary function dichotomy (see §4.12) to the discretionary-ministerial act dichotomy (see §4.13). Comparative negligence was enacted in a few states, allowing an individual to recover an award even though contributorily negligent (see §5.23). But, still, insurance was the prime management technique to transfer the financial burden of liability, although risk management became a management technique not only for financial management but also for programmatic management. In this era, also, to limit liability, there were a few statutes directed at specific functions (see §4.5). The statutory approaches taken by the various states to governmental agency immunity and liability and the interplay of the courts and the legislatures reflected society's changing social philosophy and political climate.

Era #5 — insurance and tort reform

In the mid-'80s there was an insurance "crisis"; insurance premiums for coverage of torts escalated so much until public entities, as well as non-profit and private-commercial entities, felt that services must be restricted, that the premiums could not be afforded for many services. This burden directly affected the people, both in terms of financing public services and as participants in activities. A primary management response was risk management planning. The tort claims acts, for the most part, remained intact, as far as legislative response was concerned. In some states, the legislatures passed immediate relief for only a given summer or activity. But the tort reform movement, which had started in the preceding era, accelerated greatly. Tort reform affected not only public entities, but all entities (see §4.26). Not only did special focus legislation continue, but also increased use of exculpatory clauses was utilized as a way to limit liability (see §4.5).

This chapter discusses the various aspects of these five eras, specifically: §4.1 the doctrine of governmental/sovereign immunity, including governmental-proprietary function and discretionary-ministerial act dichotomies; §4.2 tort claims acts and tort reform; §4.3 doctrine of charitable immunity; §4.4 nuisance; §4.5 special focus statutes limiting liability and exculpatory clauses as a strategy to limit liability.

§ 4.1   Doctrine of governmental/sovereign immunity

The development of the doctrine to the late '70s, when tort claim acts statutorily extensively modified the doctrine, is presented in section one. The governmental-proprietary function dichotomy, a basic element of the doctrine, is discussed in section two, while the discretionary-ministerial act dichotomy, which changed the focus of immunity from nature of the public entity's function to the nature of the act of the official or employee of the public entity, is described in section three.

§ 4.11   Historical development

While often the words sovereign and governmental are interchanged when reference is made to the doctrine of sovereign/governmental liability, sovereign immunity and governmental immunity, as concepts, should be distinguished and are distinguished in a number of states. Sovereign immunity usually refers to the immunity of the state and its agencies, departments, boards, institutions, et al. Governmental immunity is the protection afforded local governing entities, such as municipalities (cities, towns, villages) and schools. Counties, although an "arm of the state," because of their changing role in public services, are generally considered a local government entity in the comprehensive tort claims acts. Sovereign immunity as a doctrine usually has been retained longer by a state than has governmental immunity. In some states sovereign immunity exists, whereas governmental immunity does not (see §4.2 — Table 4.1).

Under the common law doctrine of respondeat superior (see Chapter 3), the entity of the person occasioning an injury compensates the injured; but, under the doctrine of sovereign and governmental immunity, the governmental agencies are immune from liability; that is, they are not liable for any damages that their personnel (persons acting on their behalf) may cause under circumstances which ordinarily would make a private party liable. When an action is brought before the court, inquiry into the merits of the claim is not made and the substantive issue of negligence is not addressed. *The protection afforded the governmental entity, however, is not extended to the officers, agents, or employees of the entity.* This fact is often misunderstood. Because immunity extends only to the governmental entity, injured persons began suing officers, administrators, and employees as persons. Reaction to this came legislatively in the tort claim acts (see §§4.234 and 4.242).

The origin of this concept distinguishing public and private corporation functions dates back to old English common and case law. The very early English law denied liability of corporations in general because of technical difficulties in securing evidence against such entities. Later, the creation of corporations, without distinguishing public or private, involved contract theory in the issuance of charters. For the special privileges granted by charter to the corporation by the "crown," the corporation assumed tort liability.[4]

Later, a distinction was drawn between "crown authority" and the corporations under charter. Although the "crown" was not to be sued, for "the king can do no wrong," it did pay damages for acts of its servants when acting in an official capacity. This "crown authority" is not comparable to the concept of "public authority" held today, although some people try to make it so.[5] "Crown authority" was much more narrow in scope. The old medieval theory "that the king can do no wrong" is often glibly quoted today as the basis for not making public corporations liable. Justice Holmes has stated the principle in a manner more specific to the American system: "A sovereign is exempt from suit, not because of any formal conception of an obsolete theory, but on the logical and practical ground that there can be no legal right as against the authority that makes the law on which the right depends."[6] Although the Supreme Court in *Chisholm v. Georgia*, 2 Dall. 419, 1 L. Ed. 440 (1792) did not adhere to the concept, it has been supported by many jurisdictions.[7] Perhaps more properly, however, immunity from suit has been based upon performance of a service essential to the welfare of the people. Nevertheless, sovereign immunity in the United States seems to have been incorporated into state constitutions, in that a government must consent before it can be sued. Failure to consent through legislation makes the state completely immune to tort claims. A good number of state constitutions do provide that the state may sue and be sued; however, this overall provision frequently is applied primarily to contract claims and is not considered a waiver of tort immunity.

Russell v. Men of Devon, 2 Term. Rep. 667, 100 Eng. Rep. 359 (1788), often is cited as the case upon which the doctrine of governmental immunity is based; however, some legal writers feel that the case was misapplied and should have been distinguished from later situations. This case involved a duty running to the sovereign and not to the individuals of the realm. No corporation was involved, but rather a county, termed in the case as a quasi-corporation, which would more nearly parallel an unincorporated county in the United States, rather than an incorporated municipality.[8]

In the United States, the first reported cases, which were in Connecticut in 1790, followed the *Russell v. Men of Devon* case in granting immunity for quasi-corporations. Other early American cases assumed without argument that a corporation was subject to actions for tort. *Mower v. Leicester*, 9 Mass. 247, 6 Am. Dec. 63 (1812), an early

---

[4] Barnett, "The Foundations of the Distinctions Between Public and Private Functions in Respect to Common Law Liability of Municipal Corporations," 16 *Ore. L. Rev.* 250 (1936).
[5] Ibid.

[6] Kawananakoa v. Polyblank, 250 U.S. 349 (1907).
[7] "Municipal Liability — A Proposal," 23 *Iowa L. Rev.* 392 (1937).
[8] David, "Municipal Liability in Tort in California," 7 *So. Cal. L. Rev.* 48 (1933).

leading case, tried to distinguish quasi-corporations and other corporations, but without clarity. North Carolina, in *Meares v. Wilmington*, 31 N.C. 61, 9 Ired. L. 73, 49 Am. Dec. 412 (1848), refused to distinguish any corporations and made them all liable; however, this was modified as time went on. To the other extreme was South Carolina, which, in *White v. Charleston*, 2 S.C. 571 (1835), gave full immunity for all functions of corporations, except "money corporations" or corporations for profit which remained liable for their acts of negligence.[9]

A New Hampshire case, *Dartmouth College v. Woodward*, 8 Am. L. Rev. 189 (1874), is the leading case on the distinction between private and public corporations; while *Bailey v. New York*, 3 Hill 531, 38 Am. Dec. 669 (1842), was the first to apply the governmental-proprietary test to municipal functions.[10] The first application of the test to park and recreation functions of municipalities came in two 1880 Massachusetts cases. In *Clark v. Inhabitants of Waltham*, 128 Mass. 467 (1880), an individual was injured due to a walk defect in a park and, in *Steele v. City of Boston*, 128 Mass. 583 (1880), the injury occurred in a park due to a coasting incident. There was no recovery in either case.

The law establishing immunity for schools became quite firmly planted during the latter part of the nineteenth century, with cases such as those in Ohio and Massachusetts.[11] In 1890, the Pennsylvania court very clearly said that "school districts are different from municipalities...and belong to the class of quasi-corporations."[12] Application of the doctrine was brought to bear in two early-1900 cases involving university athletic associations. In the Michigan case[13] recovery was allowed, holding the operation of the football stadium to be a proprietary function; but at the University of Minnesota, the court found adequate control by the university to bring the athletic association under the umbrella of the immunity rule.[14]

In the first fifty years of the twentieth century there were relatively few cases brought to court in relation to physical education, playground, or athletic activities of the schools, except for some cases in New York, where the court was allowing recovery, and in California, after the passage of the Public Liability Act. However, after 1950, there was a flurry of cases testing the old doctrine of governmental immunity and other bases for liability, such as nuisance, in relation to the schools and their recreation, physical education, or athletic function. (For some early cases see next section §4.12, under Purpose of Function.)

From the beginning, the courts throughout the United States have used, to one degree or another, the doctrine of governmental immunity from liability predicated on the distinction of function of the governmental unit. By the beginning of the 1970s, the governmental-proprietary test had been adopted by nearly every state in the Union. Because of the importance of the role this test (distinction) has played in the doctrine of

[9] Barnett, op. cit.
[10] Barnett, op. cit.
[11] Finch v. Board of Education, 30 Ohio St. 37, 27 Am. Rep. 414 (1876); Hill v. Boston, 122 Mass. 344, 23 Am. Rep. 332 (1877).
[12] Briegel v. City of Philadelphia, 135 Pa. 451, 19 A. 1038 (1890).

[13] Scott v. University of Mich. Athletic Assn., 152 Mich. 684, 116 N.W. 624 (1908).
[14] George v. University of Minn. Athletic Assn., 107 Minn. 424, 120 N.W. 750 (1909).

governmental immunity, the next section (§4.12) discusses governmental-proprietary functions. However, only a few states at the mid-'80s still utilized this distinction in determining governmental liability for negligent acts (see §4.21). During the last half of the decade of the '70s, the distinction, between acts for which there would be liability and those for which there would not be, focused upon discretionary and ministerial acts of the official, administrator, or employee, rather than function of the service (governmental-proprietary). However, the concept of immunity for discretionary acts had its roots early in the century. (See §4.13 for discussion of discretionary-ministerial acts.)

Laws regarding liability date back before 1900 in two states. Five more states passed laws before the 1940s; nine in the '40s; and sixteen in the 1950s. Most of the latter were permissive insurance laws, for the most part. Probably four of the best known earlier laws are the 1923 Public Liability Act of California, the Wisconsin Safe-Place Statute, the protective statute for schools of Washington, and the New Jersey teacher indemnification statute.

The change from the common law doctrine of governmental immunity came first for municipalities and later for schools. In 1949 Dyer and Lichtig[15] reported that slightly more than one-half (26) of the states still held the common law doctrine of governmental immunity for municipalities. Nearly two decades later there were still 39 states adhering to some aspect of the governmental immunity rule for schools.[16] The modification of the doctrine of sovereign immunity as related to states came even later in time.

The decade of the '60s saw extensive legislative activity, particularly in the area of insurance authorizations with waiving of immunity to the extent of coverage, as well as continuing judicial abrogation of the doctrine. The 1973 Restatement of Torts[17] categorized the status of the states as follows:

Common Law	Judicially Abrogated	Statutorily Abrogated	Modified	Insurance-Waiver Theory
Alabama	Alaska	Hawaii	Connecticut	Georgia
Arkansas	Arizona	Iowa	So. Carolina	Kansas
Delaware	California	New York	Texas	Maine
Maryland	Colorado	Oklahoma		Mississippi
Massachusetts	Florida	Oregon		Missouri
Pennsylvania	Idaho	Utah		Montana
South Dakota	Illinois	Washington		New Hampshire
Virginia	Indiana			New Mexico
	Kentucky			North Carolina

[15] Dyer, Donald B., and J. G. Lichtig. *Liability in Public Recreation*. C. C. Nelson Publishing Company, 1949.

[16] van der Smissen, Betty. *Legal Liability of Cities and Schools for Injuries in Recreation and Parks.*

Cincinnati: W. H. Anderson Company, 1968. This reference provides additional historical information.

[17] *Restatement, Second, Torts* §895A, 12-20 (tentative draft March 30, 1973).

Common Law	Judicially Abrogated	Statutorily Abrogated	Modified	Insurance-Waiver Theory
	Louisiana			North Dakota
	Michigan			Ohio
	Minnesota			Tennessee
	Nebraska			Vermont
	Nevada			West Virginia
	New Jersey			Wyoming
	Rhode Island			
	Wisconsin			
	Dist. of Columbia			

Tort claims acts were the major legislative activity of the 1970s. Some of these were comprehensive acts, while others attempted to unify the law in the state, but did not do a complete recodification into a comprehensive treatment of governmental immunity. While about a dozen states had some form of tort claims act or statutes relating to the doctrine of governmental immunity before 1970, more than one-half enacted statutes during the 1970s with 20 of these from 1975, through 1981. This approach to governmental immunity/liability continued in the early 1980s and is summarized in §4.2. The constitutionality of the tort claims acts has been tested and upheld in the 1980s in a number of jurisdictions.[18] Of the eight common law states indicated in the 1973 Restatement of Torts listing, four judicially abrogated the doctrine of governmental immunity and then reinstated some immunity through statutes; two enacted tort claims acts and two statutes authorizing insurance. About two-thirds of the states listed as judicially abrogating the doctrine followed up after the court decision with some type of statutory response. One-third of these states returned to some immunity. Although each state already had some statutes, slightly more than one-half of the states indicated under the insurance-waiver theory enacted tort claims acts. One of the three states under the "modified" category also enacted a tort claims act.

When it comes to stating the status of the states, as related to the doctrine of governmental/sovereign immunity, very few generalizations can be made, since the law varies widely. There are as many approaches as there are states! Bischoff, in his article "The Dynamics of Tort Law: Court or Legislature?" stated:

> In the last two decades ('60s and '70s), changes in the doctrine of governmental immunity from suit in torts have resulted in dramatic interaction between courts and legislatures. Because the changes involve fundamental policy in as sensitive an area as sovereignty, these changes best exemplify action, reaction, and synthesis between the two governmental institutions.[19]

[18] e.g., Arkansas, Georgia, Indiana, New Hampshire, Pennsylvania.

[19] Bischoff, Ralph F. The Dynamics of Tort Law: Court or Legislature? 4 *Vermont Law Review* 35, at p. 46 (1979).

Most judicial action concerning governmental immunity has been followed by legislative reaction. Following judicial abrogation, governmental immunity has been restored, partially restored, or comprehensive torts schemes have been enacted.[20]

§ 4.12   Governmental-proprietary function

The utilization of the governmental-proprietary test of function in determining whether or not a governmental agency was subject to the doctrine of governmental immunity changed extensively in the decade of the '70s. Whereas nearly every state used it as the basis of governmental immunity prior to that time, by 1980, only a few states still retained the test. The distinction was disregarded in favor of the discretionary-ministerial acts distinction (see §4.13). This change came about primarily because of the extensive statutory activity of the states (see §4.2).

At the turn of the '80s, 20 states made reference to the governmental-proprietary function distinction in their statutes. Five states indicated that they abolished the distinction,[21] while eight stated either that there was liability for both functions or that there was liability whether the tort arose out of a proprietary or a governmental function.[22] North Carolina made reference specifically to waiving immunity to the extent of insurance coverage for governmental functions, while West Virginia authorized insurance for proprietary functions. The distinction between governmental and proprietary functions was made by Texas and indicated that the tort act did not apply to proprietary functions. Michigan, Ohio, and Utah had statutes providing for immunity for governmental functions, although the Ohio statute application was through case interpretation. Indiana indicated that museums, zoos, and cultural activities were governmental functions, but this statute was repealed in 1981. Quite a number of states by enacting tort claims statutes or insurance authorization laws have de facto abolished the distinction between governmental and proprietary functions, although no reference was made in the statutes themselves. Others have done so by court decision. However, in *Oien v. Sioux Falls*, 393 N.W. 2d 286 (S.D. 1986), the court held that the park immunity statutes which attempted to expand sovereign immunity to municipalities acting in a proprietary capacity thereby defeating cause of action for negligence were unconstitutional. They violated the State constitution which had an "open courts" provision. Under the common law in South Dakota, sovereign immunity only extended to state and its agencies and subdivisions. In this situation, a child came into contact with chemical solution used to treat water in the municipal swimming pool when she sat down at the pool's edge.

Michigan courts continued into the 1980s to discuss the distinction between

[20] Persson, Darrold E. Municipal Corporations — Governmental Immunity — Political Subdivisions Liable for Non-Discretionary Tortious Conduct, 51 *North Dakota Law Review* 885 at p. 891 (1979).

[21] Colorado, New Mexico, South Carolina, Tennessee, and Wyoming.

[22] Florida, Idaho, Minnesota, Montana, North Dakota, Oklahoma, Oregon, Washington.

governmental and proprietary function as a basis of governmental immunity. In 1984,[23] the court reviewed the governmental immunity doctrine with particular attention to this dichotomy and formulated this "new" definition of governmental function:

> . . . a governmental function is an activity which is expressly or impliedly mandated or authorized by constitution, statute, or other law. When a governmental agency engages in mandated or authorized activities, it is immune from tort liability unless the activity is proprietary in nature or falls within one of the statutory exceptions to the governmental immunity act . . . .

This definition was applied in a subsequent 1985 case.[24] It was held that the zoo was a governmental function and not a proprietary function, for purposes of exception to immunity. For the status of the governmental-proprietary test in the latter years of the 1980s, see §4.2. Notwithstanding the statutory impact on the governmental-proprietary test for governmental immunity in the 1970s and its changing role in the decade of the '80s, it is important that individuals understand this test, because of its prior importance and continued application in some jurisdictions.

The governmental-proprietary dichotomy is not as simple to define as some writers would lead one to believe. Governmental function is frequently defined as the action of the municipality in discharge of a public duty in behalf of the state for the general public welfare and a proprietary function as the municipality's action in discharge of a private duty primarily in behalf of its own inhabitants, although the general welfare may be benefited. Generally, liability ensues with the latter, but immunity attaches with the first. The U.S. Supreme Court had this to say:

> The basis of the distinction (between governmental and proprietary functions) is difficult to state, and there is no established rule for the determination of what belongs to the one or the other class. It originated with the courts. Generally it is applied to escape difficulties, in order that injustice may not result from the recognition of technical defenses based upon the governmental character of such corporations. . . .[25]

Although there is no established rule as to which functions are governmental and which are proprietary, it is generally accepted that police, fire, and educational functions are governmental, while the water works and light-plants are proprietary.[26] Also, liability usually attaches to actions arising out of the functions related to streets and sidewalks.

The stand on education as a governmental function was without dispute for many

---

[23] Ross v. Consumers Power, 420 Mich. 567, 363 N.W. 2d 641 (1984). See also Richardson v. Jackson County, 159 Mich. App. 766, 407 N.W.2d 74 (1987) leave to appeal granted 420 N.W.2d 828 (1988) failure to obtain permit prior to marking off section of lake as safe swimming area; at issue, did such omission render operation of public beach ultra vires so as to abrogate township's and county's immunity with respect to accident occuring in swimming area.

[24] O'Keefe v. Detroit, 616 F. Supp. 162 (1985). See

also Eichhorn v. Lamphere School Dist., 166 Mich. App. 527, 421 N.W.2d 230 (1988) student fell from float in homecoming parade; Murphy v. Muskegon County, 162 Mich. App. 609, 413 N.W.2d 73 (1987) motorcyclist hit cable on abandoned co. road.

[25] Trenton v. State of New Jersey, 262 U.S. 182 (1922).

[26] "Municipal Liability — A Proposal," 23 *Iowa L. Rev.* 392 (1937).

years and school boards enjoyed immunity from liability in tort law, with the exception of several states where this immunity was abrogated by statute and in New York where courts have consistently held school agencies responsible in damages for the torts of their officers and agents, committed while in the performance of duties imposed by law upon the board. At the turn of the '60s, there were supreme court decisions which gave some indication that the immunity enjoyed so widely was coming to an end.[27] With the extension of the school function into recreational services for the community and athletic programs for many spectators, there was real question as to whether these functions were true educational functions and should be included under the immunity umbrella or whether they were proprietary in nature and the school should be held liable for torts committed in relation to such activities. Also, humanitarians questioned the justification of denying restitution to an injured individual because the agency is a so-called "public good" agency.

Where the parks and recreation function belonged was a particularly difficult question, with no definite and sure line of demarcation evident. Because Massachusetts was the first to hold that parks and recreation are a governmental function, such view is sometimes referred to as the "Massachusetts view," while those adhering to the view that parks and recreation are a proprietary function are sometimes said to hold the "New York view."

The courts have used as the basis of their decisions various elements and reasoning. They fall into two major categories—purpose of the function and authority for performance of the function.[28]

Purpose of function. Six primary purposes are discussed in the cases—public welfare, health, education, amusement, benefit of specific inhabitants, and monetary consideration or the test of competitive enterprise.

Public benefit and welfare. The primary, typical, and most frequent basis for holding recreation to be a governmental function is that it contributes to the public benefit and welfare of the people. The courts have said the following about public welfare as a purpose of function:

> The most general test of governmental function relates to the nature of the activity. It must be something done or furnished for the general public good..., that is, of a "public or governmental character," such as the maintenance and operation of public schools, hospitals, public charities, public parks or recreational facilities.[29]

> The constitutionally authorized function this municipality was exercising was...for purposes essentially public and of a beneficial character in

---

[27] Holytz v. City of Milwaukee, 17 Wis. 2d 26, 115 N.W. 2d 618 (1962); Lipman v. Brisbane Elementary School Dist., 55 Cal. 2d 224, 359 P. 2d 465 (1961); Molitor v. Kaneland Community Unit Dist. No. 302, 18 Ill. 2d 11, 163 N.E. 2d 89 (1959), rev'd. 24 Ill. 2d 467, 182 N.E. 2d 145 (1962); Spanel v. Mounds View School Dist., 264 Minn. 279, 118 N.W. 2d 795 (1962); see later discussions and the appendix.

[28] See for more detailed discussion and cases related to schools and to municipalities (parks and recreation), van der Smissen, Betty. *Legal Liability of Cities and Schools for Injuries in Recreation and Parks.* Cincinnati: W. H. Anderson Company, 1968.

[29] Ramirez v. Ogden, 3 Utah 2d 102, 279 P. 2d 463 (1955), in citing Griffin v. Salt Lake City.

furtherance of the common welfare in harmony with the general policy of the
state, and was in its nature a governmental activity…, whether it be put upon
the ground of health, education, charity, social betterment by furnishing the
people at large free advantage of wholesome recreation and entertainment, or
all of them.[30]

A school's function of teaching also comes under the heading of public benefit, being
immaterial whether it is performed by the municipality or the school district.[31] Since
education is compulsory in the United States, it is seldom questioned that public
education is for the public benefit and welfare. Additional cases which refer to the
public welfare in discussing the reasoning behind holding of recreation as a
governmental function are cited in the footnotes.[32]

Health. Very closely allied to the preceding basis for governmental function
holdings, and often spoken of together, is that of the health of the people. *Cornelisen v.
Atlanta*, 146 Ga. 416, 91 S.E. 415 (1917), early in the century, held that where a city
maintains a park primarily for the use of the public, intended as a place of resort for
pleasure and promotion of health of the public at large, its operation is regarded as the
exercise of governmental powers of the municipality.

> The maintenance of children's playgrounds and recreational centers for the
> general use of the children of the city are referrable solely to the duty of
> maintaining public health which is one of the delegated functions of
> sovereignty.[33]

> It affords the public, especially the young, the means of healthy recreation and
> athletic exercise.[34]

> …we are in accord with those authorities which hold such a duty a public one,
> based on the obligation of the municipality, as a branch of the state
> government, to guard, preserve, and maintain the public health. Parks, in
> crowded cities, are eminently conducive to this purpose, as places which the

[30] Heino v. Grand Rapids, 202 Mich. 363, 168 N.W. 512 (1918).

[31] Antin v. Union High School Dist. No. 2 130 Or. 461, 280 P. 664 (1929).

[32] Alder v. Salt Lake City, 64 Utah 568, 231 P. 1102 (1924); Baltimore v. State, 168 Md. 619, 179 A. 169 (1935); Bernstein v. Milwaukee, 158 Wis. 476, 149 N.W. 382 (1914); Bolster v. Lawrence, 225 Mass. 387, 114 N.E. 722 (1917); Caughlan v. Omaha, 103 Neb. 726, 174 N.W. 220 (1919); Cleveland v. Walker, 52 Ohio App. 477, 3 N.E. 2d 990 (1936); Emmons v. Virginia, City of, 152 Minn. 295, 188 N.W. 561 (1922); Etter v. Eugene, 157 Or. 68, 69 P. 2d 1061 (1937); Fahey v. Jersey City and Williams v. Red Bank (two cases), 52 N.J. 103, 244 A. 2d 97 (1968); Garza v. Edinburg Consol. Indp. School District, 576 S.W. 2d 916 (Tex. 1979); Hack v. Salem, 174 Ohio St. 383, 23 Ohio Op. 2d 34, 189 N.E. 2d 857 (1963); Heino v. Grand Rapids, 202 Mich. 363, 168 N.W. 512 (1918); Hoffman v. Scranton School Dist., 67 Pa. D. & C. 301, 51 Lack.

Jur. 25 (1949); Kerr v. Brookline, 208 Mass. 190, 94 N.E. 257 (1911); List v. O'Connor, 21 Ill. App. 2d 399, 158 N.E. 2d 103 (1959); Louisville v. Prinz, 127 Ky. 460, 105 S.W. 548 (1907); Lythell v. Waverly, 335 Ill. App. 397, 82 N.E. 2d 207 (1948); Mathis v. Dothan, 266 Ala. 531, 97 So. 2d 908 (1957); Mocha v. Cedar Rapids, 204 Iowa 51, 214 N.W. 587 (1927); Monfils v. Sterling Heights, 84 Mich. App. 330, 269 N.W. 2d 588 (1978); Parr v. Birmingham, 264 Ala. 224, 85 So. 2d 888 (1955); Ramirez v. Cheyenne, 34 Wyo. 67, 241 P. 710 (1925); Russell v. Tacoma, 8 Wash. 156, 35 P. 605 (1894); Smith v. Birmingham, 270 Ala. 681, 121 So. 2d 867 (1960); Tillman v. District of Columbia, 58 U.S. App. D.C. 242, 29 F. 2d 442 (1928); Vanderford v. Houston 286 S.W. 568 (Tex. Civ. App. 1926); Williams v. Birmingham, 219 Ala. 19, 121 So. 14 (1929).

[33] Farrell v. Long Beach, 132 Cal. App. 2d 818, 283 P. 2d 296 (1955).

[34] Mocha v. Cedar Rapids, 204 Iowa 51, 214 N.W. 587 (1927).

people may go and enjoy pure air, and sight of trees, grass, and flowers, and find the means of release for a time from the weight of care, rest from labor, relaxation for body and mind, and the recuperation of exhausted energies — all aids to health of incalculable value.[35]

Physical education and athletics are probably more directly related to the health of a student than any other phase of the educational program. As to whether physical development is in the same category as mental development, as far as being a governmental function, *Howard v. Tacoma School District No. 10, Pierce County*, 88 Wash. 167, 152 P. 1004 (1915) said:

We are asked, "How can it be said that the physical development of children is a function of government?" The answer seems obvious: Just for the same reason that it can be said that mental development is a function of government. Both are intended to raise the standard of citizenship. The state is certainly as much interested in the physical standards of its citizens as in their mental standards. Condemnation of land for playgrounds in connection with the public schools is a public use.

Although this court opinion was written more than half a century ago, it well could have been written in the 1980s with the emphasis upon physical fitness.

Those jurisdictions holding recreation to be a proprietary function usually refer to health as incidental to the function, and not integral, and, therefore, may not be considered controlling in determination of the nature of the function.[36] Some of the cases which discuss health as a justification for holding a governmental function are cited in the footnotes.[37]

Education. In regard to education as a function for government, there are two aspects which must be considered: (1) recreation as education, and (2) physical education and athletics as education. In both of these there is the distinction of education as required by law and education in a general sense. Although the recreation profession does hold that one of its functions is education for leisure, education is usually not considered a prime purpose, but more a by-product of good recreational activity.[38] The proponents of the

---

[35] Nashville v. Burns, 131 Tenn. 281, 174 S.W. 1111 (1915).

[36] Baltimore City v. State, 173 Md. 267, 195 A. 571 (1937); Edinger v. Buffalo, 213 N.Y. 674, 107 N.E. 1076 (1914).

[37] Alder v. Salt Lake City, 64 Utah 568, 231 P. 1102 (1924); Baltimore v. State, 168 Md. 619, 179 A. 169 (1935); Bernstein v. Milwaukee, 158 Wis. 476, 149 N.W. 382 (1914); Bolster v. Lawrence, 225 Mass. 387, 114 N.E. 722 (1917); Burnett v. San Diego, 127 Cal. App. 2d 191, 273 P. 2d 345 (1954); Caughlan v. Omaha, 103 Neb. 726, 174 N.W. 220 (1919); Clark v. Louisville, 273 Ky. 645 117 S.W. 2d 614 (1938); Cleveland v. Walker, 52 Ohio App. 477, 3 N.E. 2d 990 (1936); Cornelisen v. Atlanta, 146 Ga. 416, 91 S.E. 415 (1917); Etter v. Eugene, 157 Or. 68, 69 P. 2d 1061 (1937); Gebhardt v. LaGrange Park, 354 Ill. 234, 188 N.E. 372

(1933); Hannon v. Waterbury, 106 Conn. 13, 136 A. 876 (1927); Hoffman v. Scranton School Dist., 67 Pa. D. & C. 301, 51 Lack. Jur. 25 (1949); Kellar v. Los Angeles, 179 Cal. 605, 178 P. 505 (1919); Love v. Glencoe Park Dist., 270 Ill. App. 117 (1933); Lythell v. Waverly, 335 Ill. App. 397, 82 N.E. 2d 207 (1948); Pollock v. Albany, 88 Ga. App. 737, 77 S.E. 2d 579 (1953); Reid v. Atlanta, 39 Ga. App. 519, 147 S.E. 789 (1929); Stein v. West Chicago Park Comm., 247 Ill. App. 479 (1928); Vanderford v. Houston 286 S.W. 568 (Tex. Civ. App. 1926).

[38] Hannon v. Waterbury, 106 Conn. 13, 136 A. 876 (1927); McKinney v. San Francisco, City and County of, 109 Cal. App. 2d 844, 241 P. 2d 1060, 1061 (1952), in reference to Chafor v. Long Beach; see also Cleveland v. Lausche, 71 Ohio App. 273, 49 N.E. 2d 207 (1943).

proprietary function in relation to recreation draw the distinction between education as required by law and general education.[39]

The question in relation to school districts is whether physical education, not being one of the traditional "three R's," is actually a part of the curriculum and "true education." A Montana court expressed the majority opinion when it said that physical training is part of the educational duty entrusted to public schools and constitutes a governmental function.[40] Therefore, the courts seem to hold that the school is liable for negligent acts in physical education classes and activities only if it also is liable for acts occurring in other instructional situations of the school. When it comes to athletics, though, the courts differ in their opinions and reasonings. The decision seems to turn primarily upon the basis of profit or commercial enterprise and whether a player or spectator was involved.[41] See later paragraph subsection on monetary considerations.

Pleasure, amusement, entertainment. The terms "pleasure and amusement," when used to mean the enjoyment and well-being of the public, give justification for immunity as a governmental function;[42] but, when "amusement and entertainment" refer to amusement enterprises, which are of a commercial nature or competing with private enterprises, the activity or function is considered proprietary.[43] In this latter meaning, as California states, where activities are primarily for the amusement and entertainment of the public as distinguished from being for the public health and education, such activities are considered to be of a proprietary nature.[44] This distinction has arisen primarily since 1950.

Benefit for particular inhabitants. Inasmuch as municipalities are established by a specific group of people for the services it can render them, a reason for holding recreation to be a proprietary function is that the service is for the benefit of the municipal inhabitants primarily and not for the general public. Cases which discuss the distinction as to whether the act is for the common good of all without the element of special corporate benefit or pecuniary profit or whether it is for the special benefit of the inhabitants of the municipality are cited in the footnotes.[45]

[39] Byrnes v. Jackson, 140 Miss. 656, 105 So. 861 (1925).

[40] Bartell v. School Dist. No. 28, 114 Mont. 451, 137 P. 2d 422 (1943); Howard v. Tacoma School Dist., 88 Wash. 167, 152 P. 1004 (1915).

[41] Garza v. Edinburg Consol. Indp. School Dist., 576 S.W. 2d 916 (Tex. 1979); Hoffman v. Scranton School Dist., 67 Pa. D. & C. 301, 51 Lack. Jur. 25 (1949); Martini, Jr. v. Olyphant Borough School Dist., 83 Pa. D. & C. 206 (1952); Page v. Regents of University System of Ga., 93 F. 2d 887 (1937); Watson v. School Dist. of Bay City, 324 Mich. 1, 36 N.W. 2d 195 (1949).

[42] Cornelisen v. Atlanta, 146 Ga. 416, 91 S.E. 415 (1917); Love v. Glencoe Park Dist., 270 Ill. App. 117 (1933); Pollock v. Albany, 88 Ga. App. 737, 77 S.E. 2d 579 (1953); and others cited in footnote 32 supra.

[43] Blake v. Madison, 237 Wis. 498, 297 N.W. 422 (1941); Reid v. Atlanta, 39 Ga. App. 519, 147 S.E. 789 (1929).

[44] Guidi v. State, 41 Cal. 2d 623, 262 P. 2d 3 (1953); Litzmann v. Humboldt County, 127 Cal. App.

2d 86, 273 P. 2d 82 (1954); Plaza v. San Mateo, 123 Cal. App. 2d 103, 266 P. 2d 523 (1954).

[45] Backer v. West Chicago Park Comm'rs., 66 Ill. App. 507 (1896); Bernstein v. Milwaukee, 158 Wis. 576, 149 N.W. 382 (1914); Davis v. Provo City Corp., 1 Utah 2d 244, 265 P. 2d 415 (1953); Felton v. Great Falls, 118 Mont. 586, 169 P. 2d 229 (1946); Fort Worth v. Wiggins, 5 S.W. 2d 761 (Tex. Civ. App. 1928); Grover v. Manhattan, 198 Kan. 307, 424 P. 2d 256 (1967) states that in order for a function to take on a proprietary character, some special benefit accruing to the city itself and its inhabitants rather than to the public at large must be shown. Actual pecuniary profit or gain is no longer required, but whether or not the activity is commercial in nature is a matter of significance; Gorsuch v. Springfield, 43 Ohio L. Abs. 83, 61 N.E. 2d 898 (1945); Hannon v. Waterbury, 106 Conn. 13, 136 A. 876 (1927); Lythell v. Waverly, 335 Ill. App. 397, 82 N.E. 2d 207 (1948); Maio v. Ilg, 98 R.I. 71, 199 A. 2d 727 (1964); Waco v. Branch (Tex. Civ. App.) 8 S.W. 2d 271 (1928).

Monetary considerations or the test of competitive enterprise. Whereas the foregoing purposes are given by the courts in their opinions as reasons for support of either the governmental or proprietary view, the key facet in decisions is that of monetary considerations. Yet, the effect of the question of whether recreational activities and athletic events are free to participants, whether a nominal or incidental fee is charged, or whether profit is made, in determination of whether a function is governmental or proprietary, is *inconsistent and indecisive.* Most of the cases are prior to 1970,[46] and

---

[46] *No charge.* Bolster v. Lawrence, 225 Mass. 387, 114 N.E. 772 (1917); Chafor v. Long Beach, 174 Cal. 478, 163 P. 670 (1917); Emmons v. Virginia, 152 Minn. 295, 188 N.W. 561 (1922); Heino v. Grand Rapids, 202 Mich. 363, 168 N.W. 512 (1918).

Fee charged. Baltimore City v. State, 173 Md. 267, 195 A. 571 (1937); Boyer v. Iowa H.S. Athletic Assoc., 127 N.W. 2d 606 (Iowa, 1964), rev'd. 138 N.W. 2d 914 (Iowa 1965) aff'd. 260 Iowa 1061, 152 N.W. 2d 293 (1967); Burton v. Salt Lake City, 69 Utah 186, 253 P. 443 (1926); Caughlan v. Omaha, 103 Neb. 726, 174 N.W. 200 (1919); Carsten v. Wood River, 344 Ill. 319, 176 N.E. 266 (1931); Gebhardt v. LaGrange Park, 354 Ill. 234, 188 N.E. 372 (1933); Gorsuch v. Springfield, 43 Ohio L. Abs. 83, 61 N.E. 2d 898 (1945); Handley v. City of Hope, 137 F. Supp. 442 (1956); Hannon v. Waterbury, 106 Conn. 13, 136 A. 876 (1927); Hendricks v. Urbana Park Dist., 265 Ill. App. 102 (1932); Hoepner v. Eau Claire, 264 Wis. 608, 60 N.W. 2d 392 (1953); Kellar v. Los Angeles, 179 Cal. 605, 178 P. 505 (1919); Mathis v. Dothan, 266 Ala. 531, 97 So. 2d 908 (1957); Matthews v. Detroit, 291 Mich. 161, 289 N.W. 115 (1939); Mocha v. Cedar Rapids, 204 Iowa 51, 214 N.W. 587 (1927); Mokovich v. Independent School Dist., 177 Minn. 446, 225 N.W. 292 (1929); Nissen v. Redelack, 246 Minn. 83, 74 N.W. 2d 300 (1955); Reed v. Rhea County, 189 Tenn. 247, 225 S.W. 2d 49 (1949); Rhoades v. School Dist. No. 9, Roosevelt County, 155 Mont. 352, 142 P. 2d 890 (1943); Rogers v. Oconomowoc, 24 Wis. 2d 308, 128 N.W. 2d 640 (1964); Rome v. London and Lancashire Indem. Co. of America (La. App.) 169 So. 132 (1936); St. John v. St. Paul, 179 Minn. 12, 288 N.W. 170 (1929); Thrasher v. Cincinnati, 28 Ohio Op. 97, 13 Ohio Supp. 143 (1944); Vaughn v. Alcoa, 194 Tenn. 449, 251 S.W. 2d 304 (1952); Walker v. Forest Preserve Dist. of Cook Co., 27 Ill. 2d 538, 190 N.E. 2d 296 (1963); Weeks v. Newark, 62 N.J. Super. 166, 162 A. 2d 314 (1960).

Profits or income realized. Blake v. Madison, 237 Wis. 498, 297 N.W. 422 (1941); Brooks v. Bass, 184 So. 222 (La. App. 1938); Cleveland v. Walker, 52 Ohio App. 477, 3 N.E. 2d 990 (1936); Cornelisen v. Atlanta, 146 Ga. 416, 91 S.E. 415 (1917); Flowers v. Board of Comm'rs., 240 Ind. 668, 168 N.E. 2d 224 (1960); George v. University of Minnesota Athletic Assn., 107 Minn. 424, 120 N.W. 750 (1909); Glenn v. Raleigh, 246 N.C. 469, 98 S.E. 2d 913 (1957); Griffin v. Salt Lake City, 111 Utah 94, 176 P. 2d 156 (1947); Handley v. Hope, 137 F. Supp. 442 (1956); Heitman v. Lake City, 225 Minn. 117, 30 N.W. 2d 18 (1947); Hoepner v. Eau Claire, 264 Wis. 608, 60 N.W. 2d 392 (1953); Hoffman

v. Scranton School District, 67 Pa. D. & C. 301, 51 Lack. Jur. 25 (1949); Jones v. Atlanta, 35 Ga. App. 376, 133 S.E. 521 (1926); Morris v. School Dist., 393 Pa. 633, 144 A. 2d 737 (1958); Orrison v. Rapid City, 76 S.D. 145, 74 N.W. 2d 489 (1956); Page v. Regents of University System of Ga., 93 F. 2d 887 (1937); Pollock v. Albany, 88 Ga. App. 737, 77 S.E. 2d 579 (1953); Ramirez v. Ogden, 3 Utah 2d 102, 279 P. 2d 463 (1955); Rich v. Goldsboro, 15 N.C. App. 534, 190 S.E. 2d 229 (Aug. 1972), cert. allowed 281 N.C. 758, 191 S.E. 2d 362, 282 N.C. 383, 192 S.E. 2d 824 (Dec. 1972) held that where it was less than 1 percent of budget for operating park, city's receipt of $1,200 donated was incidental income and insufficient to constitute waiver of immunity; Scott v. University of Michigan Athletic Assn., 152 Mich. 684, 116 N.W. 624 (1908); Smith v. Caney School Dist., 204 Kan. 580, 464 P. 2d 571 (1970) stated that the profit, benefit, or advantage of the board of education in charging a nominal $3.00 charge for services for replacement of furniture, *et al.,* and with the fund kept separately was not sufficient to cause the function to be proprietary in nature; Smith v. Marietta, 119 Ga. App. 441, 167 S.E. 2d 615 (1969) held that rental of auditorium to private school for dance recital was governmental function because primary purpose was not for rental revenue but for use and benefit of public, incidental revenue did not affect purpose; Upton v. Chattanooga (Tenn. App. 1953); Watson v. School District of Bay City, 324 Mich. 1, 36 N.W. 2d 195 (1949); Williams v. Morristown, 32 Tenn. App. 274, 222 S.W. 2d 607 (1949).

Rental profits. Carta v. Norwalk, 108 Conn. 697, 145 A. 158 (1929); Davis v. Atlanta, 84 Ga. App. 572, 66 S.E. 2d 188 (1951); Kilbourn v. Seattle, 43 Wash. 2d 373, 261 P. 2d 407 (1953); Sawaya v. Tucson High School Dist., 78 Ariz. 389, 281 P. 2d 105 (1955); Scott v. University of Mich. Athletic Assn., 152 Mich. 684, 116 N.W. 624 (1908); Scroggins v. Harlingen, 131 Texas 237, 112 S.W. 2d 1035 (1938); Shoemaker v. Parsons, 154 Kan. 387, 118 P. 2d 508 (1941); Smith v. Hefner, 235 N.C. 1, 68 S.E. 2d 783 (1952).

Taxation. Department of Treasury v. Evansville, 223 Ind. 435, 60 N.E. 2d 952 (1945); Department of Treasury v. Tipton, 223 Ind. 373, 60 N.E. 2d 952 (1945); Griffin v. Salt Lake City, 111 Utah 94, 176 P. 2d 156 (1947); Handley v. City of Hope, 137 F. Supp. 442 (W.D. Ark. 1956); Purser v. Ledbetter, 227 N.C. 1, 40 S.E. 2d 702 (1946); Yoes v. Fort Smith, 207 Ark. 694, 182 S.W. 2d 683 (1944).

Additional cases discussing profits and charges. Aaser v. Charlotte, 265 N.C. 494, 144 S.E. 2d 610

only a few are in the decade of the '70s.[47]

Incidental to primary operation. Sometimes the location of the activity is controlling in determining whether the function is governmental or proprietary; however, the cases are also early ones. In Illinois[48] the city rented boats on its water works lake; this was held to be a proprietary function, with the inference that if the lake had been a recreational facility it would have been a governmental function. A similar result was reached in a Michigan and a Tennessee case.[49] A contrary decision[50] was reached when an injury occurred in a park when the plaintiff stepped in the "cut off" hole for water furnished to the pool by the water works system — there the governmental function was retained. However, a California case[51] held that the location of the activity was immaterial; the nature of the activity determined whether it was governmental or proprietary.

Authority for performance of function. Authority for performance of a function by a municipality or school district may come from implied, as an "arm of the state," or express authorization, as through a charter grant or enabling legislation. The latter may be mandatory or permissive and discretionary. Some courts use as a basis for determining whether a function is proprietary or governmental the nature of this authority for performance.

Whereas municipalities are organized primarily by a specfic group of people to serve their own needs, schools and counties are considered subdivisions of the state and perform the functions of the state. Sometimes they are referred to as quasi-corporations. As such, they are said to be the "arms of the state" or an extension of the state, and the governmental immunity of the state also applies to the school and county.[52] The municipality when performing the educational function of the state also becomes an "arm of the state." This immunity of the state, which also applies to the school and county, is generally said to be founded in the sovereignty of the state. The authority to perform the function is not being challenged, but rather the right of the state to evade liability.[53]

(1965); Augustine v. Brant, 249 N.Y. 198, 163 N.E. 732 (1928); Austin v. Selter, 415 S.W. 2d 489 (Tex. 1967); Petty v. Atlanta, 40 Ga. App. 63, 148 S.E. 747 (1929); Reid v. Atlanta, 39 Ga. App. 519, 147 S.E. 789 (1929); Rumsey v. Salt Lake City, 16 Utah 2d 310, 400 P. 2d 205 (1965).

[47] Collison v. Saginaw, 84 Mich. App. 325, 269 N.W. 2d 586 (1979); Cronin v. Hazel Park, 88 Mich. App. 488, 276 N.W. 2d 922 (1979); Daugherty v. State, Dept. of Natural Resources, 91 Mich. App. 658, 283 N.W. 2d 825 (1979); Feliciano v. State Dept. of Natural Resources, 97 Mich. App. 101, 293 N.W. 2d 732 (1980); Garza v. Edinburg Consol. Indp. School District, 576 S.W. 2d 916 (Tex. 1979); Knapp v. Dearborn, 60 Mich. App. 18, 230 N.W. 2d 293 (1975); Lovitt v. Concord School District, 58 Mich. App. 593, 228 N.W. 2d 479 (1975); Rohrabaugh v. Huron-Clinton Metro. Authority, 75 Mich. App. 677, 256 N.W. 2d 240

(1977); Smith v. Huron-Clinton Metro. Authority, 49 Mich. App. 280, 212 N.W. 2d 32 (1973).

[48] Cates v. Bloomington, 333 Ill. App. 189, 77 N.E. 2d 46 (1947).

[49] Carlisle v. Marysville, 373 Mich. 198, 128 N.W. 2d 477 (1964); Williams v. Morristown, 32 Tenn. App. 274, 222 S.W. 2d 607 (1949).

[50] Autrey v. Augusta, 33 Ga. App. 757, 127 S.E. 796 (1925).

[51] Rhodes v. Palo Alto, 100 Cal. App. 2d 336, 233 P. 2d 639 (1950).

[52] Buck v. McLean, 115 So. 2d 764 (Fla. 1959); Ft. Worth v. Wiggins, 5 S.W. 2d 761 (Tex. App. 1928); Wolf v. Ohio State Univ. Hospital, 170 Ohio St. 49, 9 Ohio Op. 2d 416, 162 N.E. 2d 475 (1959).

[53] Hoffman v. Scranton School Dist., 67 Pa. D. & C. 301, 51 Lack. Jur. 25 (1949); Morris v. School Dist., 393 Pa. 633, 144 A. 2d 737 (1958).

Florida and West Virginia, in cases involving parks and recreation, have held that if the specific function of operations of parks and recreation is a charter grant to the municipality, then the city is held to the same degree of care as a private person. Other cases which discuss charter grants are cited in the footnote.[54]

The dicta in *Boyer v. Iowa High School Athletic Assn.*, 127 N.W. 2d 606 (Iowa, 1964), says in regard to home rule that it is legislative recognition of the governmental immunity of the cities and towns.

Whereas charter grants are rights to specific municipalities, the state legislatures, in their power to municipalities or in recreation and park enabling acts, give municipalities, in general, the right to conduct park and recreation activities. The court may look at the nature of this general authorization to determine whether the function is governmental or proprietary.

Summarization. Generally speaking, schools, which include physical education and some extra-curricular physical activites, as well as playground activities, are operated for the public welfare, including health and education, and are an extension of the function of the state, and as such, are a governmental function. It must be pointed out, however, that any common law immunity from being a governmental function may be modified or totally negated by statutes and court decisions. Furthermore, when athletics becomes a business enterprise, there is some question as to its remaining a govermental function.

It is impossible to give a statement of the law or a "rule of thumb" that can be applied generally to the park and recreation function of municipalities in determining whether such function is governmental or proprietary, as the application to the tests by the states is not consistent. The preponderance of decisions would tend toward saying that, if the function is operated without profit, although a small charge may be made from which the city receives incidental revenue, it is governmental; and that, if a profit is derived therefrom, if the city is in competition with private enterprise, or if the service is for specific inhabitants, the function is proprietary.

Although the foregoing discussion deals primarily with the tests in determining whether a function is governmental or proprietary, some consideration should be given to the result of such determination. The basic assumption appears to be that the doctrine of governmental immunity applies to a governmental function and that a municipality is responsible for its negligent acts when the function is declared proprietary. This generally is true; however, the liability picture is complicated by certain courts holding

---

[54] Backer v. West Chicago Park Comm'rs., 66 Ill. App. 507 (1896); Belton v. Ellis, 254 S.W. 1023 (Tex. Civ. App. 1923); Boise Development Co. v. Boise City, 30 Idaho 675, 167 P. 1032 (1917); Cornelisen v. Atlanta, 146 Ga. 416, 91 S.E. 415 (1917); Emmons v. Virginia, 152 Minn. 295, 188 N.W. 561 (1922); Honaman v. Philadelphia, 322 P. 535, 185 A. 750 (1936); Hyde v. Utica, 259 A.D. 477, 20 N.Y.S. 2d 335 (1940); Ide v. St. Cloud, 150 Fla. 806, 8 So. 2d 924 (1942), aff'd. 13 So. 2d 448 (1943); Kellar v. Los Angeles, 179 Cal. 605, 178 P. 505 (1919); Lisk v. West Palm Beach, 160 Fla. 632, 36 So. 2d 197 (1948); LePitre v. Chicago Park Dist., 374 Ill. 184, 29 N.E. 2d 81 (1940); Pickett v. Jacksonville, 155 Fla. 439, 20 So. 2d 484 (1945); Pollock v. Albany, 88 Ga. App. 737, 77 S.E. 2d 579 (1953); Reid v. Atlanta, 39 Ga. App. 519, 147 S.E. 789 (1929); Rome v. London & Lancashire Indem. Co. of America, 169 So. 132 (La. App. 1936); Vaughn v. Alcoa, 194 Tenn. 449, 251 S.E. 2d 304 (1952); Warden v. Grafton, 99 W. Va. 249, 128 S.E. 375 (1925);

no liability, although the function is declared to be proprietary, where the *duty* being performed is governmental.[55] This duty in all three cases cited is the police function to preserve order or give protection.

There also are other exceptions which negate the seemingly safe condition in states which generally hold to the doctrine of governmental immunity. 150 A.L.R. 21 says:

> These exceptions may be summarized as permitting recovery 1) for a tort arising out of, or committed in the performance of a proprietary as distinguished from a governmental function or activity; 2) for damage or injury to private real property or property rights in respect thereto or consequential injuries thereon, resulting from a trespass or the creation of a nuisance; 3) for the taking or damaging of private property for public use without compensation; 4) for personal injury or death caused by the creation or maintenance of a nuisance; 5) for personal injury or death caused by an active or positive wrong, or a willful or intentional act; 7) where recovery may be predicated upon breach of contract rather than tort; and 8) the view has been adopted by some courts, notably those of New York, that a school district or a school board may be liable for its own acts or omissions as distinguished from those of its officers, agents, or employees. (Note: 6) not in ALR text.)

§ 4.13 Discretionary acts

In the decade of the '80s, performance of discretionary acts is **the** exception to liability of governmental agencies. Of the states which statutorily make governmental agencies liable and then set forth exceptions, nearly all have as the sole or one of the exceptions discretionary acts. Additionally, several more states specifically have indicated immunity for discretionary acts. (See §4.21 for Status of the states.)

The distinction of discretionary acts as a basis for determining liability, however, is not new. *Norberg v. Hagna*, 46 S.D. 568, 195 N.W. 438 (1923) in citing another case said:

> ...municipal corporations have certain powers which are discretionary or judicial in character, and also certain powers which are ministerial. They will not be held liable in damages for the manner in which they exercise good faith their discretionary powers of a public character, but are liable for damages caused by their negligence when their duties are ministerial.

Additional cases decided earlier, which uphold this view are cited in the footnote.[56]

---

[55] Prickett v. Hillsboro, 323 Ill. App. 235, 55 N.E. 2d 306 (1944); Williams v. Longmont, 109 Colo. 567, 129 P. 2d 110 (1942); Woodford v. St. Petersburg, 84 So. 2d 25 (Fla. 1955).

[56] Baltimore v. State, 168 Md. 619, 179 A. 169 (1935); Boucher v. Fuhlbruck, 26 Conn. Sup. 79, 213 A. 2d 455 (1965); Burford v. Grand Rapids, 53 Mich. 98, 18 N.W. 571 (1884); Cornelisen v. Atlanta, 146 Ga. 416, 91 S.E. 415 (1917); Diker v. St. Louis Park, 268 Minn. 461, 130 N.W. 2d 213 (1964); Felton v. Great Falls, 118 Mont. 586, 169 P. 2d 229 (1946); Gorsuch v. Springfield, 43 Ohio L. Abs. 83, 61 N.E. 2d 898 (1945); Hoggard v. Richmond, 172 Va. 145, 200 S.E. 610 (1939); Morgan v. Yuba County, 230 Cal. App. 2d 1009, 41 Cal. Rptr. 508, (1965); Norman v. Chariton, 201 Iowa 279, 207 N.W. 134 (1926); Pennell v. Wilmington, 23 Del. 229, 78 A. 915 (1906); Pollock v. Albany, 88 Ga. App. 737, 77 S. E. 2d 579 (1953).

While the governmental-proprietary dichotomy was gaining favor and nearly every state applied it in the 1960s (see §4.12), there were a few states which, at the turn of the decade of the '60s, became disenchanted with the dichotomy as a basis of liability and immunity and turned toward the concept of discretionary acts. With the 1961 California cases,[57] it appeared that it may be immaterial whether or not the governmental agency function was proprietary or governmental and that the pertinent question would be the distinction of discretionary and ministerial duties.

By around 1970, there were cases in Illinois, Oregon, Maryland, Missouri and Michigan, and more cases in California. In 1971, an *Iowa Law Review* article[58] stated:

> The discretionary exception has become the central feature of efforts to fashion a new standard of government tort liability.... The most common basis for distinguishing discretionary (immune) from ministerial (potentially liable) acts is categorization by level of decision. As such the distinction is cast in terms of "planning" versus "operational" levels of decision-making in the implementation of a given government function. This distinction has been and continues to be extremely difficult to apply in practice, since very few acts are completely devoid of discretion.... The hub of the argument against judicial review in areas of discretion (planning) is that considered judgment of a legislative or judicial nature culminating in a lawful administrative decision to act should not be subject to reconsideration by either judge or jury as to its reasonableness.... Government can reasonably require some sacrifices to be made as a result of its decisions, without paying compensation.

The Illinois court[59] discussed the rationale in saying that quasi-judicial immunity rests upon the principle that the public decision-maker should be shielded from personal liability or other factors extraneous to a judgment based on best perception of public need, and that choices or decisions should be made without fear of personal liability or the second guessing of courts and juries when powers confided to him are so far discretionary that he can exercise or withhold them according to his own judgment as to what is necessary and proper. Government officials should be permitted the freedom to perform their duties without fear of individual liability; limited liability is essential if competent individuals are to be attracted to positions of public trust.[60] The court further stated that a public employee of a local public entity is not liable in tort for injuries arising out of exercise of powers or authority vested in him in good faith if powers are discretionary as opposed to ministerial in nature, except where such acts are performed wantonly or maliciously by the employee. The Oregon court[61] tried to establish some guidelines for what is "discretion" and discussed the planning (discretionary)-

[57] Lipman v. Brisbane Elem. School Dist., 55 Cal. 2d 224, 359 P. 2d 465 (1961); Muskopf v. Corning Hospital Dist., 55 Cal. 2d 211, 359 P. 2d 457 (1961); NeCasek v. Los Angeles, 233 Cal. App. 2d 131, 43 Cal. Rptr. 294 (1965).

[58] "Notes — Separation of Powers and the Discretionary Function Exception: Political Question in Tort Litigation Against the Government." 56 *Iowa L. Rev.* 930-993, April 1971.

[59] Fustin v. Board of Educ., 101 Ill. App. 2d 113, 242 N.E. 2d 308 (1968).

[60] Dahl, Richard. Sovereign Immunity — Discretionary Function Exemption to the Tort Claims Act. 4 *Hamline L. Rev.* 103-121, 116 (1982).

[61] Smith v. Cooper, 256 Ore. 485, 475 P. 2d 78 (1970).

operational dichotomy of the federal system. California endeavored to establish a series of factors to determine discretionary acts (factors test). And, in a non-recreation/park case, the California court[62] stated that to be entitled to discretionary immunity, it must be shown that a policy decision took place. The Missouri and Maryland courts[63] held that teachers were not performing discretionary functions, but rather ministerial for which they were liable. Deciding to build a pool was deemed a discretionary act by the Michigan court.[64] By 1974 more than a dozen states referred by statute or case decision to the distinction of discretionary-ministerial duties, with immunity for the first and liability for the second.[65] Ten years later, in the mid-'80s, the discretionary act concept was well entrenched in nearly all states.

§ 4.131   Concept definition

Whereas the governmental-proprietary dichotomy is directed toward the nature of the function of the **services** provided by the governmental **agency** (see §4.12), the discretionary-ministerial distinction focuses on the **acts** of the **employee** (the person carrying out the function). It is the nature of the employee act that determines the liability of the governmental agency. If the employee (officer, administrator, employee) was engaged in a discretionary act, regardless of whether the function was governmental or proprietary, then the agency is not liable; but, if the employee was performing a ministerial act, then the negligence of the employee would be imputed to the agency and the agency would be liable. Of course, the performance of the act must be within the scope of responsibility and authority and not be done with either malice or willful and wanton misconduct (see §4.234). A consequence of the application of the discretionary-ministerial act concept is that certain activities once considered clearly proprietary in nature are now shielded, if the governmental entity can convince a court that the actions are discretionary; and, functions once viewed as clearly governmental may be subject to liability, if the injury occurred as a result of a ministerial act by an employee.

Critical to proper application of the concept is the definition of a discretionary and a ministerial act. The discretionary act concept existed when Congress enacted the Federal Tort Claims Act; and, therefore, one may look to those pre-Act cases, as well as interpretations of the court since then.[66] The leading case is *Dalehite v. United States*, 346 U.S. 15 (1953), which stated that:

> ...discretionary function or duty...includes more than the initiation of programs and activities. It also includes determinations made by executives or administrators in establishing plans, specifications or schedules of opera-

[62] Ramos v. Madera Co., 89 Cal. Rptr. 312, vac. 94 Cal. Rptr. 421, 484 P. 2d 93 (1971).

[63] Duncan v. Koustenis, 260 Md. 98, 271 A. 2d 547 (1970); Smith v. Consolidated School Dist., 408 S.W. 2d 50 (Mo. 1966).

[64] Brent v. Detroit, 27 Mich. 628, 183 N.W. 2d 908 (1970).

[65] e.g., Arkansas, California, Connecticut, Flor-ida, Idaho, Indiana, Iowa, Maryland, Massachusetts, Missouri, Nebraska, New Jersey, Oregon, South Dakota; also D.C., Illinois, Tennessee, Wisconsin.

[66] Hageman, John A. and Lee A. Johnson. Governmental Immunity. The Kansas Tort Claims Act. 19 *Washburn Law Review* 260 at p. 272 (1980). W.D.H. Case Comment: Discretionary Function Exception to the F.T.C.A., 15 *Georgia L. Rev.* 1125-1141 (1981).

tions. Where there is room for policy judgment and decision there is discretion. It necessarily follows that acts of subordinates in carrying out the operations of government in accordance with official directions cannot be actionable.

In *State v. I'Anson*, 529 P. 2d 188, (Alaska 1974), citing another case, ministerial or operational acts were defined as those which concern routine, everyday matters, not requiring evaluation of broad policy factors. And, a ministerial act, within the purview of the Indiana Tort Claims Statute, was described in *Maroon v. State Dept. of Mental Health*, 411 N.E. 2d 404 (Ind. App. 1980), as one which a person performs in a prescribed manner, in obedience to mandate of legal authority without regard to, or exercise of, his own judgment upon propriety of act being done. The planning level notion of a discretionary act, referring to decisions involving questions of policy, involves the evaluation of factors such as financial, political, economic, and social effects of a given plan or policy.[67] In a 1986 Michigan case,[68] the court, quoting a previous decision, defined discretionary and ministerial acts as:

Discretionary acts have been defined as those which require personal deliberation, decision and judgment. This definition encompasses more than quasi-judicial or policy-making authority, which typically is granted only to members of administrative tribunals, prosecutors, and higher level executives. However, it does not encompass every trivial decision, such as "the driving of a nail," which may be involved in performing an activity. For clarity, we would add the word "decisional" so the operative term would be "discretionary-decisional" acts.

Ministerial acts have been defined as those which constitute merely an obedience to orders or the performance of a duty in which the individual has little or no choice. We believe that this definition is not sufficiently broad. An individual who decides whether to engage in a particular activity and how best to carry it out engages in discretionary activity. However, the actual execution of this decision by the same individual is a ministerial act, which must be performed in a nontortious manner. In a nutshell, the distinction between "discretionary" and "ministerial" acts is that the latter involves the execution of a decision-making. Here too, for clarity, we would add the word "operational" so the operative term would be "ministerial-operational" acts.

The rules governing discretionary functions are more easily stated than applied, and where discretion ends and actionable negligence begins must ultimately be determined on a case by case basis. In the next section (§4.132) are a number of physical education and recreation/park cases in application to the discretionary-ministerial act concept.

Efforts have been made to establish "tests" or bases for determining what constitutes

[67] Swanson v. U.S., 229 F. Supp. 217 (1964).
[68] Webber v. Yeo, 147 Mich. App. 453, 383 N.W. 2d 230 (1985) lv. app. denied 425 Mich. 865; see also

Moreland v. LaPlata Co. Board of Co. Comm'rs., 725 P. 2d 1 (Colo. App. 1985) plaintiff fell off cabin deck, question of building code enforcement.

a discretionary and a ministerial act, rather than just trying to define the words. Scott,[69] in analyzing patterns of reasoning in the federal and state court decisions, identified five tests for finding an exception to governmental liability. The two most applicable to discretionary acts definition were the "undertaking" test and the "planning-operational" test. As implied, there is no duty to initially perform a function, but once it is "undertaken," then there is liability for doing the function with due care. You choose to do the function at your "discretion" and you are not liable for choosing or not choosing to do so, but you are liable for the conduct of the function once you have decided to perform it. In *Connelly v. State*, 3 Cal. App. 3d 744, 84 Cal. Rptr. 257 (1970), there was no duty on the part of the State Department of Water Resources to issue flood forecasts, but when it undertook to do so, it was held to a standard of reasonable care. Thus, the discretionary immunity exception to liability not only protects affirmative discretionary acts, but also protects the discretionary decision not to act, such as a decision not to provide police protection.[70] However, failure to act in the face of a known dangerous situation (e.g., vicious dogs) is decision-making at the operational level and is not protected as a discretionary act.[71] In a seemingly contrary decision,[72] the court held that the government was not liable for failing to exercise its discretion and provide safety features, such as board walks and rails on an undeveloped trail, inasmuch as courts have traditionally held that the government's decision to develop or not to develop certain areas within the national parks is a discretionary activity within the Federal Tort Claims Act, 28 USC 2680(a). However, this case should be distinguished from the preceding *Hanson* case, in that it involved a natural area with the conditions perfectly obvious to the user and there was no eminent danger. (See additional cases in next subsection.)

The "planning-operational" test is the most common. Under this test, decision-making, consideration of **basic** policy factors, executive or administrative level, is indicative of a discretionary function. A ministerial act implements the decision at the operational level and is not immune. Most courts seem to place emphasis upon the level of government at which the particular negligence or wrongful act occurred. A distinction is drawn between actions at the planning or policy-making level and those at a subordinate or operational level. Only the former are exempt.[73] The problem is, of course, that one usually can find implementation aspects at the planning level and planning elements at the subordinate level. Nevertheless, several of the states, in speaking of discretionary duties, refer to "public officials," and, when discussing ministerial duties, talk about "employees." A member of a policy board or planning commission would be performing a discretionary function; an administrator might be performing both types of duties, but primarily ministerial. An employee normally performs almost entirely ministerial duties. Most of the acts performed by professional personnel concerned with physical education and sport or recreation and parks are

[69] Scott, Donald G. Recent Cases: Torts — Abrogation of Sovereign Immunity — Scope of Retained Immunity. 43 *Missouri Law Review* 387 (1978).

[70] Silver v. City of Minneapolis, 284 Minn. 266, 170 N.W. 2d 206 (1969).

[71] Hanson v. City of St. Paul, 298 Minn. 205, 214 N.W. 2d 346 (1974).

[72] Henretig v. U.S., 490 F. Supp. 398 (1980).

[73] Rupp v. Bryant, 399 So. 2d 417, aff'd./rev'd. in part 417 So. 2d 658 (Fla. 1982); see also Commerical Carrier Corp. v. Indian River Co., 342 So. 2d 1042, aff'd. 371 So. 2d 1010 (Fla. 1979).

operational or ministerial in nature. A discussion of some cases is in the next section
(§4.132).

With the focus now on the acts of the employees as the determinant of liability, there
has been consideration that the official or employee should be cloaked, too, in
immunity. However, an agent (administrator), acting beyond statutory authority, cannot
then be protected under discretionary act immunity. In a federal case[74] the agent
destroyed horses grazing on lands, although he knew to whom they belonged. Also,
there is no protection from liability while performing a discretionary act, if such act
involves willful and wanton negligence.[75] (See §4.234 and Chapter 3.)

There are many cases, interpretations of statutes, and law review articles on the
subject of definition of discretionary acts.[76] Just as the body of legal literature grew
extensively regarding the governmental-proprietary function concept (see §4.12), a
defining body of literature developed in the decade of the '80s for the discretionary-
ministerial distinction.

§ 4.132   Application of concept (cases)

The cases appear to fall into three types: (1) the initial decision is of a discretionary
nature with no operational actions; (2) the initial decision is discretionary in nature, but
the injury occurred from a subsequent operational action; and (3) the decision is
ministerial, not discretionary in nature, as alleged.

Initial decision discretionary, no operational action. In several mid-1980s
cases,[77] the decision initially was of a discretionary nature and there was no subsequent
operational element; the defendant was held immune from liability. In *Wysinger* the
district forest ranger made the policy decision not to employ lifeguards at the swimming
facility, a lake, and action for subsequent drowning, alleging failure to provide adequate
supervision and safeguards, was dismissed. The discretionary act in the *Chrisley* case
was to restrict or not restrict access to a portion of the river bank below the dam on
federal lands. The court held that there was no duty to provide safe premises or give
warning of obvious dangerous conditions, when plaintiff sued for wrongful death,
drowning from fall into river. A third case also found immunity for a discretionary
decision of the County Commissioners not to provide supervisory personnel at the
public park and swimming area dock, even though they knew that children frequented
the park and roughhoused and played on the dock.

The following cases give a similar definition of duty and discretionary acts. In
Jackson v. Wilson, 581 S.W. 2d 39 (Mo. App. 1979), the plaintiff was injured while
diving into the river from a large boulder which was located near an area that was
maintained for swimming on the park grounds. The court held that the actions of the
Director of Parks and Recreation in determining whether to place a warning near the

---

[74] Hatahley v. U.S., 351 U.S. 173 (1956).

[75] Neal v. Donahue, 611 P. 2d 1125 (Okla. 1980).

[76] See especially citations and discussions in case
notes in the annotated statutes of the various states.

[77] Avallone v. Board of Co. Comm'rs. of Citrus

Co., 467 So. 2d 826 (Fla. App. 1985); Chrisley v. U.S.,
620 F. Supp. 285 (1985), aff'd. without op. 791 F. 2d
165 (1986) S. C. law applied; Wysinger v. U.S., 621 F.
Supp. 773 (1985), aff'd. 784 F. 2d 1252 (1986).

boulder from which the swimmer dived, to guard the area, and to prohibit persons from diving in the area related to a discretionary function for which the Director enjoyed official immunity. A 1987 situation in California, *Judd v. U.S.*, 650 F. Supp. 1503 (1987), also involved a decision not to post a warning sign. The plaintiff attempted to dive off rocks at a height of 35 feet into a small pool near waterfalls in an undeveloped area of the national forest. The court said that where the Forest Service Manual set forth the policy of posting warning signs at "developed" areas, but was silent regarding "undeveloped" areas, the Forest Service administrators were vested with discretion to post or not to post signs. Thus, the decision not to post warnings was held to be a discretionary act. However, the failure to post warning signs was found not to be the cause of injury; the danger was held to be obvious. Another California federal situation a year earlier held similarly. In *Schieler v. U.S.*, 642 F. Supp. 1310 (1986), plaintiff was injured by lightning while standing on a high rock in a national park. Visitors were not warned of the danger of lightning strikes. (However, see next bold faced paragraph subsection for contrary holdings regarding warnings.)

In a Yellowstone Park situation, the court held that to close garbage dumps in the national parks was related to management of the grizzly bears and therefore a discretionary function, a decision made at the planning level, rather than at the operational level. There was no evidence that the park service willfully failed to warn campers of dangerous conditions.[78]

A young girl was injured late at night in a city-owned park when a young boy threw at her a piece of copper coil which he had pulled free from a park water fountain. The plaintiff alleged that the city's failure to supervise the park at night despite its knowledge that it was frequented by minors was the proximate cause of her injury. The court held that the decision by the city to provide no supervision in the park at night was a planning or discretionary governmental decision for which the city could not be held liable in tort.[79] However, where there is a special relationship which gives rise to a duty to protect (supervise), to supervise is considered a ministerial act.[80] The Florida court, though, has attempted to distinguish inadequacy of supervision and insufficient personnel based upon budgetary and other judgmental criteria, inadequacy being ministerial in nature and insufficiency due to other controlling factors discretionary in nature.[81] In another Florida case[82] the budgetary considerations, also, were pointed out, when the court said that whether to provide security guards, parking attendants, security gates, and the numbers thereof, are clearly discretionary decisions, partially based upon budgetary limitations controlled by the Legislature. In a 1988 case,[83] a spectator was struck and burned by fireworks ignited by someone in a crowd attending a concert and fireworks display sponsored by the city. The court held that failure by the city to prohibit possession and detonation of fireworks by individuals was within the planning-level,

[78] Martin v. U.S., 392 F. Supp. 243 (1975), rev'd. 546 F. 2d 1355 (1976) rehearing denied 432 U.S. 906 (1977).

[79] Jenkins v. Miami Beach, 389 So. 2d 1195 (Fla. App., 1980); see also *Brown* case in next bold-faced paragraph sub-section.

[80] Rupp v. Bryant, 399 So. 2d 417, aff'd./rev'd. in part 417 So. 2d 658 (Fla. 1982).

[81] Cottone v. Broward Co. School Board, 431 So. 2d 355 (Fla. App. 1983).

[82] Relyea v. State, 385 So. 2d 1378 (Fla. App. 1980); see also Turner v. U.S., 473 F. Supp. 317 (1979).

[83] Delgado v. City of Miami Beach, 518 So. 2d 968 (Fla. App. 1988).

discretionary act of government. While the foregoing five cases are all from Florida, they do give some idea of the definition of discretionary and ministerial acts facing all states which have put in place this dichotomy, replacing the governmental-proprietary function approach to governmental immunity.

In *Boucher v. Fuhlbruck,* 26 Conn. Supp. 79, 213 A. 2d 455 (1965), a seven-year-old drowned in a river in the city park. The court stated that maintenance of parks and playgrounds has to do with supervisory or discretionary functions as distinguished from ministerial functions; and, therefore, held that failing to place barriers around the river, to supervise the river area, to post warning signs, to have railings or safety devices along the banks of the river, and to provide adequate supervision or guidance were discretionary acts without liability. It should be noted that this was an early (1965) case and still invoked "governmental function" as well as discretionary acts. (See next bold-faced subsection for later trends.)

There have been cases in a variety of situations in a number of different states, addressing the discretionary act as an exception to liability. A few illustrative cases[84] from the latter '80s are cited. The Minnesota court held that discretionary governmental policy decisions are not subject to judicial review and that such discretionary acts, which require a balancing of competing factors at planning, policy level, are insulated against liability by statutory immunity. In this situation the city's decision to close its ice skating rinks on a holiday weekend was a discretionary act. However, it also was pointed out that the city had provided reasonable notice to the skater, who was injured when she fell and her hand was cut on a piece of jagged glass frozen in an upright position, that the rink was closed. The notice was in the form of lack of lighting, general weather conditions, absence of other skaters, and closed recreation building. In the *Cimino* case, a spectator was seriously injured when struck by a goalpost pulled down at conclusion of a college football game. The court said, citing a previous Connecticut decision, that even where the duty of an official is not ministerial, but involves the exercise of discretion, he or she is subject to liability if the duty to act is clear and unequivocal, such as when a failure to act would be likely to subject an identifiable person to imminent harm. The issue in this case was whether the crowd which attacked goalposts was a "mob," "riotous assembly" or "assembly engaged in disturbing the peace," so that the city had a duty to protect spectator under Connecticut statute. The Illinois case also was one restricting immunity for discretionary acts. The court held that public officials' immunity for discretionary acts does not extend to (1) public employee's acts based on corrupt or malicious motives, or (2) public employee's willful and wanton acts. This situation involved emergency medical attention for a child injured on the schoolyard while playing kickball. In the Florida case, the decision not to take measures to prevent alligators from moving from the state park to adjoining university recreational park and not providing alligator spotters was held to be a discretionary

[84] Barth by Barth v. Board of Education, 141 Ill. App. 3d 266, 95 Ill. Dec. 604, 490 N.E. 2d 77 (1986); Cimino v. Yale Univ., et al., 638 F. Supp. 952 (1986); Palumbo v. State of Florida Game & Fresh Water Fish Commission, 487 So. 2d 352 (Fla. App. 1986); Robinson v. Indianola Mun. Separate School Dist., 467 So. 2d 911 (Miss. 1985) choice of location and construction of school building; Spillway Marina, Inc. v. U.S., 445 F. 2d 876 (1971); Seyler v. U.S., 643 F. Supp. 1027 (1986), rev'd. 832 F. 2d 120 (1987); Stucci v. City of St. Paul, 403 N.W. 2d 850 (Minn. App. 1987).

decision, not supporting liability. A student had used the university facility for three years and on this day, when he noticed one of the sailboats had capsized and had its mast stuck in the mud, he decided to swim out to help the occupants right it. During his swim from the boat launch area, he was attacked and severely injured by an alligator. Plaintiff had disregarded clear warnings and regulations regarding alligators. A marina owner sued the U.S. for damage to his marina from drawdown of water level of flood control reservoir. The court held that in this 1971 situation, drawdown by the Corps of Engineers was within its discretionary function exception of federal tort claims act. There was an opposite result, though, in the *Seyler* case, when the court held that the failure of the government to erect speed limit signs on reservation roadway was not within discretionary function exception of the FTCA. The plaintiff motorcyclist was riding on the Indian reservation for pleasure when he failed to negotiate a turn on a road maintained by the Bureau of Indian Affairs. Plaintiff alleged that the road was negligently designed, maintained and marked by the Bureau.

Initial decision discretionary, subsequent action operational. The majority of the cases find that while the initial decision may have been one of a discretionary nature, planning policy, the injury tended to occur in the maintenance and operational aspects of a second decision. So, whereas the policy decision is immune from liability, the operational decision is not; and, the court determines whether there was negligence in carrying out the operational aspect.

Most of the outdoor-related situations differ from those cited in the preceding bold-faced paragraph subsection; that is, where there was a known hazardous or dangerous condition, a duty to warn existed. In a case[85] involving a 14-year-old visitor to Yellowstone National Park, which was brought under the Federal Tort Claims Act, it was held that to leave an area of clear water springs in which a superheated thermal pool was located in an undeveloped state was a discretionary function, but that the decision not to post warning signs in the area could not be considered a discretionary function. The court stated that the government, as landowner, has a duty under state law to warn about dangerous conditions which have been left undisturbed as a policy matter. However, it also was held that a 14-year-old child owes a reciprocal duty to exercise ordinary care to avoid injuring oneself. There was a similar holding in a 1984 case.[86] While the decision to dredge a riverbed was discretionary, the carrying out of the contract and the adequate provision of warning signs was operational. And, in a 1985 Alaska case[87] it was held that while the decision to build and operate a sea plane dock was discretionary, the keeping of the dock operationally was not.

In *Marlow v. City of Columbia Heights*, 284 N.W. 2d 389 (Minn. 1979), a water skier severely cut the bottom of his foot when he stepped on an object in the lakebed near the city's public boat-launching site. The city tried to bring the decision to search or not search the waters for sharp objects in as a discretionary act for which there was immunity under the state law; however, the discretionary act was the decision to put in the boat launching site and there was then a duty to maintain the facilities in a safe condition or to warn of hazards. There was a similar decision in another water skiing

[85] Smith v. U.S., 383 F. Supp. 1076 (1974), aff'd. 546 F. 2d 872 (1976).

[86] Butler v. U.S., 726 F. 2d 1057 (1984).
[87] Plancich v. State, 693 P. 2d 855 (Alaska 1985).

situation. The operation of the dam was a discretionary function, but where there was knowledge of recreational use of the river and of hazards posed to such users, warnings should be posted concerning the dangerous condition of the river.[88]

The same application of responsibility was made to a reservoir used for swimming. Plaintiff dived into the reservoir lake and allegedly hit his head on a submerged tree stump. It was held that while the decision not to remove submerged tree stumps from the lake was a discretionary act, the failure to warn of a hidden danger was an operational act. The court went on to say that in view of the government's knowledge, the probability and gravity of harm, the total failure to warn, and the ease with which a warning could have been made, the government was guilty of willful and wanton misconduct under Illinois law.[89] The federal court also came to the same decision in a Texas situation.[90] The initial decision by the Corps of Engineers to designate a swimming area and beach on a flood control reservoir was a discretionary act for which there was no liability, but then the Corps was obligated to operate the swimming area in a safe manner. The plaintiff struck an underwater obstruction (concrete block anchor which had become detached), breaking his neck and rendering him a quadriplegic.

A similar finding resulted when the court held that where the manager knew of the condition of the terrain of a recreational area to which the public was invited, he had a ministerial duty to either place warning signs or advise his supervisor of a dangerous situation existing, especially when he was in position to take action to take precautions.[91]

In an Ohio case[92] it was held that the decision to permit sledding was a discretionary function, but the conduct of sledding as an activity was operational with attendant liabilities. A 1987 Florida case[93] held similarly. A 20-year-old student, while attending a picnic at a lake maintained and controlled by the University, was issued a canoe and life vest by an attendant at the boat house. The canoe almost immediately overturned and the student drowned. The complaint stated that the University had implemented a policy regarding the safe use of the lake as a recreational facility, including the provision of lifeguards and the certification of swimming as a prerequisite for the use of certain boating equipment, but not canoes, and the furnishing of life vests to students using canoes. The court held that the University (governmental unit) had the discretion to operate or not operate swimming facilities and that it was immune for that decision, but that once the university decided to operate the facility, it assumed a common law duty to operate the facility safely.

In a 1983 Florida case[94] it was held that while traffic control was a discretionary act, the city had a duty to warn of the hazardous condition. The plaintiff alleged that she was sunbathing on the beach within the limits of the city and that while so engaged, she was run over by an automobile driven by the co-defendant, suffering injuries. The plaintiff

[88] Lindgren v. U.S., 665 F. 2d 978 (1982).
[89] Stephens v. U.S. & State of Illinois, 472 F. Supp. 998 (1979).
[90] Denham v. U.S., 646 F. Supp. 1021 (1986), aff'd. 834 F. 2d 518 (1987).
[91] Cords v. Anderson, 80 Wis. 2d 525, 259 N.W. 2d 672 (1977), rehearing denied, 82 Wis. 2d 321, 262 N.W. 2d 141 (1978).
[92] Marrek v. Cleveland Metro. Board of Comm'rs. 9 Ohio St. 3d 194, 459 N.E. 2d 873 (1984).
[93] Brown v. Florida State Board of Regents, 513 So. 2d 184 (Fla. App. 1987).
[94] Ralph v. City of Daytona Beach, 412 So. 2d 875 (Fla. App. 1982), rev'd. 471 So. 2d 1 (Fla. 1983).

contended that by virtue of a charter provision making that portion of the beach within the city limits a public highway and authorizing the city to regulate traffic thereon, the city had a duty to make the beach reasonably safe for sunbathers invited thereon in the same manner as would private persons owning a place of recreation and amusement.

A pedestrian brought action against the park and recreation district when she was struck by a car backing up in a single-lane driveway adjacent to the swimming pool's entrance and exit. The court held that although the design and construction of sidewalks and the stationing of guards dealt wholly with discretionary matters, the failure to maintain in a reasonable manner existing traffic direction signs could be categorized as "maintenance" and thus "merely ministerial" for which there is liability.[95]

A 14-year-old fell from a slide in the city park. The court held that the city's decision to establish a park and equip it was a discretionary function of local government, emanating from which was the ministerial duty to use reasonable care in carrying out that decision; that is, once the city opted to provide a playground and to equip it, a ministerial duty arose to provide reasonably safe premises.[96] Similarly, in another Indiana case, *City of Bloomington v. Kuruzovich*, 517 N.E. 2d 408 (Ind. App. 1987), the court held that the decision to put a ball field into a park was discretionary, but the design and maintenance of the softball field were ministerial. A softball player sustained injuries, when he tripped over a manhole cover standing approximately 9 inches above ground and about 19 feet outside the first base line, while he was warming up.

A student drowned in a school swimming class, when he dived off the edge of the pool and did not resurface. The class instructors decided that resuscitation efforts would be more effective by first removing the student from the water, rather than attempting resuscitation in the deep end of the pool. The court held that this was a discretionary act cloaked with immunity; however, all subsequent acts performing the resuscitation, which included failure to properly administer mouth-to-mouth resuscitation and cardiopulmonary resuscitation procedures after removing student from water, were deemed to be operational-ministerial acts for which there was liability. Other instructor acts were deemed ministerial also, including failing to properly observe each child enrolled in the swimming class, failing to immediately provide assistance and first aid in the event of an accident, and failing to refrain from activities which would distract their attention from their suspervisory responsibilities.[97]

Action was brought by a child to recover damages for permanent injury suffered while attending an "Indian Powwow" conducted within the fairgrounds arena under authority and supervision of the defendant State Board of Higher Education pursuant to a lease agreement with the defendant county.[98] The public was invited to the Powwow. The area of the fairgrounds immediately adjacent to the arena, owned and controlled by the county, was used for boarding of horses, stalls being rented to private parties who are provided with rules for the use of the premises. While attending the Powwow, the plaintiff was attracted to an unattended horse kept on the fairgrounds adjacent to the

[95] Jones v. Chehalem Park and Recreation Dist., 28 Or. App. 711, 560 P. 2d 686 (1977).

[96] Mills v. American Playground Device Co., 76 Ind. Dec. 535, 405 N.E. 2d 621 (Ind. App., 1980). See also McClendon v. Norwood, 179 Ga. App. 176, 346 S.E.2d 1 (1986) defective playground equipment.

[97] Webber v. Yeo, 147 Mich. App. 453, 383 N.W. 2d 230 (1985) lv. app. denied 425 Mich. 865.

[98] Baker v. State Board of Higher Education, 20 Or. App. 277, 531 P. 2d 716 (1975).

arena. The horse was tied by a rope to a fence. The plaintiff took hold of the rope and his fingers were pulled against the fence by the horse, causing the middle three fingers to be severed. In respect to discretionary acts, it was held that the act of selecting a site was a discretionary function for which no liability may attach. It was stated further that this was the kind of decision requiring the exercise of technical judgment which neither a judge nor a jury is capable of evaluating in terms of "negligent or unreasonable behavior." It was conceded that once the fairgrounds arena had been chosen as the site for the proposed Powwow, the Board had a duty to maintain it in a safe condition and would have been liable for any injuries resulting from a defect in the building itself, since the duty of maintenance is one of a ministerial nature. The plaintiff, however, did not allege negligence related to building defects, since the injury did not occur in the building.

In a situation particularly related to therapeutic recreation, it was held that to determine which youth at the institution for the mentally retarded should be released was a discretionary act and that there was no duty to warn plaintiffs of the dangerous propensities of the youth when released for a holiday home leave. This was a professional decision comprising discretionary choice among alternatives.[99]

In a playground case,[100] plaintiff was injured while playing the game "kill" during a recess period. The game consisted of one participant having possession of the football, while all other participants attempted to obtain the ball by means of tackling and jumping. The plaintiff characterized the game as ultra-hazardous. Inadequate supervision was alleged on behalf of both the principal and the classroom teacher. The teacher was not held liable because he had no duty to be on the playground at this time, nor were the children in his charge. As for the principal, she was apprised of the dangerous condition and had a duty to reasonably exercise her supervisory powers (inferred discretionary) in such a way as to minimize injury to students in her charge (the implementation of supervision inferred ministerial).

There have been several additional cases relating to supervision and discretionary function. All cases[101] have held assignment of supervisory personnel to be a ministerial act. In the 1984 *Longo* case, the court said that decisions of principal involving assignment of school personnel for supervision were "discretionary operational" or less than high-level planning decisions involving the allocation of personnel for which principal would be granted immunity under the Tort Claims Act.

Additional cases concerned with physical education or recreation and discretionary acts are cited in the footnote.[102]

[99] Cairl v. State, 323 N.W. 2d 20 (Minn. 1982).

[100] Cook v. Bennett, 94 Mich. App. 93, 288 N.W. 2d 609 (1979).

[101] Ballard v. Polly, 387 F. Supp. 895 (1975) D.C. situation; Longo v. Santoro, 195 N.J. Super. 507, 480 A. 2d 934 (1984).

[102] Brent v. Detroit, 27 Mich. 628, 183 N.W. 2d 908 (1970); Fraser v. Henninger, 173 Conn. 52, 376 A. 2d 406 (1977); Law v. Newark Board of Education, 175 N.J. Super. 26, 417 A. 2d 560 (1980); Lindgren v. U.S., 665 F. 2d 978 (1982); McIntosh v. Becker, 111 Mich. App. 692, 314 N.W. 2d 728 (1981); Otteson v. U.S., 622 F. 2d 516 (1980); Stephens v. U.S., 472 F. Supp. 998 (1979); Tango v. New Haven, 173 Conn. 203, 377 A. 2d 284 (1977); Thomas v. Chicago Board of Education, 60 Ill. App. 3d 729, 17 Ill. Dec. 865, 377 N.E. 2d 55 (1978), rev'd. 77 Ill. 2d 165, 32 Ill. Dec. 308, 395 N.E. 2d 538 (1979); Whitney v. Worcester, 373 Mass. 208, 366 N.E. 2d 1210 (Mass. 1977); Willis v. Dade Co. School Board, 411 So. 2d 245 (Fla. App. 1982).

Decision ministerial, not discretionary. The plaintiff, who became a quadraplegic after he was injured in his physical education class while performing a gymnastic exercise, brought action against the superintendent of schools, the principal of the high school and the physical education instructor. In respect to discretionary acts, it was held that the instructor's determination of how to spot and teach an advanced gymnastic exercise was not decision making entitled to protection under the doctrine of discretionary immunity. It further was held that the principal's responsibility for developing and administering the teaching of the physical education curriculum in a safe manner was not at the decision-making planning level and thus also was not protected. The superintendent was insufficiently involved to be found negligent.[103] Defendant was not entitled to governmental immunity in *Hyman v. Green*, 157 Mich. App. 566, 403 N.W. 2d 597 (1987), because physical education instructor's alleged failure to adequately supervise and instruct physical education class and to intervene when players began to use excessive force during touch football game were ministerial acts for which there was no immunity from tort liability.

The Board of Education and the physical education instructor were sued by a tenth grade student, who was struck in the right eye by a flying hockey puck, causing a retinal detachment and eventual removal of the eye, on the basis that he was required to participate as a member of the class with an excess number of players on each team in a playing area that was too small for the purpose and, further, that the proper protective equipment was not provided. The court held that such decision to play the game with that many participants in that size space was not the type of high-level policy decision contemplated by the State Tort Claims Act in providing immunity with respect to a discretionary act.[104] Similarly, when the University drama professor decided to use an actual, breakable drinking glass in dress rehearsal rather than safer glass substitute often used in theatre productions, the court held that the decision was not a determination of governmental policy but, rather, one of professional or occupational discretion not protected under the discretionary function exception to liability.[105]

In *Staton v. U.S.*, 685 F. 2d 117 (1982), defense alleged that park ranger's shooting of hunting dogs was a discretionary act, and, thus, the U.S. was immune from liability. Even though the regulation provided that dogs running at large in the wildlife sanctuary and observed by an authorized person in the act of killing, injuring or molesting humans or wildlife may be disposed of in the interest of public safety and protection of wildlife, the court held that it was not a discretionary act. The ranger's superiors had interpreted such regulation to eliminate the rangers' discretion by setting forth the policy that such dogs should be captured and impounded.

Failure of park rangers, employees of the U.S., to maintain a danger buoy off the tip of a peninsula during boating season was held not to be a discretionary act, but willful failure to guard and warn against danger at that point and the cause of injuries to passenger in one of two boats which collided when rounding the peninsula.[106]

---

[103] Larson v. Indp. School Dist. No. 314, Braham., 312 Minn. 583, 252 N.W. 2d 128 (1977), 289 N.W. 2d 112 (Minn. 1979); see also, Kringen v. Shea, 333 N.W. 2d 445 (S.D. 1983).

[104] Sutphen v. Benthian, 165 N.J. Super. 79, 397 A. 2d 709 (1979).

[105] Christilles v. Southwest Texas State Univ., 639 S.W. 2d 38 (Tex. App. 1982).

[106] Davidow v. U.S., 583 F. Supp. 1170 (1984) Pennsylvania law applied.

Plaintiff sued for death of her daughter, who drowned while swimming off the beach in the ocean. The court held that allegations of negligence on the part of the lifeguards or members of beach patrol on duty at time of drowning were acts at the operational level, which were not barred by sovereign immunity.[107]

§ 4.133   Design immunity — a definition of discretionary act

The specification of design immunity by a number of states[108] in their tort statutes relating to governmental immunity is really only a further definition of discretionary acts. There is immunity against claims for injuries resulting from a plan or design of public property when such plan has been officially approved by an authorized body or official. Such an approval of plans or designs is peculiarly a function of the executive or legislative branch of government and is an example of the type of high discretionary activity which the courts should not second-guess.[109] There are three elements required for immunity: (1) a causal relationship between the plan or design and the accident; (2) approval of the design in advance of construction by the legislative body or officer exercising discretionary authority; and (3) the court finding of substantial evidence of the design's reasonableness.[110]

There is difference of opinion regarding whether the immunity should be in perpetuity or not. In the N.J. Stat. Ann. §59:4-6 annotated statutory comments, it is stated that the section on design immunity is intended to grant a public entity and a public employee complete immunity for injuries. The comment goes on to justify this view partially on the basis that not to do so would provide a very broad and extensive amount of exposure to liability against which there would be difficulty providing economical and adequate protection. The comment concludes, recognizing that to provide immunity in perpetuity is contra to decisions in California (it specifically rejected the California view as unrealistic and inconsistent with the thesis of discretionary immunity), that a coordinate branch of government should not be second-guessed by the judiciary for high level policy decisions. However, in *Costa v. Josey*, 83 N.J. 49, 415 A. 2d 337 (1980), the court held that the New Jersey statute immunizing for injury relating to design did not immunize from responsibility for dangerous conditions arising from maintenance.

Design immunity was not a part of the Public Liability Act of 1923 of California. California, however, did place a special section (§830.6) in the 1963 revised tort claims and actions statutes, which apparently New Jersey and other states have patterned. But, on the basis of experience with cases,[111] this section was amended in 1979 to provide limitation on design immunity. This is sometimes referred to as the *Baldwin* standard or the doctrine of changed circumstances.[112] Under this doctrine, and as incorporated into

[107] Cutler v. Jacksonville Beach, 489, So. 2d 126 (Fla. App. 1986).

[108] For example, California, Illinois, Idaho, Kansas, New Jersey.

[109] Hageman, John A., and Lee A. Johnson. Governmental Liability. The Kansas Tort Claims Act. 19 *Washburn Law Journal* 260 at p. 275 (1979).

[110] Davis v. Cordova Recreation and Park District, 24 Cal. App. 3d 789, 101 Cal. Rptr. 358 (1972); Weddle v. State of Calif., 94 Cal. App. 3d 940, 152 Cal. Rptr. 886 (1979), rev'd. new trial 156 Cal. Rptr. 692 (1979).

[111] For example, Baldwin v. State of California, 6 Cal. 3d 424, 99 Cal. Rptr. 145, 491 P. 2d 1121 (1972).

[112] Bell, Steven S. XI Torts. A. Effect of Changed Conditions or a Nonapproved Design on Statutory Immunity. 61 *California Law Review* 627 (1973).

the California statute, it is recognized that public entities should not be permitted "to shut their eyes to the operation of a design once it has been transferred from blueprint to blacktop."

> To come within the *Baldwin* standard, plaintiffs must show the governmental entity had notice that changed physical conditions created a dangerous condition on public property and did not act reasonably to correct or alleviate the hazard. The notice may be actual or constructive, but must be a sufficient time prior to the injury to have permitted the public entity to take measures to protect against the danger. When it has notice, the entity can avoid liability if its response was reasonable under the circumstances or, in at least some situations, if all possible responses were so costly or otherwise impractical that inaction was justifiable.

> The *Baldwin* rule....is a proper balance between the state's interest in not having to constantly reexamine and improve public property and the interest of those who are injured on public property in being compensating.... Moreover, *Baldwin* does not unduly interfere with discretionary decision-making because, by definition, the changed conditions doctrine will arise only when the design is operating in a way that could not have been contemplated by the governmental entity at the time the design was approved.

> ...Generally, governmental entities are not liable if they actually approve a plan that later causes injury. Courts will not inquire into such discretionary approval. When the design functions as a trap upon the public, however, and a warning sign would permit the public to avoid the trap, liability may be imposed. Furthermore, when there are changed circumstances that make the design dangerous, liability may be imposed.[113]

The California view is consistent with the exception of dangerous conditions to the doctrine of governmental immunity. (See §4.2 and Chapter 20.)

The 1972 *Davis* case illustrates the application of the elements of design immunity in the recreation field. In 1961, the defendant Park District adopted a master plan for recreation and parks. An architect was engaged to prepare detailed plans and specifications for a park, which in turn were approved by the defendant's board of directors. In the park was a pond, and one critical feature of the pond design was a certain "fish hold" or sump to be constructed near the middle of the pond. The purpose of the fish hole was to provide a deeper sanctuary for fish which, otherwise lacking oxygen, would be unable to survive the temperatures of the summer in the shallow water that characterized the rest of the pond. The dimensions of the fish hole were to be 27½' in diameter at the bottom. During construction of the facility, however, and because the area park site was smaller than originally conceived, the dimensions of the hole in question were changed so that its size was reduced. The resultant dimensons were 12' in diameter at the top, 6' to 8' at the bottom and 5½' to 6' in depth. This alteration was

[113] Ibid. at pp. 633-634.

approved during construction by both the defendant's administrator and a supervisor of the defendant. The net effect of this structural change was to increase substantially the steepness of the sloping sidewalls of the hole from 45° as designed to about 80°. The question: Was the change appropriately approved to bring the design within the statutory design immunity? The plaintiff's son, a four-year-old, went out to play with his sister and the neighbor's children. Within 15-20 minutes the daughter came in and excitedly told her parents that "Larry's hiding in the water." The father found him in the deep "hole," rushed him to the hospital, but Larry died within 24 hours from irreversible brain damage caused by lack of oxygen. The plaintiff-father and children frequently played kickball in the park. The neighborhood had many young people, and especially small children, who frequented the park and used its facilities. The perimeter of the lake had a flat cement walkway, level with the lawn area and elevated a few inches above the water. The lake was generally shallow, ranging from 3″ to 4″ to about knee deep on an adult. The bottom was largely obscured. In playing kickball, the ball frequently went into the water and the plaintiff-father would wade into the lake to retrieve the ball. The question: Was there a causal relationship between the design and the accident? And, related is the third element — Was there evidence of the design's reasonableness? Design immunity being an affirmative defense, the defendant had the burden of pleading and proving the defense and each of the essential elements of it. This the defendant was unable to do. There was not proof to the satisfaction of the court of the reasonableness of the design inasmuch as there was actual notice (knowledge) of the concentration of young children engaged in activity which made the construction and maintenance of an open, abrupt and unguarded hole in the pond dangerous, hazardous and of high risk. The court referred to it as a "trap." While the plan was appropriately approved initially and drafted by an architect, the change in the slope of the "fish hole" was deemed by the court to be a "substantial," in contrast to a trivial, change. Also, there was in essence a different use than that which was contemplated by the park designers, from aesthetics and a fishing hole to a pond used by children for wading, which made the fish hole a hazard to children by its abrupt drop-off.

Although design immunity statutes have been referenced in this section as a definition of discretionary act, it should be recognized that other states also may adhere to design immunity as an application of the concept of immunity for discretionary acts.[114] It should be noted, further, that the defense of design immunity should not be confused with limitation of actions relating to deficiencies in construction of improvements.[115] These limitations tend to be six to ten years. Nor should the defense be considered the same as limitations of actions for design professionals.[116] In two 1982 cases[117] the Florida court held that a municipal corporation is not liable for defects inherent in plans for improvement merely because they approved the plans, for approval of plans is at the judgmental planning level for which there is immunity; however, it is the operational duty to warn of hazards, particularly when a governmental entity creates

[114] For example, New York.
[115] For example, Alaska, Indiana, Nevada, Oklahoma.
[116] For example, Maine, Missouri.
[117] (Two cases in consolidated oral arguments) St.

Petersburg v. Collom, 400 So. 2d 507 (1981), aff'd. Fla., 419 So. 2d 1082 (1982); St. Petersburg v. Mathews, 400 So. 2d 841 (1981), aff'd. Fla., 419 So. 2d 1082 (1982).

a known dangerous condition that is not readily apparent to persons who could be injured by the condition.

§ 4.2　Tort claim acts

The fourth era related to public entity immunity, as described in the introduction of this chapter, is that of tort claims acts. This section deals with the content of the tort claims acts primarily, although related statutes in states that have acts, as well as statutes in states that do not have full comprehensive acts, are included. A summary by states is set forth in Tables 4.1 and 4.1-A.

Table 4.1 Tort Claims Acts and Doctrine of Government/Sovereign Immunity—Summary Status of the States

This is a summary table with key elements and must be read in conjunction with both the text, which is keyed to each column, and the actual state statutes and cases (see Appendix). There are many exceptions and ramifications of the statutory and case law in each state which cannot be displayed in either a summary table or the text. See your local attorney for your own state peculiarities. This table was compiled from data available as of mid-1980s in the University of Toledo Law Library. The footnotes at the end of the table provide explanatory information regarding the various columns. This table is in two parts because of the number of elements being summarized. Table 4.1-A is an extension of provisions of statutes indicated in column entitled Tort Claims Act.

State	Status[1]	Tort Claims Act[2]	Approach[3]	Exceptions	Jurisdictional Scope[4]			
					State	School	County	Cities
Alabama	Judicial/statutory C	Tort Claims and Judgments Against Local Government Entities 1977	immunity	as provided by various statutes		X	X	X
			immunity	"moral obligation"	X			
Alaska	Judicial/statutory J		liability	discretionary duty or function				X
Arizona	Judicial/statutory J	Actions Against Public Entities or Public Employees 1984	liability	discretionary acts; criminal felony by employee; lists "absolute" and "qualified" immunity	X	X	X	X
Arkansas	Statutory C	(Liability of Political Subdivisions) 1969 (Liability of the State) 1977	immunity		X	X	X	X
California	Judicial/statutory J	Claims & Actions Against Public Entities & Public Employees 1963	immunity	dangerous conditions; employee liable as private person except discretionary acts, recreation hazardous act, and entity liable in covering employee; limited emotional distress liability	X	X	X	X

179

State	Status[1]		Tort Claims Act[2]	Approach[3]	Exceptions	Jurisdictional Scope[4]			
						State	School	County	Cities
Colorado	Judicial/statutory	J	Colorado Governmental Immunity Act 1963	immunity	dangerous conditions of public building or facility	X	X	X	X
Connecticut	Insurance	M		liability (statute)	discretionary acts; natural land or unimproved property; access trail or footpath when no notice of defect	X	X		X
Delaware	Statutory	C	Tort Claims Act 1979	immunity discretionary acts	construction, operation, maintenance public building except for use public outdoor recreation	X	X	X	X
District of Columbia	Judicial	J		liability	discretionary acts; board of education personally immune, official duties				X
Florida	Judicial	J		liability (statute)	discretionary acts (cases)	X	X	X	X
Georgia	Insurance/statutory	I		insurance not waiver immunity		X	X	X	X
Hawaii	Statutory	S	State Tort Claims Act 1957	liability	discretionary function (lists 6 exceptions)	X	X		
			(Actions by and against the state) 1894	liability	officer not authorized	X			
Idaho	Judicial/statutory	J	Tort Claims Against Governmental Entities (Idaho Tort Claims Act) 1971, 1984	liability (see comments)	discretionary function; design immunity (lists 7 exceptions)	X	X	X	X
Illinois	Judicial/statutory	J	Local Government and Governmental Employees Tort Immunity Act 1965	immunity -condition public property for park, playground, open area recreation purposes -design immunity -condition of access road for fish, hunt, et al. -failure to supervise an activity on public property	notice of dangerous condition; where swim notice posted hours, supervision failure during hours	see notes other columns	X		X

State	Status[1]	Tort Claims Act[2]	Approach[3]	Exceptions	Jurisdictional Scope[4]			
					State	School	County	Cities
Indiana	J	Tort Claims Against Governmental Entities and Public Employees 1974	immunity for (lists 15) including: -discretionary function -natural conditions -unimproved property -unpaved access way		X	X	X	X
Iowa	S	State Tort Claims Act 1965	liability	discretionary function and others	X			
		(Tort Liability of Governmental Subdivisions) 1967	liability	4 listed		X	X	X
Kansas	I	Kansas Tort Claims Act 1979	liability	18 exceptions including: -discretionary duty -design immunity -use of public property—park, playgrounds, open area for recreation -natural condition on unimproved property	X	X	X	X
Kentucky	J							
Louisiana	J	(1980 act) (Local Government Subd. Self-insurance Act 1979)	liability	discretionary acts	X	X		X "other public bodies"
Maine	I	Maine Tort Claims Act 1977	immunity including: (listed 10 "examples") -discretionary acts -construction, ownership, maintenance or use of unimproved land, historic sites, primarily public outdoor recreation	liable motor vehicles, snowmobile, et al. moving vehicles -public buildings except primarily public outdoor recreation -5 listed	X	X	X	X

State	Status[1]	Tort Claims Act[2]	Approach[3]	Exceptions	Jurisdictional Scope[4]			
					State	School	County	Cities
Maryland	Statutory C	Local Government Tort Claims Act 1987	liability	-mun. corp. officials discretionary acts immune		comm. colleges	X	X
		Maryland Tort Claims Act 1981	liability, immunity waived to extent of insurance	-state officers and employees not liable except gross negligence and malicious conduct; -dangerous condition, building, structure, public improvement; -super. act, state park or rec. facility	X			
Massachusetts	Judicial/statutory C	Claims & Indemnity Procedures for the Commonwealth, Its Municipalities, Co., & Districts & the Officers & Employees Thereof 1978	liability	discretionary function	X	X	X	X
Michigan	Judicial/statutory J	Liability for Negligence of State & Political Subdivisions 1964	immunity for governmental functions (see comments)	-dangerous or defective condition of building if notice reasonable time and failed to remedy; -proprietary function, nuisances	X		X	X
Minnesota	Judicial/statutory J	Tort Liability, Political Subdivisions 1963 (separate law for state including colleges, but similar to Act)	liability	-discretionary acts (and several others); -(state) 12 exceptions including discretionary acts and outdoor recreation systems	X	X	X	X
Mississippi	Statutory I	Immunity of State & Political Subdiv. for Liability & Suit for Torts & Torts of Employees 1984	immunity (waived to extent of insurance)	not liable for discretionary act -plan or design for constr. -dangerous condition if not caused by negligence and no notice to give time to warn -failure to warn of dangerous condition when obvious	X		X	X
		(series of separate acts authorizing insurance for different agencies)	liability (immunity waived) to extent of insurance			X		X

State	Status[1]	Tort Claims Act[2]	Approach[3]	Exceptions	Jurisdictional Scope[4]			
					State	School	County	Cities
Missouri	Statutory/insurance I	(Sovereign Immunity) 1978	immunity	property in dangerous condition, reasonably foreseeable harm, notice in time to protect	X	X	X	X
			carry insurance on gov't. functions, but waive immunity to extent of coverage	schools keep buildings in good repair and grounds belonging thereto				X
Montana	Statutory I	Liability Exposure & Insurance Coverage 1973	liability	legislative and judicial acts	X	X	X	X
Nebraska	Judicial/statutory J	Political Subdivisions Tort Claims Act 1969, amended 1984	liability	discretionary function (and 5 other exceptions)		X	X	X
		State Claims Act 1969, amended 1984	liability	discretionary function	X			
Nevada	Judicial/statutory J	Liability of and Actions Against the State, Its Agencies & Political Subdivisions 1977, amended 1983	liability	discretionary function (and several others)	X	X	X	X
New Hampshire	Judicial/statutory I	Bodily Injury Actions Against Governmental Units 1975	immunity including injury arising from inclement weather	injury arising from ownership, occupation, maintenance, or operation — all premises except public sidewalks, streets, highways		X	X	X
		Claims Against the State 1985	liability	discretionary acts, intentional acts of employees	X			
New Jersey	Judicial/statutory J	Claims Against Public Entities (N.J. Tort Claims Act) 1972	immunity for: -discretionary acts -failure to provide supv. of public recreation -design or plan -condition of unimproved property	-ministerial functions -dangerous conditions	X	X	X	X

State	Status[1]	Tort Claims Act[2]	Approach[3]	Exceptions	Jurisdictional Scope[4]			
					State	School	County	Cities
New Mexico	I Judicial/statutory	Tort Claims Act 1978	immunity	operation or maintenance of buildings, public park, machinery, equipment, or furnishings -and several others	X	X	X	X
New York	S Statutory	Liability of Political Subdivisions 1977 (not regular act) -a series of statutes for the various jurisdictions is reported in the aggregate	liability	co. not liable for discretionary acts	X	X	X	X
North Carolina	I Insurance	(Tort Claims Act 1951; Defense of State Employees 1967; Defense Public School Employees 1979)	-state - sovereign immunity not wavied by insurance -cities, co. - purchase of insurance waiver of immunity to extent of insurance for gov't. function	board of educ. and board of trustees of institutions waiver to extent of insurance	X	X	X	X
North Dakota	I Judicial/statutory	Liability of Political Subdivisions 1977	liability	discretionary function and several others	see comment	X	X	X and park dists.
Ohio	I Judicial/statutory	(Ohio Court of Claims Act 1975) Political Subdivision Tort Liability 1985	waived immunity immunity (both governmental and proprietary functions)	to extent of insurance -motor vehicles -negligence performance of proprietary functions -public grounds in repair, free of nuisance	X	X	X	X

184

State	Status[1]	Tort Claims Act[2]	Approach[3]	Exceptions	Jurisdictional Scope[4]			
					State	School	County	Cities
Oklahoma	**S** Statutory	The Governmental Tort Claims Act 1978, repealed, new 1984 eff. Oct. 1985	liability Act applies to both gov't. and prop. func.	lists 30 including: -discretionary act -attractive nuisance -natural condition of unimproved property -participation in or practice for any interscholastic or other athletic contest sponsored or conducted by or on the property -acts done in conformance with current recognized stds. -mfg. product liability -act of indp. contractor	X	X	X	X
Oregon	**S** Statutory	(Tort Claims Against Public Bodies) 1967	liability	lists 6 including: -discretionary function	X	X	X	X
Pennsylvania	**C** Judicial/statutory	Actions Against Commonwealth Parties 1980	sovereign immunity generally	lists 9 including: -dangerous conditions of real estate	X			
		Actions Against Local Parties 1980	immunity	lists 8 exceptions including: -real property except intentional trespassing		X	X	X
Rhode Island	**J** Judicial/statutory	Governmental Tort Liability 1970	liability		X	X	X	X
South Carolina	**M** Judicial/statutory	Tort Claims Act 1986	immunity	lists 26 including: -discretionary act -nuisance -natural condition of unimproved property, unless defect/condition not corrected within reasonable time after notice -maintenance, security, supv. of park, playground, or open area for recreation, public boat ramps, unless defect/condition not corrected after notice	X	X	X	X

185

State	Status[1]	Tort Claims Act[2]	Approach[3]	Exceptions	Jurisdictional Scope[4]			
					State	School	County	Cities
South Dakota	I Insurance	(a number of different statutes)	waiver of immunity to extent of insurance		X	X	X	X
Tennessee	I Statutory	Governmental Tort Liability Act 1973	immunity both gov't and prop. functions, however, really liable except for discretionary acts (see next column)	lists 12 exceptions including: -dangerous structures negligence acts unless discretionary		X	X	X
Texas	M Statutory	Texas Tort Claims Act 1969, 1985	liability (act does not apply to proprietary functions; see comments)	-discretionary acts -attractive nuisance -intentional torts by employees	X	X	X	X
Utah	S Statutory	Governmental Immunity Act 1965	immunity for governmental function (recreation not gov't func.)	waiver of immunity except 11 listed including: -discretionary acts -natural cond. state lands	X	X	X	X
Vermont	I Insurance	(Tort Claims Against the State) 1961	liability	list 7, including discretionary function	X			
		(1974) act	waives immunity to extent of insurance coverage		X	X	X	X
Virginia	C Statutory	Virginia Tort Claims Act (1981, eff. July 1, 1982)	liability	legislative & judicial functions	X			
		(1950) act	no liability for operation of recreation facilities, including pools, beaches, parks, playgrounds	gross negligence or willful and wanton act		X	X	X
Washington	S Statutory	(Actions Against Political Subdivisions, Municipal Corporations and Quasi-Corp.) 1967 (co., town, school actions for & against) (state) many insurance-authorizing statutes	liability for both gov't. and proprietary functions	discretionary acts	X	X	X	X

186

State	Status[1]	Tort Claims Act[2]	Approach[3]	Exceptions	Jurisdictional Scope[4]			
					State	School	County	Cities
West Virginia	Statutory I	Governmental Tort Claims and Insurance Reform Act 1945, 1975 amend, 1986 new act	liability (applicable to both governmental and proprietary functions)	natural conditions of unimproved property; product liability; natural conditions due to weather on public way or place	X	X	X	X
Wisconsin	Judicial J	Claims Against Governmental Bodies, Officers, & Employees 1975	personal individual liable ministerial, not disc. acts			X	X	X
		Claims Against State Employees 1973	liability	discretionary function				
Wyoming	Judicial/statutory I	Wyoming Governmental Claims Act 1979	immunity	operation or maintenance of any building, recreation area or public park -and several other exceptions	X	X	X	X
		(several different statutes)	immunity waived to extent of insurance -by case law, state retains immunity in amount not covered by insurance			X		X

[1]Status — status of the doctrine of governmental immunity. The word "judicial" refers to abrogation by court decision; "statutory" means that the legislature enacted law abrogating, usually; "judicial/statutory" is when the courts abrogated and the legislature responded; "insurance" indicates that the legislature provided insurance as a way to cope with liability, rather than specifying liability directly. The bold-faced letters in the corner are codes designating the status as listed by the *Restatement of Torts* 1973, so that one may know the change in approximately 15 years: J - judicially abolished doctrine; S - statutorily abrogated; I - insurance waiver theory; M - modified; and C - common law.

[2]If the state has a tort claims act, the title and date of enactment are given and the provisions of the Act are specified. Most statutes have been amended. If the state has a "chapter" or "title," but does not label the statutes an Act, this chapter or title is considered an act. If the state has statutes, but not an act, the provisions are given. Parentheses means not referred to as an act, but is a chapter, section, or series of statutes similar to an act.

[3]Usually a tort claims act approaches torts of governmental agencies either as the agency is liable with exceptions or is immune with exceptions. Only selected "exceptions" are listed — those most apropos to the focus of this book.

[4]An x indicates the governmental entity to which the statute is applicable; cities includes generally local municipalities, towns, villages, et al. Sometimes a statute will refer to municipalities and mean all local government entities; reference also may be to political subdivisions or local agencies. In such instances, the various classifications are checked.

Table 4.1-A Summary Status of States, continued

State	Maximum Award[5]	Insurance Authorization[6]	Indemnification[6]	Claims Settlement[7]	Notice[8]	Comments
Alabama	$100,000/300,000 recoverable	to cover employees	X defense counsel required except intentional or willful act	to max. amounts		school — risk mgmt. cooperative co. immunity abolished
Alaska			Board of Adjustment			1980 case — const. provision state immunity not absolute
Arizona	no punitive damages	X joint agreements self-insurance	colleges, schools			case law — no immunity for public officials
				X		one year statute of limitations risk management officer, agent, or employee not personally liable for discretionary act in good faith
Arkansas	negotiated settlement amount of insur.	school liability insurance, self-insurance fund minimum $2M, self-insurance act for elem. & sec. schools	X	X		constitutionality upheld
	actual, no punitive damages	also Risk Management Act	X	X		state officers & employees immune, except liable to extent of insurance carried by employee
California	certain exemplary damages may be paid for employee	X joint agreements self insurance	X	X	100 days	courts seem to be holding generally liability notwithstanding statute and its exceptions special hazardous recreational activities statute immunity especially for natural conditions & unimproved lands
Colorado	$150,000/400,000 employees no punitive damages	X self insurance state required to insure	X public entities except states if no immunity, & employee within scope of duty & not willful act	X	180 days	state risk management division public employee not liable unless willful & wanton act

188

State	Maximum Award[5]	Insurance Authorization[6]	Indemnification[6]	Claims Settlement[7]	Notice[8]	Comments
Connecticut			X no state officer or employee liable unless wanton, malicious or reckless		6 months cities	
Delaware	$300,000 or more, if insurance	X	X		political subd. may enact min. 1 year	employee liable if outside scope of employment or willful
District of Columbia				X		status based primarily on court decisions
Florida	$100,000/200,000 no punitive	X self-insurance authorized	X defense of public officer & employee at public expense			school risk management program, appears to be conflict between statutory and case law
Georgia		X	X			by statute, mun. corp. liable for ministerial duties; case law not liable for gov'tal. func.; parks gov'tal. func., golf prop.
Hawaii		X				
Idaho	$500,000 single occurence or to extent of insurance, no punitive damages	X policy not less than $500,000	X	X	180 days; minor-6 years or 120 days after reaching majority 2 years S/L	not Act, separate statute — city not liable for damages ... accident on the parks & lands set apart for such purpose, except gross negligence employee liable if outside scope of employment or with malice and criminal intent
Illinois	state risk mgmt. plan, $2M motor vehicle, $100,000 per person other	X risk pools	not by Act, but by municipal & school codes (1977) and state as covered by self-insurance by state (1980)	under state self-insurance plan	1 year	employee not liable if property used for parks and recreation unless willful & wanton conduct, local gov't. risk care management program, hazardous recreational activity act
Indiana	$300,000/$5M no punitive	X self-insurance, risk sharing/pools; political subd. catastrophic liability fund and risk mgmt. fund	X	X	180 days	employees included with gov't entity immunities

189

State	Maximum Award[5]	Insurance Authorization[6]	Indemnification[6]	Claims Settlement[7]	Notice[8]	Comments
Iowa		reference to, not specific	X	X		employees of mun. & state not personally liable unless malice, willful
	no punitive damages	self-insurance, local gov't risk pool	X		90 days	statute-risk management, div. entities other than state; officers, employees not personally liable exempt for entities
Kansas	$500,000 no punitive	pooling, interlocal agreements	X also defense	X		employee immune for same exceptions as entity
Kentucky	$50,000 Board of Claims	co. & city may insure employees & officials 1979, schools liability insurance		X (state)		municipal liability in state of change
Louisiana		X	X	X Small Claims Settlement Act 1977		interlocal risk management agency's state office of risk management; special procedural statute
		X self-insurance	teachers if innocent-defense const. only			
Maine	$300,000	X self-insurance	X	X	180 days	personal liability of employees limited
Maryland	$200,000/500,000 no punitive	schools at least $100,000 self-insurance, colleges self-insurance minimum $100,000/500,000				
	$100,000/500,000 no punitive	park & planning comm. self-insur.			1 year S/L	
Massachusetts	$100,000 punitive damages	$500,000 self-insurance; carry insurance for excess	not to exceed $1M	X present claim with 6 months		

190

State	Maximum Award[5]	Insurance Authorization[6]	Indemnification[6]	Claims Settlement[7]	Notice[8]	Comments
Michigan		X self-insurance pools, intergovernmental contracts between municipal corp., including schools; aggregate excess insurance minimum $5M	X Idemnification Reserve Fund for higher educ. inst. incl. risk mgmt. sys.	regarding dangerous conditions 120 days		operation of recreation & park gov't. function, but activities within may be proprietary; employees & volunteers immune unless gross negl.; holdings unsettled and inconsistent
Minnesota	$200,000/600,000 applies also to employees and officers, no punitive damages, insurance may exceed limit & include punitive damages	X self-insurance and pooling	X		180 days wrongful death 1 year	1986 amend. provided limited immunity for parks & recreation; limits joint & several liability of state or municipality
Mississippi	$500,000 per occurence may purchase insurance in excess of limit no punitive	X creation of Tort Claims Fund self-insurance pooling	X municipalities defense, satisfaction of judgment against employees		2 years S/L 90 days	
		cities — errors & omissions; schools — liability coverage for employees	school professional liability			also park commissions, waterways
Missouri	$100,000/800,000 no punitive or exemplary damages	X joint self-insurance entity, political subdivisions	X			legal expense fund created public entities risk mgmt. fund act
						state legal expense fund for officials and employees
Montana	$300,000/$1M no punitive damages (not liable for non-economic damages)	X comprehensive state insurance plan; political subd. self insur., jointly, deductible plan	X	X	repealed 120 days (1977)	

State	Maximum Award[5]	Insurance Authorization[6]	Indemnification[6]	Claims Settlement[7]	Notice[8]	Comments
Nebraska				X	notice 1 year 2 years S/L	this act really procedures of State Claims Board and Risk Management Program
Nevada	$50,000 no punitive or exemplary	X local gov't. self-insurance, cooperative agreements	X	X	2 years S/L	"Essential Insurance" act; risk management division
New Hampshire	$100,000	X			60 days 4 years S/L	
	$250,000/$2M	X self-insurance	X	X	180 days 6 years S/L	
New Jersey	no punitive or exemplary damages	X joint co. school municipality risk mgmt. services	X	may establish fund to pay claims	varied but maximum 2 years S/L	
New Mexico	$300,000/500,000 no punitive or exemplary	X political subd. self-insurance; insurance pooling; also public liability fund	X	X including punitive damages	90 days 2 years S/L	public school insurance authority created 1986; state risk management division employees also immune as entity
New York	no punitive	X for officers & employees	X	State Court of Claims	90 days (public officers) 1 year (school) & court may extend	liability and casualty reserve fund, schools & municipalities
North Carolina	$100,000 state	X also group plan for professional liability	Board of Educ. carry insurance 1979 counties	Tort Claims Act provides for state & its agencies & institutions	expressly prohibits local units establishing notice limits	
North Dakota	$250,000/500,000	X self-insurance	X		3 years S/L	specifically states sovereign immunity of state not waived or abrogated, but agencies et al. authorized to purchase; employee not liable

State	Maximum Award[5]	Insurance Authorization[6]	Indemnification[6]	Claims Settlement[7]	Notice[8]	Comments
Ohio	compensatory damages only, no punitive damages; $250,000 wrongful death	X X self-insurance	X X defense	X X	2 years S/L	schools may carry insurance on employees recreation & parks proprietary function; employee immune unless outside scope of employment or malicious, wanton or reckless act
Oklahoma	no punitive or exemplary; $25,000 property loss; $100,000/$1M; state or political subd. liable only for percentage of total in ratio of percentage of total negligent	X self-insurance	X	X cannot initiate suit unless claim denied; up to $10,000 without district court approval	90 days 1 year S/L; claim reduced 10% if after 90 days	employees also have immunity but state or pol. subdiv. may recover for employee if conduct giving rise to claim outside scope of employment or failure to cooperate in defense
Oregon	$100,000/300,000; no punitive damages	X self-insurance; intergovernmental agreements	X	X	180 days	state risk management and insurance program
Pennsylvania	$250,000/$1M $500,000	X X	X			both laws held constitutional
Rhode Island	$100,000 except proprietary functions; or where state has agreed to indemnify fed. gov't. no limit; legislature may authorize more for cities & towns	X joint agreements, self-insurance, cooperative risk mangement programs	X separate act, schools & univ. idem. for supv., adm., teachers; State reserves right to determine whether to indemnify but if it does limited to $50,000	state aribitration of claims		cities & towns cooperative risk management programs authorized
South Carolina	$250,000/500,000 no punitive damages	X self-insurance, intergovernmental agreements		X	1 year to file claim 2 years S/L or 3 years if claim filed	employee immune if within scope of employment

193

State	Maximum Award[5]	Insurance Authorization[6]	Indemnification[6]	Claims Settlement[7]	Notice[8]	Comments
South Dakota	$10,000, over authorized by legislature	X risk sharing	X		60 days with 1 year max. disability (municipality claim)	state employees immune disc. & minst. acts to extent of insurance
Tennessee	$130,000/350,000 minimum insurance coverage	X (other statute authorizes state) self-insurance; pooling agreements	X if qualify city & co. board member & employee have immunity; principals and teachers	state claims (other statute authorizes)	120 days	
Texas	state, municipalities — $250,000/500,000; other local gov't. — $100,000/300,000; no punitive or exemplary damages	X including employees & officers; self-insurance; co. gov't. risk mgmt. pool	X unless gross negligence or willful act	X	6 months	gov'tal. functions include parks, zoos, museums, convention centers, comm. & sr. citizen centers, pools, beaches & marinas, recreational facilities, fireworks displays; amusements are proprietary
Utah	insurance policy not less than $250,000/500,000	X	X	X	1 year	Risk Mgr. and Risk Mgmt. Fund, State (including schools)
Vermont	$75,000/300,000 $300,000/500,000 (school shall insure) judgment restricted to insurance agreement	X(AGO)		X		
Virginia	$25,000 or max. insurance coverage; no punitive damages	X	defense costs	X	1 year 18 months S/L after filing claim	state office of risk mgmt. established (in another statute)
		X for employees & officials, too; self-insurance, pools			6 months	schools deleted by 1980 amend.; but by separate statute, insurance or self-insurance authorized for school and employees; local gov't. officials immune for discretionary acts

194

State	Maximum Award[5]	Insurance Authorization[6]	Indemnification[6]	Claims Settlement[7]	Notice[8]	Comments
Washington		X insure officers & employees authorized		X	120 days	for municipalities & state, risk mgt. services authorized and joint self-insurance pool; schools insurance reserve fund
West Virginia	$500,000 non-economic losses; no punitive damages	X self-insurance	X also defense		2 years S/L	joint & several liability against defendants 25% or more attributable negligence; employee immune from liability, but political subd. can recover from employee if act outside scope of employment
Wisconsin	$250,000 and 50,000 gov't. bodies; no punitive damages	X state & mun. authorized risk mgt. services & liability, entity & officers, employees; municipality liability reserve fund	X	X	120 days	
Wyoming	$250,000/500,000 or amt. of insurance coverage; no punitive or exemplary damages $50,000/500,000 schools	X self-ins. & joint powers agreement authorized, pool fund or purchase insurance	X schools	X Uniform Arbitration Act	2 years	

[5]Maximum award may be either specified by the statutes or indicated in terms of insurance coverage allowable. Only when actual dollar amounts were indicated was this column completed. The figures refer to maximum amount per claimant/maximum per incident. Some jurisdictions have other provisions relating to amount of award.

[6]Insurance authorization refers to general authorization to purchase insurance, while indemnification usually refers to either authorization to purchase insurance covering employees or specification that employees shall be indemnified.

[7]May be provisions for either claims court or procedures for claims settlement out of court.

[8]This is notice of claim, and frequently it is accompanied by statute of limitations designated, not often designated in chart; when it is S/L, is used.

The presentation is in four aspects: (1) §4.22 the approaches to immunity and liability, based on Table 4.1 column headings "Approach" and "Exceptions"; (2) §4.23 the jurisdictional scope; (3) §4.24 insurance and risk management, utilizing the table headings "Maximum Award," "Insurance Authorization," and "Indemnification"; and (4) §4.25 procedural elements of claims, as indicated in columns "Claims Settlement" and "Notice."

The summarization presented in the next four sections should be taken as an indication of the trend and status overall of the immunities and liabilities of governmental agencies in the latter-1980s. Specific citations for statutes and cases by state are presented in the Appendix. **The reader is cautioned that the summarization and the individual state comments are made without benefit of knowledge of local practices and interpretations and is based solely upon material of supreme court cases, law review articles, and annotated statutes.** Further, the law always being an active, changing body, subsequent court decisions or statutory enactments may materially change the analysis of individual states given here. **Consult your local attorney to update your own state.** The commentary, however, provides an overview of the states as a whole.

§ 4.22 Statutory approaches to immunity and liability

Basically, two approaches are used by the legislatures in constructing tort claims statutes, referred to as the "open-ended" approach and the "closed-ended" approach. Under the "open-ended" approach the legislature provides for liability and cites exceptions to that liability, while under the "closed-ended" approach immunity is the rule and exceptions for which the governmental agencies would be liable are enumerated.

In view of principles of statutory construction, this difference in approach can be significant. Since statutes in derogation of sovereignty traditionally are construed narrowly, courts will view "closed-ended" acts conservatively, in favor of immunity. Under the "open-ended" approach courts may rule that, given the absence of general immunity, a narrow statutory construction is inapplicable.... To a legislature seeking to protect its municipalities, a "closed-ended" approach offers obvious advantages. On the other hand, an "open-ended" scheme more closely follows the modern equitable trend requiring governments to redress their torts.[118]

The two approaches are further discussed in the *Maryland Law Review*:

...the closed-end approach,...expressly retains immunity except for enumerated areas in which it is waived. Such a statute restricts the opportunity for judicial policy making, and its certainty would enable private citizens and the government to plan their activities more effectively. A closed-end statute

[118] Leonard, Steven L. Municipal Tort Liability: A Legislative Solution Balancing the Needs of Cities and Plaintiffs. 16 *Urban Law Annual* 305 at p. 324 (1979).

constitutes a legislative declaration that immunity is the general rule and liability is the exception. Such a statute reflects a determination by the legislature that broad exposure to liability is financially impracticable or otherwise undesirable. This system of liability would require the legislature to review each element of the state's exposure to liability....

...The selection of an open-end statute by the legislature would achieve the objective of circumscribed liability, but would avoid the meticulous consideration that a closed-end scheme demands; it is easier for a legislature to specify those areas in which sovereign immunity is to be retained than to sift through the numerous areas in which immunity might be waived. Moreover, because this approach avoids the detailed enumeration of a closed-end statute, the courts possess more flexibility for dealing with new and unusual situations. ...the exceptions to the waiver of immunity under the open-end approach outline the perimeters within which a court, in the context of a specific factual situation, can balance the policies in favor of governmental immunity against the social value of distributing individual losses among the body of taxpayers. Furthermore, the jurisdictions that have adopted open-end liability have not experienced disastrous financial consequences; the open-end scheme therefore appears to present a reasonable financial alternative to complete immunity.[119]

Of the 41 states[120] which have enacted comprehensive tort claims acts or comparable statutes, 21 (identified under the Approach column, Table 4.1 by "liability") took the open-ended or "liability is the rule, immunity the exception" approach, while 20 (identified by "immunity") have closed-ended legislation. The distribution according to date of enactment showed little difference between the two approaches, with 7, 5, and 8 states enacting closed-end statutes before 1970, 1970-75, and after 1975, respectively, and 8, 4, and 9 states, respectively, with open-ended statutes.

§ 4.221   "Closed-ended" approach

There are four forms of closed-ended statutes. The legislature may enact a statute which provides for "blanket coverage immunity" with no exceptions. Alabama and Arkansas are such states. Or, the legislature may state the policy as immunity and enumerate those functions for which the governmental agency is immune. Delaware, Illinois, Indiana, and Utah are illustrations of this form. The third form states a blanket immunity policy and then sets forth the exceptions for which there is liability. New Hampshire, New Mexico, Pennsylvania, and Wyoming take this form of closed-ended approach. Other states (e.g., California, Colorado, Maine, Michigan, New Jersey, Tennessee) use a combination, giving the general policy as immunity with specification

[119] The State as a Party Defendant: Abrogation of Sovereign Immunity in Tort in Maryland. 36 *Maryland Law Review* 653 at pp. 671-673 (1977).

[120] The nine states not included are Alaska, Connecticut, Florida, Georgia, Kentucky, Louisiana, Missouri, New York, South Dakota, and the District of Columbia.

of functions and then also enumerating some exceptions for which there is liability.

Specification of functions for which there is immunity may be as many as 15, such as Indiana's statute. The most commonly specified function is that of discretionary acts. Three states (Michigan, Ohio, Utah) indicate that governmental functions are immune from tort claims by the injured.

Almost all states that enumerate exceptions list dangerous conditions as an area for which a municipality may be liable, notwithstanding the general policy of immunity. This is in accord with the definition of duty as an element in negligence — a duty is owed to protect an individual against unreasonable hazards; or, to say it the other way, a duty is owed to provide a safe environment. (See §2.1.) For further description of what is considered a dangerous environmental condition, see Chapter 20.

§ 4.222   "Open-ended" approach

Most of the statutes provide for liability "as a private person." In contrast to the "closed-ended" approach statutes, except for this phrase, there is usually no listing of functions for which the governmental agency is liable. It is a broad authorization of liability. The commentary quoted in the introductory paragraphs of §4.22 discusses this characteristic.

Nearly all of the "open-ended" states enumerate exceptions to liability, and these may be statutes other than the tort claims act. **All** states listing exceptions cite discretionary acts. "Three basic rationales are commonly asserted in support of discretionary immunity: (1) fairness to the decision maker; (2) encouragement of enthusiastic, aggressive public service; and (3) separation of powers."[121] "...the immunities scope should be no greater than is required to give legislative and executive policy makers sufficient breathing space in which to perform their vital policymaking functions."[122] A number of the states, in their enumerations of exceptions, list in addition to discretionary acts, legislative and judicial functions. Because of the importance of discretionary acts as an exception to liability, there is a separate section on discretionary acts. (See §4.13.)

§ 4.223   Reference to athletics, recreation and parks

For the most part, physical education and athletics in the schools and recreation and parks in the municipalities and states are not specifically set out in the enumerations for either liability or immunity exceptions. However, three states using the "open-ended" approach and six states adhering to the "closed-ended" approach did make reference thereto. The only reference to physical education or athletics was in Oklahoma, which provided that interscholastic athletics was an exception to the broad policy of liability.

The exceptions related to parks are influenced by public policy considerations in addition to involving no duty. This is particularly true in many states, both those following the "open-ended" and the "closed-ended" approaches, with the immunizing

[121] Leonard, Steven L. Municipal Tort Liability: A Legislative Solution Balancing the Needs of Cities and Plaintiffs. 16 *Urban Law Annual* 305 at p. 318 (1979).

[122] Peterson, Clifford J. Governmental Immunity: Has a Change Finally Come? 2 *Western State University Law Review* 209 at p. 218 (1975).

of claims arising from the natural condition of any unimproved public property.

Nine states specifically listed parks, playgrounds, open area recreation and/or outdoor recreation — seven immune from liability and two liable. Kansas stated that a governmental entity shall not be liable for damages resulting from the use of any public property intended or permitted to be used as a park, playground or open area for recreational purposes, unless the governmental entity or an employee thereof is guilty of gross and wanton negligence proximately causing such injury. Minnesota included outdoor recreation systems in the enumeration of immune functions by the state.

Of the "closed-ended" approach states, Illinois' provision is quite similar to that of Kansas when it provided that neither a local public entity nor a public employee is liable for an injury where the liability is based on the existence of a condition of any public property intended or permitted to be used as a park, playground or open area for recreational purposes unless such local entity or public employee is guilty of willful and wanton negligence proximately causing such injury. Illinois also provides for immunity related to conditions of access roads to fishing, hunting, or primitive camping, recreational or scenic areas and also hiking, riding, fishing, and hunting trails. Special provision was made for immunity for an injury caused by a failure to supervise an activity on or the use of any public property, and specifically mentioned swimming — where a local entity or public employee designates a part of public property to be used for purposes of swimming and establishes and designates by notice posted upon the premises the hours for such use, the entity or public employee is liable only for an injury proximately caused by its failure to provide supervision during the said hours posted.

Swimming pools also are specifically mentioned by Colorado, but with provision for liability — the operation and maintenance of any swimming facility by such public entity or a dangerous condition existing therein. Liability for specified dangerous conditions of any public building and any public facility, except roads and highways located in parks or recreation areas, is also a part of the Colorado Governmental Immunity Act. Liability as an exception to the general policy of immunity also was designated for injuries caused by negligence in the operation or maintenance of any building or public park in New Mexico. Wyoming, another "closed-ended" approach state, stated that there was liability for operation or maintenance of any building, recreation area, or public park.

New Jersey, a general immunity state, sets forth in a separate section of its Tort Claims Act that a public entity is not liable for failure to provide supervision of public recreation facilities; provided, however, that nothing shall exonerate a public entity from liability for failure to protect against a dangerous condition. (Here's that dangerous condition exception to immunity.) Maine cited as an example of a function for which there was immunity the construction, ownership, maintenance or use of land, buildings, structures, facilities, or equipment designed for use primarily by the public in connection with public outdoor recreation.

§ 4.23   Jurisdictional scope

True to the term "comprehensive tort act," 23 states with such acts covered the state, schools, and municipalities. The statutes in an additional 11 states also covered all three jurisdictional types. Eleven states had acts specific to states only; however, of these states, nine also have statutes for schools and municipalities. Five states had only statutes directed toward schools and municipalities. In some states there were a variety of statutes for different jurisdictions. See Table 4.1, column headed "Jurisdictional Scope" for state by state indication of the coverage.

Four subsections are presented because the jurisdictional scope is not evidenced in Table 4.1. Although tort law lies primarily in the domain of the states, and the status of the states deals with state law, no discussion of jurisdictional scope would be complete without brief commentary on the federal government. Then, with the importance of sport and athletics in the colleges and universities, a subsection is directed toward institutions of higher education. The third subsection deals with counties. The last subsection assesses the involvement and impact of the public official and employees in order to give a more accurate indication of the focus of the statutes concerned with liability and immunity of the state, schools, and municipalities.

§ 4.231   Federal government

The Federal Tort Claims Act (28 U.S.C. §§2671-2680 (1976)) was enacted in 1946. "The theory which espoused the enactment of the Federal Tort Claims Act was that governmental efforts should achieve a reasonable level of efficiency and responsibility, and that failure to meet this standard should result in liability exposure similar to that which exists in the private sector."[123] There are a series of exceptions, but most do not relate to the conduct of recreation and parks, physical education and athletics, or camping and adventure activities, although there are federal cases in these areas. A number of the states followed somewhat the Federal Tort Claims Act in designing their own statutes, and the experience with the Act (case opinions) has been used sometimes as basis of interpretation for state cases. The immunity of federal officials when they act in performance of their discretionary functions within their scope of responsibility is one of the key provisions, and one which nearly all states have.[124]

A second facet is the recognition that when a tort is performed or a law violated, even though on federal property, state law may apply in certain circumstances. This is because the federal law says that there shall be liability as if the federal government were an individual. Most common and consistent application is with the recreational user laws (see §12.1).

The impact of civil rights legislation and regulatory law is a third facet. It has been discussed briefly in §1.3. Also to be considered are other statutes which may take precedence over the Federal Tort Claims Act. Such was the situation in *U.S. v. James,* 740 F. 2d 365 (1984) rev'd. 760 F. 2d 590 (1985) rev'd 478 U.S. 597, 92 L. Ed. 2d 483, 106 S. Ct. 3116 (1986). It was held that §702c of the Flood Control Act of 1928 barred recovery where the federal government would otherwise be liable under the FTCA for

---

[123] Willig, Sidney. The Breadth of the Tort Perspective: Judicial Review for Tortious Conduct of Governmental Agencies and Agents. 44 *Missouri Law Review* 621 at pp. 636-637 (1980); Euler, J. L. and John J. Farley, III. Federal Tort Liability: Reform in the Wind. *Federal Bar News & Journal,* vol. 31, no. 2 January, 1984. Reprinted in *Trends,* vol. 21, no. 3, 1984, pp. 42-46. Discusses reform as related to federal employee (individual) as defendant.

[124] Dalehite v. United States, 346 U.S. 15 (1953).

personal injury caused by the government's negligent failure to warn of the dangers from the release of flood waters from federal flood-control projects. Two separate accidents raised the issue of precedence. In one accident, two water-skiers on the reservoir were injured when they were swept through the floodgates, and in the other accident, two fishermen in a boat were drawn through the drainage gates and one was drowned.

§ 4.232 Colleges and universities

Colleges and universities come under the same laws of liability as other agencies. A distinction, however, must be made between private and governmental institutions. Whereas some courts have held colleges sponsored by private organizations are not liable as a charitable institution, the doctrine of charitable immunity has been abrogated in most jurisdictions (see §4.3) and charitable institutions, including colleges, are being held liable for their negligence.[125] It has been alleged that judgments could not be paid out of trust funds; however, liability insurance can protect such funds and negates that allegation.

As for public institutions of higher education, those which are state supported come under the immunity of the state as recognized in that specific state[126] (see Table 4.1). Almost all of the statutes when indicating the scope of coverage for the state will indicate "...institutions...", meaning educational institutions, hospitals, et al. About two-fifths of the states have specific reference in their statutes to colleges and universities. The majority of these authorize liability insurance[127] or indemnification of the board members, officials, or employees.[128] Ohio authorizes insurance specifically for student teachers and supervisors. Institutions may provide coverage through regular insurance or self-insurance. Michigan sets up an Indemnification Reserve Fund and directs that there be a risk management system. Alabama also retains immunity, but provides for a Board of Adjustment to settle claims. Tennessee also has a Board of Claims. Georgia states that the doctrine of governmental immunity is applicable to the Board of Regents. New Mexico provides that members of the Board of Regents are not personally liable.

Even where there may be immunity in general for a state institution, especially an educational institution, this immunity is greatly jeopardized by commercial enterprises, such as "big-time football," which is more than a million dollar business![129] While it is true that some injured individuals have failed to recover in holdings that athletic boards were under the control of the school governing body, to rely on such immunity potential is hazardous as the decade of the '80s ends. With the extensive

125 Moore v. Moyle, 405 Ill. 555, 92 N.E. 2d 81 (1950).

126 Brittan v. New York State, 200 Misc. 743, 103 N.Y.S. 2d 485 (1951); Davis v. Provo City Corp., 1 Utah 2d 244, 265 P. 2d 415 (1953); Gardner v. State (two cases), 281 N.Y. 212, 22 N.E. 2d 344 (1939); Hanson v. Reedley Joint Union High Sch. Dist., 43 Cal. App. 2d 643, 111 P. 2d 415 (1941); Reynolds v. New York State, 207 Misc. 963, 141 N.Y.S. 2d 615 (1955); Rook v. State (two cases), 254 A.D. 67, 4 N.Y.S. 2d 116 (1938).

127 For example, Alaska, California, Florida, Maryland, Nevada, North Carolina, Oklahoma, Wisconsin.

128 For example, Michigan, New York, Washington.

129 George v. University of Minn. Athletic Assn., 107 Minn. 424, 120 N.W. 750 (1909); Scott v. University of Mich. Athletic Assn., 152 Mich. 684, 116 N.W. 624 (1908).

athletic scholarship programs, there is also consideration that there may be liability of a college or university on the basis of contract (see §1.1).

Because the principles of law are the same when it comes to trial for negligence, the cases involving colleges and universities have been integrated into other substantive sections (Parts B and C). See Part D for risk management. Coaches, physical education instructors, et al. should give special attention to their own personal liability (see §§3.3 and 3.4).

§ 4.233   Counties

Historically, counties have been a political subdivision of the state, and therefore, as "an arm of the state" came under whatever immunity or liability the state had, usually immunity under the doctrine of sovereign immunity.[130] However, as counties have assumed more services, they have become more like municipalities, and, thus, frequently take the liability or immunity of municipalities in the state.[131] In *James v. Prince George's County*,[132] a 1980 case, it was held in Maryland that a county is liable to the same extent as a private person, except that it is immune for discretionary acts. In recognition of this, many of the tort claims statutes include counties in enumeration of "municipalities," and in case interpretation of the term in the last decade, the courts usually have done so, too. Thirty states in their comprehensive tort claims statutes or similar statutes incorporate counties by specific reference or a broader term defined to include counties. An additional ten states have liability insurance authorization specifically for counties.

As with colleges and universities, cases have been integrated into the other substantive parts of this volume.

§ 4.234   Board members, officials, and employees

More than one-half of the states with comprehensive tort claims acts or comparable statutes have included in the scope of the act "officers, employees, and servants," and also usually board members. Most of the statutes provide that such officers and employees are covered whether they are elected or appointed, full or part-time, or compensated or volunteer.

Individual personal immunity for employees and officers in some form is provided by a number of states.[133] A number of statutes amended in the late '80s added the immunity of employees when acting within their scope of employment and not willfully and wantonly. Pennsylvania states that the employee is liable only to the extent of the employer, while California indicates that the governmental entity can be held

[130] Still held this view in the late '70s — see Coleman v. McNary, 549 S.W. 2d 568 (Mo. App., 1977); McPhee v. Dade County, 362 So. 2d 74 (Fla. App. 1978).

[131] Buck v. McLean, 115 So. 2d 764 (Fla. 1959); Keenan v. Midland County, 377 Mich. 57, 138 N.W. 2d 759 (1966); Litzmann v. Humbolt County, 127 Cal. App. 2d 86, 273 P. 2d 82 (1954); Petersen v. Bannock

County, 61 Idaho 419, 102 P. 2d 647 (1940); Ward v. County Park Board, 143 W. Va. 931, 105 S.E. 2d 881 (1958); Wilcox v. Erie County, 252 A.D. 20, 297 N.Y. 287 (1937).

[132] James v. Prince George's Co., 288 Md. 315, 418 A. 2d 1173 (1980).

[133] For example, Arizona, Florida, Maryland, New Jersey.

vicariously liable if the employee is liable. A number of states[134] specifically state that to defend and indemnify an employee does not make the governmental entity further liable, nor is it a waiver of immunity or defenses.

Montana and North Dakota provide that if a suit is brought against an employee, the governmental entity may be joined as a party. Similarly, Nevada states that a suit cannot be brought against an employee unless the governmental entity is named as a party. On the other side, Utah provides that an employee may be joined but that no employee is personally liable unless one acted with gross negligence, fraud, or malice. New Mexico indicates that there is no right of contribution against the employee unless there was fraud or malicious acts. Recovery against the employee is stipulated in the Nebraska statute.

It should be noted that the foregoing discussion is on the basis of statutory provision of these aspects. This is not to say that other states do not hold similarly. **Consult your local attorney for the practices in your state in the jurisdiction of your interest, whether it be state, school, county, or municipality.** For further discussion of the liability and immunity of board members, officials, employees, volunteers, et al., see Chapter 3.

§ 4.24   Insurance and risk management

Insurance and maximum dollars awarded are two methods that the legislatures have selected to cope with negligence liability. There are four different approaches: (1) the authorization of insurance so that the individual injured may recover, yet the governmental entity retain theoretically some essence of governmental or sovereign immunity; (2) the authorization of insurance covering public officials and employees, or specifying that employees may be/should be indemnified, since suits were being filed against them, to keep and recruit good public employees without their constant fear of having to pay a large judgment for acts done in the line of duty; (3) the placing of maximums on the amount of damages that may be recovered by the injured, thus protecting the public financial structure; and (4) the provision and requirement of risk management, including self-insurance and other forms of financial reserves for claims. Each of these four is discussed in subsequent subsections. This section discusses only the provisions in the state statutes dealing with governmental entities and their liabilities and immunities. For more detailed information on insurance and risk management, see Part D. **See your local attorney for insurance provisions for your agency in your state.**

§ 4.241   Insurance authorization

There was extensive legislative activity in the 1960s related to authorization of insurance for governmental agencies to cover injuries from negligent acts of employees (see chapter introduction on eras). Authorization for insurance was deemed necessary in states adhering to the doctrine of governmental immunity or at least to the immunity

[134] For example, Maine, Michigan.

for governmental functions because to carry insurance for acts for which the governmental entity was deemed not liable would be illegal use of public funds. With the concerns indicated in the foregoing paragraph, the statutes of the 1960s have been extended in jurisdictional scope, functions covered, and amount of coverage. Nearly all states have specific insurance statutes or provision in the comprehensive tort claims acts for insurance. (See column heading "Insurance Authorization" on Table 4.1-A.) The few which do not seem to authorize insurance either infer such authorization or appear to feel that specific authorization is not necessary. In the statutes there was no evidence of prohibiting the carrying of insurance, as had previously been indicated by Attorney Generals' Opinions or case law.

Whether a state follows the "open-ended" or "closed-ended" approach to the doctrine of governmental/sovereign immunity (see §4.22), it does not seem to make much difference for under both approaches the recovery prospects for the injury are nearly the same, subject to the maximum amounts specified in that particular state. There are, however, several different theoretical bases or rationales as related to immunity and insurance. A number of states specifically state that the defense of immunity is waived by carrying of insurance,[135] and most of these indicate that the liability is only to the extent of the insurance coverage. Some states, such as North Carolina and Wyoming, provide that the waiver to the amount of coverage is for governmental functions only. Wyoming also states that if insurance coverage exceeds the maximum amount authorized, there is liability to that amount. That the carrying of insurance does not change the basic immunity status of the governmental entity is inferred in a number of states by statute or case law. Michigan specifies such by statute. The importance of the theoretical argument is that if a judgment should exceed the amount of insurance, if there has not been waiver of governmental immunity, the injured would receive only the amount of insurance coverage, while if the state does not adhere to immunity or the carrying of insurance abrogates such immunity, then the injured may receive the full amount of the judgment. The excess between insurance coverage and the award would have to be paid by the governmental entity.

While insurance is authorized, few states require or mandate such insurance. The theoretical question then arises that if the governmental entity does not carry insurance does that mean there is no recovery at all for the injury? With the provision in many states that recovery is to the extent of insurance, "to permit a political subdivision to decide whether to insure, and therefore, whether to waive its sovereign immunity, would be like trusting the cat to guard the bird cage."[136] However, there is a "moral burden upon a political subdivision by the knowledge that they could purchase insurance and compensate persons injured as a result of their negligence."[137] New Mexico is one of few states which state that insurance must be carried for every risk for which immunity is waived.

[135] For example, Colorado, Minnesota, Mississippi, Missouri, New Hampshire, South Dakota, Tennessee, Vermont, West Virginia.
[136] Anderson, Michael Steven. Notes: Sovereign Immunity in Missouri: Judicial Abrogation and Legis-lative Reenactment. 1979 *Washington University Law Quarterly* 865 at p. 890 (1979).
[137] Bay, Jeffrey S. Sovereign Immunity: Application of Missouri's 1978 Sovereign Immunity Legislation to School Districts. 45 *Missouri Law Review* 771 at p. 784 (1984).

§ 4.242   Insurance coverage of employees[138]

Because of the societal tendency to sue not only the corporate entity, but also the individual board member, official, or employee, one of the changes from the '60s is to authorize insurance coverage for those persons who work in behalf of the governmental agency. Of the states indicating insurance authorization (see Table 4.1-A), almost all specifically provide for officer and employee insurance of some type; also, most all of the states provide for indemnification of employees or officials in one or more jurisdications in the state. (See column heading "Indemnification," Table 4.1-A.) However, the application of the statutes for protection of the employee or official in nearly all states so providing protection rests upon the act of the official or employee. There is no protection when the official or employee acts without the scope of duty or responsibility, willfully and wantonly, recklessly or ruthlessly, or with malice or fraud. Some states, such as Nevada and Rhode Island, further state in their statutes that indemnification is contingent upon the employee cooperating in the defense of a suit. The new enactments or amendments in the late '80s reflect particular concern for protecting employees financially against law suits (defense) and judgments when they act within the scope of their employment.

§ 4.243   Maximum dollar amounts authorized for damages

Damages are often the forgotten chapter in torts.... Recently we have become a very litigious society with a great emphasis on rights rather than responsibilities. When this litigiousness is combined with the knowledge that the defendant is insured, the result has been enormous jury awards with little control by the courts....

Damage awards...combined with reactions from the insurance companies, have resulted in a few dynamic interchanges between courts and legislatures. The interaction has been confined to attempts to limit excessive awards,...[139]

Many of the states have provided specifically for such award limits through statutes. (See "Maximum Awards" column on Table 4.1-A.) However, there is very little consistency in terms of maximum amount authorized among the states; each has its own approach. Bodily injury amounts only are reported with designation $ per person/$ aggregate per incidence.

In the mid-'80s, the lowest authorized is $10,000 in South Dakota; however, the statute does provide that amounts over that may be authorized by the legislature. In Nevada, $50,000 is the specified maximum, and $75,000/$300,000 by Vermont (state). Most of the states, however, provide for maximum awards of $100,000, $250,000-300,000, and some $500,000 per person single occurrence with the aggregate per incident ranging from $300,000 to $800,000, and a few states[140] having

[138] Hassman, Phillip E. Validity and Construction of Statute Authorizing or Requiring Governmental Unit to Procure Liability Insurance Covering Public Officers or Employees for Liability Arising Out of Performance of Public Duties. 71 A.L.R. 3d 6-84.

[139] Bischoff, Ralph F. The Dynamics of Tort Law: Court of Legislature? 4 *Vermont Law Review* 35 at pp. 70-71 (1979).

[140] E.g., Massachusetts, Montana, Oklahoma, Virginia.

$1M. The highest maximum states are New Hampshire at $2M and Indiana at $5M per occurrence (see Table 4.1-A, column "maximum awards"). Most of this legislation putting on maximum awards came in the 1980 or 1981 legislative enactments. One state increased its maximum amount in each year 1979, 1980, and 1981, while several other states also have increased amounts over previous maximums specified — this is in recognition of the increasing costs and judgments in respect to an individual's right to appropriate level of compensation. The amount of awards authorized has been tested for constitutionality in several states and has been held to be constitutional,[141] primarily on the basis that to recover against a governmental entity is a "privilege" in contrast to a "right." In a 1984 case,[142] the Oklahoma court held that, while the cause of action arose from the same negligence causing injury, the parents' and the child's right of action are separate claims and each entitled to the $50,000 statutory maximum. The maximum stated in the statute, in a 1985 Alabama case,[143] was held to be the maximum recoverable against the public entity and not the amount of the judgment. If there are other sources, such as individual employees, insurance, and additional sponsors, who are not protected under the statute, then an additional amount may be recovered by the injured beyond the statutory maximum. (For further discussion of this point, see §2.4.)

There are a number of other stipulations in the statutes. Georgia gives the amount to the discretion of the board. Idaho permits more insurance to be carried than the limits and then there is liability to the extent of coverage; however, if the judgment is greater than insurance coverage, the award is to be reduced to the amount of coverage. Arkansas, Colorado, and Hawaii also indicate that any awards should be reduced to the amount of insurance, but that the amount of settlement is negotiated. (See next section §4.251 for claims settlement.)

While there normally are not punitive or exemplary damages awarded in negligence cases, 25 states specify in their tort claims act that such damages shall not be paid. Massachusetts and Utah permit punitive damages, but limit them to $100,000 and $10,000, respectively (see §2.4).

In addition to the bodily injury limits described in this section, a number of states also provide limits on property damage.

§ 4.244 Self-insurance and risk management

As a number of claims increased in both quantity and amount of awards, insurance premiums rose extensively and the legislatures sought alternatives. More than one-half of the states[144] by 1981 had provided by specific reference in the statutues for self-insurance, pooling, joint powers agreement, et al. Further, because of the overall concern for the risks to which governmental entities were subjected, at the turn of the

[141] e.g., New Hampshire, Nevada.

[142] Indp. School Dist. v. Crawford, 688 P. 2d 1281 (Okla. 1984).

[143] Nowlin v. Druid City Hospital Board, 475 So. 2d 469 (Ala. 1985).

[144] Arizona, California, Colorado, Florida, Georgia, Illinois, Indiana, Louisiana, Maryland, Massachusetts, Missouri, Montana, New Jersey, New Mexico, New York, North Dakota, Ohio, Oklahoma, Oregon, South Dakota, Tennessee, Utah, Virginia, Washington, Wyoming and perhaps others.

'80s planning for risk management became recognized as essential. Seventeen states[145] by 1981 made provision for such in the statutes, some states making mandatory a risk management system, others authorizing risk management consultants, et al. Five years later nearly all states had spoken legislatively authorizing or mandating self-insurance, joint powers agreements, risk management, et al. The Illinois court held that a city did not waive its immunity from tort liability with respect to its summer recreational program through its membership in an inter-governmental risk management agency in *Ramos by Ramos v. City of Countryside*, 137 Ill. App. 3d 1028, 92 Ill. Dec. 607 485 N.E. 2d 418 (1985). Further discussion of both self-insurance (and other forms of financial responsibility) and risk management is in Part D.

§ 4.25 Procedural elements of claims

There are primarily two procedural approaches to tort claims acts and other statutes to the processing of claims — one is concerned with making available a procedure for settlement without going to court, which saves both court costs and expedites the time of settlement; and the other relates to limiting the time of the plaintiff in giving notice to the governmental agency that one intends to file suit.

§ 4.251 Claims settlement

About three-fourths of the states (see column "Claims Settlement" in Table 4.1-A) provide one form or another for claims settlement. This may be a Claims Board or just authorization for the governmental entity to settle such claims. The states providing for such settlement are equally divided between those states which adhere to the "closed-ended" approach (immunity) and those which practice the "open-ended" approach (liability) (see §4.22), thus giving further credence to the fact that individuals may recover compensation for injuries although the state may be basically one which wishes to retain the doctrine of governmental immunity. In establishing such claims procedure, those states basically practicing immunity do so on the basis of such settlement being a "privilege" in contrast to a "right."

Some states only authorize the settlement of claims, while other states specify the limits of such settlement. These limits range from $500 for Maine and Vermont to $25,000 in Kansas, Nevada, and Wisconsin. By the statutes of Hawaii and Louisiana, $2,000 is provided, while Massachusetts stipulates $2,500. Oregon, Iowa, and New Mexico have $5,000 as the upper limit of claims settlements, and New Mexico, Oklahoma and New Hampshire make it $10,000. The person or board authorized to settle such claims varies state to state. Also, some states provide that with further approval by certain officials or boards, higher amounts may be settled out of court.

There are additional requisites regarding claims settlement, such as if the agency does not dispose of the claim filed within 90 days (e.g., Idaho), 120 days (e.g., Maine) or six months (e.g., Iowa), the injured party filing may consider the claim denied and file in court.

[145] Arizona, Florida, Iowa, Illinois, Idaho, Kansas, Louisiana, Michigan, Montana, Nebraska, New Mexico, Pennsylvania, Utah, Virginia, Washington, West Virginia, Wisconsin, and perhaps others.

§ 4.252   Notice of claim filing

Notice of claim should be distinguished from statutes of limitation or limitation of action statutes. All states have the latter, but the notice of claim statutes were initiated to force the injured person to indicate to the governmental entity whether or not one intends to sue within a "reasonable" time, rather than waiting sometimes until the very last days before the statute of limitations has run. The tort claims acts do provide for some interaction between notice of claim and running of the statutes of limitation.

Slightly more than one-half of the states have included notice of claim in their statutes as related to liability of governmental entities. (See column "Notice" in Table 4.1-A.) The most common length of time in which notice must be filed is 180 days or six months, with nine states having such provision. Four states provide 120 days, and three states each make the limit 90 days and one year. New Hampshire and South Dakota have the shortest time with 60 days (N.H. claims against state 180 days) and Wyoming and Nevada the longest with two years.

Montana repealed its provision of 120 days in 1977; and, there has been some question in certain states regarding the constitutionality of such statutes. West Virginia by case law has held notice of claim unconstitutional. North Carolina expressly prohibits local units from establishing notice limits.

§ 4.26   Tort reform

The cornerstone of the tort claims statutes is insurance. However, in 1985 and 1986 the "insurance crisis" occurred, at which time liability insurance for both public and private agencies either became unavailable for recreation and sport pursuits or the premiums were so high that it became almost impossible to finance desired insurance. To have this "security blanket" or cornerstone knocked out caused a re-thinking of both the desirability of the governmental immunity policy and certain tort processes. While there had been some tort reform discussion in the early 1980s, primarily due to the very large awards being handed down, this situation with insurance gave some urgency to tort reform studies. But, reform takes time. To deal with the "emergency crisis," some state legislatures in 1986 passed legislation hastily drafted to give some relief both to municipalities and schools; but, for the most part, the basic tort claim acts, as reported in §§4.21 to 4.25, were not changed in fundamental concept or approach. These special actions, for the most part, are not reflected in the status of states chart. The emergency measures, for the most part, dealt with reduction of costs of insurance or alternatives and with reducing the liability of the sponsoring or administering organization or agency. None of the emergency measures none was concerned with the responsibilities of the participant or the societal causes of the situation.

Most of the legislative tort reform considerations passed or proposed have been of one or more of the following types, with each state having its own approach. Undoubtedly many enactments will be tested in the courts.

1. Lowered the standard of care required to recover against a municipality or school from ordinary negligence to gross negligence or willful, wanton, or malicious conduct on the part of the employee.

2. Endeavored to deal with the insurance industry by instituting premium cost regulations, cancellation of policies restrictions, et al.; permit payments of large awards to be spread out (installments).

3. Reduced the amount of insurance coverage required, where high ($1M or more) insurance coverage was required to obtain a permit, such as for amusement rides.

4. Instituted or extended limited liability for certain recreational activities or volunteers working with public entity and non-profit organization programs, especially sport organization volunteer coaches and officials.

5. Provided alternative financing to commercial insurance companies, such as self-insurance, pooled insurance, joint agreements among municipalities, intergovernmental contracts for risk management systems, et al. (many states already had this authorization).

6. Required risk management services/system to be established, of which alternate financing (#5) was a part.

7. Established "caps" on the awards, *i.e.*, maximum dollars that could be recovered for injury, especially non-economic awards for "pain and suffering;" and, re-enforced no punitive damages for negligence claims.

8. Provided greater protection for the employee by providing for indemnification and/or limited liability if acting within the scope of employment and without willful, wanton, or malicious misconduct; re-enforced immunity for discretionary acts and made it more difficult to recover against officials and board members.

9. Modified joint and several liability, so responsible only for one's portion of fault.

10. Assessed plaintiffs with costs for "frivolous" law suits.

11. Shortened time in which law suits can be filed.

12. Limited the percentage of award that can be paid to plaintiff's lawyers in cases where the total award exceeds a certain designated amount, such as $200,000.

What must be emphasized is that tort reform is not something that is particular to parks and recreation, sport and physical education, or adventure activities and camping. The impact relates to all entities. At the end of the 1980s and as the decade of the '90s begins, the meaning of the various components of tort reform must be assessed.

§ 4.3   Doctrine of charitable immunity[146]

The doctrine of charitable immunity frees eleemosynary institutions of educational, charitable, or religious purpose from any civil liability that may attach as a consequence of the institution's tortious (negligent) acts. This immunity is based primarily on four premises:

1. Public policy. A charity exists for the benefit of the public; thus, it is against public policy to stifle charities. Although a charitable institution may receive

[146] Collin, Robert W. Toward a New Theory of Nonprofit Liability, Administration in Social Work, vol. 11(1), Spring 1987, pp. 15-24, discusses theories of liability and defenses of nonprofit organizations and especially the directors; Fairchild, Janet. Tort Immu-nity of Nongovernmental Charities — Modern Status. 25 A.L.R. 4th 517-561; Korpela, Allan E. Immunity of Private Schools and Institutions of Higher Learning from Liability in Tort. 38 A.L.R. 3d 480-520.

payment for services from some of its beneficiaries, this does not affect the character of the institution as long as money is used for charitable purposes and not for profit. Also, donors should not be discouraged with the fear that gifts might go toward paying tort claims.

2. Trust fund theory. The money held by an eleemosynary institution for the purposes designated by the donor should not be diverted to payment of tort claims, but is held in trust for the purposes for which donated.

3. Implied waiver theory. The recipient of benefits of an eleemosynary institution accepts them as they are given and assumes the risk of negligence. By implication, the recipient agrees to waive the liability and assert no tort claim against the benefactor.

4. The doctrine of respondeat superior. Does not apply (see Chapter 3); the agency is not liable for the torts of its agents and employees because it does not benefit or gain from service rendered. The "Good Samaritan" should not be held to undue responsibility for one's efforts.

The doctrine of charitable immunity arises only in regard to negligent acts.

Just as the doctrine of sovereign/governmental immunity has been abrogated or modified in response to the rights of injured individuals for compensation and the responsibilities of those conducting activities, so has the doctrine of charitable immunity changed, and in a similar pattern. Prior to 1942, only two or three states had rejected the immunity of charities outright; but, with the landmark opinion[147] of Judge Rutledge in the District of Columbia in 1942, which effectively repudiated most arguments in favor of immunity, the states began to hold that charities were liable for their torts to the same extent as any other defendant. By the turn into the decade of the '70s, three-fourths (31) of the states had overturned by court decision or statute the doctrine of charitable immunity. During the decade of the '70s, state courts and legislatures[148] continued to overturn the doctrine or greatly limit its application. Only a few states as of mid-'80s have remnants of charitable immunity.

At the beginning of the 1980s, South Carolina[149] modified the doctrine so as not to include hospitals, but to continue covering other eleemosynary institutions. Several states[150] have specifically provided for waiver of immunity to the extent of insurance coverage. In this, the action is very comparable to that provided in modification of the doctrine of sovereign/governmental immunity. Illinois provides for risk pooling, and Massachusetts[151] placed a limit of $20,000 recovery. North Dakota and Indiana, as do some other states, reference the indemnification of officials and employees. Georgia[152]

---

[147] Georgetown College v. Hughes, 76 U.S. App. D.C. 123, 130 F. 2d 810 (1942).

[148] e.g., statutes in Connecticut, North Carolina, and Nevada; see also cases: Bentley v. Hamden Post 88, 27 Conn. Sup. 56, 229 A. 2d 32 (1967); Darsie v. Duke Univ., 48 N.C. App. 20, 268 S.E. 2d 554 (1980).

[149] See cases: Fitzer v. Greater Greenville S.C. YMCA, 277 S.C. 1, 282 S.E. 2d 230 (1981); Terry v. Boy Scouts of America, 471 F. Supp. 28 (1978), aff'd. without op. 598 F. 2d 616 (1979); see also statutes in North Carolina, Maryland, South Carolina.

[150] See statutes in Maine, Maryland, South Dakota, West Virginia; see also case: Wood v. Abell, 268 Md. 214, 300 A. 2d 665 (1973).

[151] See also case: Mason v. Southern New England Conf., 696 F. 2d 135 (1982) Mass. law applied.

[152] See also cases: Mack v. Big Bethel A.M.E. Church, 125 Ga. App. 713, 188 S.E. 2d 915 (1972); YMCA v. Bailey, 107 Ga. App. 417, 130 S.E. 2d 242 (1963).

and Louisiana provide that such personnel shall not be liable. Protection of directors and officials of non-profit organizations from liability, usually on the rationale that their acts are of a discretionary nature, has been subject to legislative action, especially in the late '80s. (See state statutory citations in Appendix.)

Nebraska, while providing that charitable and fraternal societies (a long list enumerates such societies) may sue and be sued, specifically exempts the Boy Scout leadership when the Scouts are performing certain activities.

New Jersey specifies in its statute that there is no liability when the injured person is a beneficiary of the works of the nonprofit corporation, but that there is liability to a person outside of such benefaction. However, the court[153] held that a member who was a resident in the YMCA building and entitled to use its recreational facilities did not prevent the corporation (YMCA) from availing itself of protection under the statute. The YMCA was not protected under the statute, though, when a non-member was injured while skiing at the Y's ski area. She had rented equipment and alleged disrepair and not properly fitting the equipment; her fee, also, was higher than for members. The court said that the immunity statute was not intended to immunize eleemosynary organizations from claims by fee-paying non-members arising from commercial activities geared to generate profit, even though the profits were to be used for charitable purposes.[154] A 1988 case[155] further interpreted the New Jersey law. The court held that the Charitable Immunity Act did not preclude church-operated school from being held liable to pedestrian who slipped on abutting sidewalk, which had not been cleared of ice and snow. For purposes of determining duty to remove snow and ice, school, although operated by a nonprofit religious institution, was deemed to be a "commercial" landowner. A number of New Jersey cases has arisen regarding the right to recovery.[156]

Additional cases relating to recreation and sport are cited in the footnotes.[157]

Often when charitable institutions are considered, the volunteer serving the institution is immediately thought of in terms of both personal liability of the volunteer and liability of the organization for the acts of the volunteer. This point is discussed in §3.5 Volunteers. A number of statutes granting limited immunity to both the individual and the organization have been passed by the legislatures, particularly in the mid to late '80s, to encourage people to volunteer in light of a litigious society.

[153] Hauser v. YMCA, 91 N.J. Super. 179, 219 A. 2d 532 (1966).
[154] Kasten v. YMCA, 173 N.J. Super. 1, 412 A. 2d 1346 (1980).
[155] Brown v. St. Venantius School, 111 N.J. 325, 544 A. 2d 842 (1988).
[156] Bixenman v. Christ Episcopal Church Parish, 166 N.J. Super. 148, 399 A. 2d 312 (1979); Book v. Aguth Achim Anchai of Freehold, 101 N.J. Super. 559, 245 A. 2d 51 (1968); Gabin v. Skyline Cabana Club, 54 N.J. 550, 258 A. 2d 6 (1969); Mayer v. Fairlawn Jewish Center, 38 N.J. 549, 186 A. 2d 274 (1962); Pomeroy v. Little League Baseball of Collingswood, 142 N.J. Super. 471, 362 A. 2d 39 (1976); Sommers v. Union Beach First Aid Squad, 139 N.J. Super. 425, 354 A. 2d 347 (1976); Stoolman v. Camden Co. Council of Boy

Scouts, 77 N.J. Super. 129, 185 A. 2d 436 (1962); Wiklund v. Presbyterian Church, 90 N.J. Super. 335, 217 A. 2d 463 (1966); Wuerffel v. Westinghouse Corp., 148 N.J. Super. 327, 372 A. 2d 659 (1977).
[157] Brown v. Church of the Holy Name of Jesus, 105 R.I. 322, 252 A. 2d 176 (1969); Cabbiness v. North Little Rock, 228 Ark. 356, 307 S.W. 2d 529 (1957); Gibbon v. YWCA, 159 N.E. 2d 911, rev'd. 170 Ohio St. 280, 10 Ohio Op. 2d 334, 164 N.E. 563 (1960); Malloy v. Fong, 37 Cal. 2d 356, 232 P. 2d 241 (1951); Mendall v. Pleasant Mountain Ski Development, 191 A. 2d 633 (Me. 1963); Roman Catholic Church v. Keenan 74 Ariz. 20, 243 P. 2d 455 (1952); Wood v. Abell, 268 Md. 214, 300 A. 2d 665 (1973); Young v. Boy Scouts of America, 9 Cal. App. 2d 760, 51 P. 2d 191 (1935).

§ 4.31   Food donors

Notwithstanding the general demise of charitable immunity just discussed, to encourage charitable giving of food donations to organizations for re-distribution to the needy, in 1980 and 1981 at least 60% of the states[158] passed limited liability laws covering both the individual donor and the recipient organization which distributes the food. Subsequently, additional states also passed legislation. Most of the laws are very similar in terminology and content, providing that neither individual nor organization will be subject to damages if the food was apparently fit for human consumption and the distribution is free of charge, unless there was injury arising from the food caused by negligence, recklessness or intentional conduct. (See also §21.1 Products liability.)

§ 4.4   Nuisance

Nuisance is a legal action of long standing, both in the courts and in the statutes, dating back to the turn of the century.[159] Nuisance is a field of torts. A common definition found in a number of statutes[160] is "anything which is injurious to health, indecent or offensive to the senses, or an obstruction to the free use of property, so as to interfere with the comfortable enjoyment of life or property, or which unlawfully obstructs the free passage or use, in the customary manner, of any navigable lake, river, bay, stream, canal, or basin or any public park, square, street, or highway."[161] Nuisance is considered a **continuing danger or permanent condition**.[162] In a New York case,[163] it was held that an occasional errant golf ball is not sufficiently continuous to be a nuisance. In this case, a resident adjacent to a golf course was hit by a ball.

> While a lawful thing or act may be a nuisance by reason of its negligent use or operation, nuisance is a condition, and not an act or failure to act of person responsible for condition; it does not necessarily depend on degree of care used, but rather on danger, indecency, or offensiveness existing or resulting even with best of care.[164]

Negligence tends to be considered an act of an individual which occasions bodily injury. Where a nuisance is based in negligence, negligence must be proven. Because the doctrine of governmental immunity is based primarily in the tort of negligence, some courts hold that nuisance founded in negligence comes within the immunity accorded by the doctrine or by the comprehensive tort claims act which sets forth "immunity is the rule; liability the exception" or "closed-ended" approach to liability

---

[158] Alabama, Arizona, Arkansas, Colorado, District of Columbia, Florida, Georgia, Idaho, Illinois, Indiana, Iowa, Louisiana, Maine, Maryland, Missouri, Montana, Nebraska, Nevada, New Mexico, Ohio, Oklahoma, Pennsylvania, Rhode Island, South Carolina, South Dakota, Tennessee, Utah, Wisconsin.

[159] Small v. Harrington, 10 Idaho 499, 79 P. 461 (1904); for example, statutes of Indiana (1881) and Montana (1895).

[160] For example, Arizona, Idaho, Indiana, Minnesota, Montana.

[161] Mont. Rev. Codes Ann. §27-30-101.

[162] Bush v. Norwalk, 122 Conn. 426, 189 A. 608 (1937); Kerr v. Brookline, 208 Mass. 190, 94 N.E. 257 (1911); Morin v. City of Valdosta, 140 Ga. App. 361, 231 S.E. 2d 133 (1976); Porter v. Gainesville, 147 Ga. App. 274, 248 S.E. 2d 501 (1978).

[163] Nussbaum v. Lacopo, 306 N.Y.S. 2d 658 (1969), aff'd. 27 N.Y. 2d 311, 317 N.Y.S. 2d 347, 265 N.E. 2d 762 (1970).

[164] Dean v. Bays Mt. Park Assoc., 551 S.W. 2d 702 (Tenn. App. 1977).

(see §4.22). On the other hand, in some courts, primarily Michigan, it has been held that "intentional" nuisance defeats immunity,[165] and also that comparative fault principles are inapplicable.[166] The intentional nuisance classification requires that the defendant knew of the dangerous condition, but did not take steps to make the area safer or keep individuals from the area, thus inferring that the defendant intended to create the condition.[167] To hold liability in such situations is consistent with the dangerous condition exception to immunity (see §4.22). In a 1981 case,[168] the court upheld liability for a nuisance as an exception to municipal immunity. Constitutional conflict is another basis for exception to statutory grant of immunity. When an activity or condition, possibly termed a nuisance, occurring on a defendant's property reaches across the property line to trespass upon or otherwise interfere with the use or enjoyment of property without just compensation, it may preclude application of the statutory grant of immunity.[169] Further, in *Sanders v. City of Ansonia*,[170] the court held that the plaintiff could bring joint actions of two counts against the city on the basis of nuisance and two counts against the employees on the basis of negligence. The court further held that the notice of claim statutory requirement for negligence actions did not apply to the nuisance action. So, it seems that if one can distinguish negligence and nuisance, then perhaps the defense of immunity can be defeated.[171]

It is important also to distinguish within nuisance between private and public nuisances and between nuisance *per se* and nuisance in fact, since these distinctions are germane to liability as related to governmental entities. A nuisance *per se* is an act, occupation or structure which is a nuisance at all times and under all circumstances, while a nuisance in fact is an act, occupation or structure which becomes a nuisance because of circumstances and surroundings. In two baseball cases,[172] it was held that the playing of baseball or a baseball park is not a nuisance *per se*, but baseball could be a nuisance in fact depending upon how it was conducted. In a Connecticut case,[173] it was held that a swimming pool or recreational center is neither a nuisance *per se* nor a nuisance in fact. The court determines what constitutes a nuisance *per se*, but a nuisance in fact is resolved by the trier of fact, the jury. Thus, the distinction between a nuisance *per se* and a nuisance in fact is an evidentiary one; however, governmental immunity does not bar liability for a nuisance *per se*, but a nuisance in fact may or may not survive the claim of governmental immunity.[174]

---

[165] Eichhorn v. Lamphere School Dist., 166 Mich. App. 527, 421 N.W.2d 230 (1988); Ford v. City of Detroit, 91 Mich. App. 333, 283 N.W. 2d 739 (1979); Garcia v. City of Jackson, 152 Mich. App. 254, 393 N.W. 2d 599 (1986); Taggie v. Dept. of Natural Resources, 87 Mich. App. 752, 276 N.W. 2d 485 (1979).

[166] Crest Chevrolet-Oldsmobile-Cadillac, Inc. v. Willemsen, 129 Wis. 2d 129, 384 N.W. 2d 692 (1986).

[167] Matthews v. Detroit, 141 Mich. App. 712, 367 N.W. 2d 440 (1985) drowned at fountain in park; Rosario v. City of Lansing, 403 Mich. 127, 268 N.W. 2d 230 (1978); Veeneman v. State, 143 Mich. App. 694, 373 N.W. 2d 193 (1985) dune buggy at state park; see also Garcia case, in preceding footnote.

[168] Banks v. City of Brunswick, 529 F. Supp. 695 (1981) applying Georgia law.

[169] Buddy v. Dept. of Natural Resources, 59 Mich. App. 598, 229 N.W. 2d 865 (1975); Dionne v. City of Trenton, 79 Mich. App. 239, 261 N.W. 2d 273 (1977).

[170] Sanders v. City of Ansonia, 33 Conn. Sup. 195, 369 A. 2d 1129 (1976).

[171] Silver, 842-3; Dean v. Bays Mt. Park Assoc., 551 S.W. 2d 702 (Tenn. App. 1977).

[172] Amdor v. Cooney, 241 Iowa 777, 43 N.W. 2d 136 (1950); Carter v. Lake City Baseball Club, 218 S.C. 255, 62 S.E. 2d 470 (1950).

[173] Marco v. Swinnerton, 22 Conn. Sup. 335, 171 A. 2d 418 (1960).

[174] Buddy v. State, 59 Mich. App. 598, 229 N.W.

Robinson v. Indianola Municipal Separate School District, 467 So. 2d 911 (Miss. 1985) set forth the interrelation of discretionary authority and nuisance, saying that "settled rule shields state and its subdivisions, including school districts, from suits at law or in equity based on exercise of discretionary governmental authority, and it remains true that, under such rule, private citizens cannot maintain action against governmental subdivision such as school district to enjoin alleged nuisance arising out of exercise of discretionary governmental authority such as choice of location and construction of school building on school property, but where public nuisance existed in the form of obstruction of street by traffic, such condition being directly traceable to school district's non-compliance with city off-street parking ordinance, injunctive relief was available to abutting landowner whose right of ingress and egress was obstructed." It was stated further that "violation of municipal ordinance does not constitute public nuisance, as such, but continuing violation of valid ordinance may constitute nuisance. Private individual cannot ordinarily maintain action with respect to enforcement of zoning regulation except where use constitutes nuisance *per se* or the individual has suffered or is threatened with special damage." In this situation, the school district was planning to replace a gymnasium destroyed by fire with a combined gymnasium and auditorium on a location directly across from the plaintiffs' property. The change in location meant a violation of the off-street parking zoning regulation.

The distinction between public and private nuisance is found in both the statutes and in cases. The Georgia statute states that "A public nuisance is one which damages all persons who come within the sphere of its operation, though it may vary in its effects on individuals. A private nuisance is one limited in its injurious effects to one of a few individuals." In 1986 the Connecticut court[175] said that there are two types of nuisance — public and private, and went on to define each:

A private nuisance exists only where one is injured in relation to a right which he enjoys by reason of his ownership of an interest in land. In the modern authorities (private nuisance) includes all injuries to an owner or occupier in the enjoyment of the property of which he is in possession, without regard to the quality of the tenure. In contrast, nuisances are public where they violate public rights, and produce a common injury, and where they constitute an obstruction to public rights, that is, the rights enjoyed by citizens as part of the public. If the annoyance is one that is common to the public generally, then it is a public nuisance. The test is not the number of persons annoyed, but the possibility of annoyance to the public by the invasion of its rights. A public

2d 865 (1975); Collison v. Saginaw, 84 Mich. App. 325, 269 N.W. 2d 586 (1979), rev'd. 406 Mich. 944, 277 N.W. 2d 643 (1979); Ford v. City of Detroit, 91 Mich. App. 333, 283 N.W. 2d 739 (1979); Garcia v. City of Jackson, 152 Mich. App. 254, 393 N.W. 2d 599 (1986); Gerzeski v. State, 68 Mich. App. 91, 241 N.W. 2d 771 (1976); Indiana Motorcycle Ass'n. v. Hudson, 399 N.E. 2d 775 (Ind. App. 1980); Stoughton v. Fort Worth, 277 S.W. 3d 150 (Tex. Civ. App. 1955).

[175] Couture v. Board of Education, Town of Plainfield, 6 Conn. App. 309, 505 A. 2d 432 (1986); see also Cimino v. Yale Univ., et al., 638 F. Supp. 952 (1986) Conn. law applied, spectator seriously injured when struck by goalpost pulled down at conclusion of college football game, held that condition at stadium was not a public nuisance.

nuisance is one that injures the citizens generally who may be so circum-
stanced as to come within its influence.

In this case the court held that a spectator could not recover under theory of public or
private nuisance. The spectator was injured while serving as sideline official ("chain
team") at a high school football game when he was overrun by a player and was driven
into an unprotected grandstand. Plaintiff alleged defendant had created a nuisance by
failing to pad the stands or to erect a barrier between the stands and playing field, and
also by failing to prevent players from congregating along the sidelines, thus impairing
the plaintiff's ability to avoid a collision with players who might overrun the sidelines.
The plaintiff alleged maintenance of a private nuisance in a Georgia case,[176] but the
court did not so hold. Plaintiff was injured when he was walking around a small pond
while fishing and slipped on the pathway falling into overgrown weeds and vegetation
wherein a roll of rusty metal fencing with sharp metal points was concealed; one of the
spikes punctured his abdomen. The Idaho statute also refers to "a moral nuisance." The
remedies are set forth in the Montana statute as indictment or information, a civil action,
or abatement for public nuisances and civil action or abatement for private nuisances. A
private person affected by a private nuisance has standing to bring action to abate it,
while a public nuisance may be subject of action to abate by private person only when
the nuisance is specifically injurious in kind to him.[177] Sovereign/governmental
immunity usually will be abrogated by a private nuisance, but may or may not be
abrogated by a public nuisance.[178]

Although damages are sought for destruction of property and other inconveniences,
the usual remedy for nuisance is abatement of the nuisance or injunction. The
determination of a nuisance and the decision regarding abatement by a governmental
entity is considered a discretionary act, for which there usually is immunity.[179] In the
Mitchell case, a father and son drowned while fishing in Lake Erie, when one stepped
off a sandbar and was apparently caught in the undertow (caused by discharge from
electric plant) and the other dived in to try to rescue, but was unable to do so. The
plaintiffs alleged that the city was aware of the dangerous nature of the undertow, but
failed to erect fences, post warning signs, or take other measures in the park to inform
persons of an alleged nuisance outside the park. The plaintiff asserted that while the
discharge channel itself was not under the city's control, it still had a duty to abate the

176 North v. Toco Hills, 160 Ga. App. 116, 286 S.E.
2d 346 (1981).

177 Buchanan v. Los Angeles Co. Flood Control
District, 128 Cal. Rptr. 770, 56 Cal. App. 3d 757
(1976).

178 Arachy v. Schopen, 22 Conn. Sup. 20, 158 A.
2d 604 (1960); Hillcrest Golf & Country Club v.
Altoona, 135 Wis. 2d 431, 400 N.W. 2d 493 (1986);
Kerlinsky v. Commonwealth, 7 Mass. App. 910, 388
N.E. 2d 717 (1979).

179 Mitchell v. Cleveland Electric Illuminating Co.,
30 Ohio St. 3d 92, 507 N.E. 2d 352 (1987); Randall v.
Delta Charter Township, 121 Mich. App. 26, 328 N.W.
2d 562 (1983); see also Eyde Brothers Development Co.

v. Roscommon Co. Board of Road Comm'rs., 161
Mich. App. 654, 411 N.W. 2d 814 (1987) alleged that
road dedicated to public use was being used as an
unsupervised and unmaintained park with a condition
resulting in litter, noise and congestion which inter-
fered with plaintiffs' use of their own properties, a
nuisance, held that actions of public in such use were
not so outrageous as to require closing of street, the
court did note that there had been occasions, particularly on summer weekends, when the public had
engaged in activities constituting nuisance, and encouraged plaintiffs to contact defendants when such behavior occurrred so that existing laws and ordinance could
be enforced.

purported nuisance since the generating plant was located within its municipal boundaries. The court held that the statute providing that municipalities "may" abate any nuisance did not affect the nature of the municipality's decision in determination of what was or was not a nuisance; such determination was held to be a discretionary, basic policy decision for which the municipality is given immunity. The Michigan case held similarly, that the ordinance authorizing the township to abate a nuisance involved a discretionary decision and thus failure to abate a nuisance (enforce the ordinance) was protected by immunity. Plaintiffs alleged that an inlet into the river, in which a five-year-old child drowned, constituted a common-law nuisance, which the township should have identified and abated.

Before 1968[180] approximately 15 percent of the cases related to physical education and athletics and parks and recreation had allegations of nuisance as a basis of liability. Twenty-nine states were represented among these cases. Recovery was had by the plaintiff in approximately one-fourth of the cases. Although at least 18 states had direct indications that nuisance is a basis for liability, in only 10 of these states were cases actually held for the plaintiff. This number of cases with nuisance allegations was undoubtedly an effort to circumvent the doctrine of governmental immunity prevalent at that time.

The court in rejecting the argument of nuisance in *Kilbourn v. Seattle*, 43 Wash. 2d 373, 261 P. 2d 407 (1953), expressed the sentiments of many courts and legal writers of that time when it said:

> In recent years (turn into decade of '50s) there has been a great increase in the number of personal injury actions brought against municipalities on the theory that the city had created, maintained, or permitted a nuisance. It was said in an article entitled, "Recent Substantive Developments Affecting Municipal Tort Liability," 21 Cin. L. Rev. 31, 48 (1952), that where negligence is present but the defense of governmental functions subsists, a wise advocate may seek to present his case upon the theory of public nuisance. There are many cases involving the claimed exception to the governmental immunity rule; and we are impressed by the aptness of a statement found in *Ramirez v. Cheyenne*, 34 Wyo. 67, 241 P. 710 (1925), that "nuisance is a good word to beg a question with."

The court went on to say that in most cases involving injuries sustained in city parks that the nuisance relied upon originated in negligence and the nuisance label was used for the obvious purpose of circumventing the defense of governmental immunity. Some courts took the label at face value without regard of the negligence origin, but others made it clear that nuisance is a condition and not an act or a failure to act of a person responsible for the condition, and pointed out the distinction between a violation of an absolute duty to protect the public from dangers inherent in a condition itself (nuisance) and a violation of a relative duty to use the degree of care required in the particular

---

[180] van der Smissen, Betty. *Legal Liability of Cities and Schools for Injuries in Recreation and Parks.* Cincinnati: W. H. Anderson Co., p. 103 (1968).

circumstances, which violation may also result in a dangerous condition (negligence). Thus, the success of the allegation of nuisance in park and recreation suits remained at the discretion of the court in what it chose to apply to the theory of nuisance.

In contrast, the decade of the '70s produced comparatively few cases brought on the theory of nuisance; and, most of these were in states which had not made provision for compensation for injuries in some form. Thus, the allegations were still seeking to circumvent the doctrine of governmental/sovereign immunity. In the mid-'80s, there were again cases alleging nuisance as an exception to immunity, and which were generally successful against governmental immunity, but not as against recreational user statute immunity. Cases are summarized in subsequent paragraphs in three categories — bodies of water; playgrounds, parks, and outdoor recreations; and adjacent residences.

§ 4.41 Bodies of water

In addition to the general statutes of nuisance, California has a law[181] stating that "any public swimming pool constructed, operated, or maintained contrary to the provisions of this article is a public nuisance, dangerous to health."

A series of cases alleged nuisance where the depth of the water seemed to be too shallow for the diving height provided;[182] while others sought to recover on faulty construction or layout being a nuisance.[183] In a 1979 case,[184] the plaintiff alleged maintenance of a public nuisance when she struck an underwater rock while swimming in a public park; while in a 1981 case,[185] it was held that constructing a dock into shallow, murky water for use of guests without posting no-diving signs or depth markers could reasonably be found to create a dangerous condition which might result in injury, and thus be a nuisance. Another case,[186] regarding an injury in a pond in a public park, which was used for swimming, was brought on nuisance against the city, summer program director, swimming program supervisor, and lifeguards. A gravel pit lake was alleged to be a nuisance when the plaintiff was injured when the bank on which he was standing crumbled as he began his dive.[187] An obstruction of an estuary through constructing a fish farm consituted a nuisance in an Idaho case.[188] Three persons

[181] See also statutes in Nebraska, Nevada and Oregon.

[182] Cabbiness v. North Little Rock, 228 Ark. 356, 307 S.W. 2d 529 (1957); Caughlan v. Omaha, 103 Neb. 726, 174 N.W. 220 (1919); Hoffman v. Bristol, 113 Conn. 386, 155 A. 499 (1931); Macy v. Chelan, 59 Wash. 2d 610, 369 P. 2d 508 (1962); Sansone v. Cleveland, 31 Ohio L. Abs. 246 (1940); Selden v. Cuyahoga Falls, 132 Ohio St. 223, 7 Ohio Op. 511, 6 N.E. 2d 976 (1937); Walker v. Forest Preserve Dist. of Cook Co., 27 Ill. 2d 538, 190 N.E. 2d 296 (1963).

[183] Gilliland v. Topeka, 124 Kan. 726, 262 P. 493 (1928); Maio v. Ilg, 98 R.I. 71, 199 A. 2d 727 (1964); Mola v. Metropolitan Park Dist., 181 Wash. 177, 42 P. 2d 435 (1935); Schneider v. Lake George, 254 A.D. 909, 5 N.Y.S. 2d 635 (1938), aff'd. 280 N.Y. 507, 19 N.E. 2d 918 (1939); Shoemaker v. Parsons, 154 Kan. 387, 118 P. 2d 508 (1941); Vaughn v. Alcoa, 194 Tenn.

449, 251 S.W. 2d 304 (1952); Virovatz v. Cudahy, 211 Wis. 357, 247 N.W. 341 (1933).

[184] Kerlinsky v. Commonwealth, 388 N.E. 2d 717 (Mass. App. 1979).

[185] Melendres v. Soales, 105 Mich. App. 73, 306 N.W. 2d 399 (1981).

[186] Sanders v. Ansonia, 33 Conn. Sup. 195, 369 A. 2d 1129 (1976).

[187] Anderson v. Brown Bros., Inc., 65 Mich. App. 409, 237 N.W. 528 (1975); see also Iseminger v. Black Hawk Co., 175 N.W. 2d 374 (Iowa 1970) drowned when lost footing in gravel pit maintained by co. conservation board.

[188] Ritter v. Standal, 98 Idaho 446, 566 P. 2d 769 (1977); the holding of an obstruction in a navigable river as a nuisance is of long-standing, see Small v. Harrington, 10 Idaho 499, 79 P. 461 (1904).

drowned when they fell through the ice covering the water in a pond which had been created by a borrow pit dug by the State; and, action was brought on the basis of nuisance.[189] Shallow water in a reservoir used for skiing was held not to be a nuisance.[190] Wading pools were involved in two cases alleging nuisance.[191] An Iowa case[192] held that a school is not immune from action relating to a nuisance (school sewage lagoon). Increased noise, traffic and parking problems were the grounds of nuisance in a Michigan case.[193] Unreasonable interference with use of a lake, also, was the basis of nuisance when a water ski school in the manner it conducted its activities deprived the resident home owners and renters and their children and guests from proper use of the lake for fishing, swimming, skiing, and boating.[194]

Generally, as stated in an early Illinois case,[195] "ponds and lagoons in parks have become too well recognized as means of decoration and recreation to be considered a public nuisance." However, they must be made reasonably safe. Concerned with an old homemade boat along a bank of a canal, a Connecticut case[196] said about nuisance: "Nuisance is a word often very loosely used; it has been not inaptly described as a catch-all of ill-defined rights. In its proper use, however, it involves as an essential element that it be the natural tendency of the act or thing complained of to create danger and inflict injury upon person or property. To constitute nuisance in the use of land, it must appear not only that a certain condition by its very nature is likely to cause injury, but also that the use is unreasonable or unlawful. Whether or not the particular condition of which the plaintiff complains constitutes a nuisance does not depend merely upon the inherent nature of the condition, but involves a consideration of all relevant facts, such as location, and its adaptation to beneficial operation of property."[197]

Generally, recreational user statutes bar counts of nuisance *per se* and nuisance in fact, in addition to barring general negligence counts; however, if the act is willful and wanton, whether nuisance or negligence, the recreational user statute does not provide immunity[198] (see also §12.1). In the *Hill* case, a man drowned in a pond behind a trailer park; plaintiff alleged that the pond was a nuisance and should have been fenced off or a warning sign posted, Not so, the court said; further, these were not willful and wanton acts, an exception under the statute. The holding was opposite in the *Garcia* situation, another Michigan case. The decedent drowned in the river near a dam when he was sucked into an unguarded open pipe and dragged by the water through the 2,000-foot conduit. Another boy had drowned similarly approximately 18 months earlier and the residents of the city had signed a petition urging defendant city to correct and improve

[189] Gerzeski v. State, 68 Mich. App. 91, 241 N.W. 2d 771 (1976).

[190] Larsen v. Santa Clara Valley Water Cons. Dist., 218 Cal. App. 2d 515, 32 Cal. Rptr. 875 (1963).

[191] Clark v. Seattle, 102 Wash. 228, 172 P. 1155 (1918); Vanderford v. Houston, 286 S.W. 568 (Tex. Civ. App. 1926).

[192] Kriener v. Turkey Valley Community School, 212 N.W. 2d 526 (Iowa 1973).

[193] Brent v. Detroit, 27 Mich. 628, 183 N.W. 2d 908 (1970).

[194] Florio v. State, 119 So. 2d 305 (Fla. App. 1960).

[195] Stein v. West Chicago Park Comm'rs., 247 Ill. App. 479 (1928); see also Capp v. St. Louis, 251 Mo.

345, 158 S.W. 616 (1913); Robbins v. Omaha, 100 Neb. 439, 160 N.W. 749 (1916); Sailor v. Columbus, 23 Ohio L. Abs. 417 (1936); Toft v. Lincoln, 125 Neb. 498, 250 N.W. 748 (1933); Toledo v. Cummings, 121 Ohio St. 37, 166 N.E. 897 (1929).

[196] Laspino v. New Haven, 135 Conn. 603, 67 A. 2d 557 (1949).

[197] Further discussion of swimming pools as a nuisance may be found in 49 A.L.R. 3d 652.

[198] Garcia v. City of Jackson, 152 Mich. App. 254, 393 N.W. 2d 599 (1986); Genco v. Conn. Light & Power Co., 7 Conn. App. 164, 508 A. 2d 58 (1986); Hill v. Guy, 161 Mich. App. 519, 411 N.W. 2d 757 (1987).

the dam, but it did not. The court held that an act of omission may constitute intent to create nuisance in fact and that the state of the pipe was an intentional nuisance, not subject to either governmental immunity or recreational user statute defense. In the Connecticut case, plaintiff was seriously injured when she dived into a lake owned by the defendant, and which was directly accessible from the abutting state park and its beaches. The lake was used by the general public. Plaintiff alleged that the defendant failed to maintain a safe recreational level of water in the lake, to warn adequately the users of the lake's unsafe depth, and to abate a nuisance. The court held that the defendant was protected by statute and, further, that the recreational user statute was constitutional exercise of legislative power.

§ 4.42   Playgrounds, parks, and outdoor recreation

A number of sledding and coasting area cases alleged nuisance,[199] but only one of these was successful.[200] In a 1975 case[201] a toboggan slide was held improperly constructed and hid dangers, but it was held that it was a nuisance in fact, not a nuisance *per se*, and, thus, did not survive the claim of governmental immunity. Another action[202] did not survive the claim of governmental immunity, when the plaintiff alleged nuisance due to failure to maintain a trail properly. As plaintiff and his family were walking on a marked trail, an old and decayed tree fell, striking and instantly killing the wife and severely and permanently injuring others. A contrary result was reached, that is, governmental immunity is not a bar to a claim based on an intentionally created nuisance in fact, when plaintiff wife was struck by falling rock in a state park. The Department allegedly knew that rock slides had previously occurred in the area and that future slides would occur, but took no steps to make the area safe, and, at the same time, created appearances of safety, which led plaintiff and others to the danger area in ignorance of the risk.[203] The Tennessee court[204] held that maintenance of a log chain across an access road to bicycle trails in a park did not constitute a nuisance. There was no evidence of inherent danger to those properly using the park. The nuisance theory was argued unsuccessfully, also, regarding a turkey trot.[205] Two cases involved shooting ranges,[206] and another the fall of an ornamental cannon in a public park.[207] In a 1981 Michigan case,[208] two boys entered a National Guard firing range, found an unexploded grenade, and took it back to their campsite at the campground. It exploded when it fell

[199] Balaas v. Hartford, 126 Conn. 510, 12 A. 2d 765 (1940); Mingo Junction v. Sheline, 130 Ohio St. 34, 3 Ohio Op. 78, 196 N.E. 897 (1935); Pohland v. Sheboygan, 251 Wis. 20, 27 N.W. 2d 736 (1947); Wilcox v. Erie County, 252 A.D. 20, 297 N.Y. S. 287 (1937), aff'd. 277 N.Y. 604, 14 N.E. 2d 184 (1938) reh. denied 278 N.Y. 567, 16 N.E. 2d 106.

[200] Devine v. Cincinnati, 68 Ohio App. 241, 22 Ohio Op. 393, 40 N.E. 2d 176 (1941).

[201] Buddy v. State, 59 Mich. App. 598, 229 N.W. 2d 865 (1975); see also Collison v. Saginaw, 84 Mich. App. 325, 269 N.W. 2d 586 (1979), rev'd. 406 Mich. 944, 277 N.W. 2d 643 (1979).

[202] Bracht v. Conservation Comm., 118 Ind. App. 77, 76 N.E. 2d 848 (1948).

[203] Taggie v. Dept. of Natural Resources, 87 Mich. App. 752, 276 N.W. 2d 485 (1979).

[204] Dean v. Bays Mountain Park Association, 551 S.W. 2d 702 (Tenn. 1977).

[205] Blackaby v. Lewistown, 265 Ill. App. 63 (1932).

[206] Dionne v. Trenton, 79 Mich. App. 239, 261 N.W. 2d 273 (1977); Gaines v. Wyoming, 147 Ohio St. 491, 34 Ohio Op. 406, 72 N.E. 2d 369 (1947).

[207] Prifty v. Waterbury, 133 Conn. 654, 54 A. 2d 260 (1947).

[208] Beard v. State, 106 Mich. App. 121, 308 N.W. 2d 185 (1981).

off a table. The court said that, while the claim of governmental immunity is defeated where there exists an intentionally created or continued nuisance in fact or the maintenance of a nuisance *per se*, the liability for nuisance does not extend to where a dangerous object is removed from the premises and results in damages elsewhere. Additional cases alleging nuisance are concerned with a variety of situations and conditions.[209]

In regard to playground apparatus, except for two, a Minnesota and a Texas case involving a swing and a slide,[210] defective playground apparatus has not been held to be a nuisance.[211] A hole at the end of a slide in a park[212] and an unblocked 6″-diameter, 20′-long corrugated metal pipes, which crushed a four-year-old boy,[213] were held to be nuisances. An allegation of nuisance was unsuccessful where a 16-year-old boy crashed into a merry-go-round pivot post while playing football on a playground; he knew of the danger and was contributorily negligent in not caring for his own safety.[214] Frequently there is confusion regarding nuisance and attractive nuisance (see §2.1231), particularly as related to playground apparatus. This confusion is present in two cases, one from Georgia[215] and one from Iowa,[216] involving a cable device (similar to a "zip line") and a teeter totter, respectively.

Both absolute and qualified nuisance were discussed by the Ohio court[217] in considering a cable fence in the outfield of a ball diamond, but the court had insufficient facts to hold on either basis. The court said that absolute nuisance had strict liability or liability without fault imposed, while a qualified nuisance was dependent upon negligence; that is, lawfully done but so negligently done as to create a potential or

[209] Baker v. Lexington, 310 S.W. 2d 555 (Ky. App. 1958); Bingham v. Board of Educ., 118 Utah 582, 223 P. 2d 432 (1950); Briggs v. Grand Rapids, 261 Mich. 11, 245 N.W. 555 (1932); Buckeye Union Fire Ins. Co. v. State, 13 Mich. App. 498, 164 N.W. 2d 699, rev'd. 383 Mich. 630, 178 N.W. 2d 476 (1970), 38 Mich. App. 155, 195 N.W. 2d 915 (1972); Decatur v. Parham, 268 Ala. 585, 109 So. 2d 692 (1959); Fort Worth v. Wiggins, 5 S.W. 2d 761 (Tex. Civ. App. 1928); Foss v. Maine Turnpike Authority, 309 A. 2d 339 (Maine 1973); Gableman v. Dept. of Conservation, 309 Mich. 416, 15 N.W. 2d 689 (1944); Grover v. Manhattan, 198 Kan. 307, 424 P. 2d 256 (1967); Guzzi v. New York Zoological Soc., 192 A.D. 263, 182 N.Y.S. 257 (1920), aff'd. 233 N.Y. 511, 135 N.E. 897 (1920); Hensley v. Gowrie, 203 Iowa 388, 212 N.W. 714 (1927); Jabs v. Burlington, 23 Conn. Sup. 158, 178 A. 280 (1962); Jones v. Kansas City, 176 Kan. 406, 271 P. 2d 803 (1954); King v. Blue Mt. Forest Assoc., 100 N.H. 212, 123 A. 2d 151 (1956); Larson v. Calder's Park Co., 54 Utah 325, 180 P. 599 (1919); McDonell v. Brozo, 285 Mich. 38, 280 N.W. 100 (1938); Prickett v. Hillsboro, 323 Ill. App. 235, 55 N.E. 2d 306 (1944); Rector v. Nashville, 23 Tenn. App. 495, 134 S.W. 2d 892 (1939); Roberson v. D.C., 86 A. 2d 536 (D.C. 1952); Sestero v. Glastonbury, 19 Conn. Sup. 156, 110 A. 2d 629 (1954); Townsley v. State, 6 Misc. 2d 557, 164 N.Y.S. 2d 840 (1957); Ward v. School Dist., 157 Or. 500, 73 P. 2d 379 (1937); Wysocki v. Derby, 140 Conn. 173, 98 A. 2d 659 (1963).

[210] Emmons v. City of Virginia, 152 Minn. 295, 188 N.W. 561 (1922); Ford v. Detroit, 91 Mich. App. 333, 283 N.W. 2d 739 (1979); Lubbock v. Green, 201 F. 2d 146 (1953).

[211] Anderson v. Board of Educ., 49 N.D. 181, 190 N.W. 807 (1922); Bernstein v. Milwaukee, 158 Wis. 576, 149 N.W. 382 (1914); Fowler v. Winfield, 286 F. 2d 385 (1960); Grinde v. Watertown, 232 Wis. 551, 288 N.W. 196 (1939); Malchow v. Leoti, 95 Kan. 787, 149 P. 687 (1915); Piasecny v. Manchester, 82 N.H. 458, 136 A. 357 (1926); Royston v. Charlotte, 278 Mich. 255, 270 N.W. 288 (1936); Stuver v. Auburn, 171 Wash. 76, 17 P. 2d 614 (1932); Williams v. Primary School Dist., 3 Mich. App. 468, 142 N.W. 2d 894 (1966).

[212] Schmitt v. Cheviot, 31 Ohio N.P. 12 (1933).

[213] Gottesman v. Cleveland, 142 Ohio St. 410, 27 Ohio Op. 353, 52 N.E. 2d 644 (1944).

[214] Iacono v. Fitzpatrick, 61 R.I. 28, 199 A. 689 (1938).

[215] Porter v. Gainesville, 147 Ga. App. 274, 248 S.E. 2d 501 (1978).

[216] Smith v. Iowa City, 213 Iowa 391, 239 N.W. 29 (1931).

[217] Kubitz v. Sandusky, 176 Ohio St. 445, 27 Ohio Op. 2d 422, 200 N.E. 2d 322 (1964); see also Curtis v. State, 29 Ohio App. 3d 297, 504 N.E. 2d 1222 (1986) football player injured when foot went through glass door in field house, use of wire-reinforced glass in door rather than another type of safety glass was not absolute nuisance.

unreasonable risk of harm. The Tennessee court[218] said that a nuisance is a condition which is dangerous, but held for the defendant on other grounds. The plaintiff alleged that when bleacher seats were removed and the cinder block foundation was left, a nuisance was created. A hole in a park, where a small pipe which was used to water the park grass arose, was held to constitute actionable nuisance because it was an affirmative act.[219] Recovery was denied on failure of the nuisance allegation for an unprotected basement stairwell[220] and a bridge over a stream.[221] The negligent operation of a power mower did not constitute a nuisance,[222] and neither did leaving a truck unattended on a park pathway.[223] The striking of a five-year-old child by a thrown discus was held not to be a nuisance.[224] Use of unslaked lime to line a football field was held not to be a nuisance.[225]

Successful allegations of negligence *per se* relate to injuries due to fireworks.[226] However, not all courts so hold, stating that fireworks are not a nuisance *per se* when properly used.[227] Other opinions hold that there must be notice.[228] In two dynamiting cases located in parks,[229] it was held that blasting is neither a nuisance *per se* nor an absolute nuisance, but may become such when of such intensity as to damage property.

The court gave a permanent injunction against the use of the fairgrounds for night stock car racing, in that "everyone in vicinity of racetrack had their eardrums hammered away at during night stock races...aftermath of dust accumulation on their property,...lived in fear for their continued safety."[230] The court opinion also stated that while almost any form of amusement or recreation can constitute a nuisance, as long as it is lawfully conducted it is not a nuisance *per se*, but further said that the fact that the racetrack was being lawfully conducted and was not in violation of zoning ordinances did not preclude attack on racetrack's operation as a public nuisance. Another consideration was that the racetrack was essentially a recreational operation that employed few people and had a capital investment at the most of only $15,000. A permanent injunction, also, was issued by the court in Louisiana to restrain motorcycle riding on a nearby property. The court found that the noise was excessive and disturbing.[231]

[218] Sewell v. Knoxville, 60 Tenn. App. 86, 444 S.W. 2d 177 (1969).

[219] Johnson v. Tennessean Newspaper, Inc., 192 Tenn. 287, 241 S.W. 2d 399 (1951).

[220] Barnett v. Memphis, 196 Tenn. 590, 269 S.W. 2d 906 (1954).

[221] Cohen v. Morristown, 15 N.J. Misc. 288, 190 A. 851 (1937).

[222] Ballinger v. Dayton, 66 Ohio L. Abs. 388, 117 N.E. 2d 469 (1952).

[223] Husband v. Salt Lake City, 92 Utah 449, 69 P. 2d 491 (1937).

[224] Ainslee v. Bellevue, 73 Ohio App. 577, 29 Ohio Op. 196, 57 N.E. 2d 279 (1943).

[225] Mokovich v. Independent School Dist., 177 Minn. 446, 225 N.W. 292 (1929).

[226] Cleveland v. Ferrando, 114 Ohio St. 207, 150 N.E. 747 (1926); Harris v. Findlay, 59 Ohio App. 375,

13 Ohio Op. 172, 18 N.E. 2d 413 (1938); Treadgill v. State of Texas, 275 S.W. 2d 658 (Tex. Civ. App. 1955).

[227] Haddon v. Lotito, 399 Pa. 521, 161 A. 2d 160 (1960); Hassett v. Thurston, 43 R.I. 47, 110 A. 394 (1920); Pope v. New Haven, 91 Conn. 79, 99 A. 51 (1916); Whittaker v. Franklinsville, 265 N.Y. 11, 191 N.E. 716 (1934).

[228] Schwarz v. Cincinnati, 55 Ohio App. 123, 8 Ohio Op. 390, 9 N.E. 2d 3 (1936).

[229] Crino v. Campbell, 68 Ohio App. 391, 23 Ohio Op. 119, 41 N.E. 2d 583 (1941); Crisafi v. Cleveland, 169 Ohio St. 137, 8 Ohio Op. 2d 125, 158 N.E. 2d 379 (1959).

[230] State v. Waterloo Stock Car Raceway, Inc., 96 Misc. 2d 350, 409 N.Y.S. 2d 40 (1978).

[231] Easterly v. Carr, 361 So. 2d 279 (La. App. 1978).

§ 4.43   Adjacent residences

It is this group of cases which is usually first thought of in relation to nuisance —
activities creating excessive noise[232] or having glaring lights[233] which disturb the
neighbors, trespass on adjacent property by participants to retrieve balls,[234] operation of
activities at unreasonable hours,[235] and balls hit onto adjacent property with subsequent
property damage or injury to persons.[236] In general, the courts have held that a person
who lives adjacent to a recreational facility submits oneself to reasonable noises and
activity, but that excessive interference with the peace of the adjacent residents will be
held a nuisance and enjoined.[237] In a Georgia case,[238] it was held that a recreation
building could become a nuisance only if there was abuse of the privilege of exercising
and playing therein. Several suits attempted to hold such facilities nuisance *per se*; but
such allegations have not been upheld,[239] if the activity is lawful and conducted in a
reasonable manner.

In 1970 the Florida court[240] held, regarding the installation of floodlights on a
playground in a park, that the municipality can put such area to any lawful use so long as
it does not deprive adjoining landowner of any right of enjoyment of property and is not a
nuisance. Similarly, the New Hampshire court[241] stated that a municipality is liable as
any other owner, if use of its property results in a nuisance.

Applying Kentucky law, the court[242] held that the one exception to the doctrine of
governmental immunity is nuisance by city or county and that it is a substantial
interference with another's use of property. In this instance, the TVA entered a license
agreement with the county whereby the county was obligated to operate property
adjoining plaintiff for recreation purposes for all members of the general public.
Plaintiff alleged that the county operated a nuisance by permitting drinking parties,
screaming, bottle smashing, refusal to collect refuse, failure to provide restrooms, nude
swimming, etc., which caused the value of his property to diminish. Plaintiff recovered
$15,000. In one case[243] plaintiff was unsuccessful in seeking an injunction against the
city for building an outdoor swimming pool in the park near his property, when he

[232] MacArtor v. Graylyn Crest III Swim Club, 41
Del. Chan. Rptr. 26, 187 A. 2d 417 (1963) loudspeaker;
Warren Company v. Dickson, 185 Ga. 481, 195 S.E.
568 (1938).

[233] Board of Educ. v. Klein, 303 Ky. 234, 197 S.W.
2d 427 (1946); Downey v. Jackson, 259 Ala. 189, 65 So.
2d 825 (1953); Neiman v. Common School District No.
95, 171 Kan. 237, 232 P. 2d 422 (1951).

[234] Hennessy v. Boston, 265 Mass. 559, 164 N.E.
470 (1929); Ness v. Independent School Dist., 230 Iowa
771, 298 N.W. 855 (1941); Woodford v. St. Petersburg,
84 So. 2d 23 (Fla. 1955); see also §6.15 baseball/
softball.

[235] Blake v. Madison, 237 Wis. 498, 297 N.W. 422
(1941); Hansen v. Independent School Dist., 62 Idaho
614, 114 P. 2d 736 (1941); Peters v. Moses, 171 Misc.
441, 12 N.Y.S. 2d 735 (1939).

[236] Hennessy v. Boston, 265 Mass. 559, 164 N.E.
470 (1929); Robb v. Milwaukee, 241 Wis. 432, 6 N.W.

2d 222 (1942) (two cases); Salevan v. Wilmington Park,
45 Del. 290, 72 A. 2d 239 (1950); see also §7.145 golf.

[237] Castell v. Afton, 227 Iowa 61, 287 N.W. 245
(1939); Vanderford v. Houston, 286 S.W. 568 (Tex. Civ.
App. 1926); Sans v. Ramsey Golf & Country Club, 50
N.J. Super. 127, 141 A. 2d 335 (1958).

[238] Talmadge v. Harvey, 55 Ga. App. 621, 190 S.E.
926 (1937).

[239] Board of Educ. v. Klein, 303 Ky. 234, 197 S.W.
2d 427 (1946); Briggs v. Grand Rapids, 261 Mich. 11,
245 N.W. 555 (1932); Warren Company v. Dickson,
185 Ga. 481, 195 S.E. 568 (1938).

[240] Rogers v. Miami Springs, 231 So. 2d 257 (Fla.
1970).

[241] Ferguson v. Keene, 111 N.H. 222, 279 A. 2d 605
(1971).

[242] Brown v. Marshall County, 394 F. 2d 498 (1968).

[243] Brent v. Detroit, 27 Mich. 628, 183 N.W. 2d 908
(1970).

alleged that the increased noise, traffic and parking problems created a nuisance. And, an adjacent resident was unsuccessful in alleging that the lights, noise, and traffic for the summer Pee Wee baseball programs were a nuisance.[244] Similarly, a church softball field lighted by high-intensity lights was held not to be a nuisance where use was restricted to the hours between 7 a.m. and 10 p.m.[245] A different result was reached in regard to a bowling alley, when the plaintiff alleged that it constituted a nuisance because it was excessively noisy, was kept open until very late at night, was a rowdy place where minors hung out, etc.[246]

Additional cases related to interference with adjacent residences include a school situation wherein students trespassed on property and harassed the occupant, allegedly due to the layout and design of the school area,[247] and the failure of the park to provide appropriate sanitary facilities.[248]

§ 4.5 Special focus statutes and exculpatory clauses

Another approach of legislatures to limiting liability is that of enacting "special focus" statutes, that is, statutes which address a specific concern or situation. Each state has its own particular needs and concerns, and hence, statutes, so it is important that one consult with local attorneys and state organizations and agencies for such statutes. (Some statutes are cited in the Appendix.) The more universal statutes among the states are included in this reference book at the appropriate sections. These statutes should be distinguished from the legislative actions regarding tort reform (see §4.26), consumer protection (see §17.41), and products liability (see §21.1).

"Good Samaritan" laws were enacted to encourage individuals to render first aid when coming upon an injury. Such laws have been directed not only toward citizens in general, but also toward medical and health personnel, team physicians, certain rescue personnel, et al. See §17.1 for discussion of emergency care statutes and the manner in which they limit liability.

Again, to encourage individuals to render service, a number of states have enacted statutes which limit liability of volunteers in the activities of non-profit organizations and public entities. Some of these, especially in the mid-80s, were initiated in regard to amateur sport leadership. See §3.5 Volunteers, for discussion of these statutes. Also, there has been legislation in the late '80s providing immunity for directors and officials of non-profit organizations (see §4.3).

With great interest in outdoor recreation, but also with increased litigation, the legislatures in nearly all states have enacted landowner limited liability or recreational user laws, which provide limited immunity to the landowner who permits a person to use one's property gratuitously for outdoor recreation purposes. These special laws for

---

[244] Kasala v. Kalispell Pee Wee Baseball League, 151 Mont. 109, 439 P. 2d 65 (1968); also, Lieberman v. Township of Saddle River, 37 N.J. Super. 62, 116 A. 2d 809 (1955).

[245] Corp. of the Presiding Bishop ex rel. Ashton v. Idaho Falls, 92 Idaho 571, 448 P. 2d 185 (1968).

[246] O'Quinn v. Homerville, 157 S.E. 109 (Ga. App. 1931).

[247] Stein v. Highland Park Indp. School District, 540 S.W. 2d 551 (Tex. Civ. App. 1976).

[248] Newport News v. Hertzler, 216 Va. 587, 221 S.E. 2d 146 (1976).

recreation should not be confused with the long-standing responsibilities of landowners to those who come upon their premises or of commercial enterprises to their patrons. For detailed analysis of these recreational user laws, see §12.1. There are some additional statutes in some states, such as the California and Illinois hazardous recreation acts, which address specifically the adventure activities (see §13.3).

When the court awarded a large amount for damages to a novice skier who was injured on a Vermont ski slope, the legislatures, in most all states with skiing, reacted with Ski Responsibility Laws, in which the operator's responsibilities are set forth and also what responsibilities the skier has when skiing. See §8.4 for further information.

The providers of leisure services, including public, nonprofit, and commercial entities, have endeavored to limit their own liability through the use of exculpatory clauses, particularly in the mid and late '80s. The elements for a valid clause, and thus limiting liability, and other aspects of exculpatory agreements are set forth in Chapter 16. The use of such clauses as a part of risk management is addressed in §24.81.

Chapter 5.   Defenses

If a suit is filed against a person, what are the defenses which can be used? Defenses fall into three categories — those which are concerned with the act(s) of the defendant, those which focus on the act(s) of the plaintiff, and those which utilize tactics in which the act(s) of neither the defendant nor the plaintiff is material. Table 5.1 depicts the various defenses by category.

Table 5.1   Defenses[1]

Defendant's Act	Plaintiff's Act	Act Immaterial

1. Negligence elements not proven
   + standard of care
   + duty
   + proximate cause
	1. Contributory negligence
	
	2. Assumption of risk
	
	3. Comparative negligence
		1. Immunity doctrines
		   + governmental/sovereign
		   + charitable
		2. Procedural non-compliance, e.g.
		   + statute of limitation
		   + notice of claim

2. Last clear chance doctrine		
3. Ultra vires act		3. Exculpatory clause
4. Nature of activity eligible for statutory immunity		
5. Discretionary act		

[1]Insurance and indemnification are not listed as defenses because they are **NOT** a defense, but a method of managing risk of financial loss. See §§25.3 and 25.21 for further discussion.

§ 5.1   Defenses related to defendant's acts

There are essentially five defenses related to defendant's acts. The primary defense is

225

that the elements of negligence have not, cannot be proven. The last clear chance doctrine in essence creates a new duty for the defendant in protecting the plaintiff, requiring the defendant to take action to extricate the plaintiff from peril. An *ultra vires* defense is used by a defendant employer against an employee in an effort to negate the doctrine of *respondeat superior*. The fourth defense concerns the nature of the activity, endeavoring to bring it under a limited liability law. Discretionary act, the fifth defense, is a bar to liability in states which have a Tort Claims Act. (See §4.13 where it is discussed in detail). Comparative negligence also has to do with the defendant's act as related to apportionment of fault, and thus damages, but is discussed in the next section under Defenses related to plaintiff's acts.

§ 5.11   Elements of negligence not proven

The best defense is that one or more of the four elements of negligence, as described in Chapter 2, have not been proven — that a duty was not owed the injured, that reasonable care was exercised in performance of the act, that the act was not the proximate cause of the injury, or that there was not in fact injury to the plaintiff. This defense is available to all parties sued, public and private. Because of the detail in Chapter 2, no further discussion is given in this chapter.

§ 5.12   Last clear chance, discovered peril, and sudden emergency doctrines[1]

The **doctrine of last clear chance** is not a defense for a defendant, but rather an allegation by the plaintiff that the defendant should be held liable in spite of the plaintiff's contributory negligence. In this it is a modification of contributory negligence. What is the last clear chance doctrine? If the injured (plaintiff) through one's own negligence puts oneself into a dangerous position from which one could not help oneself out of danger (contributorily negligent), and the defendant seeing the plaintiff's peril ("discovered peril") and having the "last clear chance" or opportunity to avoid the inflicting of the injury by ordinary care, fails to so exercise such care, that person is responsible. Or, as stated in *Gardner v. Heldman*,[2] a golf case, "The doctrine of 'last clear chance' is predicated on premise that plaintiff by reason of his negligence has placed himself in position of peril, but by subsequent action has caused the contributory negligence to disappear, but is still subjected to peril by his former acts and has a right to require defendant to use ordinary care to protect him from results of such former negligence." Differences in plaintiff and defendant pleadings are explained in a Rhode Island case,[3] thusly: "Where plaintiff traditionally pleads negligence and defendant responds with contributory negligence, plaintiff can still plead last clear chance because defendant, despite plaintiff's own negligence, still owes a duty to him; however, where plaintiff pleads negligence and defendant pleads assumption of risk, that

---

[1] See also §2.1122.

[2] Gardner v. Heldman, 82 Ohio App. 1, 37 Ohio Ops., 347, 51, Ohio L. Abs. 169, 80 N.E. 2d 681 (1948); see also Schweitzer v. Gilmore, 251 F. 2d 171 (1958) a swimming from raft to shore situation.

[3] Kennedy v. Providence Hockey Club, 119 R.I. 70, 376 A. 2d 329 (1977).

is end of chain, because once plaintiff accepts risk, defendant no longer owes a duty to him."

The doctrine is a true exception of the contributory negligence rule, but is justified on a public policy basis. On this rationale it is sometimes also referred to as the "humanitarian doctrine." The reasoning is that it would be unjust to allow the defendant to escape liability for one's actions, to deny plaintiff's recovery or protection of the law because of contributory negligence which preceded the defendant's negligence — the defendant's acts being later in time makes one the more culpable party. This also relates to proximate cause, where the plaintiff's contributory negligence would be the remote cause and the defendant's act the immediate cause. The strength of the reasoning is somewhat limited.

With consequent demise of contributory negligence, the doctrine of last clear chance is no longer viable; last clear chance and comparative negligence are not compatible.[4] Oregon[5] left no doubt by passing a statute abolishing the doctrine, and at least six other states have specifically abrogated it. Some cases which allege the doctrine of last clear chance are cited in the footnotes.[6]

The **doctrine of sudden emergency** is related to the doctrine of last clear chance, but should be distinguished. In *Egede-Nissen v. Crystal Mountain*[7] the court stated that the doctrine of sudden emergency cannot be invoked by one who at own conduct brought about, in whole or part, the emergency with which he is confronted.

The sudden emergency doctrine is a nonstatutory principle under which the law recognizes that a person suddenly and unexpectedly placed in a position of impending peril usually will not, and should not be expected to, exercise the judgment and discretion of a person acting under normal circumstances....

Although the sudden emergency doctrine makes allowances for the imperfections of human behavior, it is subject to significant limitations which serve to restrict its general application. Of paramount importance is the fact that the doctrine does not provide for a different standard of care in an emergency than in any other situation. In order to avoid negligence in any circumstance, the actor must conduct himself as would a reasonable and prudent person under the same or similar circumstances, and he may still be found negligent, despite the emergency, if his actions are deemed to be unreasonable....

...many other state courts have criticized the doctrine....the prospect of

[4] Brown v. George, 294 S.E. 2d 35 (S.C. 1982); Ratlief v. Yokum, 280 S.E. 2d 587 (W. Va. 1981).

[5] Hall v. Northwest Outward Bound School, 280 Or. 655, 572 P. 2d 1007 (1977) construes meaning of Oregon statute.

[6] Chapman v. State, 6 Wash. App. 316, 492 P. 2d 607 (1972); Cox v. Barnes, 469 S.W. 2d 61 (Ky. 1971); Keating v. Arthur Treacher's Fish and Chips, 77 A.D. 2d 616, 430 N.Y.S. 2d 364 (1980); Massey v. Scripter, 64 Mich. App. 561, 236 N.W. 2d 143, rev'd. 401 Mich. 385, 258 N.W. 2d 44 (1977); Vaughn v. Alcoa, 194 Tenn. 449, 251 S.W. 2d 304 (1952); Whittington v. Sowela Tech. Inst., 438 So. 2d 236 (La. App. 1983), cert. den. 443 So. 2d 591 (1983); Williams v. Baton Rouge, 252 La. 770, 214 So. 2d 138 (1968). See annotations for comparative negligence statutes in additional states, such as Nevada and Wyoming, for citations of cases not specific to the fields included in this reference book.

[7] Egede-Nissen v. Crystal Mountain, Inc., 584 P. 2d 432 (Wash. App. 1978), 93 Wash. 2d 127, 606 P. 2d 1214 (1980); Ratlief v. Yokum, 280 S.E. 2d 587 (W. Va. App. 1981).

additional courts abrogating the doctrine is not at all unlikely....the doctrine has, in many instances, proved to be unworkable and counterproductive.[8]

§ 5.13   Defense of Ultra Vires Act[9]

The defense of *ultra vires* act is used by a corporate entity to negate the doctrine of respondeat superior. In essence, what the corporate entity is maintaining is that it should not be held responsible for the alleged negligent act of its employee because the employee acted outside the scope of responsibility or authority. Most of the Tort Claims Acts (see §4.2) which provide for indemnification or insurance coverage for employees also specify that such protection is given only when the employee (paid or volunteer) is acting within the scope of responsibility. Thus, with increasing frequency, insurance companies seek to avoid defense or awards on the basis that the insurance covered the corporate entity and the employee's *ultra vires* act placed the employee outside the coverage.

§ 5.14   Nature of activity — limited immunity/liability

A fourth defense is that the activity is protected by limited liability laws. For example,[10] in order to encourage individuals with emergency care (first aid) competencies, a few state legislatures have passed limited immunity statutes, which state that persons are not liable for acts of negligence unless they were grossly negligent or acted willfully and wantonly to injure the victim (see §17.16). Then, there are the statutes limiting the liability of volunteers (see §3.5). Another effort on the part of state legislatures to limit liability and encourage landowners to permit use of their lands and waters for recreational purposes are the recreational user statutes (see §12.1). Most of the downhill skiing states have skier responsibility laws which limit the liability of the operator (see §8.4). See also §4.5 special focus statutes.

§ 5.2   Defenses related to plaintiff's acts

The two most common defenses prior to the 1970s were contributory negligence and assumption of risk, one dealing with the acts of the plaintiff which contributed to the injury and the other concerning the acceptance of the risks of injury inherent in the activity by the plaintiff. During the decades of the '70s and '80s, contributory negligence as a primary defense was gradually replaced in nearly all states by the doctrine of comparative negligence, which considers the apportionment of fault between plaintiff and defendant as the basis of assignment of damages. Whereas contributory negligence and assumption of risk are part of the common law of negligence, comparative negligence concept has been instigated, for the most part, by state legislatures. Contributory negligence is presented in a major section because it

---

[8] Gunn, Douglas J., Recent Decisions: Torts — Negligence — The Sudden Emergency Doctrine is Abolished in Mississippi. 51 *Mississippi Law Journal* 310-313 at pp. 302, 304, 312 (1980).

[9] See also discussion of *ultra vires acts* in §§3.411 and 3.1, introduction to chapter.

[10] See also §4.5.

continues, even under comparative negligence, as a critical determinant of fault and the pro rata of damages; and, it still is a valid defense in a limited number of jurisdictions,[11] barring any recovery by the plaintiff. It is essential to understand what contributory negligence is and how one can utilize it as related to risk management to ameliorate damages. The role of assumption of risk in comparative negligence is discussed in the section on assumption of risk §5.22. Assumption of risk remains a vital component of a defendant's defense. An exculpatory clause (agreement) also is an act of the plaintiff, inasmuch as it is the plaintiff who signs away one's rights; however, since the effect bars plaintiff from recovery of any damages and the acts are not considered on their merits, the defense of exculpatory clause was placed in the third category of defenses (see §5.33).

§ 5.21   Contributory negligence

Contributory negligence is conduct on the part of the plaintiff, contributing as a legal cause to the harm suffered, which falls below the standard to which plaintiff is required to conform for one's own protection.[12] The doctrine of contributory negligence is a common law defense and if a plaintiff sustained injury as the result of one's own negligence, however slight, plaintiff was said to have contributed to one's own harm and in most jurisdictions was denied recovery. This often caused a very harsh result, especially when the defendant's negligence played a substantial role in the injury. The basis for the doctrine of contributory negligence seems to have been predicated upon (1) the uneasy distrust of the plaintiff-minded jury in the nineteenth century and the desire to keep liabilities within bounds, (2) the tendency of the courts to look for a dominant or single "cause" of the injury, and (3) the inability of the courts to conceive a satisfactory method for damages apportionment.[13] To mitigate the harshness of the bar to recovery of the contributory negligence rule, the courts began not to apply the rule where the defendant engaged in willful misconduct, violated a safety statute,[14] or where the last clear chance to avoid accident (see §5.12) was with the defendant. These exceptions were based on a theory of inequitable denial to recovery where the defendant was so clearly at fault. To more adequately remedy the situation where both the defendant and plaintiff were at fault, many of the state legislatures enacted comparative negligence statutes; some courts have held that they will not judicially abrogate the doctrine of contributory negligence[15] (see §5.23 comparative negligence discussion).

The defense is available only in negligence cases; it is not pertinent to intentional acts. Regardless of the fault of the plaintiff, where injury has occurred due to willful, wanton, or reckless acts of the defendant, the plaintiff has a right to recover. The court held that contributory negligence was no defense to charge of willful misconduct in a situation in which a 16-year-old man broke his neck and was rendered a quadriplegic after diving into a river from a railroad trestle despite warnings. Defendant had

[11] For example, North Carolina.
[12] Second Restatement of Torts §463.
[13] Keeton, W. Page, editor. *Prosser and Keeton on Torts*. St. Paul: West Publishing Company, 5th ed. 1984 at p. 452.
[14] Potter v. N.C. School of Arts, 37 N.C. App. 1, 245 S.E. 2d 188 (1978).
[15] For example, Harrison v. Montgomery Co. Board of Education, 456 A. 2d 894 (Md. App. 1983).

knowledge that serious injury to another would probably result.[16] The defense also usually is not available in situations of strict liability;[17] however, in an early Oklahoma case,[18] absolute liability was modified by permitting contributory negligence to be pleaded; it was an issue for the jury. A 14-year-old was bitten on the foot while playing near a pet bear's cage. The court held that the owner was negligent in keeping an animal belonging to a class that is dangerous.

The use of the word negligence with contributory negligence may be a bit of a misnomer in that negligence infers failure to protect another from undue risk of harm. Perhaps it would be more appropriate to call it "contributory fault." Nevertheless, the standard of conduct the plaintiff is held to is the same as that for the defendant. And, the rule of avoidable consequences denies recovery for any damages if injury could have been avoided by reasonable conduct on the part of the plaintiff. This does not mean identical conduct on the part of the plaintiff and defendant, for it may be modified by the circumstances surrounding each, such as one having more information about the situation than the other. In *Smith v. U.S.*, 383 F. Supp. 1076 (1974), aff'd. 546 F. 2d 872 (1976) the court held that a 14-year-old boy owed a reciprocal duty to exercise ordinary care to avoid injuring himself and that his conduct failed to conform to standards of conduct required for his own protection, because he did not behave as a "reasonable man" of his age, learning and experience. In this situation the plaintiff fell into a thermal pool at Yellowstone National Park after both warnings and obvious direct observation of the condition of the thermal pools. It also was held in a water skiing situation that the minor plaintiff failed to exercise ordinary care for his own safety and, thus, could not recover from either camp operator or occupants of motor boat when he fell from skis. He could have kicked rope and tow bar free and avoided injury, but failed to do so because he would have fallen and received unsuccessful mark in competition.[19]

The avoidable consequences rule, however, seems to be modified by the "momentary inattention" rule. The plaintiff, an adult playing softball in a league using the small field of an elementary school, pursued a fly ball in left field and ran into a nearby concrete incinerator. The court said that contributory negligence rests upon constructive knowledge that a reasonable man should or could discover danger by ordinary care. Where victim (player) momentarily forgot the known danger (knew of incinerator but when he began chasing fly, forgot about it) it may be found that he acted reasonably and was not contributorily negligent, applying the "momentary inattention" rule.[20] However, in a 1985 case[21] the plaintiff did not recover an award on the basis of "distraction theory." The plaintiff, during the course of a tennis match, left her court to follow a lob shot into the adjacent court and sustained injuries when she collided with a trash bin containing protruding jagged wood. The trash bin was located immediately adjacent to the only gate in the fence surrounding the two tennis courts and the plaintiff

[16] Lostritto v. Southern Pacific Transportation Co., 73 Cal. App. 3d 737, 140 Cal. Rptr. 905 (1977).

[17] Franken v. Sioux Center, 272 N.W. 2d 422 (Iowa 1978) zoo case; see also Anthony Pools v. Sheenan, So. Md. App. 614, 440 A. 2d 1085 (1982) aff'd. 295 Md. 285, 455 A. 2d 434 (1983) plaintiff fell off diving board onto concrete coping of alcove from which board projected.

[18] Tonkawa v. Danielson, 166 Okla. 241, 27 P. 2d 348 (1933).

[19] Polsky v. Levine, 73 Wis. 547, 243 N.W. 2d 503 (1976).

[20] Chase v. Shasta Like Union School Dist., 259 Cal. App. 2d 612, 66 Cal. Rptr. 517 (1968).

[21] Anderson v. Dunwoody North Driving Club, 176 Ga. App. 210, 335 S.E. 2d 451 (1985).

had approached her playing area by going through this gate. She had reviewed the area prior to beginning play for any hazards; the trash bin was in no way obstructed from view at any time. The court held that plaintiff failed to exercise ordinary care for her own safety.

Contributory negligence is a viable defense, too, where the plaintiff intentionally exposed oneself to risk. In such cases the plaintiff's conduct may be such as to indicate one's consent or willingness to encounter the danger and relieve the defendant of responsibility.[22]

Can there be contributory negligence *per se*? In an Illinois golf club situation involving a fall on a pathway, the court addressed briefly whether plaintiff was contributorily negligent as a matter of law. It said that contributory negligence is a determination preeminently for the jury and that the issue becomes a question of law only when undisputed evidence conclusively proves that the accident resulted from the negligence of the injured party and that injuries could have been avoided by use of reasonable precautions.[23]

Some cases have held that there can be no contributory negligence if the plaintiff was not aware of one's own danger to take precautionary measures.[24] For example, an 11-year-old boy was held not contributorily negligent when he was struck in the eye with a rubber tipped badminton shuttlecock batted by a companion while playing in an inadequately lighted room.[25] Never having played before, he did not know the dangers of playing in such a room. In a 1988 case, *Russell v. Board of Regents, Univ. of Nebr.*, 423 N.W.2d 126 (Neb. 1988), the court stated that "one who is capable of understanding and discretion, and who fails to exercise ordinary care and prudence to avoid dangers is negligent or contributorily negligent." It went on to say that "among matters which must be considered in determining whether invitee is guilty of negligence is effect of distracting events or circumstances." In this situation, the university was negligent in creation of a dangerous condition by placing a pile of snow in such a position that normal temperature changes would result in the formation of ice on the parking lot; and, further, it was determined that the danger was not obvious and the student (plaintiff) used ordinary care, and thus was not contributorily negligent when he slipped and fell. The distracting event was an approaching vehicle.

The issue of contributory negligence is one of fact and for the jury to determine.[26] But, just what is conduct that gives rise to holding of contributory negligence? A Florida court[27] stated:

[22] Campbell v. Montgomery Co. Board of Educ., 73 Md. App. 54, 533 A. 2d 9 (1987) group sexual molestation of junior high girl in boys' locker room.

[23] McCarthy v. River Forest Golf Club, 62 Ill. App. 3d 483, 19 Ill. Dec. 504, 379 N.E. 2d 19 (1978); see also Friedman v. Park Dist. of Highland Park, 151 Ill. App. 3d 374, 104 Ill. Dec. 329, 502 N.E. 2d 826 (1986) eight-year-old girl, sledding.

[24] Robb v. Milwaukee, 241 Wis. 432 6 N.W. 2d 222 (1942) (two cases); Stolpe v. Duquesne, 337 Pa. 215, 9 A. 2d 427 (1939).

[25] Styer v. Reading, 360 Pa. 212, 61 A. 2d 382 (1948).

[26] Albuquerque v. Redding, 93 N.M. 757, 605 P. 2d 1156 (1980) front tire of bike slipped through drain grate in bicycle path; Benton v. YMCA, 27 N.J. 67, 141 A. 2d 298 (1958) shower room steps; Buchanan v. Newport Beach, 50 Cal. App. 3d 221, 123 Cal. Rptr. 338,(1975) surfer on beach; Marques v. Riverside Military Academy, 87 Ga. App. 370, 73 S.E. 2d 574 (1952) discus thrown; Morehouse College v. Russell, 109 Ga. App. 301, 136 S.E. 2d 179 (1964) swimming instruction.

[27] Cutler v. St. John's United Methodist Church of Edwardsville, 489 So. 2d 123 (Fla. App. 1986) drowned swimming in ocean.

In determining whether a particular individual has been guilty of contributory negligence at a particular time, it is necessary to consider (1) the characteristics of that individual — age, intelligence, experience, knowledge, physical condition, etc. — which would affect his ability to detect dangerous conditions or appreciate the degree of hazards involved in conditions actually observed; (2) the physical facts — the extent to which the particular hazard is noticeable and the degree of alertness to avoid such a hazard reasonably called for by surrounding circumstances; and, (3) the action taking place — the incidents of movement, sound and physical activities of the individual charged with contributory negligence and other persons and objects, animate and inanimate.

In a 1980 case[28] a volunteer participant in a March of Dimes walkathon stumbled in front of the bus leading the walk; contributory negligence barred recovery. And, contributory negligence was held to be an appropriate defense when a student on a band field trip dived into a pool when he could not swim.[29] These acts were alleged to be contributory negligence: a girl in physical education class failed to do an exercise as she had been taught and was thereby injured;[30] a softball player carelessly and dangerously slid into a post being used as a base;[31] a small boy had his feet crossed under a teeter-totter and when it came down quickly, he was injured;[32] a girl tried to feed a bear chained to a tree and was bitten;[33] an experienced skater skated on rough ice with a four-year-old child suspended between her and her husband;[34] a college student should have perceived danger of hopping on wooden floor in plastic bag;[35] a nine-year-old in manner rode and dismounted merry-go-round;[36] a prison inmate failed to follow instructions as to proper operation of table saw.[37]

No contributory negligence was found in a 1981[38] case when the plaintiff fell on a concrete floor in a golf club house and broke her leg. It was alleged that wearing of steel-spiked golf shoes constituted contributory negligence. There also was no contributory negligence found when the plaintiff was injured on a protruding bolt on a mechanical device used to raise and lower a tennis net.[39] In a theatrical production, the plaintiff received second degree burns when the faculty supervisor substituted carbon dioxide from the fire extinguisher for dry ice in the fog-making machine causing an explosion. It was alleged that the explosion was foreseeable, but the court did not hold contributory negligence.[40] A safety ordinance also had been violated. In a Wisconsin 1976 case,[41]

[28] Keating v. Arthur Treacher's Fish and Chips, 77 A.D. 2d 616, 430 N.Y.S. 2d 364 (1980).
[29] Powell v. Orleans Parish School Board, 354 So. 2d 229 (La. App. 1978).
[30] Bellman v. San Francisco High School Dist., 11 Cal. 2d 576, 81 P. 2d 894 (1938).
[31] Bennett v. Scranton, 54 Lack. Jur. 81 (Pa. 1953).
[32] Bruenn v. North Yakima School Dist., 101 Wash. 374, 172 P. 569 (1918).
[33] Byrnes v. Jackson, 140 Miss. 656, 105 So. 861 (1925).
[34] Cassady v. Billings, 135 Mont. 390, 340 P. 2d 509 (1959).
[35] Yarborough v. City University of New York, 520

N.Y.S. 2d 518 (1987).
[36] Rollins v. Concordia Parish School Board, 465 So. 2d 213 (La. App. 1985).
[37] Hicks v. State of New York, 124 A.D. 2d 949, 509 N.Y.S. 2d 152 (1986).
[38] Jones v. Recreation & Park Comm., 395 So. 2d 846 (La. App. 1981).
[39] Baytown v. Townsend, 548 S.W. 2d 935 (Tex. Civ. App. 1977).
[40] Potter v. N.C. School of Arts, 37 N.C. App. 1, 245 S.E. 2d 188 (1978).
[41] Treps v. Racine, 73 Wis. 2d 611, 243 N.W. 2d 520 (1976).

the plaintiff was held not contributorily negligent when he fell into a hole in a parking lot adjoining the softball field where softball players customarily warmed-up. He did not have knowledge of the hole. A number of other cases[42] have alleged contributory negligence, including cases related to proceeding on stairs or hallways in darkness;[43] exceeding a proper speed;[44] doing something after being warned or forbidden to do so;[45] walking on steps known to be wobbly;[46] failure to be cautious when a reasonable person might anticipate a dangerous condition, such as entering a shower room;[47] diving into water[48] and water activities;[49] a drunk on the beach;[50] no protective mask in softball game;[51] an explosion;[52] fallen stall bars in gym class;[53] jumping off springboard with low clearance;[54] running into glass window behind basketball goal;[55] sleigh riding;[56] golf;[57] line soccer;[58] whitewater rafting;[59] volleyball standards;[60] and ice hockey.[61]

Warnings have played a role in contributory negligence. All five cited cases[62] had to

[42] Bartell v. Palos Verdes Peninsula School Dist., 83 Cal. App. 3d 492 (1978) skateboard on playground; Guidroz v. Travelers Ins. Co., 99 So. 2d 916 (La. App. 1958) step to platform; Jeswald v. Hutt, 15 Ohio St. 2d 224, 239 N.E. 2d 37, aff'd. 17 Ohio Misc. 3, 243 N.E. 2d 790 (1966) ice and snow in parking lot; Macon v. Stevens, 156 S.E. 718 (Ga. App. 1931) cannon over sidewalk; Meyer v. State, 92 Misc. 2d 996, 403 N.Y.S. 2d 420 (1978) footbridge railing; Nelson v. Duluth, 172 Minn. 76, 214 N.W. 774 (1927) park roadway; O'Brien v. Middle Rio Grande Cons. Dist., 94 N.M. 562, 613 P. 2d 432 (1980) motorcycle; Riddle v. Ins. Co. of N.A., 290 So. 2d 470 (La. App. 1974) dinner theater premise; Shannon v. Addison Trail H.S., 33 Ill. App. 3d 953, 339 N.E. 2d 372 (1975) dimly lit muddy shortcut; Wight v. State, 93 Misc. 2d 560, 403 N.Y.S. 2d 450 (1978) snowmobile struck dock; Wilkinson v. Hartford Acc. and Indem. Co., 400 So. 2d 705 (La. App. 1981) racing in hallway — glass panel.

[43] Cheyney v. Los Angeles, 199 Cal. App. 2d 75, 258 P. 2d 1099 (1953); Sanders v. Long Beach, 54 Cal. App. 2d 651, 129 P. 2d 5ll (1942).

[44] Nelson v. Duluth, 172 Minn. 76, 214 N.W. 774 (1927); Rockett v. Philadelphia, 256 Pa. 347, 100 A. 826 (1917).

[45] Carey v. Kansas City, 187 Mo. 715, 86 S.W. 438 (1905); Howard v. Tacoma School Dist., 88 Wash. 167, 152 P. 1004 (1915); Rice v. School Dist., 140 Wash. 189, 248 P. 338 (1926); Rome v. London & Lancashire Indem. Co. of America, 169 So. 132 (La. App. 1936); Turner v. Moberly, 224 Mo. App. 683, 26 S.W. 2d 997 (1930).

[46] Woodard v. Des Moines, 182 Iowa 1102, 165 N.W. 313 (1917).

[47] Orrison v. Rapid City, 76 S.D. 145, 74 N.W. 2d 489 (1956); Tweedale v. St. Petersburg, 125 So. 2d 920 (Fla. 1961).

[48] Cardinali v. New York, 1 A.D. 2d 1018, 151 N.Y.S. 2d 514 (1956); Carta v. Norwalk, 108 Conn. 697, 145 A. 158 (1929); Cooper v. New Braunfels, 264 S.W. 2d 448 (Tex. Civ. App. 1954); Druding v. Philadelphia, 374 Pa. 202, 97 A. 2d 365 (1953); Hoffman v. Bristol, 113 Conn. 386, 155 A. 499 (1931); Liguori v. Philadelphia, 351 Pa. 494, 41 A. 2d 563 (1945); Rogers v. Oconomowoc, 24 Wis. 2d 308, 128

N.W. 2d 640 (1964).

[49] Dendy v. Pascagoula, 193 So. 2d 559 (Miss. 1967); Ferguson v. Marrow, 210 F. 2d 520 (1954); Herring v. Mathis Cert. Dairy, 121 Ga. App. 373, 173 S.E. 2d 716 (1970); Larsen v. Santa Clara Valley Water Cons. Dist., 218 Cal. App. 2d 515, 32 Cal. Rptr. 875 (1963); Mendez v. State, 56 Misc. 2d 143, 288 N.Y.S. 2d 680 (1968); Rumsey v. Salt Lake City, 16 Utah 2d 310, 400 P. 2d 205 (1965); Williams v. Baton Rouge, 200 So. 2d 420 (La. App. 1967); see also Chapters 9 and 14.

[50] Ferrell v. Santa Monica, 26 Cal. App. 3d 374, 102 Cal. Rptr. 705 (1972).

[51] Hanna v. State, 46 Misc. 2d 9, 258 N.Y.S. 2d 694 (1965).

[52] Maki v. East Tawas, 385 Mich. 151, 188 N.Y. 2d 593 (1971).

[53] Quigley v. School Dist., 446 P. 2d 177 (Ore. 1968).

[54] Grant v. Lake Oswego School District, 515 P. 2d 947 (Ore. App. 1973).

[55] Clary v. Alexander County Board of Education, 19 N.C. App. 637, 199 S.E. 2d 738 (1973), 285 N.C. 188, 203 S.E. 2d 820 (1974).

[56] Romanchuk v. County of Westchester, 337 N.Y.S. 2d 926 (1972).

[57] Alexander v. Wrenn, 158 Va. 486, 164 S.E. 715 (1932); Jackson v. Livingston Country Club, 55 A.D. 2d 1045, 391 N.Y.S. 2d 234 (1977).

[58] Keesee v. Board of Educ., N.Y., 37 Misc. 2d 414, 235 N.Y.S. 2d 300 (1962).

[59] Harmon v. U.S., 532 F. 2d 669 (1975).

[60] Santee v. Orleans Parish School Board, 430 So. 2d 254 (La. App. 1983).

[61] Parsons v. Nat'l Dairy Cattle Congress, 277 N.W. 2d 620 (Iowa 1979); Sawyer v. State of N.Y., 127 Misc. 2d 295, 485 N.Y.S. 2d 695 (1985).

[62] Clem v. U.S., 601 F. Supp. 835 (1985); Dandurand v. Chebanse Recreation Center, 8 Ill. App. 3d 508, 290 N.E. 2d 276 (1972); Markowitz v. Arizona Park Board, 146 Ariz. 260, 705 P. 2d 937, rev. 146 Ariz. 352, 706 P. 2d 364 (1985); Rodrigue v. Ponchatoula Beach Development Corp., 151 So. 2d 157 (La. App. 1963); Rosa v. U.S., 613 F. Supp. 469 (1985).

do with water accidents. In the *Rosa* and *Markowitz* cases, both 1985 opinions, the plaintiff recovered. The court held in the *Rosa* case that the defendant willfully failed to guard or to warn against a dangerous condition and thus was liable for drowning death of a nonswimming child, while in the *Markowitz* case the adequacy of warnings regarding the depth of the water was at issue. The decedent in the *Clem* case, also 1985, was held to be contributorily negligent in that he had received information via brochure and film that the waters could be treacherous and he did not exercise the proper degree of care for his own safety. In both of the two earlier cases, the court held that warning signs were adequate, that persons 19 and 17-years-old who were non- or poor swimmers should have been aware and able to avoid danger.

Can a child be contributorily negligent? The majority position holds that a child of "tender years" is capable of contributory negligence. A child must exercise a degree of care for one's own safety commensurate with one's capacity, age, experience, and intelligence.[63] This is sometimes referred to as the "Massachusetts rule." A 12-year-old girl, while engaged in horseplay with a friend, injured her right hand when she rushed toward a door with three glass panels and, in looking back toward her friend, missed the "panic bar" and broke the glass with her hand. The court held that a girl of normal intelligence should have been aware of the danger of taking such action, and that her action constituted contributory negligence against which she could not recover.[64] In another Louisiana case[65] in 1985 there was a similar holding regarding a nine-year-old on a merry-go-around; child was found 50% contributorily negligent. In *Goss v. Allen*,[66] involving a 17-year-old novice skier who hit plaintiff while plaintiff was standing to take pictures, the court stated that certain activities engaged in by minors are so potentially hazardous as to require that the minor be held to an adult standard of care. Driving a motor vehicle, operating a motorboat and hunting also are so classified.

Some courts would hold that a very young child, such as a four-year-old boy who was killed playing in the park on some corrugated metal pipes when they rolled down crushing his head,[67] is not capable of contributory negligence because the child does not realize or understand the degree of care which must be exercised to save oneself from injury. Other courts, however, hold to the Massachusetts rule even though a child may be six[68] or nine[69] years old. The North Carolina court,[70] however, stated that a six-year-old is incapable of contributory negligence as a matter of law. Under California law a four-year-old is incapable of contributory negligence, and in Wisconsin it is seven years of age. Illinois holds to seven years of age and this arbitrary age is sometimes known as the

[63] Fusilier v. Northbrook Excess & Surplus Ins. Co., 471 So. 2d 761 (La.App. 1985), writ denied 472 So. 2d 918 (1985); Garreans by Garreans v. Omaha, 216 Neb. 487, 345 N.W. 2d 309 (1984); Hyde v. Utica, 259 A.D. 477, 20 N.Y.S. 2d 335 (1940); Lottes v. Pessina, 174 S.W. 2d 893 (Mo. Ct. App. 1943); Melerine v. State of Louisiana, 505 So. 2d 79 (La. App. 1987), writ cert. denied 507 So. 2d 226 (1987); Rosa v. U.S., 613 F. Supp. 469 (1985); Smith v. Harter, 84 Cal. App. 2d 361, 191 P. 2d 25 (1948); Suarez v. Omaha Public Power Dist., 218 Neb. 4, 352 N.W. 2d 157 (1984).

[64] Tyler v. Jefferson Parish School Board, 258 So. 2d 206 (La. App. 1972).

[65] Rollins v. Concordia Parish School Board, 465 So. 2d 213 (La.App. 1985); see also Richards v.

Marlow, 347 So. 2d 281 (La. App. 1977) writ denied 350 So. 2d 676 (La. 1977) full knowledge and appreciation of danger that wet feet could slip on a metal pipe, formerly part of pier substructure, 13-year-old.

[66] Goss v. Allen, 134 N.J. Super. 99, 338 A. 2d 820 (1975), rev'd. 70 N.J. 442, 360 A. 2d 388 (1976).

[67] Gottesman v. Cleveland, 142 Ohio St. 410, 27 Ohio Op. 353, 52 N.E. 2d 644 (1944).

[68] Grace v. Kumalaa, 386 P. 2d 872 (Hawaii 1963).

[69] Robertson v. Travis, 393 So. 2d 304 (La. App. 1980).

[70] Crawford v. Wayne Co. Board of Educ., 275 N.C. 354, 168 S.E. 2d 33 (1969); see also Kopera v. Moschella, 400 F. Supp. 131 (1975) Mississippi law applied.

"Illinois rule." Five cases[71] held that children of two, five, and nine could not be guilty of contributory negligence. Some states use a guideline of below 7 years of age not capable of contributory negligence, over 14 years of age capable of contributory negligence, and the between ages (8-13) dependent upon the circumstances and individual.[72]

And what about the contributory negligence of parents? It was held that the parents were not contributorily negligent for not supervising their children at play when the park undertook such duty.[73] Nor was a parent contributorily negligent, when a child wandered away while the mother was preparing the picnic lunch on the basis that it is not reasonable to have the child in mind every moment while preparing the lunch.[74]

§ 5.22   Assumption of risk and doctrine of volenti non fit injuria

The doctrine of assumption of risk means that a plaintiff may not recover for an injury to which one assents, *i.e.*, that a person may not recover for an injury received when one voluntarily exposes oneself to a known and appreciated danger.[75]

Assumption of risk was one of the two most common defenses until the advent of comparative negligence in the 1970s, when considerable confusion began regarding the applicability of the defense of assumption of risk. In some states[76] the defense was abolished by statute, while in others,[77] usually by judicial decision, the validity of assumption of risk was not affected by comparative negligence statutes. In some states[78] it is held that assumption of risk is subsumed into comparative negligence and is on one end of the continuum of acts by the plaintiff (see §5.23). Some courts make a distinction between implied and express assumption of risk (see §5.222), such as Nevada, which held in a 1987 case[79] that assumption of risk doctrine has been subsumed by comparative negligence statute, except for express assumption of risk; on the other hand, the Ohio and Florida courts[80] held that implied assumption of risk was merged

[71] Akins v. Sonoma Co., 60 Cal. Rptr. 499, 430 P. 2d 57, 67 A.C. 209 (1967); Brown v. Alexandria, 225 So. 2d 157 (La. 1969), mod. 226 So. 2d 600 (La. App. 1969), appeals den., 254 La. 844, 227 So. 2d 591 (1969); Denver v. Kennedy, 476 P. 2d 762 (1970); Latimer v. Clovis, 83 N.M. 610, 495 P. 2d 788 (1972); Randall v. Harrold, 328 N.W.2d 622 (Mich. App. 1982).

[72] Berman v. Philadelphia Board of Educ., 456 A. 2d 545 (Pa. Super. 1983) floor hockey after school; McGarr v. Boy Scouts of America, 74 Md. App. 127, 536 A. 2d 728 (1988) 11-year-old Scout fell over precipice into partially frozen stream during camping excursion on Scout property; Melerine v. State of Louisiana, 505 So. 2d 79 (La. App. 1987) writ denied 507 So. 2d 226, ten-year-old boy not contributorily negligent when he fell from tree platform on state-owned property because he lacked intelligence of average 10-year-old, had history of coordination problems, and failed to understand danger confronting him; Meyer v. Smith, 428 S.W. 2d 612 (Ky. App. 1968) golf club swung by 10-year-old hitting 13-year-old; Randall v. Harrold, 121 Mich. App. 212, 328 N.W. 2d 622 (Mich. App. 1982) five-year-old drowned in lagoon; Wallace v. Evans, 298 S.E. 2d 193 (N.C. App. 1982)

bicyclists.

[73] Demarco v. Albany, 17 A.D. 2d 250, 234 N.Y.S. 2d 94 (1962).

[74] Williams v. Morristown, 32 Tenn. App. 274, 222 S.W. 2d 607 (1949); see also Guillot v. Fisherman's Paradise, 422 So. 2d 1194 (La. App. 1982) 437 So. 2d 840 (1983) two-year-old wandered into sewage oxidation pond; see also §2.1231 attractive nuisance.

[75] *Black's Law Dictionary,* Fifth edition.

[76] For example, Connecticut, Massachusetts, Oregon, Utah.

[77] For example, Arkansas, Georgia, Kansas, Mississippi, Nebraska, Oklahoma, Rhode Island, Texas; Kennedy v. Providence Hockey Club, 119 R.I. 70, 376 A. 2d 329 (1977).

[78] e.g., Arizona.

[79] Mizushima v. Sunset Ranch, Inc., 103 Nev. 259, 737 P. 2d 1158 (1987).

[80] Collier v. Northland Swim Club, 35 Ohio App. 3d 35, 518 N.E. 2d 1226 (1987); Robbins v. Dept. of Natural Resources, 468 So. 2d 1041 (Fla. App. 1985) diving into shallow water. See also Smith v. Ferrel, 852 F.2d 1074 (1988) applying Iowa law, diving into shallow water.

into the defense of contributory negligence and is governed by the principles of comparative negligence. In New York, the court stated that comparative negligence melded contributory negligence and assumption of risk into "culpable conduct."[81] In a footnote of the *Rutter* case[82] opinion (1981) it was stated that 19 other jurisdictions have either seriously modified or abolished the assumption of risk doctrine; however, reports of the demise of the defense of assumption of risk are exaggerated, as evidenced in this section, in respect to sport in general, and particularly to skiing. A number of states have enacted assumption of risk statutes specific to skiing (see §8.4 skiing). Vermont law states "notwithstanding (comparative negligence statute)..., a person who takes part in any sport accepts as a matter of law the dangers that inhere therein insofar as they are obvious and necessary."[83] The essence of assumption of risk remains, even when subsumed by comparative negligence and is at one end of the continuum. The principles of assumption of risk must be understood, especially by those conducting activity and providing services. Normally, assumption of risk acts as a complete defense, while comparative fault mitigates damages.[84] Notwithstanding, some believe as the 1988 Louisiana court[85] stated: "Assumption of risk terminology should no longer be utilized... Adoption of comparative negligence statute eliminates assumption of risk as total bar to recovery,...instead, comparative negligence principles apply, and plaintiff's awareness of the danger is among the factors to be considered in assessing percentages of fault." *Because of the great diversity among states, check your own state for its approach.*

Much of the confusion on the status of assumption of risk as a defense comes from failure to distinguish primary and secondary assumption of risk.[86] A Minnesota court[87] stated it thusly: "Primary assumption of risk is assumption of well-known risks inherent

[81] Akins v. Glens Falls City School Dist., 75 A.D. 2d 239, 429 N.Y.S. 2d 467 (1980), rev'd. 441 N.Y.S. 2d 644, 53 N.Y. 2d 325, 424 N.E. 2d 531 (1981); Arbegast v. Board of Educ., 65 N.Y. 2d 161, 490 N.Y.S. 2d 751, 480 N.E. 2d 365 (1985); Locilento v. John A. Coleman Catholic H.S., 134 A.D. 2d 39, 523 N.Y.S. 2d 198 (1987) intramural tackle football; McCabe v. Easter, 516 N.Y.S. 2d 515 (1987); Mesick v. State of New York, 118 A.D. 2d 214, 504 N.Y.S. 2d 279 (1986) rope swing, swimming hole; O'Connor v. State, 126 A.D. 2d 120, 512 N.Y.S. 2d 536 (1987) bicycle race; Turcotte v. Fell, 123 Misc. 2d 877, 474 N.Y.S. 2d 893 (1984) considerable discussion.

[82] Rutter v. Northeastern Beaver Co. School Dist., 283 Pa. Super. 155, 423 A. 2d 1035 (1980), rev'd./ remanded 496 Pa. 590, 437 A. 2d 1198 (1981). For commentary on the doctrine of assumption of risk, specifically as related to the Rutter case opinion, see Joseph, Kenneth, Tort Law — Negligence — Assumption of Risk — Sports Injuries, 21 *Duquesne Law Review* 815-833, 1983; Champion, Walter T., and H. Patrick Swygert. Nonprofessional Sport-related Injuries and Assumption of Risk in Pennsylvania: Is There Life After *Rutter? Pennsylvania Bar Association Quarterly,* January 1983, pp. 43-52. Both commentaries set forth what is deemed the confusion of the doctrine of assumption of risk and state that in most instances similar results could have been reached without it. It is

acknowledged that under several circumstances the doctrine should persist.

[83] Rhode Island also has an additional section related to comparative negligence — "in any legal action against the state... or any political subdivision thereof, an operator or passenger of (1) a recreational vehicle... or (2) a snowmobile... or (3) an All Terrain Vehicle (A.T.V.) or (4) a motor vehicle primarily designed for use off public roads shall, while on state property assume as a matter of law the risks inherent in such operation insofar as they are obvious and necessary."; Carpenter v. Mattison, 300 Minn. 273, 219 N.W. 2d 625 (1974) held that operation of a snowmobile involves secondary assumption of risk.

[84] McPherson v. Sunset Speedway, Inc., 594 F. 2d 711 (1979).

[85] Murray v. Ramada Inns, 821 F. 2d 272, 514 So. 2d 21, 521 So. 2d 1123 (La. 1988), 843 F. 2d 831 (1988) swim pool; see also Stephens v. Henderson, 741 P.2d 952 (Utah 1987) roller rink.

[86] Becker v. Beaverton School Dist., 25 Or. App. 879, 551 P. 2d 498 (1976); Blackburn v. Dorta, 324 So. 2d 287 (Fla. 1977); Seidl v. Trollhaugen, 305 Minn. 506, 232 N.W. 2d 236 (1975); Sunday v. Stratton Corp., 136 Vt. 293, 390 A. 2d 398 (1978); Swagger v. City of Crystal, 379 N.W. 2d 183 (Minn. App. 1985).

[87] Wagner v. Thomas J. Obert Enterprises, 384 N.W. 2d 477 (Minn. App. 1986) roller skater.

in activity voluntarily undertaken by injured person and differs from secondary assumption of risk which is assumption of risk arising from negligence of others." Secondary assumption of risk is concerned with the plaintiff's contributory negligence, and it is this aspect which is affected by comparative negligence statutes. The negligence of the plaintiff mitigates the damages in accord with whether the state adheres to the pure or modified form of comparative negligence (see §5.23). Some would hold that secondary assumption of risk is a misnomer, since there is no acceptance of risk, but rather the plaintiff acts unreasonably and thus contributes to one's own injury. Secondary assumption of risk goes to the *conduct* (unreasonable) of the plaintiff, whereas primary assumption of risk is concerned with plaintiff's voluntary *consent* to encounter a known danger or risk of the activity in which the plaintiff wishes to participate.[88] There is no negligence involved on the part of the plaintiff in primary assumption of risk, whereas the plaintiff is negligent in secondary assumption of risk.

Primary assumption of risk[89] relates to the doctrine of *volenti non fit injuria* "no harm is done to one who consents," and is directly applicable to sport and adventure activities. The doctrine means that if one, knowing and comprehending the danger, voluntarily exposes oneself to it, but without negligence in so doing, one is deemed to have assumed the risk and is precluded from recovery for an injury resulting therefrom.[90] Simply, one who takes part in sport accepts the dangers that are inherent in so far as they are obvious and necessary.[91] "Precisely what dangers inhere in sport depends, of course, on the sport in question.... Inhere refers to those dangers that are the sport, the challenges without which the activity would not be sport at all, the intrinsic risks that the participants would not dispense with even if they could."[92] It is held that consent by plaintiff to assume these inherent risks of injury, as evidenced by voluntarily participating, relieves the defendant of an obligation to exercise care for the plaintiff's safety, that is, the defendant has no duty and with no duty to breach, there exists no basis for recovery by the plaintiff.[93] *However, a participant does not assume all risks, only*

[88] Kionka, Edward J. *Torts in a Nutshell*. St. Paul: West Publishing Co., 1977, at p. 138-9; see also Renaud v. 200 Convention Center, Ltd., 728 P. 2d 445 (Nev. 1986).

[89] Indiana refers to "incurred risk" and states it is a defense separate and distinct from contributory negligence and requires voluntary acceptance of known and understood risks. See Beckett v. Clinton Prairie School Corp., 494 N.E. 2d 988 (Ind. App. 1986) aff'd. 504 N.E. 2d 552 (1987) high school baseball player collided with infielder during practice; Clem v. U.S., 601 F. Supp. 835 (1985) drowning unguarded beach; St. Mary's Byzantine Church v. Mantich, 505 N.E. 2d 811 (Ind. App. 1987) church member fell on ramp from church kitchen to storeroom.

[90] *Black's Law Dictionary*, Fifth Edition.

[91] Cambareri v. Board of Educ., Albany, 246 A.D. 127, 284 N.Y.S. 892, aff'd. 283 N.Y. 741, 28 N.E. 2d 968 (1936); Dee v. Parish, 160 Tex. 171, 327 S.W. 2d 449 (1959); Ft. Worth v. Barlow, 313 S.W. 2d 906 (Tex. Civ. App. 1958); Kanofsky v. Brooklyn Jewish Center, 241 A.D. 739, 270 N.Y.S. 951 (1934), aff'd. 265 N.Y. 634, 193 N.E. 420 (1934); Murphy v. Steeplechase

Amusement Co., 250 N.Y. 479, 166 N.E. 173 (1929); Scala v. New York, 200 Misc. 475, 102 N.Y.S. 2d 790 (1951); Westborough Country Club v. Palmer, 204 F. 2d 143 (1953); Williams v. Lombardini, 38 Misc. 2d 146, 238 N.Y.S. 2d 63 (1963).

[92] Manby, C. Robert. Assumption of Risk After Sunday v. Stratton Corporation: The Vermont Sports Injury Liability Statute and Injured Skiers. 3 Vermont Law Review 128-146 at 141 (1978).

[93] Abee v. Stone Mountain Memorial Assoc., 169 Ga. App. 167, 312 S.E. 2d 142 (1983), aff'd. 252 Ga. 465, 314 S.E. 2d 444 (1984); Dailey v. Nationwide Demolition Derby, 18 Ohio App. 3d 39, 480 N.E. 2d 110 (1984) states additionally "primary assumption of risk...has nothing to do with doctrine of assumption of risk as a defense against negligence of defendant who has a duty to plaintiff."; Dorry v. Lafleur, 387 So. 2d 690 (La. App. 1980), 394 So. 2d 614 (1980), rev'd. on other grounds 399 So. 2d 559 (La. 1981) "Assumption of risk does not merely bar a plaintiff from recovery but rather says in effect that because of relationship voluntarily engaged in by plaintiff, as to plaintiff defendant has done nothing wrong; Grisim v. Tapemark

those inherent in the activity. The defendant still has responsibilities related to those aspects not inherent.[94]

In order for assumption of risk to be successful as a defense, three elements must be present: (1) nature of the risk must be inherent to the activity; (2) voluntary consent to be exposed to the risk; and (3) knowledge, understanding, and appreciation of the risk. Each of these three elements is discussed in subsequent sections.

§ 5.221   Nature of risks inherent to activity (sport)

What risks are inherent? First, the activity must be a normal, integral part of the sport, not extraneous to it. For example, the court held that when a third party was doing flip-flops with a girl on the pool deck, this was not inherent in swimming.[95] Likewise, injuries caused when a water skier sitting on a float was thrown off the float when a rope tow failed to "flip over" her were considered not a part of the normal risks of water skiing.[96] On the other hand, injuries occurring during an informal basketball warm-up,[97] on a trampoline,[98] in an extracurricular game of pushball,[99] losing control of a toboggan and running into a clump of trees,[100] being hit by a golf ball which was hooked or sliced by another golfer,[101] falling from some apparatus,[102] possibility of fracture on a wrestling maneuver,[103] dangers inherent in swimming, such as cramps, or slipping on wet surfaces,[104] bat slipping out of batter's hand,[105] scrimmage in football,[106] and a

Charity Pro-Am Golf Tournament, 394 N.W. 2d 261 (Minn. App. 1986) rev'd. 415 N.W. 2d 874 (Minn. 1987) golf spectator; Vines v. Birmingham Baseball Club, Inc., 450 So. 2d 455 (Ala. 1984) baseball spectator.

[94] Manby, at pp. 138-9; Moschella v. Archdiocese of New York, 48 A.D. 2d 856, 369 N.Y.S.2d 10 (1975), aff'd. 52 A.D. 2d 873, 383 N.Y.S. 2d 49 (1976).

[95] Stilwell v. Louisville, 455 S.W. 2d 56 (Ky. 1970).

[96] McDonald v. Hanneson, 563 Or. 612, 503 P. 2d 674 (Or. 1972).

[97] Albers v. Independent School Dist., 94 Idaho 342, 487 P. 2d 936 (1971).

[98] Chapman v. State, 6 Wash. App. 316, 492 P. 2d 607 (1972).

[99] Rubtchinsky v. State University, 46 Misc. 2d 679, 260 N.Y.S. 2d 256 (1965).

[100] Williams v. Poughkeepsie, 266 A.D. 874, 42 N.Y.S. 2d 495 (1943); see also Meyer v. Val-Lo-Will Farms, 14 Wis. 2d 616, 111 N.W. 2d 500 (1961).

[101] Benjamin v. Nernberg, 102 Pa. Super. 471, 157 A. 10 (1931); Campion v. Chicago Landscape Co., 295 Ill. App. 225, 14 N.E. 2d 879 (1938); Trauman v. New York, 208 Misc. 252, 143 N.Y.S. 2d 467 (Sup. Ct. 1955). Additional golf cases: Alexander v. Wrenn, 158 Va. 486, 164 S.E. 715 (1932); Allen v. Pinewood Country Club, 292 So.2d 786 (La.App. 1976); Barrett v. Pritz, 42 Ill. 2d 529, 248 N.E. 2d 111 (1969); Curran v. Green Hills Country Club, 24 Cal. App. 3d 501, 101 Cal. Rptr. 158 (1972); Getz v. Freed, 377 Pa. 480, 105 A. 2d 102 (1954); Jackson v. Livingston Country Club, 55 A.D. 2d 1045, 391 N.Y.S. 2d 234 (1977); Jenks v. McGranaghan, 316 N.Y.S. 2d 648 (1970), aff'd. 30 N.Y. 2d 475, 334 N.Y.S. 2d 641, 285 N.E.2d 876

(1972); Johnson v. Blanchard, 301 N.Y. 599, 93 N.E. 2d 494 (1950); Kelly v. Forester, Ky. 311 S.W. 2d 547 (1958); Mazzuchelli v. Nissenbaum, 355 Mass. 788, 244 N.E. 2d 729 (1969); McWilliams v. Parham, 269 N.C. 162, 152 S.E. 2d 117 (1967); Nesbitt v. Bethesda Country Club, 20 Md. App. 226, 314 A. 2d 738 (1974); Oakes v. Chappman, 158 Cal. App. 2d 78, 322 P. 2d 241 (1958); Pouliot v. Black, 341 Mass. 531, 170 N.E. 2d 709 (1960); Rindley v. Goldberg, 297 So. 2d 141 (Fla. App. 1974); Robinson v. Medling, 163 A. 2d 272 (Del. 1960); Schmidt v. Orton, 190 Neb. 257, 207 N.W. 2d 390 (1973); Turel v. Milberg, 10 Misc. 2d 141, 169 N.Y.S. 2d 955 (1957); Slotnick v. Cooley, 166 Tenn. 373, 61 S.W. 2d 462 (1933); Walsh v. Machlin, 128 Conn. 412, 23 A. 2d 157 (1941).

[102] Miller v. Board of Educ. (two cases), 249 A.D. 738, 291 N.Y.S. 633 (1936); Sayers v. Ranger, 16 N.J. Super. 22, 83 A. 2d 775 (1951).

[103] Reynolds v. New York State, 207 Misc. 963, 141 N.Y.S. 2d 615 (Ct. Cl. 1955).

[104] Cunningham v. Niagara Falls, 242 A.D. 39, 272 N.Y.S. 720 (1934); Payne v. Clearwater, 155 Fla. 9, 19 So. 2d 406 (1944); Pierce v. Ravenna, 174 Misc. 774, 22 N.Y.S. 2d 32 (1940), rev'd. 264 A.D. 457, 36 N.Y.S. 2d 42 (1942).

[105] Lutzker v. Board of Educ., 262 A.D. 881, 28 N.Y.S. 2d 496 (1941), affirmed without opinion in 287 N.Y. 822, 41 N.E. 2d 97 (1942). Additional baseball/softball cases: Dudley v. William Penn College, 219 N.W. 2d 484, Iowa (1974); Klinsky v. Hanson Van Winkle Munning Co., 38 N.J. Super. 439, 199 A. 2d 166 (1966); Richmond v. Employers' Fire Insurance Company, 298 So. 2d 118 (La. App. 1974); Tavernier v. Maes, 242 Cal. App. 2d 532, 51 Cal. Rptr. 575 (1966).

karate "leg sweep"[107] were all considered normal risks of the sport and were assumed
by the participant. For further description by sport, see specific sport in Part B.

Second, risk does not mean danger caused by negligence of the defendant. *For
assumption of risk to be a defense, and bar to recovery, the situation must be without
negligence on the part of the defendant.* Poor instruction, defective equipment, lack of
safety devices, faulty layout or construction, poor officiating, and dangerous environmental conditions are all aspects of participation which occasion an undue risk of harm
(and, hence, are negligence), which the participant does *not* assume. For example, the
courts held that the particpant did not assume the risks of the sport when injuries were
caused from positioning of diving board over too shallow water[108] an underwater anchor
on a diving raft which was not visible because of unclear water,[109] a diving platform
which broke under a 250-pound person,[110] ordinary glass instead of safety glass in a
door behind a basketball goal,[111] poor officiating,[112] poor instruction on basketball
drill,[113] a bench which had been moved into the playing area,[114] improper moving of an
injured player,[115] unsafe bobsled run,[116] nonregulation-sized baseball diamond.[117]

Further, as related to defendant's duty, in *Smith v. Ferrel,* 852 F. 2d 1074 (1988), the
court stated that the lake operators were not negligent inasmuch as it was not reasonably
foreseeable that a person would dive in shallow water so as to require placing of warning
signs or stationing of additional lifeguards, but that the one engaged in water sport was
deemed to assume reasonably foreseeable risks inherent in activity and that swimmer
had duty to take precautions commensurate with potential dangers involved which he
knew or should have known existed at lake under all circumstances. In this situation, the
plaintiff died into a man-made lake where the shallow depth of the water was easily
observable. Similarly, in *Perretti v. City of New York,* 132 A.D.2d 537, 517 N.Y.S.2d
272 (1987), the court said that by electing to play softball on a wet grassy field, the
plaintiff assumed the risk of the dangers inherent in the game, thereby limiting the
defendants' duty to exercise of reasonable care to make the conditions as safe as they
appeared to be.

It should be mentioned that in some instances the participant has the right to assume,
not a risk, but that there will be no undue risk.[118] Such is the case of an initiate in a letter
club who was electrocuted in a stunt.[119] He had the right to assume that all precautions

[106] Hale v. Davies, 86 Ga. App. 126, 70 S.E. 2d
923 (1952); Martini, Jr. v. Olyphant Borough Sch.
Dist., 83 Pa. D. & C. 206 (1952); Vendrell v. School
Dist., 233 Or. 1, 376 P. 2d 406 (1962); Whipple v.
Salvation Army, 261 Or. 453, 495 P. 2d 739 (1972).

[107] Kuehner v. Green, 406 So. 2d 1160 (Fla. App.
1981), aff'd. 436 So. 2d 78 (Fla. 1983) karate.

[108] Cummings v. Nazareth, 427 Pa. 14, 233 A. 2d
874 (1967), aff'd. 430 Pa. 255, 242 A. 2d (1968). See
also diving cases: Boll v. Spring Lake Park, Mo. 358
S.W. 2d 859 (1962); Englehardt v. Philipps, 136 Ohio
St. 73, 15 Ohio Ops. 581 (1939).

[109] Mendez v. State, 56 Misc. 2d 143, 288 N.Y.S.
2d 680 (1968).

[110] Starke v. Long, 221 Pa. Super. 338, 292 A. 2d
440 (1972).

[111] Stevens v. Central School Dist., 25 A.D. 2d
871, 270 N.Y.S. 2d 23 (1966), aff'd. 21 N.Y. 2d 780,
288 N.Y.S. 2d 475, 235 N.E. 2d 448 (1968).

[112] Carabba v. Anacortes School Dist., 72 Wash.
2d 939, 435 P. 2d 936 (1967).

[113] Strauch v. Hirschman, 40 A.D. 2d 711, 336
N.Y.S. 2d 678 (1972).

[114] Domino v. Mercurio, 17 A.D. 2d 342, 234
N.Y.S. 2d 1011 (1962), aff'd. 13 N.Y. 2d 922, 193 N.E.
2d 895 (1963).

[115] Welch v. Dunsmuir Joint Union H.S. Dist., 326
P. 2d 633 (Cal. App. 1958).

[116] Kaiser v. State, 55 Misc. 2d 576, 285 N.Y.S. 2d
874 (1967), rev'd. 30 A.D. 2d 482, 294 N.Y.S. 2d 410
(1968).

[117] McGee v. Board of Educ., N.Y.C., 16 A.D. 2d
99, 226 N.Y.S. 2d 329 (1962), app. dism'd. 12 N.Y. 2d
1100, 240 N.Y.S. 2d 165, 190 N.E. 2d 537 app. denied
19 A.D. 2d 526, 240 N.Y.S. 2d 242 (1962).

[118] Burgert v. Tietjens, 499 F. 2d 1 (1974).

[119] DeGooyer v. Harkness, 70 S.D. 26, 13 N.W. 2d
815 (1944).

had been taken for his safety. The same assumption for safety was made by an applicant for a position in taking a test.[120] And, in *Thomas v. St. Mary's Roman Catholic Church*, 283 N.W.2d 254 (S.D. 1979), the court held that the plaintiff did not assume the risk that the glass panel, in close proximity to a basketball goal, would be of ordinary glass unable to withstand impact; and, that reasonably assuming that the glass was safe, the plaintiff, thus, was unappreciative of the danger produced by the use of window glass. The pane itself, being opaque, did not give any indication that a hazard existed. See subsequent discussion (§5.222) regarding voluntary assumption of risks (dangers) known.

§ 5.2211   Violence by players/violation of rules

Is violence by players an assumed risk inherent in the sport? In the latter part of the '70s and early '80s there was increasing violence by players and concern over such actions. (See also §1.41322.) This violence has been noted particularly in professional sports;[121] however, this section deals primarily with amateur sports and violation of rules/violence by players. The rules of the game are designed for protection of the players, as well as the flow of the game itself, and, thus, violence by players and violation of rules resulting in injury usually are not considered inherent in playing a sport. The New Mexico court[122] said that "voluntary participation in football game constitutes an implied consent to normal risks attendant to bodily contact permitted by the rules of the sport; however, participation in a game involving bodily contact does not constitute consent to contacts which are prohibited by the rules or usages of the sport if such rules are designed for protection of the participants and not merely to control the mode of play of the game." Further the New York court[123] distinguished players are not held to have consented to acts which are reckless or intentional; however, where players understand and accept dangers of the sport, including carelessness, the player cannot recover. And, the Louisiana court[124] held that a participant in a game or sport does not assume the risk of injury from fellow player's acting in an unexpected or unsportsmanlike way with a reckless lack of concern for others participating.

In *Nabozny v. Barnhill*, 31 Ill. App. 3d 212, 334 N.E. 2d 258 (1975) a violation of a rule was integral to the injury. The plaintiff in an amateur soccer game remained in the penalty area, after receiving a pass, pulling the ball to his chest, and dropping to one knee; however, the defendant ran into the penalty area and delivered a kick which struck the plaintiff in the head, causing severe injuries. The court remanded the case after setting forth conditions under which a participant in an athletic competition might be held liable for injury resulting from infraction of a safety rule. In an earlier Illinois case[125] involving two players in a basketball game, the defendant struck the plaintiff

[120] Bard v. Board of Educ., 140 N.Y.S. 2d 850 (1955).

[121] Hackbart v. Cincinnati Bengals, Inc., 435 F. Supp. 342 (Colo. 1977); see Baicker-McKee, Steven. Comment — Violence in Athletics: A Judicial Approach, 3 *Entertainment & Sports Law Journal* 223-242 (1986).

[122] Kabella v. Bouschelle, 100 N.M. 461, 672 P. 2d 290 (1983) friendly game of tackle football.

[123] O'Neill v. Daniels, 523 N.Y.S. 2d 264 (1987) softball player struck in eye during warmup.

[124] Novak v. Lamar Ins. Co., 488 So. 2d 739 (La. App. 1986) cert. denied 491 So. 2d 23 (La. 1986).

[125] Griggas v. Clauson, 6 Ill. App. 2d 412, 128 N.E. 2d 363 (1955).

with his fist, who lay unconscious for about 15 minutes with the defendant standing over him swearing profusely and challenging the plaintiff to get up. The court found for the plaintiff.

Some sports such as baseball and softball permit some contact, such as breaking up a slide or blocking at home plate, but the question is really one of intent, although intent to injure may be difficult to prove. In *Borque v. Duplechin*, 331 So. 2d 40 (La. App. 1976) a base runner, presumably attempting to break up a double play, went full speed and standing upright into the second baseman, who was standing 4' to 5' outside the base path. As contact was made the runner brought up his forearm forcefully under the baseman's chin and severely injured the baseman's chin. While the court said that a participant does not assume the risk of injury from fellow players acting in an unexpected and unsportsmanlike way with a reckless lack of concern for others participating, it did hold for the defendant and in favor of the baserunner. Presumably intent to injure was not proven. An opposite result was reached in *Niemczyk v. Burleson*, 538 S.W. 2d 737 (Mo. App. 1976), when in a girls' softball game the plaintiff was running from first to second when the defendant shortstop suddenly ran into the base path and they collided.

A 1984 ice hockey case, *Overall v. Kadella,* 138 Mich. App. 351, 361 N.W. 2d 352 (1984), held that although participation in a game involves a manifestation of consent to those bodily contacts which are permitted by the rules of the game, an intentional act causing injury, which goes beyond what is ordinarily permissable, is an assault and battery for which recovery can be had. In this situation, the fight occurred immediately after the game in a bench-clearing melee. In a much earlier Canadian case,[126] a similar principle was stated, violent bodily contacts will not give rise to an action of negligence even though injuries may have resulted from an infraction of the rules of the game, but where there is a retaliatory blow struck in anger, even though provoked, it may have gone beyond the immunity conferred by participation.

§ 5.222   Voluntary (express or implied) consent

While the injury to the participant may have occurred due to something inherent in the sport, there is a second element which must be present to succeed with assumption of risk as a defense — the element of voluntary consent or assumption of the risk. It may be remembered that assumption of risk is based on the legal theory of *volenti non fit injuria,* no harm is done to one who consents. This consent may be express or implied.[127] These terms have been defined by a 1988 Louisiana case,[128] thusly:

---

[126] Agar v. Canning, 54 W.W.R. 302 (Manitoba 1965), aff'd. 55 W.W.R. 384 (1966).

[127] Keeton, at pp. 482-486; see law review article cited in footnote 121.

[128] Murray v. Ramada Inns, 821 F. 2d 272, 514 So. 2d 21, 521 So. 2d 1123 (La. 1988) cert. Q. adhered to 843 F. 2d 831 (1988) case opinion discusses origin of assumption of risk, the various common law categories, et al., states that it appears that 16 states have totally abolished the defense and 17 more have eliminated the use of assumption of risk terminology in all

cases except those involving express or contractual consent by the plaintiff; see also Collier v. Northland Swim Club, 35 Ohio App. 3d 35, 518 N.E. 2d 1226 (1987) diving from side of pool; Kirk v. Washington State Univ., 109 Wash. 2d 448, 746 P. 2d 285 (1987) same definitions, but terms "implied secondary" as "implied unreasonable assumption of risk", cheerleader injured on astroturf; Mesick v. State of New York, 118 A.D. 2d 214, 504 N.Y.S. 2d 279 (1986) rope swing, swimming hole.

"Express assumption of risk," otherwise known as express consent, waiver, or release, includes cases in which plaintiff expressly contracts with another not to use for any future injuries that may be caused by that person's negligence, and such contracts usually bar recovery by plaintiff, absent statute or established public policy against them.

"Implied primary assumption of risk," is alternate expression of proposition that defendant either owed no duty or did not breach duty owed, and involves cases in which plaintiff has made no express agreement to release defendant from future liability, but is presumed to have consented to such release because he has voluntarily participated in particular activity or situation that involves inherent and well-known risks.

"Implied secondary assumption of risk," or contributory negligence, is plaintiff's conduct in voluntarily choosing to encounter known unreasonable risk created by defendant's conduct.

Usually an express assumption is a matter or contract, where the parties expressly agree in advance that the defendant is under no obligation of care for the benefit of the plaintiff. Such agreement may take the form of a release or disclaimer.[129] The agreement must be made knowingly and voluntarily. Where the plaintiff is at such obvious disadvantage in bargaining power that the plaintiff would in effect be put at the mercy of the defendant's negligence, the exempting from liability for such negligence is usually considered against public policy and void. Such contracts, too, will not be enforced as to risks of willful and wanton misconduct or intentional torts. However, the doctrine of express assumption of risk, including express covenants not to sue and situations of actual consent such as voluntary participation in contact sports, may act as a compete bar to plaintiff's recovery against a negligent defendant.[130] Missouri enacted a statute[131], regarding consent as a defense, when there is joint participation in a lawful athletic contest or competitive sport. Does the purchase of a ticket represent a contract with express consent? Maryland,[132] regarding carnivals and amusement rides, enacted a law expressly stating that purchase of such ticket is not an assumption of risk on the part of the purchaser. Under express assumption of risk (see also §16.11) a plaintiff may undertake to assume all the risks of a particular situation, whether they are known or unknown to the plaintiff, but under implied assumption of risk, plaintiff's specific knowledge of a particular risk is required, so stated the court in *Madison v. Superior Court*, 203 Cal. App. 3d 589, 250 Cal. Rptr. 299 (1988), a situation involving scuba diving.

Implied assumption may come from the conduct of the plaintiff which infers consent to relieve the defendant from liability. Usually the situations may be divided into three

[129] Gary v. Party Time Co., 434 So. 2d 338 (Fla. App. 1983); O'Connell v. Walt Disney World Co., 413 So. 2d 444 (La. App. 1982); Provence v. Doolin, 91 Ill. App. 3d 271, 46 Ill. Dec. 733, 414 N.E. 2d 786 (1980); see also Chapter 16.

[130] Potter v. Green Meadows, Par 3, 510 So. 2d 1225 (Fla. App. 1985) golfer; see also Ashcraft v. Calder Race Course, Inc., 464 So. 2d 1250 (Fla. App. 1985) jockey.

[131] Mo. Ann. Stat. §565.080. See, however, interpretation of statute.

[132] Md. Code Ann. 56 §158A. See also Russo v. The Range, Inc., 76 Ill. App. 3d 236, 32 Ill. Dec. 63, 395 N.E.2d 10 (1979).

groups and in all three, the plaintiff would be denied recovery.[133] The first is that most common in sport and adventure activities — the participants and spectators voluntarily and knowingly enter into a relationship accepting certain inherent, but common risks of the sport. In such situation there is no negligence on the part of the defendant, and there is no assumption of the risks from negligent harm — acceptance only of those inherent risks of the sport, and the plaintiff acted reasonably in assuming the risk. The fact of participation in a sport is usually sufficient to establish implied consent to assume those risks which are inherent in the sport. Even where the judgment may not be as reasonable as it might, if obviously voluntarily engaged in, plaintiff is held to have assumed the risk.[134] Two 1984 cases caution, however, that engaging in a specific activity some may consider "dangerous" does not make the person negligent. In a jockey situation the court said that "the court accepted without question the reasonableness of the participant's decision to engage in the sport implicitly determining that such decision was in no way negligent or culpable."[135] And, in a mini-trampoline situation, the defendant failed to show that there was negligence on the part of the plaintiff, that is, that there was misuse of the equipment; the fact of use was insufficient.[136] In each situation the participant assumed the risks inherent in the sport, but not the negligence or willful conduct of the defendant. This first type of implied consent is what was previously described as primary assumption of risk; the other two types really fall into the secondary assumption of risk or contributory negligence category.

In the second situation of implied consent, the plaintiff voluntarily enters into some relationship with the defendant with foresight of the consequences, with the knowledge that there is a substantial risk that the defendant will act negligently; for example, taking a ride with an intoxicated driver, the driver being the eventual defendant.[137] The true basis of defense, however, is the unreasonable conduct of the plaintiff, or contributory negligence. While an act done under direction of superior or teacher and under economic or quasi-economic compulsion is not considered voluntary for assumption of risk purposes, decision to follow such direction still may be so unreasonable as to constitute contributory negligence.[138]

The third type of implied consent is when the plaintiff was fully aware of a risk which had already been created by the negligence of the defendant and voluntarily proceeded to encounter it; for example, a spectator who sits in an area that should be screened for protection, but obviously was not. If the risks lie outside the usual range of inherent risks, the participant's assumption of risk depends upon obtrusiveness of the risk in part, and in part upon personal recognition of the danger imposed (see next section on knowledge and appreciation).[139] The defense of assumption of risk was upheld where the

---

[133] Mizushima v. Sunset Ranch, Inc., 103 Nev. 259, 737 P. 2d 1158 (1987) horseback rider.

[134] Maddox v. City of N.Y., 90 A.D. 2d 535, 455 N.Y.S. 2d 102 (1982), 121 Misc. 2d 358, 467 N.Y.S. 2d 772 (1983), 103 A.D. 2d 900, 478 N.Y.S. 2d 923, rev'd. 108 A.D. 2d 42, 487 N.Y.S. 2d 354 (1985); Perretti v. City of New York, 132 A.D. 2d 537, 517 N.Y.S. 2d 272 (1987); Smith v. Ferrel, 852 F.2d 1074 (1988) Iowa law applied; Smith v. Seven Springs Farm, Inc., 716 F. 2d 1002 (1983) Pennsylvania law applied.

[135] Turcotte v. Fell, 123 Misc. 2d 877, 474 N.Y.S.

2d 893 (1984).

[136] Pell v. Victor J. Andrew H.S., 123 Ill. App. 3d 423, 78 Ill. Dec. 739, 462 N.E. 2d 858 (1984).

[137] Cooper v. Lunsford, 234 Cal. App. 2d 554, 44 Cal. Rptr. 530 (1965).

[138] Yarborough v. CUNY, 520 N.Y.S. 2d 518 (1987) college physical education for elementary schools, plastic sack race.

[139] Chase v. Shasta Lake Union School, 259 Cal. App. 2d 612, 66 Cal. Rptr. 517 (1968).

injured knew of the hazard: playing softball on an area formerly used for tennis with an old post bracket still remaining in the field,[140] skating with a young child on rough ice with saw-teeth skates,[141] colliding with a door jamb in a brick wall 2′ from a basketball backstop,[142] and tripping on a curb around a ball diamond field which was used to retain water for ice skating in winter.[143] The court also has held voluntary assumption of risk in situations such as sand on volleyball court,[144] wet spot from leaky roof,[145] crack in ice,[146] bubbles in synthetic surface of tennis court.[147] Assumption of risk was denied as a defense when the injured stepped on a broken bottle in a dressing room,[148] when a nine-year-old girl fell when the ring holding a swing broke,[149] and when a pedestrian in the park, using a short-cut walk, fell into a hole covered by snow,[150] and when an adult in an evening softball league using an elementary school field ran into a nearby concrete incinerator.[151] Also, there was no recovery where a 17-year-old high school girl was injured when participants in a football game she was watching, in the course of play, ran into her as she stood on the sidelines; the court held that obvious and necessary risks incidental to the game were assumed, especially when the spectator chose to view from an unsafe place despite availability of protected seating.[152] Similar results were recorded in two aquatic cases,[153] both involving diving into water. A participant does not assume the risk of delayed medical attention.[154]

The plaintiff's consent must be a free and voluntary one. There must be some manifestation of consent to relieve the defendant of the obligation of reasonable conduct. It should be recognized, however, that while the plaintiff may have made a voluntary choice, it is not conclusive that the risk has been assumed. There may be other mitigating factors. Further, even though the conduct may indicate consent, risk is not assumed if it appears from words or facts of the situation that the plaintiff does not in fact consent. If the plaintiff proceeds to enter voluntarily into a situation which exposes him to risk notwithstanding his words of not consenting, he does *de facto* consent. But, if the plaintiff surrenders against his better judgment upon an assurance that the situation is safe or that the unsafe situation has been remedied or there is a promise of protection, then the plaintiff does not assume the risk unless the danger is so obvious that the

[140] Bennett v. Scranton, 54 Lack. Jur. 81 (C.P. 1953).
[141] Cassady v. Billings, 135 Mont. 390, 340 P. 2d 509 (1959). See also ice skating cases: McCullough v. Omaha Coliseum Corp., 144 Neb. 92, 12 N.W. 2d 639 (1944); Moe v. Steenberg, 275 Minn. 448, 147 N.W. 2d 587 (1966); Rauch v. Penn. Sports & Enterprises, 367 Pa. 632, 81 A.2d 548 (1951).
[142] Maltz v. Board of Educ., 114 N.Y.S. 2d 856 (1952).
[143] Scala v. New York City, 200 Misc. 475, 102 N.Y.S. 2d 790 (1951). Additional baseball cases include: Domino v. Mercurio, 17 A.D. 2d 342, 234 N.Y.S. 2d 1011 (1962); McGee v. Board of Educ., 16 A.D. 2d 99 (1962).
[144] Podvin v. Somerton Springs Swim Club, 406 Pa. 384, 178 A. 2d 615 (1962).
[145] Dawson v. R.I. Auditorium, 104 R.I. 116, 242 A. 2d 407 (1968).
[146] Filler v. Stenvick, 79 N.D. 422, 56 N.W. 2d 798 (1953).
[147] Heldman v. Uniroyal, Inc., 53 Ohio App. 2d 21, 371 N.E. 2d 21 (1977).
[148] Orrison v. Rapid City, 76 S.D. 145, 74 N.W. 2d 489 (1956).
[149] Kelley v. School Dist., 102 Wash. 343, 173 P. 333 (1918).
[150] Stolpe v. Duquesne, 337 Pa. 215 9 A. 2d 427 (1939).
[151] Chase v. Shasta Lake Union School, 259 Cal. App. 2d 512, 66 Cal. Rptr. 517 (1968).
[152] Cadieux v. Board of Educ., 25 A.D. 2d 579, 266 N.Y.S. 2d 895 (1966).
[153] Fuller v. State, 125 Cal.Rptr. 586, 51 C.A.3d 926 (1975); Warner v. Bay St. Louis, 408 F.Supp. 375, motion denied, 526 F.2d 1211 (1975).
[154] Clark v. State, 276 A.D. 10, 93 N.Y.S. 2d 28 (1949), aff'd. without opinion, 302 N.Y. 795, 99 N.E. 2d 300.

plaintiff was unreasonable in relying upon such assurance. Even where the plaintiff does not protest, the risk is not assumed if the defendant left the plaintiff no alternative.[155] The doctrine of assumption of risk can apply only where a person may reasonably elect whether or not he shall expose himself to a particular danger, and it has no application where continued exposure to risks is due to lack of reasonable opportunity to escape after danger is appreciated.[156] Where there is a reasonably safe alternative available, the plaintiff's choice of a dangerous way is a free one, it will usually be considered consent or assumption of the risk.[157] In a Pennsylvania case,[158] it was a question for the jury to determine whether the student had a reasonable alternative course of action. The football coaches announced prior to summer vacation that there would be preseason football conditioning practice and implied that boys not participating would not be likely to make the team, and "jungle" football was a part of the conditioning practice drills and participation was expected in all aspects of practice, including "jungle" football. The question was whether the student was compelled to accept the risk of playing "jungle" football in order to exercise or protect his right or privilege to play football.[159]

The risk one assumes may be affected, too, by the plaintiff's status, whether an invitee or licensee. In a 1981 Oregon case[160] it was stated that if the skier left the trail on his own and not due to negligent marking of the trail route, then his status changed from that of invitee to licensee with an implied assumption of risk different as a licensee than as an invitee. (See §2.122 for further discussion of duty owed licensees.)

Where the defendant's negligence consists of a violation of statute, the plaintiff may still assume a risk. Certain statutes, however, clearly are intended to protect the plaintiff against one's own ability to protect oneself, including one's own lack of judgment or inability to resist various pressures. Since the fundamental purpose of such statutes is defeated if the plaintiff were permitted to assume the risk, generally the plaintiff cannot do so, either express or implied. Connecticut and California hold that the risk cannot be assumed on the ground that the obligation and right so created are public ones, which is not within the power of any private individual to waive. Policy of statutes overrides private agreements and undertstandings. A doctrine of public policy excludes assumption of risk in certain actions based on violation of safety statutes or orders. A Physical Education in the Elementary School Manual, however, was held not to be such orders with binding safety regulations adopted under authority of law.[161]

---

[155] Stearns v. Sugarbush Valley Corp., 130 Vt. 472, 296 A. 2d 220 (1972) skiing, path from restaurant to parking area.

[156] Elias v. New Laurel Radio Station, Inc., 245 Miss. 170, 146 So. 2d 558 (1962) bowling, substance on floor.

[157] Smith v. Seven Springs Farm, Inc., 716 F. 2d 1002 (1983).

[158] Rutter v. Northeast Beaver County School District, 283 Pa. Super. 155, 423 A. 2d 1035 (1980), rev'd./remanded 496 Pa. 590, 437 A. 2d 1198 (1981).

[159] The case held further that the doctrine of assumption of risk was abolished except where specifically preserved by statute, in cases of express assumption of risk, or cases brought under 402A (strict liability theory). See for commentary: Joseph, Kenneth. Tort Law — Negligence — Assumption of Risk — Sports Injuries, 21 Duquesne Law Review 815-833, 1983; Champion, Walter T., and H. Patrick Swygert. Nonprofessional Sport-related Injuries and Assumption of Risk in Pennsylvania: Is There Life After *Rutter? Pennsylvania Bar Association Quarterly,* January 1983, pp. 43-52.

[160] Blair v. Mt. Hood Meadows Development Corp., 48 Or. App. 109, 616 P. 2d 535 (1981), rev'd. 291 Or. 293, 630 P. 2d 827 (1981), rehearing denied, opinion modified 291 Or. 703, 634 P. 2d 241 (1981).

[161] Chase v. Shasta Lake Union School, 66 Cal. Rptr. 517 (1968).

§ 5.223   Knowledge, understanding, appreciation of risk

A third and important element of successful application of assumption of risk defense is that of knowledge, understanding, and appreciation. It is not sufficient to have knowledge — the old axiom of "advise and consent" is no longer viable. The standard as stated in *Prosser and Keeton on Torts,* at p. 487, is that "Under ordinary circumstances the Plaintiff will not be taken to assume any risk of either activities or conditions of which he has no knowledge. Moreover, he must not only know of the facts which create the danger, but he must comprehend and appreciate the nature of the danger he confronts." Since assumption of risk is based on theory of consent, actual knowledge and appreciation of danger assumed are essential elements.[162]

In a 1985 case,[163] it was held that in raising the defense of assumption of risk, the country club and golf association had to prove that a spectator, who was struck in the eye by a golf ball while attending a golf tournament, appreciated danger of being struck by a golf ball while in presumed area of safety at the concession stand on the golf course. Knowing danger exists is not knowledge or appreciation of the amount of danger, so the court[164] held when a 15-year-old girl failed to leave the auditorium where a "light show" was to be presented by students after she learned that no teacher (supervising) was present and a small group of students became noisy. The plaintiff was struck by a metal object thrown by the rowdy group, suffering permanent eye damage. Further, it is not enough to claim that plaintiff assumed the risks ordinarily incident to a game or activity, but that the particular risk was assumed. For example, not the risks incident to the game of racquetball, but the particular risk of playing racquetball with improper footwear.[165]

Rather than using the standard of "the reasonable man" of ordinary prudence, which contributory negligence does, the standard is specific to a particular plaintiff and the situation; assumption of risk is governed by the subjective standard of the plaintiff himself.[166] If because of age or lack of information or experience, one does not comprehend and appreciate the risk involved in a known situation, one will not be taken to consent thereto. For instance, the court held that there must be actual knowledge and that a beginning skier, although a university student, was inexperienced and, therefore, did not know the danger to which she was being subjected when the student employee did not test the release mechanism on the ski bindings when the skis were rented.[167] Actual knowledge (of the pilings) also was at issue when a water skier suffered fatal injuries when he fell and struck pilings.[168] And, in *Tepper v. City of New Rochelle School Dist.,* 531 N.Y.S.2d 367 (1988), although the student's parents had signed a consent form to allow student to participate on the lacrosse team, issue of fact existed as

---

162 Berman v. Radnor Rolls, Inc., 542 Pa. Super. 525, 542 A.2d 525 (1988) roller skating; Kuehner v. Green, 406 So. 2d 1160 (Fla. App. 1981) aff'd. 436 So. 2d 78 (Fla. 1983) karate; Renaud v. 200 Convention Center, Ltd., 728 P. 2d 445 (Nev. 1986) free fall simulator. See also *Second Restatement of Torts* §496D.

163 Duffy v. Midlothian Country Club, 47 Ill. Dec. 786, 415 N.E. 2d 1099, 92 Ill. App. 3d 193 (1980), aff'd. 135 Ill. App. 3d 429, 90 Ill. Dec. 237, 481 N.E. 2d 1037 (1985) golf spectator.

164 Viveiros v. State, 54 Hawaii 611, 513 P. 2d 487

(1973).

165 Cornell v. Aquamarine Lodge, 12 Ohio App. 3d 148, 467 N.E. 2d 896 (1983).

166 Cota v. Harley Davidson, 141 Ariz. 7, 684 P. 2d 888 (1984); DePew v. Sylvia 265 So. 2d 75 (Fla. App. 1972); Everett v. Bucky Warren, Inc., 376 Mass. 280, 380 N.E. 2d 653 (1978); Van Tuyn v. Zurich Amer. Ins. Co., 447 So. 2d 318 (Fla. App. 1984).

167 Meese v. BYU, 639 P. 2d 720 (Utah 1981).

168 Spivey v. Vaughn, 182 Ga. App. 91, 354 S.E. 2d 870 (1987).

to whether student comprehended nature of risk when he opted to join team and thus assumed risk of injury. There is, however, a "reasonable man" standard when things are quite clear and obvious.[169] The court held that the danger of using a trampoline was obvious, entirely voluntary, and for personal thrill involved as related to the 19-year-old plaintiff. Also, if plaintiff has been for a substantial length of time in the immediate vicinity of a dangerous condition, plaintiff will be taken to have discovered and to understand the normal ordinary risks involved in that situation.

Appreciation of risk works both ways; that is, the inexperience of a participant requires greater effort on the part of the leader, teacher, or coach to communicate the risks; and on the other hand, if a performer is young but experienced, such performer is held to assume those risks of which there is knowledge. For example, in the *Chapman* case[170] the court held regarding an 18-year-old that a proficient performer must exercise the same judgment and discretion in care for his own safety when on the trampoline as a person of more advanced years. Similarly, in *Hanna v. State*[171] the court said that the plaintiff was an intelligent young man who had played softball without a protective eyeglass guard for several years and had proper warnings of the dangers regarding not only failure to use the protective equipment but also the batting cage screen which would "give" when a ball hit it, and thus assumed the risks in participation. Due to experience, actual knowledge of a risk and its magnitude may be inferred from the circumstances. Such was the situation in regard to an experienced diver and the diving site.[172] Experience also was a factor in playing on a synthetic surface tennis court,[173] diving into a shallow pool,[174] skiing a trail,[175] riding horseback,[176] wrestling,[177] water skiing in a narrow cove,[178] and a 10,000 meter road race.[179] In the *Williams* case, experience knowledge was enhanced by written information on the entry form (see §16.133).

Comprehension of a risk also may be a factor of age. The court held that due to the child's age (11 years) and lack of comprehension and experience in her use of the cross-bar, there was not such an obvious and open dangerous condition impressed upon the child's mind as to result in assumption of risk.[180] There are not a large number of cases involving children and assumption of risk. One limitation on a child's right to assume a risk is the *in loco parentis* relationship of a teacher/coach/leader/counselor and participant; the child must not be permitted to decide to involve himself in considerable risk. This does not mean that there can be no risk. See §2.1112 for further discussion of *in loco parentis*.

A father brought action regarding injuries sustained by his 13-year-old daughter, who was seated approximately 35' from defendant watching the defendants toss horseshoes.

[169] Williams v. Lombardini, 38 Misc. 2d 146, 238 N.Y.S. 2d 63 (1963).

[170] Chapman v. State, 6 Wash. App. 316, 492 P. 2d 607 (1972).

[171] Hanna v. State, 46 Misc. 2d 9, 258 N.Y.S. 2d 694 (1965).

[172] Fuller v. State, 125 Cal. Rptr. 586, 51 Cal. App. 3d 926 (1975).

[173] Heldman v. Uniroyal, 53 Ohio App. 2d 21, 7 Ohio Op. 3d 20, 371 N.E. 2d 21 (1977).

[174] Benjamin v. Deffet Rentals, Inc., 66 Ohio St. 2d 86, 419 N.E. 2d 883 (1981); Christman v. Senyk, 63 Ohio Op.2d 37, 293 N.E. 2d 126 (1972).

[175] Leopold v. Okemo Mountain, Inc., 420 F. Supp. 781 (1976).

[176] Baar v. Hoder, 482 P. 2d 386 (Colo. App. 1971).

[177] Kluka v. Livingston Parish School Board, 433 So. 2d 302 (La. App. 1983).

[178] Knowles v. Vikery, 323 S.E. 2d 841 (Ga. App. 1984).

[179] Williams v. Cox Enterprises, Inc., 159 Ga. App. 333, 283 S.E. 2d 367 (1981).

[180] Robbins v. Camp Sussex, 28 Misc. 2d 16, 216 N.Y.S. 2d 176 (1960), aff'd. 218 N.Y.S. 2d 695 (1961).

The horseshoes slipped from the 14-year-old defendant's hand, rolled on its edge, bounced and struck plaintiff minor on the side of her head near the temple. Defendant had yelled "Look out," but at this specific time the girl was not watching and was unable to avoid being hit. The court discussed duty and foreseeability, as well as injury of a child while playing the games of youth. It was held that children must abstain from negligent acts and exercise a degree of care to which children of their age, experience, intelligence and ability are capable. There was nothing unusual or deviant from the game of horseshoes and it was held that the spectator plaintiff assumed the risks.[181] And, in a Tennessee case,[182] the court held that a 15-year-old honor student with no known physical or mental defects was charged with the same degree of care as an adult when she voluntarily submitted to ride in the dune buggy which was not equipped with any body, doors, or any device to hold onto or to restrain passengers.

The appreciation of risks extends not only to children of young age but also to persons of less mental capacity, as was held in *Brevard County v. Jacks*[183] where a mentally retarded girl was held not to appreciate the dangers of deep water in a swimming area.

Even where there is knowledge and appreciation of a risk, the plaintiff may not be barred from recovery where the situation changes to introduce a new element, such as where there were several balls in the air at one time in a baseball park.[184]

Since the basis of assumption of risk is not so much knowledge of risk as consent to assume it, plaintiff can assume risks of whose specific existence plaintiff is not aware; for example, a licensee who enters another's premises.

Assumption of risk (whether or not called contributory negligence) may bar recovery in an action founded on strict liability where plaintiff's ordinary contributory negligence may not.[185] Fault of victim (plaintiff) in context of strict liability means conduct of victim was substantial factor in causing injury. Assumption of risk is an aspect of victim fault.[186]

A number of other cases also involved assumption of risk as an allegation for participants.[187]

Just as players assume certain risks involved in participating in a game, spectators also assume certain risks.[188] Cases involving spectators at baseball or softball

[181] Carrillo v. Kreckel, 43 A.D. 2d 499, 352 N.Y.S. 2d 730 (1974).

[182] Walker v. Hamby, 503 S.W. 2d 118 (Tenn. 1973).

[183] Brevard Co. v. Jacks, 238 So. 2d 156 (Fla. App. 1970).

[184] Cincinnati Baseball Club v. Eno, 112 Ohio St. 175, 147 N.E. 86 (1925).

[185] Everett v. Bucky Warren, Inc., 376 Mass. 280, 380 N.E. 2d 653 (1978) hockey helmet case.

[186] Brown v. Harlan, 468 So. 2d 723 (La. App. 1985) motion to dismiss granted 472 So. 2d 26 (1985) motel pool.

[187] Brevard Co. v. Jacks, 238 S.2d 156 (Fla.App. 1970); Dendy v. Pascagoula, 193 S.2d 559 (Miss. 1967); Felgner v. Anderson, 375 Mich. 23, 133 N.W. 2d 136 (1965); Hanna v. State, 46 Misc.2d 9, 258 N.Y.S.2d 694 (1965); Latimer v. Clovis, 83 N.M.610, 495 P.2d 788 (1972); Ziegler v. Santa Cruz City H.S. Dist., 168 Cal.App.2d 277, 335 P.2d 709 (1959); Austin

v. Selter, 415 S.W.2d 489 (Tex. 1967); Campbell v. Peru, 48 Ill.App.2d 267, 198 N.E.2d 719 (1964); Larsen v. Santa Clara Valley Water Consv. Dist., 218 Cal.App.2d 515, 32 Cal.Rptr. 875 (1963); Rumsey v. Salt Lake City, 16 Utah.2d 310, 400 P.2d 205 (1965); Carroll v. Askew, 119 Ga.App. 224, 166 S.E.2d 635 (1969); Eddy v. Syracuse Univ., 78 A.D.2d 989, 433 N.Y.S.2d 923 (1980); Gregory v. Heater, 123 Ga.App. 406, 181 S.E.2d 104 (1971); Jolley v. Chicago Thoroughbred Enterprises, 275 F.Supp. 325 (N.D.Ill. 1967); Lincoln v. Wilcox, 111 Ga.App. 365, 141 S.E.2d 765 (1965); Stafford v. Catholic Youth Org., 202 So.2d 333 (La.App. 1967); Burgert v. Tietjens, 499 F.2d 1 (1974); Diker v. St. Louis Park, 286 Minn. 461, 130 N.W.2d 113 (1964); Nussbaum v. Lacopo, 27 N.Y.2d 311, 265 N.E.2d 762 (1970).

[188] Adonnino v. Village of Mount Morris, 171 Misc. 383, 12 N.Y.S. 2d 658 (Sup. Ct. 1939); Bennett v. Board of Educ., 16 A.D. 2d 651, 226 N.Y.S. 2d 593 (1962); Colclough v. Orleans Parish School Board, 166

games,[189] who were not behind protective devices, and were injured by flying balls or bats frequently deal with this principle. See §15.11 for further discussion on spectators.

§ 5.23 Comparative negligence

Dissatisfaction with the "all or nothing" rule of contributory negligence in the harshness of the result has resulted in a switch from common law to the civil law doctrine of comparative negligence. Comparative negligence eliminates the need for court-formulated exceptions to contributory negligence; and, since the plaintiff is no longer barred from recovery, the blameworthiness of the defendant's conduct need only be a factor for jury consideration in assessing proportion of fault.

The shift from contributory negligence to comparative negligence has been done largely by the legislatures. The courts have been reluctant because of the necessity to apportion damages without hard criteria. Each case must turn upon all its own circumstances — there can be no definite rules. Changing by judicial decision have been Florida[190] in 1973 and California[191] in 1975. Alaska[192] also made the change by court in 1975, and Michigan[193] several years later in 1979.

However, as early as 1910[194] the legislatures began adopting the doctrine of comparative negligence; but, the transition was very slow. Although Georgia[195] in 1913 by judicial action amalgamated two statutes, one which had been enacted in 1860, it was not until 1931 that the next state, Wisconsin, joined the side of comparative negligence. Nebraska and South Dakota had adopted in 1913 "slight-gross" negligence statutes, which both still have in the late '80s. But, it took about 25 years after Wisconsin's action for another state to make the shift, when Arkansas did so in 1955, and then there was another gap of about 10 years before another state (Maine 1964) overturned contributory negligence. By 1968, more than 50 years after the first state, Mississippi, had turned to comparative negligence, only seven states had made the shift. But, in the next five years 20 more states overthrew the common law doctrine of contributory negligence, and by 1980 another 10 had done so. Thus, by the latter years of the '80s, approximately four-fifths of all the states had accepted the comparative negligence doctrine, virtually eliminating contributory negligence as a defense barring recovery.

The doctrine of comparative negligence goes to the computation of amount of damages; comparative negligence statutes do not establish criteria for liability. The common law principles of negligence, as modified by statutes, continue to determine whether the plaintiff and defendant acted in accord with the proper standard of care. Under the doctrine of comparative negligence the plaintiff's damages are reduced in proportion to the extent of plaintiff's contributory fault, whereas the doctrine of

So. 2d 647 (La. Ct. App. 1964); Jones v. Kane & Roach, Inc., 182 Misc. 37, 43 N.Y.S. 2d 140 (Sup. Ct. 1943); Perry v. Seattle School Dist. No.1, 66 Wash. 2d 800, 405 P. 2d 589 (1965).

[189] Gordon v. Deer Park School Dist., 71 Wash. 2d 119, 426 P. 2d 824 (1967); Hoke v. Lykens School Dist., 69 Pa. D. & C. 422, 60 Dauph Co. 226 (1949); Kozera v. Hamburg, 337 N.Y.S. 2d 761 (1972); Robert v. Deposit Central School Dist., 18 A.D. 2d 947, 237 N.Y.S. 2d 680 (1963), aff'd. 13 N.Y. 2d 709, 241 N.Y.S. 2d 843, 191 N.E. 2d 901 (1963); Springer v. East

Noble School Corp., 495 N.E.2d 250 (Ind. App. 1986).
[190] Hoffman v. Jones, 280 So. 2d 431 (Fla. 1973).
[191] Li v. Yellow Cab Co., 13 Cal. 3d 804, 119 Cal. Rptr. 858, 532 P. 2d 1226 (1975).
[192] Kaatz v. State, 540 P. 2d 1037 (Alaska 1975).
[193] Placek v. Sterling Heights, 405 Mich. 638, 275 N.W. 2d 511 (1979).
[194] Mississippi.
[195] Elk Cotton Mills v. Grant, 140 Ga. 727, 79 S.E. 836 (1913).

contributory negligence bars any recovery by a plaintiff based on the mere existence of such fault. It should be noted that this is a rule of comparative fault and not comparative damages and that the apportionment is on the basis of fault or negligence, not on how much of the damage was occasioned by that fault. There seems to be a trend toward use of the word "fault," rather than negligence. Minnesota has entitled its statute "comparative fault" and embodies the term contributory fault, as does Florida, New Hampshire and Washington. The Arizona and Arkansas statutes compare "fault" and not negligence; and Iowa and Maine also refer to comparative fault. In 1987 Texas amended its statute heading from comparative negligence to comparative responsibility. New York compares the "culpable conduct" attributable to the claimant or decedent. The doctrine of comparative negligence presupposes that there is independent negligence or fault on both the part of the plaintiff and the defendant which is to be compared one to the other. Apportionment of fault is usually determined by the jury.[196] Factors influencing degree of fault assigned in determining comparative negligence include whether conduct resulted from inadvertence or involved awareness of danger, how great risk was created by conduct, significance of what was sought by conduct, capacities of actor, any extenuating circumstances which might require actor to proceed in haste, and relationship between fault/negligent conduct and harm to plaintiff.[197]

There are several different approaches which have been taken to the extent to which damages may be apportioned. The "pure" form provides for reduction of plaintiff's damages in proportion to the amount of negligence attributed to the plaintiff, even though it should exceed that of the defendant. Pure comparative negligence fully implements the principle of liability based on fault. About one-fifth of the states[198] adhere to the "pure" form. Impetus was given to the "pure" form when this approach was adopted in 1977 in the Uniform Comparative Fault Act by the Commissioners on Uniform State Laws. Fault is defined as including "acts or omissions that are in any measure negligent or reckless toward the person or property of the actors or others, or that subject a person to strict tort liability. The term also includes breach of warranty, unreasonable assumption of risk not constituting an enforceable express consent, misuse of a product for which the defendant otherwise would be liable, and unreasonable failure to avoid an injury or to mitigate damages."[199] Wisconsin enacted a statute supporting the modified version in 1931, but in 1962[200] by judicial decision changed to the "pure" form.

Most states have taken the "modified" form as their approach to apportionment of damages, which really is a compromise with contributory negligence. The states fall essentially into two categories — (1) those which state in the law that the plaintiff may recover if one's fault is "not greater than" the defendants (this permits recovery if the fault is determined equal), and (2) those which use the term "not as great as" or "less

[196] Fredette v. City of Long Beach, 187 Cal. App. 3d 122, 231 Cal. Rptr. 598 (1986) dived from pier in final construction stage; Taylor v. Tolbert Enterprises, 439 So. 2d 991 (Fla. App. 1983) slippery wooden steps due to water and sand in walkway across dunes to beach.
[197] Ladner v. Firemen's Ins. Co. of Newark, 519 So. 2d 1198 (La. App. 1988) 12-year-old motorcyclist

hit barbed wire fence.
[198] Alaska, Arizona, California, Florida, Illinois, Louisiana, Mississippi, New York, Rhode Island, Washington, Wisconsin.
[199] Iowa and Washington have this definition verbatim in their statutes.
[200] Bielski v. Schulze, 16 Wis. 1, 114 N.W. 2d 105 (1962).

than" (does not permit recovery if the fault is found by the jury to be equal). The "not greater than" or 50-50 apportionment has become the most popular at the mid-'80s, with 20 states[201] adhering to this form, and the "less than" states[202] numbering 8. There are some variations among the "less than" states. Idaho applies the "individual rule," also known as the Wisconsin rule, which compares the plaintiff's negligence with each defendant being sued and recovery can be maintained against any defendant where plaintiff's negligence is less. This is in contrast to the "unit rule" of most states where for recovery the plaintiff's negligence must be less than the aggregate of all defendants' negligence. In 1986 Minnesota modified its "joint and several" statute to provide that if the state or a municipality is jointly liable, and its fault is less than 35%, it is jointly and severally liable for an amount no greater than twice the amount of fault. Then, as previously mentioned, Nebraska and South Dakota use the criterion of "slight negligence," wherein the plaintiff can recover damages if one has exercised only slight contributory negligence in comparison to gross negligence of defendant. Kentucky case law[203] holds somewhat similarly in stating that the doctrine of comparative negligence does not mean that the plaintiff is entitled to a recovery in some amount in every situation in which some negligence of the defendant can be shown; plaintiff must show defendant's negligence was a substantial factor. Further, if defendant's negligence is overwhelming in comparison to plaintiff's, defendant may be 100% liable on the basis that plaintiff's negligence was not a substantial factor. Georgia by statute applies the "avoidance doctrine" or rule of avoidable consequences, whereby recovery for any damages which could have been avoided by reasonable conduct on the part of the plaintiff is denied.

There is argument regarding which of the forms is best, the "pure" form or the "modified" form with its two versions. As social philosophy regarding the right of the plaintiff to recover changes and the courts have experience in applying one or the other form, there will be changes. *Check your local attorney for current status of your state.* (See Appendix for citations of state statutes.)

How do the different forms work? Under the slight negligence modification of Nebraska and South Dakota, in *Wentink v. Traphagen*, 138 Neb. 41, 291 N.W. 884 (1940), it was held that anyone who voluntarily walks about in total darkness in a strange place, where no special circumstances require him to proceed, does so at his own risk and is guilty of more than slight negligence as a matter of law. Such negligence bars recovery.

In the "pure" form, the defendant may recover something as long as the defendant was negligent. The plaintiff, a child, was held 100% at fault in *Wilson v. Stephens,* 757 S.W.2d 297 (Mo. App. 1988). The jury found that the child playing football on the school playground ran into car while driver was looking for place to park, rather than that child was struck by driver's car. The driver was going very slow. The suit was against the driver, city school district and board of education, but the plaintiff received

<hr>

[201] Colorado, Connecticut, Delaware, Hawaii, Indiana, Iowa, Massachusetts, Michigan, Montana, Nevada, New Hampshire, New Jersey, Ohio, Oklahoma, Pennsylvania, Oregon, Texas, Vermont, Wyoming.

[202] Arkansas, Georgia, Idaho, Kansas, Maine, Minnesota, North Dakota, Utah.

[203] Carlotta v. Warner, 601 F. Supp. 749 (1985) Ky. law applied.

no award at all. In *Metzger v. Barnes*, 141 Cal. Rptr. 257, 74 Cal. App. 3d 6 (1977), the plaintiff water skier sued the boat operator and another water skier for injuries received. The plaintiff was in the water adjusting his ski without any flag or arm extended to indicate a skier was in the water. The defendant skier took off and not seeing plaintiff skier crossed the tow rope and not only severed it but also got the thumb of the plaintiff skier, who was holding onto the rope handle. The plaintiff had directed the boat operator not to pull in the tow rope. The court held that the plaintiff was apportioned 90% of the negligence and defendants 10%, thus under the "pure" form, the plaintiff did recover 10% of the damages.

In a 1981 New York case[204] the claimant, 18 years of age, was severely injured when a boulder fell from above and struck him on the left shoulder as he was standing behind a waterfall at the state park. While there was proof that signs warned park users of the dangers of falling rock and swimming was prohibited at the site where plaintiff was injured, it also was established that the path plaintiff took to reach the waterfall, used often by park employees and the general public, was one along which there were no signs. People had been swimming in the prohibited area. However, the conduct of the plaintiff placed him in an area of danger which should have been obvious to a reasonably prudent observer; in addition, he acknowledged awareness of signs which permitted swimming only in designated areas. The negligence was apportioned at 50% plaintiff and 50% defendant. The plaintiff's award was $400,000. A second 1981 New York case[205] involved a spectator who was hit on the head by a foul ball while sitting in the stands about 60' behind home plate and 10' to 15' beyond the third base end of the backstop. There was a 3' high, chain link fence for crowd control. Plaintiff alleged improper screening. The jury awarded damages of $100,000, apportioning fault 65% to the school district and 35% to the plaintiff. And, in a 1988 New York case,[206] the court awarded damages were $1.25M with apportioned liability (fault) 30% against student and 70% against school. A high school football player brought action against board of education and city public school athletic league, alleging negligence on part of coach and principal in permitting student to play in "mismatched" game in fatigued condition. The 30% against student was because he was a voluntary participant and did not complain of being tired.

The township was adjudged 66% liability and the plaintiff 34% in a case[207] where the plaintiff sustained serious eye injury when he fell on glass debris while playing behind a backstop of a municipally-owned baseball field near his home. In another New Jersey case,[208] an employee sued employer for injury sustained when playing softball on field owned and maintained by employer. Plaintiff employee allegedly tripped over a rock while fielding balls in right field. Jury found plaintiff and defendant each 50% negligent, and with $80,000 assessed damages, plaintiff recovered $40,000.

---

[204] Terry v. State, 79 A.D. 2d 1069, 435 N.Y.S. 2d 389 (1981); see also Grant v. City of Duluth, 526 F. Supp. 15 (1981) rev'd. 672 F. 2d 677 (1982) trespass in amusement park onto 30' slide, much effort by defendant to keep out people and to warn, plaintiff 30% at fault in wrongful death action.

[205] Akins v. Glens Falls City School Dist., 75 A.D. 2d 239, 429 N.Y.S. 2d 467 (1980), rev'd. 53 N.Y. 2d 325, 424 N.E. 2d 531, 441 N.Y.S. 2d 644 (1981).

[206] Benitez v. N.Y.C. Board of Educ., 530 N.Y.S. 2d 825 (1988).

[207] Williams v. Phillipsburg, 171 N.J. Super. 278, 408 A. 2d 827 (1979).

[208] Russell v. Merck & Co., Inc., 211 N.J. Super. 413, 511 A. 2d 1247 (1986).

A nine-year-old girl was riding the merry-go-round on the school playground during physical education class. While facing inward, she tried to get off the still moving merry-go-round and broke her leg. Child was held 50% contributorily negligent and, thus, damages were reduced by 50%. The school was held 50% negligent for failure to properly supervise.[209] In a Minnesota case,[210] a seven-year-old who ran into the street alongside the school bus and slipped and fell under the wheel was held to be 35% negligent.

In *Gerlat v. Christianson*, 13 Wis. 2d 31, 108 N.W. 2d 194 (1961), a 12-year-old boy and the neighbor's (defendant's) son had been given air rifles for Christmas and instructed in their use by the father of the neighbor boy in his basement. The plaintiff was struck in the eye by a pellet. The court apportioned the negligence: 20% neighbor boy (defendant's son), 35% defendant (father who gave instruction), 20% defendant's mother, and 25% plaintiff (12-year-old boy).

A 14-year-old student, with 48 other 14 to 16-year-old boys, reported to physical education class and began shooting baskets; the teacher left the gym, and the "game" developed into "roughhouse," resulting in injury to the plaintiff. It was alleged that plaintiff was contributorily negligent for knowingly participating in a "dangerous game" and for not following instructions not to engage in horseplay. Court held the apportionment of negligence between the rowdy 14-year-old plaintiff and absent teacher a matter for jury to decide. The student's negligence was decided to be at least 50% of total negligence.[211]

A hunter was accidentally shot by a companion while duck hunting. The jury found both negligent in failing to keep such a lookout as a person using ordinary care would have kept. The plaintiff was found 50% negligent, so was not entitled to recover.[212] One of the largest percentages of fault allocated was in a motorcycle situation, *Murphy v. Muskegon Co.*, 162 Mich. App. 609, 413 N.W.2d 73 (1987), where intoxicated motorcyclists hit a cable on a deserted county road, although there were visible signs. The two riders were found by the jury to be 96% and 99% at fault.

A licensee on the church premises was injured when she caught her foot at the base of a coatrack and fell. She had previously walked around the coatrack, which was in plain sight and not in a confined area, as well as being of standard type and mechanically in satisfactory condition. The court held that her negligence was at least equal to if not greater than the owner of the premise, precluding the right to recover.[213] In a 1984 New York case[214] the State was held to be 60% liable in a situation where the student at the University was aware of a wet floor in the men's locker room on other occasions, but the institution had notice of persistent accumulation of water on the floor which created a foreseeable risk.

In a golf course construction case,[215] the jury found that the golf course owner was

[209] Rollins v. Concordia Parish School Board, 465 So. 2d 213 (La. App. 1985). See also Mayer v. Tulane Medical Center, 527 So. 2d 329 (La. App. 1988) as exiting supervised playroom, 2-year-old child fell over wooden stick toy, child held 20% at fault, supervising clinic 80%.
[210] Faber v. Roelofs, 298 Minn. 16, 212 N.W. 2d 856 (1973).
[211] Cirillo v. Milwaukee, 34 Wis. 2d 705, 150 N.W. 2d 460 (1967).
[212] Lee v. Howard, Tx., 483 S.W. 2d 922 (1972).
[213] Stapleman v. St. Joseph the Worker, 295 Minn. 406, 205 N.W. 2d 677 (1973).
[214] Van Stry v. State of N.Y., 104 A.D. 2d 553, 479 N.Y.S. 2d 258 (1984).
[215] Loup-Miller v. Brauer, 40 Colo. App. 67, 572 P. 2d 845 (1977).

50% negligent with respect to defects in the golf course and also found that the owners had assumed risk of construction negligence. The defendants knew that the ground was not properly prepared for planting of grass seed in the fall, but nonetheless directed that seeding proceed. Such contributory negligence barred recovery against the architect and contractor on negligent construction of the golf course. In another golf case,[216] a golfer's ball went astray and hit plaintiff in a boat on a river (slow moving stream) which flowed through the golf course. The jury found the boater 30% negligent, the Golf Club 70% negligent, and the defendant golfer not negligent. A woman, who had slipped on algae on a boat launching ramp at a recreational facility operated by the county, sued for damages. The jury found her 60% negligent, but in her favor.[217]

A bowling alley patron examined 7-10 bowling balls and selected one which she considered to be of an appropriate weight, and also determined that the holes in the ball fit her fingers. She made the selection without assistance from defendant bowling alley personnel. She noted that most of the balls were scratched and chipped, but the one she selected, though chipped, she thought was in better condition than most. During the evening, plaintiff was injured when she fell and a chipped portion of the ball cut her finger. The jury allocated 80% of the negligence to the plaintiff, 20% to the defendant.[218]

For additional cases regarding contributing fault, see those cited for contributory negligence (see §5.21), since under comparative negligence the plaintiff must first be contributorily negligent or at fault and then the contribution is apportioned.

The shift to comparative negligence requires a number of adjustments regarding other defenses. In most cases, the effect depends in part on the wording of the particular statute, as well as the interpretation of the court; and, thus, the effect varies from state to state. Many issues are unresolved. First, inasmuch as the doctrine of comparative negligence was developed in response to the "all or nothing" rule of the doctrine of contributory negligence, the doctrine of contributory negligence, as a total bar to recovery for damages, is abolished by comparative negligence. While there are some differences, generally the doctrine of last clear chance (see §5.12) also is abolished. Texas court has said that "discovered peril" doctrine is incompatible with comparative negligence doctrine. There are a number of states which have abolished the doctrine in the statute, including Arkansas, Connecticut, Florida, Maine, Oregon, Texas, and Wisconsin; and, Wyoming says that it is "unnecessary." The effect of comparative negligence upon the doctrine of assumption of risk depends primarily upon the definition of assumption of risk (see §5.22). Comparative negligence statutes usually do not intend to negate common-law rule whereby parties may allocate liability by express contract.

As regarding the recreational user statutes (see §12.1), the Ohio court[219] stated that such statute was not merged into or modified by comparative negligence statute. And,

---

[216] Kirchoffner v. Quam, 264 N.W. 2d 203 (N.D. 1978).

[217] Metro. Dade Co. v. Yelvington, 392 So. 2d 911 (Fla. App. 1980), rev. denied 389 So. 2d 1113 (1980).

[218] Dixon v. Four Seasons Bowling Alley, 176 N.J. Super. 540, 424 A. 2d 428 (1981).

[219] Florek v. Norwood, 25 Ohio App. 3d 47, 25 OBR 180, 495 N.E. 2d 585 (1985) plaintiff dived into pool where shallow water not marked.

the Wisconsin court[220] held that comparative principles were inapplicable to intentional nuisance.

The question, also, has been raised when the comparison is the contributory negligence of the plaintiff and the willful and wanton misconduct of the defendant. The Illinois court addressed this in a 1983 case.[221] The court noted that historically contributory negligence barred plaintiff from recovering anything, while willful and wanton misconduct by the defendant permitted plaintiff to recover everything, even though negligent[222] — an all or nothing situation. But, the purpose of comparative negligence is to compare "degree of negligence" by the plaintiff and defendant, and thus it would seem appropriate to compare the two, contributory negligence and willful and wanton misconduct. However, the Illinois court found both parties with willful and wanton misconduct. The $4,047,000 award was apportioned and plaintiff received only one-third of the award. The plaintiff had dived into a lake, hitting a rock outcropping, with resultant becoming a quadraplegic. The California court[223] also addressed the issue of willful and wanton misconduct, holding that willful misconduct does not bar application of comparative negligence doctrine. Plaintiff fell off a balcony; court held plaintiff's voluntary intoxication was willful misconduct and apportioned 20% against plaintiff. On the other hand, Minnesota[224] held that the principles of comparative negligence do not apply to an intentional tort, but did apply where there was negligent misrepresentation.

Oklahoma, Oregon, New Jersey, and Texas are among the states discussing exemplary damages and gross negligence as related to comparative negligence. The result is mixed. Some take the view that with apportionment, the degrees of negligence are not applicable any longer. Others indicate that there can be gross negligence, which is not a bar to exemplary damages,[225] nor is a willful tort a bar to exemplary damages. Generally under negligence common law, punitive or exemplary damages are not assessed.

There is considerable controversy as to the application of comparative negligence doctrine in strict liability situations, particularly product liability. The greater number of states[226] would have the doctrine and its apportionment among tortfeasors and plaintiff apply, while others[227] would hold no application. At issue is whether a product liability suit is brought on the theory of breach of warranty or theory of strict liability in tort. Texas by statute provides that for plaintiff to recover, on basis of strict liability, the plaintiff's percentage of responsibility must be less than 60%. (See §21.1 for further discussion of Product Liability.)

[220] Crest Chevrolet-Oldsmobile-Cadillac, Inc. v. Willemsen, 129 Wis. 2d 129, 384 N.W. 2d 692 (1986) plaintiff alleged development of adjoining property had caused accumulation of surface water.

[221] Davis v. U.S., 716 F. 2d 418 (1983) Illinois law applied.

[222] Melendres v. Soales, 105 Mich. App. 73, 306 N.W. 2d 399 (1981) plaintiff dived from dock into shallow murky water, court said that where defendant intentionally commits a tort, comparative negligence is no defense which can serve to reduce his potential liability.

[223] Zavala v. Regents of the Univ. of Cal., 125 Cal. App. 3d 646, 178 Cal. Rptr. 185 (1981).

[224] Florenzano v. Olson, 358 N.W.2d 175 (Minn. App. 1984) rev'd. 387 N.W. 2d 168 (Minn. 1986).Social Security situation, not sport or recreation.

[225] e.g., Pedernales Elec. Co-op, Inc. v. Schulz, 583 S.W. 2d 882 (Tex. Civ. App. 1979) mast of sailboat came in contact with power line, comparative negligence statute did not abolish gross negligence and an award of punitive damages was allowable.

[226] For example, Alaska, Arizona, California, Connecticut, Hawaii, Iowa, Kansas, Louisana, Nebraska, New Jersey, Rhode Island, Washington.

[227] For example, Colorado, Nevada, North Dakota, Oklahoma, Washington.

Another element at issue with comparative negligence is its effect on the right to contribution among joint tortfeasors and the joint and several liability of joint tortfeasors, especially since damages are apportioned. There does not seem to be any effect at all — that the rule of the state is still operative.[228] One of the most extreme cases is *Walt Disney World Co. v. Wood,* 489 So. 2d 61 (Fla. App. 1986) aff'd 515 So. 2d 198 (Fla. 1987), in which the plaintiff was held to be 14% at fault and Walt Disney World only 1% at fault, but because of the joint and several doctrine operative in Florida, Walt Disney World had to pay 86% of the damages awarded. (See §2.43 Apportionment of damages.) The general rule is that the plaintiff may collect against one or all, but may not exceed the amount awarded. If one defendant comes under governmental immunity, the other must pay the apportioned amount for defendants. In a football case,[229] jury found plaintiff's actual damages $1.8M with plaintiff's comparative fault 40% and the Oregon State Athletic Association (OSAA) 60%. The school district was immune, but had paid a $100,000 settlement. Court reduced the $1.8M by 40%, then deducted the settlement to arrive at the damages plaintiff was entitled from OSAA. Out-of-court settlements also were taken into account by the court in a snow-slide case in a national park.[230] Prior to the trial, the plaintiff settled for $50,000 with one defendant ($25,000 each the plaintiff and her mother); and, during the trial settled with another defendant for $200,000 (of which only $5,000 was for the mother). The lower court found another defendant negligent and a fourth one not negligent. The jury found plaintiff had sustained $851,000 total damages, deducted the amount ($220,000) which had already been paid and took 40% (comparative negligence amount) of that figure $252,400 (rather than taking 40% of the total, then subtracting the amount paid, as in the *Peterson* case) to assess against the defendant the court found negligent.

A defendant who has paid more than one's apportioned fault may ask for contribution from other tortfeasors. A number of states[231] specifically state the rule regarding joint tortfeasors as part of the comparative negligence law. For further discussion, see §2.43 Apportionment of damages (joint tortfeasors.)

§ 5.3   Defenses in which acts of plaintiff or defendant immaterial

The defenses in this category are not concerned with the nature of the act of either the plaintiff or defendant, whether it is negligent or not, but seek to have the suit dismissed on some basis that would bar the action. The case is never decided "on its merits" for the issue of negligence is never decided. There are three types — (1) immunity doctrines, either governmental/sovereign or charitable; (2) procedural noncompliance, which includes the statute of limitations, notice of claim, and wrong party sued; and (3) exculpatory clauses.

---

[228] American Motorcycle Ass'n v. Superior Court, 20 Cal. 3d 578, 146 Cal. Rptr. 182, 578 P. 2d 899 (1978).

[229] Peterson v. Multnomah Co. School Dist., 60 Ore. App. 81, 668 P. 2d 385 (1983).

[230] Jones v. U.S., 693 F. 2d 1299 (1982). This citation is the appeal — plaintiff appealed on the defendant found not negligent; lower court decision affirmed.

[231] For example, Idaho, Montana, Nevada, New Jersey, North Dakota, Ohio, Oregon, Pennsylvania, Texas.

§ 5.31   Immunity as a defense — governmental/sovereign and charitable

The doctrine of governmental/sovereign immunity as a bar to liability is available only to a governmental entity, such as a school or municipality or the state; it is not available to an individual or to a semi-public organization or private enterprise. This doctrine is discussed in detail in §4.1. Blanket governmental immunity is no longer available in most jurisdictions. Immunity has been modified by the Tort Claims Acts (see §4.2). The states have certain immunity to suit under the Eleventh Amendment to the Constitution (see intro. to Chp. 4). The doctrine of charitable immunity, discussed in §4.3, as related to eleemosynary organizations, also has been abolished in most jurisdictions. A specific immunity, however, is afforded certain food donors (see §4.31).

§ 5.32   Procedural noncompliance and jurisdictional issues

A court must have jurisdiction, the power of a court to hear and decide a case. Thus, a case brought in a court without proper jurisdiction is subject to dismissal. There are two primary types of jurisdiction, jurisdiction in personam and substantive jurisdiction. Jurisdiction in personam or personal jurisdiction is the power which the court has over the defendant's person. There must be some contact with the defendant in the geographical area which that particular court services. Common ways to establish personal jurisdiction are residency, driver's license, and business activity. But also, jurisdiction can be established when a defendant may injure a person within the geographical boundaries, for example, an automobile accident which occurs while a group is on a field trip to another state. When state boundaries are crossed and plaintiff and defendant are from different states, this usually is referred to as diversity of citizenship. The federal court can take jurisdiction of cases between citizens of two different states or between a citizen of a state and an alien.

A court may have jurisdiction in personam, but still not be the appropriate court because it lacks substantive jurisdiction or jurisdiction of the subject matter. That is, the court lacks power or authority to hear the type of case being brought. For example, a state court is not the proper court to hear a case involving federal law, such as a violation of human rights under the U.S. Constitution or federal statutes. Some courts require a certain minimum amount of money, such as $10,000, to be at stake in the litigation. And, some courts have limited jurisdiction, being established to hear only cases of a particular type, such as a probate or juvenile court might be.

The plaintiff or entity bringing the suit also has certain restrictions regarding the right to bring suit. The plaintiff must have "standing to sue"; that is, the plaintiff must have a legally protected and tangible interest at stake in the litigation. Usually to have standing a plaintiff must meet three criteria: (1) that the action in question did in fact cause an injury, whether economic or otherwise, to the plaintiff; (2) that the interest to be protected is substantial to the plaintiff, that is, the plaintiff must be involved directly and not have only a peripheral interest; and (3) that the interest at issue is within the zone of interests to be protected by the Constitution, legislative enactments, or judicial principles. Standing to sue may be in issue when a student-athlete brings action, or a sport association such as the NCAA or an amateur sport association; or, when citizens bring action on environmental concerns. For example, in *Georgia H.S.A.A. v. Waddell*, 248 Ga. 542, 285 S.E. 2d 7 (1981) the court held that courts of equity in Georgia do not have authority to review decisions of football referrees because such decisions do not present judicial controversies. And, players who were not members of a baseball corporation did not have standing to sue regarding the corporation's rule in *Assmus v. Little League Baseball, Inc.*, 70 Misc. 2d 1038, 334 N.Y.S.2d 982 (1972). A spectator was successful in bringing suit for an injunction preventing the state high school athletic association from enforcing a ruling that prohibited her high school team from playing any athletic contests for one year if she was in attendance as a fan because of a dispute she had had with a referee, in *Watkins v. Louisiana* H.S.A.A., 301 So. 2d 695 (La. App. 1974). And, in *Florida H.S.A.A. v. Bradshaw*, 369 So. 2d 398 (Fla. App. 1979), it was determined that neither the coach nor team players had standing to assert a denial of equal protection to an individual player.

In addition to jurisdictional issues, there often are procedures with which the plaintiffs and defendants must comply. The Tort Claims Statutes have set forth a number of procedures to be followed (see §4.25). One of these is notice-of-claim, which is discussed in a subsequent sub-section. Statutes of limitation, too, is a procedure with which the plaintiff must comply in order to bring a law suit successfully. This procedure also is discussed more fully in a sub-section.

§ 5.321   Statutes of limitation or limitation of actions

All states have statutes related to limitation of actions by restricting the length of time in which a suit may be filed after injury. The defense would be that the statute of limitations has run, which means, too long a time has lapsed between date of injury and filing the claim. The general statutes of limitation are applicable to all, except as otherwise defined by other statutes. Actions for damages can arise from many sources, such as contract, real property, tort, and many other more specific sources, and the length of time (number of years) will vary according to nature of the claim, ranging from one year to as many as 15 in certain situations. Claims related to real estate tend to have a longer time, such as six to ten years. Tort claims, more specifically, personal injuries, normally have a two- or three-year statute of limitation, with two years being more predominant.

The statute of limitation period begins running when the injury is sustained. For example, in *Nelson v. Twin Bridges High School*, 181 Mont. 318, 529 P. 2d 722 (1979), the plaintiff was injured in a student-faculty basketball game on April 29, 1974. Plaintiff alleged that he filed a claim for damages with "the proper officials of defendant" on March 3, 1977, but no suit was filed until October 31, 1977. Defendants alleged that the action was barred by the three-year statute of limitations and the court so held. Time began to run at the time of injury, that is, the date of the player's cause of action and not on the date he presented his claim to the school officials.

Most states provide for extending the time period for certain disabilities, such as being physically or mentally incapable, and for being under the age of majority, whether it be 18 or 21 in the specific state. It is this latter extension of time that is of concern to personnel in recreation and parks, physical education and athletics, and camping. A child may be injured when 10 years of age and the two-year statute of limitations would not begin running until the child reached the age of majority, let's say 21, which would mean that a suit could be filed up to 13 years after the injury occurred. It is for this reason that excellent accident reports must be maintained on file until the statute of limitations has indeed run (see § 24.823 on accident forms.) *Be sure to check your own state to determine the various lengths of time limiting actions.*

Most Tort Claims Acts (discussed in §4.25) make some provision for limiting the time in which claims may be filed. Most of the states[232] specifying the time indicate two years, although a few[233] have three years, and New Hampshire gives four years. Wyoming has a slightly different approach with one year after claim is filed and if the injured is seven years or younger, two years or eighth birthday, whichever is greater (longer). About three-fourths of the states, however, have another provision limiting the time for indicating intention of suing. This is the notice-of-claim, which is discussed more fully in a following paragraph subsection. (In looking up length of time in which claims can be presented to a governmental entity, whether municipality, school, or state, money claims should be distinguished from personal injury or property actions.)

There are a number of specialized acts which usually indicate limitations for bringing actions, such as Product Liability Acts[234] and professional malpractice, particularly medical malpractice.[235] There are a few special acts relating to sport, such as a one-year statute of limitation in skiing[236] (see §8.4).

The courts do not favor the defense of statute of limitations, and where there may be two statutes involved, the one giving the litigant the longer period of time is preferred.[237] In a Utah case[238] it was held that the statute of limitation defense should not protect one who fraudulently conceals another's right of action against him. A Florida case[239] distinguished a 12 month statute of limitation relating to liability of cities and villages for damage to person or property and trespass upon real property, from a three year statute of limitation relating to recovery of real property.

§ 5.322   Notice-of-claim statutes

Notice-of-claim statutes are founded on the doctrine of sovereign/governmental immunity. Typically, notice requirements are written into the legislation waiving or modifying immunity. More than one-half of the states have included such requirements in their statutes. (See §4.25 and Table 4.1 for states and length of time designated.) The notice of claim statutes are in essence statutes of limitation. They require a condition

---

[232] For example, Idaho, Illinois, Iowa, Kansas, Maine, Nebraska, New Jersey, New Mexico, Oregon, Virginia.

[233] For example, Massachusetts, Montana, North Dakota.

[234] Number of years varies quite widely (see §21.1); e.g., Nichols v. Swimquip, 171 Cal. App. 3d 216, 217 Cal. Rptr. 272 (1985) ten years, diving platform; Wentworth v. Kawasaki, Inc., 508 F. Supp. 1114 (1981) N.H. law applied, four years, snowmobile.

[235] For example, Indiana, New Hampshire.

[236] For example, Vermont. Atkins v. Jiminy Peak, Inc., 401 Mass. 81, 514 N.E. 2d 850 (1987); Weiner v. Sherburne Corp., 348 F. Supp. 797 (1972).

[237] Lunday v. Vogelmann, 213 N.W. 2d 904 (Iowa 1973); Sprung v. Rasmussen, 180 N.W. 2d 430 (Iowa 1970); Vermeer v. Sneller, 190 N.W. 2d 389 (Iowa 1971).

[238] Rice v. Granite School Dist., 23 Utah 2d 22, 456 P. 2d 159 (1969).

[239] Visconti v. Titusville, 269 So. 2d 693 (Florida 1972).

precedent to the right to maintain a suit.[240] Instead of giving a statutory remedy, they are a statutory limitation on the remedy. Because the effect of the notice requirements in fact negates the usual statutes of limitation,[241] reducing the amount of time an injured person had to file a claim, the issue of constitutionality has been raised. Five states[242] have held favorably toward the contentions of unconstitutionality, while other states[243] held the statutes constitutional. Montana[244] held the time limit of 120 days as unconstitutional, in violation of the statute of limitation, but retained the requirement that a claim must be filed. The arguments center on elements of due process and on equal protection.[245] Inasmuch as suing the government is usually deemed to be a privilege, rather than a right, to place certain limitations on suits against governmental agency, that is, the notice of claim provisions, was held not to involve fundamental rights. In some jurisdictions the unconstitutional issue was mitigated somewhat by extensions of time for incapacitated persons and minors,[246] and New York[247] in 1981 gave discretionary power to the court to extend the time. The Georgia court held that purchase of insurance waiver of sovereign immunity did not abrogate the special tort claim notice provisions.[248]

The primary reasons given for allowing governmental agencies to limit their tort liability through the notice requirement are that (1) notice provides an opportunity to investigate claims while facts are fresh and witnesses readily available; (2) notice protects against stale or fraudulent claims and connivance of public officials; (3) rather immediate action enables the correction of deficient facilities and functions before more people suffer injuries; (4) notice affords an opportunity for negotiation and settlement without litigation; (5) governmental agencies can plan better for fiscal needs; and, (6) damages may be minimized by prompt intervention. While the reasons for the notice requirements are equally valid for private as well as public entities, the provisions are generally part of the governmental tort claims act or statutes and are not applicable to institutions such as private schools.[249]

Notice-of-claim statutes essentially provide that notice of intent to file suit must be given within a specified number of days (see Table 4.1 for number of days by states) and,

[240] Campbell v. Lincoln, 195 Neb. 703, 240 N.W. 2d 339 (1976); D'Andrea v. City of Glen Cove Public Schools, 533 N.Y.S. 2d 456 (1988); Madore v. Baltimore County, 34 Md. App. 340, 367 A. 2d 54 (1976); Rodgers v. Martinsville School Corp., 521 N.E.2d 1322 (Ind. App. 1988).

[241] Johnson v. Fairbanks, Alaska, 583 P. 2d 181 (1978).

[242] Michigan, Montana, Nevada, Washington, West Virginia.

[243] For example, Alabama, Indiana, Iowa, Nebraska, South Dakota, Wisconsin.

[244] Noll v. City of Bozeman, 166 Mont. 504, 534 P. 2d 880 (1975).

[245] For discussion, see Fleming, John B., Jr. Notice of Claim Requirements: Judicial and Constitutional Limitations, 14 Wake Forest Law Review 215-230 (1978); Notice of Claim Requirement under the Minnesota Municipal Tort Liability Act, 4 William Mitchell Law Review 93-118 (1978); Case Notes: Torts —

Municipal Tort Liability — Kossak v. Stalling, 277 N.W. 2d 30 (Minn. 1979), 6 William Mitchell Law Review 490-499 (1980).

[246] Antonopoulos v. Telluride, 187 Colo. 392, 532 P. 2d 346 (1975); Boise City Indp. School Dist. v. Callister, 97 Idaho 59, 539 P. 2d 987 (1975); Mount v. City of Vermillion, S.D. 250 N.W. 2d 686 (1977); Langevin v. City of Biddeford, 481 A. 2d 495 (Maine 1984).

[247] Gen. Mun. Law §50-e (1,5); Bureau v. Newcomb Cent. School Dist., 74 A.D. 2d 133, 426 N.Y.S. 2d 870 (1980); Coonradt v. Averill Park Cent. School Dist., 75 A.D. 2d 925, 427 N.Y.S. 2d 531 (1980); Matey v. Bethlehem Central School Dist., 89 Misc. 2d 390, 391 N.Y.S. 2d 357 (1977).

[248] Cobb v. Board of Comm'rs., 151 Ga. App. 472, 260 S.E. 2d 496 (1979).

[249] Cooney v. Society of Mt. Carmel, 61 Ill. App. 3d 108, 18 Ill. Dec. 464, 377 N.E. 2d 1101 (1978).

in most states, set forth the specific procedures which must be followed. Just as under the Statutes of Limitation, a common exception to the running of the time is that of incapacitation and, in some states, being a minor.[250] While it is generally held that interpretation and application of a provision limiting a remedy should be strictly and narrowly construed, the courts have held that "substantial compliance"[251] is adequate and that if there were actual notice of knowledge[252] in the absence of formal notice that the notice requirement is satisfied; since the primary reason for the notice is to enable the governmental agency to conduct a timely investigation. Procedural requirements[253] usually include to whom the notice should be given and the information required and the format in which it should be presented. The information required usually is the place, time, and circumstances of the injury. Usually certain defects in compensation or other relief demanded may be corrected after notice is given. Each state's provisions are different, and a local attorney for a school or municipality can assist in understanding the particular statutory requirements. Citations of statutes by state may be found in the Appendix; most notice-of-claim provisions are within the Tort Claims Acts. Additional cases in which notice-of-claim was at issue are cited in the footnotes.[254]

§ 5.33   Exculpatory clause

The third type of defense in which the actual act of either the defendant or plaintiff is immaterial is the exculpatory clause. The exculpatory clause is a contract, a contract between the plaintiff and the defendant, signed prior to participation in activity, that the plaintiff, if injured, will not hold liable the defendant for any negligence of the defendant. Thus, there would be no determination of fault, but defendant would be "excused" from any negligence which may have resulted in injury and damages to the plaintiff on the basis of contract. The requirements for a valid contract are stringent inasmuch as the plaintiff is "signing away" rights of redress for injury. Exculpatory agreements, particularly as to the criteria for validity, are detailed in §16.1.

---

[250] See footnote 220.

[251] Anske v. Palisades Park, 139 N.J. Super. 342, 354 A. 2d 87 (1976); Shearer v. Perry Community School Dist., Iowa, 236 N.W. 2d 688 (1975); Simmon v. City of Bluefield, 225 S.E. 2d 202 (W. Va. App. 1976).

[252] Almich v. Indep. School Dist., 291 Minn. 269, 190 N.W. 2d 668 (1971); Johnson v. City of Memphis, 699 S.W. 2d 179 (Tenn. App. 1985) constructive notice upheld; Pepe v. Somers Central School Dist., 485 N.Y.S. 2d 315 (1985); Vasys v. Metro. Dist. Comm., 387 Mass. 51, 438 N.E. 2d 836 (1982).

[253] Bailey v. Mobile, 292 Ala. 436, 296 So. 2d 149 (1974); Boas v. San Diego Co., 113 Cal. App. 3d 355, 169 Cal. Rptr. 828 (1980); Hunnicutt v. Tuscaloosa, 250 Cal. App. 2d 856, 58 Cal. Rptr. 763 (1967); Sanders v. Ansonia, 33 Conn. Sup. 196, 369 A. 2d 1129 (1976).

[254] Adonnino v. Mount Morris, 171 Misc. 383, 12 N.Y.S. 2d 658 (Sup. Ct. 1939); Allen v. Los Angeles City Bd. of Educ., 173 Cal. App. 2d 126, 343 P. 2d 170 (1959); Almich v. Independent School Dist., 291 Minn. 269, 190 N.W. 2d 668 (1971); Barajas v. San Dieguito

High School Dist., 151 Cal. App. 2d 709, 312 P. 2d 282 (1957); Benedict v. Union Free School Dist., 184 Misc. 671, 54 N.Y.S. 2d 560 (1945); Canon City v. Cox, 55 Colo. 264, 133 P. 1040 (1913); Cleary v. Catholic Diocese of Peoria, 10 Ill. App. 3d 224, 293 N.E. 2d 195 (1973) rev'd. 57 Ill. 2d 384, 312 N.E. 2d 635 (1974); Colburn v. Ozaukee County, 39 Wis. 2d 231, 159 N.W. 2d 33 (1968); Cole v. Los Angeles Unified School Dist., 177 Cal. App. 3d 1, 222 Cal. Rptr. 426 (1986); Cotham v. Board of County Comm'rs, 260 Md. 556, 273 A. 2d 115 (1971); Crowe v. Doyle, 6 Ill. App. 3d 1098, 287 N.E. 2d 99 (1972); Dixon v. Mobile, 280 Ala. 419, 194 So. 2d 825 (1967); Ford v. Black Mountain Tramways, Inc., 110 N.H. 20, 259 A. 2d 129 (1969); Fry v. Willamalane Park & C. Dist., 481 P. 2d 648 (Ore. App. 1971); Grubaugh v. St. Johns, 384 Mich. 165, 180 N.W. 2d 778 (1970); Holsman v. Village of Bigfork, 284 Minn. 460, 172 N.W. 2d 320 (1969); Jackson v. Board of Educ., 58 Cal. Rptr. 763, 250 Cal. App. 2d 856 (1967); Kelly v. Rochester, 304 Minn. 328, 231 N.W. 2d 275 (1975); Lorton v. Brown Co. Comm. Unit School Dist., 35 Ill. 2d 362, 220 N.W. 2d 161

(1966); Lubbock v. Green, 201 F. 2d 146 (5th Cir. 1953); Martini, Jr. v. Olyphant Borough School Dist., 83 Pa. D. & C. 206 (1952); Meli v. Dade Co. School Board, 490 So. 2d 120 (Fla. App. 1986); Nelson v. Twin Bridges H.S., 181 Mt. 318, 593 P. 2d 722 (1979); Novak v. Delavan, 31 Wis. 2d 200, 143 N.W. 2d 6 (1966); Pattermann v. Whitewater, 32 Wis. 2d 350, 145 N.W. 2d 705 (1966); Price v. Mount Diablo Unified School Dist., 2 Cal. Rep. 23 (1960); Redlands High School Dist. v. Superior Court, 20 Cal. 2d 348, 125 P. 2d 490 (1942); Rice v. Granite School Dist., 23 Utah 2d 22, 456 P. 2d 159 (1969); Sandak v. Tuxedo Union School Dist., 308 N.Y. 226, 124 N.E. 2d 295 (1954); Shaeffer v. Canton, 337 F.S. 479 (S.D. 1972); Sherfey v. Brazil, 213 Ind. 493, 13 N.E. 2d 568 (1938); Skiris v. Port Washington, 223 Wis. 51, 269 N.W. 556 (1936); Sprung v. Rasmussen, 180 N.W. 2d 430 (Iowa 1970); Vermeer v. Sneller, 190 N.W. 2d 389 (Iowa 1971); Wibstad v. Hopkins, 291 Minn. 206, 190 N.W. 2d 125 (1971); Wilson v. Denver, 168 Colo. 43, 449 P. 2d 822 (1969); Zipser v. Pound, 69 Misc. 2d 152, 329 N.Y.S. 2d 494 (1972).

Part B
Activities and the Law

Part B is omitted from the Paperback Edition, however, cases related to various activities in Part B also are cited in Part C, in the appropriate situation chapter. For example, cases concerned with spectators for the various sports (Chapters 6 and 7) are included in Chapter 15 on spectators; or, cases involving areas and facilities are aggregated for all activities in Chapter 20.

The law and lawsuits pervade every aspect of sport, athletics, and physical education, of recreation and parks, and of camping and adventure activities. Part B presents the nature of lawsuits by activities. For the most part, the text is narrative description of activity circumstances which gave rise to the action in court. Frequently the court decision is not given because either it was based on the doctrine of governmental immunity, state tort claims act, or recreational user statute, rather than the facts surrounding the activity, or an issue of law was determined and the case was remanded for decision on the facts regarding negligence. Nevertheless, pointers found in these cases should give some insight to the conduct of activities. Old cases also are cited, even though the basis of decision, such as governmental immunity, may have changed and the decision may well be different in the late '80s, because they give illustration of the type of situations which give rise to lawsuits, as well as past thinking of the courts and the trends in the law. Cases prior to 1970, for the most part, are cited in the footnotes only and the situation not described in the text. Additional cases often may be found in case opinions.

Is there one recreational activity or sport more dangerous than others? Are there sports and games which are inherently dangerous? Which activities have been involved most frequently in lawsuits? What circumstances surround various activities which lead to court actions? From this part, you may draw some conclusions as to the answers; however, it must be pointed out that the cases included are those which have reached state supreme courts and, therefore, are not necessarily representative of the multiplicity of cases which remain on the lower levels of the court system or injuries which are settled through insurance claims. Cases against individuals, except for some illustrative cases in a sport like golf, are not included. Further, it must be cautioned that mere frequency does not necessarily reflect either the dangerousness of the activity or the likelihood for suit. Also, no claim is made for the exhaustiveness of case listings. And, one additional aspect must be kept in mind — the complete scope and ramifications of legal liability for any one activity will not be embodied in the cases cited, especially for the activities which have few cases. The next accident in a given activity could well involve a legal issue not represented among the cited cases. *For better understanding of legal principles in accord with various situations, regardless of activity, see Part C.*

The activities are presented by chapter groupings. Chapters 6 and 7 are the team and individual/dual sports. Most of the team sport cases involve football, baseball/softball, and basketball, while the individual and dual sports with the most cases are gymnastics, golf, and wrestling. However, cases for 17 other sports are cited. Ice and snow sports and activities are included in Chapter 8. Ice hockey and skiing predominate. Physical education instructional programs, games of low organization, and physical testing are in Chapter 10, along with school activities of intramurals and club sports, school clubs, special events, class excursions, and cheerleading. Also in Chapter 10 is playgrounds, including equipment, recreational sports and games, and special events on playgrounds. Recreation and urban park activities are in Chapter 11 and encompass the cultural arts (dramatics, dance, music, arts and crafts), special events (parades, bingo, exhibitions, fairs, carnivals, holidays and festivals, amusement devices, and fireworks), general recreational activities (miniature golf, indoor activities, outdoor park activities), zoos, and roller skating.

Aquatic activities are divided into swimming in pools (Chapter 9) and water-based recreation (Chapter 14). Water-based recreation includes water sports (fishing, scuba, snorkeling, skin-diving, surfing, water skiing), watercraft (sailing, rowing and canoeing, whitewater rafting, motorboating), and boat concessionnaires and marinas, swimming in lakes and ponds, river activities, and situations related to canals and drainage ditches. The three final chapters in Part B, including the aforedescribed Chapter 14, focus on the outdoor natural environment. Chapter 12 presents the landowner limited liability laws (recreational user statutes) and the activities of motorized vehicles (ORVs, dune buggies), airborne activities, hunting, sightseeing, and campgrounds. Organized camping, adventure activities and challenge courses, interpretive services and gardening, outings/field trips/excursions, mountain climbing/backpacking/hiking and tripping, firearms ranges, horseback riding, and the outdoor sports of caving and bicycling are all in Chapter 13.

Part C
Situations Which Give Rise To Lawsuits

While it is interesting to review cases specific to an activity (Part B), in terms of legal concepts and an understanding of the situations which give rise to lawsuits, it is more important to look at cases across activities. The legal principles and the standard of care required, as set forth in the cases, are applicable to all activities, programs, and services. By seeing how such principles and standard are applied in a variety of situations and settings, one can gain a greater understanding of negligence and its ramifications in the leisure industry, in parks and the outdoor field, in sport and the schools, et al. Thus, Part C takes the cases presented in Part B and re-categorizes them according to situations which give rise to lawsuits. Some cases have been added specific to the situations, but which were not appropriate to any of the chapters in Part B.

Eight major topic areas or situations have been selected. The focus is primarily upon the participant in activity or the user of areas, facilities, and services; however, the first chapter in Part C, Chapter 15, is directed toward those persons who enjoy watching others participate, the spectators, those who facilitate sport, the officials, and those who just happen to be going by, the passers-by. Chapter 16 addresses a real concern of all providers of programs and services, as well as areas and facilities, how one can limit liability through participant/user forms. If persons did not get injured, there would be no lawsuits — but it is important to be prepared for injury, as well as to enhance one's own physical condition, and Chapter 17 includes both post-injury emergency care and physical fitness and conditioning. The responsibilities of administrators, supervisors, and those directly conducting activity are set forth in Chapters 18 and 19, General Supervision and Conduct of Activity, respectively. Those persons who are concerned especially about areas and facilities, both urban and natural environment, will find cases describing layout/design/construction of facilities and areas, condition of facilities and areas (maintenance), and the care required for natural areas in Chapter 20. Equipment-related concerns are in Chapter 21 and Transportation and Traffic Control in Chapter 22.

It must be remembered that negligence law is based in the states and, therefore, one must consult local attorneys for specific application of principles of law and the standard of care required to a particular state. Also, the law is indeed everchanging, and there must be continual vigilance for reversals and overturning of case precedence, for changed interpretations, and for statutory modifications. This reference does not purport to be exhaustive in its coverage of cases, but the cases should be considered as guideposts to further study of the legal concepts being applied in various situations and different settings.

Chapter 15.   Spectators, Passers-by, and Sport Officials

While cases[1] do date back to the early 1900s, there has been increasing concern in the 1970s and 1980s by management for injuries to persons other than the individual directly participating in the activity, particularly in sport activities. This includes injuries by a player to a spectator, by a spectator to another spectator, and by premise

[1]E.g., Stewart v. Cobalt Curling & Skating Assoc., 19 Ont. L. 667 (1909); Wells v. Minneapolis Baseball & Athletic Ass'n, 122 Minn. 327, 142 N.W. 706 (1913).

1

defects or activity operations to spectators or passers-by. Injuries to an official or caused by an official, too, are of special concern into the decade of the '80s.

The cases are presented according to similar circumstances or issues. However, as an overview, it should be noted that most of the cases have arisen from professional sports and commercial enterprises; but, in the '70s and '80s there have been increasingly more suits by persons injured when in attendance at non-professional sport events. Baseball[2] has by far the greatest number of cases, but then professional baseball is indeed an old sport. Ice hockey[3] and professional wrestling[4] together have approximately the same number of cases cited as baseball; and, these three sports account for about two-thirds of the cited cases. Football and golf are next in number, and then a variety of sports have a few cases each, including basketball, polo, jai-alai and bowling. A few cases cited are related to dances and other recreational activities. The commerical field of amusements, specifically dance and theatre, are not included. The listing of cases is not exhaustive, merely illustrative of the principles being discussed.

This chapter is presented in three primary sections: spectators, passers-by, and sport officials. For violence of one player against another, see §1.41; for cases related to gender discrimination and civil liberties, see §§1.311 and 1.332, respectively; for impact of exculpatory agreements on tickets, see §16.13; and §18.324 for denying attendance at an event as discipline.

§ 15.1 Spectators

First, everyone who is not a player is not necessarily a spectator. *Martini, Jr. v. Olyphant Borough School Dist.*, 83 Pa. D & C 206 (1952), distinguishes a player from a spectator, holding that a player assumes the risks of the game, but that a duty is owed the spectator particularly to provide a safe environment for viewing the game. A spectator is distinguished from a pedestrian or passer-by, called a casual spectator, in *Jones v. Kane and Roach, Inc.*, 182 Misc. 37, 43 N.Y.S. 2d 140 (1943). In this case it was held that the casual spectator, the pedestrian passing by, was expected to assume the risk of balls going off the diamond, but should be protected in a reasonable manner, whereas the spectator did assume certain risks of the game in balls going into the stands. Attending athletic games as mere spectators has been held not a constitutionally protected right for either students or the public.[5]

Situations which give rise to law suits related to spectators include participatory risks, crowd control, safe premises, operations, and injuries to spectators by players or employees.

---

[2] Rigelhaupt, James L. Liability to Spectator at Baseball Game Who is Hit by Ball or Injured as Result of Other Hazards of Game. 91 A.L.R.3d 24-132.

[3] Shipley, W.E. Liability for Injury to One Attending Hockey Game or Exhibition. 14 A.L.R.3d 1018-1028.

[4] Shipley, W.E. Liability for Injury to One Attend-

ing Wrestling or Boxing Match or Exhibition. 14 A.L.R.3d 993-1007.

[5] Boster v. Philpot, 645 F. Supp. 798 (1986) Kansas law applied, attendance prohibited as student disciplinary action; Watkins v. Louisiana H.S. Athletic Assoc., 301 So. 2d 695 (La. App. 1974) see §15.3 intro.

§ 15.11   Participatory risks

Participatory risks are those risks which arise from the act of spectating. At issue is what risks are inherent in the game for the spectator and thus assumed by the spectator (see §5.22 Assumption of risk). Also, can a spectator waive certain rights (see §16.1 Exculpatory agreements), and what constitutes contributory negligence by the spectator (see §5.21 Contributory negligence). In contrast, what is the duty of the owner/sponsor to warn the spectators regarding the nature of the game and to protect against certain participatory risks?

Because baseball spectating with foul balls is an unique situation, §15.111 deals with such situations, while §15.112 focuses upon other types of baseball spectator risks and the spectator risks of other sports. Cases where spectators are injured due to race cars going out of control and entering an area of spectators,[6] unmanageable horses in polo injuring spectators,[7] a wrestler thrown out of the ring in professional wrestling,[8] or similar activities are not included in this section.

§ 15.111   Balls batted into the stands

Since the turn of the century, spectators have sued for injuries sustained when hit by a batted ball at a baseball game, but few have won any damages. The court stated back in 1913[9] that baseball is the national game, and the rules governing it, the manner in which it is played, and the risks and dangers incident thereto are matters of common knowledge. It makes no difference if the spectator has not played baseball nor attended a baseball game before; and, a knowledge of rules is not necessary.[10] As a general rule, the spectator assumes the risks.[11] (See discussion in §15.1121 regarding efforts of two states to apply recreational user and governmental immunity criteria.)

The courts have held that the management is not an insurer of safety[12] and that it is required only to exercise ordinary care to protect patrons against such injuries by providing screened seats for those portions (behind home plate) of the stands that are

---

[6] E.g., Alden v. Norwood Arena, Inc., 332 Mass. 267, 124 N.E. 2d 505 (1955); Capital Raceway Promotions v. Smith, 22 Md. App. 224, 322 A. 2d 238 (1974); Dailey v. Nationwide Demolition Derby, 18 Ohio App. 3d 39, 480 N.E. 2d 110 (1984); Fitchett v. Buchanan, 2 Wash. App. 2d 965, 472 P. 2d 623 (1970); Grahn v. Northwest Sport, 310 P. 2d 306 (Ore. 1957); LaFrenz v. Lake Co. Fair Board, 360 N.E. 2d 605 (Ind. App. 1977); McPherson v. Sunset Speedway, 594 F. 2d 711 (1979); Watford by Johnston v. Evening Star Newspaper Co., 21 F. 2d 31 (1954) D.C., soap box derby. There are some speedway cases cited in the section on waivers and releases, §16.1.

[7] Douglas v. Converse, 248 Pa. 232, 93 A. 955 (1915).

[8] See 14 A.L.R.3d 993.

[9] Wells v. Minneapolis Baseball & Athletic Ass'n, 122 Minn. 327, 142 N.W. 706 (1913).

[10] Anderson v. K.C. Baseball Club, Mo., 231 S.W.

2d 170 (1950); Keys v. Alamo City Baseball Co., 150 S.W. 2d 368 (Tex. Civ. App. 1941).

[11] Adonnino v. Mt. Morris, 171 Misc. 383, 12 N.Y.S. 2d 658 (1939); Hunt v. Portland Baseball Club, 207 Or. 337, 296 P. 2d 495 (1956); Iervolino v. Pittsburgh Athletic Co., 212 Pa. Super. 330, 243 A. 2d 490 (1968); Ivory v. Cincinnati Baseball Club Co., 62 Ohio App. 514, 15 Ohio Ops. 357, 24 N.E. 2d 837 (1939); Leek v. Tacoma Baseball Club, 38 Wash. 2d 362, 229 P. 2d 329 (1951); Schentzel v. Philadelphia Nat'l. League Club, 173 Pa. Super. 179, 96 A. 2d 181 (1953); Shaw v. Boston American League Baseball Co., 325 Mass. 419, 90 N.E. 2d 840 (1950); Stradtner v. Cincinnati Reds, Inc., 39 Ohio App. 2d 199, 316 N.E. 2d 924 (1972).

[12] Curtis v. Portland Baseball Club, 130 Or. 93, 279 P. 277 (1929); Hudson v. K.C. Baseball Club, 349 Mo. 1215, 164 S.W. 2d 318 (1942); Williams v. Houston Baseball Ass'n., 154 S.W. 2d 874 (Tex. Civ. App. 1941).

most frequently subject to hazards of foul balls[13] and for as many spectators as may be reasonably expected to call for them on any ordinary occasion.[14] The spectator should voluntarily occupy the seat.[15] This assumption of an inherent risk extends only to seating of the usual custom and balls which are batted and thrown in the normal progress of the game or pre-game activity.[16] There is no duty to warn by signs or otherwise, if the spectator is aware of the danger or it is so obvious that a person of ordinary intelligence would readily sense it and take measures to avert it.[17] However, there is a duty to maintain protected areas in a manner such that the spectator is protected. This means that screening must be of appropriate size[18] and in good condition (no holes for the balls to go through).[19] A 1982 case,[20] however, pointed up the role of inspections and requirement of actual or constructive notice of a hole. The case also was brought on the theory of *res ipsa loquitur* (see §2.242), the plaintiff endeavoring to obtain judgment on the fact that the injury occurred due to a situation over which the defendant had exclusive control.

A 1982 case[21] took a slightly different approach to the duty of the management and assumption of risk by the spectator. Plaintiff acknowledged that generally there is no duty to warn, but alleged that this particular area of the stands represented an unexpectedly high risk, of a magnitude much greater than common and thus the management owes a duty to warn. (Area of location not specified in opinion.) The defendant countered that even if there were a duty to warn, such duty was fulfilled by the disclaimer printed on the back of each ticket and the announcement at the beginning of the game. The court stated that such disclaimers did not fulfill an owner's duty to warn of unexpectedly high risk; however, it held for the defendant on the basis that the plaintiff failed to show any evidence that if a proper warning had been given she would have taken precautions to prevent the injury; that is, she presented no evidence in showing that failure to warn was the proximate cause of her injury.

Baseball spectator injuries due to batted balls focus upon the location of seating and the protective screening.[22] Some illustrative cases follow.

The court held that there was a duty to provide seat locations for the spectators with a

13 Anderson v. K.C. Baseball Club, 231 S.W. 2d 170 (Mo. 1950).

14 Erickson v. Lexington Baseball Club, 233 N.C. 627, 65 S.E. 2d 140 (1951); Knebel v. Jones, 266 S.W. 2d 470 (Tex. Civ. App. 1954); Williams v. Houston Baseball Ass'n., 154 S.W. 2d 874 (Tex. Civ. App. 1941).

15 Ivory v. Cincinnati Baseball Club Co., 62 Ohio App. 514, 15 Ohio Ops. 347, 24 N.E. 2d 837 (1939); Keys v. Alamo City Baseball Co., 150 S.W. 2d 358 (Tex. Civ. App. 1941); Stradtner v. Cincinnati Reds, 39 Oh. App. 2d 199, 316 N.E. 2d 924 (1972).

16 Cincinnati Baseball Club v. Eno, 112 Ohio St. 175, 147 N.E. 86 (1925).

17 Anderson v. K.C. Baseball Club, 231 S.W. 2d 170 (Mo. 1950); Curtis v. Portland Baseball Club, 130 Or. 93, 279 P. 277 (1929); Hudson v. K.C. Baseball Club, 349 Mo. 1215, 164 S.W. 2d 318 (1942); Ivory v. Cincinnati Baseball Club Co., 62 Ohio App. 514, 15 Ohio Ops. 347, 24 N.E. 2d 837 (1939); Keys v. Alamo City Baseball Co., 150 S.W. 2d 368 (Tex. Civ. App.

1941); Shaw v. Boston American League Baseball Co., 325 Mass. 419, 90 S.E. 2d 840 (1950).

18 Jackson v. Atlanta Braves, 227 So. 2d 63 (Fla.App. 1969), cert. dism'd 237 So. 2d 540; Leek v. Tacoma Baseball Club, 38 Wash. 2d 362, 229 P. 2d 329 (1951).

19 Buck v. McLean, 115 So. 2d 764 (La. App. 1959); Edling v. K.C. Baseball & Exhibition Co., 181 Mo.App. 327, 168 S.W. 908 (1914); Pollan v. Dothan, 243 Ala. 99, 8 So. 2d 813 (1942).

20 Uzdavines v. Metro. Baseball Club, Inc., 115 Misc. 2d 343, 454 N.Y.S. 2d 238 (1982).

21 Falkner v. John E. Fetzer, Inc., 113 Mich. App. 500, 317 N.W. 2d 337 (1982).

22 See 91 A.L.R. 3d 24 at 56-84 for additional early cases: Crane v. K.C. Baseball & Exhibition Co., 168 Mo. App. 301, 153 S.W. 1076 (1913); Hull v. Okla. City Baseball Co., 196 Okla. 40, 163 P. 2d 982 (1945); Johnson v. Houston Sports Ass'n, 615 S.W. 2d 781 (Tex. Civ. App. 1980).

choice between screened and open seats in *Cates v. Cincinnati Exhibition Co.*, 215 N.C. 64, 1 S.E. 2d 131 (1939). However, seats do not have to be provided for an unusually large crowd. In *Swagger v. City of Crystal*, 379 N.W. 2d 183 (Minn. App. 1985), a softball game was part of a "Frolics" sponsored by the Parks and Recreation Department. The crowd far exceeded the capacity of the bleachers. The plaintiff and husband found a spot to watch the game about 6′ past first base towards the outfield and about 30′ from the first base line. Plaintiff had never played softball, but had watched Little League and softball games her husband had played. She was struck in the face by a wildly thrown softball, suffering severe and permanent injuries to her nose and right eye. The jury found plaintiff 49% at fault and the city 51%; however, notwithstanding comparative negligence, the court held the doctrine of primary assumption of risk was still active and was appropriate for spectators of inherently dangerous sporting events. Further, the court stated that management is not required to provide screened-in seats for an unusual crowd, as long as it provides screen for the most dangerous part of the grandstand and for those who may be reasonably anticipated to desire protected seats. Based on the doctrine of assumption of risk, the city owed plaintiff no duty and thus the court held for defendant.[23]

When a spectator voluntarily chooses to sit in an unscreened area, that spectator assumes the risk of being hit by a batted ball. In a 1984 New York case,[24] the court said that since it is common knowledge that in baseball games balls are thrown and batted with swiftness and that they are liable to be thrown or batted outside the lines of the diamond, spectators who are so positioned that they may be reached by such balls assume the risk of being hit and injured, since they can follow the ball and can thus usually avoid being hit when a ball is directed toward them. The court further held that the theory of assumption of risk can be used only if the spectator had knowledge that the seating was unprotected, that the exposure was patently dangerous, and that such seating was occupied voluntarily. The Alabama court in the *Vines* case held similarly. Additionally, the court said that although there was no duty to warn, the signs warning spectators posted in obvious and open places were adequate.

If a spectator desiring a seat behind a screened area accepts a seat, even temporarily in an unscreened area, one assumes the risk of being hit by a batted ball. This includes pre-game warm-up.[25] In an early case,[26] the spectator was being ushered in and was told that she should take a seat in an unscreened area, since there were no seats available in the screened area and since the game had started she must sit down and the usher would see what he could do about finding a seat in a screened area. The plaintiff admitted that she knew at the time she took her seat that she would be in danger of being hit by batted

[23] See also Brisson v. Minneapolis Baseball & Athletic Ass'n., 185 Minn. 507, 240 N.W. 903 (1932); Rudnick v. Golden West Broadcasters, 156 Cal. App. 3d 793, 202 Cal. Rptr. 900 (1984).

[24] Davidoff v. Metro. Baseball Club, Inc., 92 A.D. 2d 461, 459 N.Y.S. 2d 2 (1983), aff'd 61 N.Y. 2d 996, 475 N.Y.S. 2d 367, 463 N.E. 2d 1219 (1984); see also Clapman v. N.Y.C., 97 A.D. 2d 990, 469 N.Y.S. 2d 832 (1983) aff'd. 63 N.Y. 2d 669, 479 N.Y.S. 2d 515, 468 N.E. 2d 697 (1984); Grimes v. American League Baseball Co., 78 S.W. 2d 520 (Mo. App. 1935); Hoke v.

Lykens School Dist., 69 Pa. D & C 422, 60 Dauph Co. 226 (1949); Ivory v. Cincinnati Baseball Club Co., 62 Ohio App. 514, 15 Ohio Ops. 357, 24 N.E. 2d 837 (1939); Stradtner v. Cincinnati Reds, Inc., 39 Ohio App. 2d 199, 316 N.E. 2d 924 (1972); Vines v. Birmingham Baseball Club, Inc., 450 So. 2d 455 (Ala. 1984).

[25] Brummerhoff v. St. Louis National Baseball Club, 149 S.W. 2d 382 (Mo. App. 1941).

[26] Quinn v. Recreation Park Assoc., 3 Cal. 2d 725, 46 P. 2d 144 (1935).

balls. The court held that the spectator assumed the risk of being hit by accepting the unscreened seat, even though temporarily, since she had full knowledge of the danger. There was a similar holding in *Baker v. Topping*,[27] but in this situation the spectator was hit while being ushered through an aisle to his reserved seat, which was in an unprotected area on the first base line. The plaintiff alleged that the usher was negligent in conducting him to his seat at a time and place when it was dangerous and without warning of possible batted balls. The court noted that it would be impractical, if not impossible, to require movement in the stands at a time only when there was no action on the field. Further, the spectator was held to be knowledgable of the risks of a batted ball coming anywhere in the stands (except in protected areas) and the spectator had not specified only behind screening, only a "good seat."

If the spectator chooses to watch from an area other than the stands, the same risk is assumed of being hit by a batted ball. Plaintiff was struck in the eye at a high school baseball game, as she stood behind a fence along the third base line. The court held that the proprietor of the ball park need only provide screening for an area of field behind home plate where danger of being struck by a ball is the greatest and with screening to be of sufficient extent to provide adequate protection for as many spectators as may reasonably be expected to desire such seating in the course of an ordinary game. The school had provided a backstop behind home plate which was 24' high and 50' wide. There was no evidence that the backstop was inadequate. The school was not required to provide additional screening along the base lines of the field. The owner of a baseball field is not an insurer of safety of its spectators, but only is under duty to exercise reasonable care under the circumstances to prevent injury to those who come to watch games played on its field.[28]

At a Little League baseball game, a father, who could have taken a seat behind the screened area behind home plate, chose to seat himself on the players' bench about 10' outside the third base foul line. Just a few moments before he was hit, he had been compelled to duck to avoid being hit. The court held that the father assumed the risks incidental to batting practice when he seated himself on the players' bench.[29]

The plaintiff in *Mayntier v. Bush*[30] desired and obtained a front row seat near the players' dugout. The plaintiff (spectator) was struck on the head and injured by a ball thrown from the bullpen. Protective screens were customarily positioned in front of both first baseman and pitcher during batting practice when more than one ball was simultaneously being played. The spectator was hit with a ball from his left (from bullpen) while he was looking to his right at the pitcher and batter in the game. The court held that even where the plaintiff has knowledge and appreciation of a risk, the plaintiff is not barred from recovery where the situation changes to introduce a new element of risk. The management is not an insurer of safety, but must exercise reasonable care for the protection of invitees on the premises. In a little earlier case[31] the plaintiff spectator

[27] Baker v. Topping, 15 A.D. 2d 193, 222 N.Y.S. 2d 658 (1961), app. den. 11 N.Y. 2d 644, 228 N.Y.S. 2d 1026, 182 N.E. 2d 620.

[28] Akins v. Glen Falls City School District, 75 A.D. 2d 239, 429 N.Y.S. 2d 467 (1980), rev'd. 441 N.Y.S. 2d 644, 53 N.Y. 2d 325, 424 N.E. 2d 531 (1981).

[29] Kozera v. Town of Hamburg, 40 A.D. 2d 934, 337 N.Y.S. 2d 761 (1972).

[30] Mayntier v. Bush, 80 Ill. App. 2nd 336, 225 N.E. 2nd 83 (1967).

[31] McNiel v. Ft. Worth Baseball Club, 268 S.W. 2d 244 (Tex. Civ. App. 1954).

was hit by a foul ball during batting practice shortly after the batting cage had been removed; batting practice had continued without the cage for 10 minutes until plaintiff was struck. The court again said that the baseball club is not an insurer of safety and that spectator was fully aware that the batting cage as protection had been removed and he was subject to foul balls.

Plaintiff, also, may allege violation of a statute, but plaintiff was not successful in either *Pollan v. Dothan*, 243 Ala. 99, 8 So. 2d 813 (1942), or *Shaw v. Boston American League Baseball Co.*, 325 Mass. 419, 90 N.E. 2d 840 (1950). Neither was the plaintiff successful in *Powless v. Milwaukee County*, 6 Wis. 2d 78, 94 N.E. 2d 187 (1959); the court, however, held the plaintiff was contributorily negligent, in that she ignored the on-going activities of the game and failed to take any precaution for her own safety.

§ 15.112   Missiles emanating from players

Whereas a ball batted in baseball into the spectators is inherent and natural to the sport of baseball/softball, this is not true of other projectiles emanating from the player participants, such as bats, bodies, pucks, etc. Just what risks does the spectator assume and from what risks must the spectator be protected?

While most of the situations involve baseball, ice hockey, golf and basketball, one spectator was injured when the ski of a contestant, freed in course of jump, slid into a group of spectators standing in a roped off area. Judgment for defendant; evidence was insufficient to show that such an event was reasonably foreseeable.[32]

§ 15.1121   Bats and thrown balls (baseball/softball)

Additional cases related to baseball/softball involve balls thrown into spectator areas and bats which break or slip from the hands of the batter. Whether or not plaintiff recovers is situational—if the situation is one of a regular part of the game, then plaintiff usually does not recover unless there is a defect in the protective screening. On the other hand, if the use of a bat or a thrown ball is part of play, then it is a matter of whether the injured should have been protected. However, two states[33] have endeavored to apply landowner duty criteria. In the Pennsylvania case, parents and infant were attending a high school baseball game. An infielder overthrew first base and the ball hit the infant, who suffered serious head injuries. Plaintiffs alleged negligence in regard to the design of the field and spectator protection, failing to warn spectator of risks, and failing to supervise or control player's conduct (throwing wildly). Court held that school district of visiting team, borough which leased field, and township in which field located was protected by governmental immunity, but as to liability of home school district, it was a question to be decided whether the ball field was real property, an exception to immunity under Tort Claims Act. Further the court held that baseball was a recreational activity and the fence, backstop and bleachers "land" under the Recreation Use of Land

[32] Merenoff v. State, 283 A.D. 1134, 131 N.Y.S. 2d 491 (1954), denied 307 N.Y. 942 (1954).

[33] Lowman v. Indiana Area School District, 96 Pa. Cmwlth. 389, 507 A. 2d 1270 (1986); City of Milton v. Broxon, 514 So. 2d 1116 (Fla. App. 1987).

and Water Act and, thus, the electric company which leased the field to the borough was protected under the Act. (This is an unusual holding, see §12.1.) The Florida situation was that 18-year-old plaintiff, watching a softball game, walked over to an area behind third base dugout and as he appeared to be heading back to the bleachers, he was struck in the head by a softball thrown by one of the players warming up. The warming up was near (about 5') an area adjacent to the bleachers where spectators sat in their lawn chairs, although plaintiff was not sitting there. No area had been designated for players for warming up while waiting for the prior game to end. The court discussed who had superior knowledge of danger, the plaintiff or the city, and if the city, then the city owed a duty to warn. The court also discussed the duties to an invitee, which the plaintiff was, and applied what it termed the "invitation test" distinguishing invitee and business invitee. Also, a landowner owes a duty to an invitee to maintain the premises in a reasonably safe condition. Held: city owed no duty to warn, whether premises were in reasonably safe condition for the jury, and city not entitled to sovereign immunity. (See also §4.2.)

There are a number of cases[34] in which the bat slipped from the person's hands, injuring plaintiff. The situations are quite varied. For example, one of the plaintiffs, while an invitee at a family outing staged by the defendant athletic association for employees of defendant company at an amusement park, operated by another defendant, was struck in the face by a softball bat which had slipped from the defendant batter's hands and sailed through the air 90'. Plaintiff was standing 30' beyond first base and 15' outside the foul line. The court said that the plaintiff will be held not to have assumed risk of danger unless plaintiff actually appreciated the danger or unless an ordinarily prudent person in same position and with experience would have appreciated it. Further, the court indicated that in such circumstances the defendant has the burden of proving assumption of risk, that is, lack of duty, notwithstanding that plaintiff usually has burden of proving that the defendant owes him duty; and, that the plaintiff has the burden of proving, among other things, that the danger is not of normal sort.[35]

After a Little League game, two young players found a broken bat and fit it together. When it was swung, it came apart and one part flew through a hole in the screen and hit a spectator. The court held for the plaintiff, saying that the owners of a softball field had permitted the screen to become damaged and worn to the extent the holes existed, which wire screen was to have protected spectators in the grandstand. The owner's contention was that they owed no duty of protection as to acts by others who might be playing on the field. The court held that the injury was reasonably foreseeable. Evidence showed that the plaintiff did not have knowledge of the hole and was not required to examine the

---

[34] Benedetto v. Travelers Ins. Co., 172 So. 2d 354 (La. App. 1965), appl. den. 247 La. 872, 175 So. 2d 108; Bennett v. Board of Education, 16 A.D. 2d 651, 226 N.Y.S. 2d 593 (1962), aff'd. 13 N.Y. 2d 1104, 246 N.Y.S. 2d 634, 196 N.E. 2d 268; Easler v. Downie Amusement Co., 125 Me. 334, 133 A. 905 (1926) watching ball game played by circus employees after work hours near the circus main tent, plaintiff struck by tent stake being used as a bat, held for plaintiff, manner in which being played jeopardized plaintiff's safety; Heim v. Mitchell-Harlee Camps, 236 A.D. 835, 259 N.Y.S. 1007 (1954), men. dec. 260 N.Y.S. 983 (1932),

aff'd. 262 N.Y. 523, 188 N.E. 48 (1933) seven-year-old camper watching ball game, bat slipped from batter's hands, flew about 10'-12', then slid on the ground, and then apparently striking something bounded up and hit plaintiff in abdomen, judgment for camper; Lutzker v. Board of Education, 262 A.D. 881, 28 N.Y.S. 2d 496 (1941), aff'd. 287 N.Y. 822, 41 N.E. 2d 97.

[35] Klinsky v. Hanson Van Winkle Munning Co., 38 N.J. Super. 439, 119 A. 2d 166 (1955), cert. dism'd. 20 N.J. 534, 120 A. 2d 661, aff'd. 43 N.J. Super. 166, 128 A. 2d 4 (1956).

safety of the facilities, but is entitled to rely on the fact that they are provided for her safety.[36]

An eight-year-old boy obtained a judgment for injuries sustained when he was struck by a baseball bat that slipped out of the hand of an older boy, who was playing a game of "fast-pitch" baseball. A rubber ball was being used in the summer recreational program. There were 50' between the injured eight-year-old and the teenagers playing ball. Inadequate supervision and defective bat were alleged.[37] In *Gordon v. Deer Park School Dist.*[38] a student was injured while watching a teacher bat a softball on the school grounds. The bat slipped out of the teacher's hands and flew 23' behind the batter. The court held that an experienced ball player could not have reasonably foreseen that the bat would have slipped out of the hands and fly toward the rear of the batter, since they usually went the other direction. In another youth incident,[39] a 14-year-old boy was sitting on a large steel drum located inside the fence of a Little League field 25' from where the defendant batter swung at a pitched ball and the bat flew out of his hands, striking the plaintiff in the face. Action dismissed against the Little League organization on the basis that lack of supervision was not the proximate cause.

There also are cases where spectators were injured by thrown balls, but in each of these five cases[40] there was no liability on the part of the defendant. There was a similar holding in a 1985 New York case.[41] A father (plaintiff) brought his adult son to ball field to introduce him to some of the players. They were leaning on a perimeter fence and talking to several persons during warmup when an errant ball hit the father on the left side of the face, causing an eye injury. The court held that one who remained standing near the field during warmup was a "spectator" and that neither the pitcher warming up whose ball went wild nor the softball league had a duty to warn such spectator of potential danger. An opposite result was held in a number of early cases.[42]

[36] Berrum v. Powalisz, 73 Nev. 291, 317 P. 2d 1090 (1957); see also Ratcliff v. San Diego Baseball Club, 27 Cal. App. 2d 733, 81 P. 2d 625 (1938).

[37] Stanley v. Board of Education, 9 Ill. App. 3d 963, 293 N.E. 2d 417 (1973).

[38] Gordon v. Deer Park School Dist., 71 Wash. 2d 119, 426 P. 2d 824 (1967).

[39] O'Bryan v. O'Connor, 59 A.D. 2d 219, 399 N.Y.S. 2d 272 (1977).

[40] Brown v. San Francisco Ball Club, 99 Cal. App. 2d 484, 222 P. 2d 19 (1950) voluntarily occupied a seat in an unscreened area; Hunt v. Thomasville Baseball Co., 80 Ga. App. 572, 56 S.E. 2d 828 (1949); Lang v. Amateur Softball Assoc., Okla. 520 P. 2d 659 (1974) hit by wild pitch that came over a 10' fence separating a warmup area from the bleachers at a city park field; Robert v. Deposit Central School Dist., 18 A.D. 2d 947, 237 N.Y.S. 2d 680 (1963), aff'd. 13 N.Y. 2d 709, 241 N.Y.S. 2d 843, 191 N.E. 2d 901 (1963); Zeitz v. Cooperstown Baseball Centennial, 31 Misc. 2d 142, 29 N.Y.S. 2d 56 (1941) wild pitch; see also Swagger v. City of Crystal, 379 N.W. 2d 183 (Mich. App. 1985) struck by wildly thrown ball while watching from place about 30' from first base line, city owed no duty, spectator primary assumption of risk.

[41] Clark v. Goshen Sunday Morning Softball League, 493 N.Y.S. 2d 262 (1985).

[42] Aldes v. St. Paul Ball Club, 251 Minn. 440, 88 N.Y. 2d 94 (1958) spectator struck by thrown ball after requested to change seats from grandstand to a box seat; Barnecut v. Seattle School Dist., 63 Wash. 2d 905, 389 P. 2d 904 (1964) plaintiff injured by ball thrown by high school player warming up; Blakeley v. White Star Line, 154 Mich. 635, 118 N.W. 482 (1908) spectator standing with back to ball players near dance pavilion when ball thrown toward pavilion struck him, players had been chased from baseball diamond so began to play between diamond and dance pavilion in which dance was in progress, held such a game in proximity of a crowd was hazardous condition; Dean v. Martz, Ky. 329 S.W. 2d 371 (1959) gone to park for employee picnic, sitting in ball grandstand just to rest, boys playing on diamond using a soft, spongy, rubber ball about 2" in diameter purchased from proprietor who also had given them a bat, protective heavy wire screening immediately behind home plate and chicken fence wire of 2" mesh on extension toward first and third bases, proprietor knew boys played on diamond with a small ball which had gone through the chicken wire, held plaintiff had right to rely on the protective nature of the fencing.

And, what is the risk by the spectator when a ball is retrieved and thrown back onto the field? In *Emhardt v. Perry Stadium*,[43] just that happened. The spectator plaintiff was injured by being hit on the head by a fly ball that another spectator attempted to throw back into the playing field after it had been fouled into the stand. The spectator tried to say to the court that play on the field should not have been resumed until the ball had been retrieved because the game diverted her attention and she did not see the returning ball come toward her. It was the practice of the home team to have an employee attempt to retrieve the ball when fouled into the stands by offering a pass to a game for its return. The court held that the ball thrown by the spectator was an ordinary hazard of the game.

§ 15.1122   Ice hockey pucks and sticks[44]

While there are those who would argue a parallel with the baseball cases where injury occurs to a spectator by a batted ball, there are some fundamental differences. First, the puck in hockey is supposed to be moved along the surface of the ice, whereas in baseball the ball is frequently batted in the air as part of the game. Second, while certainly there are avid and knowledgable ice hockey spectators, baseball has a great deal more familiarity by the general public, an important factor in assumption of risk. (See §15.111.) A 1981 case[45] discusses and summarizes the issues in liability for flying hockey pucks which hit spectators. They focus on the duty of care owed by the owners and occupiers of premises and the assumption of risk by the spectators. Regarding duty of care, the *Benjamin* case[46] opinion stated that there is a duty to exercise reasonable care under the circumstances, and if provision of protected seating along the sidelines was undertaken, then it must be certain that such area is reasonably safe for its intended purpose. Plaintiff recovered when an errant puck found its way through the open area in front of the players' bench, passed behind the protective fence, and struck him on the left side of his forehead.

The courts have consistently found that there is a duty to exercise ordinary care for the safety of spectators at hockey games by the management. In most of these cases the plaintiff is given judgment. Such situations include allegations that the screens to protect spectators did not extend as far as they did in other areas or that the seats were screened only at the ends, and that there were no warning signs or other warning of the possibility of danger to those seated in unscreened seats.[47] Two arguments are

[43] Emhardt v. Perry Stadium, 113 Ind. App. 197, 46 N.E. 2d 704 (1943).

[44] See Shipley, W.E. Liability for Injury to One Attending Hockey Game or Exhibition. 14 A.L.R.3d 1018-1028; Payne v. Maple Leaf Gardens, Ltd., 1 D.L.R. 369 (1949 Ont. Ca.).

[45] Riley v. Chicago Cougars Hockey Club, 100 Ill. App.3d 664, 56 Ill. Dec. 210, 427 N.E. 2d 290 (1981).

[46] Benjamin v. State of N.Y., 115 Misc. 2d 71, 453 N.Y.S. 2d 329 (1982).

[47] James v. R.I. Auditorium, 60 R.I. 405, 199 A. 293 (1938); Lemoine v. Springfield Hockey Assoc., 307 Mass. 102, 29 N.E. 2d 716 (1940); M.J. Uline v. Neely, 103 App. D.C. 131, 255 F. 2d 540 (1958); Morris

v. Cleveland Hockey Club, 157 Ohio St. 225, 47 Ohio Ops. 147, 105 N.E. 2d 419 (1952); Parsons v. Nat'l Dairy Cattle Congress, Iowa, 277 N.W. 2d 620 (1979); Schwilm v. Pennsylvania Sports, 84 Pa. D & C 603, 100 Pittsb. Log. J. 423 (1938); Shanney v. Boston Madison Square Garden Corp., 296 Mass. 168, 5 N.E. 2d 1 (1936); Shurman v. Fresno Ice Rink, 91 Cal. App. 2d 469, 205 P. 2d 77 (1949); Thurman v. Ice Palace, 36 Cal. App. 2d 364, 97 P. 2d 999 (1939), aff'd. Thurman v. Clune, 51 Cla. App. 2d 505, 125 P. 2d 59 (1942); Tite v. Omaha Coliseum Corp., 144 Neb. 22, 12 N.W. 2d 90 (1943); Uline Ice, Inc. v. Sullivan, 88 App. D.C. 104 187 F. 2d 82 (1950).

frequently made by the defendant, namely, that the rink conformed in size, construction, and equipment to the general custom and usage and that additional screening is not feasible because spectators would object to the interference with the viewing.

The other legal issue on which there is denial to plaintiff (spectator) of recovery is based on the principle that spectators, with knowledge of the dangers incident to the playing of the game, assume the risk of being injured.[48] A 1977 case,[49] where the spectator was injured from a flying hockey puck which struck her in the eye, discussed the doctrine of assumption of risk, the maxim *volenti non fit injuria* (he who consents cannot receive an injury), and contributory negligence. The court held that assumption of the risk by definition means voluntary and that there is no distinction between the doctrine of assumption of risk and the maxim *volenti non fit injuria*. In regard to assumption of the risk, concern is with knowingly encountering danger, which is to be contrasted with negligently encountering risk; in the former instance plaintiff can be said to have consented to possibility of harm, whereas in the latter situation he has failed to assess accurately his situation and ramifications of his own action. Where one knowingly accepts a dangerous situation, he essentially absolves defendant of creating the risk or, to put it another way, duty defendant owes plaintiff is terminated. The court further said that contributory negligence and assumption of risk do not overlap; the key difference is exercise of one's free will in encountering risk. Assumption of risk is not a variant of contributory fault. In this case the plaintiff spectator was knowledgable about the game of ice hockey and was aware that there was a risk that a puck would take flight and possibly injure her. No recovery. Whereas the *Kennedy* case put the emphasis upon assumption of risk by spectator plaintiff, an Iowa case[50] also in the late 1970s, held that the defense of contributory negligence was available to the defendant, even though there may have been some assumption of risk (see §5.2).

Another issue was raised in the *Riley* case as to the duty owed by the team, the arena, and the league toward the spectator. The court held that the professional hockey league had no legal duty to protect spectators at hockey games between its member teams, and that the arena, also, did not owe a duty by terms of its lease with the hockey team. The hockey team had expressly agreed to take on the responsibility of protecting the crowd, and, further, the lease required that the team provide "plastic walls for crowd protection"; however, it did not specify how high the walls should be or what part of the stands should be protected. Herculite glass panels had been erected, higher behind the goals, but none to protect the balcony spectators, which the plaintiff was.

The situation in the 1981 *Riley* case[51] was that the plaintiff spectator was seated in the

[48] In addition to cases cited in preceding footnote, see Anderson v. Green Bay Hockey, 56 Wis. 2d 763, 203 N.W. 2d 79 (1973) employee; Elliott v. Amphitheater Ltd., 3 West Week 225 (Manitoba 1934); Gervais v. Candian Arena Co., Rap. Jud. Quebec 74 C.S. 389 (1936); Hammel v. Madison Square Garden Corp., 156 Misc. 311, 279 N.Y.S. 815 (1935); Ingersoll v. Onondag Hockey Club, 245 A.D. 137, 281 N.Y.S. 505 (1935); Kennedy v. Providence Hockey Club, R.I., 376 A. 2d 329 (1977); Modec v. Eveleth, 224 Minn. 556, 29 N.W. 2d 453 (1947); Rich v. Madison Square Garden Corp.,

149 Misc. 123, 266 N.Y.S. 288, aff'd. 241 A.D. 722, 270 N.Y.S. 915 (1933); Shannon v. Boston Madison Square Garden, 296 Mass. 168, 5 N.E. 2d 1 (1936).

[49] Kennedy v. Providence Hockey Club, 119 R.I. 70, 376 A. 2d 329 (1977).

[50] Parsons v. Nat'l Dairy Cattle Congress, Iowa, 277 N.W. 2d 620 (1979).

[51] Riley v. Chicago Cougars Hockey Club, 100 Ill.App.3d 664, 56 Ill.Dec. 210, 427 N.E.2d 290 (1981).

first row of the balcony near one of the goals. During the third period, one of the players took a slipshod slapshot toward the goal. The puck deflected off one of the players' sticks and soared on an angle to the first row of the balcony. The puck struck the plaintiff on the left side of his head and knocked him unconscious. Plaintiff immediately suffered a Jacksonian seizure which rendered him unable to speak and caused his hands, arms and legs to violently shake. As a result of the accident, plaintiff sustained a permanent brain lesion. Subsequently, he periodically experienced epileptic seizures. Plaintiff received judgment of $90,000 against the team.

Height of the protective barrier and assumption of risk, also, were at issue in a 1985 New York case.[52] A 13-year-old spectator was struck on lip and cosmetically disfigured when a puck was deflected from the goalie's stick, to the seventh row behind the glass barrier at the goal end of the arena. Just one month prior to the accident, spectators there had been protected by a chain link fence mounted atop the boards; however, the tempered glass installed was 1' less in height than the fence. The protective netting, which had been installed behind each goal, had been drawn to the ceiling, leaving much of the area behind the goal unprotected. The court held that the spectators should have been warned about the lower protective barrier, and that the spectator could not be said to have assumed the risk. It also was stated that an arena has the duty to provide protected seats behind each goal where the danger is the greatest, and that the extent of protection depends on the number of spectators who may reasonably be expected to avail themselves of such seating in the course of an ordinary game.

In the 1979 *Parsons* case[53] the plaintiff was struck by a hockey puck while returning to her seat after intermission. She alleged that defendants failed to erect barriers to protect her from errant hockey pucks and thus provide her a safe place from which to watch the game, while defendants stated that plaintiff was an experienced hockey fan and based their defense on assumption of risk and contributory negligence. In another late 1970s case (*Kennedy* case),[54] the plaintiff was attending the game with her fiance seated in the fourth row up from the arena floor. Protection of spectators consisted of a wooden "dasher" that rose to a height of approximately 18″ to 24″ above the ice plus a 5' sheet of ½″ thick plexiglass which was attached to the top of the "dasher." This shield, however, only protected spectators in the first three rows. During a face-off, the puck was lofted from the ice and struck plaintiff in the left eye. She was treated in the first aid room and thereafter incurred substantial medical expenses and loss of work for several months. Plaintiff had attended 30-40 games at this arena and had seen many games on television, and, thus, was knowledgeable of the risks incurred by spectators.

In an early case[55] the missile which hit a spectator was a hockey stick which flew out of the hand of a player when he collided with another player. No liability. However, when the hockey puck went outside the seating area, liability was found. A spectator was struck by a puck as she was walking on the promenade to the rest room.[56]

[52] Sawyer v. State of New York, 127 Misc. 2d 295, 485 N.Y.S. 2d 695 (1985).

[53] Parsons v. Nat'l Dairy Cattle Congress, 227 N.W.2d 620 (Iowa 1979).

[54] Kennedy v. Providence Hockey Club, 119 R.I. 70, 376 A.2d 329 (1977); see also Gilchrist v. City of Troy, 67 N.Y. 2d 1034, 503 N.Y.S. 2d 717, 494 N.E. 2d 1382 (1986) municipal hockey rink, child struck in face

by puck while standing along dasher boards during game, owner not negligent.

[55] Rich v. Madison Square Garden Corp., 149 Misc. 123, 266 N.Y.S. 288, aff'd. 241 A.D. 722, 270 N.Y.S. 915 (1933).

[56] Lemoine v. Springfield Hockey Assoc., 307 Mass. 102, 29 N.E. 2d 716 (1940).

§ 15.1123   Golf balls hitting spectators

While most of the injuries from golf balls are to another player (see §7.11), there are a few cases of spectator injuries. In a 1985 case,[57] the plaintiff, her son, his friend, and his friend's mother went to the golf tournament held at the country club. This was her first tournament. She and the friend's mother went to the first tee to watch Arnold Palmer, while the boys went off on their own. As they went along, the two stopped at a concession stand, which was set up between two fairways, which were roped off. As plaintiff was watching, an unidentified golfer lined up a shot, and she was struck. No warning was heard. Plaintiff lost all sight in her right eye and wears a prosthetic shell over the eye for cosmetic purposes. Plaintiff alleged that defendant failed to give timely warning, to restrict plaintiff from place they knew or should have known was a place of danger, to provide individuals trained in crowd control and prevention of injury to spectators, to provide unobstructed views to the playing area at the location where plaintiff was standing, and to warn the plaintiff of the dangerous condition existing at the location. Plaintiff sued the player who hit the ball, the country club on whose course the tournament was being held, and the golf association, which was sponsoring the tournament. The court said that the owner of a business premise has the duty to discover dangerous conditions existing on the premises and to give sufficient warning to invitee to enable the invitee to avoid harm. The court further said that in raising the defense of assumption of risk, the defendants had to prove that the spectator appreciated the danger of being struck by a golf ball while in presumed area of safety at concession stand on golf course. Foreseeability at such location was indicated a factor.

In a case[58] about the same time as the *Duffy* case, plaintiff was a spectator in a charity golf tournament and, having followed the golfers, was now resting with other spectators under a large tree approximately 30'-35' from the edge of the green and 10'-15' from the base of the tree. There were bleachers, which were very crowded. The tee shot hooked and struck plaintiff in the eye, requiring it to be surgically removed. She heard no warning or the ball coming through the tree leaves above her. Defendant alleged that they had provided appropriate seating, which plaintiff chose not to use and thus assumed the risks. Court held that spectator barred by primary assumption of risk and that the promoters and club owed duty only to provide reasonably safe area for watching tournament.

In *Fink v. Klein*[59] the plaintiff was a member of the rules committee for the junior tournament and was on the golf course as such member. Further, she had instructed the junior player whose golf ball hit her and was aware of the type of golf he played and his ability. The court held that the plaintiff was contributorily negligent. No recovery for plaintiff.

§ 15.1124   Basketball hitting spectators

The plaintiff spectator was struck by a basketball thrown toward the spectators by a

[57] Duffy v. Midlothian Country Club, 47 Ill. Dec. 786, 92 Ill. App. 3d 193, 415 N.E. 2d 1099 (1980), aff'd. 90 Ill. Dec. 237, 135 Ill. App. 3d 429, 418 N.E. 2d 1037 (1985) comparative negligence does not affect express assumption of risk or primary implied assumption of risk, but abolishes secondary implied assumption of risk.

[58] Grisim v. Tapemark Charity Pro-Am Golf Tournament, 394 N.W. 2d 261 (Minn. App. 1986), rev'd. 415 N.W. 2d 874 (Minn. 1987).

[59] Fink v. Klein, 186 Kan. 12, 348 P. 2d 620 (1960).

member of the defendant's basketball team. The court found that the player was acting in the course of his employment, where there was no evidence upon which the jury could have found that the act arose wholly from some external, independent and personal motive of the player to do the act on his own account, rather than as an act incident to the game. In giving judgment to the plaintiff, it was held that there is a duty of ordinary care to spectators and that the rule as to assumption of risk applicable to baseball games was not applicable to spectators at a basketball game.[60]

§ 15.113   Football players running out-of-bounds

When spectators choose to sit or stand next to a football field, such persons assume the risks obvious and incidental to the game of football. In a New York case[61] a 17-year-old student was injured when the players in a football game left the marked field during the course of play. She was viewing the game from the sidelines, although she was aware that players occasionally left the field of play and also knew that seats were available in adjacent bleachers. No recovery; plaintiff assumed the risks.

In a Washington case[62] about the same time, a similar result was reached. The spectator plaintiff was a 67-year-old grandmother who was invited to the game by her grandson, who was playing. She had never been to a third team high school football game before and had attended only one other football game in her life. Although there were bleachers available, the spectators were not requested to sit in them, so the grandmother went with all the other spectators to stand on the sideline. At the time of the accident, she was standing with her daughter (the boy's mother) in the front row of a four-deep crowd about a foot or two back from the playing field boundary line. The two were conversing and not paying too much attention to the game. The game had been in progress about ten minutes when one of the players was hit by two opposing team players and knocked him into the plaintiff, throwing her violently to the ground and severely and permanently injuring her. Although the court said that the school district could have roped off an area some yards back from the boundary to make safe the place to stand or could have provided seats, it found the school not negligent and that the plaintiff had a duty to protect herself from dangers incident to the game as would be apparent to a reasonable person in exercise of due care, even if she did not have actual knowledge of dangers of the game. Judgment for defendant on the basis of contributory negligence by the plaintiff. However, the court did indicate that there is a higher degree of care required toward spectators for games with large crowds than for informal third team games or intramural contests where largely friends and relatives attend and there is no admission charged. The court also indicated that ignorance of the game by a spectator should not be a controlling factor, for spectators are not able to assume risks about which they are not knowledgeable; however, risks apparent to an "ordinary and prudent" person are assumed, such as in this case.

[60] McFatridge v. Harlem Globetrotters, 69 N.M. 271, 365 P. 2d 918 (1961).
[61] Cadieux v. Board of Education, 25 A.D. 2d 579, 266 N.Y.S. 2d 895 (1966).
[62] Perry v. Seattle School District No. 1, 66 Wash. 2d 800, 405 P. 2d 589 (1965); see also Ingerson v. Shattcuk School, 185 Minn. 16, 239 N.W. 667 (1931).

And in another case[63] involving informal football games, the court stated that with the extensive viewing of football on television, it is common knowledge that players frequently run out of bounds. In this Louisiana case, the injured person was a father, a physician, who was watching his son play in a local public high school football team scrimmage in spring practice. He was also a former football player and should have been well aware of the dangers.

Plaintiff, a professional photographer, was taking action pictures for the high school yearbook from the sidelines of a football game. He sustained injury to his left leg when he was struck by the players running out of bounds during play. No recovery on the basis of state immunity statute.[64] Plaintiff, who went to the high school football game as a spectator, was asked to serve on the sideline "chain-team." While serving in such capacity he was injured when a player forced out of bounds drove him into the grandstand. Defendants were protected by governmental immunity.[65]

§ 15.12   Crowd control

What is the duty owed a spectator to protect against injury by another spectator? The nature of the duty appears to relate to the act and its foreseeability (including actual and constructive notice), whether the act by the spectator who injured the plaintiff arose from the exuberance of the game, from rowdyism and lack of discipline, from allegations of intoxication, or from an intent to injure, and the reasonableness of the measures taken to protect against such acts. It is clear, however, that management does owe a duty to protect a spectator from unreasonable risk of harm from other spectators. What is an unreasonable risk, of course, is dependent upon each situation. In addition to the cases presented in this section, see also the next section on safe premises (§15.13).

While the cases in the subsequent sub-sections do not address this issue, not to be overlooked is disorderly conduct for the purpose of disturbing lawful assembly. Many states have laws related thereto,[66] as well as disorderly conduct on the land or property of another.[67] One such law pertaining to disturbing lawful assembly was applied to a basketball game; the court said that such game constituted a "meeting of the people" under the statute.[68] During the presentation of colors and playing of the national anthem, various objects were thrown toward the playing surface of the basketball court and others hit spectators. The start of the game was delayed 35 to 40 minutes while the surface of the court was restored to playing conditions. Disorderly conduct includes abusive language. The court held that plaintiff's conviction for disturbing a place of assembly, based on evidence that accused gestured obscenely and loudly uttered a lewd chant at a high school basketball game, did not violate the Constitutional right of free speech.[69]

[63] Colclough v. Orleans Parish School Board, 166 So. 2d 647 (La. App. 1964).

[64] Winston v. Reorganized School Dist. 2, 636 S.W. 2d 324 (Mo. 1982).

[65] Couture v. Board of Education, Plainfield, 6 Conn. App. 309, 505 A. 2d 432 (1986).

[66] For example, State v. Smith, 46 N.J. 510, 218 A. 2d 147 (1966) interpreting N.J. statute.

[67] For example, Maryland.

[68] State v. Orzen, 83 N.M. 458, 493 P. 2d 768 (1972); some states also have laws regarding throwing objects at athletic events, such as Maryland.

[69] State v. Morgulis, 110 N.J. Super. 464, 266 So. 2d 695 (La. App. 1974).

And, it has been held that to attend athletic events is not a Constitutional right.[70] A spectator, who was involved in a dispute with a basketball referee at a high school athletic contest, was effectively barred from attending events for a year when the State high school athletic association barred the school from participating in association games if this person were present. (See §1.3 Civil liberties.)

Ejection and exclusion of individual spectators as a means of crowd control are appropriate and usually upheld, as indicated in the foregoing paragraph;[71] however, there should be written guidelines instructing ushers and security guards as to proper procedures and grounds for ejecting or excluding persons whose behavior may be disruptive. The authority of ushers/ticket takers-sellers, et al., who essentially facilitate an event and maintain order, and security guards, who have the primary responsibility for law enforcement and may be deputized law officers, should be distinguished. Undue use of force may result in assault and battery charges (see §1.4132).

§ 15.121   Student discipline

A student's misbehavior may involve throwing objects. Teachers were attempting to supervise students, who were in attendance as paying spectators. During the game, the students behind the plaintiff were engaged in rowdyism and dangerous conduct, throwing objects upon those seated below. Plaintiff was hit by a heavy glass bottle. Judgment for defendant; however, plaintiff failed to allege employees had knowledge of the rowdyism.[72] An opposite result was held when plaintiff lost her eye sight due to being hit by pebbles being thrown by another student while she was a spectator on an athletic field. Twenty eighth-grade girls were directed by the teacher to sit on a log on the third-base line of a baseball field being used by the eighth-grade boys. The teacher returned to the building; about five minutes after she left some of the boys waiting to bat began pelting the girls with pebbles. Although the girls protested, the pebble throwing continued for three or four minutes until plaintiff was struck in the right eye. Plaintiff alleged lack of supervision. The court held that it was necessary to prove that a general danger was foreseeable, not the particular accident, and that supervision would have prevented the accident.[73]

General rowdiness is a matter for supervisory concern. A 64-year-old woman school bus driver, as she was walking to her seat through a grassy area behind the stands, noticed a crowd of boys and girls playing near the NW end of the stadium. Next thing she knew, she had been knocked to the ground by a "big boy," who fell on top of her, fracturing her foot. The boy apologized and left. Off-duty police and teachers had been hired to keep order. The children had been engaged in horseplay there the previous game and police were in the area. The school owed a duty to exercise reasonable care in supervising children attending the football game.[74] (See also §18.322.)

[70] Watkins v. Louisiana H.S. Athletic Assoc., 301 So. 2d 695 (La. App. 1974); see also Boster v. Philpot, 645 F. Supp. 798 (1986) Kansas law applied.

[71] Propriety of Exclusion of Persons from Horse-racing Tracks for Reasons Other Than Color or Race, 90 A.L.R. 3d 1361-1371.

[72] Weldy v. Oakland H.S. Dist., 19 Cal. App. 2d 429, 65 P. 2d 851 (1937).

[73] Sheenan v. St. Peter's Catholic School, 188 N.W. 2d 868 (Minn. 1971).

[74] Tanari v. School, 69 Ill. 2d 630, 14 Ill. Dec. 874, 373 N.E. 2d 5 (1977).

Student control in waiting for tickets was at issue in two cases. An 18-year-old student went with others to the gymnasium to attend a public dance. He found a long line waiting for tickets, and subsequently went around to a side door which was chained shut; went back to the front; then returned to side. The officer at the side door, seeing the crowd was in a belligerent mood and had been drinking, drew his .38 calibre revolver and fired toward the ground two times. One of the bullets rebounded, hitting plaintiff. The court held that although the officer did not act appropriately, the plaintiff was contributorily negligent in joining the mob crowd and thus assumed the risks of such mob action.[75] In the other case[76] the plaintiff student claimed that she was injured, while waiting to purchase football tickets, due to the negligence of the University. The plaintiff had crawled into a sleeping bag and settled in for a long wait; a large crowd collected. Abruptly, the place of sale was changed, announced over loud speakers. This precipitated an uncontrolled mass rush by the crowd, during which time the plaintiff was trampled and severely injured.

Control of students, also, was at issue in an action brought by a father who was injured at a father-son event at school. Plaintiff father was on the gymnasium floor watching a basketball game with his son, when another student went to retrieve a basketball and collided with him, causing injury to his leg. Plaintiff alleged failure to properly supervise and exercise care to protect those in attendance from injury. The court did not find that supervisory personnel could have prevented the injury which occurred.[77]

§ 15.122   Rowdyism and disorderliness

Spectators can be injured in many different circumstances due to rowdyism of fellow spectators, including jostling on a stairway without handrails when going for refreshments,[78] standing on a bench and pushed off backward,[79] crowding concessionaire in stands and causing him to lose his balance,[80] throwing soft drink bottle,[81] and pushing in aisle.[82] A baseball player was injured when the spectators congregated too close to the third base foul line and pushed a bench into a dangerous position near the foul line. The plaintiff, a catcher, going after a foul ball fell over the bench and broke his

[75] Braswell v. North Carolina A & T State Univ., 5 N.C. App. 1 158 S.E. 2d 24 (1969).

[76] Shriver v. Athletic Council, 222 Kan. 216, 564 P. 2d 451 (1977); see also Maro case in next section.

[77] Borushek v. Kincaid, 33 Ill. Dec. 839, 78 Ill. App. 3d 295, 397 N.E. 2d 172 (1979).

[78] Bacon v. Harris, 221 Ore. 553, 352 P. 2d 472 (1960) basketball game, alleged lack of supervision to control running and jostling by the crowd, held: no negligence.

[79] Waterman v. President & Fellows of Harvard College, 290 Mass. 535, 195 N.E. 717 (1935) no recovery, not anticipated that crowd would surge against such a spectator, who was not required to stand on bench.

[80] Klish v. Alaskan Amusement Co., 153 Kan. 93,

109 P. 2d 75 (1941) ice hockey game, to permit crowding is not in itself negligence.

[81] Sample v. Eaton, 145 Cal. App. 2d 312, 302 P. 2d 431 (1956) operator of refreshment stand did not owe a duty to spectator to protect from act of another spectator since neither owned nor controlled the wrestling exhibition, wrestling club proprietor did owe a duty; see also Philpot v. Brooklyn Nat'l League Baseball Team, 303 N.Y. 116, 100 N.E. 2d 164 (1951).

[82] Futterer v. Saratoga Assoc., 262 A.D. 675, 31 N.Y.S. 2d 108 (1941) returning to seat between races pushed into a private box adjoining the main aisle, plaintiff alleged chains or other barriers should be across entrances to private boxes, held certain amount of jostling by patrons at race track ordinary risk of attendance.

leg. Plaintiff recovered.[83] Often one sees fans, after a "big" football game converge on the goal posts, trying to take them down. A spectator was seriously injured at a Harvard-Yale game when she was struck by a goal post being pulled down. Plaintiff alleged inadequate crowd control. Yale and city (police officers) had agreed to let the goal post be torn down and not to try and stop the crowd.[84]

In an early New York case,[85] the court extended the concept that negligence is gauged by the ability to anticipate to a hotel, which was serving as headquarters for one of the teams in an Army-Notre Dame game. It was held that the hotel management had a duty toward patrons when the lobby became congested with hilarious persons. When one assembles a crowd for financial gain, care must be given to protect patrons.

The sufficiency of attendants, guards, or ushers to control may be at issue. In trying to remove a disorderly spectator, a police officer bumped into plaintiff who was standing directly in front of the chair he had occupied during the event, knocking him backwards and across the edge of the chair. While the plaintiff acknowledged the correctness of the trial court's ruling that the police officer was not in the employ of the defendant and the police officer was not responsible for the proprietor's negligence, the plaintiff alleged that the defendant should have erected a railing or barrier between the ring and the front seat which he was occupying and inadequacy in number of ushers, guards, or attendants. The court found no evidence that an increase in number would have prevented the accident. Judgment for defendant.[86]

Plaintiff was knocked down by two "unknown" juveniles running through the crowd at a professional football game. The professional team rented and presumably controlled the stadium and had allowed some automobiles to park inside the stadium fences, blocking certain exits, restricting egress, and causing the crowd to become unruly.[87]

In a 1985 case,[88] a patron, who was knocked down by horseplay of boys at stadium while leaving a football game, brought action against state sports authority and private security agency. The court held that the activities of the boys playing "touch football" in the absence of security guards following the game did not constitute "dangerous condition" within the meaning of the Tort Claims Act, so defendants were immune under the Act. The private security agency contract with the sport authority also brought it under the immunity of the Act.

In a very old case,[89] plaintiff had entered the enclosure of a baseball stadium to purchase tickets. Finding there were none left, he attempted to exit, but because of the crowds, the police prevented him from doing so through the regular exits and he was detained for some hours. The court held that while to redirect egress was an appropriate

---

[83] Domino v. Mercurio, 17 A.D. 2d 342, 234 N.Y.S. 2d (1962).

[84] Cimino v. Yale University, et al., 638 F. Supp. 952 (1986) a number of other issues involved — Connecticut laws, public nuisance, indemnification.

[85] Schubart v. Hotel Astor, Inc., 168 Misc. 431, 5 N.Y.S. 2d 203 (1938).

[86] C. & M. Promotions v. Ryland, 208 Va. 365, 158 S.E. 2d 132 (1967).

[87] Jung v. Tulane Univ. and Caruso v. Tulane Univ.

of Louisiana, 300 So. 2d 542 (La. App. 1974); see also Howard v. Village of Chisholm, 191 Minn. 245, 253 N.W. 766 (1934); Lee v. Nat'l League Baseball Club of Milwaukee, 4 Wis. 2d 168, 89 N.W. 2d 811 (1958); Porter v. Calif. Jockey Club, 285 P. 2d 60 (Cal. App. 1955).

[88] Vanchieri v. N.J. Sports & Exposition Authority, 201 N.J. Super. 34, 492 A. 2d 686 (1985).

[89] Talcott v. Nat'l Exhibition Co., 128 N.Y.S. 1059 (1911).

police measure, defendant owed plaintiff an active duty to point out other means of egress, and was guilty of falsely imprisoning him in failing to do so.

Injury also may occur in special events. In a Fourth of July parade situation, plaintiff spectator was injured when struck by some plywood sheathing, which had been loosened by some other spectators climbing a scaffolding onto a wooden covered walkway. The broadcasting corporation which legally sponsored the parade on public streets along a route specified in a municipal permit was not liable for injury where it had committed no negligent act, was not in control of the building or construction around it, and had no actual knowledge of alleged defective and unsafe condition of scaffolding.[90] (See §11.21 parades.)

In *Delgado v. City of Miami Beach,* 518 So. 2d 968 (Fla. App. 1988), plaintiff, a spectator, was struck and burned by fireworks ignited by someone in crowd attending a concert and fireworks display sponsored by the city. The court held that failure by city to prohibit possession and detonation of fireworks by individuals fell within planning-level, discretionary function of government for which no liability attached and thus city was protected from liability to spectator. (See §4.13 Discretionary act, and §11.26 Fireworks).

§ 15.123   Fighting and assaults[91]

When spectators get out of control, there often is fighting, which may result in physical injury. This is particularly true when spectators are intoxicated. There also may be attacks on spectators by third parties (see §1.4132).

§ 15.1231   Attacks on spectators

In a 1980 case[92] against the Chicago Park District, defendant obtained summary judgment. The District owned the stadium and football club. The plaintiff was assaulted and robbed. There was no evidence of prior incidents of violence showing that attack was reasonably foreseeable and consequently defendant owed no duty to protect spectator from such unforeseeable violence.

The lack of foreseeability, also, was the basis of holding for the defendant in a 1987

[90] Armburst v. Cox Broadcasting Corp., 117 Ga. App. 381, 160 S.E. 2d 609 (1968); see also F.W. Woolworth v. Kirby, 302 So. 2d 67 (Ala. 1974) parking lot promotional event, plaintiff knocked down and trampled by crowd.

[91] Pearson, James O., Jr. Liability of Owner or Operator of Theatre or Other Amusement to Patron Assaulted by Another Patron. 75 A.L.R.3d 441-483. For additional cases, particularly in commerical establishments.

[92] Gill v. Chicago Park District, 85 Ill. App. 3d 903, 41 Ill. Dec. 173, 407 N.E. 2d 671 (1980); see also McDonald v. Chicago Stadium Corp., 336 Ill. App. 353, 83 N.E. 2d 616 (1949) ice hockey game, assault not foreseeable, assaulted over right to a seat; Nance v.

Ball, 134 So. 2d 35 (Fla. App. 1961) patron had tendency to assault others while engaged in competitive bowling; Shayne v. Colliseum Bldg. Corp., 270 Ill. App. 547 (1933) stadium proprietor (boxing) not insurer of spectator safety, spectator shoved out of balcony during altercation in which weapons drawn and panic in audience ensued; Shtekla v. Topping, 23 A.D. 2d 750, 258 N.Y.S. 2d 982, app. dism'd. 18 N.Y. 2d 961, 277 N.Y.S. 2d 694, 224 N.E. 2d 116 (1965) baseball, fight broke out, alleged insufficient guards and guards arrived too late; Stevenson v. Kansas City, 187 Kan. 705, 306 P. 2d 1 (1961) plaintiff on ramp to restroom forcibly assaulted by unidentified man who struck plaintiff with a heavy metal object, not foreseeable.

school case.[93] Plaintiff was injured when attacked by three students at a basketball game sponsored by the two school districts, and alleged lack of proper supervision at the game. The court stated that the schools did owe a duty to take precautions to protect plaintiff from reasonably foreseeable acts of third parties; however, it found no evidence of prior assaults or misconduct by students or that such a basketball game was likely to inspire violence. A similar result was reached in *St. Pierre v. Lombard,* 512 So. 2d 1206 (La. App. 1987), when a boy was fatally stabbed while attending a high school football game. Parents sued the school board which had rented stadium to private high school for the game. Court held that the school board assumed no duty under contract to provide security for event. The case opinion stated further, however, that as a general rule while an owner of business is under duty to take reasonable care for safety of patrons on premises, this duty to protect does not extend to unforeseeable or unanticipated criminal acts of independent third person.

A college student brought an action against a state college to recover damages when he left the basketball game at half time, because a riot between black and white students had broken out, and was leaving the door when he was accosted, resulting in an altercation and stabbing. Held that under the State tort act that the college was not liable in tort for failure to protect against the criminal propensity of a third person on the premises.[94] In a 1983 case,[95] also in New Jersey, the State sports authority was held immune for failure to provide adequate security protection. Plaintiff was assaulted and robbed in the parking lot at a racetrack. There was a similar result in a 1983 Pennsylvania case.[96] Plaintiff was assaulted when he left a city-owned stadium after a professional football game. The court held that generally a municipality acting in its governmental capacity for protection of public will not be held liable for failure to provide adequate police protection to particular individual absent some special relationship. No special relationship was shown in this situation; further, there was no indication that spectator was exposed to special danger of which police were aware or undertook to prevent.

The defendant was on the teaching staff of the high school and was assigned the duty of keeping the crowd away from the fence between the stands and the playing field during a night football game. Shortly before half-time a player was injured and carried from the field on a stretcher. He was put down near the fence just below where plaintiff was sitting. Plaintiff and a number of others went to the fence to learn something about the seriousness of the injuries. The defendant came along and ordered them back to their seats. The plaintiff testified that the crowd started back, and as he also turned to go, the defendant took hold of him, turned him around, and started hitting him on the face, first with his fist, then with the flat of his hand. Another man (campus policeman) stepped between them. There was a difference of opinion as to just what happened in terms of the blow with the fist and whether plaintiff was in fact turning to go back when hit. While the court held that determination of whether the teacher used unreasonable force

---

[93] Cook v. School District UH3J, 83 Or. App. 292, 731 P. 2d 443 (1987).

[94] Setrin v. Glassboro State College, 136 N.J. Super. 329, 346 A. 2d 102 (1975).

[95] Rodriguez v. N.J. Sport & Exposition Authority, 193 N.J. Super. 39, 472 A. 2d 146 (1983).

[96] Duffy v. City of Philadelphia, 580 F. Supp. 164 (1983) Pennsylvania law applied; see also Boyd v. Gulfport Municipal Separate School District, 821 F. 2d 308 (1987) Mississippi law applied, governmental immunity, patron attacked in parking lot after attending football game.

on the 15-year-old boy was for the jury, the teacher was convicted of violating a city ordinance prohibiting fighting.[97]

§ 15.1232   Intoxication or alleged intoxication[98]

With increased concern for intoxicated persons and injuries caused thereby at the turn of the decade of the '80s, the responsibilities of the proprietor/operator of sporting events, amusements, and recreational activities may find in the courts a more strict duty to protect participants and spectators from such intoxicated persons than some of the cited cases have held. Intoxication, however has been a problem of longstanding in terms of crowd control and protecting spectators/participants from the acts of third persons.[99] (See also §1.221 Intoxication.)

Crowd control is one of the primary problems when there are persons who are intoxicated.[100] Protection of spectators extends to "tailgate" parties at football games. In a 1983 case[101] a husband and wife were going through the parking area to their car when the wife was knocked down from behind by a drunk, with resultant broken leg. The court held that where the University knew of the intoxication and the threat of safety to others, it was under a duty to take reasonable precautions to protect those who attended football games from injury caused by acts of third persons.

The standard of care which must be exercised by those who serve liquor must be recognized, and increasingly, both by statute[102] and case law the responsibility is being placed on the person (organization, business) who sells the liquor. Situations specific to leisure services are many, for example, as related to a community evening cruise,[103] a bait shop on the pier,[104] in a parking lot outside a bowling alley,[105] and ticket holders in a sports complex.[106] Also, pre-existing duties are not relieved by intoxication, as a member of a fraternal organization found when sued.[107] Further, the exact manner of the harm need not be foreseen; only that the injuries were reasonably foreseeable from consumption by spectators of alcohol.[108]

§ 15.13   Safe premises

This section deals with injuries to spectators in relation to bleachers and other seating

---

[97] Macomb v. Gould, 104 Ill. App. 2d 361, 244 N.E. 2d 634 (1969).

[98] See 75 A.L.R. 3d 441-483.

[99] e.g. Mastad v. Swedish Brethren, 83 Minn. 40, 85 N.W. 913 (1901) picnic at a lake to which tickets were sold, liable for assault and injury; Maksinczak v. Salliotte, 140 Mich. App. 537, 364 N.W. 2d 737 (1985) plaintiff attacked by intoxicated woman while attending fireworks display.

[100] e.g., Reynolds v. Deep South Sports, 211 So. 2d 37 (Fla. App. 1968); Warner v. Florida Jai Alai, Inc., 221 So. 2d 777 (Fla. App. 1969), cert. dism'd. 235 So. 2d 294; Whitfield v. Cox, 189 Va. 219, 52 S.E. 2d 72 (1949).

[101] Bearman v. Univ. of Notre Dame, 453 N.E. 2d 1196 (Ind. App. 1983).

[102] More than 20 states now have "dram shop"

laws, which this section does not detail — check your own state. Some laws are specific to leisure services, e.g., Conn. P.A. 83-283 (Jan. session 1983), serving alcoholic beverages in racquetball facility.

[103] Torres v. Salty Sea Days, Inc., 36 Wash. App. 668, 676 P. 2d 512 (1984).

[104] Estate of Starling v. Fisherman's Pier, 401 So. 2d 1135 (Fla. App. 1981), cert. denied 411 So. 2d 381 (Fla. 1981).

[105] Bishop v. Fair Lanes Georgia Bowling, 803 F. 2d 1548 (1986) Georgia law applied.

[106] Maro v. Potash, 220 N.J. Super. 90, 531 A. 2d 407 (1987).

[107] Hovermale v. Berkeley Springs Moose Lodge, 271 S.E. 2d 335 (W. Va. 1980).

[108] Ollison v. Weinberg Racing Assoc., 69 Or. App. 653, 688 P. 2d 847 (1984).

construction, rest rooms, walkways, and parking. See also §20.2 on Environmental conditions, and §22.2 Parking. Lease arrangements for maintenance, too, will affect liability (see §3.11). For fireworks going into spectators, see §11.26.

§ 15.131   Bleachers and other seating arrangements

Injuries related to bleachers occur primarily from defective bleachers, that is, the construction of the bleachers, or from the behavior of the spectators. Proximity to utility lines, also, has given rise to spectator injury. At a race track, the contractor built metal bleachers within 2′ of the electric line, which had been located in that place for a number of years. The new bleachers replaced smaller temporary stands, which had been erected out of reach of the power line. The utility company had not been notified of the new higher and wider bleachers. A slight deflection of the utility pole caused the line to touch the bleachers and cause injury to the plaintiff. While the National Electric Code required insulation where public contact and there was a duty to inspect lines, held that the company was not required to keep the lines under constant surveillance. Judgment for defendant.[109]

§ 15.1311   Defective bleachers

Except for those cases where the defendant was protected by charitable immunity,[110] governmental immunity,[111] or recreational user statutes,[112] most of the suits have held in favor of the plaintiff, inasmuch as negligent construction was found in most situations. The standard of care is high regarding inspection and appropriate repair for the safety of the spectators. Most cases turn on whether there was actual or constructive notice of the defect. Several cases especially mention the importance of inspection.[113] In *Parker v Warren*, 503 S.W. 2d 938 (Tenn. App. 1973), the court held that the spectator is entitled to assume that the premises are in a safe condition and no inspection is required by the spectator; the duty to inspect is upon the proprietor. However, if one inspects and reports, something should be done about defects. In the *Bruss* case[114] the sporting goods company employee inspected the folding bleachers and reported several defects to the company (which had sold the bleachers), but the company did not repair

[109] Pilkington v. Hendricks County Rural Electric Membership Corp., 460 N.E. 2d 1000 (Ind. App. 1984).

[110] Pomeroy v. Little League Baseball of Collingsworth, 142 N.J. Super. 471, 362 A. 2d 39 (1976). See §4.3 on charitable immunity status of states.

[111] Gravely v. Lewisville Indp. School Dist., 701 S.W. 2d 956 (Tex. App. 1986); Plemmons v. Gastonia, 62 N.C. App. 470, 302 S.E. 2d 905 (1983), denied 309 N.C. 322, 307 S.E. 2d 165 (1983); Sewell v. Knoxville, 444 S.W. 2d 177 (Tenn. 1969); see §4.2 on governmental immunity status of states.

[112] Rodrigue v. Firemen's Fund Ins. Co., 449 So. 2d 1042 (La. App. 1984). See for further discussion §12.1.

[113] Coughlon v. Iowa H.S. Athletic Assoc. et al.,

260 Iowa 702, 150 N.W. 2d 660 (1967); Guymon v. Finicum, 265 P. 2d 706 (Okla. 1953); Harllee v. Gulfport, 120 F. 2d 41 (5th Cir. 1941); Novak v. Delavan, 31 Wis. 2d 200, 143 N.W. 2d 6 (1966); Rice v. Granite School Dist., 23 Utah 2d 22, 456 P. 2d 159 (1969); Scott v. University of Mich. Athletic Assn., 152 Mich. 684, 116 N.W. 624 (1908); Southern Methodist Univ. v. Clayton, 172 S.W. 2d 197 (Tex. Civ. App. 1943) rev'd./remanded, 142 Tex. 179, 176 S.E. 2d 749 (1943); Taylor v. Hardee, 232 S.C. 338, 102 S.E.2d 218 (1958) speedway bleachers collapsed; Tyler v. Ingram, 139 Tex. Sup. Ct. R. 600, 164 S.W. 2d 516 (1942); Witherspoon v. Haft, 157 Ohio St. 474, 106 N.E.2d 296 (1952).

[114] Bruss v. Milwaukee Sporting Goods Co., 34 Wis. 2d 688, 150 N.W. 2d 337 (1967).

the bleachers, nor did they notify the school of possible danger. It was known at least four days before the accident that the row locks needed repairing. Judgment for plaintiff.

Spectator injuries have been caused by: temporary seats giving way when constructed with improper nails and insufficient bracing;[115] collapse of bleachers due to general construction of the bleachers;[116] loose planks that get moved when the spectators stand up;[117] overloading with people;[118] unsatisfactory selection of site for foundation;[119] bracing removed by mischievous boys;[120] inadequate bracing;[121] makeshift seats;[122] cadence swaying of exuberant fans;[123] as spectators leaving, stands folded up;[124] crack between planking of standing platform;[125] and crowd getting excited and standing up.[126]

Defendants have endeavored to shift responsibility on the basis of lessor-lessee relationships or independent contractors responsible for erection of the bleachers.[127] A 1976 Alabama case[128] was brought on the theory of implied contract, specifically that the athletic ticket purchased by plaintiff constituted a contract with the county board of education that a safe and proper place from which to observe the game would be provided.

Two cases were brought on product liability. In the *DiPerna* case,[129] the plaintiff pushed against the end of a metal railing protruding from the end of folding bleachers, during a basketball game. The court held that neither the architects, who designed the gymnasium, nor the manufacturers of the bleachers were liable for injuries, in the absence of proof that the complaint of danger or defect in the bleachers was either hidden or concealed. In the other case,[130] the architect, also, was sued, along with the

[115] Adams v. Schneider, 71 Ind. App. 429, 124 N.E. 718 (1919); Connor v. Meuer, 232 Wis. 656, 288 N.W. 272 (1939); Tyler v. Ingram, 139 Tex. Sup. Ct. R. 600, 164 S.W. 2d 516 (1942).

[116] Alder v. Salt Lake City, 64 Utah 568, 231 P.1102 (1924); George v. Univ. of Minn. Athletic Assn., 107 Minn. 424, 120 N.W. 750 (1909); Leeds v. Atlantic City, 13 N.J. Misc. 868, 181 A. 892 (1935); Penix v. St. Johns, 243 Mich. 259, 92 N.W. 2d 332 (1958); Reed v. Rhea County, 189 Tenn. 247, 225 S.W. 2d 49 (1949); Shaw v. Board of Educ., 17 Ohio L. Abs. 588 (1934).

[117] Bent v. Jonet, 213 Wis. 635, 252 N.E. 290 (1934); Smith v. Camden, 115 N.J.L. 503, 181 A. 160 (1935).

[118] Chafor v. Long Beach, 174 Cal. 478, 163 P. 670 (1917); Hoffman v. Scranton School Dist., 67 Pa. D & C 301 (1949); Jackson v. McFadden, 180 Miss. 78, 177 So. 755 (1938); Kallish v. Amer. Baseball Club of Phila., 138 Pa. Super. 602, 10 A. 2d 831 (1940); Novak v. Delavan, 31 Wis. 2d 200, 143 N.W. 2d 6 (1966); Scott v. University of Mich. Athletic Assn., 152 Mich. 684, 116 N.W. 624 (1908).

[119] Denver v. Spencer, 34 Colo. 270, 62 P. 590 (1905).

[120] Guymon v. Finicum, 265 P. 2d 706 (Okla. 1953).

[121] Harllee v. Gulfport, 120 F. 2d 41 (5th Cir. 1941).

[122] Hoffman v. Scranton School Dist., 67 Pa. D & C 301 (1949).

[123] Richards v. School Dist., 348 Mich. 490, 83 N.W. 2d 643 (1957).

[124] Boyer v. Iowa H.S. Athletic Assoc., 138 N.W. 2d 914 (Iowa 1965) aff'd. 260 Iowa 1061, 152 N.W. 2d 293 (1967); Board of Educ.v. Fredericks, 113 Ga. App. 199, 147 S.E. 2d 769 (1966); Schweikert v. Palm Beach Speedway, 100 So. 2d 804 (Fla. App. 1958).

[125] Scott v. William M. Rice Institute, 178 S.W. 2d 156 (Tex. Civ. App. 1944).

[126] Gallin v. Polo Grands Athletic Club, 126 Misc. 550, 214 N.Y.S. 182 (1926); Parker v. Warren and Warren v. Nailling (two cases), 503 S.W. 2d 938 (Tenn. App. 1973); Waterman v. Pres. Fellows of Harvard College, 290 Mass. 535, 195 N.E. 717 (1935).

[127] Arnold v. State, 163 A.D. 253, 148 N.Y.S. 479 (1914) landmark case, although activity under auspices of indp. contractor, owner has responsibility of safe premises, in this situation rail insufficiently guarded; Brown v. Cleveland Baseball Co., 158 Ohio St. 1, 106 N.E. 2d 632 (1952); Johnson v. Zemel, 109 N.J.L. 197, 160 A. 356 (1932); Lawson v. Clawson, 177 Md. 333, 9 A. 2d 755 (1939).

[128] Sims v. Etowah Co. Board of Educ., Ala. 337 So. 2d 1310 (1976).

[129] DiPerna v. Roman Catholic Diocese of Albany, 30 A.D. 2d 249, 292 N.Y.S. 2d 177 (1968).

[130] Lukowski v. Vecta Educational Corp., 401 N.E. 2d 781 (Ind. App. 1980).

contractor. Injury was sustained when spectator fell from top of balcony bleachers, which contained no back railing. The school had elected to use the bleachers in partially finished condition without approval of the contractor. Further, there was no evidence of breach of duty by the architect. Judgment for defendants; the school settled out of court.

Violation of legal requirements may also bring liability. Plaintiff obtained judgment when injured on portable seating at a wrestling match, when a condition of the license was that the seating be fastened to the floor.[131]

§ 15.1312   Spectator falling from bleachers

Some spectators were injured in the bleachers, but not due to collapse of the bleachers. These include falling on an unlighted concrete ramp which resulted in a fatal injury,[132] falling on stairs,[133] slipping through between the footboards of the seats and falling 15',[134] and falling off a grandstand when a railing in disrepair broke.[135] In another situation,[136] a spectator was killed when a pile of cement blocks fell on him while seated and waiting for a baseball game to begin. Lack of supervision of youngsters has been alleged to be the cause of injury in falling from the bleachers.[137] Falls also may be caused by ice and snow on the bleachers.[138]

In *Brand v. Sertoma Club of Springfield*,[139] the plaintiff voluntarily chose a seat in the top row of a set of bleachers. A rail some 24" high extended across the back of the facility. At the end of the event, when the plaintiff stood up on the top seat to move toward the aisle, "a large woman" pushed against the plaintiff and plaintiff fell over the rail injuring his shoulder. There was no premise defect and the roller derby exhibition was not under control of the school.

§ 15.1313   Seating structures and railings

Plaintiff, a paying spectator at a school basketball game, went to the school cafeteria after the game for some refreshments. While seated, the chair gave way and she was thrown to the floor, sustaining a herniated intervertebral disc and some injuries to the muscles. *Prima facie* showing of negligence of school district was made out when it was testified that the chair collapsed in ordinary use.[140]

During intermission at a wrestling tournament, plaintiff was sitting on a table in a hallway of the school, when defendant employee of school intentionally pulled the table

131 Camp v. Rex, Inc., 304 Mass. 484, 24 N.E. 2d 4 (1939).

132 Watson v. School Dist., 324 Mich. 1, 36 N.W. 2d 195 (1949).

133 Ludwig v. Board of Educ., 35 Ill. App. 2d 401, 183 N.E. 2d 32 (1962); Pollock v. Albany, 88 Ga. App. 737, 77 S.E. 2d 579 (1953).

134 Nielsen v. Sarasota, 110 S. 2d 417 (Fla. 1960).

135 Juntila v. Everett School Dist., 178 Wash. 637, 35 P. 2d 78 (1934); Sawaya v. Tucson High School Dist., 78 Ariz. 389, 281 P. 2d 105 (1955).

136 Smith v. Hefner, 235 N.C. 1, 68 S.E. 2d 783 (1952).

137 Akins v. Sonoma County, 55 Cal. Rptr. 785,

vac. 60 Cal. Rptr. 499, 430 P. 2d 57 (1967); Decker v. Dundee Cent. School Dist., 4 N.Y. 2d 462, 151 N.E. 2d 866 (1958); Strond v. Bridges, 275 S.W. 2d 503 (Tex. Civ. App. 1955).

138 Cleary v. Catholic Diocese of Peoria, 10 Ill. App. 3d 224, 293 N.E. 2d 195 (1973), rev'd. 57 Ill. 2d 384, 312 N.E. 2d 635 (1974).

139 Brand v. Sertoma Club of Springfield, 39 Ill. App. 3d 330, 349 N.E. 2d 502 (1976); Bole v. Pittsburgh Athletic Club, 205 F. 468 (1913) jostling & pushing of crowd knocked patron through open trap door.

140 Raffa v. Central School Dist., 16 A.D.2d 855, 227 N.Y.S.2d 723 (1962).

out from under her, causing her to fall and suffer injuries. The court held that the alleged negligence of the school was failure of supervision rather than failure to correct a dangerous condition of the table itself; and, therefore, the act does not fall within the real property exception of the tort claim act of the State, giving immunity. However, the tort claim act did not bar action against the employee in his individual capacity for willful tortious conduct, which was outside scope of his employment.[141]

The railing at rink side collapsed from outward pressure of spectators. Judgment for ice hockey plaintiff spectator.[142]

A music fan brought suit against the concert promoter, city and two insurers for injuries allegedly sustained by him in a fall from the second floor balcony of the city auditorium during a rock music concert. Plaintiff had gone several hours early to get a good seat, but lost it when he went to the rest room. While he was standing in the darkened balcony in the overcrowed auditorium, he saw a man leave a seat in the first or second row. Intending to take that vacated seat, plaintiff descended the stairs, and in so doing, tripped and fell into and over the balcony railing to the first floor. Although an ambulance was sent for, he left the concert with friends. In relating the incident to his treating physician initially, plaintiff had indicated that he had smoked two or three joints of marijuana and was "high" at the time and he had been leaning against the wall; when he started to take a step, he had lost his balance. Judgment for defendants; the fall was the result of a voluntary action of the plaintiff.[143]

§ 15.132   General premises

Most of the general premises injuries to spectators have occurred due to holes and obstructions on the grounds, parking and in parking lots, and the condition of steps and walkways; however, many of these are fairly old cases. See Chapter 20 for more detailed discussion of liability related to premises. Also see §11.26 for cases concerning spectators and fireworks going astray.

Not a spectator, but a person frequently found at sport events — a cameraman was injured when he fell from a ladder going to the roof of the press box in the football stadium. As he was descending he fell approximately 60' to his death. In addition to the school, the contractor and architect of the stadium were sued on failure to inspect and discover a dangerous condition. The stadium was built nine years earlier. No recovery.[144]

§ 15.1321   Holes and obstructions

The plaintiff spectator was with her husband at a professional golf match. She saw the ball coming toward her and was injured when she fell backward into a hole about 3' from the fairway in an area of higher grass called the "rough." The hole was about 3' deep and

[141] Acker v. Spangler, 500 A. 2d 206 (Pa. Cmwlth. 1985).

[142] Stewart v. Cobalt Curling & Skating Assoc., 19 Ont. L. 667 (1909); see also Greene v. Seattle Athletic Club, 60 Wash. 300, 111 P. 157 (1910); Howard v. Village of Chisholm, 191 Minn. 245, 253 N.W. 766 (1934).

[143] Adams v. Concerts West, 323 So. 2d 493 (La. App. 1975).

[144] Hall v. Rapides Parish School Board, 491 So. 2d 817 (La. App. 1986).

3' in diameter, lined with rocks and stones. The golf club corporation controlled the golf course and hence was liable for the condition of the premises.[145] And, in another golf case,[146] plaintiff spectator following the tournament play tripped on a rock which was concealed by tall grass. The court held that while reasonable care must be taken for the safety of the spectator, the proprietor is not an insurer of safety and the burden of showing that plaintiff had been subjected to some danger not reasonably incident to the game and that the proprietor knew or should have known of such danger in exercise of ordinary care rests on the plaintiff. Judgment for defendant.

A spectator passing through a corridor, while waiting for friend at the ticket window, fell over projecting sawhorse legs which were used for making a temporary aisle. While it was held that negligence could properly run against the lessor, the court stated that it was the lessee's nondelegable duty to exercise ordinary care to protect invitees.[147] (See also §20.2341.)

§ 15.1322   Parking and parking lots

Plaintiff, while walking across a parking lot adjacent to a stadium, tripped and fell over some railroad ties which had been concealed by tall grass and shrubbery. Plaintiffs alleged that the Dolphins maintained the premises in a dangerous condition, failed to warn business invitees, and the parking lot was poorly lit. Court held for defendants, stating that the City, and not the Dolphins, had retained control of the parking lot.[148] See also next section on steps and walkways, and §22.2 Parking areas, streets, connecting walkways.

The court held a university liable for injuries which occurred in the parking lot following a football game. Two men were fighting and one fell down, whereupon they walked away from each other. They were drunk and in an area of "tailgating." The plaintiff and her husband were walking through the area to their car, when one of the men fell on plaintiff from behind, causing a fractured leg. The court in awarding damages to the plaintiff said that the university was aware of the consumption of alcoholic beverages and that persons so consuming pose a general threat to safety of others, and that it was under a duty to take reasonable precautions to protect those who attended football games from injury from acts of third persons.[149] (See also §15.1232 and §1.221.)

Spectator was assaulted and stabbed in the parking lot at a jai-alai club. The court held that such assault was foreseeable in that defendants had knowledge of similar crimes occurring in the parking lot and the premises were in a high crime area. Judgment for plaintiff.[150]

[145] Buck v. Clauson's Inn, Mass. 211 N.E. 2d 349 (1965); see also Douglas v. Lang, 124 S.W. 2d 642 (Mo. App. 1939) stake protruding few inches above ground at carnival; Pollock v. Albany, 88 Ga. App. 737, 77 S.E. 2d 579 (1953).

[146] Thompson v. Sunset Country Club, 227 S.W. 2d 523 (Mo. App. 1950).

[147] Brown v. Reorganization Inv. Co., 350 Mo. 407, 166 S.W. 2d 476 (1942); see also Murray v. Pittsburgh Co., 324 P. 486, 188 A. 190 (1936) gate moved, injuring spectator.

[148] Rodgers v. Miami Dolphins, Ltd., 469 So. 2d 852 (Fla. App. 1985), pet. for rev. dism. 475 So. 2d 695 (Fla. 1985); see also Hemmingway v. Janesville, 275 Wis. 304, 81 N.W. 2d 492 (1957); Jenson v. Juul, 66 S.D. 1, 278 N.W. 6 (1938).

[149] Bearman v. Univ. of Notre Dame, 453 N.E. 2d 1196 (Ind. App. 1983).

[150] Fernandez v. Miami Jai-Alai, 386 So. 2d 4 (Fla. App. 1980); see also Olds v. St. Louis National Baseball Club, 232 Mo. App. 897, 104 S.W. 2d 746, later app. 119 S.W. 2d 1000 (Mo. App. 1937).

In *Ziginow v. Redford Jaycees,* 133 Mich. App. 259, 349 N.W.2d 153 (1983), plaintiffs were struck by "speeding" car as they left fireworks display at park. The court held that the organization which held the fireworks at the park, the county commissioners which owned the park, and the officers and members of the township police which agreed to handle crowd control were not liable in negligence to plaintiffs; plaintiffs were unable to demonstrate that any of these defendants owed them any duty and failed to present any evidence establishing any violation of a standard of care, proximate causation or foreseeability. As for the county road commission, plaintiffs did not prove a prima facie case of willful and wanton misconduct, namely, knowing of dangerous condition with crowds at the park and failing to avoid the danger by closing the road, which would have been the prudent thing to do.

§ 15.1323   Steps and walkways[151]

Weather conditions, such as ice and snow, can be a factor in falls. In two football cases,[152] the plaintiff did not recover. In the 1980 Caesar case, plaintiff spectator was injured (fractured leg) as a result of a fall sustained while leaving the University stadium at the end of the game. On the evening prior to the game, it had snowed and there had been subfreezing temperatures and high winds. There was conflicting testimony concerning the slippery condition of the stadium's walkways during the game. As plaintiff attempted to exit in the stairwell, members of the crowd fell, carrying plaintiff to the bottom of the stairwell. The stairwell, instead of having handrails, was protected by a 36″ high concrete wall on either side; the walls were 8″ thick. At issue was the Boise City Building Code, which required installation of handrails in stairwells. The court held that the state-owned stadium was not subject to a local ordinance, since State statutes empowered the Commissioner of Public Works to provide and secure all plans and specifications for public buildings. On the issue of negligence, the plaintiff had alleged that the state knew or should have known of the slippery and dangerous condition of the stadium's concrete steps and passageways. The other football case also dealt with ice and snow on a stairway. The court held that the government's efforts to remove ice and snow from the stairway prior to the football game were reasonable and that its failure to warn spectators of an obvious condition of stairway was not unreasonable. Further, it was found that the spectator's preexisting back condition was not aggravated by the fall in the stadium.

Litter and debris, as well as water, on steps and walkways, often cause falls and injury; unevenness and obstructions also can cause falls.[153] In a Kentucky case,[154] the spectator sustained injuries when she stepped on a paraffin cup on a stairway at the ball park. Beverages were dispensed in cups in accordance with the usual and customary business practice. The spectator had the burden to prove that such practice constituted negligence, that is, that the cup was an inherently or obviously dangerous object.

[151] Habeeb, W.R. Liability of owner or operator of theater or other place of amusement for injury to patron using stairway or steps. 55 A.L.R.2d 866-929.

[152] Caesar v. State of Idaho, 101 Idaho 158, 610 P. 2d 517 (1980); Hartzell v. U.S., 539 F. 2d 65 (1976).

[153] Burke v. State Fair of Texas, 93 S.W. 2d 765

(Tex. Civ. App. 1936); Martin v. Angel City Baseball Assoc., 3 Cal. App.2d 586, 40 P. 2d 287 (1935); Rowell v. Wichita, 162 Kan. 294, 176 P. 2d 590 (1947).

[154] Burriss v. Louisville Baseball Club, 317 S.W. 2d 855 (Ky. App. 1958).

Judgment for defendant. In a second baseball case,[155] the spectator slipped on steps filled with pools and puddles of water. The court held that there was no negligence on the part of the club for failing to sweep or remove the pools of water so soon after the game was called on account of rain. Two additional baseball cases[156] concerned substances on the walkways. In the 1980 case, both the school and Little League were sued by the plaintiff spectator when she fell on the ramp when leaving the game. The ramp was clear of dust and gravel when the husband and wife went to the game, but there was an unusual amount of vehicular activity in the alley which caused dust and some gravel to settle on the ramp. While the husband walking slightly ahead noticed the dust on the ramp from the footprints of people preceding him on the ramp, the wife did not and fell from the slipperiness due to the dust and gravel. The court found for the defendants, holding that the spectator was aware that the ramp had been slippery in the past and continued to use it (although there were alternative exits) and the ramp was not unreasonably dangerous; and, the Little League did not have possession and/or control of the ramp so that it owed a duty to spectators related to the maintenance of the ramp. In the earlier case, plaintiff slipped on a sticky substance on the runway of the grandstand. The court held that spectator's contributory negligence was for the jury.

Lighting also can be a factor in falls on steps and walkways.[157] In a 1980 case,[158] the plaintiff decided to leave during the curtain call and slipped on the steps leading from her seat to the main floor and broke her shoulder. The sufficiency of light was a matter for the jury. In an earlier theatre case,[159] the plaintiff stepped on a hat on the stairs, causing a fall. The usherette violated a rule requiring her to light the way of patrons to their seats in the darkened theatre.

Sufficiency of light in order for a baseball spectator to reasonably be able to see and follow the course of balls batted or thrown into the unscreened portion of the grandstand[160] and sufficient light on hallways and stairways[161] also have given rise to law suits. In a 1975 case[162] the plaintiff spectator (father going to son's high school wrestling match) was injured (broke her wrist) when he slipped on a muddy area of dimly lit grassy slope as he took a shortcut to reach doors at the side of the school. There were alternatives, although longer, paved surfaces to reach the school. Court held that plaintiff was contributorily negligent.

Safety on the walkways and corridors also is a responsibility of management. The plaintiff spectator while walking on the promenade to the rest room was struck by a puck which had left the ice. Judgment for plaintiff.[163] Another spectator in *Aaser v. Charlotte*,[164] was injured (broken ankle) when hit by an ice hockey puck while walking

[155] Lappin v. St. Louis National League Baseball Club, 33 S.W. 2d 1025 (Mo. App. 1931).

[156] Cincinnati Baseball Club Co. v. Hines, 264 F. 2d 60 (1959); Jackson v. Cartwright School Dist. and Little League, 125 Ariz. 98, 607 P. 2d 975 (1980), see also Fazio v. Dania Jai-Alai Palace, 473 So. 2d 1345 (Fla. App. 1985) foreign liquid substance in aisle.

[157] See Liability of theater owner or operator for injury to or death of patron resulting from lighting conditions on premises, 19 A.L.R. 4th 1110; and Liability to baseball spectator, 91 A.L.R. 3d 24 at 91.

[158] Upham v. Chateau De Ville Dinner Theatre, 403 N.E. 2d 384 (Mass. 1980).

[159] Beal v. Blumenfeld Theatres, 177 Cal. App. 2d 192, 2 Cal. Rptr. 110 (1960).

[160] Paxton v. Buffalo International Baseball Club, 256 A.D. 887, 9 N.Y.S. 2d 42 (1939).

[161] Dively v. Penn-Pittsburgh Corp., 332 Pa. 65, 2 A. 2d 831 (1938).

[162] Shannon v. Addison Trail H.S., 33 Ill. App. 3d 953, 339 N.E. 2d 372 (1975).

[163] Lemoine v. Springfield Hockey Assoc., 307 Mass. 102, 29 N.E. 2d 716 (1940).

[164] Aaser v. Charlotte, 265 N.C. 494, 144 S.E. 2d 610 (1965).

along a corridor in the coliseum. A group of boys were playing with sticks and pucks in the corridor. While the management knew that boys played in the hallways, they were not aware that they were playing with sticks and pucks in this dangerous manner. Plaintiff had the burden of proof and failed to show negligence. And, in a 1977 Jones case[165] the court held for the plaintiff. The spectator was struck in the eye during a pregame batting practice while using an interior walkway on the outer concourse. This concourse had openings for patrons to look out onto the playing field, which she had just been doing; but, then, she turned back to get some food and as she did so someone cried, "Watch" and she turned again toward the field and was struck in the eye. The question was whether this was a "common, frequent and expected" risk inherent and thus the risk assumed by the spectator. The court held that the "no duty" rule did not apply because of the location and nature of the situation.

Suit was brought against the golf course operator and tournament sponsors for injuries sustained by plaintiff spectators when the suspension bridge on which they were standing collapsed, dropping them into river below. The bridge capacity was 25, but 80-100 people had crowded on it; there was no warning regarding capacity, and no supervisory personnel to oversee proper use. Court held that not only must care be used not to injure a visitor and to warn of latent dangers of which owner knows, but also precautions must be taken to protect against foreseeable dangers due to use or arrangement; the obligation extends to the original construction of the premises, where it results in a dangerous condition.[166]

§ 15.14   Operations and services (concessions, emergency service)

Operations and services to spectators include concessionaires and emergency medical care. See §3.11 lessor/lessee relationships. There, also, are a few cases in other sections regarding concessionaires.

In *Fish v. Los Angeles Dodgers Baseball Club*[167] the parents of a 14-year-old decedent brought action against the physician and professional baseball club for the death of their son when struck by a foul ball while watching a baseball game. One of the allegations was provision of emergency medical services in a negligent manner, and another was malpractice of the doctor who operated the emergency medical facility at the stadium. The court reversed and remanded for determination by jury to consider the relationship between the physician and the club and the cause of death. (See §§17.1 and 17.2 on emergency care.)

Patron was injured when ball park concession stand door came loose from hook and struck him. The court held that plaintiff could recover even though he failed to establish that owner had actual or constructive knowledge of defect in hook, as owner had exclusive control over concession stand door at time of accident and the doctrine of *res ipsa loquitur* was applied.[168] (See §20.2 Condition of premises.)

[165] Jones v. Three Rivers Management Corp., 251 Pa. Super. 82, 380 A. 2d 387 (1977), rev'd. 483 P. 75, 394 A. 2d 546 (1978).

[166] Rockwell v. Hillcrest Country Club, 25 Mich. App. 276, 181 N.W. 2d 290 (1970).

[167] Fish v. Los Angeles Dodgers Baseball Club, 56 Cal. App. 3d 620, 128 Cal. Rptr. 807 (1976).

[168] Higgins v. White Sox Baseball Club, 787 F. 2d 1125 (1986).

§ 15.15   Players injuring spectators

There is a responsibility to control players as related to spectators. The plaintiff was one of 20 eighth-grade girls who were escorted by the teacher to an athletic field during the morning recess. The girls were directed to sit on a pole or log on the third base line of the field being used for softball by the eighth-grade boys. The teacher returned to the building and did not reappear until the accident. About five minutes after the teacher left, some of the boys waiting for their turn to bat started to pelt the girls with pebbles. Although the girls protested, the throwing continued for three or four minutes, until the plaintiff was struck in the right eye, causing her to lose the sight of that eye. The plaintiff recovered on the basis of inadequate supervision of a foreseeable general danger; the specific type of accident which occurred was not necessary to be proven.[169] (For general supervision, see Chapter 18.)

Most all of the injuries occurring to spectators as a result of the acts of players are in professional sports, and, also, such acts are usually intentional torts. (See §1.41 Intentional torts.) Because of the intentional nature of the act, the question is raised as to whether such acts are within the scope of employment, a requirement under the doctrine of respondeat superior (see §3.4). Another theory advanced for holding the owner liable for intentional torts of the players is that of negligent hiring and supervision (see §3.3), that is, that management knows of the violence propensities of the player.[170]

That cases of players injuring spectators is a phenomenon of the decades of the '70s and '80s is an erroneous statement. Professional wrestling has long catapulted wrestlers into spectators and wrestlers assaulted patrons.[171]

§ 15.16   Employees injuring spectators

Most situations involving employees come under the doctrine of respondeat superior (see §3.4) and are discussed in sections related to the nature of the situation. When injury is intentional, usually the doctrine is not applicable. (See §1.41 Intentional torts.)

In an early Missouri case,[172] the plaintiff was awarded compensation (from the stadium owner) when his arm was broken by the rough play of some boys hired to pick up seat cushions after the game.

§ 15.2   Passers-by

The errant ways of baseballs form the basis of law suits by passers-by. Passers-by

[169] Sheehan v. St. Peter's Catholic School, 188 N.W. 2d 868 (Minn. 1971).

[170] Bluver, Howard C. Owner liability for intentional torts committed by professional athletes against spectators. 30 Buffalo Law Review 565-586, 1981; USAA Casualty Ins. Co. v. Schneider, 620 F. Supp. 246 (1986) McEnroe, tennis player, assaulted spectator.

[171] Shipley, W.E. Liability for injury to one attending wrestling or boxing match or exhibition, 14 A.L.R.3d 993-1007. For example, Caldwell v. Maupin, 61 Ohio App. 161, 22 N.E. 2d 454 (1939);

Camp v. Rex. 304 Mass. 484, 24 N.E. 2d 4 (1939); Davis v. Jones, 100 Ga. App. 546, 112 S.E. 2d 3 (1959) timekeeper; Dusckiewicz v. Carter, 115 Vt. 122, 52 A. 2d 419 (1947); Langness v. Ketonen, 42 Wash. 2d 394, 255 P. 2d 551 (1953); Pierce v. Murnick, 265 N.C. 707, 145 S.E. 2d 11 (1965); Ramsey v. Kallio, 62 So. 2d 146 (La. App. 1952); Silvia v. Woodhouse, 248 N.E. 2d 260 (Mass. 1969); Wiersma v. Long Beach, 41 Cal. App. 2d 8, 106 P. 2d 45 (1940).

[172] Hughes v. St. Louis National League Baseball Club, 359 Mo. 993, 224 S.W. 2d 989 (1949).

cases related to baseball are of longstanding, dating back to the turn of the century.[173] Most of the cases cited are quite old, but still set forth principles.

A passers-by, who also may be a pedestrian, is distinguished from a spectator in *Jones v. Kane and Roach*, 182 Misc. 37, 43 N.Y.S. 2d 140 (1943). In this case the pedestrian passing by, called a casual spectator, was not expected to assume the risk of balls going off the diamond, but should be protected in a reasonable manner. A similar result was reached when plaintiff was struck in the back by a baseball while walking past the ballpark. The requirement for protection is not that of an insurer of safety, but rather that reasonable precautions under the circumstances must be taken. In this situation the management had notice that balls went into the street and that precautions taken (a 10' fence) were inadequate. The public has a right to use the highways safely.[174] On a similar basis, the plaintiff recovered judgment where an 11-year-old boy was struck in the face by a foul ball as he went by on the sidewalk. The catcher stood 8' to 10' from the sidewalk running near the diamond. The court held that there is a duty to erect appropriate barriers to protect those passing by.[175]

Injury was caused by a baseball coming from a game being played on a vacant lot surrounded by public streets. The action was dismissed in that this type of ballplaying was not attended with such degree of danger to make it hazardous to those using the streets. It was customary for the boys and men of the town to "knock up fly balls." However, the court did recognize a duty if inherent danger could be shown to those passing by.[176]

Plaintiff employee of the defendant was struck by a baseball coming from a game being played by other employees during the lunch hour on a lot owned by the defendant. Plaintiff was struck while standing in a public street; she had seen games played there daily during warm months, and she had seen balls come into the street previously. Judgment for defendant.[177] Employees played after work on a diamond with home plate approximately 200' from the public highway. There was an 8' fence erected on a 3' base. The ball which hit plaintiff cleared the fence by only 1'. The ball did not normally go over the fence and the court held for the defendant saying that ordinarily the fence would have been sufficient.[178]

A 12-year-old girl was struck in the face by a foul ball line drive coming from a baseball diamond in an amusement park as she and her mother were walking on a highway which led from the entrance to the picnic tables. Plaintiff received judgment on the basis that it was reasonably foreseeable that a foul ball might reach the highway which visitors were invited to use. There was no protection of any kind around the diamond to contain the balls.[179] In another case,[180] a passer-by was struck in the eye

[173] Blakeley v. White Star Line, 154 Mich. 635, 118 N.W. 482 (1908); Brann v. Hudson Falls, 169 A.D. 874, 155 N.Y.S. 796 (1915); Corley v. American Baptist Home Mission Society, 97 S.C. 460, 81 S.E. 146 (1914).

[174] Salevan v. Wilmington Park, 72 A. 2d 239 (Del. 1950).

[175] Louisville Baseball Club v. Hill, 291 Ky. 333, 164 S.W. 2d 398 (1942).

[176] Young v. New York, N.H. & H.R.R., 136 A.D. 730, 121 N.Y.S. 517 (1910).

[177] Harrington v. Border City Mfg. Co., 240 Mass. 170, 132 N.E. 721 (1921).

[178] Dwyer v. Edison Electric Illuminating Co., 273 Mass. 234, 173 N.E. 594 (1930).

[179] Wills v. Wisconsin-Minnesota Light & Power Co., 187 Wis. 626, 205 N.W. 556 (1925).

[180] Robb v. Milwaukee, 241 Wisc. 432, 6 N.W. 2d 222 (1942).

when a batted baseball carromed off the top of a woven fence 6' high just outside the walk. Balls were frequently batted over the fence. There were no warning signs. It was held that the city owed a duty to protect pedestrians. A similar holding to protect pedestrians was held when balls batted by players were apt to drop into the road striking travelers.[181]

All injuries to passers-by or bystanders are not due to batted balls. Plaintiff was struck by a ball thrown out of the park by a team member. Judgment for plaintiff on the basis that the player was "an agent of the sponsor;" and, he had acted within the scope of his employment when he threw the ball out of the park immediately after having dropped it with consequent loss of game.[182] In a New Jersey case[183] plaintiff, a bystander, was hit in the face by a softball bat which sailed through the air 90' to where she was standing, 30' beyond first base line and 15' outside foul line. The plaintiff recovered; court held that this was not a normal and reasonably expected incident, distinguishing a spectator in a grandstand and one in this informal, unsegregated area. In *Snowden v. Kittitas*,[184] a six-year-old boy was injured when he crossed a diamond and the backstop fell on him. There was no recovery (statutory protection); the boy was on the playground as a passer-by. Two New York cases involve non-spectator injuries, although injured are not exactly pedestrians. In *Wildman v. New York City*,[185] a girl standing by an open window on the second floor of the school building watching the boys play ball in the street was struck in the eye by a rubber ball, resulting in removal of the eye. It was held that this accident was not reasonably foreseeable. A visiting aunt in a residence adjacent to the same street was hit in the head by an object she claimed was a baseball from boys playing catch on the adjoining playground. There was insufficient evidence to prove that the object which hit her was a baseball.[186]

Golf is the other sport most frequently involved in injuries to passers-by or bystanders, since a golf ball tends to fly uncontrolled at times. In *Kirchoffner v. Quam*, 264 N.W.2d 203 (N.D. 1978), a minor was struck in the eye by a golf ball while boating on the river which flowed through the golf course. It was for the jury to determine whether the golf club had failed to provide adequate notice to boaters on the river, a public waterway, of danger from flying balls; the club was on notice that golfers hit balls into the river and that boaters used the river for recreation. Plaintiff was struck by a golf ball while driving her car on a public highway along which ran one of the fairways of a golf course. The golf course was held liable on the basis of failure to use reasonable care to prevent injury to persons lawfully on the highway.[187] Plaintiff also was operating a motor vehicle in *Townsley v. State*, 6 Misc. 2d 557, 164 N.Y.S. 2d 840 (1957). She was struck on the left wrist by a golf ball as she signaled to make a turn by extending her arm from the car window. The court held that where the State had notice of the golf balls landing on or across the highway and it failed to make such known or erect protective

---

[181] Lamm v. Buffalo, (two cases) 225 A.D. 599, 233 N.Y.S. 516 (1929).

[182] Bonetti v. Double Play Tavern, 126 Cal. App. 2d 848, 274 P. 2d 751 (1954).

[183] Klinsky v. Hanson Van Winkle Mining Co., 38 N.J. Super. 439, 119 A. 2d 166 (1955), cert. denied 20 N.J. 534, 120 A. 2d 661 (1956), aff'd 43 N.J. Super. 166, 128 A. 2d 4 (1956).

[184] 38 Wash. 2d 691, 231 P. 2d 621 (1951).

[185] 254 A.D. 591, 3 N.Y.S. 2d 37 (1938).

[186] Lane v. Buffalo, 232 A.D. 334, 250 N.Y.S. 579 (1931).

[187] Gleason v. Hillcrest Golf Course, 148 Misc. 246, 265 N.Y.S. 886 (1933).

devices to lessen the danger, it maintained a public nuisance and was liable for injuries resultant from the hazardous condition (see §4.4 Nuisance). The defendant also was liable when the plaintiff was injured in her car as she was on her way to the club's swimming pool and the road on which she was driving crossed the fairway about 60' from the tee. The golfers normally drove across the road.[188] And, in another case[189] the plaintiff was struck in the mouth by a golf ball as she was standing in the parking area provided in connection with the course. She had just completed a round of golf. The court held that the municipality owed its invitees the duty of exercising ordinary care for their safety.

A 13-year-old, together with about 15 classmates, was working on a float for the school homecoming parade after school. The group then went to a classmate's home for pizza. They began to play "tackle-the-football" and when the pizza was ready, most left to go eat, but defendant continued to play catch with the football, with another person. Plaintiff was near a table sitting or crouching talking with two girls when defendant, going out for a pass ran him over, falling on his back and crushing his head and chest to the ground between his legs. Defendant, however, alleged that plaintiff was hurt during the game play. The court held for the bystander plaintiff, saying that participant owed bystander a duty of care to refrain from playing catch with football in area congested with nonparticipants. The defendant owed a duty and the plaintiff was not contributorily negligent, although the court did recognize that a bystander could be negligent due to inattentiveness.[190]

A bystander also recovered the maximum under the State tort claims act of $300,000 in a Texas fireworks situation.[191] (See §11.26 Fireworks.)

In a very different situational circumstance, liability to a bystander is set forth as related to witnessing a traumatic event, the death of a sister[192] (see §17.225).

§ 15.3   Sport officials

Sport officials are involved in law suits both as defendants and as plaintiffs. An official also may be directly involved in the situation, but neither a defendant nor plaintiff, as was so in a Louisiana case.[193] A spectator was involved in a dispute with a basketball referee at a high school basketball game, and sued the State high school athletic association, seeking an injunction against its ruling that the local high school could not play any association games if this person (plaintiff) was a spectator. The effect of the ruling was to bar the plaintiff from being a spectator for a year. The plaintiff argued that he had a constitutional right under the 14th amendment to attend. The court held that even if there were a constitutional right, such right was subject to reasonable nondiscriminatory limitations established by the association, a private unincorporated entity.

[188] Westborough Country Club v. Palmer, 204 F. 2d 143 (1953).

[189] Plaza v. San Mateo, 123 Cal. App. 2d 103, 266 P. 2d 523 (1954).

[190] Osborne v. Sprowls, 84 Ill. 2d 390, 50 Ill. Dec. 645, 419 N.E. 2d 913 (1981).

[191] Genzer v. City of Mission, 666 S.W. 2d 116 (Tex. App. 1983).

[192] Landreth v. Reed, 570 S.W. 2d 486 (Tex. Civ. App. 1978).

[193] Watkins v. Louisiana H.S. Athletic Assoc., 301 So. 2d 695 (La. App. 1974).

In another case,[194] constitutional right was at issue, when parents of high school football players brought action against the state high school association, challenging the association's denial of their protests to a referee's penalty call. The court held that the official's error did not deny equal protection to the players.

In a 1984 Iowa case,[195] a college basketball referee sued a novelty store owner who was marketing T-shirts critical of him, seeking injunction and damages. The official had called a foul in a last-minute of a game; the player made the shot, and some fans blamed the official for the loss, asserting that the foul call was clearly in error. It was in relation to this event that the T-shirt was made up. When the official sued the novelty store, the store counterclaimed, alleging malpractice. The court held that the store owners' damages were not a reasonably foreseeable consequence of referee's acts and that the store owners were not direct beneficiaries of contract between the athletic conference and referee and thus could not maintain the cause of action; there was no privity of contract.

§ 15.31 Officials as defendants

An official may be a defendant either when a player is injured in a sport which the person is officiating or when an intentional injury occurs by an official injuring a spectator. Players or others also may sue when a decision by an official is perceived to be incorrect and such decision has subsequent ramifications considered detrimental to the person. However, the courts are reluctant to review officials' decisions. The Georgia court[196] said that courts of equity are without authority to review decisions of high school referees because those decisions do not present judicial controversy.

§ 15.311 Player sues official

Liability of an official rests in the duty of care required toward the player and may be established by statute, contract, or common practice. The primary basis of suits by a player is the common functions of an official which are promulgated both to conduct an orderly game and to protect the players. There is a duty on the part of the official to control the nature of the game from checking the apparatus and the equipment being worn or used by the players to properly enforcing the rules of the game and keeping the ebb and flow of the game from "getting out-of-hand" and endangering players' (and spectators') safety.

A senior member of the school's varsity wrestling squad was wrestling another senior from a neighboring school at the 145-pound weight. Near the end of one of the rounds, the other boy, who was well ahead on points, attempted to pin plaintiff's shoulders to the mat for additional points. To do so he was alternating half nelsons,

[194] Georgia H.S.A.A. v. Waddell, 248 Ga. 542, 285 S.E. 2d 7 (1981).

[195] Bain v. Gillispie, 357 N.W. 2d 47 (Iowa App. 1984).

[196] Georgia H.S.A.A. v. Waddell, 248 Ga. 542, 285 S.E. 2d 7 (1981); see also State ex rel Durando v. State Athletic Comm., 272 Wis. 191, 75 N.W. 2d 451 (1956) commission rule which did not permit it to reverse boxing referee decision in absence of fraud valid; Shapiro v. Queens County Jockey Club, 184 Misc. 295, 53 N.Y.S. 2d 135 (1945); Tilelli v. Christenberry, 1 Misc. 2d 139, 120 N.Y.S. 2d 697 (1953) boxing officials.

which process had taken the boys to a corner of the main mat near where small side mats were placed against the main mat. The referee noticed a separation between the main mat and the side mat and moved to close the gap to protect the boys should they roll in that direction and off the main mat. In so doing, his attention was diverted from the boys momentarily. At this time eyewitnesses said that the opponent applied a full nelson for one to ten seconds; the time estimated varied. Almost simultaneously the buzzer sounded the end of the round, the referee blew his whistle, and the opponent broke the hold on plaintiff after a final lunge. Plaintiff slumped to the mat, unable to move due to the severance of a major portion of his spinal cord, resulting in permanent paralysis of all voluntary functions below the level of his neck. The court held that the referee was the agent of the school and that a player does not assume the risk of another's negligence or incompetence. Plaintiff alleged that the referee was negligent in the following particulars: (1) failing to supervise adequately the contestants; (2) allowing his attention to be diverted from the actions of the boys; (3) allowing an illegal and dangerous hold to be applied; (4) failing to immediately cause the said hold to be broken; (5) allowing the said hold to be prolonged for a substantial period of time; and (6) violating the provisions of the official Wrestling Guide of the NCAA. The referee was not sued as an individual.[197]

Plaintiff, playing in an invitational basketball tournament, was injured when he slipped on an allegedly dangerously wet playing surface. Germane to this discussion was the fact that the condition of the floor was witnessed to by the referees who stated that "the floor was definitely playable." The coaches and the referees were responsible for inspecting and approving the playing conditions. Plaintiff did not recover.[198]

The city park department supervisor also was acting as umpire for a city and newspaper sponsored softball tournament. The games were being played on a cement field, and evidence indicated that its surface was strewn with shards of glass from numerous broken bottles. Prior to the game, upon complaint of the condition of the field, the infield was swept with a big broom, but not the outfield. After the first inning, player again requested the outfield be swept, but the supervisor/umpire refused saying that the brooms had been put away and it was getting dark, so just get out there and play. In the fifth inning the two players collided in the outfield, alleged due to one tripping on a piece of glass. Injured players sued the city, since the city had furnished the umpire.[199]

A student was officiating in a required physical education wrestling class, when plaintiff was thrown to the ground and his left ankle broken. An instructor was supervising at the time and the teacher was in the vicinity of the match at the time of injury, too. No substantive decision; summary judgment granted on the basis of sovereign immunity.[200]

Action was brought against the University (SUNY, Albany) for failing to adequately instruct and supervise the referees who officiated an intramural floor hockey game played in the University gymnasium. Plaintiff had successfully gotten the puck from an opponent and was moving along the gymnasium wall towards his own goal, when

[197] Carabba v. Anacortes School District, 72 Wash. 2d 939, 435 P. 2d 936 (1967).

[198] Nunez v. Isidore Newman High School, 306 So. 2d 457 (La. App. 1975).

[199] Forkash v. City of N.Y., 27 A.D. 2d 831, 277 N.Y.S. 2d 827 (1977).

[200] Merrill v. Birhanzel, S.D., 310 N.W. 2d 522 (1981).

another player pushed him against the wall and knocked the puck away from him. He got to his feet and from a crouched position grabbed his opponent by the legs, just above the knees, and attempted to tackle him. As plaintiff's head struck opponent's knees, opponent grabbed plaintiff, flipped him onto the floor, and fell partially on his neck, causing fracture of cervical spine. The court held that the cause of the injury was due to the two players attacking each other and was not attributable to the lack of supervision and training by the University relative to referee's officiating.[201]

§ 15.312   Official injures spectator

A spectator sued the referee and promoters for injuries sustained at a wrestling event when the referee, who was en route to the dressing room, when touched by the plaintiff whirled around with arms outstretched, causing plaintiff to fall and break his leg. The court held that injury was not caused by promoters' alleged failure to provide adequate crowd supervision, exposure of referee to plaintiff when he left ring, or employment of referee with dangerous propensities. An employer-employee relationship between promoters and referee was not established as a matter of law. The actions of the referee were the cause of the damage to the plaintiff.[202] In an earlier Nebraska case,[203] the referee was knocked out of the ring by one of the wrestlers and onto the plaintiff spectator.

§ 15.32   Officials as plaintiffs

An official may become a plaintiff due to injuries sustained in the performance of duties or to being assaulted. There may be other actions, too, such as in a 1987 case[204] where the baseball umpire brought defamation action against the owner of a professional baseball team for statements made to the media (see §1.4122 Defamation).

§ 15.321   Officials injured "in line of duty"

A number of cases involved injuries to officials working baseball/softball games. A softball umpire brought action against a player and his team sponsor for injuries incurred when a three-pound bat ring flew off a bat, with which the player was taking practice swings, and hit him. The court stated that the duty of care owed by a softball player to an umpire during course of game is same as that owed to another player. The plaintiff alleged that the player had a reckless disregard for his safety by failing to properly set the bat ring on the bat, although he knew or should have known that the bat ring was of improper size for the bat then being used.[205] In another baseball case,[206] the

[201] Pape v. State, 90 A.D. 2d 904, 456 N.Y.S. 2d 863 (1982).

[202] Ulrich v. Minn. Boxing & Wrestling Club, 268 Minn. 328, 129 N.W. 2d 288 (1964).

[203] Klause v. Nebraska State Board of Agriculture, 150 Neb. 466, 35 N.W. 2d 104 (1948).

[204] Parks v. Steinbrenner, 520 N.Y.S. 2d 374 (1987).

[205] Stewart v. D & R Welding Supply Co., 9 Ill. Dec. 596, 51 Ill. App. 3d 597, 366 N.E. 2d 1107 (1977).

[206] Dillard v. Little League Baseball, 55 A.D. 2d 477, 390 N.Y.S. 2d 735 (1977), motion denied 41 N.Y. 2d 801, 396 N.Y.S. 2d 1026 (1977).

plaintiff umpire (volunteer) brought action against the Little League when struck in the groin by a pitched baseball. The court held that the umpire assumed the risk of his injury. The plaintiff also was a volunteer umpire in *Hanna v. State*, 46 Misc. 2d 9, 258 N.Y.S. 2d 694 (1965). Plaintiff, a college student, was standing behind the batting cage net when he was struck in the eye by a foul-tipped ball; it did not come through the netting, but the netting had "give." The netting was purposely kept slack to absorb the force of passed balls; the plaintiff did not wear a protective mask, although one was apparently available. The court held that the plaintiff should have realized the danger of standing too close to the net under the circumstances and assumed the risks. While suit was not against the umpire, the dictum in a New York case[207] stated that an official assumed the risk of injury. In this situation a non-regulation sized diamond was being used.

In two 1970s cases,[208] the softball umpire sought workman's compensation for injuries. In the *Gale* case a player, who was not even directly involved in the disputed play, began striking the plaintiff umpire about the neck, hip, and leg with a baseball bat; while in the *Daniels* case the umpire was struck in the eye by a ball while umpiring a company intramural league game. In both of these cases the court held that the umpire was not an employee, but an independent contractor. There was a similar holding in a basketball situation, where the plaintiff while officiating was accidentally struck in the mouth and sustained damage to his teeth (see §25.343 Workers' compensation and §3.121 Individuals as independent contractors).

In a 1980 case[209] a high school football official was injured when he became trapped in a play and was accidently struck by one of the players. In this situation, contrary to the previous baseball cases, the court held that plaintiff was an employee of the school district, having been paid by the district and several other factors of control.

Plaintiff was refereeing a basketball game in the school gymnasium, when he slipped and fell, allegedly because moisture had accumulated on the floor surface from a leak in the ceiling. It was further alleged that the defendant school knew of the wet condition of the floor, but failed to notify or apprise the plaintiff of such fact. Defendants countered that the plaintiff was contributorily negligent and that he had assumed the risk. Under the state statute, the plaintiff did not recover.[210]

A volunteer track and field official was injured when he was struck in the head by a shot during a shot-put event. He alleged failure to properly supervise the event and use by athletes of the shots themselves, as well as failure to adopt rules and regulations for safe conduct of the shot-put event. The meet was in charge of the head track coach at the University, who had appointed another volunteer as head official. Both were acting within the scope of their responsibilities and hence were acting for the University. Plaintiff was not precluded from recovery under the state Tort Claims Act.[211]

[207] McGee v. Board of Educ., NYC, 16 A.D. 2d 99, 226 N.Y.S. 2d 329 (1962).

[208] Gale v. Greater Washington Softball Umpires Assoc., 19 Md. Ap. 481, 311 A. 2d 817 (1973); Daniels v. Gates Rubber Co., 479 P. 2d 983 (Colo. App. 1970).

[209] Ford v. Bonner Co. School Dist., 101 Idaho 320, 612 P. 2d 557 (1980).

[210] Studley v. School Dist., 210 Neb. 669, 316 N.W. 2d 603 (1982).

[211] Smith v. Univ. of Texas, 664 S.W. 2d 180 (Tex. App. 1984).

While not exactly "in the line of duty" injury, the decedent had been asked to officiate an interfraternity basketball game after school hours, but on school premises. While so doing, he collapsed at age 38 of a heart attack. Held that Workers' Compensation applied.[212]

A spectator was asked to serve as sideline official (chairman) at a high school football game. He sustained injuries when a player forced out of bounds hit him, driving him into an unprotected grandstand. Plaintiff sued the town and school, alleging negligence for failure to pad and fence off bleachers and in permitting benched players to congregate along the sidelines. The plaintiff further claimed that a nuisance had been created by failing to pad the stands or erect a barrier between the stands and playing field. Held: governmental immunity for both school and town, and no recovery under theory of public or private nuisance.[213] (See §4.4 Nuisance.)

§ 15.322   Officials assaulted[214]

In an effort to curb attacks on persons at athletic contests, some states, such as Oklahoma (Okla. Stat. Ann. 21§650.1) have passed a statute:

> Every person who, without justifiable or excusable cause and with intent to do bodily harm, commits any assault, battery, assault and battery upon the person of a referee, umpire, timekeeper, coach, player, participant, official, sports reporter or any person having authority in connection with any amateur or professional athletic contest is punishable by imprisonment in the county jail not exceeding one (1) year or by a fine not exceeding one thousand dollars ($1,000), or by both such fine and imprisonment.

The defendant fan was convicted of assault upon a sports official in *Carroll v. State of Oklahoma*, 620 P. 2d 416 (Ct. Criminal App. Okla. 1980), under the foregoing cited Oklahoma statute. The court held that the statute was not unconstitutionally vague and indefinite nor void for uncertainty. The assault took place in the parking lot after a baseball game when the home plate umpire (victim) was at the open trunk of his car changing uniforms in preparation for the next game. Surrounding the umpire were a group of players from the losing team, who were criticizing his calls as an umpire. The assistant coach of the losing team approached the group, exchanged words with the umpire, and struck him on the jaw with his fist.

In *Toone v. Adams*, 262 N.C. 403, 137 S.E. 2d 132 (1964), a baseball umpire sued the baseball club, manager, and baseball fan for injuries sustained as a result of an assault by a fan while he was proceeding, with another umpire and two policemen, from the exit from playing field to the dressing room. The umpire had made several decisions against the home team which the manager had protested vigorously and after being ejected from the game stated to the plaintiff that he would receive no help from him or his players in getting off the field. When the game ended fans did pour over the fence, challenging the

[212] Warthen v. Southeast Okla. State Univ., 641 P. 2d 1125 (Okla. App. 1981), rehearing denied 1982.
[213] Couture v. Board of Education, Town of Plainfield, 6 Conn. App. 309, 505 A. 2d 432 (1986).
[214] See §1.4132 Assault and battery.

plaintiff to fight. Without any provocation or warning the defendant spectator struck plaintiff a blow on his head. The court held that the manager's conduct was not the proximate cause of the fan's attack on the umpire and that there had been no violation of protection, since two police did in fact accompany the umpire. The fan defendant had default judgment rendered against him.

A high school football official was assaulted by a spectator. Plaintiff sued high school and its principal; however, since the game (football jamboree) was promoted, sponsored, organized by and in control of high school's lessee, it was held that there was no action against the school and principal. Plaintiff alleged lessees should have checked out better the lessor, who served alcoholic beverages, for crowd control measures[215] (see §1.221 Intoxication).

[215] Litomisky v. St. Charles H.S., 482 So. 2d 30 (La. App. 1986).

Chapter 16.   Participant Forms Endeavoring to Limit Liability

Private entrepreneurs, schools and municipal corporations, and voluntary and non-profit agencies and organizations are all concerned about limiting liability for negligent acts related to the services rendered, activities conducted, and facilities provided. One approach is to use participant forms. Participant waivers and releases and parental permissions are the most common for public and non-profit entities. In the private sector, exculpatory agreements and indemnification clauses have been common in the conduct of business enterprises. If the forms are to be used effectively, one must distinguish them as to function or purpose, to whom applicable, effect on liability, and when void. (See Table 16.1.) Unfortunately, many of the terms are used interchangeably and incorrectly, and with great misunderstanding as to effectiveness as concerns liability. Frequently one will find lengthy and all encompassing terminology in one form. While several terms may be used, each should be used appropriately.

Table 16.1 Comparison of Participant Forms Endeavoring to Limit Liability

Field of Law	Based in Tort Law — Participant Assumes Risks Inherent in Activity as Understood / Plaintiff Can Recover Damages for Injuries due to Negligence				Based in Contract Law — Must Meet Criteria for Valid Contract / Contract Specifies Relationship			
						Exculpatory Clauses		
Type of Document	(no document)	Agreement to Participate	Informed Consent	Parental Permission	Covenant Not to Sue	Waiver	Release	Indemnification Clause
Definition	Defense: assumption of risk do not need written agreement or formal contract criteria for assumption of risk (see §5.22) · knowledge · understanding · appreciation	formalizes into written form common law assumption of risk must include criteria for assumption of risk; usually includes other responsibilities and understandings (see §24.812)	full disclosure of facts to inform or specify the nature of the treatment and expected outcomes, usually in the medical field, including fitness, but also for human subjects experimentation (see §17.23)	a signed statement by parent/guardian that minor can participate in stated activity recommend be attached to agreement to participate	a contract not to bring any legal actions whatsoever	the basic premise is that injured plaintiff understands risks inherent in activity (if does not, contract may not be valid—see §16.114) and that by the exculpatory clause, plaintiff goes beyond assuming such inherent risks, to assuming any injury occasioned by ordinary negligence of defendant — future liabilities, prospective in nature	already existing liabilities	also referred to as "save harmless' clauses shifts financial responsibility of any award to someone other than the party being sued; someone else will reimburse the defendant who paid out
Function or Purpose		one documentary evidence of defendant trying to meet criteria for assumption of risk violation of responsibilities useful for contributory negligence (see §5.21)as bar or as part of comparative negligence (see §5.23) good public relations and an effort to teach participant responsibility	so that participant can make an intelligent decision to allow something to happen in respect to one's person, physically or psychologically	to give permission if attached to agreement to participate, serves as public relations device to inform regarding the nature of the activity, expected responsibilities of participant, and possible type of injuries which may occur	to prevent the filing of law suits	lowers the standard of care for defendant to gross negligence or even willful/wanton misconduct		way of financial risk management often used in lease or rental arrangements or when services have been contracted

Field of Law	Based in Tort Law — Participant Assumes Risks Inherent in Activity as Understood; Plaintiff Can Recover Damages for Injuries due to Negligence				Based in Contract Law — Must Meet Criteria for Valid Contract; Contract Specifies Relationship			
						Exculpatory Clauses		
Type of Document	(no document)	Agreement to Participate	Informed Consent	Parental Permission	Covenant Not to Sue	Waiver	Release	Indemnification Clause
Effect on Liability	bars any recovery by plaintiff (see comments)	assists in assumption of risk and contributory negligence defenses	not a waiver; assists in assumption of risk defense	really no effect on liability as related to injured; may help in establishing unforeseeability	presumably no one to sue	presumably no one from whom to recover for injuries due to negligence, although can still sue defendant for negligent conduct		still have someone to sue for injuries due to negligent conduct; affects who ultimately has to pay the award
To Whom Applicable	all ages	all ages	only persons of majority age	parents/guardians	only persons of majority age	only persons of majority age		only persons of majority age
When Void or Not Available	criteria for assumption of risk not met; defendant "sponsor" should make special effort to fulfill criteria	assumption of risk criteria not met; or responsibilities, such as rules and regulations, not communicated, then contributory negligence not available as defense	not full disclosure of facts or fraud/misrepresentation	if "hold harmless" clause attached, may be held invalid for conflict of interest		mutual mistake; void when gross and/or willful and wanton misconduct or against public policy		as part of parental permission, may be invalid as conflict of interest (see text)
Comments	in some states subsumed by comparative negligence, then part of plaintiff fault continuum at "no fault" end (see §5.23)	if exculpatory clause included for minors, clause invalid for adults may attach or incorporate valid exculpatory clause	exculpatory clause may be attached or incorporated, but probably invalid as against public policy	may attach or incorporate exculpatory clause; valid only to rights of parents; parents cannot sign away right of minor				

43

The forms are divided into two categories, those based in tort law and those based in contract law. Those based in tort law are useful in establishing the defenses of assumption of risk and contributory negligence and may result either in barring recovery or ameliorating damages. The agreement to participate form may be used with minors, and is the only form to be able to be so used. Those forms based in contract must meet all criteria for a valid contract, and, thus, are available only for persons of majority age.

An exculpatory agreement is one between the provider of the service, activity, or facility and the participant, signed prior to participation, stating that the participant, if injured, will "excuse" or clear, from any fault or guilt, the provider. In essence, the participant is saying that regardless of the negligence of the provider, the provider will not be held liable for damages caused by such negligence. (Some question the moral and professional ethics of a provider asking a participant to do so.) The participant agreement in an exculpatory agreement should be distinguished from a participant's primary assumption of risk (see §5.22, §18.2). Ordinarily, assumption of risk in sport/ physical education, recreation/parks, and camping/adventure activities is thought of as the participant assuming only those risks inherent in the activity, not any situation occasioned by the negligence of the provider. However, there may be an "express assumption of risk"[1] wherein the participant actually contracts or otherwise expressly agrees to accept a risk of harm arising from the defendant's (provider) negligence or reckless conduct, unless the agreement is invalid as contrary to public policy (see §16.2). There are different criteria for the use of assumption of risk of inherent dangers in an activity and of exculpatory agreements as defenses. These are discussed in this chapter and Chapter 5.

Most people use the terms "waiver" and "release" interchangeably; and, in this chapter the terms are used as referenced in the cases cited. However, there is a technical difference as pointed out in *Cash v. Street & Trail, Inc.*, 136 Ga. App. 462, 221 S.E. 2d 640 (1975). The court, in its discussion of terminology, said that "in its purest sense, a release does not relate to a future or contingent claim.... a 'release' must come after a cause of action has arisen. It operates to release a tortfeasor on the theory that there should be a just satisfaction and there has been a complete accord and satisfaction." On the other hand, the court continued, a waiver is really an agreement not to sue, given in exchange to lawful consideration. At the time an agreement is given, there is no claim in existence to be released; it speaks of the future, not of the present or past. Since no liability exists, none can be released. The Pennsylvania court[2] in 1987 stated similarly regarding the distinction between a waiver and a release: "...the release is prospective in nature, *i.e.*, it purports to exculpate the defendants from future liability, as opposed to a release compromising and settling an already existing claim for damages." Also to be distinguished are "release" and "satisfaction."[3] Satisfaction is usually full compensation and goes to the extent of compensation, whereas a release may or may not have full

[1] Restatement of Torts, Second, Chp. 17A, §496B.
[2] Simmons v. Parkette National Gymnastics Training Center, 670 F. Supp. 140 (1987).
[3] Lee v. State of Alaska & Johnson, 490 P. 2d 1206 (Alaska 1971).

compensation, but the plaintiff "releases" the tortfeasor from any further liability. (See §2.43 for further discussion.)

Being held not liable on the basis of an exculpatory agreement should be distinguished from immunity based on statutes. An exculpatory agreement is a contract between two parties, the provider and the consumer participant; while statutory immunity is the provider not being held accountable for the provider's own negligence through legislative enactment (see §4.4, §12.1, §17.1), a process in which the participant is not involved at all in terms of consent or agreement. It is an immunity given to all who can come within the "protected class" set forth in the statute.

Agreements "to hold harmless" or indemnification contracts, also, should be distinguished from exculpatory agreements.[4] An exculpatory agreement precludes any recovery by the injured participant, while an indemnity agreement ordinarily shifts the burden of paying a claim, damages having been determined. In this chapter, discussion focuses upon the participant's agreement to indemnify the provider as related to participation.

A covenant not to sue is a contract not to bring any legal action against the person with whom so contracted. The court said in *Lincoln v. Gupta*, 142 Mich. App. 615, 370 N.W.2d 312 (1985), that under common law, there is distinction between covenant not to sue and release of liability, and that covenant not to sue agent does not release principal from liability. Some hold that a waiver is in essence a covenant not to sue.[5] For the most part, the same principles of validity and unenforceability as for an exculpatory clause apply;[6] and, therefore, no separate section is included to discuss covenants not to sue.

Informed consent should not be construed as a waiver based in contract. Informed consent is based in tort and is an assumption of risks inherent in the "treatment" based upon full disclosure of the facts as to the procedures and expected outcome. The purpose of the form is to provide information for an intelligent decision by the one who is to engage in the treatment. Such forms usually are used in the medical field, including fitness programs, and experimentation on human subjects; and, thus, further discussion is in §17.4. However, an exculpatory clause may be attached to such forms. To be valid, such clause would have to meet criteria set forth in §16.1. There is indication that exculpatory clauses in informed consent forms used for prescriptive and rehabilitative fitness and conditioning programs (see Table 17.1), are invalid as against public policy.

This chapter discusses first exculpatory agreements as a matter of enforceable contract and factors of unenforceability, as well as specific application to programs and services; then, parental permissions and agreements to participate, indemnification contracts by the participant, and statutes which impact upon exculpatory agreements are presented. Most cases cited have several points of law pertinent to a number of subsections, but because of text length are not cited in all appropriate sections. Read

---

[4] Cash v. Street & Trail, Inc., 136 Ga. App. 462, 221 S.E. 2d 640 (1975) demonstration motorcycle ride.

[5] Cash v. Street & Trail, Inc., 136 Ga. App. 462, 221 S.E. 2d 640 (1975).

[6] For example, Doster v. C.V. Nalley, 95 Ga. App. 862, 99 S.E. 2d 432 (1957) and Thurston Metals & Supply Co., Inc. v. Taylor, 230 Va. 475, 339 S.E. 2d 538 (1986) covenant not to sue applied only to defendants' part of contract and not other joint tortfeasors; Wade v. Watson, 527 F. Supp. 1049 (1981) Georgia law applied, covenant not to sue barred wrongful death action.

case opinions for further applications. For situational description of cases, see appropriate chapter in Part B.

§ 16.1 Exculpatory agreements (waivers and releases)[7]

Action on exculpatory agreements is based in contract law, whereas action for injuries due to negligence is based in tort law. An exculpatory agreement is a contract which endeavors to alter tort common law, resulting in a conflict between traditional principles of tort law where the individual is responsible for one's actions which injure another person and contract law where parties have the right to define their relationship. Because the contract would curtail individual rights and insulate a party from liability for its own negligence, the courts have repeatedly looked with disfavor on such agreements and held that such contracts must be closely scrutinized and strictly construed,[8] particularly as against the party asserting validity and the drafter of the form. Further, an exculpatory agreement being a contract, the principles of contract also are applied. The court stated in a 1983 Ohio case[9] that "a participant in a recreational activity is free to contract with the proprietor of such activity so as to relieve the proprietor of responsibility for damages or injuries to the participant caused by the negligence of the proprietor, except when caused by willful or wanton misconduct."

A Georgia court in *Lovelace v. Figure Salon, Inc.*, 179 Ga. App. 51, 345 S.E.2d 139 (1986) stated it thusly: "Generally, parties are free to contract about any subject matter, on any terms, unless prohibited by statute or public policy, and injury to public interest clearly appears.... Exculpatory clause containing assumption of risk clause, disclaimer of liability clause, and covenant not to sue is not prohibited by statute, and is neither illegal, immoral, nor in contravention of law of Georgia." And, the Wisconsin court in *Merten v. Nathan*, 103 Wis.2d 693, 310 N.W.2d 653 (1981) rev'd./remanded 108 Wis.2d 205, 321 N.W.2d 173 (1982), phrased the right to contract: "Law of contracts is based on the principle of freedom of contracts, on the principle that individuals should have the power to govern their own affairs without governmental interference; courts protect each party to a contract by ensuring that the promise will be enforced; law protects justifiable expectations and security of transactions....Freedom of contract is premised on a bargain freely and voluntarily made through a process of bargaining which has integrity."

§ 16.11 Requirements for a valid contract

The court in *Blide v. Rainier Mountaineering, Inc.*, 30 Wash. App. 571, 636 P. 2d

[7] Sumner, C. D. Validity, Construction, and Effect of Agreement Exempting Operator of Amusement Facility from Liability for Personal Injury or Death of Patron. 8 A.L.R.3d 1393-1401.

[8] Doyle v. Bowdoin College, Maine, 403 A. 2d 1206 (Me. 1979); Franzek v. Calspan Corp., 78 A.D. 2d 134, 434 N.Y.S. 2d 288 (1980); Geise v. Co. of Niagra, 117 Misc.2d 470, 458 N.Y.S. 2d 162 (1983); Gervasi v. Holland Raceway, Inc., 40 A.D. 2d 574, 334 N.Y.S. 2d 527 (1972); Gross v. Sweet, 64 A.D. 2d 774, 407 N.Y.S. 2d 254 , aff'd. 49 N.Y. 2d 102, 424 N.Y.S. 2d

365, 400 N.E. 2d 306 (1979); Hine v. Dayton Speedway Corp., 20 Ohio App. 2d 185, 252 N.E. 2d 648 (1969); Jones v. Dressel, 582 P. 2d 1057 (Colo. App. 1978), aff'd. 623 P.2d 370 (1981); Leidy v. Deseret Enterprises, Inc., 252 Pa. Super. 162, 381 A. 2d 164 (1977); Rosen v. LTV Recreational Development, 569 F. 2d 1117 (1978); Schlobohm v. Spa Petite, Inc., 326 N.W. 2d 920 (Minn. 1982).

[9] Cain v. Cleveland Parachute Training Center, 9 Ohio App.3d 27, 457 N.E. 2d 1185 (1983).

492 (1982) held that absent statute to contrary, contracts against liability for negligence are generally valid except (1) where public interest is involved, (2) the negligent act falls greatly below standard established by law for protection of others against unreasonable risk of harm, (3) the hazard was within contemplation of release and the release clause was clear, unambiguous and conspicuous, and (4) individual knowingly agreed to terms of release.[10] In this situation, defendant employed the plaintiff, a physician, to conduct the medical portion of a mountain climbing seminar. The physician, not having any previous mountain climbing experience, also enrolled in the seminar as a student. While being lowered into a crevasse during the rescue practice on Mount Rainier, the plaintiff suffered a serious leg injury. Before coming to the seminar, plaintiff filled out an application for participation as a student which contained a release and assumption of risk. The application was contained on one page and the release on another. When plaintiff sent the form in, his letter of transmittal stated: "Enclosed you will find my signed release...." and at his deposition he testified that he had signed the release, but in fact he had not, merely having filled in his name on the application portion. The text of the release was:

> I am aware that during the mountain trip, or other trim (*sic*), that I am participating in under the arrangements of Rainier Mountaineering Inc., certain dangers may occur, including but not limited to, the hazards of traveling in mountainous terrain, accidents or illness in remote places, without medical facilities, and the forces of nature.
>
> In consideration of, and as part payment for, the right to participate in such mountain trips or other activities and the services and food arranged for me by RMI I have and do hereby assume all the above mentioned risks and will hold them harmless from any and all liability, actions, causes of action, debts, claims, demands of every kind and nature whatsoever which may arise of or in connection with my trip or participation in any activities arranged for me by RMI. The terms thereof shall serve as a release and assumption of risk for my heirs, executor and administrators and for all members of my family, including any minors accompanying me. (Parent or legal guardian must also sign for all persons under 21 years of age.) We recommend that the summit climb not be attempted by anyone under 15 years of age.
>
> Date:
>
>   Signature:

This case illustrates a number of the elements assessed by the courts. The court held that although mountaineering, like scuba diving, was a popular sport in the State of Washington, it does not involve public interest and at no time did the plaintiff allege negligence that fell greatly below the standard established by law and hence held that the exculpatory clause was valid and enforceable. The plaintiff also sought to hold the

---

[10] Each exception is discussed in a subsequent section of this chapter.

clause invalid because it did not specifically refer to negligence, but the court held that failure to use the word "negligence" did not render the release ineffective. Further, the court held that the accident was within the contemplation of the clause which was clear, unambiguous and conspicuous. There was no question that the plaintiff knowingly agreed to the terms, for he read it and believed that he signed it. Further, he accepted the benefits; there was objective manifestation of his understanding and intent to execute the release in the prescribed form.

In determining whether an exculpatory agreement is valid, a Colorado case[11] stated that there are four factors which the court must consider: (1) existence of duty to public; (2) nature of service performed; (3) whether contract was fairly entered into; and (4) whether intention of parties is expressed in clear and unambiguous language. In this skydiving case, the plaintiff suffered serious injuries in an airplane crash which occurred shortly after takeoff; the defendant furnished the airplane as part of its skydiving operation. The court found that the duty to the public factor was not present in this case, and that the service provided was not an essential service. And, on the other two factors, it was noted that there was no disagreement between the parties, that it was entered into fairly, and that the agreement was in clear and unambiguous language.

The *Simmons* case[12] set forth Pennsylvania law for criteria for an exculpatory agreement to be valid and enforceable: (1) does not contravene policy of law, *i.e.*, not a matter of interest to public or state; (2) must relate to individuals in their private dealings; (3) each party must be a free bargaining agent and is not a contract of adhesion; (4) agreement must be strictly construed against the party asserting it; and (5) it must spell out the intent of the parties with particularity.

§ 16.111 Expressed in clear and unequivocal terms[13]

The contract must state in clear and unambiguous terms that the person is waiving liability for injuries occurring from negligence of the provider of the service. Some courts hold that the word negligence should be specified; and that the omnibus term "any claim" is not adequate;[14] however, other courts hold the contract valid if the terminology is clear what is meant, whether or not the term "negligence" is used.[15] If there is just reference to risks of the activity, most frequently the form will be held to mean only those risks inherent in the activity and not the additional risks occasioned by negligence (see §16.1111). Where there is contradictory phraseology, such as in *Williams v. U.S.*, 660 F. Supp. 699 (1987), the attempted release will not be held valid. In this situation, swimming on an air force base, the court held that the release not only

[11] Jones v. Dressel, 582 P. 2d 1057 (Colo. App. 1978) aff'd. 623 P. 2d 370 (1981); see also Boehm v. Cody Country Chamber of Commerce, 748 P.2d 704 (Wyo. 1987).

[12] Simmons v. Parkette National Gymnastics Training Center, 670 F. Supp. 140 (1987).

[13] See also §16.13 for statements on admission tickets, membership applications, entry blanks, et al.

[14] Scroggs v. Coast Community College Dist., 239 Cal. Rptr. 916 (1987) college scuba class.

[15] Diedrich v. Wright, 550 F. Supp. 805 (1982)

skydiving, Illinois law; Hertzog v. Harrison Island Shores, Inc., 21 A.D. 2d 859, 251 N.Y.S. 2d 164 (1964) beach and yacht club; Phibbs v. Ray's Chevrolet Corp., 45 A.D. 2d 897, 357 N.Y.S. 2d 211 (1974) motorcycle racetrack; Sivaslian v. Rawlins, 88 A.D. 2d 703, 451 N.Y.S. 2d 307 (1982) parachute-jumping school; Smith v. Golden Triangle Raceway, 708 S.W. 2d 574 (Tex. App. 1986) race track pit area; Solodar v. Watkins Glen Grand Prix Corp., 36 A.D. 2d 552, 317 N.Y.S. 2d 228 (1971) sports car race driver.

failed to clearly indicate that the Government sought to abandon responsibility for its own wrongful conduct by terms of release but also served to induce confidence of its care and custody of child by use of the terms "supervised" activities and "in the unlikely event of injury." There are many different phraseologies on the forms which can be held valid in terms of clarity, as the following cases illustrate. Readability, also, can be a factor. Two California cases[16] had 5 ½ point print. *In re Conservatorship of Link* said the form must be easily read by persons of ordinary vision and recommended the typeface be no smaller than 8-10 point type generally required by the California Civil Code for various contracts, but the *Bennett* case said that type-size was just one of the factors of validity, and in this particular form the release was conspicuous and legible, practically the only language on the document, and did not have to compete with other less important information for the entrant's attention.

Franzek v. Calspan Corp.[17] stated that agreements exculpating a party from the consequences of its own negligence are disfavored and subject to close judicial scrutiny. Although such agreements are enforceable, their validity is measured by an exacting standard. Unless the intention of the parties is expressed in clear and unequivocal terms, a negligent party will not be relieved of liability. Broad exculpatory provisions, which do not specifically refer to the negligence of a party, do not insulate that party from liability. Where the waiver extends to claims arising out of the negligence of a party, whether by use of the term "negligence" or by words of similar import, it provides the negligent party with a valid defense.

In the *Franzek* case, 29 persons were aboard a rubber raft going down the "white water" of the lower Niagara River to determine the feasability of offering regular passenger trips to the general public. Plaintiff learned of the raft ride from the local newspaper. He claims he was given no instructions prior to boarding the raft and only after he boarded was he handed the waiver, which he signed without reading. However, according to the defendant, all persons boarding the raft were required to sign the release in order to go on the trip, and in the substantial interval of time while the passengers were on the dock prior to embarkation, each was required to execute the release. The release, after reciting the dangerous nature of the trip and representations as to the undersigned's age, condition and state of mind, provided:

> The undersigned understands and expressly assumes all the dangers of the trip. The undersigned waives all claims arising out of the Trip, whether caused by negligence, breach of contract or otherwise, and whether for bodily injury, property damage or loss or otherwise, which he may ever have against Niagara Gorge River Trips, Inc., its successors and assigns, and its officers, directors, shareholders, employees and agents, and their heirs, executors and administrators.

[16] Bennett v. U.S. Cycling Federation, 193 Cal. App. 3d 1485, 239 Cal. Rptr. 55 (1987); In re Conservatorship of Link, 158 Cal. App. 3d 138, 205 Cal. Rptr. 513 (1984) printed in 5 ½ point type, so lengthy and convoluted that not comprehendable, stock car auto racing pit crewman; see also McAtee v. Newhall Land & Farming Co., 169 Cal. App. 3d 1031, 216 Cal. Rptr. 465 (1985) clear, black type easily read.

[17] Franzek v. Calspan Corp. and Niagara Gorge River Trips v. Zodiac (two cases), 78 A.D. 2d 134, 434 N.Y.S. 2d 288 (1980); see also, Hine v. Dayton Speedway Corp., 20 Ohio App. 2d 185, 252 N.E. 2d 648 (1969), and VanTuyn v. Zurich American Insurance Company, 447 So. 2d 318 (Fla. App. 1984).

The court held that this statement was clear and unequivocal, and thus a valid agreement.

In another whitewater rafting case, *Delaney v. Cascade River Holidays, Ltd.*, 19 C.C.L.T. 78 (B.C.S.C.), 16 B.L.R. 114 (1981), the court held that the exclusion was clear and unambiguous. The statement read:

STANDARD LIABILITY RELEASE
TRIP NAME: 2 Day Fraser TRIP NO. C10 TRIP DATE May 5-6 1979

DISCLAIMER CLAUSE: Cascade River Holidays Ltd. is not responsible for any loss or damage suffered by any person either in travelling to the location of the trip, before, during or after the trip, for any reason whatsoever including negligence on the part of the company, its agents or servants.

AGREEMENT: I agree to assume all risks involved in taking the trip including travelling before and after, and agree to pay the cost of any emergency evacuation of my person and belongings that may become necessary. I agree to Cascade River Holidays Ltd. its agents and servants relieving themselves of all liabililty for losses and damages of all and every descriptions. I acknowledge having read this Liability release and that I am of the full age and my acceptance of the above disclaimer clause by my signature and seal.

(Parents or Guardians please sign for minors)

A Vermont skiing case[18] held that failure to include in the release agreement, expressly and literally, the word "negligence," as being within scope of parties' intent, did not preclude other language from having that effect. The following excerpts were held to be sufficiently clear, and thus a freestyle skier who had entered a freestyle skiing event was not entitled to recover damages for a permanently paralyzing spinal injury:

(He agreed) to release, hold harmless and forever discharge (defendants) from any and all claims, demands, liability, right or causes of action of whatsoever kind of nature which (plaintiff) may have, arising from or in any way connected with, any injuries, losses, damages, suffering.... which (he might sustain as a result of his participation in the competition).

The case of *Jones v. Dressel*[19] focused on a contract which had a covenant not to sue and a clause exempting the defendant (Free Flight) from liability, stated thusly:

2A. **EXEMPTION FROM LIABILITY.** The (plaintiff) exempts and releases the Corporation, its owners, officers, agents, servants, employees, and lessors from any and all liability, claims, demands or actions or causes of action whatsoever arising out of any damage, loss or injury to the (plaintiff) or

---

[18] Douglass v. Skiing Standards, Inc., 142 Vt. 634, 459 A. 2d 97 (1983).

[19] Jones v. Dressel, 582 P. 2d 1057 (Colo. App. 1978), aff'd. 623 P. 2d 370 (1981).

the (plaintiff's) property while upon the premises or aircraft of the Corporation or while participating in any of the activities contemplated by this Agreement, whether such loss, damage, or injury results from the negligence of the Corporation, its officers, agents, servants, employees, or lessors or from some other cause.

The contract also contained an alternative provision which would have permitted plaintiff to use Free Flight's facilities at an increased cost, but without releasing Free Flight (defendant) from liability for negligence. However, the alternative provision was crossed out when plaintiff signed the contract, but it was not established that defendant would have prohibited plaintiff from participating in skydiving activities if the alternative provision had not been crossed out. The alternative provision stated:

> 2B. **ALTERNATIVE PROVISION.** In consideration of the deletion of the provisions 2A, 3, 4 and 5 herein regarding **ASSUMPTION OF RISK, EXEMPTION FROM LIABILITY, COVENANT NOT TO SUE, INDEMNITY AGAINST THIRD PARTY CLAIMS, AND CONTINU-ATION OF OBLIGATIONS,** the Participant has paid the additional sum of $50.00 upon execution of this agreement, receipt of which is hereby acknowledged by the Corporation.

> 2C. It is understood that acceptance of this **ALTERNATIVE PROVISION** does not constitute a contract of insurance, but only waives Corporation's contractual defenses which would otherwise be available.

The court held that the contract expressed the parties' intention in clear and unambiguous language, and used the word "negligence" and specifically included injuries sustained "upon aircraft of corporation." The plaintiff was injured in an airplane crash related to skydiving activities.

In a parachute instruction case[20] the plaintiff paid his fee and signed a form entitled "Responsibility Release." He was then given the standard introductory lesson, which consisted of approximately one hour of on-land training, including oral instruction as well as several jumps off a 2½' table. Plaintiff then was equipped with a parachute and flown to an altitude of 2,800' for his first practice jump. Upon coming in contact with the ground on his descent, plaintiff suffered serious injuries. Plaintiff alleged he had informed defendant that several years earlier an orthopedic pin had been inserted in his leg, and the school must have known landing in a parachute puts special stress on one's legs. The statement plaintiff had signed read:

> I, the undersigned, hereby, and by these covenants, do waive any and all claims that I, my heirs, and/or assignees may have against Nathaniel Sweet, the Stormville Parachute Center, the Jumpmaster and the Pilot who shall operate the aircraft when used for the purpose of parachute jumping for any personal

---

[20] Gross v. Sweet, 64 A.D. 2d 774, 407 N.Y.S. 2d 254, aff'd. 49 N.Y. 2d 102, 424 N.Y.S. 2d 365, 400 N.E. 2d 306 (1979).

injuries or property damage that I may sustain or which may arise out of my learning, practicing or actually jumping from an aircraft. I also assume full responsibility for any damage that I may do or cause while participating in this sport.

The court held that assuming that this language alerted the plaintiff to the dangers inherent in parachute jumping and that he entered into the sport with apprehension of the risks, it does not follow that he was aware of, much less intended to accept, any enhanced exposure to injury occasioned by the carelessness of the very persons on whom he depended for his safety. Specifically, the release nowhere expresses any intention to exempt the defendant from liability for injury or property damages which may result from his failure to use due care either in his training methods or in his furnishing safe equipment. The court further stated that thus, whether on a running reading or a careful analysis, the agreement could most reasonably be taken merely as driving home the fact that the defendant was not to bear any responsibility for injuries that ordinarily and inevitably would occur, without any fault of the defendant, to those who participate in such a physically demanding sport. In short, the court continued, instead of specifying to prospective students that they would have to abide any consequences attributable to the instructor's own carelessness, the defendant seems to have preferred the use of opaque terminology rather than suffer the possibility of lower enrollment.

Two 1985 cases[21] involving parachute jumping held exculpatory agreements valid, as having language which was clear and unambiguous. In the California case, the plaintiff was a beginner, just ready for his first jump. Being unable to steer toward the target area successfully, he attempted to land in a vacant lot but collided with electric power lines as he neared the ground. He was knocked unconscious, but sustained only a broken wrist. The agreement and release of liability statement was on the reverse side of the registration form. Some of the key parts included, in bold-faced type:

I am aware that parachute instruction and jumping are hazardous activities, and I am voluntarily participating in these activities with knowledge of the danger involved and hereby agree to accept any and all risks of injury or death. Please initial.

in the third paragraph:

(the subscriber will not sue EPC or its employees) for injury or damage resulting from the negligence or other acts, howsoever caused, by any employee, agent or contractor of (EPC) or its affiliates, as a result of my participation in parachuting activities.... (will) release and discharge (EPC and its employees) from all actions, claims or demands.... for injury or damage resulting from (the subscriber's) participation in parachuting activities.

and in the fourth paragraph, also in bold-face type:

---

[21] Hulsey v. Elsinore Parachute Center, 168 Cal. App. 3d 333, 214 Cal. Rptr. 194 (1985); Poskozim v. Monnacep, 131 Ill. App. 3d 446, 86 Ill. Dec. 663, 475 N.E.2d 1042 (1975); see also Ferrell v. Southern Nevada Off-Road Enthusiasts, 147 Cal. App. 3d 309, 195 Cal. Rptr. 90 (1983).

> I have carefully read this agreement and fully understand its contents. I am aware that this is a release of liability and a contract between myself and Elsinore Parachute Center and/or its affiliated organizations and sign it of my own free will.

In the Illinois situation, the plaintiff was a student in an adult education program offered by the school district and community college. During the second class period, plaintiff read and executed a document entitled "Adult Release and Indemnity Agreement" with the provisions, thusly:

> In consideration of the permission extended to me by Sky Sports, Inc., to participate in a course of parachuting instruction, parachuting training, flying activities, ground or air operations incidental to parachuting and flying, and for other valuable consideration, hereby acknowledge, I _____ of _____.... do hereby fully and forever release and discharge the said Sky Sports, Inc. and their employees, servants, stockholders, agents, successors, assigns, and all persons whomsoever directly or indirectly liable, from any and all other claims.... in any way resulting from, personal injuries.... substained by me, arising out of.... parachute jumps.... or arising out of the ownership, operation, use, maintenance or control of any vehicle.... and meaning and intending to include herein all such personal injuries, conscious suffering, death or property damage resulting from or in any way connected with or arising out of instructions, training, and ground or air operations incidental thereto.

Students had to bring boots which were approved; plaintiff's boots were approved and he made his first jump. At the completion of his descent, he broke his leg upon impact with the ground. The court held the agreement unambigous and exonerated all defendants (Sky Sports, school district, community college, instructor).

The court said in *Empress Health & Beauty Spa v. Turner*, 503 S.W. 2d 188 (Tenn. 1973) that one must look to the intent and clarity of the statement, which was:

> 7. Member fully understands and agrees that in participating in one or more of the courses, or using the facilities that shall be maintained by the Spa, there is the possibility of accidental or other physical injury. Member further agrees to assume the risk of such injury and further agrees to indemnify the Spa from any and all liability attributable to the Spa by either the Member or Third Parties as a result of the use by the Member of the facilities and instruction as offered by the Spa.

The court held that the plaintiff was barred by "an assumption of risk provision" contained in the customer's contract with the club, inasmuch as the contract was not ambiguous. There was no uncertainty in meaning, nor could it be understood in more ways than one; the word "negligence" need not appear in the clause.

The document signed by the father in *Doyle v. Bowdoin College*, 403 A. 2d 1206 (Me. 1979), relating to an injury to minor son at hockey clinic, was held not to be a release of liability on the basis that it contained no express reference to defendants' liability for their own negligence, and such must expressly "spell out with the greatest particularity" the intention of the parties contractually to extinguish negligence liability. The document in question read:

> I understand that neither Bowdoin College nor anyone associated with the Hockey Clinic will assume any responsibility for accidents and medical or dental expenses incurred as a result of participation in this program.... I understand that I must furnish proof of health and accident insurance coverage acceptable to the College....
>
> (signed by father)

> I fully understand that Bowdoin College, its employees or servants will accept no responsibility for or on account of any injury or damage sustained by *Brian* arising out of the activities of the said **THE CLINIC**. I do, therefore, agree to assume all risk of injury or damage to the person or property of Brian arising out of the activities of the said **THE CLINIC**.
>
> (signed by mother)

The Florida court in a camp case[22] held that the language in the exculpatory clause in the enrollment contract signed by the mother was ineffective because it did not explicitly state that the camp would be absolved from liability for injuries resulting from its negligence. The language just indicated that the camp operators agreed to take precautions to assure the safety and health of the child. The exculpatory clause in the contract signed was:

> It is further agreed that reasonable precautions will be taken by Camp to assure the safety and good health of said boy/girl that Camp is not to be held liable in the event of injury, illness or death of said boy/girl, and the undersigned, does fully release Camp, and all persons concerned therewith, for any such liability.

The court held in a scuba diving case[23] that the following document signed was valid and a bar to plaintiff for alleged negligence in that it conspicuously acknowledged possibilities and explicit reference to negligence was not necessary.

SAFETY AFFIRMATION AND RELEASE

SAFETY AFFIRMATION AND RELEASE (Read carefully, then sign) I **Don F. Hewitt** hereby affirm that I have previously completed a certified beginning course of instruction in **SCUBA** diving prior to enrolling in this course. By enrolling in this course I certify that I am cognizant of all of the inherent dangers of skindiving and **SCUBA** diving, and of the basic safety rules for underwater activities.

I understand that it is not the purpose of this course to teach safety rules, nor is it the function of the instructors to serve as the guardians of my safety. I also

---

[22] Goyings v. Jack & Ruth Eckerd Foundation, 403 So. 2d 1144 (Fla. App. 1981).

[23] Hewitt v. Miller, 11 Wash. App. 72, 521 P. 2d 244 (1974).

understand that I am to furnish my own equipment and I am responsible for its safety and good operating conditions regardless of where I obtain it.

I understand and agree that neither this class nor its owners, operators, agents, or instructors, including but not limited to...., may be held liable in any way for any occurrence in connection with the Advanced SCUBA diving class which may result in injury, death, or other damages to me or my family, heirs, or assigns, and in consideration of being allowed to enroll in this course, I hereby personally assume all risks in connection with said course, and I further release the aforementioned instructors, program, agents and operators, including but not limited to the persons mentioned, for any harm, injury or damage which may befall me while I am enrolled as a student of the school, including all risks connected therewith, whether foreseen [sic] or unforeseen [sic]: and further to save and hold harmless said program and persons from any claim by me, or my family, estate, heirs, or assigns, arising out of my enrollment and participation in this course.

I further state that I am of lawful age and legally competent to sign this affirmation and release: that I understand the terms herein are contractual and not a mere recital: and that I have signed this document as my own free act.

I HAVE FULLY INFORMED MYSELF OF THE CONTENTS OF THIS AFFIRMATION AND RELEASE BY READING IT BEFORE I SIGNED IT. I have had a medical examination to assure myself, and assume my own responsibility of physical fitness and capability to perform under the normal conditions of an advanced diving program, and am physically fit as attested to by the aforementioned medical examination.

While one must understand the risks assumed (see next subsection), if the document is stated clearly and unequivocally, the injured person does not have to have knowledge of the specific risk subjected to by defendant's negligence, but the document acts as an express assumption of risk for all related negligence. So the court held in 1988 in *Madison v. Superior Court,* 250 Cal. Rptr. 299 (1988). The following statement was upheld as valid for scuba diving:

MAUI WAIVER, RELEASE AND INDEMNITY AGREEMENT

For and in consideration of permitting (1) _____ to enroll in and participate in diving activities and class instruction of skin and/or scuba diving given by (2) _____, in the City of _____, County of _____, and State of _____, beginning on the _____ day of _____, 19___, the Undersigned hereby voluntarily releases, discharges, waives and relinquishes any and all actions or causes of action for personal injury, property damage or wrongful death occurring to him/herself arising as a result of engaging or receiving instructions in said activity or any activities incidental thereto wherever or however the name may occur and for whatever period said activities or instructions may continue, and the Undersigned does for him/herself, his/her heirs, executors, administrators and assigns hereby release, waive, discharge and relinquish any action or causes of action, aforesaid, which may hereafter arise for him/herself and for his/her estate, and agrees that under no circumstances will he/she or his/her heirs, executors, administrators and assigns prosecute, present any claim for personal injury, property damage or wrongful death against (2) _____ or any of its officers, agents, servants or employees for any of said causes of action, whether the same shall arise by the negligence of any of said persons, or otherwise. IT IS THE INTENTION OF (1) _____ BY THIS INSTRUMENT, TO EXEMPT AND RELIEVE (2) _____ FROM LIABILITY FOR PERSONAL INJURY, PROPERTY DAMAGE OR WRONGFUL DEATH CAUSED BY NEGLIGENCE.

The Undersigned, for him/herself, his/her heirs, executors, administrators or assigns agrees that in the event any claim for personal injury, property damage or wrongful death shall be prosecuted against (2) _____ he/she shall indemnify and save harmless the same (2) _____ from any and all claims or causes of action by whomever or wherever made or presented for personal injuries, property damage or wrongful death.

The Undersigned acknowledges that he/she has read the foregoing two paragraphs, has been fully and completely advised of the potential dangers incidental to engaging in the activity and instructing of skin and/or scuba diving, and is fully aware of the legal consequences of signing the within instrument.

WITNESS: _____   _____
                                  Signature of participant

DATED: _____   _____
                                  Signature of Parent or
                                  Guardian — when applicable

The plaintiff had hired a horse from the defendant and before riding signed a brief agreement "I am hiring your horse to ride today and all future rides at my own risk." Plaintiff was injured while riding when a defective stirrup strap broke. The court held that subject to certain exceptions (none of which were present), parties may contract that one shall not be liable for his negligence to another, but that such other shall assume the risk incident to such negligence.[24]

§ 16.1111   Enumerating risks not sufficient; distinguish assumption of risk[25]

In a 1983 New York tobogganing case,[26] the court said that although the first paragraph of the agreement lists a series of risks that the plaintiff acknowledges can be

---

[24] Moss v. Fortune, 207 Tenn. 426, 340 S.W. 2d 902 (1960).

[25] See also §16.13 for admission ticket et al. statements; §5.22 assumption of risk.

[26] Geise v. Co. of Niagra, 117 Misc. 2d 470, 458 N.Y.S. 2d 162 (1983).

part of tobogganing, the plaintiff was never explicitly informed that he was accepting as part of the danger inherent in the activity, the enhanced risks resulting from defendant's negligence in operating or maintaining the facility. The necessary clarity and precision regarding the defendant's exemption of itself from liability for its own negligence was lacking. Any ambiguities must be resolved against the party who drafted the agreement. The court held that the agreement did not release defendant from the consequences of its own negligence.

The injured person must understand or comprehend the nature of the risk. In *Tepper v. City of New Rochelle School District,* 531 N.Y.S.2d 367 (1988), the student's parents had signed a consent form to allow him to participate on the lacrosse team; however, he had never played lacrosse before. Thus, an issue of fact existed as to whether the plaintiff comprehended the true nature of the risk when he opted to join the team.

The parents, on their own behalf, signed a form and one on behalf of the nine-year-old child who was injured before going on a horseback ride. The two releases were very similar. The child's release stated:

> I consent to the renting of a horse from Walt Disney World Co. by *Frankie*, a minor, and to his/her assumption of the risks inherent in horseback riding. I agree, personally and on his/her behalf, to waive any claims or causes of action which he/she or I may now or hereafter have against Walt Disney World Co. arising out of any injuries he/she may sustain as a result of that horseback riding, and I will hold Walt Disney World Co. harmless against any and all claims resulting from such injuries.

The court did not decide whether the parent could waive the minor child's right to recovery, but it did say that the only risks referred to in the agreement were those "inherent in horseback riding," and thus this agreement would not bar recovery for injuries resulting from defendant's negligence because it is not so expressly stated.[27] Six years earlier, Walt Disney World Co. had another horseback riding case[28] against them and the court held that the exculpatory clause was not valid and enforceable because the intent to indemnify the indemnitee for his own negligence must be specifically provided for in the contract, and it was not. The contract stated:

WAIVER AND HOLD HARMLESS AGREEMENT

> In renting a horse from Walt Disney World Co., I agree to assume the risks inherent in horseback riding. I hereby waive any and all claims or causes of action which I may now or hereafter have against Walt Disney World Co., arising out of any injuries I may sustain as a result of that horseback riding, and I will hold Walt Disney World Co. harmless against any and all claims resulting from such injuries.

> This waiver and agreement to indemnify shall be binding upon me and my heirs, personal respresentatives and assigns.

/ss/

---

[27] O'Connell v. Walt Disney World Co., 413 So. 2d 444 (Fla. App. 1982).

[28] Jones v. Walt Disney World Co., 409 F. Supp. 526 (1976).

The plaintiffs were injured when they were thrown from the horses they were riding at a private riding stable. The attendants who conducted the rides also collected the fees from the patrons. Before anyone was permitted to ride, he was required to sign a "Waiver and Hold Harmless Agreement" by virtue of which he assumed the risks inherent in horseback riding. Usually, the waiver was identified as such, but not in any way explained to the patrons. The court found that there was no negligence on the part of the defendants; there was no exposure to an unreasonable risk not inherent in riding.[29]

Assumption of risk also was at issue in a 1981 drag racing situation in Louisiana. The court held that the driver did knowingly assume the risk of injuring himself, and discussed the requirements for assumption of risk, citing other cases involving sport. The driver had signed a "tech-card" on the day of the accident with this clause:

RELEASE OF LIABILITY

This release limits your right to recovery of damages in case of accident. Read it before signing.

In applying to enter this race I promise that I will inspect the track prior to running on it, will assure myself that the track and adjacent areas are properly designed and maintained and further agree that I will not participate in this race until I have completed an inspection which satisfies me that these areas are safe for race purposes. I will further note existing weather conditions and do agree that I voluntarily assume all risks arising from conditions related to use of the track area of myself or others.

I do agree to hold harmless and indemnify the owners and possessors of this track for any loss, cost, expense, damage or injury arising from my participation in this event.

The court held that such statement was not contrary to public policy. It further found that the defendant was not negligent toward plaintiff and that the injury occurred from the inherent dangers involved in drag racing of which the plaintiff was knowledgeable and appreciated as an experienced driver.[30] In *Celli v. Sports Car Club*, 29 Cal. App. 3d 511, 105 Cal. Rptr. 2d 904, (1973), the court held that the release on the pit pass was insufficient to absolve defendants from active negligence, not clear and explicit, and that issue of assumption of risk was excluded in absence of evidence that plaintiffs had actual knowledge of the particular danger (car left race track and skidded into infield where plaintiff had been admitted as a spectator) as well as an appreciation of the risk involved and the magnitude thereof. The plaintiffs were clearly invitees to whom defendants owed a duty to exercise reasonable care in management of property; paying patron of recreation facility is not obliged to make critical examination of area about to be used to determine whether or not it is safe. Plaintiff has right to assume that those in charge have exercised due care in matter of inspection and have taken proper precautions

[29] Alfonso v. Market Facilities of Houston, 356 So.2d 86 (La. App. 1978), cert. writ denied 357 So. 2d 1169 (1978) memorandum decision.

[30] Robillard v. P & R Racetracks, 405 So. 2d 1203 (La. App. 1981).

for the safety of the patrons. Defense of assumption of risk and contributory negligence are discussed in other auto racing cases.[31]

In a 1983 snow ski club skit incident in Florida, the court held that a release executed gave evidence of actual consent to assumption of risk. The release signed by plaintiff was stated:[32]

> The release signed by Ms. Gary provides that I, (Dale Gary) do hereby release and hold harmless the Miami Snow Ski Club and its officers and members for any injury, loss or damage upon my person and/or my property that should occur during any audition, rehearsals and/or performance of "The Great Fashion Put-On" comedy [sic] show. I understand that my participation is voluntary and at my own risk and expense. I further consent to the use of my photograph(s), picture(s), caricature(s) and/or the like without compensation in the promotional, advertising and publicity activities associated with the aforesaid event.

The court held further that the assumption of risk did not merge into the principles of comparative negligence. (See §5.23 Comparative Negligence.)

There was an exculpatory clause on the back of an amusement park ticket, but the court said such was not a valid written contract and that one had to make an inference from the facts of the situation. There, also, was a sign on the giant slide that said "slide at your own risk." The court said that there could be no valid waiver if the person signing did not know, understand, comprehend the danger; further, it appeared that there was an abnormal occurrence of something causing plaintiff's body to fly into the air, and such abnormality risk would not be assumed, and thus could not be waived.[33]

A fitness club member brought action against club to recover for injuries caused when he slipped on wet tile floor. At issue was the release on the membership form, which stated:

> I _____ voluntarily enter the Westend Racquet Club.... to participate in the athletic, physical and social activities therein. I have inspected the premises and know of the risks and dangers involved in such activities as are conducted therein and that unanticipated and unexpected dangers may arise during such activities. I hereby and do assume all risks of injury to my person and property that may be sustained in connection with the stated and associated activities in and about those premises. In consideration of the permission granted to me to enter the premises and participate in the stated activities, I hereby, for myself, my heirs, administrators and assigns, release, remise and discharge, and owners, operators and sponsors of the premises and its activities and equipment and their respective servants, agents, officers, and all other participants in those activities of and from all claims, demands,

---

[31] See also §5.22 assumption of risk in other activities; for example, Provence v. Doolin, 91 Ill. App. 3d 271, 46 Ill. Dec. 733, 414 N.E. 2d 786 (1980).

[32] Gary v. Party Time Co., 434 So. 2d 338 (Fla. App. 1983).

[33] Russo v. The Range, 76 Ill. App. 3d 236, 32 Ill. Dec. 63, 395 N.E. 2d 10 (1979).

actions and causes of action of any sort, for injury sustained to my person and/ or property during my presence on the premises and my participation in those activities due to negligence or any other fault.

The court held that the release did not absolve fitness club of liability for its negligence, where release did not spell out intention of parties with necessary particularity and did not unambigously state intent of member to absolve club of liability for club's negligence, and where release could more clearly be interpreted to relieve club of liability as result of member's injuries sustained while participating in activities of club. It further stated that contracts providing for immunity from liability from one's negligent acts are disfavored and require strict adherence to standards requiring specification of intention of parties with necessary particularity and statement of intent to absolve releasee of liability for releasee's negligence.[34]

§ 16.1112   Unwittingly or ignorantly signed; signed without reading; fraud

In upholding a health club membership form in *My Fair Lady of Georgia v. Harris*, 185 Ga. App. 459, 364 S.E.2d 580 (1987), the court said that "One who can read, must read, for he is presumed to have read and understood provisions in contracts he executes, and is bound by them."

In the *Franzek* case, the plaintiff claimed that he neither read nor understood the waiver; however, the signer of an instrument is conclusively bound by it and it is immaterial whether he read it or subjectively assented to its terms[35] in the absence of fraud or misrepresentation or that a special relationship existed between the parties which would render such rule inapplicable. The court held in a bicycle rental agreement situation that the "only dispositive factor in determining the parties' intention is whether the contract was signed,...the signature attests to assent." The court found no merit in the plaintiff's argument that he "couldn't" read the contract before he signed it, for although he did not have his glasses with him, he could have requested that either the friend who accompanied him or the defendant's employee read the agreement to him before he signed it.[36]

Similarly, in *Delaney v. Cascade River Holidays, Ltd.*,[37] the court said that it is sufficient if deceased (Delaney) knew it was contractual in nature, in the absence of fraud or misrepresentation. It was held that reasonable steps were taken to ensure that the exemption from liability provision was drawn to the notice of Delaney. Whether or not he read it was irrelevant. In this situation the deceased was one of 11 participants on the raft, 8 paying passengers and 3 employees. They had gone the night before the trip was to start and stayed overnight in a local hotel. The next morning the party assembled in the hotel parking lot where they were met by the company employees. The reservation manager of the company contacted each member of the group, including Delaney, and

[34] Brown v. Racquetball Centers, Inc., 534 A. 2d 842 (Pa. Super. 1987).

[35] Broderson v. Rainier National Park Co., 187 Wash. 399, 60 P. 2d 234 (1936); see also Mayer v. Howard, 220 Neb. 328, 370 N.W. 2d 93 (1985) and Adams v. Roak, 686 S.W. 2d 73 (Tenn. 1985) both

motorcycle racing situation, failure to read document before signing does not invalidate document.

[36] Gimpel v. Host Enterprises, Inc., 640 F. Supp. 972 (1986).

[37] Delaney v. Cascade River Holidays, Ltd., 19 C.C.L.T. 78 (B.C.S.C.), 15 B.L.R. 114 (1981).

requested each to read and sign a liability release form. It was indicated that those who refused to sign would not be permitted to participate in the white water adventure. All members of the party signed. The document to which the signature and addresses were appended had at the top the words "Standard Liability Release" in bold conspicuous type. It was comprised of two parts, a disclaimer edged in black and a three-sentence agreement. Further, the brochure describing the trip read in part:

LIABILITY

Cascade River Holidays Ltd. does not guarantee safe passage and assumes no responsibility for patrons' safety or property. Patron must sign our liability release before departure. Cascade River Holidays has operated since 1973 without major loss and uses all the standard safety devices. We recommend the patron purchase personal insurance to protect himself.

The issue in *Kubisen v. Chicago Health Clubs*[38] was whether lack of knowledge could be presumed from the contract itself. In this instance, the clause in question appeared on the reverse side of the contract with other provisions; the contract was signed on the front with no reference to the exculpatory clause on the back; and, the clause was set forth in small or fine print. The court said that in absence of any assertion by plaintiff of lack of knowledge, a presumption from the contract itself was untenable, especially since there was no indication the plaintiff did not read before signing and just above the signature were the words clearly printed "NOTICE TO THE BUYER," and adjacent thereto, the following: "Do not sign this agreement before you read it or if it contains any blank spaces." And, further, provision A on the front side stated "….the terms and conditions hereinafter set forth (including the terms and conditions contained on the reverse side hereof) a membership… ."

Several cases[39] dealing with horses had in issue the waiver, which either was not read or was alleged to be a misrepresentation or deception. In the *Carrion* case, the customer, who was injured after falling from the horse, alleged that the stable's employee saddled the horse in a negligent manner. Plaintiff had signed a waiver and indemnification agreement before the ride, but admitted he had not read it. The court held that one signing written document, unless there is fraud, is chargeable with knowledge of its contents. A false statement regarding insurance was made in the *Merten* case. The stable had been using the release when they were uninsured, then when they got insurance coverage, they just did not bother to change the form. The fraudulent representation made the release invalid. The court said, though, the release itself was not void on public policy and that "instructors of dangerous sports" can shift the risk to the participant.

The plaintiff, wishing to gain entrance to the pit area of a race track, represented himself as a mechanic in order to gain such entrance. The court held that subsequently

---

[38] Kubisen v. Chicago Health Clubs, 69 Ill. App.3d 463, 26 Ill. Dec. 420, 388 N.E. 2d 44 (1979).

[39] Adams v. Roark, 686 S.W.2d 73 (Tenn. 1985); Carrion v. Smokey, Inc., 164 Ga. App. 790, 298 S.E. 2d 584 (1982); Erickson v. Wagon Wheel Enterprises, Inc., 101 Ill. App. 2d 296, 242 N.E. 2d 622 (1968); Merten v. Nathan, 103 Wis. 2d 693, 310 N.W. 2d 653 (1981) rev'd./remanded 108 Wis. 2d 205, 321 N.W. 2d 173 (1982); Palmquist v. Mercer, 263 P. 2d 341 (Cal. App. 1953), 43 Cal. 2d 92, 272 P. 2d 26 (1954).

he could not then say that he was not an entrant within the meaning of the release he signed as part of the application for membership which gave him the right to enter. Only entrants were to be mechanics, drivers, and owners, none of which the plaintiff was. Secondly, the plaintiff alleged that he did not understand and was not aware of the meaning of the paper he signed. There was no fraud or misrepresentation on the part of the defendant. While there was a line of people at the table on which the release sheets were located, there was no evidence that plaintiff was denied the opportunity to read the release and it certainly was not concealed from him. The court held that failing to avail himself of the opportunity to read it, yet gaining the admission to which his signature on the sheet was a condition precedent, he could not complain that he had no notice of the import of the paper which he signed.[40]

RELEASE SHEET

TRACK Westboro   DATE May 20/60

LIABILITY: The entrant in signing this release elects to use said track at his own risk and thereby releases and discharges the track owners,.... . from all liabilities that may be accrued from personal injuries that may be received by said entrant, from all claims and demands for damages to personal property and employee growing out of or resulting from this race meet. The undersigned hereby acknowledges and represents that he is of sound mind and over 21 years of age.

§ 16.112   Valid consideration[41]

One of the requirements for a valid contract is that of consideration. Seldom is consideration in issue; it usually is obvious. The plaintiff alleged lack of valid consideration in *French v. Special Services*, 107 Ohio App. 435, 159 N.E. 2d 785 (1958); however, the court held that the privilege of competing in races for prizes was a valuable one and met the criterion for consideration. The right to participate in a racing event, also, was held to be valid consideration in a 1984 case.[42] Similarly, permission to enter the infield area of the racetrack was deemed consideration for signing the release.[43]

In *Delaney v. Cascade River Holidays, Ltd.*, 19 C.C.L.T. 78 (B.C.S.C.) 16 B.L.R. 114 (1981), the court held that the deceased (Delaney) had paid his money on the morning at or about the time the release was signed; and, that it would be unreasonable

---

[40] Lee v. Allied Sports Associates, 349 Mass. 544, 209 N.E. 2d 329 (Mass. 1965); see also Hoffman v. Sport Car Club of America, 180 Cal. App. 3d 119, 225 Cal. Rptr. 359 (1986); Sexton v. Southwestern Auto Racing Ass'n, 75 Ill. App. 3d 338, 31 Ill. Dec. 133, 394 N.E. 2d 49 (1979); Smith v. Golden Triangle Raceway, 708 S.W. 2d 574 (Tex. App. 1986); Theroux v. Kedenburg Racing Assn., 50 Misc. 2d 97, 269 N.Y.S. 2d 789 (1965) aff'd. without opinion 28 A.D. 2d 960, 282 N.Y.S. 2d 930 (1967).

[41] See also Hewitt v. Miller, 11 Wash. App. 72, 521 P. 2d 244 (1974).

[42] Rhea v. Horn-Keen Corp., 582 F. Supp. 687 (1984) Virginia law applied.

[43] Church v. Seneca County Agricultural Society, 41 A.D. 2d 787, 341 N.Y.S. 2d 45 (1973); aff'd. without opinion 34 N.Y. 2d 571, 354 N.Y.S. 2d 945, 310 N.E. 2d 541 (1974); see also Kotary v. Spencer Speedway, Inc., 47 A.D. 2d 127, 365 N.Y.S. 2d 87 (1975) admission to pit area on auto speedway.

to conclude that he did not have actual or imputed knowledge at the time he paid his fee and received a ride ticket that a liability waiver would be required before embarkation. Such constituted valid consideration. The plaintiff had alleged past consideration making the contract not valid and enforceable.

The defendant had leased certain premises, Ostend Shore and Beach Club, from the City of New York, and by terms of the lease he was required to reserve, free of all charges, certain bathing lockers for guests of the hotel. Plaintiff's wife was a guest at the hotel and was permitted to use one of the lockers so reserved, issuing her a written pass on which appeared the following statement:

> In consideration of the use of.... Club, premises, without charge, the person whose name appears on this ticket or any person using this ticket, hereby releases.... Club, from any and all claims for personal injuries or property damage whether the said injury or damage shall be caused by or be due to negligence of.... Club, its agents, servants or employees, or otherwise.

It was held that since the plaintiff had the right to use the club facilities without charge, the defendant had no authority to prescribe conditions under which she might exercise that right. The pass issued to plaintiff by defendant was not supported by the consideration necessary to make it a contract. The recited consideration that plaintiff might use the premises without charge conferred nothing on her, since she already had the right to use the club without charge. In the absence of consideration, a release must be in writing and signed by the party against whom it is sought to be enforced.[44]

§ 16.113   Parties to the contract

Who can sign an exculpatory agreement? Because it is a contract, a person must be of majority age, and a parent cannot sign for a minor child. When a person signs, what types of actions are barred? And, who is protected by the agreement contract?

§ 16.1131   Of majority age; ratifying or voiding upon reaching majority

A valid contract requires that a person be of majority age; and, for that reason, exculpatory agreements cannot be made with a minor being one of the parties. When they are, the minor may ratify or void the contract upon reaching majority, either expressly or impliedly. Also, if a parent signed for a minor child, such child also has the right of affirming or voiding at time majority age is reached. Further, a parent or guardian cannot sign away the rights of a minor; they do not have the authority to release present claims or waive potential claims of a child merely because of the parental relationship. Such minor has the right to bring action upon reaching age of majority until the statute of limitations has run.[45] There may be, however, other bases for curtailment of the minor's right to bring action.

[44] Cohen v. N.Y., 190 Misc. 901, 75 N.Y.S. 2d 846 (1947).

[45] Apicella v. Valley Forge Military Academy and Junior College, 630 F. Supp. 20 (1985) Pennsylvania law applied, sued for medical treatment at infirmary; Reliance Insurance Co. v. Haney, 54 Mich. App. 237, 220 N.W.2d 728 (1974); Williams v. U.S., 660 F. Supp. 699 (1987).

The plaintiff when 17 years of age (approximately five weeks before eighteenth birthday) signed a contract with the defendant Free Flight Sport Aviation, which allowed him to use Free Flight's recreational skydiving facilities, which included use of an airplane to ferry skydivers to the parachute jumping site. Within a year after signing, plaintiff was seriously injured in plane crash. After stating that, as a matter of public policy, the courts have protected minors from improvident and imprudent contractual commitments by declaring that the contract of a minor is voidable at the election of the minor after he attains majority, the court in *Jones v. Dressel*, 582 P. 2d 1057 (Colo. App. 1978), aff'd. 623 P. 2d 370 (1981) further stated that a minor may disaffirm a contract made during his minority within a reasonable time after attaining his majority or he may, after becoming of legal age, by acts recognizing the contract, ratify it. In this situation it was held that the plaintiff ratified the contract made while a minor after reaching majority by accepting the benefits of the contract.

In a 1987 Pennsylvania case,[46] the court also considered the ratification of the contract by a minor. Both the minor gymnast and her mother had signed this "release":

> In consideration of my participation in Parkettes, I, intending to be legally bound, do hereby, for myself, my heirs, executors, and administrators, waive and release any and all rights and claims for damages which I may hereafter accrue to me against the United States Gymnastic Federation, the Parkette National Gymnastic Team, their officers, representatives, successors, and/or assigns for any and all damages which may be sustained and suffered by me in connection with my association with the above gymnastic program, or which may arise out of my traveling to or participating in and returning from any activity associated with the program.
>
> Gymnast's Signature   _____/s/_____
>
> Signature of Parent   _____/s/_____
> or Guardian   (Father)
>
>   _____/s/_____
>   (Mother)

Plaintiff minor sought to disavow the contract by bringing this action, although she had continued after reaching majority to receive the "benefits" of the association (gymnastics). However, the benefits in this situation were "prospective," waiving any cause of action for future injuries, while the exception to disavowing is when a release is signed as a compromise and settlement of an already existing claim, such as an out-of-court settlement for a personal injury claim. The court also noted as a problem that the statement was written in the first person and signed by minor. In its deliberation, the court was cognizant that such releases were common among many youth organizations, such as Little League, Scouting, and Midget Football, and that this case could be precedent setting. It held that minor gymnast may disavow the contract, affirming the

---

[46] Simmons v. Parkette National Gymnastic Training Center, 670 F. Supp. 140 (1987); see also Crew v. Bartels, 27 F.R.D. 5 (1961) parents cannot waive liability for negligence to minor children.

common law rule that minors, with certain exceptions, may disaffirm their contracts, based upon the public policy concern that minors should not be bound by mistakes resulting from their immaturity or the overbearance of unscrupulous adults. The court also indicated the desirable public policy of judicious and effective settlement of tort claims. The mother was barred from any claims by signing the release, but her signature did not bar her minor child from bringing actions against defendants. As to the minor, the contract was not void, but voidable, which plaintiff minor chose to do.

Fifteen-year-old daughter of plaintiff was fatally injured in a fall during a mountain climb. She and her parents had signed an agreement prior to the trip purporting to release the AYH from liability. The lower court stated that the words of the agreement were sufficiently clear and explicit to show that personal injuries occasioned by the defendant's negligence were intended to be included; however, the waiver was struck down as a defense as related both to the child and the parents. It was stated that the text of the agreement was in the first person singular and therefore it was questioned as to whether the parents' signatures meant anything more than giving permission for the child to participate in the trip. As for the signature of a minor, it was held that the right of the child (through the administrator of the child's estate) to disaffirm the agreement by reason of being a minor was effectively exercised by the act of commencing this action.[47] Another New York case[48] gave rights to a minor. Minor was injured while attending an ice hockey clinic. His father had signed a release of claims on his behalf, purporting to exempt the city and the hockey league from liability for injuries. The release stated:

> Acknowledging that the sport of ice hockey is a hazardous activity, I agree that neither The Greater NYC Ice Hockey League nor the City of N.Y., Dept. of Parks, Recreation and Cultural Affairs Administration shall be liable to me for any injury or damage resulting directly or resulting indirectly from my participation in the.... program, whether incurred on the ice or otherwise.

Neither the minor nor his father were held to be bound by the release. The city and the league were held liable for failure to properly provide general supervision over the hockey drill.

It was the practice to let persons at the racetrack into the pit and paddock areas by issuing a pit pass that each person had to sign prior to entering. Although the sponsoring organization rules let children over 12 in when accompanied by a parent, about 50 percent of the children were under 12. Plaintiff, at the time of the accident, was only nine years old. The court held that his release agreement was invalid and unenforceable inasmuch as a contract of a minor made while under the age of 18 may be disaffirmed by the minor himself either before his majority or within a reasonable time thereafter. Disaffirmance may be made by any act or declaration, and express notice to the other party is unnecesary.[49]

---

[47] Kaufman v. American Youth Hostels, 13 Misc. 2d 8, 174 N.Y.S. 2d 580 (1957), as modified & aff'd., 6 A.D. 2d 223, 177 N.Y.S. 2d 587 (1958), granted motion to appeal 6 A.D. 2d 1016, 178 N.Y.S. 2d 623; aff'd./rev'd. in part, 5 N.Y.S. 2d 1016, 185 N.Y.S. 2d 268, 158 N.E. 2d 128 (1959).

[48] Santangelo v. City of N.Y., 66 A.D. 2d 880, 411 N.Y.S. 2d 666 (1978).

[49] Celli v. Sports Car Club, 29 Cal. App. 3d 511, 105 Cal. Rptr. 2d 904 (1973).

The plaintiff was injured when his car skidded and rolled over but remained on the racetrack and then was hit by another car causing the injury. The plaintiff had misrepresented his age when he signed a release on September 1, but did not become of age until the next February. The injury occurred on July 16 following. The court held that the bringing of the action constituted an effective repudiation of the release and was timely. Under the State law at that time, a minor was not prevented from asserting his disability by the fact that he misrepresented his age.[50]

(See also §16.2 Parental permissions.)

§ 16.1132   Parties protected and barred[51]

The actions of the injured minor and of the parent are two separate actions. Parents' signatures on an exculpatory agreement will be enforced as to their right to action for pecuniary loss, such as medical claims, but if they have not signed, they do have a cause of action. The child's and the parents' causes of action are separate.[52]

Where there has been a death, it has been held that a wrongful death claim is not barred by execution of an exculpatory agreement by the decedent;[53] however, an opposite result was reached in two auto racing cases.[54]

Can a spouse bring action, if the exculpatory agreement was signed by the husband or wife? The courts have held that a release signed by a husband or wife does not bar the spouse's action for loss of consortium;[55] however, there was an opposite result in a health club situation when the wife signed an enforceable clause in the membership contract, which included an assumption of risk clause, disclaimer of liability clause, and covenant not to sue. The court said that the right of the husband to recover for loss of consortium was dependent upon the right of the wife to recover.[56]

The 1987 Wyoming court[57] stated that agreements between employee and employer were unenforceable.

And, applying Illinois law, in a sky diving incident, the court held that a release form did not bar plaintiff's suit for product liability based on strict liability.[58]

A seaman seeking damages against the owner of the vessel under the Jones Act and

[50] Del Santo v. Bristol Co. Stadium, 273 F. 2d 605 (1960).

[51] An exculpatory agreement is a contract, and as such, the principles of contract law apply, including those related to the parties to the contract. This section only illustrates a few of these, with some cases from the leisure industry field. There are many legal aspects with which your local attorney can help and certainly which may be raised in a law suit where the validity and/or application of the agreement is challenged.

[52] Apicella v. Valley Forge Military Academy & Junior College, 630 F. Supp. 20 (1985); Kotary v. Spencer Speedway, Inc., 47 A.D. 2d 127, 365 N.Y.S. 2d 87 (1975); Simmons v. Parkette National Gymnastic Training Center, 670 F. Supp. 140 (1987); see also Tepper v. City of New Rochelle School Dist., 531 N.Y.S. 2d 367 (1988).

[53] Madison v. Superior Court, 250 Cal. Rptr. 299 (1988); Scroggs v. Coast Community College Dist., 239 Cal. Rptr. 916 (1987); Wade v. Watson, 527 F. Supp. 1049 (1981).

[54] Grbac v. Reading Fair Co., 521 F. Supp. 1351 (1981); Thomas v. Sports Car Club of America, 386 So. 2d 272 (Fla. App. 1980).

[55] Gillespie v. Papale, 541 F. Supp. 1042 (1982); see also Arnold v. Shawano County Agric. Society, 106 Wis. 2d 464, 317 N.W. 2d 161 (1982); Barker v. Colo. Region-Sports Car Club of America, 35 Colo. App. 73, 532 P. 2d 372 (1975).

[56] Lovelace v. Figure Salon, 345 S.E. 2d 139 (Ga. App. 1986).

[57] Boehm v. Cody Country Chamber of Commerce, 748 P. 2d 704 (Wyo. 1987).

[58] Diedrich v. Wright, 550 F. Supp. 805 (1982).

general maritime laws sought to void the exculpatory agreement on the basis of having signed under the influence of medication and duress.[59]

And, what about the defendants? Who is protected when there is a valid exculpatory agreement? The parties must be specifically enumerated or come within the category of persons specified in the agreement.[60] In a health spa situation, it was held that the agreement, although personal in nature, could be assigned to the successor owner, based on contract law that rights can be assigned.[61]

As for joint tortfeasors, when either there has been an out-of-court settlement with some but not all of the joint tortfeasors or when only some of the joint tortfeasors are sued, it is dependent upon the situation and state in which the case is brought as to its contribution of joint tortfeasor law (see §2.43). In a 1986 Virginia case,[62] where a golfer lost an eye, the agreement by negligent golfer's homeowners insurer to pay its full coverage to injured golfer in return for the execution of a covenant not to sue and a nonsuit of the negligent golfer individually did not operate as a release of the negligent golfer's corporate employer deemed jointly liable and jointly suable.

§ 16.114   Activity/situation within contemplated coverage

The activity or situation which occasioned the injury must be within the contemplated coverage of the exculpatory agreement when signed. A bicyclist's collision with an automobile on a barricaded course was alleged by the plaintiff not to have been a foreseeable hazard contemplated by the bicyclist when he signed the release from liability.[63] The plaintiff was not barred from suing the parachute center for injuries which occurred when the parachute failed to fully open. The court stated it was following a New York case in holding that while the language alerted plaintiff to dangers inherent in parachute jumping, it did not follow that plaintiff was aware of, much less intended to accept, any enhanced exposure to injury occasioned by the carelessness of the very persons on which he was dependent for his safety.[64] The plaintiffs also argued that injury from alleged malfunctioning of equipment in an exercise facility (YMCA and health spa) was outside the scope of injuries contemplated when the exculpatory agreement was signed.[65] In the health spa situation, the court held that plaintiff did read,

---

[59] Stalnaker v. McDermott Corp., 505 So. 2d 139 (La. App. 1987).

[60] Church v. Seneca County Agricultural Society, 41 A.D. 2d 787, 341 N.Y.S. 2d 45 (1973) aff'd. without opinion 34 N.Y. 2d 571, 354 N.Y.S. 2d 945, 310 N.E. 2d 541 (1974); Kircos v. Goodyear Tire & Rubber Co., 70 Mich. App. 612, 247 N.W. 2d 316 (1976) aff'd. 108 Mich. App. 781, 311 N.W. 2d 139 (1981).

[61] Petry v. Cosmopolitan Spa, Int'l., 641 S.W. 2d 202 (Tenn. App. 1982).

[62] Thurston Metals & Supply Co. v. Taylor, 230 Va. 475, 339 S.E. 2d 538 (1986); see also Carr v. Karkow Rodeos, 610 F. Supp. 25 (1985) vacated with direction 788 F. 2d 485 (1986) South Dakota law applied.

[63] Bennett v. U.S. Cycling Federation, 193 Cal.

App. 3d 1485, 239 Cal. Rptr. 55 (1987) whether a foreseeable hazard was for jury determination.

[64] Diedrich v. Wright, 550 F. Supp. 805 (1982) Illinois law applied, but followed Gross v. Sweet, 64 A.D. 2d 774, 407 N.Y.S. 2d 254, aff'd. 49 N.Y. 2d 102, 424 N.Y.S. 2d 365, 400 N.E. 2d 306 (1979); see also Randle v. Hinckley Parachute Center, Inc., 141 Ill. App. 3d 660, 96 Ill. Dec. 5, 490 N.E. 2d 1041 (1986) skydiving.

[65] Calarco v. YMCA of Greater Metro. Chicago, 149 Ill. App. 3d 1037, 103 Ill. Dec. 247, 501 N.E. 2d 268 (1986), cert. denied 508 N.E. 2d 725; Neumann v. Gloria Marshall Figure Salon, 149 Ill. App. 3d 824, 102 Ill. Dec. 910, 500 N.E. 2d 1011 (1986).

understand and sign the form, and that injuries from improper use of an exercise machine were included in the membership contract which stated:

> Patron specifically assumes all risks of injury while using any equipment or facilities at the salon and waives any and all claims against Gloria Marshall Management Company and the owners and employees of the salon for any such injury.

In the YMCA situation, plaintiff was using weight-lifting equipment when weights in the machine fell on her hand. The court held that the language on the membership form was not explicit enough to relieve the facility from liability. The form stated:

> In consideration of my participation in the activities of the Young Men's Christian Association of Metropolitan Chicago, I do hereby agree to hold free from any and all liability the YMCA of Metropolitan Chicago and its respective officers, employees and members and do hereby for myself, my heirs, executors and administrators, waive, release and forever discharge any and all rights and claims for damages which I may have or which may hereafter accrue to me arising out of or connected with my participation in any of the activities of the YMCA of Metropolitan Chicago.
>
> I hereby do declare myself to be physically sound, having medical approval to participate in the activities of the YMCA.

The court suggested that a phrase, such as "use of gymnasium or facilities and equipment thereof" needed to be included to clearly indicate that injuries resulting from negligence in maintaining facilities or equipment would be covered by the release.

A signed liability waiver was deemed not sufficient as a matter of law to show that appellant subjectively understood the risks inherent in horseback riding and actually intended to assume those risks.[66]

Plaintiff had signed a membership contract with a health club which had an exculpatory clause. The injury, however, occurred due to inhaling dangerous gaseous vapor generated by combining certain cleaning compounds. The court held that this type of danger was not foreseeable by plaintiff and for which the contract provided an assumption of risk.[67]

In an ice hockey player's contract there was a "release," which the court held did not apply to negligence actions brought by a player against the club, but was limited to those aspects related to compensation provided in the playing contract.[68]

Mutual mistake of material fact may be a basis for voiding an exculpatory agreement. This may be at the time the agreement was signed, such as in a racetrack case.[69] Both parties were operating under a mutual mistake of fact regarding the

---

[66] O'Connell v. Walt Disney World Co., 413 So. 2d 444 (Fla. App. 1982); see also Renaud v. 200 Convention Center, Ltd., 728 P. 2d 445 (Nev. 1986) free-fall simulator.

[67] Larsen v. Vic Tanny, Int'l, 85 Ill. Dec. 769,130 Ill. App. 3d 574, 474 N.E. 2d 729 (1984).

[68] Robitaille v. Vancouver Hockey Club, Inc., 19 B.C.L.R. 158, aff'd. 124 D.L.R. 3d 228 (1981).

[69] Schlessman v. Henson, 80 Ill. App. 3d 1139, 36 Ill. Dec. 459, 400 N.E. 2d 1039 (1980); aff'd. 83 Ill. 2d 82, 46 Ill. Dec. 139, 413 N.E. 2d 1252 (1980).

condition of the racetrack. Subsequently, plaintiff was injured when a portion of the upper track embankment collapsed, causing his car to crash. Mutual mistake also may occur at time of signing a release after injury has occurred when the intent was to release for known injuries and not for future unknown injuries or later consequences of known or unknown injuries not contemplated by either party. One must, however, distinguish mistaken diagnosis and prognosis from mutually thought consequences.[70]

The question in the *Seymour* case[71] was whether a release signed one day for an event was valid for a subsequent event. The release was so stated that it did not contain any time limit but applied to any competition at that track for prize money so offered. And, in another track case,[72] the court held that the agreement was effective the same day as signed, as soon as signed.

§ 16.12   Unenforceability as contrary to public policy

Public policy does not oppose private, voluntary contracts in which one person for a consideration can agree to accept a risk which the law would otherwise place upon the other party; however, where the public interest is involved, generally an exculpatory clause is invalid where it exempts a person from one's own negligence or willful injury to another.[73] The courts look with disfavor on exempting a person from liability for future negligent acts, particularly where it relieves an individual of a legal duty to protect. The court[74] applied to a bicycle race and a scuba diving situation the six areas to consider to determine whether or not the public interest is affected as set forth in the *Tunkl* case, namely:

1.   A business of a type generally thought suitable for public regulation
2.   The service is of great importance to the public
3.   The service is open to any member of the public
4.   As a result of the essential nature of the service, in the economic setting of the transaction, the party invoking exculpation possesses a decision advantage of bargaining strength against any member of the public who seeks the services
5.   Superior bargaining power confronts the public with a standardized adhesion contract of exculpation; no provision whereby a purchaser may pay additional reasonable fees and obtain protection against negligence
6.   The person or property of the purchaser is placed under the control of the seller

In 1988 these six factors, as set forth in the *Tunkl* case and applied in the *Okura* and

---

[70] Gleason v. Guzman, 42 Colo. App. 284, 598 P. 2d 145 (1979), aff'd. 623 P. 2d 378 (Colo. 1981); see also Casey v. Proctor, 22 Cal. Rptr. 531, rev'd. 59 Cal. 2d 97, 28 Cal. Rptr. 307, 378 P. 2d 579 (1963) car accident.

[71] Seymour v. New Bremen Speedway, 31 Ohio App. 2d 141 287 N.E. 2d 111 (1971).

[72] Gervasi v. Holland Raceway, Inc., 40 A.D. 2d 574, 334 N.Y.S. 2d 527 (1972).

[73] Tunkl v. Regents of Univ. of Calif., 60 Cal. 2d 92, 32 Cal. Rptr. 33, 383 P. 2d 441 (1963) not a recreation/sport case, hospital patient against charitable hospital — but an early case frequently cited as setting forth basic law.

[74] Okura v. U.S. Cycling Federation, 186 Cal. App. 3d 1462, 231 Cal. Rptr. 429 (1986) bicycle race; Madison v. Superior Court, 250 Cal. Rptr. 299 (1988) Scuba diving.

Madison cases, were the basis of the holding in *Wagenblast v. Odessa School District*, 110 Wash. 2d 845, 758 P.2d 968 (1988). The Washington court held that releases which public school students were required to sign as condition of engaging in school-related activities such as interscholastic athletics and which released school districts from consequences of all future school district negligence were invalid as violating public policy. The Seattle School District standardized release form as a condition to participation in interscholastic sports and cheerleading was specifically cited. Public school students and their families brought suits challenging school districts' policies requiring, as condition for participating in interscholastic athletics, that students and families sign a standardized form releasing school district from liability for negligence. The court said that school districts owe a duty to their students to employ ordinary care and to anticipate reasonably foreseeable dangers so as to take precautions for protecting children in its custody from such dangers. It was further stated that to extent release portion of forms represented consent to relieve school districts of duty of care, they were invalid whether they were termed releases or express assumptions of risk. Chief among the grounds for the decision, the court said, was that the release form is an unconscionable contract of adhesion. The court also discussed briefly the recitation (in the forms) of risks associated with participation in interscholastic sports, and quoted the Superior Court opinion in saying that generalized assumption of risk such as this is not effective since any such risk should be considered on a case-by-case basis. Such statement, the court said, is consistent with the court's previous decisions "that in order to prove an express assumption of risk, the evidence must show that the plaintiff (1) had full subjective understanding, (2) of the presence and nature of the specific risk, and (3) voluntarily chose to encounter that risk." (See §24.81 Participation forms as a part of risk management).

The application the court made could be generalized to the leisure field as a whole; specifically, recreational activity is not usually subject to public regulation directly; may be a public service in terms of providing an opportunity, but not in terms of public importance or necessity; participation open to those who wish to participate and can meet the requirements (whether entrance fee, physical condition, or other); people are not compelled to participate, but are invited to participate, and if they wish to do so must sign release form (in this situation); voluntary relationship between parties and, thus, not a contract of adhesion; and participant retains complete control of oneself and may withdraw at any time. (In subsequent sections, some of these elements of public interest are set forth.) The Wyoming court in 1988 was very direct as to whether recreation was an essential public service, when it said in *Milligan v. Big Valley Corp.*, 754 P.2d 1063 (Wyo. 1988): "Types of services thought to be subject to public regulation, and therefore demanding a public duty or considered essential,...Generally, a private recreational business does not qualify as a service *demanding* a special duty to the public, nor are its services of a special, highly necessary or essential nature.... Further, contracts relating to recreational activities do not fall within any of the categories above where the public interest is involved." Some of the categories enumerated included common carriers, hospitals, public utilities, innkeepers. The *Milligan* case affirmed the 1986 skydiving case of *Schutkowski v. Carey*, 725 P.2d 1056 (Wyo. 1986), which established the Wyoming law relating to exculpatory clauses.

Some states, such as Washington,[75] state in their Uniform Commercial Code that disclaimers in commercial transactions must be in writing and conspicuous and it is against public policy not to do so (see §16.111).

The plaintiff alleged that there was a fundamental breach of an implied covenant to transport safely, and consequently the contract was brought to an end and ceased to exist, including the exemption clause. The court found the corporate defendant negligent in failing to provide adequate personal flotation devices, but ruled that even so, the plaintiff was barred from obtaining relief by the liability release executed by the deceased.[76] A contrary point of view was expressed in a racehorse barn fire situation. In discussion, the court distinguished between failure to perform the contracted services at all and the inadequate or negligent performance of such services. In this instance, the service to be provided was fire protection. It further said that were there no liability because of the exculpatory clause, then it would be an illusory contract. Breaching a contract for services should not enable the party to void the contract regarding negligence.[77]

In *Kubisen v. Chicago Health Clubs*[78] plaintiff alleged that enforcement of the contractual agreement (clause) was contrary to public policy, such enforcement being a violation of due process (U.S.C.A. Const. Amend. 14). The court rejected this argument. The court[79] in Oklahoma, regarding State constitutionality of exculpatory agreements, said that the Constitutional provision that the right of action to recover damages for injuries resulting in death shall never be abrogated meant abrogated by the legislature and did not mean it could not be by private contract.

§ 16.121   Public service duty

The question is whether the service being offered is a public or essential service, and therefore the type generally thought suitable for public regulation; and, under such circumstances, an exculpatory clause would be considered against public policy. *Public service should not be considered synonymous with public sponsorship. A public entity may offer services not considered public or essential services. This is especially true for leisure services; and, in regard to such services, exculpatory clauses are not against public policy.* The following cited cases are illustrative of the court's determination of what is regarded as a public policy concern or of public interest and application of the "public policy test." See also, especially, further discussion of the first three factors of the six in the *Tunkl, Okura,* and *Wagenblast* cases, as presented in the preceding subsection.

The court held that generally the furnishing of health spa services is not an activity of great public importance nor of a practical necessity; such services do not fall in the category of public interest; hence, the exculpatory clause was found not against public policy in *Schlobohm v. Spa Petite, Inc.*, 326 N.W. 2d 920 (Minn. 1982). In *Hewitt v.*

[75] RCW 62A.2-316(2); Baker v. Seattle, 2 Wash. App. 1003, 471 P. 2d 693 (1970), rev'd./remanded, 79 Wash. 2d 198, 484 P. 2d 405 (1971).

[76] Delaney v. Cascade River Holidays, Ltd., 19 C.C.L.T. 78 (B.C.S.C.), 15 B.L.R. 114 (1981).

[77] Rutter v. Arlington Park Jockey Club, 510 F.2d 1065 (1975) applying Illinois law.

[78] Kubisen v. Chicago Health Clubs, 69 Ill.App.3d 463, 26 Ill.Dec. 420, 388 N.E.2d 44 (1979).

[79] Trumbower v. Sports Car Club of America, Inc. 428 F. Supp. 1113 (1976).

Miller, 11 Wash. App. 72, 521 P. 2d 244 (1974), it was held that the activity involved, instruction in scuba, was not a public service which would prevent the release from being operative; it was only a private contract between the parties. And, similarly, skydiving was held not to be a public or essential service in *Malecha v. St. Croix Valley Skydiving Club*, 392 N.W.2d 727 (Minn. App. 1986).

The court held in *Haynes v. Co. of Missoula*, 163 Mont. 270, 517 P. 2d 370 (1973), that a county is precluded from disclaiming liability by virtue of a release when performing an act in the public interest. In this situation the plaintiff's horses were being exhibited at the county fairgrounds when they were destroyed by a barn fire. The general release, which appeared at the bottom of the entry blank, was held illegal and unenforcible. The release stated:

> I hereby release the Missoula County Fair Board from any liability by loss, damage or injury to livestock or other property, while said property is on the Fairgrounds.

The court did distinguish exculpatory clauses and indemnification agreements (see §16.3). In an Illinois case,[80] also dealing with racehorses burned in a barn fire, but under private auspices, the court discussed public policy as one of two exceptions for enforcement of contractual clauses exempting a party from liability for its own negligence, where such intent was clear. It stated that a strict test should be applied and that such test is not satisfied merely by showing that the state regulates the business which made the contract.

In a riding case,[81] the plaintiff had signed a release prior to rental of the horse. The issue involved was whether the release is void by law as being against public policy. The court refused to rule until a determination "of fact" was made as to whether the riding academy was a business having a public service character, for if it did, then the release would be void, and if not, it would be valid. The commentary pointed toward not having a public service character, likening it to outdoor recreation, sports, and recreational events.

An exculpatory agreement related to auto racing, as a general rule, is held by the courts not to be contrary to public policy.[82] In the *Gore* case, in stating that agreements which related to public utilities or quasi-public situations were against public policy, the court made this observation:

> … It should be noted that participation in automobile races *and other sporting events is a voluntary undertaking* (emphasis added). If a prospective participant wishes to place himself in the competition sufficiently to

---

[80] Rutter v. Arlington Park Jockey Club, 510 F.2d 1065 (1975) applying Illinois law.

[81] Duszynski v. B & T Riding Academy, 32 Wis. 2d 464, 145 N.W. 2d 736 (1966).

[82] Bruce v. Heiman, 392 So. 2d 1026 (Fla. App. 1981); Gore v. Tri-County Raceway, Inc., 407 F. Supp. 489 (1974) applying Alabama law; Johnson v. Thruway Speedways, Inc., 63 A.D. 2d 204, 407 N.Y.S. 2d 81 (1978); LaFrenz v. Lake Co. Fair Board, 172 Ind. App. 389, 360 N.E. 2d 605 (1977); Mayer v. Howard, 220 Neb. 328, 370 N.W. 2d 93 (1985) even for latent track defect; Morrow v. Auto Championship Racing Assoc., 8 Ill. App. 3d 682, 291 N.E. 2d 30 (1972); Schlessman v. Henson, 80 Ill. App. 3d 1139, 36 Ill. Dec. 459, 400 N.E. 2d 1039 (1980), aff'd. 83 Ill. 2d 82, 46 Ill. Dec. 139, 413 N.E. 2d 1252 (1980); Tope v. Waterford Hills Road Racing Corp., 81 Mich. App. 591, 265 N.W. 2d 761 (1978); Trumbower v. Sports Car Club of America, 428 F. Supp. 1113 (1976) Oklahoma law applied; Winterstein v. Wilcom, 16 Md. App. 130, 293 A. 2d 821 (1972).

voluntarily agree that he will not hold the organizer or sponsor of the event liable for his injuries, the courts should enforce such agreements. If these agreements, voluntarily entered into, were not upheld, the effect would be to increase the liability of those organizing or sponsoring such events to such an extent that no one would be willing to undertake to sponsor a sporting event. Clearly, this would not be in the public interest.[83]

It should be noted again that the test as related to public policy is not whether the activity is sponsored by a public entity or a private enterprise, but the nature of the activity and the relationship of parties. In the *Gore* case, applying Alabama law, and in a 1984 case,[84] applying Virginia law, the term is "public utility" and the court opinion does not equate this to public-sponsored activity, but with common carrier, et al. An Illinois case,[85] stated that it would be against public policy to enforce an exculpatory clause and thus protect the owner-defendant in violation of a law, in this instance violation of the Dram Shop Act. Some states have laws voiding exculpatory clauses in leases. As indicated in *Owen v. Vic Tanny's Enterprise*,[86] though, such enactments did not evidence legislative intent to extend provisions of statute to other types of contracts. A 1981 Georgia case,[87] in reference to waivers and public policy, stated that "a contract cannot be said to be contrary to public policy unless the General Assembly has declared it to be so, or unless consideration of contract is contrary to good morals and contrary to law, or unless contract is entered into for purpose of effecting an illegal or immoral agreement for doing something which is in violation of law." The court went on to say that participants in sporting or recreational events may make contractual waivers of liability. It was held that a waiver of liability by a participant in a 10,000 meter race was not contrary to law or morality, and, thus, was valid. A 1985 California case[88] held that a parachute jumping course contract was not against the public interest. The California statute declares contracts which exempt anyone from responsibility for his own fraud or willful injury as against the policy of the law and such contract is invalid.

§ 16.122   Dilutes the standard of care law developed for protection of others

One of the concerns is that if an individual has contracted not to be held liable, this will then result in less care being taken for the protection of the individual. In *Williams v. U.S.*, 660 F. Supp. 699 (1987), the court said that "the rationale behind the numerous decisions invalidating so called releases given before liability arises is based upon the strong public policy of encouraging the exercise of care." The courts have held that an exculpatory agreement is valid only if the act does not fall greatly below the standard established by law for the protection of others against unreasonable risk of harm.[89] In the *Garretson* case, one in which the plaintiff was injured while participating in a ski-

[83] 407 F. Supp. at p. 492.
[84] Rhea v. Horn-Keen Corp., 582 F. Supp. 687 (1984) Virginia law applied.
[85] Scheff v. Homestretch, Inc., 60 Ill. App. 3d 424, 18 Ill. Dec. 152, 377 N.E. 2d 305 (1978).
[86] Owen v. Vic Tanny's Enterprises, 48 Ill. App. 2d 344, 199 N.E. 2d 280 (1964).
[87] Williams v. Cox Enterprises, 159 Ga. App. 333,

283 S.E. 2d 367 (1981); see also, Cain v. Cleveland Parachute Training Center, 9 Ohio App. 3d 27, 457 N.E. 2d 1185 (1983).
[88] Hulsey v. Elsinore Parachute Center, 168 Cal. App.3d 333, 214 Cal. Rptr. 194 (1985).
[89] Garretson v. U.S., 456 F. 2d 1017 (1972) Washington law applied; see also Hewitt and McCutcheon cases.

jumping tournament, the court held for the defendant on this point. The plaintiff alleged negligence on the part of the defendants for letting him jump when the prevailing weather conditions made it unsafe for jumping. However, the plaintiff was an experienced ski jumper, being a member of the U.S. Nordic Team and the U.S. National Team.

The standard of care can be set by case precedent or by statute. Idaho has a statute setting forth the areas of responsibility and affirmative acts for which outfitters and guides shall be liable for loss, damage, or injury, and to define those risks which the participant expressly assumes and for which there can be no recovery. It says that there are inherent risks which a participant must assume and that the outfitter shall not be liable unless damage or injury was directly or proximately caused by failure to conform to the standard of care expected of members of its profession. In *Lee v. Sun Valley Company,* 107 Idaho 976, 695 P. 2d 361 (1984), the court held that the exculpatory contract was valid except to the extent the outfitter may have failed to conform to the professional standard of care; the plaintiff failed to so show and judgment was for defendant.

Where plaintiff was seriously injured in a plane crash while engaged in skydiving activities, the plaintiff argued that defendant (Free Flight) was acting as a common carrier when it carried Jones for compensation to an altitude from which he could make a parachute jump, and that a common carrier by air cannot compel a passenger to release or limit the carrier's legal liability for its own negligence. He further contended that a private air charter business operates under the FAA regulations which impose standards of safety upon the pilot of an airplane and that Free Flight cannot contract away its liability for negligence in performance of a duty imposed by law or where the public interest requires performance. The court did not so hold. The defendant flight service was not operating as a common carrier and it was not subject to the regulations for private air charter services.[90]

In another parachute jumping case,[91] the plaintiff alleged that defendant violated FAA regulations governing parachute jumping schools and student parachutists by not requiring a medical certificate as prerequisite to enrollment in a parachute jumping course. Plaintiff alleged that this was critical in that he had had, several years earlier, an orthopedic pin inserted in his leg and the school must have known that landing in a parachute puts special stress on one's legs.

The violation of rules was on the part of the plaintiff in an apartment swimming pool case. The court held that the release in the lease of landlord's liability for damages arising out of tenant's violations of rules and regulations of apartment was controlling. The tenant's violation of pool regulations created contractual bar to liability of landlord.[92]

A race driver brought action against the Stock Automobile Racing Association and others for injuries sustained when his auto burst into flames at the end of the race,

[90] Jones v. Dressel, 582 P. 2d 1057 (Colo. App. 1978), aff'd. 623 P. 2d 370 (1981); see also Hammerlind v. Clear Lake Star Factory Skydiver's Club, 258 N.W. 2d 590 (Minn. 1977) also held private carrier.
[91] Gross v. Sweet, 64 A.D. 2d 774, 407 N.Y.S. 2d 254, aff'd. 49 N.Y. 2d 102, 424 N.Y.S. 2d 365, 400 N.E. 2d 306 (1979).
[92] George R. Lane & Associates v. Thomasson, 156 Ga. App. 313, 274 S.E. 2d 708 (1980).

allegedly because the association failed to inspect the auto, which did not comply with safety regulations. The defendants sought to use as their defense the release and a benefit plan registration. The court held that the release and benefit plan registration, both of which limited liability of the association, were invalid as against public policy. Prescribed safety requirements of statutes dealing with motor vehicle racing may not be contracted away by racers, since, if safety requirements could be contracted away, salient protected purposes of the legislation would largely be nullified.[93]

§ 16.123   Special relationship

A special relationship was held to exist in *Fedor v. Manwehu Council, Boy Scouts of America*, 21 Conn. Sup. 38, 143 A. 2d 466 (1958). The court stated that in this situation, attending a camp, there was a relationship requiring of one party greater responsibility than that of the ordinary person and that it is public policy to attempt in every way possible to protect infants. The public interest required performance.

Plaintiff argued in *Gross v. Sweet*[94] that, as a matter of policy, the release should not be enforceable as between a student and his teacher, a relationship in which one of the parties holds himself out as qualified and responsible to provide training in a skill and the other party relies on this expertise, particularly in the context of an activity in which the degree of training necessary for safe participation is much greater than might be apparent to a novice. The court held that the defendant's occupation did not fall within any of the classes to form a special relationship that would make the release clause unenforceable. In this situation, the instruction was for parachute jumping.

In a racehorse barn fire situation, the court stated that the law of Illinois provided for two exceptions for enforcement of contractual clauses, public policy and social relationship. In this situation there was no special relationship, such as employer-employee or common carrier-passenger, but the relationship was that of businessmen dealing at arm's length.[95]

§ 16.124   One party clearly dominant; adhesion contract[96]

Consent is an essential element to a contract, and this consent must be free and deliberate exercise of the contracting party's will. A release required of students going on a field trip was held unenforceable in a 1983 Louisiana case.[97] While the document signed stated that plaintiff agreed to voluntarily participate in the trip, the context surrounding the execution of the documents negated such statement. Double the number of credit hours were earned for otherwise comparable time; no alternative for going on

---

[93] McCarthy v. Nat'l Assoc. for Stock Car Auto Racing, 87 N.J. Super. 442, 209 A. 2d 668, aff'd. 90 N.J. Super. 574, 218 A. 2d 871; aff'd. 48 N.J. 539, 226 A. 2d 713 (1967).

[94] Gross v. Sweet, 64 A.D. 2d 774, 407 N.Y.S. 2d 254, aff'd. 49 N.Y. 2d 102, 424 N.Y.S. 2d 365, 400 N.E. 2d 306 (1979); see also Wagenblast v. Odessa School Dist., 110 Wash. 2d 845, 758 P. 2d 968 (1988).

[95] Rutter v. Arlington Park Jockey Club, 510 F. 2d

1065 (1975) applying Illinois law.

[96] Rosen v. LTV Recreational Development, 569 F. 2d 1117 (1978); Kubisen v. Chicago Health Clubs, 69 Ill. App. 3d 463, 26 Ill. Dec. 420, 388 N.E. 2d 44 (1979).

[97] Whittington v. Sowela Technical Institute, 438 So. 2d 236 (La. App. 1983), cert. denied 443 So. 2d 591 (La. 1983).

the trip was offered; students were expected to go on the trip as part of the program requirement. And, the instrumentalities were in the exclusive control of the defendant, making it not possible for defendant to prospectively absolve itself of liability for injuries negligently caused through such instrumentalities.

A 1958 case,[98] for its emphasis upon opportunities for the economically disadvantaged, might well be a case in the '80s. The general policy is to construe against agreements which has the two parties of unequal bargaining power. In the *Fedor* case, the court stated that low-income families desiring to take advantage of the opportunity to give their sons the advantages of a Boy Scout camp have no choice other than to sign a waiver absolving the camp from liability for acts of negligence of those responsible for the safety and lives of their sons. It would not be in the public interest to countenance a policy which would deprive families of low income, otherwise eligible, of the opportunity. The defendant had argued unsuccessfully that if the meritorious function (summer camp) was to be kept within the financial means of the greatest number of boys, then some concessions had to be made. The concession, in this case, was the waiver of liability provision in the camp contract for which was substituted a personal accident insurance policy to protect the boys and their parents from unfortunate casualties.

An adhesion contract is a contract drafted unilaterally by a business enterprise and forced upon unwilling and often unknowing public for services that cannot readily be obtained elsewhere. It is generally not bargained for, but is imposed on the public for necessary service on a "take-it-or-leave-it" basis. In this Colorado skydiving case,[99] the court held that the parachute-jumping agreement with the air service was not an adhesion contract where the record established no disparity in bargaining power, and did not show that services provided by the air service could not be attained elsewhere, even if the contract was in printed form offered on a "take-it-or-leave-it" basis. On similar reasoning, the court held that a membership contract for a health spa was not an adhesion contract, nor was there greatly disparate bargaining power between the two parties.[100] Also, no disparity in bargaining power was found between entrant and sponsors of a 10,000 meter race.[101]

In a car racing case,[102] the plaintiff alleged an adhesion contract. Plaintiff was injured when a portion of the racetrack caved in on a bank. While it is obvious that plaintiff would not have been allowed to use the racetrack had he not signed the release, plaintiff was under no economic or other compulsion to sign the release in order to engage in amateur auto racing. No substantial disparity between the two parties' bargaining position was found.

[98] Fedor v. Manwehu Council, Boy Scouts of America, 21 Conn. Sup. 38, 143 A. 2d 466 (1958).

[99] Jones v. Dressel, 582 P. 2d 1057 (Colo. App. 1978), aff'd. 623 P. 2d 370 (1981); see also Milligan v. Big Valley Corp., 754 P. 2d 1063 (Wyo. 1988) ski resort race.

[100] Schlobohm v. Spa Petite, Inc. 326 N.W. 2d 920 (1982); see also, Owen v. Vic Tanny's Enterprises, 48 Ill. App. 2d 344, 199 N.E. 2d 280 (1964).

[101] Williams v. Cox Enterprises, Inc., 159 Ga. App. 333, 283 S.E. 2d 367 (1981).

[102] Schlessman v. Henson, 80 Ill. App. 3d 1139, 36 Ill. Dec. 459, 400 N.E. 2d 1039 (1980); aff'd. 83 Ill. 2d 82, 46 Ill. Dec. 139, 413 N.E. 2d 1252 (1980); see also Smith v. Golden Triangle Raceway, 708 S.W. 2d 574 (Tex. App. 1986); Trumbower v. Sports Car Club of America, Inc., 428 F. Supp. 1113 (1976); U.S. Auto Club, Inc. v. Woodward, 460 N.E. 2d 1255 (Ind. App. 1984).

§ 16.125   Willful, wanton, malicious act; intentional tort; gross negligence

While an exculpatory agreement might pass scrutiny and be held valid and enforceable to deny party an action in negligence, that party may still pursue action in damages caused by willful and wanton misconduct, so held a 1987 case,[103] in which the city was not held liable for a mock gunfight on the street. The case went on to say that willful and wanton misconduct was not negligence, but a form of intentional misconduct which tends to take on aspects of highly unreasonable conduct or an extreme departure from ordinary care in a situation where high degree of danger is apparent.[104] An attempt by a defendant to exonerate himself from liability for an intentional tort is against public policy.[105]

The Illinois court[106] also has defined willful and wanton misconduct — "an intentional injury or an act committed under circumstances exhibiting a reckless disregard for the safety of others, such as a failure, after knowledge of impending danger, to exercise ordinary care to prevent it, or failure to discover the danger through recklessness or carelessness when it could have been discovered by exercise of ordinary care." In this skydiving situation, the defendant was held not to have exhibited willful and wanton conduct, and the exculpatory agreement was held valid. In *Jones v. Dressel*,[107] another skydiving situation, the plaintiff, who was seriously injured in an airplane crash, alleged negligence and willful and wanton misconduct as the cause of the airplane crash. The court said that an exculpatory agreement, which attempts to insulate the party from liability from its own negligence, must be closely scrutinized, and in no event will such an agreement provide a shield against claim for willful and wanton negligence. No willful and wanton negligence was found.

There have been a number of cases,[108] especially car racing situations, alleging willful and wanton misconduct in an effort to void the exculpatory agreement.

As for gross negligence voiding exculpatory agreements, the courts have held that agreements are unenforceable,[109] are against public policy,[110] and do not release defendants from liability.[111] Of course, the acts must be proven to be gross negligence, rather than ordinary negligence.[112]

§ 16.13   Participation forms and tickets

For convenience, the exculpatory clause often is incorporated into the participation

---

[103] Boehm v. Cody Country Chamber of Commerce, 748 P. 2d 704 (Wyo. 1987).

[104] See §12.152 for further definition of willful and wanton acts.

[105] Goyings v. Jack & Ruth Eckerd Foundation, 403 So. 2d 1144 (Fla. App. 1981); see also Cain v. Cleveland Parachute Training Center, 9 Ohio App. 3d 27, 457 N.E. 2d 1185 (1983).

[106] Randle v. Hinckley Parachute Center, Inc., 141 Ill. App. 3d 660, 96 Ill. Dec. 5, 490 N.E. 2d 1041 (1986); see also Milligan v. Big Valley Corp., 754 P. 2d 1063 (Wyo. 1988) ski resort race.

[107] Jones v. Dressel, 582 P. 2d 1057 (Colo. App. 1978), aff'd. 623 P. 2d 370 (1981).

[108] Gross v. Sweet, 64 A.D. 2d 774, 407 N.Y.S. 2d 254, aff'd. 49 N.Y.S. 2d 102, 424 N.Y.S. 2d 365, 400 N.E. 2d 306 (1979); Hewitt v. Miller, 11 Wash. App. 72, 521 P. 2d 244 (1974); Schlobohm v. Spa Petite, Inc., 326 N.W. 2d 920 (Minn. 1982); Wade v. Watson, 527 F. Supp. 1049 (1981) Georgia law applied.

[109] Adams v. Roark, 686 S.W. 2d 73 (Tenn. 1985).

[110] Smith v. Golden Triangle Raceway, 708 S.W. 2d 574 (Tex. App. 1986).

[111] Gillespie v. Papale, 541 F. Supp. 1042 (1982) Mass. law applied.

[112] Lee v. Beauchene, 337 N.W. 2d 827 (S.D. 1983).

process, such as on admission tickets, season passes, entry forms, membership applications, or rental agreements. In such use, the "agreement" still must meet all the requirements set forth in §§16.11 and 16.12.

§ 16.131   Admission tickets/season passes

In *Falkner v. John E. Fetzer, Inc.*, 113 Mich. App. 500, 317 N.W. 2d 337 (1982), the admission ticket to the baseball game had a disclaimer printed on the back. The plaintiff spectator was struck by a batted ball. The defendant did not attempt to invoke the disclaimer in its defense; however, the court did hold that the stadium owner's duty to warn spectator of risk of being hit by batted balls was not fulfilled by the disclaimer, nor by an announcement at the beginning of the game, since neither amounted to a warning as such. (See also *Vines v. Birmingham Baseball Club, Inc.*, 450 So. 2d 455 (Ala. 1984)).

When plaintiff paid defendants' cashier 50 cents for the privilege of using his own toboggan on the slide for an hour, she informed him that he would have to sign up first. Plaintiff didn't say anything; just signed. The ticket signed consisted of two parts — the part signed by the plaintiff and retained by the cashier had on it in relatively small print:

> I agree to return all equipment in the same condition as when received, ordinary wear and tear excepted, and do release Touhy Playfield Winter Sports Co. and employees from all liability for any and all injuries or damages, or both, it being my intention to assume all risk, which may be sustained, whether arising from the use of such equipment, or otherwise.

No actual notice was given of the language claimed by defendants to constitute a release; but, the cashier testified that if a patron asks, she tells them it is a release. In addition, there was a sign about 38½" x 23" in size behind the counter on the wall of the warming room where the ticket was purchased which said: "Warning. You Ride at Your Own Risk — Be Careful!" The plaintiff said he did not see the sign. It was a matter for the jury whether the release was obtained knowingly and fairly or whether it was deceptive in appearance and itself constituted a misrepresentation.[113]

There must be opportunity for a person of average intelligence to observe what is on the ticket. In *Kushner v. McGinnis*, 289 Mass. 326, 194 N.E. 106 (1935), the admission ticket was taken four to five steps after purchase and torn up. This in itself made the release defective. Further, the plaintiff was unable to read English on the ticket, knowing only Russian. The admission ticket was for a "Dragon Ride" in the amusement park. Plaintiff was injured sliding down a chute. In another amusement park ride (roller coaster) case[114] of the same date, the court said it was for the jury as to whether the release on the back of the ticket was called to the patron's attention properly. In this situation, the ticket resembled a token or check; the plaintiff admitted not having read it although he knew about the printing on the reverse side. Properly bringing to the attention of the purchaser the release on the admission ticket also was at issue in *O'Brien*

---

[113] Moore v. Edmonds, 316 Ill. App. 453, 45 N.E. 2d 190, aff'd. 384 Ill. 535, 52 N.E. 2d 216 (1943).

[114] Brennen v. Ocean View Amusement Co., 289 Mass. 587, 194 N.E. 911 (1935).

v. Freeman, 299 Mass. 20, 11 N.E. 2d 582 (1937). It was held that a person of ordinary intelligence would not have been aware of the attempted release where the purchase of ticket and taking of ticket were a few feet apart. In dicta, however, the court did say that were proper attention of the patron brought to the statement, it could be held valid. The court was directly contra in *Hook v. Lakeside Park Co.*, 142 Colo. 272, 351 P. 2d 261 (1960), which concerned the amusement park ride "Loop-O-Plane," stating "that it attached no legal significance to the express waiver which was printed on the back of the ticket." The Illinois court held similarly, saying that a ticket for the giant slide in the amusement park, which had an exculpatory clause on the back, was not a written contract and that one must infer from the facts whether or not the ticket holder waived an assumed risk.[115] Maryland, in 1976, passed a statute (Ann. Code of Md. Art. 56 §158A) which provided that "the purchase of a ticket to a carnival or an amusement ride does not constitute an assumption of risk on the part of the purchaser."

The plaintiff spectator had purchased a ticket for a golf exhibition, and, while watching the celebrity golfer, was struck by a golf ball hit by one of the accompanying foursome. The defendant argued that the purchase of the ticket was a contractual assumption of the risk. The court did not so hold.[116]

In *Rosen v. LTV Recreational Development*, 569 F. 2d 1117 (1978), a skier collided with another, then crashed into a metal pole set in concrete in the ski area. The statement on the plaintiff skier's season pass read:

> I understand that skiing is a hazardous sport and that hazardous obstructions, some marked and some unmarked, exist on any ski area. I accept the existence of such dangers and that injuries may result from the numerous falls and collisions which are common in the sport of skiing, including the chance of injury resulting from the negligence and carelessness on the part of fellow skiers.

The court held that the statement does not contain any express consent on the part of the signer to exonerate the ski area for negligent conditions. It is true that it exonerates the ski area for injuries resulting from the negligence and carelessness of fellow skiers, but it does not promise to waive injuries resulting from the negligence of the ski area. The court concluded that the agreement was ambiguous and that it did not expressly provide for the waiver which is asserted by the defendant. Acknowledgment of the existence of a hazard, and even acceptance of dangers, falls short of saying that the ski area may be negligent toward the signer free of liability.

§ 16.132   Entry forms

Many entry forms, especially for races, have an exculpatory clause as part of the form, but few of these have reached the courts. A number of the national organizations or their state affiliates, have recommended forms for sponsors of local races. This statement on the race entry form was held valid:[117]

[115] Russo v. The Range, 76 Ill.App.3d 236, 395 N.E. 2d 10 (1979).

[116] Baker v. Mid Maine Medical Center, 499 A. 2d 464 (Me. 1985).

[117] Okura v. U.S. Cycling Federation, 186 Cal. App. 3d 1462, 231 Cal. Rptr. 429 (1986).

SOUTHERN CALIFORNIA CYCLING FEDERATION
STANDARD ATHLETE'S ENTRY BLANK AND RELEASE FORM

In consideration of the acceptance of my application for entry in the above event, *I hereby waive, release and discharge any and all claims for damages for death, personal injury* or property damage which I may have, or which may hereafter accrue to me, *as a result of my participation in said event. This release is intended to discharge in advance the promoters, sponsors, the U.S.C.F., the S.C.C.F., the promoting clubs, the officials, and any involved municipalities or other public entities* (and their respective agents and employees), from and against any and all liability arising out of or connected in any way with my participation in said event, *even though that liability may arise out of negligence or carelessness on the part of the persons or entities mentioned above.*

I further understand that serious accidents occasionally occur during bicycle racing: and that participants in bicycle racing occasionally sustain mortal or serious personal injuries, and/or property damage, as a consequence thereof. Knowing the risks of bicycle racing, nevertheless, I hereby agree to assume those risks and to release and hold harmless all of the persons or entities mentioned above who (through negligence or carelessness) might otherwise be liable to me (or my heirs or assigns) for damages.

It is further understood and agreed that this waiver, release and assumption of risk is to be binding on my heirs and assigns.

I agree to accept and abide by the rules and regulations of the United States Cycling Federation. (emphasis added in court opinion)

Plaintiff ski jumper alleged that he did not read the waiver before signing it and that he signed it unwittingly and therefore should be relieved from the consequences of his act. The court[118] rejected this contention on the basis that the plaintiff was under a duty to inform himself as to what he was signing, being a man of intelligence, able to read and understand the document (a college student), and further, no fraud or deception was practiced upon him. Plaintiff had signed similar forms before. The release was conspicuous and there was evidence he had read it because he had added his jumping class, which was on the printed listing. The Entry Blank release stated: In consideration of the acceptance of my application, I hereby release the Leavenworth Winter Sports Club, U.S. Ski Association, Ski Patrol, U.S. Forest Service, their members or agents and any person officially connected with this competition from all liability for any injuries or damages whatsoever arising from participation in or presence at this competition.

The plaintiff was required to sign and did sign an "entry blank" as a condition of entering the horse show. Directly above his signature was a paragraph:

[118] Garretson v. U.S., 456 F. 2d 1017 (1972)
Washington law applied.

OWNER'S STATEMENT, NAME, AGENT, ADDRESS, ASSUMPTION AND RELEASE OF LIABILITY

I, as owner and/or exhibitor of the horse(s), equipment, product(s) or goods hereby entered by me in the Madison Imperial Horse Show, do hereby, in consideration of the acceptance of this entry, covenant and agree to be personally liable for any and all injury, damage or loss caused by or resulting from the presence, use or operation of any animal(s), vehicle(s), equipment, product(s) or goods owned and/or exhibited by me at said show. I do further hereby covenant and agree that the sponsors of the Madison Imperial Horse Show shall not under any circumstances be liable or responsible for any injury, damage or loss to any person, animal, vehicle, building, fixture or any other property, caused by or resulting from the presence, use of operation of any animal(s), vehicle(s), equipment, product(s) or goods owned and/or exhibited by me at said show.

In holding this exculpatory clause not valid, the court found that it was deficient in that it did not specifically state that the release was to cover the Club's own negligence and it failed to specifically identify parties who were to be released from liability. It indicated "sponsors," but not all defendants could be classified as sponsors.[119]

§ 16.133 Membership applications/forms/bylaws

The wife of a member of the Windham Mountain Club, a private not-for-profit corporation, was injured while using the club's skiing facilities. The Club's bylaws provided that members would "hold harmless" the Club (see §16.3 Indemnification). The court held that the wife, not being a member, was not subject to the bylaws, and further, that the New York statute was applicable to a private, not-for-profit corporation.[120] (See §16.4.)

In a 1982 Minnesota case[121] the plaintiff had signed a membership contract with this clause:

ACCIDENTS

It is further expressly agreed that all exercises and treatments and use of all facilities shall be undertaken by member at member's sole risk and that Spa Petite shall not be liable for any claims, demands, injuries, damages, actions or causes of action, whatsoever to member or property arising out of or connected with the use of any of the services and facilities of Spa Petite or the premises where same are located, and member does hereby expressly forever release and discharge the said Spa Petite from all such claims, demands, injuries, damages, actions or causes of action, and from all acts of active or

---

[119] Ruppa v. Amer. States Insur. Co., 91 Wis. 2d 628, 284 N.W. 2d 318 (1979).

[120] Blanc v. Windham Mt. Club, 115 Misc. 2d 404,

454 N.Y.S. 2d 383 (1982) aff'd. 92 A.D. 2d 529, 459 N.Y.S. 2d 447 (1983).

[121] Schlobohm v. Spa Petite, Inc., 326 N.W. 2d 920 (Minn. 1982).

passive negligence on the part of such company, corporation, club, its servants, agents, or employees.

While the membership contract was four pages long, the regulations and policies were all on one page. There were 11 and each was headlined by a word or phrase in uniform bold-faced type. The print was of uniform size with other clauses on the page. Before signing, plaintiff had opportunity and did "somewhat" read the context of the contract. The court held that the exculpatory clause was not invalid in that it was not ambiguous, was for acts of negligence only (in contrast to willful and wanton acts), was not an adhesion contract, and did not violate public policy.

There were a number of cases in the '60s in New York dealing with clauses in membership forms. In one case,[122] the court held that a membership contract provision granting immunity from liability for plaintiff's injury allegedly caused by the defendant's negligence was valid on its face as a covenant not to sue; however, it was for the jury to determine whether the provision in fine print on reverse side of instrument had been called to plaintiff's attention when he signed the contract (instrument). In another New York case,[123] the court held that a private operator could require, as a condition of membership, a clearly expressed provision relieving him from liability for his own negligence.

A beach club membership application clause, which read:

I hereby make application for membership in the....for the season of 1963. If accepted, I agree to become bound by any and all laws of the club and by all rules and regulations as they now exist, or if they may be amended and waive claim for any loss to personal property, or for any personal injury while a member of said club.

was held to be invalid as an exculpatory agreement inasmuch as the language did not meet the test of clarity or explicitness required.[124] The language, also, in *Bernstein v. Seacliff Beach Club*, 228 N.Y.S. 2d 567 (1962), was held to lack clarity; but, in addition, and the determining factor in holding the exculpatory clause not valid, the application read in the first-person singular and the person who signed for the member did not properly indicate that he had the authority to do so. Thus, it was held that the plaintiff was an invitee and the exculpatory clause did not affect his right to recover. An opposite result was reached in an Illinois case[125] decided about the same time. The exculpatory clause required as a part of the membership was held valid. The clause stated:

Member, in attending said gymnasiums and using the facilities and equipment therein, does so at his own risk. Tanny shall not be liable for any damages arising from personal injuries sustained by Member in, on or about the

[122] Putzer v. Vic Tanny Flatbush, Inc., 20 A.D. 2d 821, 248 N.Y.S. 2d 836 (1964); see also Whalen v. Vic Tanny Hicksville, Inc., 23 A.D. 2d 778, 258 N.Y.S. 2d 562 (1965).

[123] Ciofalo v. Vic Tanny Gyms, Inc., 13 A.D. 2d 702, 214 N.Y.S. 2d 99, aff'd. 10 N.Y. 2d 294, 220 N.Y.S. 2d 962, 177 N.E. 2d 925 (1961).

[124] Hertzog v. Harrison Island Shores, 21 A.D. 2d 859, 251 N.Y.S. 2d 164 (1964).

[125] Owen v. Vic Tanny's Enterprises, 48 Ill. App. 2d 344, 199 N.E. 2d 280 (1964).

premises of any of the said gymnasiums. Member assumes full responsibility for any injuries or damages which may occur to Member in, on or about the premises of said gymnasiums and he does hereby fully and forever release and discharge Tanny and all associated gymnasiums, their owners, employees and agents from any and all claims, demands, damages, rights of action, or causes of action, present or future, whether the same be known, anticipated or unanticipated, resulting from or arising out of the Member's use or intended use of the said gymnasium or the facilities and equipment thereof.

Twenty years later, in the '80s there were several cases in various states concerned with health club/spa membership forms. In another Illinois Vic Tanny case,[126] the club membership contract also was indicated to be valid as long as the danger which occasioned injury was foreseeable, that is, not beyond reasonable contemplation of the parties. In this case, it was held outside the range of foreseeable dangers when injury was caused by inhaling dangerous gaseous vapor generated by combining certain cleaning compounds. Plaintiff, a health club member in Georgia, was barred from recovery by a valid membership contract containing an exculpatory clause. Injury was sustained during a fitness test.[127] And, plaintiff did not recover damages for injury due to misuse of an exercise machine due to valid exculpatory clause in the membership application.[128] However, an opposite result was reached when plaintiff was injured on a weight lifting machine. The court said the form was not sufficiently clear, explicit, and unequivocal to show an interest to protect facility from liability arising from use of its equipment under circumstances presented.[129] And, the agreement was held similarly, ambiguous and did not "spell out" intention of parties with necessary particularity, in a 1987 Pennsylvania case.[130] The plaintiff slipped on a wet tile floor.

In *My Fair Lady of Georgia v. Harris*, 185 Ga. App. 459, 364 S.E.2d 580 (1987), a health club membership agreement was held valid and precluded suit against the club. The contract signed by plaintiff contained the following exculpatory paragraph:

Use of Facility by Members — Member agrees...use of all club facilities shall be undertaken at the member's own risk... and that the corporation which owns the club and/or any affiliated companies and/or their respective agents and employees shall not be liable for any claims, demands, injuries, damages, actions or causes of action ... which arise wholly or partially due to the negligence of the corporation which owns the club and/or any affiliated companies and/or their respective agents and employees to member... arising out of or connected with the use of any of the services and/or facilities of such

---

[126] Larsen v. Vic Tanny, Int'l, 130 Ill. App. 3d 574, 85 Ill. Dec. 769, 474 N.E. 2d 729 (1984).

[127] Lovelace v. Figure Salon, 345 S.E. 2d 139 (Ga. App. 1986); see also Leidy v. Deseret Enterprises, Inc., 252 Pa. Super. 162, 381 A. 2d 164 (1977) also postoperative treatment, agreement held valid.

[128] Neumann v. Gloria Marshall Figure Salon, 149 Ill. App. 3d 824, 102 Ill. Dec. 910, 500 N.E. 2d 1011 (1986).

[129] Calarco v. YMCA of Greater Metro. Chicago, 149 Ill. App. 3d 1037, 103 Ill. Dec. 247, 501 N.E. 2d 268 (1986) cert. denied 508 N.E. 2d 725.

[130] Brown v. Racquetball Centers, Inc., 534 A. 2d 842 (Pa. Super. 1987).

corporation ... and the member does hereby expressly forever release and discharge said corporation and any affiliated companies and their respective agents and employees, from all such claims, demands, injuries, damages, actions or causes of action. ...

In another 1987 case,[131] at issue was the membership form of the gun club. The court held the language sufficient waiver of negligence action arising out of eye injury which occurred during mock gunfight sponsored by club. The statement provided for holding harmless and releasing members and club from any and all claims and damages which may occur from participating in any and all activities sanctioned by the club.

§ 16.134   Rental agreements for use of equipment and leases

Rental agreements are commonly used for golf carts and ski equipment. At issue in the *Zimmer* case[132] was this rental agreement:

RENTAL AGREEMENT AND RECEIPT

I accept for use as is the equipment listed on this form and accept full responsibility for the care of the equipment while it is in my possession, and agree to reimburse Mitchell and Ness Ski Shop for any loss or damage other than reasonable wear resulting from use.

I understand that insurance coverage applies to equipment breakage only, not lost, misplaced or stolen equipment.

I understand that so-called safety bindings furnished herewith are releasable bindings designed to reduce the risk or degree of injuries from falling and that these bindings will not release under **ALL** circumstances and are no guarantee of my safety.

I furthermore release Mitchell and Ness from any liability for damage and injury to myself or to any person or property resulting from the use of this equipment, accepting myself the full responsibility for any and all such damage or injury.

The defendant argued that the agreement was not enforceable because of lack of clarity, specifically, the title did not indicate that the contract contained a release and the text did not include the word "negligence." The court held that while one must construe strictly such agreements, one also must use common sense; and, therefore, stated that the text clearly stated in laymen's terms the release from liability. The defense also put forth the argument that the negligence, if any, occurred prior to the signing of the agreement. The court said that if there was negligence as alleged, in renting equipment without first testing and fitting the bindings, then that negligence occurred simultaneously with plaintiff's acceptance of the rental agreement and receipt and the exculpatory clause was valid and enforceable.

[131] Boehm v. Cody Country Chamber of Commerce, 748 P. 2d 704 (Wyo. 1987).

[132] Zimmer v. Mitchell & Ness, 253 Pa. Super. 474, 385 A. 2d 437 (1978) aff'd. 416 A. 2d 1010 (1980).

In a Washington case,[133] the plaintiff signed a printed form entitled "Golf Cart Rental Agreement" and took possession of an electric golf cart. When returning the cart, plaintiff alleges the brakes failed and the cart overturned, causing injuries to him. The disclaimer was about in the middle of the agreement paragraph and did not stand out; one would have had to read the agreement to be consciously aware of it. The entire text in which the clause was embodied was quite small print, but that in itself was not a determinant. However, the State legislature had announced a public policy with regard to disclaimers of liability in commercial transactions by enacting the Uniform Commercial Code, [particularly RCW 62A.2-316 (2) and -719(1); (3)] which required that exclusions must be in writing and conspicuous and that consequential damages may be limited or excluded "unless the limitation or exclusion is unconscionable." The court held that in this situation to allow the respondent to completely exclude himself from liability by such an inconspicuous disclaimer would truly be unconscionable. The clause in question was:

> ...Lessee agrees that in using said cart, he does so at his own risk. It is expressly understood and agreed that the lessor shall not be liable for any damages whatsoever arising from injuries to the person and/or property damage or loss, of the lessee arising from the use of, operation of, or in any way connected with said cart or any part thereof, from whatever cause arising....

In another golf cart rental agreement, the court held that the exculpation clause contained in the rental ticket did not preclude imposition of strict liability on lessor.[134] (See §21.1 Product liability.)

Plaintiff was injured while using a "jet ski" which he had rented from defendant. A release was signed prior to his injuries. The question was whether the defendant corporation came under the New York statute voiding such releases (see §16.4).[135] In another jet ski rental agreement case[136] the issue was the indemnification clause which was in the agreement and signed by the father of the injured (see §16.3). See also §3.11 Lessor/lessee relationships.

A bicycle rental agreement was at issue when plaintiff was injured, allegedly due to malfunction of bicycle brakes. The agreement read:

RIDE CHARGE AGREEMENT

> User agrees to return said item in the same condition as when received, ordinary wear and tear excepted. *User agrees to indemnify and hold Host free and harmless from all injuries to person or persons, including death, damages to property, loss of time, and/or any and all other loss or damages, whether caused or occasioned by the negligence of Host, its employees or*

[133] Baker v. Seattle, 2 Wash. App. 1033, 471 P. 2d 693 (1970), rev'd./remanded 79 Wash. 2d 198, 484 P. 2d 405 (1971).

[134] Sipari v. Villa Olivia Country Club, 63 Ill. App. 3d 985, 20 Ill. Dec. 610, 380 N.E. 2d 819 (1978).

[135] Dumez v. Harbor Jet Ski, Inc., 117 Misc. 2d 249, 458 N.Y.S. 2d 119 (1981).

[136] Salts v. Bridgeport Marina, Inc., 535 F. Supp. 1038 (1982) Missouri law applied.

servants, or any other person whatsoever, arising or flowing from the use, operation or rental of the said item by User. User agrees to pay or reimburse Host for all charges incidental to all breakages, shortages, damages, or losses other than such ordinary wear to said item caused by User.

The exculpatory agreement was held valid and released lessor from liability for injuries. The preprinted rental agreement contravened no policy of law and was entered between free bargaining agents.[137]

In *Continental Insurance Co. v. Washeon Corp.*, 524 F. Supp. 34 (1981), applying Missouri law, the court held that the exculpatory and indemnification provisions of the lease agreement were valid and enforceable where there was insufficient evidence to establish yacht club's breach of lease agreement as would estop yacht club from asserting such provisions. This case dealt with property damage, rather than personal injury. The yacht owner leased dock space from the yacht club (doing business as the Washeon Club) and fire damaged the hull of the yacht.

The defendant (Federal Government) had leased the recreation area at Lake Hasty near a dam to the Southeastern Colorado Recreation Association. A part of the Lake was used as a swimming pool and the Government had constructed a diving pier adjacent to the pool. A 16-year-old girl drowned and plaintiff alleged inadequate lifeguarding. The Government contended it was not liable based upon this clause in the lease:

5.   That the United States shall not be responsible for damages to property or injuries to persons which may arise from or be incident to the use and occupation of the said premises, nor for damages to the property of the lessee, nor for damages to the property, or injuries to the person of the lessee's officers, agents, servants or employees, or others who may be on said premises at their invitation or the invitation of anyone of them, arising from or incident to the flooding of the said premises by the Government or flooding from any other cause, or arising from or incident to any other Governmental activities; and the lessee shall hold the United States harmless from any and all such claims, except as otherwise provided in Condition No. 18.

The court held that such clause has been held to be against public policy, but further, the Government was not relieved from liability because it retained control over the premises in spite of the lease.[138] (See §3.11 Lessor/lessee relationships.)

Plaintiff and her friend had been asked to put their names, addresses and riding ability on a "sign-up" sheet when renting horses from the stable in *Mizushima v. Sunset Ranch, Inc.*, 103 Nev. 259, 737 P.2d 1158 (1987). The following language appeared at the top of the form:

I, the undersigned, assume all responsibility for horse and equipment, and all liability. It is understood that the management is not liable in case of accident.

---

[137] Gimpel v. Host Enterprises, Inc., 640 F. Supp.
972 (1986) Penn. law applied.
[138] Ward v. U.S., 208 F. Supp. 118 (1962).

I also agree to pay for damage to horse or equipment and special charge for overridden horse.

Below this language, in larger type, there was a statement which said "all patrons ride at their own risk." The court held that plaintiff did not expressly assume risk of injury caused by ranch's own negligence by signing registration or sign-up sheet containing assumption of risk language before riding horse. (See §5.22 Assumption of risk).

§ 16.2   Parental permissions and agreements to participate

Although frequently combined into one instrument, parental permissions and agreements to participate by the participant should be distinguished (see Table 16.1). Each is discussed in subsequent sections. California has an unique statute (Cal. Educ. Code §1081.5 and §72640) enacted in 1976, which states that all persons making the field trip or excursions (related to schools) are deemed to have waived all claims. And, it further states that all adults taking such trips and all parents or guardians of students on trips or excursions shall sign a statement waiving such claims. However, in the absence of statute, the common law rule is as stated in *Reliance Insurance Co. v. Haney,* 54 Mich. App. 237, 220 N.W.2d 728 (1974): "Parent has no authority merely by virtue of parental relation to waive, release or compromise claims by or against child. Status of a parent is one of guardian by nature. Generally, guardian has no authority to do any act which is detrimental to his ward."

§ 16.21   Parental permissions

Many persons feel that to secure a permit from the parents for a child, whether in school, on the city playground, at camp, or in private instruction, relieves them of possibilities of a law suit, that the parent has consented and therefore assumes the risks inherent in the activity being engaged in. This, however, is false security. While the parents may waive their own rights to sue, they cannot waive the right of a minor to sue upon reaching majority age (see §16.1131). While one does not see many permission forms with a specific exculpatory clause for the parents, a parent could sign such a clause, but it would bind only the parent. It should be noted that for many activities in which children participate and parents are asked to sign a permission form, it would be against public policy to so contract away one's rights to recover on the negligence by another under the criteria set forth in §16.12. Parental forms, however, are recommended, not as a device to limit liability, but as a public relations effort and the courtesies a sponsoring organization should exhibit to the parents in awareness of the nature of the participation of their children (see §24.811). Following are a few cases related to the legal effect of parents signing in behalf of their children.

In *Powell v. Orleans Parish School Board,* 354 So. 2d 229 (La. App. 1978), a 17-year-old high school student drowned in a hotel pool while on a band trip. The plaintiff parents had given permission for him to use the swimming pool on this trip. The court stated that if the son could not swim and was afraid of water, as plaintiff alleged, then the father should not have given written permission for him to use the pool. If the permission was intended to have been a conditional permission, the condition should have been made known to the school authorities, but was not. No evidence of negligence was shown on the part of the defendant School Board.

In a camp case[139] the young boy and his father signed a waiver regarding claims for damages. The court held that such agreement was contrary to public policy and in the dictum stated that it is doubtful that either the mother or father of this minor plaintiff had the power or authority to waive his rights against the defendant arising out of acts of negligence on the part of the defendant.

In a skydiving case[140] there was no signature by the parent, but the court held that approval by a parent does not necessarily validate an infant child's contract. An indemnification clause in a rental agreement signed by the father was at issue in a jet ski injury case[141] (see §16.3). A parent signed a release statement on behalf of the nine-year-old child, who was injured in a horseback riding situation. The court held that the release, even if valid, was a statement only related to "inherent risks" and did not void defendant's negligent acts; thus, the issue of right of a parent to sign a release for a child was not determined.[142]

The father and mother at time of enrollment each signed separate statements (see §16.1111 for statements) on behalf of their minor son, who was attending a hockey clinic when he was injured. The court held that the statements were invalid releases, but in the dictum stated that even if it were assumed that the documents were releases, the results would remain unchanged because this court has held that a parent or guardian cannot release the child's or ward's, cause of action.[143]

The Washington court held that the release form required to be signed by the parents to be an "unconscionable contract of adhesion" and void as against public policy, in *Wagenblast v. Odessa School District,* 110 Wash. 2d 845, 758 P.2d 968 (1988). See §16.12).

§ 16.22   Agreements to participate

Often it is heard that the signing of a "release" or participation form is not "worth the paper it is written on" — it depends on what one expects that form to do. If it is to release one from liability, in effect to be an exculpatory agreement, then, if a minor signs, it is not worth the paper it is written on, because a minor cannot execute a valid exculpatory agreement (see §16.1131). If a person of majority age signs, then, if the document meets the criteria for a valid exculpatory agreement (§16.11), then it indeed is a contract and will be upheld in court. For this reason, increasingly, agreements to participate in events, such as skydiving, mountain climbing, bicycle racing, road running, et al.,

[139] Fedor v. Manwehu Council, Boy Scouts of America, 21 Conn. Sup. 38, 143 A. 2d 466 (1958); see also §16.3 Goyings v. Jack & Ruth Eckerd Foundation, 403 So. 2d 1144 (Fla. App. 1981).

[140] Jones v. Dressel, 582 P. 2d 1057 (Colo. App. 1978), aff'd. 623 P. 2d 370 (1981).

[141] Salts v. Bridgeport Marina, Inc., 535 F. Supp. 1038 (1982) Missouri law applied.

[142] O'Connell v. Walt Disney World Co., 413 So. 2d 444 (Fla. App. 1982).

[143] Doyle v. Bowdoin College, Maine, 403 A. 2d 1206 (Me. 1979); Tepper v. City of New Rochelle School Dist., 531 N.Y.S. 2d 367 (1988); see also §16.3 Indemnification.

include an exculpatory clause. This may be particularly useful in limiting liability for private enterprises offering services in sport, recreation, and camping/adventure activities; however, many of these activities and areas/facilities are offered by public entities, such as schools and municipalities, or voluntary non-profit organizations, and the issue of public policy is a dominant one (see §16.12). In such instances, an agreement to participate can be a useful document, both as a defense in a law suit and as an information/public relations instrument to deter law suits or modify operational practices for better safety. While it is recommended that a parent sign a minor's agreement form, it carries no legal force, but is useful as a public relations effort.

Based upon legal concepts, it is recommended that an agreement to participate have three elements embodied within it — nature of the activity, expectations of the participant, and condition of participant. The legal concept rationale for the first element is assumption of risk (see §5.22). Under the defense of assumption of risk, the participant assumes those risks which are inherent in the activity — of which the participant is knowledgeable, understands and appreciates in terms of possible consequences. The courts have been particularly strong in emphasizing the importance of appreciating the potential consequences of participation. By describing the nature of the activity in which the participant will be engaged, including potential risks for injury, particularly if the type of injuries which may occur are very clearly stated, this signed document can be a very important piece of evidence in the court room. Some sponsors of activities have been reluctant to indicate the ultimate potential dangers, such as loss of life, fearing that individuals then will not participate. Decline in participation does not seem to be a result of printing the realities of what might happen.

The second element finds its rationale in the legal concept of contributory negligence (see §5.21) and comparative negligence (see §5.23). In this portion of the agreement to participate should be the directive that it is expected the participant will obey the leader, supervisor, or person in charge and will follow the rules and regulations set forth. If there are some special safety rules and regulations, it might be well to have them printed on the reverse side of the agreement form or have some indication that they have been received and/or read. Further, it should be stated that the participants are expected to alert the leadership to any hazards they see, including condition of the equipment or premises, difficulties they may be having in performing a skill, or the fact that they are unduly fatigued or do not feel well, which might affect safe participation. An award under comparative negligence is reduced in accord with the plaintiff's contributing negligence; failure to follow rules and regulations or the leadership or to be informed about dangerous conditions could be construed as acts contributing toward one's own injury.

To get information on the condition of the participant is the aim of the third element and is based upon the duty owed an invitee. The leadership must be knowledgeable about a participant if they are to adequately protect the participant as an invitee (see §§17.3 and 19.1). This portion of the agreement form might include an affirmation of being in proper physical condition to participate, indicate a condition of which the leadership should be aware (e.g., epilepsy, allergic to bee stings, temporary physical illness or disability), verification of skill level required for participation, et al. To withhold pertinent information can be considered misrepresentation and fraudulent; to not know and therefore not be able to be aware of possible needs would be taken into consideration when determining foreseeability of the injury and the reasonableness of the care given to the participant.

No model agreement to participate forms are set forth, since the content is so specific to individual situations (see §24.712).

§ 16.3   Indemnification contracts or "hold harmless" agreements[144]

Exculpatory clauses and indemnification clauses are technically different (see Table 16.1). An exculpatory agreement purports to deny an injured party the right to recover damages from the person negligently causing his injury, while an indemnity clause endeavors to shift the responsibility for the payment of damages to someone by contract.[145] In this section, the shift of responsibility is back to the injured party, and in respect to such party's recovery of damages, an indemnity clause would have the same result as an exculpatory provision. However, unless otherwise stated, an indemnity clause also may mean that the person signing may be liable for damages which he occasioned directly or indirectly.

Since both an exculpatory agreement and an indemnity clause have the same purpose of attempting to shift ultimate responsibility for negligent injury, they are generally construed by the same principles of law.[146] Indemnity clauses, however, usually are not held contrary to public policy and the construction tends to be a bit more broad or liberal than an exculpatory agreement.[147] This liberalization, though, is primarily because most indemnification agreements are viewed as merely allocating risk of liability to third parties, essentially through employment of insurance, and thus are considered negotiated at arm's length between business entitites, rather than individuals closely related as a participant and sponsor in an exculpatory agreement.[148] Nevertheless, and particularly where the purpose is as a substitute for an exculpatory agreement, an indemnity agreement must clearly and unequivocally provide for indemnification for the indemnitee's own negligence; the obligation will not be inferred.[149] Further, some courts have held that one who is actively negligent has no right to indemnification.[150]

A statement a mother signed for her son's participation in a hockey clinic read:

> I fully understand that Bowdoin College, its employees or servants will accept no responsibility for or on account of any injury or damage sustained by Brian

---

[144] This section discusses only an individual participant signing a form which contains an indemnity clause. See §4.2 for statutory authorization of governmental entities to indemnify officials and employees, and §25.21 for indemnification agreements as part of risk management, especially indemnification through transfer by insurance coverage. The use of an indemnity clause as an exculpatory agreement is not recommended, therefore, this section (§16.3) is brief as an informational element only. See also §16.1111 assumption of risk.

[145] O'Connell v. Walt Disney World Co., 413 So. 2d 444 (La. App. 1982).

[146] Schlobohm v. Spa Petite, Inc., 326 N.W. 2d 920 (Minn. 1982).

[147] Haynes v. Co. of Missoula, 163 Mont. 270, 517 P. 2d 370 (1973).

[148] Gross v. Sweet, 64 A.D. 2d 774, 407 N.Y.S. 2d 254, aff'd. 49 N.Y. 2d 102, 424 N.Y.S. 2d 365, 440 N.E. 2d 306 (1979).

[149] O'Connell v. Walt Disney World Co., 413 So. 2d 444 (Fla. App. 1982).

[150] Celli v. Sports Car Club, 29 Cal.App.3d 511, 105 Cal.Rptr.2d 904, (1973); Ehehalt v. Nyars O'Dette, Inc., 481 A. 2d 365 (Pa. Cmwlth. 1984); Gartside v. YMCA, 87 Mich. App. 335, 274 N.W. 2d 58 (1978); Johnson v. Hoover Water Well Service, 64 Ill. Dec. 476, 108 (Ill. App. 3d 994, 439 N.E. 2d 1284, (1982); Vinnell Co. v. Pacific Elec. Ry. Co., 52 Cal. 2d 411, 340 P. 2d 604 (1959).

arising out of the activities of the said **THE CLINIC**. I do, therefore, agree to assume all risk of injury or damage to the person or property of Brian arising out of the activities of the said **THE CLINIC.**

The court held that the agreement was not an indemnity contract because it contained no express reference to defendants' liability for their own negligence; terms such as indemnify, reimburse, or hold harmless are absent.[151]

Often parents are asked to sign a form, including an indemnification or exculpatory clause, in order for their children to go on a trip. This was the situation with a newsboys' trip to Bear Mountain. The actual statement to be signed was not in the case opinion, but it included both a release and an indemnification clause. It was signed by both the minor plaintiff and the father. While on the trip, plaintiff was accosted by a group of teenagers and allegedly injured by them. The court held that the form was void as against public policy, stating that:

> Contract wherein father, as a condition to his infant son being allowed to go on trip sponsored by corporate defendant agreed to release defendant from any and all claims for injuries sustained by son on trip and also to indemnify defendant for any and all injuries claimed by son forced father into a position whereby his personal interest came, or might come, into conflict with his duty to his son and, as such, was void as against public policy that a fiduciary may not undertake an obligation inconsistent with his duties.

The court said further that a parent has no authority to compromise or release claims or causes of action belonging to the child; a parent has at least a moral duty to see that child's property rights are fully protected. If the indemnification agreement were enforced, it would be for the benefit of the father to prevent the bringing of any suit on the claim of the minor no matter how advantageous such suit might be for the minor child.[152]

Sometimes an organization will try to use an indemnity clause in a membership application or rental agreement to shift responsibility to the participant/user for any damages which may result from activities or use of facilities or equipment, rather than taking out insurance.[153] In its membership contract, a health spa had the following clause:

> 7.   Member fully understands and agrees that in participating in one or more of the courses, or using the facilities that shall be maintained by the Spa, there is the possibility of accidental or other physical injury. Member further agrees to assume the risk of such injury, and further agrees to indemnify the Spa from any and all liability attributable to the Spa by either the Member or Third Parties as a result of the use by the Member of the facilities and instruction as offered by the Spa.

---

[151] Doyle v. Bowdoin College, 430 A. 2d 1206 (Maine 1979).

[152] Fitzgerald v. Newark Morning Ledger Co., 111 N.J. Super. 104, 267 A. 2d 557 (1970).

[153] This policy is questioned as being sound either fiscally or public relations-wise. See Part D on risk management.

This is a combination of an assumption of risk statement and an indemnity clause. The court held that the contractual provision has "an inescapable certainty of meaning that requires no construction or interpretation beyond the clear import of the words used. There is nothing inconsistent or uncertain in plaintiff assuming the risk of injury and agreeing to indemnify defendant, in the same sentence."[154]

A father signed a rental agreement for his 14-year-old son so that he could rent jet skis. One of the terms provided that

> [Gary Salts] agrees to assume all and full responsibility and liability of the jet ski against neglect, damages or personal injuries to others, thereby releasing the [Marina] of all damages or obligations.

The court held that under Missouri law the marina could not claim contractual right to indemnification, "where marina did not assert that it intended for rental agreements which it entered into with its customers to replace liability insurance for negligent acts, and where it was not asserted that individual customers of marina were on an equal footing with marina, in that the rental agreement did not manifest a clear and unequivocal intent on the part of father to act as liability insurer for negligent acts of marina."[155]

In another illustrative case, the Club bylaws had a provision whereby members agreed to hold the Club harmless from claims of any kind, including claims arising from employee negligence arising out of use of any of the club's facilities by a member of his family. Member's wife sustained serious personal injuries while using the skiing facilities at the Club. The member plaintiff denies that he had seen the bylaws until after the suit was brought, although they were adopted four years prior to the accident and four years after he first became a member. He further stated that he had requested, but had not received a copy of the Club's rules and regulations; however, there had been a general mailing to members advising them that there was in effect a limitation of liability. The dictum of the court set forth requirements for such bylaws provision to be in effect. "Assuming that the by-laws had been properly adopted.... members must be afforded notice of such by-laws to which they were to be held accountable. Otherwise, a member would be improperly denied the opportunity of electing to remain within the Club, subject to the exculpatory provision, or to withdraw therefrom by refusing to remit membership dues for the enusing fiscal year.... the absence of proper notification is crucial, since the viability of the defense is dependent upon the consensual nature of the agreement to exonerate one from liability for one's own negligence....Noticeable is the absence of any allegation that adoption occurred at a duly constituted meeting, after sufficient notice had been sent to the members. Such notice essential...." The court held that the agreement was unenforceable; and, further, that it was contrary to public policy as set forth in the State statute (N.Y. Gen. Oblig. Law §5-326) and, thus, was invalidated, rendering the clause void and unenforceable.[156]

---

[154] Empress Health & Beauty Spa, v. Turner, 503 S.W. 2d 188 (Tenn. 1973).

[155] Salts v. Bridgeport Marina, Inc., 535 F. Supp. 1038 (1982) Missouri law applied.

[156] Blanc v. Windham Mt. Club, 115 Misc. 2d 404, 454 N.Y.S. 2d 383 (1982), aff'd. 92 A.D. 2d 529, 459 N.Y.S. 2d 447 (1983).

Just what is being indemnified is important. The county had a long-term lease agreement for its use and maintenance of a building. Plaintiff was allegedly injured due to the slick condition of the front doorway-sidewalk area, which was part of the initial building construction. He sued the building lessor, the producer of the substance on the walkway, and the county lessee. The county had a "hold harmless" agreement in its lease. It was held that the contract was not intended to indemnify for third party negligence, but rather only the negligence of the county. The county was protected by governmental immunity.[157]

In a 1984 North Dakota case,[158] a dancer was rehearsing for the dance performance scheduled for that evening, when a University employee negligently raised the stage lift after being warned to stop and lower the lift. The University brought a third-party action against the YMCA and Smith, an employee of the Y, the person who had signed the lease, which provided for indemnification of the University. The court held that the lease contract reflected the unmistakable intent that the University lessor be held harmless. An opposite result was reached, however, in a 1984 Louisiana case.[159] The high school had leased the auditorium, also for a dance program, to a private dance school. Two youngsters attending the dance revue had gone to the hallway to get a drink, and seeing lights on and the door open to the gymnasium, went in. One was injured in a fall from the rings. The court held that indemnification in the lease was against consequences of one's own negligence, and the open gymnasium was not negligence of the dance school, but of the school itself, the lessor. School, but not the dance school, was held liable. The indemnification agreement, also, was not upheld in another 1984 case[160] applying Mississippi law. The court held that while the county agreed to indemnify the U.S., the latter was not entitled to indemnification because it (Corps of Engineers) had been negligent in its dredging operations while repairing a hurricane-damaged seawall in an area where resulting depression would be hazardous to swimmers, yet would not permit warnings.

§ 16.4   State statutes

New York[161] enacted a statute in 1976 voiding agreements stating:

Every covenant, agreement or understanding in or in connection with, or collateral to, any contract, membership application, ticket of admission or similar writing, entered into between the owner or operator of any pool, gymnasium, place of amusement or recreation, or similar establishment and the use of such facilities, pursuant to which such owner or operator receives a fee or other compensation for the use of such facilities, which exempts the said owner or operator from liability for damages caused by or resulting from the negligence of the owner, operator or person in charge of such establishment, or

157 Davis v. Board of Co. Com'rs of Co. of Carbon, 495 P. 2d 21 (Wyo. 1972) note date and changing status of governmental immunity, see §4.4.

158 Bridston v. Dover Corp., 352 N.W. 2d 194 (N.D. 1984).

159 Dunne v. Orleans Parish School Board, 444 So. 2d 1317 (La. App. 1984), review granted 447 So. 2d 1074 (1984).

160 Butler v. U.S., 726 F. 2d 1057 (1984).

161 N.Y. General Obligations Law §5.326.

their agents, servants or employees, shall be deemed to be void as against public policy and wholly unenforceable.

The court held a parachute and recreation center was a "place of recreation" within the meaning of the statute. The plaintiff broke a vertebra in his back while taking parachuting instruction. Plaintiff had executed a waiver and hold harmless agreement and had agreed not to commence any action for personal injuries. Defendants admitted that they agreed to instruct the plaintiff properly with regard to his parachute jump. Under the statute the agreement was void and unenforceable.[162] The statute was held inapplicable in connection with tobogganing at a county state park where the injured plaintiff was not issued a ticket of admission and did not pay a fee before entering the park, notwithstanding that plaintiff paid compensation for refreshments or that other users paid fees for different activities. The plaintiff had signed a release agreement.[163] And, in a Powder Puff derby, the court held that when plaintiff responded to a call for participants from the grandstand, the injury was in connection with the release signed and not her admission ticket, making the Statute inapplicable to void the release.[164]

In a ski situation[165] the statute was held applicable to recreation facilities of private, not-for-profit corporations. In this case the exculpatory clause was in the membership bylaws. Applicability of the statute focused on the control of environment in the jet ski case.[166] The defendant had rented equipment to the plaintiff. If the defendant merely rented the equipment and the plaintiff were free to use such equipment anywhere on the public lake, the necessary control factor would not be present so as to bring this situation within the statute; however, if the jet ski were used in close proximity to and under some kind of supervision by the defendant, then such would be considered adequate control of environment to bring the case under the statute and the exculpatory agreement in the lease (rental agreement) would be void as against public policy.

In a much earlier New York case,[167] a statute[168] specific to use of the bobsled run owned by the State required the signing of a waiver, but specifically provided "... injuries sustained in the use of the said bobsled run, except such as might arise from the negligence of the State of New York, its agents, servants or employees." The court held that once the negligence of the State was established, any waiver lost efficacy and that signature of such waivers did not make the injured assume any risk or waive any claim for damages as a matter of law in connection with injuries received on the bobsled run.

---

[162] Wurzer v. Seneca Sport Parachute Club, 66 A.D. 2d 1002, 411 N.Y.S. 2d 763 (1978); agreements also held void under statute in Gaskey v. Vollertsen, 110 A.D. 2d 1066, 488 N.Y.S. 2d 922 (1985) auto race spectator, and Meier v. Ma-Do Bars, Inc., 106 A.D. 2d 143, 484 N.Y.S. 2d 719 (1985) mechanical bull at tavern; Ward v. Dunn, 136 Misc. 781, 519 N.Y.S. 2d 307 (1987) hairstyling salon with tanning bed held not "similar" to place of entertainment or recreation for purpose of statute.

[163] Geise v. County of Niagara, 117 Misc. 2d 470, 458 N.Y.S. 2d 162 (1983).

[164] Beardslee v. Blomberg, 70 A.D. 2d 732, 416 N.Y.S. 2d 855 (1979).

[165] Blanc v. Windham Mt. Club, 115 Misc. 2d 404, 454 N.Y.S. 2d 383 (1982); aff'd. 92 A.D. 2d 529, 459 N.Y.S. 2d 447 (1983).

[166] Dumez v. Harbor Jet Ski, Inc., 117 Misc. 2d 249, 458 N.Y.S. 2d 119 (1981).

[167] Kaiser v. State, 55 Misc. 2d 576, 285 N.Y.S. 2d 874 (1967), rev'd. 30 A.D. 2d 482, 294 N.Y.S. 2d 410 (1968); see also Cunningham v. State, 32 N.Y.S. 2d 275, modified as to damages 264 A.D. 811, 34 N.Y.S. 2d 903 (1942).

[168] New York Laws of 1932, Chapter 273 §3.

The plaintiff raised the issue of enforcement of the exculpatory clause in the health club contract being against public policy by reason of statute in Illinois. This statute (Ill. Rev. Stat. 1977, Ch. 80, 91) voided certain exculpatory clauses in leases, but the court held that the statute did not encompass this type of agreement, and that if the legislature had intended all exculpatory clauses to be voided, it would have so provided.[169]

A California law[170] relating to field trips was at issue in *Castro v. L.A. Board of Education*, 54 Cal. App. 3d 232, 126 Cal. Rptr. 537, (1976). In this situation a high school student died while participating with his R.O.T.C. unit on a field trip, organized by and under the supervision and control of the school. The law provides that a statement waiving claims against the school district or the State by reason of injury occurring during or by reason of the field trip or excursion must be signed. The court held plaintiff had a cause of action notwithstanding the claim of immunity under this particular statute. The court distinguished those activities which were required for school purposes and those which were voluntary, although educational in nature.

---

[169] Bers v. Chicago Health Clubs, 11 Ill. App. 3d 590, 297 N.E. 2d 360 (1973); Kubisen v. Chicago Health Clubs, 69 Ill. App. 3d 463, 26 Ill. Dec. 420, 338 N.E. 2d 44 (1979).

[170] Calif. Educ. Code §1081.5; also §72640 applicable to community colleges.

Chapter 17.   Emergency Care and Physical Condition

Whereas other chapters (Chapters 18, 19, 20) focus upon the cause of the injury in terms of supervision, the conduct of the activity, and the environmental conditions, all circumstances preceding the injury, in this chapter are discussed the treatment of the injury and preparations which should have been made for emergency care. Attention, also, is given to the persons who render the emergency care, as well as to the physical condition and the conditioning of participants. Concerns relating to programs and services of health spas and fitness centers are set forth, too.

§ 17.1 The "Good Samaritan" concept[1]

What is the liability of the person who renders the emergency care to the injured? Is there unlimited liability, limited liability, or immunity? Several legal concepts in Part A must be referenced. Basically, there are two common law doctrines influencing the status of the persons rendering emergency care — the doctrine of respondeat superior and the doctrine of governmental immunity (see Chapters 3 and 4, respectively). Under the first doctrine there is liability, while under the second there may be immunity for employees of governmental entities, depending on how the state statutes have modified the doctrine. One must distinguish between litigation immunity and liability immunity. Under some state governmental immunity statutes (State Tort Claims Acts) there is litigation immunity, that is, the suit is not to be brought against the person (tortfeasor); however, the most common practice is to bring suit and then use as a defense "liability immunity" under the Tort Claims Act[2] or one of the statutes limiting liability for rendering emergency care discussed in this section.

Also integral to negligence liability is that a duty must be owed by the defendant (one who rendered aid) to the plaintiff; duty often is said to be the first element of negligence and without it there can be no negligence (see §2.1). The concept of misfeasance and nonfeasance (see §2.21) is germane to liability, too; and, consideration of the duty to rescue (or render aid to) another when there is no inherent duty owed is based in moral responsibility, rather than legal.[3]

The "Good Samaritan" concept is that an individual does not owe any legal responsibility to render aid in that there is no relationship by which a duty is owed;[4] but, the individual comes upon an accident or situation wherein a victim needs emergency care of an injury or rescue from that situation, and there is incumbent upon the individual a moral responsibility to render aid. Excluding motor vehicle laws,[5] only Minnesota,[6] as part of its Good Samaritan Law, actually places upon the person coming

[1] Mason, Robert A. Good Samaritan Laws - Legal Disarray: An Update, 38 *Mercer Law Review* 1439-1475 (1987).

[2] For example, Garza v. Edinburg Consolidated Indp. School Dist., 576 S.W. 2d 916 (Tex. Civ. App. 1979).

[3] Weinrib, Ernest J. The Case for a Duty to Rescue. 90 *Yale Law Journal* 247-293, December 1980; Woozley, A.D. A Duty to Rescue: Some Thoughts on Criminal Liability. 69 *Va. L. Rev.* 1273-1300 (1983). See also §2.1122.

[4] Lee v. State of Alaska & Johnson, 490 P. 2d 1206 (Alaska 1971). Duty was owed by state trooper; therefore, Alaska Good Samaritan law not applicable. Hovermale v. Berkeley Springs Moose Lodge, 271 S.E. 2d 335 (W. Va. 1980). Good Samaritan statute was designed to encourage those persons owing no duty to render aid in emergency circumstances and was not intended to relieve one of liability for breach of preexisting duty. Fraternal organization failed to comply with its ordinary duty of care to render aid to member after it knew or had reason to know that member was ill or injured.

[5] Many states require motorists coming upon an accident to stop and render aid; several states have a similar law regarding watercraft accidents.

[6] Minn. Stat. Ann. §604.05 was amended in 1983 to include this provision: Subdivision 1. Duty to assist. Any person at the scene of an emergency who knows that another person is exposed to or has suffered grave physical harm shall, to the extent that he can do so without danger or peril to himself or others, give reasonable assistance to the exposed person. Reasonable assistance may include obtaining or attempting to obtain aid from law enforcement or medical personnel. Any person who violates this section is guilty of a petty misdemeanor. This duty to render assistance should be distinguished from the duty which arises because of the relationship of parties, the duty which is an element of negligence. For further discussion of Minnesota statute, see Theisen, Dave. The Duty to Rescue and the Good Samaritan Statute. 8 *Hamline Law Review* 231-253 (1985). See also, §2.212 Nonfeasance and §2.1122 Rescue doctrine. Note: some credit Vermont with being the first state to impose a duty on the general citizen with its 1967 "Duty to Aid the Endangered

upon a scene of emergency a duty to render assistance. Because of the proliferation of lawsuits, even against those who render aid "from the goodness of their heart," and the societal attitude of not wanting to "get involved," many individuals refuse to render aid. The legislative response to encourage the voluntary rendering of aid has been to enact "Good Samaritan" statutes to provide either full liability immunity or limited liability. All states and the District of Columbia have some type of statute. The state legislation is cited in Table 17.1.

There are 39 states and the District of Columbia which have a "Good Samaritan" statute which is applicable to "anyone," while 33 states have statutes which are directed toward one or more health care pesonnel (physicians, dentists, nurses, EMTs, etc.). Nine states have a statute specific to rendering aid for injuries involving watercraft. Those persons who hold a valid certification or have received training in CPR or first aid have limited liability in 12 states. Twelve states give protection to persons rendering aid to victims who are choking. The nature of these statutes is discussed in the following subsections. One should not overlook the fact that in some states employees may have limited immunity under the State Tort Claims Acts, which could encompass rendering emergency care. The following discussion does not include related areas of hospital and community emergency services, rendering aid at vehicle accidents, or the various aspects of liability of health care providers/personnel. Liability as related to intoxication and drug abuse is in §§1.221 and 1.232, respectively.

Act." See State v. Joyce, 139 Vt. 638, 433 A. 2d 271 (1981) which holds statute does not create duty to intervene in a fight.

Table 17.1 Emergency Care Statutes Limiting Liability

State[1]	"Good Samaritan" All Citizens	CPR/1st Aid	Watercraft "Good Samaritan"	Food Service Choking	Specific Situations or Activities	Health Care Personnel "Good Samaritan"[2]
AL						Doctors, dentists, nurses, rescue squad
AK	X					Physicians, nurses
AZ	X				Amateur athletic events, health care providers	
AR	X			X	School grounds, normal school hours Athletic event—physicians insect sting	
CA	X	X	X	X	Field trips—1st aid and snake bite kits, medical services Athletic event—physicians, medical services Lifeguards Search and rescue-training Child health care training	Physicians, nurses
CO						Physicians, volunteer/rescue unit
CT		X				Physicians, dentists, nurses, LPN, EMT
DE	X				Nonprofit sports	EMT, nurses
D.C.	X					EMT
FL	X			X	School health services Athletic team physicians	Physicians
GA	X		X	X	Public school or nonprofit org. requesting service	Physicians (case law)
HI	X		X			
ID	X				Fitness center CPR	EMT
IL		X		X	Employer/employee	Physical therapists, physicians
IN	X	X		X		Paramedic or EMT
IA	X					EMT

State[1]	"Good Samaritan" All Citizens	CPR/1st Aid	Watercraft "Good Samaritan"	Food Service Choking	Specific Situations or Activities	Health Care Personnel "Good Samaritan"[2]
KS		X			Competitive sports health care providers	"Providers" — physicians, dentists, P.T., optometrists, nurses, podiatrist
KY		X				
LA	X					EMT, physicians
ME	X				School program/teacher	
MD	X		X	X	Charitable organizations—physicians, volunteers / Racquet sports / Ski patrol	Physicians, EMT
MA		X		X	Interscholastic football games / Ski patrol / Teachers / Lifeguards	EMT, health dist. employee, physicians, nurses
MI			X	X		EMT
MN	X					
MS	X		X			
MO		X				Physicians, nurses, LPN
MT	X					
NB	X					EMT
NV	X					Physicians, nurses, EMT
NH	X					EMT, physician, nurse
NJ	X					
NM	X					
NY	X			X	Athletic coaches	Physical therapist, EMT
NC	X				Teachers	
ND	X					Physicians, nurses
OH	X		X	X	School athletics/physicians, nurses volunteering services	EMT
OK	X					Licensed practitioner of healing arts

State[1]	"Good Samaritan" All Citizens	CPR/1st Aid	Watercraft "Good Samaritan"	Food Service Choking	Specific Situations or Activities	Health Care Personnel "Good Samaritan"[2]
OR		X			Teachers Insect stings Athletics/physicians	Physician, EMT government personnel
PA		X				Physicians
RI	X	X			Coaches	Physicians
SC	X		X	X		
SD	X		X			EMT and related, physicians, nurse, LPN
TN	X					
TX	X				Teachers (medication)	
UT	X					Physicians, nurses, life support personnel
VT	X					Emergency medical services volunteers
VA	X	X	X		Insect stings	
WA	X					
WV	X					Government emergency service worker
WI	X					
WY	X				Amateur rodeos	

[1]For statute citations, see appropriate state in Appendix.
[2]Not all inclusive, only selected statutes cited; emergency service of hospitals and communities and ambulance services not included; primarily physicians and nurses included, but not whole spectrum of health care personnel.

§ 17.11 "Anyone" Good Samaritan statutes

While a few states[7] enacted statutes prior to the 1960s, it was the decade of the '60s that saw the most legislative activity related to protection of those citizens rendering aid to injured persons at an accident or emergency situation.[8] Another nine states[9] enacted laws in the 1970s and a few since 1980.[10] Most laws have been amended one or more times since initial enactment. It should be noted that the initial law often did not include "anyone," but was limited to physicians and other licensed medical professionals.

Most of the laws are very similar in phraseology and content; but, as with all legislation, each state has its own peculiarities and one should check the law of the appropriate state. This law from Indiana is illustrative:

> Any person, who in good faith gratuitously renders emergency care at the scene of an accident or emergency care to the victim thereof, shall not be liable for any civil damages for any personal injury as a result of any act or omission by such person in rendering the emergency care or as a result of any act or failure to act to provide or arrange for further medical treatment or care for the injured person, except acts or omissions amounting to gross negligence or willful or wanton misconduct. (Ind. Code Ann. §34-4-12-1)

The elements in Good Samaritan laws are each discussed in subsequent paragraphs; however, there are very few cases interpreting the statutes. In a number of states the Attorney General has issued opinions and these are cited in the various annotated state statutes. Since the statutes are not applicable for the most part to professionals with a duty to protect participants (see next paragraph), discussion has been limited in this subsection.

Who is the protected class of persons? The primary purpose of the "anyone" Good Samaritan laws is to encourage those persons who do not have a relationship to the injured, but are merely "passing by," to stop and render aid. Few[11] of the statutes address even indirectly the issue of applicability if there is an antecedent duty to aid. In an Alaska case[12] it was held that the defendant did owe a duty to aid the injured and thus could not come under the Good Samaritan law. *Persons owing a duty because of a professional relationship should not presume they can use the Good Samaritan laws for limited liability or immunity.* Alabama in 1987 added public education employees to the list of protected persons, along with doctors, nurses, policemen, firemen, et al., but with the same provisions of gratuitously, good faith, et al., thus inferring, like the other professional groups, immunity is not given when in the line of duty, although the statute merely says "at the scene of an accident." However, if professionals are off-duty and owe no responsibility (duty) to the injured, then as a citizen they may be protected by the

---

[7] e.g., California, Delaware, Virginia.

[8] e.g., Alaska, Arkansas, D.C., Florida, Georgia, Hawaii, Indiana, Iowa, Maine, Montana, Nebraska, Nevada, New Hampshire, New Jersey, Ohio, South Carolina, South Dakota, Tennessee, Vermont, West Virginia, Wyoming.

[9] Arizona, Louisiana, Minnesota, North Carolina, Oklahoma, Texas, Washington, Wisconsin.

[10] e.g., Maryland, New York, North Dakota, Rhode Island, Utah.

[11] e.g., Alaska, Maine, North Carolina, Oklahoma, South Carolina, Vermont, West Virginia.

[12] Lee v. State of Alaska & Johnson, 490 P. 2d 1206 (Alaska 1971).

statute.[13] For special situations in which a person owing a duty has limited liability, see §17.16.

Almost all states include the phrase "in good faith" in their statutes, indicating the state of mind of the person rendering aid. The Washington statute defines "in good faith":

> .... a state of mind denoting honesty of purpose, integrity, and a reasonable opinion that the immediacy of the situation is such that the rendering of care should not be postponed until the injured person is hospitalized. (Wash. Rev. Code Ann. §4.24.310)

The designation of location, too, is set forth in nearly all of the state statutes. Some used the words "at the scene of an emergency"[14] or "at the scene of an accident,"[15] while others reference both terms "at the scene of an accident or emergency."[16] The inference is that one comes upon a person who needs emergency care, stops, and renders such care. What emergency care is usually is not specified in the statutes; however, Washington did define it, thusly:

> .... care, first aid, treatment, or assistance rendered to the injured person in need of immediate medical attention and includes providing or arranging for further medical treatment or care for the injured person. Except with respect to the injured person or persons being transported for further medical treatment or care, the immunity granted by (the statute) does not apply to the negligent operation of any motor vehicle. (Wash. Rev. Code Ann. §4.24.310)

This definition seems to apply generally, particularly the non-applicability to vehicle accidents.

Almost without exception, the statutes state as a condition of liability immunity that the aid must be rendered gratuitously. This term "gratuitously" may be used or the phrase "without remuneration or the expectation of remuneration." A few statutes may expressly specify both direct and indirect remuneration; however, whether or not specified, both direct and indirect remuneration are generally applied. The logic seems to be as related to persons covered that if one does receive compensation for performing a duty owed, which includes the protection of the victim (injured), then such persons are not performing the act gratuitously and cannot come under the immunity umbrella of the Good Samaritan statutes. A few statutes do except certain public service persons.

A sixth element of the statutes is the requisite standard of care. The standard of care seems to be variant to the standard required when one voluntarily assumes a duty (see §2.112), which is that where there is no duty inherent in the relationship

---

[13] Held v. Rocky Road, 34 Ohio App. 3d 35, 516 N.E. 2d 1272 (1986) off-duty fireman assisting at a fire held under Good Samaritan statute.

[14] e.g., Arizona, California, Louisiana, Maryland, Minnesota, Mississippi, Nevada, New Hampshire, Ohio, South Dakota, Texas, Utah, Washington.

[15] e.g., Delaware, Idaho, North Dakota, Tennessee, West Virginia.

[16] e.g., Arkansas, D.C., Georgia, Hawaii, Indiana, Iowa, Montana, Nebraska, New Jersey, New Mexico, South Carolina, Texas, Virginia, Wisconsin, Wyoming.

and one voluntarily performs, then there is a duty to perform with the same care as if the duty initially existed. Several states[17] do indicate that the care must be rendered in a reasonably prudent manner, with reasonable care, or as a reasonable and prudent person. Such standard, which is in accord with the voluntary assumption of a duty, would seem to preclude the immunity intended by most of the Good Samaritan statutes, which is immunity for ordinary negligence. There are some states[18] which specifically indicate that immunity is precluded for the gross negligence of the one rendering the aid, while other states[19] specifically preclude immunity for the willful, wanton, reckless, or intentional acts of the one rendering aid. And, a number of states[20] use both gross negligence and willful and wanton acts as precluding immunity.

A few statutes have some unique provisions, such as Florida,[21] which states that the aid is rendered without objection of the injured; Maine, which references religious beliefs as related to giving aid; and, Louisiana which states that the immunity is personal to the one rendering aid. North Dakota specifies that the statute does not relieve a person from liability for damages resulting from intoxication of the one rendering the emergency care.

§ 17.12   Watercraft Good Samaritan statutes

The duty of the operator of a vessel involved in a collision, accident or other casualty to render to other persons affected such assistance as may be practicable (which are similar to the motor vehicle statutes requiring a person to stop for an accident) should be distinguished from the act of rendering first aid and accorded immunity by the statutes (which are similar to the "Anybody Good Samaritan" statutes discussed in the preceding section). There is a large number of states which have either statutes or regulations relating to the duty to stop, but only nine states[22] which have watercraft "Good Samaritan" laws. Of course, it is true that persons rendering first aid in water accident situations could also come under the "Anybody Good Samaritan" statutes.

All of the statutes are very similar, such as this California law:

Any person who complies with subdivision (a) [duty to render aid] or who gratuitously and in good faith renders assistance at the scene of a vessel collision, accident, or other casualty without objection by any person assisted shall not be held liable for any act or omission in providing or arranging salvage, towage, medical treatment, or other assistance, where the assisting person has acted as an ordinary, reasonably prudent man would have acted under the same or similar circumstances. (Calif. Harbors & Nav. §656(b))

---

[17] e.g., Maryland, Arkansas, Mississippi.
[18] e.g., Arizona, D.C., Idaho, Nevada, New Mexico, Tennessee, Utah, Vermont.
[19] e.g., Iowa, Minnesota, Ohio, South Dakota, Texas.
[20] e.g., Alaska, Delaware, Hawaii, Indiana, Louisiana, Maine, Montana, North Carolina, North Dakota, South Carolina, Washington, Wyoming.
[21] Botte v. Pomeroy, 438 So. 2d 544 (Fla. App. 1983) immunity negated when certain "aid" given over objection of injured.
[22] California, Georgia, Hawaii, Maryland, Michigan, Mississippi, Ohio, South Carolina, Virginia.

Ohio has an exception clause, similar to most "Anybody Good Samaritan" statutes —
"...except that such person shall be liable for willful or wanton misconduct in rendering
assistance" — and another clause — "Nothing in this section shall preclude recovery
from any tortfeasor causing a collision, accident, or other casualty, of damages caused or
aggravated by the rendering of assistance." This latter also is true for "Anybody Good
Samaritan" situations, although not specified in most of the statutes. Maryland
references the exception of most "Anybody Good Samaritan" statutes, "is not liable...
if the act or omission does not amount to gross negligence." The phrase, "in the
exercise of reasonable care," is used in the Mississippi law.

§ 17.13   Rendering aid to victims choking

Many sport establishments and some park and recreation operations have food
service operations. In the late 1970s particularly, quite a number of states passed
statutes or promulgated regulations requiring the posting of instructions on rendering
aid to patrons who were choking. A dozen states[23] accompanied this requirement with
statutes providing immunity for those who did render aid to persons who were choking.

The basic provisions of the statutes are similar to this Illinois statute:

> Except as provided by law, no person shall be obligated to remove, assist in
> removing, or attempt to remove, food from another person's throat, nor shall
> any person who in good faith removes or attempts to remove such food in an
> emergency occurring at a food-service establishment be liable for any civil
> damages as a result of any acts or omissions by such persons in rendering such
> emergency assistance. (Ill. Rev. Stat. 56½ §605)

There are slight variations in a number of states, such as: in Arkansas and Ohio the aid
must be rendered in accordance with the instructions supplied by the State; in Florida
and Michigan the statute provides immunity only to the management and employees,
not to "any person"; in Maryland, Michigan and New York, immunity is precluded
when there is gross negligence, but in Rhode Island the statute just states no liability for
"negligently rendering aid"; in New York the wording "nonnegligently" appears and in
Florida the phrase "acts as an ordinary reasonably prudent man"; and, in Indiana the
common element in "Anybody Good Samaritan" statutes of "in good faith gratuitously" is used, while in New York it states "without expectation of monetary
compensation."

§ 17.14   Training in first aid/CPR

To encourage individuals who may have taken first aid and/or cardiopulmonary
resuscitation training to use their training, particularly in the 1970s, a number of states
(see Table 17.1) enacted statutes limiting the liability of such trained persons. Five

---

[23] Arkansas, California, Florida, Georgia, Illinois, Indiana, Maryland, Massachusetts, Michigan,
New York, Ohio, and Rhode Island.

states[24] passed statutes specific to CPR, while three[25] also referenced first aid; three[26] cited first aid training only, but in a subsequent legal opinion it was held that the term first aid also included CPR. Most of the statutes state that the training must be in accord with standards promulgated by either the American Heart Association or the American National Red Cross. As with the "anybody" Good Samaritan statutes, the emergency aid must be rendered gratuitously and the immunity does not apply to acts of gross negligence or willful/wanton negligence.

The Pennsylvania law states that the holder of a current certificate "must be performing techniques and employing procedures consistent with the nature and level of the training for which the certificate has been issued." The Pennsylvania law also includes within the exemption from civil liability the holders of advanced life saving. The Connecticut law makes specific reference to teachers or other school personnel, a member of a ski patrol, a lifeguard, and a conservation officer (see subsequent §17.21). Oregon defines "medically trained person" as meaning: a person who has completed successfully, within three years prior to the date on which emergency medical assistance is rendered by the person, a course sponsored by the American Red Cross and is qualified to render emergency first aid and who shows proof of the completion of such first aid training. Oregon, also, provides special limited liability to government personnel (see subsequent §17.15). Kansas, similar to Oregon, defined "health care provider" as a person who holds a valid certificate for the successful completion of a course in first aid offered by the American Red Cross or the American Heart Association. As for the Missouri statute passed in 1973, the attorney general issued an opinion that it violated the Missouri constitution and therefore was void; however, in 1986 the legislature repealed the 1973 law, but re-enacted essentially the same law, only adding the words "without compensation."

A couple states,[27] in order to encourage individual certified instructors and organizations to offer CPR and first aid training, provide for immunity when offering training courses.

§ 17.15   Health care personnel

Approximately two-thirds of the states have statutes which provide limited liability for health care personnel (see Table 17.1).[28] In only two states is this the only statute providing for immunity to those rendering emergency care; all other states have one or more statutes related to the categories of persons described in the preceding sections, §17.11-14. The focus of these statutes is primarily on physicians and nurses and/or EMTs, the latter particularly in relation to emergency rescue squads. The statutes do not cover physicians or nurses in malpractice, only when rendering aid at the scene of an accident or emergency to encourage such medical personnel to stop and give aid.[29] There are the same restrictions as for the "anybody" Good Samaritan statutes —

[24] California, Illinois, Indiana, Massachusetts, Rhode Island.

[25] Connecticut, Kentucky, Pennsylvania.

[26] Kansas, Missouri, Oregon.

[27] e.g., California, Illinois.

[28] A few of the "Anybody Good Samaritan" statutes specifically exclude health care personnel, while a few also have a clause pointing up inclusion.

[29] Stiepel, Henry R. Good Samaritans and Hospital Emergencies. 54 *So. Calif. L. Rv.* 417-445 (1981).

without remuneration or expectation of remuneration (gratuitously) and without gross negligence or willful and wanton misconduct. The emergency medical technicians are covered essentially when following the orders of a physician, and also in certain situations relating to consent by the victim. Other personnel, such as physical therapists, dentists, rescue squads, ambulance personnel, paramedics, et al., may also be covered in the statutes. Each state has its own variations!

A few of the statutes have provisions which are particularly germane to physical education and athletics or recreation and parks (see also next subsection). Missouri provides:

> Any physician or surgeon, registered professional nurse or licensed practical nurse licensed to practice....

> In good faith render emergency care or assistance, without compensation, to any minor involved in an accident, or in competitive sports, or other emergency at the scene of an accident, without first obtaining the consent of the parent or guardian of the minor, and shall not be liable for any civil damages other than damages occasioned by gross negligence or by willful or wanton acts or omissions by such person in rendering the emergency care. (Mo. Rev. Stat. §537.037)

Kansas, also, makes similar provision for "health care providers" rendering aid to those injured in competitive sports. Connecticut gives immunity from liability for emergency medical assistance, first aid or medication by injection to teachers and other school personnel when on the school grounds, in the school building, or at a school function, to a member of a ski patrol, to a lifeguard, and to a conservation officer who has completed a course in first aid. Maryland also covers ski patrol personnel. And, in Oregon certain government personnel are given some liability protection.

§ 17.16   Limited liability for specific situations/activities

A few states provide limited liability for individuals rendering first aid or CPR in certain situations or activities. (See Table 17.1.) In Connecticut the statute specifically states that teachers are not required to render first aid. In Massachusetts exemption from civil liability is given to teachers, principals, and nurses who "in good faith, renders emergency first aid or transporation... a public school building or on the grounds thereof...nor...liable to a hospital for its expenses...causes the admission of...injured or incapacitated student...." However, the Maine law states that "any nonlicensed agent or employee of a school or school adminstrative unit who renders first aid, emergency treatment or rescue assistance to a student during a school program may not be held liable for injuries...or for the death....This subsection does not apply to injuries or death caused willfully, wantonly, or recklessly or by gross negligence on the part of the agent or employee." Under the statutory section how a school may spend its money, in an Attorney General's Opinion, Arizona states that school districts are responsible for any treatments necessary to render first aid for accidents or sudden illnesses occurring on school property.

Increasingly states are giving immunity to teachers related to drugs. For example, Rhode Island provides immunity from civil liability for reporting, when there is reasonable cause to suspect the abuse of a controlled substance or alcohol or is under the influence of a dangerous drug or alcohol or has in his or her possession a controlled substance or alcohol. And, Texas grants immunity, except for gross negligence, in the administering of medications to students under the policies set forth by the school. A few states[30] provide immunity when administering drugs for insect stings.

Whereas the foregoing is related to schools and teachers in general, a number of states do have statutes specific to athletics (see also preceding subsection). The most common is that statute which endeavors to encourage volunteer physicians by giving immunity from liability. For example, Arkansas states that:

> No physician or surgeon who in good faith and without compensation renders voluntary emergency medical assistance to a participant in a school athletic event or contest at the site thereof, or during transportation to a health care facility, for an injury suffered in the course of the event or contest, shall be liable for any civil damages as a result of any acts or omissions by the physician or surgeon in rendering the emergency medical care. The immunity granted by this paragraph shall not apply in the event of an act or omission constituting gross negligence.

Florida's law is very similar in reference to a person acting in the capacity of a volunteer team physician. The Ohio law covers registered nurses as well as physicians, and the immunity is general except for willful or wanton misconduct. The physician is covered whether at the event and renders aid or whether a team physician under Oregon law. Arizona and Kansas give immunity to "health care providers," except when there is gross negligence. California also has a physician Good Samaritan law. There are some more encompassing immunities for nonprofit sports (Delaware) and charitable eorganizations as related to physicians and volunteers (Maryland); and, Georgia protects the sponsoring organization (public school, nonprofit organization) which requests, sponsors or participates in rendering emergency services, including acts of omission.

Rescue and search as used in this section refers to outdoor peril rescue and search operations and should be distinguished from emergency rescue/ambulance squads (see §17.15). A Good Samaritan-type statute provides immunity from civil damages in California[31], thusly:

> No person who is summoned by a county sheriff, city police department, fire department, park ranger, or other local agency to voluntarily assist in a search and rescue operation, who possesses first aid training equivalent to the Red Cross advanced first aid and emergency care training standards, and who in good faith renders emergency services to a victim prior to or during the

---

[30] e.g., Arkansas, Oregon, Virginia; see also §1.232.

[31] Calif. Gov't. Code §50086; a number of states provide for disaster rescue, in contrast to search and rescue for outdoor recreationists.

evacuation or extrication of the victim, shall be liable for any civil damages as a result of any acts or omissions by such person in rendering such emergency services.

New Mexico has a Search and Rescue Act, which provides for a state-wide plan and for the training of personnel, but there is no reference to the nature of the training nor does it give immunity in rendering aid while on a rescue mission.

In both Maryland and Massachusetts there is a Good Samaritan ski patrol statute.

§ 17.2   Treatment of injuries

There are two aspects of treatment of injuries — the duty to provide emergency care and medical services and the nature of the treatment/care given to the participant. These are discussed in subsequent sections. The condition of participants to participate and conditioning of participants are in §17.3. The provision of medical care as related to professional player contracts, for the most part, are not included in this section.[32] See also §24.33 as related to emergency procedures as a part of risk management planning.

§ 17.21   Duty to provide emergency care and medical services

Emergency care and medical services must be distinguished. In an early case[33] the court held that the teacher had acted in a situation which was not an emergency and also rendered improper first aid. A ten-year-old child had an infected finger and the teacher immersed the finger in scalding water against his will for about 10 minutes, causing intense pain and 28 days of hospital treatment and permanent disfigurement of the hand. The court held that treatment of the infected finger, not being an emergency, was a matter for the parents. And, in a New Jersey case[34] it was held that there was no urgent need of medical attention before the boy reached home and his parents could make the decision. In this situation, at high school football practice, the plaintiff was injured, a shoulder knocked out of place. It was "snapped back in place" and the next day the physician said he could play in about two weeks. At that time he did practice and his shoulder came out of place again. When he got up, the shoulder snapped in place, but he was told to go in to change his clothes. Then another coach, who had snapped the shoulder in the first time, told plaintiff he would not be able to play football for the remainder of the year and put his arm in a sling. Then, the boy walked home; the boy was suffering pain, but was fully possessed of his faculties and walked unattended.

---

[32] For example, Rivers v. N.Y. Jets, 460 F. Supp. 1233 (1978) alleged club breached contract by wrongfully concealing from the player the true nature of his physical condition and injury; Robitaille v. Vancouver Hockey Club, Ltd., 19 B.C.L.R. 158, aff'd. 124 D.L.R. 3d 228 (1981) slight spinal injury, asks to see team doctors but is not seen, suffers a further injury of same kind 10 days later and again not examined by doctors, and then suffers permanent spinal cord injury two games later; Sielicki v. N.Y. Yankees, 388 S.E. 2d 25 (Fla. App. 1980) ulnar neuritis.

[33] Guerrieri v. Tyson, 147 Pa. Super. 239, 24 A. 2d 468 (1942).

[34] Duda v. Gaines, 12 N.J. Super. 326, 79 A. 2d 695 (1951).

§ 17.211   Statutory requirements[35]

The duty to provide emergency care may be inferred by statute, such as providing immunity (see §17.16) or requiring an individual to hold a first aid/CPR certificate or a first aid kit to be carried. The duty of teachers, including substitute teachers, teacher aides, student teachers or any other public school employee, to give emergency health care when reasonably apparent circumstances indicate that any delay would seriously worsen the condition or endanger the life is set forth by North Carolina. Arkansas requires that every public elementary and secondary school in the State shall have in its employ at least one person who is certified by the American Red Cross or approved by the State Department of Education as qualified to administer emergency first aid, and such person shall be on the school ground during normal school hours. As part of the school health services program in Florida, a school is required to "meet emergency health needs." This term is defined as on-site management and aid for illness or injury pending student return to classroom or release to parent, guardian, designated friend, or designated health care provider. The Florida Act also provides that "in the absence of negligence, no person shall be liable for any injury caused by an act or omission in the administration of school health services." A teacher within 90 days after receiving an initial teaching certificate in the State of Oregon shall obtain a recognized first aid card, unless unable to do so by virtue of a physical handicap. By 1985 law, California "encourages" a person who provides child health care to have CPR and pediatric first aid.

In addition, California specifically authorizes medical and hospital services for athletic programs, including accident insurance. Both Rhode Island and New York require coaches to hold first aid certificates; Ohio also requires volunteer coaches in order to be certified to have first aid, but a certificate is not specified. (See §17.3 for more on sports medicine.) A number of states[36] provide specifically for coverage of medical costs, usually through accident insurance, for athletics.

In California there also are first aid requirements for field trips and excursions. The law requires that a first aid kit be taken on field trips and that the kit include medically accepted snakebite remedies when the trip is conducted into an area known to be infested by poisonous snakes. For trips into such snake-infested areas, the law further requires that the group be accompanied by a teacher, employee, or agent of the school who has completed a course in first aid, certified by the American Red Cross, which emphasizes the treatment of snakebites. The State also provides for medical or hospital service, including accident insurance, for excursions and field trips.

Several states have statutes specific to the sport activity. For example, California requires lifeguards at public swimming pools and beach and ocean swimming areas to be trained to administer first aid, including cardiopulmonary resuscitation. Massachusetts similarly requires persons appointed permanent or temporary lifeguards to be

---

[35] For statute citations, see respective state in Appendix.

[36] e.g., California, Missouri, Mississippi.

trained in first aid and CPR. Racquet sports facilities personnel in Maryland must be certified to administer CPR. The law requires that "at all times during business hours, each privately owned and commercially operated indoor racket sports facility shall have on the premises" such personnel. Illinois mandates that a physical fitness center shall have available on the premises at all times at least one person who holds a valid CPR certificate, and that such person is not liable in rendering assistance unless willful or wanton misconduct. State regulatory bodies, such as the New York Athletic Commission, may require provision of services. An oxygen tank and stretcher are required at the facility where boxing matches are held. Provision of such equipment and its state of working condition was at issue in *Classen v. Izquierdo,* 137 Misc. 2d 489, 520 N.Y.S. 2d 999 (1987).

It should be noted that except in the few states where limited liability (immunity) is provided to those who hold a certificate, *the fact that an individual holds a certificate of first aid or CPR does not reduce the liability. An individual still must render the first aid/ CPR with ordinary care.*

There has been concern regarding the costs of emergency response, and some agencies have established regulations regarding such costs when they issue permits for use of natural environments. California, however, enacted in 1985 its Costs of Emergency Response law. The statute defines costs as including "reasonable costs incurred by a public agency," including the cost of providing police, firefighting, rescue, and emergency medical services at the scene of the incident, but only those costs directly arising because of the response. Included in the statute are negligent operation of motor vehicle, boat or vessel, or civil aircraft and the influence of alcoholic beverage or drug or the intentional wrongful conduct; also, incidents where influence of alcoholic beverage or drug creates inability to operate such modes of transportation. The limit of liability is placed at $500.

§ 17.212   Common law (case precedents)

The duty to render emergency care arises out of the relationship of the injured and the one in charge, whether it be the teacher, coach, recreation leader, park ranger, camp counselor, et al., wherein there is a duty to provide an environment which is safe and in which there is no unreasonable risk of injury or enhancement of injury. (See §2.1 for discussion of duty owed and §2.2 for standard of care in terms of elements of negligence.) There are not many cases which specifically set forth the duty to render emergency care; however, there are more which relate to the standard of care for the treatment of injuries, which are described in a subsequent section, §17.22.

Utilizing some case law in other states and the Restatement of Torts, the Texas court in a 1984 case[37] discussed the duty to render first aid. In this situation a two-year-old boy was at a day care center. The children were outdoors in free play and the youngster also was playing. Then as the children began lining up to come inside, one of the employees noticed him with his head on a piece of playground equipment, feet touching the ground

---

[37] Applebaum v. Nemon, 678 S.W. 2d 533 (Tex. App. 1984).

and his hands near his head. She could not rouse him and called for assistance, after laying him down on the platform. An ambulance was summoned and mouth-to-mouth resuscitation applied until the ambulance arrived. He was brain dead at the time he first received treatment at the hospital. Several issues were set forth. While there is some early case law which holds that a person owes no duty to render aid to one for whose initial injury he is not liable (and in this situation there was no evidence that any injury had occurred on the playground), the Restatement and other case law hold that when certain relationships are created, there is often both an implied agreement and a duty to render reasonable assistance to a person within that setting who becomes imperiled. This includes a passenger on a common carrier, a possessor of land to the public who enter upon such land, a school, et al. Sometimes state regulations will give direction regarding such duty. The standard of duty generally requires (1) to give first aid when needed, (2) to call the physician named by a child's parent, if a minor, in the case of critical injury or illness, and (3) to take the child to the nearest emergency room when necessary. An individual is not an insurer of the life of a person and is required only to take that action reasonable under the circumstances. Establishing without question that there is a duty to render aid, the next question addressed was whether employees should be given instruction in skills not commonly known and which must be acquired through training, such as CPR. The court suggested that there was no such duty, and that if such training were desirable, such requirement should be imposed by the legislature (see preceding section §17.211); however, this point of view does not seem to be predominant in most jurisdictions which have addressed the issue of duty to render aid. Related to this topic of training is the matter of the duty to prepare beforehand for emergencies. Again, the view of the Texas court does not seem to be the predominant view — the Texas opinion stated that the duty to render aid does not arise until after the emergency has occurred, and all that is required is that the aid be rendered reasonably, and that adequacy of preparation is irrelevant. (For case law supporting the contra-Texas view, see cases in this chapter particularly, and the concept of foreseeability, §2.23.)

In *Ogando v. Carquinez Grammar School Dist.*[38] it was implied that had a supervisor been nearby she would have rendered first aid. In this case a girl had run her arm through a glass pane in a door at school and the children could not find the person on duty. And, in a 1981 case[39] involving women's intercollegiate softball, the court held that the college had a duty to provide medical assistance. The coach had put ice on the eye, which had been hit by hard impact of the ball, but did not direct the player to the school's health center, which was just across the road, or to a physician. And, a Canadian case,[40] stated that a professional hockey club is under a duty to exercise reasonable care to ensure the safety, fitness and health of its players.

Certainly it is clear that swimming pool operators have a duty to rescue and resuscitate, that is, to give emergency care.[41] For further discussion, see §9.4 Lifeguarding in pools and §14.35 Lifeguarding in natural bodies of water.

[38] Ogando v. Carquinez Grammar School Dist., 24 Cal. App. 2d 567, 75 P. 2d 641 (1938).
[39] Stineman v. Fontbonne College, 664 F. 2d 1082 (1981); for further description, see §17.341.
[40] Robitaille v. Vancouver Hockey Club, Ltd., 19 B.C.L.R. 158, aff'd. 124 D.L.R. 3d 228 (1981).
[41] Sneed v. Lions Club of Murphy, 273 N.C. 98, 159 S.E. 2d 770 (1968).

In a New Mexico case[42] the U.S. Forest Service required as part of the conditions in a Special Use Permit that the permittee, Taos Ski Valley, agreed to provide emergency care services. Failure to maintain lifesaving equipment was held to be negligence in a 1988 case, *O'Keefe v. State of New York,* 104 A.D.2d 43, 481 N.Y.S.2d 920 aff'd. 530 N.Y.S.2d 911 (1988). A father and his two sons (16 and 9 years old) and the older son's girl friend went fishing at the marina at a state park. While walking on a boardwalk above one of the marina walls, the younger boy fell in. The father jumped in the water to attempt a rescue. After searching unsuccessfully for some form of equipment to pull his brother and father from the water, the older boy and his girl friend also entered the water to attempt a rescue. All three (father and two sons) drowned when they apparently were swept under by the cold, swift current. The girl friend was rescued by another fisherman. The court held that failure to provide lifesaving equipment was the proximate cause of the three deaths, and held the State liable. Further, the court said that there was a duty during off season to provide lifesaving equipment, since the State encouraged persons to come and fish there and it had knowledge of swift currents; the landowner (State) has duty to exercise reasonable care in the maintenance and control of parks to prevent injury to foreseeable users of its facilities. The drowning victims were not reckless, wanton or rash in attempting to rescue the 9-year-old who fell into the water, after their attempt to find lifesaving equipment failed. The victims were unaware of the swift current and did not assume risk of drowning. In an earlier case[43] in a situation which involved an accident on a State-owned bobsled run, the court held that

> ... the State was under a duty to exercise ordinary, reasonable care commensurate with the circumstances... largely responsible for enticing both spectators and contestants to this somewhat remote spot... exercised almost exclusive control over the run and its surroundings... owed something more... than the duty assumed by a volunteer.... State, having been put on notice of the hazardous and dangerous propensities of the bobsled run,... could not remain aloof and leave the task of succor to such Good Samaritan as happened by... duty... to furnish reasonable facilities for the care of the injured... do not think... to furnish an ambulance... nor... provide a doctor or a nurse... State discharged its full duty... when it provided stretchers, blankets and transportation to the nearest hospital.... Unreasonable delay in transporting... might well constitute a violation of this duty.

And, in a still earlier case[44] the court of West Virginia held that the school is without authority to pay for medical services beyond that of immediate first aid which is for the welfare of the student, where not to do so may result in serious delay in receiving appropriate emergency care.

A college football player sued several years after leaving the college for medical expenses, alleging that as part of his football scholarship, the college had agreed

[42] Taos Ski Valley v. Elliott, 83 N.M. 575, 494 P. 2d 1392 (1972), aff'd. 83 N.M. 763, 497 P. 2d 974 (1972); see also Tobey v. State, 454 So. 2d 144 (La. App. 1984) campground.

[43] Clark v. State, 195 Misc. 581, 89 N.Y.S. 2d 132 (1949), aff'd. 276 A.D. 10, 93 N.Y.S. 2d 28 (1949), aff'd. 302 N.Y. 795, 99 N.E. 2d 300 (1951).

[44] Jarrett v. Goodall, 168 S.E. 763 (W. Va. App. 1933).

verbally to provide him with all necessary medical treatment. When injured while playing, the institution did cover the medical expenses; however, this suit was for additional expenses incurred. Evidence indicated that the player had become dissatisfied with the treatment by the team physicians and had sought treatment elsewhere. Held for defendant; player failed to show that the physical infirmities for which medical bills were submitted had as their probable cause his prior football injury.[45] Medical care also was at issue in another 1987 football case.[46] The college player became ill at practice and was admitted to the on-campus infirmary and later transferred to a hospital where he died. Mother plaintiff alleged breach of contract against head football coach, team physician, and head trainer, as individuals, for failure to provide medical care, that is, they were negligent in treating player after he collapsed at football practice. The court held that while the institution and board members were protected under the Eleventh Amendment, that under Mississippi law a claim of action was stated against the three specified individuals.

In general, facility operators and those sponsoring mass gatherings must provide a reasonable response to life-threatening situations. In a situation involving a fraternal organization, the court said that the organization failed to comply with its ordinary duty of care to render aid to member after it knew or had reason to know that member was ill or injured.[47] The court held in a 1981 Florida case[48] that "when an invitee comes upon commercial premises of another and passes out cold on floor, whether through illness, injury or drunkenness, the owner or operator of premises cannot ignore the inert figure lying in a dangerous place and has an affirmative duty to take at least some minimal steps to safeguard the inert figure."

A question sometimes raised is that by training employees to render first aid services is that not creating a duty that would not otherwise be present. *The duty to render emergency care is either there or is not there, dependent upon the relationship between injured and employee (see §2.1), and does not depend upon the training of the personnel.* However, the competence of the person rendering the emergency care may be in issue in respect to how the emergency care was rendered (see next subsection §17.22). The training of personnel is a prudent administrative response to provide quality emergency care.

§ 17.22   Nature of the emergency care

What is negligent emergency care? The cases focus upon the competence of the person giving the emergency care, moving or transporting the injured person, the promptness with which care is given, the availability of equipment, and the appropriateness of the treatment. Usually there are several allegations of negligence, such as failure to provide person with prompt medical attention, to employ trained

45 Eberhart v. Morris Brown College, 181 Ga. App. 516, 352 S.E. 2d 832 (1987); see also Barile v. Univ. of Virginia, 2 Ohio App. 3d 233, 441 N.E. 2d 608 aff'd. 30 Ohio App. 3d 190, 507 N.E. 2d 448 (1986).

46 Sorey v. Kellett, 673 F. Supp. 817 (1987) Mississippi law applied.

47 Hovermale v. Berkeley Springs Moose Lodge, 271 S.E. 2d 335 (W. Va. 1980).

48 Personal Rep. of Estate of Starling v. Fisherman's Pier, 401 So. 2d 1136 (Fla. App. 1981); see also §1.221 Intoxication.

personnel and supervise them properly, to promulgate and enforce staff rules for procedures to be taken when a person is injured, et al.[49]

§ 17.221   Competence of personnel

Competence of personnel in this section should be distinguished from medical malpractice (see §17.3 relating to physicians); included only are those persons rendering the first aid/CPR. In a drowning accident, it was alleged that artificial respiration was ineffectively applied due to the lack of training.[50] The one rendering the aid may go beyond the qualifications one possesses, as was the case in *Clayton v. New Dreamland Roller Skating Rink*.[51] When taken to the first aid room, the injured person was attended by an officer of the rink (corporation), who attempted to set the injured's arm. This officer, when asked if he was a doctor, said he had been a prize fight manager and had experience in such matters. It was held that he acted in a capacity for which he did not have the skill. In *O'Brien v. Township H.S. Dist. 214*[52] a student attempted to treat another student's knee. The student was not under the personal supervision and control of the teacher. It was alleged that the school was negligent in having an incompetent and untrained student administer the treatment.

The appropriateness of the person in charge (scoutmaster) was at issue in an early California case.[53] The scoutmaster was physically crippled; however, the court held that where a scoutmaster of perfect physique could not have timely removed a boy from the path of an on-coming vehicle, the fact of physical disability of the scoutmaster was not negligence on the part of the Scout Council in providing competent supervision. Where the Scout Council and church sponsoring the troop provided leadership in the form of the assistant scoutmaster who was a fireman trained in first aid, the court found this to be competent leadership on the part of the Council and church and did not hold them liable.[54]

A volunteer camp director was injured while participating in a game of water basketball, which was being played rather roughly. Immediately after the incident, the injured informed the camp nurse that his eye hurt. She examined the eye and advised him to lie down and rest. The pain subsided and the nurse asked if he wished to see a doctor, but he said "no." The accident happened on June 21 and on August 6 plaintiff saw his doctor because of a burning sensation in his right eye and blurred vision. The doctor then diagnosed the problem as a detached retina. The plaintiff alleged that the defendant was negligent in its failure to take proper care of him and have available competent medical attention. Judgment for defendent was on basis that plaintiff assumed the risks and dangers inherent in this situation.[55]

---

[49] For example, Wimbish v. School Dist. of Penn Hills, 59 Pa. Cmwlth. 620, 430 A. 2d 710 (1981).

[50] DeSimone v. Philadelphia, 380 Pa. 137, 110 A. 2d 431 (1955).

[51] Clayton v. New Dreamland Roller Skating Rink, 14 N.J. Super. 390, 82 A. 2d 458 (1951).

[52] O'Brien v. Township H.S. Dist. 214, 29 Ill. Dec. 918, 73 Ill. App. 3d 618, 392 N.E. 2d 615 (1979), aff'd/

rev'd in part 83 Ill. 2d 462, 47 Ill. Dec. 702, 415 N.E. 2d 1015 (1980).

[53] Young v. Boy Scouts of America, 9 Cal. App. 2d 760, 51 P. 2d 191 (1935).

[54] Davis v. Shelton, 33 A.D. 2d 707, 304 N.Y.S. 2d 722 (1969), app. dism'd 26 N.Y. 2d 829, 309 N.Y.S. 2d 358, 257 N.E. 2d 902.

[55] Jeffords v. Atlanta Presbytery, Inc., 140 Ga. App. 456, 231 S.E. 2d 355 (1976).

§ 17.222 Moving the injured person

Part of the "art" of first aid is being able to ascertain whether or not a person injured should or should not be moved, and if so, the proper method of moving must be used so as not to aggravate the injury or even cause paralysis. In a California case,[56] it was alleged that further injury was sustained in moving the plaintiff, who had suffered a fractured leg in wrestling, to a sitting position in an auto in that a nerve was severed which permanently crippled his foot. At the college pool a young man went down and four student swimmers, three with previous lifesaving experience, were in the process of lifting decedent out of the water when the lifeguard joined them. One of the four rescuing persons said that there was some "panic" and each had a leg and arm, but no one held the head. In the haste to get him on the deck to begin artificial respiration, the decedent's head "slapped" against the side of the pool or deck. The probable cause of death was found to be the blow on the head received after being lifted out onto the tile or concrete deck.[57] When the young man was turned over for administration of artificial respiration, it was noticed that the ear and nose were bleeding.

Improper moving of a football player was at issue in a landmark case, *Welch v. Dunsmuir Joint Union High School Dist.*[58] After a football play, the plaintiff was lying on his back on the field and unable to get to his feet. The coach suspected that plaintiff might have a neck injury and had him take hold of his hands to see if there was any grip in them. Plaintiff was able to move his hands at that time. The plaintiff was moved by eight boys, four on each side but no one directed the moving. It appeared that after the moving off the field that plaintiff could not move his hands, fingers, and feet, giving reason to believe that the plaintiff sustained additional damage to the spinal cord after being tackled. The court held that there is liability for damages if the injuries suffered in an athletic event are aggravated by the player's being moved from the scene of the accident in a negligent manner.

§ 17.223 Immediacy of emergency care

Plaintiff sought to recover in a New Jersey case[59] on the alleged negligent medical attention given a broken arm sustained in leap-frog jumping over a gym horse. The instructor directed the 14-year-old boy to walk a short distance to the principal's office where he was given first aid and taken to the hospital. Court said that this action was better than waiting for a doctor to come to the school. In another case[60] an 11-year-old boy sustained a fracture and dislocated elbow. He was taken to the principal's office. The principal called the family physician and took him to the physician. Recovery was allowed, but not on the basis of inappropriate medical attention.

An eighth grader was injured; he sat on the sidelines for a couple of plays and then was sent to the first aid room where he lay down and was covered with a blanket. The

[56] Price v. Mount Diablo Unified School Dist., 177 Cal. App. 2d 312, 2 Cal. Rep. 23 (1960).
[57] Durham v. Commonwealth of Kentucky, 406 S.W. 2d 858 (Ky. App. 1966).
[58] Welch v. Dunsmuir Joint Union H.S. Dist. 326 P. 2d 633 (Cal. App. 1958).
[59] Sayers v. Ranger, 16 N.J. Super 22, 83 A. 2d 775 (1951).
[60] Briscoe v. School Dist., 32 Wash. 2d 353, 201 P. 2d 697 (1949).

accident happened at noon; at the end of the day the physical education instructor noted blood in the injured boy's urine and took him home. Five hours later his spleen and kidney had to be removed. The court held that no injury occurred due to the delayed medical attention.[61] Similarly, in a New York case,[62] it was found that the defendants did not unreasonably delay the administration of medical treatment. Plaintiff's son was accidently kicked during his gymnasium class. The accident occurred at 12:55 p.m. The youngster had pain and was dizzy, but did not lose consciousness. Within about 50 minutes he and a friend left the school for his private physician who sent him to a hospital, where he was admitted at 2:55 p.m., two hours after the accident. A neurosurgeon testified that x-rays did not reveal the skull fracture and clot which had been sustained. Further, the symptoms evidenced at school were "soft" symptoms and not crucial signs; the nurse had checked for pupillary changes and found none. In a 1985 Louisiana case,[63] there was delay in taking a child, who had broken her leg, to the hospital because the school authorities could not reach the parents. Swelling had taken place and the cast could not be put on for several days; however, it was held that the swelling could have manifested itself even if the girl had been transported immediately. The immediacy of attention also was in issue in two Michigan cases,[64] but both were not decided on the merits of the case, but came under governmental immunity.

The opposite result, that medical attention was delayed too long, was found in a high school football suitation.[65] A young man died of profound heat exhaustion with shock to an advanced degree. The high school football team began practice about 3:45 p.m., when near the end of the session, about 4:20 p.m., during wind sprints the deceased staggered and became faint. The coach removed him from the workout and sent him to the school bus. About 20 minutes later when the bus arrived at the school, deceased was assisted into the school, placed on a blanket on the floor, his clothing removed, and immediately given a shower with water at room temperature, then covered with a blanket, and was offered a drink of salt water, but was unable to drink. The mother was phoned about 6:45 p.m. and a physician arrived at 7:15 p.m. The diagnosis indicated heat stroke and the boy was taken to the hospital where a leading specialist examined him about 8:00 p.m. The court held that the coach's delay of medical aid for two hours after the symptoms appeared was too long, and in addition, they applied ill-chosen first aid. The court awarded the parents $40,000 against the school and coaches. The case was dismissed as to the principal, superintendent and supervisor of physical education.

Prompt care also was in issue in a 1987 Texas case.[66] During the day, while the students were left unsupervised, the child was pushed into a stack of chairs and sustained a head injury and developed cold sweat and was dazed and incoherent. The teacher did not send her to the nurse, but later an O.T. noticed her and did take her to the

[61] Pirkle v. Oakdale Union Grammar School Dist., 238 P. 2d 57, rev'd 40 Cal. 2d 207, 253 P. 2d 1 (1953).

[62] Peck v. Board of Education, Mount Vernon, 35 A.D. 2d 978, 317 N.Y.S. 2d 919 (1970), aff'd 30 N.Y. 2d 700, 283 N.E. 2d 618 (1972).

[63] Rollins v. Concordia Parish School Board, 465 So. 2d 213 (La. App. 1985).

[64] Cody v. Southfield-Lathrup School Dist., 25 Mich. App. 33, 181 N.W. 2d 81 (1970); Picard v. Greisinger, 2 Mich. App. 96, 138 N.W. 2d 508 (1965); see also more recent case in Pennsylvania, Wimbish v. School Dist. of Penn Hills, 59 Pa. Cmwlth. 620, 430 A. 2d 710 (1981).

[65] Mogabgab v. Orleans Parish School Bd., 239 S. 2d 456 (La. App. 1970).

[66] Hopkins v. Spring Indp. School Dist., 706 S.W. 2d 325, aff'd 736 S.W. 2d 617 (Tex. 1987).

nurse. No one contacted the mother. At the end of the school day, the child, who had cerebral palsy, was put on the school bus. On her way to the day care center, she suffered severe convulsions. The bus driver contacted a supervisor, requesting a school nurse at the next stop, but none was provided. The driver was told to take her on to the day care center where she did receive medical treatment. Two years later the child's mother brings suit against the school district, the bus supervisor, the principal, the school nurse, and the teacher. She alleged gross negligence in failing to provide adequate care which dramatically decreased child's life expectancy. All defendants were protected by State Tort Claims Act.

The immediacy of emergency care was in issue in several non-school situations. Plaintiff was one of a four-man bobsled team racing on a bobsled run owned and maintained by the State. He was injured when the sled failed to negotiate a curve, suffering several fractures of his left leg, a collapsed lung, bruises, contusions and profound shock. Plaintiff alleged that unreasonable delay in removing him from the scene of the accident and in transporting him to the hospital in an unheated open vehicle aggravated his condition of shock and caused a failure in the circulatory system bringing on the ensuing gangrene and resultant amputation. Following the accident, the State employees provided stretchers and blankets and transported plaintiff down the mountainside and, in a pickup truck with canvas top took him to the hospital eight miles away. A volunteer physician was at the scene from almost the time of the accident; however, the court said that the State was not required to furnish one on-site. The case was held for the State, saying that reason and common sense demand that the State do no more.[67]

The court also held for the defendants, a tour planner and seller, in a 1981 case.[68] Plaintiff alleged inadequate medical care; however, the facts revealed that she was attended to by a physician and two nurses immediately following her injury and that she was under constant medical attention until transported to hospital by local ambulance.

The immediacy of getting emergency transportation was at issue in a drowning case.[69] A 14-year-old son of a country club member was brought up by his 12-year-old brother and after yelling at a pool maintenance man, 18 years old, assisted in removing the brother from the pool and began to administer artificial respiration. About 45 minutes to an hour lapsed before an ambulance and fire truck arrived, and 20 minutes later a doctor arrived and pronounced the boy dead. In the interim, a golf pro from the adjoining golf shop and two deputy sheriffs took turns administering artificial respiration. While a private pool (country club), it was operated in a manner so as to bring it under the state statutes as a public pool. Such statutes required that the names and phone numbers of agencies to call in case of an emergency were to be posted — the names were, but not the phone numbers. The court held that every small delay is important when time is of the essence, as it is in a drowning situation. Delay in

[67] Clark v. State, 195 Misc. 581, 89 N.Y.S. 2d 132 (1949), aff'd 276 A.D. 10, 93 N.Y.S. 2d 28 (1949), aff'd 302 N.Y. 795, 99 N.E. 2d 300 (1951).

[68] Lavine v. General Mills, 519 F. Supp. 332 (1981).

[69] Lucas v. Hesperia Golf & Country Club, 255 Cal. App. 2d 241, 63 Cal. Rptr. 189 (1967); for immediacy of treatment, see also Corda v. Brook Valley Enterprise, Inc., 63 N.C. App. 653, 306 S.E. 2d 173 (1983); Johnson v. YMCA, 201 Mont. 36, 651 P. 2d 1245 (1982); Stein v. Lebowitz-Pine View Hotel, Inc., 111 A.D. 2d 572, 489 N.Y.S. 2d 635 (1985).

dispatching an ambulance after the "911" emergency number was called, as well as the delay in obtaining medical attention, was at issue in an Illinois case.[70] A sixth grade child had been injured during morning recess while playing kickball, when he collided head-on. One of the teacher's aides walked the boys from the playground to the principal's office. The principal's secretary phoned the plaintiff's father, who was at home, but had to phone the mother at work and left a message for the mother to call back, which she did in about 15 minutes. The mother instructed to take her son to the hospital where she would go directly. At this time, the "911" emergency number was called, but after one-half hour and the ambulance had not arrived, another call was made — still no action after 15 minutes, so request was made to be put through directly to the fire department. The ambulance arrived in two minutes, as it was parked just across the street in front of the hospital. The physician testifed that the delay of one hour in transporting allowed the hematoma atop plaintiff's brain to grow from the size of a walnut to the size of an orange when removed. The court held for plaintiff; both the employee responding to the "911" emergency call and the school employees were found to have acted willfully and wantonly in failing to obtain prompt attention, especially since the hospital was just across the street, and thus they lost their statutory immunity.

Key aspects are whether the lack of immediacy and availability if emergency care is the proximate cause in enhancing the seriousness of the injury and whether the defendant has a special relationship giving rise to a duty to provide the immediate care. In *Hanson v. Kynast*, 24 Ohio St. 3d 171, 494 N.E.2d 1091 (1986) aff'd. 38 Ohio App. 3d 58, 526 N.E. 2d 327 (1987) Ashland College was not held liable for failure to have an ambulance and medical personnel and for permitting an illegally parked car to block the playing field's entrance at a lacrosse game.

Two cases[71] dealt with the immediacy of treatment for persons with physical disabilities. (For description of cases, see subsequent §17.341.) In both instances, there was failure to obtain appropriate follow-up medical care.

§ 17.224   Appropriateness of the treatment

An eighth grade student was playing "crack-the-whip" on the playground when the whip cracked and she went flying through the air, landing on her left leg and thigh — the left hip was fractured with some displacement which required surgery. A complication known as avascular necrosis of the hip bone occurred; it usually is caused because the blood supply to the ball part of the hip is disrupted when a fracture is displaced or comminuted. With the bone deprived of blood, it becomes softened and gradually collapses, deforms and dies. A bone graft was attempted. Upon injury two of the teachers on the playground asked plaintiff if she was all right; she said "no," complaining of pain in her left leg. One of the teachers attempted to raise her from behind to a standing position, and when weight was placed on plaintiff's left leg, she felt a crumbling or tearing sensation in left hip with excruciating pain. The leg collapsed

---

[70] Barth by Barth v. Board of Education, 141 Ill. App. 3d 266, 95 Ill. Dec. 604, 490 N.E. 2d 77 (1986).
[71] Whitney v. City of Worcester, 373 Mass. 208, 366 N.E. 2d 1210 (1977); Stineman v. Fontbonne College, 664 F. 2d 1082 (1981).

and she fell to the asphalt surface of the playground. Two teachers each took hold of one arm, lifted plaintiff up and placed her in a chair during which time the child was crying. Another teacher, indicating she either was a nurse or had nursing experience, pulled the leg outward and when plaintiff screamed, pushed it back in. She then manipulated her leg and plaintiff experienced a terrible, sharp, grinding pain in her left hip. Thereon, plaintiff's mother was called and the girl was removed to the hospital by ambulance summoned by her mother. The doctor testified that in examination at the hospital there were two classic symptoms of a fracture.[72]

A broken hip also was involved in a much earlier case.[73] The roller skating rink patron fell and was taken to the first aid room where defendant falsely represented himself as a medical doctor. He stretched, pulled and rubbed the patron's leg and pounded her thigh, then informed patron that her injury was not serious. In this case there also was disturbance of the circulation, and a shortening of the leg took place. Plaintiff had three operations. Expert testimony indicated that patron should not have been moved from the spot where she fell until splints or a substitute had been applied to the fracture to prevent movement.

A former air force cadet sued the government for alleged negligence by the Air Force team physician who prescribed an anti-inflammatory drug so that he could play football with a hurt knee. He claims the drug caused damage to his bone marrow and developed other ills, but that it was only after being retired for disability five years later his personal physician discovered that the drug was the cause of the disability. Plaintiff also alleged that his informed consent had not been obtained prior to administering the drug. The court held that plaintiff had a cause of action.[74]

Other cases involved rescue operations by lifeguards (see §9.412) and adequacy of rescue equipment at pools (see §9.23).

§ 17.225   Bystanders

Is one liable to bystanders observing emergency care being rendered? Yes, according to the *Landreth* case.[75] A 14-month-old child fell into the swimming pool, which was a part of the day nursery which the child and her infant sister attended. The child was brought to an adjacent room; her sister witnessed the unsuccessful efforts to resuscitate her. Among the damages sought was an amount of dollars for sister's emotional injury. It was alleged that as a result of the emotional trama that the sister experienced hyperactivity, distractability, loss of weight, extreme nervousness and difficulty in sleeping. The plaintiffs were awarded $25,000. (See §2.4 for further discussion of emotional stress.)

Plaintiff's wife had been taken by ambulance for emergency treatment at the hospital. Plaintiff was on crutches, having recently had hip and knee surgery. He stood beside her bed awhile, but tired and took a wheelchair nearby; however, after an hour, an orderly

[72] Bernesak v. Catholic Bishop of Chicago, 87 Ill. App. 3d 681, 42 Ill. Dec. 672, 409 N.E. 2d 287 (1980).
[73] Thomas v. Studio Amusement, 50 Cal. App. 2d 538, 123 P. 2d 552 (1942).
[74] Fischer v. U.S., 451 F. Supp. 918 (1978).

[75] Landreth v. Reed, 570 S.W. 2d 486 (Tex. Civ. App. 1978); discussed in Boone, Billy. Torts — Bystander Recovery is Determined by a Pure Negligence Standard. 10 Texas Tech Law Review 1167-1180 (1979).

took the wheelchair (needed for another patient) and left him a physician's stool (12" to 14" high). Plaintiff would sit by his wife's bedside and occasionally pull himself up by the bed rail so they could talk better. In the course of some "unexpected movement," he lost his balance when his hand slipped off the rail. He fell over backward fracturing a vertebra. Court held no liability to invitee when the stool was not defective, nor was there a duty to warn about the open and obvious perils of the stool.[76]

§ 17.23   Consent for treatment (informed consent)

The doctrine of informed consent is a part of our society's concern about human rights and the right to self-determination. More than half a century ago (1914) in the case of *Schloendorff v. The Society of New York Hospital*,[77] Judge Cardoza stated that "Every human being of adult years and sound mind has a right to determine what should be done with his own body;....This is true except in cases of emergency where the patient is unconscious and it is necessary to operate before consent can be obtained." Failure to obtain consent has traditionally brought liability on the theory of battery, although there are those[78] who believe that the negligence theory of liability more accurately characterizes the tort when the wrong does not involve touching the patient.

There are three forms of consent which should be distinguished. First is the adult informed consent, which normally is required in all circumstances, except the emergency noted in the foregoing paragraph or in the case of mental disability or other incapacitation. Consent may be express or written or it may be implied by the actions of the individual. Normally a matter of physician and patient relationship, informed consent is a requirement as a matter of law in good medical practice. In 1988 the New Jersey court (*Largey v. Rothman,* 104 N.J. 415, 517 A.2d 413 (1986) rev'd/remanded 110 N.J. 204, 540 A.2d 504 (1988)) redefined the standard for informed consent. It set forth the "prudent patient" standard, focusing on what a physician should disclose to a reasonable patient in order for that patient to make an informed decision, rather than the more common "professional" standard, focusing on what information a reasonable doctor should impart to patient. The "prudent patient" standard emphasizes the patient's right to self-determination. The court traced and commented on the development of informed consent standards, giving rationale for the "prudent patient" standard and stating that California, Connecticut, Louisiana, Ohio, Pennsylvania, Rhode Island, South Dakota, Vermont, Washington, West Virginia, and Wisconsin also have adopted by case law the "prudent patient" standard, also known as "materiality of risk" standard. A medical consent may be withdrawn at any time before the act consented to is accomplished, and a fraudulent misrepresentation overcomes the presumption of a valid consent. (*Valcin v. Public Health Trust of Dade County,* 473

[76] Sutherland v. Saint Francis Hospital, Inc., 595 P. 2d 780 (Okla. 1979).

[77] Schloendorff v. Society of N.Y. Hospital, 149 A.D. 915, 133 N.Y.S. 1143 (1912), aff'd 211 N.Y. 125, 105 N.E. 92 (1914); see also Canterbury v. Spence, 464 F. 2d 772 (1972) laminectomy; Pauscher v. Iowa Methodist Medical Center, 408 N.W. 2d 355 (Iowa

1987) intravenous pyelogram diagnostic procedure; Strachan v. John F. Kennedy Memorial Hospital, 209 N.J. Super. 300, 507 A. 2d 718 (1986) organ transplant program.

[78] Heckert, Lynne. Informed Consent in Pennsylvania — The Need for a Negligence Standard. 28 Villanova Law Review 149-172, 1982-83.

So.2d 1297 (Fla. App. 1984). As to conditions regarding joint tortfeasors, see *Lincoln v. Gupta*, 142 Mich. App. 615, 370 N.W.2d 312 (Mich. App. 1985).

As for rendering of emergency care, if the injured is able to give consent, it must be obtained and this can be implied by the injured not objecting to the treatment. However, if the injured objects and there is not a life-threatening situation, then one must not continue with emergency treatment or a charge of assault and battery may be made against the one rendering the treatment. For example, in *Clayton v. New Dreamland Roller Skating Rink*,[79] the plaintiff's consent allegedly had not been obtained by the person who manipulated her fractured arm and thus suit was brought on an allegation (among others) of assault and battery. Assault and battery was not alleged in *Botte v. Pomeroy*, 438 So. 2d 544 (Fla. App. 1983), but action was brought stating that the immunity provided by the Florida "Good Samaritan" statute was negated because the first aid had been rendered over the objection of the injured. And the court so held, but criticized the way in which the statute was written. In this situation, it appeared that the injured person's "accident" was self-inflicted as a result of excessive use of alcohol and drugs. About 5 a.m. he had gone outside, fell down, and passed out. Later while lying on the ground, he yelled for help and awoke the "good samaritan," who got out of bed and came to his assistance. Apparently the injured told the "good samaritan" to call an ambulance, but not to move him because he had no feeling in his arms and legs or from the waist down. Ignoring this request, the "good samaritan" did move him and removed his pants, rendering the injured person a quadriplegic. Most Good Samaritan laws do not have this restrictive provision (see §17.1).

The second form of consent is that related to minors and the majority of states have statutes which set forth the provisions therefore in terms of parental consent,[80] life-threatening situations,[81] and circumstances under which a minor can give one's own consent.[82] As with adults, rendering of emergency care without proper consent can lead to an allegation of willful battery or willful and wanton misconduct, as was the situation in *Bernesak v. Catholic Bishop of Chicago*,[83] where the teachers endeavored to render aid when the girl had a fractured hip and was in excruciating pain as they attempted to manipulate her leg and hip and she cried out. Is there any time when force may be used to administer emergency treatment? Some states[84] do provide by statute such authorization, but usually under specified limitations. For example, the Alaska statute provides that

§11.81.430. Justification: Use of force, special relationships. (a) The use of force upon another person that would otherwise constitute an offense is justified under any of the following circumstances:

....

[79] Clayton v. New Dreamland Roller Skating Rink, 14 N.J. Super. 390, 82 A. 2d 458 (1951).

[80] For example, Arizona, Arkansas, Georgia.

[81] For example, Alabama, Florida, Georgia, Maryland, Massachusetts, Michigan, Mississippi, Missouri, Montana, North Carolina, Tennessee, Washington.

[82] For example, Alaska, Alabama, Georgia, Mary-land, Mississippi, Montana, New Jersey, Oklahoma; see also Schere, David G., and N. Dickon Reppucci. Adolescents' Capacities to Provide Voluntary Informed Consent. 12 (2) *Law and Human Behavior* 123-141 (1988).

[83] Bernesak v. Catholic Bishop of Chicago, 87 Ill. App. 3d 681, 42 Ill. Dec. 672, 409 N.E. 2d 287 (1980).

[84] For example, Alaska, Kentucky.

(5) A licensed physician, paramedic, or registered nurse; or a person acting under the direction of a licensed physician, paramedic, or registered nurse; or any person who renders emergency care at the scene of an emergency, may use reasonable and appropriate nondeadly force for the purpose of administering a recognized and lawful form of treatment which is reasonably adapted to promoting the physical or mental health of the patient if

(A)   the treatment is administered with the consent of the patient....

(B)   the treatment is administered in an emergency... no one competent to consent can be consulted... safeguard the welfare of the patient....

(C)   ... person upon whom force was used was an incompetent person....

It is important to obtain parental consent for emergency treatment prior to the need for such a form, inasmuch as usually it is not practical to obtain the consent in the time frame of an emergency. Ohio has enacted in its statutes the actual parental emergency medical authorization. The statute requires that all schools annually before October 1 distribute the form to parents. The form is in two parts — granting consent and refusal to consent. Michigan, as part of its children's camp licensing act requires a parent or guardian of a minor child to execute a written instrument investing the camp with authority to consent to emergency medical and surgical treatment of the child; and parent consents to routine, nonsurgical medical care. Kansas does provide by statute that any health care provider may render emergency care to any minor requiring such care as a result of having engaged in competitive sports without first obtaining the consent of the parent. (For further information on forms, see §24.8.)

The third form of consent is where research is being conducted. Because of the abuse of individuals in certain types of scientific research and the right of an individual to be informed, researchers using human subjects are required to obtain the signature of such subjects consenting to the research being done with them. Sometimes this is referred to as "Use of Human Subjects Form" and in universities and colleges there is usually a committee or board which reviews studies and the adequacy of the forms/consent. Subjects "at risk" have a right to know. As with the consent for emergency treatment, parents' signature are needed for minors. In a 1987 case,[85] a participant in a study involving simulated deep sea dives in a hyperbaric chamber sued, alleging misrepresentation and fraud in his signing an informed consent form. The court held that the plaintiff, an experienced diver educated in oceanographic technology, did not rely on any false information, nor was any information concealed.

For further discussion related to consent and disclosure of information, see §17.33 The Physician. Informed consent should not be confused with exculpatory agreements (contract), as it neither absolves defendant of any wrong-doing (negligence) nor waives any of plaintiff's rights. See introduction to Chapter 16 for distinguishing information. An exculpatory contract between a patient and doctor will be considered against public policy and invalid (1) if it concerns business of a type suitable for public regulation, (2)

---

[85] Whitlock v. Duke University, 637 F. Supp. 1463 (1986), aff'd 829 F. 2d 1340 (1987).

if party seeking exculpation is engaged in performing service of importance to public and holds oneself out as willing to perform service, (3) if party invoking exculpation possesses decisive advantage of bargaining strength and, in exercising superior bargaining power, confronts public with standardized adhesion contract of exculpation, and (4) if member of public, as result of transaction, is placed under control of party seeking exculpation subject to risk of carelessness by such person or agents.[86] (See also §16.1 Exculpatory agreements.)

§ 17.3   Condition of participants

This section deals with the physical condition of participants as they engage in on-going activity, whether it be in physical education class or sport competition. Physical condition in this context is a present status of condition at the time of engagement in activity, in contrast to physical conditioning, which is a process by which one attains better physical condition. Consideration of the present condition is one of the responsibilities of the person in charge, whether instructor or coach; the same responsibility adheres to the leadership in a private club or public recreation program (see §19.13). Conditioning, also, should be distinguished from rehabilitation. Both of these are further presented in §17.4. In addition to physical condition as related to activity involvement, this section includes subsections on athletic trainers and the physician. The last subsection concerns persons with disabilities, meaning more or less permanent disabilities, in contrast to physical condition. Some of the cases on specific sports (Chapters 6 and 7), as well as other activities, (e.g., §13.33) have pertinent cases to physical condition and conditioning or involving physicians; see also §17.45 Fitness testing. For the law as related to drugs, see §1.232 and §17.33. Further, in the latter years of the decade of the '80s, AIDS (Acquired Immune Deficiency Syndrome) took its place with other life-threatening conditions. Both case law and legislation are unsettled.[87]

§ 17.31   Participation in class activities or sport competition

In one situation[88] a 17-year-old high school junior was injured when performing the exercise, "jumping the back." She alleged that she had weak wrists and had told the teacher, but she was forced to do the exercise anyway, whereupon her wrists collapsed and she pitched forward, causing injury to herself. In a second case[89] another high school girl was performing an exercise known as "knee walk" when she noticed a dull ache and tiredness in her left knee. The next exercise, "inch worm," was performed and she felt a sharp pain in her left side, and collapsed sideways upon the floor. The pain

[86] Olson v. Molzen, 558 S.W. 2d 429 (Tenn. 1977) abortion; see also Apicella v. Valley Forge Military Academy & Junior College, 630 F. Supp. 20 (1985) Pennsylvania law applied; Emory Univ. v. Porubiansky, 282 S.E. 2d 903 (Ga. 1981).

[87] For some general background, see Dalton, Harlon, and Scott Burris, editors. Aids and the Law, A

Guide for the Public. Yale AIDS Law Project. New Haven: Yale University Press, 1987.

[88] Cherney v. Board of Educ. White Plains, 31 A.D. 2d 764, 297 N.Y.S. 2d 668 (1969).

[89] Ostroski v. Board of Educ. Coxsacki Athens Central School Dist., 31 A.D. 2d 571, 294 N.Y.S. 2d 871 (1968).

seemed to localize in the left knee. The court found no negligence in supervision and held that happening of an accident is not negligence.

In a New York case,[90] an 11-year-old girl had suffered two previous fractures of her right forearm in accidents unrelated to school activities, one year apart. Due to the second fracture she returned to school in the fall with her arm in a cast and was excused from physical education by her family physician. During the following term, the physician apparently gave permission for her to return to physical education. The mother told the instructor about the fractures and advised no "rough games." In playing "jump the stick" relay, the girl did not jump when the stick came toward her and she fell, breaking her arm again. Plaintiff alleged that the instructor did not exercise reasonable care to prevent injury and also that knowing the previous condition of the fractures, no undue risks should be taken. In a somewhat similar case,[91] a high school girl, when attempting to do a "roll over two" gymnastic exercise in her tumbling class was injured (skull fracture) due to improperly executing the exercise. In doing this exercise she had fallen many times and also had a bad knee that "went out" at times. This the instructor knew. The jury held this to be an improper exercise for the condition of the participant.

Other gymnastic exercise cases involved physicians. In one[92] the plaintiff alleged a physical disability because of a prior injury, at which time (quite some years before) the doctor had sent three notes to the teacher. Over the plaintiff's protests the teacher insisted that she do broad jumps as part of an exercise, resulting in injury. The court held that medical proof was required before recovery could be awarded. In another case[93] the school district required all students to earn a certain number of physical education credits unless they had a physician's excuse. The plaintiff, when a freshman, was excused the last half year for a back condition; during the sophomore year she was excused from sit-ups because of a back disability. These excuses were a part of her permanent record. In December of her junior year, plaintiff complained of back pain and her doctor asked for a list of exercises and the type of gymnastics plaintiff was required to perform at school. The request was given to the counselor at school, rather than directly to the physical education teacher. The request was made four times, the last about one week prior to the accident. No list was ever provided. The doctor testified in court that the plaintiff should not have been doing the exercise causing the accident because she was not coordinated enough to do it correctly, and had he known he would have recommended that she not participate. The court held that teachers are bound not only by what they know but also by what they might have known had they exercised ordinary diligence. Here the harm was held to be reasonably foreseeable.

Excuses from physical education also were at issue in a 1988 case, *Hopwood v. Elmwood Comm. H.S. Dist.,* 171 Ill. App. 3d 280, 121 Ill. Dec. 441, 525 N.E.2d 247 (1988). Plaintiff claimed she informed the physical education teacher about her previous knee injury, in addition to her doctor submitting a written excuse to plaintiff's former physical education teacher a year earlier. The doctor's excuse at the time precluded plaintiff from participating in physical education for two weeks, and thereafter allowed

[90] Luce v. Board of Educ., 2 A.D. 2d 502, 157 N.Y.S. 2d 123 (1956).

[91] Bellman v. San Francisco High School Dist., 11 Cal. 2d 576, 81 P. 2d 894 (1938).

[92] Lowe v. Board of Educ., 36 A.D. 2d 952, 321 N.Y.S. 2d 508 (1971).

[93] Summers v. Milwaukie Union H.S. Dist., 481 P. 2d 369 (Or. App. 1971).

such activity as plaintiff was able to tolerate. The teacher and principal both said they had not received the doctor's note, whereupon the plaintiff alleged administrative negligence because certain nonteaching personnel failed to properly forward the doctor's note. The physical education teacher requested plaintiff to provide a written excuse from her mother, which she did, and the plaintiff was not required to perform those exercises which plaintiff indicated caused her pain. On the day of injury, plaintiff did not indicate to the teacher that the activity (hoccer) caused her pain. Her knee did not hurt prior to her injury and apparently plaintiff had played hoccer earlier and did not think it would endanger her knee. The court held that the teacher's behavior was not willful and wanton misconduct, and under Illinois' teachers' immunity statute, the physical education teacher was not liable. The principal and the administrative task of recordkeeping fell within immunity conferred upon school personnel from claims for ordinary negligence.

In another school physical education situation, the class of approximately 40 students was doing various tumbling maneuvers, including the backward somersault. To familiarize the students with the exercise, another student performed the backward somersault while other students observed. The plaintiff had received no personal attention or instruction from the instructor prior to the accident. According to the plaintiff, the day before the injury, she went to the instructor's office after class and told the instructor that she was afraid to do the maneuver and that she did not know how to perform it. She said she'd done it improperly six or seven times as a child, but that the activity had given her headaches and bothered her back. She further indicated that she did not want to do the somersault because she was big and heavy (5'6" tall, 180 pounds). The instructor offered to help plaintiff after school, but this was not possible since the girl rode the bus. The instructor told plaintiff to see her the next day. There was no discussion concerning plaintiff's weight or whether she was strong enough to do the stunt. (See further discussion of case in §19.131.) On the second attempt to do the maneuver in class the next day, at the point where all of her body was suspended above the neck, plaintiff was unable to push her weight over with her arms; she heard her neck snap. Her neck injury was diagnosed as a subluxation. When conservative therapy failed, a surgeon successfully performed a posterior cervical fusion. The court held that the teacher was aware of dangers presented to the student because of the student's fear and obesity and that her actions amounted to willful and wanton misconduct within the Illinois statute relating to teachers.[94]

A high school boy had heart disease from the time of his birth. The school authorities had examined him and prescribed no activity. He was, however, allowed to engage in basketball scrimmage. Shortly thereafter he collapsed and died. It was known that outside of school he played basketball with teams not school-connected and in the summer played softball. The injury held for the school; the evidence showed that any form of exercise would have a tendency to hasten his death and that in no event could he have lived more than four to six years. The plaintiff failed to prove any fault of the defendant school.[95] A six-year-old boy was found unconscious beneath a horizontal

[94] Landers v. School Dist. No. 203, O'Fallon, 66 Ill. App. 3d 78, 22 Ill. Dec. 837, 383 N.E. 2d 645 (1978).

[95] Mancini v. Board of Educ., 260 A.D. 960, 23 N.Y.S. 2d 130 (1940).

ladder on a black-topped playground. He died three hours later. He had been subject to seizures and had been instructed not to climb on things. While his teacher knew of the seizures, his mother had asked that others not be told. The plaintiff alleges inadequate supervision for the condition. No recovery. The school is not an insurer of safety at play; the supervision law requires regulation of disorderly conduct only. There was no negligence proved. While there appears to be a higher degree of care required in selection of activities for students with limiting physical conditions in an instructional setting as seen in later illustrations, this same degree of specific individual attention does not appear to be required while the child is at play. Individuals at play must assume some responsibility and self-discipline for themselves.[96]

Aneurism of a cerebral artery, congenital in origin, was the cause of death in an early California case.[97] A 16-year-old boy was engaged in basketball free-play during physical education class when he was hit on the forehead with the ball. He left the game and sat on a bench. The instructor did not observe the accident and nothing was said about it. Later he was found unconscious in the dressing room and was taken to the hospital where he died the next day. Lack of proper supervision was alleged by the plaintiff; however, the instructor had no knowledge of the condition, the boy knew the dangers of the game, and the instructor was in the vicinity properly giving general supervision.

A heart condition was involved in a case concerning a 14-year-old boy assigned as stockroom monitor. Because of the physical strain caused from lifting heavy boxes, he suffered heart damage. The court held that the school was negligent in failing to notice the student frailty before assigning him to such a job.[98]

An unreported previous "black-out" was at issue in a swimming case.[99] A 14-year-old drowned while participating in the first session of the fall swimming class at school. He was at the shallow end of the pool with a group of non-swimmers who were directed to become acquainted with the water and to practice holding their breath. He was discovered unconscious lying on the pool floor. Evidence was presented that in the prior school year, while a junior high student, the deceased had suffered a lapse of consciousness during a gym class rope climbing exercise. Although the incident was known to both the boy and his parents, it was not reported to the high school before he entered the swimming class. This was held to be contributory negligence and incurred risk of swimming. In another swimming pool case,[100] plaintiff nearly drowned in a private swim club pool while on an outing with his school club. One of the issues was permitting a consulting physician to testify regarding a statement on plaintiff's medical record that plaintiff said he had eaten a large dinner before swimming. However, proximate cause was inability to swim.

[96] Rodrigues v. San Jose Unified School Dist., 157 Cal. App. 2d 842, 322 P. 2d 70 (1958); see also Braun v. Board of Education, 151 Ill. App. 3d 787, 104 Ill. Dec. 416, 502 N.E. 2d 1076 (1986) cert. denied 511 N.E. 2d 426, student manager with epilepsy "blacked out" while on ladder to change basketball scoreboard, failure to provide scaffold instead of ladder not proximate cause, coach believed epilepsy controlled.

[97] Kerby v. Elk Grove Union High School Dist., 1 Cal. App. 2d 246, 36 P. 2d 431 (1934).

[98] Feuerstein v. Board of Educ., 202 N.Y.S. 2d 524 (1960), aff'd 13 A.D. 2d 503, 214 N.Y.S. 2d 654 (1961).

[99] Stephens v. Shelbyville Central Schools, 162 Ind. App. 229, 318 N.E. 2d 590 (1974).

[100] Morrison v. Comm. Unit School Dist., Payson, 44 Ill. App. 3d 315, 3 Ill. Dec. 222, 358 N.E. 2d 389 (1976).

In another school case,[101] plaintiff sought to recover on wrongful death of son against the superintendent, principal, physical education instructors, and school nurse. The son was thrown to the floor by a classmate while both were participating in physical education class, suffering a head injury. After being seen by the nurse he returned to further participate in physical education. He thereafter became ill, but was directed to remain at school until his father could be contacted. He was taken to a local physician's office and several hours later died as a result of the injuries sustained at school.

Two cases[102] involved death from heat. The *Mogabgab* case, described in §17.223, and the *Lovitt* case both were football practice situations in which the players suffered profound heat exhaustion, and heat stroke and heat exhaustion, respectively. In each case a player died. To allow players to become so affected and not identify symptoms and remove appropriately with proper treatment was held to be negligence on the part of the coaches.

The jury entered a verdict of $1.25M for negligence on the part of the coach and principal in permitting a high school football player to play in a mismatched game in a fatigued condition, in a 1988 case, *Benitez v. N.Y.C. Board of Educ.*, 530 N.Y.S.2d 825 (1988). The injury occurred just before half time of the football game when plaintiff blocked an opponent. Plaintiff had played virtually the whole time, on both offense and defense, because there was no adequate substitute and he was one of the best athletes; thus, plaintiff was greatly fatigued at time of injury. The mismatch was really between the schools, rather than players. The year before the plaintiff's school had lost many games and asked to be moved back to the B Division because they felt they could not be competitive in the A Division and that it was "unsafe" for the players. There had been more injuries the preceding year playing in the A Division than when they were in the B Division. The court held that the school unreasonably enhanced or increased risk of injury to student by keeping him in the game in a fatigued condition, and that the student did not complain of being tired and was a voluntary participant did not defeat his claim on the basis of assumption of risk. The court, however, did apportion liability 30% against student and 70% against school board.

How soon an injured player can be active again is often at issue in competitive athletics. A 16-year-old football player had been injured 12 days previously. On returning to practice he aggravated the old injury and suffered a severe shoulder separation. The coach and school were sued on the basis that they knew of the previous injury, yet permitted the boy to work out with the team. The boy did not recover an award inasmuch as he voluntarily participated; the coach did not require or coerce participation. The boy thought he was ready to play and he did.[103] Coercion was involved and the school held liable in an earlier Washington case.[104]

In another football case,[105] plaintiff was paralyzed from below the chest due to

[101] Kersey v. Harbin, 531 S.W. 2d 76 (Mo. App. 1975), aff'd/rev'd in part 591 S.W. 2d 745 (Mo. App. 1979); see also Peck v. Board of Educ., Mt. Vernon, 35 A.D. 2d 978, 317 N.Y.S. 2d 919 (1970).

[102] Mogabgab v. Orleans Parish School Board, 239 So. 2d 456 (La. App. 1970); Lovitt v. Concord School District et al., 58 Mich. App. 593, 228 N.W. 2d 479 (1975).

[103] Hale v. Davies, 86 Ga. App. 126, 70 S.E. 2d 923 (1952).

[104] Morris v. Union High School Dist., 160 Wash. 121, 294 P. 998 (1931).

[105] Cramer v. Hoffman, 390 F. 2d 19 (1968).

cervical injuries which he sustained while making a tackle. Only a few days prior he had been released from the hospital where he had been confined with German measles. The plaintiff alleged that the physician discharged him in a weakened and ill condition and failed to notify the school authorities, he was improperly lifted and carried from the field, the ambulance driver was negligent, radiologist was negligent in taking and reading x-rays, and negligence was involved in his transfer to the second hospital. The court held no recovery against the University since the physician's negligence could not be imputed to it when the physician was an independent contractor and the injury had not been aggravated by the institution.

Plaintiff sustained injuries in a high school football game. He alleged negligence by the coach in directing plaintiff to participate although he had not participated in the minimum amount of practice sessions required by the State high school athletic association and in violation of doctor's orders. Coach held immune.[106] In a professional football situation, plaintiff player alleged that he was required to engage in contact football drills before he had fully recovered from off-season knee injury. Claim was barred by failure to comply with mandatory contract arbitration requirements.[107] And, in another high school football situation, a player died while playing football. He had a history of heart illness which was serious enough to preclude the playing of football. The student had been permitted to play without the required physical examination and without parental permission.[108]

While all of the foregoing cases related to school situations, the prior physical condition of a patron at a health salon was one of the issues in the *Shugar* case.[109] When slenderizing treatments began, plaintiff signed a written instrument, which in part said that she was not under any disability to prevent receiving such services, was not being attended by any physician for an ailment which would be aggravated by such treatments, and had not been informed by any physician not to take such treatments. Plaintiff alleged that defendants should have done more to assess her physical condition, while the defendants argued they had fulfilled their duties, particularly since there were no prior injuries related to this machine. (For further description of case, see §17.44.) In another health club setting, the plaintiff was intoxicated when he dived into shallow end of the pool.[110] (See §1.221 Intoxication.)

§ 17.32   Athletic trainers

A number[111] of states have enacted legislation registering or licensing athletic trainers. There are few cases involving trainers, although they may be sued along with coaches and other school personnel, as the trainer was in a Texas case.[112] In this

[106] Kain v. Rockridge Comm. Unit School Dist. #300, 117 Ill. App. 3d 681, 72 Ill. Dec. 813, 453 N.E. 2d 118 (1983). One should distinguish when defendant is immune from not being held negligent; when one is held immune, negligence has not been determined.

[107] Ellis v. Rocky Mountain Empire Sports, 602 P. 2d 895 (Colo. App. 1979).

[108] Monaco v. Raymond, 471 N.Y.S. 2d 225 (1984).

[109] Shugar v. Pat Walker Figure Perfection Salons, Int'l, 541 S.W. 2d 511 (Tex. Civ. App. 1976).

[110] Mullery v. Ro-Mill Constr. Corp., 76 A.D. 2d 802, 429 N.Y.S. 2d 200 (1980).

[111] For example, Massachusetts, Missouri, North Dakota, Tennessee.

[112] Garza v. Edinburg Consolidated Indp. School Dist., 576 S.W. 2d 916 (Tex. Civ. App. 1979); see also Greening v. School Dist. of Millard, 223 Neb. 729, 393

situation plaintiff was injured as a member of the high school freshman team. It alleged that the three football coaches and the trainer were negligent in their supervision, instruction, and coaching. Case was not decided on its merits, but was held that football was governmental function protected by governmental immunity. In another Texas case[113] three years earlier, the focus, again, was governmental immunity under the Texas Tort Claims Act; however, the situation is pertinent. Plaintiff alleged that, although the tape was available, the trainer failed to tape or tape properly his knee, and further that the coaching staff, management and trainers of the University refused to furnish and permit plaintiff to wear proper and correctly prescribed equipment, braces and supporting devices following a knee injury and because of such the knee was reinjured.

In a 1983 Utah case,[114] the question was whether tight taping of injured student's ankle by trainer, in conjunction with ice immersion treatments and failure to elevate ankle, contributed to student's injuries. Student was injured at a basketball practice scrimmage and treatment was turned over to student trainer for the College. Apparently because of the impropriety of the icing done by the player himself, he sustained frostbite and other ills, resulting in amputation of a gangrenous toe, removal of some tissue and muscle of the right foot, and osteomyelitis of the right foot. There was question as to whether the foot would have to be amputated. The court said that a trainer at college, by providing treatment for an injury to student that would have healed by itself if left alone, did not thereby become a guarantor of good results so as to hold the college strictly liable without fault. Was for jury to determine negligence; there was a cause of action.

§ 17.33   The physician[115]

Physicians are involved in physical examinations, on-site medical attention to injured athletes, and medical services subsequent to injury. There is no specific subsection on the legal responsibilities of nurses, especially nurses in camp or school, as no cases in point were identified. See the references in footnote for general legal aspects related to the nurse.

§ 17.331   Physical examinations

New York requires its school districts to test pupils for scoliosis. In *Bello v. Board of Education, Frankfort-Schuyler Central School Dist.*, 527 N.Y.S.2d 924 (1988),

N.W.2d 51 (1986) school physical therapy program, fractured leg.

[113] Lowe v. Texas Tech Univ., 530 S.W. 2d 337 (Tex. Civ. App. 1975), rev'd/remanded 540 S.W. 2d 297 (1976).

[114] Gillespie v. Southern Utah College, 669 P. 2d 861 (Utah 1983).

[115] King, Joseph H. The Duty and Standard of Care for Team Physicians. 18 *Houston Law Review* 657-705 (May 1981); Pozgar, George D. Legal Aspects of Health Care Administration, Rockville, Md.: Aspen Systems

Corp., 2nd ed. 1983, 265 pp. (non-lawyer oriented); George, James E. Law and Emergency Care. St. Louis: C.V. Mosby, 1980, 283 pp. Mancini, Marguerite R., and Alice T. Gale. Emergency Care and the Law. Rockville, Md.: Aspen Systems Corp., 1981, 255 pp. Special issue on emergency medicine and the law — Legal Aspects of Medical Practice, vol. 11, no. 12, December 1983 (published by the American College of Legal Medicine).

plaintiff sued for school's failure to report results of the test to student's parents for 14 months, alleging that as a result of the delay the student's condition was aggravated. The court held that under the law it was provided that the school in making such test would not have any liability which did not otherwise exist, and thus held no liability on the part of the school. A required test also was at issue in *Calandra v. State College Area School Dist.*, 99 Pa. Cmwlth 223, 512 A.2d 809 (1986). As a condition for participation in interscholastic sports (baseball), students were required to receive tetanus immunization. Plaintiff filed complaint in trespass alleging that student's religious beliefs were violated by such requirement. The court held that the school board's requirement did not place impermissible burden on student as participation in interscholastic sports did not rise to level of an important government benefit.

An almost universal practice is the pre-season physical examination given to athletes on all levels of competition. These may be given by family physicians, a crew of volunteer physicians, or compensated physician(s). The legal implications of giving or not giving a physical examination are not clear (see also §17.16). Two early New York cases[116] involving boxing deal with the issue. In the *Iacona* case, it was held that evidence was insufficient to establish that the board of education was liable for the death of a 13-year-old boy who died from meningitis shortly after boxing one or two rounds in a tournament in public school wherein the board conducted a community center. Each bout consisted of three two-minute rounds, with one and a half minute rest periods. The bouts were informal with the participants in street clothes and sneakers or shoes. One of the three plaintiff allegations was that the defendant failed to examine the boy physically before permitting him to engage in the boxing bout. The court held that the defendant is under no duty to examine physically every participant in an athletic activity, where the evidence clearly indicates that there were no signs of illness prior to the bout and the boy appeared to be normal and healthy, even to his own father, who saw him for several hours shortly before the accident.

The other boxing case involved professional boxing and the state law requiring physical examinations under certain circumstances, and the status of examining physicians. The fighter had been examined by a physician following each of two fights in which he had suffered a technical knockout, and both pronounced him in appropriate physical condition to fight again. The physician present at the third (this fight), knowing of the previous knockouts, indicated he had taken extra time in giving a thorough examination; his opinion was that the deceased was in "excellent condition" to fight. For this reason he felt that the boxer met his death as a result of injury sustained during the fight itself. The injury was caused by a devastating left hook to the head. Plaintiff's allegation was that the State knew or should have known that the boxer was not in proper physical condition to fight. The case was decided on the technical basis that the physicians were not employees of the State.

In a Canadian case[117] the doctor employed to treat hockey players for hockey injuries, after examining a mole on a player's upper arm at his request, failed to tell the player that

---

[116] Iacona v. Board of Education, N.Y.C. 285 A.D. 1168, 140 N.Y.S. 2d 539 (1955); Rosensweig v. State, 208 Misc. 1065, 146 N.Y.S. 2d 589 (1955), 5 A.D. 2d 293, 171 N.Y.S. 2d 912 (1958), rev'd on other grounds 5 N.Y. 2d 404, 158 N.E. 2d 229 (1959).

[117] Wilson v. Vancouver Hockey Club, 5 D.L.R. 4th 282 (1983).

he suspected the possibility of cancer and did not refer him immediately to a specialist for a biopsy. The court held that the club was not liable, since the physician was an independent contractor, and, also, the disability suffered by the player as a result of the cancerous mole was not a hockey injury.

In a 1980 Michigan case[118] the plaintiff was participating in wrestling in his physical education class. A physician had examined him in September and this accident occurred in February following. Plaintiff suffered a subluxation of two vertebrae which resulted in quadriplegia. The school was held immune from tort liability, but the determination of the physician's negligence was a matter for the court. The question was whether the physician was negligent in not finding a defect in plaintiff during the physical examination.

A college football player was killed in practice in another 1980s case.[119] The physician who gave the physical examination and the university medical director, among others, were sued; however, the suit was dismissed as to the physician and focused upon the functions of the medical director. The young man collapsed during football practice and was taken to the hospital where he died the next day of sickle cell crisis. The opinion focused, not on the merits of the case, but upon technicalities of jurisdiction and timeliness of filing.

One of the questions often asked is "what happens if a participant does not disclose certain ailments?" While this case is not one of sport or recreation, it does give some insight. The plaintiff was referred to the defendant physician, an orthopedic surgeon, by her family physician for treatment of a persistent pain in her wrist. The surgeon testified that he had asked her during the examination whether she had any allergies and her response was "no," and he thereupon prescribed a particular drug to which she was allergic. Upon admission to the hospital two weeks later, she listed numerous medications and contact substances to which she was allergic. The surgeon stated that had he known of this history of allergies he would not have prescribed the previous drug. The court held that failure to disclose information could constitute contributory negligence; defendant could not be found negligent on basis of assessment of patient's condition, which only later or in hindsight proved to be incorrect.[120]

The high school football team was informed that physical examinations would be available free of charge from a physician and that each would have to get transportation to the physician's office in a neighboring town. The examination was required before a person could participate. Three of the boys decided to ride together and on the return trip had an accident. None of the boys had any history of irresponsible driving behavior. The court held that the doctrine of respondeat superior would not be expanded to apply to the school whose student athletes negligently injured another while driving from doctor's office after having a required physical examination.[121]

A number[122] of states regulate professional boxing by either statutes or regulation, with most requiring physical examinations. There, also, is legislation authorizing

[118] Deaner v. Utica Comm. School Dist., 99 Mich. App. 103, 297 N.W. 2d 625 (1980).

[119] Brown v. Prairie View A & M University, 630 S.W. 2d 405 (Tex. Civ. App. 1982).

[120] Haynes v. Hoffman, 164 Ga. App. 236, 296 S.E. 2d 216 (1982).

[121] Rawls v. Dugas, 398 So. 2d 630 (La. App. 1981), cert. denied 400 So. 2d 1378 (1981).

[122] For example, Maryland, specifically exempts intercollegiate or interscholastic boxing.

schools to provide medical services; and, for example, in Ohio by Attorney General's Opinion the physical examinations must be given by school physicians, but the teacher of physical education has no duty and cannot be given authority to make such examinations.

§ 17.332   On-site treatment

For a discussion of the liability of a physician serving as a Good Samaritan on-site and in special situations as defined by statute, see §§17.15 and 17.16 in this chapter.

In the landmark case of *Welch v. Dunsmuir Joint Union H.S.Dist.*,[123] evidence was conflicting as to the actions of the physician, who was present at the scrimmage. One team member testified that the physician was 20 to 25 yards away when the plaintiff was injured, but did not go to the young man until he had been brought to the sidelines. Other witnesses testified that the physician went immediately to the injured boy. The court opinion said that under the evidence of the case the jury could reasonably have inferred that both the doctor and the coach were negligent in the removal of the plaintiff from the field to the sidelines; the coach in failing to wait for the doctor and allowing plaintiff to be moved, and the doctor in failing to act promptly after plaintiff's injury.

A 14-year-old was killed when he was struck by a line drive foul while watching a professional baseball game. The ball club allegedly provided emergency medical services in a negligent manner, and the doctor who operated the emergency medical facility at the stadium was named for malpractice. Upon being hit above and behind the left ear, decedent slumped forward for about a minute, then stretched and commenced speaking unintelligibly. An ice pack was furnished by someone inside the visitors' dugout. An usher came and returned with two ambulance attendants, but by this time the boy's condition was somewhat improved and his speech normal. He was, nevertheless, escorted to the first aid station, where the doctor had already arrived, having seen that it appeared as if someone had been hit by the foul ball. The doctor had been in the press box. He took the boy's pulse, felt his head and examined site of impact; examined eyes, ears and throat with flashlight and tested reflexes. He did not, however, ask about manner decedent had reacted since being hit, nor did he take blood pressure. The boy went back to the game for remaining six innings and during the time chased another foul ball and went to the concession stand. On way out to the camper (car), the boy grabbed his companion's arm and commenced to cry and shake; speech disability reappeared. He laid down in the camper and the drive home took approximately 40 minutes. The parents immediately took him to the emergency room of a hospital, but they couldn't attend to him for an hour; so drove on to the medical center, a ride of 30 minutes, but they couldn't see him either, and so he was taken to Children's Hospital, another couple blocks distance. It was an hour and a half before treatment was given, and then an hour later a neurosurgeon was summoned. He monitored his condition and gave directions. About 9:30 the night after the injury the decedent suffered a convulsion which rendered him decerebrate and made his condition terminal. He died three days later when artificial support systems were turned off. An autopsy showed that when the

[123] Welch v. Dunsmuir Joint Union H.S. Dist., 326 P. 2d 633 (Cal. App. 1958).

boy was struck by the baseball, he suffered a hairline fracture of the outer plane of his skull and a depressed fracture of the inner plane, portions of which protruded through the covering membrane and into the brain tissue. A small artery was severed... intracerebral hemorrhage. The court held that the emergency treatment of the physician at the game was improper.[124]

With so much discussion in the mid-'80s regarding the use of drugs to enhance performance, Florida in 1985 enacted a law regarding prescription of such drugs by physicians, as grounds for disciplinary action, thusly:

> Prescribing, ordering, dispensing, administering, supplying, selling, or giving growth hormones, testosterone or its analogs, human chorionic gonadotropin (HCG), or other hormones for the purpose of muscle building or to enhance athletic performance. For the purposes of this subsection, the term "muscle building" does not include the treatment of injured muscle. A prescription written for the drug products listed above may be dispensed by the pharmacist with the presumption that the prescription is for legitimate medical use. (Fla. Stat. Ann. §458.331(1)(33)).

There are similar statutes related to an osteopathic physician, podiatrist, naturopath, or dentist also prescribing drugs for muscle building or to enhance athletic performance. See also §1.232.

§ 17.333 Malpractice

This section does not endeavor to discuss physician malpractice, but only give some illustrative cases related to recreation and sport. A few additional cases are in previous subsections. A good number of states have Malpractice Acts.[125] See also physician as independent contractor, §3.12.

At that time, the largest verdict for personal injury to a single individual in United States legal history was handed down on February 5, 1973, in a California Superior Court. Kelley Niles, a 13-year-old boy, was permanently paralyzed as a result of a fight during a supervised school baseball game. The boy was hit on the head by another boy during an argument over whose turn it was to bat. He was taken to the hospital several hours later after he complained of illness and pain. The hospital emergency room crew, as well as a pediatrician, examined the boy and sent him home. The boy's condition worsened several hours later and he returned to the hospital. It was determined that he had an extradural hematoma or bleeding inside the skull, and brain surgery revealed a skull fracture which had severed an artery causing a blood clot in the skull to put pressures on the brain, damaging the brain stem. He became paralyzed from the neck down and was mute; however, his mentality was not affected. The suit was brought against the hospital and pediatrician from which $4 million was recovered.[126]

[124] Fish v. Los Angeles Dodgers Baseball Club, 56 Cal. App. 3d 620, 128 Cal. Rptr. 807 (1976).

[125] For example, Pennsylvania Health Care Services Malpractice Act.

[126] Niles v. City of San Rafael, 42 Cal. App. 3d 230, 166 Cal. Rptr. 733 (1974).

A racquetball player injured her ankle and was diagnosed at the medical center after x-rays as a sprained ankle. Although plaintiff expressed fear she had ruptured her Achilles' tendon, the doctor wrapped her ankle with an Ace bandage and told her to see an orthopedic surgeon if her ankle did not improve. Two months later she did go to an orthopedic surgeon, who repaired the Achilles' tendon. However, two days after surgery she experienced pain with the cast. An employee changed the cast, but there was no inspection of the operative site. Two weeks later after being discharged from the hospital, during a follow-up exam, infection was noted. An antibiotic was prescribed, but the infection worsened and further surgery was required. Plaintiff claims that as a result of defendant's treatment, she was so disfigured and disabled that she had to discontinue her veterinary practice with large animals. Medical center was held not liable; as to physician, remanded.[127]

A varsity basketball player developed an upper respiratory infection which persisted. The athletic trainers gave him cold tablets. He also developed a toothache and a headache. An oral surgeon extracted two seriously decayed teeth, and prescribed codeine and aspirin for pain. The headache, nevertheless, became worse that night and was accompanied by nausea. He was ill through the weekend and on Monday morning a friend took the player back to Oral Surgery, but everything seemed in order and placebos (vitamins) were prescribed, which were given by athletic trainers. In the afternoon another trainer picked up the player from his apartment and took him to the Student Health Infirmary where he was instructed to be given fluids and Bufferin; no laboratory tests were ordered. That night his condition deteriorated and about 5:30 a.m. Tuesday morning he could no longer carry out a chin-to-chest test without experiencing stiffness and pain, a symptom of meningitis. A physician on duty was called and he had a resident in Neurology examine the player. Tuesday afternoon surgeons operated on plaintiff and during the next several days he received intensive medical care. However, although his life was saved, he became permanently blind. The plaintiff alleged (among other allegations) that the team physician failed to employ appropriate tests and examinations and this negligence proximately caused the blindness. The court so held in that the intracranial infection would probably have been disclosed and prompt large dosage of antibiotics might have prevented the blindness.[128]

The administration of an anti-inflammatory drug prescribed by the football team physician so that the player could play with a hurt knee was at issue in a case against the U.S. (Air Force). Plaintiff alleged that his informed consent had not been obtained and that the drug caused damage to his bone marrow and other ills, resulting in disability retirement about five years later.[129] A consent form also was involved in a situation involving skiing. Plaintiff injured his shoulder and an arthrogram revealed a tear in the rotator cuff. A recommended operation (two opinions) was unsuccessful, as was a second. Plaintiff declined when a third was suggested. At the time of the first operation, plaintiff was told there was 90% success rate and 10% no improvement, but nothing was said about possibility of being worse off. Plaintiff testified that had he been informed

---

[127] Wozny v. Godsil, 474 So. 2d 1078 (Ala. 1985).
[128] Speed v. State, 240 N.W. 2d 901 (Iowa 1976).
[129] Fischer v. U.S., 451 F. Supp. 918 (1978); see also Watkins v. U.S., 589 F. 2d 214 (1979) not a sport

situation, valium usage was found to be proximate cause of injury, notwithstanding a .16% blood alcohol, prescribed without taking adequate history or checking records of psychiatric clinic.

his chance of success was in the 70-80% range with the possibility of deterioration, he would not have had the operation. The plaintiff had signed an informed consent form which indicated be had been informed of possible consequences of the operation. Court held that a medical malpractice suit is not barred by a signed informed consent. However, evidence was insufficient to enable jury to determine whether it was more probable than not that conduct of physician brought about the injury.[130]

In a professional sport situation, the football player alleged that he had had wrongfully concealed from him the true nature of his physical condition and injury.[131] A similar allegation was made by a San Francisco Forty-Niner. The plaintiff player said the team physician did not fully inform him of possible consequences if he continued to play with a profoundly damaged knee or of the effect of steroid injections. This case is different from others in that the team was liable for what the doctor had done, rather than the doctor solely. The case was remanded for determination of award.[132]

An injury in physical education class occasioned on the still rings also brought an allegation of medical malpractice. The School, against whom the plaintiff brought suit on allegations of improper equipment, instruction, and supervision, joined as defendants the hospital and physicians where the student was treated for brain damage. The opinion focused on the technicality of jurisdiction.[133] And, an action on malpractice was brought for wrongful death of a person who allegedly died of lack of oxygen after surgery for a shoulder separation sustained in a neighborhood park football game.[134]

In a bit different case,[135] the person handling the injured patron at the roller skating rink in the first aid room was held to the standard of care of a physician, although he was not one, because he assumed the role and duties of a doctor.

A junior high student brought action against school physician alleging negligence and negligent infliction of emotional distress. The physician had determined that the student was not physiologically mature enough to try out for the high school tennis team. This determination was based on results of a screening test designed under the auspices of the State Education Department. There was no allegation that the test had been improperly conducted. Held: no cause of action; physician not liable for medical malpractice.[136]

Fitness assessments also have given rise to malpractice suits. Plaintiff sued her health spa for injuries allegedly sustained during participation in aerobic dance class, and the health spa brought third party action against the individual's chiropractor, alleging that his advice had directly contributed to the individual's injury. Court held that health spa's

130 Gordon v. Neviaser, 478 A. 2d 292 (D.C. App. 1984); see also Pauscher v. Iowa Methodist Medical Center, 408 N.W. 2d 355 (Iowa 1987) not a sport case; Olson v. Molzen, 558 S.W. 2d 429 (Tenn. 1977) exculpatory agreement held invalid as against public policy, abortion, see introduction §17.3.

131 Rivers v. N.Y. Jets, 460 F. Supp. 1233 (1978); see also Brousseau v. Jarrett, 73 Cal. App. 3d 864, 141 Cal. Rptr. 200 (1977) alleged too conservative prognosis report on residual disability, not a sport situation.

132 Krueger v. San Francisco Forty Niners, 189 Cal. App. 3d 875, 234 Cal. Rptr. 579 (1987) on remand, judge awarded plaintiff $2.36 million.

133 Staub v. S.W. Butler Co. School Dist., 263 Pa. Super. 413, 398 A. 2d 204 (1979), aff'd 489 Pa. 196, 413 A. 2d 1082 (1980).

134 Foster v. Englewood & Hospital Assoc., 19 Ill. App. 3d 1055, 313 N.E. 2d 255 (1974).

135 Thomas v. Studio Amusement, 50 Cal. App. 2d 538, 123 P. 2d 552 (1942).

136 Sitomer v. Half Hollow Hills Central School Dist., 133 A.D. 2d 748, 520 N.Y.S. 2d 37 (1987).

allegation stated a claim of action.[137] A second case[138] involved a man who had a heart attack when taking a stress test (see §§17.45 and 17.46).

§ 17.34   Persons with disabilities

This section does not discuss the "right to participate," which topic is addressed in §1.321. There are few cases brought on negligence for injuries related to disabilities. However, the teacher, coach or leader must be aware of the physical, intellectual, and emotional condition and capability of the participants (see §19.1). For example, a coach was sued when he asked the student manager to change the scoreboard and a ladder was used rather than an available scaffold. The student manager "blacked out." No liability; the coach was aware of the epilepsy and it was thought to be under control.[139]

§ 17.341   Physical disabilities

The American Medical Association published guidelines for permitting persons of various physical disabilities to participate in sport, which have been used widely by schools and youth organizations; however, there is indication that the guidelines are being "overruled" by the right to participate (see §1.3). Further, recognizing that the AMA guidelines were becoming "increasingly obsolete because of changes in both safety equipment and society's attitudes towards the rights of athletes to compete despite a medical condition that may increase the risk of sustaining an injury or aggravating a preexisting medical condition," the Committee on Sports Medicine of the American Academy of Pediatrics re-studied the situation and compiled a list of recommendations.[140] The Committee stated that the recommendations should be used as a guideline only and that one must recognize that most, if not all, sports have some risk, a risk which must be weighed by physician, the athlete, and the parents in relation to the advantages gained by participation. Utilizing these recommendations, it behooves a school, public recreation, community organization, or private enterprise to establish guidelines for participation. To ameliorate liability, informed consent (see §17.23) and agreements to participate should be utilized (see §24.81). Participation with a disability should be distinguished from permitting participation when injured or not in physical condition (see §17.31).

In a 1987 school situation, a junior high school student sued the school physician and school district for negligent infliction of emotional distress for physician's determination that student was not physiologically mature enough to try out for the high school

[137] Contino v. Lucille Roberts Health Spa, 125 A.D. 2d 437, 509 N.Y.S. 2d 369 (1986); for further detail, see §17.46.

[138] Tart v. McGann, 697 F. 2d 75 (1982); see §17.45 for further detail.

[139] Braun v. Board of Educ., Red Bud Comm. Unit School Dist., 151 Ill. App. 3d 787, 104 Ill. Dec. 416, 502 N.E. 2d 1076 (1987).

[140] Recommendations for Participation in Competitive Sports. Committee on Sports Medicine, American Academy of Pediatrics, in *Pediatrics*, vol. 81, No. 5, May 1988, pp. 737-739, updates and replaces Disqualifying Conditions for Sports. A Guide for Medical Evaluation for Candidates for School Sports. American Medical Association. Revised, 1976. See also DeSantis, Kathleen. The Disabled Student Athlete: Gaining a Place on the Playing Field. Comm/Ent, vol. 5, no. 3, spring 1983, pp. 517-548 (Journal of Communications and Entertainment Law).

tennis team. This determination was based upon results of a screening test designed under the auspices of the State Education Department. No liability.[141]

In a very early case[142] the question of a person who had a physical disability being "competent personnel" in charge of a group of young Boy Scouts was raised. The boys were riding bicycles, when an on-coming car on the wrong side of the road struck a boy. The court held that the scout master being "crippled" was not a factor inasmuch as a person of "perfect physique" could not have timely removed the boy from the path of the on-coming automobile.

Four cases[143] dealt with impaired vision. In the *Whitney* case a six-year-old first grader was totally blind in his left eye and had limited vision in his right eye due to congenital glaucoma. He became totally blind as a result of being struck on the head by a defective door at school, holding that the defendants failed to provide any special supervision or assistance for handicapped children who were integrated into the public school system. On this day, although the teacher was advised that the child was suffering from hemorrhaging on his sighted eye which further impaired his vision, he was directed to proceed to afternoon recess in the school yard. On his way, passing through the school corridors, downstairs, and out through the allegedly defective door, he was hit on the head due to the door's faulty closing mechanism which caused it to swing shut. He was ordered to remain in the classroom and no immediate medical attention was obtained for him. It was alleged that the total blindness which ensued was the result of the delay.

In the *Torres* and *Green* cases, the impaired vision was not really related to the injury. In the first, a 17-year-old student who was blind drowned in a swimming class. The defendant had violated its own safety rules calling for implementation of a buddy system and failure to make a periodic count of children in the pool, which failure constituted a breach of duty to provide adequate supervision. And, in the *Green* case, a young man with impaired vision was not allowed to engage in football, but was placed in a class which had a unit on wrestling. It was in the process of wrestling that his neck was injured and he became paralyzed.

The fourth case (*Swiderski* case) was concerned with protection of a visually impaired person's eyes. The suit was brought on the "right to participate," the parents seeking the right of their first year high school student to participate in high school athletics. The student had defective vision in her right eye because of a congenital cataract and an undeveloped optic nerve. The court held that it was in the best interests of the student to participate and that it was reasonably safe for her to do so, provided that her eyes were at all times protected by protective eye shields prescribed by her doctor.

One situation involved a person who was deaf and, similar to the *Whitney* case, had in issue the immediacy of first aid. Plaintiff had been deaf since infancy and had to rely upon lipreading to communicate. As a college freshman she was playing on the school's

[141] Sitomer v. Half Hollow Hills Central School Dist., 133 A.D. 2d 748, 520 N.Y.S. 2d 37 (1987).

[142] Young v. Boy Scouts of America, 9 Cal. App. 2d 760, 51 P. 2d 191 (1935).

[143] Whitney v. City of Worcester, 373 Mass. 208, 366 N.E. 2d 1210 (1977); Torres v. State, 476 S.W. 2d 846 (Tex. Civ. App. 1972); Green v. Orleans Parish School Board, 365 So. 2d 834 (La. App. 1978), cert. denied 367 So. 2d 393 (1979); Swiderski v. Board of Education, Albany, 95 Misc. 2d 931, 408 N.Y.S. 2d 744 (1978).

intercollegiate softball team. She was injured during practice when a ball thrown by another player struck her in the right eye. The impact could be heard 80 to 100 yards away, according to players in the outfield. Ice was applied, but neither coach directed or suggested that she should see a doctor, although both were aware of the hard impact and that plaintiff was dependent on her eyesight. The player returned to her dormitory room where she remained that evening and the next day, but in the evening of the next day she went to a dance. The following day after the dance she began experiencing dizziness and severe blurring and coloring of her vision. She phoned home and her parents directed her to an internist who immediately referred her to an ophthalmologist, since there was blood in the anterior chamber of the eye. While traumatic hyphemoa is a relatively common injury, according to the doctor, it also can have a 90 percent or greater success rate when treatment is promptly given. The eye was drained, but began to bleed again two days later and infection developed, resulting in complete loss of vision in the eye. The court allowed $800,000 damages on failure to provide medical assistance. The school's medical center was across the street from the softball field. There was no holding by the court on the allegation that the coaches did not properly instruct other players to be cautious in throwing the ball to plaintiff.[144]

A 14-year-old deaf camper alleged that contracted rheumatic fever was not timely detected or treated, resulting in other medical problems, specifically a slightly enlarged heart and a significant heart murmur. Although she responded well to medical treatment, there was not full recovery and her activities were limited. Judgment for plaintiff. The condition, however, had nothing to do with the camper's deafness, although in awarding damages it was stated that now instead of coping with one handicap, she now had to cope with two.[145]

In another failure to treat case, but with an opposite result, a 14-year-old asthmatic complained to the school nurse that she was feeling ill, but was denied treatment and directed back to class. Instead the student chose to leave school, apparently without permission. On the way home a neighbor suggested she visited defendant Community Medical Clinic, where she was denied treatment for lack of funds. Shortly after returning home, her mother decided it was necessary to call for an ambulance, and while she was using the phone, the student, unable to breathe, opened her bedroom window, apparently lost consciousness, and fell to the ground. In addition to the Clinic, the school was sued for failing to supervise and care for the girl while in school and the Housing Authority for failing to equip the apartment windows with window guards. The court held in *Griffith v. N.Y.C.*, 123 A.D.2d 830, 507 N.Y.S.2d 445 (1986), that even if the school violated a duty to student, school's conduct was not proximate cause of student's injuries due to the fall from the open window, inasmuch as it was not foreseeable, and further, that at the time of accident, the school owed no duty to protect student because student's mother had assumed control over her.

---

[144] Stineman v. Fontbonne College, 664 F. 2d 1082 (1981).

[145] Berman v. Nat'l Council of Beth Jacobs Schools, Inc., 119 A.D. 2d 787, 501 N.Y.S. 2d 413 (1986).

§ 17.342   Mental retardation

A particular duty is owed to individuals who are mentally retarded when they participate in activity. In *Rodriquez v. Board of Education,* 104 A.D.2d 978, 480 N.Y.S.2d 901 (1984), a special class for 16 trainable mentally retarded youngsters were taken outside to the kindergarten playground to engage in a supervised play period. The purpose of this period was to "normalize" each child's experience as much as possible and allow the child to independently select games or playground equipment. The teacher's function was to encourage the children to exercise. While the teacher was talking to a small group of children, the injured child (12 years old) and another were running and chasing each other; the children were two to three feet from the teacher at the time, but then continued to run and disappeared from the teacher's view for about 10 to 15 seconds. When the teacher turned around, she saw plaintiff child lying face down at the foot of a set of steps leading back to the kindergarten room. He did not speak. No one saw what had happened. He suffered extensive head injuries. The children often played a chasing game called "monster" during the supervised play periods; there never had been any injury as a result of this activity previously. The teacher was aware that the injured child's manner of running was "a clumsy, lumbering gait" and that he had perceptual motor difficulties and poor eye-hand coordination. An expert witness from the field of special education, who was familiar with the teaching policies of various school districts, testified that "purposeless, freestyle running" during school hours was dangerous and never permitted for any child, but was especially hazardous where mentally retarded children were concerned. She further testified that the proper procedure for a teacher to follow under the circumstances of this situation would have been to stop the children, either by word or physical act. There was no set school policy with respect to the type of running activities permitted during school hours in the defendant school. The court held that the plaintiffs established a prima facie case of negligence in the teacher failing to supervise.

In *Foster v. Houston General Insurance Co.,*[146] the mother sued for wrongful death of her mentally retarded youngster, who was killed when he impulsively dashed out into a street at a heavily traveled intersection. The decedent was 17 years of age, but with a mental age of 7 years 4 months. He had been selected for the Special Olympics basketball team, a school sanctioned activity for which they held practice sessions during the regular physical education class period. Because of lack of facilities, the players usually practiced on an adjacent dirt court outdoors; but, since the teacher felt it desirable for the team to have experience playing indoors on a wood floor, she arranged a practice in a municipal facility three blocks from the school. The 10 or 11 players assembled and were waiting for the regular physical education teacher, who was in class. They were getting fidgety, so the assisting teacher, a mathematics teacher, departed alone with the team to the municipal facility in the park along the planned

[146] Foster v. Houston General Insurance Co., 407 So. 2d 759 (La. App. 1981), writ denied 409 So. 2d 660 (1982).

route. He had discussed with the players, while they waited, safety precautions, particularly directed at street crossing. Enroute five or six of the boys broke away from the group and started running ahead, not heeding the admonishments of the accompanying teacher; however, the teacher stayed with the remaining group of five, which included the decedent. As they were lined up to cross the street, the decedent dashed between a line of cars, in mid-street looked to his right, and seeing a car coming stopped suddenly, at which time his feet slid out from under him. The youngster was run over by the oncoming automobile, suffering the serious injuries from which he died three days later. The court held that because a special relationship exists between teacher and students, there is a general duty to conduct classes so as not to expose the students to unreasonable risk of injury, and such duty becomes more onerous when the student body is composed of mentally retarded youngsters. It further stated that on-campus care does not require continuous supervision, but when the decision was made to take the team off-campus walking across heavily traveled thoroughfare, there was a duty to maintain closer supervision over the youngsters. This affirmed the earlier decision[147] where a moderately to severely retarded young man drowned in a pond on the premises of the School. He had been a student for three and one-half years. The court held that where the retarded student had been at the school for that length of time and had given no indication that he was dangerous to himself or that he did not understand the nature of the pond he worked near and walked by frequently, no duty had been breached.

In *Brevard County v. Jacks*,[148] another case involving drowning, a mentally retarded 18-year-old girl with a history of epileptic seizures requiring daily medication drowned while wading with a retarded girl friend. The lifeguard did not know the condition of the girl. The plaintiff could not read the sign "Swim at your own risk." The court held that the girl did not assume risks for she could not comprehend the danger.

A 14-year-old had finished her lunch and was passing by the concession stand located on the school playground, when two 13-year-old nonretarded students engaging in horseplay while waiting in the concession line bumped her. She fell and fractured her hip, resulting in 25% permanent disability of her leg. The court held that failure to provide direct supervision for the retarded youngster was not negligence.[149]

In another 1987 case,[150] a ten-year-old boy fell from a tree platform or "tree house" on State-owned land which was a part of the vocational training school. Hanging near the platform was a rope tied to a higher limb and extending down to a distance a few feet above the ground. While playing with some neighborhood children, in attempting to reach for the rope, he lost his grip and fell more than 6' to the ground, breaking his femur. The State was held liable under attractive nuisance doctrine; because of the child's lack of intelligence he failed to understand the danger and thus was not held to be contributorily negligent.

In two other cases,[151] the decision was made on the basis of immunity under statute

---

[147] Hunter v. Evergreen Presbyterian Vocational School, 338 So. 2d 164 (La. App. 1976).

[148] Brevard County v. Jacks, 238 So. 2d 156 (Fla. App. 1970).

[149] Brooks v. St. Tammany Parish School Board, 510 So. 2d 51 (La. App. 1987).

[150] Melerine v. State of Louisiana, 505 So. 2d 79

(La. App. 1987) writ cert. denied 507 So. 2d 226 (1987).

[151] Schumate v. Thompson, 580 S.W. 2d 47 (Tex. Civ. App. 1979); Plemmons v. Gastonia, 62 N.C. App. 470, 302 S.E. 2d 905 (N.C. App. 1983). Statute under which decision made subsequently repealed.

and not on the merits of the case. In the Texas case, the parent sued the teacher, who had directed her teacher's aide to take the class outside to play. The aide was allowed to determine the activities in which the children engaged. She directed a youngster, who was retarded, to high jump a stick and his head struck the ground when he tripped and fell, resulting in a fractured vertebra of the neck. Plaintiff alleged that the teacher was negligent in failing to supervise the activities. The statute provided for immunity of the teacher under these circumstances. In the North Carolina case, a mildly retarded child fell 8' from the gymnasium bleachers to the floor. The school leased the facility from the city. The plaintiff alleged that as a result of the fall, the child suffered serious and permanent brain damage. Court held that the school was immune, but that there was an action against the city.

The issues were supervision and self-defense in a situation which involved two members of a special education class[152] (see §18.142).

In *Cairl v. State*, 323 N.W. 2d 20 (Minn. 1982), plaintiffs brought action against the State, a county welfare department, and certain state and county employees for alleged breach of a duty to warn plaintiffs of the dangerous propensities of a mentally retarded youth released from a state institution on holiday home leave. There was a history of fire setting, and while on this home leave he started a fire in the living room couch of his mother's apartment, resulting in the death of one and severely burning another family member. The court held that the temporary release was a discretionary decision giving immunity that no statute, court order, or regulation had been violated, and that there was not duty to warn.

The standard of care required in a state development center was at issue in an Ohio 1987 case, *Johnson v. Dept. of Mental Retardation and Developmental Disabilities,* 35 Ohio Misc. 2d 18 520 N.E. 2d 29 (Ohio 1987). A 66-year-old profoundly retarded man, who also had severe eyesight problems (cataracts), was hard of hearing, and had an unsteady gait, was injured when he apparently was pushed into a door by another resident at the developmental center. An attendant was within 30 feet, and the person who did the pushing had no history of such behavior. The court held that the act was an unforeseeable behavior by a third party for which the center was not liable. The standard of care being given by the institution was held to be that appropriate to such institutions; there was neither misfeasance nor nonfeasance proven. Further, appropriate medical attention had been given and all medical bills had been paid by the state.

§ 17.343   Emotional disturbance

No cases were identified which involved injury of an emotionally disturbed person in physical activity.[153] The principles of negligence applied are the same as for situations not involving persons who are emotionally disturbed, although there is a greater responsibility for the actions of the emotionally disturbed person in terms of injuring

[152] McDonald v. Terrebonne Parish School Board, 253 So. 2d 558 (La. App. 1971), writ or review denied 260 La. 128, 255 So. 2d 353 (1971).

[153] For legal liability in psychotherapy, see Schutz, Benjamin M. *Legal Liability in Psychotherapy.* San Francisco: Jossey-Bass Publishers, 1982; for a more broad scope of services, see Woody, Robert Henley and Associates. *The Law and the Practice of Human Services.* San Francisco: Jossey-Bass Publishers, 1984.

another.[154] The validity of an exculpatory clause in the enrollment contract of a camp which served children with emotional problems was at issue in a 1981 Florida case.[155] (See §16.1 exculpatory clauses and §13.112 camp activities.) Denial of psychiatric attention was at issue in a 1984 Michigan case against a county youth home.[156]

§ 17.4   Fitness, conditioning and rehabilitation

As evidenced in this section, most of the cases involving fitness and conditioning have emanated from health spas and fitness centers, rather than fitness programs by voluntary agencies, municipalities, or schools. The cases represent situations concerned with the maintenance of the facility, the exercise machines, fitness testing, and the fitness program or activity itself. The first two subsections deal with consumer protection laws and exculpatory clauses in contracts for services. There is a final subsection on rehabilitation.

The cases presented in the sub-sections §§17.43 to 17.46 do not represent the scope of legal concepts applied to such topics, nor are all cases in which the setting is a health or fitness club in this section; there are additional cases in appropriate chapters, specific to the activity, facility or situation, e.g., health club swimming pool cases are in Chapter 9 on Pools. The legal concepts as related to liability for fitness, conditioning, and rehabilitation programs and services, in general, are the same as for any other program or service. However, there are three types of programs — the recreational fitness program, the prescriptive exercise program, and the rehabilitation program — which should be distinguished. There are differences in the standard of care required for each of these programs, according to the nature of the program. For ease of comparative understanding of the differences and the operational requirements as related to liability, Table 17.2 contrasts 12 characteristics for the three types of programs. Other sections in this book which give more information on applicable legal concepts are referenced for each of the characteristics in the left-hand column of the table. See footnote at end of table regarding school programs.

[154] Bradley Center v. Wessner, 161 Ga. App. 576, 287 S.E. 2d 716, aff'd. 250 Ga. 199, 296 S.E. 2d 693 (1982); Evans v. Morehead Clinic, 749 S.W. 2d 696 (Ky. App. 1988).
[155] Goyings v. Jack & Ruth Eckerd Foundation, 403 So. 2d 1144 (Fla. App. 1981).

[156] Mosqueda v. Macomb County Youth Home, 132 Mich. App. 462, 349 N.W. 2d 185 (1984) also discusses governmental immunity in Michigan as related to intentional tort and building exception.

Table 17.2   Fitness and Rehabilitation Programs[1]

Characteristic Referral Citation[2]	Recreational	Prescriptive	Rehabilitative
Objective	Fun! enjoyment Get some exercise General health maintenance	Effect change, e.g., weight, cardiovascular, strength, muscle tone To enhance health and reduce risk factors	Remedial, therapeutic
Clientele §19.1 §24.3	Apparently "healthy" — the "normal" person All ages	May have "high risk" factors Generally wants to "shape up" Primarily adult	A disability, disease where therapeutic exercise program as part of medical treatment plan All ages, but tend to be adult
Leadership Chp. 18 §24.1	Activity leader — knowledge about conduct of activities being sponsored or offered; ability to observe, in general, the condition of individual Improper leadership usually negligence action, in contrast to malpractice suit	Exercise "specialist" — knowledgeable about physiology, kinesiology, et al.; the conduct of exercise related to intensity, et al., which changes impact and possesses level of expertise appropriate to health-disease status of clientele **Beware** unathorized practice of medicine; malpractice suits use physician standard of care! Consulting physician mandatory	Physician — directed and monitored Exercise specialist one of health team Improper performance — practice of medicine — results in malpractice suit
Program or Activity Chp. 19 §§17.46, 17.47 §24.2	Any organized competitive-oriented or other recreational activity May have facility available for individual or group informal participation May be special event or on-going program	Generally aerobic and/or strength-oriented While done individually or in groups, prescription is for individuals after testing or classifying in other manner Physician specified parameters (intensity, nature, type of movement, et al.) and exercise specialist selects and conducts the exercises within such parameters	Activity selected specifically for its therapeutic value to a particular individual (part of medical treatment)
Testing §17.45	Not usually part of program Informal self-testing, e.g., weight, timed runs, pulse count	Essential for determination exercise prescription Exercise protocol recommended by ACSM, AHA, AMA, APTA Must be done by certified athletic trainer, exercise specialist	Under physician monitoring and at physician's direction

145

Characteristic Referral Citation[2]	Recreational	Prescriptive	Rehabilitative
		Direct physician monitoring depends on clientele condition and nature of testing and prescription Where prescription calls for exercise "on own" and self-monitoring (e.g., take pulse) client must be trained in technique and be capable of recognizing conditions of danger	
Physical Exam §3.12 §17.331 §24.82	Usually not necessary For particularly strenuous activity desirable to have "verification of condition" statement	Normally physical exam required; given by family/personal physician	Under physician's care who would have knowledge of physical condition so separate physical exam for exercise program not necessary (total health awareness)
Emergency Care §§17.1, 17.2	"Good Samaritan" law does not apply Must have CPR and first aid appropriate to the activity	Full emergency support must be available for untoward events	Full emergency support...
Records Required §24.82	None Most would keep general attendance/participation records Accident report on all injuries	Full records of test results and exercise prescriptions Accident report	Full medical records
Signed Statements Chp. 16 §§17.23 §17.42 §24.81	Depending on activity and setting, agreement to participate may be desirable Exculpatory clause may be valid for non-minors	Informed consent essential (must fully inform, then person consents) Exculpatory clauses probably not valid	Informed consent essential Exculpatory clauses probably not valid
Assumption of Risk §5.22	General instructions and warning as for any activity	Must have specific instruction, related to intensity of exercise and capability of individual related thereto Must understand any dangers and possible consequences Fully knowledgeable about equipment utilized	Must have specific instruction... (same as prescriptive)

146

Characteristic Referral Citation[2]	Recreational	Prescriptive	Rehabilitative
Statutory Control §17.41	In majority of states health spas under Consumer Protection Laws		Some states have definitions of what the "practice of medicine" is, and may have special medical malpractice laws
Facility and Equipment Chp. 21 §§17.43, 17.44 §20.2 §24.4	Must be kept in repair and good maintenance	Must be kept in repair and good maintenance	Must be kept in repair and good maintenance

[1]Note: This table is for independent fitness programs and services and is not meant to be used for school programs. However, in general, school physical education and club programs would fall between Recreational and Prescriptive; such programs are under direct supervision of teacher or club adviser, who must be aware of the condition and changes in participants (see Chapter 19). Conditioning of athletes would be between Prescriptive and Rehabilitative inasmuch as the conditioning program should be under the guidance of educated persons with expertise in conditioning and the program objective is to increase physical condition. Rehabilitation of athletes would be the same as that set forth in the Rehabilitative column. Full information as to the nature of injury, alternative treatments and short and long term ramifications is absolutely essential.

[2]Citations to sections and chapters in this book.

§ 17.41   Consumer protection laws--health spas, fitness clubs

In the late '80s, approximately two-thirds of the states[157] and the District of Columbia had legislation directly regulating health spas and similar businesses by whatever name referenced. About two-thirds of these laws were enacted in the mid-'80s from 1982 to 1987. Many of the statutes require licensing, registration, or posting of bonds with the State. The statutes are directed toward the commercial enterprises, and thus a number of the statutes specifically exempt nonprofit entities, schools, state and political subdivisions. The focus of the laws is upon the rights of the buyer, specifically upon provisions of the contract for services, which must be written and have very specific rights related to cancellation of the contract. Most laws restrict the length of time for which a contract can be written. Only one state[158] had specific provision related to the health of the consumer and stated that the contract should state that if a consumer has a history of heart disease, a physician should be consulted before joining a spa. Inasmuch as these statutes are not directly related to injuries and negligence, no further details on the statutes are given in this section. See specific statute for your state (citation in respective state in Appendix).

A member of a health spa, in a 1985 Georgia case,[159] sought damages for alleged breach of contractual promise to afford her protection and tortious negligent failure to protect premises. The court held that the concept of contract requires a meeting of the minds upon same subject matter and in the same sense, and that the membership contract was only to keep premises in a reasonably safe condition and not for unanticipated criminal act by a stranger.

A number of states have either within the same law or by a separate law similar provisions for protection of consumers purchasing dance studio[160] and campground[161] membership services. In *Brownridge Inst. of Karate v. Dorris,* 162 Ill. App.3d 483, 113 Ill. Dec. 564, 515 N.E.2d 373 (1987), the court held that a martial arts school, which advertised the physical fitness benefits of its programs and provided exercise equipment for its students, qualified as a "physical fitness center" subject to the Illinois Physical Fitness Services Act; and, in accord therewith, the school was liable for failing to honor alleged oral promise to consumer regarding customer's right to withdraw.

§ 17.42   Exculpatory clauses in membership contract

It is clear from the cases cited in subsequent paragraphs that exculpatory clauses in membership agreements can be valid if they meet the criteria established for validity of such clauses for any situation. See detailed discussion of exculpatory agreements in Chapter 16. The situations giving rise to the law suits in the cited cases may be found in

[157] Alabama, Arizona, Colorado, Connecticut, Delaware, District of Columbia, Florida, Georgia, Illinois, Indiana, Kentucky, Louisiana, Maryland, Massachusetts, Minnesota, Mississippi, Nevada, New Hampshire, New Jersey, New York, North Carolina, Ohio, Oregon, Rhode Island, South Carolina, Tennessee, Texas, Utah, Virginia, Washington, Wisconsin.

[158] Georgia
[159] Donaldson v. Olympic Health Spa, 175 Ga.App. 258, 333 S.E. 2d 98 (1985).
[160] e.g., California, Mississippi.
[161] e.g., Tennessee, Virginia.

the appropriate subsections, such as maintenance of facility, use of equipment, fitness testing, and fitness activities.

A number of cases have been brought in which the defendant sought to be relieved of any liability on the basis of an exculpatory clause in the membership contract. These date back to three cases[162] against Vic Tanny operations in the 1960s. All New York cases, the court held that the membership contract provision releasing defendant from liability for injuries caused by defendant's negligence was valid on its face as a covenant not to sue. Such a clause in the early 1970s was held not void as against public policy in an Illinois decision;[163] and, this was affirmed six years later with the court adding that the exculpatory clause was not to be denied enforcement on the basis of public policy in absence of any facts in the record indicating a disparity of bargaining power of sufficient magnitude.[164] A 1982 case[165] in Minnesota also upheld an exculpatory clause in a health spa membership contract, stating that there was no ambiguity in the clause, the contract was not one of adhesion, and the clause did not violate public policy. But, in an Illinois case[166] when plaintiff was injured on a weight machine, the exculpatory clause was held to be not sufficiently clear, explicit and unequivocal to show intent to protect facility from liability arising from use of equipment. However, the same year in Illinois in another equipment situation, the exculpatory clause was upheld and it barred plaintiff's recovery of any award.[167]

In a 1984 Vic Tanny case,[168] the court held that the dangers to be covered by the exculpatory clause must be within the range of possible dangers foreseeable by the plaintiff. In this situation, plaintiff sustained internal injuries allegedly sustained as a result of inhaling dangerous gaseous vapor generated by combining certain cleaning compounds. This danger was not within those contemplated under the clause in the health club membership agreement. The court further stated that such dangers must be foreseeable to enable plaintiff to minimize the risk by altering his conduct in order to employ a proportionately higher degree of caution.

The membership agreement with its exculpatory clause was held assignable to successor owner, although of a personal nature, since generally contractual rights can be assigned. The release was held valid.[169]

---

[162] Ciofalo v. Vic Tanny Gyms, Inc., 13 A.D. 2d 702, 214 N.Y.S. 2d 99, aff'd. 10 N.Y. 2d 294, 220 N.Y.S. 2d 962, 177 N.E. 2d 925 (1961); Putzer v. Vic Tanny Flatbush, Inc., 20 A.D. 2d 821, 248 N.Y.S. 2d 836 (1964); Whalen v. Vic Tanny Hicksville, Inc., 23 A.D. 2d 778, 258 N.Y.S. 2d 562 (1965). New York passed a law some years later voiding exculpatory clauses in particular business contexts. A hairstyling salon with tanning bed was held not similar to place of entertainment or recreation for purpose of statute voiding releases, hence release was held valid in Ward v. Dunn, 136 Misc. 2d 781, 519 N.Y.S. 2d 307 (1987).

[163] Bers v. Chicago Health Clubs, 11 Ill. App. 3d 590, 297 N.E. 2d 360 (1973).

[164] Kubisen v. Chicago Health Clubs, 69 Ill. App. 3d 463, 26 Ill. Dec. 420, 388 N.E. 2d 44 (1979).

[165] Schlobohm v. Spa Petite, Inc., 326 N.W. 2d 920 (Minn. 1982).

[166] Calarco v. YMCA of Greater Metro. Chicago, 149 Ill. App. 3d 1037, 103 Ill. Dec. 247, 501 N.E. 2d 268 (1986) cert. denied 508 N.E. 2d 725; see also Brown v. Racquetball Centers, Inc., 534 A. 2d 842 (Pa. Super. 1987) slipped on wet floor, clause held ambiguous and intent not clear.

[167] Neuman v. Gloria Marshall Figure Salon, 149 Ill. App. 3d 824, 102 Ill. Dec. 910, 500 N.E. 2d 1011 (1986).

[168] Larsen v. Vic Tanny, Int'l, 85 Ill. Dec. 769, 130 Ill. App. 3d 574, 474 N.E. 2d 729 (1984).

[169] Petry v. Cosmopolitan Spa, Int'l, 641 S.W. 2d 202 (Tenn. App. 1982) collapse of exercise machine.

A Georgia court[170] held that a husband, whose wife was precluded from recovering from owner of health club, was not entitled to recover from owner for loss of consortium. (This holding is not true for all jurisdictions.)

The effect of a professional employee (P.T.) allegedly acting outside scope of employment on an exculpatory clause was at issue in a Pennsylvania case.[171] The court stated that although exculpatory contracts are not favored, if they meet certain criteria, they are valid — but questioned that a physical therapist could come under such agreement with a health spa.

§ 17.43 Maintenance of fitness facility

Slippery floors and whose responsibility to take care was at issue in most of the cases. The general rule is that the operator owes a duty to an invitee to exercise reasonable care in inspecting the premises to discover any conditions which may be unreasonably dangerous and correct such conditions or warn the user thereof. The user's awareness and appreciation of the danger is essential to avoid liability; however, the user must exercise reasonable care for one's own safety.

The plaintiff slipped and fell inside a whirlpool bath, injuring her back. The court took judicial cognizance that areas of a spa with a swimming pool, showers, whirlpool bath, and cold dip bath by their very nature contribute to moisture and water in the areas surrounding those facilities. While an employee cleaned the area with a solution which formed suds, the plaintiff, a member of the club, could not identify any foreign substance on the steps or present to cause the fall or show improper maintenance. Judgment for the defendant.[172] Similarly, the court held that where a member slipped on an alleged foreign substance on the surface of the steam room, the plaintiff failed to establish that the surface was unusually slippery or dangerous. The court held further that the operator is not the insurer of safety of its patrons and the mere fact that the room might have been safer if adhesive strips, hand rails, or other safety devices had been installed did not warrant recovery.[173]

Where a club member allegedly slipped on a foreign substance while entering a shower, she was barred from recovery on the basis of contributory negligence, having heedlessly exposed herself to the risk presented without ever having protested the danger and without ascertaining the condition of the showers on the day in question. Plaintiff had used the facilities on several occasions prior to her fall and on each occasion the showers were slippery, filthy and dirty and she had slipped on some of these occasions due to these conditions, so she stated. On the day in question, she did not look down at the condition of the shower step or floor, but simply took a step and fell. While an operator must warn of unsafe conditions known to the operator, the court stated that it is equally well settled that one who, with knowledge of conditions, goes into danger, that

[170] Lovelace v. Figure Salon, Inc., 345 S.E. 2d 139 (Ga. App. 1986) fitness test.

[171] Leidy v. Deseret Enterprises, Inc., 252 Pa. Super. 162, 381 A. 2d 164 (1977).

[172] Sevin v. Shape Spa for Health & Beauty, Inc., 384 So. 2d 1011 (La. App. 1980).

[173] Gatti v. World Wide Health Studios of Lake Charles, 323 So. 2d 819 (La. App. 1975); see also Shumway v. Milwaukee Athletic Club, 247 Wis. 393, 20 N.W. 2d 123 (1945) floor of steam room.

person assumes the consequences. By her own admission, plaintiff knew, firsthand, the usual condition of the showers and the danger posed.[174] In another case,[175] the court distinguished the duty of a landlord toward a tenant and the operator of a club toward a club member in regard to condition of the premises, stating that the invitee did not have a relationship equal to that of a tenant whose landlord is under a contractual obligation to make needed repairs. In this situation the plaintiff slipped and fell on wet tile floor in the hallway on her way to the swimming pool, as she passed by the whirlpool. The whirlpool sometimes overflowed onto the hallway. There were no mats on the floor, but there was "a little sign, a very small sign" in the hallway which said "Slippery When Wet." This was the fifth visit of the plaintiff to the spa. The court held it was for the jury to determine whether the member had knowledge and appreciation of the slippery condition of the floor, the adequacy of warning, and the actual knowledge by member of the specific dangers.

It, also, was a matter for the jury to determine whether the defendant used reasonable diligence to remove water from a tile floor in the locker room, when it knew that tile was hazardous with water on it and that water was not uncommon in the area, especially when many of the patrons were there for treatment and suffered from physical infirmities. The plaintiff was a 42-year-old woman who had received surgery for slipped disc in her cervical spine and following laminectomy had joined the spa for swimming and other exercise.[176] Fitness club member also slipped on wet tile floor when coming out of the shower area. Court held that the exculpatory clause in the membership agreement did not absolve the club of liability for its negligence, as the agreement did not spell out intention of parties clearly enough.[177]

In *Ciofalo v. Vic Tanny Gyms*[178] the plaintiff alleged excessive slipperiness at the edge of the pool; however, an exculpatory clause in the membership contract barred recovery.

Member of a health spa sought to recover for injuries when a false ceiling collapsed, and the health spa filed a third party complaint for indemnification against the contractor. Held against the spa on both actions, in that the condition of the ceiling was known or had existed for a sufficient length of time that spa management should have known of the condition; the condition was discoverable by inspection. The contractor would have been liable if the defect had been hidden; however, evidence indicated that not only was the defect discoverable by inspection, but also the ceiling plan had been approved by the spa's maintenance supervisor and the supervisor had observed some of the construction and accepted the work upon completion after inspection.[179]

For further discussion of maintenance and condition of premises, see Chapter 20.

§ 17.44 Fitness/conditioning equipment

While health spas and exercise machines became very popular among the American

[174] House v. European Health Spa, S.C., 239 S.E. 2d 653 (1977); see also My Fair Lady of Georgia v. Harris, 185 Ga. App. 459, 364 S.E. 2d 580 (1987) fall in shower, exculpatory clause valid.

[175] Adam Dante Corp. v. Sharpe, 468 S.W. 2d 167 (Tex.Civ.App. 1971), aff'd. 483 S.W.3d 452 (1972).

[176] Bertrand v. Palm Springs & European Health Spa, Or., 480 P. 2d 424 (1971).

[177] Brown v. Racquetball Centers, Inc., 534 A. 2d 842 (Pa. Super. 1987).

[178] Ciofalo v. Vic Tanny Gyms, 13 A.D. 2d 702, 214 N.Y.S. 2d 99, aff'd, 10 N.Y. 2d 294, 220 N.Y.S. 2d 962, 177 N.E. 2d 925 (1961).

[179] Roman Spa, Inc. v. Lubell, 334 So. 2d 298 (1976), rev'd./remanded 362 So. 2d 922 (Fla. 1978), op. after remand 364 So. 2d 115 (Fla. App. 1978).

people in the '70s, law suits regarding exercise machines were not unknown prior to that time. In 1957 the court held for the defendant when the user of an "elastic exerciser" was injured and sued the manufacturer. The exerciser was made of rubber rope, in shape of a child's skipping rope, which was pushed by the foot. The elastic cord slipped off plaintiff's foot and struck her in the eye, causing detachment of the retina. There was no defect found in the exerciser.[180]

On June 25 the plaintiff, a 15-year-old high school student, reported for the first of a scheduled series of weight lifting training sessions in preparation for high school football team tryouts in the fall. Allegedly urged on by the coach to perform to the utmost, plaintiff pushed himself to and beyond his limits, and, while lifting a 250 to 300 pound weight, he fell and received injuries resulting in paraplegia. It is alleged, further, that the two spotters failed to react quickly enough to seize the barbell before the fall. The court held that the school principal and athletic director were not immune from liability for they induced, suggested, encouraged, intimidated, and coerced plaintiff to attend weight lifting session without inquiring as to experience or capabilities, without properly instructing as to techniques for safety and, further, that they failed to stop football program contrary to athletic association rules, to promulgate adequate rules and regulations, procedures and safeguards, and to properly instruct and train coach. The possible negligence of the coach and other school employees could not be imputed to the school superintendent merely because he was in a supervisory position and there was no evidence of personal neglect as superintendent. Remanded for jury determination of negligence.[181]

The plaintiff entered the health spa with a friend, who was a member and an experienced athlete. The friend had urged plaintiff to join him in a workout. They did not stop to check in with any supervisory personnel, but went directly to the main exercise room and after a workout there went into an adjoining room where the leg press was located. Plaintiff had never used a leg press before and in fact had not done any weightlifting with anything other than barbells. There were already some weights on the machine and the friend put on additional weights. The friend said he was accustomed to using a similar machine at his college and demonstrated the use of the machine to plaintiff. Then the plaintiff tried and on the second lift when the weight came down, one of the weights flipped off the top of a spindle and hit plaintiff in mouth. The spa manager testified that when he examined the machine shortly after the accident, there was more than 500 pounds on it; and, he testified further that it would not be difficult for an average person to push such a large amount of weight upward, but he surmised that when the weight was being let down, the strain was too much for plaintiff and caused the platform to descend rapidly, hitting the stops, jarring the weight off. The machine was not found defective. It was also thought that the spindles were improperly loaded to within a quarter of an inch or less of the top. In addition, there were rules and regulations concerning members bringing guests, and members were so notified. Defendant

[180] Jamieson v. Woodward & Lathrop, 101 App. D.C. 31, 247 F. 2d 23 (1957), mem. dec. cert. denied, 2 L. Ed. 2d 63, 78 S. Ct. 84, 355 U.S. 855 (1957); see also Heggbloom v. John Wonamaker New York, 178 Misc. 792, 36 N.Y.S.2d 777 (1942) "Stretch-a-way," representation as to the rubber strap.

[181] Vargo v. Svitchan, 100 Mich. App. 809, 301 N.W. 2d 1 (1980).

testified that no guest was allowed to use any equipment without instructions on its use. The court discussed the status of the guest, as whether he was a trespasser, licensee, or invitee, and determined he was an invitee because he was a prospective purchaser of defendant's services. The duty owed is not that of insurer of safety, but to protect against reasonably discoverable hazards created by a third party and an obligation to inspect premises and make them safe for visitors. It was held that it was not foreseeable that an inexperienced athlete would utilize a piece of advanced athletic equipment without proper supervision and instruction. The equipment itself was not deemed inherently dangerous, but was rendered so by the intervening unauthorized acts of plaintiff and his friend. Thus, plaintiff did not recover.[182]

As plaintiff was in the weight room using a Universal machine, weights fell on her hand, causing broken bones and permanent injury. She alleged the YMCA was negligent in failing to inspect and repair the machine and to warn users that machine was in a state of disrepair and unsuitable for use. The YMCA sought summary judgment on the basis of an exculpatory clause in the membership agreement, but it was held to be insufficiently clear as to what activities were covered and the general language was deemed not to have indicated an intention to absolve defendant from liability for negligence. Remanded for determination of negligence.[183]

In another weight lifting case, a 14-year-old was engaged in an exercise known as "curling," which involved lifting a weight attached to a bar with a cable, on a device described as a Universal Gladiator "70", the property of the high school. While so involved, a portion of the machine became disengaged from the rest of the device and struck him in the mouth and teeth, resulting in loss of his two front teeth and necessitating considerable dental treatment. At the time the physical education instructor was in the room and the injury was immediately reported and cared for. The manufacturer and distributor also were sued, but were not part of this appeal, which focused upon the constitutionality (due process and equal protection) of the required written notice required by the State Tort Claims Act. The statute was held valid and the plaintiff was barred from recovery, even though a minor.[184]

Plaintiff was using a "Gravity Gym," a machine designed to permit the user to suspend oneself upside down. When performing the exercise known as "crunches," his Velcro-attached footpads came loose, he fell onto the floor, suffering permanent partial paralysis. Plaintiff settled with manufacturer on products liability out of court, and was now suing only the Club. Plaintiff alleged that the machine was unreasonably dangerous and that the Club failed to instruct and warn. Held for Club, the jury finding the Club had properly instructed and supervised activities of plaintiff.[185]

Injury occurred when the exercise machine on which plaintiff was sitting collapsed. Plaintiff alleged maintenance of the machine in a dangerous condition. The exculpatory clause in the membership agreement was held, as a contract, to be assignable by the spa

[182] Duncan v. World Wide Health Studios, Inc., 232 So. 2d 835 (La. App. 1970).

[183] Calarco v. YMCA of Greater Metro. Chicago, 149 Ill. App. 3d 1037, 103 Ill. Dec. 247, 501 N.E. 2d 268 (1986) pet. denied 508 N.E. 2d 725 (1987).

[184] Shearer v. Perry Community School Dist., 236 N.W. 2d 688 (Iowa 1975).

[185] Burkart v. Health & Tennis Corp. of Amer., 730 S.W. 2d 367 (Tex. App. 1987).

owner to successor owner.[186] In another case, a valid exculpatory agreement also barred recovery by plaintiff when she injured her back on an exercise machine. Employee started the machine; plaintiff alleged employee did not check whether plaintiff was lying properly on the machine.[187] And in a third case,[188] plaintiff was barred from recovery because of the provision contained in the membership contract (exculpatory clause). A member of the health club brought action against the club for damages for injuries sustained when the belt on a vibrating machine being used broke.

Suit was brought against a physical fitness salon as a result of an injury while using a reducing machine. Plaintiff described the machine as a "large couch type machine" with a rod that one holds onto over your head; your feet are propped up on things that look like pedals of some sort; it has platforms in the center that move, and the pedal-like things go like a bicycle, and that rod is pulled. She added that it pulls you back and forth, stretches you back and forth at the same time. Before beginning her slenderizing treatments, she had signed a statement certifying her physical condition. Plaintiff alleged that she had not been provided with accurate and true information as to the extent of danger in using the machine, and relied on misrepresentations to her detriment. While lying on the machine near the end of a second 30-minute session, plaintiff started to feel faint and weak. The machine was in its final stages when everything was moving and plaintiff did not know how to turn it off, so remained on the machine until it turned off automatically. She called out for help, but no one heard her. She had been told by defendants not to get off the machine while it was in motion or she could hurt herself. When she got off, plaintiff went to the bathroom and found she was passing blood. She, then, directly went to her doctor's office and found that she had kidney stones, which she had not known before. Defendants argued that they had discharged their duty to make reasonable inquiry into plaintiff's health and physical condition before beginning treatments and had no further duty to discover the preexisting kidney condition. Remanded for determination of negligence.[189]

The plaintiff had been a member of the Club about a month when she was thrown from one of the exercise machines known as a "pony roller," when it allegedly all of a sudden increased speed. Held for defendant who had given proper and adequate instruction, appropriate supervision, and had maintained the premises, including inspection of equipment, in safe condition.[190]

Injuries have occurred on other equipment than exercise machines. An athlete was electrocuted while using the whirlpool bath. The coach had modified the wiring and the ground fault interrupter was absent in violation of the National Electrical Code. The absence of the ground was held the last and only substantial factor causing death.[191]

It was alleged that cause of child being born with cerebral palsy was mother's exposure when pregnant to superheated water in a hot tub owned and operated by

---

[186] Petry v. Cosmopolitan Spa, Int'l, 641 S.W. 2d 202 (Tenn. App. 1982).

[187] Neuman v. Gloria Marshall Figure Salon, 149 Ill. App. 3d 824, 102 Ill. Dec. 910, 500 N.E. 2d 101 (1986).

[188] Empress Health & Beauty Spa v. Turner, 503 S.W. 2d 188 (Tenn. 1973).

[189] Shugar v. Pat Walker Figure Perfection Salons, Int'l, 541 S.W. 2d 511 (Tex. Civ. App. 1976).

[190] O'Pry v. World Wide Health Studios, 268 So. 2d 319 (La. App. 1972).

[191] Massie v. Persson, 729 S.W. 2d 448 (Ky. App. 1987).

defendant resort. Plaintiff alleged that owner of premises had duty to warn; the court stated that such allegation must include that owner had actual or constructive knowledge of dangerous condition.[192]

Plaintiff was injured when using a tanning bed available on a fee basis at a hairstyling salon. At issue was an exculpatory clause in contract for use.[193]

For further discussion on equipment and products liability, see Chapter 21, and on exculpatory clauses, see Chapter 16.

§ 17.45   Fitness testing

Plaintiff was an 18-year-old high school student who sought admission to college as a physical education major. A prerequisite for admission was taking certain mental and physical tests, including physical fitness index tests, known as P.F.I. tests. The battery of strength tests included seven tests, among which was the leg lift. The leg lift test was fifth in the series and was administered by one senior student, while another recorded the results. A physical education instructor was in charge, but was not in the foyer where the test was being administered at the time of the injury. Plaintiff alleged a serious injury to her left knee due to the incompetence of the student, since proper administration of the test required a person of experience with the testing machine (apparatus). The senior had a tests and measurements course during which he was instructed in the administration of the test, and also there had been general group instruction to the student assistants helping with the new student testing. The record was not clear on the instruction, but it appeared from the testimony of the senior that it was not too comprehensive, and he stated that he had not been taught that there was possibility of injury to the cartilages and ligaments of the knees from the leg lift test. Judgment for plaintiff.[194]

In a 1983 case[195] a 14-year-old girl dislocated her right elbow when she struck the gymnasium wall while running the speed test portion of the State physical fitness test in a gym class at the junior high school. Plaintiff alleges that the defendant was negligent in failing to follow the recommendations in the State manual for designing the course and failing to provide adequate instructions and supervision for the students performing the test. The manual required at least 14' of unobstructed space, and there were only 8'. Although the race was taking place in an area much smaller than standard called for in the manual, no warnings were given by the instructor to the girls of possible safety hazards. The danger was foreseeable. Judgment for plaintiff. (See also §10.13 Physical tests as a part of physical education.)

In a third case[196] a young Scout was injured when he participated in the rope and ladder climb as part of a physical fitness test conducted as one of the demonstrations at the Boy Scout exposition. The exposition was sponsored to demonstrate scouting

[192] Leenen v. Ruttgers Ocean Beach Lodge, Ltd., 662 F. Supp. 240 (1987) also at issue was application of Florida's limited partnership law.

[193] Ward v. Dunn, 136 Misc. 2d 781, 519 N.Y.S. 2d 307 (1987).

[194] Brittan v. State, 200 Misc. 743, 103 N.Y.S. 2d 485 (1951).

[195] Ehlinger v. Board of Education, New Hartford, 96 A.D. 2d 708, 465 N.Y.S. 2d 378 (1983).

[196] Stoolman v. Camden Co. Council Boy Scouts, 77 N.J. Super. 129, 185 A. 2d 436 (1962).

activities to the general public. At that time, the Scouts came under the New Jersey law of charitable immunity, and the case was not decided on its merits.

The Harvard Step Test was the fitness test at issue in a 1986 case.[197] As part of her training program for crew, a 15-year-old girl was participating in the testing program. The test requires that one step briskly up and on a 16″ high bench, step back to the ground and repeat the process rapidly for two minutes. The testing was being done on a field and apparently the bench had been placed on uneven ground, so that when plaintiff was performing the test she fell. A girl in the preceding group also had lost her balance and fell backwards. The coach did not see either fall because he was mainly looking at a stop watch and counting cadence. The case was remanded for determination of negligence as to whether the bench was improperly positioned by her coach and adequacy of supervision.

Plaintiff and husband had been a member of the health club for approximately six years. She was advised by the doctor to strengthen her abdominal muscles prior to undergoing some surgery. She informed one of the employees what her doctor had recommended, and the employee said she would have to undergo a "fitness test" first which consisted of various stretching and lifting exercises. One of the tests was on the leg curling machine, performing repetitions with increasing tension to 80 pounds. She suffered injury to the lumbar region of her back. Plaintiff alleged incompetent personnel and failure to properly supervise and warn of dangers/consequences. Held that exculpatory clause barred recovery by plaintiff.[198]

Three cases[199] in the '80s concerned a treadmill. In the *Tart* case, plaintiff suffered a heart attack, and sued on malpractice. Plaintiff's employer required him to take an annual physical exam, including a stress test, and he had done so for six years. This time, about 15 to 20 minutes after the test, while still at the Institute where all the tests had been given, plaintiff suffered a heart attack. As a result, he lost his pilot's license and his job as pilot for his employer. Plaintiff alleges defendants failed to properly monitor and administer the stress test and should have stopped the test during the fourth stage when he complained of "heavy fatigue." Instead, the test continued for several minutes until the fourth stage was completed. Remanded on technical issues of trial procedure. Plaintiff suffered a stroke while taking a stress test at a VA hospital in the *Hedgecorth* case. The court found that there had been a departure from the proper standard of care, that is, the stress test never should have been given based on medical and other records; one pertinent record had not been obtained. And, there was failure to fully disclose certain risks during the informed consent process. In the *Figure World* case, plaintiff, a new member of the Club, fell from a jogging treadmill when an employee shouted instructions "suck in that stomach" as she was attempting to master the treadmill. Held for plaintiff; evidence was sufficient to establish that employee's shouting was a breach of duty.

[197] Hornyak v. Pomfret School, 783 F. 2d 284 (1986).
[198] Lovelace v. Figure Salon, 345 S.E. 2d 139 (Ga. App. 1986).

[199] Figure World, Inc. v. Farley, 680 S.W. 2d 33 (Tex. App. 1984); Hedgecorth v. U.S., 618 F. Supp. 627 (1985) Missouri law applied; Tart v. McGann, 697 F. 2d 75 (1982).

§ 17.46   Fitness activities

Few cases have been identified which have involved activities in a health spa or fitness program; however, where such clubs/facilities and programs utilize activities, such as racquet sports, swimming, et al., the nature of the suits would be the same as for those activities, see Part B, which describes situations which have given rise to suits in specific activities. See also §17.44 for use of exercise machines.

The plaintiff joined the defendant health spa and about one week later he worked out in the exercise room for 1 to 1 ½ hours and then took a shower; continued to the steam bath, the sauna, and the whirlpool bath all in the period of 45 minutes and took a cold shower; then, proceeded to the swimming pool where he shortly lost consciousness. He was found on the bottom of the pool by a passing patron who pulled him from the pool and administered first aid, saving his life. Plaintiff was in the medical center about ten days, but is now unable to pronounce words clearly, has emotionally induced stuttering, and has trouble remembering recent events. The plaintiff's petition listed 12 breaches of duty, including failure to give instruction on the proper and safe use of facilities, unqualified personnel and lack of adequate supervision, et al. Court remanded for determination of negligence on part of defendant. It did state, however, that the duty owed by the defendant to patrons who use its swimming pool is the same duty owed by the public swimming pool operator to its patrons.[200]

A highway patrolman was struck in the neck with a racquetball while playing the game at a private health spa during his lunch hour. He suffered partial facial paralysis and loss of hearing. The details of the accident were not described; the point at issue was whether the injured qualified under Workers Compensation.[201]

A chiropractor treated the plaintiff for back problems and advised her to take an aerobic dance class to relieve her tension headaches. About a month later she did enroll at the defendant's health spa. After several months, plaintiff now sued; she had fallen and injured her back during an aerobic dance class. She alleged that the class was overcrowded, improperly supervised, and conducted negligently by defendant's personnel. Defendant also was charged with failing to use due care in screening plaintiff to determine if she was physically capable of taking the class, and also failed to warn plaintiff of the dangers of aerobics to people with back problems. The health spa (defendants) countersued the chiropractor who had advised taking the class. Held that health spa's allegation that chiropractor's advice directly contributed to individual's injury stated a claim for contribution.[202]

Another case,[203] while focusing on an exculpatory clause, also involved a health-related professional (a physical therapist) and a back problem. Plaintiff had been referred to the health spa by her doctor as part of post-operative treatment following surgery on the lumbar area of her spine. But, in fact, the plaintiff alleged, the treatment

[200] Keating v. Arthur Treacher's Fish and Chips, 77 A.D. 2d 616, 430 N.Y.S. 2d 364 (1980).

[201] Roberts v. Dept. of Public Safety, 654 P. 2d 1088 (Okla. App. 1982); see §25.34 Workers compensation.

[202] Contino v. Lucille Roberts Health Spa, 125 A.D. 2d 437, 509 N.Y.S. 2d 369 (1986).

[203] Leidy v. Deseret Enterprises, Inc., 252 Pa. Super. 162, 381 A. 2d 164 (1977).

given by the health spa was directly contrary to her doctor's instructions. The health spa joined its employee, the P.T., on the theory that she had acted outside the scope of her employment in her treatment of the plaintiff. The court stated that an exculpatory contract, although not favored, could be held valid. And, it further commented that the P.T.'s status was comparable to that of a druggist, and if therapy is performed in direct contradiction to a doctor's orders, there is breach of the duty imposed by law to avoid acts dangerous to life or health and could be held liable, notwithstanding the exculpatory clause.

A third back-problem case, *McKinley v. Slenderella Systems*, 63 N.J. Super. 571, 165 A.2d 207 (1960), also related to treatments at a health spa. A 51-year-old secretary, having read newspaper advertisements and saw television commercials, signed up for 50 treatments on the "Slenderella machine," paying $100. The contract she signed contained a statement that the person signing was in good health and could undertake and complete the program outlined. Relying on this representation, defendant made no physical examination of plaintiff. The treatments were twice a week and required plaintiff to stretch out on a table with her shoulder blades resting on two oscillating pads and her arms extended to grasp a bar above her head. After three or four treatments, plaintiff reported to the attendant that she experienced "great soreness" in her back, but the attendant urged her on and supplied a sponge pad for under her hips, which was subsequently removed by the attendant, although plaintiff asked for it. After about 24 treatments, plaintiff stopped taking the treatments because of her vacation and family illness, but resumed again about five months later. After a couple visits, her back pain resumed and became severe and continuous, so that she called her physician and was admitted to the hospital where she was placed in traction. An orthopedic surgeon recommended a heavy spinal support garment. Her physician testified that plaintiff had a preexisting condition known as lumbar lordosis and that the treatments had definitely magnified her condition into a ligamentous disorder of the lumbosacral joint. The orthopedic surgeon found that X-rays revealed a preexisting degenerative arthritis and that the treatments caused an acute irritation of the arthritic process. The court stated that where the reducing salon had made specific inquiry as to physical condition and received assurance that plaintiff was in good health and able to undergo the reducing treatments, it was not negligent because it did not investigate patron's condition by a physical examination; it was not charged with the duty required of one providing medical treatments. However, the court further stated that once having learned of patron's sore back, the salon must use reasonable care to prevent reasonable risk of harm by continuing treatments and telling her they could not harm her, but would benefit her; salon was under duty to use reasonable care to avoid any further risk of harm to plaintiff.

There are not many laws related to fitness activities *per se*. Arkansas has a statute prohibiting endurance contests. An Illinois law, however, requires that a physical fitness center shall have available and on its premises at all times when members are engaging in activities or receiving services at least one person who holds a valid certificate in basic CPR. Such a person in rendering services is protected with immunity except for willful or wanton misconduct. The law applies to not-for-profit entities which offer services, as well as commercial fitness centers (see §17.16).

§ 17.461   Racing, jogging, walking

Although there is extensive participation in road races, jogging and walking, it may be the individualized nature of participation which has resulted in few cases being identified related to such activities. In a 1980 New York case,[204] a volunteer participant in a March of Dimes walkathon stumbled in front of the double-decker bus leading the walk. The participants were repeatedly instructed not to march in front of the bus; therefore, plaintiff's own contributory negligence barred recovery. Plaintiff also alleged "last clear chance" doctrine, but there was insufficient evidence to indicate that either the supervisor of the walkathon or the driver of the bus failed to take any possible action once the volunteer stumbled in front of the bus.

An entrant in a 10,000 meter running event sued sponsors of the event, claiming that their negligence in failing to adequately warn resulted in his hospitalization and permanent impairment of some motor functions. He was hospitalized for heat stroke, heat prostration, renal failure, and several other disorders. The court held that he was aware of the dangers of overheating and dehydration and thus was precluded under assumption of risk, as well as a valid exculpatory clause in the entry form, from recovery.[205]

Hiking is included in the recreational user statutes; however, walking has been distinguished from hiking (see §12.13 and also §13.32). Tennessee passed a "Jogging Act of 1980," which sets forth requirements related to designation, posting, and maintenance of trails.

Two cases[206] in 1985 related to jogging. In the *Eddings* case, the plaintiff was struck by a car while he was running on the township road. While local governments have an obligation to maintain public property in a reasonably safe condition for those for whom the property is intended, it did not have a duty owed this jogger to maintain foilage along road in condition which allowed clear visibility, to construct and maintain pavement and shoulder of road of sufficient widths to allow safe passage of vehicles and pedestrians, or to place and maintain traffic control devices to warn of dangerous conditions just specified. The Florida situation involved a shirtless runner who brought action challenging the town ordinance restricting shirtless running or jogging. The court held that the ordinance was a reasonable exercise of police power and that its restrictions bore rational relationship to the town's general welfare.

And, two cases[207] in 1986 dealt with jogging. In the federal case, a jogger was injured (broken hip) when he fell into a ditch at storm sewer outfall on a federally owned recreation area. He alleged failure of the government to warn of ditch. The ditch was 4' to 8' wide and 5' deep. The ditch was caused by water flow after the season's first hard rain earlier in the evening. Plaintiff was jogging on the sandy beach on an overcast and moonless night. Similar ditches had formed in the past, but no warnings had ever been

204 Ely v. Northumberland General Ins. Co., 378 So. 2d 1024 (La. App. 1979).

205 Williams v. Cox Enterprises, 159 Ga. App. 333, 283 S.E. 2d 367 (1981).

206 De Weese v. Town of Palm Beach, 616 F. Supp. 971, 688 F. 2d 731, (1985); Eddings by Eddings v. Dundee Tp. Highway Com'r., 135 Ill. App. 3d 190, 88 Ill. Dec. 397, 478 N.E. 2d 888 (1985).

207 Smith v. Perlmutter, 145 Ill. App. 3d 783, 99 Ill. Dec. 783, 496 N.E. 2d 358 (1986); Spires v. U.S., 805 F. 2d 832 (1986) California law applied.

posted. The government was aware of joggers along the beaches at night, often without flashlights. Court held for defendant under the California recreational user statute (see §12.1); it found the government lacked actual or constructive notice of the ditch, and thus, could not be liable for willful or malicious failure to warn. The other case involved medical malpractice. Plaintiff (administrator of estate) alleged defendant negligently failed to diagnose, properly treat or refer decedent to a specialist for medical treatment for his coronary heart disease; and, as a result, decedent was found dead at the YMCA shortly after jogging in the late afternoon. Autopsy revealed death by severe coronary artery disease. Judgment for defendant, who asserted he met applicable standard of practice in care and treatment of decedent.

§ 17.47   Rehabilitation

This section deals only with rehabilitation as would be conducted in a fitness program by professional physical education or recreation personnel, and does not include malpractice cases which may be brought against physical therapists or physicians. At least one state, North Carolina, has provided through legislation for certification of cardiac rehabilitation programs delivering services in environments other than hospitals. The American College of Sports Medicine has a program of professional certification at different levels of responsibility/competence, primarily for fitness programs and operation of fitness laboratories.

Following surgery for slipped disc in her cervical spine, the plaintiff had joined a health spa in order to swim and have other exercise. She was injured in a fall when she stepped in water on the floor of the locker room. The court stated that in determining negligence involving an unreasonable risk of harm, the type of people that might be affected must be considered. Thus, it was for the jury to decide whether the operator of the health spa failed to keep premises in reasonably safe condition, in view of its knowledge that many of its customers were there for treatment and suffered from physical infirmity.[208]

Of particular interest in rehabilitation is cardiac rehabilitation.[209] A 1982 case,[210] although not rehabilitation, involved a heart attack while the person was engaged in physical activity. The decedent at age 38 collapsed while officiating an interfraternity basketball game. And in New York a football player died while playing in high school.

[208] Bertrand v. Palm Springs & European Health Spa, Inc., 257 Or. 532, 480 P. 2d 424 (1971).
[209] Karnezis, Kristine Cordier. Heart Attack Following Exertion or Exercise as Within Terms of Accident Provision of Insurance Policy. 1 A.L.R. 4th 1319-1348. Herthel v. Time Ins. Co., 221 Wis. 208, 265 N.W. 575 (1936) pulling boat; Mass. Mut. Life Ins. Co. v. Pistolesi, 160 F. 2d 668, cert. denied. 332 U.S. 759, 68 S. Ct. 59 (1947) yacht rigging; New Amsterdam Casualty Co. v. Johnson, 91 Ohio St. 155, 110 N.E. 475 (1914) horseback ride, then cold water plunge; Schmid v. Indiana Travelers' Acci. Ass'n., 42 Ind. App. 483, 85 N.E. 1032 (1908) trip going from low to high altitude; Shopp v. Prudential Ins. Co., 115 N.J.L. 162, 178 A. 724 (1935) swim pool; Tanner v. Life Ins. Co., 217 Va. 218, 227 S.E. 2d 693 (1976) physical education teacher wrestled with student creating disturbance; Underwriters at Lloyd's, London v. Lyons, 248 F. 2d 149 (1957) hunting, applying Oregon law; Trueblood v. Maryland Assur. Co., 129 Cal. App. 102, 18 P. 2d 90 (1933) fell into whirlpool of water. Although these cases did not involve a determination of negligence, but rather relate to whether or not the situation was within terms of insurance accident policy, the situations involve physical education, sport or recreation; it will be noted that many of the cases are quite old.
[210] Warthen v. Southeast Okla. State Univ., 641 P. 2d 1125 (Okla. App. 1982).

He had a long history of heart illness which was serious enough to preclude the playing of football, but the student had been permitted to play without the required physical examination and without parental permission.[211] (See preceding subsection for other heart-related cases.)

The *Cardamone* case[212] is related to rehabilitation. After plaintiff was permanently paralyzed in an accident on gymnastic equipment, as a member of the gymnastic team, the University had been paying for his medical costs, until it was sued on negligence, then it stopped. This suit was filed in equity seeking mandatory preliminary injunction to compel the University to continue to defray medical costs. The court held that there was no contract in that the services rendered by the student as a student athlete were neither rendered or bargained for in exchange for the University's promise to pay the medical bills given the fact that such services were rendered prior to execution of agreement in question, nor was University's promise to pay given in consideration for student's forbearance in instituting suit for damages. Judgment for University.

---

[211] Monaco v. Raymond, 471 N.Y.S. 2d 225 (1984); see also McAdams v. Windham, 208 Ala. 492, 94 So. 742 (1922) blow with bare fist over the heart in a boxing match; on examination found bruised place on heart and surmised blow on that place resulted in the death; no liability as lawful, friendly combat "volenti non fit injuria."

[212] Cardamone v. Univ. of Pittsburgh, 384 A. 2d 1228 (Pa. 1978).

Chapter 18.   Supervision

Lack of or inadequate supervision is the most common allegation of negligence. It is estimated that of cases which involve programmatic situations, approximately 80 percent of the plaintiff's allegations involve supervision. Because supervision permeates so many case situations, this chapter endeavors only to set forth some of the principles of supervision with limited case illustrations. Supervisory situations for pools, water-related recreation, and spectators are not included in this section; see §§9.4, 14.35, and 15.12, respectively. Parental responsibilities, as related to supervision, for the most part, are not included in this Chapter, nor addressed elsewhere in this book, inasmuch as the focus is upon community organizations and agencies.

It should be noted that lack of supervision or inadequate supervision may not necessarily create liability; it must be shown that the lack of supervision is the proximate cause of the injury (see §18.4). Further, for the plaintiff to recover there must be a duty to supervise the plaintiff on the part of the defendant. The duty to supervise is set forth in the first section. A key element is the distinction between a duty to render specific supervision and a duty to provide general supervision. Who should render supervision? The second section deals with the supervisor — the competence of the person, the location of the supervisor at time of injury, and the number of supervisors on duty.

What is adequate or proper supervision? To determine the standard for supervision is most difficult. *Miller v. Griesel*[1] commented, thusly: "What constitutes due care and adequate supervision...depends largely on the circumstances, such as the number and age of the students...,the activity in which they are engaged, the period for which they are left without supervision, the ease of providing some alternative means of supervision...." The nature of supervision is presented in the third section. It includes the supervisory plan, the management of behavior, and other functions of supervision. Additional insights as to the standard for supervision are included in the first section under "duty inherent in the situation."

With the importance of the dichotomy of discretionary and ministerial acts of the employee to the tort claims acts (see §4.13), it should be noted that supervision is a ministerial act for which liability attaches.[2]

§ 18.1   Duty to supervise

The duty to supervise may arise in the same manner as any duty owed — by statutory requirement, by voluntary assumption of a duty, and by the duty being inherent in the situation. As set forth in *Univ. of Denver v. Whitlock*, 712 P. 2d 1072 (Colo. App. 1985), rev'd. 744 P. 2d 54 (Colo. 1987), the basis of duty is whether or not there is a special relationship between plaintiff and defendant which requires that the defendant take affirmative action to provide a reasonably safe environment. (See §2.1 The duty.) However, inasmuch as one is not an insurer of safety[3] and all situations do not give rise to a duty, there are a considerable number of cases where the allegation is failure to supervise, but in fact there is no duty to supervise. The duty to supervise should be distinguished from the authority to control the conduct of participants under the doctrine of *in loco parentis*. (See §2.1112 Doctrine of *in loco parentis*.) When one employs an independent contractor for transportation or program services, supervisory responsibilities must be specified. Generally, responsibility for supervision cannot be delegated to a premises repair contractor, as indicated in an early Canadian playground case, *Ellis v. Board of Trustees*, 2 W.W.R. 19 (1946). (See §§3.12 and 22.1).

§ 18.11   No duty to supervise

The circumstances which give rise to no duty to supervise are quite diverse. The most common circumstance is that of the use of the natural environment and undeveloped lands for outdoor recreation. The landowner does not have to provide supervision of the participants engaged in activity when on the land. The duty owed the user may be determined by the recreational user statute (see §12.1) or the tort claim statute (see §4.2); but, the duties specified in these statutes do not encompass supervision of activities. Even though a natural body of water or land area, there may be

---

[1] Miller v. Griesel, 297 N.E. 2d 463 (Ind. App. 1973), aff'd. 308 N.E. 2d 701 (Ind. 1974).

[2] See, for example, Comuntiz v. Pinellas Co. School Board, 508 So. 2d 750 (Fla. App. 1987); Ross v. Consumers Power, 420 Mich. 567, 363 N.W. 2d 641 (1984).

[3] Patterson v. Orleans Parish School Board, 461 So. 2d 386 (La. App. 1984); Rollins v. Concordia Parish School Board, 465 So. 2d 213 (La. App. 1985). See also §2.2, introduction to section.

a duty to supervise if there is high density use which gives rise to foreseeable dangers. Certainly warnings are essential regarding the conditions of the natural area (see §14.3 and §20.3). However, where the activity is sponsored by either a public or a private entity, the activity must be supervised by that sponsoring entity (see Chapters 12, 13, and 14), or if the owner/lessor voluntarily assumes a duty to supervise, it must perform such supervision in a professional manner (see §18.13).

The Bureau of Land Management granted permission to hold a European-style scrambles motorcycle race on its lands and supervision was the responsibility of the sponsor of the race holding the lease, not the BLM.[4] However, in *Ward v. U.S.*,[5] the government had retained control over the premises, and, thus, was required, in accord with a statute (Colorado), to provide reasonable supervision of swimming facilities leased by the government to an association. Lessor is not completely and automatically absolved of liability for injury sustained on premises merely through execution of a lease. (See §3.11 Lessor/lessee.) Plaintiff was injured while snorkeling in a portion of the bay not designated for public swimming when he was hit by a motorboat. Held: no duty to supervise that portion of the bay not designated as public swimming area.[6] In another case[7] the campground owners had not provided lifeguard supervision at a small swimming lake. While the court held that while there is a duty to take reasonable precautions for safety, based upon custom, it is not necessary to provide lifeguards.[8]

Urban areas, such as playgrounds, at certain seasons and times of week and day may be programmed and staffed with supervisors. This does not mean, however, that to avoid liability playgrounds need to be locked when not staffed; playgrounds are considered in continuous invitation to people to use them.[9] Generally there is no duty to supervise playgrounds at times other than those when the school is using it for the students or an agency is conducting activity on the playground. But, while there may not be a duty to supervise at the non-programmed hours, a duty to protect from dangerous conditions of area and facility, including equipment, remains (see §§20.2, 21.2 and 18.141). The duty to supervise areas and facilities should be distinguished from the duty to maintain such free from dangerous conditions (see §4.2) and nuisance (see §4.4).

An 8-year-old was struck by a 12-year-old on a bicycle while riding on the playground. The accident happened on a Saturday. The court held that where the activity drawing the spectators was not a school-related activity, there was no requirement for supervision by the school. Further, the school did not have knowledge that bicycles had been ridden in that area in a negligent or dangerous manner prior thereto.[10]

[4] Thompson v. U.S., 592 F. 2d 1104 (1979).

[5] Ward v. U.S., 208 F. Supp. 118 (1962) Colorado law applied.

[6] Cruz v. Metro. Dade Co., 350 So. 2d 533 (Fla. App. 1977).

[7] McClure v. Suter, 63 Ill. App. 3d 378, 20 Ill. Dec. 308, 379 N.E. 2d 1376 (1978).

[8] Swimming pools come under their own principles of law (see §9.4) as to when motel and resort pools do not need to be staffed with a lifeguard, however, any pool open with an admission charge certainly has an obligation to provide lifeguards. Pools most commonly are controlled by regulations and statutes.

[9] Davis v. Provo City Corp., 1 Utah 2d 244, 265 P. 2d 415 (1953); Diele v. Board of Educ., 1 A.D. 2d 676, 146 N.Y.S. 2d 511 (1955); Dolan v. N.Y.C., 5 A.D. 2d 300, 171 N.Y.S. 2d 724 (1958); Kantor v. Board of Educ., 251 A.D. 454, 296 N.Y. Supp. 516 (1937); Lutzker v. Board of Educ., 262 A.D. 881, 28 N.Y.S. 2d 496 (1941), aff'd. w/o op. 287 N.Y. 822, 41 N.E. 2d 97 (1942); Shields v. School District, 408 Pa. 388, 184 A. 2d 240 (1962).

[10] Orsini v. Guilderland Central School Dist. No. 2, 46 A.D. 2d 700, 360 N.Y.S. 2d 288 (1974); see also Diele v. Board of Education, 1 A.D. 2d 676, 146 N.Y.S. 2d 511 (1955) child struck by playmate on bicycle when

There may be no duty to supervise because of the nature of the activity and the expectations of the participants. In a 1986 Tennessee case,[11] while on a school field trip, a 13-year-old, eighth grade boy was injured when struck by an automobile when he crossed the street after lunch to go to the park. Plaintiff alleged that the two teachers were negligent in not personally escorting the student across the street. The court held that teachers do not have such duty where there was nothing to suggest that the student would not use ordinary care for his own safety or that the street was unreasonably dangerous to cross.

If an injury is not foreseeable, there is no duty to supervise.[12] Further, in a D.C. case,[13] in holding the school had a duty to a child who wandered off public school kindergarten playground through a gap in the fence and was struck and killed in street by a truck, the court said that if no special dangerous condition exists, a school is not under a duty to supervise all movements of its students at all times, but where such a condition does exist, and the school has knowledge of its existence, greater supervision is required to insure the safety of the students. Also, there has to be an activity which needs supervising, if lack of supervision is an allegation. The father of a student was injured at a father-son event, when another student went to retrieve a basketball and collided with him. It was alleged that the school failed to properly supervise events on premises in order to protect parent against injury; however, there was no indication of what activity needed to be regulated or supervised, and thus it was held that there was no basis for concluding that supervisory personnel could have prevented injury. The gymnasium was apparently overcrowded, but the plaintiff did not give evidence for the jury to draw such conclusion of fact.[14] Further, there is no duty to supervise unless there is a special relationship which gives rise to the duty to protect (see §2.1). In a Pennsylvania college situation, class picnic off-campus, the court held that no special relationship existed imposing upon the college either a duty to control conduct of student or to extend to plaintiff right of protection. Although there was a regulation prohibiting possession or consumption of alcohol at college-sponsored activities, this did not place college in custodial relationship with its students for purposes of imposing duty of protection to plaintiff.[15] (See also §1.2213 regarding duty related to intoxication.)

While the use of buildings tends to require at least general supervision, the principle of foreseeability may be applied as related to management of behavior of users; also, as with the outdoor areas, dangerous physical conditions must be taken care of and this is one of the functions of a supervisor (see §18.332).

about ready to leave playground — no duty; Kantor v. Board of Educ., 251 A.D. 454, 296 N.Y.S. 516 (1937) no duty, boy playing tag on bicycle injured child.

[11] King v. Kartanson, 720 S.W. 2d 65 (Tenn. App. 1986).

[12] Grant v. Lake Oswego School Dist., 515 P. 2d 947 (Ore. App. 1973); Hanley v. Hornbeck, 127 A.D.2d 905, 512 N.Y.S. 2d 262 (1987).

[13] Ballard v. Polly, 387 F. Supp. 895 (1975); see also Abdur-Rashid v. Consolidated Rail Corp., 135 A.D. 2d 208, 524 N.Y.S. 2d 716 (1988) child injured on tracks near playground, no duty to child who left playground absent any defect or condition of playground making danger foreseeable.

[14] Borushek v. Kincaid, 33 Ill. Dec. 839, 78 Ill. App. 3d 295, 397 N.E. 2d 172 (1979).

[15] Bradshaw v. Rawlings, 464 F. Supp. 175 (1979), 612 F. 2d 135 (1979), cert. denied. 100 S. Ct. 1836 (1980).

§ 18.12 Statutory duty to supervise

There are no generalized statutes which require supervision for physical education and sports, parks and recreation, or camping and adventure activities. Any statutes specific to a particular activity, which have been identified, are in Part B under the specific activity. Some states have statutes regarding the right of teachers to discipline.[16] (See §18.324 on discipline.)

There are several cases in point that construe the statutes, such as *Decker v. Dundee Cent. School Dist.*[17] in New York regarding adequate supervision. In this case it was held that lack of supervision breached a statutory duty. *Forgnone v. Salvadore Union Elem. School Dist.*,[18] also, was based upon a school law requiring supervision on school playgrounds. Illinois has a statute relating to discipline/supervision in schools that is the basis of a number of cases, inasmuch as it relates to teacher immunity.[19] The court held the federal government liable, based upon a Colorado statute requiring that the lessor provide or require reasonable supervision of swimming facilities.[20] And, in an early Kansas case,[21] the allegation was based upon failure to comply with a statutory duty to keep control of the student body.

§ 18.13 Voluntary assumption of duty to supervise

Particularly where natural environments are involved, there frequently is no duty to supervise (see §18.11 no duty); however, if supervision is undertaken, then that supervision must be performed with reasonable care. The New Jersey statute provides for immunity of a public entity for an injury caused by a condition of any unimproved public property, including natural conditions of beaches; but, it was indicated that if the defendant public entity undertook to provide supervision, then there was not immunity for negligent supervision.[22] There were similar holdings in two 1982 cases.[23] In the Hawaii situation, plaintiffs sued when their son drowned in the surf at a city beach. The court said that where a municipality is under no duty to provide lifeguard services, if it voluntarily assumes this protective responsibility, it has a duty to perform these services with reasonable care. On this particular day of the accident, there was no negligence in the performance of the lifeguards. Death came in the surf, too, in the California

[16] For example, California, Illinois, Kentucky, Louisiana, Maryland, Montana, South Dakota.

[17] Decker v. Dundee Cent. School Dist., 4 N.Y. 2d 462, 151 N.E. 2d 866 (1958).

[18] Forgnone v. Salvadore Union Elem. School Dist., 41 Cal. App. 2d 423, 106 P. 2d 932 (1940); see also Ogando v. Carquinez Grammar School Dist., 24 Cal. App. 2d 567, 75 P. 2d 641 (1938); Reithardt v. Board of Educ. of Yuba County, 43 Cal. App. 2d 629, 111 P. 2d 440 (1941).

[19] For example, Amer. States Ins. Co. v. Flynn, 102 Ill. App. 3d 201, 57 Ill. Dec. 889, 429 N.E. 2d 587 (1981); Hadley v. Witt Unit School Dist., 123 Ill. App. 3d 19, 78 Ill. Dec. 758, 462 N.E. 2d 877 (1984); Hilgendorf v. First Baptist Church of Danville, 157 Ill.

App. 3d 428, 109 Ill. Dec. 659, 510 N.E. 2d 527 (1987); Holsapple v. Casey Community Unit School Dist., 157 Ill. App. 3d 391, 109 Ill. Dec. 631, 510 N.E. 2d 499 (1987); Prest v. Sparta Comm. Unit School Dist. 140, 157 Ill. App. 3d 569, 109 Ill. Dec. 727, 510 N.E. 2d 595 (1987).

[20] Ward v. U.S., 208 F. Supp. 118 (1962).

[21] Koehn v. Board of Educ., 193 Kan. 263, 392 P. 2d 949 (1964).

[22] Kleinke v. Ocean City, 163 N.J. Super. 424, 394 A. 2d 1257 (1978).

[23] Kaczmarcsyk v. City & Co. of Honolulu, 656 P. 2d 89 (Hawaii 1982); Gonzales v. San Diego, 130 Cal. App. 3d 882, 182 Cal. Rptr. 73 (1982).

situation, where there was a dangerous riptide. The city had voluntarily provided lifeguard and police protection on the beach, which it owned, and the court stated that therefore the city would be held to the same standard of care as a private individual or entity. As indicated in *Avallone v. Board of Co. Com'rs,* 467 So. 2d 826 (Fla. App. 1985) 493 So. 2d 1002 (1986), the decision to provide or not to provide supervision may be a discretionary act protected by immunity (see §4.13), but the actual performance of supervision is a ministerial or operational act for which there is liability.

A 20-year-old university student drowned while attending a picnic at a lake maintained and controlled by the Board of Regents. An attendant at the boat house issued a canoe and life vest to decedent, who almost immediately overturned in the canoe and drowned because he could not swim. The Board had implemented a policy regarding safe use of the facility, including providing lifeguards (none were at dock and no warning given not on duty), certification of swimming ability as prerequisite to use certain boating equipment (but not canoes), and no instruction given regarding use of life vest or canoe (no warning of inherent instability of canoes). Held: once Board assumed responsibility for operating lake facility and distributing recreational equipment, it is no longer protected by sovereign immunity.[24]

Plaintiff was injured while playing hockey on the public ice skating rink, but held for the defendant, stating that the municipality making the rink available without charge had no duty to provide supervision of those participating in games on ice, but if it assumed such duty, it must apply reasonable care to perform it adequately. Supervision of the warming house was distinguished from supervision of activities on the ice.[25]

Schools, too, can by their actions give rise to a duty to supervise. Whereas normally a school would not need to supervise the playground after the school day had closed, on this day a Tambourine and Fan Club not only had been given permission to conduct a track practice at 3:30, but the school also had distributed a flyer to the parents saying that their children would be under tight supervision, creating a duty to supervise at this time. Some children had laid a tetherball pole on its side and were rolling it around when the child doing this fell and the tire rolled on his head, injuring him. The court held that the school owed a duty to supervise.[26]

In a 1984 Minnesota case,[27] which involved an activity of the high school cheerleaders during which an automobile accident occurred, the court held that a school district is not liable for safety of all students while in transit to or from a school activity; however, a school district may be liable where it has undertaken to provide supervision. It further said that where a school district has assumed control and supervision of all activities of a school club operated under its auspices, parents of participants have a right to rely upon such assumption. There is, though, no requirement of constant supervision of all movements of students at all times.

[24] Brown v. Florida State Board of Regents, 513 So. 2d 184 (Fla. App. 1987).

[25] Diker v. St. Louis Park, 286 Minn. 461, 130 N.W. 2d 113 (1964).

[26] Augustus v. Joseph A. Craig Elem. School, 459 So. 2d 665 (La. App. 1984).

[27] Verhel v. Indp. School Dist. No. 709, 359 N.W. 2d 579 (Minn. 1984).

In *Walker v. Garris*[28] the court held that although there was no obligation to hold a hayride for a group of children, once the activity was undertaken, there was a duty to conduct the hayride properly by providing a suitable conveyance for the hayride and by controlling and supervising the children so as to protect them from injury. In this situation plaintiff's daughter fell from the flatbed trailer being used for the hayride and was run over.

§ 18.14   Duty inherent in the situation — general, transitional, and specific supervision

Most of the situations within the fields of sport and physical education, parks and recreation, and camping and adventure activities have inherent the duty to supervise the participants, when such participants are engaged in sponsored activity. Sponsored activity includes any pursuit or involvement under the auspices of a public or private entity, such as free play in the parks or on the playground, whether at school, a resort, a motel, "fast food" place, camp, or wherever; "open" recreation in the school gymnasium, community center, or the facilities of the Y or other organization; and use of swimming, sport and fitness facilities, or other member leisure services, whether informal participation or instruction. Three 1988 cases affirmed this duty. In *Benitez v. N.Y.C. Board of Education*, 530 N.Y.S.2d 825 (1988), a situation involving a high school football player, the court said that the "school has a duty to supervise activities of students in its charge; that student is engaged in supervised interscholastic varsity sports does not lessen school's duty." And, in a Boy Scout activity, the court stated "Scoutmaster of Boy Scout troop had legal responsibility to take reasonable precautions for ... Boy Scout's safety during camping expedition." In *McGarr v. Boy Scouts of America*, 74 Md. App. 127, 536 A.2d 728 (1988). The duty toward a handicapped person (cerebral palsied) was set forth in *Funez v. Jefferson Parish School Board*, 528 So. 2d 1057 (La. App. 1988). Failure to perform such duty to supervise may be against the school or organization policy and result in dismissal from employment, as occurred in *Westbrook v. Board of Educ., City of St. Louis*, 724 S.W.2d 698 (Mo. App. 1987), when five sixth-grade teachers did not properly supervise the students during a field trip on which one student drowned.

The question is not so much whether there is a duty to supervise, but rather whether such supervision must be specific or can be general in nature, or whether it is transitional in nature. By specific is meant that the supervisor is directly with the individual or small group; whereas general supervision is when the supervisor "oversees" activity which is going on in a facility or on an area. Transitional supervision is when within a given activity timeframe supervision may change from specific to general and back, perhaps even several times during the session. Each of these three types of supervision has several dimensions.[29]

[28] Walker v. Garris, 368 So. 2d 277 (Ala. 1979) private party.

[29] Since the allegation of inadequate supervision is very common and a considerable number of cases are

A. Specific supervision
   1. Instruction
   2. Participant incapability, physically or mentally
   3. Participant behaviors
B. Transitional supervision
   1. From specific to general
   2. From no supervision to general
C. General supervision
   1. Individual-oriented supervision in an activity
   2. Group behaviors-oriented supervision in a facility or on an area

Specific supervision is required when there is instruction, participant incapability, or certain participant behaviors. Specific supervision is most often thought of in the instructional mode.[30] From a legal perspective, instruction is being given so that the individual can gain that knowledge of the activity, understanding in terms of one's own capabilities, and appreciation of the potential injuries required to have the participant assume the inherent risks of the activity. As the participant gains in knowledge, understanding, and appreciation, the degree of specific supervision required is reduced, and, in fact, the participant is provided with transitional supervision and then general supervision. Specific supervision, or what some persons refer to as "close" supervision, is **not** a function of the activity, but of the individual participating. Some people talk about "high risk activities" or "hazardous activities"[31] — it is not the activity which is hazardous or high risk, for the courts have not held any activity but boxing inherently dangerous, but the people and how they participate; in other words, reference should be made to "people hazards" rather than "activity hazards"! The determinant of likelihood of injury is directly related to the participant's skill capability, physical and mental condition to do the activity, and knowledge/understanding/ appreciation of the activity itself. (See also Chapter 19 Conduct of activity.)

When there is inability to perform the activity, due to physical disability or lack of mental capacity, then specific supervision is required. This most usually is in regard to recreational or educational activities provided in special/adapted physical education or therapeutic recreation programs offered for selected special populations, including both children and adults (see also §§19.1 and 17.34).

The third situation in which specific supervision is required is when participant behaviors so indicate, i.e., when the leadership of the activity (or the sponsor) has notice of the "propensity" of the individual to behave in the manner which either is self-injurious or injurious to others. This notice can be either actual or constructive.

A retarded student had been at the school for three and one-half years and had given no indication that he was dangerous to himself. He had many times worked near and

---

presented in other sections of this chapter, only a few illustrative cases are given in describing each of the three types of supervision briefly.

[30] Price v. Mount Diablo Unified School Dist., 177 Cal. App. 2d 312, 2 Cal. Rptr. 23 (1960); Reisman v.

Los Angeles City School Dist., 123 Cal. App. 2d 493, 267 P. 2d 36 (1954); Sayers v. Ranger, 16 N.J. Super. 22, 83 A. 2d 775 (1951).

[31] The Illinois and California legislatures passed statutes with such reference.

walked by the pond in which he drowned. Thus there were insufficient acts by the decedent to dictate continuous supervision.[32]

In a mountain climbing situation where the decedent plunged to his death from a precipice while practicing mountain climbing on an outing, it was held a matter for the jury as to whether the actions of the child were reasonably foreseeable and thus required additional precautions by the scoutmaster. The scoutmaster was aware that the scout was compulsively adventuresome, required strict supervision, and frequently disregarded instructions when they impeded his search for adventure; also, that he was keenly interested in rope climbing and the scoutmaster had allowed the scout to use his climbing equipment earlier without supervision.[33]

It was held in *Kersey v. Harbin*[34] that there was constructive knowledge of the quarrelsome propensities on the part of the student who occasioned the fatal injury of plaintiff's son as he went from the locker room to the gym. Whether the care exercised in supervision was adequate was a matter for the jury.

Transitional supervision means "a change from one state to another," usually from specific supervision to general supervision, and perhaps back and forth between the two forms several times. Many of our instructional activities, particularly, require this type of supervision. There is instruction (specific supervision) then there is practice in small groups or individually of the skill taught (general supervision). One can place participants under general supervision when the instructor feels comfortable that the individuals have adequate knowledge, understanding, and appreciation of that particular skill or activity as a whole so that they can perform it appropriately. The participant also must understand and adhere to the safety practices and procedures set forth. The supervisor in shifting to general supervision must be alert to any changing conditions which may cause possible hazardous situations, such as inability to execute a skill, fatiguing, not adhering to a safety procedure, and upon noting any such changed conditions must resume specific supervision as to that particular participant. The criteria for specific supervision apply when in specific supervision mode, and the criteria for general supervision when in that mode.

One might also refer to the type of supervision as transitional when there is either no duty to supervise or there is general supervision and because of the behaviors of the participants one must change to general supervision or specific supervision, respectively; however, this is not truly the transitional supervision of the preceding definition because such situations are not a "back and forth" shifting of supervision, integral to appropriate conduct of the activity, but a behavioral orientation which requires a change in the nature of supervision.

General supervision has two dimensions — individual-oriented supervision in an activity and group behaviors-oriented supervision in a facility or on an area. When engaged in individual-oriented supervision the focus of the supervisor is on the

[32] Hunter v. Evergreen Presbyterian Vocational School, 338 So. 2d 164 (La. App. 1976).

[33] Coffey v. Hilands, 42 Or. App. 193, 600 P. 2d 466 (1979).

[34] Kersey v. Harbin, 531 S.W. 2d 76 (Mo. App. 1975), aff'd., rev'd./in part 591 S.W. 2d 745 (Mo. App. 1979); see also Gammon v. Edwardsville Comm. Unit School Dist. No. 7, 82 Ill. App. 3d 586, 38 Ill. Dec. 28, 403 N.E. 2d 43 (1980).

individual's manner of engaging in the activity. For example, a supervisor of a weight room watches if individuals are properly using the equipment; a lifeguard (yes, lifeguarding is general supervision) is alert to any problems individuals have in the water. In contrast, when one supervises the use of a facility or an area (athletic fields, parks, recreation center, outdoor recreation area, et al.), one is aware of the behaviors of people and dangerous conditions. The extent of general supervision which must be given depends upon the density of use of the area or facility; the greater the density, the greater the extent of general supervision.

A nine-year-old girl fell 40-50 times on the roller skating rink. It was held that if there had been reasonable watchfulness (supervision), the total inability of the child to skate would have been noted and action taken before injury.[35]

In *Brady v. Buffalo*,[36] a six-year-old was injured when struck by another sled while waiting in line for his turn to go up the slide. There were a lot of people in front of him; he was near the end of the line and some other child started to run, did a belly flop on the sled and rammed into the young child (plaintiff). The court held that an adequate degree of general supervision should be exercised, but failure to furnish this supervision will result in liability only if violation of duty had a causal relation to the accident. It was held in a resident camp situation that the tent counselor was not required to be constantly in attendance with his campers and had no reason to anticipate any disturbance during rest hour, thus was found not negligent when plaintiff was injured by act of another boy at a time when the counselor was temporarily absent from the tent.[37] In another outdoor winter activity, ice hockey, the court held that general supervision was required for the hockey drill and that the league which was conducting the clinic and the city, which received a fee to enter the city-owned rink, shared the responsibility. Although the city had no control over the drill itself, the court said the city had a duty to provide general supervision to protect park invitees from foreseeable danger while using the facilities.[38] (Note: this latter holding is contra to some other cases.)

If there is a duty inherent in the situation and the participant refused the supervision, what then? Such a situation occurred in a horse trail ride.[39] The injured girl was 14 years of age. Her friend was experienced, but plaintiff had never been on a horse before. They were advised that they should take a guide, but a male friend of one of the mothers persuaded the attendant to let them ride alone, since the friend had ridden alone several times before. Plaintiff had difficulty in making her horse go and before they even reached the trail, they dismounted and walked the horses back to the stable. Then, the day of the accident, the two girls wanted again to ride alone and after much persuasion, they were permitted to do so; and, the wife of the owner disclaimed any liability for any injuries. When on the trail the plaintiff did not see a tree hazard in time and she was struck, fell from her horse, and sustained injuries. The court found the plaintiff contributorily negligent in failing to accept the services of a guide; however, the stables also was found negligent as related to maintenance of the trail.

---

[35] Blizzard v. Fitzsimmons, 193 Miss. 484, 10 So. 2d 343 (1942).

[36] Brady v. Buffalo, 34 A.D. 2d 877, 312 N.Y.S. 2d 447 (1970).

[37] Goldberger v. David Roberts Corp., 139 Conn. 629, 96 A. 2d 309 (1953).

[38] Santangelo v. City of N.Y., 66 A.D. 2d 880, 411 N.Y.S. 2d 666 (1978).

[39] Willenbring v. Borkenhagen, 29 Wis. 2d 464, 139 N.W. 2d 53 (1966).

§ 18.141 Playgrounds

Almost all playground cases allege lack of supervision; however, except as indicated in §18.11 (the circumstances which have no duty to supervise), most all cases hold that general supervision is all that is required.[40] While the school is not an insurer of safety, there must be supervision when children are on the playground during times when the school is in charge of the playground (*e.g.*, recess, lunch time);[41] the duty owed is that of a reasonable, prudent parent.[42] The fact that each student is not personally supervised every moment of each school day does not constitute fault, nor does spontaneous and/or planned acts of violence by students on school grounds create liability if the school ground is otherwise well supervised.[43] However, supervisors should be alert for prohibited or dangerous activity.[44]

The New York court extended the concept of general supervision. It said that generally a municipality is under a duty to maintain its park and playground facilities in reasonably safe condition, which goes beyond mere maintenance of physical condition of park and playground; and, although strict or immediate supervision need not be

[40] Older cases supporting this view: Bartell v. Palos Verdes Peninsula School Dist., 83 Cal. App. 3d 492, 147 Cal. Rptr. 898 (1978) death of 12-year-old playing skateboard version of "crack-the-whip"; Benedetto v. Travelers Ins. Co., 172 S. 2d 354 (La. App. 1965) bat hit softball player sitting along third baseline; Brackman v. Adrain, 63 Tenn. App. 346, 472 S.W. 2d 735 (Tenn. App. 1971) softball catcher injured when batter slung her bat after hitting ball; DeSimone v. Philadelphia, 380 Pa. 137, 110 A. 2d 431 (1955); Dolan v. New York City, 5 A.D. 2d 300, 171 N.Y.S. 2d 724 (1958); Fagen v. Summers, 498 P. 2d 1227 (Wyo. 1972) seven-year-old injured when fellow student threw small rock which hit larger rock and rebounded into him; Fein v. Board of Educ., 305 N.Y. 61, 111 N.E. 2d 732 (1953); Ferrill v. Board of Educ., 6 A.D. 690, 174 N.Y. 2d 91 (1958); Gallo v. Surf & Pool Corp., 4 A.D. 2d 762, 164 N.Y.S. 2d 880, reh. & app. denied 4 A.D. 2d 835, 166 N.Y.S. 2d 1017 (1957) playground adjacent to swimming pool, six-year-old slipped from rung of monkey bars, wet from swimmers, general supervision required but no supervision had been provided; Longmont v. Swearingen, 81 Colo. 246, 254 P. 1000 (1927); Lopez v. New York City, 3 Misc. 2d 603, 152 N.Y.S. 2d 700 (1956), 4 A.D. 2d 48, 163 N.Y.S. 2d 562 (1957), aff'd. 4 N.Y. 2d 738, 171 N.Y.S. 2d 860, 148 N.E. 2d 909 (1958); Miller v. Board of Educ., Oyster Bay, 249 A.D. 738, 291 N.Y. Supp. 633 (1936); Monell v. New York City, 5 Misc. 2d 321, 160 N.Y.S. 2d 321 (1957); Nestor v. New York City, 28 Misc. 2d 70, 211 N.Y.S. 2d 975 (1961); Peterson v. New York City, 267 N.Y. 204, 196 N.E. 27 (1935); Schuyler v. Board of Educ., 18 A.D. 2d 406, 239 N.Y.S. 2d 769 (1963), aff'd. 15 N.Y. 2d 746, 205 N.E. 2d 311 (1965) sixth grade student falling off a fence on the playground during recess; Shanahan v. St. James Roman Catholic Church, 11 A.D. 2d 584, 200 N.Y.S. 2d 798 (1960), aff'd. 10 N.Y. 2d 906, 223 N.Y.S. 2d 519, 179 N.E. 2d 519 (1961) student injured when playing King of the Mountain on pile of

snow was pushed off, landing on some stalks which pierced his body; Turano v. N.Y., 17 A.D. 2d 191, 233 N.Y.S. 2d 330 (1962) seven-year-old catcher at stickball game hit by bat because too close; Webber v. New York, 30 A.D. 2d 831, 292 N.Y.S. 2d 575 (1968) student injured when another student playing basketball, on a court laid out adjacent to an area designated for noon-recess-waiting, ran into her in an attempt to retain possession of the ball. However, case reversed and remanded on basis of layout of areas; Wilber v. Binghampton, 271 A.D. 402, 66 N.Y.S. 2d 250 (1946), aff'd. 296 N.Y. 950, 73 N.E. 2d 263 (1947) eight-year-old returning from lunch, hit by batted stone while walking along a fence on playground.
[41] Miller v. Board of Education, Albion, 291 N.Y. 25, 50 N.E. 2d 529 (1943); Miller v. Griesel, 297 N.E. 2d 463, aff'd. 261 Ind. 604, 308 N.E. 2d 701 (1974).
[42] Toure v. Board of Education, N.Y.C., 127 A.D. 2d 759, 512 N.Y.S. 2d 150 (1987).
[43] Nicolosi v. Livingston Parish School Board, 441 So. 2d 1261 (La. App. 1983) cert. denied 444 So. 2d 1243 (1984).
[44] Norman v. Turkey Run Community School Corp., 274 Ind. 310, 411 N.E. 2d 614 (1980) supervised recess, running is not an unreasonably dangerous activity, so no duty to warn; Totan v. Board of Education, N.Y.C., 133 A.D. 2d 366, 519 N.Y.S. 2d 374 (1987) cert. denied 70 N.Y. 2d 374, 524 N.Y.S. 2d 432 (1987) lunch recess, playing prohibited activity Red Rover, no notice game being played; Santee v. Orleans Parish School Board, 430 So. 2d 254 (La. App. 1983) students allowed access to stands used for volleyball nets or tetherball for purpose other than playing the games, students rolled base on one of stands over fingers of eight-year-old who was playing jacks at lunchtime, held inadequate supervision; see also Augustus v. Joseph A. Craig Elem. School, 459 So. 2d 665 (La. App. 1984).

provided, municipality may be obliged to furnish adequate degree of general supervision, which may require regulation or prevention of such activities that endanger others utilizing park. In this situation an infant was bitten by a dog running at large on a housing project playground; the court said that the city had constructive notice of the danger, which had existed for sometime, and the injury was foreseeable.[45]

There were similar holdings in three cases involving playground apparatus,[46] two concerned with playground slides and one with monkey bars.[47] In the *Chimerofsky* case a three and one-half-year-old fell from a slide. It was held that the cost and burden of supervising or maintaining each of the public playgrounds and public recreation facilities that provide slides and of requiring children to be sorted out according to age, height, weight, and attitude, and directed to and from higher and lower playground slides would be an unreasonable burden to impose on school districts. It was further held that the risk that children will climb upon and fall from nondefective standard playground slides at school playgrounds is not an "unreasonable risk" so as to impose a duty on the school district to fence, guard, or supervise playground slides or warn children against their use.

In a 1985 (apparatus) case,[48] a kindergartner was injured in a fall from the horizontal bar during recess. The court held that constant supervision is not necessary to discharge the duty of adequate supervision. The Louisiana court held similarly in another 1985 case related to an injury caused by a youngster getting hit with a bat. The court stated further "that duty depends on particular circumstances involved and does not extend to constant and undeviating supervision, which would be prohibitive and probably impossible."[49]

In a private playground case,[50] the injured child, almost two, was attending a birthday party at McDonald's Restaurant. The party was coordinated and supervised by a McDonald's employee, and included 15-20 minutes of play on the playground before eating. The employee announced the party was over and the children could return to the playground if supervised by the parents. The youngster fell from the merry-go-round. The playground was free of unreasonable risks, safely maintained and the employee had discharged her supervisory responsibilities.

Efforts have been made by defendants to break the causal relationship between the duty to supervise and the injury, when the injury was done willfully by another person on the basis of intervening act of third party, usually unforeseeable. This was the situation in a 1983 case[51] when a kindergarten student was struck in the eye by a stick thrown by another student during a supervised playground period. Judgment for defendant on the basis that there was no evidence that violation of reasonable standard of

[45] Rhabb v. N.Y.C. Housing Authority, 51 A.D. 2d 1036, 381 N.Y.S. 2d 323, aff'd. 41 N.Y. 2d 200, 359 N.E. 2d 1335 (1976).

[46] Chimerofsky v. School Dist., 121 Ill. App. 2d 371, 257 N.E. 2d 480 (1970); Hillman v. Greater Miami Hebrew Academy, 72 So. 2d 668 (Fla. 1954); Saracino v. New York, 30 A.D. 2d 853, 293 N.Y.S. 2d 29 (1968).

[47] Hillman v. Greater Miami Hebrew Academy, 72 So. 2d 668 (Fla. 1954).

[48] Collins v. Bossier Parish School Board, 480 So.

2d 846 (La. App. 1985) writ denied 481 So. 2d 1350 (1986)

[49] Ferguson v. DeSoto Parish School Board, 467 So. 2d 1257 (La. App. 1985), writ cert. denied 469 So. 2d 978 (1985), recon. writ denied 470 So. 2d 883 (1985).

[50] Gayden v. George, 513 So. 2d 515 (La. App. 1987).

[51] District of Columbia v. Cassidy, 465 A. 2d 395 (D.C. App. 1983).

care was proximate cause of injury, but rather that the injury was the consequence of an unforeseeable, intervening act of a third party which could be neither anticipated nor prevented (see §18.4).

Duty to control rowdiness was also at issue in two playground cases[52] (see §18.322). The *Sly* case concerned supervision of known troublemakers and white-black friction prior to opening of school doors in the morning. The court held that the school was not an insurer of safety and that in this given instance, lack of supervision would not have been the proximate cause. In the Louisiana playground case, some boys pushed the plaintiff into the street, but the court held that there was no duty to supervise after school hours or during vacation time, and even if there were a duty, there was no showing that supervisory personnel could have prevented the incident. Another aspect of the playground is whether there must be supervision when students are waiting, either waiting for the school bus or waiting for someone else to pick the children up. A third grader was injured when he peddled by a group waiting to be picked up for Cub Scout meeting. One of the boys grabbed at his bicycle, causing him to fall. The court held that there was no duty to provide supervision for the specific activity in question. The activity was not a part of the school program and the school authorities were unaware that the scouts met on the premises to await transportation.[53] Plaintiff's son was injured while waiting for the school bus. He was playing with or teasing a little girl when another girl struck him in the eye with a stick. Plaintiff failed to prove that there was a dereliction of duty by the school teachers or bus driver or that there was a causal connection between the failure to provide adequate supervision and the accident[54] (see §20.1 Transportation).

See other sections of this chapter and §10.3 Playgrounds for additional cases related to playgrounds.

§ 18.142 Gymnasium/classroom and locker room supervision

Inadequate supervision is almost always alleged in class settings when there are injuries on apparatus.[55] However, teachers are not the insurers of safety of the students, although they must give reasonable care; nor can teachers be expected to personally supervise every moment each school day.[56] Of particular concern as related to liability is the effect of leaving the classroom or gymnasium or athletic field during which time the students are unsupervised. Whether or not a teacher is liable depends upon two questions — was the likelihood of such injury occurring foreseeable? And was the

[52] Sly v. Board of Education, 213 Kan. 415, 516 P. 2d 895 (1973); Ulm v. Gitz, 286 S. 2d 720 (La. App. 1973); see also McStravick v. City of Ottawa, 4 D.L.R. 492 (1929).

[53] Hill v. Board of Education, 18 A.D. 2d 953, 237 N.Y.S. 2d 404 (1963).

[54] Nash v. Rapides Parish School Board, 188 So. 2d 508 (La. App. 1966).

[55] Barrera v. Dade Co. School Board, 366 So. 2d 531 (Fla. App. 1979); Fein v. Board of Educ., 305 N.Y. 61, 111 N.E. 2d 732 (1953); Reynolds v. State, 207 Misc. 963, 141 N.Y.S. 2d 615 (1955).

[56] Beechy v. Oak Forest, 16 Ill. App. 3d 240, 305 N.E. 257 (1973); Clary v. Alexander Co. Board of Educ., 19 N.C. App. 637, 199 S.E. 2d 738 (1973), 285 N.C. 188, 203 S.E. 2d 820 (1974) 286 N.C. 525, 212 S.E. 2d 160 (1975); Sly v. Board of Educ., 213 Kan. 415, 516 P. 2d 895 (1973); James v. Charlotte-Mecklenburg Board of Educ., 300 S.E. 2d 21 (N.C. App. 1983); Simonetti v. School Dist. of Philadelphia, 454 A. 2d 1038 (Pa. Super. 1982), reargument denied 1983; Swaitkowski v. Board of Educ., City of Buffalo, 36 A.D. 2d 685, 319 N.Y.S. 2d 783 (1971) (last three not phy. educ.).

absence of the teacher (lack of supervision) the proximate cause (see §18.4) of the injury?

A fourth grade teacher was held not negligent in leaving the classroom for a few minutes while the class was engaged in a program of calisthenics. A nine-year-old girl was injured when a nine-year-old boy left his assigned place and did not do his push-ups as he had been instructed to do them with result that a girl's head was struck by the boy's feet and two of her front teeth were badly chipped. The boy's act was held unforeseeable and the teacher's absence was not the proximate cause of the injury.[57] Twenty-two kindergarten youngsters were on the playground for physical education. The physical education teacher had them jumping rope and at the end of the class period permitted the children to engage in free play on the swings, slides, jungle gyms, and other playground equipment. The plaintiff, still in possession of a jumping rope, climbed to the top of a jungle gym, tied the rope to the top of the apparatus, started to swing down, fell and broke his arm. The court held that the teacher's obligation to exercise ordinary care did not require that each of the children be constantly and continuously in sight.[58]

The seventh and eighth grade students were playing "bench ball," a game of elimination where students try to hit one another below the shoulders with the ball. The teacher responsible for supervision was not present; the teachers were instructed not to leave classes unsupervised. The cafeteria manager and a former cafeteria worker wanted to cross the gymnasium floor and called out to the students asking that they discontinue the game until they had crossed. When the women were approximately two-thirds of the way across the floor, one or two of the students bumped into the plaintiff, knocking her to the floor, resulting in a broken hip. The court held for the plaintiff. Plaintiff was lawfully on the premises and there was an obligation to exercise reasonable care in conduct of activities; school was chargeable with negligence in that it was unsupervised students in the gymnasium who bumped into plaintiff, causing her to fall.[59]

The tennis coach/instructor, before going to his office to work on some bracketing for a school tennis tournament, told his class, composed of varsity team, team's managers, and those who aspired to make the team, to remain in the vicinity of the gymnasium dressing room or foyer. Plaintiff's eye was severely damaged when he ran into line of flight of tennis ball which was being thrown by another class member and batted by a third class member. The ball struck his eye, breaking his rimless glasses. The court held that proper supervision did not require him to prevent the activity in the first place or to stop the game. The game (a version of handball) was not considered inherently dangerous.[60]

In another gymnasium case,[61] the plaintiff, a 14-year-old student, with 48 other 14- to 16-year-old boys reported to physical education class. After checking attendance, the instructor told the boys to "shoot around" with basketballs; the plaintiff began shooting

[57] Segerman v. Jones, 256 Md. 109, 259 A. 2d 795 (1969).
[58] Clark v. Furch, 567 S.W. 2d 457 (Mo. App. 1978).
[59] Ragnone v. Portland School Dist., 44 Or. App. 347, 605 P. 2d 1217 (1980), 289 Or. 339, 613 P. 2d 1032 (1980), aff'd. 47 Or. App. 656, 615 P. 2d 1077 (1980), rev'd. 633 P. 2d 1287 (1981).
[60] Wright v. San Bernadino H.S. Dist., 121 Cal. App. 2d 342, 263 P. 2d 25 (1953).
[61] Cirillo v. Milwaukee, 34 Wis. 2d 705, 150 N.W. 2d 450 (1967).

with a classmate. The instructor then left the class unattended with no explanation why. The two boys were joined by two others and after about ten minutes the game deteriorated to "keep away." The game ranged over at least one-half of the gym floor, and one witness said it covered the entire floor. The game became rougher, including pushing and tripping, being characterized as a "rough-house" game. The instructor had been absent about 25 minutes when plaintiff was injured as he was pushed into another student and fell to the floor. The instructor (defendant) alleged contributory negligence on the part of the boy, for he knew he was participating in a dangerous game and he failed to follow instructions not to engage in horseplay. The court held that a teacher is neither immune from liability nor an insurer of his student's safety, but is liable for injuries resulting from failure to use reasonable care. Even if the teacher is found to be negligent in absenting himself, when injury is the result of rowdyism and intentional conduct, a question of intervening and superseding cause arises.

Dramatic activities were the situations of two additional cases.[62] In the *Ferreira* case, the script for the senior play called for the firing of blank cartridges. The student firing the gun furnished his own gun and kept it in a safe in school when not being used, and only two persons had access thereto. Just prior to the final performance, one of the cast not authorized took the gun, inserted a live bullet and fired it, injuring another cast member. The gun was picked up when lying on the table on stage while the rest of the cast were putting on make-up. The court held that because the cast had conducted themselves in an exemplary manner prior thereto, this act was not foreseeable, and that it was impossible for the teacher to supervise every detail during preparation and presentation. In the other case, a 17-year-old was working on the scenery for the school play, when the auditorium lights went out; she ran heedlessly to and from, rather than using the readily accessible and safe means of exit. As a result, she fell into an open hatchway in the stage injuring herself. Again, the court held that it was unreasonable to expect the supervising teacher to be in continual attendance and that this act was not reasonably foreseeable.

A similar holding that a teacher cannot be expected to personally supervise every moment each school day was accorded the defendant in a situation where the teacher left the classroom and a scuffle ensued ten minutes later between two boys. One retreated to the hallway; the other followed. A household broom was thrown at the plaintiff's feet; the broom bounced up on its straws and struck plaintiff under the left eye in a manner as to cause loss of sight. The plaintiff was the instigator and the defendant had the right of self-defense, but not excessive violence. The fact that the principal knew of the tendency of the class to fight did not bar recovery inasmuch as defendant was no worse than other boys in regard to fighting.[63]

Before and after class. What about supervision before and after the regular class period? The court held for the defendant physical education instructor and the school board when an eighth grader was injured prior to the beginning of the physical

[62] Ferreira v. Sanchez, 79 N.M. 768, 449 P. 2d 784 (1969); Tennenbaum v. Board of Educ., 22 A.D. 2d 924, 255 N.Y.S. 2d 522 (1964), aff'd. 16 N.Y. 2d 499, 267 N.Y.S. 2d 217, 214 N.E. 2d 378 (1966).

[63] McDonald v. Terrebonne Parish School Bd., 253 S. 2d 558 (La. App. 1971), writ denied 260 La. 128, 255 So. 2d 353 (1971).

education class. Contrary to school rules and regulations and the teaching of the instructor, the injured boy and several fellow students were engaged in a tumbling activity, which consisted of a diving roll over two or three folding-chairs stacked on top of each other on the gymnasium floor. The students in turn would approach the stacked chairs, hit a springboard, and dive head first over the chairs, landing on a mat on the other side, where they tumbled over the landing area. On this occasion, the foot of the injured boy apparently struck the chairs causing him to hit the landing mat on his head rather than on his feet, resulting in a slight subluxation of the cervical spine, which responded to conservative treatment. The class had already been properly taught tumbling.[64]

Following a college swimming class one of the students stayed to practice a dive on which the instructor had given adequate instruction in class. A classmate was aiding him; the instructor remained as lifeguard. Plaintiff hit head on the bottom of the pool. The court held no negligence in supervision.[65]

A university student remained after class to work on the trampoline. While doing so he lost his balance and fell while attempting to perform a double-forward somersault. At the time the instructor was 30' to 40' away assisting another student. The performer had participated on the trampoline in high school and had become quite proficient; therefore, he was held to exercise judgment for his own safety commensurate with his experience. Judgment for defendant.[66] Judgment also was for the defendant in a 1983 Louisiana trampoline case.[67] The court held that the instructor exercised reasonable supervision over the students, who were jumping on the trampoline on the stage of the auditorium (gym). Appropriate instruction had been given. The court also stated that a greater degree of care is required when students are required to use or come in contact with an inherently dangerous object, or to engage in an activity where it is reasonably foreseeable that an accident or injury may occur, but held that the trampoline was not an inherently dangerous object. In another Louisiana case[68] the same year, involving a table saw in a class at school, the court further stated that teachers must exercise reasonable supervision over students, commensurate with the age of the children and the attendant circumstances, with the same statement regarding the greater degree of care required.

Locker room. Supervision of students as related to the locker room also gives rise to law suits. Most of these cases involve discipline of the students. Two physical education classes were combined for the day, since one of the instructors was away at a workshop. As plaintiff's son, aged 14, went from the locker room to the gym with another student, in the hallway the other student began stepping on the heels of the shoes of plaintiff's son, whereupon he retaliated by elbowing the other student's genitals. Plaintiff's son was then picked up and either fell or was dropped on the floor, suffering a skull fracture and massive cerebral hemorrhage. He died shortly after being taken to the physician.

[64] Banks v. Terrebonne Parish School Board, 339 So. 2d 1295 (La. App. 1976).

[65] Perkins v. State Board of Educ., 364 So. 2d 183 (La. App. 1978), cert. denied. 366 So. 2d 563 (1979); see also Frankel v. Willow Brook Marina, 275 F. Supp. 320 (1967) instruction at private pool, not school setting, lifeguard instructing, no lifeguard provided for various activities going on at same time prior to opening of pool.

[66] Chapman v. State of Washington, 6 Wash. App. 316, 492 P. 2d 607 (1972).

[67] Smith v. Vernon Parish School Board, 442 So. 2d 1319 (La. App. 1983).

[68] Theriot v. St. Martin Parish School Board, 434 So. 2d 668 (La. App. 1983).

Court affirmed summary judgment for nurse and the absent instructor, but remanded the case regarding principal, superintendent, and instructor on duty to determine if any negligence related to supervision. The opinion of the court did state that the tort liability of supervisory public school employees and teachers for inadequate supervision of their students is highly subjective and the scope of their duty extremely narrow. Further, it was indicated that the 45 students per class was a recommendation from the State which was advisory only and an administrator has considerable latitude. There were 40-50 in the combined classes. There also seemed to be lacking notice of the assaultive propensities of the boy who injured plaintiff's son, the deceased.[69]

In the *Ruggerio* case[70] a 17-year-old was injured in a fight in the locker room. The two seniors and varsity teammates knew the rules governing the locker room. The argument was over who would use an unassigned locker. The plaintiff was of age and experience to know the consequences of his conduct. He took off his glasses and coat and moved out to a more suitable location and threatened defendant student by squaring off with him. The plaintiff could have secured intervention of the instructor at any time, since he was readily available. Judgment for the defendant. In another assault case,[71] both the school district and the individual employees were protected by governmental immunity. The situation, however, was that plaintiff, a member of the girls' varsity basketball team which had just finished playing, was assaulted by a student from the opposing team's school. Both teams were using the same locker room. Both high schools were sued.

Plaintiff was attacked by a non-student in a school restroom where he was changing his clothes before wrestling practice. The court, in *Leger v. Stockton Unified School Dist.*, 249 Cal. Rptr. 688 (1988), held that while neither school districts nor their employees are insurers of safety of their students, they do have a duty toward students to use a degree of care which persons of ordinary prudence, charged with comparable duties, would exercise in same circumstances involving assault of student by non-student in unsupervised restroom of school where injury was allegedly foreseeable. Plaintiff alleged that the school district and its individual employees knew or should have known that members of junior varsity wrestling team were changing clothes before wrestling practice in unsupervised boys' restroom and that it was unsafe for students for attacks were likely to occur. School authorities who know of threats of violence that they believe are well-founded may not refrain from taking reasonable preventive measures simply because violence has yet to occur. Judgment for plaintiff. (See §§18.323 and 1.4132).

Special note: Caution is given regarding the use of Illinois teacher supervision cases[72] for either precedent or illustration of a teacher's duty to supervise. Teachers in

[69] Kersey v. Harbin, 531 S.W. 2d 76 (Mo. App. 1975), aff'd./rev'd. in part 591 S.W. 2d 745 (Mo. App. 1979).

[70] Ruggerio v. Board of Educ., City of Jamestown, 31 A.D. 2d 884, 298 N.Y.S. 2d 149 (1969) aff'd. 26 N.Y. 2d 849, 258 N.E. 2d 92 (1970).

[71] Grames v. King & Pontiac School Dist. and Grames v. King & Walled Lake School Dist., 123 Mich. App. 573, 332 N.W. 2d 615 (Mich. App. 1983).

Michigan law related to governmental immunity is unsettled, court opinion discussion could be useful.

[72] For example, Albers v. Community Consolidated #204 School, 155 Ill. App. 3d 1083, 108 Ill. Dec. 675, 508 N.E. 2d 1252 (1987) teacher following routine of watching children in classroom itself and those getting water and using bathroom, child injured in classroom during an absence; Hadley v. Witt Unit School Dist., 123 Ill. App. 3d 19, 78 Ill. Dec. 758, 462

Illinois are immune by statute[73] from liability for negligent supervision; they are liable only when there is willful and wanton conduct. Whereas initially this protection was primarily in regard to discipline, it has been extended to activities directed by teachers as part of school program. Illinois is the only state which so specifically clothes a teacher in immunity, although there is governmental immunity in limited situations in certain states under the Tort Claims Acts (see §4.2).

For additional cases see other sections of this chapter and Chapters 10 and 19.

§ 18.2   The supervisor

While most of the situations describe the act of the supervisor, negligence may be occasioned by the characteristics of the supervisor, such as the supervisor's competence to handle the situation, the location of the supervisor in respect to the danger and the participant, and the number of supervisory personnel in relation to the type of activity and numbers of participants. See also cases cited in other subsections of this chapter.

§ 18.21   Location of supervisor

In several cases, it has not been the number of supervising staff at issue, but rather the location of such supervisors and whether or not the presence of a supervisor could have prevented the injury from occurring.[74] In what proximity must the supervisor be? Most of the cases involving location of the supervisor relate to general or specific supervision.

The teacher and children (ranging in age from five to eight) were on the school playground during lunchtime recess. There were 40 children with approximately one-half each involved in a softball game and on the playground apparatus. The teacher was no more than 45' from the game, engaged with a kindergarten student, when plaintiff was struck in the head by a bat. The court held that the teacher was not negligent in her supervision.[75]

In an after-class activity, it was held that an instructor who was at the time of the accident 30' to 40' away was in proper location for the activity. An 18-year-old was working on the goliath trampoline with only one spotter when he went off the trampoline, sustaining permanent injury. General supervision in the vicinity was adequate; student was experienced and understood safety practices, no recovery was awarded.[76] Particularly in school cases at the beginning or ending of class or in between classes, it has been held that supervision is adequate if the teacher is in the vicinity, engaged in duties connected with the class function.[77]

N.E. 2d 877 (1984) industrial arts class; Hilgendorf v. First Baptist Church of Danville, 157 Ill. App. 3d 428, 109 Ill. Dec. 659, 510 N.E. 2d 527 (1987) private day care center under statute, ladder of slide on playground; Holsapple v. Casey Community Unit School Dist., 157 Ill. App. 3d 391, 109 Ill. Dec. 631, 510 N.E. 2d 499 (1987) altercation in locker room; Prest v. Sparta Community Unit School Dist. 140, 157 Ill. App. 3d 569, 109 Ill. Dec. 727, 510 N.E. 2d 595 (1987) during physical education, student fell against unpadded concrete bleachers.

[73] Illinois Ann. Stat. ch. 122 ›4-24.

[74] For example, Grams v. Independent School Dist., 176 N.W. 2d 536 (Minn. 1970); Kaufman v. New York, 30 Misc. 2d 285, 214 N.Y.S. 2d 767 (1961); Ziegler v. Santa Cruz City H.S. Dist., 168 Cal. App. 2d 277, 335 P. 2d 709 (1959).

[75] Ferguson v. DeSoto Parish School Board, 467 So. 2d 1257 (La. App. 1985).

[76] Chapman v. State, 6 Wash. App. 316, 492 P. 2d 607 (1972).

[77] Kerby v. Elk Grove Union High School Dist., 1

In *Law v. Newark Board of Education*[78] two children were run over by a fire truck while participating in a recreation program on the playground. The children were drawn to the excitement by the fire and jumped on and off the truck until ordered off by the firemen. As the hook and ladder truck left the school yard, the two boys jumped back on, out of the sight of the firemen. Just after it passed through the school yard gate, in attempting to jump off, the boys slipped and fell underneath. The playground supervisors were not near the gate when the truck left, despite the number of children around the truck and the obvious danger. Held: negligent supervision.

Location of supervisors, as related to plans for supervision, is discussed in §18.31. In the *Dailey* case,[79] cited there, it was held that one cannot provide general supervision from an office which does not have a view of the area to be supervised.

§ 18.22   Competence of supervisors

What does it mean to provide supervision, to provide a competent supervisor?[80] The competence of a teacher, a lifeguard, and other personnel has been in issue in several law suits.[81] Experience is often one criterion of competence,[82] as is age; and the two may be interrelated.

In a case[83] in which a private day camp used school facilities, the court held that although the two counselors, 14 and 15 years of age, were young, they did have a year's experience and had been briefed on safety, and that there was no negligence in supervision. In this case, the children, 20 to 30 five-year-olds, were changing to bathing suits in a classroom which had unsecured school desks. The plaintiff, climbing on one with another girl, toppled over, injuring her hand so that she was left with a permanent club-like protrusion at the end of her middle finger. The young campers had been warned repeatedly about the desks and not to climb on them; the counselors were in the room, but their attention had been directed elsewhere at the specific time.

The age of the counselor also was brought into issue in the *Crohn* case.[84] A 15-year-old counselor was employed to supervise the activities of the small children. A camper, age seven, was injured when she was struck in the face by a baseball bat being swung by a boy, age ten, who also attended the camp. Held that the appropriateness of employment of such aged counselor was for the jury. And, in a drowning situation, the

Cal. App. 2d 246, 36 P. 2d 431 (1934); Reithardt v. Board of Educ. of Yuba County, 43 Cal. App. 2d 629, 111 P. 2d 440 (1941); Woodsmall v. Mt. Diablo Unified School Dist., 188 Cal. App. 2d 62, 10 Cal. Rep. 447 (1961); Wright v. San Bernardino High School Dist., 121 Cal. App. 2d 342, 263 P. 2d 25 (1953).

[78] Law v. Newark Board of Educ., 175 N.J. Super. 26, 417 A. 2d 560 (1980); see also, Smith v. Harger, 84 Cal. App. 2d 361, 191 P. 2d 25 (1948) truck backed over child.

[79] Dailey v. Los Angeles Unified School Dist., 4 Cal. App. 3d 105, 84 Cal. Rptr. 325, rev'd. 2 Cal. 3d 741, 87 Cal. Rptr. 376, 470 P. 2d 360 (1970).

[80] Graff v. Board of Educ., 258 A.D. 813, 15 N.Y.S. 2d 941 (1939); Kolar v. Union Free School

Dist., 8 N.Y.S. 2d 985 (Madison Co. Ct. 1939); Mauer v. Board of Educ., 266 A.D. 1007, 44 N.Y.S. 2d 431 (1943).

[81] Glirbas v. Sioux Falls, 64 S.D. 45, 264 N.W. 196 (1936); Norman v. Chariton, 201 Iowa 279, 207 N.W. 134 (1926); Kolar v. Union Free School Dist., 8 N.Y.S. 2d 985 (Madison Co. Ct. 1939); Sayers v. Ranger, 16 N.J. Super. 22, 83 A. 2d 775 (1951).

[82] Reynolds v. State, 207 Misc. 963, 141 N.Y.S. 2d 615 (1955); Govel v. Board of Educ. (two cases), 267 A.D. 621, 48 N.Y.S. 2d 299 (1944).

[83] Comeaux v. Commercial Union Ins. Co., 269 S. 2d 500 (La. App. 1972).

[84] Crohn v. Congregation B'nai Zion, 22 Ill. App. 2d 625, 317 N.E. 2d 637 (1974).

only lifeguard on duty for more than 50 persons was a junior lifeguard, 16 years of age.[85]

Competence also is a matter of knowledge.[86] The quality of instruction was in question when an eighth grade boy was injured while participating in wrestling for the first time. The instructor was the coach who had wrestled in school and the service, but his only coaching experience was one season seven years earlier. The court held that it is not a single act of the instructor which establishes a breach of duty but a series of acts that establishes the quality of instruction.[87]

Where someone other than a qualified instructor or leader attempts to supervise activity, the competency of the substitute may be questioned, such as in the case of students,[88] a bathhouse attendant,[89] a WPA (government welfare) worker,[90] a teacher's aide,[91] a handicapped person,[92] a janitor,[93] or watchman.[94] The criterion is the experience of the individual for handling the situation at hand. The characteristics indicated alone will not disqualify a person for competent supervision.

The competence of personnel also has been questioned relating to credentials and other requirements, particularly in the aquatics field, such as "qualified lifeguard service" as required by statute,[95] scuba certification,[96] and "properly trained."[97] The competence of supervisors at roller and ice skating rinks, too, has been raised in terms of being able to cope with the maintenance of order and conduct among skaters.[98]

Attentiveness to duty is another criterion of competence and adequacy of supervision. Most of the cases have to do with lifeguarding;[99] however, it does apply to other supervision responsibilities.[100]

[85] Sneed v. Lions Club of Murphy, 273 N.C. 98, 159 S.E. 2d 770 (1968).

[86] Gordon v. Deer Park School District, 71 Wash. 2d 119, 426 P. 2d 824 (1967) teacher's bat slipped from his hands, competence in regard to safe practices, teacher had three years of teaching and was experienced in baseball; Morris v. Douglas Co. School Dist., 241 Or. 23, 403 P. 2d 775 (1965) teacher should have known about tidal wave action; Nordgren v. Strong, 110 Conn. 593, 149 A. 201 (1930) resort, persons on duty were experienced and skilled swimmers, lifesaving course.

[87] Stehn v. Bernarr MacFadden Foundations, Inc., 434 F. 2d 811 (1970).

[88] Brittan v. State, 200 Misc. 743, 103 N.Y.S. 2d 485 (1951); DeMauro v. Tusculum College, 603 S.W. 2d 115 (Tenn. 1980); Gardner v. State, 281 N.Y. 212, 22 N.E. 2d 344 (1939); O'Brien v. Township H.S. Dist. 214, 29 Ill. Dec. 918, 73 Ill. App. 3d 618, 392 N.E. 2d 615 (1979) aff'd./rev'd. in part, 83 Ill. 2d 462, 47 Ill. Dec. 702, 415 N.E. 2d 1015 (1980). See §3.6 for description of cases.

[89] McDonnell v. Bronzo, 285 Mich. 38, 280 N.W. 100 (1938).

[90] Fritz v. Buffalo, 277 N.Y. 710, 14 N.E. 2d 815 (1938).

[91] Schumate v. Thompson, 580 S.W. 2d 47 (Tex. Civ. App. 1979). See §3.6.

[92] Young v. Boy Scouts of America, 9 Cal. App. 2d 760, 51 P. 2d 191 (1935). See §17.341.

[93] Garber v. Central School Dist., 251 App. Div. 214, 295 N.Y.S. 850 (1937).

[94] Williams v. Longmont, 109 Colo. 567, 129 P. 2d 110 (1942).

[95] Lucas v. Hesperia Golf & Country Club, 255 Cal. App. 2d 241, 63 Cal. Rptr. 189 (1967).

[96] Leno v. YMCA, 17 Cal. App. 3d 651, 95 Cal. Rptr. 96 (1971).

[97] Davis v. Shelton, 33 A.D. 2d 707, 304 N.Y.S. 2d 722 (1969), app. dism'd. 26 N.Y. 2d 829, 309 N.Y.S. 2d 358, 257 N.E. 2d 902.

[98] Rice v. Amusement Enterprises, 461 S.W. 2d 490 (Tex. Civ. App. 1970).

[99] Carter v. Boys' Club of Greater K.C., 552 S.W. 2d 327 (Mo. App. 1977); Collins v. Riverside Amusement Park Co., 61 Ariz. 135, 145 P. 2d 853 (1944); Fowler Real Estate Co. v. Ranke, 497 P. 2d 1268 (1972), 181 Colo. 115, 507 P. 2d 854 (1973); Lipton v. Dreamland Park Co., 121 N.J.L. 554, 3 A. 2d 571 (1939); Manganello v. Permastone, 30 N.C. App. 696, 228 S.E. 2d 627 (1976), rev'd. 291 N.C. 666, 231 S.E. 2d 678 (1977); Naber v. Humbolt, 197 Neb. 433, 249 N.W. 2d 726 (1977); Newport v. Ford, 54 Tenn. App. 667, 393 S.W. 2d 760 (1965); S & C Co. v. Horne, 281 Va. 124, 235 S.E. 2d 456 (1977); Wong v. Waterloo Comm. School Dist., 232 N.W. 2d 865 (Iowa 1975). See Chapters 9 and 14 for case descriptions and additional cases.

[100] Stanley v. Board of Educ., Chicago, 9 Ill. App. 3d 963, 293 N.E. 2d 417 (1973); Nestor v. City of N.Y., 28 Misc. 2d 70, 211 N.Y.S. 2d 975 (1961) distributing milk on playground; Johnson v. Co. Arena, 29 Md. App. 674, 349 A. 2d 643 (1976) roller skating.

§ 18.23   Number of supervisors

The adequacy of supervision in terms of sufficiency of supervising personnel has been raised in a number of situations.[101] Inadequacy and insufficiency should not be taken as synonomous. One can have a sufficient number of staff, but they may not be adequate in competence or location. The number of personnel required depends upon the nature of the situation and is determined by the jury upon hearing evidence, particularly from expert witnesses. In 1985 the Louisiana court discussed ratio of students to teacher on the school playgrounds, citing a number of cases. The instant situation had approximately 85 students to one supervising teacher. A child was injured when he fell from the horizontal bar. In regard to the ratio the court commented that there was nothing in the evidence to show that had there been more teachers on duty that this unfortunate incident would not have still occurred.[102]

The preponderance of cases involve swimming pool lifeguards.[103] However, the number of students per teacher in classroom/gymnasium has been in issue. In *Rodrigues v. San Jose Unified School Dist.*,[104] one supervisor for 75 to 100 students in a space 75' x 100' was alleged, but not proven, inadequate. Six to eight adults was held a reasonable number of supervisors for 250 to 300 students at noon recess,[105] and three teachers observing 170 students, also, was held adequate in another Louisiana recess case.[106] In the *Kersey* case, one instructor took two classes when the other teacher was attending a workshop. The classes combined were 40-50 students. There was an advisory State recommendation of 45 maximum class size per instructor. The injury occurred on the way from the locker room to the gymnasium. In a similar Louisiana case[107] three years later, two regular physical education classes were combined to allow one teacher a free period. The boys were playing basketball on a court adjacent to the playground apparatus, which the girls were using. The supervising teacher, a substitute for the day, walked back and forth between the two groups. She observed the merry-go-round was being made to spin too fast and just as she was admonishing the girls, telling them to slow down and get off, she heard two boys arguing over a basketball and one of them yelled for her. She had walked toward the boys about 20' when she heard one of the girls yell that someone was injured. Plaintiff had fallen off the merry-go-round and broken her leg. The court held that the supervision was inadequate, especially in light of the fact that another teacher was available, but not used to supervise.

The sufficiency of the number of guards was in issue for crowd control at a baseball game;[108] and, the court held that there were an insufficient number of guards on the

[101] Carr v. San Francisco, 170 Cal. App. 2d 48, 338 P. 2d 509 (1959); Cooper v. Pittsburgh, 390 Pa. 534, 136 A. 2d 463 (1957); Estate of Cruz, 63 A.D. 2d 862, 405 N.Y.S. 2d 867 (1978); Ferrill v. Board of Education, 6 A.D. 2d 690, 174 N.Y.S. 2d 91 (1958); Nicolos v. Livingston Parish School Board, 441 So. 2d 1261 (La. App. 1983) cert. denied 444 So. 2d 1243 (1984).

[102] Collins v. Bossier Parish School Board, 480 So. 2d 846 (La. App. 1985).

[103] Bartley v. Childers, 433 S.E. 2d 130 (Ky. App. 1968); Brumm v. Goodall, 16 Ill. App. 2d 212, 147 N.E. 2d 699 (1958); Mullen v. Russworm, 169 Tenn. 650, 90 S.W. 2d 530 (1936); Stilwell v. Louisville, 455 S.W. 2d

56 (Ky. App. 1970); YMCA of Metro. Atlanta v. Bailey, 107 Ga. App. 417, 130 S.E. 2d 242 (1963).

[104] Rodrigues v. San Jose Unified School Dist., 157 Cal. App. 2d 842, 322 P. 2d 70 (1958).

[105] Capers v. Orleans Parish School Board, 365 So. 2d 23 (La. App. 1978).

[106] Hampton v. Orleans Parish School Board, 422 So. 2d 202 (La. App. 1982).

[107] Rollins v. Concordia Parish School Board, 465 So. 2d 213 (La. App. 1985).

[108] Shtekla v. Topping, 23 A.D. 2d 750, 258 N.Y.S. 2d 982, app. dism'd. 18 N.Y. 2d 961, 277 N.Y.S. 2d 694, 224 N.E. 2d 116 (1965).

roller rink to control the patrons.[109] The number of counselors per camper also has been questioned for adequacy of supervision[110] as has the number of supervisory personnel who accompanied a Special Olympics team on an off-campus trip to the park.[111]

The foregoing are illustrative situations in which the number of supervisors has been discussed in relation to the adequacy of supervision. See description of these cases and others in Part B.

§ 18.3   Nature of supervision

Once a duty to supervise is established and there are appropriate supervisory personnel, then the question is "what is the nature of supervision required?" In other words, what is the standard of care as related to supervisory practices. First, there must be a supervisory plan. The nature of supervision focuses upon the management of the behavior of the participants and spectators and upon the various functions the supervisor must perform.

§ 18.31   Supervisory planning

In providing supervision, a plan is desirable. In *Dailey v. Los Angeles Unified School Dist.*,[112] the court showed its displeasure at the plan for supervising large groups of students during lunch hour, saying that the plan was defective because of lack of specificity as to the use of the physical education personnel. It said that the responsible department head had failed to develop a comprehensive schedule of supervising assignments and had neglected to instruct his subordinates as to what was expected of them while they were supervising. Instead, it appeared that both the time and manner of supervision were left to the discretion of the individual teacher. There was no formal scheduling. (See also *Broward* and *Comuntzis* cases in §18.323).

In the foregoing case two boys, after finishing lunch, went toward the gymnasium about 1 p.m. (the next class was at 1:16 p.m.). They stopped outside the north side of the gym building where the two engaged in "slap boxing" (using open hands). They "boxed" for five to ten minutes and about 30 students gathered. Then, one boy fell backwards, hitting his head on the asphalt paving, and suffered a fractured skull. He died a few hours later. There was no supervisor present in the immediate area. In this school, some 2,700 children ate in one session at noon with three administrative personnel and two teachers supervising. The area around the gymnasium was assigned to the physical education teachers. At the time of the accident, the chairman of the department was playing bridge in the dressing room. The person on duty for the physical educators was in the gym office, eating lunch and preparing for his afternoon classes.

---

[109] Hairston v. Studio Amusements, Inc., 86 Cal. App. 2d 735, 195 P. 2d 498 (1948).

[110] Cherry v. State, 42 A.D. 2d 671, 344 N.Y.S. 2d 545, aff'd. 34 N.Y. 2d 872, 359 N.Y.S. 2d 276, 316 N.E. 2d 713 (1973); Goldberger v. David Roberts Corp., 139 Conn. 629, 96 A. 2d 309 (1953).

[111] Foster v. Houston Gen. Ins., 407 So. 2d 759 (La. App. 1981), writ denied 409 So. 2d 660 (1982).

[112] Dailey v. Los Angeles Unified School District, 4 Cal. App. 3d 105, 84 Cal. Rptr. 325, rev'd. 2 Cal. 3d 741, 87 Cal. Rptr. 376, 470 P. 2d 360 (1970).

His desk faced away from the office windows and a wall obscured his view of the area in which the "slap boxing" occurred. It was agreed that "slap boxing" was an activity which could lead to something dangerous and normally was stopped when observed by the teachers.

A supervisory plan was the basis for holding the supervision of the teacher adequate when plaintiff was struck in the eye by a sharp object as he entered the teacher's classroom. The teacher, however, was at that time not in the classroom, but supervising the hall and cafeteria, pursuant to the school's supervisory plan. Generally the students were not in the classroom at this time, lunchtime. The court held that mere absence of the teacher was insufficient to establish negligence, particularly where there was a plan which sought to provide for maximum safety and order through deployment of teachers in various positions and locations.[113]

In supervisory planning, there are two responsibilities of the administration and, if not appropriately discharged, the appropriate administrator/supervisor can be held liable. The administrator, such as a principal or superintendent in a school system, has the obligation to provide for adequate supervisory personnel in order to provide the individuals participating with the prerequisite supervision fulfilling the duty owed.[114] In a 1984 New Jersey case[115] the court held that the assignment of supervisors is a "discretionary operational" or ministerial act not protected by governmental immunity, unless it can be demonstrated that the decision was made in the face of competing demands and involved the utilization or application of existing resources. In this situation the principal was sued related to assignment of supervisors when eighth grade plaintiff was injured on an athletic field adjacent to the school due to being struck in the face by a rock thrown by a seventh grade student.

The second responsibility is that of establishing appropriate rules and regulations, particularly for off-premises trips and activities. If these are established, then it is the responsibility of the person in charge of the group to follow such rules and regulations.[116] The rules and regulations promulgated by the administration may be slightly different from those established by the teacher, recreation leader, or other person in charge in that the administrative regulations may specify conditions under which the trip may be taken or activity held. (See also §18.331 Rules and regulations.)

§ 18.32 Management of behavior

There are three aspects of behavior management — crowd control, individual participants, and intervening acts of third parties. Cases dealing with crowd control and other spectator-related cases which have an allegation of inadequate or lack of supervision are discussed in Chapter 15. Also, for further discussion of third party

[113] Butler v. D.C., 417 F. 2d 1150 (1969).
[114] Cook v. Bennett, 94 Mich. App. 93, 288 N.W. 2d 609 (1979); Cianci v. Board of Educ., Rye, 18 A.D. 2d 930, 238 N.Y.S. 2d 547 (1963); Kersey v. Harbin, 531 S.W. 2d 76 (Mo. App. 1975), rev'd./aff'd. 591 S.W. 2d 745 (Mo. App. 1979); Krueger v. Bailey, 406 N.E. 2d 665 (Ind. App. 1980).
[115] Longo v. Santoro, 195 N.J. Super. 507, 480 A.

2d 934 (1984). See also Ballard v. Polly, 387 F. Supp. 895 (1975). For further discussion of discretionary/ ministerial function, see §4.13 and for administrative liability, see §3.3.
[116] Bryant v. School Board of Duval Co., 399 So. 2d 417 (Fla. App. 1981) aff'd./rev'd. in part 417 So. 2d 658 (Fla. 1982); Cox v. Barnes, 469 S.W. 2d 61 (Ky. App. 1971).

behavior, see §2.31 Intervening acts. This section discusses behavior as characterized by horseplay, rowdyism, assaults, and discipline. Hazing is in §10.22.

§ 18.321 Horseplay

Cases in this section, which reference "horseplay" as the situation in which the injury occurred, come primarily from the recreational setting, in contrast to the school setting, although there are a considerable number of general school cases not specific to physical education. One is not an insurer of safety, but whether or not the plaintiff obtains a judgment depends primarily upon the foreseeability of injury and the responsibility of the supervising person.

The situations are quite varied.[117] A four-year-old child was injured at a summer school when she was pushed into a hot fireplace by a playmate at a picnic. There was "horseplay" by the youngsters just prior to the accident and the court held that the injury was foreseeable and the breach of duty the proximate cause.[118] In two Louisiana cases[119] the defendant was held to have had appropriate supervision. In the *Brooks* case, two students were engaged in horseplay while in the concession waiting line on the playground at noon. They bumped a mentally retarded youngster (14 years old) enrolled in the special education program. Held that direct or specific supervision for such retarded child was not required. In the other case, a teacher's aide saw two 12-year-old students jumping up and down outside window of her classroom and one thrust his fist through the window, injuring himself. She had asked them to go on to their next assignment.

Horseplay in extracurricular activities may account for injuries.[120] In the *Arnold* case, involving an extracurricular activity, the plaintiff, a sophomore high school student, was injured by a fellow student while participating in a lettermen's outing at the coach's mountain cabin. He alleged that he was pushed off a 6′ retaining wall into a shallow stream, fracturing his leg, and attempted to recover on the basis that the coach and principal condoned the activities leading up to the injury and thus were negligent in supervision. No recovery was awarded. At a school-sponsored show created by the students, while the only supervisor (an educational assistant) was out for a coffee break, a small group of students in the corner of the hall became noisy and were told by a student-in-charge to keep quiet. Shortly thereafter, plaintiff (15 years old) and two

---

[117] Ford v. Brandan, 51 Tenn. App. 338, 367 S.W. 2d 481 (1962) 16-year-old using trampoline at center, proprietor of a public place of amusement liable to patron for injuries sustained as a result of horseplay, boisterous conduct, or other act of playfulness provided there is sufficient notice, held: not timely notice, judgment for defendant.

[118] Brown v. Knight, 362 Mass. 350, 285 N.E. 2d 790 (Mass. 1972).

[119] Brooks v. St. Tammany Parish School Board, 510 So. 2d 51 (La. App. 1987); Henix v. George, 465 So. 2d 906 (La. App. 1985).

[120] Arnold v. Hafling, 474 P. 2d 638 (Colo. 1970); Baum v. Reed College Student Body, Inc., 240 Or. 388,

401 P. 2d 294 (1965) dance at student union, took seat on bench just below stage, 200-pound boy balancing back and forth near the edge of platform fell backward off the stage onto plaintiff; Viveiros v. Hawaii, 54 Hawaii 611, 513 P. 2d 487 (1973); Ziegler v. Santa Cruz City H.S. Dist., 168 Cal. App. 2d 277, 335 P. 2d 709 (1959) deceased poked ninth grader in ribs, then when students dismissed proceeded to stair landing, sat with one foot on landing and one dangling, ninth grader raised arms as if to strike him, deceased lost his balance and fell into the stairwell, died from injuries, three teachers assigned supervisory duty and one teacher in area at the time, no recovery.

others who were standing about 35' away were struck by a metal object apparently thrown by the rowdy group. Permanent damage was done to the eye. In appeal, the Hawaii court held that the child is required only to use that degree of care appropriate to one's age, experience, and mental capacity.

There are quite a number of cases involving horseplay and swimming.[121] In *Manganello v. Permastone*[122] the court said that supervision required by a proprietor of a swimming facility to which the public is invited is not merely for purpose of warning those who are in imminent danger or rescuing those who have already been injured, but includes a duty to guard swimming facility and surrounding area for potentially dangerous activities. It went on to say, though, that if rough or boisterous play is to be permitted at a swimming facility to which the public is invited, it should be confined to a restricted area or, at a minimum, closely guarded. In this case a group of young men had been doing flips by standing on the shoulders of one another and jumping backwards into the water. Plaintiff was a father, who, after getting his children out of the water, swam behind them toward the dock and was hit by one of the young men. The lifeguards were 16 to 17 years of age and at times appeared to be paying more attention to the young female patrons than to the swimmers. They neither stopped the horseplay, nor came to the plaintiff's aid after he was injured.

Flipping, also, was the horseplay in *Stillwell v. Louisville*.[123] A 17-year-old girl was being flipped by an acquaintance. Such flipping under applicable safety standards was to be controlled by the lifeguards. At other pools such flipping was not permitted, but at this pool it was considered "normal fun." The injured had been flipped three separate times that day and each time had sufficient injury to require her to leave the pool. Also, only one lifeguard, rather than the three which the city's safety standards required, was on duty at the time.

There are several cases[124] in which judgment was for the defendant. In the Louisiana case an 11-year-old was running and playing with his brother near the pool, and thinking a clear glass sliding door was open, tried to go through it. The Club rules prohibited horseplay, including running, and they were posted, had been mailed to members, and the child was aware of the rules. The child carelessly ran through the door without attempting to determine whether it was open or not. In the Minnesota case the municipality was not liable for injuries sustained when plaintiff was pushed from the diving platform at the municipal bathing beach by another boy on allegation that the beach was inadequately supervised. The third situation came under the Washington recreational landowner statute and defendant was immune. However, the situation was that a number of teenagers in the swimming area of the park were engaged in a game called "rag tag." The decedent either fell or was pushed from the diving tower during the

[121] Quinn v. Smith Co., 57 F. 2d 784 (1932) water carnival, at end horseplay and pushed one another from platform, plaintiff alleges defendant failed to provide anyone to maintain order. See also §9.42 Supervision of swimmers and §14.35 Supervision.

[122] Manganello v. Permastone, 30 N.C. App. 696, 228 S.E. 2d 627 (1976), rev'd. 291 N.C. 666, 231 S.E. 2d 678 (1977).

[123] Stillwell v. Louisville, 455 S.W. 2d 56 (Ky. App. 1970).

[124] Williamson v. Travelers Ins. Co., 235 So. 2d 600 (La. App. 1970), cert. denied 256 La. 818, 239 So. 2d 345; Smith v. Village of Pine River, 305 Minn. 65, 232 N.W. 2d 241 (1975); McCarver v. Manson Park & Recreation District, 92 Wash. 2d 370, 597 P. 2d 1362 (1979).

activity. Plaintiffs alleged inadequate supervision, among other allegations.

Another series of cases involve horseplay at summer camp. In all five cases cited,[125] judgment was for the defendant. The basic issue was whether there was activity of the type which should have given notice (foreseeability) to the camp operator of dangerous propensities against which he must guard. Plaintiff, aged 14, on leaving the bunk room after some teasing or horseplay, fell, putting his arm through a glass panel in the upper part of a door between the bunk room proper and a vestibule which led to an outer screened door. There was no showing of causal connection between the hazing and the accident in this Massachusetts case. And, in the *Ramos* case, plaintiff died as a result of a fall from the roof of the dormitory at summer camp. There was a rule forbidding going on the roof. The two counselors were in the dormitory at all times, and at this time they had gone below to the sleeping quarters to shave. No proof of inadequate supervision evidenced.

The same principles apply to supervision and horseplay for private leisure industry as for public recreation and schools. In *McCormick v. Maplehurst Winter Sports, Ltd.*, 166 Ill. App. 3d 93, 116 Ill. Dec. 577, 519 N.E. 2d 469 (1988), a 10-year-old, while snow tubing (sliding down a hill while reclining in a truck inner tube), was injured when he released his grip on the tow rope as he was ascending the hill and he started to coast downhill in the path of other tubers moving upwards with the rope. Among other allegations, plaintiff stated that defendant failed to properly supervise in that there had been a group of youngsters about 10-13 years old engaging in horseplay on the slope; however, there was no evidence that the horseplay in any way was the proximate cause of the accident or was creating a dangerous situation although the injured boy previously had been bumped by the boys engaged in horseplay.

§ 18.322   Rowdiness

To differentiate rowdiness and horseplay is not easy. Generally, however, included within the category of horseplay are those activities which are done for "the fun of it" with no intent to interfere with anyone else and certainly not to hurt someone; whereas, rowdyism tends to be assailing others in a negative way; one might refer to it as "deviant behavior." Whatever, see also the preceding section on horseplay and the following section on discipline.

---

[125] Kosok v. YMCA, 24 A.D. 2d 113, 264 N.Y.S. 2d 123 (1965), aff'd. 19 N.Y. 2d 935, 281 N.Y.S. 2d 341, 228 N.E. 2d 398 (1967) practical joke older campers attempted to play on plaintiff during rest period, rigged up with a fishing line and rod over a rafter a galvanized pail that they hoisted toward the roof, when a boy passed by, one of the boys let out the line, the pail descended striking passer-by; Ramos v. Salesian Junior Seminary, 40 A.D. 2d 655, 336 N.Y.S. 2d 542 (1972), mem. dec., appeal dism'd. 33 N.Y. 2d 640, 347 N.Y.S. 2d 587 (1973); Rivera v. Columbus Cadet Corps, 59 N.J. Super. 445, 158 A. 2d 62 (1960), mem. dec. pet. denied 32 N.J. 349, 160 A. 2d 847 (1960) during clean-up detail, plaintiff struck in eye by a broom which he had himself placed on the upper bunk across the aisle from his own, broom handle hit his left eye piercing his glasses and causing severe damage to the eye; Sauer v. Hebrew Institute of Long Island, 33 Misc. 2d 785, 227 N.Y.S. 2d 535 (1962), rev'd. 17 A.D. 2d 245, 233 N.Y.S. 2d 1008 (1962), aff'd. without op. 13 N.Y. 2d 913, 243 N.Y.S. 2d 859, 193 N.E. 2d 642 (1963) water pistol fight between groups of campers of similar age played on a grass-covered area, plaintiff slipped on wet grass, struck head on concrete walk, held: water fight no more hazardous than any ordinary camp activity involving running; Soares v. Lakesville Baseball Camp, 343 N.E. 2d 840 (Mass. 1976). See also §13.1 Organized camping.

One of the responsibilities of a supervisor is to stop rowdiness because there is a duty owed (see §2.1) to participants to provide an environment which is relatively safe and free from undue risk of harm; and, since most deviant behavior does in fact tend toward harm of others, it is essential that such behavior (rowdiness) be curtailed before serious injury results. A key element is that of notice, both actual and constructive. Did the defendant have notice of the ensuing rowdyism and its impending potential for harm, and, if so, what was done about it? However, as with horseplay, the defendant is not an insurer of safety.[126]

A 12-year-old seventh grader fractured his right femur in physical education class when a fellow student fell on his leg. A teacher's aide was sent to take over the class while the regular teacher had a conference with the principal. The accident took place near the end of the class period and presumably the regular teacher had returned. During the class period instead of walking around the track as instructed, some of the boys, including plaintiff, engaged in a makeshift football game being played with a paper cup. They knew not only that they were disobeying the teacher's instructions, but also that they were not to play such "rough games." However, the game was said to be an ordinary activity for boys and most of them had played it in their own yards. Although the injured had never played the game, he did not view the game as particularly dangerous. The court found the school board and regular teacher 5% negligent (under comparative negligence determination) because the teacher testifed that she considered it her duty to prevent "rough-housing" and she would have stopped the game had she seen it; the game had continued for 10-20 minutes before the accident, and teacher should have noticed the activity within that time. The teacher's aide owed no duty of care to students after regular teacher returned to resume control of class.[127]

One type of rowdyism which often brings injury to others is that of throwing objects at another person.[128] The situations include acts such as the eighth grade boys throwing pebbles at the eighth grade girls sitting and watching a ball game, one girl suffering loss of an eye;[129] several boys throwing rocks at two girls on way home, but still between school buildings, resulting in eye injury and necessity for an artificial eye;[130] a fellow student throwing a small rock which hit a larger rock and rebounded hitting plaintiff in the eye;[131] and in a lecture hall where a student presentation was being given, the throwing of a metal object by a member of a rowdy group, with permanent damage being done to plaintiff's left eye.[132] The plaintiff recovered in the first and fourth cases, while the defendant won the judgment in the second and third cases. The plaintiffs won on the basis that the injury was foreseeable and the defendant's had notice. On the *Miller* case

[126] Aaser v. Charlotte, 265 N.C. 494, 144 S.E. 2d 610 (1965) ice hockey, no notice of rowdiness.

[127] Marcantel v. Allen Parish School Board, 484 So. 2d 322 (La. App. 1986) 490 So. 2d 1162 (La. App. 1986) writ denied 496 So. 2d 328 (1986).

[128] Carroll v. Fitzsimmons, 371 P. 2d 441 (Colo. 1962) aff'd. 153 Colo. 1, 384 P. 2d 81 (1963); Cioffi v. Board of Educ., N.Y.C., 27 A.D. 2d 826, 278 N.Y.S. 2d 249 (1967); Mandelowitz v. N.Y.C., 277 A.D. 1134, 101 N.Y.S. 2d 166 (1950); Weldy v. Oakland H.S. Dist., 19 Cal. App. 2d 429, 65 P. 2d 851 (1937); Whiteford v.

Yuba City Union High School Dist., 117 Cal. App. 462, 4 P. 2d 266 (1931).

[129] Sheehan v. St. Peter's Catholic School, 188 N.W. 2d 868 (Minn. 1971).

[130] Miller v. Yoshimoto, 536 P. 2d 1195 (Hawaii 1975).

[131] Fagen v. Summers, 498 P. 2d 1227 (Wyo. 1972).

[132] Viveiros v. State, 54 Hawaii 611, 513 P. 2d 487 (1973).

there was no supervision, but the area in which the injury occurred was not considered a dangerous area where constant supervision was required. In the *Fagen* case, the time was so short that defendants did not have notice of the danger. In a 1988 case, *McQuiggan v. B.S.A.,* 73 Md. App. 705, 536 A.2d 137 (1988), a Scout was injured when he joined in a game of shooting paper clips prior to the meeting. The court held that he voluntarily assumed the risk of injury and that the scoutmasters did not have the "last clear chance" where they were setting up for the meeting at the far end of the room from where the boys were playing.

Another form of rowdyism to which supervisers must be responsive is that of fighting and general scuffling.[133] Perhaps the best known case is the landmark case of *Niles v. San Rafael*.[134] An 11-year-old boy got into a fight with another boy over whose turn it was to bat in a softball game on the school playground, but under supervision of the city park and recreational department. He was hit on the head with a bat and suffered a skull fracture and intracranial bleeding. The court held that there were two separate acts of negligence — the failure to stop the fight (the supervisor was inside the school building, but came out immediately), and the improper medical attention by the hospital for which $25,000 and $4 million, respectively, were awarded in damages.

Other cases include fighting in or on the way to or from the locker room,[135] dances,[136] gang interfering with activity,[137] and general disorder.[138] Injuries due to broken glass, too, have occurred due to rowdyism, either when a bottle was thrown[139] or there was glass debris when a person was knocked down.[140]

Rowdiness in and around pools have occasioned injuries allegedly due to lack of supervision.[141] Playgrounds often are the site of rowdiness. (See §18.141.)

§ 18.323 Assaults (physical, sexual)

The cases in this section differ from horseplay and rowdyism in that there is intent to harm and an attack on another person, who may be another participant/player, a person in the vicinity such as another student, or the one in charge (e.g., teacher). Notice of circumstances which might lead to violence or likelihood of attack is essential. Both criminal (see §1.24) and civil (see §1.4132) are included. The term assault in this

[133] Beck v. San Francisco Unified School Dist., 225 Cal. App. 2d 503, 37 Cal. Rptr. 471 (1964); Charonnat v. San Francisco Unified School Dist., 56 Cal. App. 2d 840, 133 P. 2d 643 (1943); Cianci v. Board of Educ., 18 A.D. 2d 930, 238 N.Y.S. 2d 547 (1963); Forgnone v. Salvadore Union Elem. School Dist., 41 Cal. App. 2d 423, 106 P. 2d 932 (1940); Hoose v. Drum, 281 N.Y. 54, 22 N.E. 2d 233 (1939); Raleigh v. Indp. School Dist. No. 625, 275 N.W. 2d 572 (Minn. 1978). See also §15.122 spectators.

[134] Niles v. City of San Rafael, 42 Cal. App. 3d 230, 116 Cal. Rptr. 733 (1974).

[135] See §18.142.

[136] Howard v. Rogers, 19 Ohio St. 2d 42, 48 Ohio Ops. 2d 52, 249 N.E. 2d 804 (1969); Tanner v. Life Ins. Co., 217 Va. 218, 227 S.E. 2d 693 (1976).

[137] Caldwell v. Island Park, 304 N.Y. 268, 107

N.E. 2d 441 (1952); DeMarco v. Albany, 17 A.D. 2d 250, 234 N.Y.S. 2d 94 (1962).

[138] Koehn v. Board of Educ. 193 Kan. 263, 392 P. 2d 949 (1964).

[139] Barakos v. Kollas, 433 Pa. 258, 249 A. 2d 568 (1969); Crossen v. Board of Educ., N.Y.C., 45 A.D. 2d 952, 359 N.Y.S. 2d 316 (1974).

[140] Parness v. City of Tempe, 123 Ariz. 460, 600 P. 2d 764 (1979).

[141] Jeffords v. Atlanta Presbytery, Inc., 140 Ga. App. 456, 231 S.E. 2d 355 (1976); Morris v. School Dist., 393 Pa. 633, 144 A. 2d 737 (1958); Phoenix v. Anderson, 65 Ariz. 311, 180 P. 2d 219 (1947); Zeman v. Cannonsburg, 423 Pa. 450, 223 A. 2d 728 (1966); Jeffords v. Atlanta Presbytery, Inc., 140 Ga.App. 456, 231 S.E.2d 355 (1976). See also §9.42 and §14.35, and §18.321 Horseplay.

section is used in its general usage to mean assault and battery, physical harm. Sexual assault also is included in this section. For child abuse, see §18.325.

Attacks may take place in the context of the physical education class. Plaintiff, an 11-year-old, was in his physical education class playing softball on the playground. There were 50 to 60 students. Another student allegedly hit him in the head with a baseball bat. He suffered a concussion and permanent hearing loss in the right ear. Several weeks prior to the assault, the father had talked with the assistant principal and the principal about others picking on the injured child. Judgment for plaintiff.[142] And, in a 1987 New York case,[143] the eighth grade boys were playing wiffleball in physical education class when two boys became involved in an altercation. While the court stated that the school is liable for foreseeable injury related to absence of supervision, in this incident, the teacher responded immediately and need for closer supervision could not have been known prior to the fight breaking out. A teacher, also, may commit assault and battery in disciplining a student (see next section §18.324).

Intentional injuries may be referenced as "willful and wanton conduct," rather than assault. Most frequently this is a player injuring another player. For example, plaintiff was injured when kicked while playing basketball in a required high school physical education class. Plaintiff alleged violation of rules and that defendant owed a duty to enforce such rules.[144] In a golf case[145] it was alleged that violation of rules and customs also inflicted injury on another golf player. And, it was a similar allegation in a soccer situation.[146]

Altercations may occur in locker rooms and restrooms used for changing of clothes by athletes (see *Leger* and *Holsapple* cases, respectively, in §18.142), as well as in other areas of a school facility or grounds. In *Broward County School Board v. Ruiz*, 493 So. 2d 474 (Fla. App. 1986), the court held that the school breached its duty to provide adequate security to its students, where student waiting for ride after school in cafeteria, where no supervision was provided, was attacked and beaten by three other students. The school had recognized the need for supervision by adopting a comprehensive system of supervision and patrols designed to prevent students from being left alone on campus either during the school day or during after-school activities. A year later the Florida court held similarly in *Comuntzis v. Pinellas County School Board*, 508 So. 2d 750 (Fla. App. 1987), when a high school student was physically beaten during school lunch hour just outside the school cafeteria. No teacher was posted to keep order in the cafeteria, and the beating was near enough, loud enough, and prolonged enough to alert

[142] Brown v. Calhoun Co. Board of Educ., 432 So. 2d 1230 (Ala. 1983); see also *Niles* case in §18.322 for another baseball bat situation; Pope v. McIntyre, 124 Mich. App. 144, 333 N.W. 2d 612 (1983) 13-year-old attacked by fellow student, governmental immunity; Silverman v. Board of Educ., New York, 15 A.D. 2d 810, 211 N.Y.S. 2d 560 (1961) 225 N.Y.S. 2d 88 (1962) on way to locker room, plaintiff was bouncing a ball when another boy seized it, he retrieved ball and continued on his way when he was brutally assaulted by three other students, two of assailants were not members of class, instructor had remained outside picking up equipment, judgment for plaintiff, questioned whether one teacher adequate for 200-250 students, including students known to be troublesome.

[143] Hanley v. Hornbeck, 127 A.D. 2d 905, 512 N.Y.S. 2d 262 (1987); see also Emery v. Chapman, 495 So. 2d 371 (La. App. 1986) no awareness of tendency of student to do violence, hit another student with fist.

[144] Oswald v. Twsp. H.S. Dist. #214, 84 Ill. App. 3d 723, 40 Ill. Dec. 456, 406 N.E. 2d 157 (1980); see also §1.41322.

[145] Allen v. Pinewood Country Club, 292 So. 2d 786 (La. App. 1976).

[146] Nabozny v. Barnhill, 31 Ill. App. 3d 212, 334 N.E. 2d 258 (1975).

teacher if one had been so posted. (See §18.31 Supervisory planning).

Physical assault and battery also may occur at sporting events. While at a professional basketball game, 17-year-old was accosted in the rest room by young males older and larger. When he was solicited for money and had none, he was struck in the face, knocking out two teeth, and beaten into a semi-unconscious condition. Held for plaintiff; the dimly lit rest room was a security responsibility.[147] There was a different result in an Oregon case.[148] Plaintiff was attacked by three students at a girls' basketball game. It was alleged that these rival school districts knew or should have known that there was a risk of violence if they did not provide proper supervision; however, the court held that defendants failed to provide evidence that prior violence had occurred or that the game was likely to inspire violence. When a black high school player was shot during a game, the court held no cause of action under §1983 (due process) resulting from failure to provide adequate security at interracial school events; plaintiff alleged no more than simple negligence and did not show that city officials knew of racial violence at previous athletic events or of an impending attack.[149]

In a 1982 case[150] a bowler was assaulted by another player while bowling. Assaults also take place on the playground.[151] And, an assault occurred on a field trip to a museum. The court held that there was no duty to guard against that type of risk, that the child would be assaulted by other children, a criminal act of a third person.[152]

As for assault and battery of the leadership, some states have enacted laws related to assault and battery upon certain "public servants," and especially teachers, such as Massachusetts and Illinois. Illinois specifically states, in addition to teachers, "supervisor, director, instructor or other person employed in any park district and such supervisor, director, instructor or other employee is upon the grounds of the park or grounds adjacent thereto, or is in any part of a building used for park purposes."

There also are sexual attacks. Injury was sustained when a student left the physical education class and went to the rest room. The class was being conducted in the park. A 14-year-old trainable mentally retarded child was sexually assaulted.[153] A second grader was abducted enroute from her homeroom to physical education class. The students were being escorted by the teacher; but, when the little girl did not arrive at class with the others the teacher went back to the classroom, but she was not there. She had been abducted from the school grounds and sexually molested. Judgment for plaintiff.[154] Just before classes began, as she was about to enter the building, a 15-year-old high school student was grabbed from behind and dragged to some nearby bushes

147 Townsley v. Cincinnati Gardens, Inc., 39 Ohio Misc. 1, 314 N.E. 2d 406 (1973) rev'd. 39 Ohio App. 2d 5, 314 N.E. 2d 409 (1974), rev'd.

148 Cook v. School Dist. VH3J, 83 Or. App. 293, 731 P. 2d 443 (1987).

149 Williams v. City of Boston, 599 F. Supp. 363 (1984), aff'd. 784 F. 2d 430 (1986).

150 Gustaveson v. Gregg, 655 P. 2d 693 (Utah 1982).

151 Cianci v. Board of Educ., Rye, 18 A.D. 2d 930, 238 N.Y.S. 2d 547 (1963); Everhart v. Board of Educ., Roseville, 108 Mich. App. 218, 310 N.W. 2d 338 (1981).

152 Mancha v. Field Museum of Nat'l Hist., 5 Ill. App. 3d 699, 283 N.E. 2d 899 (1972).

153 Corbett v. Dade Co. Board of Public Inst., 372 So. 2d 971 (Fla. App. 1979); Wallace v. Der-Ohanian, 199 Cal. App. 2d 141, 18 Cal. Rptr. 892 (1962) camp situation, judgment for plaintiff.

154 McGraw v. Orleans Parish School Board, 519 So. 2d 847 (1988); see also Randi F. v. High Ridge YMCA, 170 Ill. App 3d 962, 120 Ill. Dec. 784, 524 N.E. 2d 966 (1988) assault and sexual molestation of 3-year-old at day care center by teacher's aide, act outside scope of employment and center not liable.

where she was beaten and raped. Another rape had occurred on the school grounds 15 days earlier. The court[155] stated what appears to be the general rule:

> A school's "duty of supervision" refers not only to a student whose conduct injures a plaintiff but to students who are injured by others or by themselves; it is a special duty arising from a relationship between educators and children entrusted to their care apart from any general responsibility not unreasonably to expose people to a foreseeable risk of harm.

> Fact that school personnel assume a great deal of authority over conduct of students during the school day does not mean that schools, in absence of statute, are strictly liable for a student's injury on proof of causation alone, but it does mean that negligence toward a student is tested by an obligation of reasonable precautions against foreseeable risks beyond that which might apply to other persons.

> Scope of school's obligation under its duty of supervision includes precautions against risks of crime or torts inflicted by a third person.

A Maryland case[156] had the added element of assumed risk by the plaintiff. A female junior high school student, instead of going to her physical education class, returned to the building and entered the boys locker room, which was against the rules; she had done so on four other occasions during the preceding two months, but no teacher was aware. There was an off-limits area (old shower area) in the back of the locker room. No one was in the locker room when she entered; however, one boy came in, and then subsequently others. Plaintiff alleged group sexual molestation. Held that it was a jury question whether plaintiff was contributorily negligent or assumed risk of group molestation by her actions, which in Maryland would bar her recovery.

Parents brought action against the Boy Scouts and a charitable corporation which provided teachers for a private school for personal injuries their two sons suffered because the boys were sexually abused by an employee and for wrongful death of one son. The employee was a teacher who also served as scoutmaster; the two boys were both in employee's class and members of his scout troop. Plaintiffs alleged that one son was sexually abused while at summer camp, and that this abuse continued when they returned to school in fall; the son was threatened with harm if he revealed what had occurred. The other son also was sexually abused while on a weekend camping trip and similarly threatened. Plaintiffs claimed that as a result of such acts both boys suffered severe psychological, emotional, and mental pain and suffering and that as a result of the distress caused one to commit suicide by ingesting drugs. Plaintiffs charged both defendants with negligence in hiring and supervising, specifically in assigning employee to positions (teacher, scoutmaster) of trust where he could molest young boys and in failing to dismiss him despite actual or constructive notice that he had previously been dismissed from another Boy Scout camp for similar improper conduct. Also at issue was jurisdiction. Plaintiffs were domiciled in New Jersey, but the tortious acts in

---

[155] Fazzolari v. Portland School Dist., 303 Or. 1, 734 P. 2d 1326 (1987).

[156] Campbell v. Montgomery County Board of Education, 73 Md. App. 54, 533 A. 2d 9 (1987).

camp were committed in New York. One of the charitable corporations was domiciled in Ohio, and the other in New Jersey at time of incident. The court in *Schultz v. Boy Scouts of America,* 102 A.D.2d 100, 476 N.Y.S.2d 309, aff'd. 65 N.Y. 2d 189, 491 N.Y.S. 2d 90, 480 N.E.2d 679 (1985), said that the law of the place of wrong governs all substantive issues in the action, but when defendant's negligent conduct occurs in one jurisdiction and plaintiff's injuries are suffered in another, the place of the wrong is considered to be the place where the last event necessary to make the actor liable occurred. Thus, the law of New Jersey governed and the defendants were protected under the N.J. charitable immunity statute. (See §4.3, Doctrine of charitable immunity).

§ 18.324   Discipline and disciplining

How much and what type of disciplining can a supervising person do? Most of the cases involve school settings. The basic principle is that one has a right to discipline to maintain appropriate control of the participants, but the type of disciplining technique must not physically injure the individual. (See also §§1.2213, 1.323, 1.331, 1.41311,1.41321 and 2.1112.) Also, the discipline must not be more severe than the nature of the misbehavior; it must be proportionate.

A 16-year-old plaintiff was late for his physical education class. The instructor/coach inquired as to the reason for tardiness; plaintiff did not respond; the question was repeated. Plaintiff said he had forgotten his athletic shoes and was waiting to use those of his cousin. A verbal reprimand was concluded by the coach asking "Do you understand?" The response was "yeah," whereupon he was requested to respond correctly because the instructor required all students to address any member of the faculty with Sir or Ma'am. The student plaintiff refused and turned to walk away; the coach grabbed him by the shoulders, turned him around, and told him to say "Yes, sir." The coach admits to being irritated and to releasing him in a forceful manner. Plaintiff claims the coach was trying to provoke a fight (student black, coach white) by throwing him into some lockers to incite a violent response so that the coach could expel him. A doctor testified that the injuries were slight. In Louisiana, corporal punishment reasonable in degree, administered by a teacher for disciplinary reasons is permitted. The court held that the punishment was not excessive or unreasonable, and that the student could not recover damages.[157]

---

[157] Guillory v. Ortego, 449 So. 2d 182 (La. App. 1984); see also Frank v. Orleans Parish School Board, 195 So. 2d 451 (La. App. 1967), writ refused 250 La. 635, 197 So. 2d 653 (1967) 14 years old, 4'9" tall, 101-pound boy participating in physical education class, teacher 5'8" tall, 230 pounds, was demonstrating a technique in basketball, boy did not participate as instructed, teacher ordered him to sidelines, boy continued to misbehave, teacher grabbed him, lifted him from the floor, shook him against folded bleachers nearby, and released him so suddenly that he fell to the floor fracturing his arm, held that teacher has right of restraint but in this situation he went beyond the restraint necessary and used excessive physical force; LaFrentz v. Gallagher, 105 Ariz. 255, 462 P. 2d 804 (1969) softball in physical education class, instructor umpiring called boy out at first on a close play, while walking back boy was "kicking the dust," plaintiff alleged instructor grabbed him by the throat and slammed him into backstop with "I don't want anymore of your Little League lip, punk," instructor alleged boy said "What?" to which he replied, "You're out," boy responded "The hell I am," whereupon instructor came from third base line toward chicken-wire backstop, pushed the boy on the chest region and told him that that was not the type of language to use on

Action was brought on assault when the football coach for seventh grade team struck a player's helmet and grabbed his face mask. The coach was displeased with the player's performance of a blocking assignment. Shortly after, the player was admitted to the hospital and his condition was diagnosed as a severe cervical sprain and bruising of the brachial plexus. He fully recovered within several months, but was in the hospital eight days. The player was 12 years of age, weighing 115 pounds; the coach was 28 years old, 5'11" tall and weighed 195 pounds. The coach maintained that he had done the act for instruction and encouragement without any intent to injure. The court said that under the rule of privileged force, as applied in a civil assault case against a school teacher, any force used must be that which the teacher reasonably believes necessary to enforce compliance with a proper command issued for the purpose of controlling, training, or educating the child or to punish the child for prohibited conduct. The force or physical contact must be reasonable and not disproportionate to the activity or the offense.[158] The Education Code of Texas provides that no professonal employee of any school district shall be personally liable for any act incident to or within the scope of duties which involves exercise of judgment or discretion except in circumstances where employee uses excessive force in the discipline of students.[159]

Plaintiff brought action for damages sustained from an alleged excessive beating administered with a stick (paddle) by the physical education teacher. At the school at which the youngster who was paddled attended, paddling was a frequent form of punishment. On this day, the coach had the paddle in his pocket before the beginning of the physical education class, the last period of the day. He struck the child once because he would not line up properly for a foot racing event; and, later in the same class, he administered a whipping as punishment for an improper start in another event. After class the child went to the principal; and, his mother took him to a physician that same day. The court found for the plaintiff, saying that evidence as to a broken paddle, bruises and asserted reasons for punishment compelled a finding that the punishment was excessive and unreasonable.[160]

Plaintiff was a student in physical education class. The instructor said that because the class had made noise while leaving class the previous day, each boy should hold their hands up, palms out, and he went down the line giving each in turn three or four licks with a rubber strap. The plaintiff tried to tell him he was not in school the day before and he had not made noise, but to no avail. When he went to the doctor he had a badly bruised wrist and a broken thumb. None of the other boys complained of any injury and there was some evidence that the plaintiff may have hurt his hand previously playing sports, although he denied this. The court held for the teacher, indicating that corporal

the athletic field, boy did not fall when pushed, held instructor did what he did to maintain control in the future and that the extent of pushing was a reasonable disciplinary measure; Macomb v. Gould, 104 Ill. App. 2d 361, 244 N.E. 2d 634 (1969) teacher on duty at night football game to keep crowd away from fence between stands and playing field, struck a 15-year-old boy several times, for jury to determine whether force was unreasonable, however, court said that a teacher has right to inflict corporal punishment in the process of

enforcing discipline, but may not wantonly or maliciously inflict corporal punishment or may be guilty of battery.

[158] Hogenson v. Williams, 542 S.W. 2d 456 (Tex. Civ. App. 1976).

[159] Schumate v. Thompson, 580 S.W. 2d 47 (Tex. Civ. App. 1979).

[160] Johnson v. Horace Mann Mutual Ins. Co., 241 So. 2d 588 (La. App. 1970).

punishment, reasonable in degree, administered by teacher to pupil for disciplinary reasons, is permitted; the paddling in this case was neither excessive nor unreasonable.[161]

The court held in *Metzger v. Osbeck,* 841 F. 2d 518 (1988), that a teacher's decision to discipline a student, if accomplished through excessive force and appreciable physical pain, may constitute invasion of a child's Fifth Amendment liberty interest in his personal security and a violation of substantive due process prohibited by the Fourteenth Amendment. In this situation, the plaintiff was enrolled in a swimming class taught by defendant physical education teacher. Plaintiff was failing swimming for failure to participate in class, but had not been a source of disciplinary problems. On the last day of class, the time was being used for recreational swim. Plaintiff had a written excuse from class that day, suffering from flu and a swollen leg; so, he was sitting on the pool deck with several fellow students trading baseball cards. The teacher was standing several feet away talking to a student teacher and heard plaintiff use inappropriate language in conversation with a female student. The teacher walked to plaintiff, who now was standing, and standing behind plaintiff, placed his arms around plaintiff's neck and shoulder area. Holding plaintiff in that position, the teacher quietly asked him, "Was that you using foul language?" When there was no response, the teacher said, "That kind of language is unacceptable in this class. Do you understand me?" In the course of the questioning, the teacher's arm moved slightly upward, from plaintiff's Adam's apple to under his chin; at some point plaintiff felt pressure on the underneath portion of his chin and had to stand up on his toes. The teacher then released plaintiff, intending to turn him around. Instead, plaintiff, who had lost consciousness at some point, fell face down on to the pool deck, suffering lacerations to his lower lip, a broken nose, fractured teeth and other injuries requiring hospitalization. It was undisputed that defendant intentionally placed his arms around plaintiff's neck and shoulders, but the teacher disclaimed any ill-will toward plaintiff and stated that the action was motivated by a legitimate desire to admonish, not injure. However, the court felt that the defendant's being a wrestling coach might give reason to a jury to find that the teacher was aware of the inherent risks of restraining plaintiff in the manner done and, thus, intended the consequences of his act; therefore, the court remanded the case for jury determination of intent to harm.

There was a short supply of towels for showering after junior high physical education class, and the defendant teacher had a rule, which had been enforced, of a student taking only one towel. Plaintiff took a second when the teacher's back was turned; then the teacher turned and saw it, and requested plaintiff to return the second towel. Plaintiff responded with a burst of laughter and noncompliance. The teacher ordered him to do 25 pushups, his standard punishment for comparable behavior. Plaintiff asked if he could go to his locker and put on his shorts first, and was told to do the pushups now, which plaintiff started in a dry area of the locker room. The teacher watched him do some of the pushups, but also had to supervise other students. While doing the pushups, plaintiff alleged the teacher told him to make sure his penis touched the floor. With his

---

[161] LeBoyd v. Jenkins, 381 So. 2d 1290 (La. App. 1980).

face to the floor, plaintiff could not see who made the statement. The teacher said he did not and this was verified by a student. Student and parents sued for intentional infliction of emotional stress. Held: teacher's objective in punishment (pushups) was to ensure discipline through quick and certain punishment rather than emotionally injure child; pushups without first dressing was not "utterly intolerable in civilized community," and student suffered hurt feelings rather than severe emotional distress.[162]

Plaintiff, a 15-year-old, was playing football with a group of people on the practice football field at the high school. The school football coaches were meeting at the high school that day and two went to the practice field to move a water sprinkler. They also asked the boys to leave, which they refused to do. The coaches called the police. When the other coaches heard about the game on the field, they got into a pickup truck and drove to the field, jumped out of the truck, and went to the boys. Defendant coach pushed plaintiff to get him to leave, whereupon plaintiff started pushing back, and the two began to struggle and the coach struck plaintiff in the mouth, knocking out two of his teeth and loosening several others. Plaintiff also alleged that the coach shouted obscenities at him. The court remanded for determination of fact issues, specifically whether teacher was acting incident to or within scope of duties, whether the act involved exercise of judgment or discretion, and whether the teacher was not disciplining student at time of disturbance.[163]

Discipline, also, may take the form of suspension. In the *Hebert* case[164] high school students, who were suspended from their school hockey team because authorities suspected that the four students had obtained guardianships simply to change their legal address and thus play together on that particular school team, were held not entitled to notice and hearing prior to their suspension and that they had no property right to play interscholastic sports under Rhode Island law. The six-week suspension of the high school hockey players in the *Buhlman* case[165] was for violation of training rules. The court held that the procedures adopted by the principal gave the team members sufficient notice of the nature of the complaint and a fair opportunity to be heard; the team members were afforded due process. As noted, these two cases do not involve any negligent act. Discussion of student rights is in Chapter 1.

Appropriateness of suspension and denying attendance at athletic games was at issue in a 1986 case,[166] applying Kansas law. There were two situations within the case. In one incident several high school students and two former students vandalized school property; the students were suspended three days and the non-students were told they could not attend any high school extracurricular events (including games). In the other incident, two high school students were reprimanded for unsportsmanlike behavior at a basketball game by the athletic director; and, after ignoring the reprimand, the next day they were informed by the principal that they were not to attend the next night's game.

[162] Jackson v. City of Wooster Board of Education, 29 Ohio App. 3d 210, 504 N.E. 2d 114 (1985).

[163] O'Haver v. Blair, 619 S.W. 2d 467 (Tex. Civ. App. 1981).

[164] Hebert v. Ventetuolo, 638 F. 2d 5 (1981) Rhode Island law applied.

[165] Buhlman v. Board of Educ., Ramapo Central School Dist., 107 Misc. 2d 932, 436 N.Y.S. 2d 192 (1981).

[166] Boster v. Philpot, 645 F. Supp. 798 (1986); see also Haverkamp v. United School Dist., 689 F. Supp. 1055 (1986) head cheerleader disciplined; Webb v. McCullough, 828 F. 2d 1151 (1987) field trip behavior.

However, the students and their parents did attend that game. Plaintiffs alleged violation of due process. Held: (1) by admitting guilt, students waived right to hearing; (2) attending athletic games as mere spectator not constitutionally protected right; and (3) parents had no standing to assert their own due process rights violated, school could impose discipline without first seeking parental permission or approval.

Excessive physical discipline also can mean dismissal for a teacher. A teacher was appealing his dismissal for physically abusing two students. The specific incident occurred during a kickball game when one student threw the ball at another. The teacher accused the one student of deliberately throwing the ball at a player who already was safe on base. The teacher called the student over to the doors of the weight room where he grabbed him by the hair near the ear and pulled him into the weight room. He then threw him down on the bench. The previous incident was when a student asked the teacher if he was going to let go on some rough horseplay between two other students. The teacher then grabbed the questioning student forcefully by the arm and jabbed him in the chest a few times and then led him to the locker room, where he grasped the student by the shoulder yoke with his thumbs firmly pressing at a point above the clavicle. He then ground his fist into the boy's chin and mouth to get his chin up. There had been several prior similar incidents of teacher abuse of the students, and the plaintiff teacher had received personnel "advice" letters directing him to follow an assertive discipline plan and improve his relations with the students. One letter listed nine deficiencies. The dismissal of the plaintiff teacher was upheld.[167]

Most school discipline is controlled by state statutes[168] or state department of education regulations, with policy established by the local school system. The State of Illinois law[169] is unique and has had the most physical education and recreation litigation of any state related to state discipline statutes. These include cases related to the shot put,[170] still rings,[171] trampoline,[172] and powder puff football,[173] among others. Suit, also, has been brought in federal court on the basis that disciplinary paddling constituted cruel and unusual punishment in violation of the Eighth Amendment, and on lack of due process in violation of the Fourteenth Amendment. Not so, said the court, since there are common law legal constraints imposed.[174]

§ 18.325   Child abuse

In the mid-'80s a new dimension of discipline and concern for teacher/leader

[167] Russell v. Special School Dist. No. 6, 366 N.W. 2d 700 (Minn. App. 1985); see also Thomas v. Cascade Union H.S. Dist., 80 Or. App. 736, 724 P. 2d 330 (1986) teacher while participating in dodgeball game was hit with ball from behind, reacted in anger, lost self-control, grabbed offending student and kicked her in the thigh and had verbal exchange in the locker room.

[168] See §18.12 Statutory duty to supervise.

[169] Ill. Rev. Stat. Ann. chp. 122 §24-24, 34-84a.

[170] Amer. States Ins. Co. v. Flynn, 102 Ill. App. 3d 201, 57 Ill. Dec. 889, 429 N.E. 2d 587 (1981) discusses statute as purpose more for promoting discipline than immunity.

[171] Kobylanski v. Chicago Board of Education, 22

Ill. App. 3d 551, 317 N.E. 2d 714 (1974), aff'd. 63 Ill. 2d 165, 347 N.E. 2d 705 (1976).

[172] Chilton v. Cook Co. School Dist., 26 Ill. App. 3d 459, 325 N.E. 2d 666 (1975), aff'd. 63 Ill. 2d 165, 347 N.E. 2d 705 (1976).

[173] Lynch v. Board of Educ., Collinsville, 72 Ill. App. 3d 317, 28 Ill. Dec. 359, 390 N.E.2d 526, (1979), aff'd. 45 Ill. Dec. 96, 82 Ill. 2d 415, 412 N.E. 2d 447 (1980).

[174] Ingraham v. Wright, 498 F. 2d 248, rev'd. 525 F. 2d 909, aff'd. 430 U.S. 651, 51 L. Ed. 2d 711, 97 S. Ct. 1401 (1977) Florida common law; see also *Boster* case, supra.

behaviors with students/participants arose and that is child abuse. These statutes may define child abuse and what excessive corporal punishment is, as well as protect those who work with children with immunity for turning in to authorities suspected cases of child abuse. Some states require such persons who work with children to make reports. In the mid-'80s the law is not settled on this issue and its development should be followed by all working with children. (See also preceding two subsections, §§18.323 Assault and 18.324 Discipline).

In a 1988 case, *Randi F. v. High Ridge YMCA*, 170 Ill. App. 3d 962, 120 Ill. Dec. 784, 524 N.E.2d 966 (1988), parents of a 3-year-old child brought action against both a teacher's aide at a day care center and her employer, the YMCA which conducted the day care center. Plaintiff alleged that the child had been beaten and sexually assaulted, the counts specifically: touched her vagina and private parts, hit her with a stick on her chest and stomach, inserted a stick in her rectal area, inserted a stick in her vaginal area, and pulled her pants down and shirt up while the child protested. Plaintiff further alleged that as a direct and proximate result of these acts, the child suffered pain and physical injury, as well as severe emotional distress, which required both medical and psychiatric care. In this particular situation, the court held that the teacher's aide's actions departed from the scope of her employment having no relation to the business of the day care center or the furtherance thereof and therefor under the doctrine of respondeat superior the YMCA was not liable.

A fourth grade teacher, in *Malte v. State*, 125 A.D.2d 958, 510 N.Y.S.2d 353 (1986), was charged with third-degree assault and endangering the welfare of child when he responded to the misbehavior of a 10-year-old girl in his class by picking her up, placing her on the floor, straddling her legs, and hitting her backside approximately 12 times. The court found the teacher not guilty, which gave rise to the teacher's action for false arrest and malicious prosecution. (See §1.4131).

§ 18.33   Functions of supervision

The functions of supervision fall basically into five categories: (1) behavior management, (2) rendering of emergency care, (3) enforcement of rules and regulations, (4) alertness to dangerous conditions, and (5) responsibilities for persons "off premises." Behavior management is discussed in this chapter, §13.32, intoxication in §1.221, and crowd control in §15.12. First aid and emergency care as a duty are described in §17.2. Alertness to dangerous conditions encompasses areas and facilities (see §20.2, §20.3), equipment (see §21.2), and conduct of activities (see especially §19.221). Subcategories in this section discuss rules and regulations, alertness to dangerous conditions, and responsibilities for persons "off premises."

§ 18.331   Rules and regulations

There are several contexts in which one must consider rules and regulations, such as (1) rules which are policies made by the governing body, and for which the corporate entity and board members are immune in exercise of a discretionary act (see §3.2 and §4.13); (2) rules which are operational in nature made by administrative and supervisory personnel, and which are considered ministerial acts for which there usually is liability (see §3.3); and (3) rules and regulations of the game itself. In respect to the third context, the specific supervisor or the person in charge of the conduct of the activity is required to see that the game is played according to the rules (see Chapter 19 and specific activities in Part B). Individuals, too, such as in golf and boating must comply with the courtesy and common rules of the game. However, a general supervisor of an area or facility is not usually responsible to enforce the rules of the game among participants, such as a walleyball game in the racquetball club.[175] The second context has two aspects, those rules and regulations which are concerned with the use of an area or facility (see §1.22) and those which are set forth for the safety of the participants. It is this latter aspect which is one of the responsibilities of supervision, and which is the focus of this section. There is a supervisory responsibility to (1) establish rules and regulations, (2) communicate them to the persons affected, and (3) enforce them equitably.[176] All three components must be present for defendant to use effectively violation of rules and regulations in contributory negligence (see §5.21) defense. (See §24.22 for operational elements of rules and regulations.)

In some jurisdictions there is a statutory duty to prescribe rules and regulations for certain activities, especially in school districts (see §2.113), but also in recreation situations. Decedent was killed when struck by a boat while waterskiing on the lake. The court held that plaintiff could not recover on the theory that the county had failed to perform a mandatory duty to enforce safety laws, because no laws had been enacted to be enforced. This was in reference to the statute which provided immunity for failing to adopt an enactment or enforce a law[177] (see §4.3, 4.4). However, as indicated in subsequent paragraphs, rules and regulations for specific activities to protect the participants is a ministerial act for which there is liability. The two purposes of the enactment of rules and regulations must be distinguished.

The provision and enforcement of rules and regulations is evidence of concern for safety; for example, in skating rinks,[178] initiation hazing,[179] in locker room,[180] in

[175] Dillon v. Keatington Racquetball Club, 151 Mich. App. 138, 390 N.W. 2d 212 (1986) app. denied 425 Mich. 885.

[176] Beach v. Springfield, 32 Ill. App. 2d 256, 177 N.E. 2d 436 (1961); Becker v. Newark, 72 N.J. Super. 355, 178 A. 2d 364 (1962); Gattavara v. Lundin, 166 Wash. 548, 7 P. 2d 958 (1932); Thayer v. St. Joseph, 227 Mo. App. 623, 54 S.W. 2d 442 (1932).

[177] Osgood v. Shasta Co., 50 Cal. App. 3d 586, 123 Cal. Rptr. 442 (1975); see also Dummond v. Mattoon, 60 Ill. App. 2d 83, 207 N.E. 2d 320 (1965) city established regulations for use of water supply lake for recreation but copies of regulations had certain restrictions marked out with black crayon including the act in question regarding fishing, must be shown that there was reliance on the marked out section; Ostrowski v. Board of Educ., Coxsacki-Athens Central School

Dist., 31 A.D. 2d 571, 294 N.Y.S. 2d 871 (1968) no violation of statutory duty by Board, student injured in high school physical education class performing certain exercises; Selleck v. Board of Educ., 276 A.D. 263, 94 N.Y.S. 2d 318 (1949) failure to establish rules and regulations for safety of youngsters on school grounds after dismissal awaiting transportation was proximate cause of injury.

[178] Hildebrandt v. Univ. Denver, 482 P. 2d 403 (Colo. App. 1971); Yeater v. Decatur Park Dist., 290 N.E. 2d 282 (Ill. 1972).

[179] Chappel v. Franklin Pierce School Dist., 71 Wash. 2d 17, 426 P. 2d 471 (1967).

[180] Ruggerio v. Board of Educ., Jamestown, 31 A.D. 2d 884, 298 N.Y.S. 2d 149 (1969), aff'd. 26 N.Y. 2d 849, 258 N.E. 2d 92 (1970).

gymnastic activities,[181] and boat riding.[182] Rules and regulations also may reflect the experience of the participant and the occasion for participation.

In *Brown v. Board of Educ.*,[183] the defendant Board of Education failed to follow its own safety rules requiring implementation of a buddy system and periodic counting of children in a pool, which constituted breach of the Board's duty to provide adequate supervision. It was for the jury to determine whether the negligent act of failing to enforce its regulation prohibiting children from playing on a jungle gym on the playground while wearing mittens or gloves was the proximate cause of the injury in *Ward v. Newfield*.[184] The school also failed to enforce a regulation of prohibition in the *Tashjian* case.[185] A third grade student was injured when struck on the nose by a bat held by a fourth grade student while engaged in softball at a supervised playground during lunch recess. There was a school rule that third graders not be allowed to participate in softball games. The court held that the school's failure to enforce such rule constituted negligence, which was the proximate cause of the injury. And, it also was a matter of proximate cause in *Whorley v. Brewer*, 315 So. 2d 511 (Fla. App. 1975). In this situation a physical education teacher drove his automobile to a nearby swimming pool used for class, which was prohibited by school regulations.

In several cases it was alleged that there were inadequate or no rules and regulations for the safety of the participants. These included a gym class crossing a street,[186] informal activity in a physical education class,[187] and swimming during a class outing.[188] However, even though there may be a duty to establish rules and regulations, either by statute or a dangerous situation, the mere fact that there were no rules or regulations is not negligence per se. The lack of rules and regulations must be the proximate cause of the injury.[189]

See also §18.31 on supervisory plan and policies.

§ 18.332   Dangerous activities and conditions

One of the key responsibilities or functions of both general and specific supervision is that of identifying dangerous conditions or activities and then either stopping the

---

[181] Armlin v. Board of Educ. Schenectady, 36 A.D. 2d 877, 320 N.Y.S. 2d 402 (1971); Chapman v. State, 6 Wash. App. 316, 492 P. 2d 607 (1972); Lueck v. Janesville, 57 Wis. 2d 254, 204 N.W. 2d 6 (Wis. 1973); also see, at noontime, Miller v. Griesel, 297 N.E. 2d 463 (Ind. App. 1973), aff'd. 308 N.E. 2d 701 (Ind. 1974); nearby natural drainage ditch Whitfield v. East Baton Rouge Parish School Board, 43 So. 2d 47 (La. App. 1949).

[182] McQuire v. Louisiana Baptist Encampment, Inc., 199 So. 192 (La. App. 1940).

[183] Brown v. Board of Educ. N.Y.C., 37 A.D. 2d 836, 326 N.Y.S. 2d 9 (1971).

[184] Ward v. Newfield Central School Dist. No. One, 66 A.D. 2d 968, 412 N.Y.S. 2d 57 (1978).

[185] Tashjian v. North Colonie Central School Dist. No. 5, 50 A.D. 2d 691, 375 N.Y.S. 2d 467 (1975) motion denied 38 N.Y. 2d 708, 382 N.Y.S. 2d 1082 (1976).

[186] Flournoy v. School Dist. No. 1, Denver, 482 P. 2d 966 (Colo. 1971); Flournoy v. McComas, 488 P. 2d 1104 (Colo. 1971).

[187] Cirillo v. Milwaukee, 34 Wis. 2d 705, 150 N.W. 2d 460 (1967).

[188] Cox v. Barnes, 469 S.W. 2d 61 (Ky. App. 1971); Westbrook v. Board of Education, City of St. Louis, 724 S.W. 2d 698 (1987).

[189] Ferguson v. Payne, 306 N.Y. 590, 115 N.E. 2d 687 (1953), aff'd. 279 A.D. 968, 111 N.Y.S. 2d 531 (1953).

activity or warning of the condition. The supervisor must take appropriate action for the protection of the participants. Duty to warn contemplates opportunity to know of danger (actual or constructive notice) and to have time to communicate it.[190]

Although the majority of cases involving the nature of supervision are concerned with dangerous conditions or activities, only brief comment is made in this section. There are many citations and descriptions in both Parts B and C which provide details of dangerous activities and conditions.

A supervisor must be concerned about stopping dangerous activities in which a participant may be engaged, such as taking a teeter-totter board and placing it on a swing seat,[191] riding bicycles dangerously on the playground,[192] standing upon a swing after having wrapped the chains and letting them unwind, thereby getting dizzy,[193] playing frisbee at a day care center,[194] playing crack-the-whip on ice,[195] using electric shock as an initiation stunt,[196] running races on a gravel walk around a reservoir,[197] shooting in a park,[198] playing badminton with poor lights,[199] diving off a board into swimmers,[200] driving a motorboat into an area of fishermen,[201] and roller or ice skating on the rink so as to endanger others.[202]

Highly dangerous activities, such as the handling of firearms, require a higher degree of supervision than other activities.[203] The court also said that in respect to discus throwing that there must be due care exercised in its supervision.[204] Although the judgment was for the defendant, a dart can be a dangerous instrument if not properly used.[205]

A supervisor should also prevent use of defective equipment which would cause an activity to become dangerous.[206] This might include the correct size of rope for a game,[207] a hazardous condition of the equipment in art class,[208] and an unsteady

[190] Norman v. Turkey Run Comm. School Dist., 411 N.E. 2d 614 (Ind. 1980) second grade student was injured when she collided with a first grade student on the playground during supervised recess, children running on playground not an unreasonably dangerous condition, no duty on teachers to warn of possible injury.

[191] Bruenn v. North Yakima School Dist., 101 Wash. 374, 172 P. 569 (1918).

[192] Buzzard v. East Lake School Dist., 34 Cal. App. 2d 316, 93 P. 2d 233 (1939).

[193] Cooper v. Pittsburgh, 390 Pa. 354, 136 A. 2d 463 (1957).

[194] Drueding v. St. Paul Fire & Marine Insurance Co., 482 So. 2d 83 (La. App. 1986).

[195] Fritz v. Buffalo, 277 N.Y. 710, 14 N.E. 2d 815 (1938).

[196] DeGooyer v. Harkness, 70 S.D. 26, 13 N.W. 2d 815 (1944).

[197] State ex rel. K.C. v. Ellison, 281 Mo. 667, 220 S.W. 498 (1920).

[198] Stevens v. Pittsburgh, 329 Pa. 496, 129 Pa. Super. 5, 198 A. 655 (1938).

[199] Styer v. Reading, 360 Pa. 212, 61 A. 2d 382 (1948).

[200] Lincoln v. Wilcox, 111 Ga. App. 365, 141 S.E. 2d 765 (1965).

[201] Dellwo v. Pearson, 259 Minn. 452, 107 N.W. 2d 859 (1961).

[202] Farinelli v. La Venture, 342 Mass. 157, 172 N.E. 2d 825 (1961); Goldman v. Bennett, 189 Kan. 681, 371 P. 2d 108 (1962); Hildebrandt v. Univ. of Denver, 482 P. 2d 402 (Colo. App. 1971); Murphy v. Winter Garden & Ice Co., 280 S.W. 444 (Mo. App. 1926); Rauch v. Penn. Sports & Enterprises, 367 Pa. 632, 81 A. 2d 548 (1951).

[203] Bucholz v. Sioux Falls, 77 S.D. 322, 91 N.W. 2d 606 (1958); Wesley v. Page, 514 S.W. 2d 697 (Ky. App. 1974); Wishart v. Claudio, 207 Cal. App. 2d 151, 24 Cal. Rptr. 398 (1962).

[204] Marques v. Riverside Military Academy, Inc., 87 Ga. App. 370, 73 S.E. 2d 574 (1952).

[205] Hendriksen v. YMCA, 313 P. 2d 54 (1957), rev'd. 173 Cal. App. 2d 764, 344 P. 2d 77 (1959).

[206] Comeaux v. Commercial Union Insurance Co., 269 So. 2d 500 (La. App. 1972); Rook v. State (two cases), 254 A.D. 67, 4 N.Y.S. 2d 116 (1938).

[207] Kearney v. Roman Catholic Church of St. Paul, 31 A.D. 2d 541, 295 N.Y.S. 2d 186 (1968).

[208] Bottorf v. Waltz, 218 Pa. Super. 49, 369 A. 2d 332 (1976).

scaffold being used in dramatics.[209] Maintenance aspects, too, can initiate dangerous conditions, such as hot fireplaces at a picnic,[210] and debris on the toboggan run or around bleachers.[211]

Natural conditions, too, can be dangerous and a supervisor must be alert. Such conditions might include ants in a child care center outside play area,[212] the surf,[213] rocks in a lake swimming area,[214] weather conditions,[215] or thin ice.[216]

Extra supervision also may be required where the supervisor has knowledge of a given condition of a participant.[217]

§ 18.333 Off-premises activities

The California statute[218] regarding liability when pupils are not on school property gives the general principles for not only schools, but also other entities. It states that there is no liability for the conduct or safety of any student of the public schools at any time when such student is not on school property, **unless** the school has undertaken to provide transportation to and from the school premises, or to sponsor a school activity off the premises. In the event of such undertaking, there is liability for the conduct or safety of any student only while such student is or should be under the immediate and direct supervision of an employee of the school. If a city recreation department, a YMCA or Boys' Club, or a private racquet club or other private club sponsors an activity or trip away from the city or within the city, but away from the building or premises of the entity, then the same responsibilities for supervision are required as on-site. For a discussion of situations, see §10.2 School activities — class excursions, special events, clubs; §11.2 Special events; and §13.4 Outings, field trips, excursions; for transportation situations, see §20.1. For criminal acts by third parties, see §1.21.

As to liability for injuries occurring to persons who have left the premises without authorization, there are two factors. First, was there negligence in supervision on-site which occasioned or permitted unauthorized leaving; if so, then that breach of duty to supervise would be the proximate cause of the injury. However, there is a second mediating factor — was that type of injury foreseeable; if so, then not to properly supervise to prevent such injury would be negligence.[219] There is another aspect of unauthorized leaving of the premises which can be considered negligence — the failure to inform the parents of such unauthorized absence.[220]

In performing supervisory functions, such persons must conduct themselves

[209] Miller v. Macalester College, 262 Minn. 418, 115 N.W. 2d 666 (1962).

[210] Brown v. Knight, 362 Mass. 350, 285 N.E. 2d 790 (1972).

[211] Buddy v. State, 59 Mich. App. 598, 229 N.W. 2d 865 (1975).

[212] LaTorre v. First Baptist Church of OJUS, 498 So. 2d 455 (Fla. App. 1986).

[213] Gonzales v. San Diego, 130 Cal. App. 3d 882, 182 Cal. Rptr. 73 (1982); Kleinke v. Ocean City, 163 N.J. Super. 424, 394 A. 2d 1257 (1978).

[214] San Giacomo v. State of New York, 38 A.D. 2d 683, 327 N.Y.S. 2d 87 (1971).

[215] Garretson v. U.S., 456 F. 2d 1017 (1972) Washington law applied.

[216] Stein v. West Chicago Park Commrs., 247 Ill. App. 479 (1928).

[217] Rodrigues v. San Jose Unified School Dist., 157 Cal. App. 2d 842, 322 P. 2d 70 (1958).

[218] Calif. Educ. Code §§87706, 44807, 44808.

[219] Chavez v. Tullesun Elem. School Dist., 122 Ariz. 472, 595 P. 2d 1017 (1979); Hoyem v. Manhattan Beach City School Dist., 139 Cal. Rptr. 769 (1977), 22 Cal. 3d 508, 150 Cal. Rptr. 1 585 P. 2d 851 (1978).

[220] Levandoski v. Jackson Co. School Dist., 328 So. 2d 339 (Miss. 1976).

appropriately. The behavior of the supervising personnel may lead to not only a negligence suit for any injuries sustained thereby, but also disciplinary action against the supervisors. Two coaches were fired for immoral conduct in a Missouri case.[221] The two coaches took six high school boys to the state wrestling meet. Four female students, who were cheerleaders but not going in such capacity, and a mother of one as chaperon also went to the meet. The case opinion is descriptive of the circumstances, but evidence indicated that the coaches had left the students unsupervised while they attended a party and drank alcoholic beverages, and had allowed male and female students to sleep in same rooms. Held: coach-teachers engaged in immoral conduct which rendered them unfit to teach. (See also §1.2213 regarding responsibility toward youth and participants as related to intoxication.)

§ 18.4   Supervision and proximate cause

Proximate cause is one of the elements of negligence which must be proven before a plaintiff may recover from the defendant. (See §2.3 Proximate cause.) Thus, there must be proof of causal connection between lack of supervision or negligent supervision and the accident causing injuries.[222]

In most of the cases which have lack of supervision due to absence of a supervisor, the plaintiff alleged that if a/the supervisor had been present, the injury might not have occurred or would have been minimized.[223] In the situations where the activity was unsupervised, it must be shown how the presence of a supervisor would have prevented the circumstances which gave rise to the injury. In the *Albers* case[224] the plaintiff and some other boys were playing basketball at the school gymnasium during the Christmas holiday after having prevailed upon the custodian to open a locked door. A shot came off the backboard and headed out towards the out-of-bounds line. Plaintiff and another player ran for the loose ball and as plaintiff reached to pick it put, the two boys collided, plaintiff hitting his head against his opponent's hip. Plaintiff fell to the floor on his back in a semi-conscious state, suffering a fracture in the cervical area of the spine necessitating surgical correction and prolonged hospitalization. There was no evidence presented as to how the presence of a coach or teacher would have prevented the collision of the boys chasing the rebounding basketball. Court held for plaintiff in that there was no causative element shown, even though generally schools owe a duty to supervise activities. In a YMCA case,[225] plaintiff was participating in a volleyball

[221] Schmidt v. Board of Education, 712 S.W. 2d 45 (Mo. App. 1986).

[222] Nash v. Rapides Parish School Board, 188 So. 2d 508 (La. App. 1966).

[223] Decker v. Dundee Cent. School Dist., 4 N.Y. 2d 462, 151 N.E. 2d 866 (1958); Gattavara v. Lundin, 166 Wash. 548, 7 P. 2d 958 (1932); Lopez v. New York City, 3 Misc. 2d 603, 152 N.Y.S. 2d 700 (1956), 4 A.D. 2d 48, 163 N.Y.S. 2d 562 (1957), aff'd. 4 N.Y. 2d 738, 171 N.Y.S. 2d 860, 148 N.E. 2d 909 (1958); Lutzker v. Board of Educ., 262 A.D. 881, 28 N.Y.S. 2d 496 (1941); affirmed without opinion in 287 N.Y. 822, 41 N.E. 2d 97 (1942); McLeod v. Grant County School Dist., 42 Wash. 2d 316, 255 P. 2d 360 (1953); Stein v. West Chicago Park Commrs., 247 Ill. App. 479 (1928); Williams v. Longmont, 109 Colo. 567, 129 P. 2d 110 (1942).

[224] Albers v. Indp. School Dist., 94 Idaho 342, 487 P. 2d 936 (1971); see also Bradford v. John A. Coleman Catholic High School, 110 A.D. 2d 965, 488 N.Y.S. 2d 105 (1985) recreational football and flag football (two situations); Frazier v. YMCA, 286 A.D. 464, 144 N.Y.S. 2d 448 (1955).

[225] Hearl v. Waterbury YMCA, 187 Conn. 1, 444 A. 2d 211 (1982).

game, when he and another participant collided in mid-air. Plaintiff was knocked to the ground and suffered serious, permanent and disabling personal injuries. The court held that any failure by recreational organization to provide supervision of the volleyball game was not a substantial factor in bringing harm to plaintiff. The presence of officials would not have prevented the collision. An organization's lack of supervision also was found not to be the proximate cause in a youngsters' baseball game. Plaintiff was sitting on a steel drum 25' from the batter watching several boys play "home run derby." The bat flew out of the batter's hand and hit the 14-year-old plaintiff.[226]

A death also occurred in *Ogando v. Carquinez Grammar School Dist.*,[227] a rather well-known case, where a girl playing at noon ran into a French door, cutting her arm severely. She and her friends could not find a supervisor; by the time the bleeding was stopped by the nurse who was found later, the girl had lost too much blood and died. If a supervisor is supposed to be on duty, but cannot be found, it is the same as if the supervisor is absent. Accessibility of the supervisor is very important.

No evidence was presented for the allegation of inadequate supervision when on a band field trip one of the students drowned. He had parental permission to swim, but could not swim. The court held that there was no connection between supervision and the cause of drowning.[228] But, failure to provide or require supervision of the swimming facility by the government leasing to an association was held to be the proximate cause of drowning in *Ward v. U.S.*[229]

While the plaintiff alleged inadequate supervision, the court held that the adequacy of the supervision was not the proximate cause of injury, but rather the directions given to and followed by the student. In this situation the child had arrived for gym class without sneakers, but was instructed to take off his shoes and work out in his socks. He then began tumbling and as he ran toward the mat, from about 10' away, and was about to spring forward, his feet went from under him and he fell on his arm. There was a question as to whether or not the student had properly followed the instructor's directions.[230]

Foreseeability as related to supervision also is a factor. The court held that there was no negligence in leaving the classroom for a few minutes while the class was engaged in a program of calisthentics and that the attendant lack of supervision was not the proximate cause of injuries sustained, because it was not foreseeable that a nine-year-old boy would leave his place and assigned tasks and strike the back of the head of the plaintiff, causing her to fall and chipping two of her front teeth.[231] Similarly, due to lack of foreseeability, failure to supervise was not held to be the proximate cause of injury in a situation where plaintiff was injured while playing catcher in an unsupervised stickball game. The seven-year-old player was too close to the batter, although there was plenty of room, and was struck in the eye by the stick swung by the batter in course of the game.

---

226 O'Bryan v. O'Connor, 59 A.D. 2d 219, 399 N.Y.S. 2d 272 (1977).

227 Ogando v. Carquinez Grammar School Dist., 24 Cal. App. 2d 567, 75 P. 2d 641 (1938); see also Tymkowicz v. San Jose Unified School Dist., 151 Cal. App. 2d 517, 312 P. 2d 388 (1957).

228 Powell v. Orleans Parish School Board, 354 So. 2d 229 (La. App. 1978).

229 Ward v. U.S., 208 F. Supp. 118 (1962).

230 Passafaro v. Board of Educ., N.Y.C., 43 A.D. 2d 918, 353 N.Y.S. 2d 178 (1974).

231 Segerman v. Jones, 256 Md. 109, 259 A. 2d 794 (1969).

The physical layout of the playground did not compel the catcher to stand that close.[232]

However, in other cases, the lack of supervision has been held to be the proximate cause of injury, especially when the accident or likelihood of injury is foreseeable by the circumstances. In the *Brahatcek* case[233] the decedent had never had a golf club in his hand and was participating in a physical education class. The class was practicing swings in the gymnasium. The decedent was having some difficulty and one of the group members said he would show him and would take two practice swings, then hit the ball. The demonstrating student had observed decedent prior to taking the practice swings, but when he took the full swing at the ball, he was unaware that decedent had moved closer and hit him on the follow-through of the club. Foreseeability was also at issue in a Minnesota case.[234] The court held, where plaintiff was injured by student rowdiness at a school-sponsored film, that proximate causation is established by showing likelihood that misconduct would have been prevented had the duty to supervise been discharged. Four years earlier in a landmark case[235] it, also, was held that the injury was the reasonable and probable consequences of their negligent acts. In this situation the 11-year-old injured plaintiff was participating in a softball game at the school playground. The supervisor was inside the school building when the fight broke out; he ran back to the playground and separated the two boys, but plaintiff had suffered a fractured skull which tore an artery under the fracture.

And, in *Sheehan v. St. Peter's Catholic School*, 188 N.W. 2d 868 (Minn. 1971), a teacher escorted twenty eighth grade girls to the athletic field during the morning recess. The children were directed to sit on a pole or log on third base line of the baseball field being used by the eighth grade boys. The teacher returned to the building. About five minutes after she left, some of the boys waiting to bat began pelting girls with pebbles. Although the girls protested, pebble throwing continued three or four minutes until plaintiff was struck in the right eye, causing her to lose the sight of that eye. It was held that lack of supervision was causative, for had the supervisor been there, the accident would have been prevented by stopping the pebble throwing. It was not necessary to prove that the particular accident (loss of sight) was foreseeable. In a playground situation, temporary absence also was alleged to be proximate cause of injury. The supervisor temporarily abandoned her post on the playground at lunch time, during which time a six-year-old stood up in a "baby swing" and fell off. The court held that there was no evidence that failure to provide general supervision could have been the proximate cause of plaintiff's injuries.[236]

But proximate cause, too, can be attributable to negligent supervision, rather than lack of supervision. In two illustrative lifeguard situations, the court said in one that the lifeguards failed to keep careful lookout for decedent, knowing he was a non-

[232] Turano v. N.Y., 17 A.D. 2d 191, 233 N.Y.S. 2d 330 (1962).

[233] Brahatcek v. Millard School Dist., 202 Neb. 86, 273 N.W. 2d 680 (1979).

[234] Raleigh v. Indp. School Dist., 275 N.W. 2d 572 (Minn. 1978).

[235] Niles v. City of San Rafael, 42 Cal. App. 3d 230, 116 Cal. Rptr. 733 (1974).

[236] Nichter v. City of Buffalo, 74 A.D. 2d 996, 427 N.Y.S. 2d 101 (1980).

swimmer,[237] and in the other the court held that the lifeguard failed to observe the distress of the victim as soon as he should have.[238]

There are many illustrative cases in this chapter and throughout Part B.

---

[237] Carter v. Boys' Club of Greater K.C., 552 S.W. 2d 327 (Mo. App. 1977).

[238] S & C Co. v. Horne, 281 Va. 124, 235 S.E. 2d 456 (1977).

Chapter 19.　The Conduct of Activity

The Concept of Professional Malpractice

This chapter deals with the conduct of activity when the participants are directed in their activity by a leader, coach, teacher, or other responsible person, by whatever name that person is referred. The proper conduct of activity requires knowledge of both the participant engaged in the activity and the activity itself. The first section of this chapter presents the participant in terms of developmental stage, experience, and condition; while the second section sets forth elements related to the activity itself, such as the adequacy of instructions given, the safety directions stipulated, the manner of play (dangerous situations), the equipment and protective devices used, and the conditions of the facilities. Supervision is a very common allegation of negligence and a most integral and essential element when activity is conducted (see discussion in Chapter 18 Supervision).

As in Chapter 18, the cases cited are illustrative only; also, a case cited in one section may have pertinence to other subsections. For additional cases and case descriptions, see Part B, especially §9.5 Swimming in pools.

It is public policy to hold professionals accountable for the quality of their services; hence, the concept of "professional malpractice" is most pertinent when one discusses negligence in the conduct of activity.

Malpractice...(is the) failure of one rendering professional services to exercise that degree of skill and learning commonly applied under all the circumstances in the community by the average prudent reputable member of the profession with the result of injury, loss or damage to the recipient of those services or to those entitled to rely upon them. It is any professional

209

misconduct, unreasonable lack of skill or fidelity in professional or fiduciary duties, evil practice, or illegal or immoral conduct.[1]

The term malpractice is most often thought of in respect to "medical malpractice," including all of the health-related professions, and would include team physicians, athletic trainers, and those rendering rehabilitative services (see §§17.2, 17.3, and 17.4). The personnel field has referenced "managerial malpractice" for the lack of proper administration (see §3.3). And, a novelty store owner counterclaimed for damages, alleging "referee malpractice"; however, the court held that "absent corruption or bad faith, no independent tort exists for sports referee malpractice."[2]

"Educational malpractice" has usually been in respect to the failure to educate within the school system, and generally does not include the functions of discipline and punishment, supervision, co-curricular activities, privacy, censorship and libel/slander, equal rights, due process, et al., only the process of learning, the learning outcome of the school's responsibility to teach, to educate.[3] In this context of failure to educate, the plaintiffs' successes have been almost non-existent,[4] notwithstanding considerable legal literature most of which is pro educational malpractice.[5] In the appeal of *Thompson v. Seattle Public School District*,[6] efforts were made to apply the concept of "educational malpractice," by alleging that there was failure to properly instruct and if other methodology had been used, perhaps injured plaintiff would have "learned." The application of educational malpractice to negligent conduct of activity is an unusual application. However, in a technical definition sense, educational malpractice can be applied to those persons in educational (public and private school) settings who perform negligently their instructional responsibilities, or in the broader context, to any individual who has an instructional responsibility, including specific and transitional supervisory responsibilities (see introduction Chapter 18). This chapter focuses upon this latter concept of educational malpractice by the professional, whether in the school, community recreation, commercial enterprise, or private not-for-profit organization setting.[7]

What are the standards against which professional conduct is assessed to determine malpractice? According to a 1980 New Jersey case,[8] "a standard does not mean a

---

[1]Black's Law Dictionary./5th ed. Also citing Matthews v. Walker, 34 Ohio App. 2d 128, 63 Ohio Op. 2d 208, 296 N.E. 2d 659 (1973).

[2] Bain v. Gillispie, 357 N.W. 2d 47 (Iowa App. 1984); for discussion at case, see §15.3.

[3] See also §§1.323, 1.411 failure to educate and athlete's property right.

[4] For example, Donohue v. Copiague Union Free School Dist., 47 N.Y. 2d 440, 418 N.Y.S. 2d 375, 391 N.E. 2d 1352 (1979); D.S.W. v. Fairbanks N. Star Borough School Dist., 628 P. 2d 554 (Alaska 1981); Helm v. Professional Children's School, 103 Misc. 2d 1053, 431 N.Y.S. 2d 246 (1980); Hoffman v. Board of Education, 49 N.Y. 2d 121, 400 N.E. 2d 317, 424 N.Y.S. 2d 376 (1979); Hunter v. Board of Education, 47 Md. App. 709, 425 A. 2d 681 (1981), aff'd./rev'd. in part, 292 Md. 481, 439 A. 2d 582 (1982); Loughran v. Flanders, 470 F. Supp. 110 (1979); Paladin v. Adelphi Univ., 110 Misc. 2d 314, 442 N.Y.S. 2d 38 (1981); Peter

W. v. San Francisco Unified School Dist., 60 Cal. App. 3d 814, 131 Cal. Rptr. 854 (1976).

[5] For example, Collingsworth, Terrence P. Applying Negligence Doctrine to the Teaching Profession, 11 *J. of Law & Educ.* 479-505 (1982); Masner, Charles M. Note: Educational Malpractice and a Right to Education: Should Compulsory Education Laws Require a Quid Pro Quo? 21 *Washburn L.J.* 555-579 (1982); Tracy, Destin Shann. Comment: Educational Negligence: A Student's Cause of Action for Incompetent Academic Instruction, 58 *N. C. L.Rev.* 561-597 (1980).

[6] See footnote on Thompson case in §19.211, plaintiffs did not pursue concept of educational malpractice because of general unsuccessfulness of such allegations, according to a personal conversation with one of the attorneys.

[7] See also §25.332 Malpractice insurance.

[8] Fantini v. Alexander, 172 N.J. Super. 105, 410 A. 2d 1190 (1980).

principle which every practitioner in the applicable profession will follow but, rather, is a generally recognized standard." A professional need not be superior to others in the profession, but must possess and exercise the knowledge and skill of a member of the profession in good standing. A standard may be established by custom, an organization, or by literature. "Safety standards promulgated by organizations active in a particular field are admissable even though the defendants were unaware of the standards."[9] This usually is given by an expert witness, although a court may take notice of such printed standards.

Custom may be established by bringing in evidence of the common or customary method within the profession for conducting an activity, such as was done in cases related to attempting a head stand in physical education class by an 11-year-old,[10] the appropriateness of a basketball drill for boys of plaintiff's age,[11] the instruction in wrestling for a 15-year-old boy,[12] the operation of a trampoline center,[13] and the appropriate time in skill development for a karate student to "free fight."[14] Custom also may mean according to the accepted rules of the game. For example, such standard was applied in a soccer game[15] and a softball game.[16] In both these instances it was one player hurting another player in violation of the usual rules by which the game is played. Usually the desirable professional practice and the dangerousness of the manner in which the activity was conducted will be testified to by an expert witness.[17] Sometimes the expert witnesses testify differently — for example, one expert witness said that the activity "Ride the horse," a gymnastic stunt, did not belong in the public school system because it was inherently dangerous; a second indicated that it was not inherently dangerous; and that it was reasonable for the plaintiff's grade level; and, the third stated that the activity was a popular one which has been played since early history.

Standards, also, may be established by a school or State syllabus for that specific activity, as was done in the situation of an 11-year-old performing on rings in gymnastics class.[18] The standards may come from printed pamphlets or materials setting forth desirable practices, such as is done for the skiing industry by the National Ski Patrol (pamphlet of safe skiing suggestions) and the U.S. Ski Associaton (National Skier's Courtesty Code).[19] And, in a heat exhaustion situation, the plaintiff alleged that the defendants did not follow the recommendations of the American Medical Association for the prevention of heat stroke and heat exhaustion during football workouts.[20] The American Academy of Pediatrics and the American Alliance for Health, Physical Education, Recreation, and Dance have established standards in relation to performance on the trampoline.[21] There also are standards for equipment to be used, such as football

[9] Walheim v. Kirkpatrick, 287 Pa. Super. 130, 429 A. 2d 1134 (1981), 451 A. 2d 1033 (1982).

[10] Gardner v. State, 281 N.Y. 212, 22 N.E. 2d 344 (1939).

[11] Strauch v. Hirschman, 40 A.D. 2d 711, 336 N.Y.S. 2d 678 (1972).

[12] Stehn v. Bernarr MacFadden Found., 434 F. 2d 811 (1970).

[13] Kungle v. Austin, 380 S.W. 2d 354 (Mo. 1964).

[14] Fantini v. Alexander, 172 N.J. Super. 105, 410 A. 2d 1190 (1980).

[15] Nabozny v. Barnhill, 31 Ill. App. 3d 212, 334 N.E. 2d 258 (1975).

[16] Bourque v. Duplechin, 331 So. 2d 40 (La. App. 1976) cert. denied 334 So. 2d 210 (1976) writ rev. not considered 334 So. 2d 230 (1976).

[17] Stanley v. Board of Educ., Chicago, 9 Ill. App. 3d 963, 293 N.E. 2d 417 (1973).

[18] Armlin v. Board of Educ., Schenectady, 36 A.D. 2d 877, 320 N.Y.S. 2d 402 (1971).

[19] LaVine v. Clear Creek Skiing Corp., 557 F. 2d 730 (1977).

[20] Mogabgab v. Orleans Parish School Board, 239 So. 2d 456 (La. App. 1970).

[21] See §7.26 Gymnastics.

helmets.[22] Standards also may be a matter of professional ethics, as was the situation in *Florian v. Highland Local School District,* 24 Ohio App. 3d 41, 493 N.E. 2d 249 (1983), when the wrestling coach (and guidance counselor) was terminated for immorality when he instructed a freshman wrestler to misrepresent his status by weighing in for an older wrestler, who was overweight.

For high school interscholastic athletics, the National Federation of High School Athletic Associations and its respective state associations set standards and rules for the conduct of many sports at the high school level. In a number of law suits, they are being included as defendants.[23]

§ 19.1   The participant

The appropriate conduct of activity requires an understanding of the participant engaging in the activity. Three attributes of the participant should be distinguished: (a) those characteristics which relate to the developmental stage of the individual, including age, maturity, size; (b) the experience of the person with the activity; and (c) the condition of the participant as concerns temporary and permanent physical and emotional disabilities. These attributes are as important to adults, and especially older adults, as to children and youth. Then, there also is the matter of where the activity was required of the participant.

In *McGill v. Laurel*[24] it was held that one must distinguish age, capacity, and experience of a child of tender years in the case of contributory negligence. See §5.21 Contributory negligence, for more cases relating to expectations of children.

§ 19.11   Developmental stage of participant

A competent leader or teacher is one who selects and organizes activities in accord with the size, age, and grade level of the participants; however, just what is appropriate is not clear in the courts. There seems to be a difference between activities engaged in as free play or recreation and those which are conducted in an instructional setting. Further, the appropriateness of an activity to the size, age and skill of a participant is closely related to the degree of supervision required. (See also §2.1 on duty owed children and Chapter 18 Supervision.) It should be noted that the cases do not involve appropriateness of activity to gender of the participant; in other words, there does not seem to be any evidence that legally one activity may be considered an activity for girls or women and another for boys or men only or primarily. It appears that the other factors of development are the determinants. For the right to participate, however, in which gender appropriate sports are at issue, see §1.3.

---

[22] See §6.311 and §21.13.

[23] For example, Barrett v. Phillips, 29 N.C. App. 220, 223 S.E. 2d 918 (1976); Oswald v. Twsp. H.S. Dist. #214, 84 Ill. App. 3d 723, 40 Ill. Dec. 456, 406 N.E. 2d 157 (1980) National Federation; Peterson v. Multnomah County School Dist., 60 Or. App. 81, 668

P. 2d 385 (1983); Rutter v. Northeastern Beaver Co. School Dist., 283 Pa. Super. 155, 423 A. 2d 1035 (1980), rev'd./remanded 496 Pa. 590, 437 A. 2d 1198 (1981). See also §3.13.

[24] McGill v. Laurel, 252 Miss. 740, 173 So. 2d 892 (1965); see also Rosa v. U.S., 613 F. Supp. 469 (1985).

§ 19.111 Playground activities and apparatus

The seventh and eighth grade classes were pitted against each other in a touch football game. An eighth grader, 13 years old, 5'4", weighing 97 pounds, attempted to block a seventh grade boy, 14½ years old, 5'10" tall, weighing 145 pounds, and was struck in the abdomen by the seventh grader's knee resulting in removal of the spleen and left kidney five hours later. It was held that a class division was a logical method of organization for free play during the noon period.[25] A similar situation occurred in a physical education class. An eighth grade boy, 13 years of age, weighing about 75 pounds, collided with a sixth grade boy, 15 years old, weighing over 200 pounds, as they were playing "king king calico." This was held to be an unavoidable accident in a non-hazardous game.[26] A different result was reached, however, when a 12-year-old seventh grader was playing in the gymnasium at noon under supervision of the physical education teacher. Twenty boys were on each side of the gymnasium about 75' apart with a ball in the middle. Each boy was assigned a number; teams had corresponding numbers and when the instructor called a number, the boy who had the number from each team ran at full speed to the middle and attempted to kick the ball over the opponent's goal line. The seventh grader was kicked by his opponent, a 6' tall, 180 to 190 pound boy (much larger than the injured boy), and sustained a cerebral concussion. The court held for the injured lad on the basis of a hazardous game and unmatched opponents.[27]

There is a series of early cases relating to the appropriateness of certain pieces of apparatus to the age of the child. A first grade pupil fell while hanging from a 6' high horizontal ladder. The court held the apparatus appropriate.[28] A six-year-old girl, although told not to use the horizontal and vertical ladders, had watched the older children using them, and in trying them herself (they were 30' long, 7' high) she became exhausted and fell, breaking her arm. The court held that one could not blame the child for wishing to try the apparatus and held the school liable for maintaining a dangerous piece of equipment. The court said that the apparatus should have been so constructed that the vertical ladder could have been removed, preventing use of the horizontal ladder.[29] A nine-year-old plaintiff fell from the top of a piece of apparatus and suffered a skull fracture. The main frame of the apparatus consisted of two upright 6' x 6' posts set in the ground, with another 6' x 6' board resting horizontally on top of and flush with the sides. The top of the horizontal piece was about 14' from the ground. A ladder ran up one side of the posts. On the other side of the posts were two long iron pipes which extended from the ground to the top on an incline. There were bannisters at the top. The object was to climb the ladder to the top and slide down the pipes resting the arms and legs on them. Plaintiff recovered alleging that the apparatus was inherently too dangerous for children the age of the injured.[30] In another case a ramp was constructed

[25] Pirkle v. Oakdale Union Grammar School Dist., 238 P. 2d 57, rev'd. 40 Cal. 2d 207, 253 P. 2d 1 (1953).

[26] Ellis v. Burns Valley School Dist., 128 Cal. App. 550, 18 P. 2d 79 (1933).

[27] Brooks v. Board of Educ., 29 Misc. 2d 19, 205 N.Y.S. 2d 277 (Sup. Ct. 1960).

[28] Cordaro v. Union Free School Dist., 14 A.D. 2d 804, 220 N.Y.S. 2d 656 aff'd. 11 N.Y. 2d 1038, 230 N.Y.S. 2d 30, 183 N.E. 2d 912 (1962).

[29] Howard v. Tacoma School Dist., 88 Wash. 167, 152 P. 1004 (1915).

[30] Holt v. School Dist., 102 Wash. 442, 173 P. 335 (1918).

for use by older boys when supervised. The younger children on the playground, however, were allowed to use it, and played around it, although they were instructed not to use it. A six-year-old boy was injured when he fell from the ramp during recess when there was no supervision. He had previously used it without mishap. The court held that the ramp as constructed, maintained, and used constituted a dangerous piece of playground apparatus for small children.[31]

For children using playgrounds and public recreation facilities, it was held that it would be an unreasonable burden to impose upon school districts the requirement that children be "sorted out" according to age, height, weight and attitudes and directed to and from higher and lower playground slides. In this case[32] a three and one-half-year-old fell from a slide. Additional apparatus cases relating to the age of the child involved monkey bars and children of "tender age,"[33] a seven-year-old when he fell from a rope cargo net which hung in the gymnasium,[34] a six-year-old who fell from a 7' high jungle bar erected on a blacktop surface,[35] and a young child falling from a 12' high slide guarded by a single pipe railing 40" high.[36]

See also §§10.3 and 18.141, related to playgrounds.

§ 19.112 Non-playground activities; appropriateness according to syllabus

Wrestling is one sport in which differences among participants is important. The court discussed wrestling and inferred that for negligence one would need to allege that the opponent was larger, stronger, and more skillful — in other words, unmatched opponents.[37] Pairing was held proper, in another case,[38] when the injured plaintiff wrestled a boy ten pounds heavier, but shorter.

A defense for requiring activities (see §19.13) is sometimes the fact that they are included in a course syllabus, which is recommended by the State or school system; this also is used as a defense for appropriateness of the activity to the age or grade level of the injured plaintiff. Such was the situation in three gymnastic exercise cases.[39] In the *Govel* case the instructor assigned a student in physical education class, who was not exceptionally skilled, to perform an acrobatic feat beyond his prowess and which was not recommended in the regent's syllabus, and also with the knowledge that several boys had been injured while performing such feat. The exercise was to jump from a springboard over five' parallel bars 20" wide and turn a somersault upon landing. One

---

[31] Sullivan v. Binghamton, 271 A.D 860, 65 N.Y.S. 2d 838 (1946).

[32] Chimerofsky v. School Dist., 121 Ill. App. 2d 371, 357 N.E. 2d 480 (1970).

[33] Hillman v. Greater Miami Hebrew Academy, 72 So. 2d 668 (Fla. 1954).

[34] Tardiff v. Shoreline School Dist., 68 Wash. 2d 164, 411 P. 2d 889 (1966).

[35] Hunt v. Board of Education, Schenectady, 43 A.D. 2d 397, 352 N.Y.S. 2d 237 (1974).

[36] Vecchio v. Pittsburgh, 114 Pa. Super., 326, 173 A. 468 (1934); see also Berstein v. Milwaukee, 158 Wis. 576, 149 N.W. 382 (1914); Nashville v. Burns, 131 Tenn. 281, 174 S.W. 1111 (1915) older youth using

swings for five to seven year olds; Ramirez v. Cheyenne, 34 Wyo. 67, 241 P. 710 (1925).

[37] Smith v. Consolidated School Dist., 408 S.W. 2d 50 (Mo. 1966).

[38] Reynolds v. State, 207 Misc. 963, 141 N.Y.S. 2d 615 (Ct. Cl. 1955).

[39] Govel v. Board of Educ., 267 A.D. 621, 48 N.Y.S. 2d 299 (1944); Larson v. Indp. School Dist. No. 314, Braham, 252 N.W. 2d 128 (1977) 312 Minn. 583, 289 N.W. 2d 112 (1979); Yerdon v. Baldwinsville Academy & Cent. S.D., 50 A.D. 2d 714, 374 N.Y.S. 2d 877 (1975), motion denied 39 N.Y. 2d 705, 384 N.Y.S. 2d 1027 (1976).

foot caught and plaintiff landed where no mat had been laid. There was a conflict in expert testimony in the *Yerdon* case, as to the reasonableness of the exercise, "Ride the horse" for the tenth grade. The rationale for requiring the activity as appropriate was that it had been played "since early history days," as a matter of custom. The third case discussed the responsibility of the principal as related to curriculum and what it meant when an activity was required according to the curriculum. The court held that because the Minnesota education regulation provided that there be taught in every secondary school the prescribed course of study prepared by the State did not mean that the curriculum bulletin established mandatory affirmative duties for physical education instruction.

Two additional cases involved whether or not the activity in which the individual was participating was a part of the physical education syllabus. In the first[40] the program of studies K-6 did provide for the classroom teacher to conduct such physical activity on days when the physical education teacher was not at that school. And, in the second case[41] wrestling was suggested or recommended as part of the curriculum; that is, the state law was permissive, not prohibitive. In both cases the activity was held appropriate and there was no recovery. Two other cases were concerned with the school requirement of physical education. In both cases[42] the requirement of activity was appropriate; however, in the *Summers* case the teacher was negligent regarding the participant's physical condition. In *Keesee v. Board of Education*,[43] a 13-year-old, 110-pound student fractured her right tibia in a game of line soccer being played on a gymnasium floor area about 50' x 60'. She was required to participate. The teacher deviated from the school syllabus by having eight contenders instead of two. Plaintiff was injured when she fell from a shove and three girls piled on top of her. Held that the activity was allowed to be played in a dangerous manner. A basketball drill was held in the *Strauch* case to be dangerous and inappropriate for the age of the participants. The high school junior varsity coach had ordered the team to do the drill. Apparently five minutes after the injury, the physical education director came on the scene and scolded the coach for having ordered the drill.[44] And, in a football (tackle) case[45] the appropriateness of the play and age overmatching were in issue. In this situation, the plaintiff assumed the risks.

§ 19.12   Experience and capability of participant

The selection of activities and manner of conducting them as related to experience and skill competence is critical to liability. The nature of experience, as an indicator of the understanding and appreciation of an activity, is at the heart of the defenses of contributory negligence and assumption of risk (see §5.21 and §5.22, respectively, for discussion and additional cases).

[40] Segerman v. Jones, 256 Md. 109, 259 A. 2d 794 (1969).

[41] Smith v. Consolidated School Dist., 408 S.W. 2d 50 (Mo. 1966).

[42] Hanna v. State, 46 Misc. 2d 9, 258 N.Y.S. 2d 694 (1965); Summers v. Milwaukie Union H.S. Dist., 481 P. 2d 369 (Or. App. 1971).

[43] Keesee v. Board of Education, N.Y.C., 37 Misc. 2d 414, 235 N.Y.S. 2d 300 (1962).

[44] Strauch v. Hirschman, 40 A.D. 2d 711, 336 N.Y.S. 2d 678 (1972).

[45] Whipple v. Salvation Army, 261 Or. 453, 495 P. 2d 739 (1972).

In two horseback riding cases[46] the instructor's knowledge of the inexperience of the rider(s) was an important element. In the *Bulkin* case, a child who was almost totally inexperienced in horseback riding was placed on a horse and then left unattended; while in the *Chanaki* case, the group being led was inexperienced and unfamiliar with horses, but the defendant's agent (leader of the group) loped on ahead of the group. Skill and experience also played a part in determining liability in two gymnastics situations,[47] and in a line soccer game.[48] In line soccer the court said that there was "negligence in permitting the game to be played under such circumstances that eight relatively inexperienced girl pupils actively contended for possession of the ball."

In *Mullen v. Russworm*[49] the court held that the proximate cause of drowning was the inability of the decedent to swim and no negligence could be proven against the defendant. The plaintiff had alleged that the defendant had failed to learn whether the boy could swim before admitting him to the pool. In two Florida cases[50] involving a canoe trip and a church outing, the intelligence, experience, and knowledge of the quadriplegic plaintiff and decedent, respectively, were primary factors in the holdings. In the *Clark* case, a 21-year-old fellow dived into shallow water where they had beached the canoe, breaking his neck, resulting in quadriplegia. The court held that the danger was open and obvious and that he had sufficient intelligence, experience, and knowledge to both detect and appreciate the physical characteristics of the swimming place. The court distinguished the *Cutler* case from the *Clark* case, in that plaintiff in *Clark* case did assume responsibility for his actions, and stated the principle that the sponsoring organization had the duty to exercise ordinary care for protection of the girl (decedent), measured in accordance with the ability of the girl to care for herself.

Identifying the ability of the participant and/or classifying the participants may also be involved in allegations of negligence. It was brought out in the evidence in a senior gymnastics class that the plaintiff, a 17-year-old high school student, was tested and passed all of his stunt requirements on the still rings as a sophomore and passed all of his requirements in gymnastics his junior year, yet was still classified in the beginner's group. The stunt he was doing when he was injured was considered an elementary stunt, which he had done many times.[51] Decedent, a college freshman, was attending his first session of a required swimming class. The class was asked to divide itself into two groups, those who could swim and those who could not. Decedent went to the group which was supposed to be able to swim, although he was unskilled. The group was asked to swim from the deep end to the shallow end. About 10′ from the start, decedent went down, but no one noticed until the group was asked to swim back some 8-10 minutes later and one of the students spotted him on the bottom of the pool. Alleged that the assistant instructors, who were members of the swim team, were inexperienced in

[46] Bulkin v. Camp Nockamixon, 367 Pa. 15, 79 A. 2d 234 (1951); Chanaki v. Walker, 114 N.H. 660, 327 A. 2d 610 (1974).

[47] Govel v. Board of Educ., 267 A.D. 621, 48 N.Y.S. 2d 299 (1944); Chapman v. State, 6 Wash. App. 316, 492 P. 2d 607 (1972).

[48] Keesee v. Board of Educ., N.Y.C., 37 Misc. 2d 414, 235 N.Y.S. 2d 300 (1962).

[49] Mullen v. Russworm, 169 Tenn. 650, 90 S.W. 2d 530 (1936); see also Gilliland v. Topeka, 124 Kan. 726,

262 P.493 (1928) six-year-old boy had gone to depth beyond his capability; Morrison v. Comm. Unit School Dist., Payson, 44 Ill. App. 3d 315, 3 Ill.Dec. 222, 358 N.E. 2d 389 (1976).

[50] Clark v. Lumbermans Mutual Insurance Co., 465 So. 2d 552 (Fla. App. 1985); Cutler v. St. John's United Methodist Church of Edwardsville, 489 So. 2d 123 (Fla. App. 1986).

[51] Lueck v. Janesville, 57 Wis. 2d 254, 204 N.W. 2d 6 (1973).

watching and guarding, while instructing; it should have been noted that the decedent was having difficulty and was in the incorrect grouping.[52]

Inexperience can be with adults, as well as children. A family was climbing a mountain. The wife lived in a flat region of Georgia and had no experience in mountain climbing, thus was ignorant of the dangers of both wet and dry climbing. About two-thirds of the way up the mountain, while attempting to seek shelter from a rainstorm, she slipped on the wet rock surface and rolled 100' to 200' where she struck a boulder, severely and permanently injuring herself. Plaintiff alleged that there was failure to warn of hazards and to provide a safe path with handrailings.[53]

Experience, in contrast to inexperience, too, can be the focus of allegations of negligence and a determinant of who is liable. In *Neumann v. Shlansky*,[54] an 11-year-old child who was playing golf was held to the same standards of care as an adult because of his experience. Similarly, a high school athlete who challenged the girls' basketball coach to a wrestling match was held to be knowledgeable regarding wrestling, despite his disclaimer, because of his experience.[55] And the same was true of a football player, who received an injury resulting in his becoming a quadriplegic. He had alleged inexperience, but the evidence did not support the claim.[56]

§ 19.13   Condition of participant

The condition of participants falls basically into two types, physical condition and emotional condition, which includes being forced or required to participate. The person who conducts activity must not only be aware of the condition of the participants but also be able then to conduct activities so that the participants are not exposed to an unreasonable risk. See also §17.3 Condition of participants, including persons with disabilities, and §17.4 Fitness and rehabilitation.

§ 19.131   Physical condition

There are those physical conditions of which one should be aware, those which are obvious, and those which are undetected. A student in physical education class had a history of an "infirm back" condition. The doctor attending her requested a list of exercises which she was required to perform at the school, and the request had been made by the mother at least four times; but, the information was never furnished. She was further injured performing a springboard exercise. The court held that there was foreseeable harm, which gave rise to a duty to take reasonable care to avoid the harm.[57]

In addition to bringing action for negligence in requiring plaintiff to participate in physical education activity when she had a bad knee, plaintiff also alleged administra-

[52] Morehouse College v. Russell, 109 Ga. App. 301, 136 S.E. 2d 179 (1964).

[53] Herrington v. Stone Mountain Memorial Ass'n., 119 Ga. App. 658, 168 S.E. 2d 633 (1969), rev'd. 225 Ga. 746, 171 S.E. 2d 521 (1969), aff'd. 121 Ga. App. 20, 172 S.E. 2d 434 (1970).

[54] Neumann v. Shlansky, 58 Misc. 2d 128, 294 N.Y.S. 2d 628, aff'd. 63 Misc. 2d 587, 312 N.Y.S. 2d

951 (1970), aff'd. 36 A.D. 2d 540, 318 N.Y.S. 2d 925 (1971).

[55] Kluka v. Livingston Parish School Board, 433 So. 2d 302 (La. App. 1983).

[56] Vendrell v. School Dist., 226 Or. 263, 360 P. 2d 282 (1961), rev'd./remanded 233 Or. 1, 376 P. 2d 406 (1962).

[57] Summers v. Milwaukie Union H.S. Dist. No. 5, Clackamas Co., 481 P.2d 369 (Or. App. 1971).

tive negligence for certain nonteaching personnel failing to forward properly doctor's notes regarding the injury and participation which had been submitted the previous year to the physical education instructor, who was a different person than the present instructor, in *Hopwood v. Elmwood Comm. H.S. Dist.*, 171 Ill. App. 3d 280, 121 Ill. Dec. 441, 525 N.E. 2d 247 (1988). Approximately a year earlier, plaintiff injured her knee and the doctor wrote a note indicating that plaintiff was precluded from participating in physical education activity for two weeks, and thereafter allowed such activity as plaintiff was able to tolerate. Plaintiff had informed the present instructor of the injury and the doctor's note. Neither the present instructor nor the principal were aware of the note; however plaintiff was requested to have her mother write a note, which she did, and the instructor did not require plaintiff to participate in any activity in which plaintiff indicated pain. On this day of re-injury, a group of girls, including plaintiff, did not want to participate in "hoccer" because they thought it stupid, it was hot, and they were tired. The instructor threatened them with disciplinary action if they did not play. Plaintiff did not indicate that the activity caused pain; she apparently had played hoccer earlier and did not think it would endanger her knee. The court held that the instructor's requirement was not willful and wanton misconduct, as related to the condition of the knee.

A chiropractor, who treated plaintiff for back problems, advised her to take an aerobic dance class to relieve her tension headaches. A month later she enrolled at the defendant health spa, and shortly thereafter plaintiff fell and injured her back during class. In bringing suit, one of plaintiff's allegations was that the health spa failed to use due care in screening her to determine if she was physically capable of taking the class, and failed to warn her of the dangers of aerobics to people with back problems. Plaintiff received an award and health spa sued chiropractor for contribution; the court held that chiropractor's advice directly contributed to individual's injury and stated claim for contribution.[58]

The court held for the defendant in a swimming pool incident.[59] It was decedent's first swimming class in the fall in high school. The 14-year-old was at the shallow end with a group of non-swimmers, who were directed to become acquainted with the water and to practice holding their breath. He was found unconscious on the pool floor. There was some evidence that he had participated in activities, contrary to the instructor's direction, including diving into the pool and engaging in a breath holding contest. The court considered it contributory negligence for the decedent not to have reported that he had suffered a lapse of consciousness during a gym class rope climbing exercise.

Where a student was obese, it was held that such condition was obvious and the instructor should have been knowledgeable as to the dangers presented in the student attempting to do the backward somersault maneuver, yet had the student do it without personal attention. In holding for plaintiff, the court said that it is sufficient if a reasonable person in the position would be brought to such realization by the

[58] Contino v. Lucille Roberts Health Spa, 125 A.D. 2d 437, 509 N.Y.S. 2d 369 (1986).

[59] Stephens v. Shelbyville Central Schools, 162 Ind. App. 229, 318 N.E. 2d 590 (1974).

circumstances which one knows or has reason to know.[60] In a New York situation[61] the student also had gone to the instructor and informed of weak wrists; but, notwithstanding the knowledge, she was directed to proceed with the gymnastic exercise known as "jumping the buck."

In an early case[62] the physical education instructor was held not negligent in permitting vigorous, robust 16-year-old boy, whom no one knew to be suffering from chronic aneurism of cerebral artery, to participate in a basketball game. This decision was notwithstanding the fact that the proximate cause was deemed to be the blow from the basketball, which accelerated or aggravated the chronic aneurism, so as to cause fatal rupture thereof. However, the defect might ultimately have caused death without traumatic injury.

In two football situations[63] the results were opposite. In the *Hale* case, the player had been injured previously and was participating in practice at the coach's request, when he injured his shoulder and arm. The player, however, did not object to participation, nor did the coach force participation against the will of the player. In the other case, though, the coach "induced, persuaded, and coerced" the player to participate when in an injured condition. The coach knew well of the condition. In the third case, plaintiff sued the school and the coach for injuries sustained in a high school football game. The coach directed the plaintiff to play although he had not participated in the minimum amount of practice sessions required by the State high school athletic association. In this situation the school and coach were immune from liability under the Illinois law.

In a 1988 football case, *Benitez v. N.Y.C. Board of Education,* 530 N.Y.S.2d 825 (1988), a high school football player brought action alleging negligence on the part of the coach and principal in permitting him to play in "mismatched" game in a fatigued condition. The mismatching came when the high school was transferred to the A Division for football the preceding year. There had been more serious injuries to the players that year and the principal requested a transfer back to Division B because of what he considered an inability to compete and the risk of injury; but his request had not been granted. Thus, in this game, since the team did not have adequate players, plaintiff, a "blue-chip athlete," had been playing virtually the whole half on both offense and defense and was extremely fatigued at the time of injury. Being a competitor, he had not complained about fatigue to the coach. The court held that the school (coach) unreasonably enhanced risk of injury to student; however, liability was apportioned 30% against the student and 70% against the school.

The court held that disclosing treatment of child for an epileptic condition manifested by convulsive seizures was admissible as being relevant and material to determination

[60] Landers v. School Dist. No. 203, O'Fallon, 66 Ill. App. 3d 78, 22 Ill. Dec. 837, 383 N.E. 2d 645 (1978).

[61] Cherney v. Board of Educ., White Plains, 31 A.D. 2d 764, 297 N.Y.S. 2d 668 (1969).

[62] Kerby v. Elk Grove Union H.S. Dist., 1 Cal. App. 2d 246, 36 P. 2d 431 (1934).

[63] Hale v. Davies, 86 Ga. App. 126, 70 S.E. 2d 923

(1952), also Hale v. Davies, 86 Ga. App. 130, 70 S.E. 2d 926 (1952) [same situation, first next of friend suing for injured, second parent suing for son's services and expenses]; Morris v. Union High School Dist., 160 Wash. 121, 294 P. 998 (1931); Kain v. Rockridge Comm. Unit School Dist. #300, 117 Ill. App. 3d 681, 72 Ill. Dec. 813, 453 N.E. 2d 118 (1983).

of county's contention that child drowned as a result of an epileptic seizure. The decedent was an 18-year-old girl who was mentally retarded and with a history of epileptic seizures requiring daily medication for control. This fact had not been reported to the lifeguard. She was to be accompanied by an adult, but was in the water with a friend, also mentally retarded. Neither girl could swim.[64]

Physical examinations were the focus of two boxing cases,[65] again with opposite results. See §17.331 Physical examinations.

§ 19.132   Emotion condition (fear, required activity)

It seems to be immaterial whether the situation is instructional, cocurricular, or recreational. The question is one of voluntary participation, particularly as related to assumption of risk (see §5.22.) A 14-year-old high school freshman in a required physical education class was told "that if he didn't think he could do it, he shouldn't." He had been informed regarding the jump and assumed the risk of his trying the jump.[66]

It must be distinguished between requiring a person to participate in a course, which is mandated by the curriculum, and requiring the participation in a specific activity. There are cases in which the participant was required to participate in situations, such as floor hockey when there were allegedly an excess of players for the size of floor,[67] broad jump when student had a note from her physician regarding a disability,[68] performance on a mini-trampoline[69] and a regular trampoline,[70] weight lifting without inquiring into experience or properly instructing[71] and entrance to college physical tests.[72] In most of the cases, the requirement to participate was only one factor toward determining liability.

Fear to participate is another element with which an instructor has to deal. In the *Landers* case,[73] cited in the preceding subsection, the student also expressed fear of attempting the maneuver not only because of her obesity which would make it difficult to do the maneuver, but also because of an early childhood experience, when she had had some difficulties performing such exercises. The request was for personal instruction by the teacher, which was not given. In the *Chilton* case,[74] the class was required of all freshman students without regard to any demonstrated ability or experience on the trampoline, but the students were not forced to participate in any specific exercise. In this situation, plaintiff had experienced some difficulty in performing the specific

[64] Brevard County v. Jacks, 238 So. 2d 156 (Fla. App. 1970).

[65] Rosensweig v. State, 208 Misc. 1065, 146 N.Y.S. 2d 589 (1955) 5 A.D. 2d 293, 171 N.Y.S. 2d 912 (1958), rev'd. on other grounds 5 N.Y. 2d 404, 158 N.E. 2d 229 (1959); Iacona v. Board of Educ., N.Y.C., 285 A.D. 1168, 140 N.Y.S. 2d 539 (1955).

[66] Sayers v. Ranger, 16 N.J. Super. 22, 83 A. 2d 775 (1951).

[67] Sutphen v. Benthian, 165 N.J. Super. 79, 397 A. 2d 709 (1979).

[68] Lowe v. Board of Educ., N.Y.C., 26 A.D. 2d 952, 321 N.Y.S. 2d 508 (1971).

[69] Cody v. Southfield-Lathrup School Dist., 25 Mich. App. 33, 181 N.W. 2d 81 (1970).

[70] Talmadge v. District School Board, Lake Co., 355 So. 2d 502 (Fla. App. 1978), aff'd. 381 So. 2d 698 (1980), aff'd. 381 So. 2d 1290 (1980), rev'd. 406 So. 2d 1127 (1981).

[71] Vargo v. Svitchan, 100 Mich. App. 809, 301 N.W. 2d 1 (1980).

[72] Brittan v. State, 200 Misc. 743, 103 N.Y.S. 2d 485 (1951).

[73] Landers v. School Dist. No. 203, O'Fallon, 66 Ill. App. 3d 78, 22 Ill. Dec. 837, 383 N.E. 2d 645 (1978).

[74] Chilton v. Cook Co. School Dist., 26 Ill. App. 3d 459, 325 N.E. 2d 666 (1975), aff'd. 63 Ill. 2d 165, 347 N.E. 2d 705 (1976).

maneuver and the instructor had encouraged her not to be fearful. Then, in a trampoline situation, there was evidence that the plaintiff began his exercise just a few minutes before the end of the class period and that the coach had told the students to hurry along as they could take showers. However, there was no testimony that the plaintiff did indeed feel rushed, or was anxious, or concerned about the amount of time remaining so that it affected his performance.[75]

An instructor also must be aware of the propensity of a student or participant to act in a violent manner. In *Hanley v. Hornbeck,* 127 A.D.2d 905, 512 N.Y.S.2d 262 (1987), the students in physical education class were playing whiffleball, when a dispute arose between plaintiff and another student. As the instructor started to separate the boys, the one student hit plaintiff in the face. The court said that while the record did reveal that the student who hit plaintiff had a disciplinary record, with only one specific incident recorded, the record also showed that he had been referred to the committee on the handicapped as the result of some behavioral traits exhibited in the sixth grade. The committee, however, determined that the boy should remain with the regular students. Thus, the disciplinary record, so the court held, did not show such a strong propensity to engage in violent or physical behavior as to warrant a finding that the child should have been isolated or supervised to a greater degree than other students. The teacher was within 25 feet when the altercation broke out and responded immediately. Judgment for teacher. (See also §2.23 Test of foreseeability, and §18.323 Assaults, as part of management of behavior).

§ 19.2 The activity

If a leader, teacher, or coach is to properly handle an activity, there must be knowledge about the specific activity. This means that correct instructions as to how to play the activity must be given, that there must be special concern for the directions given as to safety, and that the manner in which the activity is done must be non-dangerous with no unreasonable risks of harm. In these three tasks there must be knowledge regarding the standards, rules, and courtesies of the game, as determined by prevailing custom and the standards of a profession. In addition, attention should be paid to the equipment and safety devices, as well as to the conditions of the facility on which the activity is played.

§ 19.21 Adequacy of instruction

There are two aspects related to adequacy of instruction. One is the actual instruction of skill technique and strategies, including methodology of teaching. The second aspect focuses upon safety, including rules and regulations and the courtesies of the game.

§ 19.211 Instruction in skill performance

Sometimes an activity becomes inappropriate and injury occurs because the

[75] Berg v. Merricks, 20 Md. App. 666, 318 A. 2d 220 (1974), cert. denied 272 Md. 737 (1974).

participants have not had adequate instruction.[76] In a 1980 case,[77] the court stated that "...unless he (one teaching) represents that he has greater or less skill or knowledge, one who undertakes to render services in the practice of a profession or trade is required to excerise the skill and knowledge normally possessed by members of that profession or trade in good standing in similar communities." This includes proper instruction.

In defining what proper instruction is, the court[78] in Louisiana said, "explanation of basic rules and procedures, suggestions for proper performance, and identification of risks"; however, in this case and another[79] about the same time, it also was stated that considerations in determining whether instructions are proper and sufficient include difficulty and inherent dangerousness of activity, and age and experience of students. Supporting this point of view is an earlier Oregon case,[80] involving the use of a springboard in class. Inadequate in-depth instruction had been given to a 12-year-old girl, as well as failure to instruct properly to provide appreciation of the danger of the activity. Appreciation of danger is a concept of the doctrine of assumption of risk. For further discussion regarding the necessity to warn and appreciation of danger, see §5.22 assumption of risk.[81]

The inadequacy of instruction allegation is found in a number of activities, such as baseball,[82] soccer,[83] speed test in a gym,[84] informal boxing,[85] golf,[86] football,[87] judo,[88] shot put,[89] and wrestling;[90] but the preponderance of cases is in the gymnastics area, including tumbling and trampolining.[91] Instruction also includes proper rescue

[76] Brittan v. State, 200 Misc. 743, 103 N.Y.S. 2d 485 (1951); Clark v. Board of Educ., 304 N.Y. 488, 109 N.E. 2d 73 (1952); Petrich v. New Orleans City Park Improvement Assn., 188 So. 199 (La. App. 1939), and others in subsequent footnotes of this section.

[77] Fantini v. Alexander, 172 N.J. Super. 105, 410 A. 2d 1190 (1980).

[78] Green v. Orleans Parish School Board, 365 So. 2d 834 (La. App. 1978).

[79] Perkins v. State Board of Educ., 364 So. 2d 183 (La. App. 1978), cert. denied 366 So. 2d 563 (1979).

[80] Grant v. Lake Oswego School Dist., 515 P. 2d 947 (Or. App. 1973).

[81] On Feb. 14, 1982, a lower court in Washington rendered a $6.3M decision against the Seattle School District. In Thompson v. Seattle School District the plaintiff made five charges of failure to warn, five charges of failure to adequately instruct, and ten charges of negligence of the District. A great deal has been said about the ramifications of this case where a high school football player was injured in an accident relating to the helmet and tackling. The manufacturer settled out of court for $95,000 (see §21.1 for product liability discussion). The case brought against the school focused upon effective instruction of partici-pants. The case has been reported in: Adams, Samuel H., Court Decision Hits Hard with New Liability Twists. Athletic Purchasing and Facilities, vol. 6, no. 5, May 1982. The Seattle Public School District appealed the decision (appeal docket #4971912) and settled out of court 1984 for $3.78M. See comment on educational malpractice in introductory section of this chapter.

[82] Passantino v. Board of Educ., N.Y.C., 52 A.D. 2d 935, 383 N.Y.S. 2d 639 (1976), rev'd. 41 N.Y. 2d 1022, 395 N.Y.S. 2d 628, 363 N.E. 2d 1373 (1977); Weiss v. Collinsville Comm. Unit School Dist., 119 Ill. App. 3d 68, 74 Ill. Dec. 893, 456 N.E. 2d 614 (1983).

[83] Darrow v. W. Genesee Cent. School Dist., 41 A.D. 2d 897, 342 N.Y.S. 2d 611 (1973).

[84] Ehlinger v. Board of Educ., New Hartford, 96 A.D. 2d 708, 465 N.Y.S. 2d 378 (1983).

[85] Iacona v. Board of Educ., N.Y.C., 285 A.D. 1168, 140 N.Y.S. 2d 539 (1955); LaValley v. Standford, 272 A.D. 183, 70 N.Y.S. 2d 460 (1947).

[86] Petrich v. New Orleans City Park Improvement Assn., 188 So. 199 (La. App. 1939).

[87] Mark v. Colgate Univ., 53 A.D. 2d 884, 385 N.Y.S. 2d 621 (1976).

[88] Klocek v. YMCA, 48 Wis. 2d 43, 179 N.W. 2d 835 (1970).

[89] Merkley v. Palmyra-Macedon Cent. School Dist., 130 A.D. 2d 937, 515 N.Y.S. 2d 932 (1987).

[90] Price v. Mount Diablo Unified School Dist., 177 Cal. App. 2d 312, 2 Cal. Rptr. 23 (1960); Smith v. Consolidated School Dist. No. 2, 408 S.W. 2d 50 (Mo. 1966); Stehn v. Bernarr MacFadden Foundation, Inc., 434 F. 2d 81 (1970).

[91] Armlin v. Board of Educ., Schenectady, 36 A.D. 2d 877, 320 N.Y.S. 2d 402 (1971); Bellman v. San Francisco High School Dist., 11 Cal. 2d 576, 81 P. 2d 894 (1938); Brown v. Quaker Valley School Dist., 31 D & C 3d 384 (1983), 86 Pa. Cmwlth. 496, 486 A. 2d 526 (1984); Fallon v. Indian Trail School, 148 Ill. App. 3d 931, 102 Ill. Dec. 479, 500 N.E. 2d 101 (1986) competence of teachers in question; Gardner v. State,

methods.[92] Commercial recreation instruction requires the same standard of performance as instruction in schools.[93] And, low organized games, too, are subject to proper instruction.[94] See Part B for description of cases.

With sport psychology a more prominent element in sport performance, the psychological aspect of instruction has been the focus of litigation. In a 1985 New Jersey case,[95] the plaintiff, a member of the high school varsity soccer team, brought action against the opposing school and its coach alleging that the coach taught his players to compete in an aggressive and intense manner and that winning the game was all important, inferring that the players were being instructed in moves that would intentionally injure an opposing player. Plaintiff was injured when he was "undercut" by a member of the opposing team. The court held that in absence of evidence that the coach instructed his players to commit wrongful acts or in moves or procedures that would increase risk of harm to opposing players, coach was not responsible to player on opposing team for injury.

What about the methods used for instruction? Not too much is said regarding methods, more on the content and adequacy of the instruction. However, in *Sayers v. Ranger*[96] a demonstration by the teacher was part of the instruction; but in another gymnastics case,[97] the failure to demonstrate raised a factual issue as to negligence. The plaintiff, though, had seen others in class perform. In the *Stehn* case[98] the court held that not a single act of instruction establishes a breach of duty, but a series of acts establishes quality of instruction. The plaintiff, a 15-year-old eighth grader, was participating in wrestling for the first time. This incident occurred in the sixth week after four lessons per week. No negligence was found regarding instruction in a football case[99] and a broad jumping situation in camp.[100] In a line soccer situation, it was found that the teacher did not adhere to the method prescribed by the syllabus.[101] In a 1980 golf situation,[102] plaintiff, a freshman student, was playing in a foursome, which had a student assistant. It was when the student assistant "shanked" the ball that plaintiff was

281 N.Y. 212, 22 N.E. 2d 344 (1939); Grant v. Lake Oswego School Dist., 515 P. 2d 947 (Or. App. 1973); Larson v. Indp. School Dist., 252 N.W. 2d 128 (1977) 312 Minn. 583, 289 N.W. 2d 112 (1979); Lueck v. Janesville, 57 Wis. 2d 254, 204 N.W. 2d 6 (1973); Montag v. Board of Educ., 112 Ill. App. 3d 1039, 68 Ill. Dec. 565, 446 N.E. 2d 299 (1983); Passafaro v. Board of Educ., N.Y.C., 43 A.D. 2d 918, 353 N.Y.S. 2d 178 (1974); Rodriguez v. Seattle School Dist. No. 1, 66 Wash. 2d 51, 401 P. 2d 326 (1965); Talmadge v. Dist. School Board, Lake Co., 355 So. 2d 502 (Fla. App. 1978), aff'd. 381 So. 2d 698 (1980); aff'd. 381 So. 2d 1290 (1980), rev'd. 406 So. 2d 1127 (Fla. App. 1981).

[92] Webber v. Yeo, 147 Mich. App. 453 383 N.W. 2d 230 1986) lv app. denied 425 Mich. 865; see also swimming instruction case Wong v. Waterloo Comm. School Dist., 232 N.W. 2d 865 (1975).

[93] Randle v. Hinckly Parachute Center, 141 Ill. App. 3d 660, 96 Ill. Dec. 5 490 N.E. 2d 1041 (1986) skydiving, exculpatory agreement barred recovery.

[94] Yarborough v. C.C.N.Y., 520 N.Y.S. 2d 518 (1987) sack race (hopping in plastic bags) in college physical education class.

[95] Nydegger v. Don Bosco Preparatory High School, 202 N.J. Super. 535, 495 A. 2d 485 (1985).

[96] Sayers v. Ranger, 16 N.J. Super. 22, 83 A. 2d 775 (1951).

[97] Lorenzo v. Monroe Comm. College, 72 A.D. 2d 945, 422 N.Y.S. 2d 230 (1979).

[98] Stehn v. Bernarr MacFadden Foundation, Inc., 434 F. 2d 811 (1970); see also Llorence v. Natchitoches Parish School, 529 So. 2d 479 (La. App. 1988) Wrestling instruction held proper.

[99] Vendrell v. School Dist., 226 Or. 263, 360 P. 2d 282 (1961), rev'd./remanded 233 Or. 1, 376 P. 2d 406 (1962).

[100] Weinstein v. Tunis Lake Properties, 15 Misc. 2d 432, 181 N.Y.S. 2d 916 (1958), aff'd. without op. 9 A.D. 2d 960, 196 N.Y.S. 2d 605 (1959), app. denied 10 A.D. 2d 711, 199 N.Y.S. 2d 437 (1960).

[101] Keesee v. Board of Educ., N.Y.C., 37 Misc. 2d 414, 235 N.Y.S. 2d 300 (1962).

[102] DeMauro v. Tusculum College, 603 S.W. 2d 115 (Tenn. 1980).

injured. The instruction book the students were supposed to purchase confirmed the general positioning of the students for safety; however, it appeared from the evidence that the plaintiff had not read the book of instructions issued to her, nor had she been assigned any readings therein. The court said that "Where students are novices and are receiving courses of instruction in sports held out and offered for credit by an educational institution, a duty of supervision and instruction arises from the relationship which is not terminated or abrogated merely by reason of the fact that one student participant injures another." In another golf instruction situation, the focus was upon the formation used indoors, when the class came inside due to inclement weather. The students were in an oval-circle, using plastic balls, and hitting toward the opposite wall or center of the oval. Plaintiff was hit in the eye with one of the balls, losing nearly all vision in the eye. The formation was found to be appropriate and no negligence was attributed to the instructor.[103]

Some activities, such as weight lifting, require special training;[104] and where young boys were playing tackle football, at issue was their preparation and training.[105] And, on the other hand, a situation involving a trampoline center stated that where the plaintiff was 26 years old and had received instruction on indoor trampolines in college, he did not need to be told where the only safe place to land on the nylon mat was.[106] The failure to perform according to instructions is a matter of contributory negligence. See §5.21 for discusson of contributory negligence.

In a membership recreation center, the court held that a guest of a member, when the director of the center undertook to instruct him in the use of the chinning bar, became entitled to reasonable care in such instruction, as would a member have.[107]

§ 19.212   Safety directives

The adequacy of instruction is not only instruction related to the technique of skill performance but also directives concerning safety. The court said that school authorities have an affirmative duty to instruct students in physical education classes on reasonable safety precautions to be observed while engaged in class activities. In this situation, the instructor had not instructed the boys as to what they should do when two players met the ball at the same time when they were engaged in indoor soccer in class.[108] Two softball cases[109] involved safety instruction, one as to safety precautions given a catcher as to stance behind the batter, and the other the care that should be taken in throwing to a deaf player. But, just as with the inadequacy of technique instruction, the preponderance of cases is also with gymnastics in relation to safety instruction. All of these concern the use of spotters. Instruction includes both how to spot and the use of spotters. Cases

---

[103] Catania v. Univ. of Nebr., 204 Neb. 304, 282 N.W. 2d 27 (1979), aff'd. 213 Neb. 418, 329 N.W. 2d 354 (1983).

[104] Vargo v. Svitchan, 100 Mich. App. 809, 301 N.W. 2d 1 (1980).

[105] Whipple v. Salvation Army, 261 Or. 453, 495 P. 2d 739 (1972).

[106] Ragni v. Lincoln-Devon Bounceland, 91 Ill. App. 2d 172, 234 N.E. 2d 168 (1968).

[107] Gregaydis v. Watervliet Civic Chest, 14 A.D. 2d 623, 218 N.Y.S. 2d 383 (1961).

[108] Darrow v. W. Genesee Cent. School Dist., 41 A.D. 2d 897, 342 N.Y.S. 2d 611 (1973).

[109] Moschella v. Archdiocese of N.Y., 48 A.D. 2d 856, 369 N.Y.S. 2d 10 (1975), aff'd. 52 A.D. 2d 873, 383 N.Y.S. 2d 49 (1976); Stineman v. Fontbonne College, 664 F. 2d 1082 (1981).

include a variety of activities, such as vaulting horse,[110] still rings,[111] tumbling,[112] unevens[113] and trampoline.[114] Safety instruction is of importance in non-sport activity, too. In a 1983 Louisiana school situation, plaintiff alleged that he had never been taught the use of a blade guard or other safety devices on a table saw.[115]

Safety directives also may include rules and regulations; in fact, there is an obligation to establish rules for safety purposes and then to carry out the rules established. This was evident in the *Bauman* case,[115a] where in playground softball situation, the supervisor established a safety rule, but the directors did not adhere to it. Many of the rules are supervisory in nature, directed toward general conduct (see §18.331), and should be distinguished from rules of safety in the conduct of a specific activity. This is particularly true for water activities (see Chapter 9). In other activities, such as golf, it is a matter of learning the "courtesies of the game," not only for the enjoyment of playing, but also for the safety precautions built into such courtesies.[116] Such regulations may be established to protect the participant from participating when there is no supervisor, such as in the *Banks* case.[117] Students were not to participate in gymnastics until after they had properly dressed and the roll call taken by the instructor. Plaintiff was engaged in unauthorized tumbling activities when he was injured.

Rules and regulations may be printed and/or posted. At a trampoline center, printed instructions were posted;[118] and in another trampoline case,[119] the plaintiff had read a notice and acknowledged that certain rules governing the use of the trampoline were posted. In a bowling situation, the owners of a bowling alley were not held negligent for failing to post signs regarding practice swings in the open area between the alleys and the ball storage room.[120] When there is violation of a rule or regulation, it may influence whether or not plaintiff is contributorily negligent (see §5.21), while the posting or distributing of printed rules and regulations may provide some documentary evidence of an effort to inform the plaintiff toward appreciation of the risks involved in participation. (See §5.22 Assumption of risk; for warning of danger in activity, see §19.22.)

[110] Montague v. School Board, 57 Ill. App. 3d 828, 15 Ill. Dec. 373, 373 N.E. 2d 719 (1978).

[111] Armlin v. Board of Education, Schenectady, 36 A.D. 2d 877, 320 N.Y.S. 2d 402 (1971); Lueck v. Janesville, 57 Wis. 2d 254, 204 N.W. 2d 6 (1973).

[112] Larson v. Indp. School Dist. No. 314, Braham, 252 N.W. 2d 128 (1977) 312 Minn. 583, 289 N.W. 2d 112 (1979).

[113] Cantwell v. Univ. of Mass., 551 F. 2d 879 (1977).

[114] Chapman v. State, 6 Wash. App. 316, 492 P. 2d 607 (1972); Chilton v. Cook Co. School Dist., 26 Ill. App. 3d 459, 325 N.E. 2d 666 (1975), aff'd. 63 Ill. 2d 165, 347 N.E. 2d 705 (1976).

[115] Theriot v. St. Martin Parish School Board, 434 So. 2d 668 (La. App. 1983).

[115a] Bauman v. San Francisco, 42 Cal. App. 2d 144, 108 P. 2d 989 (1940); similarly, Park District failed to enforce its regulations, McRoberts v. Maxwell, 40 Ill. App. 3d 766, 353 N.E. 2d 159 (1976).

[116] For example, Allen v. Pinewood Country Club, 292 So. 2d 786 (La. App. 1976); Carrigan v. Roussell,

177 N.J. Super. 272, 426 A. 2d 517 (1981); Everett v. Goodwin, 201 N.C. 734, 161 S.E. 316 (1931); Getz v. Freed, 377 Pa. 480, 105 A. 2d 102 (1954); Jackson v. Livingston Country Club, Inc., 55 A.D. 2d 1045, 391 N.Y.S. 2d 234 (1977); Jenks v. McGranaghan, 316 N.Y.S. 2d 648 (1970), aff'd. 30 N.Y. 2d 475, 334 N.Y.S. 2d 641, 285 N.E. 2d 876 (1972); Neumann v. Shlansky, 58 Misc. 2d 128, 294 N.Y.S. 2d 628 aff'd. 63 Misc. 2d 587, 312 N.Y.S. 2d 951 (1970), aff'd. 36 A.D. 2d 540, 318 N.Y.S. 2d 925 (1971); Nino v. Hight, 385 F. 2d 350 (1967); Oakes v. Chapman, 158 Cal. App. 2d 78, 322 P. 2d 241 (1958). See §7.1 Golf.

[117] Banks v. Terrebonne Parish School Board, 339 So. 2d 1295 (La. App. 1976).

[118] Daniel v. S-Co Corp., 255 Iowa 869, 124 N.W. 2d 522 (1963); Phoenix v. Anderson, 65 Ariz. 311, 180 P. 2d 219 (1947).

[119] Williams v. Lombardini, 38 Misc. 2d 146, 238 N.Y.S. 2d 63 (1963).

[120] Kincaid v. Lagen, 781 Ill. App. 2d 307, 218 N.E. 2d 856 (1966).

In talking about the safety of a program or machine, one must be careful about misrepresentations. Plaintiff alleged in the *Shugar* case[121] that she had received false and material misrepresentation as to the use and safety of a vibrating/reducing machine at the health spa. She also indicated that she had not been given instructions how to turn the machine off, so she had to remain on the machine until it stopped, since no one heard her call for help. Similarly, advertisements must be trustworthy. In a summer camp riding situation, it had stated in the brochure of the camp that the horses had been selected for gentleness and were ideally suited for work with children. The 11-year-old child was kicked by a horse of a "fractious nature."[122]

§ 19.22   Manner of play (dangerous situations)

The manner in which play is conducted by the teacher, leader, or coach has an important bearing on whether or not the defendant instructor has been negligent. The types of situations which have been alleged as dangerous conduct of activity fall into those where the manner of playing the activity itself appears to be dangerous and those which relate to the nature of a drill, the placement of players and crowdedness, and violation of rules of the game. A primary question is how well the person in charge controls the activity. (See also Chapter 18 Supervision).

In two games of bombardment, where the object is to hit members of the opposite team with a ball below the waist, thereby eliminating them, the plaintiff in one game was hit in the eye, subsequently losing sight, when a ball was hurled at her head. The ball, instead of being a volleyball, was a smaller, hard ball, more the size of a softball.[123] In the other game the plaintiff bent over to pick up a ball and an unidentified player's knee struck his face.[124] Dangerous play may be occasioned by players not matched for size, or in activities not appropriate to the skill level and experience of the players.[125] Other cases alleging dangerous activity include a jump rope situation,[126] not stopping play when youngsters were piling on in a recreational tackle football game,[127] failure to intervene when players used excessive force in touch football game in physical education class,[128] the instructor forcibly throwing a basketball at a player,[129] an exercise known as "ride-the-horse,"[130] and hurrying along the participants so they could take showers, thus making the individual on the trampoline feel rushed and not concentrating.[131] The same care regarding playing in a dangerous manner must be exercised in private as well as public school situations, as evidenced in *Bernesak v.*

[121] Shugar v. Pat Walker Figure Perfection Salons, Int'l., 541 S.W. 2d 511 (Tex. Civ. App. 1976).
[122] Burwell v. Crist, 251 F. Supp. 686 (1966), 373 F. 2d 78 (1967).
[123] Rivera v. Board of Educ., N.Y.C., 11 A.D. 2d 7, 201 N.Y.S. 2d 372 (1960).
[124] Fosselman v. Waterloo Comm. School Dist., 229 N.W. 2d 280 (Iowa 1975).
[125] Brooks v. Board of Educ., N.Y.C., 29 Misc. 2d 19, 205 N.Y.S. 2d 777 (1960), aff'd. 12 N.Y. 2d 971, 238 N.Y.S. 2d 963 189 N.E. 2d 497 (1963); see also §19.11.

[126] Wire v. Williams, 270 Minn. 390, 133 N.W. 2d 840 (1965).
[127] Whipple v. Salvation Army, 261 Or. 453, 495 P. 2d 739 (1972).
[128] Hyman v. Green, 157 Mich. App. 566, 403 N.W. 2d 597 (1987).
[129] Picard v. Greisinger, 2 Mich. App. 96, 138 N.W. 2d 508 (1965).
[130] Yerdon v. Baldwinsville Academy, 50 A.D. 2d 714, 374 N.Y.S. 2d 877 (1975) motion denied 39 N.Y. 2d 705, 384 N.Y.S. 2d 1027 (1976).
[131] Berg v. Merricks, 20 Md. App. 666, 318 A. 2d 220 (1974), cert. denied 272 Md. 737 (1974).

Catholic Bishop of Chicago, 87 Ill. App. 3d 681, 42 Ill. Dec. 672, 409 N.E.2d 287 (1980), where plaintiff was injured while playing "crack-the-whip" on the church school playground.

Dangerous conditions also may arise because of the drills in sport practices. Two boys were overcome with heat prostration, one died and the other suffered serious permanent injury. The plaintiff alleged that the proximate cause was the coaches ordering them to perform unreasonably strenuous exercises in the heat.[132] In another football case,[133] the coaches required in the summer preseason practice sessions a game called "jungle football"; the manner of playing and lack of conditioning were alleged cause of injury. In a Maine case,[134] a 14-year-old in freshman football "tryouts," after running a sprint drill, put his arm through the glass in a gymnasium door. And, a high school player sustained injuries in a football tackling drill, resulting in quadriplegia. The coach was held for misfeasance.[135] And in basketball, the drill being used by the coach was alleged to be dangerous and improper for the 15-year-old boys and considerably more dangerous than customary methods of training.[136]

A speed test in the manner in which it was administered was alleged to be dangerous. This junior high fitness test was being run with the finish line 8' from the wall, instead of the recommended 14'.[137] In a sixth grade physical education class, the children were being asked to do a vertical jump up a wall. Plaintiff had not performed the jump before, had no knowledge of the proper way to perform the jump or the danger created by the wall. There was conflict of evidence as to what the teacher instructed. Plaintiff alleged that the instructor did not demonstrate, had used a floor mat perpendicular to the wall, and had directed the students to run toward the wall; defendant teacher stated she had demonstrated, did not use a floor mat, and acknowledged that while the students were not directed to run toward the wall, they did take two to three quick steps in the direction of the wall before jumping up. In jumping and reaching, plaintiff hit her mouth on the concrete wall, injuring her tooth. The court stated that the teacher had a duty to conform her conduct as a physical education teacher to a certain standard, and expert witnesses were brought in to testify as to the safety in performance aspects.[138]

Injury also may occur due to alleged violation or non-enforcement of the rules of the game. Often these cases involve intent, that is intentional injury of one player by another.[139] In several softball cases[140] it was a matter of the players colliding, usually outside of the basepath or not in conformity with regulations and in most instances the

---

[132] Lovitt v. Concord School District, 58 Mich. App. 593, 228 N.W. 2d 479 (1975).

[133] Rutter v. Northeastern Beaver County School Dist., 283 Pa. Super. 155, 423 A. 2d 1035 (1980), rev'd./remanded 496 Pa. 590, 437 A. 2d 1198 (1981).

[134] Langevin v. City of Biddeford, 481 A. 2d 495 (Maine 1984).

[135] Marcy v. Town of Sangus, 22 Mass. App. 972, 495 N.E. 2d 569 (1986).

[136] Strauch v. Hirschman, 40 A.D. 2d 711, 336 N.Y.S. 2d 678 (1972).

[137] Ehlinger v. Board of Educ., New Hartford, 96 A.D. 2d 708, 465 N.Y.S. 2d 378 (1983).

[138] Dibortolo v. Metro. School Dist., Wash. Twshp., 440 N.E. 2d 506 (Ind. App. 1982).

[139] Moore v. Jones, 120 Ga. App. 521, 171 S.E. 2d 390 (1969); see also §1.41322.

[140] Beckett v. Clinton Prairie School Corp., 494 N.E. 2d 988 (Ind. App. 1986), 504 N.E. 2d 552 (1987); Niemczyk v. Burleson, 538 S.W. 2d 737 (Mo. App. 1976); Novak v. Lamar Ins. Co., 488 So. 2d 739 (La. App. 1986) cert. denied 491 So. 2d 23 (1986); Ross v. Clouser, 637 S.W. 2d 11 (Mo. 1982); see also Bowser v. Hershey Baseball Assoc., 357 Pa. Super. 435, 516 A. 2d 61 (1986) hit by batted ball in tryouts, no duty to warn.

players assumed the risk. In a basketball situation[141] and a soccer game[142] it was a matter of bodily contact and noncompliance with rules that was alleged proximate cause of injury. An illegal hold in wrestling brought an allegation of permitting dangerous play.[143] During orientation week plaintiff freshman was injured in a game of pushball by a clipping incident, which was alleged to be dangerous play.[144] Defendant was held 70% fault in an organized recreational flag football game when the game rules were violated and plaintiff was injured.[145] Condoning previous dangerous play also is evidence of negligence in conducting activity in a dangerous manner.[146]

A position of individuals or proximity to others has been a part of situations alleged to be dangerous. These incidents include the catcher standing too close to the batter,[147] waiting batter struck in the face with a bat,[148] children playing too close to a softball game,[149] waiting boy too close to wrestling mat and became entangled in the wrestlers when they came to edge of mat,[150] bat slipping out of hands of batter and hitting another,[151] and layout of track in relation to discus throwing.[152] Overcrowding as a cause of injury has been alleged in situations such as inexperienced skiers on a crowded ski slope,[153] too many on a bobsled,[154] excess number of players playing floor hockey for the size of floor,[155] and a large class of girls in physical education running across the gymnasium floor to get showered and to the next class.[156]

When youngsters do not come to an activity with appropriate shoes, it is tempting to have them play in socks or barefoot. Such was the situation in two cases.[157] In the *Passafaro* case the plaintiff was asked to tumble in his socks, which evidence established as a "bad practice," as it would not provide sufficient traction for the activity to be done safely. In the other case the nine-year-old plaintiff was required by the physical education teacher to participate in bounceball barefoot. The ball got away and as he ran to get it, his feet stuck to the floor, he lost his balance, and as a result of the fall, plaintiff lost two front teeth. The teacher maintained that the injury was caused by his tripping over his own feet when bouncing the ball. Judgment for plaintiff.

It should be pointed out that in the foregoing cases, the plaintiff was not always

[141] Oswald v. Twsp. H.S. Dist. #214, 84 Ill. App. 3d 723, 40 Ill. Dec. 456, 406 N.E. 2d 157 (1980).

[142] Nabozny v. Barnhill, 31 Ill. App. 3d 212, 334 N.E. 2d 258 (1975).

[143] O'Dell v. School Dist. of Independence, 521 S.W. 2d 403 (Mo. 1975) cert. denied 96 S. Ct. 125, 423 U.S. 865.

[144] Rubtchinsky v. SUNY, Albany, 46 Misc. 2d 679, 260 N.Y.S. 2d 256 (1965).

[145] Segoviano v. Housing Authority, 143 Cal. App. 3d 162, 192 Cal. Rptr. 578 (1983).

[146] Passantino v. Board of Educ., N.Y.C., 52 A.D. 2d 935, 383 N.Y.S. 2d 639 (1976), rev'd. 41 N.Y. 2d 1022, 395 N.Y.S. 2d 628, 363 N.E. 2d 1373 (1977) baseball; Peterson v. Multnomah Co. School Dist., 60 Or. App. 81, 668 P. 2d 385 (1983) football.

[147] Brackman v. Adrain, 63 Tenn. App. 346, 472 S.W. 2d 735 (1971).

[148] Ceplina v. South Milwaukee School Board, 73 Wis. 2d 338, 243 N.W. 2d 183 (1976).

[149] Stanley v. Board of Educ., Chicago, 9 Ill. App. 3d 963, 293 N.E. 2d 417 (1973).

[150] Stafford v. Catholic Youth Org., 202 So. 2d 333 (La. App. 1967).

[151] Gordon v. Deer Park School Dist., 71 Wash. 2d 119, 426 P. 2d 824 (1967); Lutterman v. Studer, 217 N.W. 2d 756 (Minn. 1974); Richmond v. Employers' Fire Ins. Co., 298 So. 2d 118 (La. App. 1974), cert. denied 302 So. 2d 18 (1974).

[152] Marques v. Riverside Military Academy, 87 Ga. App. 370, 73 S.E. 2d 574 (1952).

[153] Davis v. Erickson, 53 Cal. 2d 860, 345 P. 2d 942 (1959).

[154] Cunningham v. State, 32 N.Y.S. 2d 275, mod. as to damages 264 A.D. 811, 34 N.Y.S. 2d 903 (1942).

[155] Sutphen v. Benthian, 165 N.J. Super. 79, 397 A. 2d 709 (1979).

[156] Driscol v. Delphi Comm. School Corp., 155 Ind. App. 56, 290 N.E. 2d 769 (1972).

[157] Passafaro v. Board of Educ., N.Y.C., 43 A.D. 2d 918, 353 N.Y.S. 2d 178 (1974); Brod v. Central School Dist., 53 A.D. 2d 1002, 386 N.Y.S. 2d 125 (1976).

successful in the allegation of dangerous manner of conducting the activity. The primary defense is assumption of risk by the plaintiff. Generally, an individual does not assume any risks which arise from negligence. Further, there must be understanding and appreciation of the risk assumed; thus, if there is a risk beyond the ordinary, there must be complete awareness of such risk before the participant assumes the risk. Therefore, the warning of danger in activity becomes a critical and essential component in activity administration. The warnings of danger are of two types, the nature of the activity and the possible consequences of participation in terms of injury. It is this latter type of informing or warning that has been held in the late '70s and early '80s to void assumption of risk if not properly done. (See §§5.22, 16.22, 18.33, amd 20.332.) Pertinent is the statement in a decision involving a motorcyle hill climb: participants in sporting event are not negligent if they injure another as long as they play within rules and they reasonably believe the injured party knew of the hazards of the game.[158]

§ 19.23 Equipment and facilities

Safety devices and protective equipment are of continuing importance in situations which give rise to law suits, and their use in the conduct of activity is essential. It is not always sufficient to warn of dangers in activity; safety devices and protective equipment must be provided. This section includes only those items which are more directly related to the conduct of the activity, and does not include aspects, such as walk surfaces, fences, outdoor areas in natural state, maintenance of areas and facilities, et al. These are included in some detail in Chapter 20. However, where facility layout and condition are directly related to the activity, some illustrative cases are included. As with previous sections, case listings are illustrative only, and additional cases may be found in Part B.

§ 19.231 Safety devices and protective equipment

While one usually thinks of the sports as related to equipment, low organized games, too, must be considered in terms of proper and safe equipment. The use of three hard balls about the size of a softball, instead of a volleyball, for "bombardment" was central to the allegation of dangerous play,[159] as was the size of the rope used in an activity being played by the Scouts.[160] A jump rope with wooden handles, which when jerked from the "turner's" hand hit plaintiff's front teeth, was considered a rope of ordinary kind and the accident was unforeseeable.[161] The lack of protective equipment was alleged in two floor hockey cases,[162] a case where "jungle football" was played,[163] and a judo

[158] Franks v. Smith, 444 P. 2d 954 (Or. 1968).

[159] Rivera v. Board of Educ., N.Y.C., 11 A.D. 2d 7, 201 N.Y.S. 2d 372 (1960).

[160] Kearney v. Roman Catholic Church, 31 A.D. 2d 541, 295 N.Y.S. 2d 186 (1968).

[161] Wire v. Williams, 270 Minn. 390, 133 N.W. 2d 840 (1965).

[162] Berman v. Phila. Board of Educ., 456 A. 2d 545 (Pa. Super. 1983) mouthguard not provided;

Sutphen v. Benthian, 165 N.J. Super. 79, 397 A. 2d 709 (1979); see also Keller v. Mols, 129 Ill. App. 3d 208, 84 Ill. Dec. 411, 472 N.E. 2d 161 (1984) aff'd. 156 Ill. App. 3d 235, 509 N.E. 2d 584 (1987) game on neighbor's patio, landowner's duty.

[163] Rutter v. Northeastern Beaver Co. School Dist., 283 Pa. Super. 155, 423 A. 2d 1035 (1980), rev'd./remanded 496 Pa. 590, 437 A. 2d 1198 (1981).

situation.[164] Plastic golf balls being used indoors, although the instrumentality of injury, were not considered a dangerous piece of equipment, but appropriate.[165]

Defective equipment was alleged in three football cases.[166] (See Product liability §21.1.) In the *Thomas* case it also was alleged that defendants failed to inspect the equipment. The failure to provide protective equipment for a football drill was at issue when the plaintiff was injured as a freshman out for spring football practice. The first day of practice, equipment was issued, but plaintiff and several others did not receive helmets because of insufficient number of the correct size. No special instructions were given by any of the coaches to those who had not received helmets equipped with mouth guards as to limitations on their participation in practice. On the second day several players were instructed to do an "agility drill," which did not involve blocking or tackling, but it did involve coming into contact with other players. As plaintiff began the drill, the first lineman with whom he had contact straightened his arms or raised his head and plaintiff's face collided with the lineman's helmet, suffering facial injuries and his front teeth were shattered.[167]

There are a number of cases related to softball/baseball involving a variety of equipment and protective devices. In two face mask cases, the injured party did not recover. Basic protective equipment was provided and recommended for use when catching or umpiring in a softball game. The court held in both cases that because of the skill and experience of the injured person, he was well aware of the risks when not using protective equipment, and hence assumed such risks when he refused to wear the face mask. In the *Brackman* case[168] the court distinguished softball from baseball regarding mandatory requirement of mask wearing. In the other case,[169] an umpiring case, the injured person wore glasses; however, umpiring was done behind a portable backstop or batting cage. The backstop would "give" when a ball was fouled back into it. In this specific incident, the person's face was about one foot from the wire when a foul tip shattered his glasses. A typewritten outline of instructions included reference to use of protective equipment by those wearing eyeglasses. In a third case[170] the court said that failure to furnish the plaintiff with a mask constituted negligence. Plaintiff lost the sight in one eye when hit with a bat, while serving as catcher during a softball game in physical education class.

Several softball cases related to the condition of the bat. In the *Stanley* case[171] there was no tape on the bat and the batter's hands had become very moist; also, the knob around the handle was frayed. The bat on a hard swing slipped from the batter's hands, richocheted off the building, and struck the plaintiff in the head. In the *Stewart* case[172] a

---

[164] Miami Shores Village v. Mallicote, 421 So. 2d 662 (Fla. App. 1982).

[165] Catania v. Univ. of Nebr., 204 Neb. 304, 282 N.W. 2d 27 (1979), aff'd. 213 Neb. 418, 329 N.W. 2d 354 (1983).

[166] Thomas v. Chicago Board of Educ., 60 Ill. App. 729, 17 Ill. Dec. 865, 377 N.E. 2d 55 (1978) rev'd. 77 Ill. 2d 165, 32 Ill. Dec. 308, 395 N.E. 2d 538 (1979); Lowe v. Texas Tech. Univ., 530 S.W. 2d 337 (Tex. Civ. App. 1975), rev'd./remanded 540 S.W. 2d 297 (1976); Gerrity v. Beatty, 71 Ill. 2d 47, 15 Ill. Dec. 639, 373 N.E. 2d 1323 (1978).

[167] Leahy v. School Board of Hernando Co., 450 So. 2d 883 (Fla. App. 1984).

[168] Brackman v. Adrain, 63 Tenn. App. 346, 472 S.W. 2d 735 (1971).

[169] Hanna v. State, 46 Misc. 2d 9, 258 N.Y.S. 2d 694 (1965).

[170] Moschella v. Archdiocese of N.Y., 48 A.D. 2d 856, 369 N.Y.S. 2d 10 (1975), aff'd. 52 A.D. 2d 873, 383 N.Y.S. 2d 49 (1976).

[171] Stanley v. Board of Educ., Chicago, 9 Ill. App. 3d 963, 293 N.E. 2d 417 (1973).

[172] Stewart v. D & R Welding Supply Co., 51 Ill. App. 3d 597, 9 Ill. Dec. 596, 366 N.E. 2d 1107 (1977).

bat ring flew off the bat as the individual was taking practice swings, and hit the umpire. It was alleged that the bat ring was of the improper size. In another baseball case,[173] a defective bat broke and a piece hit plaintiff. A third grader in physical education class was hit in the face with a wooden bat swung by a classmate while he was catching. It was alleged that the bat was too heavy for the child to swing properly and that a safety helmet or face mask should have been provided.[174] The improper accessibility to baseball equipment was alleged to be the proximate cause of injury in a day camp.[175]

The provision of mats under gymnastics apparatus is essential. Usually the allegation is that no mats were provided or inadequate matting; however, not all allegations are successful.[176] Additionally, in the *Gregaydis* case it was alleged that magnesium powder should have been provided to minimize slipping on a chinning bar. The pommels had been removed from a horse in the *Tiemann* case.[177] After having vaulted successfully several times, plaintiff's finger stuck in one of the two ½" holes where the pommels had been removed, causing her to fall and receive permanent injury to her right leg. In addition to alleging injury due to inadequate matting, the reasonableness of removing the pommels and foreseeability of the injury due to the holes was at issue, notwithstanding that this was customary practice. The height of the horse was alleged to be the cause of injury in an Illinois case.[178] Plaintiff fell and fractured his arm. Judgment for defendant. And, in two trampoline cases it was a question of whether failure to attach a pad properly at the end of the trampoline was negligence and proximate cause of injury to plaintiff who lost several teeth when he hit the frame.[179] In a 1987 Pennsylvania case,[180] plaintiff alleged failure to protect sufficiently the pole vault pit with mats; plaintiff landed one foot on and one foot off the mat.

The availability of and proper instruction in use of life vests for canoeing was at issue in a situation where the University operated a canoe rental.[181]

§ 19.232   Dangerous conditions of facilities

Plaintiff was hit in the eye by a tennis ball while playing tennis in physical education class. There were two adjacent courts indoors and the ball was hit by a player on the court other than the one on which the plaintiff was playing. Plaintiff alleged negligence for failing to have sufficient nets or other safety devices between the courts to prevent

[173] Vaughn v. Commonwealth, 46 Pa. Cmwlth. 101, 405 A. 2d 1119 (1979).

[174] Ausmus v. Board of Education, Chicago, 155 Ill. App. 3d 705, 108 Ill. Dec. 137, 508 N.E. 2d 298 (1987).

[175] Crohn v. Congregation B'nai Zion, 22 Ill.App. 3d 625, 317 N.E. 2d 637 (1974).

[176] Gregaydis v. Watervliet Civic Chest, 14 A.D. 2d 623, 218 N.Y.S. 2d 383 (1961); Baird v. Hosmer, 46 Ohio St. 2d 273, 75 Ohio Ops. 2d 323, 347 N.E. 2d 533 (1976); Fein v. Board of Educ., 305 N.Y. 611, 111 N.E. 2d 732 (1953); Govel v. Board of Educ., 267 A.D. 621, 48 N.Y.S. 2d 299 (1944); Howard v. Tacoma School Dist., 88 Wash. 167, 152 P. 1004 (1915); Lueck v. Janesville, 57 Wis. 2d 254, 204 N.W. 2d 6 (1973); Montag v. Board of Educ., 112 Ill. App. 3d 1039, 68 Ill. Dec. 565, 446 N.E. 2d 299 (1983); Yerdon v. Baldwinsville Academy, 50 A.D. 2d 714, 374 N.Y.S. 2d 877

(1975), motion denied 39 N.Y. 2d 705, 384 N.Y.S. 2d 1027 (1976).

[177] Tiemann v. Indp. School Dist., 331 N.W. 2d 250 (Minn. 1983).

[178] Montague v. School Board, 57 Ill. App. 3d 828, 15 Ill. Dec. 373, 373 N.E. 2d 719 (1978).

[179] Kungle v. Austin, 380 S.W. 2d 354 (Mo. 1964); Ragni v. Lincoln-Devon Bounceland, 91 Ill. App. 2d 172, 234 N.E. 2d 168 (1968).

[180] Cestari v. School Dist., Cheltenham Twshp, 520 A. 2d 110 (Pa. Cmwlth. 1987); see also Singer v. School Dist., Phila., 513 A. 2d 1108 (Pa. Cmwlth. 1986) gymnast performing on vaulting horse missed mat, in both cases the question was whether "landing surface" is within real property exception under Pennsylvania Tort Claim Act.

[181] Brown v. Florida State Board of Regents, 513 So. 2d 184 (Fla. App. 1987).

tennis balls from crossing from one into an adjacent one.[182] In another tennis case[183] in attempting to chase a lob, the plaintiff ran into the rear wall which had a heavy plastic curtain hung against it. Apparently plaintiff slipped and fell when he planted his foot on the overlap of the curtain. Plaintiff alleged dangerous maintenance of the court.

Dangerous conditions, also, can be due to overcrowding. In an early case,[184] where 48 boys were playing basketball on eight courts in an area 80' x 43', the school was held liable on the basis that the floor was too crowded for safety. However, an opposite result was reached by an Indiana court.[185] The girls' physical education class of 45 shared the basketball floor with a boys' class, dividing the area by a canvas curtain. The girls' dressing room was located in the far corner of the boys' end of the playing floor. It was the custom of the girls, when dismissed, to run toward the locker room. In this situation, the plaintiff began to run and became entangled with some other girl and fell, breaking her left femur and cracking her right elbow. In physical education class, a game of whiffle ball was being played within close confines of the gymnasium. The first row of bleachers was open (pulled out) in locked position; plaintiff ran into the bleachers, causing his injury.[186]

Landing surfaces also can give rise to dangerous conditions. In *Singer v. School Dist. of Phila.*, 99 Pa. Cmwlth 553, 513 A. 2d 1108 (1986), plaintiff broke his elbow when he missed the mat while performing a gymnastic stunt over a vaulting horse and landed on the hardwood floor.

In a judo class, plaintiff student's back hit partly on the mat and partly on the floor during instructor's execution of hip throw on the student, resulting in permanent back injury. It was not part of the assumption of risk to have this unanticipated extraordinary hazard in instruction.[187] Judgment was for the defendant in a camp case where the plaintiff alleged negligence for failure to prepare the broad jumping landing pit area so that it would better cushion her landing.[188]

The youngsters in a day care center were playing frisbee, when a five-year-old collided with his companion and broke his leg. Plaintiff alleged cause of injury was inadequate space (15 children on 60' x 27' area), when there was other equipment on the area, and lack of supervision.[189]

The layout of the diamond was alleged to be the cause of injury in a softball case.[190] The pitcher's mound had been laid out directly in line between first and third base on a non-regulation practice field. In a family softball game in a recreational park, there were no base bags; second base was defined by a hole in the ground. The plaintiff was

[182] Zawadzki v. Taylor, 70 Mich. App. 545, 246 N.W. 2d 161 (1976).

[183] Yammerino v. Cranston Tennis Club, 416 A. 2d 698 (R.I. 1980).

[184] Bauer v. Board of Education, 285 A.D. 1148, 140 N.Y.S. 2d 167 (1955).

[185] Driscol v. Delphi Comm. School Corp., 290 N.E. 2d 769 (Ind. 1972).

[186] Tijerina by Tijerina v. Evans, 150 Ill. App. 3d 288, 103 Ill. Dec. 678, 501 N.E. 2d 995 (1986).

[187] Wells v. Colorado College, 478 F. 2d 158 (1973) Colorado law applied; see Pennsylvania cases regarding mats in preceding subsection.

[188] Weinstein v. Tunis Lake Properties, 15 Misc. 2d 432, 181 N.Y.S. 2d 916 (1958), aff'd. without op. 9 A.D. 2d 960, 196 N.Y.S. 2d 605 (1959), app. denied 10 A.D. 2d 711, 199 N.Y.S. 2d 437 (1960).

[189] Drueding v. St. Paul Fire & Marine Insurance Co., 482 So. 2d 83 (La. App. 1986).

[190] McGee v. Board of Educ., 16 A.D. 2d 99, 226 N.Y.S. 2d 329 (1962), app. dism'd. 12 N.Y. 2d 1100, 240 N.Y.S. 2d 165, 190 N.E. 2d 537, app. denied 19 A.D. 2d 526, 240 N.Y.S. 2d 24.

held to have voluntarily placed himself knowingly in danger and assumed the risk.[191]

Slippery floors, also, give rise to allegations of cause of injury, as was the situation in a high school tumbling class.[192] In a physical education class, plaintiff alleged negligence for having been directed to run on a macadam driveway on which there was loose gravel.[193] In issue in a summer day camp case was the dangerousness of a wet, sloping grass surface used to play "ring-a-levio," a run-hide-and chase game.[194]

For further discussion of conditions of areas and facilities, see Chapter 20.

[191] Tavernier v. Maes, 242 Cal. App. 2d 532, 51 Cal. Rptr. 575 (1966).

[192] Cambareri v. Board of Education, Albany, 246 A.D. 127, 284 N.Y.S. 892 (1936), aff'd., 283 N.Y. 741, 28 N.E. 2d 968 (1940).

[193] Dobbins v. Board of Educ., Henry Hudson Regional High School, 133 N.J. Super. 13, 335 A. 2d 58 (1974), aff'd. 67 N.J. 69, 335 A. 2d 23 (1975).

[194] Greaves v. Bronx YMCA, 87 A.D. 2d 394, 452 N.Y.S. 2d 27 (1982).

Chapter 20.   Environmental Conditions

Environmental conditions which surround the activity in which one is engaged can impact upon the likelihood of injury occurring. The design, layout, and construction of areas and facilities (§20.1) can provide either safe or hazardous conditions, enhancing or detracting from the activity in which one is engaged. But it is not sufficient to properly design, layout, and construct areas and facilities. The manner in which they are maintained, that is, negligent maintenance, is the number one allegation of cause of injury in the parks field. In fact, more than 90 per cent of the urban parks situations allege improper maintenance practices.

Critical to whether judgment will be for the plaintiff or for the defendant is the concept of notice. Generally the courts will give a reasonable time after notice to ameliorate a defective premise condition; however, what is a reasonable time is determined by the jury in relation to the likelihood of injury and the severity of injury which may occur. Notice is of two types — actual notice, *i.e.*, having direct information regarding the defect or hazard, and constructive notice, *i.e.*, one should have known if they were doing the proper job of inspection or otherwise be aware of what was going on. One is held accountable for both types of notice. Action to remedy dangerous conditions is of utmost importance. Section 20.2 deals with condition of premises.

A question also frequently raised is "who is liable for a premise defect?" This question is dealt with in this chapter and also in Chapter 3. Suffice it to be said at this time, however, that most pertinent is the distinction between activity-related injuries and premise-related injuries. An entity which is responsible for the premise, but not the activity is liable for injuries related to the premises, but not for those occurring due to the activity; whereas, an entity which is responsible for the activity is usually liable to the participant for both premise-related and activity-related injuries, since it owes the participant a duty not to expose to unreasonable risks of any type, including both premise and activity. The immunity statutes (see §4.2) also, often make the distinction between activity and premise-related injuries, in holding a governmental entity liable for dangerous conditions, particularly physical surroundings,[1] even though there may be immunity for activity-related injuries.

The third major section in this chapter is focused upon the natural (unimproved) areas and their condition. Again, the governmental immunity statutes often speak to the liability occasioned in use of this type of area, as well as the recreational user statutes (see §12.1). The status of the injured may determine the degree of care owed (see also §2.12).

§ 20.1 Design, layout, construction and installation of areas and facilities

This section is concerned with non-maintenance aspects of areas and facilities, that is, with the initial design, the layout of facilities, particularly proximity of different uses and utilities, and the actual construction and/or installation of a facility or element within a facility. When there is utilization of areas and facilities, there is an implied warranty that the area or facility is properly designed, laid-out, constructed, or installed for the given use. In a 1988 case, *Berman v. Radnor Rolls, Inc.*, 542 Pa. Super. 525, 542 A.2d 525 (1988), the court held for plaintiff, stating that a participant (skater), while charged with knowledge of general risks of the activity (skating), was not charged with knowledge of how risk was increased by the physical layout of the building. In this

[1] Zawadzki v. Taylor, 70 Mich. App. 545, 246 N.W. 2d 161 (1976); Morris v. Jersey City, 179 N.J. Super. 460, 432 A. 2d 553 (1981).

situation, the court said that the skater's injuries were caused by defective design of roller skating rink's facility, including vending area where skater was actually injured.

Ordinarily, when a contractor completes a job and turns the facility over to the owner, then the ensuing responsibility is that of the owner. A contractor, who had built a football stadium ten years before injury, was sued by the survivors of a cameraman who fell from a ladder in the stadium, alleging negligence in design and construction against the contractor, school board, and architects. In this case, *Hall v. Rapides Parish School Board,* 491 So. 2d 817 (La. App. 1986), the cameraman had been filming a game from the roof of the press box and as he descended a ladder, he fell approximately 60 feet to the ground, suffering fatal injuries. The court held that the contractor, which had obtained acceptance of the football stadium nine years before by the school board, owed no duty to cameraman.

While indemnity contracts is one form of risk management, a number of states, such as Indiana, have a statute holding certain types of indemnity agreements in construction or design contracts void.[2]

§ 20.11 Design and planning

Planning is generally considered a discretionary act for which there is governmental/ sovereign immunity for public agencies. Some states specifically have what is referenced as "design immunity." See §4.2 for discussion of these legal concepts.

More than one-half of the design situations giving rise to law suits involve swimming areas. The swimming pool cases are detailed in §9.1 Layout and construction of pools, and in §9.6 Locker rooms and showers, bathhouses. A shower room wall in a junior high school collapsed, and the plaintiff sued the contractor and architects, as well as the city and school board. The school had been completed and two years later the wall in question had to be completely rebuilt by workmen employed by the school system; and, it was seven years later that the wall collapsed, injuring plaintiff. Suit barred by statute of limitations.[3]

There is not a large number of cases in which design of buildings as related to recreation or physical education/sport was in issue. In *Toothe v. Wilmington*[4] a question was raised regarding design of the orchestra pit in an auditorium; and, the plaintiff in a Florida case[5] also was injured when he fell into the orchestra pit. He was a student at the University and the pit was created by a lowered area of the stage in a theater classroom auditorium. Plaintiff alleged negligent design. Plaintiff, who was injured when a jug of wood alcohol exploded in science class in high school, alleged defective design and unsafe classroom in that the class because of increased enrollment had been moved to a non-laboratory room which did not have safety shower, ventiliation or exhaust hoods,

[2] Sink and Edwards, Inc. v. Huber, Hunt, and Nichols, Inc., 458 N.E. 2d 291 (Ind. App. 1984) interprets Indiana statute.

[3] Hill v. City of Chattanooga, 533 S.W. 2d 311 (Tenn. 1975).

[4] Toothe v. Wilmington, 8 N.C. App. 171, 174 S.E.

2d 286 (1970); see also Frazier v. City of Norfolk, 234 Va. 388, 362 S.E.2d 688 (1987). Fall from pit platform through gap approx. 18' into basement.

[5] Erwine v. Gamble, 343 So. 2d 859 (Fla. App. 1976).

sinks, et al.[6] In a Kansas case,[7] action was brought against contractor, engineering company and architects for water damage to the gymnasium floor, allegedly resulting from improper design and construction.

In a 1986 case,[8] the girders used for indoor tennis courts in the Club were at issue, with the structure and position of the horizontal girders of particular importance. There were two horizontal girders, one 3'8" above the floor and the second 4'-½" above the first, or 7'2" above floor level. Each girder was U-shaped, forming a channel 7" wide and 2½" deep. Steel was approximately .6" thick. Additionally, a metal lip at the edge of the opening of the channel protruded inward ¾". The opening of the lower girder channel faced down, while the upper girder faced up. Tennis balls became trapped in this upper girder. Plaintiff had gone up to retrieve her ball, that is, her teammate boosted her onto the first girder so she could reach the ball in the second. Then, while still facing the girder, she let go with her right hand and jumped back, being careful to clear the first girder. However, as she jumped, the ring she was wearing on her left little finger caught on the girder lip and she suffered a severe avulsion of little finger. There was slight discrepancy in the sequence of events — the other version being that plaintiff lost her balance, slipped, and grasped for the girder. There was dispute as to the club policy of replacing balls so entrapped, if requested; there were no warning signs regarding climbing on the girders. An engineer testified that blocks of wood could have been put in the girder channel to block balls from being trapped there at $180 per court. The jury found defendant 75% negligent, plaintiff 25%, with total award for damages at $100,000.

Design as related to steps was at issue in two cases.[9] A 77-year-old museum visitor fell on the steps at the fountain area, fracturing her right elbow. The plaintiff recovered $30,000 on the basis that the platform steps were unreasonably dangerous because of the difficulty presented in visually detecting the presence of the steps. There were no warnings of cautionary markings. In the 1980 situation the roller skating patrons were playing "follow the leader" and were taken from the skating surface onto an elevated carpeted refreshment area. It was as plaintiff was stepping down from the elevated area back onto the skating surface that he fell. The question was the knowledge of the plaintiff regarding the step down. In another case, it was a recessed area of a kitchen in a school and plaintiff fell, not realizing the step down. The court held that it was obvious and not a hidden design defect.[10]

Windows and glass panels in doors, specifically safety glass, have been at issue in a number of cases. In six cases[11] the injury occurred in the gymnasium. In the *Stevens*

[6] Bush v. Oscoda Area Schools, 72 Mich. App. 670, 250 N.W. 2d 759 (1976), rev'd./remanded 405 Mich. 716, 275 N.W. 2d 268 (1979).

[7] Seaman Unified School Dist. v. Casson Const. Co., 3 Kan. App.2d 289, 594 P. 2d 241 (1979).

[8] Hueston v. Narragansett Tennis Club, 502 A. 2d 827 (R.I. 1986).

[9] Zambito v. Southland Recreation Enterprises, 383 So. 2d 989 (Fla. App. 1980); Watt v. U.S., 444 F. Supp. 1191 (1978).

[10] Hughes v. Chehalis School Dist., 61 Wash. 2d

222, 377 P. 2d 642 (1963); see also Jones v. Swatszel, 145 Kan. 99, 64 P. 2d 555 (1937) fell from second-story window while attending dance, alleged window sills in anteroom 13" lower than in main room, causing plaintiff to lose his balance when attempting to sit down.

[11] Clary v. Alexander Co. Board of Educ., 19 N.C. App. 637, 199 S.E. 2d 738 (1973), 285 N.C. 188, 203 S.E. 2d 820 (1974), vacated on other grounds, 286 N.C. 525, 212 S.E. 2d 160 (1975); Eddy v. Syracuse Univ., 433 N.Y.S. 2d 923 (1980); Hutt v. Etowah Co. Board of Educ., 454 So. 2d 793 (Ala. 1984); McGovern v.

case, one of two doors was almost directly behind the basketball hoop, approximately 2' from the court end line and 4'3" from the backboard. The plaintiff, running along the court at considerable speed and "going up" for a shot was carried by his momentum beyond the end line into the door, causing his arm with which he tried to brace himself to go through the pane of ordinary glass. The court held the school negligent for not using safety glass. The *McGovern* and *Hutt* cases were quite comparable in situation to the *Stevens* case. There also was a similar result in the South Dakota case when plaintiff received 15 per cent permanent disability in both arms when he was injured due to crashing into sidelight panels while playing basketball in the church gymnasium. The panels were 6' from the sideline and two of the four had previously been broken and replaced with plywood. Plaintiff lunged for a ball going out of bounds in an intensely played game. The glass shattered. Judgment for plaintiff of $125,000. In the *Eddy* case plaintiff was playing "ultimate frisbee" in the gym. The game is somewhat-like soccer and the boys were using as the goal lines the outermost sidelines of two basketball courts laid across the width of the gymnasium. Thus, the one goal line was located approximately 5' to 8' from the west wall, which was of masonry construction with glass doors in the center. Looking over his shoulder for a thrown frisbee, plaintiff was unable to stop and ran into the doors. He raised his arm to protect himself and his body struck the bar across the door, but because the door was locked, it did not open, the impact shattered the glass and as plaintiff's torso went through the door, his right arm was severely lacerated. The game was an informal one and plaintiff acknowledged that he was aware of the presence of the walls and the doors; however, the University should have foreseen the dangerous condition and such danger could be obviated without imposing an undue burden upon the University. An opposite result was reached in the fourth case. The court held that the plaintiff, knowing of the glass panels, which were only 3' from the baseline of the basketball court, was contributorily negligent when he ran wind sprints and made no effort to stop until he reached the baseline. In two others cases injury occurred in the hallway. In the *Wilkinson* case[12] the student crashed through a glass panel in the gymnasium foyer while engaged in an unsupervised race during physical education class. A visiting coach had several years previously walked into the panel which was located less than 5' from the traffic pattern of spectators and directly accessible to the basketball court. At that time, nonsafety glass was replaced in the broken panes with safety glass, but not the unbroken panes. The court held that the school board knew of the danger created by nonsafety glass. It was an opposite result when a 12-year-old severely injured her hand while rushing toward a glass paneled door and reached out for the "panic bar" while looking the opposite direction. The court held that the proximate cause of the accident was her running into the door while looking away from it.[13] The plaintiff also recovered in a Utah case.[14] Another 12-year-old

Riverdale Country School Realty Co., 51 A.D. 2d 894, 380 N.Y. 2d 687 (1976); Stevens v. Central School Dist., 25 A.D. 2d 871, 270 N.Y.S. 2d 23 (1966), aff'd. N.Y. 2d 780, 288 N.Y.S. 2d 475, 235 N.E. 2d 448 (1968); Thomas v. St. Mary's Roman Catholic Church, 283 N.W. 2d 254 (S.D. 1979); see also, Schnell v. Travelers Insurance Co., 264 So. 2d 346 (La. App. 1972).

[12] Wilkinson v. Hartford Accident & Indem. Co., 400 So. 2d 705 (La. App. 1981), rev'd. 411 So. 2d 22 (La. 1982), aff'd. 421 So. 2d 440 (La. App. 1982).
[13] Tyler v. Jefferson Parish School Board, 258 So. 2d 206 (La. App. 1972); see also, Eberle v. Benedictine Sisters of Mt. Angel, 235 Or. 496, 385 P. 2d 765 (1963).
[14] Wheeler v. Jones, 19 Utah. 2d 392, 431 P. 2d 985 (1967).

walked into a partially opened sliding glass door between the pool and a store and the ordinary glass broke. Held that defendant should have recognized the danger and corrected it.

Two 1986 cases[15] each held opposite to the other. There was a safety glass statute in Massachusetts requiring glazing material in entrance doors of public buildings, but this glass panel had been installed prior to the mandatory statute; however, the court held that at the time of installation it was widely recognized as prudent to use safety glass and held for the plaintiff, who had suffered serious injury when he put his hand through glass panel of swinging entrance doors to auditorium. In the Ohio case, a football player practicing with the team in the field house was doing an exercise, referred to as "livers," which entailed wind sprints. He proceeded beyond the area where the exercise was taking place and struck a wire-reinforced glass door with his foot. His foot and leg broke through the door resulting in serious injury. The court stated a number of points pertinent to universities: (1) State university's employment of a number of scientific and technical experts did not impose upon university a duty of care higher than ordinary or reasonable care, where nothing in record indicated that field house was managed by experts or that other than ordinary management expertise was applied; (2) student athletes training in university athletic facilities are owed ordinary standard of care to invitees; (3) university's safety policy of using tempered glass to replace broken glass, which policy was begun two years before such glass was required by federal regulations, did not establish that university knew of or considered doors of field house, which contained wire-reinforced glass, to be unreasonable risk of harm, for purposes of determining whether university was negligent in failing to replace glass prior to injuries received by football player; and (4) university's knowledge that field house doors had high window breakage rate did not, absent proof as to cause of breakage, establish that university knew of dangerous condition prior to injuries of football player; and, further, in fact there had been only one prior instance of injuries to athlete caused by impact with glass door of field house during 30 years of use of field house, and such did not establish notice of dangerous conditions or unreasonable risk of harm. The allegation of plaintiff that using wire-reinforced glass in door, rather than another type of safety glass, was an absolute nuisance was not upheld, in absence of evidence that university culpably and intentionally maintained wire-reinforced glass, the consequence of which necessarily resulted in injury; evidence indicated that the university had a policy of stocking, installing, and maintaining safer window material.

Where the boundary lines of the playing courts are right at a wall, the issue of dangerous design has been raised in several cases.[16] (See also §6.22 basketball.) There are few cases[17] involved with sport fields or courts. Most of these involve layout in

[15] Curtis v. State, 29 Ohio App. 3d 297, 504 N.E. 2d 1222 (1986); Johnson v. City of Boston, 22 Mass. App. 24, 490 N.E. 2d 1204 (1986).

[16] For example, Bradley v. Board of Educ., 243 A.D. 651, 276 N.Y.S. 622 (1935), 247 A.D. 833, 286 N.Y.S. 186 (1936), aff'd. 274 N.Y. 473, 8 N.E. 2d 610 (1937); Maltz v. Board of Educ., 114 N.Y.S. 2d 856 (1952).

[17] Berger v. Miller, 241 F.Supp. 282 (1965) camp

situation, playing basketball on outdoor court which had a low wall (maximum height 2'8") 5'1" beyond the end line of the court, players momentum carried him onto the wall, court observed that a full height wall could serve as safety factor to brace a player running over the end line, but a shorter wall would act more like a rope stretched across a path to trip the unwary; Scala v. New York City, 200 Mis. 475, 102 N.Y.S. 2d 790 (1951) softball field constructed so cement curb to

contrast to design. (See next section, §20.12.) In a golf case,[18] where plaintiff was struck in eye at golf course, the court held in respect to who is a design expert that experience alone is enough to qualify a witness as an expert, and that scientific or professional training is not a prerequisite to being an expert; however, experience obtained from playing golf did not qualify witness as expert in design.

As for park situations, again there are few, primarily zoo cases (injury by animals) concerned with the construction of the cages and barriers to keep patrons back (see §11.4 Zoos). In a California case[19] a four-year-old was drowned in a park pond "fish hole," which had been constructed near the middle of the pond to provide a deeper sanctuary for the fish. The court directed judgment for the plaintiff, holding that there was actual knowledge of the concentration of young children and this hole was hazardous. The hazard, however, came from the change in design, which was altered during construction by the defendant's administrator and a supervisor, to much steeper sloping sidewalls from 45 degrees to approximately 65 to 80 degrees. In a California case,[20] plaintiff sued the contractor, alleging negligent excavation and construction of swimming pool, leaving pool with inadequate slope and depth. Held for defendant; swimmer had complete knowledge of layout of pool and failed to exercise ordinary care for his own safety by diving into the shallow end.

In a 1984 case,[21] plaintiff alleged negligence in not installing lightning protection system on a metal-roofed picnic shelter. Defendant sought to use defense of act of God as the cause of injury to picnickers. The court said that if proper care and diligence on part of defendant would have avoided act, it is not excusable as act of God.

Boat house lessee and his guest were overcome by carbon monoxide as a result of accumulation of exhaust fumes in the boat house. Action was brought against the lessor. The court held that fact that lessor had installed vents on other boat houses in marina did not render lessor liable for not providing ventilation. Plaintiff alleged negligence in design and construction of the boat house.[22]

§ 20.12 Layout of areas

Layout of area as a premise condition should be distinguished from proximity of activity to some physical condition, such as the close confines of a gymnasium or outdoor area,[23] which is a matter of supervision and/or conduct of activity. Layout

contain water for ice skating, plaintiff in going after ball stumbled over the curbing, held for defendant.

[18] Baker v. Thibodaux, 470 So. 2d 245 (La. App. 1985).

[19] Davis v. Cordova Recreation and Park Dist., 24 Cal.App.3d 789, 101 Cal.Rptr. 358 (1972).

[20] Davis v. Larue Enterprises, Inc., 146 Ga. App. 516, 246 S.E. 2d 515 (1978); see also Nelson v. Spokane, 104 Wash. 219, 176 Pa. 149 (1918) dam in public park; St. Petersburg v. Collom, 400 So. 2d 507 (1981), aff'd. 419 So. 2d 1082 (Fla. 1982) design at issue, 20-month-old child drowned in drainage ditch in public park, judgment for plaintiff, known dangerous condition.

[21] Bier v. City of New Philadelphia, 11 Ohio St.3d 134, 464 N.E.2d 147 (1984).

[22] Charlton v. Day Island Marina, 46 Wash. App. 784, 732 P. 2d 1008 (1987).

[23] For example, Drueding v. St. Paul Fire and Marine Insurance Co., 482 So. 2d 83 (La. App. 1986) day care center, playing frisbee in crowded area; Prest v. Sparta Comm. Unit School Dist. 140, 157 Ill. App. 3d 569, 109 Ill. Dec. 727, 510 N.E. 2d 595 (1987) supervised activity in gymnasium, plaintiff fell on unpadded concrete bleachers; Tijerina v. Evans, 150 Ill. App. 3d 288, 103 Ill. Dec. 678, 501 N.E. 2d 995 (1986) whiffle ball in gym, fell against first row bleachers open in locked position; see Chapters 18 and 19.

includes not only the activity area, but also proximity to utility structures, frequently obstructions on which participant is injured. Layout also includes proximity to other persons, such as passers-by, and to other functions which may be hazardous to recreation users and, thus, require some protective measure. For example, in *Abdur-Rashid v. Consolidated Rail Corp.*, 135 A.D.2d 208, 524 N.Y.S.2d 716 (1988), a child, who had been playing on the playground, was injured on the nearby railroad tracks. However, a 6' high fence had been erected to protect the children. The court held that, in absence of any defect or condition related to the fence or playground which invited a child to use the tracks as an extension of the playground, there was no duty owed the child, once she had left the jurisdiction of the playground. (See §20.231 Fences...).

The preponderance of cases related to layout of areas involve either baseball or golf (see §6.12 baseball and §§7.11, 7.132 golf, §15.111 baseball spectators, and §15.2 passers-by). The baseball/softball situations concern primarily proximity of the diamond to walks and streets and to children's play areas. A few address the layout of the diamond itself, but small diamonds in and of themselves are not a dangerous condition. Some baseball cases involve outfield obstructions, such as a flag pole or sprinkler. Most of the golf cases find one golfer being injured when another hits the golf ball, but few golf course layouts are found to be hazardous; it is usually the hooking or slicing of a golf ball.

An outdoor basketball court was laid out adjacent to an area prescribed for children to wait in at noon. The plaintiff was injured when a student playing basketball ran off the court in an effort to retain possession of the ball and collided with him. While general supervision only was required, the court said that it was negligence to set up the court so close to the children's area.[24] Students were engaged in throwing a discus on an elliptical track which had other students playing baseball on the field adjacent. The plaintiff entered the area commonly used by students entering and leaving the baseball field, and as he advanced along this undefined way, he was struck in the head and face by a discus. The court said that while a 17-year-old at a private military academy is chargeable with diligence for his own safety as an adult, it does not relieve the academy from its duty for safety. Coaches of both sports were aware of plaintiff in the danger area. The athletic field was so laid out that students participating in one activity would, when approaching or leaving the field, be endangered by those participating in another activity on adjoining field. There was no pathway or other defined route protected by fence, shelter or otherwise.[25] The proximity of two areas, also, was in issue in a skiing injury. A novice ski slope and a sled run were separated only by a mound of dirt 10' north and parallel with the toboggan slides immediately adjacent to the sled run. The mound was about 4½' wide at the base, 2½' wide at the top and 40' long. The plaintiff had put on her skis at a point midway on the novice slope and started down in a snowplow position when she was struck from behind by a sled loaded with two or three young men. Judgment for plaintiff.[26] The Bureau of Land Management was sued for alleged

[24] Webber v. N.Y., 30 A.D. 2d 831, 292 N.Y.S. 2d 574 (1968).

[25] Marques v. Riverside Military Academy, 87 Ga. App. 370, 73 S.E. 2d 574 (1952).

[26] Morse v. State, 262 A.D. 324, 29 N.Y.S. 2d 34, app. dim'd. 287 N.Y. 666, 39 N.E. 2d 288 (1941).

negligent marking of a motorcycle race course and it owed a duty to assure that the race was conducted safely. The court held that the Government was not liable for negligence of the employees of the Association conducting the race (European-style scrambles) on federal land for which the Association had been issued a permit; the Association was responsible for laying out the course.[27]

Placement of utility wires and poles was at issue in a number of layout cases. In two 1984 cases[28] the court held that the danger of high voltage, uninsulated power lines was foreseeable. In the Illinois situation a 10-year-old boy sustained serious electrical burns while playing on a public playground when a spool of copper wire held by him came near the power lines that ran over the middle of the playground at a height of 30'. The power line also was at a height of 30' in the other case. A scaffold (33' high), being pushed into position to replace light bulbs on a tennis court, came into contact with the power line. In two Florida cases[29] power lines were hit. In the earlier case a student was electrocuted when, while flying a model airplane over the university's open field, the airplane came in contact with an uninsulated power line. Judgment for defendant University and power company. The power company did not have a duty to foresee and protect against the type of injury involved, and the University was not liable for allowing a latent hazard to persist; the power lines were clearly visible above the field. In the other case, the mast of a catamaran sailing boat touched uninsulated high tension electrical power transmission lines. The Court remanded the case to determine whether the power company knew, or should have known, that waters of the river were navigable and frequented by many sailing vessels and whether it exercised reasonable care for the safety of others in maintaining the lines. Defendant had designed and constructed the power line in compliance with accepted engineering procedures and in conformance with National Electrical Safety Code; and further, the line had been constructed and installed under authority of the County. The court said, however, that such compliance and authority did not serve to establish no negligence under the given conditions at the time of injury. And, in a 1980 case[30] a frog hunter was electrocuted when his 12'-long metal frog-catching device came in contact with an electric wire some 12' above the water. Court held for defendant under the State statute, saying that such condition did not constitute a deliberate or willful act designed to injury. (See also §20.238 electrical hazards.)

Proximity of playground to electrical hazards was at issue in two cases.[31] In the Illinois situation a seven-year-old was electrocuted when he climbed on top of transformer inside substation adjacent to public park; the fence surrounding the station was broken. In the New York situation, a youngster was injured when he came in contact with highly charged electric third rail on right-of-way of transit authority adjacent to city park. It was known to both city and transit company that the children climbed over the

[27] Thompson v. U.S., 592 F. 2d 1104 (1979).

[28] Bush v. Alabama Power Co., 457 So. 2d 350 (Ala. 1984); Nelson by Tatum v. Commonwealth Edison Co., 124 Ill. App. 3d 655, 80 Ill. Dec. 401, 465 N.E. 2d 513 (1984).

[29] Rice v. Florida Power & Light Co., 363 So. 2d 834 (Fla. App. 1978), cert. denied 373 So. 2d 460 (1979); Fries v. Florida Power & Light Co., 402 So. 2d 1229 (Fla.App. 1981).

[30] Rushing v. State of Louisiana, 381 So. 2d 1250 (La. App. 1980).

[31] Del Muro III v. Commonwealth Edison Co., 124 Ill. App. 3d 473, 79 Ill. Dec. 868, 464 N.E. 2d 772 (1984); Lederman v. N.Y. City Transit Authority, 36 Misc. 2d 571, 233 N.Y.S. 2d 425 (1962).

fence to retrieve balls. In a 1987 case,[32] a 16-year-old's rocket-propelled parachute he fired from a vacant field became entangled in a power line. While trying to retrieve the parachute, he made contact with one of the live lines causing serious body injury and death six days later. Held for defendant; though the utility company had knowledge of children playing on the field, they had no actual knowledge that children were capable of climbing pole.

A spectator was injured when struck by a batted foul ball which had rebounded off a light pole, even though he was seated behind a wired screen. Plaintiff alleged gross negligence on part of defendant by reason of its improper location of the light switch pole; however, the court did not agree.[33] A skier was injured when he collided with a utility pole on the ski slope. The court found skier 51% negligent, and under comparative negligence law of Vermont, he could not recover. The pole, however, was held to be an obvious, observable obstacle, rather than a hidden or latent danger.[34] Two snowmobilers were killed when they struck unmarked guy wires of a utility pole on the fairgrounds. The court held that there was genuine issue of fact as to gross negligence on part of electric utility and county agricultural society, which allegedly knew of utility's unmarked guy wires and threat therefrom to snowmobilers, who were using the society's land with permission. Allegedly the unmarked guy wires violated industry's safety code.[35] A skier collided with another skier and then crashed into a metal pole set in concrete in the ski area in the *Rosen* case.[36] The waiver on the skier's purchased season pass relating to hazards that exist in skiing and specifically waiving injury from carelessness or negligence of fellow skiers did not exonerate ski area for negligent conditions.

Plaintiff was injured while playing softball when he ran into a concrete incinerator while chasing a fly ball. The incinerator was a tower-like structure about 10' tall and 3' square in a grassy area in the outer reaches of center field, beyond the range of most hit balls. It stood on a base of concrete about 6" high, which protruded about 2' beyond the incinerator on all sides. Although a nearby septic tank was protected by a fence, the incinerator was unfenced. While the plaintiff knew the incinerator was there, he momentarily forgot about it as he went after the fly ball. The court held for the plaintiff. It discussed the differences between contributory negligence and assumption of risk, and then stated that public policy excluded assumption of risk when there was a violation of safety statutes or orders.[37]

In a 1985 case[38] a tennis player collided with a trash bin with protruding jagged wood when she followed a lob shot into the adjacent court. The trash bin was located immediately adjacent to the only gate in the fence surrounding the two tennis courts, and she had not only come in that gate, but also acknowledged that she had reviewed the area for any hazards before commencing play. The trash bin was in the open and in plain

[32] Lewis v. Georgia Power Co., 182 Ga. App. 375, 355 S.E. 2d 731 (1987).

[33] Jones v. Alexandria Baseball Ass'n., 50 So. 2d 93 (La. App. 1951).

[34] Green v. Sherburne Corp., 137 Vt. 310, 403 A. 2d 278 (1979).

[35] Estate of Thomas v. Consumers Power Co., 58 Mich. App. 486, 228 N.W. 2d 786 (1975), appeal 394 Mich. 459, 231 N.W. 2d 653 (1975).

[36] Rosen v. LTV Recreational Development, 569 F. 2d 1117 (1978).

[37] Chase v. Shasta Lake Union School Dist., 259 Cal. App. 2d 612, 66 Cal. Rptr. 517 (1968).

[38] Anderson v. Dunwoody North Driving Club, 176 Ga. App. 210, 335 S.E. 2d 451 (1985).

view during the entire time; at no time was the plaintiff's view of it obstructed. The court held that the player had failed to exercise ordinary care for her own safety, and that for the tournament to be held at fault she would have had to have been ignorant of the danger. Plaintiff tried to use the "distraction theory," that although she was aware of the trash bin that her playing distracted her from consciously knowing of the hazard. The court did not allow the theory in this situation.

§ 20.13   Construction and installation

The general rule is that the responsibility for performing or conducting task in safe manner rests with contractor and not premises owner where the operation is under control of contractor and danger arises out of employee's performance of task. Premises owner may be liable for injuries suffered by employee of independent contractor when owner retains right to control some part of independent contractor's work, but fails to exercise retained control with reasonable care.[39] A general contractor and subcontractor, as well as county and engineering firm, were sued with the issue of fact being whether such contractors and county had knowledge of use of area by children and exercised reasonable care regarding decedent who was killed while sledding on slope in county recreation area. The premises were not open for public use. Decedent collided with a metal post near the base of the hill, which had been set in concrete and was part of a chain link fence being erected. Engineering firm was granted summary judgment as it had no control over the work nor responsibility for what or how the work was done.[40] There are, however, certain premises repair situations which give rise to owner liability to patrons for independent contractor negligence. (See §3.122).

Several cases relate to construction of buildings. In a health club a false ceiling collapsed, the patron sought recovery against the health club, and the club against the contractor. The court held for the patron and the contractor, saying that the condition had existed for a sufficient length of time that the club knew or should have known of the condition.[41] The beam and framework toppled, causing volunteer member, who was helping, to fall off ladder and be injured. The yacht club had not hired any outside independent person to either supervise or direct the renovation work in the club building; however it was not held liable to the club member, primarily on the basis of "common" or "joint" enterprise.[42] A concrete block fell from a partition of a shower at a public swimming pool when 12-year-old plaintiff tried to climb it. The court held for the owner; no liability where there was no negligence in construction or maintenance of the wall and the climbing of the wall was in a panicky attempt to escape under a mistaken belief that an entrance door was blocked. The sticking of the door was not sufficient to find negligence.[43]

Snowmobiler sued those who had designed and installed gate into which he crashed;

[39] Gulf States Utilities v. Dryden, 735 S.W. 2d 263 (Tex. App. 1987) painting contractor.

[40] Caine v. New Castle County, 379 A. 2d 1112 (Del. 1977).

[41] Roman Spa v. Lubell, 334 So. 2d 298 (1976), rev'd./remanded 362 So. 2d 922 (1978), Op. after remand 364 So. 2d 115 (Fla. App. 1978).

[42] Farrar v. Edgewood Yacht Club, 302 A. 2d 782 (R.I. 1973).

[43] Ramadan v. Crowell, 192 So. 2d 525 (Fla. App. 1966).

summary judgment for defendant.[44] A six-year-old drowned in a swimming pool owned by the Recreation and Park Commission, when the Commission failed to equip the gates and doors of the pool with self-closing devices in violation of a city ordinance. There had been repeated acts of vandalism; however, the court said that the doors were left standing open when the locks were removed by vandalism and that the open door leading to the pool created an attraction or implied invitation to enter to children of tender years.[45] There also was code violation in the death by electrocution of a substitute guard at the pumphouse of the private swimming club pool. There had been notice, through an employee, of the unsafe condition. Wiring was not properly installed in accord with the National Electrical Code, and such violation was deemed negligence *per se*.[46] Judgment was for the defendant when the plaintiff scalded her hand by hot water when she attempted to draw cold water from a combination hot and cold faucet in the pool bathhouse. There was no evidence of defective equipment and the patron was familiar with that type of fixture.[47]

Plaintiff alleged an implied breach of warranty when paint with which pool had been painted camouflauged decedent so that his difficulty was not promptly observed, and thus could be rescued. Held that the promotional efforts of defendant which lead to the painting was not the proximate cause of injury.[48]

The owners of the golf course brought action against the architects and the person hired to perform earthmoving to recover damages for alleged negligent construction of the golf course. At issue was the contributory negligence of the owners. There was evidence that the owners knew the ground was not properly prepared for planting of grass seed in the fall, but nonetheless directed that the seeding proceed and the grass did not grow properly.[49] Piles of sand had been left on the playground as part of the reconstruction of baseball diamonds by the school and city. Plaintiff was struck by a "dirt rock" thrown by another child while playing among the piles of sand, which were not fenced in or otherwise rendered inaccessible to children. He suffered the permanent loss of sight in his right eye. Previously parents had complained about the dirt piles and dirt fights. Judgment for defendant on governmental immunity.[50] A concrete ring around a water sprinkler had been placed in the outfield of a softball diamond in the city park. It was held that the player who suffered severe injuries when he fell to the ground and struck his shoulder on the concrete knew the concrete "doughnuts" were in the outfield and knew of their uncovered, unprotected condition, and thus could not recover.[51] (See other cases of obstructions in the outfield in §6.12.) The type of fencing

[44] LaCarte v. N.Y. Explosives Corp., 72 A.D. 2d 873, 421 N.Y.S. 2d 949 (1979).

[45] Clifford v. Recreation & Park Comm., 289 So. 2d 373 (La. App. 1973), cert. denied. 293 So. 2d 168 (1974); see also Holsapple v. Casey Community Unit School Dist., 157 Ill. App. 3d 391, 109 Ill. Dec. 631, 510 N.E.2d 499 (1987) school locker room door without device to retard closing of door, no statute violated; Brookville v. Paulgene Realty Corp., 9 A.D. 2d 770, 192 N.Y.S.2d 988, 200 N.Y.S.2d 126 (1960) day camp, village zoning ordinance and building code.

[46] Ward v. Thompson Heights Swimming Club, Inc., 27 N.C. App. 218, 219 S.E. 2d 73 (1975); see also

preceding subsection regarding placement of utility poles and electric wires.

[47] Rothfield v. St. Louis Bath House Corp., 338 Ill. App. 200, 86 N.E. 2d 897 (1948).

[48] Kelly v. Koppers Co., 293 So. 2d 763 (Fla. App. 1974) cert. denied 302 So. 2d 415 (Fla. 1974).

[49] Loup-Miller v. Brauer, 40 Colo. App. 67, 572 P. 2d 845 (1977).

[50] Monfils v. City of Sterling Heights, 84 Mich. App. 330, 269 N.W. 2d 588 (1978).

[51] Rich v. City of Lubbock, 544 S.W. 2d 958 (Tex. Civ. App. 1976).

installed on a ball field was at issue in a Kansas case.[52] Plaintiff sought damages for cuts and other injuries he suffered to his face and head when he collided with a chain link fence with raw sharp cutting edges running along the top. There also are cases related to upkeep of sport areas, such as long jump pits. See §20.212.

The construction and installation of water-related facilities was at issue in several cases. In *Mendez v. State*,[53] the plaintiff recovered on dangerous condition due to anchoring of a raft with concrete blocks; and, plaintiff also recovered in *Sherman v. City of Springfield*[54] when he struck his head on a chlorinating pipe not installed at a sufficient depth to be safe for swimmers using the city lake. The failure to paint the boardwalk at the pier so as to prevent the boards from becoming water soaked and slippery and failure to cover the platform with matting of rubber of fiber to prevent it from becoming slippery were alleged to be dangerous conditions by a 13-year-old girl who slipped on a wet dock at the pier and was injured.[55] Construction of the dock was one of the allegations of danger in a Lake Placid case.[56] It was alleged that the dock was improperly constructed with its diving edge extending into an area of 3' to 5' of water depth. Plaintiff struck his head on bottom of lake and became permanently paralyzed. Held for the plaintiff. Dock construction also was at issue in *Kreiss v. Allatoona Landing, Inc.*[57] Plaintiff went upon the dock at night to go to her husband's boat in which she was to sleep. At an unlighted place, there was a 4" open space between the dock and a catwalk. She fell due to the open space. Summary judgment for defendant was precluded, and court was to determine both negligence of defendant and exercise of ordinary care on the part of plaintiff.

Judgment was for the plaintiff when the footboard of the lifeguard platform rig broke under his weight as he was participating in lifeguard lessons at the public swimming pool. The court stated that though one who dives from a lifeguard platform rig necessarily assumes some risk of danger from diving from such high altitude, it cannot logically be said that one of the risks he assumes is that the board will not withstand the stress of his dive but will break upon use and catapult him to the concrete below. There also was indication that the board should have been tested for strength by the owners.[58] And, in another case[59] five years later, the plaintiff was injured, too, on a diving platform at an outdoor pool owned by the city. Plaintiff alleged negligent installation of anti-skid pads on the steps of the ladder. He was injured while climbing the ladder between first and second levels.

§ 20.2   Condition of premises (maintenance)

Basically, this section deals with the maintenance of areas and facilities. One might well say, "but this is all common-sense maintenance." True, but unfortunately,

[52] Willard v. K.C., 235 Kan. 655, 681 P. 2d 1067 (1984); see also Edwards v. City of Birmingham, 447 So. 2d 704 (Ala. 1984).

[53] Mendez v. State, 56 Misc. 2d 143, 288 N.Y.S. 2d 680 (1968).

[54] Sherman v. City of Springfield, 77 Ill. App. 2d 195 (1966).

[55] Feirn v. Shorewood Hills, 253 Wis. 418, 34 N.W. 2d 107 (1948).

[56] Jacques v. Village of Lake Placid, 39 A.D. 2d 163, 332 N.Y. S.2d 743 (1972).

[57] Kreiss v. Allatoona Landing, Inc., 108 Ga. App. 427, 133 S.E. 2d 602 (1963).

[58] Starke v. Long, 221 Pa. Super. 338, 292 A. 2d 440 (1972).

[59] Schmit v. City of Detroit, 88 Mich. App. 22, 276 N.W. 2d 506 (1979).

somewhere along the line someone gets careless — does not make as thorough an inspection as one should, does not take time to completely put out or remove ash piles, does not repair immediately obvious defects. Perhaps the greatest deterrent to law suits in respect to premises is an excellent program of preventive maintenance; there should, without question, be periodic, regular, thorough inspections. Worn parts which may "go out at any time" should be replaced before they break and injure someone; loose parts should be tightened; decayed and rusted out supports or other parts should be replaced; all debris should be constantly kept picked up. *All equipment and structures found in disrepair should be repaired immediately.* To cut corners in maintenance is false economy and may prove very costly in the end, not only in greater repair bills, but also in liability suits — for remember, practically all law suits involving urban parks are concerned with maintenance. Of particular importance is the concept of the duty owed (see §2.12) to the injured by the defendant, as well as the knowledge the defendant had of the dangerous condition of the premises.

An inspection system is essential for risk management (§24.41), for inspections play a vital role in discovery of conditions;[60] and "notice" is a most important legal concept regarding liability for conditions of premises. Notice is information, knowledge of the existence of a fact; and, in this situation, means knowledge regarding the conditions of the premises. Two types of notice are pertinent, for defendants can be liable for those conditions of which they had either constructive notice or actual notice. Actual notice is information or knowledge positively proved to have been given to a party directly and personally, that is, the person has direct knowledge of the condition of the premises; while constructive notice is information or knowledge of a fact imputed by law to a person (although a person may not actually have it) because one could have discovered the fact by proper diligence, and the situation was such as to cast upon one the duty of inquiring into it.[61] If one could by diligent inspection or analysis of information available have learned of the premises' conditions, then one is held to have "notice" or knowledge of the condition.

What state of condition should the premises be? Usually the standard of care is that of "reasonableness," as determined by the jury. What is reasonable, however, may be determined by not only the use of the premises but also the characteristics of the clientele.[62] There is a considerable amount of legal commentary on condition of premises.[63]

[60] See, for example, Blanchard v. City of Bridgeport, 190 Conn. 798, 463 A. 2d 553 (1983); Bruss v. Milwaukee Sporting Goods Co., 34 Wis. 2d 688, 150 N.W. 2d 337 (1967); Daniele v. Board of County Comm'rs. 376 So. 2d 1 (Fla.App. 1979); Keating v. Wagner, 42 Lack. Jur. 84 (Pa. 1938).

[61] Black's Law Dictionary, Fifth edition at pp. 957-8.

[62] O'Leary v. Jacob Miller Co., 19 Mass. App. 947, 473 N.E. 2d 200 (1985).

[63] For example, Korpela, Allan E. Tort Liability of Public Schools and Institutions of Higher Learning for Accidents Occurring During Use of Premises and Equipment for Other Than School Purposes. 37 A.L.R. d 712-734; Korpela, Allan E. Tort Liability of

Public Schools and Institutions of Higher Learning for Injuries Due to Condition of Grounds, Walks, and Playgrounds. 37 A.L.R. 3d 738-765; Horpela, Allan E. Tort Liability of Private Schools and Institutions of Higher Learning for Accidents Due to Condition of Buildings, Equipment, or Outside Premises. 35 A.L.R. 3d 975-1006; Hawkins, Carl S. Premises Liability After Repudiation of the Status Categories: Allocation of Judge and Jury Functions, 15 Utah Law Review 15-63 (1981); Schopler, Ernest H. Modern Status of the Rule Absolving a Possessor of Land of Liability to Those Coming Thereon for Harm Caused by Dangerous Physical Conditions of Which the Injured Party Knew and Realized the Risk. 35 A.L.R. 3d 230-274.

Who is liable for dangerous conditions of the premises? The most frequent questions asked by an employee, whether instructor, activity leader, coach, park ranger, fitness specialist, et al., are "If I report the defective condition, am I free of personal liability?," "Must notice to my superior be in writing?," and "What if 'they' won't fix it?" The principles of the doctrine of respondeat superior apply (see Chapter 3). Thus, the answer to the first question is "NO". The employee remains personally liable, even though the condition is reported, because it is the duty of the employee working directly with the participants to provide a safe environment and the standard of care required is not to expose the participants to an unreasonable risk of injury (see introduction Chapter 2). When there is a dangerous condition, there are several alternatives: (1) discontinue activity — do not allow activity in that area where participants would be exposed to the danger; (2) modify activity — adjust the manner of play to avoid contact with the defect; or (3) temporarily repair the defect and continue the activity with care — for example, a hole in a floor board might have a temporary covering. While to warn participants of the danger and continue the activity is often done, it really is not a viable option. However, if there seems to be no alternative but to continue the activity, it is essential that there be warnings.

Must there be written notice to the supervisor/administrator? Written notice is a "two-edged sword." It is desirable to give written notice, for then there can be no question that you informed your supervisor/administrator (this will help you in court to show that you were concerned), and the nature of the dangerous condition and what you may see the problem to be are documented. On the other hand, written notice also can be used against you as documentary evidence that you were aware of the dangers, and, in fact, may be proof of a longstanding danger, but proceeded notwithstanding, with conduct of the activity. It should be noted that activity includes not only face-to-face leadership-lead activities, but also general supervision of activities, that is, permitting activities to take place on an area or in a facility (see introduction §18.3).

What about the supervisors' and administrators' liability, once they have been informed and they will not fix the dangerous condition? When there is "notice" (see a previous paragraph), if the appropriate supervisor(s) or administrator(s) does not take action, then that is one of those acts which "enhance the likelihood of injury" for which such person is personally liable (see §3.3). (The administrative/supervisory chain may involve several persons in the hierarchy, including persons such as maintenance supervisor, head lifeguard or aquatic manager, supervisor of the fitness facility, general manager of an arena or park, program director, head of athletics, et al.) They would not, however, be responsible for injury occasioned by the employee's negligence, if such employee continued to conduct the activity with a known dangerous condition, unless a directive were given to continue activity under dangerous circumstances. Then the directive would be administrative/supervisory negligence. If a directive to continue activity notwithstanding the dangerous condition is issued, what can the employee do? This is sometimes done when economics is at stake, such as in a fitness center, or the administrator may not be informed, such as a park director, supervisor of physical education, et al., and believe that the limited immunity provided the governmental/ sovereign entity protects, but, except in a few states, the employee remains liable as an individual. What most administrators do not realize is that they, too, would become liable for issuing such a directive, because it would probably be considered a ministerial act (see §4.2). If the employee has presented evidence of desirable professional practices and really feels that the activity is too dangerous and is compromising one's professionalism, where there is a teachers' union or other such organization of employees, one may file a grievance. Most organizations of such type have a provision in the collective bargaining agreement when a person is asked to perform work either for which one is not qualified or in situations which are hazardous. If no such organization for employee grievance, and appeal to the top administrator is unsuccessful, then there really are only two courses of action — conduct the activity and run the risk of injury to a participant, or resign!

Now, what about the corporate entity's liability? Usually when there is negligence on the part of employees, such negligence is imputed to the corporate entity and it is liable. However, when the repair of a premise defect is at issue, there is another factor which is taken into consideration, involving a discretionary act of the policy board (see §4.13). If the cost of the repair is not within the budget and the policy board determines that the repairs shall not be made, or shall be delayed until a later time, then the question before the court is how easy or difficult and how inexpensive or costly are the repairs in relation to the likelihood and severity of injury. There are several cases in this section which consider this issue. If the repair is not difficult to make and is relatively inexpensive, usually the court will hold that the corporate entity should have made the repair; if the cost in dollars and difficulty is great and the likelihood of injury not too great or severe, usually the court will decide that the repairs were not worth it for the danger; and, if the danger is great and the cost great, then the activity should not be permitted.

This chapter is sub-divided into those conditions which are concerned with: (a) surfaces, (b) pedestrian ways, and (c) general maintenance of buildings and of outdoor areas. The cases provide illustration of some of the basic principles discussed in this introductory section.

§ 20.21 Surfaces

So many of the injury situations are concerned with surfaces, especially playing surfaces. Because of the difference in maintenance, surfaces are divided into those which are indoors (floor surfaces) and those which are outdoors (fields, courts, and playgrounds).

§ 20.211 Indoor facilities

Indoor facilities include gymnasiums, rinks, dance floors, community buildings, et al. The floor conditions which occasion injuries include extraneous substances on the floor, slipperiness due to wetness of floor, the finish of the surface making it slippery, and defective condition of the surface. In most all instances, these aspects are a matter of proper maintenance. Notice of the hazard and what one does about it are important.

Extraneous substances on the floor was the basis of action brought by a student when he slipped on spaghetti sauce which had spilled on the cafeteria floor while carrying his food tray. The court held that the school needed to provide for more careful supervision in regard to cleaning up spills. The food had been there sufficient length of time (from circumstantial evidence), but the inspection procedure was insufficient.[64] A fronton patron, as she stepped into the aisle, slipped and fell on a foreign liquid substance, sustaining severe permanent injuries. It was alleged that the floor of the aisle was sloped and covered with linoleum and that it was customary for patrons to carry food and drink from the service area to their seats. The court said that litter in aisles was an on-going problem on the premises and was a foreseeable danger of which owner had constructive notice. Evidence showed that owner did not have reasonable inspections and did not take reasonable precautions to guard against foreseeable dangers.[65] Again, in a roller skating situation, the question of notice, how long a wad of gum had been on the floor, was at issue, as well as whether the gum actually was the cause of the fall.[66]

In the Elks Club lodge, during a social event, plaintiff slipped and fell on a soapy substance on the kitchen floor, while he was assisting with the dishes, sustaining a back injury. Witnesses testified that the accumulation of dishwashing water causing slippery conditions on the tile floor often occurred and had extended over a period of time. The cause was a leak in the drain pipe and water supply line of the dishwasher. There was a medical settlement of $815,000 prior to trial. The jury rendered a verdict of $3,163,834 and a finding that plaintiff was 25% comparatively negligent. The court said that the requirement of actual or constructive notice of the existence of an unsafe condition applies only to temporary conditions created by others, and that this condition had been in existence for a long time.[67]

In a 1985 case[68] plaintiff brought action against both the school district which owned the gymnasium and the park district which had leased it for injury when he fell to floor during basketball game. During the course of the game, plaintiff jumped up in the air to catch a pass, and when he came down with the ball, he fell to the floor with a terrible pain in one leg, a torn ligament in his knee. He alleged that the fall was caused by improperly maintaining and cleaning the floor and failing to warn of such condition. However, he could not prove that the condition actually existed, and the court held for defendants.

Falls occasioned by slipperiness of floors due to water was the subject of a number of cases. In five cases[69] the wetness was from leaky roofs. In the 1982 case, a referee of a

[64] Sansonni v. Jefferson Parish School Board, 344 So. 2d 42 (La. App. 1977); see also Cumberland College v. Gaines, 432 S.W. 2d 650 (Ky. App. 1968) "foreign, sticky substance, dark in color" on gym floor, held: a fall does not, of itself, evidence negligence on part of possessor of premises, evidence failed to show that college created or had notice of the floor condition.

[65] Fazio v. Dania Jai-Alai Palace, Inc., 473 So. 2d 1345 (Fla. App. 1985); see also West Flagler Associates, Ltd v. Jackson, 457 So. 2d 587 (Fla. App. 1984).

[66] Lindsey v. Crescent Park, Inc., 139 Ga. App. 5, 228 S.E. 2d 6 (1976).

[67] Erdman v. Lower Yakima Valley, Wash. Lodge No. 2112 of B.P.O.E., 41 Wash. App. 197, 704 P. 2d 150 (1985); see also Campbell v. Peru, 48 Ill. App. 2d 267, 198 N.E. 2d 719 (1964) failure to rinse off soap or other cleaning substances from the floor properly; §9.6

Locker rooms and showers; Kmeth v. Delehanty, 266 N.Y. 600, 195 N.E. 218 (1935) slippery matter from showers had accumulated over the drain, when plaintiff stepped on mat, which extended $\frac{2}{3}$'s over drain, mat slipped, causing him to fall; Shumway v. Milwaukee Athletic Club, 247 Wis. 393, 20 N.W.2d 123 (1945) steam room, held: pitch of floor according to common practice, discounted roughed surface and mat on sanitation basis, soapy condition was of such short time that no constructive or actual notice was given to the Club.

[68] Pedersen v. Joilet Park District, 136 Ill. App. 3d 172, 90 Ill. Dec. 874, 483 N.E. 2d 21 (1985).

[69] Albers v. Indp. School Dist., 94 Idaho 342, 487 P. 2d 936 (1971); Clancy v. Oak Park Village Center, 140 Mich. App. 304, 364 N.W. 2d 212 (1985); Dawson v. R.I. Auditorium, 104 R.I. 116, 242 A. 2d 407 (1968); Dorry v. LaFleur, 387 So. 2d 690 (La. App. 1980), cert.

basketball game slipped and fell; in the Rhode Island case it was a professional basketball player during pre-game warm-up who slipped in a puddle of water; and, in the *Albers* case plaintiff was one of six boys who during the Christmas holiday persuaded the custodian to let them play basketball in the high school gymnasium. The situation in the case against the Athletic Center involved a racquetball court. Plaintiff paid a fee for use of the court for one hour. During the first 15 minutes of play, the roof began to leak, forming a puddle of water on the floor. Plaintiff slipped while playing, crashed into the wall, and injured his foot. He alleged both negligence and breach of implied warranty of fitness (see §21.122) of the racquetball court. The *Dorry* case involved a roller skating rink in a rather old building. Two large puddles had merged into one large area of water about 20' to 25' by 6', and the court held that the plaintiff assumed the risk related to this obvious water; however, plaintiff did not assume the risk of a smaller 18" puddle in another corner of the rink of which he was unaware. The water on the basketball floor in a Louisiana case[70] came from condensation due to high humidity. Prior to the game, the floor had been mopped and someone had turned on fans and heaters in an attempt to dry the floor. The senior player from a visiting high school did not obtain judgment. The court held that since none of the coaches or referees, who were responsible for inspecting and approving the playing conditions, considered the floor's condition serious enough to even discuss the possibility of cancelling the game, it could not be said that the host school acted unreasonably in preparing and maintaining the floor.

Wetness due to water occurs logically in the locker/shower rooms around pools[71] and in steam rooms and other related facilities.[72] The use of skid-resistant wax, rubber mats and other substances or textured surfaces is usually in issue as to the reasonableness of the care taken by the proprietor. (See §9.6 Locker rooms and showers in pools; §17.43 Maintenance of fitness facility.) One, also, must be concerned about slipperiness due to mopping. Wetness after mopping the floor, onto which tumbling mats had been placed at the recreation center, was alleged to be the cause of plaintiff slipping and being injured while at summer camp.[73]

Wetness from beverage spills has resulted in accidents and law suits. The wetness in the *Elias* case,[74] which was situated in a bowling alley, came from an undetermined liquid, but apparently a beverage purchased at the snack bar adjacent to the lanes. Customers deposited drinking cups partially filled with ice and liquid substances into

granted 394 So. 2d 614 (1980), rev'd. 399 So. 2d 559 (La. 1980); Studley v. School Dist., 210 Neb. 669, 316 N.W. 2d 603 (1982).

[70] Gatti v. World Wide Health Studios of Lake Charles, 323 So. 2d 819 (La. App. 1975); Sevin v. Shape Spa for Health & Beauty, 384 So. 2d 1011 (La. App. 1980).

[71] For example, Bertrand v. Palm Springs, 257 Or. 532, 480 P. 2d 424 (1971); House v. European Health Spa, 239 S.E. 2d 653 (1977); Johnson v. Bimini Hot Springs, 56 Cal. App. 2d 892, 133 P. 2d 650 (1943); Owen v. Vic Tanny's Enterprises, 48 Ill.App. 2d 344, 199 N.E. 2d 280 (1964); Richard v. General Fire & Casualty Co., 155 So. 2d 676 (La. App. 1963), cert. den. 245 La. 82, 157 So. 2d 230; Roeland v. Geratic

Enterprises, 187 Cal. App. 2d 280, 9 Cal. Rptr. 538 (1960); Spoltore v. Gilbert, 15 Bucks Co. L.R. 240, 37 Pa. D. & C.2d 410 (1965); Tulsa v. Goins, 437 P. 2d 257 (Okla. 1967); Van Stry v. State of N.Y., 104 A.D. 2d 553, 479 N.Y.S. 2d 258 (1984).

[72] Nunez v. Newman High School, 306 So. 2d 457 (La. App. 1975).

[73] Johnson v. Atlanta, 171 Ga. App. 296, 319 S.E. 2d 506 (1984); see also Gray v. Wood, 64 A. 2d 191 (R.I. 1949) going from classroom into corridor, had been washed and left wet and slippery, teacher did not know about the slipperiness, principal not liable for the misfeasance of school employees (custodian).

[74] Elias v. New Laurel Radio Station, 245 Miss. 170, 146 So. 2d 558 (1962).

receptacles on each side of the cashier's stand, and often there was spillage on the floor. Plaintiff stepped in the liquid while wearing his bowling shoes, then went onto the lanes to bowl, where he fell due to the slipperiness of his shoes. The court said that the proprietor owed a duty to the bowler to have and keep the bowling alley in reasonably safe condition, and that a bowler assumes only those risks to which he voluntarily exposes himself and appreciates the danger. Defendant alleged that plaintiff was contributorily negligent. Liquids on dance floors, too, and the negligence of the proprietor/owner/sponsor is at issue in a number of cases. In some instances the allegation included failure to properly clean up, especially shattered glass.[75]

In a Florida case,[76] plaintiff slipped and was injured on an outdoor dance area, about 3' to 4' on the edge from a low spot which remained damp and more slick than the rest of the floor. Some silt and fungus was on this area.

Slipperiness of floors, also, may come from the finish of the floors. In two golf club cases[77] plaintiffs alleged that the floors were too slippery. In the *Lightner* case, the question was whether the failure to provide anti-skid ingredient or other surfacing and failure to warn of slipperiness as a dangerous condition were the proximate cause of the fall. Plaintiff recovered in the 1981 case when she slipped and fell on a concrete floor of the club house. The court held that the floor was unreasonably dangerous for its intended purpose. Plaintiff was wearing her steel-spiked golf shoes. The golf pro testified that 99% of the golfers enter the building wearing their golf shoes. Ten years earlier, after complaints, rubber mats had been installed inside the women's locker room. This fall occurred outside the locker room in area coming from the lounge (see §7.131 Club house - golf).

Wax may be the cause of slipperiness. In *Elmich v. Indp. School Dist.*,[78] a 17-year-old slipped on freshly waxed floor in the high school, sustaining fracture of left ankle. However, case not decided on its merits; procedural noncompliance. A seventh grade student fractured his hip when he slipped on a coat on the floor of the cloakroom and went "sailing" with force with his feet into the wall so that he turned a backward somersault. He alleges that this force and slide was occasioned by the waxing and slipperiness therefrom of the floor. The floor was linoleum, and in the Fall it was waxed and buffed; then, once a month to remove scuff marks, beeswax candles were grated onto the floor and the children were directed to stomp in the wax with their stocking feet. Plaintiff had participated in this process. Judgment for plaintiff; the school knew that the cloakroom was constantly and hurriedly used by the children.[79]

More common, however, are waxed floors for dancing.[80] Plaintiff did not recover

---

[75] Cardone v. Sheldon Hotel Corp., 160 Pa. Super. 193, 50 A. 2d 700 (1947); Hendrickson v. Brill, 45 Wash. 2d 766, 278 P. 2d 315 (1954); Roberts v. Courville, 162 So. 2d 750 (La. App. 1964); Rosensweig v. Travelers Ins. Co., 333 So. 2d 334 (La. App. 1976), Ward v. Veterans of Foreign Wars, 109 Ga. App. 563, 136 S.E. 2d 481 (1964); see also 38 A.L.R. 3d 419.

[76] Country Club of Coral Gables v. McHale, 188 So. 2d 405 (Fla. App. 1966).

[77] Lightner v. Balow, 59 Wash. 2d 856, 370 P. 2d 982 (1962); Jones v. Recreation & Park Commission,

395 So. 2d 846 (La. App. 1981), writ cert. denied 400 So. 2d 1379.

[78] Almich v. Indp. School Dist., 291 Minn. 269, 190 N.W. 2d 668 (1971); see also Smith v. Cedar Rapids Country Club, 124 N.W. d 557 (Iowa 1963).

[79] Haymes v. Catholic Bishop of Chicago, 41 Ill. 2d 336, 243 N.E. 2d 203 (1968).

[80] Turner v. Fleet Leasing, Inc., 91 Or. App. 257, 754 P.2d 614 (1988); see also Spivey, Gary D. Liability of Dancehall Proprietor or Operator for Injury to Patron Resulting from Conditions of Premises. 38 A.L.R. 3d 419-447.

when she alleged that one spot on the dance floor must have been very slippery; no such evidence was found.[81] In the *Carlin* case,[82] plaintiff alleged that the defendant carelessly applied wax to the floor. The court stated that assumption of risk was not available as a complete defense. And, in other cases, the wax was not properly mopped out,[83] the floor was freshly waxed,[84] and a polishing substance for dance floors made it too slippery,[85] et al.[86] Generally, the owner/sponsor of the dance or dance floor is not held liable unless there has been negligence in the materials used or in the manner of application.

Defective conditions of surface also have brought injuries and lawsuits.[87] A square dancer was injured when she tripped on uneven joint between two adjacent sections of plywood in the dance floor. Plaintiff was participating in a square dance festival operated by the defendant corporation. The court held that the dancer assumed the risks inherent in square dancing, such as being kicked by another dancer, but not the risk of a faulty and dangerous floor whose unevenness caused her to fall.[88] And, the owner of the dance hall in a Minnesota case[89] was liable when plaintiff fell due to a crack or hole in the floor, which had existed at least two months before the incident.

The condition of the surface of both ice skating and roller skating rinks has been the allegation as cause of injury by plaintiffs in a number of cases.[90] In a 1987 case,[91]

[81] Hammonds v. Jackson, 132 Ga. App. 528, 208 S.E. 2d 366 (1974).

[82] Carlin v. Goldman Industries, Inc., 347 So. 2d 837 (Fla. App. 1977).

[83] Koder v. Phoenix Ins. Co., 241 So. 2d 257 (La. App. 1960).

[84] Lorenz v. Santa Monica City H.S. Dist., 51 Cal. App. 2d 393, 124 P. 2d 846 (1942).

[85] Hedrick v. Tigniere, 267 N.C. 62, 147 S.E. 2d 550 (1966); McArthur v. Elad Conservat. 26 A.D. 2d 528, 270 N.Y.S. 2d 977 (1966).

[86] Brown v. Appleton Masonic Temple Assoc., 243 Wis. 147, 9 N.W. 2d 637 (1943); Cambereri v. Board of Educ., 246 A.D. 127, 284 N.Y.S. 892 (1936) aff'd. 283 N.Y.S. 741, 28 N.E. 2d 968 (1940); Champagne v. Harahan Lions Club, 243 So. 2d 292 (La. App. 1971); Custer v. St. Clair Country Club, 349 Ill. App. 316, 110 N.E. 2d 697 (1953); Fishman v. Brooklyn Jewish Center, 234 A.D. 319, 255 N.Y.S. 124, app. dismd. without op. 263 N.Y. 685, 189 N.E. 757 (1932); Jones v. Benevolent Protective Order of Elks, 17 Pa. D. & C. 2d 233 (1958); Jones v. Kansas City, 176 Kan. 406, 271 P. 2d 803 (1954); Jurden v. Dranetz, 99 So. 2d 716 (Fla. App. 1958); Robinson v. Ipswich Post 1093, V.F.W., 343 Mass. 771, 178 N.E. 2d 24 (1961); Tanner v. Columbus Lodge No. 11, Moose, 44 Ohio St. 2d 49, 73 Ohio Op. 2d 233, 337 N.E. 2d 625 (1975); Thompson v. Board of Educ., 11 N.J. 207, 94 A. 2d 206 (1953).

[87] Additional cases prior to 1970: Gerber v. White Sulphur Co., 261 A.D. 853, 24 N.Y.S. 2d 356 (1941) breaking of board in floor of bathroom at pool, no recovery; Grover v. Owens, 222 Or. 496, 353 P. 2d 254 (1960) wrestling premise; McGuire v. Valley Arena, 299 Mass. 351, 12 N.E. 2d 808 (1938) wrestling premise; Miller v. Macalester College, 262 Minn. 418,

115 N.W. 2d 666 (1962) drama student injured when 35' high scaffold mounted on wheels tipped over while plaintiff was on it removing lighting fixtures, college field house, a dirt floor, front wheels dropped into a small trench in the dirt floor, judgment for plaintiff, duty to inspect; Waxenberg v. Crystal Baths, 129 N.Y.S. 2d 71 (1954) handball, unevenness, linoleum raised to height about 1" and wavy, cracked and loose at the edge over an area about one square yard, plaintiff's partner lost balance and in swinging at ball, struck plaintiff's face causing portion of eyeglass to become imbedded in eye, held: defect neither obscure nor hidden, plaintiff should have exercised reasonable care; Wright v. Downing, 116 Utah 465, 211 P. 2d 211 (1949) appeal for Hayward v. Downing, 112 Utah 508, 189 P. 2d 442 (1948) wrestling premise.

[88] Thayer v. Oregon Fed. of Square Dance Clubs, 482 P. 2d 717 (Ore. 1971).

[89] Martin v. Veterans of Foreign Wars, 279 N.W. 2d 70 (Minn. 1979); see also Nolan v. North Hills Golf Club, 21 A.D. 2d 695, 250 N.Y.S. 2d 471 (1964) fell on dance floor at dinner dance held at golf club's lodge, alleged bump in floor held not sufficient to show existence of any actionable defect; Olson v. Weingard, 77 Ill. App. 2d 274, 222 N.E. 2d 24 (1966) heel caught in raveled carpeting tacked along a metal strip which projected above and along the edge of the dance floor; Toftoy v. Ocean Shores Properties, 71 Wash. 2d 833, 431 P. 2d 212 (1967) foot caught in crack between sections of a portable dance floor.

[90] For example, ice: Brown v. Tulsa Exposition & Fair Corp: 429 P. 2d 767 (Okla. 1967) hole in ice; Dean v. Co. of Allegheny, 209 Pa. Super. 310, 228 A. 2d 40 (1967) soft spot; Goldman v. Bennett, 189 Kan. 681, 371 P. 2d 108 (1962) holes and debris on ice; Meistrich

plaintiff was seriously injured when she fell on an outdoor ice rink and her hand went through the ice into a puddle of water. A sharp object, later found to be a 2″ piece of jagged glass frozen in upright position, slashed through plaintiff's glove and severely cut palm of hand. Held: city exercised reasonable care in inspection and maintenance of rink and did not breach duty to warn; the city's decision to close the rink (was closed at time of injury) was held to be a discretionary act. (Note: closing was not an operational decision due to weather conditions, but a policy decision due to city budgetary problems.) Unevenness of ice was the alleged cause of injury to the plaintiff in a college case. Plaintiff was playing "pick-up" ice hockey on an outdoor rink. The rink was scraped and flooded whenever the weather would permit, usually a couple times each week. Snow was removed when necessary and college employees checked the rink daily or every other day. On this day, the temperature had risen to about 35°, but as the sun went down it became colder. The ice was rather rough, but skatable; it was "snowflakey" and cut up from having been skated on. Plaintiff, while playing, noticed a small lump or ball of ice between ½″ and 1″ in height; he raised his foot to pass over it, but when he put his foot down, his skate hit the lump, causing him to fall and injure himself severely. Plaintiff had not previously seen the lump, and there is no evidence that anyone else did either. Judgment for defendant; the small lump on ice did not exist for sufficient time to render college negligent for failing to discover and eliminate the potential hazard.[92] (See §8.312 for ice rinks and §11.55 for roller skating rinks.)

§ 20.212 Outdoor playing fields and courts

For the most part, this section focuses upon the traditional sports and their playing areas in terms of the nature of the surface. For conditions of golf courses, see §7.13 Injuries due to premises; for ice rinks, see the preceding section and §8.312, and for other ice and snow courses, see §8.1 Bobsledding and §8.7 Tobogganing, as the nature of ice and snow areas is quite different from the land sports areas. For areas and facilities specific to a particular activity, see specific chapter for that activity; see also safe premises for spectators, including bleachers §15.13.

§ 20.2121 Condition of playing surface

Law suits are brought on varied playing surface conditions, the most predominant being holes and depressions, but also including loose material on the surface, rocks and other extraneous objects on the field and wet grassy areas.

In two cases[93] physical education classes were being held on asphalt or macadam

v. Casino Arena Attractions, Inc., 31 N.J. 44, 155 A. 2d 90 (1959) departed from usual procedure in preparing ice, ice too hard and hence too slippery for skater of average ability; Nierman v. Casino Arena Attractions, 46 N.J. Super. 566, 135 A. 2d 210 (1957) soft, slushy, bumpy, uneven, small holes; Shields v. Van Kelton Amusement Corp., 228 N.Y. 396, 127 N.E. 261 (1920); see also Kaufman, A.D. Liability of Owner or Operator of Skating Rink for Injury to Patron, 24 A.L.R. 3d 911-937 (contains cases for both ice and roller rinks).

[91] Stucci v. City of St. Paul, 403 N.W. 2d 850 (Minn. App. 1987); see also Madden v. Co. of Nassau, 117 A.D.2d 717, 498 N.Y.S.2d 856 (1986) 6-year-old girl amputation of part of her ring finger while skating.

[92] Mortiboys v. St. Michael's College, 478 F. 2d 196 (1973).

[93] Dobbins v. Board of Educ., 133 N.J. Super. 13, 335 A. 2d 58 (1974), aff'd. 67 N.J. 69, 335 A. 2d 23 (1975); Shelton v. Planet Insur. Co., 280 So. 2d 380 (La. App. 1973).

parking areas. In both situations, the plaintiff slipped on loose gravel. In the *Dobbins* case, the court found no negligence on the part of the teacher in the conduct of the activity and the school board regarding the facility was protected by governmental immunity. In the other situation, the teacher sued the superintendent and other executive officers on unsafe workplace, but the court held that the action could not be maintained against them because the school board had the sole authority to approve the repair and renovation of the property and provide funds therefor. Sand on a volleyball court (outdoor) at a swim club was in issue in *Podvin v. Somerton Springs Swim Club*.[94] The court held that there was no duty to warn against obvious or known danger. The plaintiff had been around the court for an hour and had been playing for twenty minutes, and had not noticed the sand. Plaintiff assumed the risks of the court.

Holes and depressions in playing surfaces also have given rise to lawsuits. While most of the cases involve softball/baseball fields, it was basketball being played on an outdoor asphalt playground (fenced in) owned by the YMCA in a Nebraska case.[95] Plaintiff (33 years old) fell as he was going in for a lay up, allegedly due to a depression in the asphalt surface, described by plaintiff as 2' to 3' long, 2" to 3" wide, and 1½" to 2" deep. He was participating in a "pick-up" game and was not a member of the Y and had not obtained express permission to play. Although the Y did not prevent persons from playing, there was no evidence of an invitation to the public to use the playground. Held, if the depression were a defect, it was open and obvious, and something the plaintiff could have readily discovered by the exercise of even slight care.

In three cases[96] where plaintiff was engaged in a recreational game of softball, leg injuries were alleged to have been caused by a hole in the playing field. The plaintiff won judgment in the *Tijerina* case, where the game was being played on a church premise. The court remanded for determination of negligence on the part of the owner in the *Garafano* case, but did state that a duty was owed to the plaintiff for a reasonable safe condition of the area. In the third case, the hole really did not play much of a factor in the injury. Several 1984 cases,[97] all in different states, dealt with the condition of ball fields. In the Nebraska situation, plaintiff was member of softball team playing in the league. While running after a pop fly, plaintiff stepped in a hole in the outfield and injured his knee. The court held that the city came under the Recreation Liability Act, and since plaintiff had paid no fee (gratuitous), and there was no willful misconduct on the part of the city, the decision was in favor of the city. The plaintiff was just playing ball in the city park in the Alabama situation, when he stepped in a hole between the left field foul line and a nearby chain link fence, causing him to fall against the fence, cutting himself on the exposed pointed edges on the top of the fence. No fee was paid for use of the field and the court considered plaintiff a licensee to whom the city owed a duty not to willfully

[94] Podvin v. Somerton Springs Swim Club, 406 Pa. 384, 178 A. 2d 516 (1962).

[95] McCurrey v. YMCA, 210 Neb. 278, 313 N.W. 2d 689 (1981).

[96] Garafano v. Neshobe Beach Club, 238 A. 2d 70 (Vt. 1967); Tavernier v. Maes, 242 Cal. App. 2d 532, 51 Cal. Rptr. 575 (1966); Tijerina v. Cornelius Christian Church, 273 Or. 48, 539 P. 2d 634 (1975); see also Luftig v. Steinhorn 21 A.D. 2d 760, 250 N.Y.S. 2d 354 (1964) resort hotel; Praetorius v. Shell Oil Co., 207 So. 2d 872 (La. App. 1968).

[97] Bailey v. City of North Platte, 218 Neb. 810, 359 N.W. 2d 766 (1984); Barker v. Tennis 59th, Inc., 99 A.D. 2d 999, 473 N.Y.S .2d 456 (1984); Edwards v. City of Birmingham, 447 So. 2d 704 (Ala. 1984).

injure him. This case came under the landowner limited liability statute. The 26-year-old policeman playing with his team in city park also did not have a favorable court ruling. As he was rounding third his foot went into a depression (rut), which was not in the diamond the preceding week, injuring himself. The court said that proof of notice was required; that is, that the city knew or should have known of the defect and that it had existed for a reasonable length of time and should have been repaired in that length of time. An opposite result was obtained by the plaintiff in a 1982 New York situation. The college women's softball team was using a makeshift diamond because of the heavy rains. As plaintiff slid into third, she caught her foot in a depression hidden by grass. Plaintiff had no prior knowledge of the depression and she was engaged in a normal activity associated with playing softball.[98]

Extraneous objects in or on a field may be considered a dangerous condition.[99] Most of the cases occur in regard to softball/baseball fields. Plaintiff was injured during physical education class when he tripped on a piece of concrete variously estimated at 12" x 12" to about 30" in diameter, about 8" thick, and imbedded in the ground directly on the base path, protruding ½" to 1" above ground. Danger related to the bases can also occur on the ball field.[100] In a 1983 Illinois case[101] first base was an unsecured rubber mat about 12 inches square and about one-half to three-fourths of an inch thick. Plaintiff alleged that this was an unsafe condition and that a secured canvas bag should have been used. Or, a base may not be set correctly, as was the situation in *Mitchell v. McArthur,* 743 S.W.2d 604 (Mo. App. 1988). Plaintiff fractured her leg when she slid into home plate, which extended 2-3" above the ground. The case focused upon the status of the player (invitee, licensee or trespasser) and the duty owed. (See §2.12).

A high school varsity baseball player was participating in a game. When he was jogging to first base after being walked, he fell and broke his leg. He alleged that the fall was caused by a metal spike which had embedded itself in the ground along the base path and was concealed from view by dirt and chalk used to designate the base line. He sued on negligent maintenance.[102]

Employee brought action against employer for injury sustained when playing softball on field owned and maintained by employer. It was employee's first time on the field; he

[98] Lamphear v. State, 91 A.D. 2d 791, 458 N.Y.S. 2d 71 (1982).

[99] Frieze v. Rosenthal, 148 Misc. 273, 264 N.Y.S. 378 (1933), rev'd. 241 A.D. 719, 269 N.Y.S. 1010 (1934) softball at country hotel, rock protruding from ground along base path third to home plate, no recovery, assumption of obvious risk; Hoepner v. Eau Claire, 264 Wis. 608, 60 N.W. 2d 392 (1953) first game played on a diamond which had just been filled and graded, running from first to second, cleat of shoe caught in imbedded strand of wire, fractured leg, surface previously had been raked, but wire had not been found; Indianapolis v. Baker, 72 Ind. App. 323, 125 N.E. 52 (1919) stone curbing as home base; Schimenti v. Nansen Properties, Inc., 20 A.D. 2d 653, 246 N.Y.S. 2d 273 (1964) metal stake to which first base canvas-covered bag was attached protruding about 2" to 3" above the ground, when slid bag moved so spike uncovered; Smith v. U.S., 337 F. 2d 237 (1964) Pony League, Air Force field, plaintiff crashed into bracket on pipe stub, formerly flag pole, lost eye, around pipe large cement collar like park bench, in warm-up time, owed invitee duty; Weitzen v. Camp Mooween, 163 Misc. 312, 295 N.Y.S. 640 (1937) 15-year-old camper broke leg while sliding into a rock being used for second base, lack of evidence showing that accident could have been avoided by use of a regulation sack.

[100] Ardoin v. Evangeline Parish School Board, 376 So. 2d 372 (La. App. 1979).

[101] Weiss v. Collinsville Comm. Unit School Dist., 74 Ill. Dec. 893, 119 Ill. App. 3d 68, 456 N.E. 2d 614 (1983); under Illinois law, act of teacher must be willful and wanton, and such act was not so held.

[102] Overcash v. Statesville City Board of Education, 83 N.C. App. 21, 348 S.E. 2d 524 (1986) Statute can waive immunity to extent of insurance, however, insurance policy excluded athletic contests, so school retained its immunity, see §4.2.

was fielding balls when he alleged that he hit a "big rock (as big as a football) among other things" and twisted his knee. He claimed the field had rocks and tree stumps and was unlevel with small rocks and stones on it. However, the maintenance supervisor testified that they had cut the grass that morning at a level 2 ½" above the ground with a vacuum mower which also picked up paper, small stones and twigs. Another employee, also playing at time of injury, testified that he had inspected the field and warned plaintiff about the field being "spongy," but did not see any large rocks and thought the field was in good condition. He saw plaintiff's foot go out from under him while chasing a ball.[103]

Plaintiff had gone to the field to practice, but since another team was still using it, he and a teammate warmed up by playing catch outside the first base line. To simulate fly balls, teammate threw ball high, and as plaintiff backpedaled the last few steps to get into position, he tripped over a manhole cover, which was approximately 19' from the field and 9" above ground level. Plaintiff suffered a back injury, including a cracked vertebrae, and was unable to continue his work as a hod carrier. Judgment for plaintiff.[104]

The landing area of a long jump was in issue in a 1985 case. The injured plaintiff was one of 30 students in the seventh grade participating in physical education class. The teacher gave instructions regarding how to run on the runway, jump and land. This was the first exercise of the class period. It was the responsibility of the teacher to check the amount of sawdust in the jump pit. Normally it was filled to the level of the surrounding ground, 12" to 14" deep. To have little or no sawdust in the pit was unusual, but on this day it contained as little as 2" to 3" inches. The teacher remained at the end of the runway, and was not at the pit. The whole class had performed the exercise once and it was on plaintiff's second try that he fractured his left ankle. Plaintiff alleged both inadequacy of supervision and unsafe condition of the long jump pit.[105]

A wet, grassy field was at issue in a 1987 case.[106] The plaintiff's team, a member of the amateur softball adult league, was scheduled to play on a field that had been inundated by water from rain earlier in the day. The team captains and umpires shifted the game to a nearby grassy area, which was wet and slippery, and the grass was 6" to 7" high rather than the usual 1" to 2" on the regular playing field. The plaintiff was allegedly injured when a base runner slipped and, unable to stop, slid into him. Defendants were alleged negligent for failing to cancel game, to provide a proper and safe area to play, and to provide supervision. Held that plaintiff, by electing to play, assumed risk of dangers inherent and that city department of parks and recreation had a duty only to exercise care to make conditions "as safe as they appeared to be." Such duty does not require that

[103] Russell v. Merck & Co., Inc., 211 N.J. Super. 413, 511 A. 2d 1247 (1986) held employee was invitee because was playing for employer's benefit (see Chapter 3 and §25.342), under comparative negligence, employer and employee each held 50% negligent.
[104] City of Bloomington v. Kuruzovich, 517 N.E. 2d 408 (Ind. App. 1987), see also §3.11, city was held liable even though written lease had expired.
[105] McInnis v. Town of Tewksbury, 473 N.E.2d 1160 (Mass. 1985) under the state tort claim act, liability could attach only for unsafe condition; see also

Weinstein v. Tunis Lake Properties, 15 Misc. 2d 432, 181 N.Y.S. 2d 916 (1958), aff'd. without op. 9 A.D. 2d 960, 196 N.Y.S. 2d 605 (1959), app. den. 10 A.D. 2d 711, 199 N.Y.S. 2d 437 (1960).
[106] Perretti v. City of New York, 132 A.D. 2d 537, 517 N.Y.S. 2d 272 (1987); see also Greaves v. Bronx YMCA, 87 A.D. 2d 394, 452 N.Y.S. 2d 27 (1982) summer day camp, playing "ring-o-levio," a roughhouse run-hide-and chase game, on a sloping grassy area wet from people coming out of pool and hosing down, held: defendant 60%, plaintiff 40% negligent.

municipality provide direct supervision or prevent adult plaintiff's use of municipality's land because of existence of readily observable but hazardous condition.

§ 20.2122   Synthetic turf

In *Heldman v. Uniroyal*,[107]a professional tennis player was injured on alleged defective condition of the synthetic surface. The court held in favor of the manufacturer on the basis that the evidence, via photographs taken two days later and of the repairs done at that time, did not show that such condition was the same as at time of injury, and it was a question for the jury as to whether the player had assumed the risk of playing on the court, being aware of the conditions. A second synthetic turf case[108] was brought by a student football player in high school. He alleged that he was required to play on the surface, which was constructed, installed and maintained improperly. The court held that on this count plaintiff had failed to state a cause of action. Another tennis surface action was brought in New York against a private tennis facility when plaintiff was injured allegedly due to a raised seam. The seam was raised $\frac{1}{16}''$ to $\frac{1}{8}''$ above the surface of the court. While the court said that the defendant was under a duty to keep the courts in a reasonably safe condition and not potentially dangerous to its users, the plaintiff failed to establish either that the raised seam was the proximate cause of the injury or that the defendant had either actual or constructive notice of the alleged defect.[109] A miniature golf course covered with outdoor carpet was at issue in *Sanders v. Stutes*, 400 So.2d 1159 (La.App. 1981). Plaintiff was unsuccessful in his allegation that a wet condition following rain constituted unreasonable risk of injury to patrons so as to render proprietors liable on theory of strict liability to customer who suffered a fractured toe allegedly from fall on premises.

A college cheerleader received slightly more than $350,000 in damages when she sustained permanent disability to her elbow, having shattered three bones when she fell onto the astroturf, in *Kirk v. Washington State Univ.*, 109 Wash. 2d 448, 746 P. 2d 285 (1987). Generally the cheerleading squad used the mat room for practices, but were told not to use that room, so began conducting its practices on the astroturf surface at the stadium. While faculty were aware that astroturf was harder and caused more injuries than nonartificial turf, the cheerleaders were given no warning of the dangers of practicing on the astroturf. At the time of injury, the cheerleaders were practicing shoulder stands; in dismounting, instead of properly releasing plaintiff's ankles, the male on whose shoulder's plaintiff was standing held on and she fell backward, landing on the astroturf with her full weight on her elbow. Also at issue were the failure to supervise properly the stunts and the assumption of risk by plaintiff.

See also §21.1 Product liability.

§ 20.2123   Appurtenances

Appurtenances are those structures which are accessory or incidental to the playing

---

[107] Heldman v. Uniroyal, Inc., 53 Ohio App.2d 21, 7 Ohio Op. 3d 20, 371 N.E. 2d 557 (1977).
[108] Thomas v. Chicago Board of Educ., Northport, 60 Ill. App. 3d 729, 17 Ill. Dec. 865, 377 N.E. 2d 55 (1978), rev'd. 32 Ill. Dec. 308, 77 Ill. 2d 165, 395 N.E. 2d 538 (1979).
[109] Katcher v. Ideal Tennis, Inc., 65 A.D. d 751, 409 N.Y.S. 2d 756 (1978).

of the game. Screening for the protection of spectators and bleachers, however, are not included in this section. They are detailed in §§15.111 and 15.13.

In *Cappel v. Board of Educ., Northport*,[110] a five-year-old was injured when he and several other children tried to lift a field hockey goal cage, which was located in the middle of playing fields of a junior high school. It was not anchored to the ground or otherwise secured, and the children previously had tipped it over, making out a case sufficient for the jury for determination of negligence of the school. It was a metal soccer goal which fell and struck student as she knelt to tie her shoe during physical education class. She was fatally injured. Plaintiff brought action on wrongful death, and also sought punitive damages for maintenance of a nuisance. Plaintiff could not recover on nuisance or for punitive damages; defendants were protected by governmental immunity for any negligence as related to the unstable condition of the goal.[111]

Tennis facilities were constructed by the city on school property pursuant to an agreement to provide a joint park-playground. Plaintiff was playing tag at noon with a classmate, who fell down on the tennis court. Attempting to avoid him, plaintiff jumped over him and hit the net post, impaling his arm (97 stitches) on a threaded bolt ½″ diameter which was protruding 2″ to 3″ from the post. The bolt was part of the turnbuckle used to raise and lower the net. The court held that the plaintiff proved that the city built and maintained an inherently dangerous mechanism on the tennis courts, and did not accept the city's allegation of contributory negligence on the part of the plaintiff for an open and obvious hazard. While the city had employed a contractor to install the courts, it could not prove that the condition at that time was different than at the time of injury.[112]

A snowmobiler hit a snow-covered bench along the third base line on a softball diamond. It had been there 11 years, was placed in concrete and had metal pole legs. The school had notice that the field was being used for snowmobiling. Judgment for defendant; plaintiff could not prove that the bench was a "trap" or inherently dangerous instrumentality.[113]

For objects on fields not an inherent part of the sport, such as utility poles and incinerators, see §20.11.

§ 20.213 Playgrounds

Although frequently the question is raised regarding proper surface for under playground equipment, there are few cases related thereto.[114] A 1985 Florida case,[115] seems to summarize the prevalent view in the mid-'80s: "Public safety and welfare demand that a public agency be responsible for meeting its own standards at the very least." This means that the U.S. Consumer Product Safety Commission (CPSC)

110 Cappel v. Board of Educ., Northport, 40 A.D. 2d 848, 337 N.Y.S. 2d 836 (1972).

111 Truelove v. Wilson et al. Dekalb Co. Board of Educ., 159 Ga. App. 906, 285 S.E. 2d 556 (1981).

112 Baytown v. Townsend, 548 S.W. 2d 935 (Tex. Civ. App. 1977).

113 Mattison v. Hudson Falls Central School Dist., 91 A.D. 2d 1133, 458 N.Y.S. 2d 726 (1983).

114 While there do not seem to be many cases, in mid-'80s there was much legal action and out-of-court settlements for injuries on hard surfaces under playground and exercise equipment. The trend in the courts is not established, but insurance settlements seem to be the practice. See also §10.31 Playground equipment.

115 Miami v. Ameller, 447 So. 2d 1014 (Fla. App. 1984), 472 So. 2d 728 (Fla. 1985).

document[116] on standards for playground equipment and other recreation, park, and school literature recommending surfaces with some resilience are the norm. Such was the holding in the Florida case. The court stated additionally, however, that a city is not the insurer of the safety of all who use its free public parks and that injury is not a matter of strict liability. Some of the cases, many before the decade of the '80s, are briefly set forth in subsequent paragraphs.

Maintenance of an asphaltic cement paving under playground apparatus was in issue in a 1987 Illinois case.[117] A six-year-old, attempting to turn around in the middle of a playground slide, fell onto an asphaltic surface, and as a result allegedly sustained a skull fracture. The court held that the asphaltic surface was not so unreasonable as to constitute a dangerous condition, rendering playground owner liable. The risk was obvious — the six-year-old should have known that were she to fall she would stand the risk of injury. In another 1987 Illinois case, *Young v. Chicago Housing Authority*, 162 Ill. App. 3d 53, 113 Ill. Dec. 794, 515 N.E.2d 779 (1987), the court held that allegations that the Authority installed "monkey bars" upon playground's concrete surface and failed to remove that surface and replace it with a softer surface after children had been injured after falling were insufficient to establish willful and wanton misconduct necessary to overcome statutory immunity.

In a camp case the alleged cause of injury was dirt and rock surface beneath a ladder bar.[118] An opposite result to that in camp was held in a 1981 North Dakota case.[119] The school was not found negligent in regard to the surface around the slide. First grader had fallen off the slide and allegedly struck a rock. The surface was earth covered with grass and the rock was somewhat buried (about 4" x 6", flat). The injury appeared to be more from the fall in extending one's arm (broken arm), than in hitting a rock, and the rock was only about 4" to 5" from a plane vertical from the slide, making it difficult to hit in a fall while in descent on the slide portion. Plaintiff alleged that a neighbor was negligent in allowing the ground surface under the monkey bars to become hard packed, rather than providing some cushioning surface for the prevention of injuries. Not so, the court said.[120] In two other monkey bar situations, the surface was in issue. A New York case[121] held that it was a jury question as to whether the school was negligent in placing a set of monkey bars over an artificially hardened, black-top surface; and, in a Florida case[122] the plaintiff was playing on the playground of a private school. Plaintiff contended that the equipment was negligently constructed in that it extended over the trunk of a coconut palm tree. No recovery by plaintiff. A child fell from a climbing device "monkey tree" in a trailer park playground onto hard asphalt paving, injuring

---

[116] U.S. Consumer Safety Product Commission, Washington, D.C. 20207. A Handbook for Public Playground Safety. Vol. I: General Guidelines for New and Existing Playgrounds, Vol. II: Technical Guidelines for Equipment and Surfacing (no date).

[117] Alop v. Edgewood Valley Community Assoc., 154 Ill. App. 3d 482, 107 Ill. Dec. 355, 507 N.E. 2d 19 (1987); see also Reisman v. Los Angeles City School Dist., 123 Cal. App. 2d 493, 267 P. 2d 36 (1954).

[118] Robbins v. Camp Sussex, Inc., 28 Misc. 2d 16, 216 N.Y.S. 2d 176 (1960), aff'd. 218 N.Y.S. 2d 695 (1961).

[119] Besette v. Enderline School Dist. No. 22, 288 N.W. 2d 67 (1980), aff'd. 310 N.W. 2d 759 (N.D. 1981).

[120] Alegre v. Shurkey, 396 So. 2d 247 (Fla. App. 1981).

[121] Hunt v. Board of Education, Schenectady, 43 A.D. 2d 397, 352 N.Y.S. 2d 237 (1974).

[122] Hillman v. Greater Miami Hebrew Academy, 72 So. 2d 668 (Fla. 1954).

nose and face. The court found in favor of plaintiff under Utah law which required motel and trailer parks maintaining playgrounds to take greater care for safety of children, particularly of tender years.[123] In another case[124] a six-year-old child fell from a pepper tree in the playground and landed on an unfilled sandbox. The plaintiff unsuccessfully attempted to recover on an allegation that a sandbox without sand was in defective condition. In a 1987 case[125] the court found the city negligent in failing to rake the sand at the landing area of a slide. From heavy use, feet of youngsters in hitting the bottom had created a pit and the pushed up sand formed a mound. However, the court said that although the city voluntarily undertook to make the area more safe by adding sand and raking daily, that under the Recreational User Statute there was no duty, except for willful and malicious acts, and hence no liability.

Plaintiff was injured on the playground by another student who threw a rock picked up from the playground surface. The court held that the unpaved (dirt) playground was not an unreasonably hazardous condition.[126] (See also §20.233 Weeds, debris, litter.)

There are a number of additional cases[127] which relate to non-supervisory playground situations. See also §10.31 Playground equipment (specific pieces of apparatus), §21.2 Negligence — maintenance and use of equipment, §18.141 supervision on playgrounds, and §19.111 Playground activities.

§ 20.22   Pedestrian ways

The owner/lessor of the premise has a duty to provide safe passageways for the participants, including steps, stairways, entrances, corridors, walkways and paths. Most plaintiffs recover when injury is due to negligent care of pedestrian ways, even in those states which provide for some form of governmental immunity (see §4.2). In most situations, notice of the dangerous condition and the amount of time which has lapsed since notice are important. Immediate repair of such dangerous conditions is essential. However, where the injured is quite familiar with the premises, there may be no recovery or under comparative negligence reduced award. See also pedestrian ways to/from parking areas §22.22, walkways, as related to spectators §15.1323, paths, walks, and trails in natural areas §20.31, swimming pool pedestrian ways §9.7, and Walkways in fitness facilities §17.43.

§ 20.221   Steps and stairways

Suits relating to steps and stairways are of longstanding, as evidenced by the 1897

[123] Hart v. Western Investment & Development Co., 417 F. 2d 1296 (1969).

[124] Holder v. Santa Ana, 205 Cal. App. 2d 194, 22 Cal. Rptr. 707 (1962).

[125] Thies v. City of Omaha, 225 Neb. 817, 408 N.W. 2d 306 (1987).

[126] Hampton v. Orleans Parish School Board, 422 So. 2d 202 (La. App. 1982).

[127] Clayton v. Penn Central Transportation Co., 176 Ind. App. 544, 376 N.E. 2d 524 (1978) train adjacent to playground; Gayden v. George, 513 So. 2d 515 (La. App. 1987) merry-go-round in MacDonal's playground area; Hilgendorf v. First Baptist Church, 157 Ill. App. 3d 428, 109 Ill. Dec. 659, 510 N.E. 2d 527 (1987) slide, day care center playground; Preston v. Pierce Co., 48 Wash. App. 887, 741 P. 2d 71 (1987) merry-go-round in county park; Springer v. St. Bernard Parish School Board, 521 So. 2d 461 (La. App. 1988) jumped over fence to retrieve softball, slipped on wet grass; Town of Big Stone Gap v. Johnson, 184 Va. 375, 35 S.E. 2d 71 (1945) road grader on playground.

O'Rourke case.[128] Plaintiff fell down the steps along the path in Central Park at night in complete darkness. The court held that it was the city's duty to maintain the walks in a reasonably safe condition. Law suits relating to steps and stairways are resultant from primarily five conditions: uneven steps, unprotected stairways/stairwells or defective railings, defective steps, unlighted steps or stairways, and cluttered steps/stairways.

Uneven steps were in issue when a woman touring a garden (park) fell while descending rough hewn stone steps,[129] while in the *Goldstein* case[130] the plaintiff alleged that she did not know the steps were of unequal height. The steps in the *Tarver* case,[131] which were leading to the beach, abutted to and were on the same level as the sidewalk. The next seven steps had a rise of approximately 12″, but then the last step was approximately 28″ to the surface of the beach. It had been the practice to remove the steps at the end of the beach season and put them in storage until the next year, when they were again positioned. The defendant officers and agents had for many years been aware of the changing level and elevation of this portion of the beach caused by the tidal currents, but they failed to adjust the structure. This was held to have continued a sufficiently long time and with actual notice so as to hold the defendant liable; this was a neglect of a ministerial duty. In a somewhat similar case,[132] plaintiff fell as she stepped off the bottom step of stairs leading from pool, alleging water seepage from the pool had caused erosion, making the distance between the bottom step and the ground greater than the distance between the other steps. However, plaintiff was barred from recovery because she was as knowledgable about the alleged defect as the defendant association. The unevenness in the *Weisman* case[133] were wooden steps which slanted from one end to the other and away from the building.

Improperly protected stairways includes both open stairways and steps and those with defective handrails.[134] In *Caesar v. State of Idaho*,[135] the city building code required installation of handrails in stairwells, but it was held that the city ordinance did not apply to state-owned buildings, in this situation, a stadium at the State University. Plaintiff fell while leaving a football game, allegedly on the slippery and dangerous condition of the stadium's concrete steps and passageways.

The preponderance of cases relating to steps and stairways allege defective steps[136]

[128] O'Rourke v. New York, 17 A.D. 349, 45 N.Y.S. 261 (1897).

[129] Lindstrom v. Mason City, 126 N.W. 2d 292 (Iowa 1964).

[130] Goldstein v. United Amusement Corp., 86 N.H. 402, 169 A. 587 (1933).

[131] Tarver v. Savannah Beach, 96 Ga. App. 491, 100 S.E. 2d 616 (1957).

[132] Purvis v. Holiday Hills Property Owners Assoc., 163 Ga. App. 387, 294 S.E. 2d 592 (1982).

[133] Weisman v. Herschend Enterprises, 509 S.W. 2d 32 (Mo. 1974).

[134] Barnett v. Memphis, 196 Tenn. 590, 269 S.W. 2d 906 (1954); Eversole v. Columbus, 79 Ohio L. Abs. 108, 154 N.E. 2d 442 (1958); Goldstein v. United Amusement Corp., 86 N.H. 402, 169 A. 587 (1933); Hovey v. State, 261 A.D. 759, 262 A.D. 791, 27 N.Y.S. 2d 195 (1941), aff'd. 287 N.Y. 663, 39 N.E. 2d 287

(1941); Martin v. Asbury Park, 111 N.J.L. 364, 168 A. 612 (1933); O'Loughlin v. State, 32 Misc. 2d 264, 224 N.Y.S. 2d 354 (1962); Sanders v. Long Beach, 54 Cal. App. 2d 651, 129 P. 2d 511 (1942).

[135] Caesar v. State of Idaho, 101 Idaho 158, 610 P. 2d 517 (1980).

[136] Marcus v. Manhattan Beach Parks Corp., 246 A.D. 331, 284 N.Y.S. 952 (1936) gradual wear and deterioration, constructive notice of condition; O'Loughlin v. State, 32 Misc. 2d 264, 224 N.Y.S. 2d 354 (1962) steps were constructed of ribbed or rough concrete, regularly cleaned and inspected, no evidence of negligent maintenance; Robinson's Tropical Gardens, Inc., v. Sawyer, 105 Ga. App. 468, 125 S.E. 2d 131 (1962) slipperiness due to wax; Slovin v. Gauger, 200 A. 2d 565 (Del. Sup. 1964) steps were of temporary nature and unfastened, amateur theatrical group using the school building, shop teacher made set

including rotten and missing steps[137] and stair treads.[138] In a 1985 case[139] an elderly woman fell and hurt herself on a carpeted step in a restaurant. The court held for the plaintiff, stating that what is reasonable care by the restaurant owner depends upon the circumstances and such risk factors as customer use of premises and characteristics of the patrons. Elderly people comprised a substantial portion of the restaurant's clientele.

Allegations of negligence come from both unlighted and inadequately lighted stairways or steps.[140] The situations encompass a variety of settings,[141] although auditoriums are a common location.

The court held in *McLaughlin v. Home Indemnity Insurance Co.*[142] that the risk created by the defendant's failure to turn lights on during intermission of a concert was unreasonable. Plaintiff attending a rock concert sought to go to the rest room. Proceeding slowly down the aisle, she stepped into something wet and slippery and fell onto the platform, and as she attempted to right herself, she slipped again and injured herself. She was taken to the hospital. Drinks were being consumed in the audience and being spilled on the floor. Employees were assigned to mop up spills reported to them, but no one was assigned to inspect the stairs for spills or debris.

In a 1980 case[143] the plaintiff left the theater during curtain call and slipped on the steps, allegedly because of the semi-darkness, breaking her shoulder. Court said that adherence to the trade standard as conclusive proof of lack of negligence would no

of steps to permit exit through stage door, plaintiff alleged school owed duty of warning that steps might move when weight was placed upon them, held that theatre group was licensee, duty only not to trap into injury through hidden defects, temporary character of step well known to plaintiff.

137 Cedeno v. Lockwood, Inc., 164 Ga. App. 34, 295 S.E. 2d 753 (1982), rev'd. 250 Ga. 799, 301 S.E. 2d 265 (1983); Cheyney v. Los Angeles, 199 Cal. App. 2d 75, 258 P. 2d 1099 (1953); Corso v. Knapp, 347 Ill. App. 556, 107 N.E. 2d 59 (1952); Jopes v. Salt Lake County, 9 Utah 2d 297, 343 P. 2d 728 (1959); Rhoades v. School Dist., 115 Mont. 352, 142 P. 2d 890 (1943); Smith v. Board of Educ., Marietta, 119 Ga. App. 441, 167 S.E. 2d 615 (1969); Weiss v. Milwaukee, 268 Wis. 377, 68 N.W. 2d 13 (1955); Woodward v. Des Moines, 182 Iowa 1102, 165 N.W. 313 (1917).

138 Benton v. YMCA, 27 N.J. 67, 141 A. 2d 298 (1958) repeated complaints about condition of stair pad going from shower to pool, but no corrective action had been taken, this was the only route to pool; Goldstein v. United Amusement Corp., 86 N.H. 402, 169 A. 587 (1933) no treads; Martin v. Asbury Park, 111 N.J.L. 364, 168 A. 612 (1933) should have been nonslip treads, steps were wet, slippery, and slimy, were handrails and a question of structural defect, design and construction was raised.

139 O'Leary v. Jacob Miller Co., 19 Mass. App. 947, 473 N.E. 2d 200 (1985).

140 Burnett v. San Diego, 127 Cal. App. 2d 191, 273 P. 2d 345 (1954); Dively v. Penn-Pittsburgh Corp., 332 Pa. 65, 2 A. 2d 831 (1938); Eversole v. Columbus, 79 Ohio L. Abs. 108, 154 N.E. 2d 442 (1958); Jopes v. Salt Lake Co., 9 Utah 2d 297, 343 P. 2d 728 (1959); Kane v. Board of Educ., 20 N.J. Misc. 7, 23 A. 2d 277 (1941); Kuenzel v. St. Louis, 278 Mo. 277, 212 S.W. 876 (1919); Roberts v. Mayor & Aldermen, City of Savannah, 188 S.E. 39 (Ga. 1936); Sanders v. Long Beach, 54 Cal. App.2d 651, 129 P. 2d 511 (1942); Smith v. Board of Educ., Caney School Dist., 204 Kan. 580, 464 P. 2d 571 (1970); Wukaloff v. Malibou Lake Mountain Club, 214 P. 2d 832 (Cal. 1950).

141 Heiden v. Milwaukee, 226 Wis. 92, 275 N.W. 922 (1937) plaintiff attending festival promoted by city in connection with summer supervised school grounds play program, injured while passing along basement corridor which was in semi-darkness because the lights therein had not been turned on, going to the rest room in building with permission of playground supervisor, fell down flight of four steps which were very close to a turn in the corridor, those in charge of festival were also in charge of lights and had been fully instructed as to their operation, plaintiff recovered; Hovey v. State, 261 A.D. 759, 262 A.D. 791, 27 N.Y.S. 2d 195 (1941), aff'd. 287 N.Y. 663, 39 N.E. 2d 287 (1941) plaintiff fell down unlighted staircase in school, having attended a musical rehearsal, State negligent in failing to provide light and for providing a faulty handrail; Miles v. Ozark Bowl, Inc., 250 S.W. 2d 849 (Mo. App. 1952) bowling, failure to have lights on, plaintiff looking at score board and under score board were a couple of steps.

142 McLaughlin v. Home Indemnity Insur. Co., 361 So. 2d 1227 (La. App. 1978).

143 Upham v. Chateau DeVille Dinner Theatre, Inc., 380 Mass. 350, 403 N.E. 2d 384 (1980).

longer be followed, but that to be considered were the patron's age, the lack of ushers, and the lack of warning to patrons to be careful going to and from their seats. Plaintiff was one of a group of elderly persons attending the dinner theatre and had made arrangements more than five weeks previous.

A state-operated theater was held not to come within the immunity of the State because the protection does not extend to a failure to correct or warn of a known dangerous condition which it (theater) created and which was not readily apparent. Plaintiff fell over a "camouflaged" step which was not visible in the darkened theater. Not only did the theater have notice of prior fall at that point, but also the state safety official who inspected recommended that warning lights be installed.[144]

Clutter on steps also may bring injury to patrons.[145] Clutter may mean an accumulation of a substance which makes steps dangerous. Guest of motel fell on wooden steps and walkway across the dunes to the beach. She alleged sand and water draining from the adjacent shower created a slippery condition. Evidence indicated that the condition had existed for sometime to afford adequate notice to defendants. On the other hand, plaintiff had observed the condition while using the walkway for several days before the incident (a comparative negligence situation).[146]

§ 20.222 Entrances

Cases involving entrances are primarily weather-related,[147] occasioned by rain[148] and ice. In a 1980 Minnesota case,[149] the court held that the municipality was held to the same duty of care required of private enterprise for the maintenance of sidewalks leading to and from the entrances of the arena auditorium complex. Plaintiff fell on a patch of glare ice obscured by a light covering of snow as he stepped from his father's auto onto a semi-circular sidewalk leading to the main entrance of the building. There

[144] Kitchens v. Asold State Theater, 465 So. 2d 557 (Fla. App. 1985).
[145] Beal v. Blumenfeld Theatres, Inc., 177 Cal. App. 2d 192, 2 Cal. Rptr. 110 (1960) usherette violated a rule requiring her to light the way of patrons to their seats in the darkened theatre; Burke v. State Fair of Texas, 93 S.W. 2d 765 (Tex. Civ. App. 1936) stadium, spectator slipped when her foot caught on protruding stick in aisle and rolled down steps colliding with plaintiff, no recovery; DeHeer v. Seattle Post-Intelligencer, 372 P. 2d 193 (Wash. 1962) plaintiff fell on littered steps as she descended flight of stairs on her way out of home show, janitor was in process of sweeping stairs, plaintiff's attention was called to litter by her daughter; Rowell v. Wichita, 162 Kan. 294, 176 P. 2d 590 (1947) stadium owner owes spectator duty to proper care of aisles and walkways and must have sufficient personnel to prevent accumulation of objects causing obstruction and potential injury.
[146] Taylor v. Tolbert Enterprises, Inc., 439 So. 2d 991 (Fla. App. 1983).
[147] Sarno, Gregory G. Liability for Injuries in Connection with Ice or Snow on Nonresidential Premises. 95 A.L.R. 3d 15-164.

[148] Harvey v. Savannah, 199 S.E. 653 (Ga. App. 1938); Gruhalla v. George Moeller Constr. Co., 391 S.W. 2d 585 (Mo. App. 1965) assistant Brownie leader tripped in depressed or recessed area in vestibule of school as entering to conduct meeting, building not quite finished yet and mat had not been put in place, held leader was a licensee, entitled to recover damages; Lappin v. St. Louis National League Baseball Club, 33 S.W. 2d 1025 (Mo. App. 1931) no liability to patron who slipped on steps filled with pools and puddles of water, since so soon after the game was called on account of rain; Wiklund v. Presbyterian, 90 N.J. Super. 335, 217 A. 2d 463 (1966) raining and no mat at the entrance, lobby floor had recently been waxed, church was not liable on basis of charitable immunity (note: few states any longer have charitable immunity).
[149] Bufkin v. City of Duluth, 291 N.W. 2d 225 (Minn. 1980); see also Dillon v. York City School Dist., 442 Pa. 103, 220 A. 2d 896 (1966) school accumulation of ice that had become glazed and ridged on the school steps; Libby v. Perry, 311 A. 2d 527 (Me. 1973) icy entrance to dance, verdict in favor of plaintiff.

was no snowfall immediately before the accident. It was held that it is the responsibility of the maintenance manager to see that the dangerous conditions on the sidewalks are remedied and normal procedure was to inspect the sidewalks prior to an event in the building; however, no one on the maintenance staff could state what the condition was prior to the accident. In another icy steps situation, the plaintiff fell on the stadium stairway, allegedly due to the accumulation of ice and snow. The court held that the efforts to remove ice and snow from the stairway prior to the football game were reasonable, and that the failure to specifically warn spectators was not unreasonable inasmuch as the condition was obvious.[150] A number of cases[151] involving ice have occurred at ski areas, including slipping on ice adjacent to a restaurant while leaving the restroom, a non-skiing visitor walking out the lodge door which led to the slopes, and crossing an icy path at a ski race.

§ 20.223   Walkways

Liability for dangerous conditions in walks is of long standing. In 1915 the Minnesota court held that a city that maintains walks and footpaths in its parks, which are used as thoroughfares in passing from one part of the city to another, is liable for injuries resulting from dangerous conditions (even if parks were held to be a governmental function and immune), if such danger is caused by the negligence of its employees. In this case, the employees had raked together a large quantity of leaves and other rubbish and burned it at the intersection of two or more of these walks. When they quit work, they left the ashes and unburned rubbish on the walk. That evening a child, less than two years of age, with his mother, stumbled and fell into the pile of ashes, burning his right hand so that he was permanently crippled.[152] In a 1988 case, *Brown v. St. Venantius School,* 111 N.J. 325, 544 A.2d 842 (1988), a private school operated by a non-profit religious organization was held liable to a nonbeneficiary pedestrian for injuries caused by the school's failure to remove snow and ice from an abutting sidewalk. The school contended that as a non-commercial landowner it had no duty to maintain the abutting sidewalk; however the court held that the school fell within the category of commercial landowner for purposes of liability for maintenance of abutting sidewalks and that it had a duty to remove snow and ice. The charitable immunity act in New Jersey was not applicable in this situation. (See §4.3 Doctrine of charitable immunity). See also §§21.22 and 21.23 Walkways to/from parking areas and Urban streets and roadways, respectively.

Immediate repair of defects is important. In *Stolpe v. Duquesne,*[153] a woman suffered fractures of both bones of her left leg, shortening the leg by ¾″, when she fell in a hole 3′ in diameter and 4″ to 6″ deep in the walk. The walk was actually a short cut, but was used

---

150 Hartzell v. U.S., 539 F. 2d 65 (1976).

151 Eisenhart v. Loveland Skiing Corp., 33 Colo. App. 120, 517 P. 2d 466 (1973); Jung v. State, 14 A.D. 474, 217 N.Y.S. 2d 405, aff'd. 12 N.Y. 2d 778, 234 N.Y.S. 2d 722 (1961); Sherburne Corp. v. Hoar, 327 F. Supp. 570 (1971), aff'd. 456 F. 2d 1269 (1972) applying Vermont law; Stearns v. Sugarbush Valley Corp., 130

Vt. 472, 296 A. 2d 220 (1972).

152 Ackeret v. City of Minneapolis, 129 Minn. 190, 151 N.W. 976 (1915); see also Birmingham v. Brasher, 359 So. 2d 1153 (Ala. 1978) for holding liability even parks governmental immunity.

153 Stolpe v. Duquesne, 337 Pa. 215, 9 A. 2d 427 (1939).

daily by many people. It had remained unrepaired for about two years. The injured woman, however, had not been through the park in that time and furthermore the defect was covered by snow, hence was not visible. The court held that the city owed a duty to maintain the walk, although a short cut, in a safe condition.

Situations on which suit is brought include sidewalks which are uneven or have cracks,[154] and walkways which have holes in the surface.[155] A teacher had accompanied her first grade on a field trip to the University campus. Carrying an ice chest, which had milk cartons for the children, she suddenly fell forward on the sidewalk. As she lay on the ground, she noticed a portion of the sidewalk had sunken down, gradually slanting to a depth of approximately 2 ½″ in one corner. She assumed that it was on this drop-off that she had tripped. The court held that the defective sidewalk posed an unreasonable risk.[156] A dangerous condition may be a corridor which has an obstruction, such as sawhorse legs of a wooden horse being used to make a temporary aisle,[157] or a pathway to the zoo which had an exposed pipe extended into it.[158] Dangerous conditions may include a slippery grass pathway on an embankment,[159] a gangplank being used as a walkway,[160] or a slippery condition from dampness and fungus on the edge of a terrazzo open-air dance floor.[161] A church member fell on ramp from kitchen to storeroom resulting in serious and permanent injuries. She was helping prepare a meal for a church function, as she had done many times before. She alleged the ramp was dangerously steep and testified she had long been afraid of the ramp. The court found that plaintiff knew the ramp was dangerously steep, she appreciated the risk of falling, and she voluntarily continued to use the ramp; thus, she incurred the risk of her injuries.[162]

Footbridges,[163] too, must be properly maintained. In the *Meyer* case, a college

[154] Barone v. City of San Jose, 79 Cal. App. 3d 284, 144 Cal. Rptr. 836 (1978); Birmingham v. Brasher, 359 So. 2d 1153 (Ala. 1978); Cygielman v. City of New York, 93 Misc. 2d 232, 402 N.Y.S.2d 539 (1978); Dixon v. Mobile, 280 Ala. 419, 194 So. 2d 825 (1967); Errante v. City of New York, 414 N.Y.S. 2d 603 (1979); Goetz v. N.Y.C., 205 Misc. 1001, 131 N.Y.S. 2d 850 (1954); Jones v. Birmingham, 282 Ala. 276, 224 So. 2d 632 (1969); Johnson v. City of Memphis, 699 S.W. 2d 179 (Tenn. App. 1985); Jones v. Deeter, 152 Cal. App. 3d 798, 199 Cal. Rptr. 825 (1984); Larson v. City of Chicago, 142 Ill. App. 3d 81, 96 Ill. Dec. 351, 491 N.E.2d 165 (1986); Miller v. Savannah, 33 Ga. App. 560, 126 S.E. 867 (1925); Olson v. Village of Oak Lawn, 104 Ill. App. 3d 501, 60 Ill. Dec. 221, 432 N.E. 2d 1120 (1982); Selph v. Morristown, 16 N.J. Misc. 19, 195 A. 862 (1938).

[155] Bisbing v. Asbury Park, 80 N.J.L. 416, 78 A. 196 (1910); Columbia v. Wilks, 220 Miss. 260, 166 So. 925 (1936); Fowler v. Board of Regents, Central Missouri State Univ., 637 S.W. 2d 352 (Mo. App. 1982); Gelhot v. Excelsior Springs, 277 S.W. 2d 650 (Mo. App. 1955); Griffin v. Chicago, 317 Ill. App. 368, 45 N.E. 2d 890 (1943); Hill v. Chicago and Chicago Park Dist., 25 Ill. App. 2d 721, 165 N.E. 2d 726 (1960); Laurel v. Hutto, 220 Miss. 253, 70 S. 2d 605 (1954); Loughran v. N.Y.C. 298 N.Y. 320, 83 N.E. 2d 136 (1948); Miller v. Savannah, 33 Ga. App. 560, 126 S.E.

867 (1925); Pensacola v. Stamm, 448 So. 2d 39 (Fla. App. 1984); Rhoades v. Palo Alto, 100 Cal.App.2d 336, 223 P.2d 639 (1950); Walker v. Birmingham, 342 So. 2d 321 (Ala. 1976).

[156] Carter v. Board of Supervisors, L.S.U., 459 So. 2d 1263 (La. App. 1985).

[157] Brown v. Reorganization Inv. Co., 350 Mo. 407, 166 S.W. 2d 476 (1942).

[158] Schenkolewski v. Cleveland Metro Park System, 67 Ohio St. 2d 31, 426 N.E. 2d 784 (1981); see also Bowman v. Richardson, 176 Ga. App. 864, 338 S.E.2d 297 (1985) plaintiff walking down pathway through amusement park slipped and fell on manhole cover made slippery by sprinkler, held plaintiff did not exercise due care for own safety when she had actual knowledge of traversing in an area where there were sprinklers throwing water.

[159] Heidt v. Lauless, 348 S.W. 2d 599 (Mo. App. 1961); see also for slippery surface Harvey v. Savannah, 59 Ga. 12, 199 S.E. 653 (1938).

[160] Hertzog v. Harrison Island Shores, 21 A.D. 2d 859, 251 N.Y.S. 2d 164 (1965).

[161] Country Club of Coral Gables v. McHale, 188 So. 2d 405 (Fla. App. 1966).

[162] St. Mary's Byzantine Church v. Mantich, 505 N.E. 2d 811 (Ind. App. 1987).

[163] Boggs v. Board of Educ., Clay Co., 244 S.E. 2d 799 (W.Va. App. 1978); Fry v. Willamalane Park &

student and his friend were on an unpaved path through the college wooded area and stopped to talk on the footbridge. As plaintiff leaned on the bridge railing, it broke, throwing him into a small creek about 3' below, which had some rocks in it and which caused injury. The plaintiff was well aware of the condition of the bridge. The court held that there was a duty to use reasonable care in maintaining the path and that there should have been an inspection, which would have disclosed the condition of the footbridge. The college had constructive notice of the situation. However, because the student knew of the rotted condition, he was held contributorily negligent, but recovered partial judgment under comparative negligence. The *Rockwell* case had a different basis of negligence. The suspension bridge was on a golf course and had a capacity of 25 people; however, for this golf tournament 80 to 100 people were on this bridge when it collapsed, dropping the plaintiff and other spectators into the river below. The court held for the plaintiffs saying that there were no warning signs regarding the capacity of the bridge and no supervisory personnel to oversee proper use of the bridge.

§ 20.23   General maintenance

General maintenance includes a great variety of situations which can bring liability. These are represented by cases regarding fences, walls, railings, gates and screenings; weeds, debris, and litter; general building maintenance; holes, depressions, and obstacles; incinerators and ash piles; trees; supplies/equipment used in maintenance; electrical hazards; and general outdoor maintenance — those areas not included in other subsections of §20.2 Condition of the premises. Bleachers and spectator accommodations are included in §15.131 and general maintenance of spectator facilities in §15.132.

There is a responsibility to have a maintenance program with an inspection system to identify both foreseeable hazards and those presently existing (see §24.4). On existing hazards, whether the plaintiff recovers is primarily determined by whether or not the park superintendent or person responsible for maintenance had actual or constructive notice and the length of time of such notice (see introduction §20.2). The court in a 1984 case[164] stated that the duty imposed upon a city is to use reasonable care under the circumstances. See also *Short v. Griffitts'* case in §20.233 in which the court set out the duty to have procedures for maintenance, including inspection. Cases in subsequent subsections give some indication of what the courts deem reasonable care for given circumstances.

§ 20.231   Fences, walls, railings, gates, screening

This subsection includes only maintenance of structures, such as fences, gates,

Rec. Dist., 481 P. 2d 648 (Ore. App. 1971); Lowe v. Gastonia, 211 N.C. 564, 191 S.E. 7 (1937); Meyer v. New York, 92 Misc. 2d 996, 403 N.Y.S. 2d 420 (1978); Rockwell v. Hillcrest Country Club, 25 Mich. App. 276, 181 N.W. 2d 290 (1970).

164 Benjamin v. City of New York, 99 A.D. 2d 995, 473 N.Y.S. 2d 450 (1984) city maintained vacant lot which youngsters used for recreation, sign was posted on a tree "the Future Home of a Park for the Community Children," children were playing softball when 14-year-old took can of inflammable substance from nearby van and poured its contents into pipe which protruded from the ground, there was an explosion and the burning liquid was sprayed over the infant plaintiffs, city was not held liable in that the elements of negligence were not proven.

railings, etc., and does not include whether barriers should be erected to protect against natural conditions perceived to be a hazard. See §20.331. Also, see §15.11 and 15.132 for fences and screening related to spectators, and §9.73 for fencing and gates at pools.

Fences are used as a protective structure for many different situations.[165] In most cases it is the same allegation — if it were not for the hole in the fence, the defective support post, the fence being down, et al., all conditions obvious to any maintenance inspection, the injury would not have occurred. For example, in *Zaepfel v. Yonkers*,[166] a nine-year-old caught his leg on a bent rusty pole which supported a portion of a fence while sledding on the school grounds. The fence had been used to contain football game spectators and normally would have been dismantled by the maintenance crew after Thanksgiving Day, but the fence had been left standing. The condition of the fence existed 30 days prior to the accident, no sign had been posted, and the school authorities had not affirmatively attempted to dissuade children from using the slope in favor of a safer one. In a similar situation, an eight-year-old girl sustained injury when she was seated in the front of the sled as she and her sister (10 years old) went down a sledding slope owned and maintained by the park district. They angled (45°) across the hill, rather than a straight descent, and hit a snow fence at the point of one of the metal support poles. The fence was erected to help control sleds going toward the woods. Under circumstances existing, plaintiff did not recover.[167]

Frequently fencing is used around playgrounds to protect youngsters from adjacent roads or railroad tracks.[168] In the *Ballard* case a kindergarten child wandered through a gap in the fence and was killed by a truck; and, in the *Lukasiewicz* case, a ten-year-old crawled through holes in the playground fence and was injured by a moving boxcar on the railroad tracks. There were paths that led to the opening and were utilized by children on the playground. Three mid-1980s cases concerned with playgrounds and railroad tracks should be compared, as each is from a different state. In *LaSalle National Bank v. City of Chicago*, 132 Ill. App. 3d 607, 88 Ill. Dec. 102, 478 N.E.2d 417 (1985), where a child was injured while attempting to jump onto a moving freight train after climbing through hole in city's fence, the court held the city liable for having "created" or contributed to a hazardous condition even though it did not own the property on which the child was injured; the city had a duty to exercise ordinary care to guard against foreseeable injuries. The holding was for the defendant, but the rationale or basis was the same in *Abdur-Rashid v. Consolidated Rail Corp.*, 135 A.D.2d 208, 524 N.Y.S. 2d 716 (1988). A child was injured on tracks nearby the playground, and the court said also that the owner of the playground owed a duty of care against foreseeable danger to all users of playground. However, the Housing Authority had erected a 6' fence to protect, and the court stated that there was no duty to the child once he had left

[165] Brown v. Scranton, 313 Pa. 230, 169 A. 435 (1933); Schneider v. Seattle, 24 Wash. App. 251, 600 P. 2d 666 (1979) park under construction surrounded by cyclone fence and Keep Out signs; Shields v. School Dist., 408 Pa. 388, 184 A. 2d 240 (1962).

[166] Zaepfel v. Yonkers, 56 A.D. 2d 867, 392 N.Y. S.2d 336 (1977).

[167] Friedman v. Park District of Highland Park, 151 Ill. App. 3d 374, 104 Ill. Dec. 329, 502 N.E. 2d 826

(1986) lengthy opinion discusses issues of witnesses, jury, appeal and error, as well as negligence, especially maintenance procedures.

[168] Ballard v. Polly, 387 F. Supp. 895 (1975); Leone v. City of Utica, 66 A.D. 2d 463, 414 N.Y.S. 2d 412 (1979), aff'd. 49 N.Y. 2d 811, 426 N.Y.S. 2d 980, 403 N.E. 2d 964 (1979); Lukasiewicz v. City of Buffalo, 55 A.D. 2d 848, 390 N.Y.S. 2d 341 (1976).

the playground "jurisdiction", absent showing of any defect or condition in playground that might invite children playing in playground to enter tracks from playground or to use railroad yard as an extension of their play area. In the third case, *Lynch v. National Railroad Passenger Corp.*, 540 A.2d 635 (Pa. Cmwlth 1988), a child fell while crossing the tracks and a train ran over his legs, severely injuring him. The child had gone to the city-owned pool in the playground, but found it closed, whereupon he went through a hole in the city-owned fence separating the playground and the railroad tracks, intending to go to a vacant lot, also owned by the city, located on the other side of the tracks. There was a clubhouse on the vacant lot where the child and his friend frequently played. The city also had a fence separating the vacant lot from the tracks through which there also was an opening. The court in Pennsylvania held opposite of the courts in Illinois and New York, saying that the city owes a duty only to those who are on city property, notwithstanding that the tracks were between two pieces of city property. The court cited its earlier holding, *Kearns v. Rollins Outdoor Advertising, Inc.*, 492 A.2d 1204 (Pa. Cmwlth 1985), in which it stated that the city had no duty as adjacent landowner to erect fence to deter persons on playground from entering adjacent property owned by transportation authority or rail corporation. In the *Kearns* situation, a 14-year-old boy drank several cans of beer in a cemetery, then crossed the baseball field of a city playground, passed through a hole in the chain link fence around the playground, and proceeded to a billboard. He climbed the billboard, fell, and was injured. The court said, further, that one who has suffered injuries as result of encountering hazardous artificial condition on another's land cannot recover damages from owner of land over which he passed to reach land on which dangerous condition existed. An unrepaired hole in a playground fence also was in issue in *Kavanaugh v. Orleans Parish School Board*, 487 So. 2d 533 (La. App. 1986). A teacher brought action against the school to recover value of property taken from her in armed robbery on school premises. The court held that the school board did not breach its statutory duty to provide a reasonably safe environment for its employees in that the board could not reasonably foresee that the unrepaired hole in the fence, through which the robbers obtained entry, would lead to armed robbery of teacher. (See also §20.3312 Fencing). Not only a fence but also a gate may be in issue.[169] However, in the *Bartell* case, where injury was caused by skateboarding, the court held that the fact that the fence and gate were in disrepair and unlocked did not create a dangerous condition as to the injury itself.

Failure to take care of old tennis court fencing was at issue in *Caltavuturo v. Passaic*.[170] Plaintiff cut his knee on a jagged, rough-edged portion of the fence as he attempted to go through a 6' by 8' hole in the chain-link fence, which enclosed the playground on one side and formerly was used for tennis. The fence was mounted on a concrete base which varied in height from a few inches to over 2'. At the point where plaintiff was injured, there was a 2' drop from the sidewalk to the concrete yard below,

169 Bartell v. Palos Verdes Peninsula School Dist., 83 Cal. App. 3d 492, 147 Cal. Rptr. 898 (1978); Boyce v. Pi Kappa Alpha Holding Co., 476 F. 2d 447 (1973); Guilmartin v. Philadelphia, 201 Pa. 518, 51 A. 312 (1902); Luna v. Needles Elementary School Dist., 154 Cal. App. 2d 803, 316 P. 2d 773 (1957).

170 Caltavuturo v. City of Passaic, 124 N.J. Super. 361, 307 A. 2d 114 (1973); see also Moloney v. Columbus, 2 Ohio St. 213, 31 Ohio Op. 2d 447, 208 N.E. 2d 141 (1965).

where they had played tennis. Painted lines remained, but apparently the court had not been used for 12 years and the net posts had been removed and the holes filled in. The street foreman of the city testified that although the maintenance crew "constantly" repaired the fence, new holes cut by children using pliers would almost immediately appear. The court held that reasonable precautions must be taken for the safety of the children; and, negligence is related to awareness of recognizable risk of harm and duty may be violated not only by commission of acts but also in neglect or failure to act.

Contrary to the holdings of many of the cases in this section, a 1985 New York case[171] held for the defendant. Plaintiff was a trespasser, who sued the pool owner and lessee school, when he became a quadriplegic due to a miscalculated dive. Plaintiff, 20 years old, had gained access to the pool about 11 p.m. through a hole in the fence surrounding the pool. The plaintiff dived from the lifeguard chair platform, but when he tried a dive with entry more perpendicular to the water, his head struck the bottom with the resultant injury. The court held that the hole in the fence and failure to repair it was not paramount to liability, but rather the sole cause of injury was the trespasser's miscalculated dive and that liability should not attach to a landowner merely because a resourceful and determined trespasser was able to find a way to gain entry.

Allegations of improper maintenance can come also on indoor facilities.[172] In the *Woodring* case, the nut and bolt which secured a railing in the gymnasium were not in place and the railing gave way when plaintiff was doing somersaults thereon. The defendant had no program of preventive maintenance or inspection. Further, the construction of the railings and posts were not in accord with proper construction practice. In the other case involving an indoor tennis facility, plaintiff was injured when he ran to the rear wall to hit a ball and as he planted his foot on the overlap of a heavy plastic curtain which hung against the court's rear wall, he slipped. In addition, there was a cement footing about 3' high, which extended out from the wall about 6".

Other situations include railings,[173] broken concrete structures,[174] and gates.[175]

§ 20.232 Building maintenance

For indoor surfaces, see §20.211, for pedestrian ways, including steps/stairways and entrances §§20.221 and 20.222, for safety glass §20.11, and for maintenance relating to cultural arts facilities §11.1.

The situations which give rise to lawsuits are, indeed, varied. They include defective gas heaters,[176] hot water faucet which malfunctioned and scalded the plaintiff,[177] colliding with a support column in an exhibit room allegedly because of inadequate

[171] Boltrax v. Joy Day Camp, 113 A.D. 2d 859, 493 N.Y.S. 2d 590 (1985), aff'd. 67 N.Y. 2d 617, 489 N.Y.S. 2d 660, 490 N.E. 2d 527 (1986).

[172] Woodring v. Board of Educ., Manhasset Union Free School Dist., 79 A.D. 2d 1022, 435 N.Y.S. 2d 52 (1981); Yammerino v. Cranston Tennis Club, 416 A. 2d 698 (R.I. 1980).

[173] Howard v. Chisholm, 191 Minn. 245, 253 N.W. 766 (1934); Levine v. N.Y.C., 2 N.Y.S. 2d 246, 140 N.E. 2d 275 (1957); Schofield v. Wood, 170 Mass. 415, 49 N.E. 636 (1898).

[174] Bonczek v. Philadelphia, 338 Pa. 484, 13 A. 2d 414 (1940); Hensley v. Gowrie, 203 Iowa 388, 212 N.W. 714 (1927).

[175] Rosenberger v. Central Louisiana Dist. Livestock Show, 312 So. 2d 300 (La. 1975).

[176] Gorsuch v. Springfield, 43 Ohio L. Abs. 83, 61 N.E.2d 898 (1945); Ramirez v. Ogden, 3 Utah. 2d 102, 279 P. 2d 463 (1955).

[177] Cohen v. Bradley Beach, 135 N.J.L. 276, 50 A. 2d 882 (1947).

lighting,[178] metal bar projecting from ceiling,[179] defective metal plate and improper lighting at exit,[180] stubbing a toe on the hearth of fireplace while being seated at a table and falling and breaking a wrist,[181] and catching foot at base of coat rack on church premises and falling.[182] Failure to provide appropriate window screening and a window guard were alleged to be the cause of injury in two cases.[183] In one instance the ping pong table had been placed quite close to the window which was unguarded and when a waiting player was pushed by an active player, his left foot went through the French window pane. Situations also include a movie screen falling on plaintiff,[184] and having fingers cut due to the blades of a ventilating fan being unguarded.[185]

Some cases have been brought by the plaintiff on allegations regarding doors, such as when a door stuck and the plaintiff kicked it to open it,[186] a door-closer came loose from the wall of gymnasium and struck the student,[187] and a piece of rusty tin sticking out of the edge of the door injured plaintiff.[188] Plaintiff was in the school's locker room for a school-sponsored athletic event, and was provoked and antagonized by another student, who closed a door on plaintiff's hand, resulting in the "traumatic amputation" of the small finger. In addition to failure to supervise, plaintiff alleged that school violated statute to maintain property in reasonably safe condition by not having a spring-loaded or pneumatic device to retard closing of door. Held: no violation of statute.[189] And, a baseball spectator recovered damages when a concession stand door came loose from hook and struck him. Even though plaintiff did not establish owner had either actual or constructive notice of defect in hook, owner had exclusive control over concession stand door at time of accident and *res ipsa loquitur* was applied.[190] In another situation, a six-year-old boy was swinging on the iron pipe holding up an awning just being installed and it came down, causing the boy to hit the plaintiff.[191] And, at a ski lodge, a stone ledge fell from the building, striking the plaintiff.[192]

In a resident camp setting, other situations included a crack in the duckboard on the floor at the dish drying area in the kitchen,[193] and a trapdoor in the caretaker's

[178] Berry v. City of Monroe, 439 So. 2d. 465 (La. App. 1983).

[179] Congleton v. Starlite Skate Center, 175 Ga. App. 438, 333 S.E. 2d 677 (1985).

[180] Wagner v. Thomas J. Obert Enterprises, 384 N.W. 2d 477 (Minn. App. 1986).

[181] Manor Country Club v. Richardson, 253 Md. 319, 252 A. 2d 847 (1969).

[182] Stapleman v. St. Joseph the Worker, 295 Minn. 406, 205 N.W. 2d 677 (1973).

[183] Wildman v. New York City, 254 A.D 591, 3 N.Y.S. 2d 37 (1938); Wysocki v. Derby, 140 Conn. 173, 98 A. 2d 659 (1953).

[184] Mason v. Southern New England Conf. Ass'n. of Seventh-Day Adventists, Town of So. Lancaster, 696 F. 2d 135 (1982).

[185] Noble v. Park Enterprise, 313 Mass. 454, 47 N.E. 2d 947 (1943).

[186] Obshatcko v. YM & YWHA of Williamsburg, 45 A.D. 2d 1023, 358 N.Y.S. 2d 43 (1974); see also

Whitney v. City of Worcester, 373 Mass. 208, 366 N.E. 2d 1210 (1977) defective door.

[187] Chavez v. Mountainaire School Board, 80 N.M. 450, 457 P. 2d 382 (1969).

[188] Phillips v. Quapan Bath House Co., 206 Ark. 816, 170 S.W. 2d 1001 (1943).

[189] Holsapple v. Casey Community Unit School Dist., 157 Ill. App. 3d 391, 109 Ill. Dec. 631, 510 N.E. 2d 499 (1987).

[190] Higgins v. White Sox Baseball Club, 787 F. 2d 1125 (1986) Illinois law applied; see also §§2.242 res ipsa loquitur and §2.244, doctrine of exclusive control.

[191] Childress v. Martens, 444 S.W. 2d 362 (Tex. Civ. App., 1969).

[192] Refson v. State, 52 Misc. 2d 498, 276 N.Y.S. 2d 176 (1966).

[193] Bernal v. Baptist Fresh Air Home Soc., 275 A.D. 88, 87 N.Y.S. 2d 458 (1949), aff'd. 300 N.Y. 484, 88 N.E. 2d 720 (1949).

cottage.[194] Plaintiff was injured when he fell through a hole in the restroom. The restroom light switch did not work, so he could not see the hole.[195]

Lockers in the dressing room were the subject of five cases.[196] In three instances the locker was insecurely fastened and it toppled over causing injury, and in another the locker at the bottom was sharp and jagged. General inspection should have given notice of both defects. In the fifth, the lockers were taken outdoors to be cleaned and one toppled over on a five-year-old boy causing his death.

A student playing a game of field dodgeball in the gymnasium slipped on the floor, fell, and struck the corner of a brick pilaster which projected from the wall of the building. Corner boards had originally been installed to guard this pilaster, but they had become loose at the corner in question and had drawn away, leaving the brick corner exposed and unguarded. Judgment for plaintiff.[197] And, in a 1987 case,[198] plaintiff was injured during supervised activity in the gymnasium when he fell against the unprotected concrete riser located in the front row of the bleachers.

In an early bowling case,[199] plaintiff sustained injuries when he slipped and fell on the alley, catching his foot in a 2″ space between the floor and the bottom of the return trough of the bowling alley structure. The court held for the defendant, saying that the proprietor is not an insurer of safety and mere fact that such accident happened does not prove the place was not safe. Plaintiff did not prove that this space made the place a dangerous one.

§ 20.233 Weeds, debris, and litter

The essence of the cases concerned with weeds, debris, and litter is contained in the plaintiff's allegation in *Short v. Griffitts*,[200] a situation in which plaintiff, while running laps around the high school outdoor track, fell on broken glass and was injured. The question of fact was whether the defendants (school board, athletic director, buildings and grounds supervisor, who also was the baseball coach) had a duty to establish procedures for the maintenance of the track and to supervise and instruct the custodial staff of the school to insure that the premises were maintained in a safe condition. This included inspection of the facilities to discover dangerous conditions. The answer is "yes"; there is a duty to have a maintenance program with an inspection system. Where

[194] Artz v. Todd, 191 Misc. 497, 77 N.Y.S. 2d 836 (1948).

[195] Pickard v. Honolulu, 51 Hawaii 134, 452 P. 2d 445 (1969).

[196] Freund v. Oakland Board of Educ., 28 Cal. App. 2d 246, 82 P. 2d 197 (1938); Gensch v. Milwaukee, 179 Wis. 95, 190 N.W. 843 (1922); Hannon v. Waterbury, 106 Conn. 13, 136 A. 876 (1927); Light v. Ohio University, 28 Ohio St. 3d 66, 502 N.E. 2d 611 (1986); Powell v. Garden Court Corp., 146 Pa. Super. 372, 22 A. 2d 605 (1941); see §9.6 for further cases regarding lockers and shower rooms.

[197] Bradley v. Board of Educ., Oneonta, 243 A.D.

651, 276 N.Y. 622 (1935), 247 A.D. 833, 286 N.Y.S. 186 (1936), aff'd. 274 N.Y. 473, 8 N.E. 2d 610 (1937).

[198] Prest v. Sparta Comm. Unit School Dist., 157 Ill. App. 3d 569, 109 Ill. Dec. 727, 510 N.E. 2d 595 (1987) held that Illinois law, vesting teachers with some immunity for disciplinary and supervision, did not apply to premises, remanded for determination of negligence.

[199] Sykes v. Bensinger Recreation Corp., 117 F. 2d 964 (1941) applied Wisconsin safe-place statute.

[200] Short v. Griffitts, 220 Va. 53, 255 S.E. 2d 479 (1979).

tall grass and weeds cover hazardous debris of whatever nature, there usually is liability. Other glass debris situations include a child who was playing behind the backstop of a municipally owned baseball field when he fell and injured his eye on glass debris.[201] And another young child also was injured on broken glass when he was playing in a broad-jumping pit on the school grounds during a baseball game (the pit was of such nature as a child might find it to be as a sand box).[202]

A 1985 case[203] also was a situation of debris covering a hazard near an athletic field. Three youths were watching the high school football team practice and when the practice was over they began playing tag along the perimeter of the field. As the injured, a six-year-old, chased his companions, he ran through an area of uncut grass near one of the light poles which illuminates the football field, and punctured his ankle bone on a section of chain link fence which was hidden by the tall grass. Although treated immediately in the hospital emergency room, he did develop a severe bacterial infection of the ankle joint and bone, and then a blood infection; he also suffered damage to the ankle's hyaline cartilage and perhaps also to the growth plate. The court held that the recreational user statute did not apply to this type of situation and that the school was negligent in maintaining an unsafe premise. The evidence was quite clear that the maintenance staff knew of the fallen fence and purposely avoided its repair or removal and allowed the grass to cover it; the school authorities had a responsibility to inspect and should have found the fence. It was reasonable to assume that a youngster might be hurt on the fence so hidden. The child was not held guilty of contributory negligence.

When a ten-year-old stepped off of the hard surface under a swing in roughhousing with another boy, on a playground near the pool to which he had come to swim and was just taking a break, he severely cut his foot on a piece of broken beer bottle. This accident occurred mid-afternoon and the condition of the broken beer bottles existed during the morning when city inspections were being made; during the day at least 12 city employees were present at the location. Held that the city had constructive notice and had a duty to make the premises safe.[204] The Arizona court also held that broken glass in a recreational area maintained by a municipal corporation was an unreasonably dangerous condition for which it had a duty. A seven-year-old boy was knocked down from behind by a couple of boys near the neighborhood recreation center, and suffered severe cuts, including nerves and tendons from broken glass to his hand. A recreation official testified that before the accident he "always" saw broken glass on the ground; this was sufficient to find that the city had actual notice of the broken glass.[205]

The court also found that defendants had notice when plaintiff stepped upon the edge of a tin can concealed in the grass about 40' south of the swimming pool; the operator knew of the patrons' habit of throwing bottles, opened tin cans and other dangerous objects into this grassy area and the grass had been permitted to grow to a height of 6" to 8".[206]

---

[201] Williams v. Town of Phillipsburg, 171 N.J. Super. 278, 408 A. 827 (1979).

[202] Brown v. Oakland, 51 Cal. App.2d 150, 124 P. 2d 369 (1942).

[203] Fusilier v. Northbrook Excess & Surplus Ins. Co., 471 So. 2d 761 (La. App. 1985), writ denied 472 So. 2d 918 (1985).

[204] Catalano v. Kansas City, 475 S.W. 2d 426 (K.C. Ct. App. 1971).

[205] Parness v. Tempe, 123 Ariz. 460, 600 P. 2d 764 (1979).

[206] Lamb v. Redemptorist Fathers of Georgia, 111 Ga. App. 491, 142 S.E. 2d 278 (1965).

A 14-year-old was injured when, wearing rubber beach sandals, she stepped on a portion of a broken-glass olive jar or bottle which was lying on a well-lighted wide concrete walkway in the amusement park. The court said that the duty is not greater than that of a storekeeper to his customers, that is, to keep passageways in a reasonably safe condition. It was further stated that the foreign substance must have been placed or left in position to cause the accident or, if placed by someone else, then there must be knowledge of it and sufficient time for removal. It is presumed that a picnicker had brought the olives for consumption on the picnic grounds nearby and dropped or threw the glass container on the walkway. All employees are directed to pick up any debris or trash and seven persons are employed to patrol for such and promptly remove, making rounds about every 25 minutes. Hence, no evidence was shown that the defendant was negligent.[207] In a Virginia case,[208] plaintiff unsuccessfully alleged that presence of trash and debris in the park was a nuisance.

A musician was injured when he fell over boulders and debris as he was approaching the bandstand where the concert was to be given. Held that there was no immunity and returned for determination of negligence.[209] A spectator following a golf tournament tripped on a rock concealed by tall grass and was injured. Judgment for defendant on the basis of insufficient evidence to show negligence of the defendant. Plaintiff has the burden of showing that she had been subjected by golf operator to some danger not reasonably incident to the game and that the operator knew of such danger, or should have known of it in the exercise of ordinary care.[210]

Weeds also concealed a danger in *Sears v. City of Springhill*.[211] Plaintiff was playing touch football on the playground and in the course of the game was running at full speed in an attempt to touch an opposing intended receiver, was unable to stop, and continued at the end of the playground into the weeds and grass, falling into a ditch, breaking both bones of his right leg below the knee. The open ditch, which was located at the end of the playground where the children were encouraged to play, was varied 5' to 10' in depth and totally concealed by the overgrowth. There were no barricades, warnings or other protective measures. Held that the school should have been aware of the danger.

A "city dweller" who rented a trailer space on the lakeshore brought suit against the owner and operator of the campsite for failure to warn of the existence of posion ivy, poison oak or other noxious weeds on the premises. In holding for the defendant, the court said that the owners of camping areas are not obligated to maintain their campsites in the same manner as a municipal park system is maintained and that a city dweller who rents a trailer space on a lake front assumes the risks of natural hazards of the outdoors, such as poison ivy.[212]

Mounds of weed-covered dirt and patches of tall weeds and brush on an unfenced, unimproved urban parcel adjacent to a park was alleged to pose risk of death or serious

[207] Simon v. Playland Amusements, Inc., 160 So. 2d 834 (La. App. 1964), writ refused 245 La. 1087, 162 So. 2d 576 (1964).

[208] Newport News v. Hertzler, 216 Va. 587, 221 S.E. 2d 146 (1976).

[209] Villanova v. American Federation of Musicians (and Essex Co. Park Comm.), 123 N.J. Super. 57, 301 A. 2d 467 (1973).

[210] Thompson v. Sunset Country Club, 227 S.W. 2d 523 (Mo. App. 1950).

[211] Sears v. City of Springhill, 303 So. 2d 602 (La. App. 1974), writ refused 307 So. 2d 371.

[212] Hersch v. Anderson Acres, Inc., 5 Ohio Ops. 2d 432, 146 N.E. 2d 648 (1957).

harm to child trespasser. Park users often wandered onto defendant's property. In this situation a ten-year-old girl was attacked, stabbed, and murdered by a third party and her body found on this parcel of land. The court did not sustain the allegation.[213]

A number of water-related cases involve debris, litter, and weeds (see §§9.71, 14.33, and 14.422). Also, litter on stairways at baseball games has been subject of lawsuits (see §15.13). Other cases which allege debris as a factor in the injury to plaintiff are cited in the footnote.[214]

§ 20.234   Holes, depressions, and surface obstructions

Most of the situations involving holes and depressions and obstructions concern playing fields (see §20.2121). Holes and depressions overgrown with weeds, but in which there are hazardous objects, such as glass and rusty fencing, also give rise to liability (see preceding section §20.233). Holes may be caused by construction work or settling of dirt around a pipe or structure.[215] Manhole covers, meter boxes, water pipe holes and sprinkler heads are also apt to cause a person to stumble and be injured.[216] Open ditches or trenches and other holes give rise to law suits when an individual is injured.[217]

Small surface obstructions protruding from the ground can give injury when a person stumbles thereon.[218] Several cases[219] involved wires or cables as the obstruction. In Pennsylvania a ten-year-old plaintiff and friends were riding their bicycles on the tennis courts, which were on the playground, when plaintiff struck a wire supporting the

[213] Thomason v. Olive Branch Masonic Temple, 156 Mich. App. 736, 401 N.W. 2d 911 (1986).

[214] Amato v. Lynbrook, 193 N.Y.S. 2d 444 (1959); Benton v. Santa Monica, 106 Cal. App. 339, 289 P. 203 (1930); Havre de Grace v. Maxa, 177 Md. 168, 9 A. 2d 235 (1939); Hedman v. City of Rochester, 64 A.D.2d 817, 407 N.Y.S.2d 300 (1978) mem. dec. aff'd. 47 N.Y. 2d 933, 419 N.Y.S.2d 969, 393 N.E.2d 1041 (1979); MacGillicuddy v. New York City, 255 A.D. 793, 7 N.Y.S. 2d 71 (1938).

[215] Aurutick v. U.S., 164 F. Supp. 585 (1958); Bisbing v. Asbury Park, 80 N.J.L. 416, 78 A. 196 (1910); Cupita v. Carmel Country Club, 252 N.C. 346, 113 S.E. 2d 712 (1960); Johnson v. Tennessean Newspaper, Inc., 192 Tenn. 287, 241 S.W. 2d 399 (1951); Sayers v. School Dist., 366 Mich. 217, 114 N.W. 2d 191 (1962); Terre Haute v. Webster, 112 Ind. App. 101, 40 N.E. 2d 972 (1942).

[216] Autrey v. Augusta, 33 Ga. App. 757, 127 S.E. 796 (1925); Cleveland v. Pine, 123 Ohio St. 578, 176 N.E. 229 (1931); Cothern v. La Rocca, 255 La. 673, 232 So. 2d 473 (1970); Dramstadt v. West Palm Beach, 81 So. 2d 484 (Fla. 1955); Edmonston v. Kansas City, 227 Mo. App. 817, S.W. 2d 690 (1933); Floyes v. Monroe, 194 So. 102 (La. App. 1939); Glase v. Philadelphia, 169 Pa. 488, 32 A. 600 (1895); Holytz v. Milwaukee, 17 Wis. 2d 26, 115 N.W. 2d 618 (1962); McKinnon v. Wash. Fed. Savings & Loan Assoc., 68 Wash. 2d 644, 414 P. 2d 773 (1966); Musetto v. Miami Beach, 82 So. 2d 595 (Fla. 1955); Stubbs v. Macon, 78 Ga. 237, 50 S.E. 2d 866 (1948).

[217] Brown v. Oakland, 51 Cal. App. 2d 150, 124 P. 2d 369 (1942); Doria v. Mamaroneck, 210 N.Y.S. 2d 897 (1961); Goodson v. Racine, 61 Wis. 2d 554, 213 N.W. 2d 16 (1973); Hale v. City of Santa Paula, 159 Cal. App. 3d 1233, 206 Cal. Rptr. 265 (1984); Landry v. State of Louisiana, 466 So. 2d 758 (La. App. 1985), writ cert. granted 468 So. 2d 567 (1985), rev'd/ remanded 477 So. 2d 672 (1985), rev'd./rendered 483 So. 2d 162 (La. App. 1986), rev'd./trial ct. J reinstated 495 So. 2d 1284 (1986); Matuson v. Camp Orinsekwa, 155 Misc. 452, 280 N.Y.S. 626 (1935); Moss v. Dept of Nat. Res., 62 Ohio St. 2d 138, 16 Ohio Op. 3d 161, 404 N.E. 2d 742 (1980); Saul v. Roman Catholic Church, 75 N.M. 160, 402 P. 2d 48 (1965).

[218] Clark v. Pierce & Norton Co., 131 Conn. 499, 40 A. 2d 752 (1945); Douglas v. Lang, 124 S.W. 2d 642 (Mo. App. 1939).

[219] Bush v. Village of Saugerties, 114 A.D. 2d 176, 498 N.Y.S. 2d 563 (1986) the Village and Town, not having placed any restrictions on bicycle riding were not immuned under the statute from rendering ordinary care; McNeil v. Philadelphia, 522 A. 2d 174 (Pa. Cmwlth. 1987) at issue was whether the tennis net was realty within Tort Claims Act, and if so, defendant was not protected by the immunity provided by the Act; Estate of Thomas v. Consumer Power Co., 58 Mich. App. 486, 228 N.W. 2d 786 (1975) aff'd./rev'd. in part 394 Mich. 459, 231 N.W. 2d 653 (1975).

tennis net, causing serious injury. Plaintiff alleged that by leaving exposed this thin wire support, an unreasonable risk of harm was created, particularly where the activity (bicycle riding) was common on the playground. A second case in New York also involved a bicyclist, who was riding along a common boundary line. Separating contiguous parks owned by Village and Town was a row of maple trees spaced 25' to 30' apart. The Town had installed a steel cable from tree to tree, attached by eye hooks screwed into the trees at a height of about 4' to 5' above the ground. While the cable was gray and unpainted, it was wrapped with orange-red surveyor's tape/ribbon and streamers of the same material hung from the cable at 4' to 5' intervals. It was not unusual for walkers and bicyclists to go from one park to another and go between the trees. Plaintiff was riding on the cross-bar of a bicycle driven by her aunt, when they decided to take a short cut and collided with the cable. The next day the Town removed the cable entirely. In the third situation, two snowmobilers, who were riding at night, were killed when they hit an unmarked and unprotected guy wire on a utility pole on the fairgrounds. Both the utility company and the fairgrounds association were sued. Snowmobilers had been given general permission to use the fairgrounds, and plaintiff argued that thus an unmarked guy line was gross negligence in maintaining a hazardous condition. If it were gross negligence, then the defendants would not be protected under the recreational user statute. Plaintiff also alleged violation of industry safety code.

§ 20.235   Incinerators, coals and ashes

Most cases involving incinerators are in regard to the incinerator being an obstacle on a playing field (see §20.2121).[220] When one burns rubbish or makes a barbecue fire, the disposition of the coals is of utmost importance. In most instances, whether on the playground, in a park, or on a beach, it is a young child who is injured and the attractive nuisance doctrine (see §2.1231) is applied, and to leave live coals open is usually considered a dangerous condition not given immunity protection by most Tort Claim Acts (see §4.2).

If employees burn leaves or other rubbish, it is important that the ashes be removed or be completely cold. And, if recreational users of a beach or picnic area are using a fire, it is equally as important that proper care be taken of the coals and ash piles. Supervision also plays a role in determination of negligence. (See Chapter 18.) In most cases where injury occurred due to being burned on such hot ash piles, the plaintiff recovered.[221]

In a 1972 Hawaii case,[222] a child just under two years old stepped on coals in or near an open barbecue pit in a park and was badly burned. The pits were frequently inspected and cleaned. The court held that children incapable of recognizing dangers presented by the pits should be closely supervised by parents. A similar holding that no dangerous condition was created by the defendant was given in *State v. San Mateo County*,[223]

[220] See also Garreans case in §20.237.
[221] Ackeret v. Minneapolis, 129 Minn. 190, 151 N.W. 976 (1915); Bingham v. Board of Educ., 118 Utah 582, 223 P. 2d 432 (1950); Howard v. Fresno, 22 Cal. App. 2d 41, 70 P. 2d 502 (1937); Sherfey v. Brazil, 213 Ind. 493, 13 N.E. 2d 568 (1938).
[222] Petersen v. Honolulu, 53 Hawaii 440, 462 P. 2d 1007 (1970), aff'd. 53 Hawaii 449, 496 P. 2d 4 (1972).
[223] State v. San Mateo County, 263 Cal. App. 2d 396, 69 Cal. Rptr. 683 (1968).

where the remains of a fire located in an alcove was in the white ash stage and thus blended with the white sand. A two and one-half-year-old was burned when he sat in the remains. The beaches were regularly inspected, and had been the day before, but no remains (live) of fires were noted. Fires were not extinguished because there was no convenient way for doing so — covering with sand could keep a fire alive for days, making it a hazard for those walking on the beach. In *Lam v. Board of Educ.*,[224] a seven-year-old was injured on live cinders which remained in the process of the school's clearing a wooded area to the rear of the regular playground. A four and one-half-year-old child was pushed into a hot fireplace by a playmate at a picnic, while attending a summer program. Held that the person in charge failed to discharge her supervisory duty because of the "horseplay" of the children and the foreseeable harm with the fireplace. Plaintiff did not sue the municipality who owned the picnic grounds.[225] On the way home from fishing, ten-year-old youngster stopped to play on some "grey hills," which were composed of hot ashes and chemical debris. He was severely burned. The court held that the Louisiana statute absolving owners from liability when they let others use their premises for listed recreational purposes, did not abolish the doctrine of attractive nuisance[226] (see §12.143).

§ 20.236   Trees

There is a duty to inspect trees closely for decay and then to remove the tree or limb so that injury will not be caused by the tree falling or limb breaking off at the decayed point. It is true that sometimes decay is not visible from the outside, but every effort should be made to ascertain the condition of the tree. A court will hold constructive notice where the condition is obvious, even if the park superintendent has not had actual notice.[227] In *Smith v. U.S.*,[228] the plaintiff, a 15-year-old boy, was injured by a falling tree limb in the Forest Service campground. The court held that the limb was visibly rotten and in an advanced state of decay, hence creating a dangerous condition for which there was a duty to eliminate it (see also §12.62 Campgrounds maintenance). If a tree has been broken off in a wind storm or due to other causes, there is also a duty to remove it, particularly if it obstructs a path or roadway.[229] In a 1982 case,[230] a hickory tree fell upon plaintiff's vehicle as he waited to launch his boat. While the State was held immune under the statute, the lessee operator of the park, who was required pursuant to the lease to maintain the property in accord with good business practices, was held liable for damages. In two other 1980's cases,[231] however, there was no immunity under

[224] Lam v. Board of Educ., 53 Misc. 2d 238, 278 N.Y.S. 2d 264 (1965); see also Rose v. Board of Education, Abilene, 184 Kan. 486, 337 P. 2d 652 (1959) six-year-old, coals from burning tree stump on school grounds.
[225] Brown v. Knight, 362 Mass. 350, 285 N.E. 2d 790 (1972).
[226] Smith v. Crown-Zellerbach, Inc., 638 F. 2d 883 (1981) Louisiana law applied; see also Lacombe v. Greathouse, 407 So. 2d 1346 (La. App. 1981).
[227] Edwards v. San Diego, 126 Cal. App. 1, 14 P. 2d 119 (1932); Kilbourn v. Seattle, 43 Wash. 2d 373, 261 P. 2d 407 (1953); Lisk v. West Palm Beach, 160 Fla. 632,

36 So. 2d 197 (1948); Lythell v. Waverly, 335 Ill. App. 397, 82 N.E. 2d 207 (1948); Pietz v. Oskaloosa, 250 Iowa 374, 92 N.W. 2d 577 (1958); Smith v. San Mateo Co., 57 Cal. App. 2d 820, 135 P. 2d 372, 62 Cal. App. 2d 122, 144 P. 2d 33 (1943).
[228] Smith v. U.S., 117 F. Supp. 525 (1953).
[229] Rockett v. Philadelphia, 256 Pa. 347, 100 A. 826 (1917).
[230] Thomas v. Jeane & State of Louisiana, 411 So. 2d 744 (La. App. 1982).
[231] McKenna v. City of Fort Wayne, 429 N.E. 2d 662 (Ind. App. 1981); Milligan v. Laguna Beach, 34 Cal. 3d 829, 196 Cal. Rptr. 38, 670 P. 2d 1121 (1983).

the statutes. In the Indiana case, plaintiff sought damages for injuries to a child resulting from a limb falling from a tree in a city-owned park. Where a picnic table had been placed under a tree, a play area was nearby, and the grass had been mowed, the court held that the park did not come under statutory immunity for "natural conditions and unimproved property." In the California case, a storm had caused a tree from the city property to fall on plaintiff's house on adjacent private property. The immunity extended only to recreational users of government (city) property and not to nonusers on adjacent property.

In three situations, the injured plaintiff was climbing/swinging in the tree. Plaintiff was using a table and bench to jump and swing from a tree limb, fell and fractured her arm. Plaintiff alleged negligence in permitting picnic table to be placed in close proximity to low extending limb of tree; however, the court held that such was not an "inherently dangerous condition," an instrumentality or product does not become inherently dangerous merely because there is abuse of it, or because it is used for wrongful purpose. Further, it was held that a child of ten must have appreciated the risk of falling when she jumped from the table to the tree limb.[232] An 11-year-old was fatally injured when he climbed a large mulberry tree on school property while waiting to be picked up. Deceased was in the tree picking mulberry blooms and throwing them down to his friend on the ground, when he lost his balance and fell to the ground. Around the base of the tree were partially exposed and visible broken pieces of brick or concrete block; decedent's head struck the broken masonry. No liability on either attractive nuisance or negligence. Mere occurrence of accident does not give rise to inference of negligence.[233]

Stumps of trees can also cause a problem if not cared for properly.[234] However, where the tree stump did not have jagged or knifelike protrusions, it was not considered a hazardous or dangerous condition so as to render the school liable when a student fell or was pushed on a tree stump in the school playground. The children had been cautioned about playing in that area.[235]

The court held that there was no duty to warn of open and obvious conditions, when plaintiff fell on a grassy incline which had sweet gum balls underfoot. The city, which was sponsoring a barbecue in the city park, did not violate any duty in failing to clean up all sweet gum balls or twigs. Such tree "debris" was an expectation under a sweet gum tree.[236]

Tree roots, also, can occasion a lawsuit. A golfer sued the golf course alleging that she tripped over an exposed tree root, injuring her foot. She was walking on a well-traveled path from one green to the next tee, and her spiked golf shoe caught the root.

[232] Bazos v. Chouinard, 51 Ill. Dec. 931, 96 Ill. App. 3d 526, 421 N.E. 2d 566 (1981); see also Shermoen v. Lindsay, 163 N.W. 2d 738 (N.D. 1968) ten-year-old swinging on rope from tree over street, a trailing piece of rope was caught by auto, rope had been tied to tree by playground supervisor for rope climbing activities.

[233] Cassel v. Price, 396 So. 2d 258 (Fla. App. 1981); see also Bryant v. Thunderbird Academy, 103 Ariz. 247, 439 P.2d 818 (1968) student standing in a

pecan tree picking nuts fell when limb broke, picking nuts as part of fund raising project for school.

[234] Bank v. Brainerd School Dist., 49 Minn. 106, 51 N.W. 814 (1892); Rose v. Board Education, Abilene, 184 Kan. 486, 337 P. 2d 652 (1959); Sapulpa v. Young, 147 Okla. 179, 296 P. 418 (1931).

[235] Partin v. Vernon Parish School Board, 343 So. 2d 417 (La. App. 1977).

[236] Shaw v. City of Lipscomb, 380 So. 2d 812 (Ala. 1980).

The court held that the protruding tree root was a natural condition of a golf course for which there was no liability.[237]

See also §20.32 regarding trees in a natural area.

§ 20.237   Maintenance equipment/supplies and chemical hazards

The courts hold that there is a high degree of care demanded in the handling and storage of explosive and poisonous substances. Often there are statutes or regulations regarding care of these substances. In the late '80s, concern extended to additional chemical hazards, such as might be in use of maintenance supplies, for employees, and a number of states[238] have enacted laws regarding labeling and safety precautions. Also, the effect of increased use of pesticides in schools on students has given rise to more strict policies regarding use. (See local health regulations.) California has a law prohibiting governmental entities from using state funds for purchase of wooden playground and recreation equipment where there is likelihood of contact by children when such equipment has been treated by pentachlorophenol, creosote, or arsenic, nor shall such funds be used to maintain or upkeep such wooden equipment, unless sealed with nontoxic and nonslippery sealers in accordance with commodity standard C-17 for playground equipment adopted by the American Wood-Preservers Association.

In *Carradine v. NYC*,[239] turpentine was stored under a bridge archway near a playground area. A nine-year-old child was killed when a match was dropped into it. A match was used in *Estate of Cargill v. City of Rochester*,[240] to see into a barrel which was in a wooden shed near the indoor swimming pool building in the municipal park. The unsealed 55-gallon drum, alleged to have contained methanol, exploded, engulfing the shed in flames. Young Cargill (aged 10) subsequently died from burns. (Note: this case challenged the New Hampshire $50,000 maximum placed on tort recovery from governmental units; held constitutional.) There was a somewhat similar situation in Nebraska.[241] Two boys entered the park to visit their grandparents who were in their camper in the campground for the weekend. Near the camper pad were trash barrels, 55-gallon drums from which the tops had been removed, painted various colors, and labled "Trash" on the side. There also was another 55-gallon drum, black, with lid still on. There was lettering on the side indicating it had contained antifreeze compound, and a red-orange 4″ square label was affixed to the top, which had the words "Flammable liquid" below a representation of a fire or flames. The lid had a 1″ diameter hole from which the plug had been removed. The boys had been given firecrackers by their fathers inspite of the fact that use of firecrackers in park was prohibited. They used a cigarette lighter to ignite the firecrackers, and the top of the drum was used as the shelf for their activities. The drum exploded when they dropped a lighted firecracker into the drum through the hole in the lid. Both boys were burned from the spraying flammable liquid. The city had not placed the drum in the park and had not purchased it, nor did it know how the drum got there. Held: boys were sufficiently contributorily negligent to bar

---

[237] Burns v. Addision Golf Club, Inc., 161 Ill. App. 3d 127, 112 Ill. Dec. 672, 514 N.E. 2d 68 (1987).

[238] For example, Michigan.

[239] Carradine v. New York City, 16 A.D. 2d 928, 229 N.Y.S. 2d 328 (1962).

[240] Estate of Cargill v. City of Rochester, 119 N.H. 661, 406 A. 2d 704 (1979).

[241] Garreans by Garreans v. City of Omaha, 216 Neb. 487, 345 N.W. 2d 309 (1984).

recovery; further, the act of the city in not removing barrel was not willful misconduct under Recreation Liability Act.

The court found for the plaintiff, holding that the city was negligent in leaving barrels of liquid fertilizer on the city golf course, which was separated from the picnic and playground area by only a single smooth wire strand fence. Decedent, a six-year-old boy, took a drink from the tank while attending a family picnic. Further held that the city failed to provide adequate fence around the barrels or to warn public of danger in the area where the barrels were kept.[242] In *Lewis v. Kehoe Academy,*[243] the court held that the operators of a day camp had a duty to exercise reasonable care in preventing a child from ingesting rat poison, but did not encompass the risk if the poison caused accentuation of subsequently incurred bruises. (The case involved a question of child abuse.) In a bit different situation, the poisonous substance was chlorine gas. A police officer was directed to the premises of a swimming pool to render aid to persons exposed to large quantity of chlorine gas, which had escaped from its containers at the pool. He inhaled a quantity of the gas while removing tank, although wearing a mask provided by the swimming club. The court held that it was the officer's duty to assist and that the Club owed a duty as to a licensee, to refrain from wanton negligence or willful conduct and to warn if not obvious. No liability to the plaintiff.[244] In *Oien v. Sioux Falls,* 393 N.W. 2d 286 (S.D. 1986), a child came into contact with a chemical solution used to treat water in the municipal swimming pool when she sat down at pool's edge. Held that plaintiff had a common law action against city.

Caustic lime used in marking lines on athletic fields was the substance of injury in two cases.[245] In the *Jacksonville* case, plaintiff received $50,000. A ten-year-old boy's eye was burned by lime spilling from the machine used to line the ballpark base lines in the public park. The boy had gone unattended to the truck containing the machine and attempted to remove it, and, as he did so, the lime spilled onto his face and into his eye. Employees had previously sustained eye injuries and inert marble dust was available as an alternative to lime. In the other case, plaintiff, a student at a church-sponsored four-year school, was voluntarily marking lines on an athletic field to be used for intramurals. As he was doing so, the marking material, which was caustic lime, was expelled into his face and eyes, causing injury. (No recovery; case before charitable immunity abolished in Missouri.)

A 12-year-old boy, while playing in the school yard, slipped and slid under the grass mower. The metal guard had been taken off the mower so that the motor could be repaired and was never replaced. The mower was of the rotary blade type and cut a swatch about 30″. The motor made the noise of "a small motorcycle." Defendant alleged that plaintiff was contributorily negligent in not hearing the motor and turning before getting to the mower as he was running; the Industrial Commission did not so find.[246] Additional cases involve negligent operation of power mowers or leaving

[242] Lampasas v. Roberts, 398 S.W. 2d 612 (Tex. Civ. App. 1966).

[243] Lewis v. Kehoe Academy, 346 So. 2d 289 (La. App. 1977).

[244] Adair v. Island Club, 225 So. 2d 541 (Fla. App. 1969); see also Morena v. Leslie's Pool Mart, 110 Cal. App. 3d 179, 167 Cal. Rptr. 747 (1980).

[245] Jacksonville v. Raulerson, 415 So. 2d 1303 (Fla. App. 1982) pet. den. without op. 424 So. 2d 760 (1982); Bodard v. Culver-Stockton College, 471 S.W. 2d 253 (Mo. 1971).

[246] Adams v. State Board of Educ., 248 N.C. 506, 103 So. 2d 854 (1958).

maintenance equipment in a hazardous condition.[247]

§ 20.238   Electrical Hazards

Defective electric wiring,[248] which has caused death in some instances, around drinking fountains, in bath houses, in open excavations, hanging from poles, etc., and short-circuited electric pump in lake[249] has been plaintiffs' allegation as to cause of injury in a number of cases.

In two 1980s cases[250] efforts by the defendants to be shielded from liability by the limited statutes were unsuccessful. In the Ohio situation, a husband and wife had paid a fee to park their camping trailer in the State park. The site offered an electrical hookup for the trailers and as the husband was attempting to connect the electrical system to the trailer, he was electrocuted. The court held that payment of the fee took the defendant out from the protection of the "recreational user" limited liability statute, and further held that defendant owed a duty to keep the premises safe for entry or use. Immunity was evaded in a Michigan case by holding that the presence of a dangling, high voltage wire was a dangerous condition which could be considered a nuisance for which the company was not shielded from liability by the recreational user statute. A storm had uprooted two tall trees that fell against defendant's power line knocking it nearly to the ground. A company repairman replaced a burned-out fuse to restore power without determining the cause of power failure or fuse blowout. Later that evening, two young couples drove into a dirt road in the area of the power line failure and parked. One couple walked into the wooded area and came into contact with the downed electric wire and were killed by electrocution.

In a Texas case,[251] the mast of a sailboat came into contact with a power line owned by the power company and maintained by a governmental entity (Lower Colorado River Authority) and plaintiff was disfigured from electrical shock. The court held that adoption of comparative negligence did not abolish gross negligence as viable ground for recovery of exemplary damages and allowed punitive damages against the power company. There was a similar situation in Florida.[252] Negligence action was brought against power company for injuries sustained when uninsulated, high tension electrical

---

[247] Ballinger v. Dayton, 66 Ohio L. Abs. 388, 117 N.E. 2d 469 (1952); Big Stone Gap v. Johnson, 184 Va. 75, 35 S.E. 2d 71 (1945); Fisher v. U.S., 534 F. Supp. 514 (1982) snowplow blade dropped on child on school field trip; Glenn v. Raleigh, 246 N.C. 469, 98 S.E. 2d 913, 248 N.C. 378, 103 S.E. 2d 482 (1958); Holt v. Moline, 196 Ill. App. 235 (1916); Husband v. Salt Lake City, 92 Utah 449, 69 P. 2d 491 (1937).

[248] Decatur v. Parham, 268 Ala. 585, 109 So. 2d 692 (1959); Irvine v. Greenwood, 89 S.C. 511, 72 S.E. 228 (1911); Lewis v. Kansas City, 233 Mo. App. 341, 122 S.W. 2d 852 (1938); Novak v. Ford City, 292 Pa. 537, 141 A. 496 (1928); Rector v. Nashville, 23 Tenn. App. 495, 134 S.W. 2d 892 (1939); Rice v. School Dist., 140 Wash. 189, 248 P. 388 (1926); Texaco Country Club v. Wade, 163 S.W. 2d 219 (Tex. Civ. App. 1942); Travelers Ins. Co. v. Stanley, 252 F. 2d 115 (1958).

[249] Morgan v. U.S., 709 F. 2d 580 (1983) Washington law applied.

[250] Crawford v. Consumers Power Co., 108 Mich. App. 232, 310 N.W. 2d 343 (1981) held in abeyance 323 N.W. 2d 8 (1982); Huth v. State of Ohio, Dept. Natural Resources, 64 Ohio St.2d 143, 18 Ohio Op. 3d 370, 413 N.E. 2d 1201 (1980); see also Colvin v. Southern California Edison Co., 194 Cal. App. 3d 1306, 240 Cal. Rptr. 142 (1987) two youths on bikes crossing creek pulled guy wire dangling from pole and wire touched electrically charged conductor, anchor of guy wire had washed out night before, power company's easement within "premises" of recreational user statute, no liability.

[251] Pedernales Elec. Co-op, Inc. v. Schulz, 583 S.W. 2d 882 (Tex. Civ. App. 1979).

[252] Fries v. Florida Power and Light Co., 402 So. 2d 1229 (Fla. App. 1981).

power lines were touched by mast of catamaran sailing boat. The question was whether the power company knew the river was navigable and frequented by many sailing vessels and took care for safety of boaters in maintaining the lines or whether the boaters were negligent in manner of sailing the boat.

A 40′ power pole carrying high voltage lines had been on the roadside edge of a vacant lot used by children for playing. This day 16-year-old decedent was firing a rocket-propelled parachute from the field adjacent to the power lines. As the parachute descended, it became entangled in the power lines. In climbing the pole, he came into contact with one of the live lines, causing his death six days later. No liability; while the power company knew children played in the lot, there was no reason for it to believe the children were capable of climbing the pole. Decedent, also, was held to be a trespasser on the pole.[253]

When new metal bleachers were built, replacing lower wooden ones, they came within 2′ of electric line. The give in the uninsulated line caused it to touch the bleachers; electricity was conducted down through the stands, into nine-year-old's right hand and out her back. Plaintiff did not recover; court held that the lines were initially properly installed and that the utility company's duty to inspect its lines did not require it to keep those lines under constant surveillance. The power company had no reason to believe the contractor would erect bleachers so close to the line.[254]

See also §20.12 Layout, §20.2121 regarding utility poles on baseball field, and §20.234 guy wires as obstructions.

§ 20.239   Other aspects of grounds maintenance

The scope of grounds maintenance encompasses many different aspects, in addition to those presented in foregoing subsections. Such aspects include structures, such as pool coping, collapse of bathhouse shed, or picnic shelter, defective plank in dock or bridge, toppling or placement of picnic or work tables/benches, and location of ventilator system and garbage containers, as well as objects which might be considered dangerous if used inappropriately.[255]

---

[253] Lewis v. Georgia Power Co., 182 Ga. App. 375, 355 S.E. 2d 731 (1987); see also Suarez v. Omaha Public Power District, 218 Neb. 4, 352 N.W. 2d 157 (1984) 12-year-old climbed to top of tree, making contact with electric transmission line on private property, held minor contributorily negligent (knew better!) and absent evidence that wires strung in defective manner, no liability. Kirschner v. Louisville Gas & Electric Co., 743 S.W.2d 840 (Ky. 1988) 15-year-old boy injured by arcing electricity after he climbed high voltage transmission tower which was located near entrance to an open field on which youth frequently played, the boy and his friends had constructed a wooden platform on the tower and was a trespasser, no recovery as the danger was not concealed, the electric company had an easement on the land.

[254] Pilkington v. Hendricks County Rural Electric

Membership Corp., 460 N.E. 2d 1000 (Ind. App. 1984).

[255] Bigelow v. Randolph, 80 Mass. 541 (1860); Bolster v. Lawrence, 225 Mass. 387, 114 N.E. 722 (1917); Brown v. Dorney Park Coaster Corp. 167 F.2d 433 (1948); Brown v. Southern Ventures Corp., 331 So. 2d 207 (La. App. 1976); Capers v. Orleans Parish School Board, 365 So. 2d 23 (La. App. 1978); Curtiss v. Chemung Co., 78 A.D. 2d 908, 433 N.Y.S. 2d 514 (1980); Gottesman v. Cleveland, 142 Ohio St. 410, 27 Ohio Op. 353, 52 N.E. 2d 644 (1944); Jacques v. Lake Placid, 39 A.D. 2d 163, 332 N.Y.S. 2d 743 (1972) motion to dismiss denied 31 N.Y. 2d 662, 336 N.Y.S. 2d 898 (1972) aff'd. 32 N.Y. 2d 739, 344 N.Y. 2d 736 (1973); Jenkins v. Miami Beach, 389 So. 2d 1195 (Fla. App. 1980); Lanclos v. Tomlinson, 351 So. 2d 1218 (La. App. 1977); McMurran v. Kansas City, 236 Mo. App. 562, 158 S.W. 2d 213 (1942); Novak v. Los Angeles

Inadequate lighting,[256] also, is an allegation brought by plaintiffs. Increasingly, such allegation relates to criminal attacks. In a 1987 case[257], plaintiff was in a state park for a camp-out. While in the bathhouse, she was attacked, suffering deep cuts about the face, neck, and head from a razor-like instrument used by the assailant. Among other allegations was inadequate lighting.

Blocked intake pipes and storm drains,[258] and conditions related to water, such as algae growth,[259] are all part of liability concerns. Natural conditions[260], if not properly taken care of, may bring liability suits, such as ants in a child care day center playground, poisonous berries on playground, and stalks under a snow pile. Maintenance in relation to snow and ice is primarily concerned with pedestrian ways (see §20.22) and parking and roads (see §22.2). Action also has been brought on behalf of spectators injured on bleachers.[261]

§ 20.3   Natural (unimproved) area conditions

Whereas the preceding section (§20.2) is concerned essentially with "man-made" conditions for urban or high density use environments, what premise conditions bring lawsuits, and what the standard of care is which is required by the court, this section focuses upon the natural environment itself, what must be done to protect users from the hazards of the environment, and the liabilities which arise in recreational use of the environment. (For municipalities, usually unimproved parcels of land are considered natural areas.) The duty owed the participants is quite different for the two environments. The duty owed in the urban environments is that of public or private invitee, or business invitee (see §2.121) and requires an affirmative act to seek out foreseeable risks to participant injury. However, the duty owed in regard to natural environments has been codified by most states through the recreational user laws, also

School Dist., 92 Cal. App. 2d 169, 206 P. 2d 403 (1949); Panoz v. Gulf & Bay Corp., 208 So. 2d 297 (Fla. App. 1968); Perry v. San Diego, 80 Cal. App.2d 166, 181 P. 2d 98 (1947); Streickler v. N.Y.C., 225 N.Y.S. 2d 602 (1962); Van Kempen v. Hayward Area Park, Recreation & Park Dist., 23 Cal. App. 3d 822, 100 Cal. Rptr. 498 (1972); Ware v. Cincinnati, 98 N.E. 2d 102 (1951) 93 Ohio App. 431, 51 Ohio Op. 184, 111 N.E. 2d 401 (1952).

[256] Board of School Directors v. Kassab, 450 A. 2d 282 (Pa. 1982); Boyce v. Pi Kappa Alpha Holding Co., 476 F. 2d 447 (1973); Calhoun v. Royal Globe Insurance Co., 398 So. 2d 1166 (La. App. 1981); Cohen v. Morristown, 15 N.J. Misc. 288, 190 A. 851 (1937); Cox v. Des Moines, 235 Iowa 178, 16 N.W. 2d 234 (1944); Davis v. Springfield Lodge No. 158, Elks, 24 Ill. App. 2d 102, 164 N.E. 2d 243 (1960); Dean v. Bartlesville, 176 Okla. 460, 56 P. 2d 140 (1936); LePitre v. Chicago Park Dist., 374 Ill. 184, 29 N.E. 2d 81 (1940); Styer v. Reading, 360 Pa. 212, 61 A. 2d 382 (1948); see also §20.2214 lighting steps and stairways.

[257] Trevathan v. State, 740 S.W. 2d 500 (Tex. App. 1987).

[258] Liguori v. Philadelphia, 351 Pa. 494, 41 A. 2d 563 (1945); Nemet v. Kenosha, 169 Wis. 379, 172 N.W. 711 (1919); Wexler v. Los Angeles, 110 Cal. App. 2d 740, 243 P. 2d 868 (1952).

[259] Brown v. Harlan, 468 So. 2d 723 (La. App. 1985) motion to dismiss granted 472 So. 2d 26 (1985); Metro. Dade Co. v. Yelvington, 392 So. 2d 911 (Fla. App. 1980) review denied 389 So.2d 1113 (1980); Sea Fresh Frozen Products v. Abdin, 374.So. 2d 1379, rev./ remanded 411 So. 2d 218 (Fla. App. 1982); Steele v. Jekyll Island State Park Authority, 122 Ga. App. 159, 176 S.E. 2d 514 (1970); Strongman v. Co. of Kern, 255 Cal. App. 2d 308, 62 Cal. Rptr. 908 (1967).

[260] Glasgow Corp. v. Taylor, 1 A.C. 44, 29 A.L.R. 846 (1922) well-known English case, protect children on park-school area from poisonous berries; La Torre v. First Baptist Church of OJUS, 498 So. 2d 455 (Fla. App. 1986) ants; Shanahan v. St. James Roman Catholic Church, 11 A.D. 2d 584, 200 N.Y.S. 2d 798 (1960).

[261] Cleary v. Catholic Diocese of Peoria, 10 Ill. App. 3d 224, 293 N.E. 2d 195 (1973) rev'd. 57 Ill. 2d 384, 312 N.E. 2d 635 (1974); see also §15.13.

referred to as landowner limited liability laws (see §12.1), and state tort claims acts or governmental/sovereign immunity statutes (see §4.2). Essentially the duty owed under the recreational user statutes by both private and public entities is that owed to a trespasser (see §2.123), while under the tort claim statutes, the governmental entity is usually immune from liability. What then is the importance of this section? Even though there may be some immunity or the standard of care required is not as high, as set forth by the foregoing statutes, when a known dangerous condition is maintained, there may be liability. Under the recreational user statutes, if the existence of the dangerous condition is considered gross negligence or willful and malicious misconduct (see §12.152), then there is liability; while under most state tort claim acts or immunity statutes for governmental entities, dangerous conditions is an exception to immunity, and it does not have to be occasioned by more than ordinary negligence. When neither statute is applicable, the principles of negligence law are applicable.

This section approaches the natural environment conditions first from maintenance responsibilities for paths/walks/trails and for trees, then the protective measures which must be taken against natural hazards. (See also §12.6 Campgrounds, including wild animals; §2.32 Acts of God (wind, et al.) as proximate cause; §13.13 Natural conditions in organized camps; and for water-based recreation injuries due to environmental conditions, see specific subsections in Chapter 14.) This section does not deal at all with outdoor recreation program and activities. (See §§12.2 through .5 for motorized vehicles, airborne activities, hunting, and sightseeing; Chapter 13 Camping, environmental education, and adventure recreation; and Chapter 14 Water-based recreation.)

§ 20.31 Paths, walks, trails

Maintenance of paths, walks, and trails include clearing of natural "debris," especially tree limbs, and protecting users as related to the terrain. Responsibilities are similar, whether the paths and trails are used by people on foot or people riding a vehicle (bicycle, snowmobile, trail bike, jeep) or a horse.

Terrain-related maintenance may require protection by erecting barriers or signs (see also §§20.331 and 20.3322). For example, at a state-owned recreational and scientific area, a preglacial gorge with unique geological features, the three plaintiffs, who were college students, were visiting the area for the first time with a group of four couples who had come for picnicking and hiking. One of the trails, at places, came within a foot of a high bluff where the bluff was undercut obliquely. The undercut was narrow, not readily discernible and within 45' of a picnic area. This cutback was at a place where one misstep of a foot would cause an uninterrupted 20' slide down a sharp incline to a direct dropoff of approximately 80' to the rock bottom of the gorge. This was the point where one of the plaintiffs fell. The other two, who were on a different trail, fell when they went to give help (it was already dark). One of them had been on the trail two or three times that day. They decided it would be safer to sit down and slide. As one started to slide, the other, thinking the first was falling, reached for her. They both fell about 60'. The court said that the manager, who knew condition of terrain, had a ministerial duty to either notify his superiors of sharp drop-off, i.e., an undercut in high bluff, located within inches of path or trail where the public was invited to walk, or to erect signs warning the public of such danger, especially after twilight.[262]

In two situations the ground "gave way" as plaintiffs were hiking above a steep slope, and they fell to the ground and rocks below, causing injury. In Ohio, a 12-year-old, who was visiting a state park with his parents, was injured. The State was protected from liability by the recreational user statute.[263] In the other situation, a group of boys were at a picnic in the state park, which had been left in its natural state. The boys followed a trail which led toward the cliff area. After about 350', as they were walking on the trail which was along the top of a steep slope which led to the cliffs, the ground gave way and the boys tumbled down toward the cliffs and then they went over the cliffs and fell perpendicularly some 60' onto soft ground covered with layers of dead leaves. The court found that the park path was an invitation from the state, that the boys were unaware of the cliff or the loose composition of soil along the slope leading thereto, and that the cause of the fall was loosening of gravel. It also said that failure of the state to warn, together with lack of any guard rails or safety measures, constituted negligence.[264]

An opposite result (judgment for plaintiff) was reached in a case[265] where the plaintiff slipped and injured her ankle while walking on a footpath in a national park. The court said that whatever dangers there might have been from the incline of the path, presence of rocks on the path or lack of boardwalks and handrails, these were or should have been known to plaintiff before she took the path and she should have watched carefully the placement of her feet as she walked along the path. The path was an unimproved dirt surface, and her slip was occasioned by loose gravel or pebbles. Her ankle twisted and upon hitting the ground, plaintiff slid about 6' down the path slope. She did have surgery on the ankle. Rangers walked the trails daily to remove rocks, branches and other obstacles; however, the pebbles were a natural part of the path. Observation immediately after the fall found no trees, roots, branches, or other obstructions which would have caused the fall. Types of surfacing and uses is briefly discussed in the opinion. The conditions of the area and the terrain dictate the type of surface to be used in a particular area of a trail, with maintenance of as natural a condition as possible.

Snow and ice may make paths and trails hazardous. In a 1987 New York case,[266] plaintiff was injured when her bicycle skidded on ice on a bicycle path at a State park. A sightseer, passenger in a jeep, while traveling down a narrow dirt logging access road was forced to return due to impassable snow and ice. On the way back, the jeep slid on an ice patch and rolled down an embankment. Sightseer was killed. Government was protected under Colorado sightseer statute; no liability in absence of willful or

[262] Cords v. Anderson, 80 Wis. 2d 525, 259 N.W. 2d 672 (1977), aff'd./rev'd. in part 82 Wis. 2d 321, 262 N.W. 2d 141 (1978); same situation — Cords v. Ehly, 62 Wis. 2d 31, 214 N.W. 2d 432 (1974).

[263] Phillips v. Ohio Dept. of Natural Resources, 26 Ohio App. 3d 77, 498 N.E. 2d 230 (1985).

[264] Burkhart v. State of New York, 50 Misc. 2d 912, 272 N.Y.S. 2d 52 (1966).

[265] Henretig v. U.S., 490 F. Supp. 398 (1980) Wyoming law applied; see also Colburn v. Ozaukee

Co., 39 Wis. 2d 231, 159 N.W. 2d 33 (1968) 11-year-old fell down bluff in county park, but decision on technical point; Rendak v. State, 18 Cal. App. 3d 286, 95 Cal. Rptr. 665 (1971) cliff arising from ocean, which was submerged at high tide, statutory immunity invoked.

[266] Leonakis v. State of New York, 126 A.D. 2d 706, 511 N.Y.S. 2d 119 (1987), held: recreational user statute not applicable to state and state subject to liability for negligence, to be determined.

malicious conduct. The court did say, however, that the Forest Service was not required to maintain logging roads to the same standard that political subdivisions must maintain public thoroughfares.[267]

Overgrown grass and weeds which conceal a hazardous object can bring liability. A fisherman on corporate property was walking along a well-worn pathway from one fishing point to another at a small pond. He ascended a slight incline, slipped and fell forward into overgrown vegetation wherein rusty metal fencing with sharpened metal points was concealed. The points were pointing upward and when plaintiff fell one of the spikes pierced his abdomen.[268] In *Guenther v. G. Grant Dickson and Sons,* 170 Ill. App. 3d 538, 121 Ill. Dec. 393, 525 N.E.2d 199 (1988), a 13-year-old girl was injured when three-wheeled all-terrain vehicle she was riding was struck by another ATV, alleging that presence of paths and "racetracks", combined with overgrown foilage, created a dangerous condition she could not have been expected to appreciate. While the landowner had not discouraged use of the property by ATVs, "no trespassing" signs had been posted. Preferring to "let nature take its course," there had been no trimming of trees, shrubs, or weeds. No recovery by plaintiff; girl admitted she was familiar with the risks, such as the changing nature of foilage and that it might obscure vision of other riders on the path and the fact that other people often drove vehicles on paths in opposite directions, and thus the landowner owed no duty. The court stated that the owner has a duty to exercise due care to remedy condition or protect children when the owner knows or should know that young children habitually frequent the property and a dangerous agency on the land is likely to injure such children because they, by reason of their immaturity, cannot appreciate the risk involved and the expenses of remedying the condition are slight compared to risk of children.

Hazards caused by tree limbs may be logs or limbs across the trail, overhanging limbs, tree stumps, or trees along the edge of the path. (See also next subsection on Trees.) The maintenance of a bridle path was at issue in *Mitchell v. Gay.*[269] An inexperienced rider was on a trail for the first time. She alleged that as she put her hand up to shield herself from a tree limb, at a point in the path where there was a downward incline, the horse took a "jump" over a log in the path. The log had been placed there purposefully for that purpose. She fell off, fracturing her back. Her allegation was failure to maintain the trail in a safe condition and failure to warn of the condition. Judgment for plaintiff. However, assumption of risk was held in another riding situation, and judgment was for defendant. Plaintiff was at a dude ranch on vacation. After riding on the trail, his party ventured off into a wooded area through unmarked terrain at a trot until they came to a clearing with fallen logs, when plaintiff, who was in the rear, quickened the pace to catch up. The horse stopped abruptly, shying at a small log in the path. He was thrown from the horse. Plaintiff had ridden previously and even experienced a similar mishap; his experience justified holding of assumption of risk.[270]

[267] Otteson v. U.S., 622 F. 2d 516 (1980) Colorado law applied.
[268] North v. Toco Hills, 160 Ga. App. 116, 286 S.E. 2d 346 (1981) recreational user statute applied, but question for jury as to whether this was a willful and wanton disregard for plaintiff's safety; see also Smith v. Goldman, 53 Ill. App. 3d 632, 11 Ill. Dec. 444, 368 N.E.2d 1052 (1977) bicyclist fell from bicycle onto sharp debris hidden in pool of standing water adjoining bicycle path, licensee, landowner had no duty to warn.
[269] Mitchell v. Gay, 111 Ga. App. 867, 14 S.E. 2d 568 (1965).
[270] Baar v. Hoder, 482 P. 2d 386 (Colo. App. 1971).

(See also §13.51 Trails and §13.53 Trail rides as related to horses.)

Plaintiffs were walking through a wildlife preserve on their way to photograph a historic attraction, Indian Caves, when they heard an "explosion" and a visibly dead tree fell on them. Both were injured. In suing, they alleged that the City had constructive notice of the tree's inert condition for a long time. The City, however, said it had no notice for this was in a remote, wooded, and undeveloped part of the area.[271] In another New York case,[272] a dead tree fell on plaintiff while bicycling on defendant's property, a private parcel of 15 to 20 acres located in suburban setting and consisting of wooded wetlands and marshlands upon which it was impossible to build. By agreement between defendant and City, property was to remain in its natural state.

Plaintiff and his family had paid a fee to enter the state park and was given a brochure describing the various trails. While walking along one of the trails, an old and decayed tree fell, striking and instantly killing the wife and severely and permanently injuring the plaintiff. Plaintiff alleged failure to use reasonable care in keeping the walks, paths, and trails in the park in a reasonably safe condition. No recovery under governmental immunity.[273] However, in a different state, a laborer who was on a work project to clear paths in the state park was injured when a tractor ran over some tree limbs, which twisted up around his legs and pulled him off the tractor. The court held that there was no immunity for such laborer work.[274]

In two camp situations, the court held in favor of the camp. In one situation a leader had just finished giving some instructions to a group of campers in broad daylight, and when she turned to go to her tent, she tripped over a tree stump in the path. This was a rustic camp with unpaved paths. The court said that the condition of the premises was incidental to the nature of the camp conducted and that the circumstances did not unnecessarily or unreasonably expose her to danger.[275] In the other, a camper who had been at the camp for a month as well as having been at the camp the previous summer, had been participating in the evening social activity. He was on his way back to his cabin to get his jacket, but had not taken a flashlight. As he started to his cabin on a well-used path, which was 2' to 3' wide, he hit a tree on the right side of the path (not on the path). The court held that there was no duty to illuminate a path, which was wide enough for two persons to walk abreast, in the absence of any peculiar danger on the path.[276]

A passenger was injured when the ORV crested a hill, became airborne and tipped over. The road in the dune area of the state park, on which they were riding, had been left in the natural condition with some steep hills. Three warning signs were posted in the dune and at the only entrance to the area a large warning sign with 2' and 3' letters was erected. Plaintiff alleged failure to warn as gross negligence; not so held. Immunity under recreational user statute.[277]

[271] Guillet v. City of N.Y., 131 Misc. 2d 578, 500 N.Y.S. 2d 946 (1986) city also sought to come under recreational user statute, with the question being were the plaintiffs hiking or walking (see §12.13).

[272] Hirschler v. Anco Builders, 126 A.D. 2d 971, 511 N.Y.S. 2d 746 (1987), held: defendant protected by recreational user statute.

[273] Bracht v. Conservation Comm., 118 Ind. App. 77, 76 N.E. 2d 848 (1948).

[274] Cuddy v. Texas Dept. of Corrections, 578 S.W. 2d 522 (Tex. Civ. App. 1979).

[275] Alcantara v. Federated Girl Scout Councils of Nassau Co., 24 A.D. 2d 585, 262 N.Y.S. 2d 190 (1965).

[276] Kimber v. Estis, 1 N.Y. 2d 399, 153 N.Y.S. 2d 197, 135 N.E. 2d 708 (1956).

[277] McNeal v. Dept. of Natural Resources, 140 Mich. App. 625, 364 N.W. 2d 768 (1985); see also